Using
OS/2.1, Special Edition,
Third Edition

Barry Nance
with
Greg Chicares
Caroline M. Halliday
Sue Plumley

que

Using OS/2 2.1, Special Edition, Third Edition

Copyright© 1994 by Que® Corporation

All rights reserved. Printed in the United States of America. No part of this book may be used or reproduced in any form or by any means, or stored in a database or retrieval system, without prior written permission of the publisher except in the case of brief quotations embodied in critical articles and reviews. Making copies of any part of this book for any purpose other than your own personal use is a violation of United States copyright laws. For information, address Que Corporation, 201 W. 103rd St., Indianapolis, IN 46290.

Library of Congress Catalog No.: 94-65144

ISBN: 1-56529-635-4

This book is sold *as is*, without warranty of any kind, either expressed or implied, respecting the contents of this book, including but not limited to implied warranties for the book's quality, performance, merchantability, or fitness for any particular purpose. Neither Que Corporation nor its dealers or distributors shall be liable to the purchaser or any other person or entity with respect to any liability, loss, or damage caused or alleged to be caused directly or indirectly by this book.

97 96 95 94   4 3 2 1

Interpretation of the printing code: the rightmost double-digit number is the year of the book's printing; the rightmost single-digit number, the number of the book's printing. For example, a printing code of 94-1 shows that the first printing of the book occurred in 1994.

Publisher: David P. Ewing

Director of Publishing: Michael Miller

Director of Acquisitions and Editing: Corinne Walls

Marketing Manager: Ray Robinson

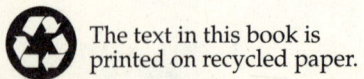
The text in this book is printed on recycled paper.

Dedication

We dedicate this book to the talented, hard-working team of people who make OS/2 2.1 a better DOS than DOS, a better Windows than Windows, and a better OS/2 than ever before.

Credits

Publishing Manager
Brad Koch

Acquisitions Editor
Angie Lee

Product Director
Bryan Gambrel

Production Editor
Mike La Bonne

Copy Editors
Geneil Breeze
Linda Seifert
Alice Martina Smith

Technical Editors
John Little

Book Designer
Amy Peppler-Adams

Cover Designer
Dan Armstrong

Production Team
Angela Bannan
Kathryn Bodenmiller
Meshell Dinn
Karen Dodson
Mark Enochs
Brook Farling
Carla Hall
Bob LaRoche
Beth Lewis
Nanci Sears Perry
Linda Quiqley
Marc Shecter
Kris Simmons
Greg Simsic
Amy Steed
Michael Thomas
Tina Trettin
Jennifer Willis
Donna Winter
Lillian Yates

Indexers
Charlotte Clapp
Michael Hughes

Composed in *Stone Serif* and *MCPdigital*
by Que Corporation

About the Authors

Barry Nance, a columnist for *BYTE* Magazine and a programmer for the past 20 years, is the author of *Network Programming in C* and *Introduction to Networking*. Barry is the Exchange Editor for the IBM Exchange on BIX, where you can reach him as "barryn."

Greg Chicares is a Fellow of the Society of Actuaries and an avid user of personal computers. Greg is an officer of a major insurance company, where he manages a group of people who develop new life insurance products. You can reach Greg on BIX as "gchicares."

Caroline M. Halliday is an electrical engineer with High Tech Aid, a Pittsburgh-area company specializing in technical documentation and training for the PC environment. She is also the author of *The First Book of AutoCAD*.

Sue Plumley, an account representative for ComputerLand of Beckley, is the author of Que's *Look Your Best with Word for Windows*, and *Look Your Best with Ami Pro*, and contributing author to *Using Ami Pro*, Special Edition. She specializes in desktop publishing.

Acknowledgments

We thank the people at IBM who helped make the writing of this book possible. In particular, we thank John Tiede, Irv Spalten, Jeff Cohen, Dave Reich, Steve Mastrianni, and John O'Hara for their assistance. We also thank Glen Horton for his timely and excellent technical editing and for his assistance in capturing screen shots in Collage Plus.

Trademarks

All terms mentioned in this book that are known to be trademarks or service marks have been appropriately capitalized. Que cannot attest to the accuracy of this information. Use of a term in this book should not be regarded as affecting the validity of any trademark or service mark.

Contents at a Glance

Introduction	1
Introducing OS/2	**11**
1 Taking a Quick Tour of OS/2 and Your Computer	13
2 Learning OS/2 If You Don't Know DOS	33
3 Learning OS/2 If You Know DOS	59
Installing and Configuring OS/2	**77**
4 Deciding How You Want to Use OS/2	79
5 Using Non-IBM Computers and OS/2	103
6 Installing OS/2	121
7 Modifying Your OS/2 Configuration	161
8 Troubleshooting OS/2	193
Using OS/2's Graphical Interface	**227**
9 Using Your Computer Screen as a Desktop	229
10 Managing the Workplace Shell	245

Learning the Basic Features of OS/2	**269**
11 Using the Drives Object	271
12 Learning the Commands You Use Most Often	301
13 Using the Built-In Help Facility	333
14 Using the OS/2 Text Editors	345
15 Printing with OS/2	373
16 Running DOS and Windows Under OS/2	393
17 Configuring Your DOS and Windows Sessions	409
18 Batch-File Programming with OS/2	447
Advancing Your OS/2 Skills	**463**
19 Programming with REXX	465
20 Using OS/2 Utilities	489
21 Using the OS/2 Time Management Applets	519
22 Using the OS/2 General Purpose Applets	545
23 Using the OS/2 Data Management Applets	579
24 Understanding OS/2 Communications and Database Tools	623
25 Networking OS/2 with NetWare	659
26 Connecting OS/2 to Other LANs	695

Using the Command Reference   **717**

Using the Command Reference   719

Command Reference

A   The Past, Present, and Future of OS/2   817
B   Workplace Shell Tasks and Keyboard Shortcuts   823
C   Enhanced Editor Keystroke Guide   827
D   OS/2 Games   837
E   OS/2 Files by Function   845
F   The Default CONFIG.SYS File   883
G   Enjoying Multimedia Presentation Manager/2   889
H   Identifying Sources of OS/2 Information   893

Index   989

Appendixes

Contents

Introduction   **1**

   Introducing OS/2 2.1 2
   Who Should Read This Book 4
   What You Need To Use This Book 4
   The Details of This Book 4
      Part I: Introducing OS/2 5
      Part II: Installing and Configuring OS/2 5
      Part III: Using OS/2's Graphical Interface 6
      Part IV: Learning the Basic Features of OS/2 6
      Part V: Advancing Your OS/2 Skills 8
      Part VI: Using the Command Reference 9
      Appendixes 9
   Conventions Used in This Book 9

I Introducing OS/2   11

1 Taking a Quick Tour of OS/2 and Your Computer   13

   Examining Presentation Manager 14
   Understanding Hardware and Software 15
      Examining Hardware Components 15
      Understanding Software Components 23
   Chapter Summary 32

2 Learning OS/2 If You Don't Know DOS   33

   Understanding Operating Systems 33
      Supporting Your Applications 34
      Supporting Your Work 35
   Starting the Operating System 36
      Understanding the Power-On Sequence 36
      Stopping the Computer 37
      Restarting from the Keyboard 37
      Restarting by Using the Power Switch 37
   Hurting the Computer or Losing Your Work 38
      Experimenting and Exploring 39
      Knowing What Hurts the Computer 39
      Saving Your Data and Making Backups 40
   Making the Computer Work for You 41
      Treating the Computer as a Tool 41
      Being Methodical 42

Understanding Disk Partitions and Disks 43
    Allocating Disk Partitions 43
    Working with Floppy Disks and Hard Disks 45
Storing Files and File Names 45
    Identifying Your Files 46
    Using File Names and Wild Cards 47
    Listing Your Files with DIR 47
    Working with Files 47
Organizing Directories 51
    Organizing Files into an Outline 51
    Creating and Using Directories 52
Formatting Hard Disks and Floppy Disks 53
    Formatting Hard Disks 53
    Formatting Floppy Disks 54
    Knowing What Can Go Wrong 54
Copying Disks and Files 54
    Copying Floppy Disks 55
    Copying Files 55
Deleting, Renaming, and Moving Files 56
Chapter Summary 57

3 Learning OS/2 If You Know DOS   59

Matching OS/2 with DOS 60
    Comparing OS/2 and DOS Files 60
    Comparing OS/2 and DOS Commands 61
    Using DOS Applications under OS/2 61
Understanding How OS/2 Expands upon DOS 62
    Providing More Memory for DOS Applications 63
    Running Multiple DOS Applications 65
    Getting More from OS/2 Applications 65
    Printing from DOS and OS/2 67
    Examining New and Changed Commands 67
    The Workplace Shell and Presentation Manager 70
Using Microsoft Windows with OS/2 70
Looking at DOS and OS/2 Incompatibilities 71
    Working with HPFS Partitions and HPFS Files 72
    Understanding INI Files and Extended Attributes 73
    Using Hard Disk Utilities 74
Chapter Summary 76

II Installing and Configuring OS/2   77

4 Deciding How You Want to Use OS/2   79

Choosing OS/2 for Windows 80
Examining Other Operating Systems 81
    Employing Dual-Boot 82
    Using the Multiple Operating System Tool
    (Boot Manager) 82

Contents xi

Considering Disks and Disk Files 83
    Installing CD-ROM Drives 83
    Offering the High Performance File System 84
    Using Buffers, Disk Caches, and Lazy Writes 85
    File Compression Utilities and Disk Space 87
    Working with RAM Disks 87
Understanding Application and General System Options 88
    Using Autofail 88
    Looking at PauseOnError 88
    Working with Input/Output Privilege Level 89
    Examining Threads 89
    Considering MaxWait 90
    Using Memory Management 90
    Working with Priority 91
    Examining SwapPath and Initial Swap File Size 92
    Using DOS Environment Control 92
Using Device Support 94
    Increasing Display Resolution and Colors 94
    Working with Printers and Fonts 96
    Connecting with Communications Ports 97
    Advanced Power Management and PCMCIA Support 97
Reflecting Personal Preferences 98
    Selecting Screen Colors and Arranging Your Desktop 98
    Specifying Mouse Usage 99
    Varying Input Methods 99
    Examining National Language Support 100
    Using On-Line Documentation 100
    Installing Tools, Games, and Utilities 100
    Working with the REXX Language 101
    Using Command History/Recall 102
Chapter Summary 102

5 Using Non-IBM Computers and OS/2   103

Working with IBM-Compatible Computers 104
    Examining OS/2 2.1 Hardware Requirements 105
    Making OS/2 Vendor-Neutral 107
Understanding CPU Chips 107
    Examining the Intel 80386 Chip 108
    Examining the Intel 80486 Chip 109
    Examining the Intel Pentium Chip 109
    Examining 80386 and 80486 CPU Chips from Other
        Manufacturers 110
Using ROM BIOS 110
    Making BIOS Criteria Compatible 111
    Manufacturing ROM BIOS Software 111
Working with Disks and Disk Controller Cards 113
    Understanding Disk Drive Types 113
    Learning about Disk Controller Cards 114

Using the Keyboards and Mice 115
    Looking at the 101-Key Keyboard 115
    Considering Serial, Bus, and PS/2 Mice 115
Working with Video Adapter Cards and Monitors 116
    Using VGA 117
    Using XGA 117
    Using CGA and EGA for OS/2 117
    Using 8514/A 118
    Using Super VGA 118
Chapter Summary 119

6 Installing OS/2   121

Installing from a CD-ROM Disk 123
Installing OS/2 for Windows 125
Setting Up the Installation Floppy Disks 126
Booting the Installation Disk 127
First Step: Text Mode 128
    Partitioning and Formatting Your Disk 130
Choosing the OS/2 Features You Want 139
    Using the Initial PM Installation Screen 139
    Confirming Your Configuration 140
    Selecting Your Features 143
    Changing Your Configuration Settings 153
    Installing Your Selected Features 154
    HPFS and Boot Manager—the Finishing Touches 159
Chapter Summary 160

7 Modifying Your OS/2 Configuration   161

Using CONFIG.SYS and AUTOEXEC.BAT 162
    Changing CONFIG.SYS Statements 163
    Changing DOS and Windows Settings 165
    Migrating CONFIG.SYS Statements 167
    Updating CONFIG.SYS Statements for Application
        Programs 167
    Executing AUTOEXEC.BAT Statements 168
    Executing STARTUP.CMD Statements 168
Upgrading Your Hardware 169
    Adding a Printer 169
    Adding and Changing Fonts 172
    Adding a Mouse 173
    Changing the Display Adapter or Resolution 173
    Adding a Hard Disk 176
Installing Features Selectively 176
Configuring Your Desktop 178
    Selecting Icon, Tree, and Details Views 178
    Using Other Notebook Settings 181
    Altering Screen Colors and Background Images 182
    Customizing with the System Object 184
    Modifying the Sound 185

  Altering the Country 186
  Customizing the Mouse 186
  Changing the Keyboard 188
  Using the System Clock 189
  Adding Applications to Your Desktop 190
 Chapter Summary 191

8 Troubleshooting OS/2   193

 Understanding Installation Errors 195
  Installation Problems by Symptom 196
  Dealing with Error Messages 197
 Preparing for Trouble 201
  Configuring Your Hard Disk 201
  Using a DOS Boot Disk 202
  Making Copies of Important OS/2 Files 202
  Working with Sensitive OS/2 Files and Directories ... 206
  Accessing the Message Files 209
 Recognizing Trouble 209
  Understanding Error Messages 210
  Understanding the `The system is stopped` Message ... 210
  Catching Application Program Errors 211
 Knowing What Steps to Take 214
  Knowing Why the Computer Fails To Boot 215
  Fixing Lost and Cross-Linked Extended Attributes ... 218
  Reacting When the Computer or Application
   Stops Suddenly 220
  Dealing with an Application that Does Not Behave ... 220
  Unscrambling a Garbled Screen 221
  Freeing a Keyboard that Fails to Work 222
  Solving Mouse Problems 222
  Checking the System When Nothing Prints 222
  Clearing Garbled Printouts 223
  Analyzing Performance Problems 223
 Using the Installation Disks in an Emergency 224
 Booting a DOS Disk 225
 Chapter Summary 225

III Using OS/2's Graphical Interface   227

9 Using Your Computer Screen as a Desktop   229

 Understanding CUA Principles 230
 Using the Workplace Shell 231
  Understanding Workplace Objects 231
  Dragging and Dropping Objects 232
  Navigating the Workplace Shell 233
 Introducing Presentation Manager 234
  Using the Keyboard in PM 234
  Using the Mouse in PM 236

Understanding the Elements of a PM Window	237
Working with Dialog Boxes	239
Chapter Summary	243

10 Managing the Workplace Shell — 245

Working with Program Objects	246
Starting a Program Object	246
Displaying an Object's System Menu	246
Viewing an Object in Different Ways	250
Viewing the Settings Notebook	250
Experimenting with Different Settings	251
Undoing Changes	252
Moving between Windows	252
Using the Window List	253
Choosing an Object View	253
Displaying More Than One Open View of an Object	253
Summarizing What You Have Learned So Far	254
Manipulating Icons	254
Selecting an Icon	255
Opening a View	255
Popping Up the System Menu	255
Moving an Object	255
Creating a Copy of an Object	256
Creating a Shadow of an Object	256
Dropping One Icon on Another	257
Canceling a Move, Copy, or Shadow Operation	257
Changing an Object's Name	257
Working with Minimized Views	257
Performing a Select, Move, Copy, or Shadow Operation with the Keyboard	258
Using a Folder's System Menu	258
Arranging Icons by Default	258
Changing Folder Settings	259
Changing the Window Background	259
Using the Workplace Shell's System Menu	260
Locking Up the System	260
Shutting Down the System	260
Saving the Arrangement of Open Objects on the Desktop	261
Customizing the Workplace Shell	262
The Mouse	262
The Keyboard	262
The System Object	263
The Sound and Country Objects	263
The Palettes	263
Setting Up Other Applications	264
Migrating DOS and Windows Applications	264
Creating Folders	264
Using the Drives Object	265
Chapter Summary	267

IV Learning the Basic Features of OS/2   269

11 Using the Drives Object   271

Understanding the Drives Object Display 271
    Icon View 274
    Tree View 275
    Details View 276
    Display Configuration 278
Expanding and Collapsing a Directory List 279
Finding Files 282
Manipulating Files 284
    Opening Files 285
    Selecting Multiple Files 285
    Canceling Selections 286
    Moving Files 286
    Copying Files 287
    Shadowing Files 288
Formatting and Copying Floppy Disks 289
    Formatting Floppy Disks 289
    Copying an Entire Floppy Disk 291
Associating a File with an Application 292
    Associating by File Type 292
    Associating by File Name 293
    Associating from the Pop-up Menu 294
Assigning Attributes to Files 297
    Flags 297
    Extended Attributes 298
Chapter Summary 300

12 Learning the Commands You Use Most Often   301

Beginning the Command-Line Interface 303
    Viewing or Changing the System Date (DATE) 303
    Viewing or Changing the System Time (TIME) 304
    Clearing the Screen (CLS) 305
    Closing the Command-line Session (EXIT) 305
Learning Commands for Managing Directories 305
    Making a Directory (MD or MKDIR) 307
    Changing the Current Directory (CD or CHDIR) 308
    Removing a Directory (RD or RMDIR) 309
Learning the Commands for Managing Files 311
    Listing Files (DIR) 312
    Using Wild Cards 313
    Using DIR with Wild Cards 314
    Deleting a File (DEL or ERASE) 315
    Changing a File Name (REN or RENAME) 316
    Copying Files (COPY) 317
    Copying Directories (XCOPY) 321

Learning the Commands to Back Up Your Hard Disk 323
    Making a Backup (BACKUP) 324
    Restoring from Backup (RESTORE) 327
Learning the Commands for Viewing and Printing Files 329
    Displaying a File On-Screen (MORE) 329
    Printing a File (PRINT) 329
Chapter Summary 331

13 Using the Built-In Help Facility   333

Understanding a Command-Line Window 334
    Turning the HELP Reminder On and Off 334
    Using HELP to Remember a Command 335
    Using HELP to Explain an Error Message 335
Learning Presentation Manager 336
    Getting Help on Help 336
    Getting Help for Menu Options 336
    Using an Application's Help Menu 337
Using the Command Reference Utility 340
    Selecting Levels of Detail in the Table of Contents 340
    Getting Help on a Command 341
Chapter Summary 344

14 Using the OS/2 Text Editors   345

Using the OS/2 Editors 346
Mastering Basic Editing Techniques 347
    Understanding the Text Cursor 348
    Understanding the Mouse Cursor 349
    Inserting or Replacing Text 349
    Deleting Text 350
    Joining, Splitting, and Inserting Lines 350
Learning Advanced Editing Techniques 350
    Understanding Blocks 351
    Finding and Replacing 352
Understanding the System Editor Menus 356
    Working with the File Menu 356
    Using the Edit Menu 358
    Using the Options Menu 359
Comparing the System Editor to the Enhanced Editor 361
Starting the Enhanced Editor 362
Understanding the Enhanced Editor Menus 362
    Working with the File Menu 363
    Using the Edit Menu 364
    Using the Search Menu 366
    Using the Options Menu 367
    Using Other Menu Options 371
    Editing Files without Typing their Names 372
Chapter Summary 372

15 Printing with OS/2 — 373

- Learning OS/2 Printer Basics 375
  - Using Multiple Applications with One Printer 375
  - Understanding Printer Differences 375
  - Seeing the Printer as an OS/2 Object 376
  - Working with the Spooler and Queue Driver 379
  - Creating Print Jobs 380
- Learning about Fonts 382
  - Understanding Font Basics 383
  - Using OS/2 System Fonts 384
  - Working with Adobe Type Manager Fonts 384
  - Installing Soft Fonts and Font Cartridges 385
- Printing with OS/2 386
  - Using Drag and Drop 387
  - Sending the Print and Copy Commands 387
  - Printing from an Application 387
  - Handling Printer Errors 389
  - Using Multiple Printer Objects 390
  - Printing to a File 390
- Chapter Summary 391

16 Running DOS and Windows Under OS/2 — 393

- Understanding DOS Sessions 394
- Opening a DOS Command-Line Session 395
  - Making Sessions Full Screen or Windowed 395
  - Moving among Sessions 395
  - Starting a Windows Session 396
- Adding DOS Programs 397
  - Creating a New Program Object 397
  - Telling OS/2 How to Run the Program 398
  - Telling OS/2 How To Recognize Files 398
  - Telling OS/2 What Kind of Session To Open 399
  - Using a DOS Session's System Menu 401
  - Running Individual Windows Applications 403
- Switching between OS/2 and DOS with Dual-Boot 404
- Booting DOS without Leaving OS/2 404
- Learning What You Cannot Do in a DOS Session 405
  - Preventing Viruses 405
  - Using Disk Utilities 405
  - Running Diagnostic Utilities 406
  - Working with Memory Managers 406
  - Using Applications that Use Obsolete DOS Extenders 406
  - Employing Windows Enhanced Mode 406
- Chapter Summary 407

17 Configuring Your DOS and Windows Sessions 409

Changing Default Settings in CONFIG.SYS 409
    Telling DOS to Make the Best Use of Memory 409
    Setting the Number of Files DOS Can Use 410
    Expanding the DOS Environment 410
Changing Settings in the System Menu 410
    Using Special Kinds of Memory 411
    Getting More than 640K of Memory for DOS 413
    Tuning the Priority of DOS Sessions 413
    Choosing Performance Enhancements 414
    Accommodating Special Needs 415
Changing DOS Settings for Each Session 418
    Making DOS Sessions Perform Better 418
    Configuring the Keyboard, Mouse, and Touch Screen 421
    Modifying Display Settings 425
    Maximizing Available Memory 428
    Tuning Other DOS Session Settings 434
Chapter Summary 445

18 Batch-File Programming with OS/2 447

Learning Batch-File Program Basics 448
    Distinguishing OS/2 and DOS Batch-Files 448
    Running a Batch-File Program 449
    Using DOS and OS/2 Commands in Batch-Files 450
Creating a Simple Batch-File Program 451
Using Batch-File Program Statements 452
    Inserting Comments with the REM Statement 453
    Writing to the Screen with the ECHO Statement 453
    Passing Parameters to a Batch Program 454
    Changing Program Flow with the GOTO Statement 455
    Testing File Existence with the IF EXIST Statement 455
    Comparing Strings with IF 456
    Processing ERRORLEVEL in a Batch-File Program 457
    Inserting FOR Loops in your Batch Programs 458
    Calling Batch-Files from Other Batch Programs 458
Halting a Batch-File Program 459
Interacting with Batch-File Programs 459
Using Startup Batch Programs That Run Automatically 460
Chapter Summary 461

V Advancing Your OS/2 Skills 463

19 Programming with REXX 465

Understanding REXX Basics 466
Displaying Information with REXX 469
Using the *PULL* and *PARSE PULL* Commands 469
    Defining Variables in REXX 469
Controlling Program Flow 471

Computing Results with REXX 476
Working with Strings in REXX 476
Reading and Writing Files in REXX 479
Passing Parameters to REXX Programs 481
Visual REXX Tools 482
    VisPro REXX 482
    GPF REXX 483
    VX/REXX 484
Testing REXX Programs 485
Chapter Summary 487

20 Using OS/2 Utilities   489

Using BOOT 490
    Instructions 491
    Warnings 492
    Return Codes 492
Using EAUTIL 493
    Instructions 493
    Examples 494
    Warnings 494
    Return Codes: 494
Using FDISKPM 494
    Instructions 497
    Warnings 497
Using MAKEINI (OS/2 Only) 498
    Instructions 498
    Example 498
    Warnings 499
Using PATCH 499
    Instructions 500
    Examples 500
    Warning 501
    Return Code 501
Using PMCHKDSK 501
    Instructions 501
    Warning 503
Using PSTAT (OS/2 Only) 504
    Instructions 504
    Examples 505
Return Codes 505
Using SETBOOT 509
    Instructions 509
    Examples 510
Using SORT 510
    Instructions 511
    Examples 511
    Return Code 511
    Warnings 512

Using SYSLEVEL 512
    Instructions 512
    Example 512
Using UNDELETE 513
    Instructions 513
    Examples 514
Using UNPACK 514
    Instructions 514
    Examples 515
    Return Codes 516
Using VIEW (OS/2 Only) 516
    Instructions 516
    Examples 516
Chapter Summary 517

21 Using the OS/2 Time Management Applets   519

Starting Time Management Applets 520
Using Daily Planner 521
    Using the File Menu 523
    Using the Edit Menu 523
    Using the Completed Menu 524
    Using the View Menu 524
    Using the Tidy Menu 525
    Using the Customize Menu 525
Using Monthly Planner 526
    Using the View Menu 527
    Using the Customize Menu 527
    Making Changes 528
Using Calendar 529
Using Activities List 531
    Using the File Menu 532
    Using the Edit Menu 532
    Using the View Menu 533
    Using the Customize Menu 533
    Using Planner Archive 534
Using Alarms 534
    Using the Alarms Menu 535
    Using the Edit Menu 538
    Using the Customize Menu 538
Setting a Default Planner File for All Time Management
    Applets 538
Using To-Do List 540
    Entering Tasks on To-Do List 540
    Using the File Menu 541
    Using the Mark Menu 542
    Using the View Menu 542
    Using the Customize Menu 543
    Using To-Do List Archive 543
Chapter Summary 544

22 Using the OS/2 General Purpose Applets 545

Starting the General Purpose Applets 546
Learning Commands Shared by Most General Purpose
    Applets 547
        Picking Colors 547
        Choosing a Font Size 548
        Printing from a General Purpose Applet 549
Using Calculator 550
        Doing Arithmetic on the Calculator 551
        Using the Tally and Customize Menus 553
Using Pulse 553
        Setting Pulse Options 554
        Running Pulse as Graphically Changing Icon 555
Using Clipboard Viewer 556
        Choosing a Display Format 557
        Sharing Information between Windows and OS/2 557
Using Tune Editor 559
        Entering a Tune 560
        Using the File Menu 560
        Using the Edit Menu 561
        Playing Your Melodies 562
Using Seek and Scan Files 562
        Searching For a File 563
        Using the File Menu 565
        Using the Selected Menu 565
        Using the Edit Menu 566
        Using the Options Menu 566
        Stopping a Search 566
Using Sticky Pad 567
        Attaching a Sticky Note 567
        Using the Edit Menu 568
        Using the Customize Menu 569
Using Notepad 569
        Creating Notes 569
        Using the File Menu 570
        Using the Edit Menu 571
        Using the View Menu 572
Using Icon Editor 572
        Creating a New Icon 572
        Using the File Menu 573
        Using the Edit Menu 573
        Using the Palette Menu 574
        Using the Options Menu 575
        Using the Device Menu 575
        Using the Tools Menu 576
        Associating Your Own Icon with a Program 576
        Modifying an Application's Default Icon 576
Chapter Summary 578

23 Using the OS/2 Data Management Applets — 579

- Using Database 580
  - Purpose 582
  - Understanding Database 582
  - Working with Database 584
  - Understanding Database Limitations 591
  - Sharing Database Information 592
- Using Spreadsheet 593
  - Purpose 595
  - Understanding Spreadsheet 595
  - Working with Spreadsheet 596
  - Understanding Spreadsheet Limitations 600
  - Sharing Spreadsheet Information 600
- Using PM Chart 601
  - Understanding PM Chart 603
  - Working with PM Chart 605
  - Understanding PM Chart Limitations 611
  - Sharing PM Chart Information 612
- Using PM Terminal 612
  - Purpose 613
  - Understanding PM Terminal 613
  - Working with PM Terminal 614
  - Understanding PM Terminal Limitations 621
  - Sharing PM Terminal Information 621
- Chapter Summary 621

24 Understanding OS/2 Communications and Database Tools — 623

- Defining the Facilities within Extended Services 624
  - Learning Extended Server Basics 624
  - Exploring Extended Services with Database Server 626
- Securing Access to Your Data 627
- Using Communications Manager 628
  - Understanding Connectivity Options 629
  - Using Terminal Emulations 631
- Learning Database Manager 635
  - Understanding Database Manager Basics 636
  - Using Database Services 638
  - Exploring Database Tools 642
  - Using Query Manager 644
  - Applying Remote Data Services 651
  - Supporting DOS and Windows Database Clients 654
- Moving Up to CM/2 and DB2/2 654
  - Communications Manager/2 655
  - Database 2 for OS/2 655
- Investigating Other OS/2-Based Products 657
- Chapter Summary 657

25 Networking OS/2 with NetWare — 659

Looking at OS/2 Workstations
   on a NetWare LAN 661
      Understanding NetWare Requester for OS/2 662
      Installing the NetWare Requester 663
Logging In and Mapping Drives 675
      Issuing Commands To Log In 675
      Setting Up OS/2 Login Scripts 676
      Mapping Drives with NetWare Tools 678
Using NetWare Utilities 680
      Using OS/2 Menu-Based NetWare Utilities 681
      Using OS/2 Command-Line NetWare Utilities 682
Knowing Your Rights 686
Printing with NetWare 687
      Using CAPTURE To Print Screens 687
Understanding NetWare Security 689
Assigning Types of Users 690
Using NetWare for OS/2 691
Chapter Summary 693

26 Connecting OS/2 to Other LANs — 695

Focusing on LAN Server and LAN Manager 696
      Considering LAN Server and LAN Manager 697
      Exploring the IBM and Microsoft Team Effort 698
      Learning LAN Server and LAN Manager Terms 699
      Understanding the Essentials of Security 701
      Contrasting LAN Server and LAN Manager 701
      Understanding LAN Server and LAN Manager 705
      Taking Advantage of Client/Server Computing 706
      Using LAN Manager or LAN Server 708
      Logging In 710
      Mapping Drives 711
      Printing with LAN Manager and LAN Server 712
      Ensuring Security 712
Connecting OS/2 to LANtastic, NetWare Lite, and
   Personal NetWare 713
Chapter Summary 715

VI Using the Command Reference — 717

Using the Command Reference — 719

Organization 719
Layout 719
Commands That Help You Work with Your Files 721
Commands That Help You Work with Your Directories 722
Commands That Help You Prepare and Maintain
   Disks and Floppy Disks 722

Commands That Support National Languages 723
Commands That Give You Information about Your
 System or Let You Change How It Works 723
Configuration Commands 725
Other Commands 728
Configuration Commands 782

A The Past, Present, and Future of OS/2   817

The Past 817
The Present 821
The Future 821

B Workplace Shell Tasks and Keyboard Shortcuts   823

Workplace Shell Keyboard Shortcuts 825

C Enhanced Editor Keystroke Guide   827

Function Key Keystroke Reference 828
Basic Editing Keystroke Reference 829
 Cursor Key Keystroke Reference 829
 Mouse Cursor Reference 830
 Editing Keystrokes 830
File Menu Keystroke Reference 832
Edit Menu Keystroke Reference 833
Search Menu Keystroke Reference 834
Options Menu Keystroke Reference 834
Command Menu Keystroke Reference 835

D OS/2 Games   837

Cat and Mouse 837
 Settings and Options 838
Jigsaw 839
 Settings and Options 839
OS/2 Chess 840
 Settings and Options 840
Reversi 841
 Settings and Options 842
Scramble 842
 Settings and Options 843
Klondike Solitaire 843
 Settings and Options 843

E OS/2 Files by Function   845

F The Default CONFIG.SYS File   883

G Enjoying Multimedia Presentation Manager/2 — 889

Defining Multimedia and Multimedia Presentation
   Manager/2 889
Knowing the Hardware Requirements 890
Installing MMPM/2 891
Using MMPM/2 892

H Identifying Sources of OS/2 Information — 893

Information Services 893
Bulletin Boards 893
The Internet 915

Index — 989

Introduction

The first edition of this book went on sale at the same time OS/2 2.0 went on sale in April 1992. For much of 1992, Que's *Using OS/2* was the only printed documentation on the subject of OS/2 (IBM itself did not provide printed documentation with OS/2 2.0).

When IBM released OS/2 version 2.1, Que continued producing the *first and best* book on OS/2, which enabled users to buy the second edition of this book the same day IBM released the software. Thanks to a great working relationship with IBM, the authors had an early, in-depth look at IBM's new desktop computer operating system and were able to finish writing the book immediately after IBM's programmers finished writing version 2.1 of the operating system. Note that IBM supplies its OS/2 technical support team with copies of this book to help answer your questions.

PC Magazine says this about *Using OS/2*: "...it's obvious that the authors did their homework and consulted system designers and beta testers; the best feature is the collection of tips and tricks on getting the best performance from OS/2...." And this: "...The combination of practical information and tips makes *Using OS/2* the best choice...." And this: "*Using OS/2* is the best comprehensive guide."

The book has expanded. The edition of *Using OS/2* you're holding covers the OS/2 for Windows product, explores networking OS/2 in more detail, provides more information about the object-oriented nature of OS/2, includes more troubleshooting and configuration tips, and gives you a look at future versions of OS/2. You get a peek at Workplace OS (Presently in the early states of development, Workplace OS is an IBM operating system with object-oriented features that will someday perhaps replace OS/2) and at the efforts of other companies such as Apple, Taligent, and even Microsoft. We feel this book is the most complete, most accurate, most reliable source of information about OS/2 you can possibly get.

Future editions of this book will continue to keep pace with IBM's development and deployment of OS/2. You might be interested to know that the authors already have a copy of the top-secret plans for the features and functions intended for later versions of OS/2.

Of course, this edition of *Using OS/2 2.1* includes all the basics. You get both a tutorial and a reference you can use to discover all the features and functions of OS/2. The early chapters introduce you to OS/2 and help you understand, install, configure, and—if necessary—troubleshoot OS/2. Later chapters fully discuss and explain the Workplace Shell, the command-line interface, the Drives object, the miniapplications (called *applets*) that come with OS/2, the use (and tuning) of the DOS and Windows components of OS/2 (Win-OS/2), and the steps you take to print with OS/2. Still later in this book, you get useful information to help make your applications run best under OS/2. You gain an understanding of how OS/2 works in a Novell NetWare, IBM LAN Server, and other local area networking environments. There is a thorough discussion of how database and communications technologies relate to OS/2. You even get programming lessons for those times you want to take charge of your computer yourself.

This book is really three books in one: First, throughout this edition of *Using OS/2 2.1*, you find *tutorial* material to bring you up to speed on topics you're unfamiliar with. Along the way, you also find *reference* material you can use if you feel comfortable with OS/2 but need to look something up. (You'll find the Command Reference section indispensable.) Finally, you find excellent discussions that help you understand the *philosophy* behind OS/2.

The authors and Que continue to work overtime to make this book your best tool for understanding and using OS/2. We hope you enjoy the results of our labors!

Introducing OS/2 2.1

OS/2 2.1 gives you more as an operating system than earlier versions of OS/2 did—for example, Windows 3.1 compatibility. You can run a Windows 3.1 application from OS/2 2.1 just as though you were running Windows 3.1.

Additionally, OS/2 2.1 adds increased hardware compatibility, including support for high-resolution video displays.

OS/2 is an outgrowth of IBM's PC DOS and Microsoft's MS-DOS operating systems that frees you from most of the constraints that DOS imposed. The most significant of these constraints is the amount of computer memory (RAM) available to the applications you run on your computer. OS/2 2.1 gives you more memory to run DOS applications, Windows applications, and OS/2 applications.

OS/2 is not an extension of DOS, however. OS/2 is a completely new operating system. From version 1.0 through version 2.1, IBM (and, to some extent, Microsoft) designed OS/2 to support sophisticated business applications with its high-performance features and its consistent, easy-to-use interface. OS/2 2.1 exploits your PC's hardware to give you multiple simultaneous DOS sessions, Windows sessions, and OS/2 sessions.

As you work your way through this book, you will see that OS/2 2.1 offers you a wide array of features, including the following:

- System integrity for applications
- Virtual memory
- Preemptive multitasking and task scheduling
- Fast, 32-bit architecture
- Overlapped, fast disk file access
- DOS compatibility
- More available memory for DOS applications (typically about 620KB of conventional memory)
- Capability to run OS/2, DOS, and Windows software concurrently and seamlessly
- Multiple concurrent OS/2, DOS, and Windows sessions
- High Performance File System (HPFS)
- Presentation Manager (PM) graphical user interface
- The object-oriented Workplace Shell (WPS)

- National Language Support (NLS)
- Boot Manager
- Small, easy-to-use applications (called *applets*) bundled with OS/2, such as notepad, diary, spreadsheet, presentation graphics software, and other productivity tools
- Interactive on-line documentation and help screens
- Capability to run OS/2 on both IBM and non-IBM hardware

If some of the terms in the preceding list confuse you or seem foreign, take heart. *Using OS/2 2.1,* Special Edition, quickly brings you up to speed with OS/2 and helps you get the most from the OS/2 operating system. This book helps you understand OS/2, guides you in learning to use OS/2, and serves as a reference when you need to look up commands or intricate procedures.

Who Should Read This Book

This book assumes little or nothing about your previous computer experience and knowledge. You will find the book useful whether you are new to OS/2 or just want a handy OS/2 reference. If you have DOS experience, you will be interested in Chapter 3, "Learning OS/2 If You Know DOS," which compares OS/2 with DOS and shows you the relationship between the two operating system environments. If you're not a DOS veteran, Chapter 2, "Learning OS/2 If You Don't Know DOS," is a friendly introduction that helps you learn how your computer can be a useful, productive tool in your work.

What You Need To Use This Book

The first few chapters use illustrations to help you visualize and understand OS/2 and your computer. Chapter 4, "Deciding How You Want To Use OS/2," and Chapter 5, "Using Non-IBM Computers and OS/2," get you involved with your computer system but don't assume that you have installed OS/2. From Chapter 6, "Installing OS/2," through Chapter 26, "OS/2 and Other Networks," you should have both your computer system and your OS/2 2.1 system disks handy so that you can give yourself on-the-job experience with OS/2 2.1.

The Details of This Book

The first five parts of this book explain how to use OS/2 2.1 effectively. Part VI is a Command Reference you can turn to when you need to know the exact usage of an OS/2 command. The appendixes contain less frequently used but still important information about OS/2.

Part I: Introducing OS/2

Part I is an introductory tutorial that helps you clearly understand what your computer and OS/2 can do for you. As you learn IBM's latest operating system, begin to think of your computer as a more useful tool. And you quickly gain self-confidence as you discover exactly how to use that tool.

Chapter 1, "Taking a Quick Tour of OS/2 and Your Computer," starts you on the road to OS/2 expertise by examining your computer and its components and showing you how they work together. The chapter also shows you what OS/2 looks like and what it can do for you.

Chapter 2, "Learning OS/2 If You Don't Know DOS," introduces you to your personal computer. If you're a first-time computer user, Chapter 2 gently but thoroughly acquaints you with the fundamentals of both DOS and OS/2.

Chapter 3, "Learning OS/2 If You Know DOS," describes the differences between DOS and OS/2. If you're one of the 60 million people who use DOS, you will quickly see the relationship between OS/2 and its predecessor. You discover the extra things you can do with OS/2 that you cannot do with DOS, such as running several large applications at one time and easily copying data from one application to another.

Part II: Installing and Configuring OS/2

Part II helps you install OS/2 on your computer so that you can begin using the operating system immediately. In Part II, you learn how to consider carefully the many configuration settings and options you need to select, how to install OS/2 on your computer, how to change your configuration, and—should it become necessary—how to make corrections to your OS/2 configuration when errors occur.

Chapter 4, "Deciding How You Want To Use OS/2," describes the options available under OS/2 so that you can decide which ones to choose during installation. For example, the chapter explains the pros and cons of installing the games, tools, and utilities that accompany OS/2.

Chapter 5, "Using Non-IBM Computers and OS/2," is for you if you use IBM-compatible hardware. If your computer system is non-IBM, or if you have a non-IBM mouse device or monitor, Chapter 5 shows you how to make OS/2 work on your hardware.

Chapter 6, "Installing OS/2," quickly gets you up and running with OS/2 by leading you carefully through the installation process.

Chapter 7, "Modifying Your OS/2 Configuration," tells you how to modify your computer's configuration safely, should it become necessary.

Chapter 8, "Troubleshooting OS/2," helps you identify and quickly fix problems you might encounter with OS/2.

Part III: Using OS/2's Graphical Interface

Part III helps you through the new language of icons, action bars, and dialog boxes. In Part III, you learn how the mouse, keyboard, and screen work together. You learn about the object-oriented nature of the Workplace Shell and how to make Presentation Manager and the Workplace Shell work for you. In addition to the chapters in Part III, you find a quick-reference guide for Workplace Shell operations on the inside front cover of this book.

Chapter 9, "Using Your Computer Screen as a Desktop," explains the latest terminology of graphical user interfaces (GUIs). Icons, action bars, push buttons, and dialog boxes will become second nature to you.

Chapter 10, "Managing the Workplace Shell," gives you an understanding of the techniques you use to manipulate the Workplace Shell. The chapter also supplies tips you can use to customize the Workplace Shell to your liking.

Part IV: Learning the Basic Features of OS/2

You earn your OS/2 wings in Part IV as you explore the full utility of the operating system. You gain practical experience with useful commands, the OS/2 on-line help facility, the OS/2 Enhanced Editor, printing, and DOS/Windows sessions.

Chapter 11, "Using the Drives Object," shows you how you can manage disk drives by using the Drives object. You learn about how the Drives object displays information and how to change the way you view files. You also learn to manage files, format disks, and associate files with application programs.

Chapter 12, "Learning the Commands You Use Most Often," explains the OS/2 commands you use every day to accomplish your work. You cannot always use Presentation Manager's graphical interface to give directions to OS/2. When you're faced with OS/2's command-line prompt, however, this chapter provides what you need to know.

Chapter 13, "Using the Built-In Help Facility," helps you access, manage, and understand the wealth of on-line help that OS/2 offers. From how to ask for help at a command-line prompt to how to get instant help for a menu option, Chapter 13 reveals the many sources of help you have at your fingertips.

Chapter 14, "Using the OS/2 Text Editors," describes the text-editing tools supplied with OS/2 2.1: the System Editor and the Enhanced Editor. You first master the basics of creating and editing text files. Next you learn how to perform operations such as cutting, copying, and pasting. This chapter also leads you through setting tab stops, setting margins and text fonts, and editing multiple files at the same time.

Chapter 15, "Printing with OS/2," ensures that your printed reports, documents, letters, memos, and charts come out looking the way you want, when you want. You learn how to tell OS/2 to recover from printer problems (such as paper jams) and how to set up your computer to print several different kinds of forms.

Chapter 16, "Running DOS and Windows under OS/2," helps you run your DOS applications easily and productively under OS/2. You gain insight into the OS/2 options that control your DOS sessions and learn what you can and cannot do in an OS/2-controlled DOS session.

Chapter 17, "Configuring Your DOS and Windows Sessions," shows you how to change global DOS settings by using CONFIG.SYS commands to get more memory and speed. You learn how to fix common DOS-session and Windows-session problems. You also learn how to modify each of the individual DOS-session and Windows-session settings that affect the performance of each of your sessions.

Chapter 18, "Batch-File Programming with OS/2," discusses the power and flexibility you can gain by using batch files. The chapter discusses the differences between OS/2 and DOS batch files and lists the batch commands you can use. This chapter also describes how you can use batch commands to automate many tasks you must otherwise perform manually.

Part V: Advancing Your OS/2 Skills

OS/2 is more than just an operating system that controls a single computer. The system comes with several applications you can use to increase your work productivity immediately. You can connect your OS/2 computer to other computers to share and use information not found on your computer. Part V teaches you REXX programming, walks you through OS/2's productivity applets, and shows you how to access information on other computers.

Chapter 19, "Programming with REXX," extends your personal control over your computer by explaining how you can easily use the REXX programming language to implement your own computer programming solutions. You may become addicted to REXX; it's easier to use than the BASIC language.

Chapter 20, "Using OS/2 Utilities," provides you with information for using advanced OS/2 utility programs. These utilities help you customize, manage, and maneuver the operating system. Some of these utilities aid in gathering information; others help correct system problems.

Chapter 21, "Using the OS/2 Time-Management Applets," teaches you to use the personal information applets that come with OS/2. Specifically, you learn about the Activities List, the Alarms, the Calendar, the Daily and Monthly Planners, and the To-Do List applets.

Chapter 22, "Using the OS/2 General-Purpose Applets," introduces you to nine of the OS/2 applets that give you varied capabilities. These applets are the Calculator, the Clipboard Viewer, the Icon Editor, the Notepad, the Pulse, the Seek and Scan Files, the Sticky Pad, the Time, and the Tune Editor applets.

Chapter 23, "Using the OS/2 Data-Management Applets," shows you how to use four useful productivity applications. You learn how to manage information using Database, create charts with PM Chart, connect to other computers using a modem with PM Terminal, and create ledger sheets (including calculations) with Spreadsheet.

Chapter 24, "Understanding OS/2 Communications and Database Tools," introduces you to the powerful capability of accessing information on larger mainframe computers. You learn to connect to these computers by using the Communications Manager and to access database information with the Database Manager.

Chapter 25, "Networking OS/2 with NetWare," describes how to use OS/2 on a local area network based on Novell's popular NetWare network operating system.

Chapter 26, "Connecting OS/2 to Other LANs," provides you with an understanding of how you can use OS/2 with other network operating systems such as IBM LAN Server, Microsoft LAN Manager, Artisoft LANtastic, Novell NetWare Lite, and Novell Personal NetWare. Also mentioned in this chapter are POWERLan and Banyan VINES networks.

Part VI: Using the Command Reference

Part VI is a comprehensive Command Reference you can use to look up specific OS/2 commands. OS/2 has three categories of commands: commands you give at a command-line prompt, commands you put into batch files, and commands you use to configure the system. Part VI groups the OS/2 commands by category and lists them alphabetically within each group. You also find an alphabetical listing of all the commands on the inside back cover of this book; a Workplace Shell quick-reference guide is on the inside front cover.

Each reference entry describes the command in detail and shows its exact syntax. (*Syntax* means the precise form that the wording of a command must be given so that the computer can recognize and process the command correctly.) You find practical examples of each command in Part VI, along with notes that tell you when to use the command, cautions you should observe, and advice on how best to use the command. Each entry prominently identifies the command as belonging to OS/2, DOS, or both environments.

Appendixes

The appendixes provide less frequently needed but still essential information about OS/2. You get the "Past, Present, and Future of OS/2," two keyboard guides, information about games that come with OS/2, a listing of OS/2 files by function, a compendium of bulletin boards and information services that offer information about OS/2, and a fun look at how OS/2 does sound and pictures through multimedia.

Conventions Used in This Book

To make the information as clear as possible, this book follows certain conventions. Filenames and OS/2 commands appear in capital letters, for example (although you can type them in either capital or lowercase letters).

When a keyboard key has a special name, such as PgUp or F1, the name appears exactly that way in the text. When you are instructed to choose a menu command, the shortcut key is in **boldface** (for example, **F**ile).

Words or phrases defined for the first time appear in *italics*. Words or phrases you are to type appear in **boldface** or indented on a separate line. All on-screen messages use a `special typeface`.

To understand an OS/2 command fully, you need to know what to type verbatim from the book (fixed, constant words and phrases) and what to type based on your knowledge of what you intend the command to accomplish (variable, fill-in words and phrases). This book shows commands in the following manner (called the command *syntax*):

CHKDSK filename.ext */switches*

In this example, the variable, fill-in items (**filename.ext**) appear in boldface, the command itself (**CHKDSK**) appears in bold uppercase letters, and the optional switch appears in italics. To use the CHKDSK command, you type **CHKDSK** and follow it with information you supply, such as the name of a file or so-called command switches to tell CHKDSK exactly what you want it to do. Not all parts of a syntax entry are essential; optional elements appear in italics. Programming code is shown in `monospace`, as is programming statements such as the REXX statement `IF..THEN...ELSE`.

The new world of OS/2 2.1 awaits you. To get started, just turn the page.

Part I
Introducing OS/2

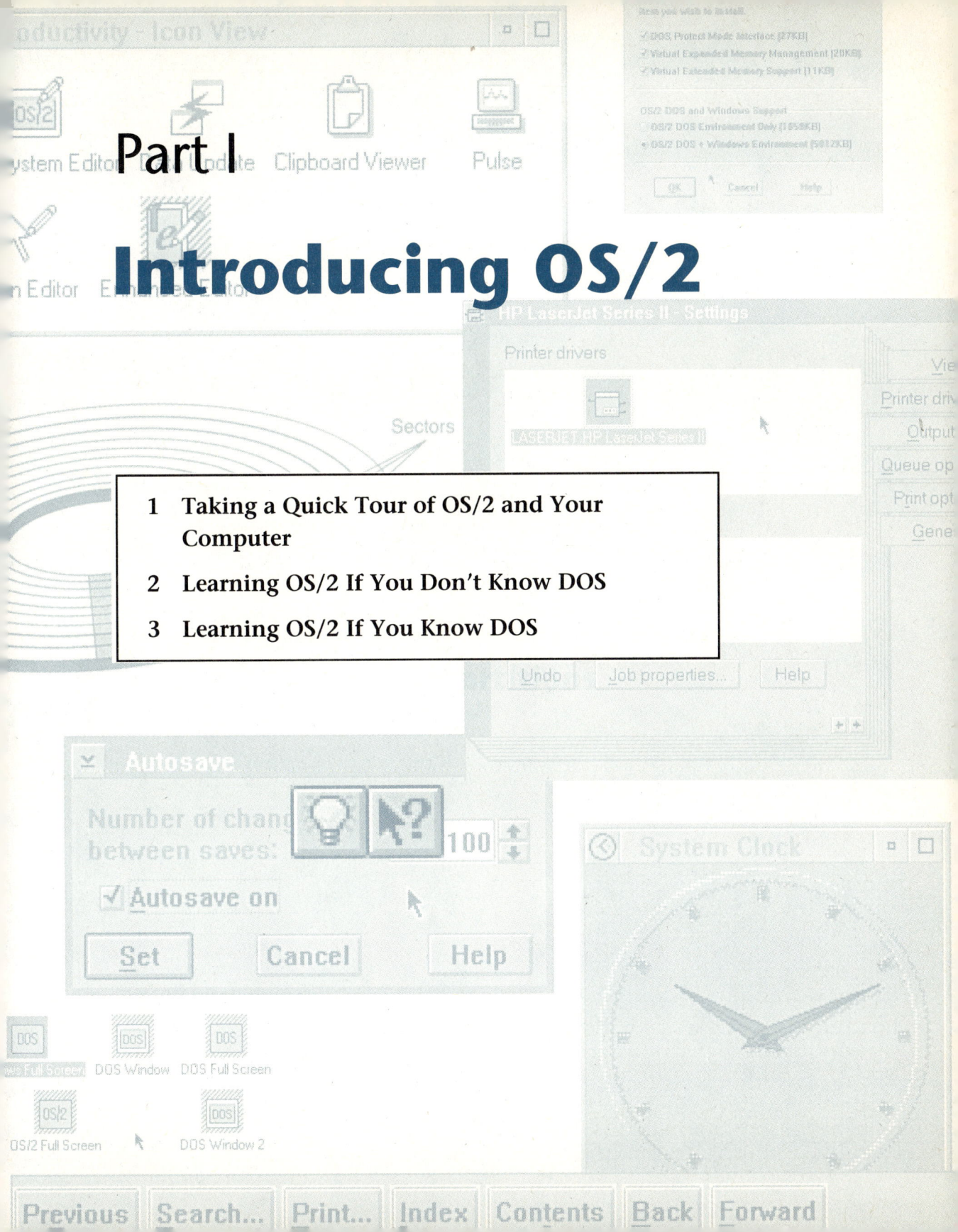

1 Taking a Quick Tour of OS/2 and Your Computer
2 Learning OS/2 If You Don't Know DOS
3 Learning OS/2 If You Know DOS

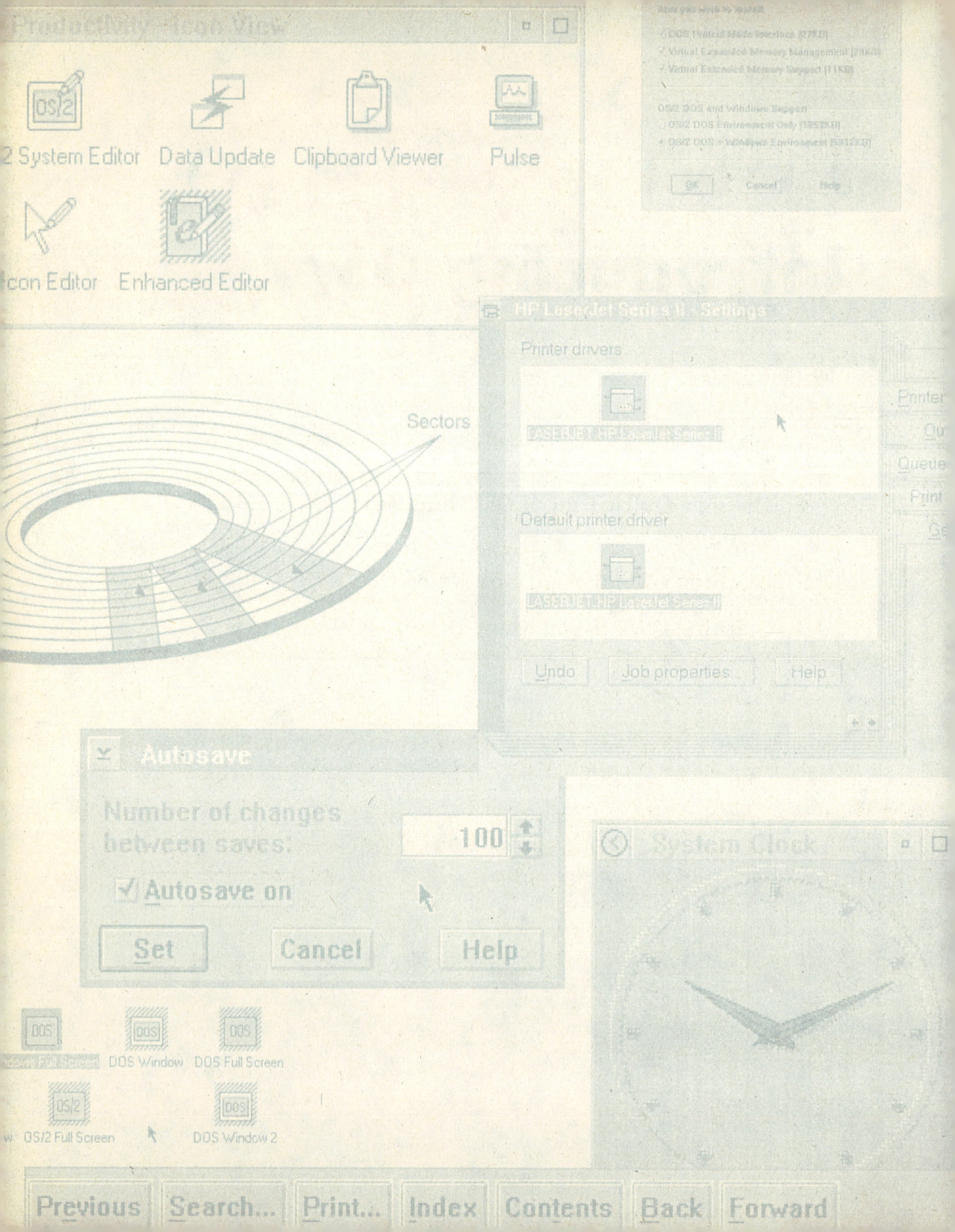

Chapter 1
Taking a Quick Tour of OS/2 and Your Computer

In the office today, personal computers are as common as telephones, fax machines, and copy machines. You can now begin to treat a personal computer just about the same way you treat your automobile. You start it up, navigate your way to your destination, and shut it off when you are done. Of course, a computer can do quite a bit more than a car. A computer is a multipurpose tool, with each application helping you to do a different kind of job.

You take for granted that cars have steering wheels, brake pedals, turn signals, and speedometers, usually located in the same place in all cars. Until OS/2 came along, personal computers didn't have this sort of consistency. The keyboard may have looked the same, but the information presented to you on-screen was nearly always different for each job you wanted to do. You had to learn how to use a spreadsheet application all over again or start learning over again how to use a word processor. If you needed to use a communications program, you had to return to square one.

OS/2 Presentation Manager brings consistency to your personal computer. Figuratively speaking, when you learn where the steering wheel, brake pedal, turn signals, and speedometer are located for one type of OS/2 application, you learn them for all OS/2 applications. OS/2 Presentation Manager's interface is easy to learn; Part III of this book, "Using OS/2's Graphical Interface," helps you become an expert.

Examining Presentation Manager

New versions of computer applications do not appear overnight, so there will be a transition period while non-Presentation Manager (inconsistent-interface) applications co-exist on your computer with the newer, consistent-interface PM applications. (You will often see the abbreviation PM for Presentation Manager in this book and in other OS/2-related documentation.) OS/2 2.1 supports these non-PM applications at the same time it supports PM applications. In fact, OS/2 2.1 enables you to run several kinds of applications at the same time, on the same personal computer.

PM is a part of OS/2. Along with a set of standards and guidelines that IBM developed called *System Applications Architecture (SAA)*, PM is the foundation for the kind of consistent interface in your personal computer that you expect from the car you drive. For you, the computer user, PM is the most important part of the operating system. OS/2 has other features in addition to PM, however.

If you have used Microsoft Windows before, you have experienced the *Common User Access (CUA)* interface, which complies with SAA. PM and Windows look very much alike, and you manipulate them in much the same ways. Versions 3.0 and 3.1 of Windows have been around for well over a year, which means that software companies have had time to develop several applications for Windows. OS/2 supports Windows applications as well as PM applications.

During the transition period mentioned earlier, you still need to run non-PM, non-Windows applications. These software tools are the ones you would have run under plain DOS. For a while, you may even find that the majority of the applications you use are DOS applications. OS/2 supports these applications the same way DOS does, but OS/2 gives DOS applications more memory in which to run than DOS does. This feature is why you will want to use OS/2 2.1 now, even if you don't have any PM applications yet.

For Related Information
- "Understanding CUA Principles," p. 230
- "Introducing Presentation Manager," p. 234

In this chapter, you take a guided tour of OS/2 2.1 and your computer. If you have used a computer before, some of the material may be familiar to you. If so, skim through the hardware descriptions until you get to the section on software, where the discussion turns to OS/2.

You don't have to turn your computer on to take the tour; you can see the sights just by studying the illustrations.

Understanding Hardware and Software

Hardware is easy to define. If you can touch it, it's hardware. Software is trickier; it exists as magnetic recordings on disks or other media. Like an audio recording on a cassette tape that you play back with your tape deck, or a video recording on a videocassette that you play back with your VCR, software comes alive when you "play it back" with your personal computer.

> **Caution**
>
> Software is subject to accidental erasure, just like other types of magnetic recordings.

Unlike these recordings, however, software is interactive—you give information to the software application, tell the software to store the information for later use, and instruct the software to collate, process, select, calculate, and print the information. With the computer hardware and software, you can do your work more quickly and accurately than you could by hand.

Examining Hardware Components

Figure 1.1 shows the hardware components of a typical computer system. The computer in the illustration may be a little different from yours, but you can easily spot the essential components (the keyboard, the monitor, and the system unit) and relate them to your own computer's appearance. With many computer systems sold today, the mouse also has become an essential component.

Using the Keyboard, Mouse, and Monitor. The keyboard and the mouse enable you to enter information into the computer and tell the computer what to do with that information. The monitor (the screen display) shows the results.

Using the Keyboard. Figure 1.2 shows the common 101-key IBM keyboard, sometimes called the Enhanced Keyboard. The original IBM AT computer came with an 83-key keyboard that had the function keys on the left of the keyboard instead of at the top. For several years, however, IBM and makers of compatible keyboards have offered the 101-key keyboard as standard equipment for desktop computers. Laptop computers use a smaller keyboard with fewer keys, which means that you sometimes have to press two keys together to get the effect of a single key on the larger keyboard. The principles are the

16 Chapter 1—Taking a Quick Tour of OS/2 and Your Computer

same for all keyboards, however. You use the center section just like a typewriter. The numeric keypad has two modes, which can be switched with the Num Lock key. The keypad behaves like the buttons on an adding machine when Num Lock is on, and like cursor control keys when Num Lock is off.

Fig. 1.1
Typical computer hardware components.

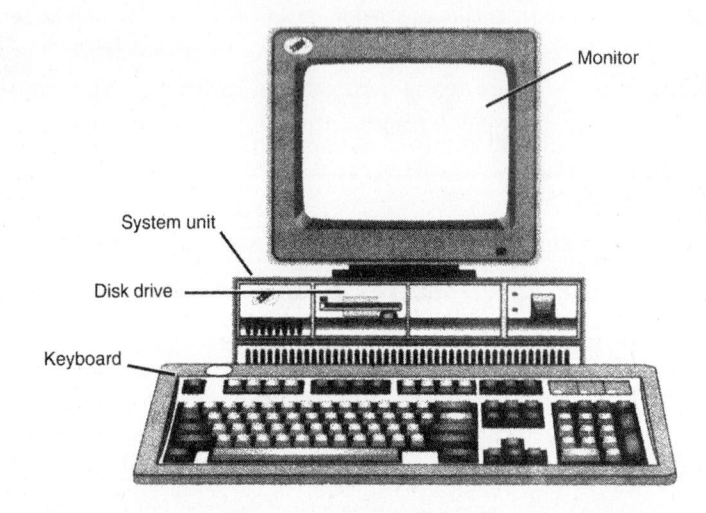

Fig. 1.2
The popular 101-key IBM keyboard.

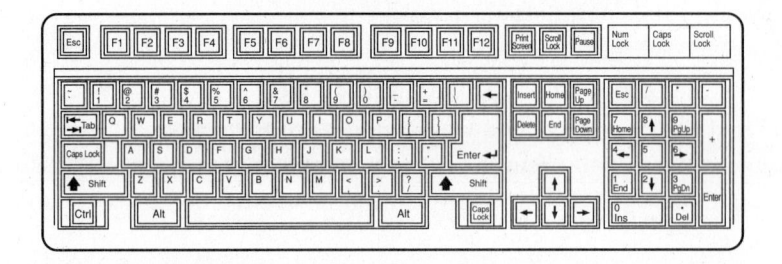

Besides those keys in the typewriter and adding machine sections, special computer keys tell the computer what actions you want it to take. For example, you often use the PgUp and PgDn (page up and page down) keys to tell the computer to show you the previous or the next screen. If the application software has no previous or next screen to show you, the PgUp and PgDn keys do nothing.

PgUp and PgDn are not difficult to decipher, but what about the keys labeled F1 through F12? Or the Home and End keys? The Ins and Del keys? Table 1.1 lists these keys and their (usual) meanings.

Table 1.1 Special Keys on the Computer Keyboard

Key	Usual Meaning
Enter	Tells the computer to perform the command you have typed, presses the highlighted button on-screen, or ends a line of text that you have entered into a word processor (similar to the function of the carriage return key on the electric typewriter).
Cursor Keys	The up-, down-, left-, and right-arrow keys move the text cursor on-screen, but do not move the mouse cursor (the section on computer screens explains cursors).
PgUp/PgDn	Shows the previous screen or the next screen.
Home/End	Moves the cursor in one big jump to the left side of the screen or to the right.
Backspace	Moves the cursor to the left one character and deletes that character.
Ins/Del	Inserts characters at the current text cursor location, or deletes characters.
Ctrl	A modifier key, like Shift, Control changes the meaning of another key pressed in combination with Ctrl.
Alt	Another modifier key; also used to activate menus in Presentation Manager applications.
Esc	Escapes from (abandons) the current operation and returns to a prior level.
Num Lock	Toggles the numeric keypad from adding-machine mode to cursor-control mode.
PrtSc	In non-PM applications, sends the current screen to the printer. Sometimes labelled Print Screen.
Scroll Lock	Tells the cursor control arrows to scroll the on-screen information instead of just moving the cursor.
Pause	Suspends display output until another key is pressed; the 83-key keyboard assigns this function to Ctrl-Scroll Lock.
Ctrl-Break	Stops the currently running program.
F1-F12	Function keys whose meaning depends on the currently running application. The 83-key keyboard lacks the last two function keys, F11 and F12.

Using the Mouse. Figure 1.3 shows two of the many types of mice available to PC users. A computer mouse is a pointing device. Some mice are optical, some are mechanical; some have one button (the Macintosh mouse); others have two or three buttons. Some kinds of pointing devices are called trackballs. Basically, all pointing devices enable you to move the cursor on-screen and click (or hold) buttons to manipulate items shown on-screen. To interact with many of the items shown on your computer screen, you roll the mouse on your desk or table, or you roll the ball in a trackball. Mice are generally optional. Except for applications that allow you to draw pictures on-screen, for example, most software products and Presentation Manager applications recognize certain keystroke combinations as equivalent to the common, standard mouse operations.

Fig. 1.3
The two-button mouse and the trackball are two types of mice available to PC users.

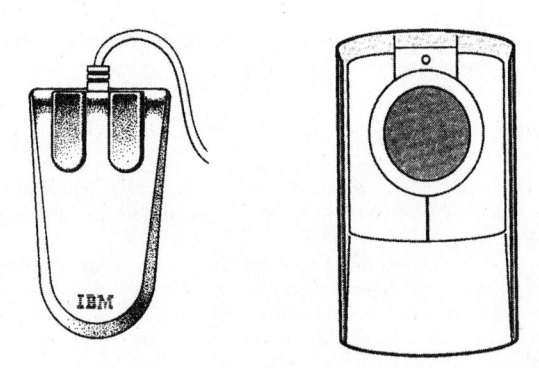

Using the Monitor. Your computer monitor, sometimes called the screen display, shows your work. More accurately and specifically, the screen shows the computer's response to your work. Many times, the screen also shows you options from which you can choose. Because the screen can sometimes look cluttered, you may find it difficult to understand what the screen is telling you. Later in this book, you learn to recognize the on-screen landmarks by which you can navigate.

What you see on the computer screen is placed there by OS/2, or Presentation Manager, or your application software, or a combination of all three. The distinction is important because when you want to look something up, you need to know whether to refer to this book (for OS/2 and PM), or to the manuals that came with your application. Chapter 10, "Managing the Workplace Shell," tells how to distinguish between on-screen elements.

Figure 1.4 shows OS/2's Workplace Shell on a computer screen. This example may differ from the appearance of the Shell on your own screen. OS/2 offers many ways for you to customize the Workplace Shell to suit your personal preferences.

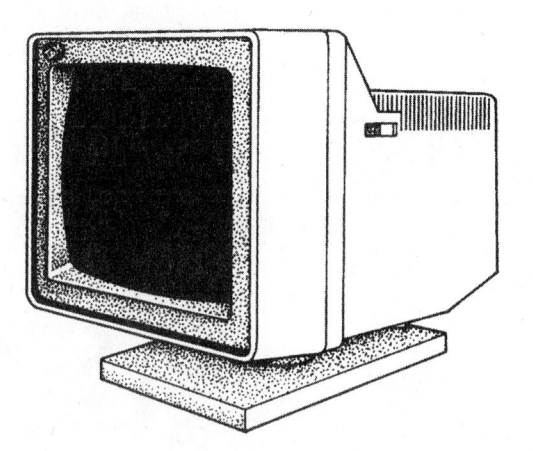

Fig. 1.4
A typical computer monitor.

Most computer screens have two *modes*: text and graphics. In graphics mode, the mouse cursor typically is an arrow pointing to the left and upward, although the mouse cursor sometimes turns into a picture of a clock or perhaps an I-beam. You see *icons* (small pictures) that represent applications and other OS/2 tasks. A thin, blinking underline (sometimes a solid one-character-wide block) is the *text cursor*.

Text mode also shows the text cursor as a thin blinking underline or as a solid block. The mouse cursor in this mode, however, is optional and appears as a solid block (if you move the mouse, the mouse cursor moves). The software application determines whether the text mode mouse cursor shows. The text mode screen is 80 columns wide, usually 25 lines high, and takes up the entire display.

OS/2 supports both modes, text and graphics, and can even display a text mode screen inside a graphics window. A *window* is a subsection of the display. A window has a rectangular border and functions almost like an entire screen, with the added benefit that you can move and resize the window to suit your own preferences.

Understanding Disks, Disk Files, and Disk Directories. The data you enter, the results, and the applications themselves reside on disks, either *floppy disks* (removable) or hard disks (nonremovable). Figure 1.5 shows the two types of floppy disks, 5 1/4-inch and 3 1/2-inch. The *hard disk* is a sealed unit, usually hidden inside your computer, although some hard disks are removable. When you turn the power off or if you suffer a power failure, the data you have stored on a hard disk remains on that disk for future use. If you have entered data into the computer but not yet saved the data on disk at the time the power fails, the data is lost and you have to reenter it later.

Fig. 1.5
The 3 1/2-inch and 5 1/4-inch floppy disks.

Using Disks. Floppy disks are sometimes called floppies or microfloppy disks. Hard disks are sometimes called fixed disks. Hard disks rotate whenever the computer is on; floppy disks rotate only when they are being accessed. In either case, a red (or perhaps orange) light on the front of your computer indicates when the disks are in use. The light on the disk drive indicates when the drive is busy; the light on the main computer indicates when the hard disk is busy. When one of these lights comes on, the computer is reading or writing data.

> **Caution**
>
> Do not remove a floppy disk from the disk drive when the disk drive light is on. You may damage the data on the floppy disk because OS/2 must also make a record of where the data can be found. Imagine adding a book to a library's collection but not making an entry in the card catalog. When you need the book (or your data) later, you cannot locate it.

Using Disk Files. To put the application software and data on disks, you copy files or you instruct an application to store (or save) your data into a file. A *file* is a single stream of data that you refer to by name; it is a named collection of information. One file might contain a single memo, letter, or spreadsheet. Figure 1.6 shows the magnetic tracks and sectors on the disk that store saved files. If you are familiar with audio cassette tapes that have songs on both sides, think of a file as one song; the number of songs the tape can hold depends on the length of the songs and the space of the tape. Like cassette tapes, disks have varying capacities.

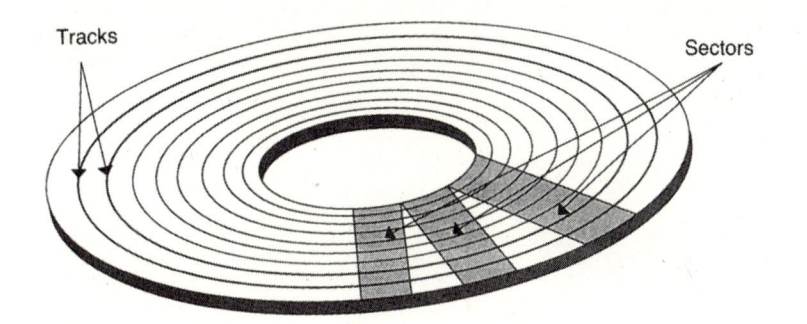

Fig. 1.6
The magnetic tracks and sectors on the disk that store saved files.

5 1/4-inch disks come in 360K (kilobyte) and 1.2M (megabyte) capacities. 3 1/2-inch disks come in 720K, 1.44M, and the relatively new 2.8M capacities. A *kilobyte* is equal to 1,024 characters; a megabyte is equal to 1,024 kilobytes. How many files can you put on a 40M hard disk? How much room do you have left on your hard disk? OS/2 provides tools you can use to monitor disk usage. Also, make sure that you use disks of the proper size and capacity in your computer. Check your computer manual to find out the specifications of your disk drive(s).

Using Disk Directories. Speaking of capacities, how do you organize files if you have hundreds (or thousands) of them? Chapter 2, "Learning OS/2 If You Don't Know DOS," explains *disk directories* in detail. Basically, you use directories to organize a disk into an outline structure. A directory can contain other directories as well as files. The structure of the directories (the outline) is up to you, so plan your organization thoughtfully. Directories are a wonderful convenience but can sometimes cause confusion. OS/2 provides tools for finding misplaced files.

Using Printers. Printers seem simple—blank paper goes in one side and the printed result comes out the other side. Printers are almost as complicated internally as the computer to which you connect them, however. A laser printer, for example, works much like a photocopy machine and contains a variety of fonts (typefaces) you can use to make your printouts look their best. Figure 1.7 shows a typical laser printer connected to its computer. Dot-matrix printers, which work by striking an inked ribbon with tiny pins, are also common.

Fig. 1.7
A typical laser printer connected to its computer.

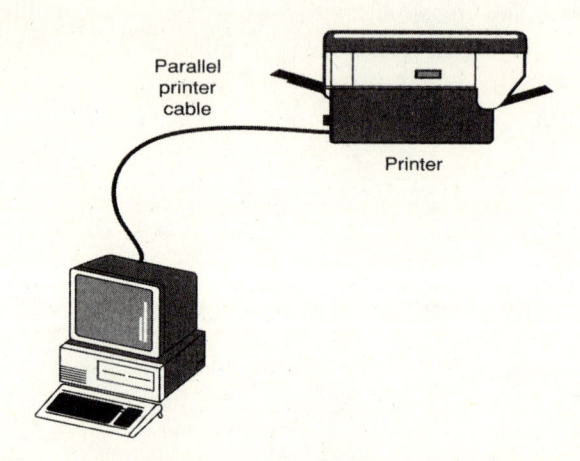

Laser, dot-matrix, and other types of printers connect to your computer through a serial interface (requiring a serial cable), a parallel interface (requiring a parallel cable), or perhaps through a local area network (LAN) cable. In this last case, several people share the same printer. Each type of interface has a device name and number. Serial cables connect to COM1, COM2, COM3, or COM4 (your computer may not have all four of these devices). Parallel cables connect to LPT1, LPT2, or LPT3. When you tell an application to print something, you specify the device name and number for your printer. On a network, for example, you still print to LPT1, but the LAN redirects your print material to the shared printer. The parallel interface is the most common type.

The care and feeding of a printer requires some work on your part. You need to buy the correct size and weight paper for your printer. You need to regularly change the ribbon or toner cartridge, and you need to clean the printer periodically. You also may need to purchase fonts and memory cards (printed circuit boards). Study the owner's manual to learn the sophisticated things your printer can do.

Using Fonts. Several companies sell add-in fonts for laser printers. These fonts come as cartridges you insert into the printer, or as disk files. You store the fonts on the disk files in your computer and download the contents into the printer. If you need numerous fonts, you may have to buy extra memory for your printer—each font is a different size and takes up space inside the printer. In general, whether the font is built into the printer, on a cartridge, or downloaded, you select fonts with instructions you give your application software.

Learning More About Printing Text and Graphics. The following table lists some other characteristics of printers you should know about. Check your printer manual to see whether your printer supports or uses any of the features described in the table.

Feature	Function
Graphics	Makes charts, pictures, digitized photographs, and other images.
Landscape	Sometimes called sideways printing, prints the page with the long edge at the bottom, instead of upright.
Duplexing	Prints on both sides of the page.
Postscript	A special language of page layout and drawing commands, developed by Adobe Systems, Inc.
PCL	Another printer control language. PCL is used mainly in Hewlett-Packard printers.

So far in this chapter, you have absorbed a considerable amount of information about your computer hardware. Your understanding of the computer as a useful tool is growing by leaps and bounds. Next, the tour of your computer and OS/2 turns to the topic of software.

Understanding Software Components

As mentioned earlier, software is more intangible than hardware, but you cannot use your computer system without it. (Some people colorfully describe a computer without software as a big, expensive paperweight.) Software exists as disk files, and sophisticated software products comprise many disk files—sometimes several disks' worth. Some of the disk files that make up a software product contain computer programs which give the computer instructions on what to place on-screen, what data to accept, and how to process the data. Other files contain information that the computer programs need to refer to when you interact with the programs and process your data.

You usually install software on your system by running a special computer program that copies the product's disk files to your hard disk. Simple software products may just ask you to use OS/2 commands to copy the disk files, however. These commands are explained later in this book.

Running a computer program is easy. If you (or the installation program) added a program to the Workplace Shell desktop, you double-click the program's icon with your mouse. If you are using the keyboard rather than the mouse, you use the cursor control keys to highlight the item and press Enter. If you have not added the program item to the Workplace Shell desktop, you run the program by typing its name at a command-line prompt. (More on Workplace Shell and command-line prompts in a moment.)

OS/2 is a type of software product known as an operating system. Utilities and applications are the other two types of software.

Learning Operating Systems. An *operating system* is the first software to run on your computer when you turn it on. An operating system loads itself into your computer "by its bootstraps" (hence the term "booting" to describe the power-on sequence). An operating system can display a set of icons from which you can choose applications or utilities that you want to run, or the system can display a command-line prompt (such as C:\>) and await your commands. OS/2 provides both icons and command-line prompts.

Any operating system, OS/2 included, provides services to utilities and applications while they run. The best example is file access. When a computer program needs the contents of a particular disk file, it asks OS/2 to open the file, read the data, and close the file. The computer program does not need to know where on the disk the file is physically located; OS/2 manages the disk at that level of detail.

OS/2 is full-featured; it provides an easy-to-use *graphical user interface*, command-line prompts, and a rich set of services to utility and application software as well as some utilities and small applications. You sometimes see the latter identified as *applets*.

Examining Presentation Manager and the Workplace Shell. Presentation Manager is the component of OS/2 that manages the computer display and provides screen-related services to utilities and applications. The Workplace Shell uses PM to enable you to select icons to run programs.

Figure 1.8 shows a Workplace Shell screen. Notice the icons at the top of the screen; they represent OS/2 programs and folders. The DOS Window is active and appears in the middle of the screen. If you use either the mouse or the keyboard to select one of the icons, the Workplace Shell uses OS/2's internal services to run the computer program represented by that menu item. In fact, figure 1.8 shows the result of choosing DOS Window.

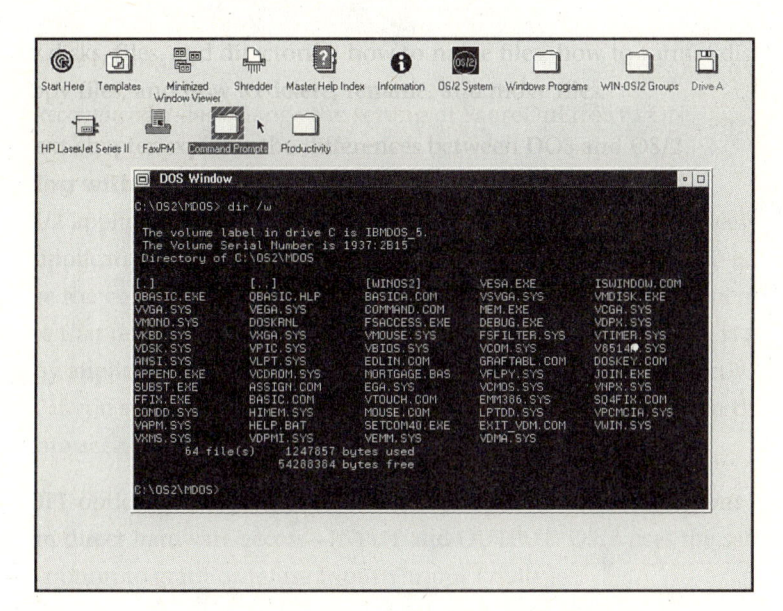

Fig. 1.8
A Presentation Manager screen, showing the Workplace Shell, several icons, and an active DOS session.

Using DOS and OS/2 Sessions. Figure 1.9 goes beyond the previous screen in several ways. First, two DOS Windows have been started and appear on-screen. One of them contains Lotus 1-2-3, and the other shows a C:\> prompt. The desktop icons remain on-screen in the background.

When you tell the Workplace Shell to open a DOS Window, OS/2 creates a Virtual DOS Machine (VDM) in your computer and shows the new DOS session to you in a window on your computer screen. You can do anything inside this window that you could have done with DOS 5.0 before OS/2 2.1. In addition, you have the following features, which DOS did not support:

- You can open multiple DOS Windows on-screen at the same time.
- You can copy and paste from one screen to another.
- You can run graphics-mode programs inside the window.

26   Chapter 1—Taking a Quick Tour of OS/2 and Your Computer

- You get considerably more memory for your programs in DOS sessions.
- You can choose the font in which text appears in the window (this also determines the size of the window on-screen).
- You can run different versions of DOS in different windows.

Fig. 1.9

Two DOS Windows open simultaneously under OS/2 2.1.

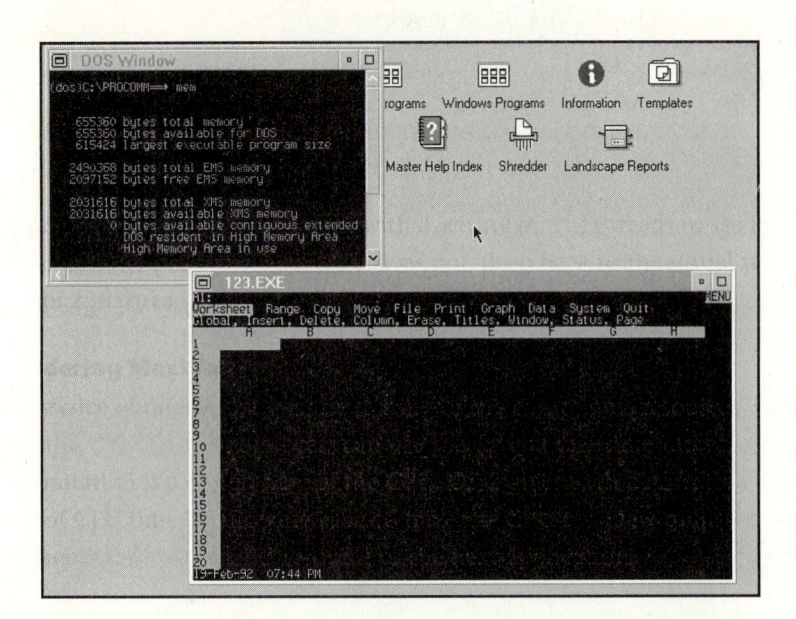

When you choose DOS Full Screen on the Main group menu, OS/2 creates a new VDM for you. Rather than putting the DOS session in a window, however, OS/2 gives the session the entire screen with which to work. You might choose DOS Full Screen for applications that do on-screen graphics so that they work a bit faster, or you might prefer to have the entire screen dedicated to a particular application.

You also can choose OS/2 Window and OS/2 Full Screen from the Command Prompts folder, which appears when you double-click the OS/2 System icon. These selections also create special sessions inside your computer system, but the sessions are not VDMs and they are not running DOS. These sessions are for the OS/2 applications you run. You might run Microsoft Word in an OS/2 Window, for example, while you are running Borland's Paradox in a DOS Window. And yes, you can perform copy-and-paste operations between DOS and OS/2 Windows.

Figure 1.10 shows a Microsoft Windows application, Word for Windows, running under Microsoft Windows, which is running under OS/2. You probably will run Microsoft Windows full-screen to enhance performance, but the figure illustrates that OS/2 is capable of running Windows on the OS/2 desktop. Microsoft Windows becomes just another DOS task for OS/2 to manage.

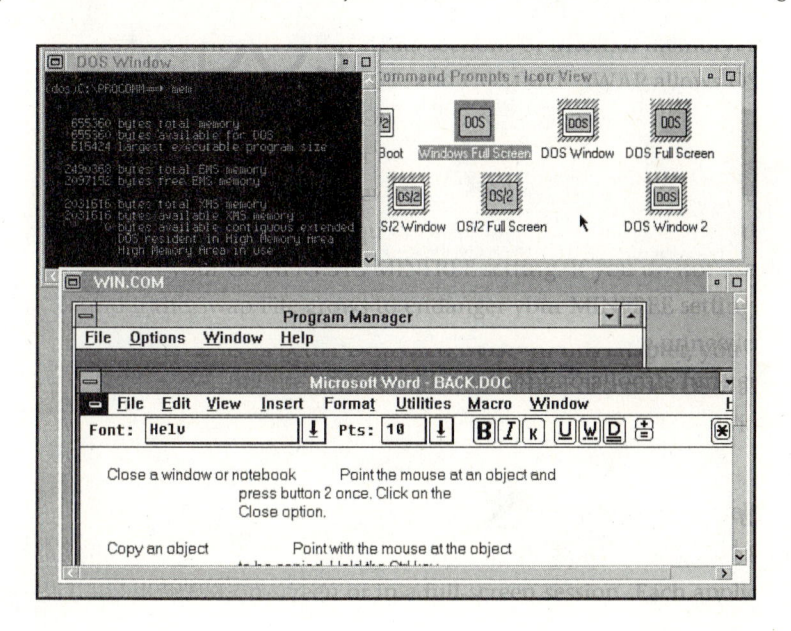

Fig. 1.10
Word for Windows running under Microsoft Windows, which in turn is running under OS/2.

Learning Utility Programs. OS/2 includes several utility programs to make your life easier. Figure 1.11 shows the OS/2 Enhanced Editor (a text editor for changing the contents of text files) in the upper right window of the screen. The folder at the top of that window is Productivity, from which the Enhanced Editor was started, and you can see that the editor's icon is highlighted to show that it is in use. Chapter 14, "Using the OS/2 Text Editors," discusses the Enhanced Editor and the System Editor.

Examining the Drives Object. The screen in figure 1.11 is busy-looking. A few clicks of the mouse closes some of those windows, and a double-click on the Drives icon in the OS/2 System folder brings up the OS/2 Drives object. Clicking the Drive D icon gives you a screen similar to the one shown in figure 1.12.

Fig. 1.11
The OS/2
Enhanced Editor.

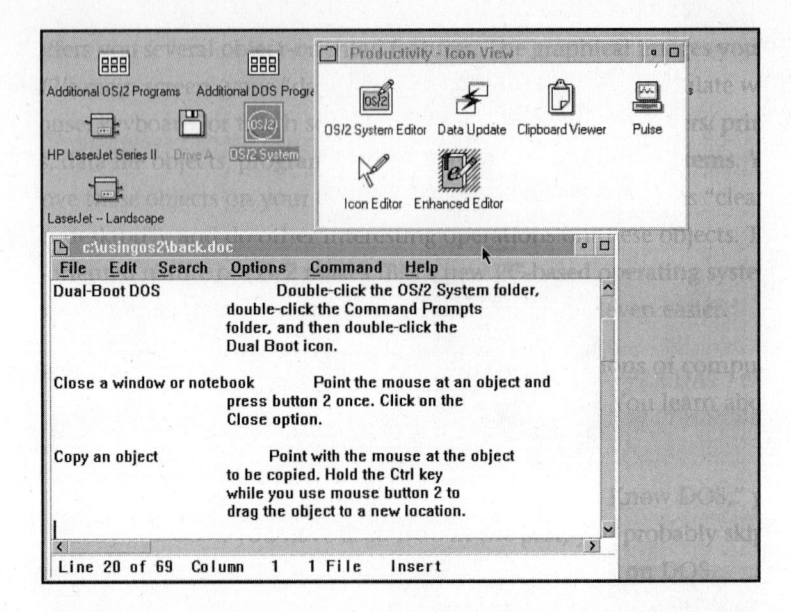

Fig. 1.12
Using the OS/2 2.1
Drives Object to
examine Drive D.

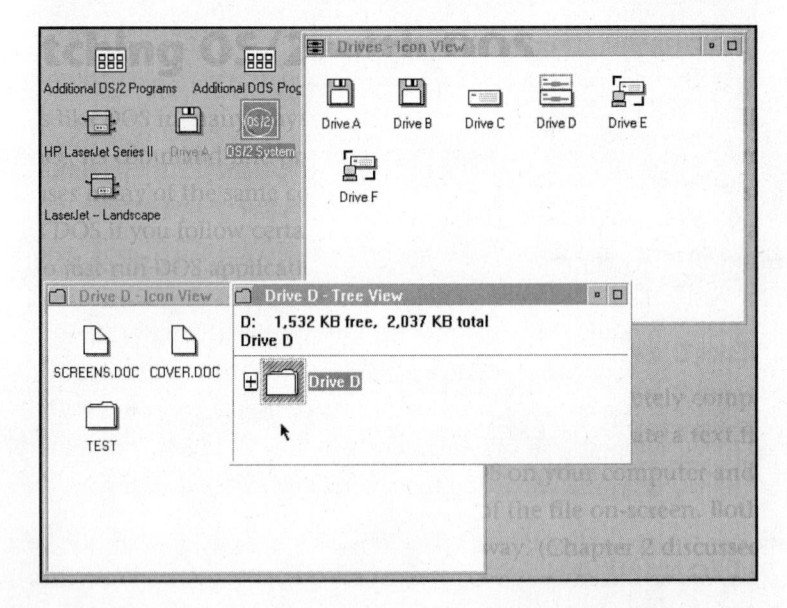

As mentioned earlier in this chapter, disk directories are a method of organizing your files into an outline structure. The Drive object shows the tree structure of your directories in graphic detail. Files can be shown by name or represented as icons (refer to fig. 1.12). You can use the Drives object to create or remove directories as well as to copy files from one disk to another.

Learning the System Setup Utility. Figure 1.13 shows the result of closing the Drive D window and then starting the System Setup utility in the OS/2 System folder. System Setup is your tool for changing many of your OS/2 configuration options. You can adjust the cursor blink rate and the mouse double-click rate here (not everyone presses the mouse buttons in exactly the same way). You also can use System Setup to install fonts (recall the discussion of downloadable printer fonts earlier in this chapter) or to tell OS/2 you added a printer to your system.

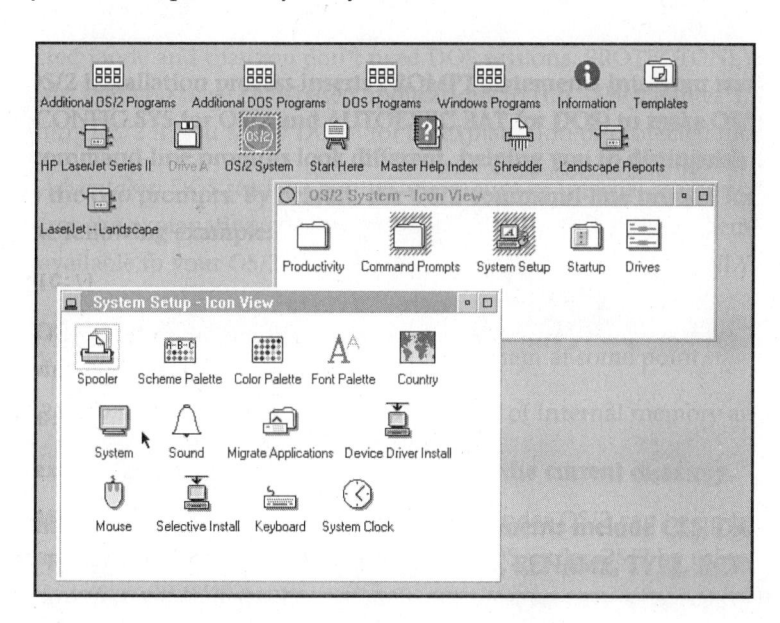

Fig. 1.13
The OS/2 2.1 System Setup utility.

Using the Printer Object. If you can run multiple applications at the same time under OS/2, what happens if all those applications try to use the printer at once? The Printer object solves this problem by putting each printout (a print job, in Printer object terms) into a queue and printing each assignment one after the other. In figure 1.14, the Printer object window, in the lower half of the screen, shows the print queues and any pending print jobs. The details for one print job appear across the window. Chapter 15, "Printing with OS/2," gives you the information you need to use Printer objects effectively.

Fig. 1.14
Using the OS/2 2.1 Printer Object.

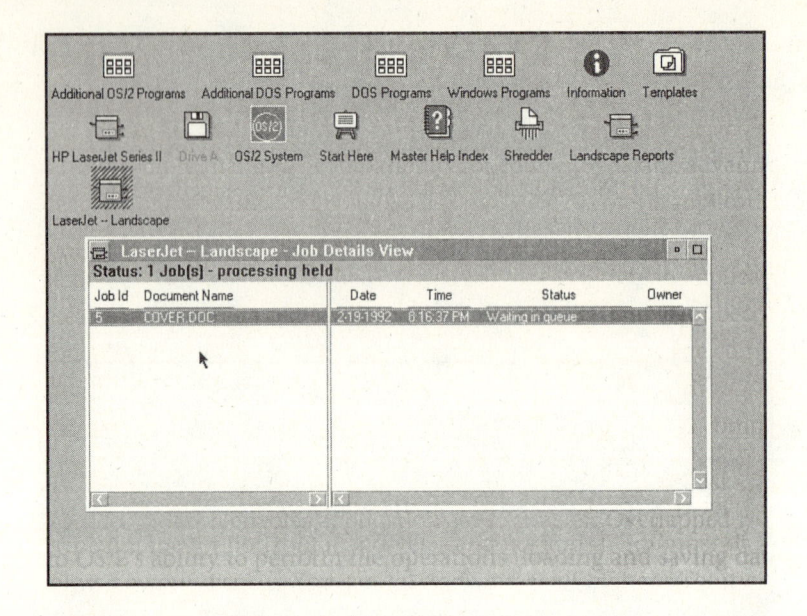

Using the Help Facility. OS/2 has basically two types of on-line help. At a command-line prompt, you can type **HELP command name** to get a brief display of information about a particular command (but you will not get help if you type **HELP ME**). You access the other type of help by choosing the Master Help Index or Information icons on the desktop. Figure 1.15 shows a screen of information you can obtain from the OS/2 Command Reference, which is inside the Information folder. Notice that the mouse cursor points to a highlighted box (containing OS/2*) on-screen. The box is a hot link; clicking it provides more information on the highlighted subject. Chapter 13, "Using the Built-In Help Facility," discusses OS/2's on-line help, including concepts such as hot links.

Learning the Workplace Shell. With its consistent, graphics-based user interface, Presentation Manager makes your computer much easier to use than DOS did. OS/2 goes a step beyond PM, though, by offering the Workplace Shell. The Workplace Shell carries the desktop metaphor farther than PM, enabling you to organize your documents, reports, memos, spreadsheets, charts, lists, and tables as objects that you file in folders. When you double-click a folder, you see the folder open on-screen. If you click a memo in the folder, for example, OS/2 runs whatever application you use to edit your memos, and your memo appears on-screen, ready for editing. If you want to print your memo, you can use the mouse to drag the memo object to a picture of a printer on-screen. When you drop the memo onto the printer icon, OS/2 prints the memo. Chapter 10, "Managing the Workplace Shell," describes this object-oriented interface in more detail.

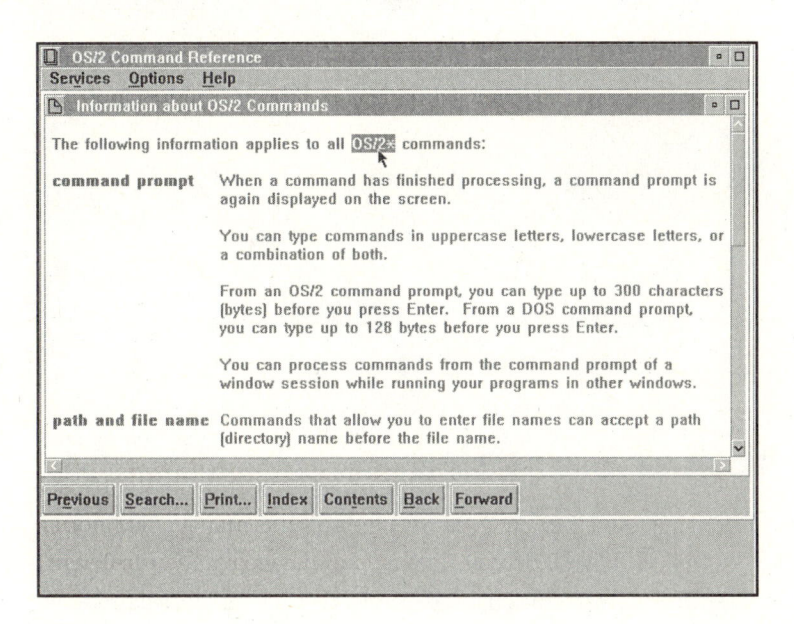

Fig. 1.15
The OS/2 Command Reference.

Examining Application Software. Your tour of OS/2 and your computer ends with a look at a popular personal computer application—1-2-3 for OS/2, from Lotus Development Corporation. Formerly called 1-2-3/G, this Presentation Manager application uses several features of OS/2 to transcend the limitations of earlier DOS-based versions of 1-2-3. In particular, you can create much larger worksheets with the OS/2 version of 1-2-3. Figure 1.16 shows what 1-2-3 for OS/2 looks like. Notice the CUA-compliant pull-down menu interface, the different fonts, and the other PM characteristics. Above the application's window, you see the normal Workplace Shell desktop icons.

For Related Information
- "Working with IBM-Compatible Computers," p. 104
- "Using The Workplace Shell," p. 231
- "Introducing Presentation Manager," p. 234
- "Working with Program Objects," p. 146

Fig. 1.16
A typical OS/2 application: Lotus 1-2-3 for OS/2.

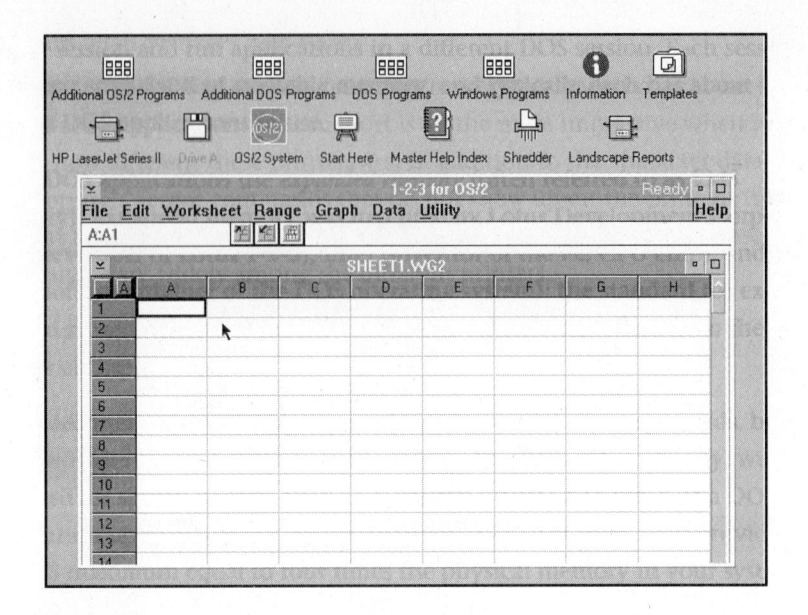

Chapter Summary

You have just ended your tour of OS/2 and your computer. Later chapters of this book go into detail to explain the features and operations of OS/2 2.1 that you saw briefly in this chapter. Your tour covered hardware such as the computer keyboard, mouse, and monitor. The chapter also covered software, including disks, files, and directories. Printers, printer fonts, and printer connections were briefly explained as well. Finally, the chapter introduced OS/2 basics, such as the definition of an operating system, Presentation Manager, Microsoft Windows, full-screen and windowed OS/2 sessions and DOS sessions, OS/2 utilities such as File Manager, Control Panel, Print Manager, and the Help facility, the Workplace Shell, and a typical OS/2 application software product.

OS/2 and DOS are somewhat alike. Especially at a command-line prompt, many OS/2 commands function much the same way as their DOS counterparts. If you have not used DOS before, however, you need to become familiar with it.

In Chapter 2, you learn about DOS—what it is, how to start it, and how to use it. If you already feel comfortable using DOS, you can move on to Chapter 3, which explains the differences between DOS and OS/2.

Chapter 2

Learning OS/2 If You Don't Know DOS

Chapter 1 was a whirlwind tour of OS/2 and your computer. If you have used DOS before, you should feel free to move on to Chapter 3, "Learning OS/2 If You Know DOS." If you're new to computers and want a little hand-holding to help you get your bearings, however, this chapter is for you.

The first thing you learn in this chapter is what makes up an operating system. Next, you learn how to start (and restart) your operating system. After you know how to get your computer system up and running, you find out why it's difficult for you to hurt the computer. You also learn how to prevent your work from being lost. You also learn techniques that make the computer a compliant and useful tool.

You then move on to practical topics, including how the operating system manages hard disks, hard disk partitions, and floppy disks. After exploring files, file names, and directories, you learn how to format disks and copy files.

Understanding Operating Systems

OS/2 is an operating system, like DOS, UNIX, and MVS. An operating system consists of one or more computer programs. These programs are the first software to run inside your computer when you turn it on, and they display a set of icons or a command-line prompt so that you can run applications (programs) and type commands. You saw some OS/2 icons illustrated in Chapter 1, "Taking a Quick Tour of OS/2 and Your Computer." A command-line prompt looks like the following:

```
C:\>
```

An application performs the work that you tell it to do. The application also uses the operating system to read and write information from and to disks, display information on-screen, find out what you are doing with the mouse, and obtain directions and information from you when you use the keyboard.

The following sections describe OS/2 and operating systems in general, but some operating systems don't have all the features discussed. DOS cannot support many new applications and cannot run more than one application at a time, for example.

Supporting Your Applications

When you choose a menu item or type the name of a computer program at a command-line prompt, the operating system starts the software (which might very well be an application you want to use). The computer program is a stream of recorded data that rotates on your disk. The stream of data has a name; you typed this name to tell the operating system what computer program to launch.

The operating system copies the computer program into internal memory from the disk and allows the program to have control of the computer. (Internal memory, which also records information like a disk does, is made of silicon chips and does not rotate; its recorded information disappears when the computer is turned off.) Every few thousandths of a second, the operating system regains control of the computer to see if other applications, previously preempted, want to have control of the computer. This round-robin scheduling of multiple computer programs is called *multitasking*.

Not only does the operating system decide which application controls the computer next, but it also offers services to those applications. If this seems contradictory, consider this example: your telephone can ring and interrupt you as you work, but at another time it can be used to make a phone call. An operating system that features preemptive multitasking is like a smart telephone—the system can call applications to wake them up (putting others on hold for a moment), and it can answer calls from applications that need its services.

Your applications use operating system services to perform the following functions:

- Open, read, write, and close files
- Create, remove, and use directories

- Use the computer's internal calendar and clock
- Display information on-screen
- Read the keyboard
- Send information to a printer
- Send and receive information to and from a modem
- Locate the mouse and detect which mouse buttons you have pressed

If the operating system did not provide these services to the applications, they would have to provide their own services. This situation would lead to inconsistency and perhaps incompatibility among the applications.

Supporting Your Work

An operating system supports you at the same time that it supports the applications you run. To manage your computer system, you must do several tasks. Most of these tasks cannot be handled by your applications. The most important of these tasks is making backup copies of your data. Other tasks you need to do include the following:

- Occasionally restoring your data from your backup copies
- Formatting disks
- Copying files that you need to share with others (or that others want to share with you)
- Editing system configuration text files
- Viewing system help files
- Removing old files and directories
- Customizing your computer system
- Finding misplaced files and directories
- Installing new applications
- Installing a new printer or new fonts

For Related Information
- "Understanding Application and General System Options," p. 88

An operating system may help you do these jobs by enabling you to choose icons on-screen and pick tasks from menus, or it may expect you to type commands. (OS/2 has all these kinds of interfaces). Step by step, this book helps you do all these tasks.

Starting the Operating System

You can start or restart the operating system in one of three ways: using the power switch, pressing the Ctrl-Alt-Del keys simultaneously (called a *warm boot*), or running a utility program called BOOT.COM.

Understanding the Power-On Sequence

When you apply power to your computer by turning on the power switch, the computer checks itself in a process known as the *Power-On Self Test* (POST). The POST makes sure that the CPU is okay; that the internal memory chips are in good health; and that the keyboard, mouse, hard disk, and other components are responding. After the computer system passes these tests, it checks your hard disk for an operating system to load and run.

The operating system ensures that it is the first software to run on your computer by inserting, at installation time, special computer instructions onto the *boot sector*, a special location of your hard disk. The computer instructions in the boot sector load the remainder of the operating system and give control to the just-loaded operating system. The operating system then displays a menu of available tasks or a command-line prompt at which you type commands.

If the computer is already running, you can reload the operating system from the keyboard or run a utility that reboots (restarts) the computer.

Before you reboot the computer, make sure that you save the information you're working on. Otherwise, you have to redo your work. Also, you might want to close and exit from all your applications before performing a reboot. Using the power switch to reboot the computer is a bad idea, as you see later in this section.

If you have installed OS/2's Boot Manager, you see an optional screen display at boot time. This screen allows you to choose which operating system you want to use next. You probably will not use Boot Manager, which is covered in detail in Chapter 7, "Modifying Your OS/2 Configuration." Boot Manager is intended for use on computers that have both OS/2 and UNIX.

Dual-Boot is another OS/2 option for starting your computer system with a different operating system. You can alternate between booting DOS and booting OS/2 with the Dual-Boot option. Chapter 16, "Running DOS and Windows under OS/2," discusses Dual-Boot in detail.

Don't worry about Boot Manager or Dual-Boot yet. You now know these options exist, and that is enough for now.

Stopping the Computer

Incidentally, OS/2 provides a menu option for shutting down (stopping) your computer system. You should form the habit of using the menu option before you turn off your computer. You learn more about OS/2's menu options in Chapter 10, "Managing the Workplace Shell." If you need to use this feature before you get to Chapter 10, however, the procedure is as follows: click the right mouse button on any vacant part of the Workplace Shell desktop. From the pop-up menu, choose the Shutdown option and wait for the message that tells you it is safe to turn the power off.

Restarting from the Keyboard

To reboot your computer system, simultaneously press the following three keys on the keyboard: Ctrl, Alt, and Del. Your computer system restarts.

If pressing these keys doesn't work the first time, try them again—you may have a sticky keyboard. After a few tries, however, you may discover that your computer has locked up. When that happens, you may want to reach for the power switch. Before you do, though, use this hint to tell whether the computer is responding to the keyboard: press the Caps Lock key (located above the numeric keypad on the enhanced keyboard). Check to see whether the green light on the keyboard labeled Caps Lock goes on or off. If pressing Caps Lock has no effect on the green light, your computer has locked up and you must use the power switch.

Restarting Using the Power Switch

Using the power switch is the most obvious way to restart your computer, but it is also the worst way for the following reasons:

- Any work you have in progress is not saved when you turn the power off.

- Even if you do not have any work in progress, the computer may not have finished storing (recording) the information on the surface of the disk.

Chapter 2—Learning OS/2 If You Don't Know DOS

- The electrical surges during power-on and power-off strain your computer; the hardware lasts longer if you infrequently use the power switch.

Use the system shutdown option mentioned earlier to ensure that the computer has finished storing information on the surface of the disk.

For Related Information
- "Using the Workplace Shell's System Menu," p. 260

Some experienced computer users would have you believe that understanding hard disks, floppy disks, files, directories, formatting, and copying is all you need to know about DOS or OS/2. This is not the whole truth. If you have watched an expert use a computer, you probably had the feeling that the person had more skills and knowledge than you would find in an encyclopedia of operating system commands and concepts. You were right, and you are about to acquire those skills and that knowledge in the following sections.

Hurting the Computer or Losing Your Work

The previous discussion on starting and stopping your computer system may have given you the idea that your computer system is fragile and that you should give up before you begin. Not so. You *do* need to observe some cautions when shutting down your system, but shutting down is an action you probably take only once a day. You can form good habits for doing it properly.

You cannot physically hurt your computer system with software or by giving wrong directions to your application software. The worst things that can happen are as follows:

Problem	Likely Cause(s)
Frozen system	The programmer made a mistake, or perhaps your computer needs repair.
Wrong results	The programmer made a mistake, or perhaps you entered the wrong data.
Acts funny	The programmer made a mistake, the keyboard/mouse/monitor connections are loose, or perhaps your computer needs repair.

You can see that the most common cause for computer error is programmer error (a *bug*). You learn to identify and solve computer system problems in more detail in Chapter 8, "Troubleshooting OS/2." In this chapter, however, the usual solutions to computer problems are to reenter the data, close and restart the application, or reboot the computer; which action you take depends on the nature of the problem.

Unfortunately, you can lose data. You might accidentally erase data, for example. You might save data and give it a name that is the same name you used for other data (thus replacing the old data with the new), or you might experience a computer failure and not have a copy of your work. In each case, the process of periodically and regularly making backup copies of your work would have saved you much grief.

Experimenting and Exploring

Power users is a term that describes computer experts. These people have two characteristics in common. They experiment and explore until they understand their computer systems thoroughly, and they use their computers a lot. You can do the same.

First, you need to set aside time to experiment with your computer. If you're naturally curious, you probaby tend to use spare moments to try out new techniques and methods. Encourage yourself to spend time with your computer.

Next, you need to find things to try, and you need to have data with which you can safely experiment. This book gives you many things to try; you can attempt these operations on data that you make up. In fact, you might want to set up "test cases" of data with which you can experiment. You may even want to have a disk directory titled TEST that contains files with pretend data on which you can try things out.

Knowing What Hurts the Computer

Compared with most electronic equipment, computers are fairly rugged—especially considering that computers contain mechanical parts such as rotating hard disks. You can find information in your computer's user manual on how to take care of your computer. In general, avoid moving your computer while it is on. Don't drop it. Don't spill things on it (particularly on the keyboard). If you plan to up-end your computer (relocating it from a horizontal desktop position to a desk-side, upright position or vice versa), you may need technical assistance in doing what is called a reformatting of your hard disk.

Also, watch out for power surges (during thunderstorms, for example)—they can cause damage to your computer's electronic circuitry. You can buy surge protectors, or you can turn off your computer during a thunderstorm.

Notice that many of these precautions are the same as the ones that apply to other electronic components you own.

Saving Your Data and Making Backups

As mentioned earlier, you should make frequent copies of your data in case something happens to your computer or the data on it. You can purchase several software utilities that help you back up and restore data—OS/2 itself supplies BACKUP and RESTORE utilities that do the job nicely if you don't mind working with floppy disks. If you have a lot of data, you may want to purchase a tape drive. If your computer is part of a local area network, however, you can copy your files to a file server and have your network administrator make backups.

If you make your own backup copies, you can choose one of three approaches depending on how often your data changes, how important it is, and how much work you would have to do if you had to reenter it. The approaches are *occasional, serious,* and *professional*, and are defined as follows:

- *Occasional*. You may get by with occasionally copying individual files to one or more floppy disks. This approach is the least secure, but it is better than nothing. If you adopt this method, make sure you label your disks. Disorganization is your enemy with this approach. Another caution is this: If you have to restore a file, you may find that your backup copy is not as recent as you would like. When this happens, you have to redo any work you have done since the backup copy was made. You may even find that the disk containing the backup copy is damaged, and you have to re-create *all* of the data.

- *Serious*. If you make backup copies regularly (perhaps more than once a day), if you use a backup utility such as OS/2's BACKUP.EXE, and if you use two sets of disks (or two tapes) to do your backups, you are in this category. You know exactly how much time has elapsed since your last backup copy was made, and you know exactly which disks to use if you need to restore a file.

- *Professional.* Data centers with multi-million dollar mainframe computers use this method. You can, too. Essentially, you always have three copies of your data on three sets of disks (or tapes). To make your backup copies, you first identify each set of disks as A, B, and C. (For safety's sake, you should actually have two A sets, two B sets, and two C sets.) Rotate your use of the three sets of disks. If today's backup is labeled C, you should have yesterday's backup copies on B and the previous day's on A. Then, tomorrow, you use the A set to make your backup copies. You might even extend this approach to a fourth set of disks and make sure the oldest copy is taken to a different location just in case something happens to the building in which your computer is located. (This backup method is sometimes known as the grandfather/father/son scheme.)

For Related Information
- "Preparing for Trouble," p. 201
- "Learning the Commands to Back Up Your Hard Disk," p. 323

Making the Computer Work for You

Make the computer work for you, not against you. This strategy is the key to getting your time and money's worth from your computer system. In this section—before the discussion turns to more practical topics such as disks, directories, and formatting disks—you investigate ways to think of the computer as a tool, similar to the way a carpenter thinks of his saw or hammer as a tool. You learn ways of being methodical in your work and methods for developing attitudes and work habits that make using your computer fun and productive.

Treating the Computer as a Tool

Longtime DOS users are familiar with their applications and know how to use those applications to get work done. They have a good idea of what software products are available and what products work with what; if they need application software to solve a problem or accomplish a task, DOS users know the cost of the software and can quickly determine whether getting the application software will save time and money. A carpenter or an auto mechanic treats his tools (and the hardware store) the same way. Armed with a little knowledge and the right attitude, you can treat your computer as a tool.

The first thing you need to learn is how to use your new operating system, and that is why you bought this book. Even after you read the narrative portions, keep this book handy so that you can refer to the Command Reference section in part VI or perhaps reread the explanations of how the parts of OS/2 work. Similarly, keep the manuals that came with your computer, printer, and other equipment in a certain place so that you can refer to them occasionally.

Talk with other people to learn more about computers and application software. Almost everyone has a personal computer these days, and discussing them is fun. Computer-related topics are good conversation-starters, and your knowledge of computers increases as you hear how other people use them.

The best way to learn more about an application software product is to try it out. If you know someone who uses a product in which you are interested, ask the person to show you how it works. Computer people invariably like to show what they have done with their applications.

The weekly and monthly trade magazines are useful for keeping up-to-date on what hardware and software products are available, how good a product is, and how much it costs. Some of the more popular magazines are *PC Magazine*, *PC Week*, *InfoWorld*, *Computer Shopper*, and *BYTE Magazine*.

The best attitude to have toward computers is curiosity. You must take the time to understand how to make your computer do what you want. If you use a cookbook approach to run through a series of steps without understanding what each step does, you probably cannot put those steps into a different sequence to do a different job. On the other hand, if you use your natural curiosity to understand the steps, you can use those steps as building blocks to do many different things.

The next best attitude is patience—with yourself and your computer system. You can avoid a great deal of frustration by patiently analyzing your interactions with the computer. By having patience, you also obtain the best results.

Being Methodical

Computers are incredibly predictable (unless they need repair, which is rare). If you use the same sequence of steps to enter exactly the same information into two equivalent computers, using the same application software, both computers function the same and produce the same results.

By methodically analyzing how the computer responds to each step in the sequence, you can use this predictability to your advantage. The key is knowing and understanding the steps you use to reach a desired result and knowing that those steps always have a predictable outcome. The next time you need to do a similar task, you can use your prior experience with those steps to figure out what your computer system is telling you and how to make it do what you want. This approach is the opposite of the cookbook approach.

Being methodical can pay big dividends. The first time you try something new, pay careful attention to the effect of each step you take. Examine the text and the on-screen prompts closely. Try to avoid making assumptions.

You know what an operating system is, you know how to start and restart your computer, you understand the necessity of making backup copies, and you have set yourself on the road to becoming a computer expert—possibly even a power user. The preceding sections covered topics (and ingrained habits) that everyday computer users take for granted. Soon you will, too. Next, you explore the more practical side of operating systems and OS/2, in particular. You learn about disks, disk files, directories, formatting disks, and copying files.

For Related Information
- "Reflecting Personal Preferences," p. 98
- "Knowing What Steps To Take," p. 214
- "Manipulating Icons," p. 254
- "Learning the Commands To Back Up Your Hard Disk," p. 323

Understanding Disk Partitions and Disks

You learned about hard disks and floppy disks in Chapter 1, "Taking a Quick Tour of OS/2 and Your Computer." You know that both the information you enter and the calculated, processed results become streams of recorded data identified by name. Each single stream of named data—a memo, letter, or spreadsheet—is a *file*.

In the following sections, you learn what a disk partition is, how OS/2 and DOS organize disk partitions, how OS/2 and DOS store files in disk partitions, and how hard disks and floppy disks differ.

Allocating Disk Partitions

A hard disk in an IBM or IBM-compatible computer contains up to four disk partitions. DOS and OS/2 organize one or more of these partitions in a method that enables them to store files you save (*write*) and retrieve files you load (*read*). DOS and OS/2 organize by subdividing the partition into many small, numbered data blocks of fixed size. For each file, DOS or OS/2 maintains a table of which data blocks belong to which file. The operating system also keeps track of unoccupied blocks (disk free space).

You (or whoever sets up your computer) allocate the partitions of your hard disk to one or more operating systems you want to use. Most people give all their hard disk space to a single operating system, such as OS/2, in one partition. The OS/2 utility program for allocating these partitions is called FDISK; the DOS utility is also called FDISK. OS/2 supplies a Presentation Manager version of this utility called FDISKPM. You learn about FDISK later in this book.

After you allocate (or re-allocate) disk partitions, you then *format* the partition. You learn more about formatting later in this chapter. Periodically, in the ongoing maintenance of your system, you run the OS/2 utility CHKDSK (Check Disk) to ensure that OS/2 (or DOS) has fully allocated all the data blocks to files or has marked them as unoccupied.

In general, an operating system in one partition cannot see data stored in other partitions. The same operating system can use more than one partition, however, and may be able to use data in the partitions (if you allocate it that way). Because of its compatibility with DOS, OS/2 can use the data on any DOS partition.

If you use multiple operating systems on your computer (UNIX and OS/2, for example), you might allocate partition 1 to the Multiple Operating System Tool utility mentioned earlier, Boot Manager. You then could allocate partition 2 to OS/2 and partition 3 to UNIX. At boot time, Boot Manager runs first and enables you to choose which of the other operating systems you want to run.

Even if you use only OS/2 (and the DOS sessions that OS/2 provides), you still must choose between two different file systems. DOS understands only a single kind of partition, called the *File Allocation Table* (FAT) file system. OS/2 understands FAT partitions and *High Performance File System* (HPFS) partitions. HPFS is faster than FAT.

Table 2.1 simplifies these rules.

Table 2.1 Partition Compatibilities

Operating System	Partition
DOS	Can use only FAT partitions
OS/2	Can use FAT or HPFS partitions
DOS under OS/2	Can use FAT or HPFS partitions
Boot Manager	Needs a small partition itself and can boot any one of the other partitions

Chapter 6, "Installing OS/2," provides more detail about disk partitions. If you use only OS/2 and the DOS sessions it provides, you don't have to worry a great deal about allocating your hard disk partitions; you should probably choose HPFS in this case. After you get your hard disk set up the way you want, you may never have to think about disk partitions again.

Working with Floppy Disks and Hard Disks

Floppy disks, which you learned about in Chapter 1, do not have disk partitions. Floppy disks *do* need to be formatted, however, before you can put files on them.

Each hard disk partition you allocate to OS/2 and each floppy disk drive installed in your computer has a *drive letter*. You use drive letters to identify on which disk a file is located. Your first floppy disk drive is drive A. Your second drive is B; but if you do not have a second floppy disk drive, drive B refers to the same drive as drive A. Your hard disk is drive C, and you can use other drive letters with your computer system, depending on the number of additional floppy disk drives and hard disk partitions you have.

Storing Files and File Names

When you save data on a hard disk or floppy disk, your application software (or the command you type) gives the data and the name of the data to OS/2 to store on the disk's surface. OS/2 records the data in one or more of the small data blocks mentioned previously, puts the name into a directory (a table of file names), and does the bookkeeping necessary to associate those particular data blocks with that named file. OS/2 also stores in the directory

For Related Information
- "Understanding the Drives Object Display," p. 271
- "Learning Commands for Managing Directories," p. 305

the date and time the file was modified and the file's exact size. OS/2 and DOS show a file's size as the number of characters (sometimes called *bytes*) in the file.

The process is analogous to filing documents in a folder and putting the folder into a file cabinet. Your disk is a file cabinet; a directory is a file folder in the file cabinet; and a file is one of the documents in the folder. The small, fixed-size data blocks are like the pages in a document: the larger the document, the more data blocks it needs.

In fact, the Workplace Shell, a part of OS/2, uses this analogy and displays file folders on-screen.

Identifying Your Files

A few applications assign file names, but most allow you to name your files the way you prefer. DOS and OS/2 impose a few restrictions on how you name your files.

Files in a FAT partition have two parts to their file names. The first part is called the *name* and the second part is called the *extension*. The name can be from one to eight characters long, and the extension, which is optional, can be up to three characters long. If an extension is used, a period separates the name and the extension, as shown in the following example:

MAY5MEMO.DOC

DOS and OS/2 consider the following characters legal in a file name or extension:

- The letters *A* through *Z* (DOS and OS/2 do not distinguish between upper- and lowercase letters, so you can use either.)

- The numbers *0* through *9*

- Special characters and punctuation marks, such as $ # & @ ! ( ) - { } ' _ ~ ^ `

If you try to name a file by typing characters other than these, you see an error message, and you have to retype the name.

In addition, certain names denote devices and cannot be used to identify disk files. If you try to use names that begin with COM1, COM2, COM3, COM4, LPT1, LPT2, LPT3, PRN, CON, or NUL to name disk files, you generally cause an error or obtain unexpected results. If you try to copy LISA_PT1.DOC to a file named LPT1.DOC, for example, the operating system sends the file to the printer (which is named LPT1).

To specify a particular file on a particular disk drive (floppy or hard), you type the drive letter, a colon, and the name of the file, as shown in the following example:

C:\MYFILE.DOC

Using File Names and Wild Cards

You also can specify which directory a file is in; a later section covers directories and directory names. Also, some commands and utilities can operate on more than one file at a time. To indicate a group of files, you can use the wild, card characters * (for any number of characters) and ? (for any single character). When you specify which files are in the group, you put one or both wild, card characters in the name. OS/2 finds the files that match the name you have typed. An asterisk matches any number of characters, and the question mark matches any single character. If you want to refer to the group of all files with the extension DOC, for example, type ***.DOC**.

Listing Your Files with DIR

The DIR command displays a list of files and, if you use command-line prompts, is the command you are likely to use most frequently. DIR shows each file's name, extension, size, last-modified date, and last-modified time. You can use wild cards with DIR to list only certain files.

File names in an HPFS partition are less restrictive than in a FAT partition. The maximum number of characters in an HPFS name is 255, and the name can contain spaces (blanks) and multiple periods. Also, you can use upper- and lowercase letters in your HPFS file names. OS/2 displays the name exactly as you typed it, but otherwise does not distinguish between upper- and lowercase. The two file names in the following example specify the same file:

Memo.of.December 1st

memo.of.December 1ST

Working with Files

Two types of files exist on your hard disk after you install OS/2 and have used OS/2 for a while. The first type is executable computer software and has a file extension of EXE, COM, BAT, or CMD. Any other file extension denotes a

Chapter 2—Learning OS/2 If You Don't Know DOS

non-executable data file. Some of these data files are part of OS/2, some are part of application software products you install, and others are files you create.

You can name your files anything you like, within the restrictions mentioned previously, but you probably want to use meaningful names that suggest the contents of the file. This practice helps jog your memory later when you need to remember the file name. (OS/2 supplies utilities you can use to locate a file if you do happen to forget its name.)

You certainly want to follow a file-naming convention that DOS users have found advantageous over the years. In essence, this convention uses the file extension to identify the type of the file. Table 2.2 lists commonly used file extensions and their customary uses.

Table 2.2 Common FileName Extensions

Extension	Common Use
ARC	Archive (compressed file)
ASC	ASCII text file
ASM	Assembler source file
BAK	Backup file
BAS	BASIC program file
BAT	Batch file
BIN	Binary program file
BIO	System file
BMP	Font and picture file
C	C source file
CBL	COBOL source file
CFG, CNF	Program configuration information
CHP	Chapter file (Ventura Publisher)
CMD	Executable program file
COM	Executable program file
CPI	Code page information file (DOS)

Extension	Common Use
DAT	Data file
DBF	Database file (dBASE)
DCP	System file
DCT	Dictionary file
DEV	Program device driver file
DIF	Data Interchange Format file
DLL	System file
DOC	Document (text) file
DRV	Program device driver file
DTA	Data file
EXE	Executable program file
FON	Font and picture file
FNT	Font file
IDX	Index file (Q&A)
IFS	System file
IMG	GEM image (graphics) file
INF	Help file
INI	System file
HLP	Help file
KEY	Keyboard macro file (ProKey)
LET	Letter
LST	Listing of a program (in a file)
LIB	Program library file
LOG	System file
MAC	Keyboard macro file (Superkey)
MAP	Linker map file
MSG	Program message file

(continues)

Table 2.2 Continued

Extension	Common Use
NDX	Index file (dBASE)
OBJ	Intermediate object code (program) file
OLD	Backup file
OVL, OVR	Program overlay file
PAK	Packed (archive) file
PAS	Pascal source file
PCX	Picture file for PC Paintbrush
PIF	Program Information File (TopView/Windows)
PRO	Profile (configuration file)
PRN	Program listing for printing
PS, PSF	PostScript program file
RC	System file
RFT	Revisable Form Text (Document Content Architecture)
SAV	Backup file
SYS	System or device driver file
STY	Style sheet (Ventura Publisher; Microsoft Word)
TIF	Picture file in tag image format
TMP	Temporary file
TST	Test file
TXT	Text file
WK1	Worksheet file (1-2-3 Release 2)
WK3	Worksheet file (1-2-3 Release 3)
WQ1	Quattro spreadsheet file
WKS	Worksheet file (1-2-3 Releases 1 and 1A)
ZIP	Compressed file (PKZIP)

Organizing Directories

As mentioned in Chapter 1, "Taking a Quick Tour of OS/2 and Your Computer," a disk directory can contain files, as well as other directories, in an overall outline structure. This structure helps you organize your files and your work. OS/2 creates a basic directory structure during the installation process; Figure 2.1 shows this initial structure for your hard disk. You see directories named SPOOL, OS2, and DESKTOP. The DESKTOP directory contains directories for the icons INFORMATION, TEMPLATES, and OS/2 SYSTEM. In this last directory, you see the icon representations for PRODUCTIVITY, GAMES, and COMMAND PROMPTS.

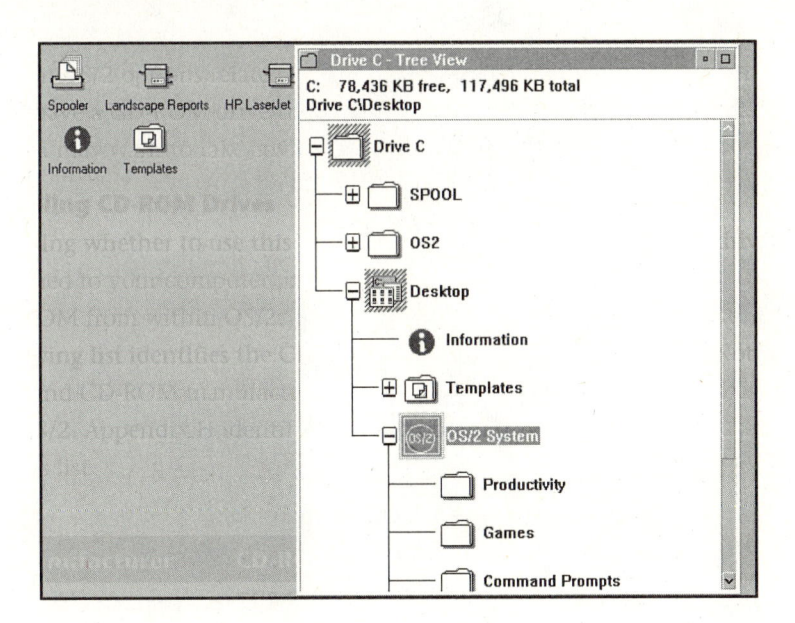

For Related Information
- "Manipulating Files," p. 284
- "Learning the Commands for Managing Files," p. 305

Fig. 2.1
The directory structure created during the installation of OS/2, displayed by the Drives object.

You have at least one directory on every formatted disk, the *root directory*. A few operating system files exist in the root directory of your hard disk. You should create other named directories on your hard disk to hold your files (instead of putting them all in the root directory). Then you have little or no clutter in your root directory.

Organizing Files into an Outline

OS/2 creates an initial directory structure on your hard disk. Each application you later install may create one or more directories to hold its files. You create any other directories you need later by using either OS/2 commands or the icons in the Drives folder. Should you create only a few directories or several that are many layers deep? How should you name your directories?

You need to decide how to structure and name your directories. In general, you should think of the work you do in terms of an outline and create directories accordingly.

If you are a commercial loan officer at a bank, for example, you might create the following structure:

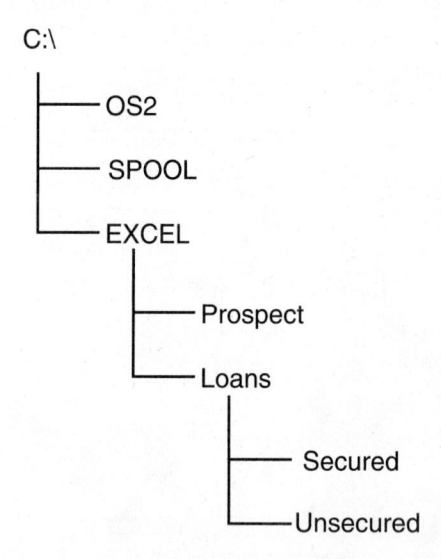

```
C:\
 ├── OS2
 ├── SPOOL
 └── EXCEL
      ├── Prospect
      └── Loans
           ├── Secured
           └── Unsecured
```

The first two directories—OS2 and SPOOL—were created by OS/2; The application Excel created the EXCEL directory during its installation.

Creating and Using Directories

You can create a directory whenever you want; you do not have to create directories all at once. You may prefer to use the icons in the Drives folder to create the directories, or you can use the OS/2 command MKDIR (or enter **MD**) at a command-line prompt. To remove a directory, first delete the files and any subdirectories in the obsolete directory. (OS/2 warns you if the directory is not empty.) Then use the icons in the Drives folder or enter RMDIR (RD, for short) to remove the directory.

To specify a drive letter, directory structure (called a *path*), file name, and extension, you use the notation shown in the following example:

C:\LOANS\SECURED\EXXON.WK1

In this example, C is the drive letter, \LOANS\SECURED\ is the directory structure (path), EXXON is the file name, and .WK1 is the extension. OS/2 requires you to use the backslash character (\) to separate each of the directory names.

You use the drive letter, path, name, and extension to refer to a file that is not in the *current directory*. For a file in the current directory, you need to specify only the name and extension. At a command-line prompt, you enter the CHDIR (or CD, for short) command to change directories. Many applications provide menus to enable you to change to a different directory without typing an OS/2 command.

Formatting Hard Disks and Floppy Disks

As mentioned earlier, a hard disk partition or floppy disk must be formatted before you can store files on it. You probably can format your computer's hard disk only once—after allocating its partitions. Formatting erases existing information on the floppy disk or hard disk partition, so the FORMAT program asks you to confirm your actions. If you do not want to run the FORMAT program from a command-line prompt, OS/2 supplies a Format Disk menu item you can choose.

You use the same FORMAT utility to format hard disks and floppy disks. Behind the scenes, however, OS/2 treats hard disks and floppy disks a little differently during the formatting process.

Formatting Hard Disks

You can instruct FORMAT to put either an HPFS or a FAT file system on a disk partition. Files in an HPFS partition can have long names, and applications generally access HPFS files faster than FAT files. You can use HPFS files with OS/2 applications and, if you do not use long names, with DOS applications you run in a DOS session under OS/2. HPFS files are invisible to DOS programs if you give them long names or if you boot your computer with DOS rather than OS/2.

For a hard disk, the FORMAT program creates the initial, empty root directory and checks the surface of the disk to make sure each of the data blocks can be read and written on. FORMAT marks questionable data blocks as unusable so that OS/2 does not later try to store your files in those blocks.

For Related Information

- "Expanding and Collapsing a Directory List," p. 279
- "Learning Commands for Managing Directories," p. 305

Formatting Floppy Disks

FORMAT creates the initial, empty root directory on floppy disks, as well. In addition, FORMAT actually electronically subdivides the disk surface into data blocks (manufacturers do this subdividing for hard disks at the factory). Finally, FORMAT checks the surface of the disk and marks defective blocks as unusable.

If you keep a supply of formatted disks, you can avoid the annoyance of having to run the FORMAT utility just to copy a few files to give to someone.

Knowing What Can Go Wrong

With early versions of DOS, reformatting your hard disk was an easy mistake to make. Early FORMAT programs did not have the built-in safeguards contained in the OS/2 FORMAT program. Even though FORMAT asks you twice for confirmation that you really want to format your hard disk, you may someday reformat by mistake. This accident is not likely, though. If you have recently backed up your hard disk, the mistake only costs you the time you must spend in copying the files back to your disk.

For Related Information
- "Formatting and Copying Floppy Disks," p. 289
- "Command Reference, p. 717

Hard and floppy disks have imperfections; FORMAT notices these defective spots and marks them accordingly. If FORMAT finds bad spots on a floppy disk, you may want to consider throwing it away (or sending it back, if the disk is under a warranty). Your data is worth much more than the cost of a disk. Because a hard disk has a greater capacity than a floppy disk, bad spots are not as significant. FORMAT and the CHKDSK utility tell you the number of bytes in bad *sectors* (data blocks). If the number is less than about 3 to 5 percent of the total disk capacity, you probably should not be concerned. A larger number may signify a malfunctioning disk or some other hardware problem.

Copying Disks and Files

You copy disks and files to share information with others, make backup copies of your application software and the work you do, and establish different versions of your work. In this last situation, you make a copy of a file that contains current information; run your application to update the copy with tentative, new information; and then later, may delete the older version if it does become out of date.

Copying Floppy Disks

The DISKCOPY command (or the Copy Disk item on the drive icon's menu) makes an exact copy of an entire floppy disk. Both the original and the copy must be the same type of disk. If the original holds 1.44 megabytes of data, the target disk also must be a 1.44 megabyte disk. DISKCOPY actually copies data blocks, not files. Copying a nearly empty disk takes the same amount of time copying a full disk takes.

The following example shows the syntax of the DISKCOPY command:

    DISKCOPY A: B:

This command tells OS/2 to copy the disk in drive A to the disk in drive B.

If you have only one floppy disk drive (A), you still give the same command. When OS/2 prompts you for the *source disk* (the original disk) and the *target disk* (the copy), you insert them into the same disk drive. OS/2 keeps track of which disk is which.

Copying Files

You can copy files by using the COPY command (which you type at a command prompt) or by using the Workplace Shell. With its menus and graphical representation of files, the Workplace Shell provides an easy way to copy files. You can use the mouse to identify which file you want (called *selecting* a file) and then drag the file to another directory or disk drive.

The following example shows the most commonly used syntax for the COPY command:

    COPY C:\PROSPECT\ACME.DOC C:\LOANS\SECURED\ACME.DOC

This example shows how to copy the ACME.DOC file from the PROSPECT directory to the SECURED subdirectory in the LOANS directory.

The following command is a slightly more complex example that uses wild cards to copy more than one file:

    COPY C:\PROSPECT*.DOC C:\LOANS\SECURED*.DOC

This second example of the COPY command shows how to copy all the PROSPECT directory files that have the .DOC extension to the LOANS\SECURED directory.

If the disk that is the target of the COPY command does not have enough room left (that is, enough unoccupied data blocks) to hold the target file, OS/2 displays an error message and stops the copy operation. You also see an error message if you try to copy a file to itself (the source and target are the same drive, same path, and same file name).

For Related Information

■ "Learning the Commands for Managing Files," p. 311

If you have only one disk drive, you can still copy files from disk to disk. You can copy the files to an empty directory on your hard disk, switch disks, and then copy the files to the target disk. Or you can use the A and B drive letters as if you did have two disk drives; OS/2 prompts you to insert the appropriate disk at the appropriate time.

Deleting, Renaming, and Moving Files

After you have used your computer for a while, it will seem like home to you. As a consequence, you may have to do some periodic housecleaning of your files. You can use commands or the Workplace Shell to tidy up your hard and floppy disks.

The ERASE (or DEL) command removes files. You can use wild cards to delete many files at once (be sure you know which files match your wild cards). If you tell OS/2 to delete all the files in a directory, OS/2 asks you if you are sure. The following is an example of the DEL command:

    DEL *.TMP

This command deletes all the files with an extension of TMP in the current directory.

Renaming a file changes the file's name but otherwise leaves it intact. You cannot rename a file onto a different disk (use COPY instead). The following is an example of the RENAME (REN) command:

    RENAME ACME.DOC ACME.OLD

For Related Information

■ "Command Reference, p. 717

Similarly, you can use the OS/2 MOVE command to move a file from one directory to another (but not to different disks). The following command moves the ACME.DOC file from the PROSPECT directory to the LOANS\SECURED directory:

    MOVE C:\PROSPECT\ACME.DOC C:\LOANS\SECURED\ACME.DOC

Chapter Summary

If you have not used DOS before, you should feel a little more at ease after reading this chapter. The basic principles and operations of personal computers were covered. You learned what makes up an operating system, how to start DOS, what attitudes you need to use your computer productively, how to protect your work by making backup copies, how DOS treats hard and floppy disks, files, and directories, how to name files, how to format disks and copy files, and how to delete, rename, and move files.

The next chapter explains the differences between DOS and OS/2.

Chapter 3
Learning OS/2 If You Know DOS

IBM describes OS/2 2.1 as "a better DOS than DOS." In this chapter, you explore how and why this statement is true. IBM further describes OS/2 as a "better Windows than Microsoft Windows." You also meet Microsoft Windows in this chapter.

OS/2 2.1 runs DOS applications compatibly, and it runs them in ways that DOS cannot. With OS/2, you can run multiple DOS applications at the same time, each in a window on-screen or in a full-screen session. Each application has more internal memory available to it under OS/2 than it had under DOS. You can start a specific version of DOS in a DOS session and manage that session separately from your other DOS sessions.

OS/2 uses the hardware features of the 80386, 80486, and Pentium Intel CPU chips to give you these advantages. The DOS inside OS/2 is a special DOS that uses the 32-bit architecture of these CPU chips, the overlapped input/output capabilities of OS/2, and the preemptive multitasking of OS/2. Your DOS applications run faster on OS/2 and have more internal memory available to them, but they assume that they are running on a regular version of DOS.

To run OS/2 2.1, you need a computer with an 80386, 80486, or Pentium CPU chip; a hard disk; a VGA-, Super VGA-, or 8514, or XGA-compatible screen and video adapter; and at least 6M (megabytes) of internal memory. Although a mouse is optional, it is strongly recommended. (If you're familiar with Microsoft Windows, note that these are close to the same requirements for running Windows in Enhanced Mode.) You learn more about these hardware requirements in Chapter 5, "Using Non-IBM Computers and OS/2."

OS/2 offers you several object-oriented features. The graphical images you see on OS/2's main screen (your "desktop") are objects you can manipulate with the mouse, keyboard, or touch screen. The objects you see are folders, printer objects, data file objects, program (application) objects, and other items. You can move these objects on your desktop, put objects in folders (thus "cleaning up your desktop"), and do other interesting operations on these objects. The object-oriented nature of OS/2 makes IBM's new PC-based operating system as easy to use as an Apple Macintosh—in some ways, perhaps even easier.

Companies selling utility software have developed collections of computer programs that extend and enhance the functions of OS/2. You learn about these utilities in this chapter.

If you just finished Chapter 2, "Learning OS/2 If You Don't Know DOS," you looked briefly at DOS. If you have used DOS in the past, you probably skipped Chapter 2. Now you're ready to discover how OS/2 improves on DOS.

Matching OS/2 with DOS

OS/2 is like DOS in many ways. If you choose to use OS/2's command-line interface, its command-line prompt looks like the one that DOS gives you. OS/2 uses many of the same commands as DOS, and OS/2 can use the same files as DOS if you follow certain rules—an important advantage. You can use OS/2 to just run DOS applications and still have many benefits beyond what DOS alone offers.

Comparing OS/2 and DOS Files

Disk files in a File Allocation Table (FAT) partition are completely compatible with DOS and OS/2. If you use the OS/2 System Editor to create a text file on a FAT disk drive, for example, you can boot DOS on your computer and use the DOS TYPE command to type the contents of the file on-screen. Both DOS and OS/2 treat FAT files exactly the same way. (Chapter 2 discussed File Allocation Table partitions.) OS/2 also offers a High Performance File System (HPFS). HPFS is a new way to format your hard drive that lets your application software store and retrieve files faster. The HPFS is somewhat compatible with DOS and OS/2, but only if you use the DOS built into OS/2, and then only if you follow certain rules. The "Looking at DOS and OS/2 Incompatibilities" section of this chapter covers these rules and restrictions fully.

Comparing OS/2 and DOS Commands

Most OS/2 commands are similar in appearance and function to their DOS counterparts. With OS/2, however, you can use Workplace Shell utilities to accomplish many of your administrative and maintenance tasks. But you will occasionally find that you have to start the OS/2 command processor, either full-screen or in a window (by using the Command Prompts icon in the OS/2 System folder). Chapter 12, "Learning the Commands You Use Most Often," and Part VI, "Using the Command Reference," explain the OS/2 commands in detail.

The OS/2 installation process inserts PROMPT statements into your startup files (CONFIG.SYS for OS/2 and AUTOEXEC.BAT for DOS) to make OS/2 and DOS command-line prompts look different, helping you to distinguish between the two prompts. By default, the OS/2 command-line prompt looks like the following example:

    [C:\]

For DOS sessions under OS/2, the DOS command-line prompt has the following appearance:

    C:\>

Both examples assume that the root directory is the current directory.

Commands that work the same in both environments include CLS, DATE, TIME, BACKUP, RESTORE, COPY, ERASE, PRINT, RENAME, TYPE, XCOPY, CHDIR (CD), MKDIR (MD), RMDIR (RD), VER, DISKCOPY, DEL, LABEL, and, except for HPFS files, DIR. If you have used these commands under DOS but without OS/2, you will be pleased to know that they operate the same way; these are the commands you use most often in a DOS or OS/2 environment.

Using DOS Applications under OS/2

The DOS inside OS/2 is highly compatible with DOS Version 5.0, and, to some extent, DOS Version 6.0. You cannot use OS/2 to access a disk partition on which you've installed the DoubleSpace option of DOS 6.0, however. This compatibility means that business-related and general purpose DOS applications run under OS/2 the same way they ran under DOS 5.0. Even most entertainment software products (games) run under OS/2. Disk utilities and disk diagnostics are one category of DOS-based software that does not run successfully under OS/2, however. The section of this chapter on DOS and OS/2 compatibility issues talks about this category of software.

For Related Information

- "Beginning the Command-Line Interface," p. 303
- "Understanding DOS Sessions," p. 394

Understanding How OS/2 Expands upon DOS

OS/2 2.1 offers more than DOS compatibility, of course. By taking advantage of the features of the 80386 and 80486 CPU chips, OS/2 protects applications in different DOS sessions from crashing into one another (*system integrity protection*). Before OS/2—under plain DOS—a bug (software error) in an application often meant that your computer would lock up, become unstable, or become unresponsive; you would have to use the power switch to reboot the computer. OS/2 catches these situations, ends the offending DOS session and its application, and enables you to continue your work without rebooting the computer.

OS/2 also implements a scheme of overlapped access to the hard disk (*overlapped I/O*), which enables applications to run faster. Overlapped I/O refers to OS/2's ability to perform file operations (loading and saving data) for one program while concurrently performing other operations or other programs. This same input/output scheme tries to anticipate what disk data your application will need next by reading ahead and putting the read-ahead data into a memory buffer. The scheme also performs *lazy writes* (if you have turned the option on). A lazy write puts the data onto the surface of the disk a few short milliseconds after an application has told OS/2 to write that data, allowing the application to continue processing in those short moments as if the data had actually been written. Lazy writes make your system more responsive, although they present a minor risk of data loss if power is interrupted before data is written.

OS/2 provides better support than DOS for different languages. Called *National Language Support (NLS)*, you set this OS/2 attribute with a configuration option at installation time. The country and language you select determine the display format of such country-dependent items as time of day, calendar date, and currency amounts and symbols.

Chapter 2, "Learning OS/2 If You Don't Know DOS," discussed the Multiple Operating System Tool, called Boot Manager, when it explained hard disk partitions. If you choose to install it, Boot Manager is an option that takes up a small disk partition of its own. When your computer boots, Boot Manager gets control first and allows you to select from OS/2, DOS, UNIX, or some other operating system. If you are upgrading your computer from UNIX and DOS to UNIX and OS/2, Boot Manager makes switching between operating systems easier. You can also use Boot Manager to switch between OS/2 and other operating systems besides UNIX.

Both DOS and OS/2 use a configuration file named CONFIG.SYS at boot time. CONFIG.SYS is a text file, which means that you can change it with a text editor (such as the OS/2 Enhanced Editor). The changes you make take effect the next time you boot your computer.

OS/2 expands upon DOS in several other ways, too. Your applications have more internal memory available to them when you run them in DOS sessions.

If you start one application that takes a long time to finish an operation (recalculating a spreadsheet, for example), you can start other applications in other sessions so that you can continue to be productive. Your DOS and OS/2 applications can share the printer without confusion about which printout is which. Your DOS, Microsoft Windows, and OS/2 applications can work alongside each other; you can often share information among your applications without having to retype it.

As you might expect, the list of OS/2 commands you can use is longer than the DOS list. Chapter 12, "Learning the Commands You Use Most Often," explains some of these commands, and the command reference in Part VI is a complete dictionary of OS/2 commands. Finally, the Workplace Shell and Presentation Manager are easy-to-use features of OS/2 that you do not find in DOS. These features are covered in chapters 9 and 10.

Providing More Memory for DOS Applications

PC users often hear and talk about the number *640 kilobytes* (or 640K). In a plain DOS environment, or DOS and Microsoft Windows environment, the *real mode address space* (also called *conventional memory*) is a maximum of 1 megabyte of internal memory. Real mode address space is the space in which DOS applications run. After allowing for video adapter cards, network adapter cards, hard disk controller cards, and the so-called ROM BIOS, only 640 kilobytes are left.

DOS takes up part of the 640 kilobytes. Each statement in the CONFIG.SYS file causes more of the 640K to be taken up. Your DOS applications have to work in the remainder. On a local area network using plain DOS, you may only have 500K in which to run applications. If your computer is also connected to a host (mainframe) computer, the communications software occupies another portion of the 640K.

OS/2 gives you back some conventional memory in two ways. The memory used by CONFIG.SYS statements (your device drivers) comes from a separate memory area, not from the 640K. In addition, because you can have several DOS sessions under OS/2, you can put your host communications software in one session and run applications in a different DOS session. Each session starts out with 640K of available memory, and typically each has about 620K free for DOS applications to use.

Some DOS applications use *expanded memory* (often referred to as EMS memory). Expanded memory was invented by Lotus Development Corporation (developer of Lotus 1-2-3), Intel (inventor of the PC CPU chip), and Microsoft (maintainer of the DOS operating system); the standard for expanded memory is called the LIM 4.0 Specification. *LIM* comes from the initials of these companies.

Expanded memory was originally provided by special memory boards, but OS/2 provides expanded memory to your applications automatically, without the need for special boards. Each DOS session under OS/2 can give a DOS application up to 32M of expanded memory. Microsoft Windows provided an EMS maximum equal to four times the physical memory in your system.

Extended memory is another type of memory that your applications may use. By supporting the Extended Memory Specification (XMS) and the DOS PRotected Mode Interface (DPMI) standards, OS/2 makes up to 16M of SMC memory and up to 512M of DPMI memory available to DOS applications.

You probably have noticed that these memory amounts exceed the physical memory in your computer. Under plain DOS, both the 640K limit and the amount of physical EMS memory in your computer were "hard" boundaries, and you would see out-of-memory error messages when your applications reached a boundary. Under OS/2 and in DOS sessions under OS/2, your hard disk becomes an extension of the internal memory in your computer. OS/2 can overcommit memory by swapping internal memory to your hard disk and back again as necessary.

Your system may seem to run more slowly when applications begin to surpass your installed physical internal memory, but you still can finish your work. The file SWAPPER.DAT, which by default resides in the \OS2\SYSTEM directory, contains the overflow; the size of SWAPPER.DAT gives you a clue as to when you need to install more memory in your computer. SWAPPER.DAT usually starts out as a 2M file. As a rule of thumb, if it increases to 2M or more, you should consider installing more internal memory in your computer.

Not all DOS applications use expanded or extended memory. Check your software products to see if they can use the special types of memory that OS/2 provides.

Running Multiple DOS Applications

Chapter 1, "Taking a Quick Tour of OS/2 and Your Computer," mentioned that you can run several DOS applications at the same time. OS/2 creates a Virtual DOS Machine (VDM) for each application, with each VDM having about 620K of internal memory free to run programs. You might have a DOS word processor in one VDM, a communications program in a second VDM, and just a command-line prompt in a third VDM so that you can easily enter DOS commands in that third session.

A DOS session under OS/2 can be full-screen or it can be windowed. In the case of a windowed DOS session, OS/2 displays the DOS command prompt or the textual output of an application in a font you choose. The size of the window depends on the font (smaller fonts cause smaller windows, which you may prefer).

OS/2 provides *clipboard services* you can use to copy information from one DOS session to another. With these services, you mark a region of one screen (OS/2 highlights that region), copy the information in that screen region to the clipboard, and then paste the information into another window.

Unless it is waiting for keyboard input, an application in a DOS session under OS/2 continues to process even while you use another application in a different DOS session. The system integrity protection afforded by OS/2, as mentioned earlier, prevents one application in a session from locking up the computer and causing you to lose the work you have not yet saved. This feature is important when you have more than one application running at the same time.

The first question most people ask about running multiple applications is, why do it? The answer is productivity. You no longer have to wait for your computer to finish a long-running operation (printing a large report, transferring a large file in a communications session, or recalculating a large spreadsheet, for example). You can go on to other tasks after starting a long-running operation.

Getting More from OS/2 Applications

The DOS sessions and DOS compatibility provided by OS/2 2.1 are important because more than 20,000 DOS applications exist today. People rely on these applications to get their work done, but a DOS application can use no more than the 640K of conventional memory when run either under plain DOS or under the DOS that is part of OS/2.

Applications written especially for OS/2 do not have this 640K memory limitation, and they can take advantage of other features of OS/2, such as the Presentation Manager interface. When they develop OS/2 applications, software developers have more operating system resources from which to draw. In general, an OS/2 application can be faster and can process more data than a similar DOS application. Some of the resources available to developers are rather complicated and technical, but you should understand three significant ones: *threads, 32-bit architecture,* and the *object-oriented interface*. Use the steps detailed in Chapter 17 to configure your DOS and Win-OS/2 sessions according to the amount of expanded and extended memory those sessions need.

- *Threads*. Not only can you run several OS/2 applications at the same time on your computer, each application may in turn run portions of itself concurrently. Each portion is a thread. Applications use threads to perform long-running tasks that do not need your attention, and you see an enormously increased performance in such applications. You might instruct your word processor to save the current document, for example, so that you can go on to the next. If the application uses a thread to do the work of saving the current document, it can immediately begin processing your request to load the next document. The saving of the first document file occurs in the background.

- *32-bit architecture*. OS/2 utilizes the 32-bit architecture of the 80386 and 80486 CPU chips, and applications can also take advantage of this architecture. Basically, these CPU chips have the capacity to process larger amounts of data at one time (the older 80286 CPU chip in the IBM AT could process only 16 bits at a time, while the original IBM PC, first released in September 1981, could process data only 8 bits at a time with its 8088 CPU chip). When software developers write computer programs based on the 32-bit architecture, the result is increased performance. Because windowed sessions operate in graphics mode rather than text mode, you'll find that windowed sessions may display information slower than you would like. However, windowed sessions offer the advantage of showing information right on your OS/2 desktop, alongside your other running applications.

- *Object-oriented interface*. While OS/2 offers a command-line interface you can use to issue commands for managing your files, launching your applications, printing your correspondence and reports, and performing other tasks, OS/2 also offers an object-oriented interface. OS/2 represents the work you do in terms of objects on your desktop, with the computer screen playing the role of your desktop. The component of OS/2 that displays your desktop and lets you manipulate objects on your desktop is the *Workplace Shell*. You see icons, open folders, notebooks, or other graphical figures on-screen. Each figure is an object you can click, double-click, and drag-and-drop with your mouse. These mouse operations are your means of selecting, opening, closing, moving, and otherwise working with the objects on your desktop. The section, "The Workplace Shell and Presentation Manager," later in this chapter, and Chapter 9, "Using Your Computer Screen as a Desktop", discuss the Workplace Shell in detail.

OS/2 applications can be text-based (as most DOS applications are), or they can be Presentation Manager-based. You can run text-based applications in an OS/2 window or a full screen. The user guide or manual that comes with your application software tells you whether that software product uses Presentation Manager.

Printing from DOS and OS/2

Multiple concurrent applications need to share the printer; you don't want pages from a spreadsheet report mixed with pages from a word processing document. To keep printouts separate, OS/2 spools each one to the hard disk and then prints each as a separate print job. OS/2 comes with a Workplace Shell utility (called the *Printer object*) for managing these print jobs. Chapter 15, "Printing with OS/2," discusses this Presentation Manager utility in detail.

In Chapter 1, "Taking a Quick Tour of OS/2 and Your Computer," you read about printer fonts and how they should match the fonts you see on-screen. Presentation Manager contains services that applications use to put characters on-screen and on the printer, but the fonts themselves—their shape, size, and other attributes of their characters—come from both Presentation Manager and a product called Adobe Type Manager (ATM), licensed by IBM and included on your OS/2 disks. The computer industry recognizes Adobe and its ATM product as having the highest quality fonts for both print and display purposes.[*]

Examining New and Changed Commands

Some commands that you type at an OS/2 command-line prompt function slightly differently from the way their DOS counterparts do. In particular, the DIR command, which displays the names of the files in a directory, shows HPFS file names in a different format so that OS/2 can show you the long file names you can use in an HPFS partition. In a FAT partition, the OS/2 DIR command functions the same way it does under DOS.

Some of the commands that accept file name options (including the wildcard characters * and ?) can process multiple options under OS/2. The DIR command in an OS/2 session is the best example. You can type **DIR *.DOC *.TXT** to see a display of those files with either DOC or TXT as the file's extension.

The on-line HELP command, introduced by IBM in DOS 5.0 and DOS 6.2, takes on an entirely new dimension under OS/2. When you type **HELP CHKDSK** at an OS/2 command-line prompt, for example, OS/2 gives you information about the CHKDSK command (just as DOS 5.0 does). The information is provided by the OS/2 on-line command reference. This reference is a Presentation Manager utility that allows you to explore OS/2 concepts, commands, and options. Chapter 13, "Using the Built-In Help Facility," describes the on-line command reference in more detail.

You may be accustomed to using the ANSI.SYS device driver supplied with DOS. ANSI.SYS processes screen color change commands, cursor positioning commands, and clear-screen commands issued from within an application. Under OS/2, ANSI.SYS functions the same in DOS sessions as it always has. In OS/2 sessions, you have a new ANSI command you can use to turn the processing of these screen commands on or off. ANSI.SYS does not affect OS/2 sessions.

The CHKDSK command, under both DOS and OS/2, verifies that file storage and file allocation on your disk are correct. Each data block within the partition must be allocated to a file or marked as unoccupied (free), and no data block can be allocated to more than one file. For an HPFS partition under OS/2, CHKDSK also verifies the internal structure of the special list of physical location information for directories and files.

The following commands are unique to OS/2 or DOS sessions within OS/2. Part VI of this book, "Using the Command Reference," describes each command in detail. This list gives you an idea of the extra commands you can use in an OS/2 session.

Command	Description
AUTOFAIL	Specifies how you want "Abort, Retry, Ignore" situations processed.
BOOT	For Dual Boot, starts the other operating system.
CACHE	In CONFIG.SYS, specifies how you want HPFS managed.
CHCP	Change Code Page (NLS).
DISKCACHE	In CONFIG.SYS, specifies how you want non-HPFS files managed.
DPATH	In CONFIG.SYS, tells applications where to look for data files, such as the system message file.
IFS	In CONFIG.SYS, tells OS/2 to use an Installable File System (such as HPFS).

Understanding How OS/2 Expands upon DOS

Command	Description
IOPL	In CONFIG.SYS, indicates whether you want applications to have I/O Privilege Level.
KEYS	In CONFIG.SYS, indicates whether you want OS/2 to keep a list of commands you have entered so that you can recall and reuse them later.
LIBPATH	In CONFIG.SYS, specifies where to find Dynamic Link Library (DLL) files.
MAXWAIT	In CONFIG.SYS, indicates the maximum number of seconds each application should have to wait before getting to use the CPU.
MEMMAN	In CONFIG.SYS, specifies how to manage memory swapping.
MOVE	Moves files from one directory to another on the same disk drive.
PAUSEONERROR	In CONFIG.SYS, specifies whether to pause when OS/2 detects errors in the CONFIG.SYS file.
PRIORITY	In CONFIG.SYS, specifies whether OS/2 can dynamically change application priorities to allow better access to the CPU.
PROTECTONLY	In CONFIG.SYS, specifies whether you want DOS sessions.
PROTSHELL	In CONFIG.SYS, specifies which command shell you want to use (Workplace Shell is common).
RMSIZE	In CONFIG.SYS, tells the memory size for each DOS session (maximum 640K).
RUN	In CONFIG.SYS, starts a program in the background at boot time.
SETBOOT	Tells Boot Manager your defaults for how you want to boot your computer.
SPOOL	Starts a Printer object; redirects print from one device to another.
SWAPPATH	Specifies where you want your SWAPPER.DAT file.
THREADS	In CONFIG.SYS, specifies the maximum number of threads OS/2 should allow.
TIMESLICE	In CONFIG.SYS, sets the minimum and maximum amounts of CPU time, in thousandths of a second, that OS/2 allots to each application and its threads.
VIEW	Interactively displays document files that have an INF extension.

The Workplace Shell and Presentation Manager

As you learn in Chapter 9, "Using Your Computer Screen as a Desktop," and Chapter 10, "Managing the Workplace Shell," Presentation Manager (PM) is OS/2's graphical interface. The Workplace Shell uses PM to make your computer look and work like a desktop. You organize your real desk by placing papers in folders and by arranging your work and your tools on top of your desk. Workplace Shell enables you to group files, tools, and other objects in the same way. For example, the Workplace Shell represents a document (text) file as an icon, a small picture that looks like a piece of paper with a folded-down corner. You can use the mouse to pick up the icon and drop it into a folder to file the document away. Or you can get a printed copy of the text file by dropping its icon onto a printer object—just like putting a real piece of paper into the office copier when you need a copy. To delete a file, you drop its icon onto a picture of a paper shredder.

For Related Information
- "Using the Workplace Shell's System Menu," p. 260
- "Introducing Presentation Manager," p. 234
- "Adding DOS Programs," p. 397
- "Switching between OS/2 and DOS with Dual-Boot," p. 404

In the Workplace Shell, everything appears as an object, just like the papers, folders, printer, and paper shredder in your office. You use all these objects in the same way; after you learn how to work with one object, using the others comes naturally. Even programs are objects. The basic keystrokes, menus, and mouse actions you use to get your work done are the same for every PM program because the interface is consistent. Best of all, with the Workplace Shell you never have to type instructions at a command prompt because you can use the mouse to manipulate objects. People who are comfortable dealing with the computer through a DOS prompt can use OS/2's command-line interface. But OS/2 gives easy-to-use alternatives to people who don't want to struggle with commands, command-line parameters, directory structures, and filename wildcard characters.

Using Microsoft Windows with OS/2

OS/2 has built-in support for both Windows 3.0 and Windows 3.1 applications. You don't have to buy a separate copy of Microsoft Windows just to run an application written for the Windows environment. Your Windows applications function the same under OS/2 as they would have functioned under Microsoft Windows. If you already purchased the regular OS/2 2.1 operating system product and you have a copy (perhaps pre-loaded) of Microsoft Windows on your computer, you may want to consider removing Windows (but not your Windows applications) to save disk space.

If you already have Windows 3.1 on your computer, you can buy OS/2 2.1 for Windows and let the OS/2 installation procedure modify your existing Windows 3.1 environment to transform Windows into Win-OS/2. The OS/2 2.1 for Windows product costs much less than the OS/2 2.1 product because you've already paid for the Windows component. OS/2 for Windows merely runs your existing copy of Microsoft Windows in the Win-OS/2 environment. After using OS/2 for Windows to upgrade your old Windows environment to become the new Win-OS/2 environment, you then have the same features and functions on your computer as if you had purchased the regular OS/2 2.1 product. Chapter 4, "Deciding How You Want to Use OS/2," provides more detail about OS/2 for Windows.

Version 3.x of Microsoft Windows operates in one of the following three modes, depending on how much internal memory you have and what type of CPU you have:

- *Real Mode*. The operating mode that provides maximum compatibility with Version 2 of Microsoft Windows. Real mode is the only mode available if you have less than 1M of internal memory (RAM). Microsoft Windows 3.0 offered Real Mode operation, but Windows 3.1 did not.

- *Standard Mode*. This mode provides access to more internal memory; standard mode enables you to run multiple large Windows applications simultaneously.

- *Enhanced Mode*. Takes advantage of the 80386 and 80486 Intel CPU chip's virtual memory capabilities, just as OS/2 does.

OS/2 runs Windows applications in either Standard Mode or Enhanced Mode.

Looking at DOS and OS/2 Incompatibilities

In general, OS/2 runs business-related DOS applications the same way plain DOS did. As mentioned earlier, however, one category of software presents a potential problem to OS/2's preservation of system integrity. This category consists of utilities that perform hard disk diagnostics, sort directory entries, and rearrange file physical location information to make each file contiguous (defragment).

For Related Information
- "Adding DOS Programs," p. 397

If you use DOS applications under OS/2 to access files in an HPFS partition, you have to be careful about how you specify your filenames. The next section of this chapter explains why. Be aware that you cannot access HPFS files at all if you boot plain DOS with a DOS system disk or with the Dual Boot feature of OS/2.

Non-IBM computer equipment *may* present you with an OS/2 compatibility problem. Chapter 5, "Using Non-IBM Computers and OS/2," goes into detail on this issue. The degree of compatibility depends on the manufacturer's adherence to IBM's standards. Most manufacturers are very careful to ensure their equipment's level of IBM compatibility.

Some DOS applications use the *Virtual Control Program Interface (VCPI)* to store information in extended memory. VCPI, by its nature, allows a DOS application to directly control and modify all of extended memory, subverting the system integrity protection that OS/2 enforces. VCPI applications cannot run under OS/2. If you have an application that uses VCPI to access extended memory, use Dual Boot to boot DOS before running that application, and set up a FAT (not HPFS) partition. In the next section of this chapter, DOS compatibility with HPFS partitions is discussed.

Working with HPFS Partitions and HPFS Files

The File Allocation Table scheme was really designed to work with the small-capacity disks that were popular when DOS was first released. Performance suffers when applications access FAT files, especially large files. DOS and OS/2 have to read and process long chains of physical disk location information to satisfy application requests for files.

OS/2 offers a High Performance File System (HPFS) option especially designed for hard disks. Outside of OS/2, DOS cannot recognize files on an HPFS partition. If you use the OS/2 System Editor to create a text file on an HPFS drive, and then reboot your computer with DOS (perhaps by using Dual Boot or a system-formatted floppy disk), DOS does not show you the HPFS disk drive. DOS reassigns your computer's drive letters, and the HPFS drive is invisible. On the other hand, if you use the DOS that is built into OS/2, your DOS applications can use files on an HPFS partition, with the exception of long file names.

HPFS enables you to use long file names (as many as 254 characters) and to include spaces and several periods in such a name. If you use long file names, your DOS applications cannot see or use those files. Your OS/2 applications can, of course, see and use these files.

If this sounds like a problem, remember that you use an application (DOS- or OS/2-based) to create most of your files. DOS applications do not allow you to create files with long names, so only rarely should you have to be careful about naming files. You probably only notice the difference when you start a DOS session under OS/2 and ask DOS to list the files in a directory on an HPFS drive. If files with long names exist in that directory, DOS shows you only the files with short names. You recall that a short name has one to eight characters of name and, optionally, an extension containing a period and one to three characters.

Now that you understand HPFS better, you'll want to consider OS/2's usage of INI files and Extended Attributes, which represent two of the most significant differences between OS/2 and DOS.

Understanding INI Files and Extended Attributes

OS/2 uses configuration files, called INI files, to remember your color scheme preferences, the positions of windows and other objects on your desktop, the name of your default printer object, and other system information. OS/2 maintains two INI files, OS2.INI and OS2SYS.INI, both in the OS2 directory. Application software can store configuration information in OS/2's INI files or the software can create INI files specific to the application.

OS/2 organizes entries in all INI files in three levels... *applications*, *keys*, and *user data*. The application level identifies the application product or OS/2 component that owns an entry in an INI file. PM_Spring_Colors, PM_Fonts, Microsoft Word, and PM_Workplace:Templates are examples of application identifiers. One or more keys, at the second level, can exist for each application. Each key is the name of a configuration option for that application. COUR.OFM, COURB.OFM, COURBI.OFM, and HELV are examples of values of keys for the PM_Fonts application. At the third level, the user data for a particular key contains the configuration option's value. "\PSFONTS\HELV.OFM" is an example of a user data entry for the HELV key for the PM_Fonts application.

OS/2 updates the INI files as you change the arrangement of your desktop or run OS/2 application software. Chapter 8, "Troubleshooting OS/2," gives you methods you can use to preserve and later restore your INI files' contents. When this chapter turns to the subject of utility programs, you'll find out about OS/2-specific utilities that help you manage your INI files.

For Related Information
- "Switching between OS/2 and DOS with Dual-Boot," p. 404
- "Learning What You Cannot Do in a DOS Session," p. 405

OS/2 uses Extended Attributes to store information about files in a manner similar to the way OS/2 uses INI files to store information about configuration preferences and choices. Each Extended Attribute has a name and an associated value. The name and value can be any information an OS/2 application programmer wishes to store about a file. The operating system itself uses Extended Attributes to remember things like the type of information in a file and the position of the file's icon in a folder. OS/2 also lets you specify which application software programs can update a particular file. OS/2 stores the name of the designated application in the file's Extended Attributes. Typical names that OS/2 uses when it stores Extended Attributes include .TYPE, .CLASSINFO, and .ICONPOS.

OS/2 stores Extended Attributes differently on a FAT-based drive from the way it stores Extended Attributes on an HPFS drive. Directory entries in a FAT-based drive are big enough to hold four file attributes: read-only, hidden, system, and archive. To hold additional information about a file (the Extended Attributes) located on a FAT-based drive, OS/2 stores the additional information in a hidden file named EA DATA. SF. The blanks (space characters) between EA and DATA and between DATA and SF make it difficult for you to inadvertently modify or erase this important file. The EA DATA. SF file exists in the root directory of the FAT-based drive. On an HPFS-formatted drive, OS/2 stores the Extended Attributes in the directory itself. OS/2 doesn't need to use the separate EA DATA. SF file on an HPFS drive.

An Extended Attribute can provide extra information about a file (a simple Extended Attribute) or can point to other Extended Attributes (a multiple Extended Attribute). If you're familiar with Apple Macintosh computers, you'll be interested to know that Extended Attributes serve much the same purpose as Resource Forks.

You can get OS/2 utility software products that will let you view, modify, back up, and restore your Extended Attributes. The next section of this chapter explains INI file utilities and Extended Attribute utilities, as well as the role of DOS utility programs in an OS/2 environment.

Using Hard Disk Utilities

Probably the most popular DOS-based hard disk utility product is Norton Utilities from Symantec Corporation. This set of computer programs enables you to set your screen colors, search for text strings in files, find files, set volume labels, test your system's performance, change file attributes, print text files, and do a number of other useful things. These other things can compromise OS/2's integrity. Norton Utilities also contains computer programs for sorting directories, un-erasing files, undeleting directories, and modifying the internal physical file allocation tables. These computer programs, while useful, are dangerous in a multitasking environment. If you sort a directory in one DOS session while another DOS session is using that same directory, you "pull the rug out from beneath" the second session. The first session's sort operation distorts the second session's view of the directory.

Other popular hard disk utilities that potentially compromise OS/2's file integrity include PC Tools Deluxe from Central Point Software, HDTest from Peter Fletcher, SpinRite from Gibson Research, OPTune from Gazelle Systems, and Mace Utilities from Symantec. If you want to use one of these products on your computer, you should use only FAT (not HPFS) partitions, and you should use Dual Boot to boot DOS on your computer before you run the utility. Better yet, you should plan to acquire utility software that works specifically with OS/2.

What if you have an HPFS partition and accidentally erase a file? Are you out of luck? No; providers of utility software are developing OS/2 utility applications to help you out of such predicaments. One of the first is GammaTech Utilities for OS/2 from GammaTech (Cary, North Carolina). Among other functions, this product enables you to restore erased files on an HPFS drive and work with both Extended Attributes and INI files. (The next section of this chapter provides more detail about HPFS.) The following list identifies the functions that GammaTech Utilities for OS/2 provides.

> Analyze - The PM Analyze utility for testing and displaying information about your disk drives
>
> Attribute - The PM Attribute utility for changing the attributes, dates, and times of files
>
> Delete - The PM file delete utility for deleting files and, optionally, obliterating any residue of what the deleted files might have contained
>
> FAT-Opt - The FAT Optimizer utility for defragmenting a disk drive formatted with the FAT file system
>
> Find - The PM file find utility for locating mislaid files
>
> Sentry - Boot sector monitor and file lock utility for protecting the integrity of your important files
>
> Sysinfo - Display system information about your computer and operating system

HPFS-Opt - The PM HPFS Optimizer for defragmenting a disk drive formatted with the HPFS file system

UnDelete - The file-undelete utility for recovering accidentally erased files

Miscellaneous utilities for editing disk sectors, flagging disk sectors as bad, recovering damaged files, backing up and restoring boot sectors, and rebooting your computer from the command line

Additionally, GammaTech sells the GammaTech Power Pack software product to help you manage OS/2's INI files (for example, the OS2.INI and OS2SYS.INI in the OS2 directory) and OS/2's Extended Attributes (EAs). You can use the Power Pack's GammaTech INI Editor to view and edit INI file entries and the GammaTech EA Editor to examine and alter the Extended Attributes that OS/2 attaches to files and directories.

Carry Associates of Marco Island, Florida, also markets an OS/2 utility for managing your INI files and Extended Attributes. You'll find a shareware version of the program, called INIMAINT, on many bulletin boards and on information services such as CompuServe, BIX, and GEnie. The commercial version of the program, SYSMAINT, offers more features than the shareware version with its support for Extended Attributes and for backing up and restoring your desktop configuration.

Chapter Summary

You now understand the differences between DOS and OS/2, and you know that OS/2 is like DOS in many ways. In this chapter, you learned that OS/2 and DOS files are usually indistinguishable and that many OS/2 commands behave just as they did under DOS. Not only can you run your DOS applications under OS/2, but when you do the applications have more of the 640K of memory available to them. OS/2 also can run multiple DOS applications at the same time. OS/2 applications are not constrained by the 640K limitation. You also learned about Microsoft Windows applications working under OS/2, why some DOS-based hard disk utilities cannot run under OS/2, and that OS/2 is highly configurable.

In the next chapter, you decide how you want to use OS/2.

Part II
Installing and Configuring OS/2

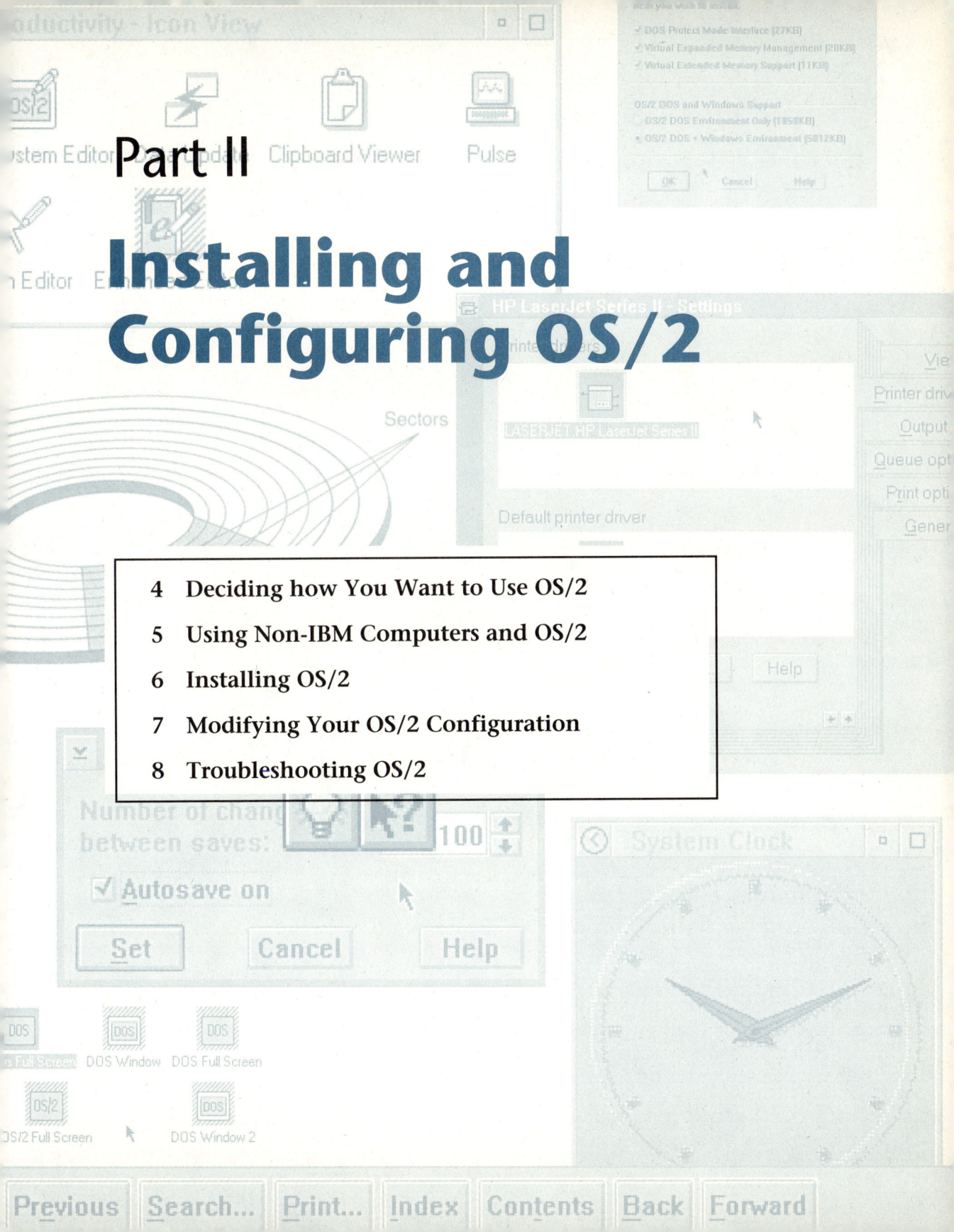

- 4 Deciding how You Want to Use OS/2
- 5 Using Non-IBM Computers and OS/2
- 6 Installing OS/2
- 7 Modifying Your OS/2 Configuration
- 8 Troubleshooting OS/2

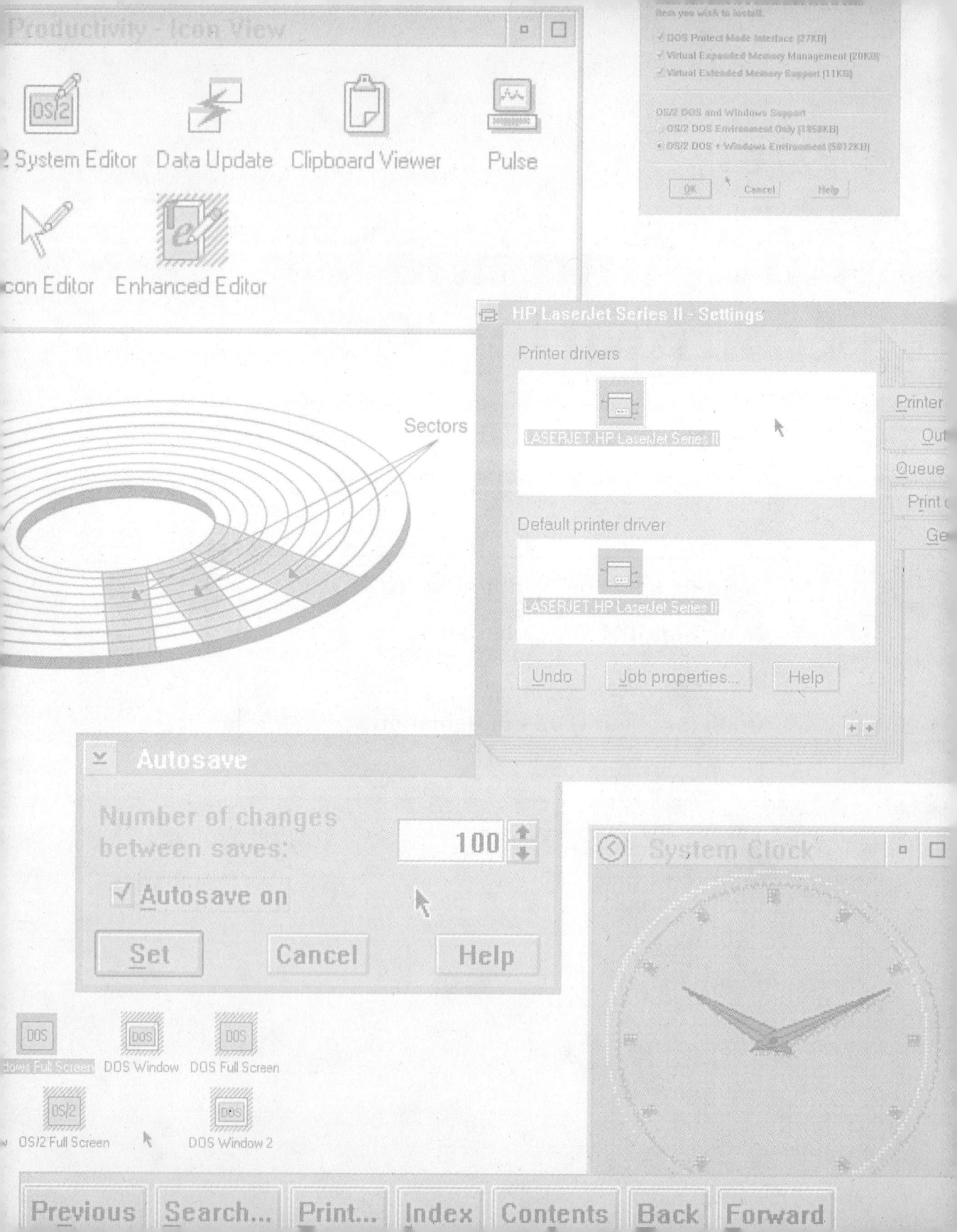

Productivity - Icon View

- OS/2 System Editor
- Data Update
- Clipboard Viewer
- Pulse
- Icon Editor
- Enhanced Editor

---

item you wish to install.

- ✓ DOS Protect Mode Interface (27KB)
- ✓ Virtual Expanded Memory Management (20KB)
- ✓ Virtual Extended Memory Support (11KB)

OS/2 DOS and Windows Support
- ○ OS/2 DOS Environment Only (1858KB)
- ● OS/2 DOS + Windows Environment (5012KB)

[OK] [Cancel] [Help]

Sectors

HP LaserJet Series II - Settings

Printer drivers

LASERJET HP LaserJet Series II

Default printer driver

LASERJET HP LaserJet Series II

[Undo] [Job properties...] [Help]

Printer
Out
Queue
Print
Ge

Autosave

Number of changes between saves: **100**

✓ Autosave on

[Set] [Cancel] [Help]

System Clock

- DOS Windows Full Screen
- DOS Window
- DOS Full Screen
- OS/2 Full Screen
- DOS Window 2

[Previous] [Search...] [Print...] [Index] [Contents] [Back] [Forward]

Chapter 4

Deciding How You Want to Use OS/2

In the last two chapters, you learned how DOS operates and you also learned that OS/2 is a superset of DOS, with capabilities that exceed those of DOS. By now, you may feel that you want to try out OS/2 immediately. If you rush ahead with the installation, however, you might miss some key points about tailoring OS/2 to your own work habits. The OS/2 installation process might even fail to complete properly. Take your time and thoughtfully work your way through this chapter before you start the installation process. You will find that the time is well-spent and that your use of OS/2 is much more productive after you learn the many ways you can customize OS/2 to work the way you want.

You can set up OS/2 in literally hundreds of different configurations. You begin making your setup choices when you install OS/2. The installation program creates disk files on your hard disk that contain your preferences; OS/2 uses these preferences when it loads itself and later while you use your computer.

The installation process asks you how OS/2 should set up your computer system's hard disk, what brand of mouse you have, and which tools and utilities to use. Also, you indicate the maximum number of threads your applications might use and the way in which OS/2 should manage your swap file. OS/2 supplies default answers to many of these types of questions, but you want to be aware of the meanings of these options so that you can determine for yourself what is appropriate. This chapter gives you that information.

If you change your mind later about how you installed OS/2, you may be able to use OS/2's configuration tools (such as Selective Install) to reconfigure your system. OS/2 is definitely not rigid and unyielding; you will find that the operating system probably functions properly even if you made an inappropriate choice during installation. Your computer system may run more slowly than it might otherwise, however, or OS/2 may not make the best use of your computer's internal memory. The worst situation is a computer that may not work at all—a remote but definite possibility. This chapter helps you prevent that from happening.

The first choice you make regarding OS/2 is whether to get the standard version of OS/2 2.1 or the special Windows version of OS/2 for Windows. If you haven't made the choice already, this chapter explains the differences between the two versions so that you can make an informed purchase.

To help you organize your thoughts, you will find the discussion of the configuration options categorized into the following areas:

- Coexistence with other operating systems
- Disk and disk file considerations
- Application and general system options
- Device support
- Personal preferences

In each area, you learn advantages and disadvantages of the various options you can choose and receive recommendations suitable for most people. Use these recommendations as a guide, but don't be afraid to experiment with other options that seem to fit your needs better.

Choosing OS/2 for Windows

Many—if not most—desktop computers come with DOS and Windows preloaded. The computer manufacturer installs the DOS operating system and the Microsoft Windows operating environment on the computer before shipping the machine to you. (Some manufacturers are beginning to preload OS/2 on their computers, if you ask for OS/2 rather than DOS-and-Windows. This is a new trend.)

If you have Windows 3.1 on your computer already and want to step up to OS/2, you can purchase the OS/2 for Windows product rather than regular OS/2 2.1. After you install OS/2 for Windows, you have exactly the same features and functions on your computer as if you had installed the regular

OS/2 2.1. OS/2 for Windows costs much less than the regular OS/2 2.1 product. The lower cost reflects the fact that you've already paid for a license to use Windows. If you were to purchase the regular OS/2 2.1 package, you'd be paying twice to use Windows 3.1 because the regular OS/2 2.1 product loads a "new" version of Windows on your computer. OS/2 for Windows, on the other hand, uses the Windows operating environment you already have on your computer.

Perhaps you don't use Windows at all. In this case, you don't care that you might have a WINDOWS directory on your hard drive (except, of course, for the disk space it consumes). You may simply want the full-featured, extra DOS sessions that OS/2 2.1 can provide. If you purchase regular OS/2 2.1, you'll be paying needlessly for a license to use Windows. You can instead purchase OS/2 for Windows and save quite a bit of money. Despite the use of the word "Windows" in the name of the product, OS/2 for Windows doesn't require that you already have Windows. OS/2 for Windows installs its DOS and OS/2 components if the installation program does not detect Windows on your computer.

> *Advantages:* OS/2 for Windows is less expensive but provides the same features and functions as the regular OS/2 2.1 product.
>
> *Disadvantages:* If you install OS/2 for Windows on a PC that doesn't have Windows, just for the DOS session support, you cannot later add Windows without reinstalling.
>
> *Recommendation:* Get OS/2 for Windows rather than the regular OS/2 2.1 if you already have Windows or if you don't use Windows at all.

Examining Other Operating Systems

OS/2 2.1 wants to be a good neighbor to the other operating systems you might use with your computer system. As Chapter 1, "Taking a Quick Tour of OS/2 and Your Computer," and Chapter 3, "Learning OS/2 If You Know DOS," discussed, you can start specific, older versions of DOS by booting them in a Virtual DOS Machine (VDM) environment under OS/2. You also can boot other operating systems on your computer, alternating between OS/2 2.1, OS/2 1.3, UNIX, and/or "plain" DOS. When you use one of these other operating systems on your computer, you reboot your entire computer rather than boot a DOS version in a VDM within OS/2.

Employing Dual Boot

If booting a specific DOS version (such as 3.3) inside a VDM under OS/2 does not allow you to run a particular application, you may have to close all your current OS/2 applications, choose Shutdown from the OS/2 desktop menu, and reboot your computer with the "real" version of DOS in order to use that finicky application. You also can reboot by inserting a DOS boot disk (system-formatted) into drive A and pressing the Del key while holding down the Ctrl and Alt keys. Or you can use OS/2's Dual Boot feature.

Dual Boot keeps a set of DOS system files on your hard disk beside the OS/2 system files. Dual Boot also stores your DOS CONFIG.SYS and AUTOEXEC.BAT files in the C:\OS2\SYSTEM directory. When you type **BOOT /DOS**, the BOOT utility saves the current OS/2 CONFIG.SYS and AUTOEXEC.BAT files, restores the DOS files, and boots DOS. When you later (under DOS) type **BOOT /OS2**, the BOOT utility reverses its previous actions and boots OS/2.

Advantages: You may want to run a DOS disk diagnostic program such as Norton Utilities on your hard disk. OS/2 does not allow the diagnostic program access to the hard disk if OS/2 currently has files open on that disk. Dual Boot lets you boot DOS, run the disk utilities, and then reboot OS/2. You don't have to keep a DOS system-formatted disk handy for such situations. Dual Boot uses very little hard disk space.

Disadvantages: None, but you may still want to keep a DOS system disk handy for emergencies, as explained in Chapter 8, "Troubleshooting OS/2."

Recommendation: Allow the OS/2 installation process to set up Dual Boot on your computer.

Using the Multiple Operating System Tool (Boot Manager)

The Multiple Operating System Tool (Boot Manager) is much more complicated than Dual Boot. Fortunately, you almost certainly will not need it. Boot Manager sets up a small portion of your hard disk with a special program that controls the boot process. At boot time, this program enables you to choose which of several different operating systems you want to use; each operating system is in a hard disk partition of its own. You might use Boot Manager for a non-OS/2 operating system such as UNIX that insists on booting from drive C, or you might use Boot Manager to boot OS/2 2.1 from drive D if you have a drive D.

Advantages: Boot Manager allows you to install a second operating system such as UNIX and then switch between OS/2 and the second system. Boot Manager is useful for operating systems too cumbersome to be booted from a single floppy disk.

Disadvantages: Boot Manager slows the boot process and requires that you partition and format your hard disk differently. Boot Manager isn't difficult to install on a new computer; however, if you already have files on your hard disk, you have to back up your files before you use Boot Manager to partition and format your hard disk. Boot Manager also takes up a little disk space.

Recommendation: Avoid installing Boot Manager unless you need to use a non-DOS, non-OS/2 operating system such as UNIX.

Considering Disks and Disk Files

Several OS/2 options relate to the disk drive or drives in your computer. You may have a CD-ROM drive that requires special driver software, for example, or you may want to take advantage of OS/2's High Performance File System.

Installing CD-ROM Drives

Deciding whether to use this option is easy. If you have a CD-ROM drive attached to your computer, install the support for it. You can access your CD-ROM from within OS/2. This option takes up very little disk space. The following list identifies the CD-ROM drives supported by OS/2 2.1. Note that IBM and CD-ROM manufacturers continue to develop new CD-ROM drivers for OS/2. Appendix H identifies ways to obtain drivers for CD-ROM drives not in this list.

Manufacturer	CD-ROM Drive Model
Hitachi	CDR-1650S, CDR-1750S, CDR-3650, CDR-3750
IBM	CD-ROM I, CD-ROM II
NEC	CDR-36, CDR-37, CDR-72, CDR-73, CDR-74, CDR-82, CDR-83, CDR-84
Panasonic	CR-501, LK-MC501S
Pioneer	various
Sony	CDU-541, CDU-561, CDU-6111, CDU-6211, CDU-7211
Texel	DM-3021, DM-5021, DM-5024
Toshiba	XM-3201, XM-3301

For Related Information
- "First Step: Text Mode," p. 128
- "Choosing the OS/2 Features You Want," p. 139
- "Switching between OS/2 and DOS with Dual Boot," p. 404

The CD-ROM drive uses a cable to attach to an adapter card in your computer. The following table lists the OS/2-supported adapter cards you can use.

Manufacturer	SCSI adapter or interface
Adaptec	AIC 6260, AHA 1510/1512/1520/1522, AHA 1540/1542/1544, AHA 1640/1642/1644, AHA 1740/1742/1744
DPT	PM2011/2012
Future Domain	TMC-850/860/875/885, TMC-1660/1670/1680, MCS-600/700, TMC-700EX, TMC-850IBM
IBM	PS/2 SCSI Adapter, PS/2 SCSI Adapter with cache Creative Labs Sound Blaster CD bundle via CompuServe, BBS, or Creative Labs

Offering the High Performance File System

DOS uses a software mechanism called a File Allocation Table (FAT) to access disks. OS/2 also can access FAT-based disks. The File Allocation Table scheme was really designed to work with small-capacity disks, however. Applications that access files (especially large files) on FAT-based hard disks run slowly. Each file access causes DOS or OS/2 to search long chains of physical disk location information inside the FAT.

OS/2 offers a High Performance File System (HPFS) option especially designed for hard disks. The HPFS works much faster than a FAT when applications access large files, directories containing many files, or large hard drives. On a FAT-based disk, your file names can be only 11 characters long—eight characters for the root name, one period, and three characters for an extension. With HPFS, you can give files longer, more meaningful names—up to 255 characters long—and your file names can include embedded spaces and lowercase letters (for example, a valid HPFS filename is **October 1st Sales Projection**).

> **Note**
>
> If you allocate your entire disk drive to HPFS, you completely lose the ability to access the drive after you boot DOS (perhaps from a system-formatted floppy disk). For those times when you might need to run the CHKDSK utility (provided with OS/2) on your HPFS drive, you'll need to boot OS/2 from the first two distribution floppy disks to get to a command-line prompt.
>
> You should instead allocate a small first partition on your disk drive, formatted FAT. This first partition becomes your bootable OS/2 drive. OS/2 will assign the drive letter C: to this first partition. You can allocate the remainder of the drive to HPFS. If you find the need to run CHKDSK on your HPFS partition, you can do so directly from OS/2. You won't have to separately boot OS/2 from the floppy disk to run CHKDSK.

Advantages: Your computer will seem much **faster**, your DOS applications can access HPFS files from DOS sessions under OS/2, long file names are convenient, and HPFS uses little disk space.

Disadvantages: HPFS files are invisible unless OS/2 is running (if you use Dual Boot to start DOS, for example, you cannot access your HPFS files). Files with long file names are invisible in DOS sessions. (In fact, the entire HPFS partition is invisible unless you are running OS/2.) The first disk partition must be FAT-based if you use Dual Boot. Your copy of Norton Utilities (or other disk utility) can't access an HPFS partition. You'll need to purchase an HPFS-aware disk utility tool, such as GammaTech Utilities for OS/2 (discussed in Chapter 3). Finally, installing HPFS requires that you format your hard disk, so you must back up and restore existing files.

Recommendation: Set up part of your hard disk as an HPFS partition for the files you access from within OS/2 (using either DOS-based or OS/2-based applications). Avoid using long file names for files you access from DOS-based applications. Make the first partition FAT (perhaps 40M to 80M worth) and allocate the remainder of the drive to HPFS.

Using Buffers, Disk Caches, and Lazy Writes

Because disks are partly mechanical, they are relatively slow in comparison to your computer's internal memory. You can make your computer faster by using some of the internal memory to hold portions of disk files while they are accessed.

Buffers. A buffer is 512 characters of internal memory. When an application reads or writes blocks of data that are not exactly the same size as a disk sector (512 characters), OS/2 uses a buffer as an intermediate holding area. Buffers also take part in OS/2's overlapped input/output feature. Data in a buffer can be processed and handed to an application even while other disk activity continues.

Advantages: You can increase the speed of your system by increasing the number of buffers OS/2 uses.

Disadvantages: When you increase the number of disk buffers, you decrease your available internal memory. Additional buffers may cause large, memory-intensive programs to run more slowly or not at all because OS/2 must perform memory-swapping to allow these applications to share the same internal memory space.

Recommendation: Experiment with the number of buffers to get the best performance. Start with the OS/2-supplied default value. Increase the number if you run many programs concurrently.

Disk Caches. You can set aside a portion of your computer's internal memory as a disk cache. OS/2 can remember previously accessed disk file data stored in a cache and give that data to an application without waiting for the relatively slow hard disk. When an application program requests hard disk data already in the cache, the disk cache sends the data directly to the application program. This procedure is much faster than if the data were read from the disk each time.

A disk cache has the same advantages and disadvantages as buffers.

Recommendation: Base your setting of the size of the disk cache on the amount of physical internal memory in your computer. The following table lists the recommended cache size per computer memory size.

Computer Memory	Cache Size
2-3M	64K
4-5M	192K
6M or more	256K

Lazy Writes. Disk caching can be applied to disk data write operations as well as read operations. When lazy writes are enabled, OS/2 uses its multitasking capability to perform physical write operations in the background while you continue to use the computer. If you turn off lazy writes, OS/2 actually places the data on the disk surface before allowing your application to continue processing.

Advantages: Lazy writes make your computer system faster.

Disadvantages: A power failure that occurs at just the wrong moment can cause data to be lost.

Recommendation: Unless you use your computer in life-or-death situations, such as running a heart/lung machine, you probably want to take advantage of lazy writes.

File Compression Utilities and Disk Space

Before you install OS/2, you'll want to evaluate the amount of available disk space on your computer's hard drive. You'll also want to consider whether to use an on-the-fly disk file compression utility with OS/2, to conserve disk space, and whether you presently use such a utility under DOS. Products such as DoubleDensity from Abacus Software, Stacker from Stac Electronics, SuperStor Pro from AddStor, XtraDrive 1.0 from Integrated Information Technologies, and DoubleSpace from Microsoft let you store more data on your hard drive by compressing data during write (save) operations and decompressing data during read (load) operations. These DOS-based products do not work with OS/2, unfortunately.

> **Note**
>
> You cannot install OS/2 on a drive that uses a DOS-based on-the-fly file compression utility. You must make backup copies of your data, uncompress the disk drive, install OS/2, and then restore your data. The good news is that two companies, Stac Electronics (Stacker) and Proportion Software (DCF/2), have begun shipping on-the-fly file compression utilities that work with OS/2.

Advantages: On-the-fly file compression utilities help your files use less disk space.

Disadvantages: File compression and decompression add a little extra time to file read and write operations. Your PC might seem to run more slowly.

Recommendation: Hard disk drives have become relatively inexpensive commodities. Consider adding another drive to your computer as you decide whether to use a file compression utility in the OS/2 environment.

Working with RAM Disks

IBM supplies what is called a RAM Disk utility (or VDISK) with OS/2. A RAM Disk utility uses internal memory to simulate the operation of a disk drive.

Advantages: The RAM Disk utility is fast and is a convenient place to put temporary files.

For Related Information

- "First Step: Text Mode," p. 128
- "Understanding the Drives Object Display," p. 271
- "Manipulating Files," p. 284
- "Learning the Commands for Managing Directories," p. 305
- "Learning the Commands for Managing Files," p. 311

Disadvantages: The files on the RAM Disk disappear when the computer's power is off. A RAM Disk large enough to be useful may preempt more internal memory than you are willing or able to allocate.

Recommendation: If your applications use temporary files and if you have more than about 12M of internal memory (a rough guideline), you should have OS/2 set up a RAM Disk, and then you should instruct your applications to use it.

Understanding Application and General System Options

You can set or change several OS/2 options to control how OS/2 functions internally and how it uses your computer's resources. These resources include the CPU (how it should be shared among the various applications), the hard disk (how OS/2 should use the hard disk when the demand for physical memory exceeds the actual amount installed, as well as how OS/2 should report disk errors), and the internal memory (whether a DOS environment should be created and what size it should be).

Using Autofail

If you have ever seen a DOS Abort, Retry, or Ignore? message, you will recognize the importance of the AUTOFAIL option. If a serious disk error occurs and AUTOFAIL is OFF, you see a pop-up window that notifies you of the error. You have the opportunity to retry the disk operation, notify the application that the operation failed, or end the application. If AUTOFAIL is ON, no pop-up window appears, and the application is automatically told the disk operation failed.

Advantages: When a computer runs unattended, you can set AUTOFAIL ON to ensure that you do not have to periodically check on the hands-off application to see if it is still running.

Disadvantages: You don't see serious disk errors when they happen. Not all applications correctly handle the FAIL notification.

Recommendation: Leave AUTOFAIL set to the default OFF.

Looking at PauseOnError

If OS/2 detects an error while it processes the CONFIG.SYS file at startup, it looks at the value of PauseOnError. If this option is ON, OS/2 displays an error message and waits for you to press Enter before OS/2 continues. If this option is OFF (the default), OS/2 continues to process the remainder of the CONFIG.SYS file.

Advantages: The ON setting may be useful for unattended computers that need to begin processing without human intervention when power is restored following a power failure.

Disadvantages: You do not get a chance to read and correct CONFIG.SYS error messages.

Recommendation: Change the setting of PauseOnError to ON.

Working with Input/Output Privilege Level

For OS/2 applications to multitask and share computer resources successfully, those applications must not try to take over the computer. OS/2's job is to manage the computer hardware. An application should ask OS/2 to perform services that require direct hardware control. When the IOPL option is set to NO, any application that tries to access the computer hardware directly is ended. If you set IOPL to YES, OS/2 allows the application to perform the hardware access and to continue processing.

The IOPL option gets its name from the names of the CPU instructions that perform direct hardware access—INPUT and OUTPUT. OS/2 uses the setting of this option to grant or refuse Input/Output Privilege.

Advantages: Setting IOPL to NO prevents a program that accesses the hardware directly and that contains programming errors (bugs) from continuing to process.

Disadvantages: A few applications exist that multitask correctly and yet require I/O privilege. Check the documentation that came with your application to see if it requires IOPL to be set to YES.

Recommendation: Set IOPL to YES.

Examining Threads

In OS/2's multitasking environment, several applications can run at the same time. In various sessions, for example, you might be entering information into a spreadsheet program, printing a report, formatting a floppy disk, and downloading a file from another computer. In turn, each application may be doing multiple things at the same time. Each of these running processes is called a *thread*. An OS/2-aware word processing program will likely have separate threads for repaginating, saving a file to disk, and printing. OS/2 supports a maximum of 4,095 simultaneous threads. The default (if no option is supplied) is 256 threads. You use the THREADS option to tell OS/2 to allow more than 256 simultaneous threads. When an application tries to exceed the allocated number of threads (to calculate results in the background, for example), OS/2 forces the process to run serially and thus more slowly.

> *Advantages:* A higher value for THREADS allows more multitasking to occur under OS/2.
>
> *Disadvantages:* Each allocated thread takes up a small amount of internal memory.
>
> *Recommendation:* Experiment with a setting of 512 threads to see if your computer performs faster. If it does not, drop back to the initial setting of 256 threads.

Considering MaxWait

The essence of multitasking is the sharing of the computer's resources, especially the CPU. Only one process can use the CPU at one time, however, and this limitation is a design flaw of the CPU. OS/2 gives each application its fair share of CPU time by allowing each to have the CPU for a few milliseconds and then handing the CPU resource to the next application.

The MaxWait option specifies the longest amount of time, in seconds, that an application has to wait for the CPU. The system default is three seconds. To help an application that has waited MaxWait seconds for the CPU, OS/2 boosts the application's priority so that it is next in line.

> *Advantages:* Setting a lower value for MaxWait causes all applications to seem to move along more smoothly.
>
> *Disadvantages:* The processing that occurs inside OS/2 when the MaxWait setting is exceeded is small but significant. A too-low value for MaxWait causes OS/2 to spend unproductive time trying to determine which application to run next.
>
> *Recommendation:* Leave the system default at three seconds; you may want to experiment with values of two or perhaps even one, however.

Using Memory Management

OS/2 can assume that you have in your computer more internal memory than is physically present. OS/2 does this by using a portion of your hard disk as an overflow area. You may have only 4M of physical memory, yet run a set of concurrent applications that together require 6M of memory. OS/2 over-commits memory by using the overflow area on the disk, called the Swap File, to temporarily hold sections of internal memory. OS/2 also can move sections of internal memory around to make more room.

The Memory Management (MemMan) CONFIG.SYS statement controls how OS/2 uses the Swap File and how it treats sections of internal memory. Setting options are SWAP/NOSWAP, PROTECT, and COMMIT. SWAP allows OS/2 to use the Swap File; NOSWAP denies OS/2 the use of the Swap File. PROTECT enables OS/2 to allocate memory for dynamic link library (DLL) software modules. COMMIT (a version 2.1 new parameter) causes OS/2 to deny an application's memory allocation request if that request would expand the Swap File beyond your CONFIG.SYS MINFREE setting. If you do not use COMMIT and if the Swap File grows to endanger your MINFREE setting, OS/2 warns you that you need to close applications and delete unneeded files. The COMMIT setting prevents OS/2 from trying to allocate further memory to applications and thus makes sure you always have free disk space equal to your MINFREE setting.

> *Advantages:* OS/2's memory management is sophisticated and well-designed, allowing you to run applications that otherwise would not fit in your computer.
>
> *Disadvantages:* Swapping and moving memory take time, and you will notice that your computer runs more slowly when OS/2 needs to use the Swap File.
>
> *Recommendation:* Leave the system defaults (SWAP, PROTECT) alone. Use COMMIT for PCs that are low on disk space and that usually run in unattended mode. If your swap file (named SWAPPER.DAT, located in the \OS2\SYSTEM directory) tends to grow to two, three, or more times its initial size, consider installing more physical RAM in your computer.

Working with Priority

As mentioned in the discussion of the MaxWait option, OS/2 can change the priority of threads waiting to use the CPU. You use the Priority option to override OS/2's manipulation of thread priorities. A setting of Absolute tells OS/2 not to change thread priorities; Dynamic tells OS/2 to do what is necessary to activate a thread and have it use the CPU. The default setting is Dynamic.

Advantages: A value of Absolute may help achieve predictable results by allowing applications to control their own priorities.

Disadvantages: Some threads may not run for a long time.

Recommendation: Use the default Dynamic value.

Examining SwapPath and Initial Swap File Size

The discussion of the MemMan option mentioned the swap file, the special disk file that OS/2 uses to temporarily hold sections of memory. You specify the disk drive and directory in which the swap file (named SWAPPER.DAT) exists by using the SwapPath option. You can also specify the starting (minimum) size of the swap file. The default location of the file is the C:\OS2\SYSTEM directory. The default initial file size is 2048K, depending on how much physical memory (RAM) is in your PC.

> **Note**
>
> You cannot erase the SWAPPER.DAT file while OS/2 is operating. You'll receive an "Access is denied" error message if you try to delete the file.

Advantages: Overcommitment of memory through the use of the swap file enables you to run more applications and larger applications.

Disadvantages: A swap file on a relatively slow hard disk severely affects performance. At times, the swap file may grow quite large.

Recommendation: Never place the swap file on a floppy disk. If you have more than one hard disk, put the Swap File on the disk you think is fastest. If the swap file grows considerably, to more than two or three times its initial size, consider putting more physical RAM in your computer.

Using DOS Environment Control

OS/2 offers extensive support for DOS-based applications. Several OS/2 configuration options (Break, ProtectOnly, and Real Mode Size) pertain only to DOS and enable you to better control and manage your DOS sessions.

BREAK. Holding the Ctrl key and pressing the Break key terminates a DOS application. BREAK instructs OS/2 to determine whether you pressed the Ctrl/Break keys before it performs an Input/Output operation for the DOS application. The default for BREAK is OFF.

Understanding Application and General System Options

Advantages: You can use the Ctrl/Break keys to more quickly stop an errant computer program if BREAK is ON.

Disadvantages: The computer may run slightly more slowly.

Recommendation: The default setting of OFF should suffice for most people.

ProtectOnly. The ProtectOnly option indicates whether you have DOS sessions. PROTECTONLY=YES tells OS/2 that all your applications run in protected mode and that you don't need DOS sessions. PROTECTONLY=NO indicates that you have DOS-based applications to run. (See Chapter 3, "Learning OS/2 If You Know DOS," for an explanation of protected mode.)

Advantages: DOS sessions require an amount of internal memory (see the explanation of the RMSIZE option). You have more memory available to your OS/2 applications if you specify PROTECTONLY=YES.

Disadvantages: More than 20,000 DOS-based applications exist, and you will probably want to run at least one of them at some point.

Recommendation: Unless you are very short of internal memory and you only run OS/2 applications, specify NO.

Real Mode Size. The size of each DOS session under OS/2 can be up to 640K. You can specify a smaller memory region for DOS under OS/2 by using the Real Mode Size (RMSIZE) option.

Advantages: If you don't have much memory, you can allocate a smaller amount to DOS and a correspondingly larger amount for OS/2 applications by using this option.

Disadvantages: When you want to run a DOS-based application that requires a substantial amount of memory, OS/2 displays an error message instead of running the application.

Recommendation: Unless you are very short on internal memory, use the default 640K. Note that the CONFIG.SYS entry for RMSIZE is a default that you specify. On a session-by-session basis, you can instruct OS/2 to use a different value by adjusting the DOS_RMSIZE setting in a DOS session's settings notebook. Chapter 17, "Configuring Your DOS and Windows Sessions," explains such DOS settings in more detail.

For Related Information
- "Choosing the OS/2 Features You Want," p. 139
- "Adding DOS Programs," p. 397
- "Command Reference," p. 717

Using Device Support

OS/2 includes built-in support for many computer devices you might connect to your system. The designers and developers of OS/2 paid particular attention to graphical displays, printers, and downloadable fonts. If you have an application that uses a communications (serial) port, the application will probably configure the COM1, COM2, COM3, or COM4 port itself. OS/2 lets you provide default startup options for devices connected to communications ports, however.

Increasing Display Resolution and Colors

Depending on the video adapter card installed in your computer, OS/2 2.1 can display more information on your monitor. You can use more and larger windows on the Workplace Shell desktop. You can increase the display resolution (the number of horizontal and vertical dots) and the number of possible colors on your display. You can take advantage of higher resolutions to see more of your work at the same time. In a graphics-based word processing application such as WordPerfect for OS/2, Microsoft Word/PM, or Ami Pro for OS/2, for example, you see a greater portion of each page of the document while you work.

The following table lists several IBM-established display standards that OS/2 2.1 supports.

Adapter	Common Name	Resolution
Color Graphics Adapter	CGA	640x200
Enhanced Graphics Adapter	EGA	640x350
Video Graphics Array	VGA	640x480
8514 Display Adapter		1024x768
Extended Graphics Array	XGA	1024x768

OS/2's support for CGA is quite limited; IBM strongly recommends that you upgrade from CGA to a more modern video adapter and monitor if you want to use OS/2. If you have an EGA video adapter, you will find the amount of information displayed on-screen is similarly limited. You should consider upgrading your video adapter and monitor if you presently use CGA or EGA.

In addition, OS/2 2.1 supports several brands of Super VGA video adapters. IBM did not create the Super VGA display standard. Several manufacturers of IBM-compatible computers and peripheral devices formed a committee, the Video Electronics Standards Association (VESA), to promote higher-resolution displays. VESA has defined a Super VGA standard that offers a resolution of 640x480 with 256 colors and a resolution of 800x600 with 16 colors. Some manufacturers go beyond the VESA specification to provide even higher resolutions, such as 1024x768. IBM built device drivers for Super VGA video adapters as well as some higher-resolution video adapters into OS/2. You select your level of video adapter support during the installation process. You can use an OS/2 configuration option, as Chapter 7, "Modifying Your OS/2 Configuration," explains, to further increase the resolution produced by your video adapter.

IBM now makes a Super VGA video adapter, the IBM VGA 256c. OS/2 2.1 supports the VGA 256c and the following video adapters or video adapter chipsets, in resolutions of 800x600, 1024x768, or higher:

ATI Technologies VGA Wonder XL

Cirrus Logic CL-GD542X

Headland Technology VRAM II

Trident Microsystems 8900

Tseng Laboratories ET4000

Video adapters based on chipsets from the S3 company

Western Digital Paradise

Recommendation: Before you install OS/2, refer to the documentation supplied with your computer system to determine the type of video adapter your computer has, as well as the amount of video memory (VRAM) on the adapter. Greater amounts of VRAM allow higher resolutions and more colors. During installation (see Chapter 6, "Installing OS/2") and configuration (see Chapter 7, "Modifying Your OS/2 Configuration"), you choose the video resolution and color possibilities that best suit the work you do. Choose the highest resolution that you can comfortably view on whatever size monitor you use.

Working with Printers and Fonts

In OS/2 2.1, IBM offers support for many makes and models of printers besides IBM's own printers. This support is all the more impressive when you realize how different these printers are. In addition to the character data they print, printers accept commands that do not show up on the printed page, but that tell the printer how to handle subsequent character data. These commands vary widely among the different printers.

OS/2 supplies printer driver software modules for the following general categories of printers:

- IBM/Epson-compatible dot-matrix printers
- PCL printers (Hewlett-Packard LaserJet and InkJet)
- PostScript printers
- IBM laser printers

In addition, OS/2 supports other printers with a generic printer driver that does not include printer command functions. The type of control you can exercise over each kind of printer driver is extensive; the Hewlett-Packard LaserJet driver allows you to specify such settings as number of copies, type of form, orientation (portrait or landscape), manual or automatic paper feed, one- or two-sided (duplexed) printing (for selected models), dots-per-inch resolution, and font cartridge selection, for example.

If you have a laser printer and a WYSIWYG (What-You-See-Is-What-You-Get) word processor application, you know that getting fonts for the printer, especially ones that match the fonts you see on-screen, can be difficult. Your application and Presentation Manager (PM) have to cooperate with each other to make the best use of your fonts. Generally, PM and the printer both choose the closest one available to match your choices.

OS/2 comes with a set of fonts, fortunately, and these fonts provide an excellent match between what you see on-screen and what is actually printed. OS/2 groups the fonts into the following typeface families: Courier, Helvetica, System (monospaced), Times Roman, Courier (Adobe), Helvetica (Adobe), and Times New Roman (Adobe).

Advantages: Installing all the fonts gives you the greatest accuracy between what you see on-screen and what is actually printed. If you use a laser (or other font-based) printer with your desktop publishing application or WYSIWYG word processor, the fonts you install save you time because you need to do fewer trial-and-error printouts. Even without a laser printer, you may just want to be able to select your on-screen fonts from the variety supplied with OS/2.

Disadvantages: The screen and printer fonts supplied with OS/2 occupy disk space. The amount of space varies according to which font families you choose to install, ranging from about 100K up to 1.5M.

Recommendation: Unless you have a shortage of disk space, install all the fonts.

Connecting with Communications Ports

You may have no communications port, one port, or a full complement of COM1, COM2, COM3, and COM4 on your computer. These serial device ports enable you to connect a modem or plotter to your system. In addition, some mice connect to computers through serial ports.

With OS/2, you can supply startup options for the communications ports; these options take effect when you boot the computer. Most applications that use these ports, however, automatically reconfigure the ports when the applications are started. If you have an application that does not initialize a communications port before using it, the options you specify to OS/2 remain in effect so that the application can successfully use the port. The options you can specify for a communications port are baud rate, number of data bits, parity, number of stop bits, and whether the computer should use a hardware handshaking protocol. Consult your application's documentation to find out what these options mean and what values to use.

Advanced Power Management and PCMCIA Support

IBM assumes that someday you may want to use OS/2 on a small, battery-operated notebook computer. The Advanced Power Management (APM) and Personal Computer Memory Card International Association (PCMCIA) specifications are two emerging standards for notebook computers. OS/2 2.1 includes support for both of these specifications. During installation, you choose to configure OS/2 for either or both of the APM/PCMCIA environments.

For Related Information

- "Choosing the OS/2 Features You Want," p. 139

- "Learning OS/2 Printer Basics," p. 375

- "Learning about Fonts," p. 382

- "Printing with OS/2," p. 386

OS/2's support for the APM specification means that OS/2 will help you run your notebook computer for a longer time on one battery charge. OS/2 detects that it's running on a computer based on the APM specification and cooperatively uses APM to consume fewer of the computer's battery-draining resources. The relatively new technology standard of PCMCIA allows add-ins such as modems, network adapters, and even disk drives approximately the size of a credit card. If your computer offers an APM feature or a PCMCIA slot, you will want to configure OS/2 2.1 to support these options.

Reflecting Personal Preferences

You're a unique person, and you like to get your work done in a style that's distinctly your own. The designers of OS/2 realize this and want OS/2 to reflect your preferences and personal tastes. OS/2, therefore, supports many categories of options you can select to tailor OS/2 in highly personal ways. These options include screen colors, mouse usage, keyboard usage, national language, on-line documentation, tools, games, utilities, a sophisticated batch processing language, command history/recall, and the Workplace Shell.

Are you the only person who uses the computer system? If not, when you consider each of these options (especially in the area of screen colors), keep in mind that the selections you make also affect other people.

Selecting Screen Colors and Arranging Your Desktop

You can express a great deal of artistry and personal taste by selecting screen colors for the different parts of each Presentation Manager window. You can easily spend an hour or two—or more—adjusting these colors, if you want. The PM window has 26 different parts you can color, and you can choose from literally thousands of colors for each part. You also can set the width of each window border.

Besides choosing a background color or picture image that you prefer for your on-screen desktop, you can place folders and other icons on your desktop in locations that make sense to you, or you can have OS/2 automatically arrange the icons in symmetrical patterns on your desktop or inside your folders. You can even drag and drop folders and other icons into other folders, thus giving your desktop a "clean" appearance. You have several options for how you want to organize your desktop. Chapter 10, "Managing the Workplace Shell," explains how to express your preferences. For now, you'll want to begin thinking about how you want your computer screen to look as you do your work.

> **Note**
>
> During installation, OS/2 asks you whether you want optional bitmaps installed. These bitmaps are amusing images and patterns that you can display on your desktop. If you're not short of disk space and if you think you'd like to see an image or pattern on your desktop (as opposed to a plain background color) while you work, choose to install the optional bitmaps.

Advantages: Color choices and adjustments are personal matters of taste. You can make your computer system look exactly the way you want.

Disadvantages: If you begin adjusting colors, you may have to remind yourself to stop playing and get back to work. On a serious note, you do need to choose some of the color combinations carefully. You might make on-screen components invisible by selecting, for example, the same foreground and background colors for a part of the screen.

Recommendation: Don't try to make all your color selections in a single session. Make a few adjustments and try out the new color scheme for a while before you make further changes. With this approach, you will not get frustrated when you attempt to make the colors come out exactly right, and you are less likely to make on-screen components invisible or hard to read.

Specifying Mouse Usage

Of all the devices ever connected to computer systems, the mouse (and its cousin, the trackball) probably undergoes the most varied techniques and styles. People double-click at different rates, people like to give the mouse buttons different meanings—and not everyone is right-handed. OS/2 allows you to configure the mouse to work the way you want.

If you are left-handed, you can tell OS/2 to reverse the meanings of the mouse buttons. You can specify which mouse button is the selection button and which is the manipulation button, and you can indicate to OS/2 which combination of buttons you want to use to pop up the Task List window.

Varying Input Methods

People type on the computer keyboard in almost as many different ways as they use the mouse. Some people have special needs when it comes to using the keyboard. With OS/2, you can enable what IBM calls input methods and then select how you want the keyboard to react to your keystrokes. You can type with one finger and still use keys such as Shift, Ctrl, and Alt—you tell

OS/2 to make these keys "sticky," for example. When you press a key, it remains active (even after you release it) until after you press the next key. With OS/2 you can specify the length of time the stickiness persists and which keys to regard as sticky. You also can change the rate at which a key repeats when you hold it down and the delay before it starts repeating.

Examining National Language Support

IBM is an international company, of course, and its products are sold worldwide. To make OS/2 easy for people in different countries to use, the designers of OS/2 provide support for different display formats for time of day, calendar date, numbers in general, and currency.

Using On-Line Documentation

OS/2 comes with a set of documentation files on disk that you can view on-screen. To learn about OS/2 in general, you choose Start Here on the Workplace Shell desktop. When you need help with an OS/2 command or utility, you type HELP at an OS/2 command-line prompt or you use a HELP menu item (or pushbutton) if one is visible on-screen. You also can choose OS/2 Command Reference in the Information folder to browse through the IBM documentation on OS/2 commands and their syntax. Chapter 13, "Using the Built-In Help Facility," describes each of these facilities in more detail.

Advantages: On-line help is quick, handy, and often context-sensitive (it shows you information that relates to the current task).

Disadvantages: The help files use 1.5M of disk space. The tutorial needs only about 200K, and the command reference occupies about 500K. You may not like the way the help windows and command reference windows pop up over your application and obscure your view of the application.

Recommendation: If you have the disk space, install the on-line documentation. Remember that you can later erase the tutorial files after you feel comfortable using OS/2.

Installing Tools, Games, and Utilities

As Chapter 1, "Taking a Quick Tour of OS/2 and Your Computer," mentioned, OS/2 is a full-featured operating system. It comes with utilities and small applications (called *applets*). With the applets, you can become productive immediately after you install OS/2. You may need to obtain and install other applications to use your computer effectively, of course. The tools and utilities will serve you well and help you manage your computer system, however.

You can choose to install or not install each component. Disk space requirements range from about 100K to 2.5M, depending on how many components you choose.

The tools, games, and utilities you can choose to install include the following:

- Calendar and Diary
- Address Book
- Mini-spreadsheet and database
- Calculator
- Alarm Clock
- Business graphics charting
- Enhanced Editor (text editor)
- Seek and Scan (file search utility)
- Cat and Mouse (cursor finder/chaser)
- Solitaire game
- A chess game that embodies artificial intelligence
- Other miscellaneous games

Working with the REXX Language

With Batch files, you can construct and run scripts of OS/2 commands on your computer. The REXX language goes a step further and enables you to write sophisticated computer programs that automate many of the repetitious tasks you need to do. REXX complies with the standards set forth in IBM's System Applications Architecture (SAA). Chapter 19, "Programming with REXX," shows you how to program with REXX, and Chapter 18, "Batch File Programming with OS/2," gives an overview of the similar, simpler batch language.

> *Advantages:* When your experience with OS/2 increases, you will find that batch file programming saves you time and effort in typing. Because batch file programming is somewhat restrictive, you may find that REXX is exactly what you need to overcome these restrictions.
>
> *Disadvantages:* REXX and its on-line help files take up about half a megabyte of disk space—only a small disadvantage. Perhaps the biggest

considerations are your own intentions and objectives for how you want to use your computer. The idea of computer programming may be not be appealing to you.

Recommendation: Install REXX and spend a little time learning to do batch file programming and REXX programming to see if you enjoy it. REXX is perhaps the simplest, easiest-to-use, yet most powerful programming language.

Using Command History/Recall

For the commands you enter at an OS/2 command-line prompt, you can save typing time and reduce typing errors by installing and using the command history/recall feature. This feature is automatically enabled at installation.

For Related Information
- "Choosing the OS/2 Features You Want," p. 139
- "Installing Features Selectively," p. 176
- "Configuring Your Desktop," p. 178

Suppose that you type a command or program name at an OS/2 command-line prompt and then you type another. Next you want to redo the first command you typed. Command history/recall enables you to scroll through previously entered commands (by using the cursor keys) and to choose one to execute again. You can edit a previously entered command before you execute it.

Chapter Summary

This chapter showed you the different options and features that you can choose during the installation of OS/2. You learned about the following options and features: Dual Boot; the Boot Manager; CD-ROM drive support under OS/2; the High Performance File System; application and general system options; printer and serial port device support; custom screen colors and mouse usage; selecting special keyboard conventions; National Language Support; on-line documentation; tools, games, and utilities; REXX programming; and command history/recall.

The next chapter discusses OS/2 considerations for non-IBM computers and non-IBM computer hardware components. If your computer system is manufactured by IBM, you can move on to Chapter 6, "Installing OS/2." If some component in your computer system is not made by IBM, go to the next chapter to learn about the compatibility issues you face when you install and use OS/2 on your non-IBM computer.

Chapter 5

Using Non-IBM Computers and OS/2

If all of your computer equipment is made by IBM, you can safely move on to Chapter 6, "Installing OS/2," and install OS/2. If you have an IBM computer and an IBM display adapter but your computer monitor is non-IBM or if you have an IBM computer but some of the internal memory chips (RAM chips) are non-IBM, you can safely move on to Chapter 6 to learn about the installation procedure. This chapter is for you if you own a personal computer made by another company or if some part of your computer system (such as a video adapter card, mouse, hard disk, hard disk controller card, or keyboard) is non-IBM.

In this chapter, you learn about the differences between true IBM and IBM-compatible computers and components that affect OS/2. You may find that your computer system supports OS/2 perfectly or, less likely, that you need to make some adjustments to your system so that you can install and use OS/2 2.1.

If you're thinking of buying a computer and you suspect that the one you choose will not be IBM-manufactured, you can follow the number-one rule for buying a computer system—purchase your software, including the operating system and initial applications, first. Then try these applications on the hardware you want to buy. You can easily save yourself some time, effort, and expense. When they can, wise computer buyers purchase software first, and then hardware. You may even want to follow this maxim if you purchase an IBM computer to see whether the model you choose performs as well as you want it to perform.

Some companies make computers and parts that look quite a bit like IBM's equipment, and you may have difficulty identifying non-IBM components in your computer. The following list gives some tips on identifying non-IBM equipment:

- When you boot your computer, you see messages (perhaps only briefly) that mention the name of a manufacturer other than IBM.

- You have user manuals and user guides for add-in boards (adapter cards) or disk drives that you or someone else has added to your computer.

- The computer case is similar to IBM's, but you cannot find an IBM logo/sticker on the front of the case.

- The FCC certification sticker on the back of the computer case identifies a manufacturer other than IBM.

Working with IBM-Compatible Computers

Legally, manufacturers cannot exactly duplicate IBM's personal computers, but they can make computers that behave and work the same (or, with respect to such things as video monitor resolution and hard disk speed, perhaps even better). The engineers at COMPAQ, Dell, Gateway 2000, CompuAdd, AST, Toshiba, Texas Instruments, and hundreds of other companies work hard to design electronic circuits that use the same chips IBM computers use but that are laid out differently. These engineers also have to write ROM BIOS software that works the same as IBM's software but looks different from it; like this book, software is copyrighted. (You learn more about ROM BIOS software later in this chapter.)

Companies in the United States are careful to design personal computers that run DOS and OS/2 applications as perfectly as possible so that the applications appear to be running on IBM hardware. These companies are equally careful to create computers that do not infringe on IBM's patents and copyrights, however. Ironically, manufacturers in places such as Taiwan and Korea have duplicated the IBM personal computers almost exactly, without as much regard for legalities, but their computers sometimes have more problems running DOS and OS/2 applications.

Most people categorize the manufacture of PCs into three tiers. IBM occupies the first tier. Companies such as COMPAQ, Dell, Tandy, Gateway 2000, AST Research, Texas Instruments, and Toshiba fall into the second tier. The third tier of manufacturers includes companies in Taiwan and Korea as well as some U.S. companies.

Some companies try to compete with IBM by producing computers that are compatible in all respects but that go beyond IBM's hardware capabilities to provide special options and features. Occasionally, some of these manufacturers get together to form standards committees that proclaim these options and features as new standards. An example is VESA, the Video Electronics Standards Association. VESA came into being to promote high-resolution computer monitors and adapter cards. Soon after the formation of VESA, IBM announced a new, high-resolution video adapter and monitor combination called XGA (Extended Graphics Array). Now the other manufacturers are working overtime to create XGA clones.

In general, OS/2 works (or works best) on computer equipment that functions exactly like IBM hardware. OS/2 2.1 doesn't support every extension and enhancement, such as the ones being promoted by VESA. Version 2.1 of OS/2 does offer support for the most popular non-IBM PC components and peripherals, however.

Before you go much further with the discussion on IBM-compatible computers, take a moment to review the hardware requirements for OS/2 2.1 as outlined in the next section. Then, when you move ahead into specific areas of compatibility (such as hard disks and video adapters/monitors), you have a solid foundation on which to judge your own computer's compatibility with OS/2.

Examining OS/2 2.1 Hardware Requirements

OS/2 is necessarily more stringent than DOS about the hardware on which it runs. Version 2.1 takes advantage of the Intel-designed 80386 or 80486 CPU chip to offer the multiple DOS sessions and the system integrity protection mentioned earlier. OS/2 cannot offer these capabilities on the older 80286 or 8088 CPU chips used in the IBM AT and the original IBM PC. Intel created two distinct types of 80386 CPU chips; OS/2 works with both the sx and dx designations.

OS/2 needs at least 4M of internal memory (RAM); the operating system performs better if you give it even more memory. You should consider putting at least 8M of RAM in your computer before you install and begin using OS/2.

Chapter 5—Using Non-IBM Computers and OS/2

OS/2 is also selective about the type of hard disk, hard disk controller, and video display that you have. While it operates, OS/2 controls these devices to an extent beyond that imposed by plain DOS. The extra control allows OS/2 to perform faster and more reliably than DOS.

OS/2 supports several types of hard disks and hard disk controllers, but you may have to obtain software device drivers from the manufacturer of the disk or controller to use a hard disk with OS/2 2.1. Usually, the types of disks known as MFM and ESDI do not require drivers; IDE and SCSI disks may require software drivers. Hard disk controllers that behave exactly like the Western Digital WA1003 and WA1006 controllers should not require software drivers, but other hard disk controllers may.

You need a high-capacity floppy disk drive to install and use OS/2. If you use 5 1/4-inch disks, the disk drive must be a 1.2M drive. If you use 3 1/2-inch disks, the disk drive must be a 1.44M or 2.88M drive. You can use the lower capacity 360K (5 1/4-inch) or 720K (3 1/2-inch) drives to store files you create, but you cannot use these drives to install OS/2.

IBM originally used a chip with the designation 8250 on its asynchronous communications adapters. This adapter contains the COM1, COM2, and/or COM3 port. You can connect a modem to this adapter when you want to dial a bulletin board or information network, for example. OS/2 does not support the now-obsolete 8250. Beginning with the IBM AT computer, IBM has installed in its personal computers chips with the designation 16450 or 16550. OS/2 works with communications adapters based on these chips.

You can use a variety of video displays (adapters and monitors) with OS/2; however, VGA (Video Graphics Array) and XGA (Extended Graphics Array) work best.

The following list summarizes the hardware requirements of OS/2 2.1:

- 80386 (sx or dx or slc), 80486 sx/dx/dx2/slc2, or Pentium CPU chip
- 4M or more of internal memory (RAM)
- MFM or ESDI hard disk; probably no software driver needed
- SCSI or IDE disk drive, possibly with a software driver
- IBM/Western Digital (or compatible) hard disk controller
- Floppy disk drive; 1.2M drive, 5 1/4-inch disk; 1.44M drive, 3 1/2-inch disk; or 2.88M drive, 3 1/2-inch disk
- A mouse and printer, optional

> **Note**
>
> OS/2 is easier to use if you have a mouse.

You can use one of the following types of video systems:

- CGA (Color Graphics Adapter)
- EGA (Enhanced Graphics Adapter), color or monochrome
- VGA (Video Graphics Array), color or monochrome
- Some Super VGA (SVGA) displays
- 8514/A, with or without memory expansion
- XGA or XGA-2 (Extended Graphics Array)

Making OS/2 Vendor-Neutral

You might think that IBM designed OS/2 2.1 to be incompatible with other vendors' personal computers. This is not the case. In fact, IBM has enlisted the aid of many PC vendors to ensure that OS/2 2.1 runs on the greatest variety of computers. These PC vendors include ALR, Apricot, AST, AT&T, COMPAQ, CompuAdd, Dell, Grid, Everex, Hewlett Packard, NCR, NEC, Netframe, Olivetti, Reply, Siemens, Tandon, Tandy/Grid, and Trichord.

Someone at IBM coined the phrase "vendor-neutral" to describe IBM's positive attitude about making sure that OS/2 2.1 runs on both IBM and IBM-compatible hardware.

Understanding CPU Chips

Intel Corporation manufactures a variety of 80386, 80486, and Pentium (80586) CPU chips. These chips provide your computer with its "brainpower." Intel is even now designing, building, and testing the next generation of personal computer CPU chips. Internally, Intel refers to the 80386, 80486, and Pentium chips as the iAPX386, i486, and P5 Microprocessors. Just as computer manufacturers have cloned the IBM personal computer, chip makers have recently cloned the Intel 80386. A computer capable of running OS/2 2.1, whether that computer is made by IBM or another manufacturer, contains an 80386, an 80486, or a Pentium (80586) CPU chip.

For Related Information
- "Understanding Hardware and Software," p. 15
- "Booting the Installation Disk," p. 127

Examining the Intel 80386 Chip

Intel rates its microprocessor chips at different running speeds. Naturally, higher speeds mean better performance and increased cost. Intel expresses the speed ratings in *megahertz* (often shortened to MHz), a unit of measurement equal to one million that tells the number of times per second the CPU chip is driven to perform its work. An 80386 chip running at 33 MHz is about twice as fast as one running at 16 MHz. Don't depend solely on this rating to measure the speed of your computer, however; other components, such as the hard disk, weigh heavily as factors in how well the computer performs.

Intel makes two kinds of 80386 chips, sx and dx. An 80386sx computer can address up to 16M of internal memory. An 80386dx computer (sometimes the dx designation is omitted when discussing these computers) can address up to 4G (G represents gigabytes, or four billion bytes) of memory. In all other respects, the two kinds of 80386 CPU chips are virtually identical. OS/2 runs equally well on sx and dx chips.

Some computers have math coprocessors installed, or you may install one as an option. Such chips are designated as 80387 chips, and you can purchase one to help your applications run more quickly. The 80387 chip helps the CPU perform certain kinds of arithmetic operations faster. OS/2 does not benefit from the presence of a math coprocessor.

Your 80386 CPU can operate in three modes. In the simplest mode (*real mode*), the CPU is a fast version of the older 8088 chip, and it can address up to 1M of memory. If you install DOS on your computer instead of OS/2, you get this mode by default.

In *protected mode*, the CPU can address up to 4G of internal memory. Practically speaking, however, you're unlikely to have a computer with this amount of RAM installed. One of the benefits of protected mode is the 32-bit architecture you read about in Chapter 4, "Deciding How You Want To Use OS/2." OS/2 and OS/2 applications run in protected mode.

Finally, *virtual 8086 mode* allows the 80386 CPU to act as if it were several real-mode computers. This mode is what OS/2 uses to give you multiple concurrent DOS sessions.

You sometimes see advertisements for 80386 accelerator cards that you can add to an existing computer. In general, these cards cannot run OS/2. An example of such a card is the Intel InBoard.

Examining the Intel 80486 Chip

The 80486 CPU chip is an enhanced edition of the 80386. The 80486 contains circuitry enabling it to operate faster than an 80386. The 80486 CPU also incorporates the functions of a math coprocessor. You don't need to purchase an 80487 math coprocessor if you have an 80486 CPU. Intel produces a particular 80486sx CPU, however, that is an 80486 chip without the math coprocessor functions. This specialized 80486 CPU chip is for unique purposes, and you probably should not consider getting one.

The clock-doubled 80486 DX2 works just like other 80486 chips, just faster. The bus interface portion of the CPU chip produces a 2-to-1 "gear reduction" action. The DX2 runs twice as fast inernally. When the DX2 CPU accesses its internal registers, refers to a memory location already in the internal cache, or performs a floating point operation, the CPU does work at the faster (double-speed) rate. The CPU only has to refer to data within itself to perform these operations. However, when the CPU has to access main memory (RAM), do I/O instructions to an adapter card, or access one of the other chips in the computer, the DX2's electrical signals through the bus occur at half-speed (25 Mhz for a 50 Mhz DX2). Intel also now makes a clock-tripled DX3 CPU.

Examining the Intel Pentium (80586) Chip

Intel found, to the company's dismay, that it could not register the number *80386* or the number *80486* as a trademark. Other companies, as explained in the next section, have produced CPU chips that function in exactly the same way as Intel's 80386 and 80486 chips. These other companies use variations of the numbers *80386* and *80486* to identify the clone CPUs. Intel wants to protect its competitive edge and keep other companies from using Intel's names for PC CPU chips. Toward this end, Intel named the latest generation of CPU chips *Pentium* rather than 80586. The situation is confusing because the 80586 designation is a natural progression from earlier CPU designations. Clone CPU makers who use the name 80586 will take advantage of the progression. Intel, on the other hand, plans a multimillion-dollar advertising campaign to bring name recognition to the Pentium.

At any rate, you should be aware that the Pentium CPU chip is the next generation CPU beyond the 80486. A Pentium CPU typically operates two to three times faster than an 80486.

Examining 80386 and 80486 CPU Chips from Other Manufacturers

At least two companies have either reverse-engineered the Intel 80386 and 80486 CPU chips or claim to have licensing arrangements with Intel that allow them to produce the chips. These companies are Advanced Micro Devices, Chips & Technologies, and Cyrix.

> **Note**
>
> *Reverse engineering* is the process of duplicating the function of a chip by carefully and thoroughly understanding that function and then creating a chip that behaves the same way without actually copying someone else's design. As you might imagine, this process is subject to interpretation; Intel, Advanced Micro Devices, and Chips & Technologies have filed lawsuits to encourage the courts to clarify such interpretations.

For Related Information
- "Understanding Hardware and Software," p. 15
- "Booting the Installation Disk," p. 127
- "First Step: Text Mode," p. 128

Interestingly, IBM has a license from Intel to produce CPU chips. Some IBM computers contain CPU chips manufactured by IBM; some contain Intel-made chips.

Using ROM BIOS

The *ROM BIOS* is software built into your computer. This software is always in the computer—even when you turn it off. The BIOS software is burned into special memory chips; the contents of those chips do not depend on the presence of electrical power. ROM stands for Read-Only Memory, and BIOS stands for Basic Input Output System.

The ROM BIOS takes control when you turn on your computer and checks out your computer with a series of diagnostic steps. It then transfers control of the computer to the operating system (OS/2, in this case), and the operating system loads into memory. Because the ROM BIOS software is always present and available, OS/2 sometimes uses the ROM BIOS functions as if they were part of OS/2.

An IBM or IBM-compatible computer is likely to contain an 80386 or 80486 CPU chip made by Intel. An IBM computer contains a ROM BIOS written and copyrighted by IBM, however. A compatible computer contains a ROM BIOS written by another company that specializes in such software. IBM designed OS/2 to take advantage of the IBM-written ROM BIOS, if it is present. Otherwise, OS/2 loads and uses its own BIOS program code.

If the ROM BIOS in an IBM computer is computer software copyrighted by IBM, how do other companies avoid infringing on IBM's intellectual property rights? They hire programmers who sign affidavits saying that the programmers have never seen or worked with IBM's software and give those programmers specifications on how the ROM BIOS should behave. The programmers write their own computer software (without copying IBM's). The result, if the specifications are accurate, is an IBM-compatible ROM BIOS. People often call this process the "clean room" approach.

> **Tip**
>
> Sometimes you find that companies that do not manufacture IBM ROM BIOS provide extra setup parameters, including such options as *ROM BIOS shadowing*. You may need to turn off shadowing, disable an external CPU cache, switch to a slower CPU speed, or perhaps make other setup changes to successfully install OS/2.

Making BIOS Criteria Compatible

Despite OS/2's loading of its own BIOS code, the computer's internal ROM BIOS does play a part in the loading and initial installation of OS/2. Non-IBM manufacturers of ROM BIOS program code are aware of this fact and have, for the past few years, developed ROM BIOS software that is compatible with OS/2.

An adapter card often contains its own ROM BIOS software that augments the BIOS built into the computer. In general, OS/2 operates these adapters through device drivers, without using the built-in ROM BIOS. In a DOS session under OS/2, you may find that your software runs okay, but OS/2 applications might not be able to use the adapter/device unless the manufacturer supplies an OS/2 device driver with the hardware. Check with the manufacturer to find out whether an OS/2 device driver is available for non-IBM adapter cards. If the adapter requires a device driver under DOS, it almost certainly needs one under OS/2.

IBM's own ROM BIOS is actually two distinct sets of ROM BIOS code. The first, called the *ABIOS*, is compatible with and used by DOS. The other, *CBIOS*, is for use by OS/2.

Manufacturing ROM BIOS Software

The biggest manufacturers of IBM-compatible ROM BIOS software are COMPAQ, Phoenix Technologies, American Megatrends (sometimes referred to as AMI), Award, and Quadtel. New versions appear from these companies all the time, so pinpointing compatibility issues with a particular manufacturer's ROM BIOS is difficult. These difficulties represent another reason why trying out your software, and even the operating system, on a computer before you buy it is important. Bugs (programming errors) in early versions of the AMI BIOS prevented OS/2 from installing successfully on machines equipped with the early AMI BIOS chips, for example. OS/2 2.1 installs on and runs successfully with recent versions of ROM BIOS software from each of the companies just mentioned, however.

AMI designed its BIOS to display a Screen ID Code, which you see each time you boot a computer equipped with an AMI BIOS. The Screen ID Code appears in the bottom left portion of the screen at boot time and has one of the following formats:

AMI BIOS and AMI BIOS Plus:

aaaa-bbbb-mmddyy-Kc

AMI Hi-Flex BIOS:

ee-ffff-bbbbbb-gggggggg-mmddyy-hhhhhhhh-c

If you have a BIOS written by AMI, make a note of the Screen ID Code. If you want to use an IDE hard disk drive in your computer (with any operating system, not just OS/2), the BIOS date (the *mmddyy* part of the Screen ID Code) should be 040990 or later. AMI modified the BIOS code on that date (April 9, 1990) to accommodate the special timing requirements of IDE drives. A BIOS date of 092588 or later allows OS/2 to install on other types of disk drives, as explained in the next section. The Keyboard Controller Revision Level (*c* in the Screen ID Code format) must be *F* or later to support OS/2 2.1.

For Related Information

- "Understanding Hardware and Software," p. 15
- "Booting the Installation Disk," p. 127

Some early Gateway 2000 computers, and computers with a BIOS written by Phoenix Technologies or Micronics, have trouble with OS/2. In particular, Gateway 2000 computers with a Phoenix BIOS version 1.10 M6 cannot run OS/2 2.1. Computers with a revision E Micronics motherboard (the *motherboard* is the main circuit board in the computer on which the CPU sits) cannot run OS/2 2.1.

If you suspect a BIOS conflict between your computer and OS/2, you should call the manufacturer of your PC to determine whether the BIOS needs upgrading. Many manufacturers offer no-cost or low-cost BIOS upgrades to make sure their customers can run OS/2 successfully.

Working with Disks and Disk Controller Cards

Hard disk drive companies manufacture several different kinds of hard disks for personal computers. The following table shows the acronyms by which these disk types are known.

Acronym	Meaning
MFM	Modified Frequency Modulation
RLL	Run-Length-Limited
ESDI	Enhanced Small Device Interface
SCSI	Small Computer System Interface
IDE	Integrated Drive Electronics

Disk drives vary not only by type but also by capacity, number of surfaces, information density, and access rate.

Understanding Disk Drive Types

As mentioned earlier, MFM and ESDI disk drives are likely to work with OS/2 2.1 without a special device driver from the manufacturer. IBM uses primarily MFM and ESDI drives, and a few types of SCSI drives, in its computers. SCSI and IDE drives may need a device driver from the disk drive or disk controller manufacturer, depending on the hard disk controller card's degree of IBM compatibility. The next section discusses hard disk controller cards. RLL drives do not work with OS/2.

A disk cylinder is made up of tracks. A track is one of the concentric circles on the surface of the disk for storing information. A cylinder is the set of tracks that, one on top of the other, are all equidistant from the edge of the disk surface (the platter). Figure 5.1 illustrates disk drive cylinders and their tracks.

Some disk drives have more than 1,024 cylinders, which may be a problem for OS/2. DOS has this problem, too, but DOS users install special device drivers to allow DOS to use these disk drives. (Two popular drivers are Disk Manager from OnTrack Computer Systems and SpeedStor from Storage Dimensions.) Under OS/2, people commonly use (or switch to) disk controller cards that do sector translation, as described in the next section. You may find that your hard disk controller vendor has written an OS/2 device driver to provide compatibility. One such vendor is Adaptec.

Fig. 5.1
A disk drive cylinder.

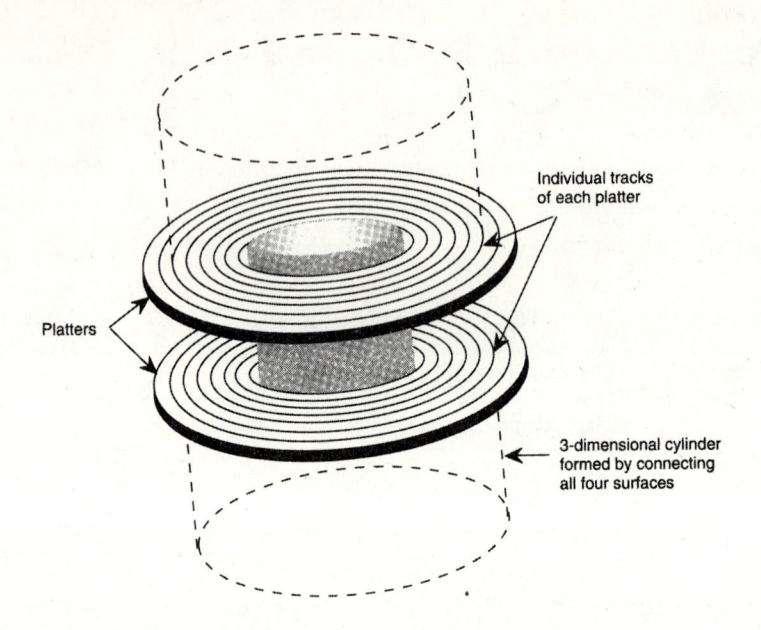

Learning about Disk Controller Cards

Each type of disk drive (MFM, SCSI, IDE, ESDI) requires its own particular kind of disk controller. For years, IBM has used controller cards made by Western Digital in addition to manufacturing its own controllers. This practice has made Western Digital controllers something of a standard. For compatibility, other manufacturers ensure that their controller cards behave the same as Western Digital cards.

MFM drives commonly place 17 sectors on each track. With their higher capacity, ESDI and other drives use more sectors per track (34 or 63, for example). Some controller cards have options that enable you to set the number of sectors per track and to set aside some sectors as spares in case bad spots develop. Bad spots on the disk surface cause disk read/write errors; some controller cards recover from these errors automatically.

The Western Digital WD1007VSE2 is an example of a controller card that enables you to use an ESDI disk with OS/2 that has up to 1,700 cylinders. This type of card employs sector translation, which enables the ROM BIOS and OS/2 to treat the disk as having fewer than 1,024 cylinders. The actual sector numbering scheme on the disk is translated into a different scheme that's acceptable to the ROM BIOS and to OS/2 (or DOS) without the need for a device driver.

On the other hand, some people have reported problems getting the SCSI Future Domain TMC 850 controller card to work successfully with OS/2. If you have doubts or questions, contact the manufacturer.

Using the Keyboards and Mice

Most non-IBM keyboards and mice are compatible with OS/2. The few keyboards that are not are older models whose electronics do not closely match IBM's. Similarly, the few incompatible mice (or other pointing devices) do not behave electronically like the IBM and Microsoft mice.

Looking at the 101-Key Keyboard

As Chapter 1, "Taking a Quick Tour of OS/2 and Your Computer," pointed out, the 101-key keyboard has become an industry standard. The number of keys on the keyboard, however, is not a compatibility issue. Notebook computers have fewer keys (you sometimes use a combination of two keys to equal a single key on the 101-key keyboard), yet are usually quite compatible with OS/2. Toshiba's computers, the CompuAdd, COMPAQ, Companion/SX, the Twinhead Slimnote, and the Texas Instruments TravelMate are examples of notebook computers that run OS/2 well.

Personal computers contain what is called a *keyboard controller chip*. You can think of this chip as part of the ROM BIOS. Some years ago, a few makers of IBM-compatible computers did not design this chip exactly right. The computers ran DOS successfully, but not OS/2. These computers also have difficulty with some DOS Extender software products and with Microsoft Windows. An earlier section of this chapter on Manufacturing ROM BIOS Software explained how to determine the proper revision level for machines equipped with AMI BIOS chips.

Considering Serial, Bus, and PS/2 Mice

IBM makes a two-button mouse that connects directly to the mouse port in an IBM computer. The IBM mouse works exactly the same as the Microsoft mouse, and the two pointing devices are interchangeable. In fact, when you purchase a Microsoft serial mouse, one of the cables in the package connects the Microsoft mouse to the mouse port on a PS/2.

Microsoft offers three kinds of mice. The most popular is the serial mouse, which connects to a serial port or to the mouse port on a PS/2 (using the special cable). Microsoft also makes a bus mouse that requires its own adapter card, and a mouse called the InPort.

For Related Information
- "Understanding Hardware and Software," p. 15
- "First Step: Text Mode," p. 128
- "Understanding Installation Errors," p. 195

During the installation process, OS/2 tries to identify the type of mouse you have (if any). In many cases, this automatic detection eliminates compatibility problems. You may find, however, that OS/2 has chosen the wrong type of pointing device. Check the documentation that came with your mouse to see whether it emulates one of the mice in the following list:

- IBM PS/2 mouse
- Microsoft serial, bus, or InPort mouse
- PC Mouse (from PC Mouse Systems)
- Visi-On Mouse (from Visi-On)
- Logitech Serial Mouse

For Related Information
- "Understanding Hardware and Software," p. 15
- "Upgrading Your Hardware," p. 169

OS/2 directly supports the mice in this list. For pointing devices that are not on the list or that do not emulate these mice, you may need to experiment by telling OS/2 that you have each of the mice on the list until you find a combination that works. You also may see that your mouse, trackball, or other pointing device connects to the computer like one of these other mice, and that may give you a clue as to what to tell OS/2. Logitech manufactures a bus mouse, for example; you would select the Microsoft bus mouse during the OS/2 installation process.

Working with Video Adapter Cards and Monitors

The IBM Video Graphics Array (VGA) specification has existed long enough that almost every manufacturer of video adapter cards and monitors is highly compatible—sometimes indistinguishably so—with IBM. The Extended Graphics Array (XGA) specification, on the other hand, is relatively new. The Radius company has obtained rights from IBM to produce versions of the XGA video adapter. Other manufacturers have not yet copied the IBM XGA design in a manner that does not infringe on the patent. Many of these manufacturers, to compete with IBM's VGA standard, formed the Video Electronics Standards Association (VESA) to promote higher-resolution, fuller-color displays. Video modes supported by VESA are often called Super VGA, and the non-IBM hardware always has two modes: standard VGA and Super VGA.

In addition, IBM has three older standards—the Color Graphics Adapter (CGA), Enhanced Graphics Adapter (EGA), and 8514/A color adapter.

Note

The video adapter card and software drivers, not the computer monitor, determine OS/2 compatibility.

Using VGA

IBM's VGA specification describes color and monochrome displays. A monochrome VGA display can show text with a resolution of 132 columns horizontally and 50 rows vertically; most people and applications use 80 columns and 25 rows. In graphics mode, a monochrome VGA display can show a resolution of 640 dots horizontally and 480 dots vertically.

A color VGA display for text has a 132-column by 50-row mode, also. Most people and applications use 80 columns and 25 rows, however. Each character on-screen has a foreground color and a background color using colors chosen from a range of 16 possibilities. In high-resolution graphics mode, a color VGA display also shows 640 dots horizontally and 480 dots vertically in 16 colors. In medium-resolution graphics mode, a color VGA display shows 320 dots horizontally and 200 dots vertically in 256 colors.

Most people use VGA color systems for OS/2, which operates in high-resolution graphics mode for Presentation Manager (PM) applications.

Using XGA

The Extended Graphics Array (XGA) is IBM's most recent specification. XGA is compatible with the earlier VGA and 8514/A video adapters from IBM. (This chapter discusses the 8514/A and other adapters in the next few sections.) With an XGA-equipped computer, you get a high-resolution mode that shows 1,024 dots horizontally and 768 dots vertically in 256 colors. You also get a medium-resolution mode that shows 640 dots horizontally and 480 dots vertically in 65,536 colors. Of course, you can still have 80 columns by 25 rows of text.

Using CGA and EGA for OS/2

The Color Graphics Adapter (CGA) and Enhanced Graphics Adapter (EGA) standards are officially obsolete, but OS/2 supports them. Basically, the CGA video adapter offers a high-resolution graphics mode that shows 640 dots across and 200 dots vertically in black and white. The EGA adapter is similar, but it can show 350 dots vertically. These resolutions are coarse. OS/2 cannot make effective use of your monitor if you have either CGA or EGA. You should consider upgrading to a higher resolution video adapter and monitor.

Using 8514/A

The 8514/A video adapter standard was IBM's highest-resolution personal computer display offering until XGA. It offers a 1,024x768-dot resolution, like XGA, but XGA operates much faster. XGA has superseded the 8514/A video standard. Some manufacturers still sell 8514/A video adapters, and OS/2 works well with these adapters.

> **Note**
>
> For some 8514/A and Super VGA video adapters, you must run a DOS utility program to set the refresh rate of the adapter to a value consistent with the resolution you choose and with the monitor itself. During the OS/2 video adapter update process, as explained later in Chapter 7, "Modifying Your OS/2 Configuration," you click a button to indicate that you need to run such a DOS utility program. You'll need to run the DOS utility if the manufacturer of your video adapter is Diamond Computer Systems, if your monitor supports only non-interlaced operation, if your video adapter does not support VESA standard refresh rates, or if your video adapter needs to be configured via software to run in DOS or with Windows. The next section discusses VESA and Super VGA in more detail.

Using Super VGA

When VESA was formed, initial participants included ATI Technologies, Genoa Systems, Orchid, Renaissance GRX, STB, Tecmar, Video-7, and Western Digital/Paradise. At the present time, members of VESA include Panacea, Western Digital, Everex, Hewlett Packard, Intel, ATI Technologies, Headland, Chips and Technologies, Mitsubishi, Genoa, Tandy, NEC, and Willow. VESA exists to promote the so-called Super VGA standard, which calls for an 800 horizontal by 600 vertical dot resolution.

Video adapters made by these companies all support VGA and should work with OS/2 in VGA mode. In some cases, a non-IBM Super VGA mode requires that you load an OS/2 device driver (you must use a text editor to change the CONFIG.SYS file). If you have a video adapter made by one of these companies, check with your manufacturer to find out whether that company has written an OS/2 device driver so that you can use the special 800 by 600 mode (or other non-IBM mode).

IBM built into OS/2 2.1 device drivers for the most popular Super VGA video adapters as well as some higher-resolution video adapters. You select your level of video adapter support during the installation process. You use an OS/2 configuration option to further increase the resolution produced by your video adapter. Chapter 7, "Modifying Your OS/2 Configuration," gives you step-by-step instructions for changing display resolutions under OS/2.

IBM now makes a Super VGA video adapter, the IBM VGA 256c. OS/2 2.1 supports the VGA 256c and the following video adapters or video adapter chipsets, in resolutions of 800x600, 1024x768, or higher:

> ATI Technologies VGA Wonder XL
>
> Cirrus Logic CL-GD542X
>
> Headland Technology VRAM II
>
> Trident Microsystems 8900
>
> Tseng Laboratories ET4000
>
> Video adapters based on chipsets from the S3 company
>
> Western Digital Paradise

For Related Information
- "Understanding Hardware and Software," p. 15
- "Upgrading Your Hardware," p. 169

Chapter Summary

This chapter helped you understand the problems you may encounter if part or all of your computer system is made by a company other than IBM. In particular, you covered what makes a computer IBM-compatible and how OS/2 runs successfully on most non-IBM computers. Other topics emphasized were the 80386, 80486, and Pentium CPU chips, the computer's ROM BIOS, non-IBM disk drives and disk controller cards, non-IBM keyboards and mice, and compatibility issues with video adapter cards.

In the next chapter, you install and begin using OS/2. Now that you know what issues you face if you have non-IBM computer hardware, you are well prepared for any problems you may encounter during the installation. In most cases, you find that OS/2 installs onto your computer without your realizing that it isn't made by IBM.

Chapter 6

Installing OS/2

You're now ready to install OS/2 or OS/2 for Windows, whether from floppy disk or CD-ROM. If you're familiar with DOS and have a computer system made by IBM, you reached this chapter quickly. You quickly toured OS/2 in Chapter 1, "Taking a Quick Tour of OS/2 and Your Computer," discovered the differences between OS/2 and DOS in Chapter 3, "Learning OS/2 If You Know DOS," and decided how you want to configure OS/2 in Chapter 4, "Deciding how You Want To Use OS/2."

On the other hand, if you haven't used DOS before, Chapter 2, "Learning OS/2 If You Don't Know DOS," brought you up to speed; if another manufacturer besides IBM made your computer system, Chapter 5, "Using Non-IBM Computers and OS/2," helped you identify potential compatibility problems.

OS/2 installation is a simple process, for the most part. The installation software preselects common choices for you, and you can install many options just by clicking buttons or pressing the Enter key. The installation of HPFS and/or Boot Manager works differently, however, and you use a multistep process to set up these optional features of OS/2. If you want to install HPFS or Boot Manager, use the instructions later in this chapter.

You can install OS/2 on a computer's hard disk that already has DOS on it, or you can install OS/2 on a "fresh" (not previously formatted) hard disk. The installation software prompts you to do the formatting step.

If you want to use HPFS or Boot Manager, you must set up new partitions on your hard disk and go through the formatting process. When you install HPFS and/or Boot Manager on a computer already formatted with DOS, you must make a backup copy of your hard disk files; the partitioning and formatting process does not preserve existing hard disk files. You then restore your files to the hard disk after installation by copying them from your backup copy.

The following list describes the basic steps you use to install either OS/2 2.1 or OS/2 for Windows. You can use this list as a roadmap when you explore the details of the installation process in this chapter.

- Insert the OS/2 2.1 Installation Disk and turn on the computer.
- When prompted, insert OS/2 Disk 1 and press Enter.
- View some introductory screens of information.
- Indicate whether you want to partition and/or format the hard disk.
- Select your type of mouse.
- Insert OS/2 Disks 2 through 5 when prompted.
- Reinsert the OS/2 Installation Disk and Disk 1 when prompted.
- Remove the floppy disk and reboot the computer into the Presentation Manager (graphical) portion of the installation.
- Select the features you want to install.
- Change configuration settings, if desired.
- Insert the remaining floppy disks, when prompted.
- Migrate your existing applications and Windows environment (optional).
- Insert the Windows 3.1 floppy disks (just for OS/2 for Windows).
- Reboot; OS/2 is installed.

The installation process takes from 40 minutes to as long as two hours, depending on the number of features you choose to install and the processing power (speed) of your computer system.

If you encounter any difficulty installing OS/2, recheck the instructions in this chapter first. Then use Chapter 8, "Troubleshooting OS/2," to fix the problem.

> **Note**
>
> The OS/2 installation software contains foreground and background threads. You learned about OS/2 threaded applications in Chapters 3 and 4. The foreground installation thread displays information on-screen and interacts with you. The background thread copies files and performs other internal tasks. During the installation process, you may notice hard disk activity even while you're inserting the next disk. This is a sign that the background thread is working, even while the foreground thread prompts you for a disk.

Installing from a CD-ROM Disk

If you have a CD-ROM drive supported by OS/2 and you purchased the CD-ROM edition of the operating system, you will have an easier time installing OS/2. You will not have to insert several floppy disks during installation. You simply boot your computer with the two floppy disks supplied with the CD-ROM disk and continue the remainder of the installation from the CD-ROM disk.

To install OS/2 from the CD-ROM drive, first make sure that your CD-ROM drive is on and ready (if the drive has a power switch). Close any open files and exit your applications to save any work you're doing. Turn off the computer.

Insert the OS/2 CD-ROM disk into the CD-ROM drive. Then insert the floppy disk labeled OS/2 2.1 Installation into the first floppy disk drive (the A: drive). Turn on your computer. When the blue IBM logo screen appears, remove the OS/2 2.1 Installation floppy disk and insert the OS/2 Disk 1 floppy disk into the first floppy disk drive. Press Enter. After a few moments, you see the Welcome to OS/2 screen shown in figure 6.1. After you press Enter, the installation program uses the CD-ROM disk for the remainder of the installation process.

You still need to read the rest of this chapter. You have choices to make during the installation and you should follow the steps and guidelines presented in this chapter to make correct choices. You don't have to insert floppy disks into your computer during the process, however. OS/2 installs from the CD-ROM disk.

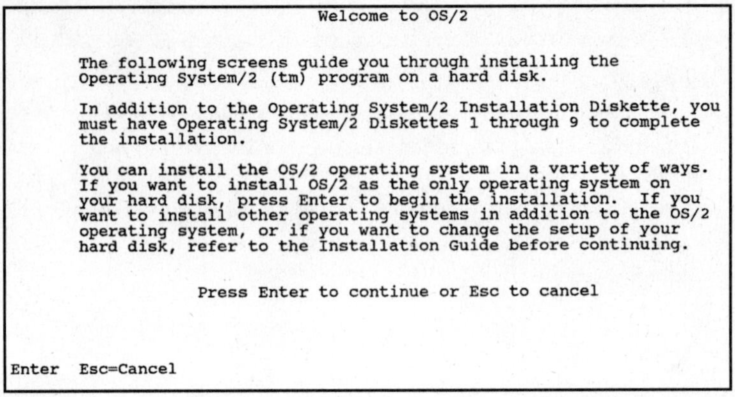

Fig. 6.1
The Welcome to OS/2 screen.

```
                       Welcome to OS/2

      The following screens guide you through installing the
      Operating System/2 (tm) program on a hard disk.

      In addition to the Operating System/2 Installation Diskette, you
      must have Operating System/2 Diskettes 1 through 9 to complete
      the installation.

      You can install the OS/2 operating system in a variety of ways.
      If you want to install OS/2 as the only operating system on
      your hard disk, press Enter to begin the installation.  If you
      want to install other operating systems in addition to the OS/2
      operating system, or if you want to change the setup of your
      hard disk, refer to the Installation Guide before continuing.

                 Press Enter to continue or Esc to cancel


   Enter   Esc=Cancel
```

If you see an error message after the OS/2 Disk 1 floppy disk loads into memory and you press Enter, you may have a CD-ROM drive that OS/2 doesn't support. To determine if this is the case, verify that you have properly inserted the CD-ROM disk into the CD-ROM drive, that the CD-ROM drive is turned on, and that all connections are tight. Restart the installation from the beginning. If the error message appears again, your CD-ROM drive is probably not supported by OS/2. You should contact the company that sold you the CD-ROM edition of OS/2 and explain the problem. You may have to obtain the floppy disk edition of OS/2 and install from floppy disks. Alternatively, a telephone call to the manufacturer of your CD-ROM drive may reveal that the manufacturer now offers device drivers to allow your CD-ROM drive to function in an OS/2 environment.

> **Caution**
>
> The OS/2 installation procedure automatically detects the presence of your CD-ROM drive and displays the name of the detected drive on the System Configuration screen (shown in fig. 6.2). *Do not put a check mark in the box labeled CD-ROM Device Support.* Viewing or changing the automatically detected CD-ROM drive value will cause the installation to fail. You can later use OS/2's Selective Install, located in the System Setup folder, to change the CD-ROM driver support.
>
> If you do inadvertently check the CD-ROM Device Support box, simply restart the installation procedure from the beginning.

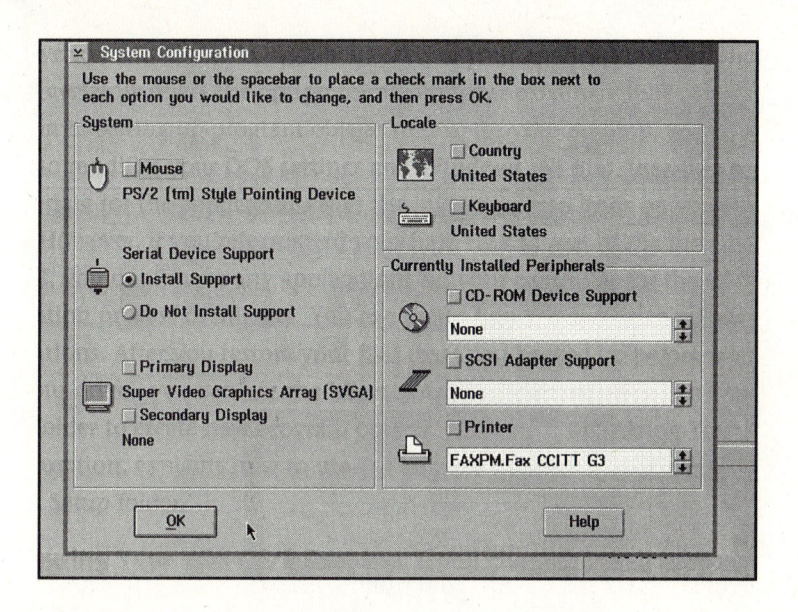

Fig. 6.2
Confirming your mouse, keyboard, display, printer, and other peripherals.

Installing OS/2 for Windows

If you purchased the OS/2 for Windows product, on either CD-ROM or floppy disk, you follow the same directions in this chapter as for installing OS/2 2.1. During the installation procedure, you also need your original Microsoft Windows 3.1 floppy disks. Toward the end of the installation procedure, you will see prompts asking you to insert your Windows 3.1 distribution disks.

If the manufacturer of your PC preloaded Windows 3.1 on your computer but did not supply you with Windows 3.1 distribution floppy disks (an all-too-common occurrence), look on your hard drive for files representing the floppy disk images or for a directory containing the Windows 3.1 distribution files. The directory usually has the name WINSTALL. If you have floppy disk images, follow the directions your computer manufacturer gave you for creating floppy disks from those images. When the OS/2 for Windows installation procedure asks you for the location of your Windows 3.1 distribution files, you can respond by inserting the diskettes that you created or by giving the WINSTALL directory name.

The labels on the OS/2 for Windows distribution disks are green.

Setting Up the Installation Floppy Disks

IBM distributes the OS/2 operating system on 3, 19, or 25 disks. (Many features of OS/2 are optional; don't be overly concerned about the number of disks. You can install as much or as little of OS/2 as you want.) Check your OS/2 distribution disks now to make sure that you have the right number of disks.

If you purchased OS/2 2.1 on CD-ROM media, you should have three disks—the CD-ROM disk plus two floppy disks labeled Installation Disk and Disk 1.

If your OS/2 2.1 floppy disks have blue labels, you should have a total of 25 floppy disks. One disk is labeled Installation Disk and 17 other disks are labeled Disk 1 through Disk 17. You should have seven other disks—three labeled Printer Driver Disk 1 through Printer Driver Disk 3, two labeled Display Driver Disk 1 and Display Driver Disk 2, and two containing the Multimedia Presentation Manager/2 (MMPM/2) software simply labeled Disk 1 and Disk 2. (Appendix G discusses MMPM/2.) In this package, the MMPM/2 disks have dark blue labels.

If your OS/2 2.1 floppy disks have salmon (pink) labels, you should have a total of 19 floppy disks. One disk is labeled Installation Disk, 13 disks are labeled Disk 1 through Disk 13, two disks are labeled Printer Driver Disk 1 and Printer Driver Disk 2, two disks are labeled Display Driver Disk 1 and Display Driver Disk 2, and the two MMPM/2 disks are simply labeled Disk 1 and Disk 2. In this package, the MMPM/2 disks have red labels.

> **Note**
>
> Shortly after it began selling OS/2 2.1, IBM found a better way to pack and compress the OS/2 2.1 files on the distribution floppy disks. IBM changed the color of the floppy disk labels from the original blue to salmon (pink) when the company switched to using the new method of putting the files on the floppy disks. The blue- and salmon-labeled floppy disks contain the same operating system code. The disks with the salmon-colored labels are simply packed differently, resulting in fewer floppy disks.

> **Note**
>
> If you bought OS/2 on floppy disk (either blue- or salmon-labeled), Disk 3 contains a file named README.INS that you should read before installing OS/2. If you bought OS/2 on CD-ROM, the README.INS file is on Disk 1. README.INS is approximately 17,000 text characters—more than a screenful of text. To read this text file prior to installation, perform one of the following options:
>
> - Use a PC that has an operating system on it already. View the README.INS file with a text editor or file browser (suggested procedure).
>
> - Boot a PC with Installation Disk 1 followed by OS/2 Disk 1. Press the Esc key when you see the Welcome to OS/2 screen (shown in fig. 6.1). Copy the README.INS file to a printer attached to your PC with the command
>
>   COPY A:README.INS LPT1
>
> - Boot a PC with Installation Disk 1 followed by OS/2 Disk 1. Press the ESC key when you see the Welcome to OS/2 screen (shown in fig. 6.1). Use the **TYPE** command to display the text file to the screen. Use the Pause key to keep the material from scrolling off the screen before you've read it. On a fast computer, you may not be able to press the Pause key quickly enough before material scrolls off the screen. Use the **TYPE** command as many times as necessary to gain an understanding of what's in the README.INS file.

Following your installation of OS/2, or perhaps even before installation if you already have a working computer, make copies of all the distribution disks in case something happens to the originals. The fastest way to copy disks is with the **DISKCOPY** command, explained fully in Part VI, "Using the Command Reference."

Booting the Installation Disk

If you already have DOS or an earlier version of OS/2 on your computer, make sure that you have a backup copy of your files before continuing. If you want to use Boot Manager or HPFS, you *must* have a backup copy of your files at this time. When you install Boot Manager or HPFS, you repartition and reformat your hard drive, which erases all existing files.

For Related Information
- "The TYPE Command," p. 777
- "The DISKCOPY Command," p. 749
- "Understanding Hardware and Software," p. 15

> **Tip**
>
> If your computer system is on, save your work and turn off the computer. On a few kinds of non-IBM hardware, the OS/2 Installation Disk has trouble initializing the computer if the previously run DOS-based application leaves the hardware in an unusual state. Installing OS/2 onto a just-powered-on computer sometimes helps the OS/2 Installation Disk boot properly because it allows the installation software to avoid the leftover hardware state.

Insert the Installation Disk into drive A and turn on the machine. The first part of the installation software takes several moments to load from the disk. After a while, you see an IBM logo and a message asking you to remove the Installation Disk and replace it with the disk labeled Disk 1. After you insert Disk 1, the next part of the installation software loads from the disk (which also takes several moments). You then see the Welcome to OS/2 screen (refer to fig. 6.1).

For Related Information
- "Understanding Hardware and Software," p. 14

> **Caution**
>
> Make sure that you follow the on-screen disk insertion instructions and prompts carefully. Removing a disk at the wrong time can cause the installation process to fail partway through.

First Step: Text Mode

You install OS/2 in two steps. The first step uses a full-screen text mode interface. The second step uses the graphical interface of Presentation Manager. OS/2 reboots your computer between these steps. Step 1 uses the OS/2 Installation Disk, the OS/2 Disks 1 through 5, and then the Installation Disk and Disk 1 again. Step 2, the graphical portion of the installation, uses the remainder of the diskettes, including the Printer Driver Disks and the Display Driver Disks. As explained in Appendix G, "Enjoying Multimedia Presentation Manager/2," you optionally install MMPM/2 in a separate, third step.

After you use the Installation Disk and OS/2 Disk 1 to reach the "Welcome to OS/2" screen shown in figure 6.1, press Enter to continue or press the Esc (escape) key to stop the installation process. Pressing Esc presents you with an

First Step: Text Mode

OS/2 command-line prompt. Because OS/2 is not yet installed, you can execute commands only from the distribution disks after you press Esc. If you press Esc by mistake at this point, restart the installation process by reinserting the OS/2 Installation Disk and rebooting your computer.

> **Note**
>
> As Chapter 8, "Troubleshooting OS/2," explains, pressing the Esc key after booting with the Installation Disk and Disk 1—to obtain an OS/2 command-line prompt—will be an important problem-solving tool in the future if you have trouble with OS/2. You may someday, for example, need to run the **CHKDSK** command on the OS/2 boot drive. If you boot OS/2 from the hard drive, **CHKDSK** won't be able to repair anything because OS/2 is using files on that drive. Booting from a floppy disk, however, lets **CHKDSK** repair the files on the hard drive.

The next screen displayed is the Introduction screen. This screen provides tips on selecting choices and obtaining help from OS/2 during the installation. You need only to read the Introduction screen, which does not ask you any questions. When you press Enter to leave the Introduction screen, the File System screen appears. This screen reminds you to repartition and reformat your hard disk to use HPFS. The File System screen also only requires that you read it. When you press Enter, you see the Installation Drive Selection screen, shown in figure 6.3.

```
                    Installation Drive Selection

        If you are interested in having multiple versions of DOS, OS/2
        or other operating systems on the same hard disk, refer to the
        Installation Guide for information on OS/2 Hard Disk
        Management before continuing.

        If you have multiple primary partitions set up on your hard
        disk, select option 2 to verify that the correct partition is
        active.

        OS/2 will be installed on drive C :

        Select an option:

           1. Accept the drive

           2. Specify a different drive or partition

        If you select option 2, the FDISK screen is displayed.
  Enter   Esc=Cancel   F3=Exit   F1=Help
```

Fig. 6.3
The Installation Drive Selection screen.

The Installation Drive Selection screen is another information display. You use this screen to confirm whether you want to install OS/2 on drive C (your first bootable partition). If you have used DOS on your computer before and don't want to install Boot Manager or HPFS, choose option 1. Choose option 2 if any of the following conditions fit your situation:

- Your hard disk has not been previously formatted by DOS or an earlier version of OS/2.

- You want to install HPFS in place of the DOS File Allocation Table formatting.

- You want to install Boot Manager.

Choosing option 2 on the Installation Drive Selection screen presents you with the Installation FDISK screen. You use this screen to indicate partition and formatting changes. Figure 6.4 shows this FDISK screen.

Fig. 6.4
The Installation FDISK screen for repartitioning your hard disk.

```
           Formatting the Installation Partition
The partitions on a hard disk must be formatted before information
can be placed on them.  If the partition in which you are going to
install the OS/2 operating system has been formatted by DOS or the
OS/2 operating system, it is not necessary to format it again.

The installation partition can be formatted to use either the High
Performance File System (HPFS) or the FAT file system.  If you have
other partitions on your hard disk, you can format them to use either
file system after you have completed installation.  Files can be
copied between partitions that use different file systems.

Formatting erases all files.  If you need these files, or if you want
to repartition your hard disk, refer to the Installation Guide before
continuing installation.

Select an option.

   1. Do not format the partition

   2. Format the partition
Enter   F1=Help
```

If your hard disk is already partitioned and formatted the way you want for OS/2, you can move on to the next section.

Partitioning and Formatting Your Disk

Because partitioning and formatting your hard disk erases any existing files on your hard disk, including application software files, data files, and operating system files, make sure that you make a backup copy of any files you want to save before you partition or format your hard disk.

If you're installing the OS/2 for Windows product and your original Windows 3.1 distribution disks are floppy disk images or files on your hard drive, make sure you copy those images or files to floppy disks before repartitioning or formatting your drive.

> **Caution**
>
> When you partition and format your hard disk, you erase *all* data on the disk. If you want to save the data on your disk, make a backup copy before you partition or format.

Installing OS/2 on a Non-Formatted Machine. If you're installing OS/2 on a new machine and you want to use the Dual-Boot feature, you first should install the appropriate version of DOS on your computer. *Que's MS-DOS 6 User's Guide,* Special Edition, leads you through booting DOS, running the DOS FDISK program, and running the DOS FORMAT program.

If you don't want Dual-Boot, you can proceed to FDISK and format your hard disk as part of the OS/2 installation procedure.

Before you tell the OS/2 or DOS FDISK programs to set up your hard disk partitions, you should decide whether to use Boot Manager or HPFS.

Installing OS/2 on a DOS-Formatted Machine. To change your partition sizes, to use Boot Manager, or to use HPFS, you first should make backup copies of the data on your computer, and then treat your computer as if it had not been formatted before (see the previous section). Remember that the FDISK and FORMAT programs erase existing data on your hard disk.

If you want OS/2 to recognize your existing version of DOS and automatically install Dual-Boot, use the instructions and guidelines presented later in this chapter.

Choosing Boot Manager. To install the Multiple Operating System Tool (Boot Manager), you must tell FDISK to create a primary disk partition for each of the operating systems you will use, in addition to the disk partition you set aside for Boot Manager. Boot Manager needs only a 1M partition. When you create partitions, make the first partition the one for Boot Manager.

To use Boot Manager and HPFS, designate the last partition on the disk as the HPFS partition. (All installable file systems for all operating systems generally should be placed in partitions at the end of the partition list.) Be aware of the disk partition restrictions, if any, for the non-OS/2 operating systems you will use. If you create a partition for use by DOS 3.3 (that you can select with Boot Manager at boot time), for example, ensure that the DOS 3.3 partition is located within the first 32 megabytes of the hard disk.

After you use FDISK, your list of allocated partitions might look like the following example:

Alias	Status	Access	FS type	Size (MB)
BOOT MGR	Startable	Primary	Boot Manager	1
DOS 3.3	Selectable	Primary	FAT 16	20
OS/2 2.1	Selectable	Primary	FAT 16	32
Common	None	Logical	FAT 16	32

In the preceding table, BOOT MGR represents the Boot Manager partition.

To set up the Boot Manager partition, first tell FDISK to delete any existing partitions on the hard disk. Use the up-arrow and down-arrow keys to select (highlight) the partition you want to delete, and then press Enter to see the Options menu. Select Delete and press Enter. Repeat these steps for all the partitions on the hard disk.

> **Note**
>
> Changes you make in FDISK take effect only after you press F3 to exit from FDISK. You then have the opportunity to accept or abandon your FDISK modifications.

After you delete any existing partitions, you can create the Boot Manager partition and the partitions for the other operating systems. Select (highlight) the unused partition entry with the up- or down-arrow keys. Press Enter to access the Options menu, and then choose the Install Most... item. You next specify whether you want the Boot Manager partition to occupy the beginning or end of the hard disk. You probably should use the first 1M of the hard disk for Boot Manager.

You have allocated your Boot Manager partition, but the OS/2 installation process has not yet copied Boot Manager to it. The installation of Boot Manager occurs later in the installation process.

You now can create partitions for other operating systems, unless that operating system requires you to use its own FDISK-type utility to allocate disk space. You can create DOS and OS/2 partitions now. Some UNIX operating systems, such as IBM's AIX, must allocate their own space. If you plan to use an operating system such as AIX, leave sufficient unallocated (unused) space in the partition table; AIX allocates the space during its installation procedure.

To create a DOS or an OS/2 partition that you can select from the Boot Manager menu when you start the computer, press Enter to see the FDISK Options menu. Choose Create and press Enter. Type the number of megabytes you want the partition to occupy on the hard disk, and specify whether the partition should be a primary partition or a logical drive within an extended partition. You should set up the first DOS or OS/2 partition as a primary partition. Tell FDISK where on the disk the new partition should exist.

After you create the partition, use the Options menu to change the characteristics of that partition. If you have multiple primary partitions, choose the Access menu item to tell FDISK which primary partition is active (you can have only one active primary partition). Use the Startable menu item to select which partition you want to have control when you start the computer. When you install Boot Manager, you normally make the Boot Manager partition the Startable partition. At boot time, Boot Manager then gives you the opportunity to select one of the other partitions. Use the Selectable menu item to designate which partitions (and therefore which operating systems) you want to see in the Boot Manager menu at boot time. You also can give each partition a meaningful name, or *alias*, at this time.

You now have told FDISK about the Boot Manager partition and about any other partitions for other operating systems you will use except for OS/2 2.1. You left unallocated space for an operating system such as AIX (UNIX operating systems supply their own FDISK equivalents).

To continue installing OS/2, you now create its partition. Choose Create from the Options menu, and specify the size of the OS/2 2.1 partition. Make sure that the new OS/2 2.1 partition is marked Installable by choosing that FDISK menu option.

Finally, before you continue with the installation of OS/2, you can configure Boot Manager by selecting the Startup Values menu option. You can tell Boot Manager whether to start one of the partitions' operating systems by default each time the computer boots, and you can tell Boot Manager how long to display its menu before booting that default operating system.

When you are satisfied with the changes you made to your partition table, press F3. FDISK asks you to confirm your changes; you then proceed with the installation of OS/2 2.1.

Selecting HPFS. You install the High Performance File System by creating a partition on your hard disk that contains HPFS data, formatting that partition with a special form of the FORMAT command, and inserting the appropriate HPFS statements in your CONFIG.SYS file. You run FDISK, and perhaps the FORMAT command, during the installation procedure.

First, use FDISK to delete any existing partitions on the hard disk. Use the up- and down-arrow keys to select (highlight) the partition you want to delete. Then press Enter to see the Options menu. Select Delete from this menu and press Enter. Repeat these steps for all the partitions on the hard disk.

> **Note**
>
> Changes you make in FDISK take effect only after you press F3 to exit from FDISK. You then have the opportunity to accept or abandon your FDISK modifications.

After you delete any existing partitions, you can create the HPFS partition. You might choose to have a combination of FAT and HPFS partitions, or you might choose to install Boot Manager and HPFS on the same computer, with perhaps a combination of FAT and HPFS partitions. You create the partitions when you run FDISK as part of the installation process. The actual formatting of the HPFS partition occurs later.

To create an HPFS or FAT partition, press Enter to see the FDISK Options menu. Choose Create and press Enter. Type the number of megabytes you want the partition to occupy on the hard disk, and select whether the partition should be a primary partition or a logical drive within an extended partition. (Your HPFS partition should be a primary partition.) Indicate to FDISK that the HPFS partition should be allocated at the end of the disk, if you are creating multiple partitions.

After you create the partition(s), use the Options menu to change the characteristics of the partition(s). If you're installing Boot Manager, follow the directions given earlier for setting these characteristics. If you want only a single HPFS partition, be sure to mark that partition primary, startable, and installable. For a combination FAT and HPFS set of partitions, tell FDISK to put the FAT partition at the beginning of the disk and the HPFS partition at the end of the disk. Ensure that the FAT partition is marked startable and installable. You also can give each partition a meaningful name at this time.

When you're satisfied with your changes to the partition table, press F3. FDISK asks you to confirm your changes, and you then continue to install OS/2 2.1.

Continuing with the Installation. Depending on the OS/2 functions, features, and mini-applications you select, OS/2 needs from about 10M of disk space to about 45M. The installation software detects an insufficient disk space condition and warns you that the installation may not succeed. Figure 6.5 shows the warning screen titled Hard Disk Space Requirement.

```
Hard Disk Space Requirement

The OS/2 operating system requires 16MB of hard disk space.
You now have less than that amount available.  If a previous
version of the OS/2 operating system is installed on your hard
disk, or if you want to reformat your hard disk later in the
installation process, you might not need as much space.

Be sure that you have 16MB of hard disk space available.


Do one of the following:

- Press Enter to continue with installation.

- Press F3 to exit to the OS/2 command prompt.


Enter  Esc=Cancel  F3=Exit
```

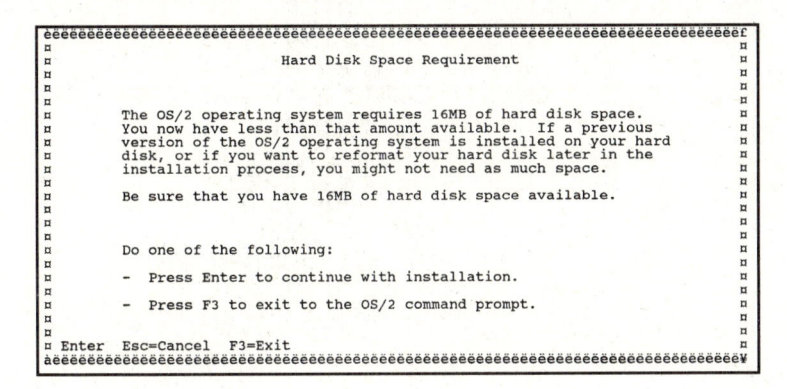

Fig. 6.5
The Hard Disk Space Requirement warning screen.

You can safely ignore the warning if you simply restart the installation process or you install version 2.1 of OS/2 over an earlier version (files are replaced in both situations).

If you're not replacing files during the installation and you truly lack the disk space to continue, you have the following three options:

- You can press F3 to exit from the installation software. An OS/2 command-line prompt appears. At the prompt, use the **DIR**, **CD**, and **ERASE** commands to perform housecleaning on your old files and directories. When you regain enough free disk space, restart the installation process by rebooting the OS/2 Installation Disk. This option appears on the Hard Disk Space Requirement warning screen.

- You can press Enter to continue with the installation. The installation of OS/2 probably will not complete if you choose this alternative. This option also appears on the Hard Disk Space Requirement warning screen.

- You can boot DOS and use your favorite file manager to do the housecleaning. Choose this option if you don't feel comfortable finding and deleting files at a command-line prompt. When you recover enough disk space, restart the OS/2 installation.

Installing Dual-Boot. OS/2 2.1 automatically installs its Dual-Boot feature if you have an existing version of DOS on your computer. If OS/2 cannot completely install the Dual-Boot feature, you may see a screen similar to the one in figure 6.6. If you see such a warning during installation, you must note the problem and fix it after OS/2 is installed. You usually can fix the problem by using the OS/2 System Editor to correct your DOS CONFIG.SYS file or by moving files to their usual directories as specified in the *DOS User's Guide and Reference*.

Fig. 6.6
The Dual-Boot Installation Warning screen.

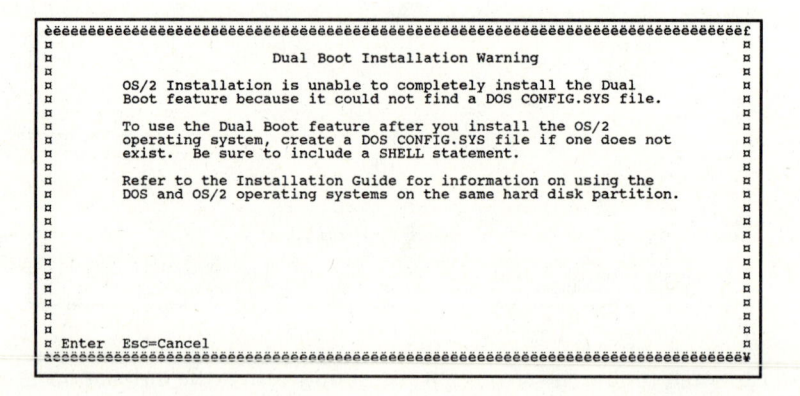

```
Dual Boot Installation Warning

OS/2 Installation is unable to completely install the Dual
Boot feature because it could not find a DOS CONFIG.SYS file.

To use the Dual Boot feature after you install the OS/2
operating system, create a DOS CONFIG.SYS file if one does not
exist. Be sure to include a SHELL statement.

Refer to the Installation Guide for information on using the
DOS and OS/2 operating systems on the same hard disk partition.




 Enter  Esc=Cancel
```

If Dual-Boot does not successfully and completely install on your computer, use the following guidelines to correct your DOS AUTOEXEC.BAT and CONFIG.SYS files and to put the files into the proper subdirectories. Dual-Boot successfully installs if the following conditions are true on your computer:

- DOS is already installed.

- The DOS operating system is version 3.3 or later.

- DOS is installed in the first partition on the hard disk and that partition is marked bootable.

- Your DOS partition has sufficient free disk space for the installation of OS/2.

- All DOS commands and utility programs exist in a subdirectory (such as C:\DOS) and not in the root directory of the disk. In particular, the file COMMAND.COM must reside in this subdirectory.

- You do not select the FORMAT option during OS/2 installation.

- The file C:\AUTOEXEC.BAT contains at least the following statements, exactly as shown:

      PATH C:\DOS
      SET COMSPEC=C:\DOS\COMMAND.COM

- The file C:\CONFIG.SYS contains at least the following statement, exactly as shown:

      SHELL=C:\DOS\COMMAND.COM C:\DOS\ /P

Your SHELL statement in the CONFIG.SYS file may also contain the /E:*XXXX* option, where *XXXX* represents the number of bytes of environment space to reserve. Your DOS CONFIG.SYS file and AUTOEXEC.BAT file may also contain other statements. The preceding entries are the minimum requirement for the correct installation of the OS/2 Dual-Boot feature.

Selecting Your Mouse. OS/2 needs to know whether you have a pointing device (a mouse) and what brand it is. You have an opportunity to change this selection later in the installation, just in case you make a mistake. You can use a mouse to choose options during the graphical second part of the installation, and so you need to tell OS/2 now what sort of mouse you have.

You can select your mouse from the following list:

- PS/2 Style Pointing Device
- Bus Style Mouse
- InPort Style Mouse
- Serial Pointing Device
- Logitech C-Series Serial Mouse
- Logitech M-Series Mouse
- IBM Touch Device
- PC Mouse Systems Mouse

- Other Pointing Device for Mouse Port
- No Pointing Device Support

If you choose Other Pointing Device, you use the mouse driver file on the disk that contains an OS/2 device driver. You received this disk from the manufacturer of your pointing device. OS/2 prompts you to insert this disk.

If your brand of mouse is not on the list, you often can choose a mouse similar to and compatible with your brand. You can choose Microsoft Mouse, Bus Version, for example, if you have a Logitech Bus Mouse.

If you select Microsoft Mouse, Serial Version, OS/2 asks you to confirm which serial port to use. OS/2 tells you how many COM ports it has found, suggests one, and allows you to change the COM port assignment.

Copying Files from the First Few Disks. After you have determined how you want to set up your disk partitions (or decided to use your already-formatted ones), selected your pointing device, and made a note of any warning screens that you see, you're ready to continue. After you select your mouse and confirm its serial port usage (if necessary), the following message appears on-screen:

```
Remove the diskette from Drive A. Insert Operating System/2
Disk 2 into Drive A. Then press Enter.
```

When the installation program prompts you, follow the instructions on-screen to insert OS/2 Disks 2 through 5 and the Installation Disk, which contains the installation software and some other OS/2 files. While OS/2 copies the files of each disk onto your hard disk, the program indicates the process is underway by displaying the message Transferring Files from Disk and by showing you the name of each file being installed.

When you install OS/2 files on your hard disk, you may see a screen that contains the following message:

```
The installation program has failed due to an error. To view the error,
you need to look at the INSTALL.LOG file that was created for you.
Press Enter to display INSTALL.LOG.
```

The OS/2 installation program suggests that you fix the problem by exiting to a command-line prompt and issuing commands. Alternatively, if you have a DOS-bootable floppy disk, you can boot DOS and use a file manager or your favorite text editor to correct any errors. An example of such an error is an AUTOEXEC.BAT or CONFIG.SYS file with a read-only attribute.

Note that most files on the distribution disks are compressed. You should let the installation software copy the files to your hard disk. If you attempt to copy them with the COPY command, your computer system will not work. If you absolutely must copy a file from one of the distribution disks by hand, use the UNPACK command described in the command reference section of this book.

When OS/2 has copied and installed the contents of the first several OS/2 distribution disks onto your hard disk, a screen with the following message appears:

```
The hard disk preparation is complete. The next step will be OS/2 system
configuration. Remove the diskette from the disk drive. Press Enter to
start OS/2 system configuration.
```

When you take the disk out of the drive and press Enter, the computer reboots (do not be surprised) and the second part of the installation begins.

Choosing the OS/2 Features You Want

After the computer reboots into the graphical portion of the installation process, the first screen displayed is an IBM OS/2 logo. You then use the Presentation Manager interface to confirm the type of mouse you have, the type of keyboard, type of computer monitor, your country, and other configuration settings. Next, you choose the OS/2 features you want—CD/ROM support, on-line documentation, printer/screen fonts, optional system utilities, tools and games, HPFS, the OS/2 DOS and Windows environment, the REXX batch programming language, serial device support, and the serviceability and diagnostic aids. Finally (and optionally), you can modify your DOS environment and OS/2 configuration parameters.

Using the Initial PM Installation Screen

The first screen of the graphical portion of the installation asks you if you want to learn how to use a mouse, if you want to install all of OS/2 (including all the mini-applications, games, options, and features), or if you want to select which features OS/2 should install. You would normally choose this last item, Select features and install because OS/2 is so feature-rich you almost certainly will not use every option or utility.

For Related Information
- "Understanding Hardware and Software," p. 14
- "Examining Other Operating Systems," p. 81
- "Considering Disks and Disk Files," p. 83

The Learn how to use a mouse option takes you through the Mouse-familiarization section of the OS/2 tutorial. If you select this option, you spend a few moments learning how to interact with OS/2 through your mouse movements and button presses. Exiting from the mouse tutorial returns you to the installation screen.

The Install all features option tells the OS/2 installation program that you want every last bit of OS/2 on your computer—no questions asked. Even if you have ample free disk space, you probably do not want to choose this option. OS/2 includes a rich set of options, features, utilities, and games that you probably will not get around to exploring or using.

The Select features and install option takes you to the System Configuration screen. The next several sections of this chapter discuss how to choose which OS/2 features you want on your computer. Before you do that, however, confirm your mouse, keyboard, country, and type of computer display (monitor) to OS/2. This step is important because it lets you and OS/2 know that you see and hear one another, in the correct language, during the remainder of the installation process.

> **Note**
>
> OS/2 has a Selective Install feature you can use after you have OS/2 up and running. If you want to install a feature you did not install initially, you can use Selective Install to add the feature later, as explained in Chapter 7, "Modifying Your OS/2 Configuration."

Confirming Your Configuration

Figure 6.6 shows an example of the screen on which you confirm your system configuration. Note that this figure is only an example; your screen will contain other values for the preselected choices if you have a different computer configuration (such as an XGA display screen or a mouse that does not connect through a serial port).

You typically will find that the preselected choices for mouse, keyboard, country, type of display, and other peripherals are correct for your computer. You can press Enter or click the OK button if this is the case.

If the Mouse Doesn't Work. If you find that the mouse cursor doesn't move when you roll your mouse on the surface of your desk, you can navigate the System Configuration screen with your keyboard. Use the up- and down-arrow keys to select (highlight) the item you want to change. Press the space bar to put a check mark next to that item and then press Enter. (Pressing Enter is equivalent to clicking the OK button.) You see a screen on which you can change the value for that item, as described in the next few sections. Choose the value you want and press Enter. The OS/2 installation program returns you to the System Configuration screen. Press Enter, with no check marks showing, when you finish.

If the OK button is highlighted and you want to go back to one of the items to put a check mark next to it, use the Tab key to move the selection highlight.

Selecting Serial Device Support. If you have a modem or plotter connected to a serial port on your computer (COM1, COM2, COM3, or COM4), you need to install OS/2's serial device support. These software driver modules take very little room on your hard disk. In most cases, you will want to check the box labeled Install Support under the Serial Device Support heading.

Setting Up Your Display. If you put a check mark in the Primary Display check box and click OK, OS/2 lets you choose your computer's video adapter and display resolution from a list. The list of adapters will look similar to that shown in figure 6.7. Click the type of video adapter your computer uses (OS/2 may already have highlighted your adapter in the list for you if OS/2 was able to automatically detect the adapter type) and click OK. On the next screen, choose the display resolution you feel you will be most comfortable using. Be aware that higher resolutions, such as 1,024 by 768, present more information on-screen at one time but require a larger screen to be readable. If your video adapter is not listed, choosing plain VGA is usually a safe choice.

> **Note**
>
> If the OS/2 installation process asks you to confirm the type of video adapter you have but doesn't ask you to choose a display resolution, continue with the installation and use the procedure described in the next chapter if your video adapter supports higher resolutions and you want to change the display resolution.

If you later upgrade or change the video adapter in your PC, or just want to change the display resolution, you can use OS/2's Selective Install feature, as explained in Chapter 7, "Modifying Your OS/2 Configuration," to reconfigure OS/2 for the different display mode.

Fig. 6.7
Choosing your video adapter.

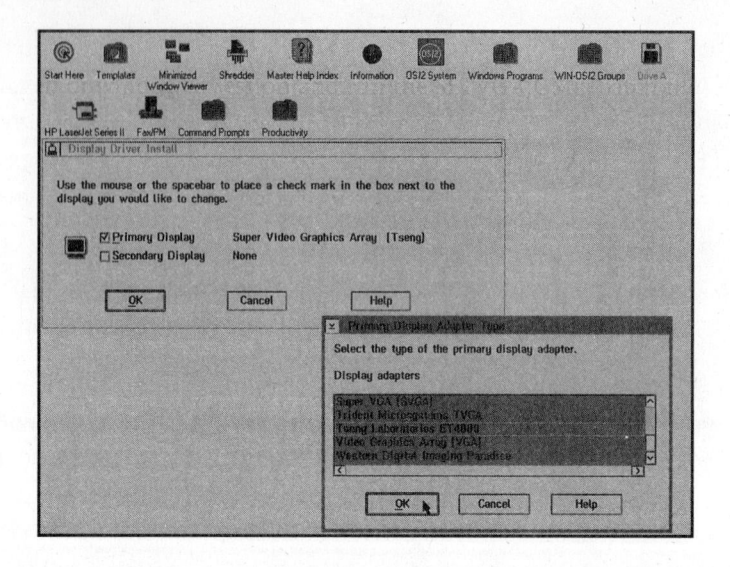

Verifying CD-ROM, SCSI Adapter, and Printer Support. Under the screen heading Currently Installed Peripherals, you see buttons, called *spin buttons*, with headings labeled CD-ROM Device Support, SCSI Adapter Support, and Printer. You use these spin buttons to see the types of these peripherals that OS/2 thinks you have attached to your computer. To operate a spin button, click the mouse button 1 (left mouse button) on the up arrow or down arrow located to the right of the current text value for that peripheral. The spin buttons let you see the list of peripherals OS/2 has detected in your computer but do not let you change those values. You click the mouse to put a check mark next to the labels CD-ROM Device Support, SCSI Adapter Support, and Printer if you want to make changes to the lists you see. Then click OK.

> **Caution**
>
> If you're installing from CD-ROM, do not click the CD-ROM Device Support or SCSI Adapter Support check box during the installation process. Use the steps given in the next chapter, after installation is complete, to make changes to your CD-ROM or SCSI device configurations. If you're installing from floppy disk media, continue reading this section.

Changing CD-ROM and SCSI Adapter Settings. If you click the check box next to CD-ROM Device Support and then click the OK button, OS/2 displays a list of the CD-ROM drives that OS/2 can access. The following list identifies these supported CD-ROM drives:

Manufacturer	CD-ROM Drive Model
Hitachi	CDR-1650S, CDR-1750S, CDR-3650, CDR-3750
IBM	CD-ROM I, CD-ROM II
NEC	CDR-36, CDR-37, CDR-72, CDR-73, CDR-74, CDR-82, CDR-83, CDR-84
Panasonic	CR-501, LK-MC501S
Pioneer	various
Sony	CDU-541, CDU-561, CDU-6111, CDU-6211, CDU-7211
Texel	DM-3021, DM-5021, DM-5024
Toshiba	XM-3201, XM-3301

By clicking the SCSI Adapter Support check box and then clicking OK, you tell OS/2 which kind of SCSI adapter you have in your computer. You can choose from the items in the following list:

Manufacturer	SCSI Adapter or Interface
Adaptec	AIC 6260, AHA 1510/1512/1520/1522, AHA 1540/1542/1544, AHA 1640/1642/1644, AHA 1740/1742/1744
DPT	PM2011/2012
Future Domain	TMC-850/860/875/885, TMC-1660/1670/1680, MCS-600/700, TMC-700EX, TMC-850IBM
IBM	PS/2 SCSI Adapter, PS/2 SCSI Adapter with cache

Selecting a Printer. If you check the Printer check box under Currently Installed Peripherals and click the OK button, a list of printers appears on-screen (see fig. 6.8). Select your printer from the list. OS/2 may ask you a few questions about your printer; you will probably have to refer to the manual that came with your printer to answer these questions.

Selecting Your Features

After you confirm or change your mouse, keyboard, display, printer, and other system configuration settings, the OS/2 installation program displays the Setup and Installation screen, as shown in figure 6.9. Choose the features and options you want by checking the items you want and by unchecking the items you do not want. These items include on-line documentation,

144 Chapter 6—Installing OS/2

fonts, system utilities, tools and games, DOS and Windows support, the High Performance File System, Advanced Power Management support (available in some notebook computers), PCMCIA Support (a new way of connecting adapter cards to computers), REXX, serviceability and diagnostic aids, and the optional OS/2 bitmaps.

Fig. 6.8
Selecting your printer.

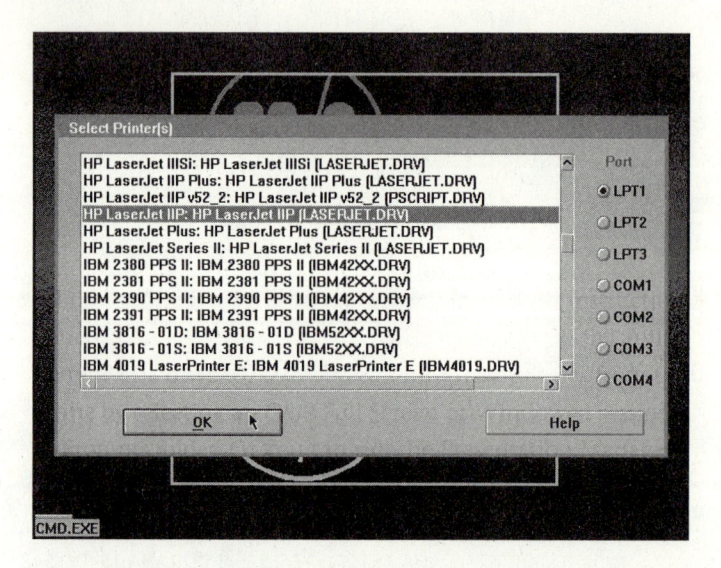

Fig. 6.9
Selecting OS/2 features.

Choosing the OS/2 Features You Want

You check and uncheck the items (also called *selecting* and *deselecting*) until you're satisfied with the set of features you want to install. When you make changes, OS/2 displays in the bottom right corner of the screen a running status of the amount of disk space your selected options require. Many items on the Setup and Installation screen have subcategories of items. These items appear with a More... button next to them. If you have selected the item and you click the More... button, you see a list of the subcategories for that item; you can make further selections of those subcategory items.

When you complete the selection process, click the Install button to continue with the installation process. OS/2 then asks if you're ready to proceed with the installation.

The next few sections of this chapter discuss each of the selectable items on the Setup and Installation screen.

Using On-Line Documentation. You certainly will want to install at least a portion of the on-line documentation for OS/2 2.1, but you may not want all the files on your hard disk. To choose the subcategories you want, put a check mark in the box labeled Documentation on the Setup and Installation screen. Click the More... button to view the screen illustrated in figure 6.10.

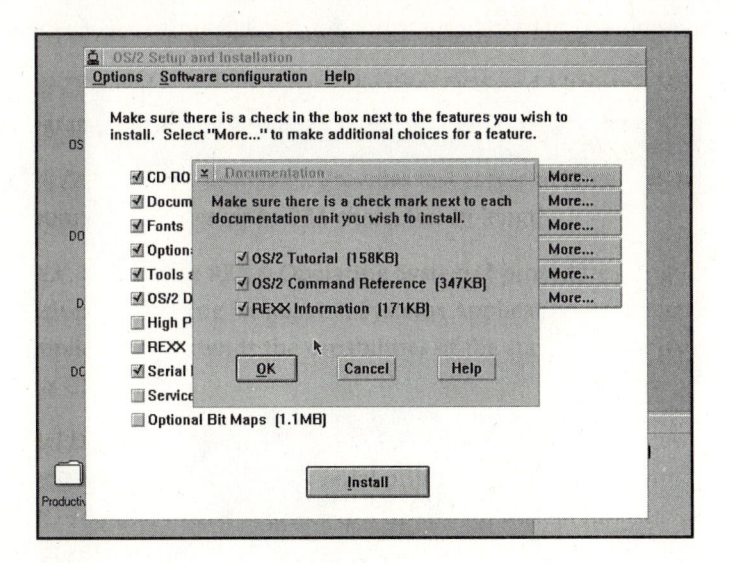

Fig. 6.10
Selecting on-line documentation.

If you're new to computers or feel the least bit timid about them, leave the OS/2 Tutorial button checked. After you install OS/2, you can run through the tutorial to strengthen your familiarity with OS/2. You also may want to install the tutorial for curiosity's sake, even if you are familiar with computers. You can remove the tutorial from your computer later, if you want to free up the disk space.

The second subcategory, the OS/2 Command Reference, is the heart of the on-line documentation. You almost certainly will want to install this part so that you can refer to the on-line help whenever you have a question. Chapter 13, "Using the Built-In Help Facility," shows you how to ask questions and receive answers from the on-line help that OS/2 supplies.

The third option, REXX Information, tells OS/2 you want the on-line help available for the REXX programming language. If you plan to do sophisticated batch file programming under OS/2, leave this box checked. Otherwise, you can safely uncheck the box.

When you have made your selections, click the OK button or press Enter with the OK button highlighted. The OS/2 installation process returns you to the Setup and Installation screen.

Installing Fonts. Chapter 4, "Deciding how You Want to Use OS/2," explained the pros and cons of installing the fonts that come with OS/2. When you check the Fonts option and click the More... button for that option, you receive an opportunity to indicate which fonts you want to use. Figure 6.11 shows the screen that appears.

Fig. 6.11
Selecting fonts.

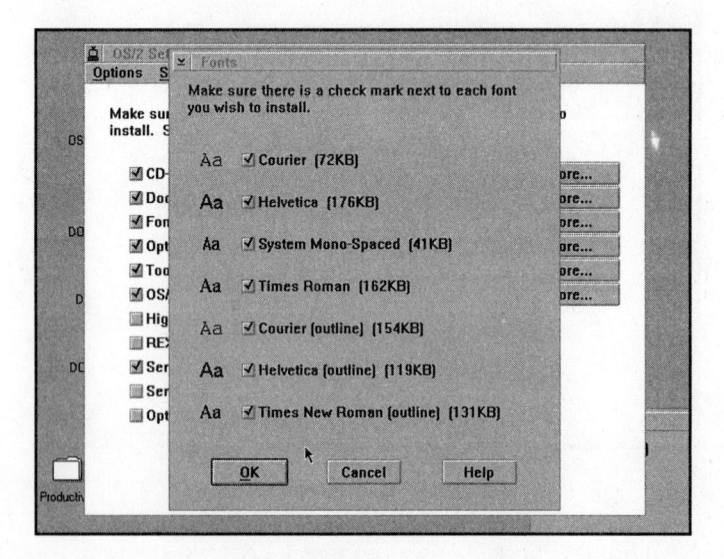

Note that if you just check the Fonts option without clicking the More... button, OS/2 installs all the fonts. If you uncheck the Fonts option, however, OS/2 doesn't install any of the fonts. The Fonts selection screen shown in figure 6.11 appears only if you check the Fonts option and click the More... button to view the subcategories for that option.

The fonts supplied with OS/2 include Courier, Helvetica, System Mono-Spaced, Times Roman, Courier outline, Helvetica outline, and Times New Roman outline. The last three fonts are products of the Adobe company and are quite handsome. These special outline fonts do take a larger amount of disk space, however. The Fonts selection screen shows you exactly what each font looks like.

After you make your selections, click the OK button, or press the Tab key to highlight the button and then press Enter.

Selecting Optional System Utilities. The Optional System Utilities Selection screen allows you to choose from the list of system utilities supplied with OS/2 (see fig. 6.12).

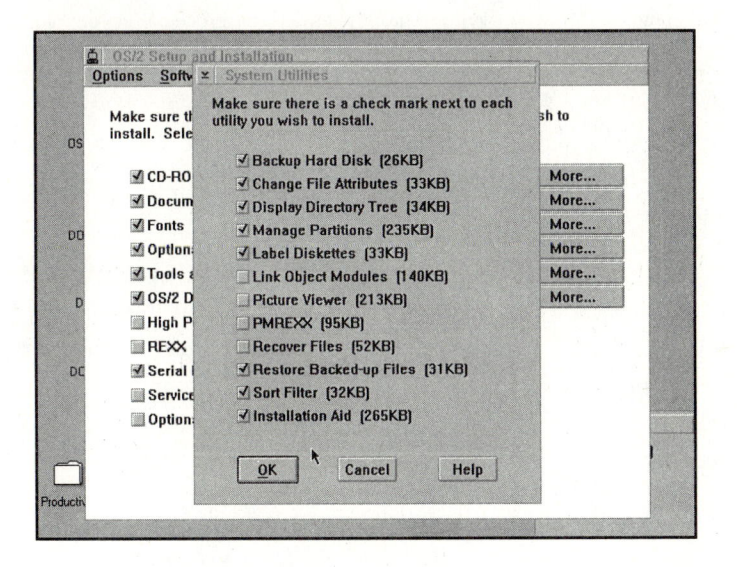

Fig. 6.12
Selecting system utilities.

The following table shows the purpose of each of these optional utilities so that you can judge whether you want to install that utility.

Utility	Purpose
Backup Hard Disk	Make backup copies of your data on floppy disks
Change File Attributes	Change a file to/from Read-Only status
Display Directory Tree	View the structure of your hard disk subdirectories
Manage Partitions	Change partition sizes
Label Disks	Record internal volume labels on your disks
Link Object Modules	A programmer development tool
Picture Viewer	View OS/2 metafiles
PMREXX	A Presentation Manager interactive REXX programming environment
Recover Files	A rarely used, CHKDSK-like command for emergency recovery of files from a badly corrupted hard disk
Restore Backed-up Files	Copy backed-up files to your hard disk
Sort Filter	Sort text files; used most within batch file programs
Installation Aid	A portion of the installation process that you might need later when you want to do a selective install

After you check the items you want to install, click the OK button (or press the Tab key to highlight OK and press Enter). You return to the Setup and Installation screen.

If you're uncertain about which system utilities to install even after looking over the preceding list, you may want to choose the same items checked in figure 6.12. You can selectively install other portions of OS/2 later, if you want, but for now the sample configuration shown in figure 6.12 will probably suffice for all your day-to-day work and for the occasional disk file administration you will do.

Adding Tools and Games. When you check the Tools and Games box and click its More... button, the screen shown in figure 6.13 appears. On this screen, you select the OS/2 tools and games components you want, just as you did on the previous screens.

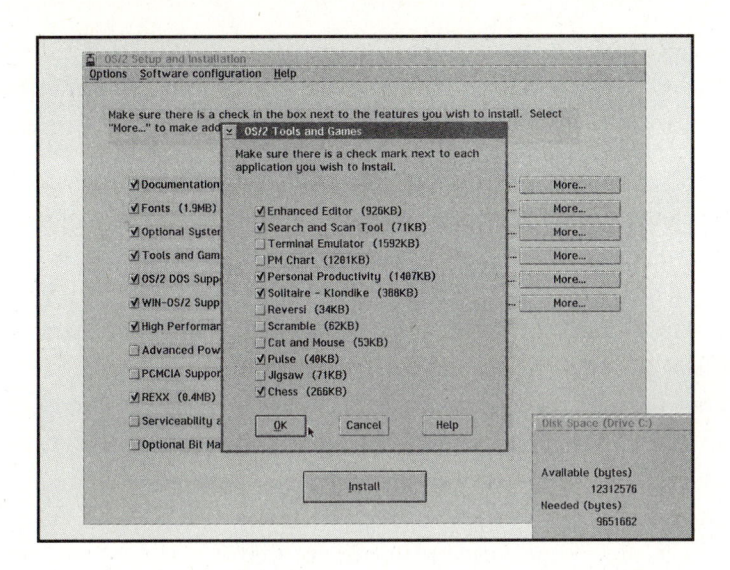

Fig. 6.13
Selecting tools and games.

To help you decide which components you want, the following table lists the purpose of each of the items on the Tools and Games Selection screen.

Tool or game	Purpose
Enhanced Editor	Edits text files
Search and Scan Tool	Enables you to search for files by name as well as search the contents of files
Terminal Emulator	Connects to other computers through your modem
PM Chart	An application for preparing graphs and charts from spreadsheet data
Personal Productivity	A collection of mini-applications (applets); includes a calendar, a calculator, to-do list, simple spreadsheet, notepad, and other helpful software
Solitaire-Klondike	The one-player card game
Reversi, Scramble	Puzzles for you to solve and play
Cat and Mouse	The animated cat follows your cursor
Pulse	Graphs how hard your computer is working
Jigsaw	Another puzzle
Chess	A 3-D chess game; play against the computer or over a local area network against another player

If you're uncertain about which tools and games to choose, select those that you think will give you a good starting point and suffice for most day-to-day computer work. You can make changes later with OS/2's selective install capability.

Working with the OS/2 DOS Environment. Figure 6.14 is the screen you see when you check the OS/2 DOS box and click the More... button. The three check boxes, labeled DOS Protect Mode Interface, Virtual Expanded Memory Management, and Virtual Extended Memory Support, enable you to install all of OS/2's built-in memory managers. If you install these three items, they provide the same functions and features as the popular DOS products QEMM (from Quarterdeck Office Systems) and 386MAX (from Qualitas). A growing number of applications take advantage of the memory management interfaces created by products such as QEMM and 386MAX. OS/2 has a built-in capability to also provide these interfaces. The DOS Memory Management section, next in this chapter, covers DOS memory management in detail.

Fig. 6.14
Selecting DOS/Windows options.

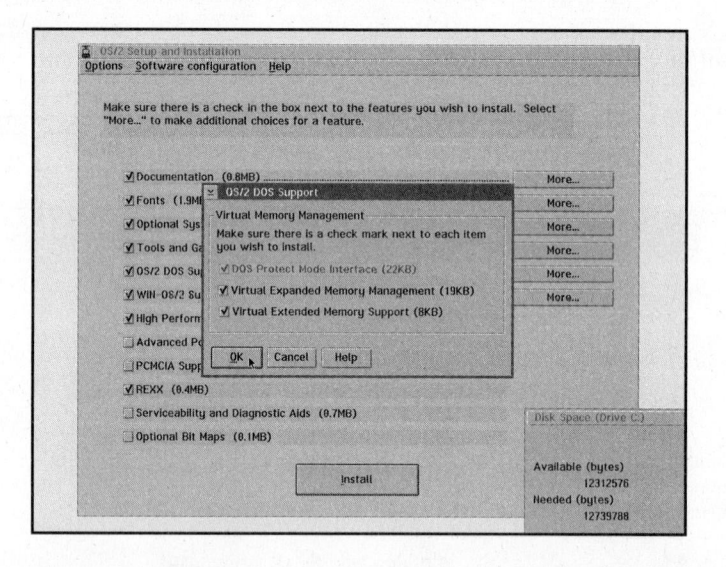

Because you will almost certainly run DOS applications under OS/2 and DOS applications now commonly use these memory management interfaces, you should leave all three boxes checked. The disk space taken by these memory management modules is minimal.

> **Note**
>
> The OS/2 installation procedure automatically checks the first box, DOS Protected Mode Interface, and does not allow you to uncheck this box. IBM made the DOS Protected Mode Interface (DPMI) an integral part of OS/2 and you cannot choose to have OS/2 operate without DPMI.

DOS Memory Management. Memory management programs work with the following types of memory:

- *Conventional memory*. The memory that is directly addressable by the CPU chip in real mode. The upper boundary is normally the well-known 640K limit, but some memory managers raise that ceiling.

- *Upper memory*. The memory between 640K and 1M. Video adapters, ROM BIOS chips, hard disk controller ROMs, and network adapters are in this region, but some memory managers can map "holes"—Upper Memory Blocks—as regular memory.

- *Extended memory*. Memory above the 1M threshold, addressable only in protected mode.

- *High memory area*. The first 64K of extended memory, minus 16 bytes, beginning at the 1M threshold. Because of a quirk in the design of the 80286, 80386, and 80486 CPU chips, you can address these 65,520 bytes in real mode.

- *Expanded memory*. Invented jointly by Lotus, Intel, and Microsoft, expanded memory enables an application to bank-switch RAM, in 16K blocks, from an EMS memory card into conventional or upper memory. The specification is the Lotus/Intel/Microsoft (LIM) Expanded Memory Specification (EMS). The most recent EMS version is version 4.0. OS/2 can transform extended memory into expanded memory.

- *EXTENDED MEMORY SPECIFICATION (XMS)*. Also developed by Lotus/Intel/Microsoft, this standard provides the means for DOS applications to use portions of extended memory.

- *VIRTUAL CONTROL PROGRAM INTERFACE MEMORY (VCPI)*. Quarterdeck Office Systems and Phar Lap Software developed the VCPI standard so that DOS applications can cooperatively share extended memory without conflict.

- *DOS PROTECTED MODE INTERFACE (DPMI).* Developed by Microsoft, DPMI offers functions similar to VCPI but allows OS/2 to enforce control over extended memory access.

Selecting the Win-OS/2 Environment. The options on the Win-OS/2 Support screen represent somewhat larger amounts of disk space than those on the DOS Support screen. For this reason, the first installation choice on the Win-OS/2 Support screen is the letter of the destination drive on which you want to place OS/2's Windows environment. If you have more than one disk partition, you can choose to install the OS/2 for Windows files on a drive other than C:.

The Readme files, Accessories, Screensavers, and Sound check boxes let you select optional components of the Win-OS/2 environment. The check box labeled Readme files installs to your hard drive informative text files that explain details of the Win-OS/2 environment. The Accessories check box puts the usual Windows 3.1 accessory computer programs on your disk...Paintbrush, Calendar, Calculator, Cardfile, and other Windows applications. The Screensavers check box puts a collection of files with the extension .SCR on your disk. Later, when you start Windows under OS/2, you'll be able to use Windows screen saver feature. The Sound check box puts a collection of .MID and .WAV files on your disk. If you have a sound card in your computer that is Windows-compatible, you'll be able to play and hear these sound files.

After you make your selections, click OK (or use the Tab key to move the selection highlight to the OK button and press Enter). You return to the Setup and Installation screen.

Adding High Performance File System Support. In Chapter 4, "Deciding how You Want to Use OS/2," you learned the pros and cons of using the High Performance File System. The next box you can check on the Setup and Installation screen, the HPFS box, enables you to choose to use HPFS. If you put a check mark in the box, the OS/2 installation process takes the following actions:

- Copies the HPFS support modules to your hard disk.

- Inserts a statement in your CONFIG.SYS file to load the HPFS software drivers at boot time.

Checking the HPFS box does not automatically format one of your disk partitions with the new file system. You must do that formatting at a later time. The HPFS check box does not have a More... button.

Installing REXX. You also learned about REXX in Chapter 4. If you want to try your hand at batch file programming, check the box marked REXX on the Setup and Installation screen. The OS/2 installation process copies the REXX modules to your hard disk.

Note that you can do simple batch file programming without REXX. REXX enhances your batch file programs by enabling you to use more sophisticated techniques in your programs. The REXX check box does not have a More... button.

Choosing Serviceability and Diagnostic Aids. If you check the box marked Serviceability and Diagnostic Aids, the OS/2 installation process copies certain optional OS/2 software modules to your hard disk. These modules enable you to "take a snapshot" of the contents of memory if you encounter an error in OS/2 that halts your computer. Such errors are rare. If you have IBM-trained support people in your company who can make sense of the "post-mortem" memory snapshot, however, you probably will want to install these optional modules. If you do not install them, you do not change the performance of OS/2.

Working with Optional Bit Maps. You may someday tire of having a computer screen desktop that appears in a solid color. If you are the flamboyant type, you perhaps will want to select a different background image for your OS/2 desktop. OS/2 comes with a variety of pictures and images you can install by checking the Optional Bit Maps box. Later, after the installation process is completed, you can choose one of these pictures (an OS/2 logo screen, a New England lighthouse, and other images) to be the background of your desktop.

Changing Your Configuration Settings

After you have checked all the boxes on the Setup and Installation screen you want (and perhaps have used the More... buttons to further select or deselect items within each category), you can modify the configuration settings for your OS/2 sessions and your DOS sessions. Making such changes is optional; you may not want to change the defaults at all.

Chapter 6—Installing OS/2

On the Setup and Installation screen, click the Software Configuration menu item (or press Alt-S) to see the configuration pull-down menu. Choose the OS/2 or the DOS menu option. The screen shows various CONFIG.SYS entries. If you have used DOS and a text editor to modify CONFIG.SYS, you will appreciate the ease with which you can change these settings. The OS/2 configuration screen, illustrated in figure 6.15, shows such items as the number of Buffers, the Diskcache size, the MaxWait option, the Swap Minfree option, the number of Threads, the settings for MemMan Protect, MemMan Swap, Priority, and SwapPath. The DOS configuration screen, illustrated in figure 6.16, shows items such as the setting of the Break switch, the amount of memory you want for each DOS session, and the number of FCBs (file control blocks).

Fig. 6.15
The OS/2 Configuration Window in which you make CONFIG.SYS changes.

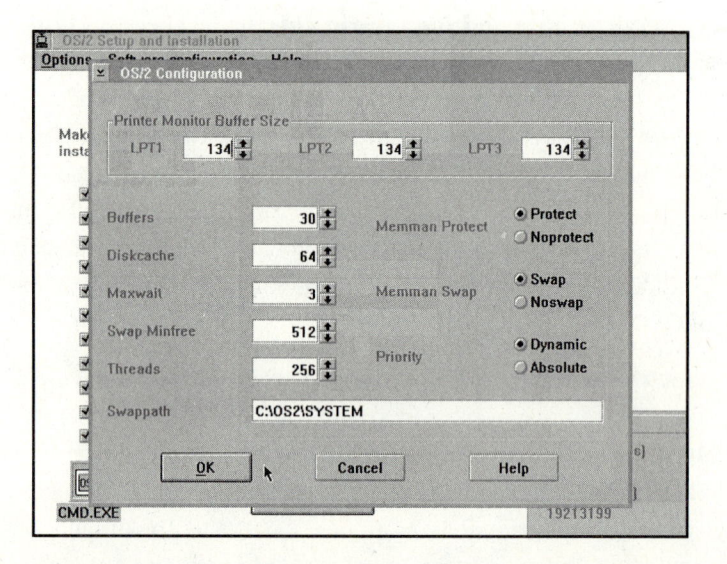

The defaults for all these settings are almost certainly correct for you. Leave them alone for now. If you discover you want to change a setting, you can go back and make changes later. Chapter 7, "Modifying Your OS/2 Configuration," discusses how to make such changes.

Installing Your Selected Features

When you finish with the Setup and Installation screen, click the Install button (or press Alt-I) to continue with the installation process. A popup message box appears; confirm that you want to proceed. The message `You're about to begin the installation of your selected configuration` appears on-screen, and OS/2 asks you to insert the remaining disks.

Choosing the OS/2 Features You Want   **155**

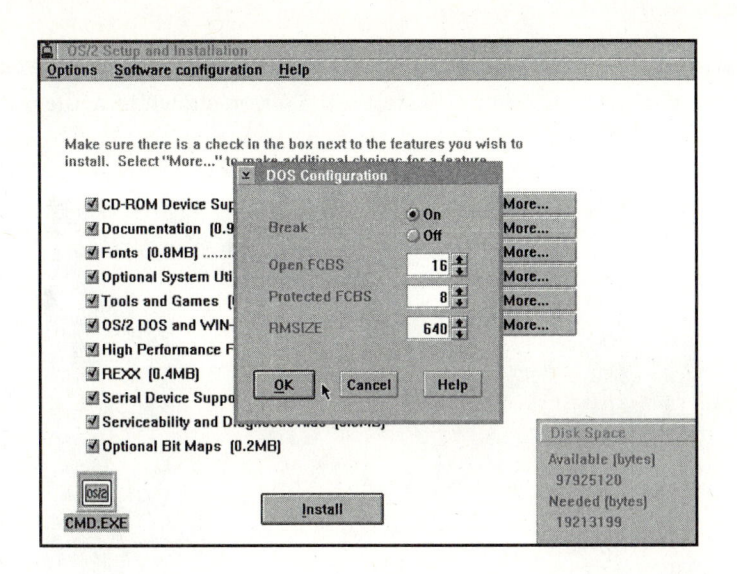

Fig. 6.16
The DOS Configuration Window, for DOS-related CONFIG.SYS changes.

While the OS/2 installation process copies the components of the operating system you selected, you see the progress of the installation on-screen. OS/2 displays a bar chart to show how much of the installation has been completed. It also displays images of the disks so that you can tell which ones you have processed. OS/2 tells you the name of each file while it installs the file on your hard disk.

After OS/2 copies the last file from the disk labeled Disk 19, the installation process displays a message box telling you OS/2 Setup and Installation is updating the system configuration. This update may take several minutes. When OS/2 finishes updating your system configuration, you're almost finished with the installation of your new multifaceted operating system. The Advanced Options window screen appears (see fig. 6.17).

Choosing Advanced Options. You next need to tell OS/2 how you want OS/2 to configure itself for your Windows applications, whether you want OS/2 to automatically make icons for your existing DOS and Windows applications, whether you have optional device support disks to install, and whether the installation process should examine your existing CONFIG.SYS and AUTOEXEC.BAT files to migrate their contents into your new environment.

On the Advanced Options menu, put check marks in the boxes for the actions you want to take and click the OK button. OS/2 leads you through all of the selections, one by one.

Migrating DOS and Windows Applications. If you checked the Advanced Option box labeled Migrate Applications, the screen shown in figure 6.18 appears.

Fig. 6.17
The Advanced Options installation window.

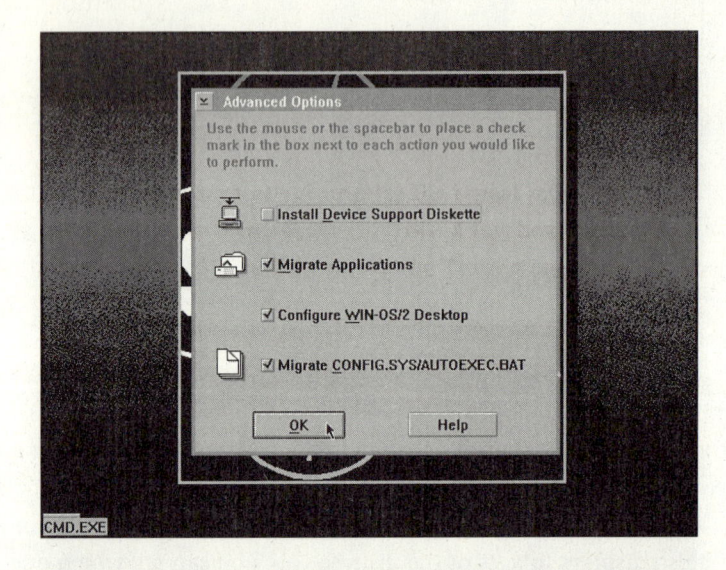

Fig. 6.18
Migrating your DOS and Windows applications.

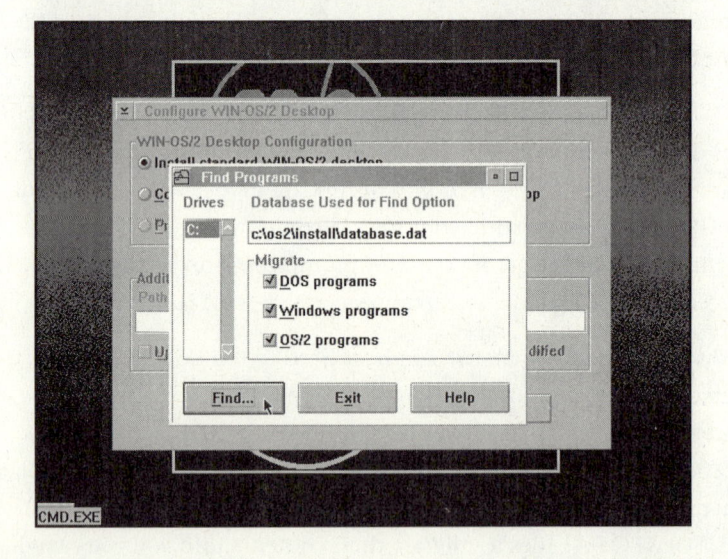

Icons (objects) represent applications, data files, and utility programs on your OS/2 desktop. You can tell the OS/2 installation process to automatically search for your existing DOS and Windows applications and make icons for them. Later, when you reboot your computer and OS/2 is running, you do not have to manually tell OS/2 about each of your applications. You should almost certainly select the option to migrate your existing applications. In addition to setting up program objects (icons) on your desktop, the migration step also modifies your DOS settings and Windows INI files, inserting entries appropriate for the applications that the migration step finds on your computer. However, if you reformatted your hard disk as part of the installation of OS/2, you don't have any applications on your computer for the OS/2 installation process to migrate. You can safely skip the option to migrate applications. After you restore your files (that you backed up before reformatting your drive), you can use the Migrate Applications object in the System Setup folder to create new program objects. Chapter 7, Modifying Your OS/2 Configuration, explains how to use the Migrate Applications object in the System Setup folder.

Configuring Your Win-OS/2 Desktop. If you chose to install support for Windows applications on your OS/2 computer, the screen shown in figure 6.19 appears.

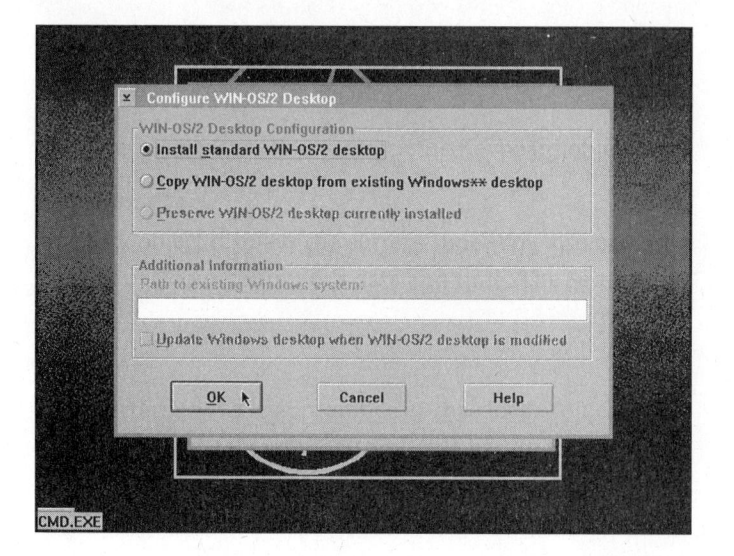

Fig. 6.19
Configuring your Win-OS/2 desktop.

You can choose the standard Win-OS/2 desktop, you can copy your existing Windows desktop, or you can preserve an existing Win-OS/2 desktop configuration. The last two options only apply if you already have Windows installed on your computer.

You also can tell OS/2 the path to your existing Windows directory, and you can instruct OS/2 to update your existing Windows desktop settings to reflect your new Win-OS/2 settings.

> **Note**
>
> If you're installing the OS/2 for Windows product, OS/2 will prompt you to insert your Microsoft Windows 3.1 distribution floppy disks or indicate where on your hard drive OS/2 can find your Windows distribution files (these files are typically in a directory named WINSTALL).

Using Optional Device Support Disks. The standard set of OS/2 distribution disks does not include device support disks. Third-party (non-IBM) manufacturers supply these disks along with hardware components. The disks contain optional software driver modules. If you have such a disk, you should follow the instructions that came with the disk to install the drivers. You probably will not have any device support disks.

Migrating CONFIG.SYS and AUTOEXEC.BAT File Contents. OS/2 can determine whether you have statements and commands in your existing CONFIG.SYS and AUTOEXEC.BAT files that OS/2 should include in your new environment. You almost certainly should select this option. OS/2 will migrate the contents of the previous files into the new CONFIG.SYS and AUTOEXEC.BAT files it creates.

The five disks labeled Printer Driver Disk 1 through Printer Driver Disk 5 contain software drivers for a variety of printer makes and models. (You have three disks if your floppy disks are the salmon-colored set. If you're installing from CD-ROM, the driver files are on the CD-ROM disk.) If you chose to install a printer earlier (in the Currently Installed Peripherals section of the System Configuration screen), OS/2 asks you to insert one or more of these disks now. (The System Configuration screen is the one illustrated in figure 6.6.) OS/2 then copies the appropriate printer to your hard disk. Next OS/2 may ask you to insert one or both of the Display Driver diskettes.

When you finish with the Advanced Options portion of the installation of OS/2, you then see the message `OS/2 Setup and Installation is complete. Remove the disk from Drive A:. Press Enter to restart your system.` When you remove the last installation disk from the disk drive and press Enter, OS/2 reboots your computer. After OS/2 loads into your computer, a screen similar to the one in figure 6.20 appears. You're now running OS/2!

Choosing the OS/2 Features You Want   **159**

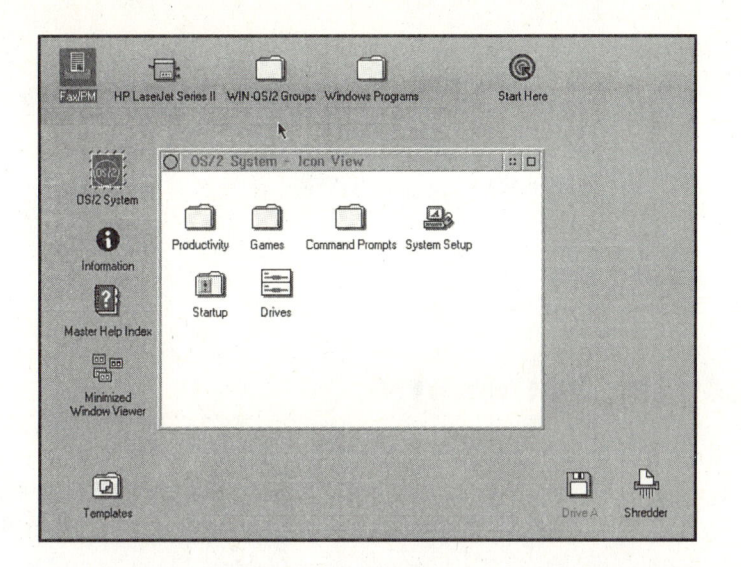

Fig. 6.20
The initial OS/2 screen, showing your new desktop.

> **Note**
>
> The first time the Workplace Shell initializes itself, it has extra work to do. OS/2 is busy creating the Extended Attributes and INI files you learned about in Chapter 3. Don't be concerned if this process takes several moments. The next time you boot your computer, the Workplace Shell will appear much more quickly.

If you asked for tutorial help during the installation process, the first software OS/2 runs will be the OS/2 Tutorial. Spend a few minutes exploring this tutorial material to make yourself more comfortable with your new operating system.

HPFS and Boot Manager—the Finishing Touches

If you chose either Boot Manager or HPFS, you have a little more work to do. For Boot Manager, you need to install the other operating system(s) that Boot Manager allows you to select each time you reboot your computer. Follow the directions that came with the operating system(s).

For HPFS, you may need to format the separate disk partition you designate for HPFS. If you chose to use HPFS for your primary OS/2 partition, the installation process formatted that partition before installing OS/2 on it. If you designated a second, separate partition for use by HPFS, however, you should format that partition now. Double-click the icon labeled OS/2 System.

For Related Information

- "Understanding Hardware and Software," p. 14

- "Examining Other Operating Systems," p. 81

- "Considering Disks and Disk Files," p. 83

- "Understanding Application and General System Options," p. 88

- "Reflecting Personal Preferences," p. 98

After the folder opens, double-click the icon labeled Command Prompts. Then double-click the icon labeled OS/2 Full Screen. When you see the command-line prompt, enter the following command:

FORMAT <drive letter:> /FS:HPFS

The <drive letter:> is the logical drive that FDISK assigned to the HPFS partition you set up.

Chapter Summary

This chapter led you step-by-step through the installation of OS/2. You found out how many distribution disks you should have, and you started the installation process. You proceeded through the text mode portion of the installation, partitioning your hard disk as necessary for Boot Manager and HPFS. You learned how to set up your computer so that Dual-Boot would install without incident. You told OS/2 what sort of pointing device you have, and you learned how OS/2 uses that device.

You next confirmed your mouse, keyboard, country, printer, type of computer display, and other peripherals to OS/2. You may have told OS/2 to install all components on your computer, or you more likely told OS/2 that you wanted to indicate which features and options you use.

You learned about the DOS and OS/2 configuration settings, which the next chapter explores in more detail. You then used the Advanced Options menu of the installation process to indicate whether OS/2 should turn your DOS and Windows applications into icons and whether OS/2 should automatically migrate your CONFIG.SYS and AUTOEXEC.BAT file contents into your new environment. If you installed the OS/2 for Windows product, you followed the usual OS/2 installation steps and then inserted your Windows 3.1 distribution disks. You may possibly have installed optional device support disks. You then completed the installation and booted your computer with its new operating system.

In the next chapter, you learn how to modify your OS/2 configuration.

Chapter 7

Modifying Your OS/2 Configuration

As part of the installation process, you may want to tailor OS/2 to your own tastes before you use your new operating system. You also may want to know about the several configuration options before you use OS/2. You should feel comfortable using the OS/2 Workplace Shell before you make changes to your new operating system, however. If OS/2 is your first graphical user interface-based operating environment, explore Chapter 9, "Using Your Computer Screen as a Desktop," and Chapter 10, "Managing the Workplace Shell," before you make any configuration changes. You can come back to this chapter later if you first want to try out OS/2 before changing anything.

If you don't have a mouse, read Chapters 9 and 10 before proceeding. OS/2 has keystrokes you can use instead of moving the mouse and pressing the mouse buttons. Chapters 9 and 10 cover these special keyboard operations.

The OS/2 installation process created new CONFIG.SYS and AUTOEXEC.BAT files. You learn in this chapter how to modify these startup files. You also learn about the OS/2 STARTUP.CMD file, an optional file of boot-time commands you can create.

> **Note**
>
> If your computer had a copy of DOS on it before you installed OS/2, the OS/2 installation process saved your old AUTOEXEC.BAT and CONFIG.SYS files in the C:\OS2\SYSTEM directory. When you use Dual-Boot (the BOOT command), OS/2 moves its AUTOEXEC.BAT and CONFIG.SYS files to C:\OS2\SYSTEM and moves the DOS versions of these files to your root directory before booting DOS. Using Dual-Boot to return to OS/2 causes the reverse actions to occur.

When you add new hardware options to your computer, you need to change your OS/2 configuration. This chapter discusses how adding a printer, a new font, a mouse, and a hard disk, as well as changing your display adapter, affect these configuration files.

During installation, you may have chosen to leave out certain features of OS/2. This chapter shows you how to selectively install OS/2 features without reinstalling all of OS/2.

The desktop is one of OS/2's most configurable elements. This chapter shows you how to express your preferences by selecting screen colors, background images (wallpaper), and different views of your system.

When you use the objects on your new OS/2 desktop, keep the following basic procedures in mind:

- Use mouse button 1 for selection (opening folders and running programs); use mouse button 2 for manipulation (drag-and-drop movement of icons).

- Click an icon with mouse button 2 to bring up that object's pop-up menu.

- Click an empty space on the desktop with mouse button 2 to bring up the system pop-up menu.

- *Always do a shutdown before powering down or rebooting.* Click an empty part of the desktop with mouse button 2 and then choose the Shutdown option on the system pop-up menu.

- When an object's icon is selected, OS/2 displays a gray backdrop around the icon. This is called *selection emphasis*.

Using CONFIG.SYS and AUTOEXEC.BAT

Each time you boot your computer, OS/2 uses the contents of the CONFIG.SYS file to load its device drivers and to configure itself for your use. At boot time, OS/2 also uses the contents of the STARTUP.CMD file to automatically execute commands and programs. Each time you start a DOS session under OS/2, your AUTOEXEC.BAT file tells DOS what programs and commands to run as part of setting up that DOS session.

> **Note**
>
> Here is a summary of when the different startup files take effect: At boot time, OS/2 uses the entries in the CONFIG.SYS file and executes the statements in the STARTUP.CMD file (if STARTUP.CMD exists in the root directory of the boot drive). Each time you start a DOS session, OS/2 executes the statements in the AUTOEXEC.BAT file.

If you have used DOS before, you may be surprised at the number of entries in the OS/2 CONFIG.SYS file. OS/2 is more sophisticated than DOS and requires many more setup options. The CONFIG.SYS file for OS/2 is correspondingly more sophisticated because it expresses these setup options.

> **Note**
>
> Remember to reboot your computer—after you first use the Shutdown option—when you make changes to CONFIG.SYS. The changes take effect only after you reboot.
>
> After rebooting, you may decide you do not like the changes. Before changing your CONFIG.SYS file, make a copy of the file (type **COPY C:\CONFIG.SYS C:\CONFIG.HLD** at an OS/2 or DOS command-line prompt). If you decide to undo your changes, you can copy the saved file (CONFIG.HLD) over the CONFIG.SYS changes and reboot.

Appendix F, "The Default CONFIG.SYS File," identifies and explains the typical contents of the initial CONFIG.SYS file that OS/2 creates for you.

Changing CONFIG.SYS Statements

To make changes to portions of the CONFIG.SYS file, you can use OS/2's Enhanced Editor or OS/2's System Editor. Chapter 14, "Using the OS/2 Text Editors," explains OS/2's built-in text editors in detail. However, the basic process of editing a text file (such as CONFIG.SYS) with the Enhanced Editor is simple.

To use the Enhanced Editor to change CONFIG.SYS, run the text editor by opening the Productivity folder and double-clicking the Enhanced Editor's icon. Choose the File, Open menu option, specify the file C:\CONFIG.SYS, and make your changes. Use File/Save when you finish, select Shutdown from the system pop-up menu, and reboot.

The following listing shows some of the CONFIG.SYS entries that you might want to change:

```
LIBPATH=C:\OS2\DLL;C:\OS2\MDOS;C:\;C:\OS2\APPS\DLL;C:\NETWARE;
SET PATH=C:\OS2;C:\OS2\SYSTEM;C:\OS2\MDOS\WINOS2;
C:\OS2\INSTALL;C:\;C:\OS2\MDOS;C:\OS2\APPS;F:\PUBLIC\OS2;
C:\NETWARE
SET DPATH=C:\OS2;C:\OS2\SYSTEM;C:\OS2\MDOS\WINOS2;
   C:\OS2\INSTALL;C:\;C:\OS2\BITMAP;C:\OS2\MDOS;C:\OS2\APPS;
SET PROMPT=[OS2] $p$g
BUFFERS=30
DISKCACHE=74,LW
BREAK=OFF
SET TEMP=C:\
PROTECTONLY=NO
SHELL=C:\OS2\MDOS\COMMAND.COM C:\OS2\MDOS /E:1024 /P
RMSIZE=740
DOS=LOW,NOUMB
DEVICE=C:\OS2\MDOS\ANSI.SYS
DEVICE=C:\OS2\VDISK.SYS 2048 512 128
```

The LIBPATH statement tells OS/2 where to find the parts of your OS/2 application programs called Dynamic Link Libraries (DLLs). The PATH statement, as in DOS, tells OS/2 where to find executable programs. The PATH statement in CONFIG.SYS refers only to OS/2 applications. You put a separate PATH statement in your AUTOEXEC.BAT file for DOS sessions and the applications you run in those sessions. The DPATH statement works for OS/2 applications and indicates where OS/2 or an OS/2 application can find data files that are not in the current directory. The OS/2 DPATH statement is similar in purpose to the DOS APPEND statement.

You can change the appearance of your OS/2 command-line prompt with the PROMPT statement. Unlike other CONFIG.SYS statements, the PROMPT statement also works at a command-line prompt. The BUFFERS entry tells OS/2 how many disk buffers to use. The DISKCACHE statement lets OS/2 know how much memory you want allocated for OS/2's disk cache feature and whether you want OS/2 to use "lazy writes." The BREAK parameter, which applies to DOS sessions, enables you to press Ctrl+C to interrupt a running program. Some OS/2 applications use the TEMP environment variable, set in the listing's example to C:\, to indicate where to store temporary files. The SET statement specifies the environment variable and its value.

PROTECTONLY tells OS/2 whether you will use DOS sessions. (PROTECTONLY = YES prevents you from starting DOS sessions, which you might want to do on a file server PC. The default is NO.) The SHELL statement expresses the location of the DOS command processor, COMMAND.COM. SHELL also enables you to allocate more memory to any DOS environment variables set in your AUTOEXEC.BAT file. The RMSIZE parameter indicates the maximum size of any DOS session you might start. The DEVICE statement loads a device driver; in the statement listing, the two DEVICE statements load the ANSI.SYS driver and the OS/2 RAM disk driver.

You now understand the basic function of each statement in the example listing. If you want to know more about one of these CONFIG.SYS statements, or about other CONFIG.SYS entries, see Appendix F of this book for a complete explanation.

Changing DOS and Windows Settings

The changes you make to CONFIG.SYS affect all future OS/2, Windows, and DOS sessions after you reboot. But you can change several DOS and Windows settings on a session-by-session basis. You can modify all the settings before you start a session. For an already started session, you can change a subset of the DOS and Windows options.

To see the list of settings, follow these steps:

1. Open the Command Prompts folder by double-clicking it. (Unless you have moved this folder, you can find it inside the OS/2 System folder.)

2. Display the pop-up menu for the DOS Full Screen object by placing the mouse cursor over the object and pressing mouse button 2.

3. Place the mouse cursor on the arrow next to the Open menu item. Press mouse button 1 once to see the Settings/Program menu.

4. Place the mouse cursor on the Settings menu item. Press mouse button 1.

5. Select the **S**ession tab on the notebook that appears on-screen.

6. Click the button labeled DOS Settings. Your screen should now look similar to the one shown in figure 7.1.

Figure 7.2 shows part of the list of settings you can change on a session-by-session basis. One of the settings, PRINT_TIMEOUT, is highlighted; the Description and Value fields you see apply only for the PRINT_TIMEOUT settings. Other settings' fields have their own descriptions and methods for changing their values. To change the current setting, you can type a new value in the text box or use the slider box to increase or decrease the value. When you finish, click the **S**ave button.

Fig. 7.1
The DOS Full Screen Settings Session notebook page.

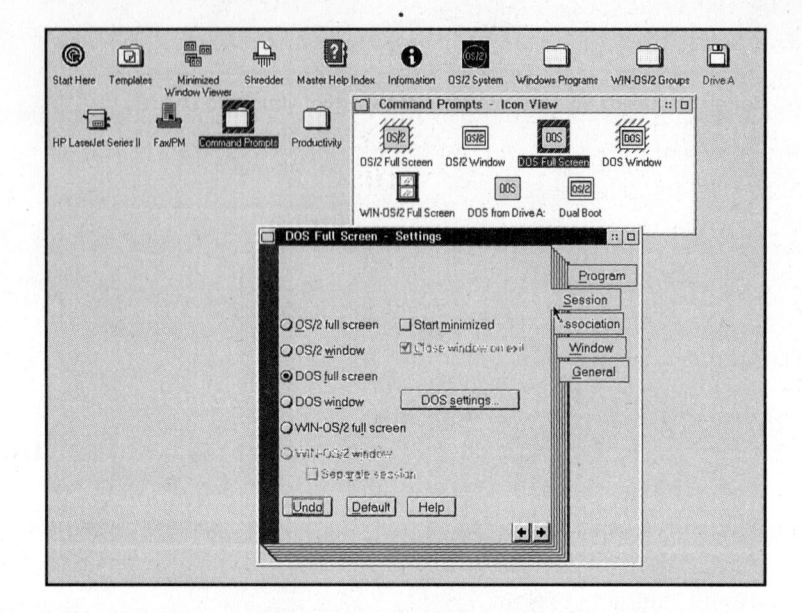

Fig. 7.2
Changing DOS/Windows settings on a session-by-session basis.

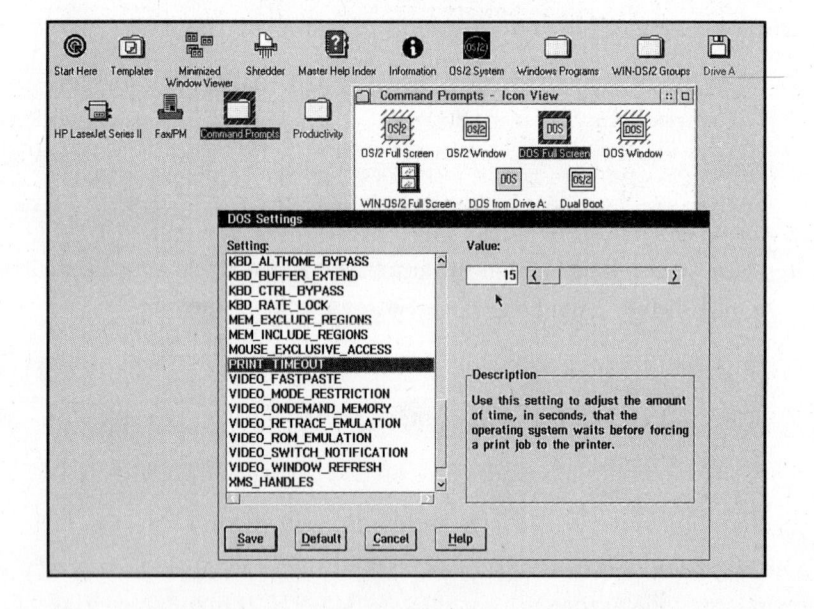

Chapter 16, "Running DOS and Windows under OS/2", and Chapter 17, "Configuring Your DOS and Windows Sessions," describe all the settings values you can change to improve and enhance the way your application software runs.

Migrating CONFIG.SYS Statements

If you use the Enhanced Editor to view the CONFIG.SYS file, you may notice that some device driver statements have been turned into comment statements because they are preceded by the word REM. The OS/2 CONFIG.SYS Migration utility may have made these changes for you during installation. Some device drivers, designed to work with DOS, may not function correctly with OS/2. The OS/2 Migration utility turns the statements that load these device drivers into comments. You can delete the word REM from these statements with a text editor and then reboot your computer to see whether the device driver operates correctly. If the driver malfunctions, you can copy your saved CONFIG.HLD file (as mentioned earlier in this chapter) over the CONFIG.SYS file and reboot again to remove the driver from memory.

If your computer doesn't boot properly after you "unremark" the device driver statement in CONFIG.SYS, you can recover by following these steps:

1. Insert the OS/2 Installation Diskette in the disk drive and reboot your computer.

2. When prompted, insert OS/2 Diskette 1.

3. At the next prompt (the Welcome to OS/2 screen), press the Esc key to obtain a command-line prompt.

4. Use the **COPY** command to overlay the CONFIG.SYS file with your saved CONFIG.HLD file.

5. Remove the floppy disk from the disk drive and reboot by pressing Ctrl+Alt+Del.

Updating CONFIG.SYS Statements for Application Programs

The installation software programs for some applications may contain their own configuration editors. For example, the Novell NetWare Requester for OS/2 versions 2.0 and 2.1 comes with such a configuration aid. If an application requires changes to CONFIG.SYS, such a configuration aid makes it easy to complete the application's installation. You indicate your preferences to the configuration aid, and the software automatically updates the CONFIG.SYS file for you.

On the other hand, some applications tell you to use a text editor to make CONFIG.SYS changes. In such cases, you need to use the OS/2 Enhanced Editor or the OS/2 System Editor to make your changes.

Executing AUTOEXEC.BAT Statements

OS/2 executes the statements in your C:\AUTOEXEC.BAT file each time you start a new DOS session. The following is an example of the statements that OS/2 automatically inserts in a new AUTOEXEC.BAT file at installation time. You can use a text editor to insert other statements. You'll find an explanation of these example AUTOEXEC.BAT statements in Chapter 17, "Configuring Your DOS and Windows Sessions," in Chapter 18, "Batch-File Programming with OS/2," and in the Command Reference.

```
@ECHO OFF
PROMPT $p$g
SET DELDIR=C:\DELETE,512;
PATH C:\OS2;C:\OS2\MDOS;C:\OS2\MDOS\WINOS2; C:\;C:\WORD;C:\DOS;
LOADHIGH APPEND C:\OS2;C:\OS2\SYSTEM;
LOADHIGH DOSKEY
SET DIRCMD=/OD /L
```

Executing STARTUP.CMD Statements

The STARTUP.CMD file is the OS/2 equivalent of the DOS AUTOEXEC.BAT file. OS/2 executes the STARTUP.CMD file at boot time. The installation process does not create a STARTUP.CMD file because the file is optional, but you can make one if you want to run certain commands and utilities each time you start your computer. Alternatively, you can create a CMD file that executes OS/2 commands and programs, make a shadow of the CMD file, and place the shadow in your Startup folder. (Chapter 10, "Managing the Workplace Shell," explains how to make shadows of objects and perform drag-and-drop operations.)

For Related Information
- "Understanding Disk Partitions and Disks," p. 43
- "Understanding DOS Sessions," p. 394
- Command Reference, p. 717

If your computer is part of a local area network (LAN), you will find that the STARTUP.CMD file is a good place to put the commands you use to log on to the network. Under OS/2, a file with an extension of CMD is a batch file program that runs in an OS/2 (not a DOS or a Windows) session. Chapter 18 describes how to create batch file programs. You might use a STARTUP.CMD file whose contents are similar to the following:

```
@ECHO OFF
C:
CD \MUGLIB
LOGON BARRY /D=TCNS
C:
CD \NETWARE
LOGIN BARRY
C:
CD \NETWARE
MAP E:=SERVER1\SYS:
C:
CD \NETWARE
capture nt nb noff s=server1 q=laserjet
```

Upgrading Your Hardware

When you add hardware options to your computer, you need to indicate the changes for OS/2. In particular, you need to give OS/2 information about a new printer, new font, new mouse, new display adapter, or additional hard disk.

> **Note**
>
> You might receive special device driver installation disks from hardware manufacturers. OS/2 provides a facility for using these disks: the Device Driver Install program. If you need to access this program, you can find it in the System Setup folder. Figure 7.3 shows the Device Driver Installation window.

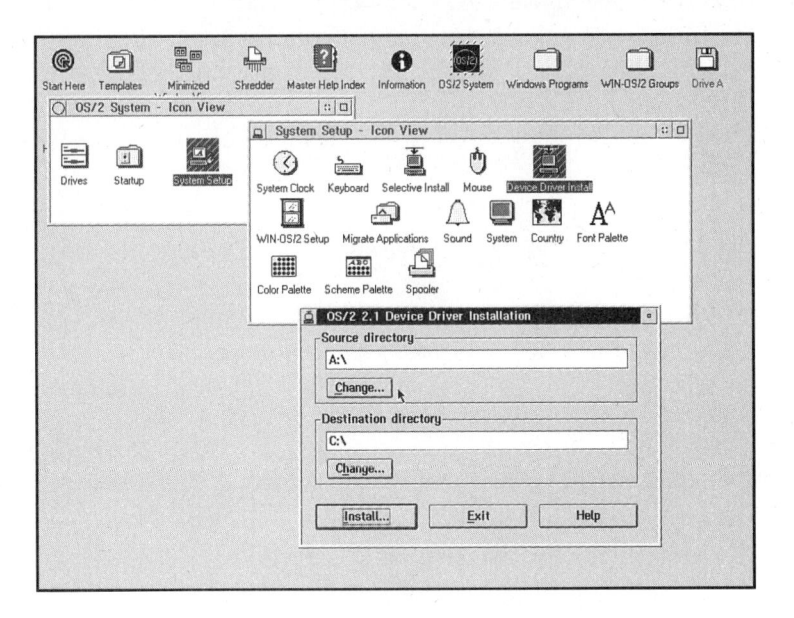

Fig. 7.3
The Device Driver Installation window.

Adding a Printer

To install a printer, first connect it to your computer according to the directions that came with the printer. These directions probably tell you to connect the device to your LPT1 or COM1 port. Note which port you use. Next, indicate to OS/2 that you have a new printer and the special things your new printer can do. You do this with a Settings notebook entry for a printer object. If you do not have a printer object on your desktop (it appears as an icon labeled Printer or labeled with the make and model of your printer), create one by following the steps below. Chapter 15, "Printing with OS/2," explains the creation of printer objects in more detail.

1. Open the Templates folder. By default, it is located inside the OS/2 System folder.

2. Use mouse button 2 to pick up the icon labeled Printer, drag it onto the desktop, and drop it (release the mouse button). The Create A Printer window opens automatically.

3. Click the Output Port to which you attached the printer. Type a name for the new printer object in the Name field. Choose one of the printer drivers in the list that OS/2 displays or click the Install New Printer Driver button and choose a printer from the list that OS/2 presents. Click the Create button.

4. If you want the equivalent Windows printer driver installed, click the Yes button that appears in the message window labeled Printer.

5. If you clicked the Install New Printer Driver button, OS/2 prompts you to insert the appropriate printer driver floppy disks (Printer Driver Diskette 1 through Printer Driver Diskete 3). Select your printer from the list of printers that OS/2 displays and follow the on-screen instructions to finish creating your printer object.

Use the remaining steps if you want to customize your printer object. You can change the printer driver associated with the printer object, specify the capabilities of your printer, and select the printer port to which your printer connects.

1. Open the settings notebook for the printer object. (Click with mouse button 2 on the printer object. Click once on the Open menu item. Click on the Settings menu item that appears.)

2. Use the **P**rinter driver tab if you'd like to install a new printer driver for your printer. Figure 7.4 shows a sample Printer Driver page of the settings notebook. Click with mouse button 2 (right button) on one of the displayed printer driver icons. The printer driver's pop-up menu appears. Choose the Install menu item. Select your printer from the list of available printer drivers that appears and follow the on-screen instructions to copy a new printer driver from the distribution floppy disks.

3. Double-click the Printer Driver icon to see the Job Properties notebook page, on which you tell OS/2 about the paper-handling and font capabilities of your new printer. Figure 7.5 shows the Job Properties notebook page for a Hewlett-Packard LaserJet printer.

Upgrading Your Hardware **171**

4. Use the tab marked **O**utput to change which port the printer uses (LPT1 or COM1, for example).

5. Close the settings notebook by clicking Close in the window's system menu.

> **Note**
>
> Some Novell NetWare network printer objects do not have settings notebooks.

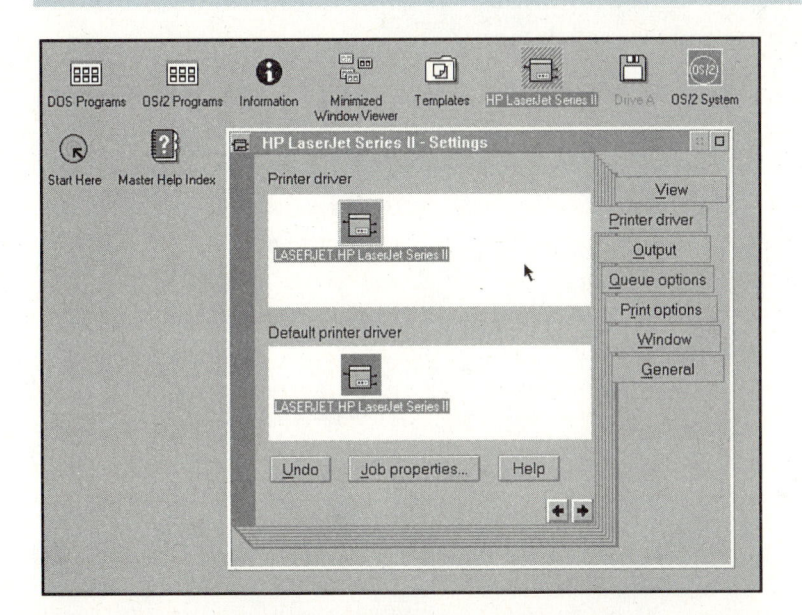

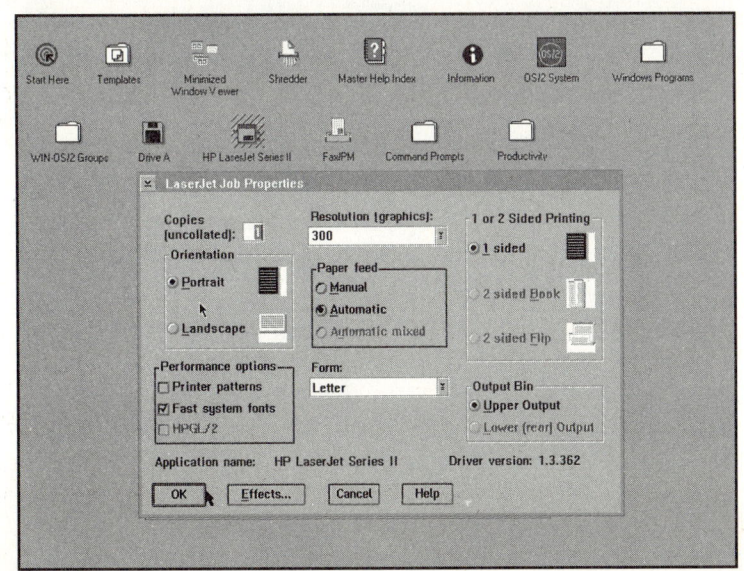

Fig. 7.4
The **P**rinter Driver page of the Settings notebook for a printer object.

Fig. 7.5
Telling OS/2 about the capabilities of your new printer on the **J**ob Properties settings notebook page.

You probably do not need to use the other tabs on the Settings notebook to specify your new printer. If you want more details on printers and fonts under OS/2, however, please see Chapter 15, "Printing with OS/2."

Adding and Changing Fonts

OS/2 comes with a wide range of printer and screen fonts, some of which are fonts supplied to IBM by Adobe Systems. You may want to selectively install some of these IBM and Adobe fonts at a later time if you did not select them during the initial OS/2 installation process. Or you may purchase additional font files and then install them.

To install a font, first open the System Setup folder (located by default in the OS/2 System folder). Then double-click the object labeled `Font Palette`. The Font Palette (the top window shown in fig. 7.6) enables you to edit the characteristics of existing fonts in your computer as well as add new fonts. Choose the Edit Font option in the Font Palette window to see the Edit Font window shown in figure 7.6.

Fig. 7.6
The Font Palette and Edit Font window.

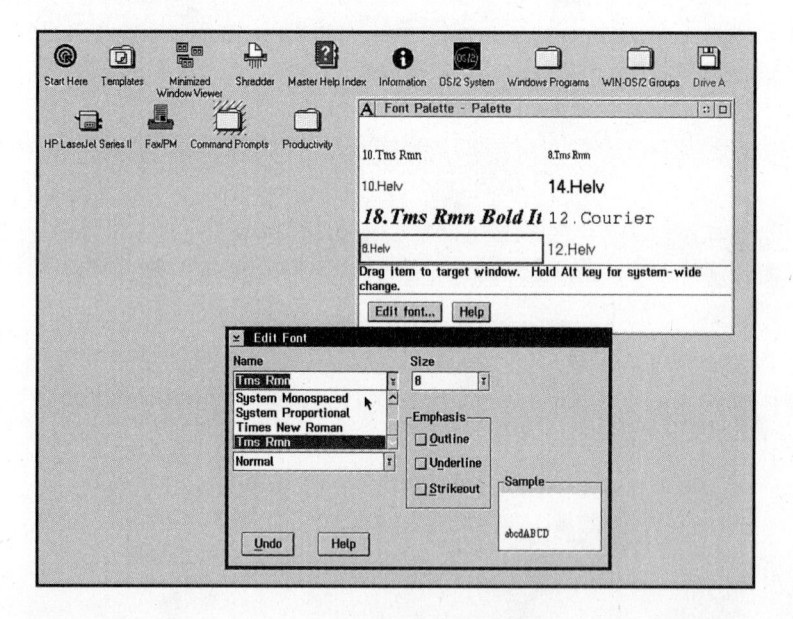

Figure 7.6 shows how to select an existing font on your computer for editing, but you can use the same window to add a new font. Click the Add button to install a new font from a floppy disk (in the figure, the Add button is hidden by the list of fonts). Choose an existing font from the list to change its characteristics.

If you click the Add button, OS/2 asks you to insert the floppy disk containing the new font file. OS/2 then adds that font to your collection. If you choose an existing font from the list, you can specify its size and emphasis (outline, underline, or strikeout).

Try this: Select a font on the Font Palette by clicking it with mouse button 1. This highlights the font item. Use mouse button 2 to drag the highlighted font to a window title bar or to the name of an icon on the desktop. Drop the font by releasing the mouse button. You have changed the appearance of the title bar or icon name.

As yet, not too many OS/2 objects display the different font when you drop a font on them. This situation will change as more applications become OS/2-aware.

Adding a Mouse

To add a mouse to your computer, or to change the type of mouse you have, first connect the mouse according to the directions that came with the pointing device. Then open the Selective Install object in the System Setup folder. You see the System Configuration window, which may look familiar to you. It is the same window you used during the installation process to confirm your mouse, keyboard, country, and display. Check the box labeled **M**ouse and press Enter. Then select your mouse from the list that OS/2 displays and click OK.

If the manufacturer of your new mouse gave you a floppy disk with an OS/2 device driver on it, use the manufacturer's instructions to install the driver.

Changing the Display Adapter or Resolution

You follow the same steps to upgrade your display adapter that you do to install a new mouse. Install your new adapter according to the manufacturer's instructions. If the manufacturer supplied a disk containing an OS/2 device driver, install that driver by using the manufacturer's instructions.

If your new display adapter does not support the video mode and resolution of the old one, you may find that simply installing the new hardware and booting OS/2 results in an incoherent screen. Before you power off your PC in preparation for the new display adapter, first reconfigure OS/2 to use a mode (such as plain VGA) supported by both the old and new display adapters. After inserting the new adapter and booting OS/2, you can reconfigure for different display resolutions.

To restore OS/2's display resolution to VGA (640 x 480), you open an OS/2 full-screen or windowed session and run the SETVGA.CMD batch file program located in the \OS2 directory. Before you run SETVGA, however, here's a tip: Drag the icons on your desktop to the center of the screen. Make sure that you don't have anything displayed near the perimeter of the desktop screen. Stop any tasks that might be running in the background, especially screen-savers, because you have to reboot the computer after SETVGA finishes to make the new screen resolution take effect. Putting desktop objects in the middle of the screen ensures they'll be visible in the new video mode.

The SETVGA program prompts you to insert the OS/2 display driver floppy disks. Make sure that you have the disks handy. After you run SETVGA, perform a Shutdown and turn off the computer in preparation for installing the new video adapter card. Follow the manufacturer's instructions to insert the new adapter in your computer and then power on your computer again.

To reconfigure OS/2's display system, click the Selective Install object located by default in the System Setup folder inside the OS/2 System folder. The Selective Install object lets you select a supported display adapter and the screen resolution you want the display adapter to use. OS/2 2.1 supports the IBM VGA 256c Super VGA adapter as well as the display adapters in the following list:

ATI Technologies VGA Wonder XL

Headland Technology VRAM II

Trident Microsystems 8900

Tseng Laboratories ET4000

Many adapters that use video chips made by S3, such as the Miro company's miroCRYSTAL adapter and the Number Nine company's GXE adapter

Western Digital Paradise

Another way to change display modes is to use the OS/2 DSPINSTL utility. Using DSPINSTL is quicker and just as reliable as using Selective Install. To run the utility, open a full-screen or windowed OS/2 session. Type the command **CD \OS2\INSTALL**, press Enter, then type the command **DSPINSTL**, and then press Enter.

When using DSPINSTL, you click the check box labeled Primary Display and then click OK to bring up a window entitled Primary Display Adapter Type (see fig. 7.7). Choose your display adapter from the list and click OK. OS/2 asks you to choose a screen resolution supported by the display adapter you selected. OS/2 asks you to insert one or both of the OS/2 distribution disks labeled Display Driver Diskette 1 and Display Driver Diskette 2. During reconfiguration, OS/2 blanks the screen and your monitor may emit a few clicks. After OS/2 reconfigures itself for the new display adapter and screen resolution, you should perform a Shutdown operation and reboot your computer. OS/2 uses the new video mode and screen resolution after the reboot.

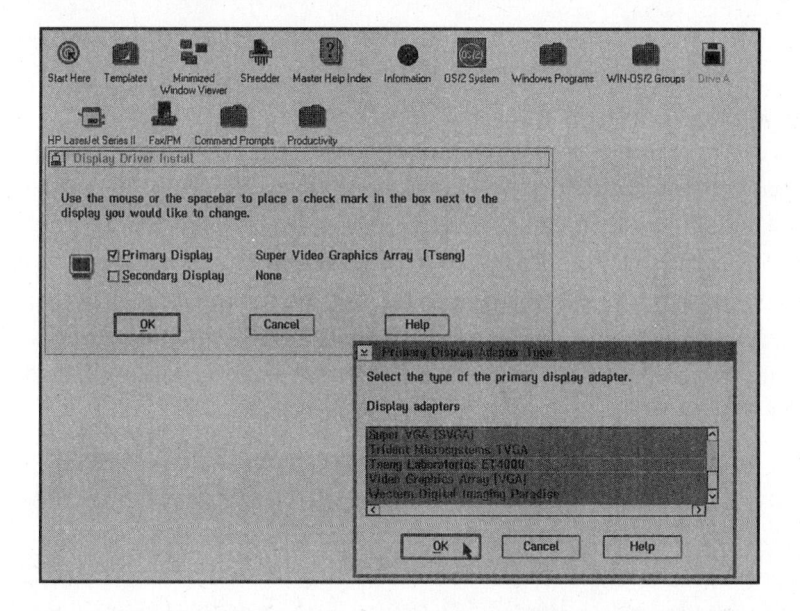

Fig. 7.7
The Primary Display Adapter Type configuration window.

Note

Some video adapters require that you run a utility program to set the refresh rate of the adapter to that of your monitor. OS/2 gives you an opportunity to run this utility midway through the DSPINSTL process. You see a button on the Monitor Configuration/Selection screen labeled *Install Using Display Adapter Utility Program*. (The default button is *Install Using Defaults for Monitor Type*.) Click the *Install Using Display Adapter Utility Program* button if the manufacturer of your new video adapter supplied you with a configuration disk and instructions to use the disk to set the refresh rate.

Adding a Hard Disk

You add a hard disk to a computer running OS/2 in much the same way you add a hard disk to a DOS-based computer. You may want to confirm with the manufacturer that the drive is compatible with OS/2 (as well as with your present hard disk controller) before you purchase the extra disk. See Chapter 5, "Using Non-IBM Computers and OS/2," for a discussion on disk drives and OS/2.

> **Note**
>
> If you're replacing your present hard drive rather than simply adding another one, you must completely reinstall OS/2.

For Related Information
- "Understanding Hardware and Software," p. 15
- "Using Device Support," p. 94
- "Reflecting Personal Preferences," p. 98
- "Working with IBM-Compatible Computers," p. 104
- "Learning about Disk Controller Cards," p. 114
- "Using the Keyboards and Mice," p. 115
- "Working with Video Adapter Cards and Monitors," p.116

First, install the new drive according to the manufacturer's instructions. Then power up your computer and run the FDISK and FORMAT utilities to prepare the new disk drive for use. You can run these utilities from the OS/2 command line by selecting an OS/2 Full Screen or Windowed session from the Command Prompts folder. Or you can run the Presentation Manager versions of these programs. To do the latter, choose PMFDISK and PMFORMAT from the OS/2 System folder, or execute these programs from an OS/2 command-line prompt. You find both programs in the C:\OS2 directory, assuming that you selected them for installation when you installed OS/2.

Installing Features Selectively

In addition to enabling you to confirm or change your mouse, keyboard, display, and country, as explained later in this chapter, the Selective Install object in the System Setup folder allows you to add the following features to your system (if you omitted them during the initial installation):

- *CD-ROM Device Support*. Provides system support for CD-ROM devices.

- *Documentation*. Adds the OS/2 Tutorial, the OS/2 Command Reference, or REXX Programming Information.

- *Fonts*. Determines the typefaces you can use on your system. The OS/2 operating system gives you both bit-map fonts and fonts in Adobe Type 1 format for displaying and printing data on many output devices. Vector devices, such as plotters, cannot use the bit-map fonts. When you haven't installed the optional fonts, OS/2 uses the system default font and the Helvetica fonts.

- *Optional System Utilities.* These utilities enable you to do the following:

    Back up the hard disk

    Change file attributes

    Display the directory tree

    Manage disk drive partitions

    Put internal labels on disks

    Link object modules (a programmer's tool)

    Convert, display, and print pictures

    Use PMREXX

    Recover files

    Restore backed-up files

    Sort files

- *Tools and Games.* Installs productivity aids, such as a simple database manager, a spreadsheet application, a calculator, a calendar, and a notepad, as well as some games.

- *OS/2 DOS and Windows Support.* Enables DOS and Microsoft Windows programs to run under the OS/2 operating system.

- *High Performance File System.* Provides fast access to large files and supports file names up to 254 characters in length.

- *REXX.* Installs the REXX Operating System/2 procedures language. This batch-programming language is Systems Application Architecture (SAA) compliant and extends the capabilities of the statements you embed in your CMD files.

- *Serial Device Support.* Provides system support for serial devices, such as a modem, a serial plotter, or a serial printer assigned to a communication port. You don't need to select this option for a serial mouse.

- *Serviceability and Diagnostic Aids.* This option provides information to a technical support person who typically forwards the information to IBM so that IBM can isolate and correct system problems.

- *Optional Bitmaps*. Provides a set of images (sometimes called *wallpaper*) you can use to change the background of the desktop.

To add one or more of the listed features after installation, open the Selective Install object in the System Setup folder. Click the **O**K pushbutton in the System Configuration window. In the OS/2 Setup and Installation window (the same window you used during the installation of OS/2), check the box for each feature you want to add to your computer. If you want to select a subset of that feature, click that feature's More... button.

After you select the additional features, click the **O**K button. When prompted, insert the installation disks to let OS/2 copy the features to your hard disk.

For Related Information
- "Choosing the OS/2 Features You Want," p. 139

Configuring Your Desktop

You can configure your OS/2 desktop in a variety of ways. You can change general system parameters and the appearance of the information the desktop presents to you. You can alter the desktop's settings for sound, country, mouse behavior, and keyboard usage. You can choose how you want the system clock to appear, and you can choose background colors and images for the desktop. You can create objects on the desktop that represent your applications. The next sections of this chapter explain these configuration settings.

To access the Settings notebook for the desktop, move the mouse cursor to an empty part of the desktop and click the right mouse button. The desktop's pop-up menu appears. Click the arrow next to the **O**pen menu option to make your screen look like the one shown in figure 7.8. Then click the **S**ettings option.

When the Settings notebook for the desktop appears, you see tabs labeled **V**iew, **I**nclude, **S**ort, **B**ackground, **M**enu, **F**ile, **W**indow, **G**eneral, and **L**ockup. Click the **V**iew tab to see a screen similar to the one shown in figure 7.9.

Selecting Icon, Tree, and Details Views

Each Settings notebook, including the one for the desktop itself, enables you to change the way objects appear on the desktop. You can select Icon View, Tree View, or Details View from the pop-up menu shown in figure 7.8.

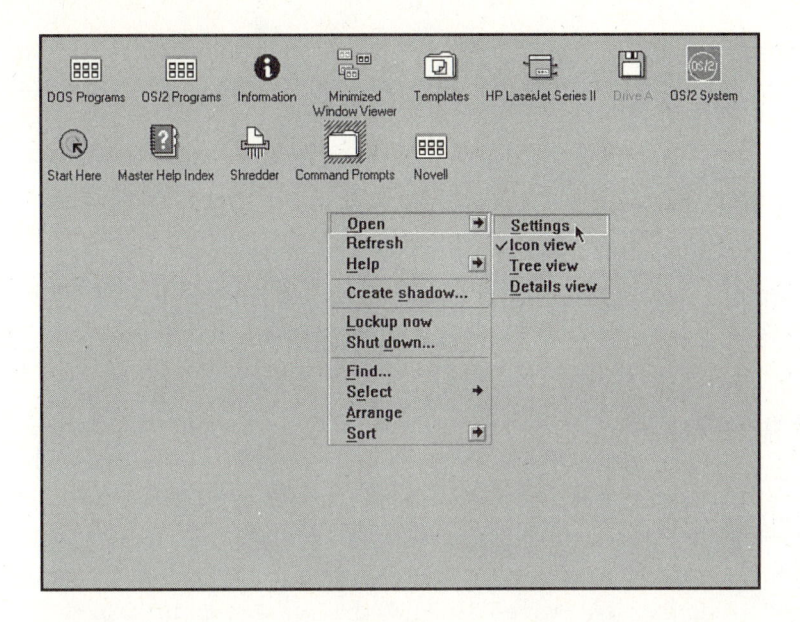

Configuring Your Desktop   **179**

Fig. 7.8
The pop-up menu for the OS/2 desktop.

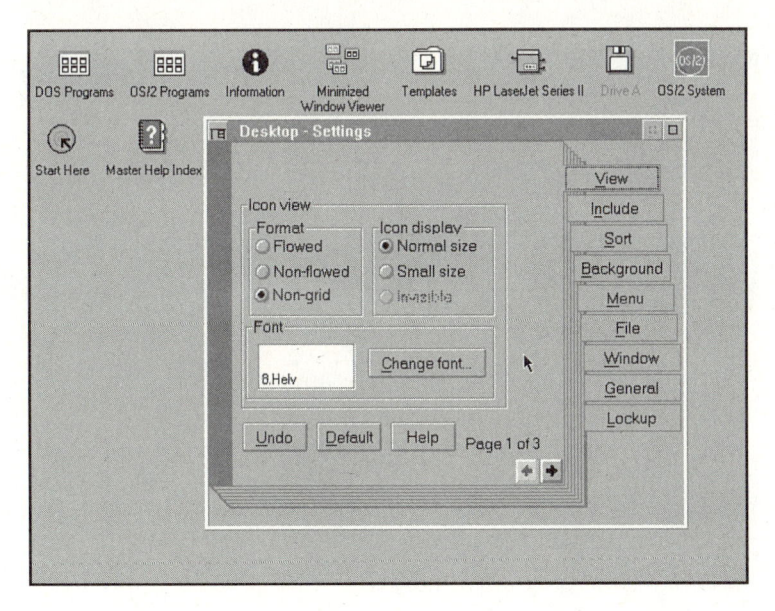

Fig. 7.9
The **V**iew page of the desktop Settings notebook.

Selecting Icon View. Icon view is the default view. Each object appears on the desktop as an icon with the icon's name positioned next to it. The **V**iew page of the Settings notebook allows you to customize the Icon view format, icon display, and font.

Icon view has three formats: *flowed*, *non-flowed*, and *nongrid*. The default is nongrid. In this mode, icons can appear anywhere on the desktop. In non-flowed mode, each object is a separate line that shows the object's icon followed by its name. Flowed mode is a multiple-column version of nonflowed mode. Each column is just wide enough to hold the longest icon's name.

You can configure the icon's size and font independently for each of the three formats, in any font and point size. Icons can be normal size (the default) or small size. In flowed and nonflowed modes, you can suppress the icon itself so that you see only the name of the icon on the desktop.

Selecting Tree View. To select Tree view, click Tree View in the pop-up menu shown in figure 7.8. Tree view shows the contents of the desktop or a folder as a directory tree. The folder is at the root of the tree. You can collapse or expand the subtrees by clicking the + (plus) and – (minus) buttons. The desktop, or each folder, shows the icon and the name for each folder contained within the view. Figure 7.10 shows the Tree view for the OS/2 desktop.

Fig. 7.10
The desktop Tree view.

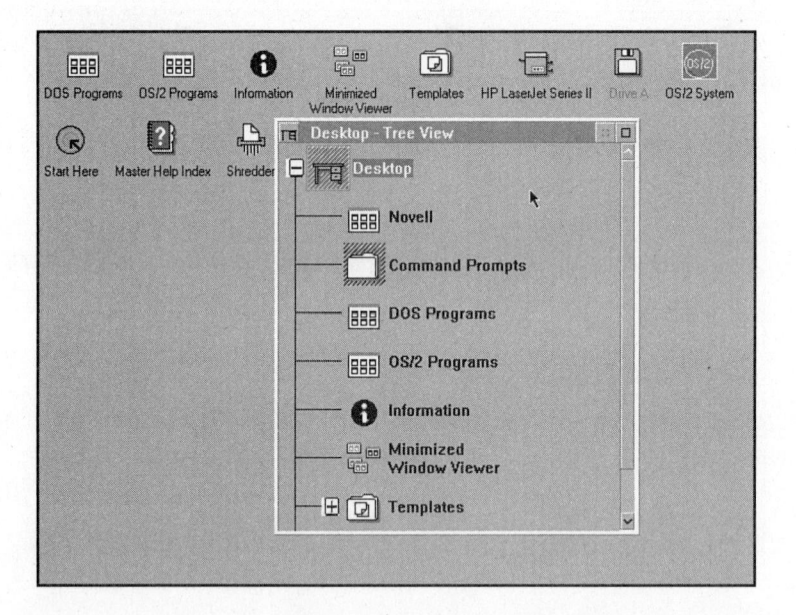

The **V**iew page of the Settings notebook allows you to customize the Tree view's format, icon display, and font. You can customize the icon display and font, just as you can for Icon view. The format can be *lines* or *no lines*. In lined mode, the tree structure is emphasized with lines that highlight the objects.

Selecting Details View. To select Details view, click Details View in the pop-up menu shown in figure 7.8. Details view uses one line for each object. The view is split vertically into two panes. The left pane shows the object's icon and descriptive name. The right window pane gives details about the object. You can adjust the placement of the boundary between the panes. Figure 7.11 shows the Details view for the OS/2 desktop.

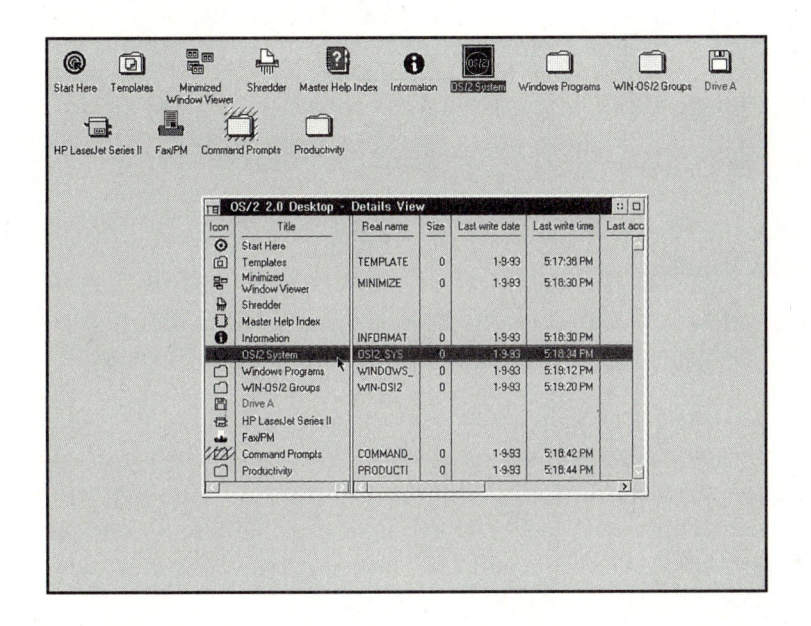

Fig. 7.11
The desktop Details view.

The **V**iew page of the Settings notebook allows you to customize the Details view display. You can select the font, and you can specify which of the object's details you want to see.

Using Other Notebook Settings

In addition to the **V**iew page, the Settings notebook has eight other pages: **I**nclude, **S**ort, **B**ackground, **M**enu, **F**ile, **W**indow, **G**eneral, and **L**ockup.

The **I**nclude page allows you to select which objects to display in the views.

The **S**ort page selects the object ordering that occurs when you perform an Arrange operation. You can choose to sort objects by name or by type.

The **B**ackground page selects the background for the views. You can select a color or a bit-map image. You learn more about configuring the desktop's screen colors in the next section of this chapter.

The **G**eneral page enables you to customize the folder's icon.

The **M**enu page enables you to customize the folder's pop-up menu.

The three **F**ile pages provide the following information about the object whose Settings notebook you have selected:

- Descriptive and physical names
- Time and date at which the object was last created, modified, or accessed
- Data and extended attribute sizes
- Attribute flags
- Subject, comments, key phrases, and history information

Some of the information you enter on the **F**ile pages applies only if you have an HPFS partition.

The **W**indow page enables you to customize window behavior in ways that seem most natural and comfortable to you.

The three **L**ockup pages allow you to specify security options. You can indicate whether OS/2 should password-protect your computer when you step away from it, what OS/2 should show on-screen while you're away, and how many minutes of no keyboard activity should cause OS/2 to activate password protection. When you return to your computer, you enter a password to regain use of the PC.

Altering Screen Colors and Background Images

You can change screen colors for the desktop and each of the folders. To choose a different color for the background of the desktop, click the **B**ackground tab of the Settings notebook for the desktop. You see a screen similar to the one shown in figure 7.12. Select the **I**mage button if you want to see a bit-map image (picture) on the desktop instead of the default solid color. You can preview and select from the bit-map images supplied with OS/2. If you want to use this option, you must first tell the installation process to install the optional bit-map files.

Click the **Ch**ange Color button if you want to select a solid color for the desktop's background. You see a palette of colors from which you can choose.

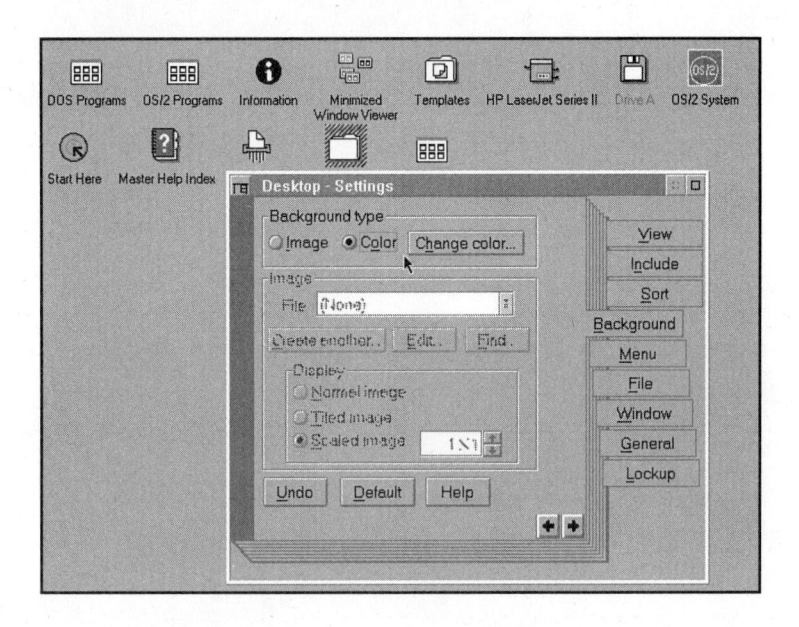

Fig. 7.12
The options on the **B**ackground tab in the desktop Settings notebook.

The Display options enable you to specify how you want an image to appear: normal, tiled, or scaled. Normal Image tells OS/2 to show the image file, in its original size, as a single picture on the desktop's background. Tiled Image instructs OS/2 to place several copies of the image on the desktop's background. Scaled Image informs OS/2 that you want the image blown up or reduced as necessary to fit on-screen.

To change the colors that appear inside each of your folders, select the Color Palette object in the System Setup folder. The Color Palette enables you to customize the screen colors of various other objects. When you select the Color Palette, you see a window that contains several circles, each a different solid color. You can edit the color of a circle if you want.

Try this: use the right mouse button (button 2) to drag a nonwhite color circle from the Color Palette window. When the circle moves out of the Palette window onto the desktop, it changes into a picture of a paintbrush. Drop the resulting paintbrush image on the background of a open folder on the desktop. The color of the folder changes.

Unfortunately, not too many OS/2 objects currently understand what to do when a color is dropped on them. This situation will change as more applications become OS/2-aware.

184 Chapter 7—Modifying Your OS/2 Configuration

Customizing with the System Object

The System object enables you to customize the behavior of certain aspects of the system. This object has only a Settings view with six pages: **C**onfirmations, **T**itle, **W**indow, **P**rint Screen, **L**ogo, and **G**eneral. To change one of these settings, select the System object located in the System Setup folder. Click the **W**indow tab of the Settings notebook that appears. You see a screen similar to the one shown in figure 7.13.

Fig. 7.13
The **W**indow page of the Settings notebook for the System object.

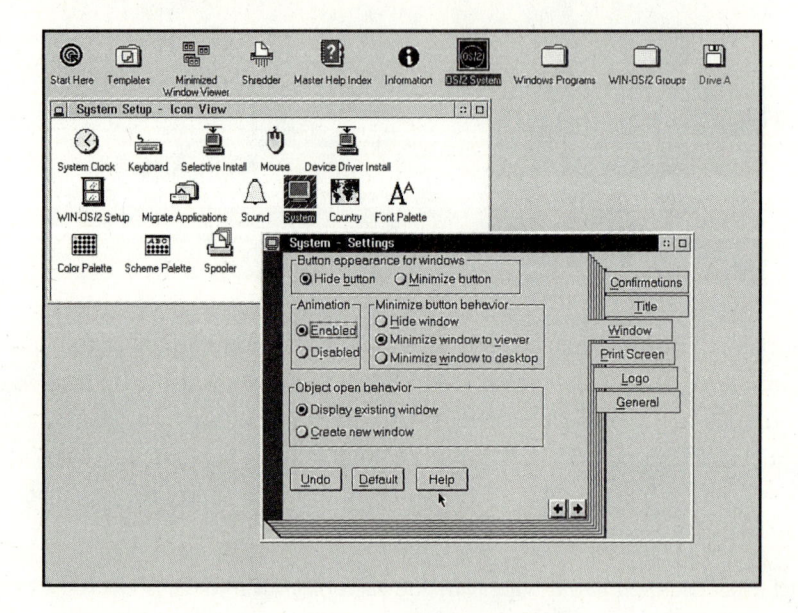

The **W**indow page of the Settings notebook allows you to enable or disable the animation that occurs when a window opens or closes. You can specify how minimized windows are to be handled and specify what happens when you open an object that already exists on the desktop. By default, the Workplace Shell resurfaces the existing object. You can tell the Shell to create a new view of the object instead of reshowing the existing object.

The **C**onfirmations page, shown in figure 7.14, allows you to enable or disable the confirmation dialog boxes you get when you attempt to shred folders and objects.

The **L**ogo page allows you to specify how long applications should display their product information window when they start up.

The **G**eneral page allows you to alter the System object's icon.

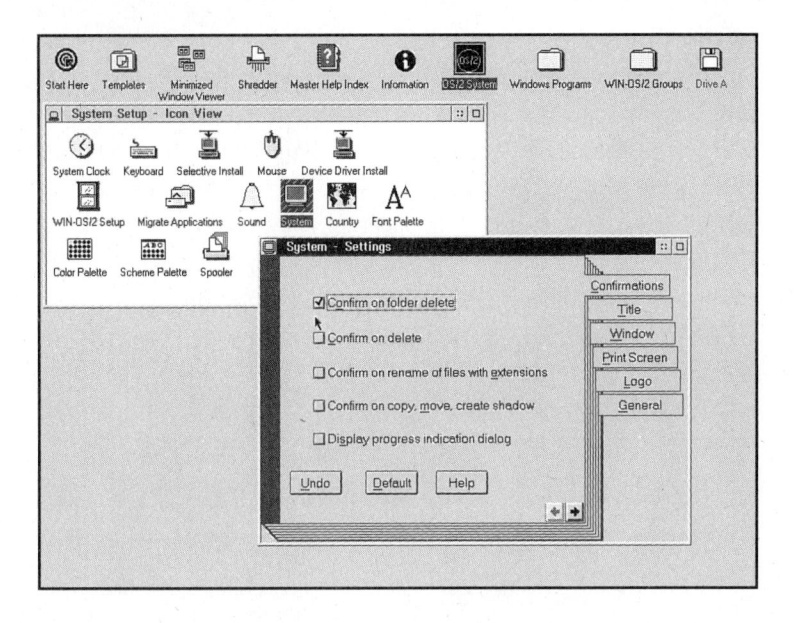

Fig. 7.14
The Confirmations page of the Settings notebook for the System object.

The **P**rint Screen page enables and disables the capability of the Print Screen key to send output to the printer.

Changes in these settings take effect immediately.

Modifying the Sound

The Sound object, shown in figure 7.15, allows you to enable or disable OS/2's warning beep. Sound has only a Settings view. You find the Sound object in the System Setup folder.

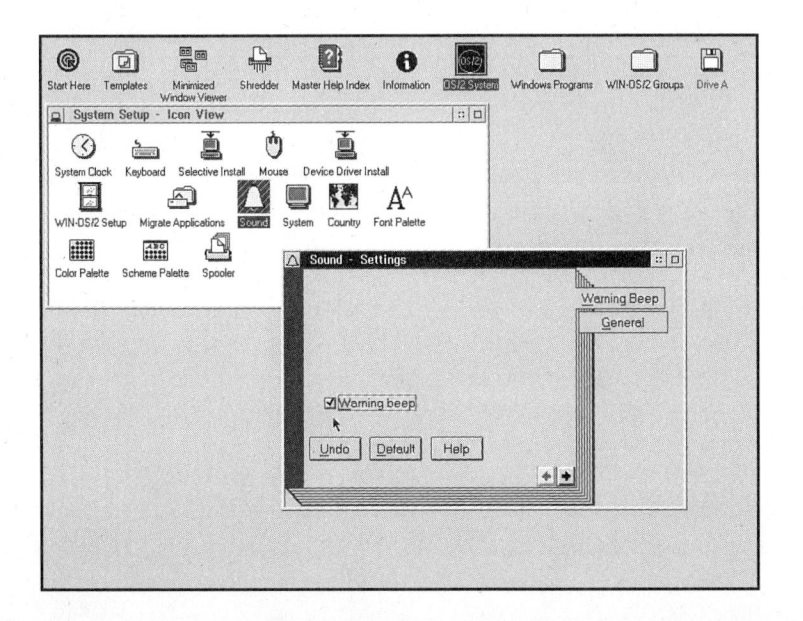

Fig. 7.15
The Sound object in the System Setup folder and its Settings notebook.

Altering the Country

The Country object, also located in the System Setup folder, allows you to customize OS/2 to use national language support. Country has only a Settings notebook, with five pages whose tabs are labeled **C**ountry, **T**ime, **D**ate, **N**umbers, and **I**con. The **C**ountry page is shown in figure 7.16. You specify your national language on the Country page. The Time and Date pages let you choose the display format for dates and times that OS/2 shows. The Numbers page of the Country Settings notebook provides options for how you want decimal points and commas to appear in the numbers you see in your OS/2 applications. And the Icon page lets you change the icon associated with the Country object.

Fig. 7.16
The **C**ountry page in the Settings notebook for the Country object.

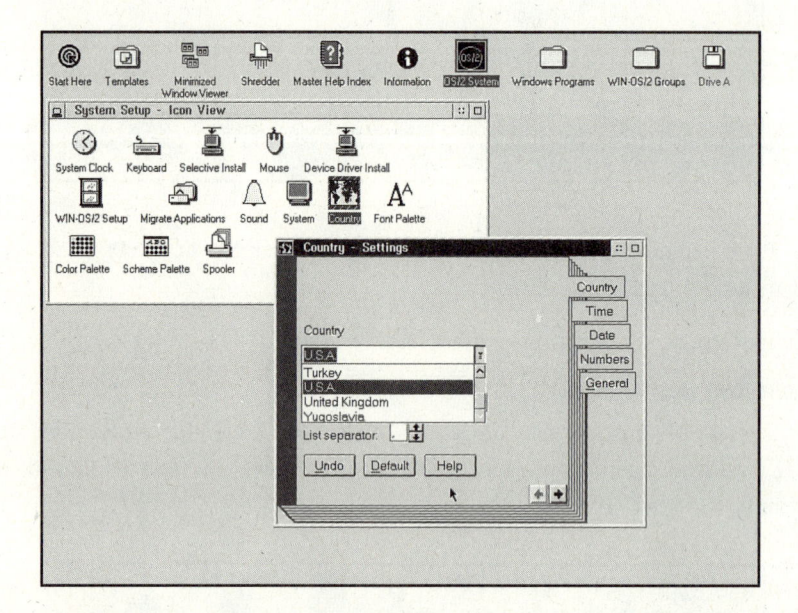

Customizing the Mouse

The Mouse object enables you to customize the behavior of the mouse. This object has a five-page Settings notebook, with tabs labeled **T**iming, **S**etup, **M**appings, **W**indow, and **G**eneral.

The **T**iming page enables you to set the double-click interval and the tracking speed. Changes take effect immediately. In fact, the tracking speed of the mouse actually changes as you manipulate the slider control to increase or decrease the tracking speed.

The **S**etup page enables you to configure the mouse according to whether you're right-handed or left-handed. Figure 7.17 shows the **S**etup page of the Mouse Settings notebook.

Configuring Your Desktop   187

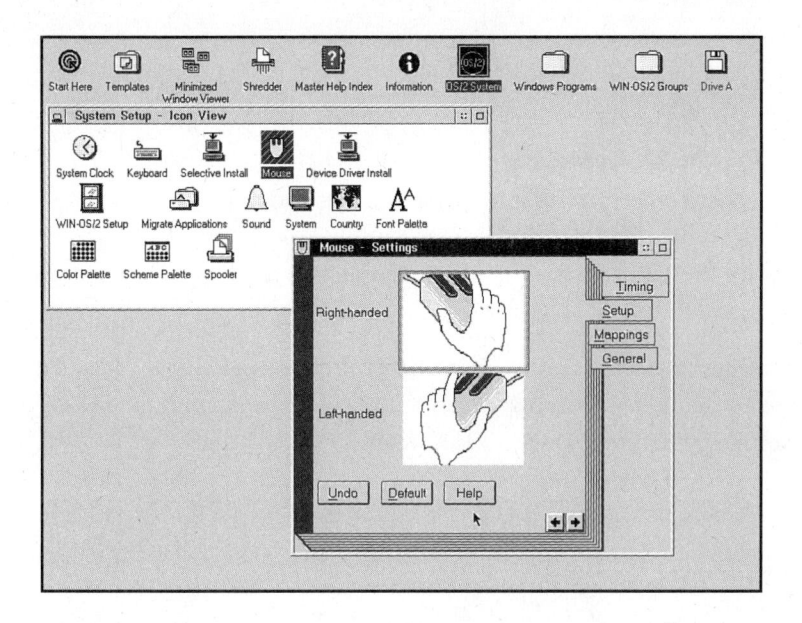

Fig. 7.17
The **S**etup page of the Settings notebook for the Mouse object.

The **M**appings page enables you to define which combination of mouse buttons, single/double-clicking, and Shift/Ctrl/Alt keys perform selection functions and other actions. You can configure which button performs a drag operation (the default is mouse button 2), which button displays pop-up menus (the default is a single click of mouse button 2), and which button enables you to edit icon and window title text (the default is a single click of mouse button 1, while holding down the Alt key). Figure 7.18 shows the **M**appings page of the Mouse settings notebook.

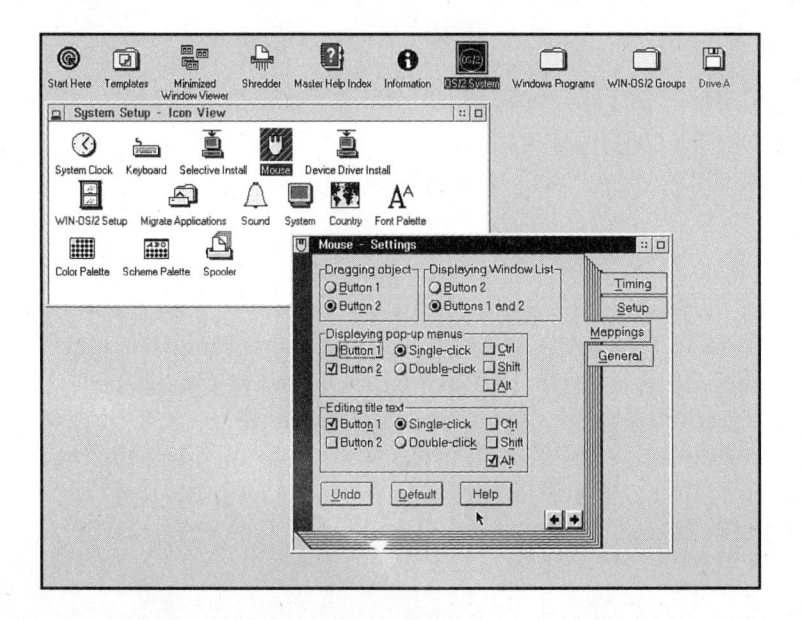

Fig. 7.18
The **M**appings page of the Settings notebook for the Mouse object.

The **G**eneral page of the Mouse Settings notebook allows you to customize the Mouse object's icon.

Changing the Keyboard

The Keyboard object in the System Setup folder allows you to customize the keyboard configuration of the system. This object only has a Settings notebook with five tabbed pages: **T**iming, **M**appings, **S**pecial Needs, **W**indow, and **G**eneral.

The **T**iming page allows you to customize the repeat rate, repeat delay rate, and cursor blink rate by using slider controls. A test box appears so that you can test your changes. Figure 7.19 shows the **T**iming page.

Fig. 7.19
The **T**iming page of the Settings notebook for the Keyboard object.

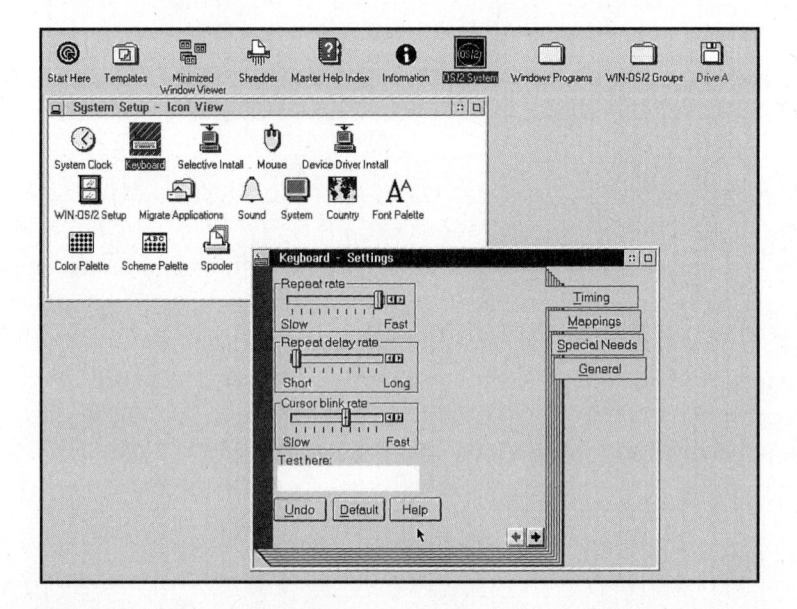

The **M**appings page provides keyboard equivalents for certain mouse operations. By default, Shift+F10 displays pop-up menus. Shift+Ins enables you to edit window-title text.

The **S**pecial Needs page allows configuration of the system for people who have special requirements. For example, if you cannot simultaneously press several keys, such as the Shift key along with a letter key, you can use the **S**pecial Needs page to tell OS/2 to treat the Shift key as a "sticky" key, which means that when you press Shift, the key remains active for a period of time you specify. This time period allows you to press another key that OS/2 deems to be shifted.

Four slider controls appear on the **S**pecial Needs page: Acceptance delay, Delay until repeat, Repeat rate, and Settings time-out. Figure 7.20 shows the **S**pecial Needs page of the Keyboard Settings notebook.

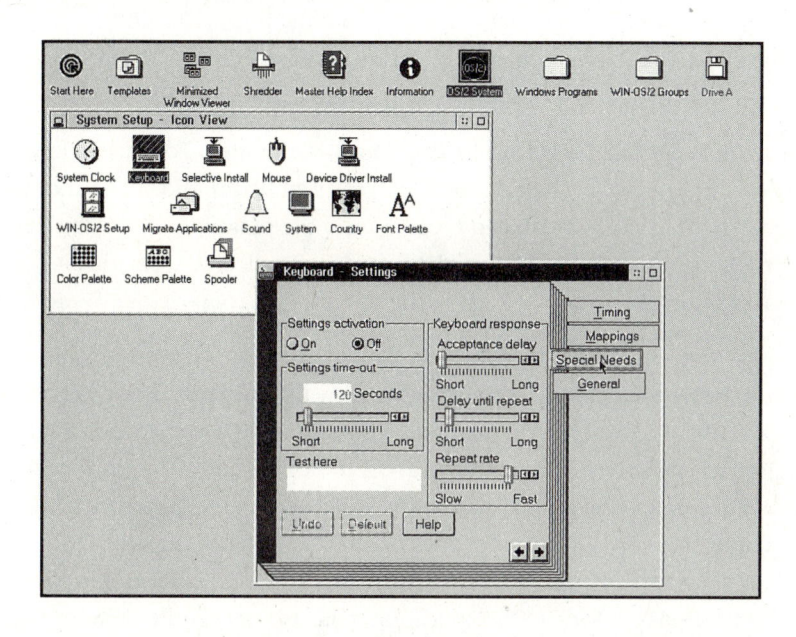

Fig. 7.20
The **S**pecial Needs page of the Settings notebook for the Keyboard object.

The **G**eneral page enables you to customize the Keyboard object's icon.

Using the System Clock

The System Clock object displays the current time. You also can use the System Clock to change your computer's date and time. The Settings notebook for the System Clock object has four tabbed pages: **V**iew, **A**larm, **D**ate/Time, and **G**eneral.

The **V**iew page determines the appearance of the clock. You can select digital or analog, time and/or date, and hide/show title bar. In analog mode, you can select hour marks, minute marks, and a second hand.

The **A**larm page allows you to set an alarm. You can specify both a time and date for when the alarm sounds; you also can specify whether you want an audible alarm or a message box.

The **D**ate/Time page allows you to change the system date and time. You change the hours, minutes, seconds, month, day, and year fields with spin buttons.

The **G**eneral page allows you to customize the System Clock object's icon.

Adding Applications to Your Desktop

Earlier in this chapter, when you learned how to install a printer, you used the Templates folder to create a new print destination object. You dragged a printer icon out of the Templates folder and configured the printer through the icon's Settings notebook. When you want to create an icon object on the desktop that represents one of your applications, you perform a similar set of steps.

Using the Program Template in the Template Folder. To place a new program object icon on the desktop, open the Templates folder. Use mouse button 2 to drag the icon labeled Program onto the desktop. (Don't double-click the Program icon in the Templates folder.) The icon automatically opens its Settings notebook for you. The tabs on the five pages are **G**eneral, **A**ssociation, **P**rogram, **W**indow, and **S**ession.

You use the **G**eneral page to specify the window title and icon for your application program. The **A**ssociation page enables you to tell OS/2 the kinds of files and file names with which your application works. Use the **P**rogram page to tell OS/2 the name and directory location of the executable file for that application. On the **S**ession page, you specify whether the application is a DOS or an OS/2 program and whether the application should run full screen or in a window on the desktop. For a DOS application, you also can specify DOS settings (as discussed earlier in this chapter) if that application requires settings other than the OS/2 defaults. Use the **W**indow page to customize window behavior.

For Related Information
- "Using the Workplace Shell," p. 231
- "Understanding the Drives Object Display," p. 271
- "Understanding DOS Sessions," p. 394
- "Adding DOS Programs," p. 397

Choosing to Migrate Applications. When you installed OS/2, you had an opportunity to migrate your DOS and Windows applications into the OS/2 environment. If you did not select this option during installation, you can select it later by choosing the Migrate Applications object in the System Setup folder. You see a screen similar to the one shown in figure 7.21. Use this screen to indicate whether you want OS/2 to search for DOS applications, Microsoft Windows applications, OS/2 applications, or all three. You tell OS/2 which drive letter to search and then click the **F**ind button. The Migrate Applications object searches your disk for applications. When it finds each application, Migrate Applications identifies that computer program in a list, by name. You can deselect items in the list that you do not want to migrate onto your desktop. You also can add to the list of applications by clicking the Add button and specifying additional computer programs. When the list meets with your satisfaction, click the OK button to cause the Migrate Applications object to create a new folder and put the migrated applications, in icon form, in the new folder.

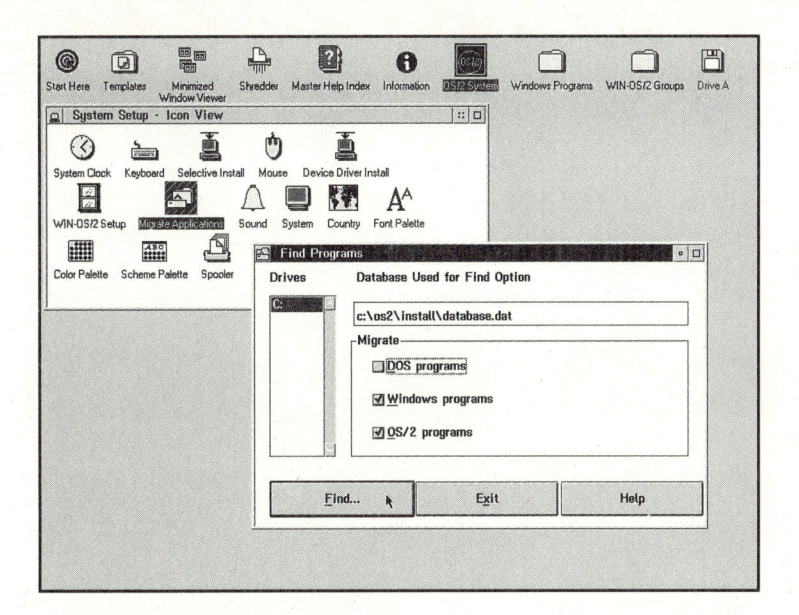

Fig. 7.21
The Migrate Applications object.

Chapter Summary

In this chapter, you learned how to configure OS/2 to suit your day-to-day work habits and your computer's particular needs. You found out how to modify the startup files AUTOEXEC.BAT, CONFIG.SYS, and STARTUP.CMD, discovered how to tell OS/2 about new hardware options you might add to your computer, and explored the selective installation of OS/2 options and features. You now know how to configure the OS/2 desktop itself.

In the next chapter, you learn how to troubleshoot OS/2.

Chapter 8
Troubleshooting OS/2

You may never have any trouble with OS/2 2.1. If you do have problems, however, this chapter explains the steps you can take to solve them; it also explains how to prevent problems.

> **Tip**
>
> **1-(800) 992-4777**. That's the telephone number of IBM's software support team for OS/2. IBM gives you 60 days free telephone support from the date you purchase OS/2. If you encounter a problem with OS/2, you should first look for a solution in this chapter and in the other chapters of this book. You also may want to explore bulletin boards or ask questions on information services such as CompuServe or BIX. However, you can use this telephone number if you need to discuss your problem with an IBM support team person. Have your OS/2 registration number handy; it's printed on the inside cover of the *Using the Operating System* manual that IBM supplies with OS/2. Be aware of two things. First, try to call during business hours. Someone will take your call late in the evening, but that person won't be able to pass a really stubborn problem along to a knowledgeable analyst. The analysts will have gone home for the day. Second, many of the support people have a copy of this book available to help answer your questions. Notice that you're already holding this book in your hands.

Computers are not foolproof. People occasionally run into problems with DOS, UNIX, and other operating systems, and OS/2 is no different from other software in that regard. OS/2 does have some built-in safeguards, however, and the OS/2 error messages are generally clear and self-explanatory. In fact, the OS/2 designers went to some lengths to make both the error messages and informational messages as easily understood as possible.

Unlike DOS and some other operating systems, OS/2 provides a great deal of on-line help and information. The OS/2 files of error messages are sizable. You can appreciate the amount of information OS/2 is prepared to give you in case of trouble by looking at the sizes of the message files and help files within the OS/2 system. Take a moment now to locate and identify these files. Open (double-click) an OS/2 Full Screen session in the Command Prompts folder. At the command line prompt, type **CD \OS2\SYSTEM**, and then type **DIR *.MSG**. OS/2 displays the names and sizes of the message files. Type **CD \OS2\HELP** followed by **DIR *.HLP**. The names and sizes of the OS/2 help files appear. Finally, type **CD \OS2\BOOK**, and then type just **DIR**. The names and sizes of the OS/2 information files appear. (Type **EXIT** to close the OS/2 Full Screen session.) The message, help, and information files exist to help you whenever you encounter problems with OS/2.

If you have used DOS before, you know that when DOS or a DOS application fails, the entire computer stops and you have to reboot. If you're logged into a local area network, booting and logging in can take a considerable amount of time away from your personal productivity. Under OS/2, when OS/2 itself, an OS/2 application, a DOS application, or a Windows application fails, OS/2 notifies you of the error, enables you to terminate the application that failed, but does not crash. Only in rare circumstances (if a device driver fails to work properly, for example) does OS/2 fail in such a way that you must reboot your computer.

The type of error that causes you to reboot OS/2, no matter how rare, is serious, so this chapter first explains how to prepare your computer system for such errors. Errors that require you to reboot your computer are easy to recognize. This chapter also helps you identify and deal with other types of less obvious errors. You learn the steps you take to gracefully recover from error situations, including diagnosing the problem, issuing commands to correct the problem, using the installation disks to reboot your computer to deal with unusual problems, and even booting a DOS disk so that you can fix the really stubborn problems.

This chapter organizes errors into the following categories:

- The Installation process encounters a problem.

- The computer fails to boot.

- An application, or the entire computer, stops suddenly.

- An application does not behave as expected.

- The screen is garbled.

- Pressing keys produces no reaction from the computer.
- The mouse fails to move the cursor, or the mouse buttons fail to select items on-screen.
- Nothing prints.
- Printouts are garbled.
- Performance is slow.

Understanding Installation Errors

Figure 8.1 shows an example of a screen displayed if the OS/2 installation process encounters a problem and cannot continue without your intervention. OS/2 may find, for example, that a sector of your hard disk is damaged and that sector cannot reliably hold the information written to it during the installation of OS/2. If a screen similar to the one in figure 8.1 appears, you must boot a DOS system-formatted floppy disk or the OS/2 Installation Disk and Diskette 1 to fix the problem (as detailed later in this chapter).

```
An error occurred when system Installation tried to
copy a file. The installation program has failed due
to an error. To view the error, you need to look at the
INSTALL.LOG file that was created for you. That file
gives the condition that caused the error.

Press Enter to display INSTALL.LOG.

To take action to correct the error, insert the Operat-
ing System/2 Installation Disk in drive A. Press and
hold the Ctrl and Alt keys, then press the Del key.

When the Logo panel appears, remove the Installation
disk, insert OS/2 Disk 1, and press Enter. When the
Welcome screen appears, press Esc.

After you correct the error, restart OS/2 Installation
by inserting the Operating System/2 Installation Disk
in Drive A. Press and hold the Ctrl and Alt keys, then
press Del.
```

Fig. 8.1
Notification that the OS/2 installation process encountered a problem.

If you have a problem during installation or immediately after installation, and if you have computer components made by a company other than IBM, review Chapter 5, "Using Non-IBM Computers and OS/2."

The next two sections of this chapter discuss installation problems in detail. The first section presents installation problems by symptom; the second section by error message number.

Installation Problems by Symptom

You may see the following behaviors from your computer during or right after installation. Along with each description of a symptom, you find suggested actions you can take to solve the problem.

Computer Stops During Diskette 1. First, be aware that Diskette 1 takes a long time to load. Wait several minutes until you are sure that the installation process has stopped before concluding that you have a problem. If the installation process halts with Diskette 1 in the floppy disk drive, OS/2 encountered a problem with your hard disk controller or CD-ROM. You may be able to circumvent the problem. If your hard disk controller has an on-board disk caching feature, turn off the feature and restart the installation. If the controller has an asynchronous memory refresh feature, turn off this feature as well. Restart the installation.

Computer Keeps Prompting for Diskette 3. If the OS/2 installation process prompts you repeatedly for Diskette 3, you have a dual-mode floppy disk drive that can act as an XT-style disk drive or an AT-style disk drive. Configure the floppy disk drive as an AT-style disk drive by changing the jumper or switch for pin 34 (refer to your computer's manual for the detailed procedure). Restart the installation.

Reboot During Installation Fails. The OS/2 installation process reboots your computer part way through the installation of OS/2. If OS/2 fails to reboot your computer into the graphical section of the installation process (see Chapter 6, "Installing OS/2"), you likely have a VGA-capable video adapter (display adapter) operating in non-VGA mode. Refer to your computer's manual for the procedure to set the adapter to 640 x 480 VGA mode and, if present, turn off the adapter's autosense feature. Restart the installation.

Computer Beeps Continuously. Your computer's floppy disk drive or disk controller may be defective; the cable connections between the controller and the floppy disk drive may be loose; or the cable may be bad if your computer beeps continuously during the installation process. Check your hardware and your cable connections before restarting the installation.

White Screen with Disk Drive Light On. This symptom usually means that your computer and OS/2 have a timing conflict. If your computer has a turbo mode, disable the turbo mode to see if you can successfully install OS/2. You may be able to restore the computer to turbo (fast CPU) mode after the installation finishes. This behavior also may signify that OS/2's video drivers and your video adapter card are not working well together. Try moving your video adapter to an 8-bit slot in your computer (refer to your computer manual). If the mode exists, set your video adapter to 8-bit mode before switching to a different slot. Try disabling the video adapter's autosense feature, if one is present.

Other Abnormal Behavior During Installation. If the installation process fails to complete successfully, your computer may have a hardware problem or you may have encountered an incompatibility between your hardware and OS/2. If you suspect the latter, contact the manufacturer of the failing PC component and ask what steps you can take or replacements you can get to solve the problem. First, however, review the next section's explanation of error messages to determine if one of the suggested actions might help.

Dealing with Error Messages

One of the following error messages may appear on-screen during the installation process. Following each message, you find suggested actions that you can take to solve the problem.

```
Only some files were copied. You may be out of disk space.
```

This message appears if OS/2 cannot install all its files because your hard drive is full. If you created a partition too small to hold the OS/2 files, you can restart the installation and (1) specify a larger partition or (2) select fewer OS/2 options on the System Configuration screen. If you're using an existing partition (perhaps because you had DOS on the machine in the past), you can (1) restart the installation, specify new partition sizes, and reformat (be sure to make backup copies of your files first); or (2) boot DOS and clean out your old files.

> **Tip**
> If your hard disk was previously formatted by DOS, you may be able to regain some disk space by booting DOS and running the CHKDSK program. If you have lost clusters, CHKDSK can return the lost clusters to the pool of available disk space.

```
An error occurred when System Installation tried to copy a file.
```

If OS/2 detects hardware or disk media errors during the installation, this message appears. Run a disk diagnostic utility on the OS/2 distribution floppy disk that was in the PC at the time of the error. If you determine the floppy disk is bad, request a replacement disk from IBM. If, on the other hand, your hard disk or PC is experiencing hardware problems, you need to repair the hardware before installing OS/2.

```
An error occurred when System Installation tried to transfer system
files to your hard disk. Your hard disk might be unusable.
```

This message indicates that the OS/2 installation process tried to create a new boot record at the very beginning of your hard disk and failed. You should first boot DOS from a system-formatted floppy disk and back up any files you want to preserve, and then format the drive. If the format operation also fails, you need to repair or replace the hard disk.

```
System Installation failed trying to load a module into memory.
```
```
An error occurred when System Installation tried to allocate a
segment of memory.
```

Both of these messages indicate you don't have enough physical memory (RAM) in your computer. Add more RAM and restart the installation.

```
FDISK unsuccessful.
```

This message usually indicates that OS/2 doesn't support the hard disk controller in your computer. If the manufacturer of your disk controller adapter supplied you with a floppy disk containing device drivers for various operating systems, you need to find the device driver for OS/2 and follow the manufacturer's instructions for using that device driver. Typically, you copy the device driver to Diskette 1 and use a text editor to insert the following line in the CONFIG.SYS file on Diskette 1 (note that some device drivers have an extension of DMD or ADD rather than SYS):

```
    :
    BASEDEV=xxxxxxxx.SYS

    xxxxxxxx is the name of the device driver file. Then you can re-
    start the installation.
```

    COUNTRY.SYS file cannot be found.

This message appears when OS/2 doesn't recognize the type of hard disk installed in your PC. If you have a PS/2 model P70, you need to request engineering change "ECA068" from IBM. If you have other devices besides the hard disk and floppy disk drives attached to your hard disk controller, disconnect the devices. Recheck your computer's IRQ assignments to ensure that the IRQs do not conflict (consult the manual that came with your computer). If you use an on-the-fly file compression utility (such as DoubleSpace), decompress the partition and restart the installation.

    TRAPxx (where xx is a letter and/or number)

Memory (RAM) failures in your computer cause almost all TRAP errors. Boot DOS and run a memory diagnostic utility to determine the problem. But even if the diagnostic program reports no errors with the RAM in your computer, OS/2 still may have trouble accessing the RAM. OS/2 operates in the CPU's protected mode. (DOS runs in real mode.) Accessing memory in protected mode requires good quality RAM chips in your computer.

You may be able to restart the installation of OS/2, however, after simply disabling your computer's shadow RAM and external CPU cache, and switching your computer from turbo to slow mode. If you cannot set these options, or if changing these options does not help the installation finish successfully, the likeliest problem is the RAM in your machine.

    SYS1475

This message indicates that OS/2 cannot find one of its system files (the hidden file OS2BOOT in the root directory of the boot drive). The problem may be a defective hard disk or that you inadvertently deleted the file. If reinstalling OS/2 does not solve the problem, run a disk drive diagnostic utility.

SYS2025

OS/2 cannot read the hard disk or a floppy disk. This error happens most often during the OS/2 boot process, and the error usually signifies a hardware problem. If the error occurs during installation, perhaps the distribution floppy disk is bad. Request a replacement disk. If the distribution floppy disk is not the culprit, run diagnostics on your computer to determine the problem. Note that SYS2025 occurs on some computers with BIOS chips made by American Megatrends (AMI). Refer to the discussion of BIOS chip compatibility in Chapter 5, "Using Non-IBM Computers and OS/2." You may need a BIOS chip upgrade.

SYS2026

The message indicates that OS/2 cannot find one of its system files (the hidden file OS2LDR in the root directory of the boot drive). The problem may be a defective hard disk or that you inadvertently deleted the file. If reinstalling OS/2 does not solve the problem, run a disk drive diagnostic utility.

SYS2027

This message usually accompanies message SYS2025. It simply indicates you should restart your computer.

SYS2028

OS/2 cannot find one of its system files (the hidden file OS2KRNL in the root directory of the boot drive). The problem may be a defective hard disk or that you inadvertently deleted the file. If reinstalling OS/2 does not solve the problem, run a disk drive diagnostic utility.

SYS2029

See message SYS2028.

SYS2030

Your computer does not have enough physical RAM to start OS/2. Add more memory.

SYS3146

For Related Information
- "Booting the Installation Disk," p. 127

OS/2 cannot find one of its system files (the file OS2LDR.MSG in the root directory of the boot drive). The problem may be a defective hard disk or that you inadvertently deleted the file. If reinstalling OS/2 does not solve the problem, run a disk drive diagnostic utility.

SYS3147

See message SYS3146.

Preparing for Trouble

Before trouble strikes, you can do certain things to prepare yourself and your computer. You can minimize the effect of some problems by configuring your computer in a way that enables you to get at the hard disk from DOS as well as from OS/2. You can further prepare yourself by keeping a DOS boot disk handy for emergencies; making copies of your configuration files in case the originals get damaged; knowing which files OS/2 considers sensitive; and making sure that you can access OS/2's files of messages.

Configuring Your Hard Disk

If you want to use HPFS, you don't have to make the entire disk a single HPFS partition. You may benefit from creating a FAT partition for the OS/2 system files and an HPFS partition on the remainder of the disk. You then can use CHKDSK to repair HPFS damage on the separate partition, or you can boot DOS to fix errors in the primary FAT partition. Depending on how much of OS/2 you decide to install, you can designate the first 50M or so as the FAT partition that holds the OS/2 system files.

While OS/2 is active, you cannot use CHKDSK with the /F parameter to repair errors in the partition containing the OS/2 system files. OS/2 keeps many of its system files open when it runs your applications and manages the desktop. Because files are open in the partition containing the OS/2 system files, CHKDSK cannot move portions of files or change Extended Attributes. If you make the entire disk a single partition, either FAT or HPFS, you have to boot the OS/2 Installation Diskette and Diskette 1 to get a command-line prompt at which you can run the CHKDSK utility. This procedure is outlined at the end of this chapter.

If you create a FAT partition for the OS/2 system files and an HPFS partition for your data files, however, you can use CHKDSK on the HPFS partition without having to reboot your computer with the Installation Disk.

Even if you don't want to use HPFS, you can use the two-partition approach to divide your disk into separate FAT partitions. You can use the second partition for your data files and manage that partition separately. You can access both partitions with either OS/2 or DOS. You can run CHKDSK from one partition, when no files are in use on the other partition, to repair damaged files.

Using a DOS Boot Disk

Perhaps a power failure occurs just when one of your applications updates a file, and you want to use a DOS-based disk diagnostic tool to inspect the damage. Perhaps you want to run a DOS-based disk reorganizer utility to defragment the files on your hard disk; or perhaps you chose not to install OS/2's Dual-Boot feature but want to use plain DOS (outside of OS/2) to play a game that is copy-protected or that reboots the computer when you finish playing the game. For these and similar situations, you should keep a DOS boot disk handy. A later section of this chapter explains how to use the DOS boot disk.

> **Note**
>
> When one of your applications writes a file to a FAT partition, both DOS and OS/2 put the contents of the file into sectors on the disk. These sectors don't have to be contiguous. The next time you access the file, DOS and OS/2 retrieve the contents of the file for your application without the application having to know that the file may have come from disk sectors that aren't contiguous.
>
> Your application seems to run slightly slower, however, because DOS or OS/2 must move the read/write mechanism of the disk drive back and forth to the various locations of the file. This phenomenon is most apparent on large files. You can speed things up by periodically running a disk utility that rearranges the files so that their sectors are contiguous. Such a utility is called a disk defragmenter or *defragger*. The DOS-based versions of such low-level disk utilities cannot run in a DOS session under OS/2; you must boot plain DOS to use them.
>
> HPFS partitions don't usually need to be defragmented. HPFS automatically organizes the contents of your files in a way that enables OS/2 to access the files quickly.
>
> Recall that Chapter 3, "Learning OS/2 If You Know DOS," mentioned some OS/2-based disk diagnostic and defragmentation utilities that you may want to acquire. You then do not have to boot DOS to diagnose or defragment your drive.

Making Copies of Important OS/2 Files

You know the importance of your CONFIG.SYS file. OS/2 uses the contents of the CONFIG.SYS file at boot time to determine how to configure the operating system for your use and what device drivers you want loaded. OS/2 uses other files to hold configuration information, too. You should make copies of these files periodically (perhaps daily or at least weekly) in case you need to recover from an OS/2 configuration error.

In addition to the CONFIG.SYS file (located in the root directory of drive C) the other files whose current state you want to preserve are the OS2.INI and OS2SYS.INI files (located in the OS2 subdirectory). You also need to make a copy of the desktop's directory structure. The desktop directory, along with all its subdirectories and associated Extended Attributes, comprise your desktop.

Backing Up Your Desktop. For a FAT-based system, OS/2 names the desktop directory either **OS!2_2.0_D** or simply **DESKTOP**. For an HPFS-based system, you may find that the name of the desktop directory is **OS!2 2.0 DESKTOP**, **OS!2_2.1_D** or **OS!2 2.1 DESKTOP**. (You can use the DIR command or the Drives object to determine the name OS/2 uses on your computer.) You should make a backup copy of your desktop directory structure. To do so, follow these steps:

1. Boot with the OS/2 Installation Diskette; insert OS/2 Diskette 1 when the prompt for the disk appears.

2. After the second part of the installation software loads from OS/2 Diskette 1, use the Esc key to obtain a command-line prompt.

3. Type **C:** and press Enter.

4. If the hard disk partition OS/2 starts from is FAT-based, insert a blank, formatted disk in the A drive and enter the following command (substituting the directory name appropriate for your computer):

    BACKUP OS!2_2.0_D A: /S

5. If the hard disk partition from which OS/2 starts is HPFS-based, insert a blank, formatted disk in the A drive and enter the following command (substituting the directory name appropriate for your computer):

    BACKUP "OS!2 2.0 DESKTOP" A: /S

6. Use the XCOPY command to also make a backup copy of the OS2SYS.INI and OS2.INI files. These two files, located in the OS2 directory, contain information about how you customized your desktop. The following command puts the backup copy of these files on the same floppy disk you used in the preceding steps:

    XCOPY C:\OS2\OS2*.INI A:

7. Putting a copy of your CONFIG.SYS file on the floppy disk is also a good idea; to do so, use the following command:

    XCOPY C:\CONFIG.SYS A:

8. You should now store the floppy disk in a safe place. This floppy disk contains a copy of your computer's OS/2 configuration, including the state of your desktop.

Restoring Your Desktop. If you need to restore your configuration files from the floppy disk, including the appearance of your desktop, follow these steps (substitute the name of the desktop directory your computer uses in each case):

1. Boot with the OS/2 Installation Diskette; insert OS/2 Diskette 1 when the prompt for the disk appears.

2. After the second part of the installation software loads from OS/2 Diskette 1, use the Esc key to obtain a command-line prompt.

3. Type **C:** and press Enter.

4. For an HPFS-based system, type the following command:

    RESTORE A: "OS!2 2.0 DESKTOP" /S

5. If your system is FAT-based, type the following command:

    RESTORE A: OS!2_2.0_D /S

6. You can make your backup copy of the OS2SYS.INI and OS2.INI files current by typing the following command:

    XCOPY A:*.INI C:\OS2*.INI

7. Make the copy of your CONFIG.SYS file on the floppy disk current with the following command:

    XCOPY A:\CONFIG.SYS C:\CONFIG.SYS

You can use a second method to back up and, if necessary, restore your OS2SYS.INI, OS2.INI, and CONFIG.SYS files. You may want to consider using this second method in addition to the first method already discussed. The OS/2 installation process copies your original OS2SYS.INI and OS2.INI files into the

\OS2\INSTALL directory. Unless you copy newer files over the original ones, the files in \OS2\INSTALL reflect the original (installed) state of your desktop.

OS/2 gives you an opportunity during the boot process to restore your desktop, INI files, and CONFIG.SYS file to an earlier state. If you simultaneously press the Alt and F1 keys during the boot process, OS/2 restores your computer's configuration to a previous state by copying OS2.INI and OS2SYS.INI from \OS2\INSTALL to \OS2, and copying CONFIG.SYS from \OS2\INSTALL to the root directory.

If the OS2.INI, OS2SYS.INI, and CONFIG.SYS files in the \OS2\INSTALL directory are the ones left by the installation process, pressing Alt and F1 during system boot puts your desktop back to its original (first time) state. You periodically can update the files in the \OS2\INSTALL directory to reflect your current desktop settings, however.

As a first step toward establishing an automated backup copy of your OS/2 desktop, use a text editor (such as the Enhanced Editor) to insert the following four lines at the end of your CONFIG.SYS file:

```
CALL=C:\OS2\XCOPY.EXE C:\OS2\INSTALL\*.INA
    C:\OS2\INSTALL\*.INB
CALL=C:\OS2\XCOPY.EXE C:\OS2\*.INI
    C:\OS2\INSTALL\*.INA
CALL=C:\OS2\XCOPY.EXE C:\INSTALL\CONFIG.SYA
    C:\OS2\INSTALL\CONFIG.SYB
CALL=C:\OS2\XCOPY.EXE C:\CONFIG.SYS
    C:\OS2\INSTALL\CONFIG.SYA
```

These four additions to the CONFIG.SYS file give you two copies of your OS2.INI, OS2SYS.INI, and CONFIG.SYS files. The files whose last character in the extension is A are the most recent copy. The files with a final extension character of B are the next most recent copy. The copies exist in the \OS2\INSTALL directory, and you automatically make new copies every time you boot your computer.

If you need to restore your desktop to an earlier state, follow these steps:

1. Boot with the OS/2 Installation Diskette; insert OS/2 Diskette 1 when the prompt for the disk appears.

2. After the second part of the installation software loads from OS/2 Diskette 1, use the Esc key to obtain a command-line prompt.

3. Type **C:** and press Enter.

4. Type **CD \OS2\INSTALL** and press Enter.

5. Type one of the following commands, depending on whether you want to use the "A" set or the "B" set of files. (You may want to start with the older "B" set, unless you know the "A" set isn't corrupted in any way.)

    COPY *.INA *.INI

    or

    COPY *.INB *.INI

6. Type one of the following commands:

    COPY CONFIG.SYA CONFIG.SYS

    or

    COPY CONFIG.SYB CONFIG.SYS

7. After you set up the "A" or "B" filesets to become the current desktop and CONFIG.SYS, press Ctrl-Alt-Del to reboot the computer. During the boot procedure, hold down Alt and F1 so that OS/2 uses the backup files in the \OS2\INSTALL directory.

Of course, you should make a separate copy of these files in addition to the regular backup procedures you use.

> **Tip**
>
> OS/2-specific utility programs, such as the ones discussed in Chapter 3, "Learning OS/2 If You Know DOS," typically automate the entire process of backing up and restoring your desktop, INI files, and CONFIG.SYS file. You may want to consider acquiring OS/2-specific utilities to help you manage your computer.

Working with Sensitive OS/2 Files and Directories

OS/2 creates and manages certain files that you should not attempt to modify or delete. Make sure that you back up these files along with the other files on your hard disk, however. In general, these files contain information about other files. OS/2 gives these special files the Hidden and System attributes so that you normally don't see them. A DIR command does not show these files. You run across the files, however, if you boot DOS and inspect your hard disk with a low-level disk utility. Depending on how you have your desktop's Detail View file criteria set up, you also may see the files in a Detail View window.

The first special file is named EA DATA. SF. Notice that the file has spaces in its name. You cannot access this file with most OS/2 and DOS software. EA DATA. SF contains extended attributes for the files on your computer system. OS/2 uses this file to hold information about other files that does not fit into a directory entry (the 32 bytes of internal directory information that OS/2 or DOS displays when you use the DIR command). OS/2 2.1 relies heavily on EA DATA. SF. If you use low-level disk diagnostic software, make sure that you do not disturb this file.

The WP ROOT. SF file is another special OS/2 file. The Workplace Shell uses this file to hold information about your desktop settings. As with the EA DATA. SF file, be careful that you do not disturb WP ROOT. SF.

> **Caution**
>
> Some defragmenters don't work with OS/2 drives, regardless of whether the disk is formatted as FAT or HPFS. The defragmenter might scramble the EA DATA. SF file. That file is critical to OS/2, as discussed in this chapter. Make sure that a DOS-based disk defragmenter is OS/2-compatible before using it on your FAT-formatted disk partitions. For both FAT and HPFS drives, you might want to consider acquiring one of the OS/2-specific utility program products discussed in Chapter 3, "Learning OS/2 If You Know DOS."

> **Caution**
>
> The C:\DELETE directory holds copies of files you have deleted. OS/2 automatically reclaims the space used by these deleted files as necessary, but maintains the copies as long as possible in the C:\DELETE directory should you want to undelete them. OS/2 also marks the copies of the deleted files with the Hidden and System file attributes. If you use a DIR command in the C:\DELETE directory, you see what appears to be an empty directory. Do not try to remove this directory.

Chapter 8—Troubleshooting OS/2

> **Note**
>
> OS/2, by default, does not enable the management of deleted files in the DELETE directory. If you want to use OS/2's movement of deleted files into the DELETE directory and OS/2's management of that directory, you must turn this option on by editing both your CONFIG.SYS file and your AUTOEXEC.BAT file. You must edit the line that begins `REM SET DELDIR` (as shown in the following example):
>
> ```
> REM SET DELDIR=C:\DELETE,512;D:\DELETE,512;
> ```
>
> Delete the characters `REM` from the beginning of the line. Shut down and reboot. The setting of the `DELDIR` environment variable enables OS/2's management of deleted files.

OS/2 creates a set of directories on your hard disk at installation time. The directory names are OS2, SPOOL, NOWHERE, DELETE, and either OS!2_2.0_D or OS!2_2.1_D. You almost certainly should leave this directory structure alone. In particular, the OS!2_2.0_D directory (perhaps named OS!2_2.1_D) holds information the Workplace Shell needs to function properly. The directories underneath the OS!2_2.0_D directory typically include TEMPLATE, MINIMIZE, OS!2_SYS, COMMAND_, GAMES, and PRODUCTI. You may find additional directories in C:\OS!2_2.0_D, depending on which applications you install on your system. You should make backup copies of this directory structure, as discussed in the previous section.

The following table identifies OS/2's use of the directories within C:\OS2.

Directory	Contents
SYSTEM	Message, swap, and Dual Boot files
DLL	Dynamic Link Library (OS/2 program) files
HELP	On-line help files
INSTALL	Installation program and data files
BOOK	The OS/2 command reference
BITMAP	Image files for your desktop
APPS	The applets that come with OS/2
MDOS	DOS and Windows environment files
WINOS2	Microsoft Windows files (WINOS2 is a subdirectory of the MDOS directory)

Appendix E, "OS/2 Files by Function," contains a complete list of files that OS/2 installs on your PC. The list groups the files by function so that you can understand why OS/2 installs a particular file.

Accessing the Message Files

Finally, before a problem happens, make sure that OS/2 can locate your message files. As the beginning of this chapter mentioned, the OS/2 installation process places the files in the C:\OS2\SYSTEM directory. For many types of errors, OS/2 retrieves the explanation for the error from one or more of the message files, and then displays the result to you. If the message files cannot be found, OS/2 cannot fully explain the error.

The DPATH entry in the CONFIG.SYS file tells OS/2 where to find the message files for errors that happen in OS/2 sessions. The APPEND statement in the AUTOEXEC.BAT file does the same thing for DOS sessions. If you make changes to either the CONFIG.SYS or AUTOEXEC.BAT files, be careful about the DPATH and APPEND entries. Make sure that you use APPEND in your DOS sessions so that your DOS sessions also get the benefit of the message files in C:\OS2\SYSTEM. For OS/2 sessions, make sure that C:\OS2\SYSTEM is in the DPATH statement in the CONFIG.SYS file.

Also make sure that you install the OS/2 on-line command reference. If trouble strikes, you may be able to solve the problem by simply referring to OS/2's on-line help.

For Related Information
- "Making the Computer Work for You," p. 41
- "Using the Command Reference," p. 719

Recognizing Trouble

When OS/2 displays an error message or error screen, the error appears as a textual response to a command you entered at a command-line prompt or as a window of explanatory information. Sometimes you notice a problem, however, and no error explanation appears. This latter situation happens when one of your applications does not behave as expected; when the screen becomes garbled and unreadable; when you press keys on the keyboard or move the mouse or press its buttons, but the computer doesn't respond; when the printer does not print your documents properly; or when performance suddenly degrades. Any of these occurrences is reason to suspect a problem.

Understanding Error Messages

When OS/2 displays an error message in response to a command you entered at a command-line prompt, you see something similar to the examples shown below:

Example 1

```
ERROR: The name specified is not recognized as an internal or
external command, operable program, or batch file.
```

This error is equivalent to the DOS Bad command or file name error message.

Example 2

```
ERROR: You tried to write to a disk, but it is write-protected.
ACTION: Make sure that the proper disk is being used, or remove
the write protection. Retry the command.
```

Example 3

```
ERROR: A file contains a reference to an extended attribute
that does not exist. Either the disk partition is damaged or the
extended attribute system file has been improperly modified.
ACTION: Run CHKDSK /F on the disk or disks.
```

Example 4

```
ERROR: The system cannot find the file "<filename>" specified in
the <statement> command on line <line number> of the CONFIG.SYS
file. Line <line number> is ignored.
```

You usually can take corrective action when you see an error message such as in the preceding examples by choosing an appropriate action from those suggested, typing the command correctly, or making sure that the appropriate files are located in the proper directories. You also can get help by typing the command **HELP <message number>** at an OS/2 command-line prompt. For example, type **HELP 32** after receiving a SYS0032 error from OS/2. OS/2 will, in this example, respond with the following information:

```
SYS0032: The process cannot access the file because it is being
used by another process.
EXPLANATION: The file is already being used by another process.
ACTION: Retry the command later.
```

Understanding the The system is stopped Message

When OS/2 detects an error that halts the entire computer, you typically see a screen similar to the one illustrated in figure 8.2. You then must reboot OS/2 with the reset button or power switch on your computer. You can report the error to IBM (perhaps through a help desk or technical support group within your organization). If you report the error, you need to write down the contents of the screen before you reboot your computer. The contents of the screen help the programmers diagnose and fix the problem.

```
Exception in device driver: TRXNET$
TRAP 000e        ERRCD=0000   ERACC=****   ERLIM=********
EAX=fdce0001  EBX=fff311c0  ECX=000000fc  EDX=ffe302e0
ESI=fd415d96  EDI=feb40008  EBP=00000000  FLG=0001026
CS:EIP=0700:00000c69   CSACC=009b   CSLM=00000fce
SS:ESP=00e8:000007dc   SSACC=0093   SSLIM=000007ff
DS=2310   DSACC=0093   DSLIM=0000fdff   CR0=fffffe1
ES=0708   ESACC=1093   ESLIM=00003fff   CR2=00015d96
FS=0000   FSACC=****   FSLIM=********
GS=0000   GSACC=****   GSLIM=********
The system detected an internal processing
error at location ##0160:fff6986f - 000d:986f.
60000, 9084
038600d1

The system is stopped. Record the location number of the
error and contact your service representative.
```

Fig. 8.2
The *The system is stopped* error screen.

Catching Application Program Errors

The safeguards built into OS/2 can catch an application program's error that otherwise would cause you to reboot your computer. Figures 8.3, 8.4, and 8.5 show such an error. You can respond to the error by clicking the button labeled End program/command/operation. Figure 8.3 illustrates the initial notification screen.

If you click the Help button shown in figure 8.3, OS/2 displays an explanation of the error (see fig. 8.4). Usually, the explanation tells the programmer what he or she did wrong. If you purchased rather than developed the application that caused the error, you may want to record the system error number (SYS3175 in the examples shown in figures 8.3 and 8.4) and send the error number to the customer support personnel at the company that makes the software.

Fig. 8.3
OS/2's notification that it has caught an application error before the application can crash your computer.

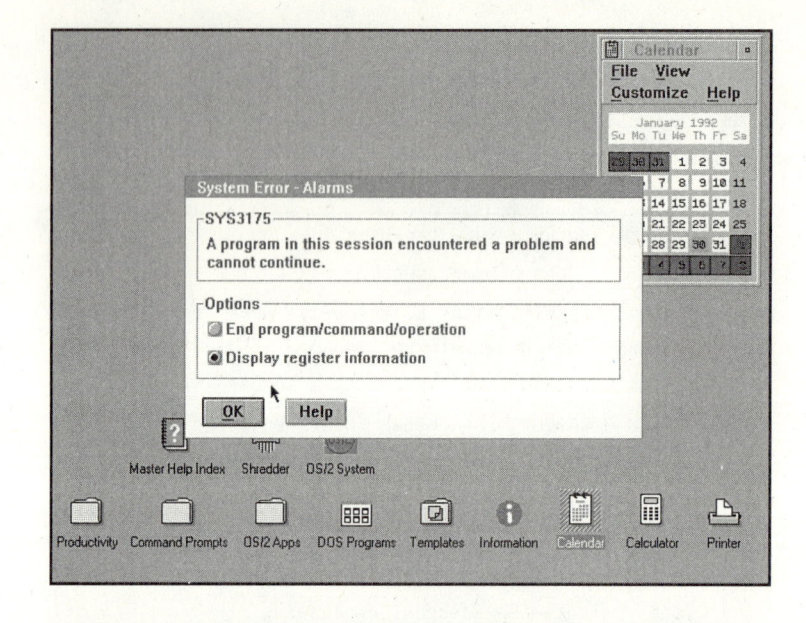

Fig. 8.4
OS/2's explanation of what the application was doing at the time of the error.

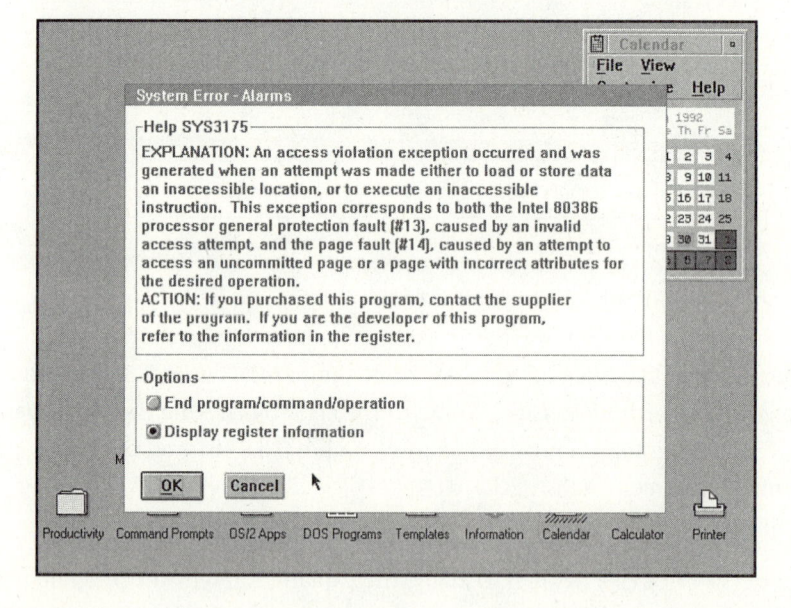

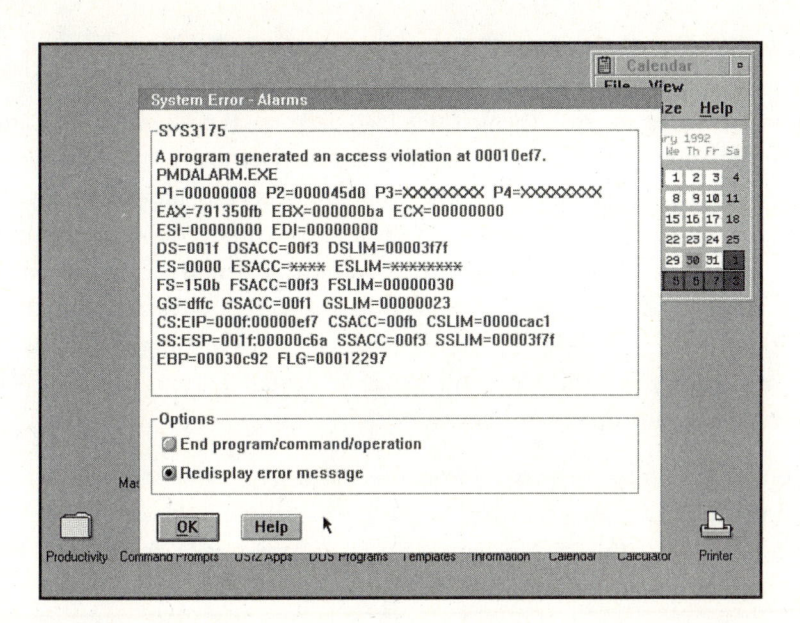

Fig. 8.5
OS/2's display of registers when an application fails.

Clicking the Display register information button shown in figure 8.3 makes the screen illustrated in figure 8.5 appear. This screen shows the contents of the CPU chip's internal registers at the time the application error occurred. Note that figure 8.5 is only an example; the actual values in the registers vary from application to application. As with the system error number information shown in figure 8.3, the register display is for the programmer who wrote the software. You may want to record the information so that you can send it to the customer support people at the company that makes the software. The system error number and the register values give the programmer enough information to fix the software.

After you end the program, you can continue using OS/2 and your other applications. You can restart the application that failed, but be aware that you have discovered a bug in that application. The application may fail again.

For Related Information
- "Understanding Operating Systems," p. 33
- "Matching OS/2 with DOS," p. 60
- "Looking at DOS and OS/2 Incompatibilities," p. 71

Knowing What Steps to Take

If you encounter an error, the first step is to diagnose the problem. You can categorize and identify the error by using the later sections of this chapter. These sections explain how to recover from problems that happen during the boot process, when an application (or the entire computer) stops suddenly, when an application does not behave as expected, when the screen becomes garbled, when pressing keys on the keyboard produces no reaction from the computer, when the mouse fails to move the cursor or the mouse buttons fail to work, when your printouts don't appear or are garbled, and when the performance of your computer suddenly becomes slow.

If your computer cannot recover from the error by your responding to an error message, changing a setting, or issuing a command, this chapter explains how to use the OS/2 installation disk, or perhaps a DOS boot disk, to fix the problem.

Getting Patches and Fixes for OS/2

IBM announces and releases patches and updates to OS/2 from time to time. The software corrections are distributed as *Corrective Service Diskettes* (CSDs). IBM does not distribute CSDs daily, weekly, or even monthly to all its customers. If IBM did this, you would be busy installing changes and wouldn't get any real work done. The changes might not even affect the type of work you do on your computer.

When a customer finds a programming error in OS/2 and reports the error, IBM often provides corrected software to that customer on a prompt basis. IBM keeps a list of all reported OS/2 problems and makes the list available to its customers (you, for example). You can download the problem lists from information services such as BIX or CompuServe or from other sources (see Appendix H, "Identifying Sources of OS/2 Information"). IBM accumulates the fixes over a time period ranging from a month to several months, and then distributes the fixes as an official, announced CSD. IBM makes the CSD available to all OS/2 customers electronically, or you can order the CSD floppy disks from IBM. There's no charge if you acquire the CSD electronically (by downloading the files through a modem and creating your own CSD floppy disks). IBM charges a nominal fee if you ask IBM to send you floppy disks containing the CSD. The fee simply covers the cost of the floppy disks.

IBM released a CSD for OS/2 2.1 shortly after 2.1 itself was released. The CSD corrected a few Workplace Shell problems, particularly in the operating system file PMWP.DLL. The following list identifies the problems fixed by the first CSD for OS/2 2.1:

- When installing 2.1 over an earlier version of OS/2 without formatting, the system may reboot to a white screen and fail to bring up the desktop.

> - The final `shutdown complete` message is displayed underneath (overlapping) the `shutdown please wait` message on some systems.
> - Mass duplication of template objects after creating a shadow.
>
> Early in 1994, IBM released another, larger CSD for OS/2 2.1 called the OS/2 2.1 *Service Pack*. The corrected and updated files in the Service Pack not only fix a number of problems, but also add support for additional CD-ROM drives from companies such as Creative Labs, Chinon, Mitsumi, Panasonic, Sony, NEC, and Texel.
>
> Watch for IBM's announcements of CSDs and Service Packs for OS/2. You'll want to apply the patches to your copy of OS/2 2.1. Carefully follow the instructions that accompany the CSD. Make sure that the CSD is appropriate for the level of operating system code on your computer.

This chapter has shown you OS/2 error messages, including the `The system is stopped` error message and application error messages. An error may appear in a different form, however. The next several sections of this chapter discuss unusual kinds of errors.

Knowing Why the Computer Fails To Boot

If your computer does not display the Workplace Shell desktop screen within several minutes after booting, look carefully at the screen for error messages that explain why the computer stopped. If no message appears, you may have a hardware problem. (Hardware problems are beyond the scope of this book. You may want to get a copy of Que's *Upgrading and Repairing PCs* by Scott Mueller.) If no message appears and you don't have a hardware problem, you may need to reinstall OS/2. First, though, try booting the OS/2 Installation Diskette and Diskette 1, as outlined later in this chapter. If the Installation Diskette and Diskette 1 boot successfully, try the CHKDSK /F command to see if it repairs your hard disk so that you can reboot.

One of the first things you can do if your computer fails to boot OS/2, boots with error messages, or boots with a corrupted desktop is restore your desktop with the procedure detailed earlier in this chapter. If you haven't made a backup copy of your CONFIG.SYS and INI files, however, you won't be able to restore from your saved copies.

Also note whether you made configuration changes recently to your computer. One of your changes may have disabled the computer's capability to boot properly.

If OS/2 displays the message Workplace desktop could not be located. The user INI file or hardfile may be corrupt on-screen during the boot process, you have a fairly serious OS/2 error on your hands. The cause of this error is usually the erosion and subsequent failure of a spot on the hard disk. If OS/2 recorded desktop information on the hard disk and now cannot retrieve that desktop information, you see this error. You may have to reinstall OS/2. First, however, try the following three procedures to see if you can solve the problem without performing a complete reinstall.

Solving Boot Problems—Quick Procedure. You can press the left Ctrl key, the left Shift key, and the F1 key simultaneously during the boot process to tell OS/2 to omit the automatic program startup feature of the Workplace Shell. You lose nothing of your desktop customization when you press these keys. Simultaneously press and hold the keys from the time you first see the OS/2 logo to the time that icons appear on your desktop. If this procedure solves your problem, you need to inspect your Startup folder and your STARTUP.CMD file before you next reboot your computer. One or more of the entries in the Startup folder or the STARTUP.CMD file is likely causing OS/2 not to boot correctly.

Solving Boot Problems—Quick Procedure. You can press the left Alt key and the F1 key simultaneously during the boot process to tell OS/2 to use the CONFIG.SYS and the INI files located in the \OS2\INSTALL directory rather than the usual CONFIG.SYS and INI files. OS/2 also will not execute the commands in the STARTUP.CMD file and will not run the program objects in the Startup folder. OS/2 renames your existing CONFIG.SYS file to CONFIG.001, and your existing STARTUP.CMD file to STARTUP.001; and renames your INI files in the \OS2 directory.

> **Note**
>
> When OS/2 uses the CONFIG.SYS and INI files from the \OS2\INSTALL directory, your desktop and general OS/2 configuration revert to the configuration represented by the earlier files. The OS/2 installation process copies your initial CONFIG.SYS and INI files to the \OS2\INSTALL directory. If you haven't copied newer versions of the files to \OS2\INSTALL, you revert to the OS/2 configuration you had immediately after you installed OS/2. If you've copied later, known-to-work versions of these files to the \OS2\INSTALL directory, you revert to that later state. An earlier section of this chapter explains how to copy later versions of the files to the \OS2\INSTALL directory.

To tell OS/2 to use the earlier versions of these files, press Alt-F1 before the OS/2 logo appears. Hold the keys for about 20 seconds. OS/2 displays a message telling you that it renamed the existing files. If this procedure solves the problem, you can delete the files renamed to *.001 from your hard disk. One or more of those files is corrupt.

Solving Boot Problems_Lengthy Procedure. If the procedures you just learned (characterized as quickest and quick) don't solve the problem, you can try recreating your INI files with the MAKEINI program. Running MAKEINI rebuilds your desktop. Follow these steps:

1. Boot your computer with the OS/2 distribution floppy disks labeled Installation Diskette and Diskette 1.

2. Press the Esc key when you see the Welcome to OS/2 screen.

3. At the A: prompt that appears next, change to the OS/2 boot drive by typing **C:** and pressing Enter.

4. Change to the OS/2 directory by typing a **CD/OS2** command.

You're now ready to run MAKEINI. Run the program twice—once for the OS2.INI file and once for the OS2SYS.INI file. Type the following command at the C:\OS2 prompt, and then type the second command after the first one finishes:

MAKEINI OS2.INI INI.RC

MAKEINI OS2SYS.INI INISYS.RC

After you run MAKEINI twice, you need to delete the hidden file WP ROOT. SF from the root directory. (Note that the file has spaces in its name.) Use the OS/2 ATTRIB command to remove the file's "hidden" attribute by typing the following:

**CD **

ATTRIB -h -s -r WP?ROOT.?SF

You can then delete the file with the following command:

ERASE WP?ROOT.?SF

Remove the floppy disk from the disk drive and press Ctrl-Alt-Del to reboot your computer.

If this first MAKEINI procedure doesn't help solve the problem, you can try a variation of the MAKEINI procedure. The MAKEINI program will merge the information in the RC files with information in any existing INI files. If the existing INI files are badly damaged, MAKEINI may not be able to fix the files. So, in a variation of the MAKEINI procedure, boot your computer with the Installation Diskette and Diskette 1. Before you run MAKEINI, however, delete the existing INI files to force MAKEINI to create brand new files. After you change to the \OS2 directory on your C drive, the following commands will delete the INI files:

ERASE OS2.INI

ERASE OS2SYS.INI

Then continue with the MAKEINI procedure.

If deleting the INI files and using the MAKEINI procedure solve the problem, OS/2 appears in the same configuration and with the same desktop as you saw immediately after installation.

Solving Boot Problems —Reinstalling OS/2. For really intractable OS/2 boot problems, you must reinstall the operating system. Before you do, however, the following tips help you to avoid the error that originally caused the problem.

Prior to the reinstall, delete any existing WP ROOT. SF and EA DATA. SF files from your root directory (if your bootable drive is FAT-based). Also delete the OS2.INI and OS2SYS.INI files from your \OS2 directory. Use the OS/2 distribution floppy disks labeled Installation Diskette and Diskette 1 to boot your computer. Use the ATTRIB and ERASE commands, as explained in earlier sections of this chapter, to delete the files. Before reinstalling OS/2, run the CHKDSK command with the /F parameter (this removes any Extended Attributes from the files on the boot drive). Then reinstall the operating system.

Fixing Lost and Cross-Linked Extended Attributes

The section of Chapter 3 entitled, "Understanding INI files and Extended Attributes," explains how OS/2 stores Extended Attributes on a FAT-based drive. Directory entries on FAT-based drives do not have enough room to store extra information about a file (beyond the file's date, time, size, and a few simple attributes). A file with Extended Attributes has a special pointer in that file's directory entry. The pointer tells where in the EA DATA. SF file the file's Extended Attributes exist. This pointer mechanism allows the relatively small FAT-based directory entry (each FAT-based directory entry is exactly 32 characters) to indirectly store more information about a file. The information is the file's Extended Attributes. The system file EA DATA. SF is a collection of Extended Attributes for all the files on the drive that have Extended Attributes.

Especially after booting plain DOS (which does not understand Extended Attributes or EA pointers) and working with files on your hard drive, the EA pointers possibly can be damaged. When you next boot OS/2, you may find that OS/2 cannot access your files normally. You may, for example, see `Access Denied` error messages when you issue commands or run programs. Running the CHKDSK utility reveals `Lost Extended Attributes` and `Cross-Linked Extended Attributes` error messages.

> **Note**
>
> In the multitasking environment of OS/2, the Access Denied error message normally means that you're trying to access a file in one session that another session already is using.

If two directory entries for two different files point to the same Extended Attributes in the EA DATA. SF file, OS/2 does not know to which file the Extended Attributes really belong. The CHKDSK program reports this situation as Cross-Linked Extended Attributes.

If a directory entry has an EA pointer but the EA DATA. SF file contains no Extended Attributes at the location the pointer refers to, CHKDSK reports this situation as Lost Extended Attributes.

Booting with the Installation Diskette and Diskette 1, and then running the CHKDSK utility with the /F parameter, can repair the Extended Attributes problem. If CHKDSK detects that two files claim the same Extended Attributes information in EA DATA. SF, CHKDSK gives the Extended Attributes to one of the files by removing the second file's EA pointer in the second file's directory entry. If CHKDSK detects an invalid EA pointer in a file's directory entry, CHKDSK removes that EA pointer. After you run CHKDSK, you should be able to reboot and use OS/2 normally.

Reacting When the Computer or Application Stops Suddenly

The computer's or application's stopping suddenly is perhaps the rarest of errors. If OS/2 does not show you even a `The Computer is Stopped` error message, and you cannot get a response from the computer, look for a hardware problem in your computer.

If you suspect your computer has stopped working entirely, the first thing to do is move your mouse. Does the cursor on-screen move with it? If so, your computer is still running, although it is perhaps not running the software you intended.

If the mouse cursor does not move, reboot the computer with the power switch or the computer's reset button. Note that with OS/2's built-in safeguards, encountering the situation in which you need to use the power switch is highly unlikely.

The problem may be that the full-screen or windowed application session you're using simply has lost the current focus; another application is using the keyboard and/or the screen. Click the title bar of the window of the application you're using. Does this action highlight (activate) the window? If so, you should be able to resume using that application.

Before you reboot your computer, try pressing Ctrl-Esc to bring up the list of active applications on your desktop. If Ctrl-Esc has no effect, reboot. Don't forget to have your computer checked for hardware malfunctions.

Dealing with an Application that Does Not Behave

If your application's behavior causes you to suspect a strange interaction between OS/2 and the application, first make sure that you followed the correct steps to obtain results from that application. You simply may have typed an incorrect file name or clicked a button unintentionally. Also, inspect the settings notebook for the session in which the application is running. Perhaps you changed a setting and need to restore it to its original value. Also, you might need to change a setting to make the session's environment better suited to your application.

This category of error is the broadest and the most difficult to pin down. You must verify whether the application is in error, OS/2 is in error, or you have a hardware problem. Perhaps you misunderstand how the application is supposed to behave. One step you can take is to see if the error is repeatable. If you cannot make the error happen a second time, the error may be the result of a typing error.

If you have a DOS application that is supposed to run in the background but that does not run properly, look at the DOS settings for that session. Make sure that running in the background is enabled, and try increasing idle sensitivity from the default 75 percent to a higher value. By increasing the idle sensitivity, you allocate more CPU time to the DOS program.

If the application is a communications program that uses one of the serial ports (COM1, COM2, COM3, or COM4), you may want to substitute the COM02.SYS file for the default serial port device driver. Change your CONFIG.SYS file to DEVICE=C:\OS2\COM02.SYS rather than DEVICE=C:\OS2\COM.SYS. Unpack COM02.SYS from Disk 5 of the distribution disks. In an OS/2 full-screen session, insert Disk 5 in your A: drive, make C:\OS2 your current directory, and type **UNPACK A:\SERIAL**. You should see a message telling you COM02.SYS is unpacked. After using the Shutdown option, reboot your computer; the change then takes effect.

If you find that a serial mouse doesn't function properly on an IBM PS/2 model 90 or model 95 computer, you may need to use the Setup/Diagnostics disk that came with the computer to disable the serial port arbitration levels.

If a DOS application requires VCPI memory, that application does not run under OS/2. You must use Dual Boot to run the VCPI application by itself and under DOS, without the benefit of OS/2's multitasking.

Perhaps the software you're trying to run is a low-level disk utility that reads and writes to disk sectors (rather than files). Or perhaps the software is copy-protected or is a game, and you need to use Dual-Boot to run the software under plain DOS.

Unscrambling a Garbled Screen

If your screen appears garbled (not just confused—actually unreadable), first ask yourself if you recently made configuration changes to your computer, especially the CONFIG.SYS file. If so, reset your changes and reboot. You also can explore the possibility that your computer has a hardware problem.

To see if OS/2 can regain control of the video adapter, try pressing Ctrl-Esc to bring up the list of active sessions on the desktop. If this action fails to work and because you cannot read the screen, try rebooting the computer. You also can verify the jumper and switch settings on your computer's video adapter. If the manufacturer of your video adapter supplied you with a floppy disk containing utilities and diagnostic programs, you may want to try running the utility that sets the adapter's default video mode. You also can run the video adapter diagnostic program.

Freeing a Keyboard that Fails to Work

If pressing keys on the keyboard produces no response from the computer, first work through the material given earlier in this chapter in the section titled, "Reacting When the Computer or Application Stops Suddenly." The problem may be that a different application is using the keyboard.

Try pressing the Caps Lock key. Does the green light on the keyboard toggle on and off each time you press Caps Lock? If so, the computer is still active, but the other keystrokes are not getting through to the intended application. Try pressing Ctrl-Esc to bring up the list of active desktop sessions. If this action is effective, select your application from the list and try to resume your work. If you still have a problem, the application is simply not looking for keyboard input (despite what may appear on-screen). The application software may have a bug in it. Consult the application documentation to pursue this further.

Solving Mouse Problems

Most of the suggestions and discussion you covered earlier in the sections titled "Reacting When the Computer or Application Stops Suddenly" and "Freeing a Keyboard that Fails to Work" apply also to the mouse. The mouse cursor should always move in response to moving the mouse, regardless of whether an application is looking for mouse input. If the mouse cursor fails to move, you probably have a hardware problem. (If the mouse cursor fails to move and you have just installed OS/2, you may have made an incorrect selection regarding the type of mouse you have. Double-check your selection before you proceed.) Also, make sure that the mouse is connected properly to the computer. A loose connection can cause the mouse to appear unresponsive.

Checking the System When Nothing Prints

Obviously, the first thing to check when the printer does not print is that it is plugged in, turned on, and selected (on-line). Also check with the documentation that came with the printer to see why it might fail to print.

If you are trying to print for the first time after installing OS/2, go back to Chapter 6, "Installing OS/2," and Chapter 7, "Modifying Your OS/2 Configuration," to make sure that you configured OS/2 for your make and model of printer. Ensure that you have a properly set up print destination object on your desktop (refer to Chapters 6, 7, and 15, "Printing with OS/2").

If your printer is connected to your serial port and you have an IBM PS/2 model 90 or model 95 computer, make sure that you set the Serial Transmit and Serial Receive Arbitration Levels to Dedicated and assign different numbers to each. Use the Setup/Diagnostics disk to make this configuration change, as outlined in the documentation that came with your computer.

Clearing Garbled Printouts

If your printer worked fine yesterday but prints unreadable characters today and you haven't made configuration changes to your OS/2 print destination object, the problem simply may be that the printer is in the wrong mode. Turning the printer off and on again or using its reset button usually clears things up. If these actions don't cure the problem, you probably have a hardware problem in the printer, or the printer cable is bad.

If your printer does not print correctly right after you install OS/2, you should review Chapters 6 and 7 to make sure that you gave OS/2 the correct data for your printer. In particular, look at the printer driver settings to see if they match the type of printer you use.

Analyzing Performance Problems

If your computer produces the correct results but slowly, you may have a performance problem. "May have" is the operative phrase because performance is a perceived thing; you may think the computer is slow, but another person may think it is fast.

Here are some tips you can use to make your computer run as fast as possible. First, look at the number and complexity of the applications you're trying to run simultaneously under OS/2. Your computer has only a certain amount of horsepower. OS/2 divides up that horsepower among the active applications on your desktop. To get better performance, try reducing the number of applications you have open at the same time.

Next, realize that OS/2 uses the hard disk as a memory-overflow device. When OS/2 begins to run out of physical memory in which to run applications, the SWAPPER.DAT file in the C:\OS2\SYSTEM directory becomes very active. Choose a command-line session and look at the size of the SWAPPER.DAT file. If the size exceeds about 2 or 3M, you probably should consider installing more physical RAM in your computer. (Under DOS, when applications reach the 640K threshold, they simply stop working altogether. Because OS/2 uses the SWAPPER.DAT file for overflow, the computer just slows down.)

You can enhance the performance of a FAT partition by using the Lazy Write (LW) parameter on the DISKCACHE statement in the CONFIG.SYS file. If you change this parameter, remember to reboot your computer so that your

For Related Information

- "Understanding Disk Partitions and Disks," p. 43
- "Working with Video Adapter Cards and Monitors," p. 116
- "Managing the Workplace Shell," p. 245
- "Introducing Presentation Manager," p. 234

change takes effect. You also can make sure that the third parameter on the DISKCACHE statement is 128, as shown in the following example:

DISKCACHE=64,LW,128

If you have a performance problem with an application that uses graphics and you're running that application in a windowed session, you can get a much better performance from the application by running it in a full-screen session. If you run Windows applications on your desktop, you should realize that OS/2 must serialize access to the screen. Windows can write to the screen or OS/2 can write to the screen, but both cannot write to the screen at the same time.

Using the Installation Disks in an Emergency

If your computer does not boot or if you need to run the CHKDSK command with the /F parameter on a partition that OS/2 is using, you usually can fix the problem by following these steps:

1. Insert the disk labeled OS/2 Installation Diskette in the disk drive and reboot your computer.

2. At the prompt for the next floppy disk, insert the disk labeled OS/2 Diskette 1.

3. At the next prompt, press the Esc key to obtain an OS/2 command-line prompt.

For Related Information

- "Beginning the Command-Line Interface," p. 303
- "Learning the Commands for Managing Directories," p. 305
- "Learning the Commands To Back Up Your Hard Disk," p. 323
- "Using the Command Reference," p. 719

If the problem is caused by errors in the CONFIG.SYS file, you can use the procedures given earlier in this chapter to restore the CONFIG.SYS file to a previous state. You also can use those procedures to restore the appearance and configuration of your desktop.

If you need to run the CHKDSK program, you can insert Diskette 2 in a floppy disk drive and type the following command at the command-line prompt to repair damaged files:

CHKDSK C: /F

After you restore files and repair the disk format, reboot your computer.

Booting a DOS Disk

You can stop OS/2 by selecting the Shutdown option from the desktop's pop-up menu, inserting a DOS boot disk in drive A, and rebooting your computer. At the DOS prompt, you can run disk diagnostic tools, disk defragmenters, copy-protected software, and games. If you have an HPFS partition, it is invisible under plain DOS. You can access your FAT partitions normally, however, after booting DOS.

You also can use the Dual-Boot feature to run DOS. Dual-Boot does need to write files on your hard disk just before it restarts your computer. You should use a DOS disk if you suspect you need to repair a Sector Not Found error or other error requiring the use of low-level disk diagnostic tools. In this case, you probably don't want to even use the Shutdown option. Your first action after seeing signs of a hard disk malfunction might be to insert the DOS system-formatted floppy disk and press Ctrl-Alt-Del.

Note that the DOS version of the CHKDSK utility cannot repair damage to OS/2's extended attributes. Running CHKDSK under DOS is not as satisfactory as running the OS/2 version.

Also note that utilities such as PC Tools and Norton's Utilities cannot repair damage to an HPFS partition.

For Related Information
- "Understanding DOS Sessions," p. 394
- "Switching between OS/2 and DOS with Dual-Boot," p. 404

Chapter Summary

This chapter covered a number of unlikely situations. Being prepared for these situations is important. You're now ready in case problems arise.

You learned what OS/2 error messages look like, including the ones that appear when you issue commands at the command line and those that appear when OS/2 detects that an application is misbehaving. You can recognize the `The system is stopped` error screen that you now know means you must reboot your computer.

You learned how to deal with installation errors; you know what to do if the computer fails to boot; and you understand the different problems causing an application (or the entire computer) to stop suddenly. When an application does not behave as expected or displays a garbled screen, you can diagnose the problem. If the keyboard or mouse produce no reaction from the computer, you know what to look for. If you have problems with your printouts, you can correct the problem. You also know ways you can deal with performance problems so that you get the most productivity from your computer system.

Part III

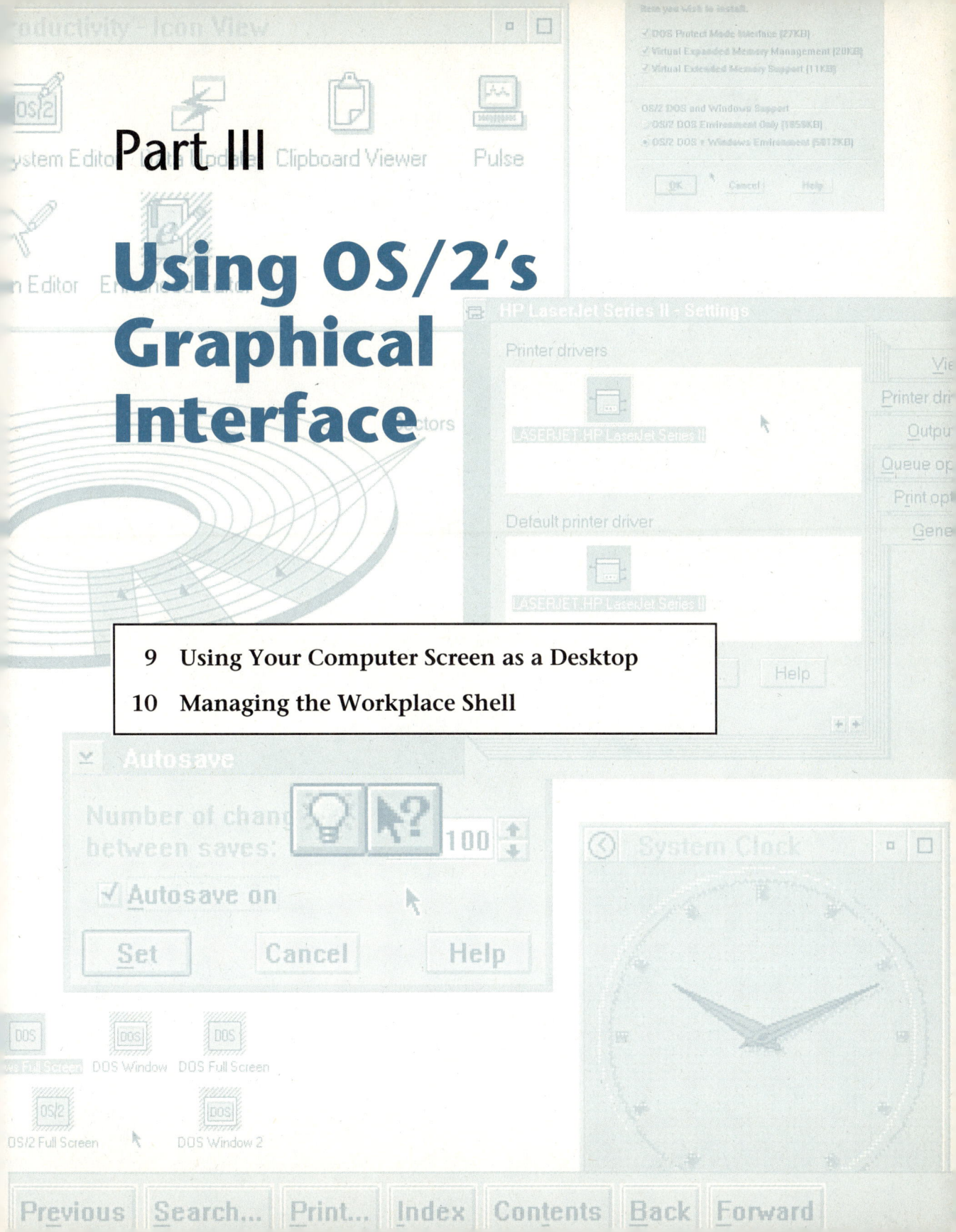

Using OS/2's Graphical Interface

> 9 Using Your Computer Screen as a Desktop
>
> 10 Managing the Workplace Shell

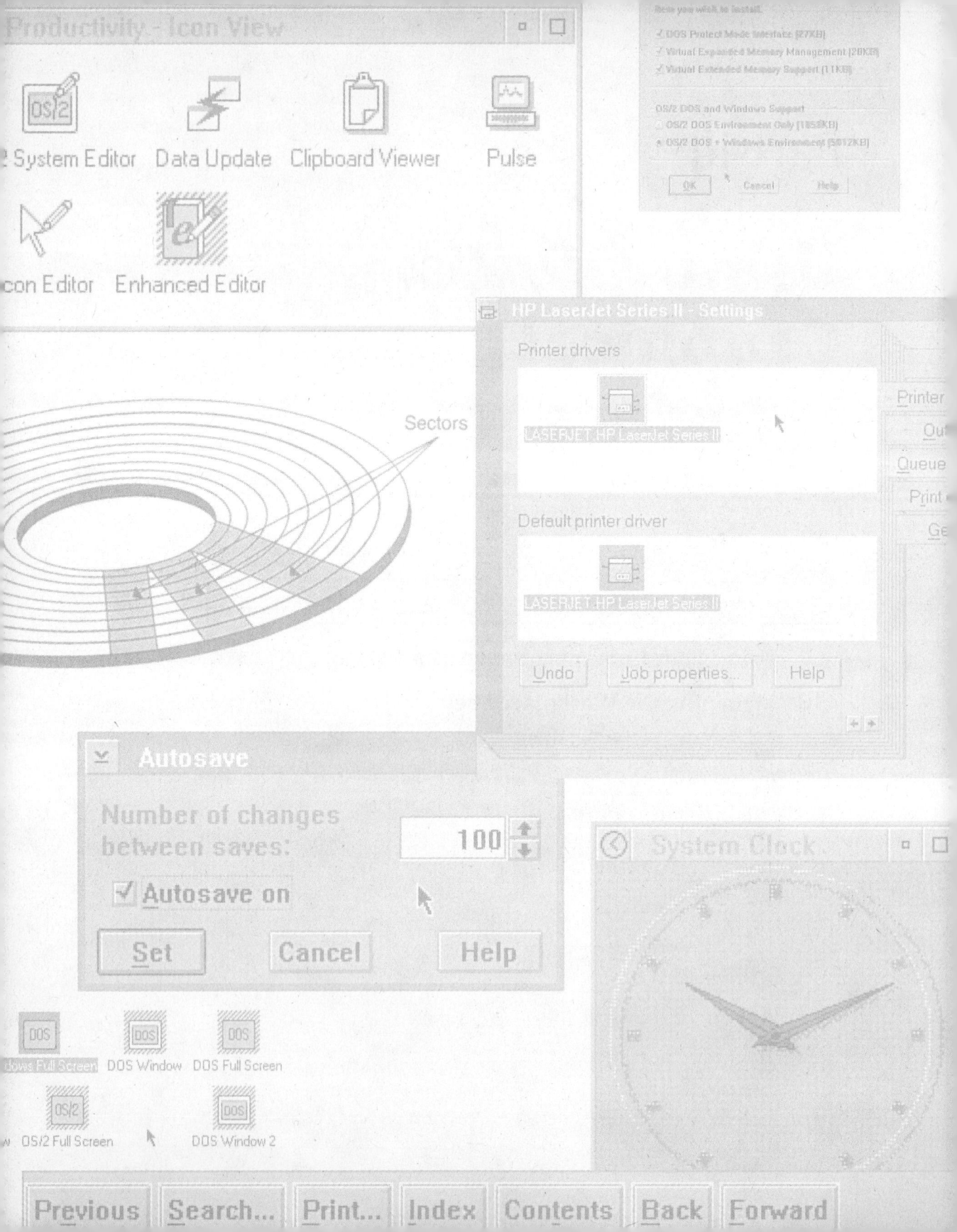

Productivity - Icon View

- System Editor
- Data Update
- Clipboard Viewer
- Pulse
- Icon Editor
- Enhanced Editor

Sectors

HP LaserJet Series II - Settings

Printer drivers

LASERJET HP LaserJet Series II

Default printer driver

LASERJET HP LaserJet Series II

Undo | Job properties... | Help

Printer
Ou
Queue
Print
Ge

Autosave

Number of changes between saves: 100

☑ Autosave on

Set | Cancel | Help

- DOS Full Screen
- DOS Window
- DOS Full Screen
- OS/2 Full Screen
- DOS Window 2

System Clock

Previous | Search... | Print... | Index | Contents | Back | Forward

Chapter 9

Using Your Computer Screen as a Desktop

You now have OS/2 2.0 up and running on your computer. If you didn't have a problem installing OS/2, you probably skipped Chapter 8, "Troubleshooting OS/2," and came directly to this chapter's explanation of the OS/2 graphical user interface. This approach is a good one; you can return to Chapter 8 when you need to (or if you just get curious).

Presentation Manager—the OS/2 graphical user interface (GUI)—is easy to learn, easy to use, and consistent. PM gives you on-screen objects that you can manipulate in several ways. In this chapter, you learn how to identify these objects readily. You also discover that PM and the Workplace Shell make these objects behave similarly to the objects on a desk, with which you are already familiar. This behavior is OS/2's *desktop metaphor*.

The PM standard for consistency and ease of use comes from a team of IBM people who spent a number of years investigating user interfaces. The team's findings parallel the findings of Xerox Corporation at the Palo Alto Research Center (PARC) and the findings of the Apple Computer, Inc., makers of the Macintosh computer. IBM published these findings in the form of suggested standards and called them *Common User Access*, or CUA. CUA is part of a larger set of standards, termed *Systems Application Architecture* (SAA) by IBM. SAA covers communications, programming, database design, and user interfaces.

When applications have a consistent appearance, operational interface, and terminology, you naturally develop a conceptual model for how to use computer software. If you encounter a new application that presents a consistent appearance, you transfer previously learned skills and experience to the new application. You accurately can predict how the new application may behave and can expect your skills to carry over to the new application. This carryover translates into productivity.

Non-PM-based applications have little or nothing in common, in terms of their appearance and interface, with other applications you use. Inconsistency costs more in training time and increases the likelihood of errors, resulting in decreased productivity and increased frustration.

Common User Access treats the computer screen as a desktop that holds as many or as few objects on your *desk* as you prefer. (Some people like a clean desk, others don't.) PM is a bit object-oriented; the Workplace Shell is even more so.

Understanding CUA Principles

IBM based the Common User Access standard on seven principles that describe how people and computers should work together. The following table describes these principles.

Principle	Description
Actions should be reversible.	In a dialog between you and the computer, the application should provide a Cancel option to return the application to a previous state. You easily should be able to undo a wrong menu choice and be able to back up more than one step. When appropriate, an application should offer a Refresh option for restoring input values to a default state.
Preserve the display context to sustain orientation.	Primary windows, window titles, secondary windows, pop-up windows, and scrolling information should appear and behave in a way that suggests the context in which the action takes place. (These terms are defined later in this chapter.)
Don't rely on a person's memorization of steps.	You shouldn't have to remember how to type commands and what every command does. Pull-down menus and other means of selection should offer available options from which you can choose.
Give immediate feedback for every action.	The application should acknowledge each step or action you take. An application should use screen colors, emphasis, and other selection indications to denote what item is chosen, what may not be chosen, and whether an error condition exists.

Principle	Description
Confirm potentially destructive actions.	An application should verify your intent and provide options to perform or cancel an action that erases or deletes information.
Common definitions enhance consistency.	Applications should use common definitions for concepts, appearance of displayed information, and interaction techniques.
The keyboard and mouse interchangeable.	You should be able to use the keyboard to perform actions that you can perform with a mouse (or with another pointing device). You should be able to switch to and from the mouse and the keyboard in the middle of an operation.

The best way to begin identifying and working with the objects on the Workplace Shell desktop or in Presentation Manager is to start with the outermost parts first. After you understand the overall screen display, you can work inward, focusing more closely on the detail of the smaller components. In the following sections, you look first at the Workplace Shell. You explore a basic PM screen, application windows, and then so-called *dialog boxes*.

Using the Workplace Shell

IBM designed the Workplace Shell to be an easy-to-use, object-oriented environment. You do some computer work directly on the Workplace Shell's desktop, but most often you probably use the Workplace Shell to run your applications. In the next few sections, you learn about the objects on your OS/2 desktop and how to manipulate them.

Understanding Workplace Objects

The icons you see when you start OS/2 are objects. You can use these objects when you use the objects on your desk—as tools and as places to file information. When you first boot OS/2, your screen should look like figure 9.1.

The icons you see on-screen and in figure 9.1 are *objects*. Those labeled OS/2 System, Information, Main, and Templates are *folders*. Place the mouse cursor over the OS/2 System folder and quickly click mouse button 1 twice. This mouse operation, known as *double-clicking*, opens the folder. Hold down the Alt key and press the F4 key to close the folder.

For Related Information
- "Examining Presentation Manager," p. 14
- "Understanding How OS/2 Expands upon DOS," p. 62

232   Chapter 9—Using Your Computer Screen as a Desktop

Fig. 9.1
The initial OS/2 screen, showing your new desktop.

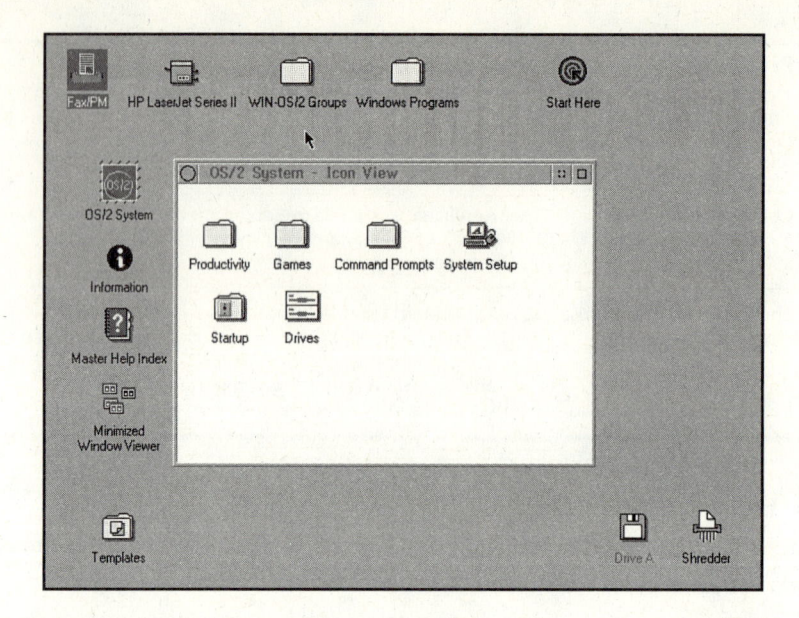

Dragging and Dropping Objects

Now you should take something out of a folder so that you can see how objects behave on your desktop. Double-click the OS/2 System folder to open it. Then follow these steps:

1. Move the mouse cursor over the icon labeled Command Prompts.

2. Press and hold down mouse button 2 and move the mouse cursor to an empty place on the desktop screen. The Command Prompts folder moves with the mouse cursor.

3. Release the mouse button. You have dragged the folder to your desktop and dropped it.

4. Double-click the Command Prompts folder. It opens to reveal objects representing the DOS, OS/2, and Windows sessions you can start under OS/2.

5. Press Alt-F4 to close the Command Prompts folder, and then press Alt-F4 again to close the OS/2 System folder. The Command Prompts folder remains on your desktop.

Navigating the Workplace Shell

The techniques you learn in this section serve you well when you use other CUA-compliant computer software. Figure 9.2 shows a typical Presentation Manager utility, the OS/2 System Editor. The System Editor is a good example of CUA compliance.

Fig. 9.2
The System Editor, a typical Presentation Manager utility.

You easily can use the keyboard to make your screen look like figure 9.2 by following these steps:

1. Press Alt-Tab until you highlight an icon. The highlight appears as a gray rectangle around the icon.

2. Press the arrow keys to move the highlight from icon to icon. Watch how the highlight moves.

3. Highlight the icon labeled OS/2 System. Press Enter to open this object (a folder).

4. You see another group of objects in the OS/2 System folder. Highlight the Productivity object and press Enter.

5. Highlight the OS/2 System Editor object and then press Enter. The System Editor screen appears.

6. Press Alt-Tab to move the Productivity folder to the foreground.

For Related Information
- "Understanding How OS/2 Expands upon DOS," p. 62
- "Configuring Your Desktop," p. 178

7. Press Alt-F4 to close the Productivity folder.

8. Press Alt-F9 to *minimize* the OS/2 System folder. (The folder is still open but doesn't take up space on your OS/2 desktop.)

9. To bring the System Editor to the foreground, press Alt-Tab again.

> **Note**
>
> The preceding steps assume that you don't have a mouse attached to the computer. You can use a mouse in several of these steps, but now you are somewhat familiar with the keystroke equivalents for some basic Workplace Shell operations.

Introducing Presentation Manager

By looking at figure 9.1, you can tell that the previously outlined CUA principles are fully effective. These principles probably seemed to be obvious, common-sense ideas when you first read about them. Now you have seen these principles put to use. The screen preserved the related display context, you received immediate feedback for each action you took, and you used the keyboard to perform actions that you may have believed would require a mouse. Not all application environments are as consistent, easy to learn, and easy to use as Presentation Manager and Workplace Shell.

Using the Keyboard in PM

In figure 9.1, the System Editor is the *active* window, and the desktop is an *inactive* window. To switch to another window and make the next window active, you can press Alt-Tab, or move the mouse cursor over the inactive window and click mouse button 1 once after the mouse cursor is in the inactive window. The keyboard and the mouse perform equivalent operations.

With the System Editor as the active window, press Alt to highlight the menu item labeled File in the upper left corner of the System Editor window. (If File isn't highlighted, you may have pressed the Alt key twice. Press Alt again.)

Now press the right-arrow key until you highlight the word Help and then press Enter. A menu appears (drops down) on-screen. Press the down-arrow key until you highlight the word Copyright; press Enter. These steps make the About dialog box (listing product information for OS/2) appear. Your screen should resemble figure 9.3. Press Enter to remove the About box from the screen.

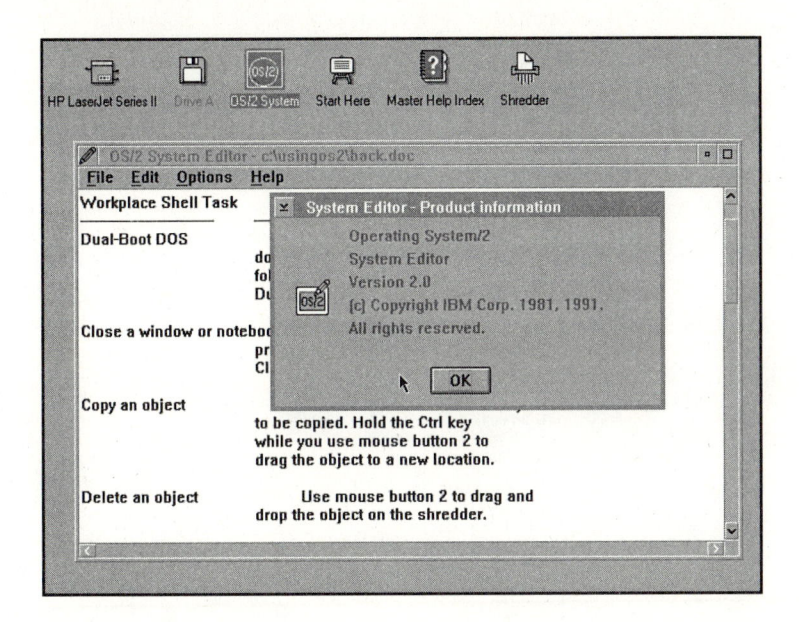

Fig. 9.3
The System Editor's About box.

You can move, maximize (to take up the entire screen), or minimize (to become icons) PM application windows. You learn more about these procedures in later sections of this chapter and in the following chapter. For now, just minimize the System Editor by pressing Alt-F9. The only objects left on the desktop are the icons.

To activate windows that you previously minimized to icons, press Ctrl-Esc. The Window List appears. Use the arrow keys to highlight the OS/2 System Editor entry in the Window List. Press Enter to bring the System Editor window to the foreground.

Now to make your screen look like figure 9.4, press Alt-space bar. You have activated the System Editor's pop-up system menu. (You can press Alt-space bar or Shift-Esc to invoke the pop-up system menu for the currently active window.)

To maximize the Editor window, press Alt-F10. To restore Editor to the former position and size, press Alt-F5. You can see that focusing on the current application (maximizing it), or making the window the same size as the other windows on-screen is a simple matter.

Fig. 9.4
The pop-up system menu.

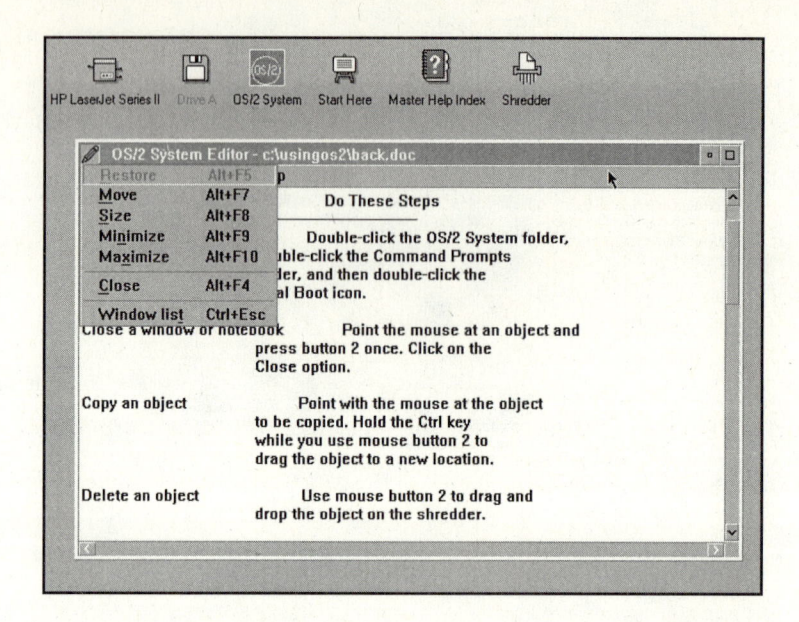

[Figure 9.4: Screenshot of the OS/2 System Editor window showing the pop-up system menu with options: Restore (Alt+F5), Move (Alt+F7), Size (Alt+F8), Minimize (Alt+F9), Maximize (Alt+F10), Close (Alt+F4), Window list (Ctrl+Esc). Desktop icons visible at top: HP LaserJet Series II, Drive A, OS/2 System, Start Here, Master Help Index, Shredder.]

Using the Mouse in PM

Up to this point, you have not used the mouse. You can use the keyboard or the mouse to perform the same operations, according to your preferences.

Study figure 9.1 again for a moment. The pencil icon in the upper left corner is the system menu icon. If you click the system menu icon, you activate the system menu. To deactivate the system menu, click mouse button 1 again.

In the upper right corner are the Minimize and Maximize icons. Clicking these icon causes the window to minimize or to take up the entire screen. In the latter case, the Maximize icon becomes a double arrow that you can use to restore the window to its former size.

> **Note**
>
> At various times and in various areas of the screen, the mouse cursor may change from an arrow into an I-beam, an hourglass, a cross, a hand, and other shapes. Each shape indicates a different mode for the application.

So far, you have concentrated on managing the desktop as a whole. In the following sections, you delve deeper by focusing on the interior of a Presentation Manager application window.

Understanding the Elements of a PM Window

Presentation Manager windows have elements in common: title bars, action (menu) bars, window borders, dialog boxes, and the Client Area. The following sections explain each element.

Title Bars. All Presentation Manager windows have a title bar, which contains the name of the application and sometimes the name of a file on which you are working. Some applications insert extra material in the title bar, such as the name of the file on which you are working.

When the screen contains several windows at the same time, title bars identify each window. As a result, title bars serve as your first line of defense against confusion on a cluttered screen.

Action Bars. Below the title bar all primary windows and many secondary windows offer *action bars* (known as *menu bars* in other applications).

Notice that for the System Editor, the action bar contains the words **F**ile, **E**dit, **O**ptions, and **H**elp. In each word, one character (for System Editor, the first character) of the word is underlined. When you use the keyboard to activate an item in the action bar, you press the Alt key and the underlined character; for example, press Alt and then E for the **E**dit item. The selection becomes a pull-down menu, an extension of the action bar item. The menu items you see for the **E**dit menu are **U**ndo, Cu**t**, **C**opy, **P**aste, Cl**e**ar, **F**ind, and Select **a**ll (see fig. 9.5). Some menu items appear in a shade of gray, which means these menu items are now unavailable. When you are ready to close the menu, press Alt or Esc.

You also can use the mouse to access the **E**dit menu by clicking the menu's name on the action bar. Then click to choose an option from the pulled-down menu.

Presentation Manager often gives you several ways to take the same action. With the System Editor, for example, you can choose the **C**opy option from the **E**dit pull-down menu with any of the following actions:

- Press Alt-E, C (the underlined letters in the menu and the option) to activate the command.

- Use the command's shortcut keystroke, Ctrl-Insert. (The shortcut is listed to the right of the command on the pulled-down menu.) With shortcut keystrokes, you don't have to access the menus.

Fig. 9.5
The System Editor, with the Edit menu pulled down.

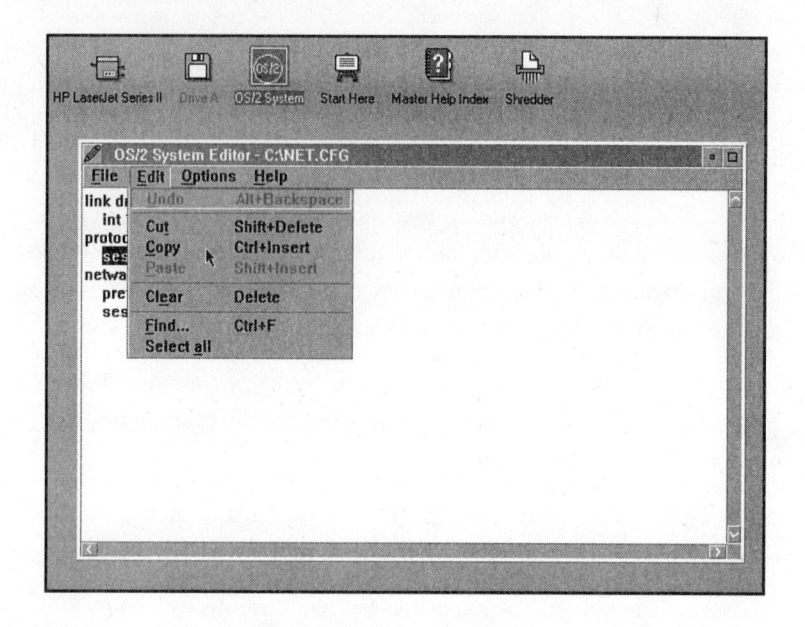

- After you pull down the Edit menu, use the arrow keys to highlight Copy and then press Enter. Alternatively, click the command.

The important thing to note about action bar menu items is that these items are consistent across all Presentation Manager applications. You used the System Editor in this example, but you just as easily can use a different utility or application.

Sizable Window Borders. So far, each window you have used has remained its original size, expanded to maximum size, or shrunk to an icon. You also can size each window the way you want, as discussed in this section. You can give a window virtually any dimensions you want.

By using the keyboard, you can size the currently active window by first pressing Alt-F8 and then using the arrow keys to move window borders inward or outward. By using the mouse, you move the mouse cursor directly over a window border until the cursor changes to a double-arrow shape. Then press mouse button 1 and drag the border until the window is the size you want it.

The Client Area. The body of a window inside the border and below the action bar is the client area. The *client area* is the workspace for viewing, entering, and selecting information.

Scroll Bars. Often, the information that an application presents to you exceeds the viewing area of the current window—vertically, horizontally, or in both directions. If you are faced with this situation, you can scroll the information on-screen. The presence of a horizontal or vertical *scroll bar* is a visual cue that more information is available, and that you can bring the unseen information into view.

Earlier in this chapter you saw and used scroll bars. If you look again at figure 9.5, you see scroll bars along the bottom and right side of the System Editor's client area. These scroll bars are *grayed* to indicate that no off-screen information is present. (If you are looking at a text file that is several lines long, the vertical scroll bar is darkened.)

In figure 9.1, however, the display of text in the System Editor window extends beyond the bottom of the window. The vertical scroll bar is active (not grayed) and you can use the up- and down-arrows and the Page Up and Page Down keys to see more of the directory list.

So far, you have become acquainted with the PM screen as a whole and have learned to manipulate objects and windows on this screen. Now, prepare to focus even more closely as you look at a type of secondary window known as the dialog box.

Working with Dialog Boxes

Most applications use pop-up windows, or *dialog boxes*, to gather information from the user. These secondary windows appear inside a primary window and contain a variety of information display, entry, and selection tools. Dialog boxes usually are movable and fixed in size. A menu option name followed by an ellipsis (for example, **O**pen...) calls up a dialog box or a secondary (cascaded) menu. Figure 9.6 shows the dialog box the System Editor uses to ask you which file you want to edit.

To bring up a dialog box, follow these steps:

1. From the System Editor window, press Alt-F to drop down the **F**ile menu.

2. Choose the **O**pen... menu command.

3. After you finish viewing the information in the dialog box, press Esc to close the dialog box.

Fig. 9.6
The System Editor dialog box for opening a file to edit.

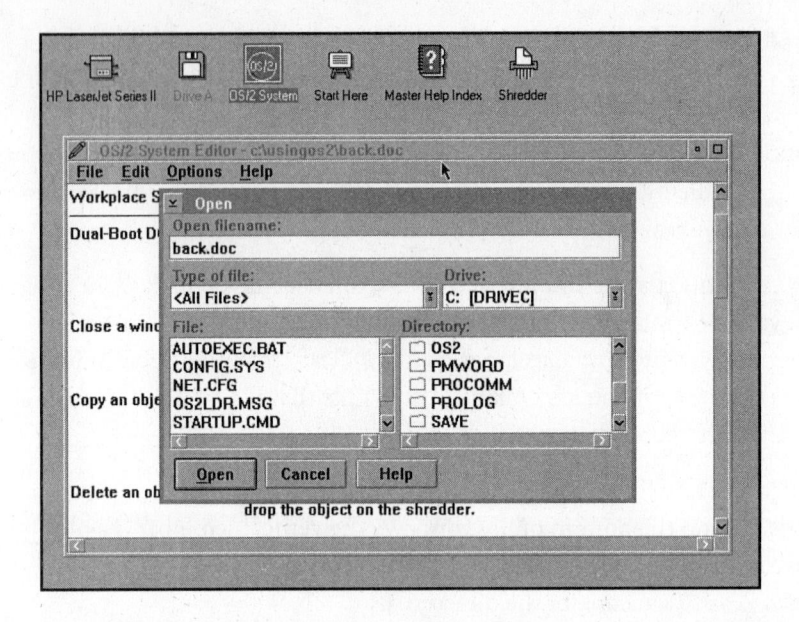

Title Bar and System Menu. Like most other windows, dialog boxes have title bars for easy identification. Some dialog boxes also have minimize/maximize icons and a system menu. Usually, the system menu for the dialog box contains only two menu items: **M**ove and **C**lose.

Buttons and Boxes. When an application directs you to specify a value (or select an option) from a list, the application displays a set of buttons. Beside or inside each button, you see a word or phrase that tells you what the button does.

You can use the mouse or the keyboard to choose a button. You can click the button with the mouse. If you're using the keyboard, press Tab and the arrow keys to move to the button you want to choose and then press the space bar. A button with a *selection highlight* (a visual emphasis) around it means that you now can choose this button.

In a dialog box, you can choose options marked with a pushbutton, radio button, spin button, slider box, or check box. Figure 9.7 shows the Autosave dialog box displayed by the System Editor. It contains pushbuttons, a spin button, and a check box.

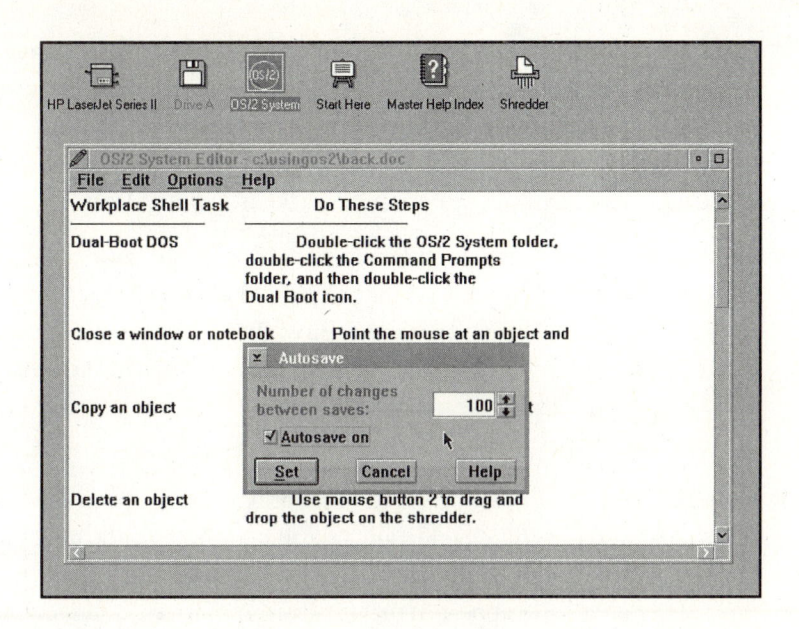

Fig. 9.7
The System Editor Autosave dialog box.

The various button types are described as follows:

- *Pushbutton.* The most common button, a pushbutton looks like a rectangle with rounded corners and text inside. When you choose a pushbutton, the application performs the indicated action. Figure 9.5 shows three pushbuttons: **O**pen, Cancel, and Help. If you choose the **O**pen button, the System Editor uses the other information in the dialog box, including the file name, to open a disk file for you to edit. The text you see in a pushbutton is application- and context-specific. You often see action-oriented words, such as OK, Accept, Save, Yes, and No.

- *Radio button.* Unlike pushbuttons, radio buttons don't cause the application to take immediate action. You use radio buttons to choose one of a mutually exclusive, fixed set of options. A radio button is a small circle with text beside it. When selected, the option has a partially filled-in circle.

- *Spin buttons.* Sometime you may need to make a choice from a consecutive list with values that don't all fit in the dialog box window. The application may use a spin button with which you can make your selection—for example, the months of the year or the hours in a day. The spin button shows the current value next to two icons and up and down arrows. Clicking the up arrow selects a previous item in the list;

clicking the down arrow selects the following item. (You also can activate the up and down buttons by pressing the up- and down-arrow keys.) This button is called a spin button because the current value "spins" if you continue to click the up or down buttons. The number of changes between saves option in figure 9.6 is a spin button.

- *Check boxes*. Pushbuttons cause immediate action, radio buttons select mutually exclusive options, and spin buttons change the current value from a range. To make one or many choices that are not mutually exclusive, you use check boxes. OS/2 displays a check mark in the *check box* when its corresponding option is selected. The **A**utosave on option in figure 9.6 is an example of a check box.

- *Slider box*. You already saw one kind of slider box when you explored scroll bars earlier in this chapter. On a scroll bar, the slider box shows you the relative position and size of the visible information in a window. Slider boxes also appear in dialog boxes so that you can select a value by positioning the slider within a range. The Mouse object (in the System Setup folder), for example, uses a slider box on the Timing page of its settings notebook to ask you how fast the mouse cursor should move.

List Boxes. Look at figure 9.6 again. The Open dialog box from the System Editor contains four list boxes (sometimes known as *selection lists*). Two of these boxes, Type of file and Drive, serve as drop-down list boxes and text boxes. The other two boxes, File and Directory, are ordinary list boxes. A list box contains a set of scrollable choices from which you can choose. You select one entry from the list with the mouse or the keyboard. The ordinary list box always shows the scrollable list, with the currently selected item highlighted in the list.

The drop-down list box shows the currently selected value in a separate text box. To pull down the list so that you can select a different value, you click the text box, or use Alt-down-arrow to display the list. You also can type the information in the text box.

Another kind of list box, the combination box, is a cross between the other two kinds of list boxes. The scrollable list always appears (it doesn't drop down). You make a selection from the list or you enter text in the text box.

Data Entry Fields. All the selection and data entry mechanisms you just covered assume that the application knows ahead of time what you may want to choose to enter. Of course, the computer cannot possibly know what you may type in the next memo or what name and phone number you may want to track next. For these kinds of situations, you use a special area on-screen known as an *entry field*. In figure 9.5, the Open filename text box is a data entry area.

One thing that the application does know about what you type in an entry field is the maximum number of characters you can type for the field. The application can gather your information from a single-line, nonscrollable entry field (much like the text box mentioned in the discussion on drop-down list boxes). The application also can offer a single-line text box that scrolls; if you reach the right side of the text box while you type, the characters to the far left disappear while you continue to type at the right edge of the text box. If the application is prepared to accept several lines of typed text, you may see a multiple-line entry field.

Of all the selection and data entry mechanisms you learned to identify, the entry field is one you sometimes see in a primary window client area, outside a dialog box.

Chapter Summary

This chapter showed you how to operate the basic elements of the Workplace Shell screen (the desktop) and a Presentation Manager application. You now should be able to understand the CUA principles on which PM is based, and identify and manipulate title bars, action bars, window borders, dialog boxes, and the client area in your PM windows. You also have learned how to drag and drop the objects on your OS/2 desktop.

In the next chapter, you learn more about "Managing Presentation Manager and the Workplace Shell."

For Related Information
- "Examining Presentation Manager," p. 14
- "Using the OS/2 Editors," p. 346
- "Mastering Basic Editing Techniques," p. 347
- "Understanding the System Editor Menus," p. 356
- "Learning Commands Shared by Most General Purpose Applets," p. 547

Chapter 10
Managing the Workplace Shell

The Workplace Shell is OS/2's graphical interface. As you learned in Chapter 9, the Shell resembles a desktop covered with objects. Nothing is mysterious about these objects; the items are just things you use to work. On a real desk, a memo and a manila folder are objects. The Workplace Shell has many objects that look and work like the things with which you are familiar, such as notebooks and a paper shredder. Because the Workplace Shell uses the 1991 Common User Access standard, you can work these objects (and also the desktop) with the keyboard or the mouse, or both. Because this interface is consistent, the way you work with one object carries over to the other objects.

In this chapter, you gain hands-on experience working with three main kinds of objects: programs, data files, and folders. Folders contain other objects, so these folders help you organize the way you work with information.

Each kind of object appears initially as an icon—a small picture that tells you something about the object. You learn how to do many things by working directly with icons. To erase a file, for example, you can click the related icon with the mouse, and drag and drop the icon on the Shredder.

When you use an object, a window on the desktop usually opens. Several windows can be open at the same time. You can change each window's size and location, and you can move between windows. After working through this chapter's examples step by step, you will know how to arrange the desktop to best fit the way you work.

You also learn how to personalize the Workplace Shell. You can control how fast the mouse moves and how fast a key repeats when held down. You find out how to choose the fonts you like best and change the color of all parts of the windows on-screen. If solid colors seem too plain, you even can put a picture in each window.

If you previously installed DOS and Windows applications, you can still use these applications. This chapter shows how to put these applications on the desktop by default.

IBM designed the Workplace Shell to be easy to learn and easy to use. If you previously used a graphical interface like Windows, you may notice that many things are easier to do in the Workplace Shell. When you want to change a program's settings, for example, you don't have to open the Windows PIF Editor and type the program's name. Instead, just click mouse button 2 on the program's icon. Invest the time to work through this chapter at the computer, and all these procedures soon will become second nature.

Working with Program Objects

Everything on the Workplace Shell desktop, even programs, is an object. The best way to become familiar with objects is to use them. In this section you start with a useful program object—the System Clock.

Starting a Program Object

When you start OS/2 for the first time, the Workplace Shell desktop is clear except for a few icons. One icon, called OS/2 System, contains many other objects. Open this icon and look inside. If you're using a mouse, move the mouse cursor to OS/2 System and double-click with mouse button 1. If you prefer to use the keyboard, use the arrow keys to move the cursor to OS/2 System and press Enter.

Inside OS/2 System, an icon labeled System Setup looks like a keyboard, mouse, and screen combined. Open System Setup like you did OS/2 System. Now, find and open the System Clock object. A window appears on-screen with a clock inside.

Displaying an Object's System Menu

Every program object has a system menu from which you control the program. To use the clock's system menu, move the mouse cursor to the clock and click mouse button 2, or press and release the Alt key.

Working with Program Objects   247

The screen should look like figure 10.1. Actually, two menus are available. These menus are *cascaded* because one menu flows from the other in a cascade. On the main menu, Window is already selected for you because this choice is probably where you want to start most of the time. The arrow to the right of Window means that a cascade menu listing several things you can do with the clock window is available. For now, you focus on the Window menu.

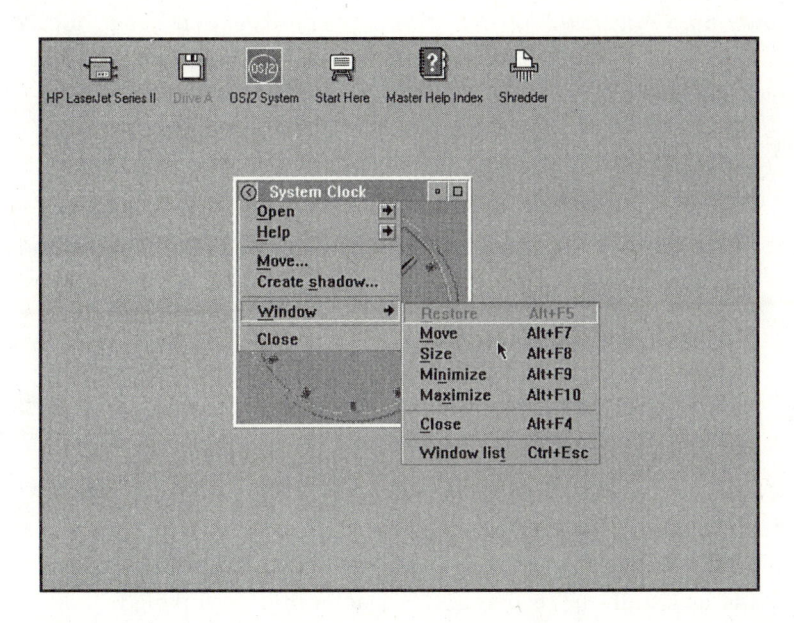

Fig. 10.1
The System Clock and its system menu.

Maximizing a Window. To expand the clock to fill the whole screen, you can maximize it (or any other icon) in the following ways:

- With the mouse button 1, click Ma**x**imize from the system menu.

- Press X. (X is the underlined letter in the word Ma**x**imize.) M would be easier to remember, but **M** already stands for **M**ove. Fortunately, Workplace Shell applications are consistent, and X always means Maximize on every application Window menu.

- Hold down Alt and press F10. You need not memorize this keystroke combination, because you always see the combination listed on the **W**indow menu beside the Ma**x**imize option.

- Double-click mouse button 1 on the clock's title bar, the shaded area at the top of the window that says System Clock. This method is faster than other ways because you can click at any time without first popping up the **W**indow menu.

- Click once with mouse button 1 on the Maximize button. This button has a large square and is located in the upper right corner of the window.

Minimizing a Window. You can go to the opposite extreme and shrink the window to an icon. As with maximizing, you can minimize a window in the following ways:

- Pop up the **W**indow menu, and click with mouse button 1 on the word Mi**n**imize.

- While the **W**indow menu is displayed, press the N key. N is the underlined letter in Mi**n**imize.

- Hold down Alt and press F9.

- Click once with mouse button 1 on the Minimize button. This button contains a small square and is located to the left of the Maximize button.

By default, a minimized window disappears into the Minimized Window Viewer. You can restore the window on your desktop by double-clicking the icon in the Minimized Window Viewer, or you can click the object's name in the Window List. In the section of this chapter titled "Working with Minimized Views," you learn how to minimize objects into icons that remain on your desktop.

Restoring a Window to Original Size. To reset the window to original size and position, choose **R**estore from the **W**indow menu. You can move the highlight to **R**estore and press Enter, but just pressing R is easier. Alt-F5 produces the same result.

To restore a maximized window with the mouse, two quick ways are available. When you maximize the clock window by clicking the Maximize button, the button changes to a Restore button, which looks like a picture of a medium-size square between two vertical lines. Click this button to restore the window to the original state. Or if you prefer, double-click the title bar in the maximized window to restore it to original size.

Moving a Window. Another choice on the **W**indow menu is **M**ove. Choose **M**ove and you can reposition the window anywhere by moving the arrow keys or the mouse. The shortcut key for **M**ove is Alt-F7.

If you're using a mouse, you have an easier way to choose **M**ove. Follow these steps:

1. Click either mouse button on the window's title bar.

2. Position the window to the desired location on-screen by moving the mouse while you hold the button down. This *drags* the window to its new location.

3. Release the mouse button when the window is at the desired location.

Resizing a Window. To change the clock window's size by using the keyboard, follow these steps:

1. Choose **S**ize from the **W**indow menu, or press Alt-F8.

2. Move either the arrow keys or the mouse. The mouse cursor changes to a double arrow.

3. Press Enter or click a mouse button when the window is the size you want.

You may find resizing windows an easier task by using the mouse directly, without going through the **W**indow menu. First, move the mouse cursor to any edge or corner of the window, and notice that the cursor changes to a double arrow. Hold down either mouse button to grab the window frame at this spot, move the mouse to get the exact window size you want, and then release the button.

Closing a Window. To close a window, click **C**lose or press **C** while the Window menu is displayed. Alt-F4 is the shortcut keystroke. The mouse shortcut is to double-click the Menu button, which is in the upper left corner of the window.

When you close the System Clock, the program ends, and the clock vanishes. If you experiment with closing a window now, remember that you must open the clock again before you go on to the following section, which tells how to change the clock display to suit your personal preferences.

For Related Information
- "Examining Presentation Manager," p. 14
- "Understanding How OS/2 Expands upon DOS," p. 62

Viewing an Object in Different Ways

You usually place a clock so that you can view the time. If you want to change the time, however, you turn the clock around to see the knobs on the back. Workplace Shell objects like the System Clock work in the same way. To change an object's display, you open a view of the object's Settings.

Viewing the Settings Notebook

To open a view of the object's Settings, follow these steps:

1. Move the clock to the far right side of the screen so that it is still visible in the background when you open the settings notebook.

2. Click the mouse button 2 on the clock. The System Clock main menu appears, with the **O**pen option at the top of the menu.

   To the right of **O**pen, you see an arrow button, which means that more than one way to open the clock program exists—more than one view is available.

3. Move the highlight to **O**pen and press the right-arrow key, or just click the arrow button.

   A cascaded menu appears, giving you a choice between Settings and Program. These selections are available for all Workplace Shell program objects. The check mark next to Program means that starting the program is the default.

4. Choose Settings. The settings notebook appears.

5. Resize this window so that you can also see the open program view of the clock, as shown in figure 10.2. The notebook contains several pages grouped in sections, and each section has a tab—just like a real notebook.

6. Choose the **V**iew tab, either by clicking mouse button 1 on the tab, or by flipping the pages with Alt-PgDn or Alt-PgUp.

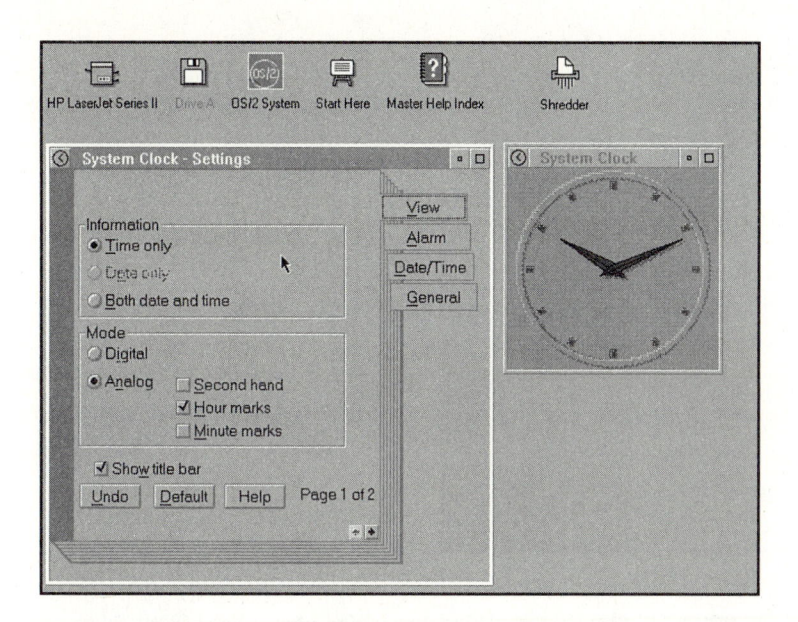

Fig. 10.2
The System Clock's Program and Settings Views.

Experimenting with Different Settings

The first page in the View section, as shown in figure 10.2, enables you to change the clock from an analog (a round clock face with hands) to a digital (numeric) face. Click D**i**gital, or use the arrow keys to select the button and press Enter. Two things happen immediately. The clock changes to a digital display; and in the settings notebook, options that don't apply to digital clocks, such as showing the second hand, are *grayed*. You still can see the grayed options faintly, but clicking them does nothing. This condition is typical of the Workplace Shell; changing an option produces a visible effect instantly. You don't have to close Settings to see the effect.

The View screen says Page 1 of 2. To go to the next page under the View tab, press Ctrl-PgDn or click the right-arrow button at the bottom of the page. Experiment with different fonts and colors. You can display the available choices by clicking the *spin buttons*—the buttons with an arrow that points downward. To activate a spin button from the keyboard, highlight the button and press Alt-down arrow.

The System Clock also is an alarm clock. You can set alarms by choosing the **A**larm tab in the settings notebook. The **D**ate/Time tab enables you to change the date and time. Experiment with these tabs now if you want. Remember, however, that the computer remembers new times or dates that you set, even after you turn off the power.

Chapter 10—Managing the Workplace Shell

For Related Information
- "Configuring Your Desktop," p. 178
- "Using the Workplace Shell," p. 231
- "Understanding the Enhanced Editor Menus," p. 362
- "Learning OS/2 Printer Basics," p. 375
- "Adding DOS Programs," p. 397
- "Understanding CUA Principles," p.230
- "Introducing Presentation Manager," p. 234

Undoing Changes

What happens if you change several settings on a page in the notebook and then decide that you prefer your previous settings? To cancel all the changes you just made, choose the **U**ndo button. To restore all options to the way you originally set them when you installed OS/2, use the **D**efault button.

Moving between Windows

By now, the desktop may be getting cluttered. The clock's settings notebook takes up much of the screen, hiding the objects beneath. To use the other open windows, you need a way to bring the windows to the top of the screen. Alt-Esc performs this job.

By pressing Alt-Esc repeatedly, you can move through all the different object views currently open on the desktop. When you move to each view, the related window appears on the top of the stack. As long as you also can see part of a window in the background, you can click the window to bring it to the top.

What happens if you close the OS/2 System folder? Should this step terminate the clock because it's contained in the folder? Many people may expect the clock to stay open, so this result is what normally happens. Later in this chapter, you learn how to change this default behavior.

For now, tidy up the screen by closing any open folders, and then minimize both open views of the clock. Alt-Esc still moves between the minimized views and by default does not restore them to the original size. Instead, this key combination shows the related system menus, and you can choose to restore the views or pick any other action you want.

Having two minimized icons may seem odd—especially if you have used another graphical interface previously. After all, only one clock exists. The explanation is that the clock is an object, and you can never actually see an object directly; you can see only a *view* of the object. The icons symbolize two different views of the clock object. This state is different from the way many other systems work. If you haven't used another interface, however, this state probably seems completely natural.

Using the Window List

At any time, you can pop up a special menu known as the Window List by pressing Ctrl-Esc. Pop up this menu, and you see a list of every open view of an object. First comes the object's name—for example, System Clock. Indented beneath this list item are the two open views—Program and Settings.

Choosing an Object View

The object view that was active when you popped up the Window List is highlighted. You can move the highlight to any other view with the up- and down-arrow keys. If you press Enter, the highlighted view surfaces on the desktop, and the Window list disappears. You also can choose a view from the Window List by double-clicking mouse button 1 on it. If you press Esc or click anywhere outside the Window List, the Window List vanishes.

A special menu for each view is available from the Window List. To display the menu, move the highlight to a view with the up- and down-arrow keys and press Shift-F10. To display a menu by using the mouse, click mouse button 2 on any view.

The menu that you pop up within the Window List is different from the view's system menu. The first choice the menu lists is Show. This does the same thing as Restore on the system menu; the name is different so that you do not confuse the two menus. The second choice, Hide, does the same thing as Minimize on the system menu.

Displaying More Than One Open View of an Object

The Tile and Cascade options are useful when you have multiple views of an object open, such as the clock's Program and Settings. The Tile and Cascade options arrange the different views either side by side with no overlap, like tiles, or in an overlapped, cascaded stack. The best way to see this is to try it. First, show both views of the clock, because Tile and Cascade do nothing if minimized. Next, pop up the Window List and select System Clock, either by clicking it with mouse button 1 or by moving there with the arrow keys. This highlights not only the clock object, but also both its open views. Pop up the menu by using Shift-F10 or mouse button 2, and choose Cascade. Try the same thing with Tile.

You also can close a view of an object from the menu in the Window List. A Help selection is available as well, in case you get lost. Some of these items will not be present on the menu for certain objects. The desktop itself shows

For Related Information
- "Examining Presentation Manager," p. 14

up on the Window List, for example, but you cannot close it. Think of it this way: you can close a folder and put it away, but you cannot close the top of the desk. The menu offers only the choices that make sense for the current object.

The Window List is especially handy for keyboard users. You also can pop up the List with the mouse by clicking both buttons at the same time on any blank part of the desktop.

Summarizing What You Have Learned So Far

Now that you are halfway through this chapter, take a break and review what you have learned. You saw how to open a folder, or start a program, by double-clicking its icon. This opens a window, giving you a view of the object. You know how to rearrange windows, change their size, and move between them. And you have learned how to view and use an object's settings notebook. In the next section, you see that you can work with objects without even opening them.

Manipulating Icons

Remember how the Workplace Shell desktop looked when you first started the system? It was blank except for a few icons at the top. Icons are graphical representations of objects, and you can do lots of things with them without opening them first. You already learned how to open a view of an object by double-clicking its icon. This section shows several other things you can do with the icons on the desktop and inside folders.

The documentation calls these actions *direct manipulations* because you are dealing directly with the icon instead of going through menus. Each form of direct manipulation gives you a distinctive kind of visual feedback.

Before you start exploring, clear off the desktop by closing all views of the clock. Then open the OS/2 System folder as you did earlier, so that you have a selection of icons to experiment with—some on the desktop, and others in the folder.

Selecting an Icon

Click any icon once to select it. Selecting does not actually do anything to the object. Instead, it means that the next action you take will apply to that object. Pressing Enter, for example, opens any object you select. The Workplace Shell gives you immediate visual feedback by highlighting the icon you select in gray. The documentation calls this *selection emphasis*.

With the keyboard, you can select an icon by moving to it with the arrow keys. Because OS/2 System is the currently open folder, however, the keys move only among the icons the folder contains. To select an icon on the desktop, use Window List to show the desktop.

Opening a View

You have already learned how to open a view. Press Enter to open a view of the currently selected object. Double-clicking mouse button 1 on an icon selects and opens the icon. The icon gets *in-use emphasis*—a horizontally shaded pattern that tells you at a glance which objects are open.

Popping Up the System Menu

As mentioned previously, clicking mouse button 2 on an icon brings up the icon's related system menu. Selecting the icon first isn't necessary.

Moving an Object

The following procedure is the first of several direct manipulations that you haven't yet used. To move an icon, press and hold down mouse button 2 on an icon while you move the mouse. This is called *dragging*. The icon moves on-screen with the movement of the mouse cursor.

Drag the Information icon to an empty place on the desktop and release the mouse button. The icon is placed there. You can arrange the icons in any way you like.

You also can move objects between folders. Drag the Information icon to an empty spot inside the OS/2 System folder. Drop the icon. The original icon on the desktop vanishes and reappears inside the folder.

You can perform the same process by dragging Information onto the OS/2 System icon. First, drag the Information icon back to the desktop and drop it. Then drag the Information icon to the OS/2 System icon and drop it on top. This icon again vanishes from the desktop and appears inside the folder.

Creating a Copy of an Object

Making a copy of an object is like putting a memo through a copy machine. You get a new object that appears to be an exact duplicate of the original, but the two are distinct. To copy an object, follow these steps:

1. Hold down the Alt key.
2. Drag the icon to any blank spot on the desktop or in a folder.
3. Drop the icon; then release the Alt key.

When you move the icon, the on-screen representation looks dimmer than usual, which gives you visual feedback that a copy is in progress.

Creating a Shadow of an Object

A shadow is a great deal like a copy, except that the shadow is just an alias for the original object. Like a reflection in a mirror, the shadow has no independent existence of its own. The advantage of using shadows rather than copies is that these objects don't take disk space, and copies do use disk space. You can delete a shadow without affecting the original object.

If you want a program object to run (execute) when you boot your computer, you can make a shadow of the object and move the shadow to the Startup folder. You also might put shadows of the objects you open and close frequently during the day right on your desktop. This makes the objects immediately accessible, yet leaves the original in an appropriate folder. You don't have to move such an object onto the desktop, then later move the object back to its proper folder.

You may have noticed that you cannot open two identical views of the same object. You cannot have, for example, two program views of a single System Clock. If you want two clocks, make a shadow of the original and open the shadow.

You create a shadow the same way you make a copy, but you hold down the Ctrl and Shift keys instead of the Alt key. To emphasize the difference, the Workplace Shell draws a line that connects the original icon to the shadow icon while you move the mouse.

The result of a drag operation—move, copy, or shadow—actually depends on whether you are holding down Alt or Shift and Ctrl when you release the icon. Holding down these keys isn't necessary when you start the operation, but the visual feedback, like the line connecting the original object to a shadow that you create, depends on the current state of these keys.

Dropping One Icon on Another

Dropping an icon on top of another icon is one of the Workplace Shell's most exciting features. As you saw previously, you can move an object to a folder by dropping the object on the folder's icon. This procedure works even if the folder isn't open. To print an object, drop the object on the printer icon. To delete an object, drop the object on the Shredder. OS/2 applications may enable you to drag a number from a phone book, drop the number on a telephone icon, and have the application place a call.

Suppose that you copied the System Setup object from the OS/2 System folder to the desktop. As mentioned earlier, the copy operation wastes considerable disk space. To clean up the disk, drag and drop the copy from the desktop to the Shredder. Be careful that you shred only the copy, not the original. If you made a Shadow, the shadow disappears when you shred the original object.

As another experiment, drop the OS/2 System icon on the icon for the Master Help Index. You see a circle with a bar through it, similar to a *do not enter* road sign. Master Help Index is a program, not a folder, and dropping the system on a program makes no sense. The *do not enter* symbol tells you that dropping the icon here has no effect.

Canceling a Move, Copy, or Shadow Operation

When dragging an icon, you may change your mind and decide not to complete the operation. If so, just press the Esc key before you drop the icon.

Changing an Object's Name

You can change the name of any object by typing the new name in the Title box, which comes under the **G**eneral tab of the related settings notebook. A shortcut is available for mouse users. Hold down Alt and click mouse button 1, either on the icon or on the Title bar of an open view. Backspace over the old name, type the new name, and then click the icon or title bar.

Working with Minimized Views

When you minimize an open view, it becomes a special kind of icon, which is surrounded by a gray box to emphasize that the view is open. Because you are working with a view and not an object, most direct manipulations don't work. You can only move the view or pop up the related system menu. You cannot create a copy or shadow, and dropping a view on another icon, such as the Shredder, has no effect.

Performing a Select, Move, Copy, or Shadow Operation with the Keyboard

Keyboard users cannot perform direct manipulation, but several operations can be done indirectly with the keyboard. These options are available as choices on an object's system menu.

Take a moment to review direct manipulation. Following chapters explain the results of dropping icons on the Printer or the Editor. The following section of this chapter discusses the system menu for Folder objects, which includes the desktop.

For Related Information
- "Examining Presentation Manager," p. 14
- "Understanding CUA Principles," p. 230
- "Introducing Presentation Manager," p. 234

Using a Folder's System Menu

Earlier in this chapter, you studied the system menu for the System Clock program object—especially the cascaded menus for Open and Window. The OS/2 System folder open on the desktop now has a system menu specific to the folder, which contains these options and also some new ones. You just covered several of the options, which are keyboard equivalents for direct manipulation with the mouse. An option to arrange icons also is available, and Open has new selections on the related cascaded menu.

First, you need to know how to pop up a folder's system menu. Keyboard users can press and release the Alt key to perform this step. Mouse users can click with mouse button 2 on any blank spot inside the folder or with either button on the menu box in the upper left corner of the window.

Arranging Icons by Default

In a random order, move around a few of the icons in the OS/2 System folder's pop-up menu inside the folder. Now, pop up the folder's system menu and select Arrange. The icons are placed in a tidy straight line.

Next, choose Resize to change the folder from a short, wide window to a tall, narrow window, so that you no longer see one or two of the icons. A scroll bar appears at the bottom of the window. You can use the scroll bar to scroll to the other icons, but a better way is available. Select Arrange again; the icons are placed regularly within the window so that you see all the icons at one time (providing that the window is large enough), and the scroll bar vanishes.

Changing Folder Settings

After you open the settings notebook for the OS/2 System folder, you see options that weren't available for program objects. Some of these options are advanced settings normally used by programmers, but you may find some of the other icons helpful.

Under Format on the View page, you see the following three settings:

- *Flowed* arranges icons in straight rows and columns.
- *Non-Flowed* puts all icons in a single column.
- *Non-Grid* enables you to place icons anywhere in the window. Non-Grid is the default.

The three radio buttons under Icon Display enable you to make icons large, small, or invisible. If you choose Invisible, the names of objects are displayed on-screen, but no icons appear next to them. Invisible icons are unavailable with the Non-Grid arrangement.

The final option on the View page enables you to change the font for the names of objects. You can choose different typefaces, styles, and sizes. Just for fun, try the Symbol Set font.

Changing the Window Background

If the normal gray background seems unexciting, flip to the Background tab and choose a different color. By choosing Change Color, you call up the Color Editor and design your own background. Drab solid colors generally work best, but choose whatever background fits your mood.

If you prefer to see a picture, select Image. If you copied pictures included with the system during installation, or if you created pictures with the built-in paint program, you can choose from these pictures. Try drawing a simple picture and then select Scaled Image 10x10. The window becomes tiled with little copies of the drawing.

For Related Information
- "Using the Workplace Shell," p.231

Using the Workplace Shell's System Menu

Because the Workplace Shell desktop also is a folder, it has a system menu. Although you don't usually see an icon for the desktop, you can get to this menu by clicking mouse button 2 on any blank spot on the desktop.

Using the keyboard is only a little more difficult. To open the Workplace Shell's system menu using the keyboard, follow these steps:

1. Pop up the Window List by pressing Ctrl-Esc.

2. Select Desktop, and press Enter.

3. Press the space bar to unselect the current icon.

4. Hold down Shift, press F10, and release both keys.

You see a menu slightly different from the system menu for other folders. The Copy, Move, and Window choices are unavailable because using these choices with the desktop makes no sense. Two extra choices that appear nowhere else are found here—Lockup and Shutdown. You need to understand how to use Shutdown, but Lockup is optional.

Locking Up the System

The computer may contain confidential files that you don't want others to examine if you step away from the computer. The LOCKUP command on the Workplace Shell's system menu provides simple protection. When you choose this option, you are asked to type a password, which can be anything you want. You type the password twice, just to ensure that you don't misspell the word accidentally.

The screen is replaced by the OS/2 logo, and a picture of a padlock appears. When you return, type the password to restore the desktop.

If you forget the password, you can restart the system by turning the power off and back on again. Of course, anyone can access the computer by flipping the power switch. If the files are really sensitive, save them on a floppy disk that you can lock in a drawer or carry with you.

Shutting Down the System

Shutting down a DOS system is easy. Just turn off the computer. Avoid taking this step with OS/2, however; instead, always use Shutdown from the Workplace Shell's system menu.

By default, OS/2 doesn't always write data to the hard disk immediately, even when you save a file. OS/2 waits until you or the programs aren't working the computer very much and then writes the data during slack times. By performing an orderly shutdown, you ensure that all open files are closed properly and saved. Shutdown also saves the state of the Workplace Shell, so that when you turn on the computer again, the screen you saw at Shutdown is the same screen you see when you re-enter OS/2.

When you use Shutdown, you may notice some disk activity. A message asks you to wait a few seconds for the activity to finish. You then see a `Shutdown has completed` message telling you that you can safely turn off the power.

Although a reliable system, OS/2 also is large and complex. No system this big is completely free of bugs. If you encounter a severe bug, the system may lock up so that you cannot even perform a shutdown. If this error occurs, wait for a minute to see if the system comes back by itself. If not, hold down the Alt and Ctrl keys at the same time, press Del, and then release all three keys. OS/2 tries to close all open files and then reboot. You also can try pressing Alt-Esc repeatedly; this sometimes will bring control back. If neither of these methods works, the only remaining option is to turn off the power.

If you have to turn off the system without running Shutdown, the CHKDSK program runs immediately after you turn back on the computer. Chances are good that CHKDSK can recover from any damage. For more information, see the instructions for CHKDSK in this book's Command Reference section.

Saving the Arrangement of Open Objects on the Desktop

When you use Shutdown, all open objects on the desktop are saved in the Startup folder, which is inside OS/2 System. The next time you turn on the system, these objects reappear in the same locations. You may never need to do anything with this folder directly because it works automatically. If you want, however, you can drag and drop extra objects into the Startup folder. To try this, use a Shadow (hold down Ctrl and Shift when you drop the object). This step leaves the object in the original location so that you can still use it without opening the Startup folder. Use Shadow rather than Copy because Copy creates a duplicate of the object, which takes up disk space.

Congratulations! You now have learned everything you need to know about running the Workplace Shell. The following section shows several settings you may want to change to fit your personal preferences.

For Related Information
- "Configuring Your Desktop," p. 178

Customizing the Workplace Shell

After studying the previous parts of this chapter, you should feel comfortable working with the Workplace Shell. Now that you have learned how to use the system the way it was installed, you are ready to explore ways to personalize the system to suit your tastes. The System Setup folder inside OS/2 System has objects that enable you to customize many details. Most of these objects have only one view—Settings. Experiment with these objects when each is discussed in the following sections.

The Mouse

The tabs in the Mouse object's settings notebook cover several aspects of using the mouse:

- *Timing* controls how fast the cursor moves when you move the mouse, and how quickly you need to double-click.

- *Setup* gives you a choice between right- and left-handed mouse operation.

- *Mappings* enables you to pick a custom combination of mouse clicks and Alt, Shift, and Ctrl keys for the different kinds of direct manipulation.

> **Caution**
>
> You should not touch these default settings if you share a computer with another person.

The Keyboard

The following Keyboard object options enable you to change the speed of the keyboard and to customize the actions that the keys perform:

- *Timing* enables you to adjust the rate at which a key repeats when held down. A short delay occurs before the key starts to repeat; you can customize this delay. You also can make the cursor blink slower or faster.

- *Mappings* is similar to the Mouse Settings tab of the same name.

- *Special needs* gives you several options that may help if you find certain keyboard actions uncomfortable. If you cannot easily hold down the Shift key and press Tab to move backward, for example, you can make Shift *sticky*, which means that you get the desired effect when you press and then release Shift, and then press and release Tab.

The System Object

The System object enables you to customize the appearance of all windows on-screen and to control the safety feature that asks you for confirmation when you drop an object on the Shredder.

- *Confirmations* determines whether you get a last chance to change your mind when deleting an object or folder. You probably want to leave this option turned on.

- *Window* enables you to turn off the *exploding window* graphical effect you see when you open a window. Window also controls whether minimized object views are visible as icons on the desktop, and whether opening a minimized icon restores the original view or opens a fresh copy.

- *Logos* gives you control over the menu button at the upper left corner of a window. If you don't want a miniature copy of the icon to appear here, you can turn off the menu button. You can even tell logos displayed by applications to show for a number of specified seconds and then to disappear, or not appear at all.

The Sound and Country Objects

The Sound object has only one useful tab—Warning Beep. If you don't like the beep, turn it off here.

The Country object enables you to tell the system in what country you live. Numbers, times, and dates are displayed in the format of that country.

The Palettes

A *palette* is the thin board that painters use for mixing colors. Using the Color Palette, you can mix colors to use with Workplace Shell objects. You can pick a color or design your own. If you drag the color somewhere, the mouse cursor turns into a picture of a paint roller. If you drop the color on the title bar of an open window, for example, the bar turns that color.

The Scheme Palette, similar to the Color Palette, works with an entire color scheme at one time. Dragging and dropping the Scheme Palette on a window sets different colors for the border, title bar, text, background, and other areas. You can choose from preset color schemes named for the seasons of the year, or you can design custom color schemes.

264   Chapter 10—Managing the Workplace Shell

For Related Information
- "Installing Features Selectively," p. 176
- "Configuring Your Desktop," p. 178

What the Color and Scheme palettes do for color, the Font Palette does for fonts. You can pick from, and change the size of, any of the previously installed fonts.

Setting Up Other Applications

The Workplace Shell includes objects for all related built-in applications, but you also probably use some other applications. You can add other applications in two ways: automatic and manual. Automatic setup was an option when you installed OS/2, but if you didn't choose the automatic setup when you installed OS/2, you can run this setup now.

Migrating DOS and Windows Applications

To set up icons for your DOS and Windows applications in the Workplace Shell, open the Migrate Applications object in the OS/2 System folder. This program creates two new folders, one folder each for DOS and Windows programs, searches the hard disk for applications, and enables you to choose the programs you want to put in the folders. When you open the folders, you find the chosen programs ready to use.

Applications written before OS/2 Version 2.0 cannot take full advantage of all the Workplace Shell's features. Many software companies, however, are writing new OS/2 versions of the old programs that will work better with the new interface.

Creating Folders

You probably want to arrange your favorite applications to fit the way you work. Suppose that you want to make a new folder for word processing. All you have to do is open the Templates object and drag the Folder template onto the desktop. As you may have guessed, Templates contains a model for each kind of Workplace Shell object. Whether you move or copy a template—or create a shadow—doesn't matter. Dragging a template always creates a new, empty object.

Using the techniques you learned previously, customize the new folder any way you like. You at least want to give the folder a name. Putting a shadow of your word processor into the new folder makes sense. You also can store memos in the folder; this procedure is shown in a following section. First, however, you should know about another useful option on the folder's Settings view.

Go to the File tab in the new folder's Settings and click Work Area. Now, whenever you close this folder, every open object it contains—for example, the word processing program—also closes. When you open the folder again, every object inside is restored to the last view. You may want to drag in and customize a printer object for the document settings you use.

The following section shows how to find programs and documents on the hard disk. You can put shadows of these files in the new folder you just created.

Using the Drives Object

Migrate Applications recognizes most popular programs, but may miss one of your favorites. You can fix this oversight by finding the program yourself.

Open Drives in the OS/2 System folder and double-click the drive you want to examine. A good place to start is drive C (usually, the main hard disk), but you can choose any drive. A folder with an icon of a hard disk appears; click the plus sign beside the icon to see more detail.

Figure 10.3 shows the Tree View of the directories on the hard disk. Directories are the same thing as folders, and indeed the directory icons are pictures of folders. This is the way your hard disk looks to the Workplace Shell—folders and icons.

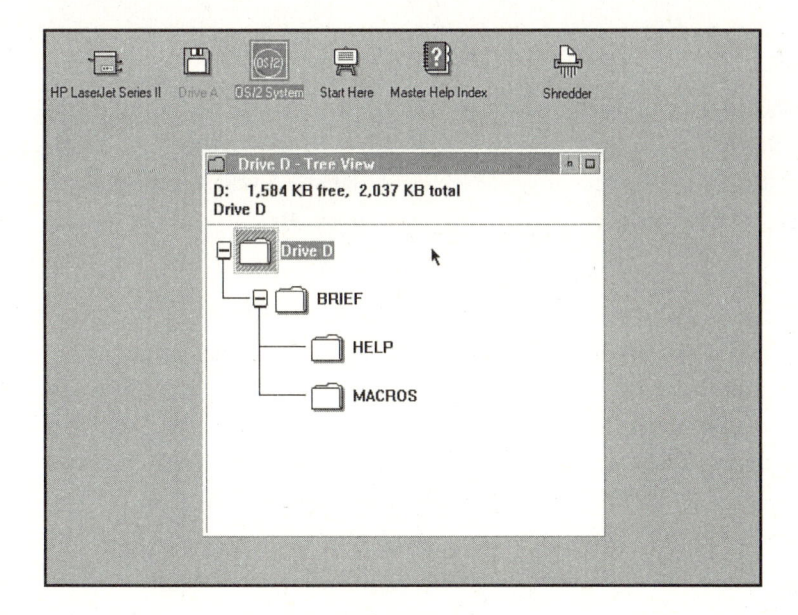

Fig. 10.3
The Tree view of a Drive object.

Chapter 10—Managing the Workplace Shell

To examine the contents of any folder, you double-click the folder. Figure 10.4 shows the Details View of the files contained in the folder. This list shows the name and size of each file, and tells when you saved the file. You can perform direct manipulations (drag-and-drop, for example) with the icons that you see on the left side of the list.

Fig. 10.4
The Details view of a Drive object.

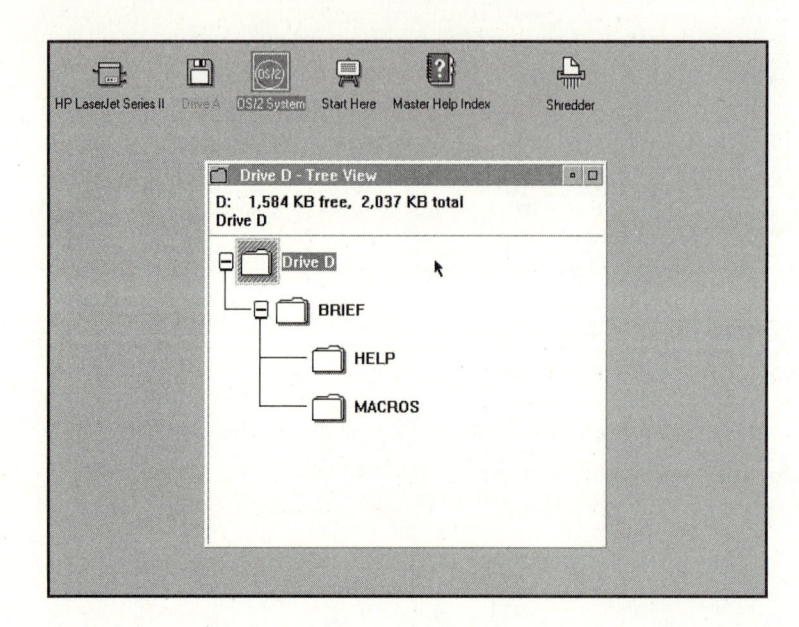

For Related Information
- "Choosing the OS/2 Features You Want," p. 139
- "Installing Features Selectively," p. 176
- "Associating a File with an Application," p. 292
- "Adding DOS Programs," p. 397

Suppose that you want to put a word processor program and documents into the folder you just created. Just drag shadows of these objects from Drives and drop them on the folder. Remember that shadows are better than copies because these items don't consume extra disk space.

The system menus for Drives objects have a Check Disk option. This diagnoses disk problems and draws a chart that shows how the disk is used and how much space is available. From time to time, run Check Disk, especially if you turn off the computer without first performing a complete Shutdown. For information on fixing disk problems, see the CHKDSK command in the Command Reference. Chapter 8, "Troubleshooting OS/2," also discusses using the CHKDSK command to repair disk problems.

Chapter Summary

In this chapter, you mastered the Workplace Shell. You learned how to arrange and customize the desktop to suit your preferences. This graphical interface is object-oriented. You choose an object, decide what to do with it, and receive immediate feedback. You briefly explored the Drives object in this chapter. The next chapter, "Using the Drives Object," explains many more ways you can use the Drives object to manage your work.

Part IV

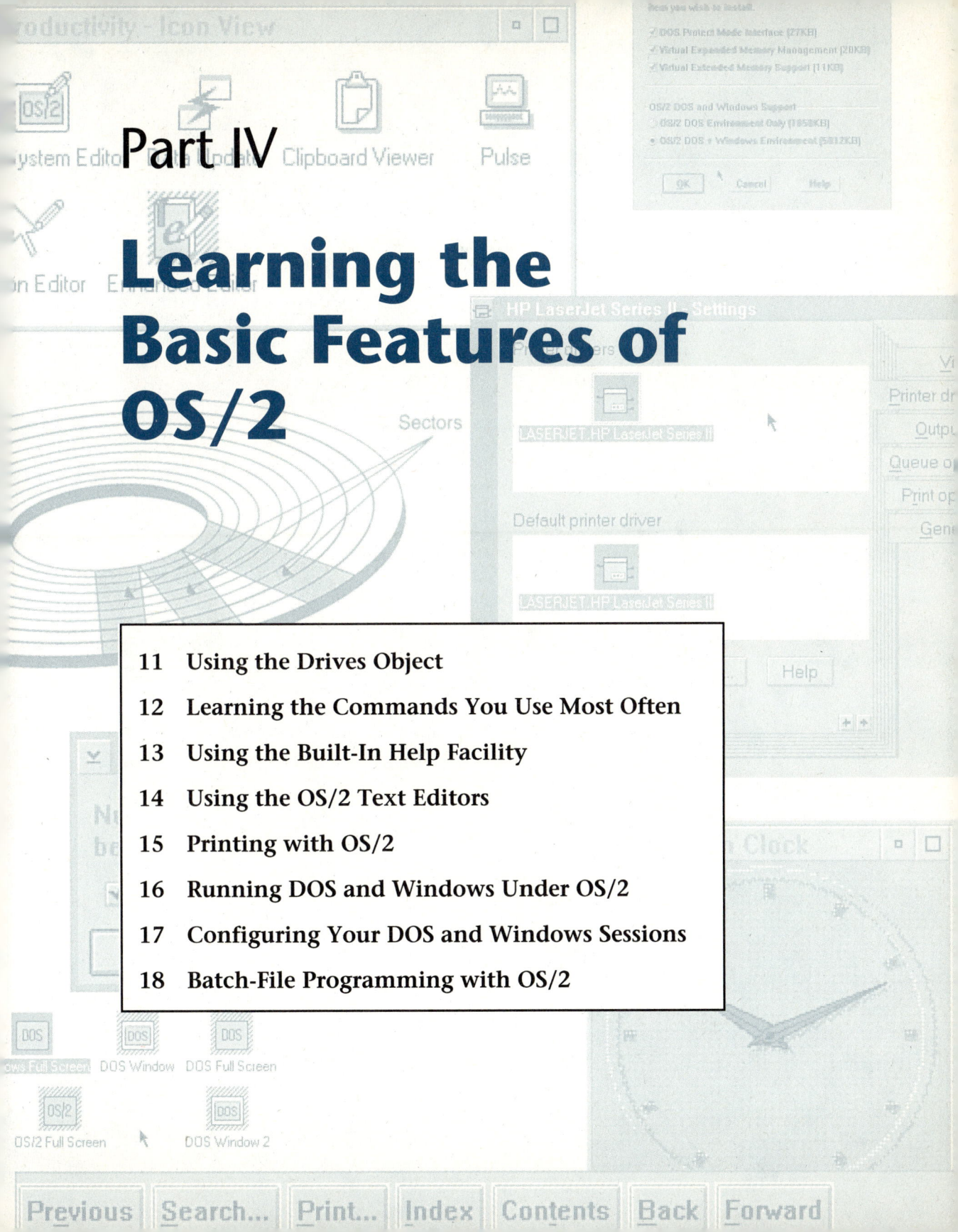

Learning the Basic Features of OS/2

- 11 Using the Drives Object
- 12 Learning the Commands You Use Most Often
- 13 Using the Built-In Help Facility
- 14 Using the OS/2 Text Editors
- 15 Printing with OS/2
- 16 Running DOS and Windows Under OS/2
- 17 Configuring Your DOS and Windows Sessions
- 18 Batch-File Programming with OS/2

Productivity - Icon View

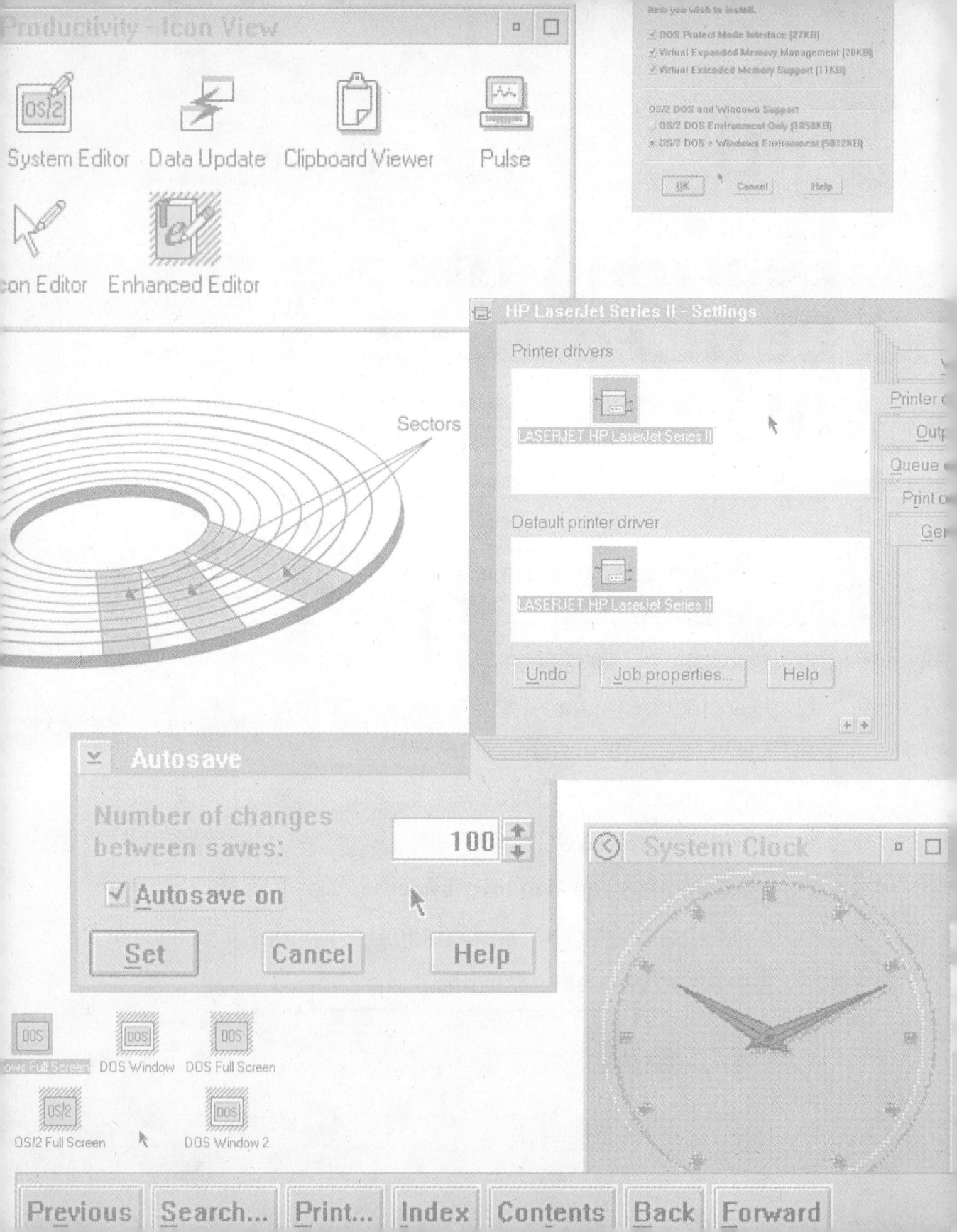

- System Editor
- Data Update
- Clipboard Viewer
- Pulse
- Icon Editor
- Enhanced Editor

Sectors

Item you wish to install.

☑ DOS Protect Mode Interface (27KB)
☑ Virtual Expanded Memory Management (20KB)
☑ Virtual Extended Memory Support (11KB)

OS/2 DOS and Windows Support
○ OS/2 DOS Environment Only (1858KB)
● OS/2 DOS + Windows Environment (5812KB)

[OK]   [Cancel]   [Help]

HP LaserJet Series II - Settings

Printer drivers

LASERJET.HP LaserJet Series II

Default printer driver

LASERJET.HP LaserJet Series II

[Undo]   [Job properties...]   [Help]

Printer
Output
Queue
Print o
Ger

Autosave

Number of changes between saves: **100**

☑ Autosave on

[Set]   [Cancel]   [Help]

System Clock

- DOS Full Screen (Windows Full Screen)
- DOS Window
- DOS Full Screen
- OS/2 Full Screen
- DOS Window 2

[Previous] [Search...] [Print...] [Index] [Contents] [Back] [Forward]

Chapter 11

Using the Drives Object

In Chapter 10, "Managing the Workplace Shell," you learned how to manage the Workplace Shell. Armed with this knowledge, you are now ready to learn how to use the basic features of OS/2. This chapter introduces the Drives object, the file management program for your disk drives. From the Drives object, you can view your files and their arrangement on the disk as well as select, copy, open, and move files. The file association features help you organize your files further by providing an association between a file's name and an application program.

This chapter first describes the parts of Drives object displays. The chapter also teaches you how to configure your file viewing options in different ways, manipulate directory lists and manage each disk drive, format and copy floppy disks, and assign attributes to files.

Understanding the Drives Object Display

When you create memos, spreadsheets, and databases, you fill your disks with files. Eventually you will need to move, copy, or delete the files to keep them organized, regardless of how many application programs you run under OS/2.

In some cases, you may need to get involved with files immediately after installing OS/2 so that your favorite application program can run. You perform file management tasks from the Drives object.

272 Chapter 11—Using the Drives Object

The Drives object is located in the OS/2 System window. To open the OS/2 System folder, double-click the OS/2 System icon. The OS/2 System window appears. Then double-click the Drives icon to view the drives available to you. The Drives window opens (see fig. 11.1).

Fig. 11.1
The drives displayed in Icon View.

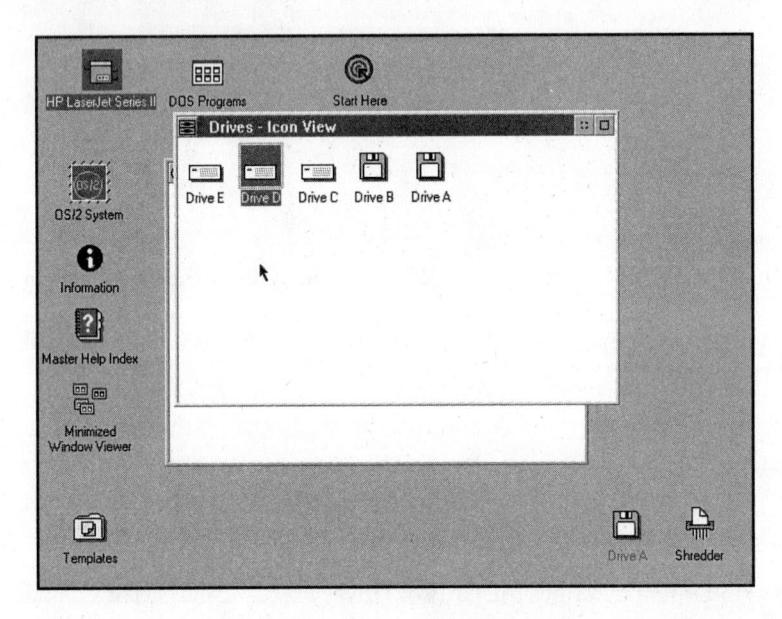

When you open the Drives object, a list of all the disk drives on your computer appears. This list includes the floppy disk drives and any networked drives. Logically, the icon for a floppy disk drive is shaped like a floppy disk, and the icon for a hard disk drive is shaped like a hard disk.

Your computer designates drives by letters. Drives A and B are floppy disk drives and hard disks are drive C and higher. The computer used to generate the figures has two floppy disk drives, as well as three hard disks or partitions, named C, D, and E. Your computer may have a different number of drives. If your computer does not have a floppy disk drive, you will not see an icon for drive A or B. If your computer only has one floppy disk drive, you will not see an icon for drive B. The first hard disk on your computer is always named drive C. In most cases, your computer boots from drive C. This chapter focuses on drive D as an example.

OS/2 can show the available drives in any of three different ways—Icon View, Tree View, and Details View. In figure 11.1, the drives are shown in Icon View. In figure 11.2, the drives are shown in Tree View, and in figure 11.3, they are shown in Details View.

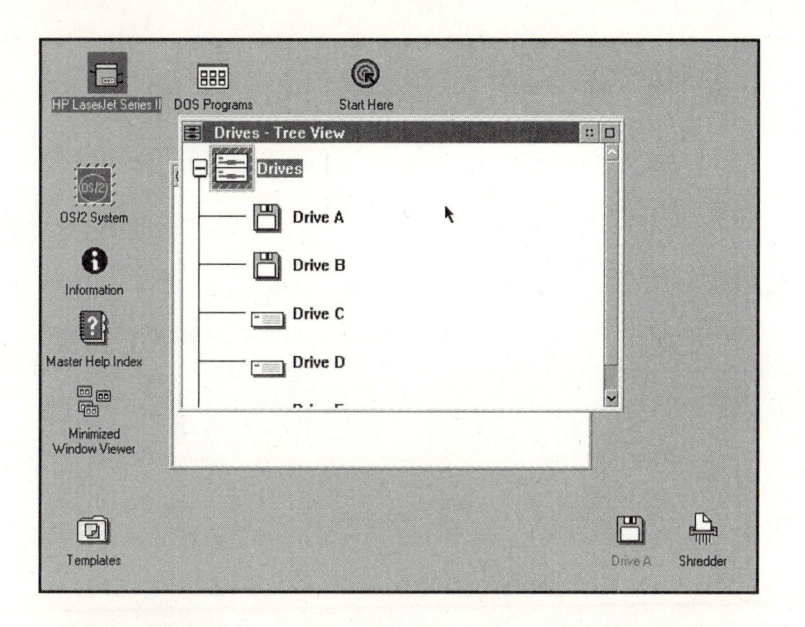

Fig. 11.2
The drives displayed in Tree View.

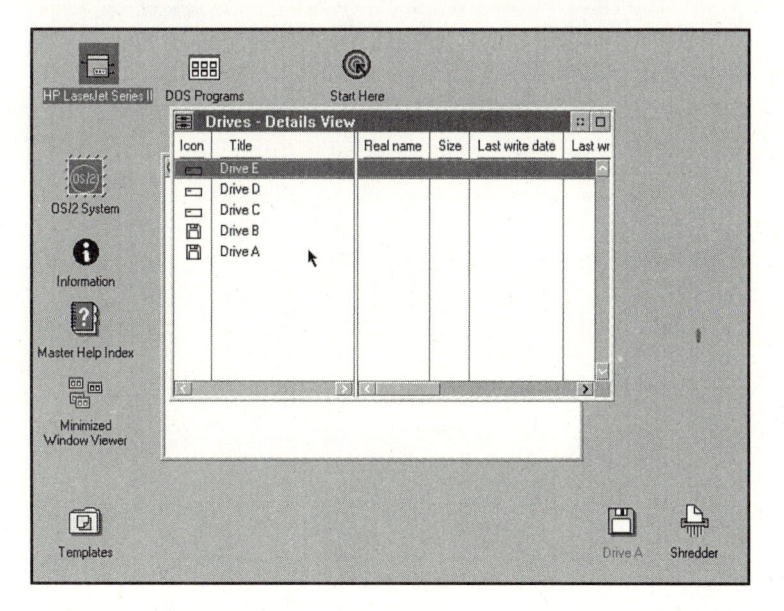

Fig. 11.3
The drives displayed in Details View.

To select the view type, choose Open from the system menu and then choose your view type from the cascaded menu by clicking the appropriate option with the left mouse button. From the keyboard, access the system menu by pressing Alt-space bar (or Shift-Esc). Then use the arrow keys to reach Open. Press the right arrow key to list the view types. Highlight your selection and press Enter.

You view your files depending on the level of detail required. For example, Icon View is generally used for viewing the drive icons themselves. Tree View is for seeing the general arrangement of your directories (or folders) on a particular disk, and Details View displays all the information on particular files within a directory or file folder.

Icon View

After double-clicking the Drives object in the OS/2 System folder, you will probably see an icon view of your drives. (If not, open Icon View as described in the preceding section.) OS/2 displays each drive that you can access from your computer.

As is typical with OS/2 icons, a drive icon's image changes depending on your selections. In figure 11.4, for example, the diagonal lines behind the Drive D icon indicate that drive D is open; the Drive E icon is highlighted, showing that drive E is your current selection.

Fig. 11.4
The Drives - Icon View showing one open drive and the currently selected drive.

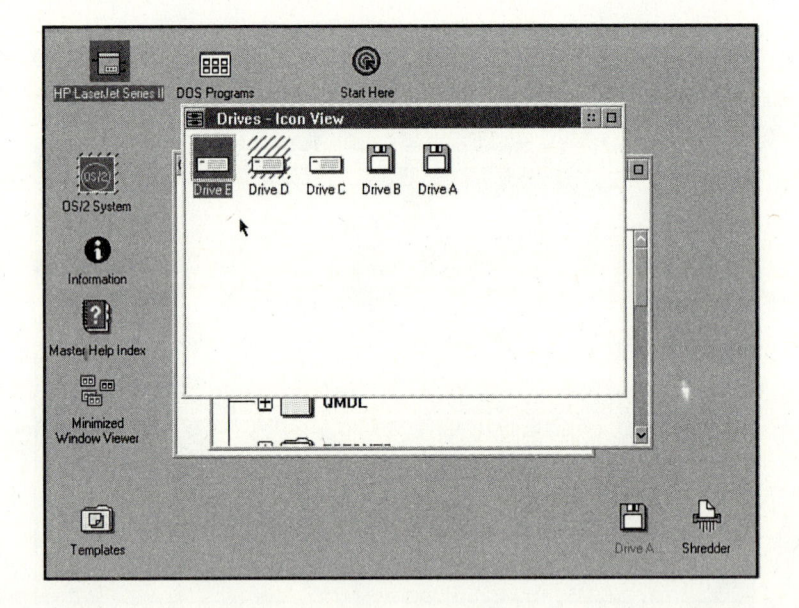

To view the contents of a drive, double-click its icon; or use the arrow keys to highlight the icon and then press Enter. You see a new window displaying the files and directories on this drive.

Tree View

After double-clicking the drive icon, you see a tree view of your chosen disk. (If you see an icon or detail view, open Tree View from the system menu as described earlier.) Figure 11.5 shows the Drive D Tree View maximized to fill the screen.

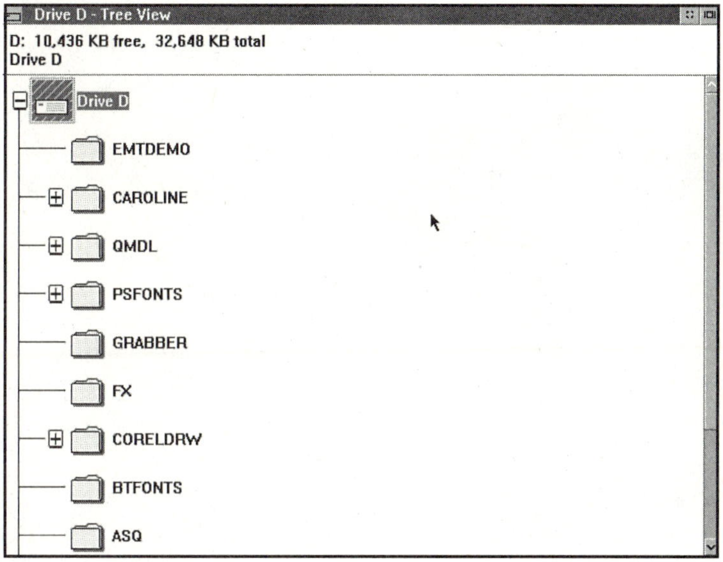

Fig. 11.5
Drive D shown in Tree View.

The Tree View window shows the directories (or folders) on your disk arranged in a tree-like form. (This form is more like a family-tree structure than the growing tree kind.) The drive icon (Drive D in figure 11.5) is at the top. All the directories found in drive D are listed below the Drive D icon. They are linked by a series of lines intended to represent branches of a tree. The directories are represented by file folder icons, and the name of each directory is beside the file folder icon. The example disk includes directories called EMTDEMO, CAROLINE, and GRABBER.

As in Icon View, any currently open object in Tree View has a background with diagonal hatching on it. The currently selected object, in this case the Drive D icon, has a shaded background.

The minus sign to the left of the Drive D icon indicates that you can see all the directory levels within drive D. A plus sign, such as the one in front of the folder named CAROLINE, indicates that there are additional levels of subdirectories that are not currently visible. A later section in this chapter, "Expanding and Collapsing a Directory List," shows how to expand and collapse the directory tree.

Details View

Details View shows a list of all the files and directories for the selected object. Double-click a file folder to open a details view. (If you are looking at a tree or icon view of a file folder's contents, open Details View from the system menu as described earlier.) Figure 11.6 shows the directory CAROLINE in Details View.

Fig. 11.6
The CAROLINE directory shown in Details View.

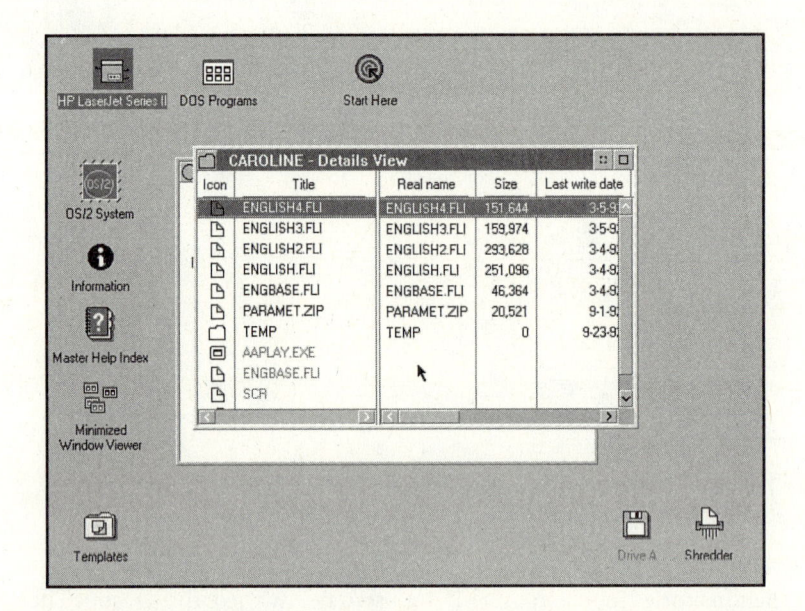

The files and subdirectories are listed in tabular form. The left column shows the file type. Notice that nonexecutable files, such as ENGLISH.FLI, have icons that resemble pieces of paper with a folded corner. The icon shape for an executable file looks like a miniature window. The shadowed items, such as AAPLAY.EXE, are shown in grayed-out text. The names of the shadowed items appear on the list, but the detailed information, such as the size and date, does not appear. See the "Shadowing Files" section of this chapter for more on shadowing.

The Title column lists the file names as they appear next to the icon; the real name column shows the file name as it is stored on the disk. For example, if you create a folder named My Scrapbook, its title is My Scrapbook but its real name is MY_SCRAP to conform with correct file-naming procedures. (If you are using the high performance file system (HPFS), the real name is the same as the title. See Chapter 4 for more information on HPFS.) As another example, your OS/2 drawing program may name its icon Best Drawing Program, but the executable file has a different name, such as BESTDRAW.EXE, on the disk. You can change the names associated with any icons without altering the file name stored on the disk.

The title and real name are separated in the Details View window by a double line. You can move this line to the left or right by pointing at it with the mouse. The cursor changes to a double-headed arrow, and you can drag the line to a new position. Moving this line to the left, for example, leaves less room for the icon and title columns but shows more of the other detail information.

You view the rest of the detail information by enlarging the window or by using the window's scroll bars.

In addition to the title and the real name, OS/2 displays the following attribute information in this window:

- Size
- Last write date
- Last write time
- Last access date
- Last access time
- Creation date
- Creation time
- Flags

The file size is given in bytes. Notice that directories do not have file sizes. A directory's name is stored on the disk, in the directory area, but the directory itself does not occupy any data area. Creating a lot of directories on your disk to make finding files easier does not result in wasted disk space.

The last write date and time indicate the date and time when the file was last changed. The last access date and time show when the file was last read, and the creation date and time show when the file was originally created. If OS/2 does not know the date and time information, typically because the file was

278 Chapter 11—Using the Drives Object

created prior to OS/2's installation, OS/2 displays a time of 12:00:00 AM and a date of 0-0-80.

The Flags column at the far right of this window has four letters or dashes in it. The letters may be R, A, S, or H, referring to read-only, archived, system, or hidden flags or indicators. A file may have any combination of these flags.

A read-only file cannot be changed or deleted while it is marked as read-only. When you back up a file or use a copy command with a suitable switch you can set (or reset) the archive switch on a file to indicate it has been backed up.

The system flag appears on files that are part of the OS/2 operating system. System files are most typically used when you boot your computer. The hidden flag appears on files that are normally hidden from view. You make them visible from the Settings menu. A typical end user never alters or moves system or hidden files.

Display Configuration

If you want to customize your drive views, you adjust the settings from the Open option on the system menu. Many of these settings are similar to the options detailed in Chapter 10, "Managing the Workplace Shell." Click the system menu icon for the drive you want; click **O**pen and then **S**ettings to reach the settings options shown in figure 11.7.

Fig. 11.7
The Drive Settings window.

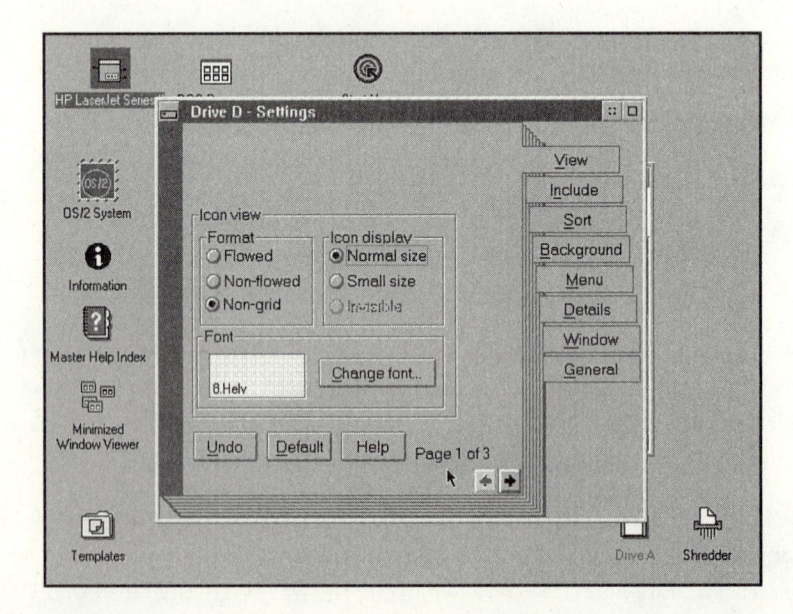

You adjust each view's appearance with the View option. As covered in Chapter 10, you can alter the format, icon size, and font for Icon View and Tree View. The first page alters Icon View. The second page alters Tree View, and the third page alters Details View. You can select the details that you want displayed in Details View, as well as alter the font size. Move from page to page by clicking the arrow buttons at the lower right corner of the page.

When set to the default, the Include option prevents hidden files from appearing in the views. You can alter this setting to limit the files that are displayed. As a beginner, however, you should avoid altering this setting because you may reveal and later erroneously delete or move important system files that have been hidden to reduce the chance of their accidental deletion or movement. You can restore the default setting at any time by clicking the Default button on the Include Settings screen. The Default button works the same way with other setting options as well.

Although you may prefer a smaller or larger font size for your views, you are unlikely to need the other settings in this menu. However, you should realize that OS/2 is fully customizable and you can alter every aspect of your views by creating, for example, special icons, limiting the file display, and altering screen colors.

For Related Information
- "Offering the High Performance File System," p. 84
- "Using a Folder's System Menu," p. 258

Expanding and Collapsing a Directory List

In order to manipulate directory lists, you first must open a tree view for the drive of interest. Figure 11.8 shows a Tree View display of Drive D.

To see the divisions within a folder, click the plus sign to the left of the folder and expand the Tree View listing. Figure 11.9 shows the subdivisions of the folder named CAROLINE, for example.

To collapse the tree view and make the subdivisions of a folder disappear, click the minus sign to the left of the folder. Experiment by clicking the minus sign to the left of your drive icon. Figure 11.10 shows a completely collapsed tree view.

Fig. 11.8
The Tree View display.

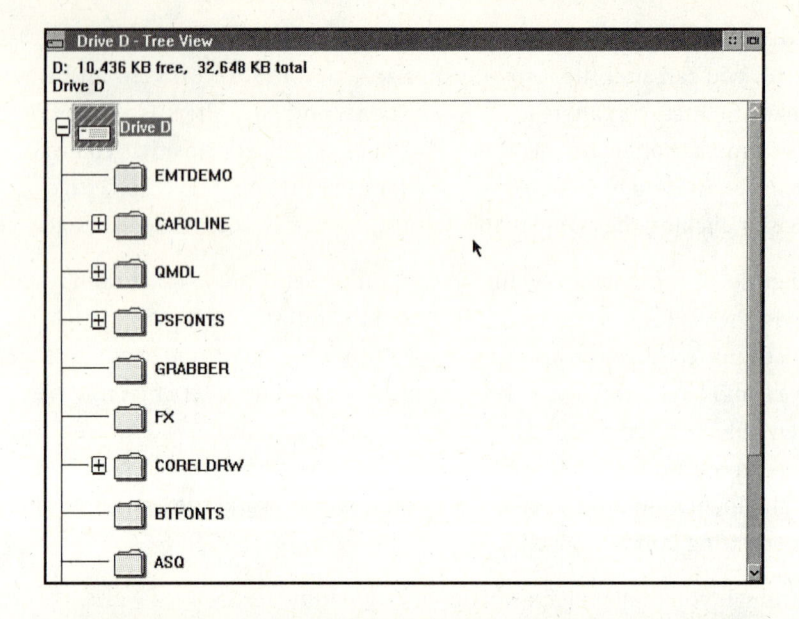

Fig. 11.9
The expanded Tree View of the folder named CAROLINE.

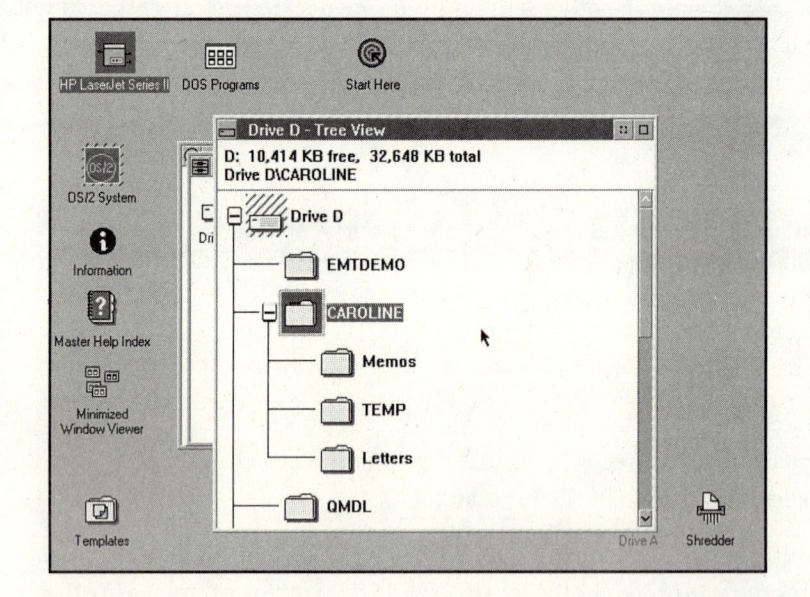

Expanding and Collapsing a Directory List   **281**

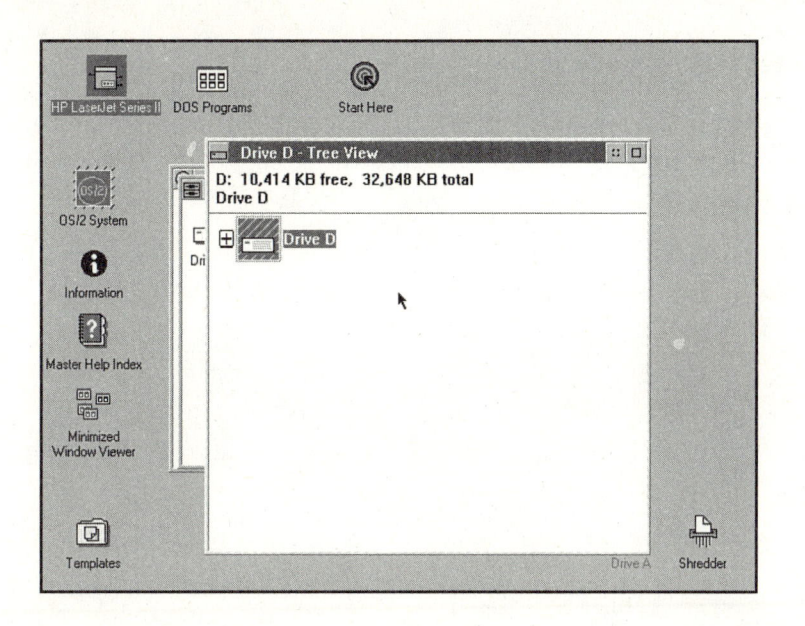

Fig. 11.10
A completely collapsed tree view of Drive D.

Expand your tree view until you can see the folder you want to examine in more detail. For example, you may want to examine the folder named Memos. When you can see the folder, double-click it to open a view of its contents. Figure 11.11 shows the contents of the Memos folder in Icon View.

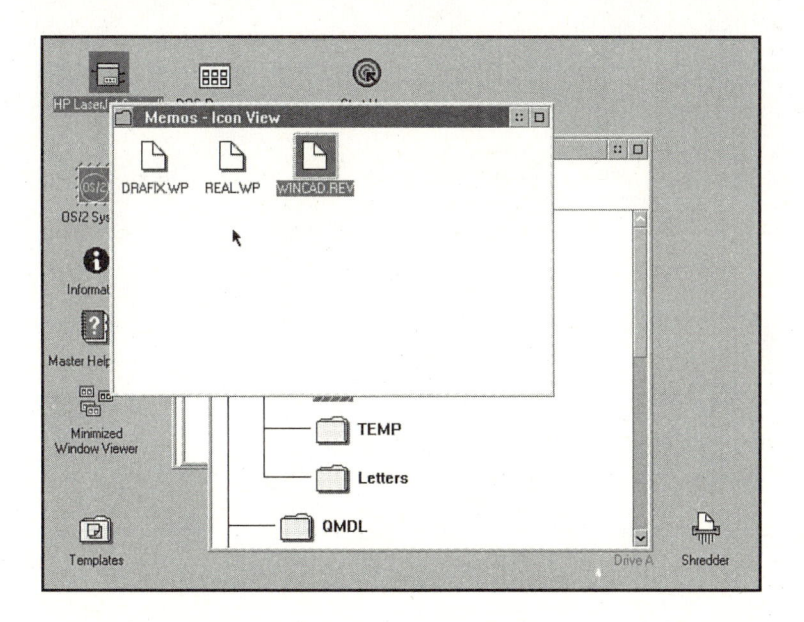

Fig. 11.11
The icon view of the contents of the Memos folder.

Finding Files

So far in this chapter, you have looked at lists of files and selected the items of choice. Sometimes, you may know a file name but not the location of the file. You can make OS/2 search for your file in a folder.

From the tree view of a drive, click a folder with the right mouse button to display its pop-up window. Your screen resembles figure 11.12.

Fig. 11.12
An Object's pop-up menu.

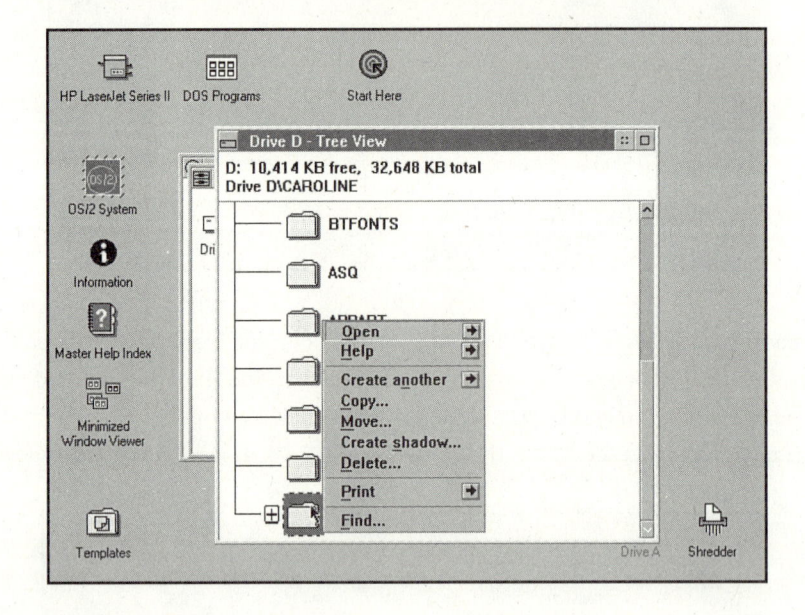

Click **F**ind to open the Find window. Your screen resembles figure 11.13.

The Folder text box lists the folder's name. If you want to pick a different folder, click the **L**ocate button and choose a new folder from the list.

You pick the items to find from the area of this window that contains the Name text box and the Type list box. The Name text box shows the file names for inclusion. An asterisk (*) is the wild card character and means all files of the specified type will be found. Wild cards are explained in Chapter 2. If you know your file's name, you type it in this box.

The Type list box lists all the possible OS/2 object types. For example, you can look for a data file, a folder, or a bit-mapped file. Notice that this list has a hierarchy. The subsets are indented from the left.

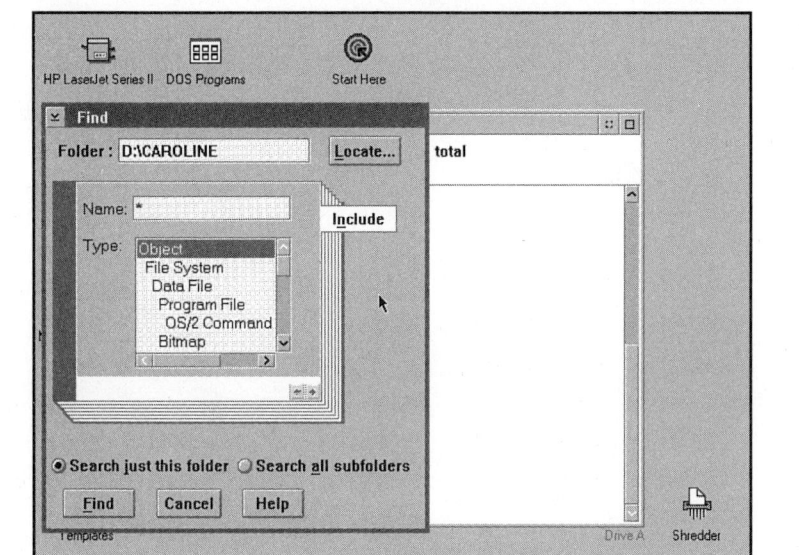

Fig. 11.13
The Find window.

When you open the Find window, the Object type is highlighted. This selection causes OS/2 to look for all objects in the folder. The File System type is indented one character to the right, showing that all the File System objects comprise a subset of OS/2 objects. If you use the scroll bars to view the rest of the list, you see that OS/2 considers Abstract objects, such as indexes, and Transient objects, which are typically temporary files, as equivalent objects to File System objects. The File System subset contains Data Files and Folder objects that have subdivisions of their own.

You can limit your search by picking one of the divisions rather than all the objects. For example, you can choose the Program File type and find only executable files, or choose Network and find only network folders. When you have highlighted the object type of interest, choose the appropriate radio button to search only within the current folder or to widen the search into all the subfolders of the current folder. Click **F**ind to start the search. Your screen resembles figure 11.14.

You can change the view of this display to Tree View or Details View, as described earlier in this chapter.

Each file that is found and its folder's name is shown in this window. If you do another search using different criteria, any additional objects found are placed in another Find Results window.

Fig. 11.14
The Find Results window.

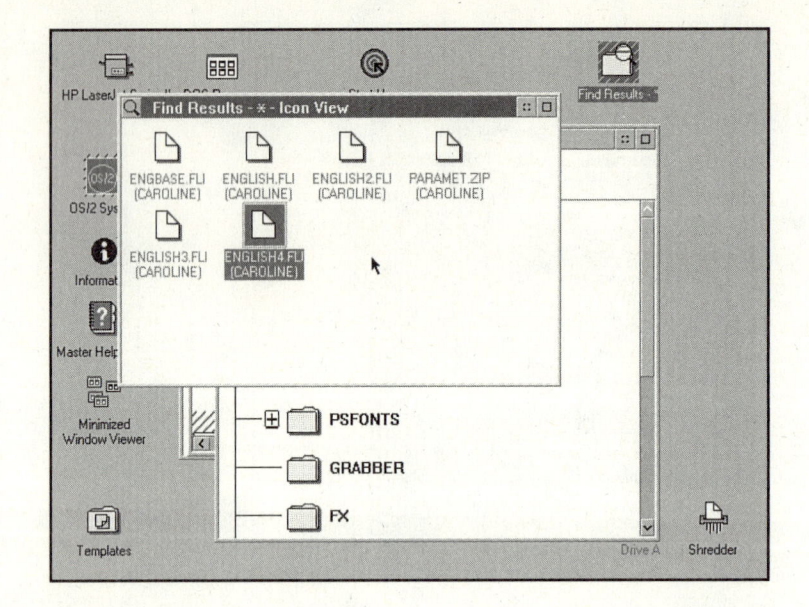

You can manipulate the found objects in the same way as objects in other windows. For example, you can move, copy, or create shadows of objects. The Find Results folders are placed on the desktop when you close them.

Delete the Find Results folders to remove them from the desktop. Deleting the Find Results folder does not delete the objects, only the found copies. To delete a folder, open its system menu and click Delete. Confirm the deletion by clicking Yes when prompted.

OS/2 also supplies a more sophisticated file finding and examining program called Seek and Scan. If you selected this program during installation, it was placed in the OS/2 System folder in the Productivity folder. Chapter 21 details how to use this powerful utility program. See Chapter 7 for information on installing selective portions of OS/2.

For Related Information
- "Using Seek and Scan Files," p. 562
- "Installing Features Selectively," p. 176

Manipulating Files

You can manipulate files in the same way as other OS/2 objects. For example, you can move one or multiple files, copy one or more files, or create shadows of one or multiple files.

This section covers the basics of working with OS/2 files: opening files, selecting files, moving files, copying files, and shadowing files. You can display the program files in any view type when you manipulate the files; however, you probably will prefer to use Icon View.

Opening Files

To open a file, double-click its icon, or use the arrow keys to highlight its icon and press Enter. When you open a file, OS/2 takes different actions depending on the file type.

For example, if the file is an executable program and you open its icon, the program starts. If the file is a text file (the file type OS/2 assumes if it cannot identify the file's type), OS/2 starts the System Editor and tries to load the file into the editor for viewing.

Selecting Multiple Files

As with any OS/2 object, you select a file by clicking it with the left mouse button. The selected item becomes highlighted. When the file is selected, you can do things to it, such as move or copy it. In many cases, however, you want to do the same action to more than one file. For example, you may want to move three files to another folder or copy a whole folder to another disk. In such cases, you need to select more than one object at a time.

If you want to select all the files in a folder, click the window's system menu. Choose Select and then choose Select All from the pop-up menu. All the objects are highlighted. From the keyboard, press Ctrl-/ to select all the objects in a folder.

To select more than one file, but less than all the files in a folder, you can use one of following methods:

- Click the first file for selection and keep the left mouse button pressed. Using the mouse, point to each of the other files you want to select. Each file becomes highlighted when you select it.

- Draw a box around the desired files. Use this method when the desired files are arranged in a rectangle. Move to a point in the window that is below and to the left of the lower left file and then press the left mouse button. Keeping it pressed, move the mouse to the upper right corner of a rectangle that encloses the desired objects.

- If the desired files are in separate places within the window, press Ctrl and then click the first file with the left mouse button. Keep Ctrl pressed and click each of the other files for selection. Many users prefer to use this method of selecting files.

Canceling Selections

To cancel all your selections, click a blank area of the window with the left mouse button or press Ctrl-\. OS/2 removes all the icon highlighting.

To cancel some of your selections, rather than all of them, you essentially reselect the icons. If you have selected only one file, select it again to remove the highlighting.

If you have selected several icons either by drawing a box or by using the Ctrl key method, but decide you do not want one of files selected, use the Ctrl key method. Hold down Ctrl and click the undesired file. Many users prefer this method of file selection.

Selecting and canceling selections can be frustrating unless you remember the Ctrl key method. Unless you are careful, it is easy to accidentally deselect all your icons by clicking a blank area of the window and have to reselect them all again.

Moving Files

To move files from one folder to another, or between a folder and the desktop, follow these steps:

1. Arrange your windows so that you can see the files you want to move and the position to which you want to move them.

2. Select the file or files that you want to move.

3. Click one of the selected files with the right mouse button. While continuing to hold down the mouse button, drag the files to their new position.

   When you start to move the mouse, the pointer changes to show that you are moving the file. Figure 11.15 shows the icon that appears when you move three text files.

   If you move a variety of file types, the pointer icon reflects these types. For example, if you move an executable file, a folder, and a text file, the pointer you see while you are dragging the files shows a stack of icons—one a text file icon, one a folder icon, and one an executable file icon.

4. Release the mouse button. Your files are moved to their new position. You can cancel the move by pressing Esc before you release the mouse button.

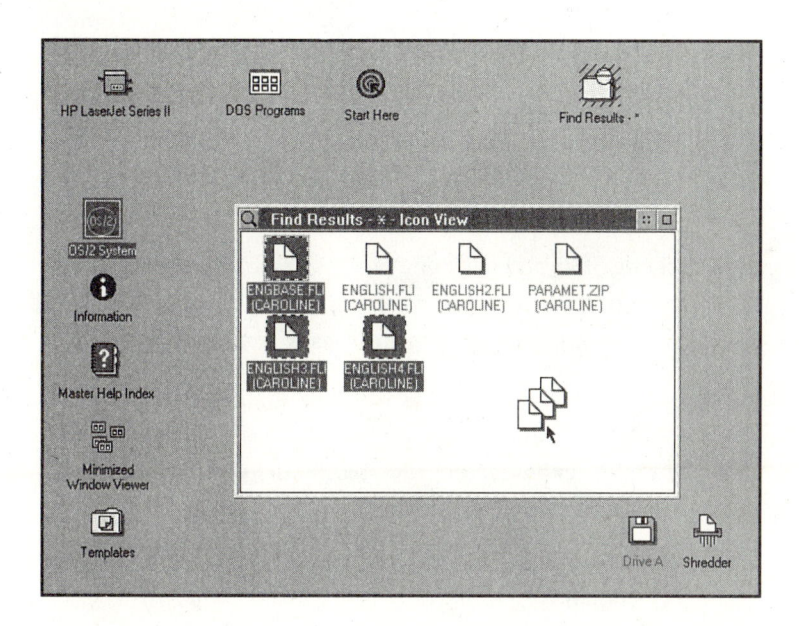

Fig. 11.15
The pointer displayed when you move figures.

Copying Files

The method for copying files is similar to the method for moving them. Follow these steps:

1. Arrange your windows so that you can see the files you want to copy and the position to which you want to copy them.

2. Select the file or files that you want to copy.

3. Press Ctrl and click one of the selected files with the right mouse button. While continuing to hold down the Ctrl key and the mouse button, drag the files to their new position.

   When you start to move the mouse, the pointer changes to show that you are copying the files. The pointer is similar to the one that appears when you move files, except the outlines of the icons are dashed lines rather than solid.

4. Release the Ctrl key and the mouse button. Your files are copied to their new position.

Shadowing Files

As explained in Chapter 10, you can create shadows of objects, including files. Shadowing creates a duplicate icon for a file but does not duplicate the file itself, thereby saving disk space. Shadowing files is similar to moving them. Follow these steps:

1. Arrange your windows so that you can see both the files you want to shadow and their potential shadow's position.

2. Select the file or files that you want to shadow.

3. Press Ctrl and Shift and click one of the selected files with the right mouse button. While continuing to hold down the Ctrl key, the Shift key, and the mouse button, drag the files to their new position.

   When you start to move the mouse, the pointer changes to show that you are shadowing the objects. The pointer is similar to when you move, but a line extends from the original file position to the new file position, as shown in figure 11.16.

4. Release the Ctrl and Shift keys and the mouse button. Your files are shadowed to their new position.

Fig. 11.16
The pointer icon showing that you are shadowing files.

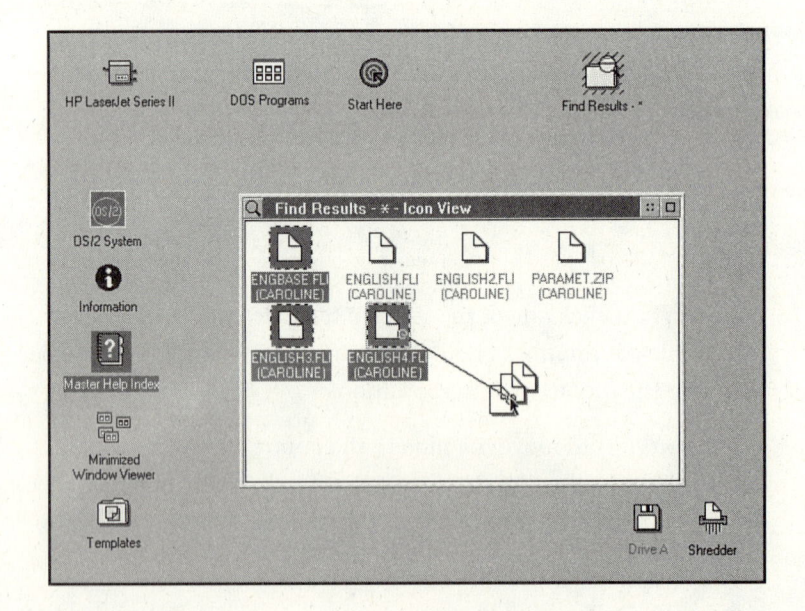

Formatting and Copying Floppy Disks

Formatting and copying disks are typical routine chores you have to do to create copes of your data. You may want to give others the disks or use them as backups for some of your data files.

Formatting Floppy Disks

You must format new floppy disks to prepare them for use. The formatting process establishes the positions for the data that you store on a disk. You can think of the formatting process as laying out and numbering the spaces in a parking lot so that when cars are parked you can easily find any car by its position.

You can reformat floppy disks. Note, however, that the formatting process prevents your accessing any data previously stored on your floppy disk. Consider formatting an irreversible procedure.

To format a blank floppy disk (or one that you are sure does not contain valuable data), insert the disk into the floppy disk drive, click the floppy disk drive icon with the right mouse button to open the system menu, and choose Format disk. If the floppy disk drive icon is not visible, open the Drives window from within the OS/2 System folder. Your screen resembles figure 11.17.

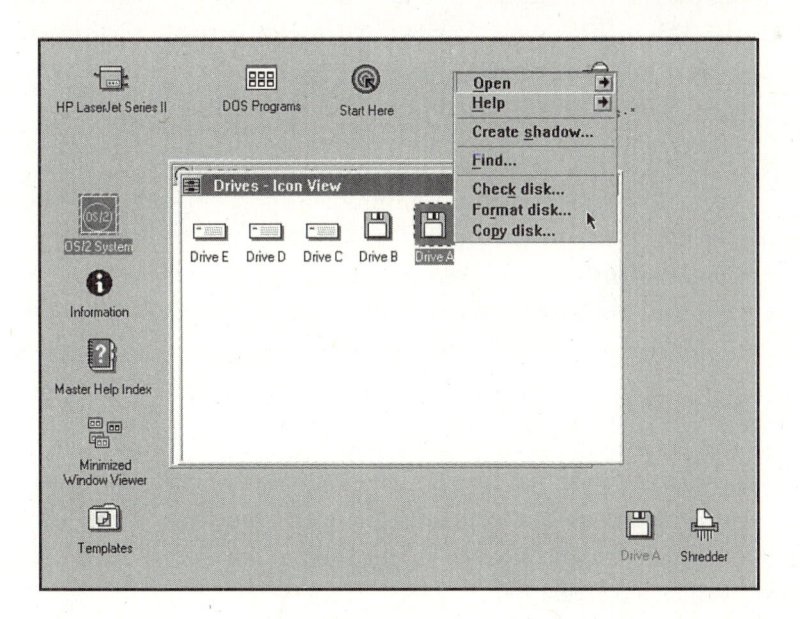

Fig. 11.17
The system menu for the Drive A icon.

Chapter 11—Using the Drives Object

When you choose Format disk, a pop-up window resembling figure 11.18 appears.

Fig. 11.18
The Format Disk A pop-up window.

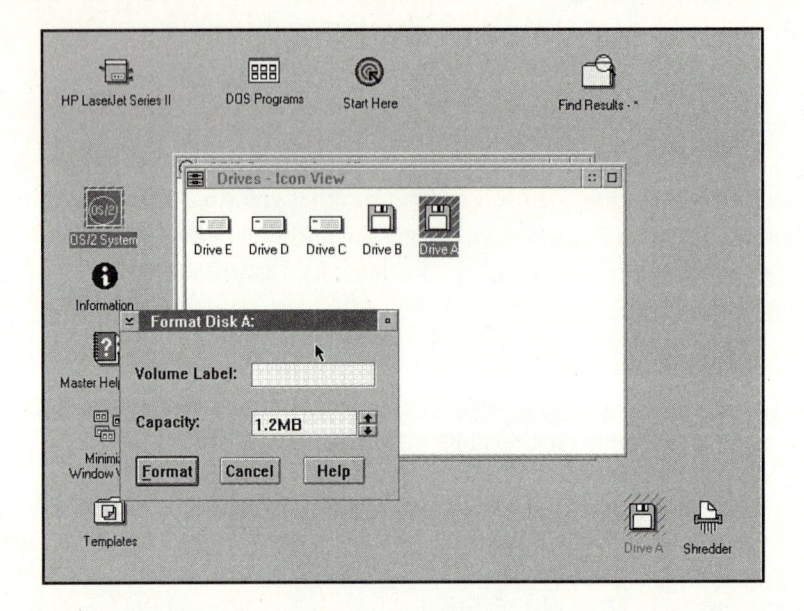

The volume label is the disk's electronic name. When you display a directory of this disk, this name is shown. You should label your floppy disks electronically as well as with paper labels so that you can still identify them even when a paper label falls off. Type in your label for the floppy disk in the Volume Label text box.

Next, select a disk capacity. Chapter 1 introduces floppy disks and their capacities. Be sure to choose the capacity that matches the physical floppy disk you insert in the drive; you choose the capacity by using the arrows at the far right of the Capacity box. Note that if you format a floppy disk at the wrong capacity, you may see a large number of data errors, depending on your error. Check your floppy disk's capacity and the formatting capacity you select carefully.

Click **F**ormat to start the formatting process. A progress window appears showing the percentage of the disk that has been formatted. When complete, this window shows the total space on the disk and the space available. Click OK to complete the operation.

If the space available differs from the total space available on the disk, OS/2 has determined that certain areas of your floppy disk are defective and has marked them as unavailable to store data. Do not use a floppy disk with many defects because you may have a marginal disk and may lose data later. Most floppy disks are warrantied to be defect-free by the manufacturer, so you may be able to exchange it for another floppy disk.

Copying an Entire Floppy Disk

You also can make copies of your floppy disks with the Copy disk command from the drive icon's pop-up menu. Note that this command copies the whole floppy disk rather than a selection of files on a floppy disk.

OS/2 refers to the floppy disk you are copying from as the *source* floppy disk and the floppy disk you are copying to as the *target* floppy disk. During the copying process, the target floppy disk is formatted, so you lose any existing data on that disk. All the files on the source disk are copied to the target floppy disk.

To copy a floppy disk, insert your source floppy disk into a floppy disk drive. Click the floppy disk drive's icon in the Drives - Icon View window with the right mouse button. The system menu opens. Choose the Copy disk command from this window. OS/2 opens a command line menu and starts the Copy command. Your screen resembles figure 11.19.

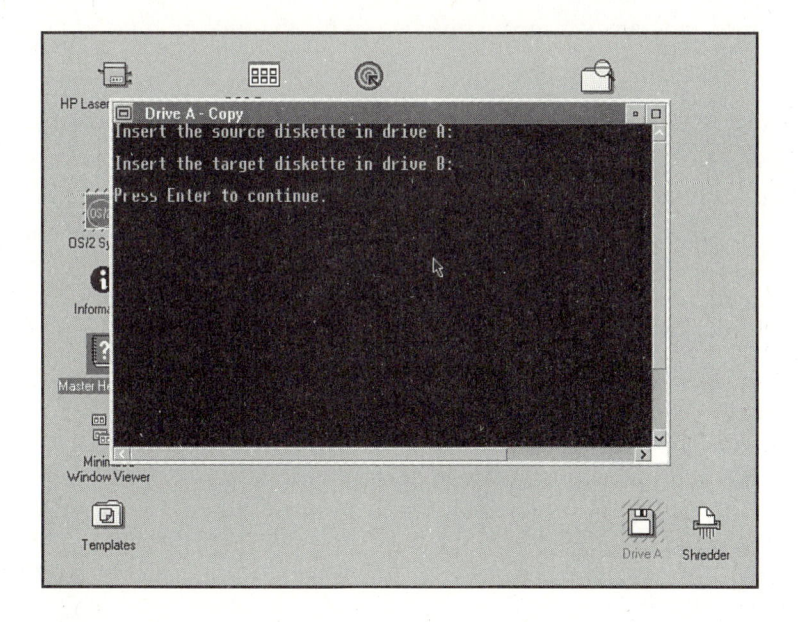

Fig. 11.19
The Copy command window.

Chapter 11—Using the Drives Object

For Related Information
- "Understanding Disks, Disk Files, and Disk Directories," p. 19

If you have two floppy disk drives, place your target floppy disk into drive B. If you only have one floppy disk drive, OS/2 prompts you to swap source and target floppy disks when necessary. Press Enter to start the copying process. OS/2 displays a status line showing the status of the copying process. Exchange floppy disks when prompted, if necessary, until the process is complete. Diskcopying between different size disks does not work.

Associating a File with an Application

OS/2 enables you to link (or associate) your data files with particular application programs. For example, if you open a text file, OS/2 automatically starts the OS/2 System Editor and loads your selected text file into it. You can create your own associations with other application programs. Three approaches are supported.

You can specify that a data file is a particular type and have OS/2 start the associated application program automatically, or you can add the application program to a data file's pop-up menu so that you can start the associated application program. Alternatively, you can create associations so that all data files with similar file names are considered associated with a particular application program. When you open a data file that fits the pattern, the associated application program starts.

Note that these processes will not be successful unless you choose appropriate file associations. If you are a beginner, you are unlikely to set up these associations. However, after you are familiar with the concepts of program files, data files, and their locations, you will probably take advantage of the power and convenience of file associations.

Associating by File Type

When you associate by file type, all files of a particular type, such as bit-map, metafile, Pascal code, or Plain Text files, are considered associated with a particular application program. You create the association by adjusting the program's settings by using its icon settings menu selection.

Click the program icon with the right mouse button to see the system menu. Click the arrow alongside Open to see the Settings menu. Click **S**ettings to open the Settings window. Figure 11.20 shows a typical program icon Settings window.

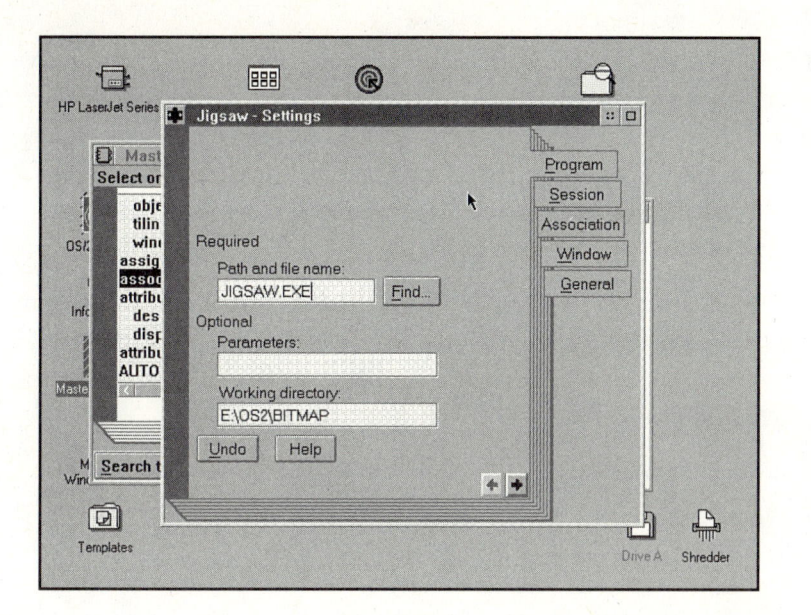

Fig. 11.20
The Settings window for the program Jigsaw.

Click Association to adjust the data file associations. To associate by file type, pick the desired file type from the Available types list at the top of the window. You can add and remove file types as desired. When complete, close the Settings window.

When you open a data file of the appropriate type, OS/2 starts the associated application program and loads your data file into it.

Associating by File Name

When you associate by file name, all files with a similar name are considered associated with a particular application program. As with associating by file type, you create the association by adjusting the program's icon settings.

Click the program icon with the right mouse button to see the pop-up menu. Click the arrow beside Open to see the Settings menu. Click **S**ettings to open the Settings window. Figure 11.21 shows a typical program icon Settings window.

Click Association to adjust the data file associations. To associate by file name, type the file name in the box labeled New Name and then click Add to add it to the Current Names list. You can use OS/2 wild cards for this association.

If you want all files with the file name extension DOC to be considered word processing documents, for example, open the Settings window for your word processor and type ***.DOC** in the New Name text box. If you want all files that have file names beginning with CAD to be considered drawing files for your CAD program, open your CAD program's settings menu and type **CAD*.*** in the New Name text box.

You can add or remove files from the Current Name list. When you are finished, close the Settings window. When you open a data file with an appropriate name, OS/2 starts the associated application program and loads your data file automatically.

Notice that although this feature is powerful, you need to use consistent file naming methods for it to be successful. For many users, particularly those users who run several different application programs, this process is intuitive, but for many beginners, the desirability of this practice is not obvious.

Associating from the Pop-up Menu

To associate a data file with an application program, you can add the application program's name to the pop-up menu. Unlike the other association methods that link a set of data files with an application program, this method links one data file with an application program. You can add several application programs to one data file and choose between them from the pop-up menu.

You alter your pop-up menus by adjusting the menu settings. Be aware in the following explanation that you are adjusting the configuration of your pop-up menu. You need to realize when you are to choose an item from the pop-up menu and when you are adjusting the items that make up the pop-up menu. You pick Open from the pop-up menu to start the adjustment and then alter the Open menu to add the association, for example.

To associate a data file with a program, follow these steps:

1. Click the data file icon by pressing the right mouse button. The pop-up menu appears.

2. Click the arrow to the right of the Open option.

3. Choose **S**ettings from the menu. The Settings window appears.

4. Choose **M**enu from within the Settings window. Your screen resembles figure 11.21.

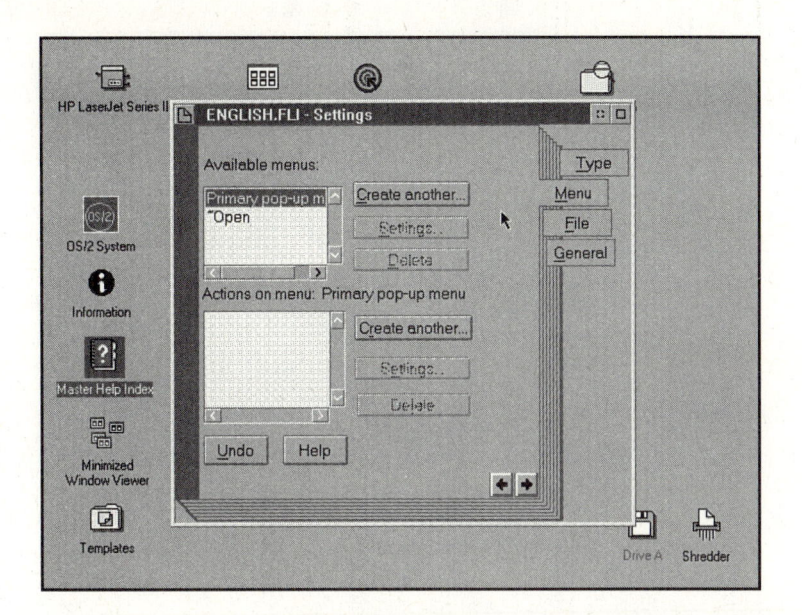

Fig. 11.21
The Settings window with Menu displayed.

5. Click ~Open in the Available menus list. Your screen resembles figure 11.22. The Actions on menu scroll bar in the lower half of the Settings window shows the items that appear when you select the Open menu.

   Before continuing, look at this window in detail to understand the lists. The Available menus scroll box shows a list of available menus—a primary pop-up menu and the Open menu—for the data file object. The tilde (~) in front of the word *Open* indicates that the Open menu contains a selection of items.

   The list of options in the Actions on menu scroll box in the bottom half of the window are the menu options you see when you click the arrow to the right of Open on the pop-up menu. In this example, you see ~Settings and OS/2 System Editor. The OS/2 System Editor appears because OS/2 assumes that all data files can be loaded into the System Editor. You want to add your application program name for the data file to this list.

6. Click C**r**eate another... in the bottom half of the window to add an application program to the pop-up menu. Your screen resembles figure 11.23.

7. In the Menu item name text box, type in the name of your application program. This name will appear in the pop-up menu.

Fig. 11.22
Settings window with Menu Open selected.

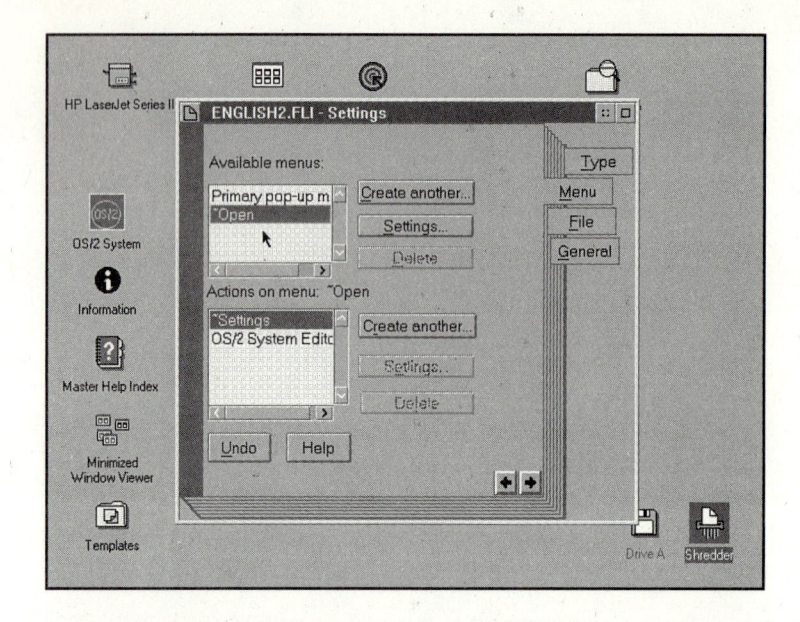

Fig. 11.23
The Menu Item Settings window.

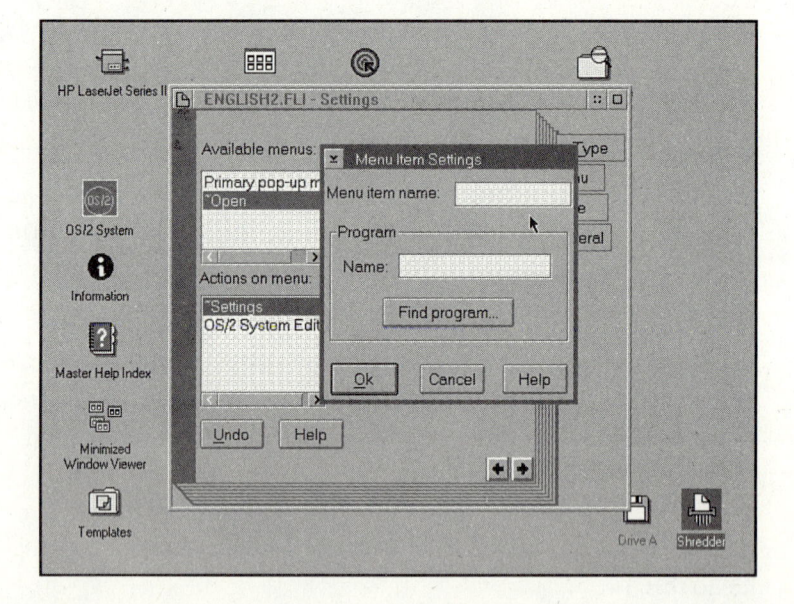

8. Type the executable file name for your application program in the Name text box. You can use the Find program option to search for your program if you are unsure where the executable file is located.

9. Click **O**K to accept the change. Your application program appears in the Actions on menu list below OS/2 System Editor.

10. Close the Settings window by double-clicking the system icon. Now when you open the pop-up menu for the data file and click the arrow to the right of Open, you see your application program name.

   You can start the application program by double-clicking its name from the pop-up menu's Open list. Alternatively, if you select Open, or double-click the data file object, OS/2 opens your application program and loads your data file into it.

You can make the application program the default setting so that the program automatically runs when you select Open. To do this from the ~Open option in the Available menus list, click **S**ettings. Then click the radio button labelled Conditional Cascade. Choose your application program's name from the text box list to make the program the default setting. Click **O**K to accept the changes. (Click **U**ndo if you want to reject any changes.)

Assigning Attributes to Files

Each file within a directory has certain attributes. For example, a file has a name and size. It was created or last modified on a particular date and at a particular time. OS/2 can store a variety of attribute information about each file on your disk. If, for example, you have two files with similar names but know that the one you want is the one you were working on yesterday, you can use the attribute information (the date the file was last modified) to find the file of interest.

You can attach two main types of attributes to your files: attributes and extended attribute flags. As covered in the "Details View" section, a file can have up to four flags associated with it. These flags are read-only, archive, system, and hidden. You also can attach descriptive information about the file by using the extended attribute features.

Flags

In practice, you are unlikely to need to change the flags for a file although you may execute a command on a set of files based on their flag settings. For example, you probably will not need to make a file read-only or a read-only file editable. However, you may use an application program that does that for you. You may, for example, make a spreadsheet data file read-only, but you will probably use the application program's features rather than set it yourself.

Chapter 11—Using the Drives Object

When you use backup or copying commands, you may choose options that only back up files that do not have an archive flag set. You are unlikely, however, to use OS/2 features to reset the archive flag for any files individually.

If you do want to alter the flags for a file, open the pop-up window for the file by clicking it with the right mouse button. Choose the arrow to the right of Open, and click **S**ettings to open the Settings window. Click the **F**ile tab to open the File Settings window.

The File Settings window consists of three pages. Page 1 contains the file's name and its icon's name. Click the right arrow to move to page 2. Your screen resembles figure 11.24.

Fig. 11.24
Page 2 of the File Settings window.

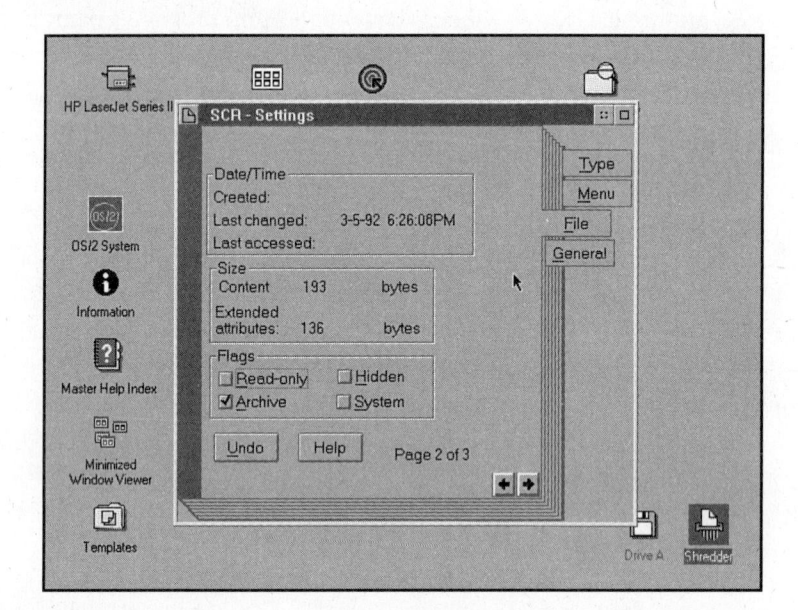

The window shows information about when the file was created and last accessed as well as the file size. Its flag settings are shown at the bottom of the window. In the example, the selected file has its Archive flag set. You toggle each of the flags by clicking the check box to the left of the flag's name.

Extended Attributes

With OS/2 you can store extra information with a file. You can add, for example, a file description in the extended attribute area.

You are much more likely to want to add descriptive information about your files than alter a file's flags. This information is known as extended attribute information. You add extended attribute information on page 3 of the File Settings window. From the second page of the File Settings window (refer to fig. 11.24), click the right arrow at the bottom of the window to move to page 3. Your screen resembles figure 11.25.

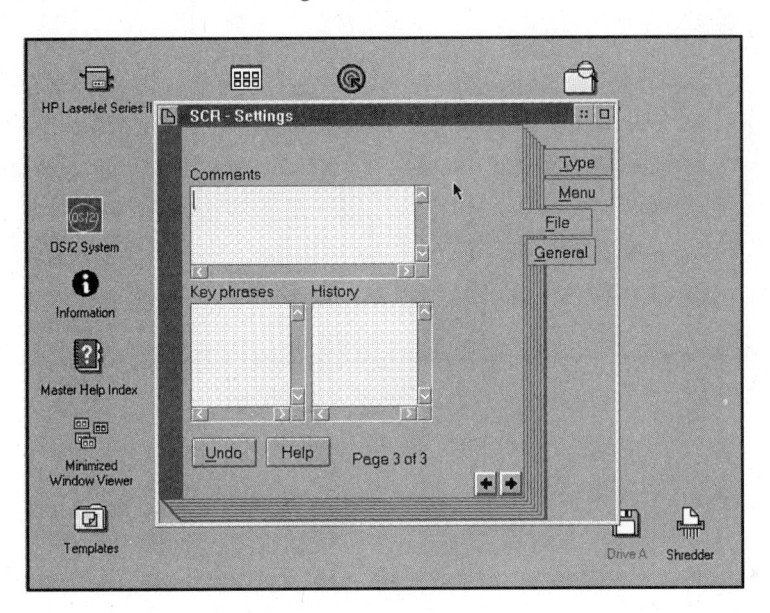

Fig. 11.25
Page 3 of the File Settings window.

You add the extended attribute information about your file in this window. You can search this information by using the Find procedure explained in an earlier section. You typically add this information to keep an audit trail or description of your files. The information is particularly valuable if more than one person will be accessing the file or if a traditional file name isn't descriptive enough.

Type any general notes you want to keep about the file in the Comments section. If the file were a preliminary budget spreadsheet, for example, you might include a couple of the assumptions you made during its creation.

In the Key phrases section, you type important words or phrases that you might want to use later in an index. Using the spreadsheet example, the key phrases might be *budget*, *five-year plan*, and *ten-percent growth*.

After adding your extended attributes, close the Settings window by double-clicking the system menu icon in the upper left corner of the window. (To undo any changes, click **U**ndo before closing the window.)

Chapter Summary

In this chapter, you learned about the Drives icon and file management features of OS/2. You now know how to use Icon, Tree, and Details Views to see your file arrangements. You also can find files by file type or by searching for key phrases previously stored in a file's extended attribute area. This chapter covered the basics of working with files, including selecting one or more files at a time, copying files, and shadowing files. Copying and formatting floppy disks from the Drives icon was described. Finally, you learned how to alter or add to a file's attributes from its Settings menu and link data files with application programs by one of three methods.

The next chapter covers the commands you use most often in OS/2.

Chapter 12

Learning the Commands You Use Most Often

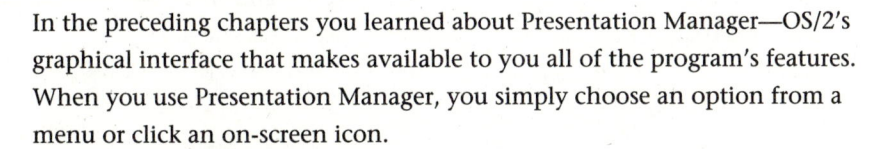

In the preceding chapters you learned about Presentation Manager—OS/2's graphical interface that makes available to you all of the program's features. When you use Presentation Manager, you simply choose an option from a menu or click an on-screen icon.

OS/2 also offers a command-line interface. Initially, you may find the command-line interface more difficult to use than Presentation Manager. Because the command-line interface has no menus, you must know the name of the command you want to use and how to use the command. When you master the command-line interface, however, you may find it quicker and easier to use than the graphical interface. Further, the command-line interface enables you to perform functions you cannot perform with Presentation Manager. Give both interfaces a try, to see which you prefer.

To explore the command-line interface, you first must start an OS/2 or DOS session under OS/2. Several session objects are in the Command Prompts folder. The names of the session objects suggest their purpose—full-screen or windowed, OS/2 or DOS. The Command Prompts folder also contains a Windows full-screen object. Chapter 17, "Configuring Your DOS and Windows Sessions," discusses the different kinds of DOS and Windows sessions.

Open an OS/2 windowed session by double-clicking the OS/2 Window object. You now have opened a window on the past—this feature was the only interface in early computers. Your computer screen is no longer a desktop; it is now a line-oriented teletypewriter. In this mode, you type a line of command text and OS/2 (or DOS, in a DOS session) responds with one or more lines of information that explain the command's action. Although the plain white text on a black background may make this interface appear less exciting than Presentation Manager's colorful graphical environment, the interface is no less powerful. You can use the command-line interface to run applications and issue commands. This chapter concentrates on issuing OS/2 and DOS commands.

You can look up commands in OS/2's on-line Command Reference (as explained in Chapter 13, "Using the Built-in Help Facility") or in the Reference section of this book. You want the most frequently used commands to become second-nature to you, however, and this chapter focuses on those commands. You actually learn the commands for two operating systems because the commands presented in this chapter work for both OS/2 and DOS sessions. You learn that some of the more powerful commands have built-in safety features that protect against accidental misuse. This chapter also explains some important concepts about using OS/2 and provides you with a variety of expert tips.

You learn best by doing, and this chapter presents many examples to reinforce the information contained in the text. Type these examples as you go, and feel free to make up your own. The following list presents a roadmap of the topics discussed in this chapter:

- Opening, clearing, and closing a command-line window
- Setting the system time and date
- Understanding, creating, removing, and navigating directories
- Listing, copying, erasing, and renaming files
- Backing up your hard disk and restoring files from the backup
- Displaying files on the screen and printer

Beginning the Command-Line Interface

To use the command-line interface, choose either OS/2 Window or OS/2 Full Screen from Presentation Manager's Main Group. When you choose OS/2 Window, you find a new menu selection available only in windowed sessions, font size, in the pull-down menu bar. Set the characters to the size you prefer and maximize the window so you can see it all at once. Alternatively, you can choose DOS Window or DOS Full Screen; the commands are basically the same in both OS/2 and DOS modes.

You begin this session by learning to use the commands for changing the system's date and time. These commands are useful in themselves, and you can practice working with them before tackling more complicated commands. The discussion concludes with commands for clearing the screen and ending the session.

Viewing or Changing the System Date (DATE)

In the OS/2 window you just opened, type **DATE** and press Enter. The information that appears on-screen should resemble the following:

DATE

The current date is: Sat 11-15-92

Enter the new date: (MM-DD-YY)

If the date is correct, just press Enter. To change the date, type a new date, such as the following, and press Enter:

4-15-93

If you prefer, you can separate the numbers with slashes instead of hyphens or type the year as a four-digit number. You even can type the date command and the new date all on one line:

DATE 4/15/1993

Try an invalid date, such as 2-31-93, and see what happens.

> **Tip**
>
> You can use the DATE command as a calendar. Suppose that you want to know on what day of the week 1995 will begin. You can type the following command to find out:
>
> **DATE 1-1-95 (this changes the date)**
>
> **DATE (this reports the date)**
>
> The system returns the following message:
>
> Current date is: Sun 1-01-95
>
> This technique tricks the system into believing that the current date is January 1, 1995. The system obligingly reports that the day of the week is Sunday. Be sure to reset the system to the true date, or your computer will remember the wrong date even after you turn the power off.

Viewing or Changing the System Time (TIME)

The OS/2 TIME command works much like the DATE command. To use the TIME command, type **TIME**. OS/2 then displays the following messages on-screen:

> The current time is: 14:31:25.78
>
> Enter the new time:

TIME uses a 24-hour clock, so that a minute before midnight is 23:59:00.00 and a minute after is 0:01:00.00. To set the clock to 3:31 p.m., for example, you add 12 to the number of hours and type the following at the `Enter the new time` prompt:

15:31

If the system shows the correct time, just press Enter.

As you saw with DATE, you can type the command and the new time all on one line, for example:

TIME 15:31

Notice that you can choose not to specify seconds and hundredths of seconds. You even can leave out the minute and type the following, for example, if you want to set the clock exactly to midnight:

TIME 0

You also can follow the custom of many countries and use periods to separate hours, minutes, and seconds, as shown in the following example:

TIME 15.31.59

Try setting an impossible time, such as 65 minutes past 25 o'clock. OS/2 recognizes that no such time exists, and asks you to try again.

Clearing the Screen (CLS)

As you practiced with the TIME and DATE commands, the screen filled, and some lines scrolled off the top. You can unclutter the screen before going on to the next section. For this action, you use the CLS command.

CLS, which stands for Clear Screen, is the simplest of all commands. To use it, just type **CLS**. Everything vanishes from the screen, and you start at the top again. Be certain you want to remove all the information on your screen before you use this command. When CLS removes information from the screen, the information is gone forever.

Closing the Command-line Session (EXIT)

When you finish using an OS/2 window and want to close it, you use the EXIT command. You type **EXIT**, the window disappears, and the system returns you to the Main Group. You also can close the window from Task Manager. If you try EXIT now, remember to open another OS/2 window before continuing with the next section.

Learning Commands for Managing Directories

As you learned in Chapter 2, "Learning OS/2 If You Don't Know DOS," OS/2 organizes its files into directories. Figure 12.1 shows an example of a directory structure for a word processor.

For Related Information
- "Understanding Disk Partitions and Disks," p. 43
- "Storing Files and File Names," p. 45

Fig. 12.1
A sample directory structure for a word processor.

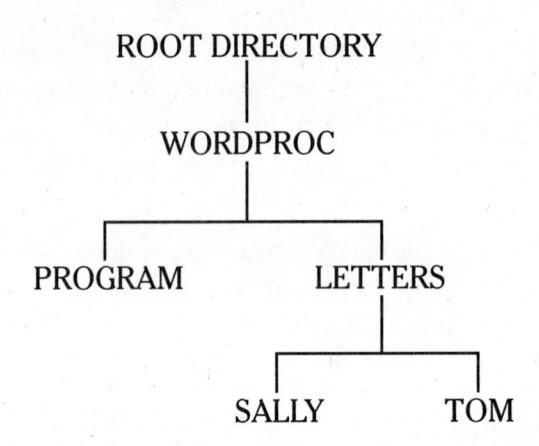

```
              ROOT DIRECTORY
                    |
                WORDPROC
                    |
         ┌──────────┴──────────┐
      PROGRAM               LETTERS
                               |
                      ┌────────┴────────┐
                    SALLY              TOM
```

This structure groups the word processor's program files in a PROGRAM directory and contains a separate branch for letters. Two people, Sally and Tom, use the word processing program, and both have a private directory for the letters they type. This section shows you how to set up, manage, and navigate this directory layout. Your first step in learning these techniques is to familiarize yourself with the following terms and concepts.

Current Working Directory. Think of the directory structure as a tree, with each directory representing a branch. You can climb up and down from one branch to another, but you are always in some directory on the tree. The prompt that OS/2 displays, such as [C:\OS2], when it waits for your next command, tells where you are. This is the current directory.

Paths. You can tell someone how to get anywhere in a tree by specifying which branches they must climb. Similarly, you can specify any directory's location by spelling out the path to that directory. A complete path starts at the root directory, but you also can use a shorter form that starts from the current working directory.

Shorthand Directory Names. You use three special abbreviations in paths:

Abbreviation	Represents
\	The root directory
.	The current working directory
..	The parent of the current working directory—the directory one level closer to the root. (In figure 12.1, WORDPROC is the parent of LETTERS, and LETTERS is a child of WORDPROC.)

Making a Directory (MD or MKDIR)

OS/2 creates several directories in which it stores its files; DOS and Windows applications do the same. You can create your own set of directories to organize your files. You create directories by using the MD (Make Directory) command. MKDIR is another name for the command, but MD is easier to type.

The first step in creating the layout for the word processing example is to open an OS/2 window and create the \WORDPROC directory. To create the directory, you type the following:

MD \WORDPROC

The backslash before the name indicates that this directory is a child of the root directory. You can create a subdirectory by typing its full path, for example:

MD \WORDPROC\PROGRAM

Both preceding examples give the full path from the root to the new directory because they start with the backslash character (\). An easier way to create children of the current directory is to use the CD command to make \WORDPROC the current directory. The next section explains the CD command in detail. For now, type the following command-lines, pressing return at the end of each line:

CD \WORDPROC

MD LETTERS

These commands create the subdirectory \WORDPROC\LETTERS. To complete the directory structure, type these commands:

CD LETTERS

MD SALLY

MD TOM

You now have created the directory structure pictured in figure 12.1.

The last command you typed is equivalent to MD \WORDPROC\LETTERS\TOM, but MD TOM is shorter and reduces the risk of typing errors. This command works, however, only if \WORDPROC\LETTERS is the current directory. Each command form has advantages, and you work most efficiently when you learn to use both forms.

Changing the Current Directory (CD or CHDIR)

Both CD and CHDIR are names for the Change Directory command. Most users prefer the shorter command name, CD. You use this command to move to any directory on a hard disk or floppy disk. The directory you move to becomes that disk's current working directory.

Suppose you want to work with the \WORDPROC\PROGRAM directory you created earlier. You can use any of several techniques to make this the current directory. To use a direct method, you type this:

CD \WORDPROC\PROGRAM

This form of the CD command gives the complete path from the root to the desired current directory. This command always works, no matter what directory you are in when you type it.

If you are already near the directory you want to make current, however, you can use a shorter command form to reach the directory. If you are in the \WORDPROC directory, for example, you can change to \WORDPROC\PROGRAM by typing the following:

CD PROGRAM

Alternatively, you can move to \WORDPROC\LETTERS\TOM with this command:

CD LETTERS\TOM

If you're in \WORDPROC\LETTERS, and you want to move to the \WORDPROC\LETTERS\SALLY directory, type the following:

CD SALLY

This method of changing directories is quick and helps you avoid typing errors.

Tip

When you want to know what directory you're in, type **CD** without any path following it. This command instructs OS/2 to tell you the name of the current directory.

Here is another shortcut to help you work faster. If you're working in the \WORDPROC\PROGRAM directory and want to move back to the \WORDPROC directory, type the following:

CD ..

Remember that the double period is shorthand for the parent directory, one level closer to the root. You can use this shorthand symbol with the name of another subdirectory that is a child of the same parent. For example, suppose that you want to move from \WORDPROC\LETTERS\TOM to \WORDPROC\LETTERS\SALLY. These subdirectories share the same parent, \WORDPROC\LETTERS, which you abbreviate with a double period:

CD ..\SALLY

You can use the double period more than once. To move to the parent directory's parent, type the following:

CD ..\..

To return to the root directory, you use this special form:

**CD **

Removing a Directory (RD or RMDIR)

As your needs change over time, you can remove directories that you no longer use. You need not keep, for example, the directories you created in the two preceding sections of this chapter. You can use the RD (Remove Directory) command to delete directories. RD has a built-in safety feature that prevents you from removing a directory that contains any files or subdirectories.

Because \WORDPROC\PROGRAM is empty, you can remove it. You can either specify the full path by typing **RD \WORDPROC\PROGRAM,** or you can move to \WORDPROC and use the short form, as shown in this command sequence:

CD \WORDPROC

RD PROGRAM

Do not attempt to use the following command:

RD \WORDPROC\LETTERS

If you try this command, you receive an error message. You cannot delete this directory because it contains two child directories. Although this safety feature may seem an inconvenient obstacle when you want to remove an entire directory, it has its benefits. The feature averts the potential disaster of mistakenly wiping out a whole branch of your directory tree. OS/2 provides this feature as a built-in safety net.

To remove the \WORDPROC\LETTERS branch, you must first remove its subdirectories by typing the following command sequence:

CD\WORDPROC\LETTERS

RD SALLY

RD TOM

Again, however, don't try typing this command:

RD \WORDPROC\LETTERS

If you type this command now, you run into another safeguard. OS/2 does not let you remove the current directory. You easily can get around this safeguard; simply switch to another directory, such as the root, and remove the remaining directories in the opposite order in which you created them, as shown in the following command sequence:

**CD **

RD \WORDPROC\LETTERS

RD \WORDPROC

You have learned how to create, move, and remove directories. Directories are just containers, however, useful only because of the files you put in them. The next section discusses several commands for managing files.

For Related Information
- "Organizing Directories," p. 51
- "Command Reference," p. 717

Learning the Commands for Managing Files

As you learned in Chapter 2, "Learning OS/2 If You Don't Know DOS," files are sets of data you store on a disk. This section covers several important commands you use to do the following:

- Obtain a list of the files in a directory
- Copy a file
- Back up a group of files to a floppy disk
- Delete a file you no longer need
- Change a file's name

In this section you learn that these commands can manipulate more than one file at a time.

Every file has a *name* and an *extension*—these are like your first and last names. Your last name tells what family you belong to, and file extensions work the same way.

Program files usually have the extension EXE, which means they are files of the executable program family. A file's name tells which member of the family it is. The file MURAL.EXE, for example, is part of the program family whose members can paint a background on the Presentation Manager screen. A period usually separates the name and extension.

If you use OS/2's High Performance File System (HPFS), you can give files very long names; other systems limit filenames to eight characters and extensions to three characters. With this bit of background, you are ready to start working with files.

> **Caution**
>
> HPFS files with long file names are invisible in DOS sessions under OS/2. OS/2 applications and OS/2 command prompt sessions can access the files, but DOS applications and DOS command prompt sessions cannot.

Listing Files (DIR)

The first question you may ask about a directory is "what files does it contain?" The DIR command answers that question. To see a list of the files in the current directory, type **DIR**. To list the files in a non-current directory, type **DIR** followed by the name of the directory, for example:

DIR \OS2\BOOK

If you type this example, the system returns the following messages:

```
The volume label in drive C is HARDDISK.
 The Volume Serial Number is 3F58:12C9
 Directory of C:\OS2\BOOK
 .            <DIR>       7-31-92    9:04p
 ..           <DIR>       7-31-92    9:04p
 REXX    INF    174936    7-03-92    4:19a
 CMDREF  INF    364447    7-03-92    3:21a
 SAMPLE       <DIR>       8-10-92    2:40p
      5 File(s)     13117440 bytes free
```

What do these messages mean? First, the directory contains two files. REXX.INF is 174,936 bytes long and was created or last modified on July 3, 1992, at 4:19 a.m. The other file, CMDREF.INF, is about twice as big as REXX.INF and was created about an hour earlier. About 13 million bytes are available on this disk.

If only two files are located on this disk, why does the last line displayed by DIR say 5 File(s)? The three extra "files" are marked <DIR>, which labels them as directories. Technically, directories are files of a special type. They have a date and time stamp but no size. The first directory name is shown as a period, meaning the \OS2\BOOK directory, and the second directory name is shown as two periods, meaning the parent directory, \OS2. If you run DIR on a drive that you formatted with the High Performance File System, DIR displays the same information, but in a different order.

Most directories have many more files than this example illustrates. The \OS2 directory, for example, contains about 100 files. If you type **DIR \OS2**, the filenames zoom by on your screen faster than you can read them. To help you manage lengthy directories, OS/2 provides two options called *switches*. A switch is an option that you type after a command; the switch always follows a slash (/). If you type the switch **/P**, for example, you tell OS/2 that you want your scrolling screen to pause after every page. To look at the files in the \OS2 directory one screen at a time, type the following:

DIR \OS2 /P

OS/2 displays as much information as it can fit on the screen, followed by the message `Press any key when ready`. When you press a key, OS/2 shows the next screen and pauses again.

If you want to see only the filenames and not the size and date information, use the /W (Wide Listing) switch. This switch makes DIR list the filenames five columns across. Type the following:

DIR \OS2\BOOK /W

The system returns the following message:

```
The volume label in drive C is HARDDISK.
The Volume Serial Number is 3F58:12C9
Directory of C:\OS2\BOOK
.              ..             REXX      INF       CMDREF
INF            SAMPLE         DIR
     5 File(s)    13117440 bytes free
```

These switches can help you wade through a large directory list, but sometimes you want to display only the names of certain files. You can narrow the scope of DIR by telling it, for example, to show only files with names containing a particular sequence of characters. The next two sections explain the techniques for producing these listings and provide some practice examples.

Using Wild Cards

In some card games, certain cards are *wild*; wild cards match any other card. In OS/2, when you want to refer to a set of computer files that have similar names, you can use wild-card characters. If the following explanations seem complicated at first, you can skim through them for now and then skip ahead to the examples in the next section. Practice is the best way to become familiar with wild cards and to appreciate their usefulness.

OS/2 uses two wild cards—the asterisk (*) and the question mark (?). The asterisk matches any *group* of characters, as you can see in the following examples:

*.EXE indicates the set of all files with the extension .EXE, regardless of the filename.

C*.EXE indicates all .EXE files with names beginning with the letter C. These files include CALENDAR.EXE but not ABC.EXE or CC.TXT (ABC.EXE does not start with C, and CC.TXT's extension is not .EXE).

C.* indicates all files whose names contain the letter C, regardless of their extension. The group includes files CONSYS, ACE.TXT, and

ABC.DEF. It does not include AAA.CCC, however, because the letter C occurs only in the file's extension, not in its name.

The question mark is OS/2's other wild card character. While the asterisk matches any group of characters, the question mark matches any *single* character, as shown in the following examples:

?.EXE indicates all files with one-character names whose extension is .EXE. This category includes the file A.EXE; it does not include file AB.EXE.

???.* indicates all files whose names are up to three characters long, regardless of their extensions. It matches ABC.DEF, but not ABCEF.GHI.

You also can combine wild cards. The example ?O*. means any file with O as the second letter of its name and no extension. This example matches COMMENTS and COOKIES but not MEMO or OOO.OOO.

In DOS sessions, the asterisk wild card works a little differently. DOS ignores characters following the asterisk. In DOS mode, therefore, A*C matches ABC, AAA, or any other name beginning with A.

You also can insert filenames containing wild cards in your command-lines. In these situations, the filename containing the wild card becomes a *file specification*. OS/2 looks for every file that matches the file specification and applies the command to each of those files in turn. The remaining sections of this chapter provide many examples that illustrate the use of wild cards with a variety of commands.

Using DIR with Wild Cards

Now that you're acquainted with wild cards, the time has come to reinforce the concepts with practical examples. Suppose that your word processing program applies the extension TXT to the documents you type. To view a list of these documents, you can type DIR and search the entire directory for TXT files. The following command, however, provides a more efficient tool:

DIR \WORDPROC*.TXT

This command produces a list of only the TXT files; you easily can compare their names, dates, and sizes. If the listing of TXT files does not fit on one screen, add a switch to the command, for example:

DIR \WORDPROC*.TXT /P

As another example, if you use Lotus 1-2-3 for Presentation Manager, you may save spreadsheets with extensions WK1, WK2, or WK3. To list them all, type the following:

DIR \123G*.WK?

If you have a series of spreadsheets with names like BUDGET1 and BUDGET2, you can display all names in the series by typing the following:

DIR \123G\BUDGET*.WK?

In OS/2 mode only, you can specify more than one set of files in a single command:

DIR \123G\BUDGET*.WK? \123G\SALES.WK?

You can create your own examples and use them to experiment with the wild cards. Practice until you feel comfortable with wild cards—they are an important tool for extending the power of many commands.

Deleting a File (DEL or ERASE)

DEL (Delete) and ERASE are two names for the command you use to delete files. If you use the delete command by mistake, it can erase a file you don't want to erase. To practice safely with the command, type the following command sequence to set up a directory of files you can afford to delete:

MD \ERASE.ME

CD \ERASE.ME

XCOPY \OS2

The last line above copies the OS/2 files into your new directory. To protect its most critical files, OS/2 does not copy them to the new directory. You can confirm with the DIR command, however, that you have enough files in the new directory to experiment with DEL. You can begin experimenting by deleting XCOPY.EXE, the program you used to copy the files. To delete it, type:

DEL \ERASE.ME\XCOPY.EXE

Alternatively, make very sure that you are in the \ERASE.ME directory first, then type:

DEL XCOPY.EXE

DEL also works with wild cards. Many of the files in \ERASE.ME begin with the letters PM. To erase them all in one operation, type the following:

DEL PM*.*

In OS/2 mode (but not in DOS mode), you can delete more than one set of files with a single command. To delete all files whose names or extensions contain the letter E, type:

DEL *E*.* *.*E*

Finally, type the following to try to delete all the files remaining in \ERASE.ME:

DEL .

Remember, the single period is shorthand for the entire current directory. Wiping out this directory is a drastic action, so OS/2 asks you to confirm that you really want to do so. For now, answer **no** to leave some practice files for the next command.

> **Caution**
> Be extremely careful when you use wild cards with the DEL command. You inadvertently may delete more files than you intended to.

Changing a File Name (REN or RENAME)

The RENAME or REN command changes the name of a file. If you worked through the examples in the previous section and are still in the ERASE.ME directory, your practice directory still has a file called CHKDSK.COM. To give it a more pronounceable name, type this command:

REN CHKDSK.COM CHEKDISK.COM

REN works with wild cards. If you find the command names DISKCOPY and DISKCOMP too long for your taste, try typing this:

REN DISK*.COM D*.COM

Now you have two new commands, DCOPY and DCOMP, which work exactly like the originals.

Copying Files (COPY)

The COPY command has many uses. In its most basic form, it duplicates a file and gives the duplicate a different name than the original, or it places the duplicate in a different directory. Before changing your CONSYS file, for example, which records the particular way you have customized OS/2, you first make a backup copy as a safeguard. To create the backup copy and name it CONOLD, you type the following:

COPY \CONSYS \CONOLD

If you're already in the root directory, you can omit the backslashes and just type the following:

COPY CONSYS CONOLD

In either situation, you first type the name of the file you want to copy, followed by the name of the file want to create. Use care when assigning names to files you create with COPY. If you create a file using a name that is already assigned to another file, COPY overwrites the original file and replaces its contents with those of the new file. The original file's contents are lost forever.

What if you want to copy the file to a different directory? You may create a directory named \BACKUP, for example, specifically for saving old files. In this case, you need not change the file name to CONOLD because two files can have the same name if they are in different directories. You can type the full path of each file with this command:

COPY \CONSYS \BACKUP\CONSYS

You must do some extra typing to specify the path and file name completely, but this command always works no matter in which directory you are currently working. If no \BACKUP directory exists, your screen displays an error message.

If the \BACKUP directory exists, you can use this shorter command form and achieve the same results:

COPY \CONSYS \BACKUP

Because this method specifies the path but not the name of the copy, OS/2 uses the name of the original file. If the \BACKUP directory doesn't exist, OS/2 interprets \BACKUP as the name of a file that you want to create in the root directory.

If \BACKUP is the current directory, you need only type the following to get the same result:

COPY \CONSYS

OS/2 sees that you have not specified a name for the new file, so it assumes that you want a duplicate, with the same name as the original file but in the current directory. If you're in the root directory, however, this command gives you an error message because you cannot copy a file onto itself.

OS/2 offers shortcuts that can help you work more quickly, but you must be aware of the dangers of using shortcuts. You always are safest when you spell out what you want in full detail. Practice that way at first until you feel proficient. The next section introduces another powerful technique—one that enables you to copy whole groups of files with a single command.

Copying with Wild Cards. Suppose that you have four Lotus spreadsheets in your \123G directory and you want to copy them all to a disk so that you can work on them at home. You can type a separate COPY command for each spreadsheet, but you have an easier option because the spreadsheets share the same file extension. You type the following to take advantage of the easy method:

COPY \123G*.WK1 A:

This single command copies all four spreadsheets because the asterisk wild card matches any file name.

If you have January sales and payroll figures in spreadsheets named JANSALES.WK1 and JANPAYRL.WK1, and you want duplicates for entering February results, type the following:

COPY \123G\JAN*.WK1 \123G\FEB*.WK1

If you're in the \123G directory, you can simplify the command to the following:

COPY JAN*.WK1 FEB*.WK1

Remember that OS/2 applies the command to every file that matches the wild-card specification. If your coworker Janet had a spreadsheet JANET.WK1 in this directory, you just made a copy called FEBET.WK1.

COPY with wild cards is a very powerful command that can save you a lot of typing. You must be careful, however—a typing mistake can mean you don't get what you want. If your finger slips, for example, and you accidentally omit the colon in this section's first example, then OS/2 interprets **A** as the name of a file:

COPY \123G*.WK1 A

OS/2 creates a file called A and copies each of your spreadsheets to it. Further, if you already had a file named A, it is gone forever. Of course this outcome is not what you intended; but the command is valid, so the system produces no error message. The more powerful the command, the more carefully you must work with it.

Copying and Combining Files. COPY also enables you to combine files. Suppose that you have used a spreadsheet to create several exhibits, which you want to print out and attach to a memo. Putting them all in one file makes this task a little easier and ensures that the files remain together. To use COPY to accomplish this task, you join the names of the files you want to combine with plus signs and then give a name for the file that is to contain them, as shown in the following example:

COPY EXHIBIT1.PRN+EXHIBIT2.PRN+EXHIBIT3.PRN EXHIBITS

If you don't supply a new name for the combined file, COPY uses the first name you listed. For example,

COPY EXHIBIT1.PRN+EXHIBIT2.PRN+EXHIBIT3.PRN

adds EXHIBIT2.PRN and EXHIBIT3.PRN to the end of EXHIBIT1.PRN.

> **Tip**
>
> Every file has a date and time stamp that shows when you last changed the file. COPY usually duplicates this information along with the file's data; but when you use COPY to combine files, the new file gets the current date and time. Here is a neat trick to change the date and time of an old file to the current date and time:
>
> **COPY MYFILE+**
>
> The plus sign means add another file at the end of MYFILE, but you have not indicated what file is to be added. The contents of MYFILE, therefore, are unchanged. You can give a file any date you want by first using the DATE command to set the computer's internal date.
>
> Consider the following command:
>
> **COPY .+**
>
> This command puts the current time and date on every file in the current directory. This unusual trick works only with OS/2 and not DOS.

Using COPY and Devices. This section contains somewhat advanced information. You may want to skip this section entirely unless you have enjoyed the expert tips in earlier sections.

COPY treats devices—such as the keyboard and the printer—as though they are files. As a result, you can use the following command to copy from the keyboard to the printer:

COPY CON PRN

This command makes your computer behave like a typewriter. PRN is the name of the printer device, and CON (short for console) represents the keyboard and screen. You also can copy a file to the PRN device. However, the PRINT command, discussed later in this chapter, is a more versatile tool for producing printouts.

When you COPY from CON, you need a way to tell COPY that you are finished typing your file, so that the command can stop copying and return you to the OS/2 prompt. You stop the copying action by pressing the special end-of-file character, Ctrl-Z, and then pressing Enter. This feature is easy to remember, because Z comes at the end of the alphabet, so Ctrl-Z marks the end of the file.

You can copy from the console to a file by using the following:

COPY CON MYFILE.TXT

You can use this command to create a new file quickly; just type the text and press Enter after each line. This feature is handy when you want to quickly copy a short file. You cannot change a line after you type it, however, so this technique does not replace your editor or word processing program. Remember to press Ctrl-Z and then Enter when you are finished typing.

What happens if you COPY a file to CON? You can try this experiment by typing the following command:

COPY \CONFIG.SYS CON

This command copies the file to your screen. Remember, the console represents the keyboard and the screen. When you COPY *from* the console, you copy from the keyboard. When you COPY *to* the console, you copy to the screen.

You also can copy a file to the printer by typing this command:

COPY \CONFIG.SYS PRN

You cannot copy *from* the printer, however, because it is not an input device like the keyboard.

Copying files to the screen and printer are such important operations that they have their own commands, TYPE and PRINT, which are discussed later in this chapter.

Copying Directories (XCOPY)

XCOPY (Extended COPY) is a specialized version of the COPY command. The XCOPY command copies groups of files more flexibly than COPY. XCOPY can even copy whole branches of a directory tree. This command is not a complete replacement for COPY, however, because it does not combine files or work with devices such as the printer.

In early OS/2 versions, XCOPY ran faster than COPY under DOS, but that advantage has all but disappeared in later OS/2 versions. Compare the speed of both commands on your system. XCOPY may be the quicker of the two commands. Even if XCOPY is not faster, the command is worth learning because of the power of its optional switches. Some of these switches tell the command to copy whole directories, including their subdirectories and all the files they contain. Other switches enable you to copy only certain files—based, for example, on the date you last changed them or whether you have backed them up. The following paragraphs describe these XCOPY switches.

/S With this switch, you can copy an entire directory tree. If you have several subdirectories on a floppy disk and want to copy them with all their contents to your hard disk, for example, type:

XCOPY A: C: /S

This command creates all the subdirectories automatically and then copies every file to its proper location. If you have two hard drives and want to move an entire spreadsheet package with all its subdirectories and files from the first drive to the second, type:

XCOPY C:\123G D: /S

/E Perhaps your spreadsheet setup includes a separate subdirectory for files you plan to create for a future project, but you have not yet put any files in the subdirectory. XCOPY with the /S switch does not copy this empty subdirectory unless you also include /E, as in the following example:

XCOPY C:\123G D: /S /E

You should make a habit of including /E whenever you use /S, because in most circumstances you want to copy all subdirectories, even those that are empty.

/P Sometimes you want to copy only certain files from one directory to another. Suppose that you have a dozen memos in your \MEMOS directory, for example, and you want to copy five of them to a disk. If you use the command

XCOPY \MEMOS A: /P

OS/2 displays the name of each file in turn, and asks whether you want to copy it.

/D This switch enables you to copy just the files that you created or changed after a certain date. For example,

XCOPY \MEMOS A: /D:1-1-92

selects every file in your \MEMOS directory that bears a date later than 1991, and copies it to a floppy disk.

/A This switch copies files that have not been backed up. Back up your files regularly by using the BACKUP command, which is discussed later in this chapter. Suppose that you do this every Friday, but this is Tuesday and you just finished an important project. You may want to copy your latest files to a disk for extra safety. Instead of running BACKUP, you type the following:

XCOPY \PROJECT A: /A

The /A switch stands for archive because backing up files is like packing papers into a box and shipping them off to an archive. Every file has an archive flag that indicates whether or not you have backed up the file; the flag is turned on when you create or change the file, and off when you run BACKUP. When you run XCOPY with /A you do not change this flag.

/M This switch works exactly like /A except that it turns off the archive flag of each file you copy. This feature is useful when you want to use XCOPY as a substitute for BACKUP. BACKUP writes files in a special format, and you must use RESTORE to convert them back to their original format before you can use them. XCOPY does not have this drawback, but because BACKUP makes more efficient use of space, it uses fewer disks than does XCOPY. BACKUP also can copy a file that is too large to fit on a single disk. You may prefer to use BACKUP rather than XCOPY, therefore, in some situations.

For Related Information
- "Copying Disks and Files," p. 54
- "Deleting, Renaming, and Moving," p. 56
- "Command Reference," p. 717

Learning the Commands to Back Up Your Hard Disk

If your hard disk stops working correctly, you can replace it. The data you have stored on the disk, however, is probably worth more to you than the computer itself. You may have to put forth enormous effort to replace the data—unless you have a backup copy. Hardware failures are rare, fortunately, and you are more likely to lose data because of a defective program or a mistaken command. In either case, however, the BACKUP command is your insurance policy against losing valuable data.

BACKUP copies data on your hard disk to floppy disks. It uses a special format for your data, so you cannot use commands such as COPY to read the data. Instead, you must use RESTORE to copy files from your backup disks back to the hard disk.

BACKUP and RESTORE intentionally refuse to work with some of OS/2's most critical files. These files are the OS2.INI, OS2SYS.INI, EA DATA. SF, and WP ROOT. SF files. When it multitasks, OS/2 keeps these files open and continually updates the files. BACKUP and RESTORE cannot access these files while OS/2 is using them. Chapter 8, "Troubleshooting OS/2," provides steps you can take to make backup copies of these critical files.

If you have a large hard disk, consider buying a tape backup unit. Tape cartridges can hold as much data as your hard disk, so you can back up your hard disk without having to continually swap floppy disks. As a rule, tape drives come with their own software; make sure that the one you get can run under OS/2 as well as DOS.

Making a Backup (BACKUP)
BACKUP copies the files on your hard disk to floppy disks. After you have a complete backup of every file, you can update the backup by directing BACKUP to affect only the files that you have changed or added. User opinions vary, but one rule of thumb is to do a complete backup every couple of months and update it weekly.

Making a Complete Backup. Most users need several floppy disks for a complete backup, because each floppy disk holds far less data than a hard disk. If you have a 60 megabyte hard disk that is half full, for example, you need about 20 floppy disks if you are using a high-density, 3 1/2-inch drive. To find out how many disks you need, follow these steps:

1. Run the CHKDSK program to find out how much space your files consume. The command's response should resemble this:

   ```
   29935872 bytes in 827 user files.
   ```

2. Look up the capacity of your disk drive in the following table:

Table 12.1 Disk Drive Capacities

Disk Drive Type	Capacity in Kilobytes
5 1/4-inch double density	360
5 1/4-inch high density	1,200
3 1/2-inch double density	720
3 1/2-inch high density	1,440
3 1/2-inch ultra density	2,880

3. Divide the number of bytes used on the hard disk by the number of bytes on each disk; divide the result by 1,000 and round up the result. If you're using 3 1/2-inch, high-density disks, 29,935,872 / 1,440 is approximately 21,000, so you need about 21 disks. Add a few extra disks to be sure you have enough. Twenty-five disks should be plenty for this backup.

To do a complete backup from your hard drive C to a high-density, 3 1/2-inch disk drive A, first prepare the necessary number of disks. You don't need to format them, but stick a label on each and number them in order. Then type the following:

BACKUP C:*.* A: /F:1440 /S

This command uses the two following optional switches:

/F This switch tells BACKUP to format each disk, so you can use new disks right out of the box. You have to include the disk capacity (in kilobytes), shown in the preceding table. If you already formatted the disks, BACKUP doesn't format them again, which makes the backup process go a little faster. Further, if you format the disks first, you can discard any that have bad sectors.

/S This switch tells BACKUP to copy not only the files in the root directory of C but also each subdirectory and all its files.

After you type the preceding command, your screen displays the following messages:

```
BACKUP C:\*.* A: /F:1440
Insert backup disk 01 in drive A:
Warning!  The files in the root directory
of target drive A: will be erased.
Press Enter to continue or Ctrl+Break to cancel.
```

The warning simply states that any data you may have on the disk will be replaced with the backup. If this condition is acceptable, press Enter. If the disk is unformatted, BACKUP takes care of that first:

```
Insert a new disk in drive A:
and press Enter when ready.
Formatting has been completed.
The Volume Serial Number is 6217-1815
Enter up to 11 characters for the volume label,
or press Enter for no volume label. BACKUP01
```

A *volume label* is similar to the paper label you stick on the disk except that the volume label is a file on the disk. This label is optional.

```
1457664 bytes total disk space
1457664 bytes available on disk
512 bytes in each allocation unit.
2847 available allocation units on disk.
Format another disk (Y/N)? N
```

After formatting the disk, BACKUP moves your files onto it.

```
The files are being backed up to drive A.
Disk number 01
```

The name of every file appears on the screen after it is backed up. When a disk is full, BACKUP asks you to remove the disk and insert the next one.

Updating the Backup. Later on, when you want to refresh your complete backup by adding newly created or modified files, type the following:

BACKUP C:*.* A: /F:1440 /S /M

Notice the new switch, */M Modified Files Only*. This switch tells BACKUP to add only the new files. OS/2 marks the files it backs up, so it can pick out those that are new or have changed. After you type the above command, the following message appears on-screen:

```
Insert backup disk 01 in drive A:
Warning!  The files in the root directory
of target drive A: will be erased.
Press Enter to continue or Ctrl+Break to cancel.
```

```
The files are being backed up to drive A.
Disk number 01
```

BACKUP lists the files on-screen, enabling you to watch its progress.

Making a Partial Backup. In some situations you may want to back up only a certain directory or a certain set of files. If you want a separate backup copy of the memos you keep in your \MEMOS directory, for example, and they all have the extension MEM, type the following:

BACKUP C:\MEMOS*.MEM A:

The following two switches can help you make selective backups:

/D Backs up files created or changed since a given date

/T Backs up files created or changed since a given time

You can use these switches together. To make a backup of the memos in \MEMOS, excluding files that were present before noon on March 1, 1992, and have not changed since then, type the following command-line:

BACKUP C:\MEMOS*.MEM A: /D:3-1-92 /T:12:00

Restoring from Backup (RESTORE)

In the preceding section, you learned how to use the BACKUP command to store the contents of your hard disk on a set of disks. You cannot use the stored data immediately, however; to put it back on the hard disk, you use BACKUP's companion, the RESTORE command.

Suppose that you backed up the hard disk you use at work and want to recreate all the files and directories on your computer at home. You first must install OS/2 at home—remember, BACKUP and RESTORE do not work with OS/2's system files. After you complete the installation, type the following:

RESTORE A: C: /S

Insert the disks in order, and OS/2 places all the files and directories on the hard disks, and your screen displays these messages:

```
Insert backup disk 01 in drive A:
Press Enter when ready.
The files were backed up on 09-28-1992.
Files will be restored from drive A:
Disk 01
```

RESTORE then displays the name of each file and prompts you to change disks as needed.

You also can restore a single file, for example,

RESTORE A: C:\CONFIG.SYS

or all the files in a single directory,

RESTORE A: C:\DATABASE*.*

or a certain set of files that you specify by using wild cards, as in

RESTORE A: C:\DATABASE\CUSTOMER.*

If you backed up files from the \DATABASE directory, however, you cannot restore them to a different directory, such as \DATA.

Several optional switches extend the flexibility of RESTORE. They enable you to restore files in all subdirectories or restore only files that you have modified or deleted since the last backup. You can limit the command to files that you modified either after or before a given time and date, and you can tell RESTORE to ask your permission before writing over a file that you have modified. The following paragraphs list and describe these switches.

/S By default, RESTORE only restores files in the hard disk's current directory. Use this switch when you want to restore files in all subdirectories.

/N With this switch, RESTORE processes only files that don't exist on the hard drive, such as files you deleted after making the backup.

/M This switch tells RESTORE to restore only those files that you have deleted or changed since the backup and to ignore all other files. Use /M if you have made accidental changes to your files and want to put them back the way they were.

/P If you want RESTORE to ask your permission before replacing any file that you have changed since its last backup, use /P. This safety feature protects you against accidentally wiping out the changes you have made after the backup.

/A and */L*   Suppose that you finished a project last Friday at 6 p.m. and then immediately did a backup. If a misguided co-worker dropped in over the weekend and deleted or changed some of the files, these switches let you undo the damage. To put your files back the way they were at a given date and time, type the following:

RESTORE A: C: /S /A:3-1-92 /L:18:00

/B and */E*   These switches correspond to /A and /L, but they tell RESTORE to replace files that you changed *before* the data and time you specify.

For Related Information
- "Formatting Hard Disks and Floppy Disks," p. 53
- "Command Reference," p. 717

Learning the Commands for Viewing and Printing Files

The preceding sections of this chapter have presented commands that treat files as sealed boxes. You have learned how to change the labels on file folders and move them from one file cabinet to another. You haven't learned, however, how to open the folders up and look at what they contain (except within the "expert" sections on using COPY to display files on-screen and the printer). The following sections examine two commands that display a file's contents.

Displaying a File On-Screen (MORE)

The MORE command displays a file on-screen. MORE uses a syntax unlike the other commands in this chapter. To use MORE to display your system configuration file, for example, one screen at a time, type the following command-line:

MORE< \CONFIG.SYS

You must type the less-than sign, because MORE is a special type of program known as a *filter*. The advanced topic of filters is beyond the scope of this book. For now, consider the less-than sign as part of the command's name.

Printing a File (PRINT)

Most OS/2 and DOS applications have built-in options for printing the files they create. You also can print files with the PRINT command. For example, to send the file \CONFIG.SYS to the printer, type the following:

PRINT \CONFIG.SYS

You can print more than one file at once, by typing the following:

PRINT \LETTERS\LETTER1.TXT \LETTERS\LETTER2.TXT

You also can use wild cards, for example:

PRINT \LETTERS\LETTER*.TXT

The PRINT command works correctly only for plain text files. If you try to print a Lotus 1-2-3 spreadsheet with a WK1 extension, you do not get a spreadsheet printout because WK1 files have a special internal file format that only the spreadsheet program understands. (You would get a garbled printout of the internal file format.) If you use 1-2-3's Print to File option, however, 1-2-3 will create a plain, unformatted file with a PRN extension that can be printed with the PRINT command. 1-2-3 in this instance converts the WK1 file contents to a plain text file format the printer can print.

The following paragraphs list and describe the optional switches you can use with PRINT.

/D If you have more than one printer, you can use this option to choose among them. Follow the /D switch with a colon and then the name of the printer. The names for the first three printers are LPT1, LPT2, and LPT3; network printers can have higher numbers. To print a file on the second printer, for example, type the following:

PRINT MYFILE.TXT /D:LPT2

If you don't use the /D switch, your files go to the first printer.

For Related Information
- "Storing Files and File Names," p.45
- "Command Reference," p. 717

/C This option tells PRINT to stop printing the file it is currently working with. PRINT goes on to print any other files you have sent to the printer.

/T This option cancels all files you have sent to the printer.

You cannot use the /C and /T switches together. You cannot cancel printing of a particular file by name.

Chapter Summary

In this chapter, you saw how to use the command-line interface and mastered its most important commands. Working through examples, you saw that this interface is very powerful, although it is harder to learn than Presentation Manager. OS/2 has more than 100 commands, and the Command Reference in Part VI, "Using the Command Reference," discusses them in detail.

Fortunately, you don't have to remember all the options and switches for each command. Chapter 13, "Using the Built-In Help Facility," explains how to obtain extensive on-line help for both command-line and Presentation Manager sessions.

Chapter 13

Using the Built-In Help Facility

In the last chapter, you learned several OS/2 commands, but you undoubtedly did not memorize every option and switch. If you did memorize them, congratulations! The rest of us, however, can use OS/2's built-in help facility to look up the command for every option and switch.

Even if you remember the exact command, the built-in help feature can be a valuable tool by deciphering OS/2 error messages for you. Suppose that you make a mistake typing a command, and OS/2 replies with an error message that you don't understand. You can use the HELP command to obtain a full explanation of the error message, including possible causes for the error and steps you can take to correct it.

The Presentation Manager application also includes a built-in help feature. This feature offers many pages of information to assist you in learning and using the program. The help feature presents its information in a book format, with a table of contents and an index. You also can search the help information for key words, or print the information if you want a paper copy.

Presentation Manager's on-line Command Reference program offers extensive help on every OS/2 command. The Command Reference includes many examples and cross-referenced related commands.

No matter how you use OS/2, you have immediate access to help in many ways and in many forms. This chapter groups the discussion of the HELP command into the following four categories:

- Understanding a Command-Line Window
- Learning Presentation Manager
- Using the Command Reference Utility

Understanding a Command-Line Window

What if you are working in an OS/2 window, and you cannot recall exactly how to use a needed command? Or what if you receive a puzzling error message and don't understand it? You easily can get assistance in both situations if you simply type **HELP**. After you type the HELP command, the following messages appear on-screen:

```
[C:\]HELP
Alt+Esc to switch to the next session.
Ctrl+Esc to switch to the Task List.
Type HELP ON for help text.
Type HELP OFF for no help text.
Type HELP message-number for message help.
Type HELP [ BOOK ] SUBJECT to receive online information.
Type EXIT to end this OS/2 session.
```

The following paragraphs discuss each of these HELP messages and how to use them. Even if you already know how to switch from one session to another, you can benefit from learning the forms of the HELP command.

Turning the HELP Reminder On and Off

You can use the HELP ON and HELP OFF commands to instruct OS/2 to display or not to display help reminders. When you opened the window, for example, you may have noticed this brief reminder at the top:

```
Ctrl+Esc = Task List   Type HELP = help
```

This reminder remains on-screen even when other text scrolls off. If you type **CLS** to clear the screen, the reminder remains. If you want to instruct OS/2 not to display the reminder, type **HELP OFF**. You can redisplay the message at any time by typing **HELP ON**.

Using HELP to Remember a Command

Suppose that you want to list your files one screen at a time. You remember that DIR is the command you need but cannot recall the necessary switch. Is it /W for *Wait* or does that stand for *Wide*? You can look up the switch in the Reference Section if you have this book handy, or you can type the following:

HELP DIR

When you type **HELP** followed by the name of a command, you bring up OS/2's on-line Command Reference and go right to the command you named. In a later section of this chapter, you learn how to use the powerful Command Reference program.

Using HELP to Explain an Error Message

If you ask OS/2 to do something impossible, such as to show the directory of a drive that doesn't exist, you receive an error message similar to the following:

```
[C:\]DIR Z:  SYS0015: The system cannot find the drive specified.
```

Perhaps you wanted drive A but typed **Z** by accident. You have no idea that you typed the wrong letter, and therefore you don't understand why the system cannot find drive A.

In the previous example, you may go back and check your DIR command line and discover your error. Many of OS/2's error messages, however, are more complex than the one just displayed. You can obtain a further explanation of any error message by typing HELP followed by the number that appears at the beginning of the message (you need not type the letters and zeroes at the beginning of the number.) HELP then repeats the error message, explains the message's meaning, and suggests other ways to issue the command.

To obtain help on SYS0015, for example, you type HELP 15 and receive the following explanation:

```
SYS0015: The system cannot find the drive specified.
EXPLANATION: One of the following has occurred:
  1. The drive specified does not exist.
  2. The drive letter is incorrect.
  3. You are trying to RESTORE to a redirected drive.
  ACTION: For situations 1 and 2 above; retry the command by using
the correct drive letter. For situation 3, you are not allowed to
RESTORE to a redirected drive.
```

In this example, the second explanation is the hint you need.

For Related Information
- "Beginning the Command-Line Interface," p. 303

Learning Presentation Manager

All Presentation Manager programs share a common user interface. As a result of this shared interface, you can get help regardless of which PM program you are using. Further, you obtain help by using the same methods in every application. You use the following methods to obtain help:

- Press F1 to bring up a Help menu or screen.
- Use the application Help selection. Every PM application has a Help selection on its action bar. Clicking that selection, or pressing Alt-H, pulls down a Help menu.
- Most dialog boxes offer Help buttons that give you specific help for that dialog box.

Getting Help on Help

OS/2's Help system is extensive. You can explore the Help system to find out what it offers, although you may spend a great deal of time doing so. Fortunately, the Help system contains information on how to use Help.

To see the Help feature in action, open the Desktop settings notebook by clicking an empty place on the desktop with the right mouse button. Click the arrow next to the word Help. Choose the menu item labeled Using Help. The window now displays Help for Using the Help Facility. If you want more information on this category, press F1 and Help for the Help Window appears.

As this exercise has demonstrated, Help has several levels. You can back up one level by pressing Esc.

Getting Help for Menu Options

Sometimes you encounter menu items whose operations are not immediately apparent to you. In most circumstances, you want to know what a menu item does before you try to use it.

Click an empty place on the desktop with the right mouse button (button 2) to bring up the desktop's pop-up menu. Click the Select menu item once to highlight it. Press the F1 key to get help for that menu option.

You can get instant help on a highlighted option only by pressing F1. If you click Help on the action bar, the Help menu replaces the pop-up menu. Not all ways of getting help work in all situations, so you benefit from mastering every technique for obtaining help.

You can use another technique to learn more about an action before you select that action. Bring up the desktop's pop-up menu again and choose the Find option. A dialog box pops up that contains a Help button you can click. You also can use F1 in this box.

In most situations, you can choose between several methods of obtaining help. If you practice them all, you find it easier to learn new applications. Most of the methods you learn also apply to other programs, because of Presentation Manager's common interface.

Using an Application's Help Menu

The Help menu mentioned in the preceding two sections deserves a detailed discussion. The menu is a gateway to extensive help on each Presentation Manager application. In many cases, the help information is so complete that you can use it to learn a new application without studying the manual. The information is tailored to each application, but the ways you use the Help feature are always the same. Any time you spend now exploring all the available Help features, therefore, is time well spent. You already have opened the desktop's pop-up menu, so it can be your first example.

A Presentation Manager application's help system is like a book. The system has an introduction that gives you an overview, and a table of contents and an index that help you easily find the information you need. Because you can search the entire help system for a key word that interests you, the system is easier to use than most books.

Introduction. The introduction is the first section many people turn to when they pick up a book. To read the introduction to the desktop's on-line manual, select the Help option on the action bar, pull down the menu, and choose General Help. This selection displays a brief summary of the OS/2 desktop.

Table of Contents. Many books have a table of contents, and so does the Help facility. Pull down the Options menu on the General Help screen you just opened, and select Contents. You can scroll through the topics to get an idea of the desktop's capabilities. You may want more information, for example, on the Help for Folders topic. You can move the highlight to that topic and press Enter to get a brief explanation of folders.

Index. You also can learn about folders by looking up the topic in the index, which you call up with the Index option on any Help menu. The Help index contains an alphabetic listing of topics. As a result of this arrangement, when you know what you want to look up, the index can be a quicker source of help than is the table of contents. Help's index works just like a book's index, except you don't have to flip through pages to find a reference. You find the reference instantly when you press Enter.

For practice, open the index and look under F to find the word folder. Highlight the word and press Enter, or double-click the word. OS/2's on-line description of folders appears.

Search. Imagine reading through an entire book and marking every occurrence of a given topic. That task may be a chore for you, but it is the type of job a computer does well.

To start a search any time you are in the Help facility, press Ctrl-S or select Search from the Services menu. A Search window pops up. Type folder, press the All Sections button, and then press Enter. A menu appears listing every topic that contains the word folder, including some topics you may not have considered. When you press Enter again to explore any topic further, Help highlights in the text the word for which you searched.

Instead of searching all sections, you can look through the current section only, or just the index. You even can search across the entire OS/2 Help system if you pick All Libraries on the Search menu. In most situations, however, you can limit your search to All Sections.

Print. On-line help is easier to explore than a printed book, but you must be at your computer to use Help. You may want information on a piece of paper, so you can make notes on the paper, then fold it up and put in your pocket. This capability is built into on-line help through the Print option.

The Print option on the Services menu gives you several choices for printing Help text. You can print the current section, or the index, or the table of contents. You can print an entire Help manual by selecting All Sections.

Copy and Append to File. OS/2 stores Help files in a special format that saves space on your hard disk. You cannot examine the files directly by using tools such as the System Editor. If you want to put help information into a file you can access with a text editor, choose Copy or Append from the Services menu. These options put the currently displayed topic into a file. The file, named TEMP.TXT, is in the root directory of your hard disk. The Copy option replaces anything that was already in this file. The Append option adds the current topic to the file and leaves the file's previous contents intact.

Previous Topics and Previously Viewed Pages. As you wander through on-line help, you may want to retrace your steps. To backtrack one screen, press Esc or select Previous on the Options menu. You also can choose Viewed Pages on the same menu to obtain a list of all topics you have viewed. You then can jump immediately back to any page you want to see again.

Shortcut Keys. The pull-down menus provide an easy way to learn how to use help because they display every option. As you become proficient at using Help, however, you may want to maneuver around the system more quickly. You can use single keystrokes, or shortcut keys, for the operations you need most often. The menu lists these shortcut keys. The Options menu, for example, shows the shortcut key Ctrl-C next to Table of Contents. You can press this key to move right to the table of contents, even if the menu is not displayed. The Keys option on the Help menu gives a list of these shortcuts.

New Window. You can view more than one Help topic at a time. The New Window option enables you to do this by placing each topic in a separate window.

As an example of this option's uses, you can search all sections for help on folders. Help for Folder sounds useful, so you highlight it and press Ctrl-N to display this help panel in a new window. You can make the window smaller and drag it to the bottom of the screen so you can see the search list again. Now, you highlight the Help for Open entry and press Ctrl-N. If you resize this new window and move it to the top right corner, your screen resembles figure 13.1.

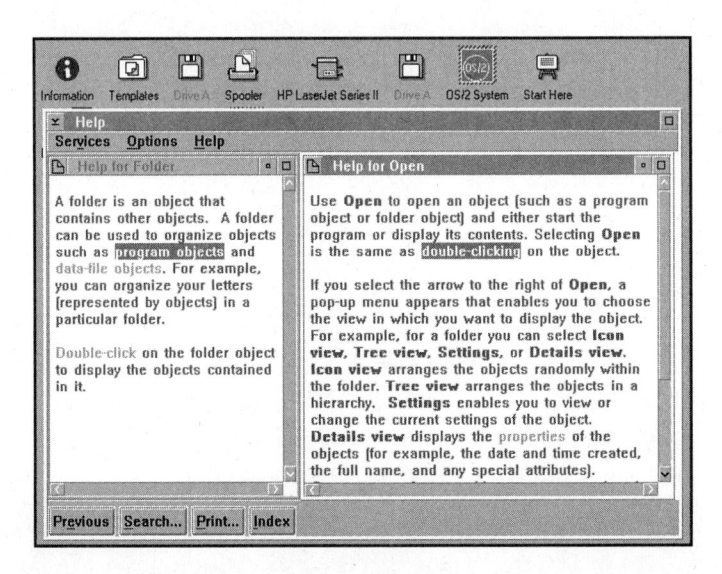

Fig. 13.1
Viewing more than one help window at a time.

The New Window option enables you to display several help panels at one time. You can maximize the Help window first, to provide more room for on-screen information. If the screen becomes crowded, you can minimize or close some of the windows.

For Related Information
- "Introducing Presentation Manager," p. 234

Branches. A table of contents is an outline and, like all outlines, it can have more than one level. Levels are like branches of a tree, in that each branch can have subbranches. The Command Reference help utility has several levels. The following section explains this program and shows how to view the table of contents in whatever level of detail you want.

Using the Command Reference Utility

The OS/2 Command Reference utility explains every OS/2 and DOS command. Because the Command Reference is a Presentation Manager program, it uses all the features you learned in the previous section of this chapter. As you learned in the first section, you can start the Command Reference from an OS/2 command-line session by typing **HELP** followed by the name of any command. You also can start it from the Information folder.

Selecting Levels of Detail in the Table of Contents

In addition to containing help for each command, the Command Reference contains general help for concepts that apply to your command-line sessions.

You can explore this utility by starting the Command Reference from the Information folder now. The table of contents appears, displaying a plus sign (+) next to the first entry, Information about OS/2 Commands. When you press the plus (+) key on the keyboard or click the plus sign in the window, you see another level of detail with three subtopics indented under the main heading. You click the first one, File and Directory Concepts, to see the screen illustrated in figure 13.2.

When you no longer want to view this branch of the outline, click the minus sign (–). The plus and minus keys are shortcut keys for the Expand One Level and Collapse Branch choices on the Options menu.

You can have more than one extra level of detail. To explore this capability, you first can expand the OS/2 Commands by Name heading. Next, scroll down a page, and you see the CHKDSK command with a plus sign before it. Click the plus sign, and yet another level of the outline appears.

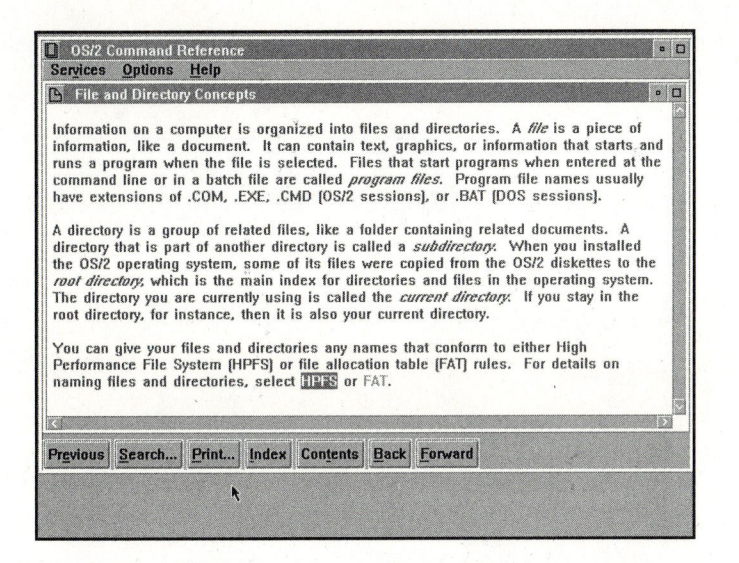

Fig. 13.2
Selecting a topic from on-line Help's table of contents.

To collapse the entire outline and see only the highest level, you press Ctrl-minus (–). To show the outline in full detail, you press Ctrl-asterisk (*).

Getting Help on a Command

To find out more about a particular command, you expand the OS/2 Commands by Name branch, move to the command, and press Enter. You can try this operation with the TIME command, located near the bottom of the alphabetical list. This command shows a Help screen with the following features (the screen is shown in figure 13.3):

- A brief description of the command's action. The TIME command, for example, sets the time on your computer's built-in clock.

- A railroad diagram that includes the command's name, (in this example, TIME), followed by several lines pointing to the options you can use with the command (here, to set the hour, minute, and second). Railroad diagrams are explained later in this section.

- An Examples button that you click to get an illustration of how to use the command. One of the examples for TIME shows how to set the clock to 6:45.

- A list of related commands. In addition to DATE, the TIME example includes COUNTRY, because the country you live in determines how OS/2 displays the time.

342   Chapter 13—Using the Built-In Help Facility

■ Notes that elaborate on what the command does and how you use it. The comments on TIME, for example, say that it uses the 24-hour clock.

Fig. 13.3
Obtaining on-line help for the TIME command.

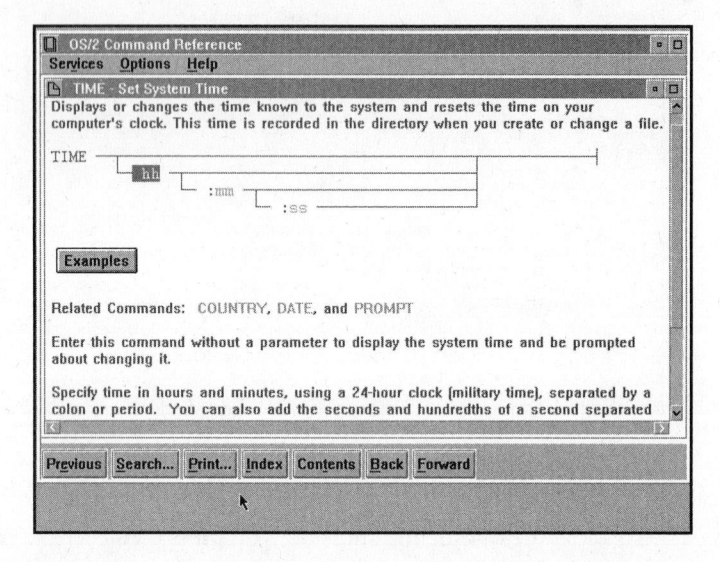

The screen in figure 13.3 shows hh in highlighted form. Highlighting indicates that more help is available for that word or phrase. Press Tab to move to a highlighted word, then press Enter to obtain more information about the word or phrase.

A few commands work only in DOS sessions or only in OS/2 sessions. The Help screen for these commands has a DOS or OS/2 icon in the top-left corner. To see an example of these icons, you can ask for help on the APPEND command, which works only under DOS. TIME has no such icon because the command is available in either operating system.

The Command Reference expresses the syntax of each command by drawing lines between each of the command's parts. These lines are railroad diagrams that help you understand how to use the command. The following section discusses these diagrams.

Railroad Diagrams. *Railroad diagrams* are a compact, graphic illustration of every valid technique for using a command. Although the diagrams initially may appear confusing, with a little practice you can learn to read them. On the left and right sides of the railroad diagram are *stations*, where a train must begin and end its trip. The train must start on the left side and end on the right side, but in between, the train can take any path. The train represents the command you type, including any parameters you can or must supply.

Paths on the Diagram. You can perform a simple exercise to learn how to use railroad diagrams. For this exercise, you use the OS/2 Command Reference screen for the TIME command (refer to fig. 13.3). You begin by typing **TIME**, because the command is at the left side of the diagram. You need not type anything else because a line (the railroad track) goes directly to the right side of the screen. That direct line indicates that the word TIME is a valid command on its own. You use the TIME command in the following manner to ask what time it is:

Suppose that the train takes the southern path whenever it comes to a junction. That situation means you type TIME hh:mm:ss to reset the clock to a certain hour, minute, and second. Whenever the train passes through capital letters or punctuation marks, like the colons here, you have to type them exactly as shown. When you come to something in lowercase letters, you have to plug in a value. TIME 13:20:59, for example, is a legal command.

Can you use TIME 13:20 as a valid setting? Yes, because the train can pass through the hh (hour setting) and mm (minute setting) stations and bypass the ss (seconds setting) station to return to the main TIME track line. The diagram illustrates, however, that you cannot reach the minute setting without first specifying the hour.

Lines and Arrows. In a railroad diagram, the train has no reverse gear; normally, it cannot move to the left. In some circumstances, however, you can backtrack through a command. The diagram marks with an arrow each command phase, or optional switch. The CHKDSK command, for example, has several optional switches, such as /F to fix any problems CHKDSK finds and /V to show the name of each file it checks (see fig. 13.4). You can use either switch, neither switch, or both switches. To see how you can use both, tell the train to pass through /F, turn left, backtrack along the upper path with an arrow, and then pass through /V.

The arrows also keep the train from running off the page. Because this route map is too wide to fit on the screen, the system breaks the map into two pieces. When the train gets to the right end of the top line, it continues at the left end of the next line, as the arrows pointing to the left show.

For Related Information
- "Using The Workplace Shell," p. 231
- "Introducing Presentation Manager," p. 234
- "Command Reference," p. 717

Fig. 13.4
Viewing the railroad diagram for the CHKDSK command.

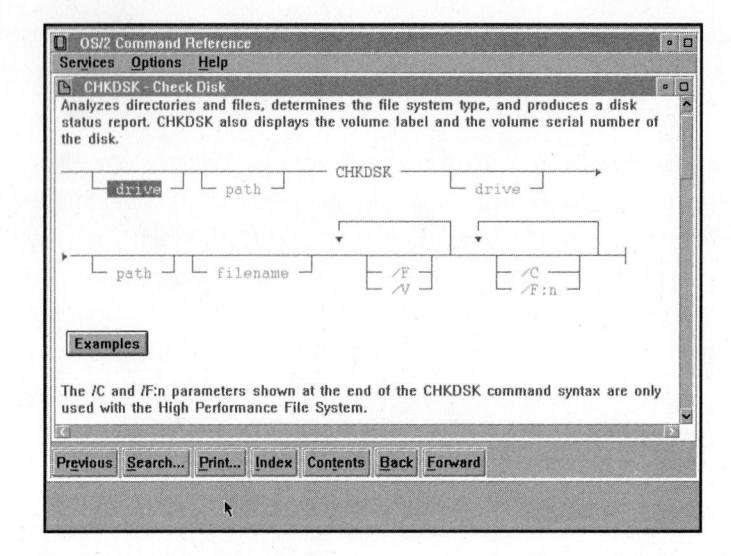

Chapter Summary

In this chapter, you learned that on-line help is always available in OS/2, and you mastered the help menus for Presentation Manager applications. Although you may not need to use the command-line interface often, you learned how to get help on error messages and how to look up information on DOS and OS/2 commands.

In the next chapter, "Using the OS/2 Text Editors," you learn how to view, create, and change text files.

For Related Information
- "Examining Presentation Manager," p. 14
- "Understanding CUA Principles," p. 230
- "Introducing Presentation Manager," p. 234

Chapter 14
Using the OS/2 Text Editors

OS/2 includes two text editors, the System Editor and the Enhanced Editor, that you can use to view, create, and change simple text files. The System Editor is simple to learn and easy to use. You can think of the Enhanced Editor for Presentation Manager (EPM) as the System Editor's bigger brother. EPM was developed by an IBM employee, and people who work at IBM have used EPM for years. Because EPM works like the System Editor but adds many extra features, IBM decided to distribute EPM free with OS/2 versions 2.0 and higher.

In this chapter, you learn how to use the System Editor and EPM. This chapter discusses all techniques—including the basic ones—you need to know in order to use a text editor. If you have some experience using a text editor, you may want to skim the first few sections quickly as a refresher.

The first sections of this chapter present a short file that contains several typographical errors, then demonstrate various ways you can use the text editor to correct the errors. You gain valuable practice as you work through these steps. The illustrations show what your screen should look like along the way.

After you master the basics, you learn advanced techniques that make your work easier and more efficient. These powerful commands enable you to do the following:

- Copy and rearrange lines and paragraphs
- Scan files for a particular phrase

- Automatically replace one word or phrase with another throughout a file
- Move and copy text
- Undo the last change you made
- Use different fonts and colors
- Wrap words at the end of a line, as you do with a word processing program

EPM provides additional commands that enable you to do the following:

- Edit several files at once
- Move and copy text between files
- Undo any or all changes you have made
- Customize the appearance of the editor

As the above lists indicate, the OS/2 editors have many useful features. You may find the text editors handy for many tasks, even if you have a word processing program.

Using the OS/2 Editors

The System Editor and the Enhanced Editor work with pure text files, also called *flat files* or *ASCII files*. The files contain only the text you put in them. Word processing programs use special format codes to keep track of paragraphs, page breaks, and more. Because the OS/2 editors do not understand these special codes, the text editors may not work well with documents produced with word processing software. Most word processing programs enable you to save documents as flat files, however, so you can edit them with tools like the System Editor or EPM.

The System Editor is handy for creating simple files like memos or to-do lists. You can use the System Editor to make changes in your system setup files, such as the CONFIG.SYS file. In addition, you can use the System Editor to display a file without making any changes. While you learn how to use the System Editor in the next few sections, remember that you can use the same techniques with EPM.

You start the System Editor by opening the Productivity folder (located inside the OS/2 System folder) and clicking the System Editor icon. Figure 14.1 shows the System Editor's initial screen.

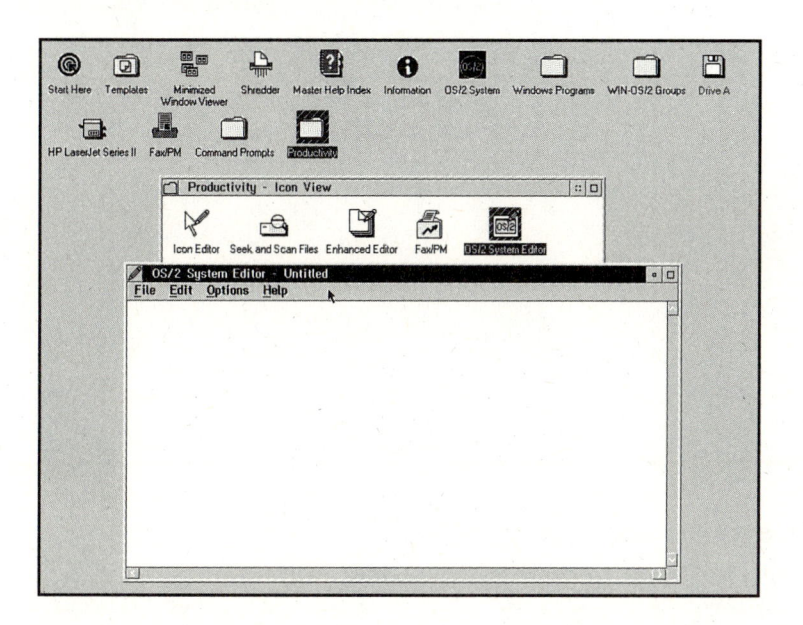

Fig. 14.1
The System Editor startup screen.

The editor window provides you with much information. The title bar displays the name of the file you are editing. In the figure, the name *Untitled* indicates that you have not yet named the file. Below the title bar is a menu bar from which you can pull down several menus. Later sections of this chapter discuss these menus in detail.

Mastering Basic Editing Techniques

After you type a memo, you may see an error that needs correction, or a sentence that you want to change. In this section, you learn how to use the text and mouse cursors to move directly to the text you want to alter and then make the alterations.

Practice makes perfect. To begin this section, therefore, you must type some erroneous text upon which you can practice the basic editing techniques by correcting the errors. You enter text simply by typing on the keyboard. Type the text shown in figure 14.2 now, pressing Enter at the end of each line. Include all the typing errors; you correct them in the following sections.

For Related Information
- "Examining Presentation Manager," p. 14
- "Using The Workplace Shell," p. 231

Fig. 14.2
A poem excerpt with typographical errors.

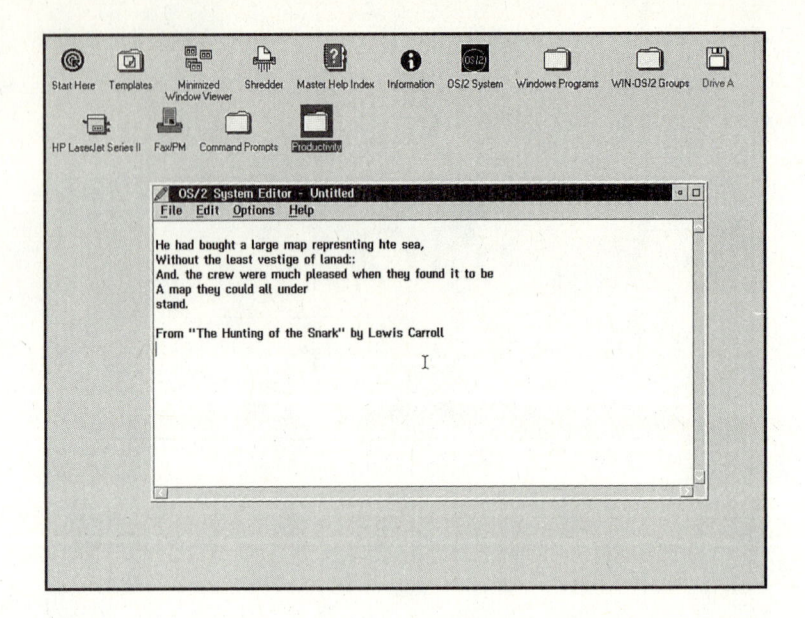

Understanding the Text Cursor

While you type, you see that a flashing vertical black line moves one space ahead of your typed characters. This line, the *text cursor*, indicates your current position in the file.

Text cursor movement is one of the most frequently performed operations you use when revising a file. The shortcut keystrokes in the following table enable you to move the cursor quickly. These shortcuts are worth learning; they can make your work easier and more efficient.

As you might expect, the PgUp and PgDn keys move the cursor up or down a page. When you press and hold down the Ctrl key, Ctrl changes the meaning of any cursor-movement key you press. For example, Home moves the text cursor to the beginning of the current line, but Ctrl-Home moves the cursor to the beginning of the file.

Table 14.1 Keystrokes to Move the Cursor

Keystroke	Action
Left arrow	Left one letter
Ctrl-Left	Left one word
Right arrow	Right one letter

Keystroke	Action
Ctrl-Right	Right one word
Up arrow	Up one line
Down arrow	Down one line
PgUp	Up one page
PgDn	Down one page
Home	Beginning of line
Ctrl-Home	Beginning of file
End	End of line
Ctrl-End	End of file

Understanding the Mouse Cursor

In Chapter 9, "Using Your Computer Screen as a Desktop," you used the mouse in conjunction with the scroll bars to scroll the screen forward or backward. You also can move around in the System Editor with the *mouse cursor*. In figure 14.2, the mouse cursor appears in the center of the screen. The mouse cursor looks like a fancy capital I. Move anywhere in the file and click once with the left button, and the text cursor moves to that place. If you click beyond the end of a line, the text cursor moves only to the end of that line.

Many people find the mouse cursor easier to learn and use than the text cursor. With the keystrokes listed in table 14.1, however, you can move the text cursor without taking your hands away from the keyboard. You can experiment with both methods to see which you prefer.

Inserting or Replacing Text

Now that you have learned how to move the cursor, you are ready to learn how to manipulate the text. Move to the first line of the file and place the cursor after the letter *s* in *represnting*. Type an **e** to correct the spelling of the word.

The text editor inserts into the text the letter you typed. Letters to the right of the insertion shifted to make room. The editor is in Insert mode, the editor's default mode.

Now, press Ctrl-right arrow to move to the beginning of the next word. Press the Ins key once, then type **th** to correct the misspelling of *the*.

When you pressed Ins, you may have noticed that the text cursor grew larger. The text cursor enlarged because you put the editor in Replace mode. In this mode, each letter you type replaces the letter to the right. You can toggle back to Insert mode by pressing Ins again.

Deleting Text

Sometimes you need to remove a letter or phrase from a document. At the end of the second line of the sample text, for example, you need to remove the second *a* from the word *lanad*. Move the cursor to the left of the extra *a*, and press the Del key to delete the letter *a*. Now go to the end of the line and press Backspace to remove the extra colon.

Both the Del and Backspace keys delete one letter at a time. You must move the cursor to the letter you want to delete. The Del key deletes the letter to the right of the cursor. The Backspace key erases the letter to the left of the cursor. If you hold down either Backspace or Del, you continue to delete letters (the key action repeats until you release the key).

Joining, Splitting, and Inserting Lines

You may want to divide a line, or join two lines together. In the sample text, line four breaks in the middle of the word *understand*. To reconnect the two parts of the word, move the cursor to the end of *under* and press Del. You also can remove the break by moving the cursor to the beginning of the word *stand* and pressing Backspace.

For Related Information
- "Understanding CUA Principles," p. 230

To break a line in two, move the cursor to the place where you want to make the break, and press Enter. If you want to insert a blank line beneath the current line, move the cursor to the end of the current line and press Enter. You can insert a blank line above the current line by pressing Enter while the cursor is at the beginning of the current line.

Learning Advanced Editing Techniques

In the last section, you learned the basic techniques of entering and revising text one letter at a time. In this section, you learn how to work with whole blocks of characters, such as paragraphs. You practice moving blocks of text within a file, and you learn how to search for words or phrases and replace them with others.

Understanding Blocks

When editing, you frequently need to move or alter whole sentences or paragraphs that span many lines. The System Editor has convenient commands to copy and paste blocks of text. The title of the poem in the sample text appears at the end of the poem selection. To move the poem's title to the beginning, follow these steps:

1. Move the cursor to the beginning of the line of text containing the poem's title.

2. Hold down Shift and press End to highlight the entire line.

3. Hold down Shift and press Del. The highlighted text disappears.

4. Move the cursor to the beginning of the first line of the sample text. Press Enter twice to insert two blank lines; then move the cursor back to the beginning of the first line.

5. Hold down Shift and press Ins. The title appears at the top of the window.

In this operation you marked and moved a block of text. The following sections discuss in detail each step of the operation you performed.

Marking a Block. Before you can delete, move, or copy a block of text, you must tell the System Editor what block you want to work with. You accomplish this task by *marking* the block. To mark a block of text, move the cursor to the beginning of the text you want to include in the block, hold down Shift, and move the cursor to the end of the text you want to include in the block. You can use any of the shortcut keys in table 14.1 to move the cursor. When you release the Shift key, the system highlights the block of marked text, as shown in figure 14.3. Note that you need not begin blocks at the beginning of a line.

You can use the mouse to mark a block of text easily. Move the mouse cursor to the beginning of the text you want to mark. Hold down the left button and move the mouse cursor across the text you want to mark. The text highlights as you move the mouse across it. Release the button when you reach the end of the text you want to include in the marked block.

Chapter 14—Using the OS/2 Text Editors

Fig. 14.3
Marking a block of text.

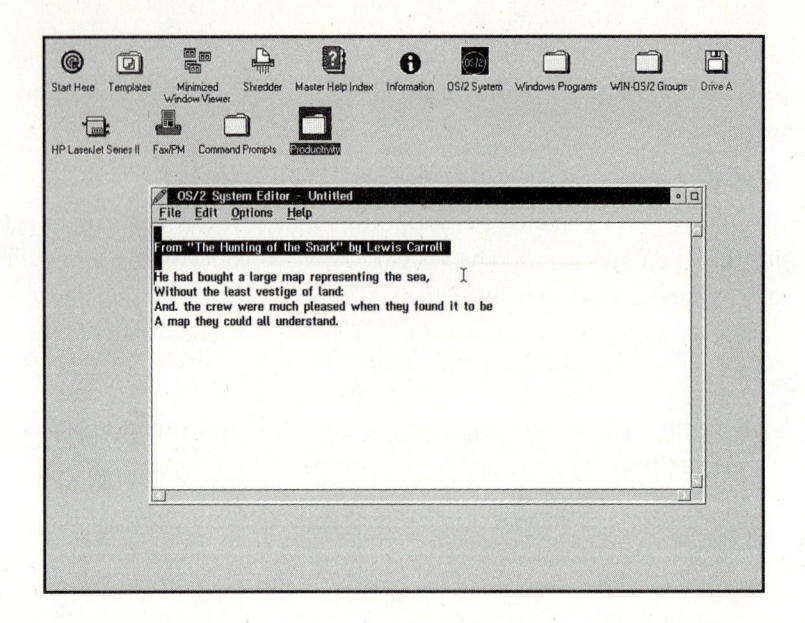

Clearing, Cutting, Pasting, and Copying Blocks. When you want to edit whole sections of text, marking a block is only the first step. With the keystrokes in the following list, you can remove or insert blocks in the editor, in a manner similar to cutting and pasting paper documents.

- *Cutting.* You press Shift-Del to remove a marked text block from the screen and into a temporary holding area called the *Clipboard*. You can insert the block elsewhere in the document by using the Paste command.

- *Copying.* You press Ctrl-Ins to copy a block of text to the Clipboard. Unlike Cutting, Copying does not delete the original block.

- *Pasting.* To paste a block of text from the Clipboard into a document, move the cursor where you want to insert the block, and press Shift-Ins. The block appears at the new location and the surrounding text moves down to make room. Pasting does not clear the Clipboard. You can press Ctrl-Ins repeatedly to insert multiple copies of the same text.

- *Clearing.* To erase a marked block of text, press the Del key. Note that a cleared block is gone forever. You cannot retrieve a cleared block.

Finding and Replacing

In some documents, you may use a single phrase repeatedly throughout the text, and later discover you want to change the phrase. Searching for and correcting each occurrence of a phrase can be a time-consuming task, particularly in a long document. To make this task easier, you can use the OS/2 text editor's find-and-replace capabilities to locate and change every occurrence of the text you designate. The following sections discuss this operation in detail.

Finding Text. The FIND command has some fancy options, and this section explores them all. The following exercise, however, demonstrates the basic use of this command.

To use the FIND command to locate *vest* in our sample text, follow these steps:

1. Move to the top of the file, to search from the beginning to end of the document.

2. Press Ctrl-F to pop up the Find menu.

3. Type **vest**. These letters then appear in the Find field.

4. Press Enter.

The System Editor finds and highlights the word. Your screen now resembles figure 14.4.

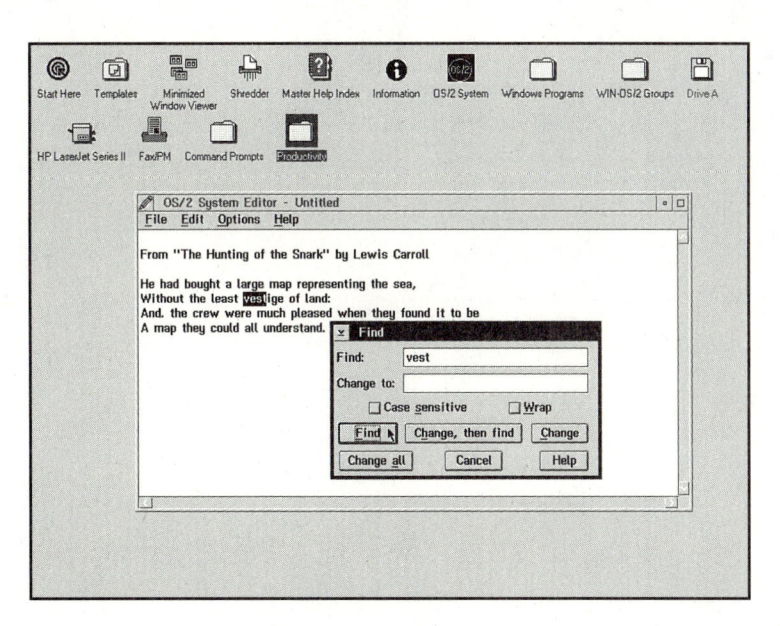

Fig. 14.4
Finding a string of letters.

354 Chapter 14—Using the OS/2 Text Editors

Note that the search was succesful, even though it located the word *vestige*. The FIND command looks for strings of letters, not whole words.

Replacing One Text String with Another. One typing error remains in our sample text—the period after *And* at the beginning of the second line. You can practice using the Replace command by following these steps to correct the error:

1. Move to the top of the file to search the document from beginning to end.

2. Press Ctrl-F to pop up the Find menu.

3. Type **And.** in the Find field (be certain to include the period).

4. Press Tab to move to the Change To field, and type **And** without the period.

5. Click the Find button to search for the text, then click the button labeled Change, then click Find again.

Your screen now resembles figure 14.5. Note that the replacement is complete.

Fig. 14.5
Replacing a string of letters.

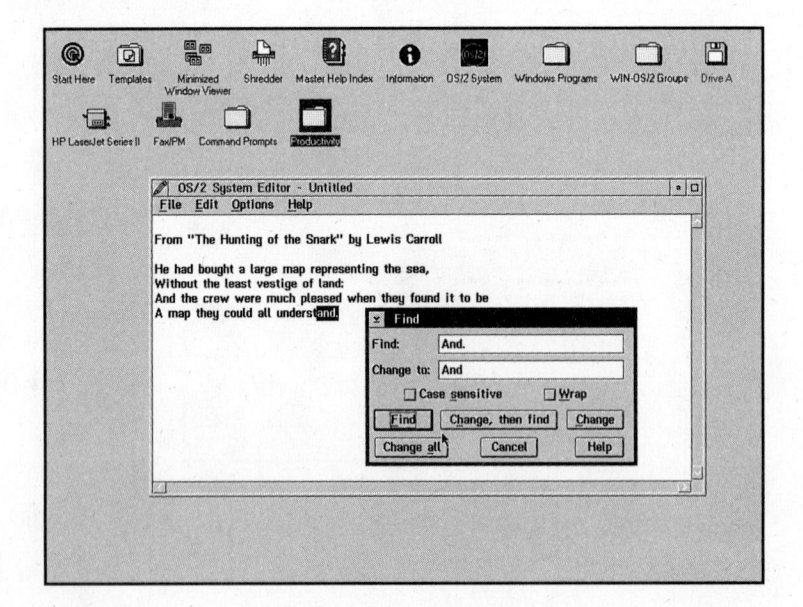

If you look again at figure 14.5, you see that something interesting has happened. The editor has found another occurrence of *and.* at the end of the fourth line. You could change this occurrence, too, by pressing the Change button, then the Find button again. In this occurrence, however, the period is correct and you need not change the word. Instead, you press Esc to clear away the Search screen.

With these operations under your belt, you are ready to study the items on the rest of the Find menu. You can customize these operations to make them work exactly the way you want.

Using Find Options. The Options section of the Find menu contains two buttons. The following paragraphs describe the function of each button.

- *Case sensitive* tells the FIND command to distinguish between uppercase and lowercase characters in its search. If you turn case sensitivity off, FIND treats all letters the same. Case sensitive is the only option the editor activates by default.

- *Wrap* tells the System Editor to search the whole file. In Wrap mode, the editor searches from the cursor to the end of the file, then wraps around and searches from the start of the file to the cursor.

Each of the six buttons at the bottom of the Find menu performs a different function. You can click them with the mouse. If you prefer to use the keyboard, move the cursor to your selection with the Tab and arrow keys, and then press Enter; or press Alt plus the letter underlined in your selection.

- *Find* locates the next occurrence of the string of letters you have typed in the Search field and draws a circle around the found text.

- *Change* locates the next occurrence of the text you typed in the Search field and replaces that text with the text you typed in the Replace field.

- *Change, then find* performs a Change operation, then finds and highlights the next occurrence of the text in the Find field. You can repeat this action to continue changing and finding the text. If you reach an occurrence of the text that you do not want to change, select the Find button to leave that occurrence unchanged and search for the next.

- *Change all* automates a Change operation. Use this option to tell the System Editor that you want to replace every occurrence of the text string you have supplied without confirming each one separately.

For Related Information
- "Introducing Presentation Manager," p. 234

- *Cancel* makes the Search menu disappear. You can press the Esc key to accomplish the same action.

- *Help* brings up the help system. This action is similar to selecting Help on the Menu bar.

Understanding the System Editor Menus

You now know the techniques for entering and editing text and are ready to tackle the menus. In this section, you learn commands that enable you to load and save files and to customize many editor options. You also learn how to undo and redo the most recent change you have made—a useful tool if you have made a mistake.

The items on the Menu bar are called pull-down menus, because they hang from the bar when you access them. To go to the Menu bar, press and release the Alt key. Now press the first letter of the menu you want to use; for example, type **F** to pull down the File menu.

The status line tells you the function of the current menu option. If you want more information on a menu item, use the arrow keys to move to that item, then press F1. F1 is the Help key, and it activates a complete on-line help system. Chapter 12, "Learning the Commands You Use Most Often," explains how to use on-line help.

As you study the menus, you see shortcut keystrokes listed next to many items. You already used one of these shortcut keystrokes when you pressed Ctrl-F to activate the Find menu. Try learning the shortcuts for the commands you use most often. The shortcuts help you work more efficiently.

Working with the File Menu

The File menu enables you to load and save files. Pull down the menu (with Alt-F or the mouse) to see the choices offered by the File menu. You can move among the items with the up-arrow and down-arrow keys. The following sections discuss each item on the menu, after enabling you to experiment with a couple of the most useful operations.

Now that you have corrected all the typing errors in the sample file, you need to save your corrections. Using the down-arrow key, move to Save As... on the File menu. Press Enter, and the Save As... window pops up, as shown in figure 14.6.

Understanding the System Editor Menus 357

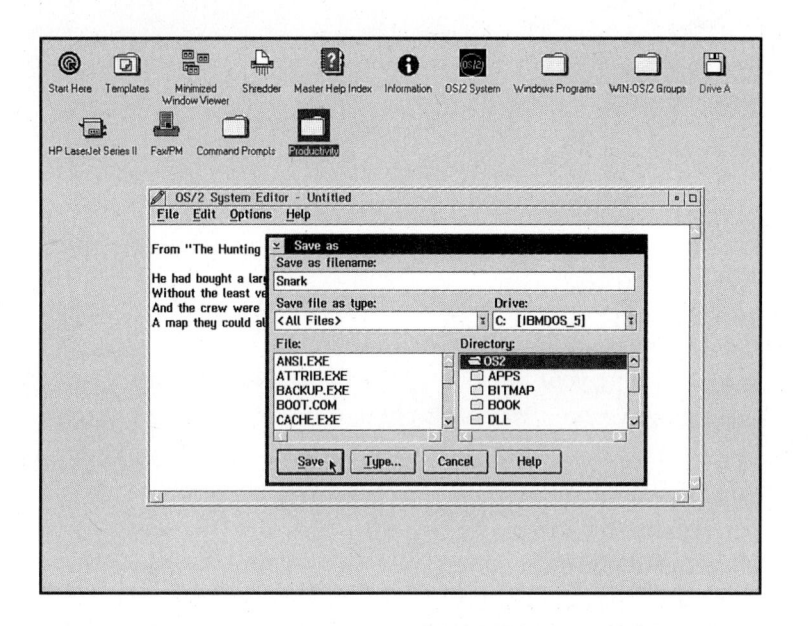

Fig. 14.6
The File Save As... menu.

The first field, Save as filename, asks what you want to call the file. *Snark* seems an appropriate name, so type the name in the first field. You can skip the next field, Save file as type, a field useful mostly to programmers. The Drive and Directory options enable you to put the file anywhere on any disk. For now, use the default, which is the root directory of the C: drive. The box labeled File shows the names of all files in the chosen directory. You could pick one of these, but avoid this option for now. This option replaces the highlighted file's contents with the poem in the editor. Now press Enter to save the file. The new name appears on the title bar.

Next, pull down the File menu again and move to Open.... This command loads a different file into the System Editor, where it replaces the file with which you previously were working. The three periods after Open indicate that this item offers you additional options. With Open... selected, you press Enter, then type the name of a new file, or pick one of the files listed.

Through the preceding excercises, you have learned to use some of the basic File functions. To better acquaint you with this versatile tool, the following paragraphs list and discuss each option on the File menu.

- *New* wipes out all the text in the current editor window, and gives you a blank screen to begin a new file. Before using this option, be certain that you really want to wipe out the text in the current window. You cannot get the original text back unless you have saved the file.

- *Open* loads a different file in the editor, where it replaces the file you were previously editing.

- *Save* writes the current file to disk. Save your files often—this operation is your best insurance against losing valuable data.

- *Save As* is a combination of Rename and Save, as you saw in the example in figure 14.6.

- *Autosave* automatically saves your file at set intervals. You protect your work by saving your files often. When you are working on a large document, however, you may not want to repeatedly interrupt your progress in order to perform frequent save operations. To avoid this problem, you can use the Autosave option to instruct the System Editor to handle the chore automatically. To take advantage of this valuable insurance, click the Autosave On button. The System Editor then saves the file after every 100 changes. You can change the save interval by clicking the arrows in the Number of Changes between Saves box.

Using the Edit Menu

The Edit menu has several options that you can use to activate the Mark, Cut, Copy, and Paste block commands you learned earlier. You may prefer using the keyboard shortcuts, however, rather than the Edit menu. The Edit menu also lists the Find command that you learned earlier.

The System Editor keeps track of the last change you made to a file so that you can undo a mistaken change if you catch the error quickly. This feature is very helpful if you accidentally delete something and want to get the original text back.

To undo your most recent change, select Undo from the Edit menu, or press Alt-Backspace. Try changing something now in the file you have loaded, then undoing your change. When you pull down the Edit menu again, a Redo option appears. Redo enables you to reverse the Undo operation.

The System Editor remembers only the last change you made (but forgets that change when you save the file). Later in this chapter, you learn that the Enhanced Editor has a more versatile Undo option. EPM enables you to undo or redo many changes, one at a time.

Using the Options Menu

In this section, you explore the three items on the Options menu. You learn how to select different fonts and colors, and how to use word wrap to make the System Editor work more like a word processing program.

Choosing Colors. Pick the Colors option from the Options menu, and a new window appears, as shown in figure 14.7. Move the text or mouse cursor up and down in the Foreground area to pick a text color. The text in the Color Sample box changes immediately, to show you how the new color scheme looks.

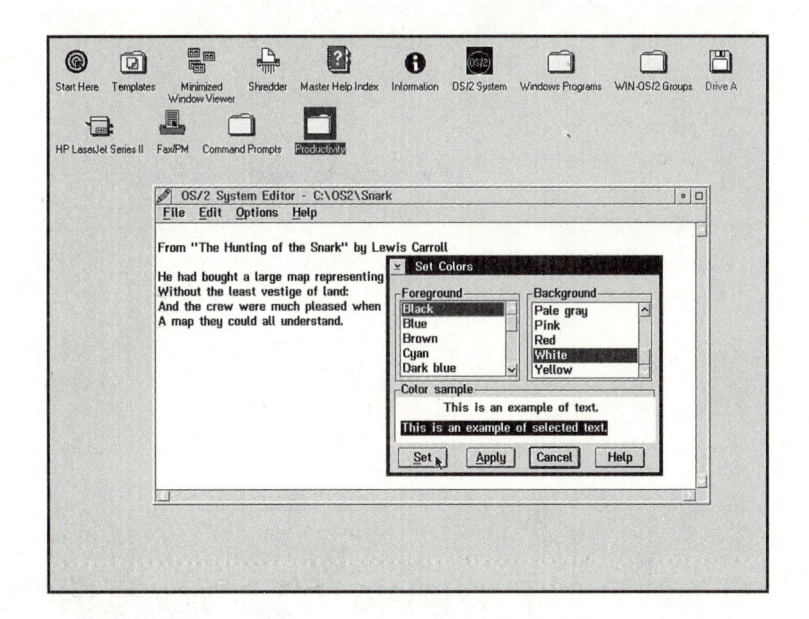

Fig. 14.7
The Set Colors pop-up window.

Now try picking a contrasting color from the Background box. You can move to this box with the Tab key, or just place the mouse cursor there and click a new color. Again, the Color Sample area displays your changes.

When you are satisfied with your new color scheme, press the Set button. The System Editor saves these colors, and uses them the next time you start your computer. If you want to see how the new colors look in the editor before making your final decision, click the Apply button. Apply has an action similar to Set, but Apply leaves the Set Colors window open and doesn't change the colors permanently.

When you select colors, try to choose colors that are different enough for easy readability but don't contrast too sharply. Many people prefer light text on a dark background, but experiment to find the combination you like best.

Selecting a Font. When you choose the Font option from the Options menu, a new window appears (see fig. 14.8). The options in this window enable you to customize the typeface of the text you see in the System Editor window. The following paragraphs list and discuss these options in detail.

Fig. 14.8
The Font pop-up window.

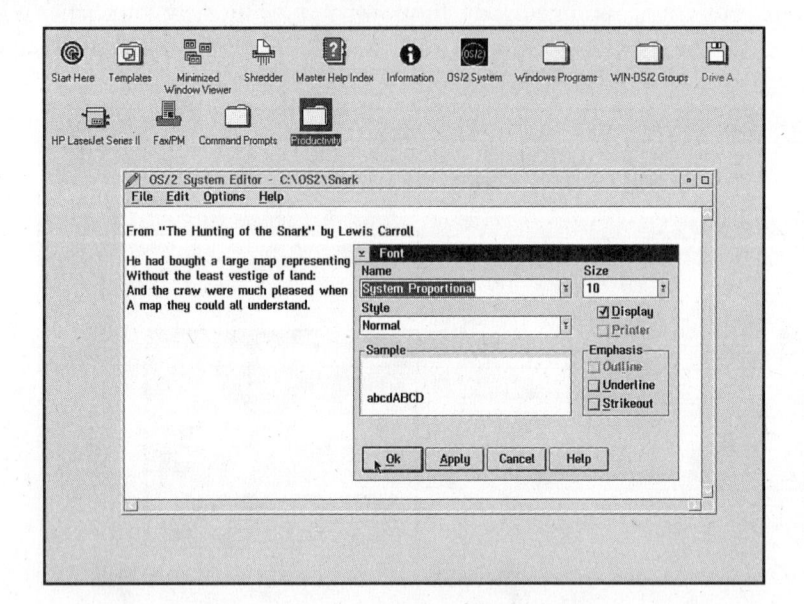

- *Font* enables you to choose from a variety of type fonts. Some fonts are proportionally spaced, so that the letter *i* takes up less room than the letter *m*. The default System Proportional font is an example. Some fonts use equal spacing between letters. Some fonts have serifs, and others do not.

- *Style* enables you to customize the font you have chosen. You can use this option to apply italics, for example, or boldface. Not all options are available with all fonts.

- *Size* enables you to control the type size. The number in this box is the size in *points*, a measurement that printers use. Seventy-two points equal one inch. Some fonts are available in only one point size.

- *Display* makes the System Editor use the font you pick to display text in the text edit window.

- *Emphasis* presents options similar to Style. You can choose Outline, Underline, or Strikeout emphasis. Some of these options are not available with every font.

The Sample box immediately reflects each of your choices. Click Apply to see how the editor screen looks with the font and options you have chosen. When you're satisfied with the results, click OK.

Using Word Wrap to Reformat Paragraphs. The System Editor isn't a full-featured word processing program. If you leave Word Wrap enabled on the Options menu, however, you can type past the end of a line, and the editor continues the text on the next line, breaking between words. If you resize the editor window, the editor rearranges the text to fit the new window size.

If you use this feature, you might be surprised when you print a file. With the System Editor, word wrap applies only to the screen display, not to printed output. The following sections of this chapter discuss the Enhanced Editor, which handles word wrap more consistently on the screen and the printed page. Better word wrap is only one of EPM's many features.

For Related Information
- "Introducing Presentation Manager," p. 234

Comparing the System Editor to the Enhanced Editor

The System Editor is handy for changing small files, and perhaps that's all you need. If you long for a more powerful tool, however, read on. EPM, the Enhanced Editor, is similar to the System Editor, but offers many more options. Although some of the menus are slightly different, EPM operates much like the System Editor, so you can be productive in EPM right away with the techniques you already have mastered.

The Enhanced Editor is similar to the System Editor, but EPM does a lot more. Like the System Editor, EPM works with pure text files, but EPM also gives you the following extra capabilities:

- You can edit several files at once, and copy text between them.

- EPM's Undo and Redo commands are much more powerful than those of the System Editor, as you learn in a later section. You can replay all the changes you make backward and forward—a very useful capability if you mistakenly delete an important block of text.

- A status line at the bottom of the EPM screen tells you at a glance the line and column where the text cursor is located, and indicates whether you are in insert or replace mode.

- EPM's message line gives a simple explanation of every menu option as you explore the menus.

- You can customize the appearance of the EPM screen to fit your own preferences.

- You can use various fonts and colors for different parts of your file.

Command names in the editors differ in two minor respects. The System Editor's Find command has a parallel in EPM's Search command, and the EPM Search shortcut key is Ctrl-S instead of Ctrl-F. When EPM finds text you have designated for a search, the editor highlights the found text by drawing a circle on the screen around the characters. Aside from the highlight, the commands work the same in the two editors. And EPM's Edit menu has a Delete option to remove a marked block of text. This EPM option works in the same manner as the System Editor's Clear option.

Starting the Enhanced Editor

For Related Information
- "Using The Workplace Shell," p. 231

You start the Enhanced Editor by opening the Productivity folder (it's inside the OS/2 System folder) and clicking the Enhanced Editor icon. Alternatively, you can type EPM at the command line in an OS/2 window to start the editor. Figure 14.9 shows the Enhanced Editor's initial screen.

Understanding the Enhanced Editor Menus

EPM's pull-down menus look very much like those of the System Editor you studied earlier in this chapter. In this section, you learn how EPM differs from the System Editor, and discover new commands to load and save files and to customize many editor options. You also explore EPM's great flexibility in undoing and redoing changes you make in your text.

The EPM status line tells you the function of the current menu option. As with the System Editor, you can get more information on a menu item by pressing F1.

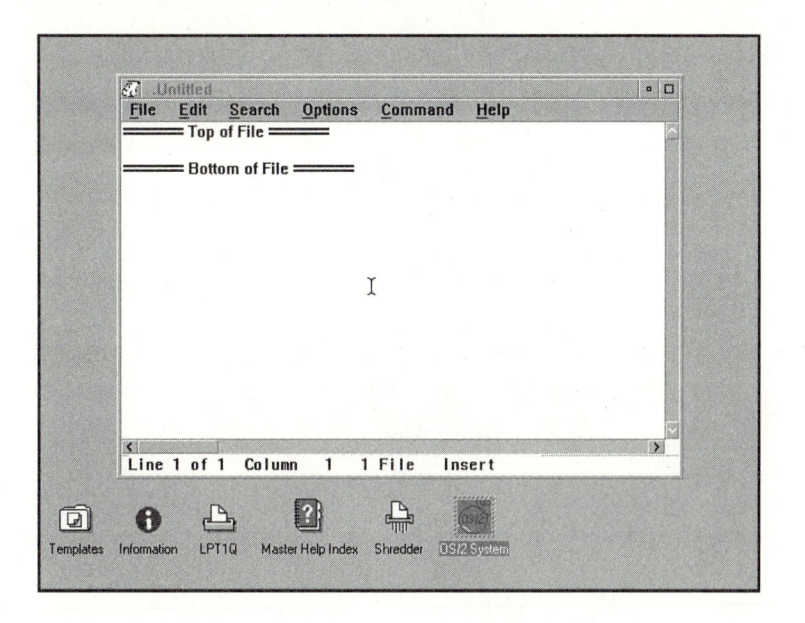

Fig. 14.9
The Enhanced Editor startup screen.

Working with the File Menu

Pull down the EPM File menu, and you see some familiar options. Previously in this chapter, you mastered the New, Open, Save, and Save as... options. The menu also contains some new options, which you learn to use in this section of the chapter.

Move the cursor to Open.... The status line message reads `Open a file in a new window`. That message tells you that you can edit more than one file at a time with EPM. The three periods at the end of this **menu** option name indicate that you can use additional options with the command.

After you select Open..., press Enter. You can type a new filename, or you can choose from the list of files you have recently edited, as shown in figure 14.10. Editing multiple files is handy, for example, when you want to Cut (or Copy) text from one window and Paste the text into another.

The following paragraphs list and describe the EPM File menu options. You used some of these options when you worked with the System Editor, but others are unique to the EPM editor.

- *New* wipes out all the text in the current editor window and gives you a blank screen to begin a new file. Use this option with care. You cannot retrieve information wiped out by this option unless you saved the file.

- *Open Untitled* opens a new, empty editor window. The new window overlaps the original one.

364   Chapter 14—Using the OS/2 Text Editors

- *Open* creates a new editor window and loads a file (refer to fig. 14.7).

- *Import Text File* inserts—at the current cursor position of the file you are editing—any file you name. You can use this option to combine files.

- *Rename* enables you to change the name of the current file.

- *Save* writes the current file to disk. Save your files often—this is your best insurance against losing valuable data.

- *Save As* acts as a combination of Rename and Save. You can use this option to save a file under a new name.

- *Save and Close* combines the functions of Save and Quit.

- *Quit* closes the current window. If this is the only open EPM window, Quit also closes the editor. If you have made changes since you last saved a file, Quit prompts you to save the file before the window closes.

- *Print File* enables you to print a copy of your file.

Fig. 14.10
The Enhanced Editor's Open window.

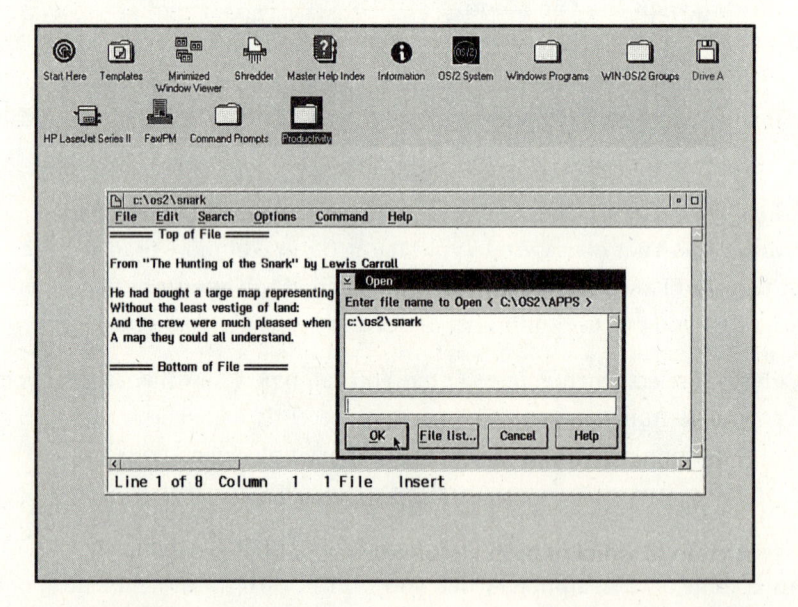

Using the Edit Menu

You are familiar with most of the functions on the Edit menu, such as Marking, Cutting, Copying, and Pasting blocks. In this section you learn to use the EPM Styles option. You also work with EPM's Undo feature, which is much more flexible than Undo in the System Editor.

Using Styles. Although EPM's style options are not as fancy as some word processing and desktop publishing programs, EPM does allow you to pick different fonts and type sizes. Figure 14.11 displays an example of EPM's versatility. In the figure, each line is set in a different style. This EPM option is similar to the System Editor's Font options, except that you can use many different Styles within an EPM file.

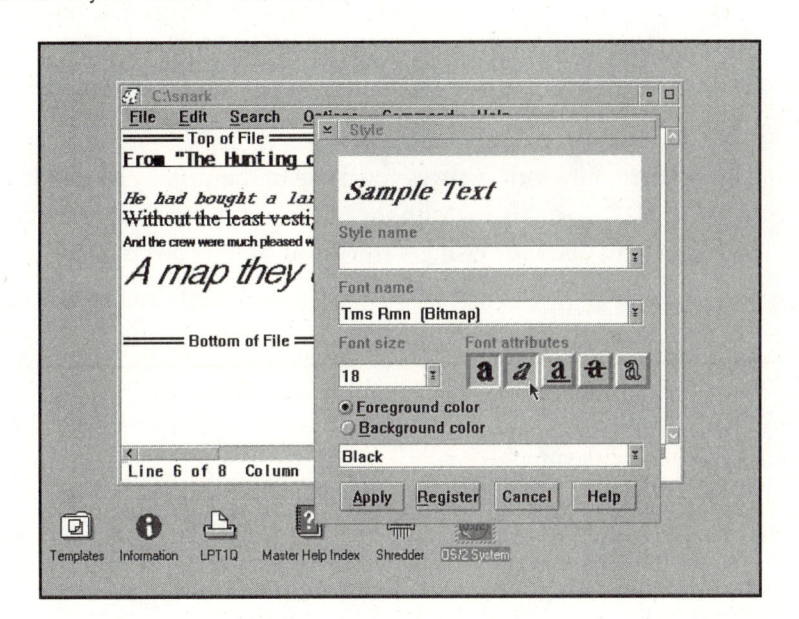

Fig. 14.11
Viewing different style selections.

To experiment with styles, mark a block of text—it need not be a whole line—and bring up the Styles screen. You then select a font, change the font's size, and choose one or more attributes, such as boldface or italic. The sample text at the top of the window immediately reflects every change you make. You can choose different colors for the text, the background, or both. When you are satisfied with the style, press the Apply button to apply the change to the marked block.

Undoing Changes. Even if you are just skimming this chapter and something has yet to grab your interest, please read this section.

The Enhanced Editor keeps track of every change you make to a file, and enables you to undo each change in reverse order. After you undo changes, EPM enables you to redo them. This undo feature is very helpful if you accidentally delete something and want to get the text back.

When you choose Undo from the Edit menu, a slider bar appears on-screen. To undo your changes one by one, press the left-arrow key repeatedly. Use the right-arrow key to reapply each change in order. You also can drag the slider with the mouse. To accomplish this action, you move the mouse cursor to the slider, hold down the left button, and move the slider back and forth.

Every change you make to a line is saved when you move the text cursor to a new line. If you type a word, for example, and then hit Enter to move the text cursor to a new line, you can use Undo to remove the word you typed. Undo will not, however, remove the letters in the word one by one.

You can use Undo only with changes you make in the current session. EPM does not save the change history with the file. If you modify and then save the file, you cannot undo the changes when you later reopen the file.

Using the Search Menu

When you need to search for or replace a string of text, use EPM's Search feature. Search works in a manner similar to the Find option on the System Editor's Edit menu. EPM includes enough additional features that Search deserves a separate menu.

> **Tip**
>
> The shortcut key for Search is Ctrl-S—not the Ctrl-F shortcut you learned for the System Editor.

The Options section of the Search menu contains five buttons. The following list describes the functions of these buttons:

- *Ignore case* directs the Search function to pay no attention to the distinction between uppercase and lowercase letters. This option is the editor's default option, and perhaps its most useful setting. This option is similar in function to the System Editor's Case sensitive option.

- *Marked area* confines the search to a marked block of text.

- *Reverse search* searches backward through the file. The default is a forward search.

- *Grep* is an advanced option that enables you to work with patterns of characters. Grep is powerful, but Grep can be subtle and tricky even for experts. The text box below gives more information about Grep. You can find complete details for using Grep in the Help system for EPM.

- *Change all occurrences* automates a Replace operation. Use this option to tell EPM that you want to replace each occurrence of the specified text string without confirming each one separately. This option is similar to the System Editor's Wrap option.

> **Note**
>
> When you check the Grep option, EPM searches for patterns of characters. If you want to find every numeric digit in a file, for example, check the Grep option and type **[0123456789]** in the Search field. EPM finds any character you included in the set between square brackets. You get the same result if you type **[0-9]** in the Search field, because EPM understands that you mean all the digits from 0-9.
>
> With the Grep option checked, you also can tell EPM to find all characters except the ones you specify, by typing ^ as the first character in the set. For example, **[^0-9 A-Za-z]** finds all characters that are neither digits, spaces, nor upper- or lowercase letters. This Search string finds all the punctuation marks and other less common characters in a file.
>
> In a Grep expression, a period represents any single character. If you type **t.e** in the Search field, for example, EPM finds *the*, *tie*, and *little*. The search is unaffected by what single character comes between *t* and *e*. The search does not identify *true* as a match, because the word has two characters between the *t* and the *e*.
>
> A potential problem exists in the previous example, because *The*, with its capital *T*, does not match the search string. To fix that, you can type your search expression as **[Tt].e**. As you can see, Grep search expressions can be quite complicated. The great power Grep makes available to you, however, repays you for the time you spend mastering its uses.

Using the Options Menu

In this section, you explore the most useful items on the Options menu. You learn how to do the following:

- Customize margins, tab stops, colors, and fonts
- Use word wrap to structure paragraphs in the manner of a word processing program
- Edit several files in a single window

368   Chapter 14—Using the OS/2 Text Editors

- Save files automatically
- Change the appearance of the editor

Using the Settings Notebook. As you learned in Chapter 9, "Using Your Computer Screen as a Desktop," you can flip through the pages of the Settings Notebook to select various options. To access these options, you choose Preferences from the Options menu, then select Settings. Figure 14.12 shows the settings notebook opened to the Margins page.

Fig. 14.12
The Margins page of the Enhanced Editor's settings notebook.

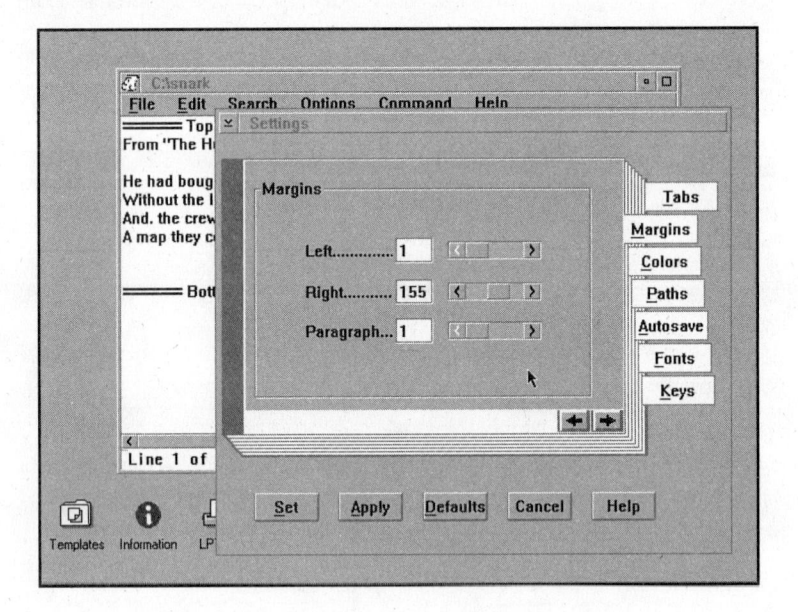

Each page of the Settings Notebook presents you with various choices. After you change options on one or more pages, press one of the following buttons at the bottom of the notebook page:

- *Set* saves the options you have selected as your personal default for all files.
- *Apply* uses the selected options only on the current file. You clear the option settings when you quit the editor.
- *Defaults* restores the original settings, clearing any you saved with Set.

The following sections describe the settings notebook pages under the Enhanced Editor's Options menu.

Setting Tab Stops. Choose Tabs and type a single number in the input field on this screen to tell EPM how many spaces to insert when you press the Tab key. The default Tab setting is eight spaces. You can use Tab stops to create table columns. This technique works best with a monospaced font, where all characters are the same width. If you want to line things up in columns 10, 15, and 28, type those three numbers on this screen.

Setting Margins. On this page of the notebook you set the left and right margins for your file. The paragraph margin controls the number of spaces that the editor indents the first line of each paragraph.

Unlike a word processing program, the Enhanced Editor formats in lines rather than paragraphs. If you use EPM to type memos, you need a way to reformat each paragraph to fit within the margins. The Alt-P keystroke performs the reformatting, based on the margins you set.

Choosing Colors and Fonts. These two tabs in the notebook resemble the Style option on the Edit menu (refer to fig. 14.11). The choices you make here apply to the entire document, not just a marked block of text. You can make the changes permanent with the Set button.

Saving Files Automatically. You protect your work best by saving your files often. The settings on the Autosave page enable you to instruct EPM to handle this chore automatically. By default, EPM saves a file after every 100 changes. This setting is generally satisfactory, but you can change the value according to your preferences. To turn off this feature, set the number to zero.

By default, EPM stores autosave files in the current directory. The settings on the Paths page enable you to place autosave files somewhere else. Don't store files on a temporary disk, however, or you could lose your work if the power goes off.

Redefining Keystrokes. With the options on this notebook tab, you can redefine several keystrokes to perform different actions. The Enter key on the numeric keypad, for example, normally adds a new line after the cursor. You can redefine the Enter keystroke to move the cursor to the beginning of the next line.

Editing Several Files in a Single Window. As you learned when exploring the File menu, the Enhanced Editor can edit several files at once and displays the files in separate windows. You may discover that viewing files side by side is convenient, but the desktop gets cluttered if you have four or five files open at the same time. EPM answers this problem by letting you edit several files in one window.

To see how this works, pick Ring Enabled from the Options Preferences menu. Two *rotate buttons* appear near the right end of the title bar. The rotate buttons look like two circles, one with an arrow pointing clockwise and the other with a counterclockwise pointing arrow. You can arrange several files in a ring pattern and move around the ring with these buttons.

Now pull down the File menu, and you notice a new option, *Add File*. This option enables you to add a new file to the ring. Use the Quit option to remove a file from the ring. If you want to see what files are in the ring, pick *List Ring*, a new choice that appears on the Options menu when you edit a ring of files. Figure 14.13 shows the List Ring dialog box. List Ring shows the names of the files you are editing and enables you to move to any one without using the mouse. With this feature, you can use the up- and down-arrow keys to move to the file you want, and then press Enter.

Fig. 14.13
Editing several files in a ring.

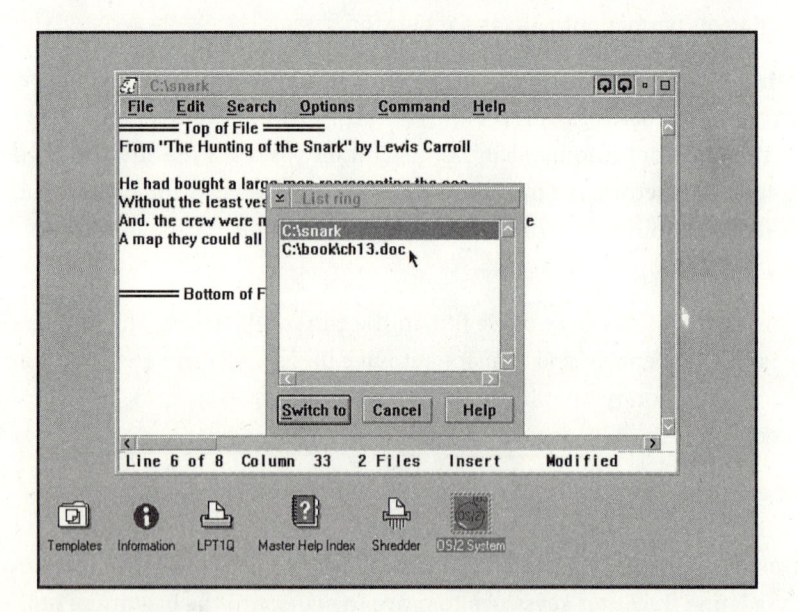

Changing the Window Display with Frame Controls. The frame surrounding EPM's main window provides useful information, such as telling you in which line and column the text cursor is located. The frame provides scroll bars so that you can move through the file with the mouse. You can customize the frame's appearance to suit your preferences. Select Frame

Controls from the Options menu. This choice brings up a menu with six items that you can turn on or off. The following paragraphs discuss the six optional Frame Control features.

- The *status line* at the bottom of the screen displays the current row and column numbers. The status line also indicates whether you are in Insert or Replace mode and whether you have modified the current file since you last saved your changes. In most situations, leave the status line turned on.

- The *message line* is the area at the bottom of the screen where EPM gives you information, such as describing the action of a menu. If you turn the message line off, the messages appear on the status line.

- You can turn the *scroll bars* off, and may want to do so if you are using the keyboard instead of the mouse.

- *Rotate buttons* enable you to move around a ring of files.

- *Info at top* puts the status and message lines at the top of the window. Most people prefer that the messages appear at the bottom of the window, but you can choose the location you like.

- *Prompting* refers to the messages you see when you move around the menus. This item is helpful to you, particularly while you learn to use the editor.

Reviewing Messages from the Editor. EPM gives you useful information on the message line, but old messages disappear to make room for new ones. You can see a list of all the messages you have received from EPM. To produce this list, pick the Messages item on the Options menu.

Saving Options. After you set the options you like best, you can preserve them so that they take effect whenever you load EPM. To save the options, select Save Options from the Options menu.

Using Other Menu Options

The Enhanced Editor has some additional capabilities that may interest programmers only. If you want to learn about these exotic options, explore the Help facility, as discussed in Chapter 12, "Learning the Commands You Use Most Often."

For Related Information
- "Introducing Presentation Manager," p. 234

Editing Files without Typing their Names

This section gives you one last tip to make your work easier. When you double-click a data file's icon, the file is automatically loaded into the System Editor. If you prefer to use the Enhanced Editor, you can drop the file icon onto EPM instead. You can accomplish this switch by using the drag-and-drop techniques you learned in Chapter 10, "Managing the Workplace Shell."

Chapter Summary

In this chapter, you learned how to use the System Editor and its more powerful cousin, the Enhanced Editor. With these versatile tools, you can examine the files on your computer and create new ones. You learned how to use the text editors' powerful features to make your work easier.

After you create a file, you may want to print it. In the next chapter, you learn the techniques for printing with OS/2 2.1.

Chapter 15
Printing with OS/2

Before the advent of OS/2, your applications dealt with the printer without asking for much help from DOS. DOS provided a device name for the printer (LPT1, LPT2, or LPT3) and offered a PRINT command. DOS did not deal with such printing issues and application options as font selection, page orientation, and two-sided printing.

Microsoft Windows was a great step forward toward device-independent printing. The Print Manager inside Windows acts as a waiting room (a queue) for your printouts, until your printer is ready to print them. The Windows Control Panel enables you to configure your printer for page orientation, fonts, and other characteristics. With Windows, your applications no longer have to provide their own interface for setting up and configuring your printer.

OS/2 includes a spooler (described later in this chapter) and a Print Manager for printouts you request in DOS and OS/2 sessions. Because Windows is a part of OS/2, OS/2 includes the Windows Print Manager for printouts you request in Windows sessions. Instead of remembering how to tell your application to change printer features, you now use OS/2's printer-awareness to control the appearance of your documents, reports, memos, and other printouts.

OS/2, like Windows, gives you more control over your printer and better enables your applications to make use of your printer's features. OS/2 can manage printing by multiple applications at the same time. OS/2 prints as easily to a network printer as it does to a local printer. Further, OS/2 understands fonts, page orientation, two-sided printing, and other printer features.

You may find that you rarely need to refer to the printer or spooler icons on your desktop to make settings changes. You may rarely open the printer icon's Icon View or Details View to see your printouts in the output queue. The information in this chapter prepares you for what you see when you do open these icons and teaches you how to gain maximum benefit from the OS/2 printing facility.

You start this chapter by learning the basics of printing with OS/2. You learn how OS/2 keeps your printouts separate when you use OS/2's multitasking feature to tell multiple applications to send printouts to the printer. You come to understand the role of the spooler. You explore the different printer features that OS/2 helps you manage and set. You may come to view your printer as just another object on your OS/2 desktop, as you learn about print jobs, print queues, and print job properties.

Your exploration of OS/2 printing leads you next to printer fonts. You cover font basics—what it means to download a font, what a font cartridge contains, and how to work with font metrics. You learn about the OS/2 system fonts and the Adobe Type Manager fonts, and you discover how to install soft fonts for your printer.

You can print from your applications or directly from the Workplace Shell. You learn in this chapter how to send files to your printer by using your mouse, either on your desktop or within your OS/2 applications.

This chapter explains what you see in the printer icon's list of print jobs, both in the Icon View and the Details View. You learn how to change the status of a print job. You find out how to set up multiple printer objects to represent different forms and multiple printers. Further, you learn how to send your printouts to a file instead of directly to the printer.

> **Note**
>
> If during OS/2 installation you did not enter information about your printer, you do not have what is called a *printer object* on your desktop. You must have a printer object before going further in this chapter. You can find step-by-step instructions for creating an initial printer object in Chapter 7, "Modifying Your OS/2 Configuration."

Learning OS/2 Printer Basics

In the next few sections, you become acquainted with printer basics in an OS/2 environment. When you have started one printout from an application, you need not wait for the printer to finish before you continue your work. This capability is the biggest advantage to printing with OS/2 rather than printing with DOS. OS/2 also enables you to use the special features of your printer—landscape or portrait printing, fonts, and duplex printing.

Each time you request a printout, you create a print job. OS/2 enables you to manage these print jobs individually. You use the printer icon on your desktop to see the list of print jobs. The *printer icon* is the object on your desktop that represents your printer. The *Spooler* is the OS/2 desktop object that holds your printouts until the printer is ready to receive them.

Using Multiple Applications with One Printer

When you tell one of your applications to print something, OS/2 accepts the print material on behalf of the printer. OS/2 begins printing the data in the background. As a result, your application "frees up" even before the printout finishes, and you can continue working in the application. If you need to print two reports or documents from two applications in a hurry, you can switch to the second application and tell it to print, even while the first application is still giving print material to OS/2. Both applications can send printouts through OS/2 to the printer, and OS/2 keeps them separate.

Understanding Printer Differences

Some years ago, dot-matrix printers could print characters in two or three sizes and produce rather coarse-looking graphics output. Dot-matrix printers are faster now, and they can print a greater variety of character sizes. Some dot-matrix printers can display italics and other special effects on the printed page.

Laser printers, which are generally faster and more expensive than dot-matrix printers, offer better-looking characters, more character shapes and sizes, the capability to accept different paper stock from separate trays, duplex (two-sided) printing, and higher-resolution (300 dots per inch) graphics. You can add extra character shapes and sizes (fonts) to most laser printers in the form of *downloadable character sets* or *font cartridges*. You learn more about these special printer features later in this chapter.

In Chapter 4, "Deciding how You Want to Use OS/2," you learned that printers accept commands that don't show up on the printed page. These commands—which vary widely among different printers—tell the printer how to handle subsequent character data.

OS/2 supplies printer driver software modules for the following general categories of printers:

- IBM/Epson-compatible dot-matrix printers
- PCL printers (Hewlett-Packard LaserJet and DeskJet)
- PostScript printers
- IBM laser printers

In addition, OS/2 supplies a generic printer driver that doesn't include printer command functions. This driver supports other printers.

In each case, the printer driver software presents a common, generic interface to your OS/2 and Windows application software. You need not configure each of your OS/2 and Windows applications to use your printer's special features. You tell the OS/2 Print Manager and the Windows Print Manager what kind of printer you have. When your Windows and Presentation Manager applications print, OS/2 handles the details of fonts, page orientation, duplexing, and other printer capabilities. If your printer doesn't support a particular capability, such as duplex print, your applications cannot take advantage of that capability.

You may have one or more DOS applications that don't use the OS/2 print driver interface. Such applications ask you what sort of printer you have and provide their own non-PM support for your printer's features. When you use these applications, follow the application software's instructions for printing. Configure the application's print environment as though you are using plain DOS rather than OS/2.

Seeing the Printer as an OS/2 Object

When you choose a printer during OS/2 installation, or if you add a printer to your computer system, your printer selection becomes an icon on your desktop. OS/2 labels the icon with the make and model of your printer or with the generic label "Printer." This printer icon is an OS/2 object that, like the other objects on your desktop, has a settings notebook and other object-like characteristics.

The printer object (icon) is OS/2's desktop representation of your printer. When you want to manage your printer's features and configuration, you manipulate the printer object. You can create and set up more than one printer object on your desktop. A second printer object may represent a second printer, or it can represent a different configuration of the same printer. A later section of this chapter explains creating multiple printer objects.

One of the settings for the printer object is the *printer driver*. The printer driver understands the features and capabilities of your printer. You can use the printer driver's *job properties* settings to tailor the default appearance of your printouts. If you want OS/2 to prompt you for specific job property settings for each printout, you can check the box marked Prompt for Job Properties on the Queue options settings page. Each printer object has its own *queue driver* as well as a setting that indicates which printer port (usually LPT1, LPT2, or LPT3) the printer object uses. Figure 15.1 shows the Queue Options page of the printer object's settings notebook.

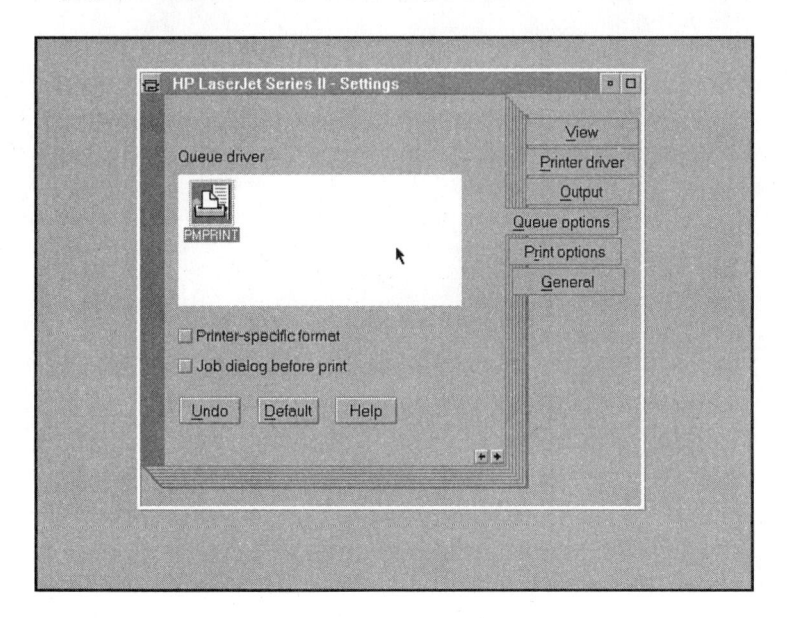

Fig. 15.1
The Queue options page in the settings notebook for the printer object.

The settings notebook for the printer object includes pages labeled View, Printer Driver, Output, Queue Options, Print Options, and General. The following list outlines the use of these pages:

- You can change the name of the printer object on the View page.

378 Chapter 15—Printing with OS/2

- The Printer driver page enables you to specify the printer driver name and properties. Figure 15.2 shows a typical Printer driver settings notebook page.

- You indicate the printer port on the Output page, as shown in figure 15.3.

- On the Print options page, as shown in figure 15.4, you can tell OS/2 to defer the printing operation until a time of day you specify. The Print options page also enables you to enter the name of a file that OS/2 is to print before each print job. OS/2 prints this file on *job separator pages* between each of your printouts.

Fig. 15.2
The Printer driver page in the settings notebook for the printer object.

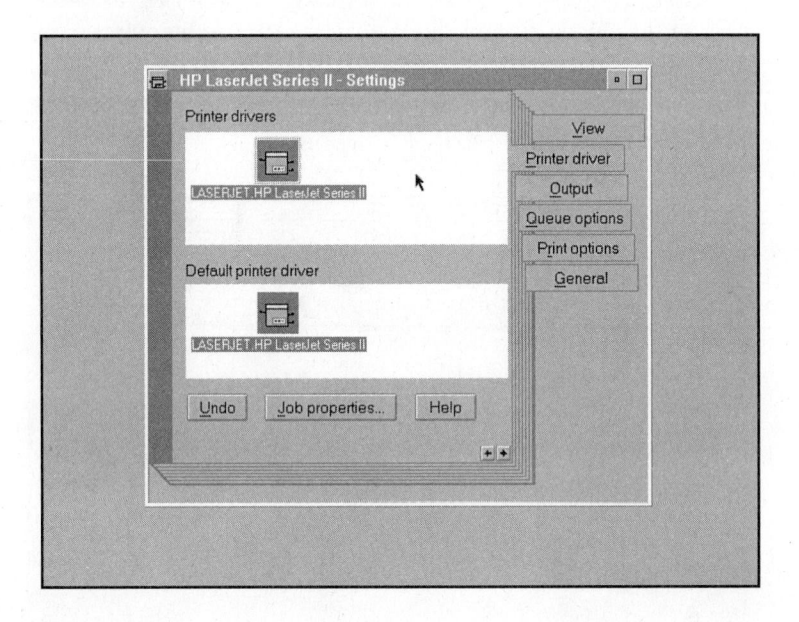

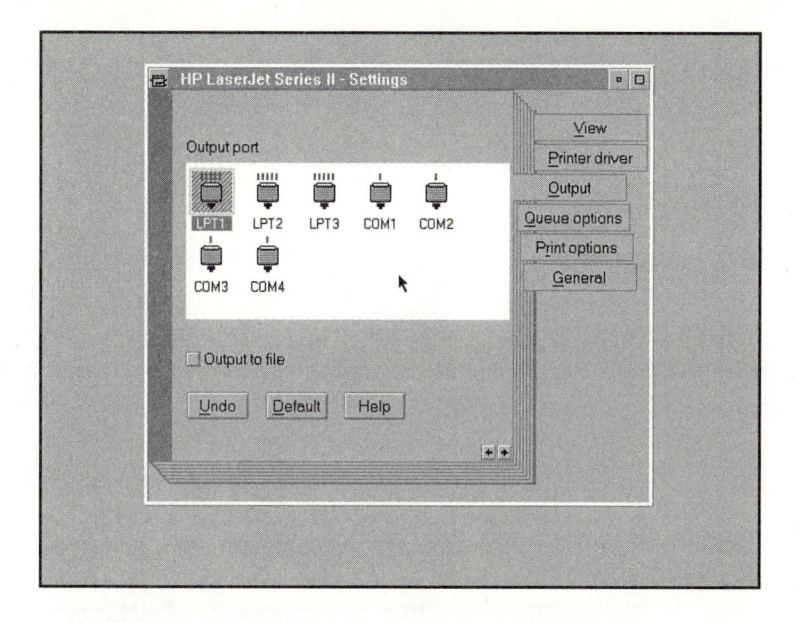

Fig. 15.3
The Output page in the settings notebook for the printer object.

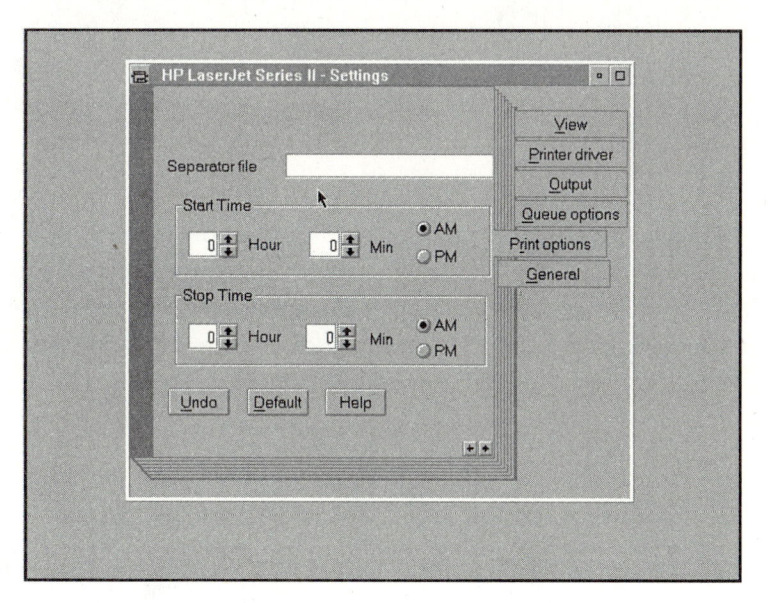

Fig. 15.4
The Print options page in the settings notebook for the printer object.

Working with the Spooler and Queue Driver

When you send data to the printer, OS/2 sometimes has to convert the data file to a form the printer can accept. OS/2 also must hold the print data in a queue until the printer is ready to receive it. Print jobs can come from multiple applications, PRINT commands, and other printer operations you initiate.

The Queue driver individually tracks each print job and sends the jobs, one by one, to the Spooler object. The Spooler object holds the print data until the printer is ready to accept it. The Spooler object receives print jobs from each of your Queue drivers. By default, the OS/2 Spooler object is in the System Setup folder.

The OS/2 Spooler object holds the material waiting to be printed in the *spool directory*. The installation process created this directory, named C:\SPOOL. You can change your spool path on the settings notebook page for the Spooler object. You also can disable the Spooler with a menu option on the Spooler's pop-up menu. If you disable the Spooler, you must be careful to not send two print jobs to the printer at the same time. You may find that the printed pages contain a confusing mixture of interspersed data from both print jobs.

Creating Print Jobs

Each printout you request, whether from an application, a PRINT command, or other print operation, is a print job. You can see a list of print jobs by double-clicking the printer object. The list shows each print job's associated properties. You may want to change some print job properties before printing starts. You can see in the list the size of the print job and when the job was submitted.

Viewing Your Print Jobs. The list of print jobs for a printer object represents the printer's output queue. To see this list, open the printer object (by default, the installation process leaves the printer object on your desktop). You can specify on the printer object's settings notebook whether you want to see an Icon View or a Details View of the print job list. Figure 15.5 is an example of the Icon View of a job list. Figure 15.6 shows the Details View of the same list.

The job list changes dynamically as the printer finishes each print job. You can change the frequency with which OS/2 updates the on-screen list of print jobs. To make this change, use the Refresh Interval field of the View page of the printer object. You also can use the Refresh menu option to cause OS/2 to update the list immediately.

Learning OS/2 Printer Basics **381**

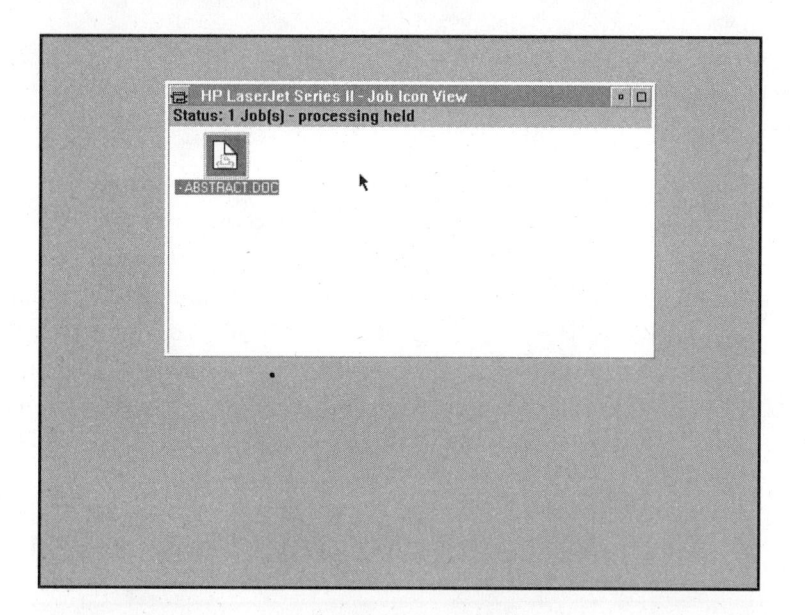

Fig. 15.5
The Icon View for print jobs that are awaiting print.

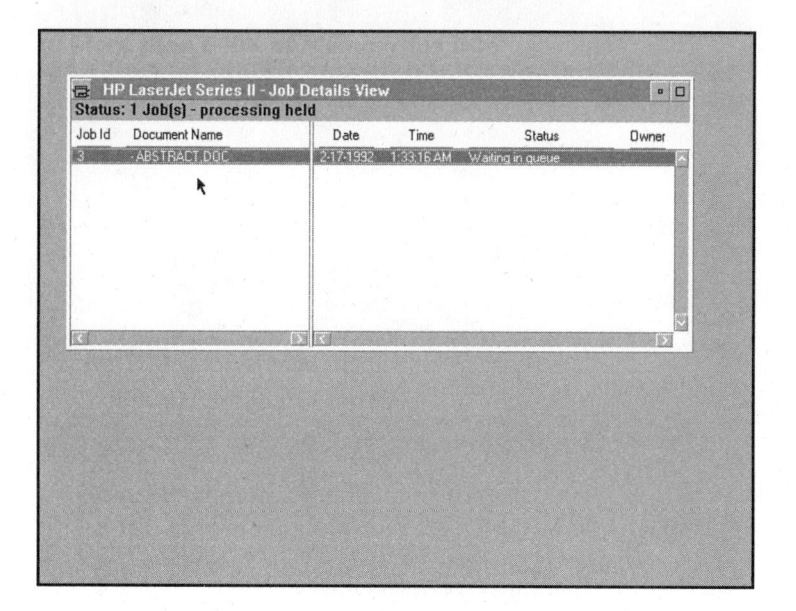

Fig. 15.6
The Details View for the print jobs in the queue.

Changing Print Job Status. The pop-up menu for the printer object contains options for changing the status of the printer driver. You can set the status to *Hold* (to hold print jobs without printing them) or *Release* (to release previously held print jobs). When you use the printer object's pop-up menu to hold or release print jobs, your action affects all print jobs in that print queue. You can use this technique to release print jobs you previously held, or hold print jobs that haven't yet printed. You also can use the printer object's pop-up menu to switch to a different default printer if you have more than one printer object defined.

For Related Information
- "Understanding How OS/2 Expands upon DOS," p. 62

The individual print job icons have pop-up menus, too. Before a print job begins printing, you can use the job's pop-up menu to change its print job properties. You can specify a new *job position*, to make the printout appear before or after other print jobs. You can tell OS/2 to print a different number of copies of the job. You can give the print job a different priority, and you can change the *form name* on which OS/2 is to print the job. If you specify a different form name from the default for that printer object's properties, OS/2 prompts you to change the paper in the printer when it is ready to print that job.

Fig. 15.7
The Print Options settings notebook page for a particular print job.

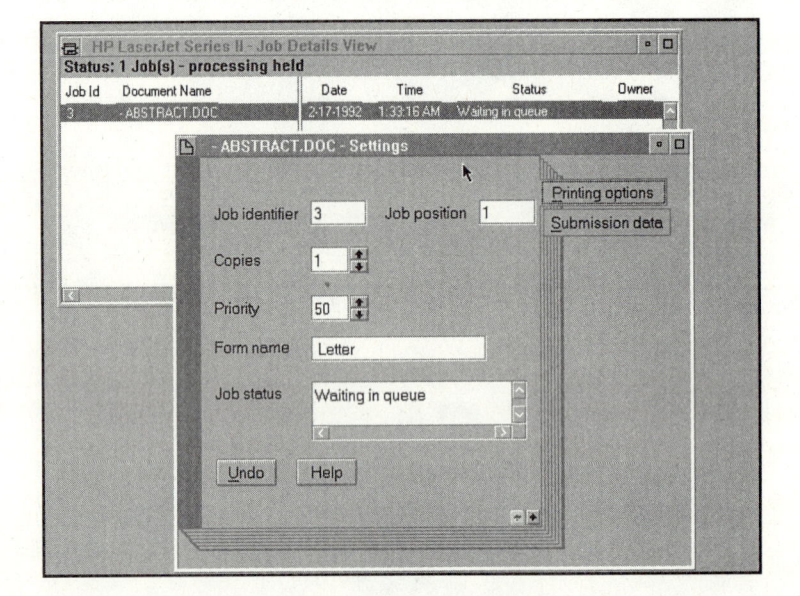

Learning about Fonts

During the OS/2 installation process, you indicated which of the optional fonts you wanted to install. The fonts you chose control the appearance of the screen and the appearance of the printouts you produce. In the next few sections, you learn more about the fonts on your computer system. You start with the basics, then move up to important details about OS/2 system fonts and Adobe Type 1 fonts. You discover how to install new soft fonts and how to tell OS/2 that you have a font cartridge in your printer.

Understanding Font Basics

A font is a set of characters that have a particular size and shape. Each font has a name, usually supplied by the font's designer. To represent a font on your computer screen and on your printouts, the computer must know how each character is shaped, and it must know the font's spacing, pitch, height, style, stroke weight, symbol set, and typeface. These characteristics of a font are, collectively, its *font metrics*.

You're looking at an example of a font right now. This book uses Garamond, a pleasant, easy-to-read font that doesn't intrude on your efforts to understand the information contained in the text.

The *spacing* characteristic determines the size of the distance between the font's letters and numbers. *Pitch* expresses the number of characters that occur per horizontal inch for a font that has equidistant (fixed) spacing. Pitch does not apply to proportionally spaced fonts, because the spacing varies in these fonts on a character-by-character basis. A font's *height* is specified in *points*, and each point is 1/72 of an inch.

Style denotes the angularity of the font's characters; popular styles are upright and *italic*. *Stroke weight* describes the thickness of the lines that make up the characters. You sometimes see a **bold** stroke weight, but most characters appear with a medium stroke weight.

A font's *symbol set* reveals the font's intended purpose. The symbols may be ordinary letters and numbers, or the symbols may be specific to a particular kind of work. Lawyers, engineers, and mathematicians use special symbol sets.

A font's *typeface* identifies its design and corresponds to the name of the font. A group of fonts that have similar characteristics make up a *font family*. Font designs are either *serif*, with characters having curved, adorned shapes, or *sans serif*, with straight characters having little or no adornment.

The fonts that come with OS/2 are *soft fonts*. Soft fonts come on a floppy disk and must be downloaded into the printer. OS/2 Presentation Manager takes care of this task automatically when you print from a PM application. The Windows Print Manager performs the same job if you use a Windows application. DOS applications, however, must use their own printer management methods to download fonts as necessary.

Using OS/2 System Fonts

You received four IBM Core Fonts with your OS/2 operating system. These fonts are Courier, Helvetica, System Monospace, and Times Roman. The installation process copied the appropriate files to your hard disk automatically. The IBM Core Fonts are *bit-map* fonts, which means each character is a simple matrix of dots.

> **Note**
>
> IBM Core Fonts can be used by PostScript printers.

OS/2 cannot arbitrarily scale (resize) or reshape bit-map fonts. A bit-map font can only be enlarged by multiplying it by a whole number scaling factor. At larger sizes, bit-map fonts look coarse, because the software is only doubling or tripling the matrix of dots. Type 1 fonts, on the other hand, can be easily scaled and reshaped. The next section discusses Type 1 fonts.

Working with Adobe Type Manager Fonts

In addition to the four IBM Core Fonts, OS/2 gives you 13 Adobe Type 1 fonts. Adobe Systems is a company well known for its font technology. Adobe created what it calls *Type 1* fonts to be easily scaled and managed by computer software. A Type 1 font file contains directions and shape information that computer programs can use to render that font, either on the computer screen or on your laser printer.

Adobe Type Manager (ATM) is built into OS/2. ATM is a font manager software module that does the job of managing, scaling, and rendering Type 1 fonts. Because each character exists in the Type 1 font file as a series of directions that tell how to draw that character, ATM can scale the character in an arbitrary fashion. Each character in the font retains its good resolution and quality when it is enlarged.

The following list shows the names of the 13 Adobe Type 1 fonts you received with OS/2. These fonts work with Hewlett-Packard laser printers (which use PCL, *Printer Command Language*) and with Postscript printers. *Postscript* is a page description language developed by Adobe.

- Times New Roman
- Times New Roman Bold

- Times New Roman Bold Italic
- Times New Roman Italic
- Helvetica
- Helvetica Bold
- Helvetica Bold Italic
- Helvetica Italic
- Courier
- Courier Bold
- Courier Bold Italic
- Courier Italic
- Symbol

Installing Soft Fonts and Font Cartridges

Adobe Systems and other companies that specialize in computer font technology offer thousands of fonts. You can add new fonts to your computer system by purchasing and installing extra Type 1 fonts (contact IBM or Adobe for more information on what fonts you can add to your system). You also may be able to install a font cartridge in your printer, if your printer supports this option.

To install soft fonts, and to tell OS/2 about a font cartridge you have installed in your printer, open the settings notebook for the appropriate printer object. Select the Printer Driver notebook page. Next, open the settings notebook for the default printer driver object.

To tell OS/2 about a font cartridge you have purchased, select the appropriate font names (up to two) in the list box of available choices.

To install soft fonts for a Hewlett-Packard or a Postscript laser printer, select the Fonts option. For an IBM laser printer, select the Download Fonts option. OS/2 displays the Font Installer window. Insert your disk of new fonts and click the Open button to display a list of fonts. Select (highlight) from the list box the fonts you want to install and click the A**d**d>> button.

> **Note**
>
> Type 1 fonts come in pairs of disk files. One file has an AFM extension and the other has a PFB extension. The Font Installer window must have both files available to it at the same time, to install a given font. If you received more than one disk containing your new fonts, create a temporary directory, copy all the disk files to the temporary directory, and install the new fonts from the temporary directory.

To delete fonts from your system, follow the preceding directions but click the Delete button after you have selected the fonts you want to remove.

For Related Information
- "Understanding Hardware and Software," p. 15

You can change your default fonts with the Font Palette (located in the Setup folder inside the OS/2 System folder). The Font Palette contains font samples and an Edit Font option. You can add or delete fonts in the Font Palette window by selecting (highlighting) a font, checking the Edit Font option, and using the Add or Delete buttons to indicate the operation you want to perform. Chapter 7, "Modifying Your OS/2 Configuration," contains more information on using the Font Palette.

Printing with OS/2

The preceding sections of this chapter introduced you to the way OS/2 and your printer work together to make your printouts look their best. You learned yet another way in which OS/2 is highly configurable—printing. To this point, however, you have yet to print anything. This chapter now turns to the different ways you can send your printouts to the printer.

You can print with OS/2 by the following methods:

- You can drag and drop a data file object onto a printer object.
- You can use the PRINT or COPY commands at an OS/2 command-line prompt.
- You can instruct your application program to print.
- You can use the Print Screen key on the keyboard.

The following sections cover these OS/2 printing techniques.

Using Drag and Drop

The printer object understands that it is to print a file that you drop on it. Remember, however, to drop only text files or other printable files on the printer object. The printer object uses its default print job properties to send your printout through the queue to the printer.

Sending the Print and Copy Commands

If you want to send a text file to the printer and you are currently looking at an OS/2 command line prompt, you can use the PRINT command. Part Five (the Reference section) of this book provides details of the PRINT command. Generally, however, you type the PRINT command as shown in the following example:

PRINT MEMO.DOC

If you prefer a command line interface over OS/2's drag-and-drop mechanism, you can use a simple COPY command, as shown in the following example, to print a text file:

COPY MYFILE.TXT LPT1

Printing from an Application

OS/2 is a multifaceted environment. You can send printouts to the printer from your Presentation Manager, Windows, or DOS applications. You can print from two or more applications at the same time. OS/2 turns each printout into a separate print job and queues each print job for printing.

Printing with PM Applications. Most PM applications have at least two printer-related menu options on the File item's drop-down menu. The Print menu item brings up a dialog box in which you can specify details about what you want to print. The application's Print dialog box enables you select which parts of the document you want to print, and enables you to change other application-related print options. In most applications, the dialog box tells you the name of the printer object it is to use for printing.

The other drop-down menu item, Printer Setup, enables you to choose a printer object. You click the Setup button to see the Printer Properties window. In this window, you can specify such things as which paper tray to use and which font cartridge is active. You also can manage your fonts, forms, and printer device defaults in the Printer Properties window, just as you can in the settings notebook pages for the printer object.

Printing with Windows Applications. You notice little or no change in the way your Windows applications print under OS/2's WIN-OS2 environment, as compared to printing with Microsoft Windows under DOS. The Print Manager controls your printouts (and you control the Print Manager). When you print from a Windows application, OS/2 routes your printouts through a printer object. The Windows Print Manager is closely tied to the OS/2 desktop's printer objects.

The Windows Print Manager enables you to pause or resume a printout, and its window shows you a list of Windows print jobs currently awaiting print. You can use the Options menu item to set the priority of your print jobs. Another setting on this menu enables you to determine how the Print Manager signals you if the printer has a problem or is off-line. The View menu item enables you to specify what information about each print job you want to see (Time/Date Sent and Print File Size). You also can remove Windows print jobs from the queue with the Windows Print Manager.

If you previously installed Windows on your computer, the OS/2 installation process migrated your Windows printer setup to your new Windows-under-OS/2 environment. If you installed OS/2's Windows support on a machine that did not already have Windows (when there was nothing to migrate), you must tell Windows about your printer. You find the Control Panel in the Main window. Double-click Control Panel and then the Printers icon to see the Printer Setup window. In this window, you can choose a default printer, you can configure Windows to use that printer to your specifications (click the Configure button), and you can toggle the Print Manager on or off.

> **Note**
>
> Toggling the Print Manager off may result in intermixed printouts if you print from more than one Windows application at the same time.

You see the Printer Configuration window when you click the Configure button on the Printer Setup window. To configure Windows for your particular printer, choose a printer port (the one labeled LPT1.OS2 is an *alias*, or synonym, for the OS/2 printer object connected to the LPT1 printer port) and click the Setup button. For now, you can leave the Device Not Selected and Transmission Retry fields set to their default values.

The Windows Printer Setup window behaves like the OS/2 desktop's Printer Properties window. You use both windows in the same way to specify your printer's features.

Printing with DOS Applications. As this chapter mentioned earlier, non-PM, non-Windows applications have their own methods of enabling you to specify printer options and of downloading fonts and printer commands to the printer. DOS applications do not use Presentation Manager to format and prepare their printouts. When you tell a DOS-based computer program to print something, that application manages the final appearance of the printed output completely without PM's help. The printout does appear, however, as a print job that you can view with the printer object's Icon View or Details View window.

Handling Printer Errors

Any mechanical process is subject to occasional errors, and this rule holds true for computer printing operations. When OS/2 sends spooled output to the printer, for example, the printer may run out of paper or develop a paper jam. OS/2 notifies you of printer errors with a screen similar to the screen in figure 15.8. After you fix the problem with the printer (consult the printer's reference manual as necessary), you can click Retry to tell OS/2 to resume the print job. Alternatively, you can click Abort to end that print job, or Ignore. The Ignore option will probably result in part of the printout not appearing.

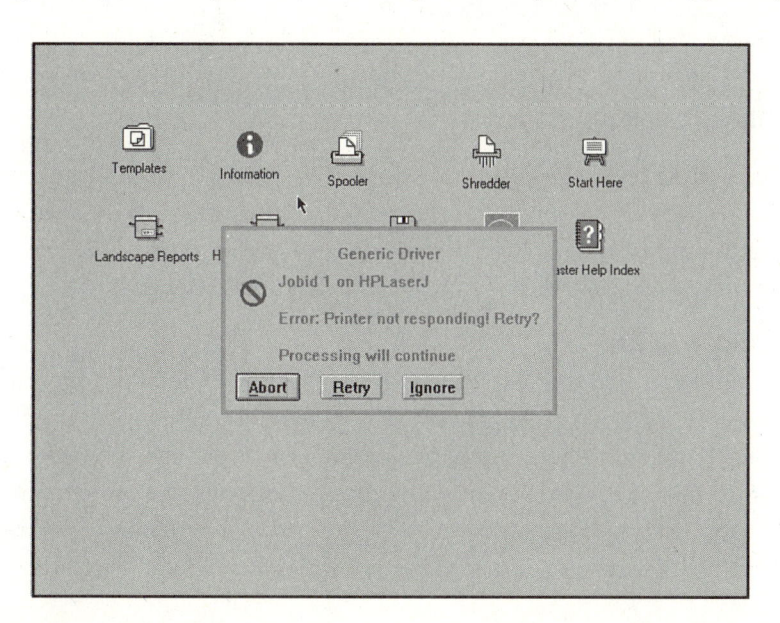

Fig. 15.8
An OS/2 pop-up window notifies you of printer errors.

Using Multiple Printer Objects

You can use multiple printer objects in a variety of ways. Each printer object can represent a different printer, or different default configuration settings for the same printer. You can use a second printer object for landscape printing, for example, if your printer supports this feature. When you drop a text file object on the printer object configured for landscape printing, your printout appears across the page instead of down the page.

To create a second printer object, open your Templates folder. Drag the Printer template onto an empty place on your desktop. When the Create Another Printer window appears, give the new printer object a unique name and choose a printer port. You also can select a different printer driver in this window. OS/2 may prompt you to insert a Printer Driver Disk after you click the Create Another button.

If you want to change the printer driver for a printer object, insert Printer Driver Disk 1 in drive A and select Drive A: on your desktop. A printer driver folder appears, from which you select the make and model of the printer driver you want to install. Drag and drop that printer driver icon onto your printer object.

If you are unsure which printer driver to select for your particular make and model of printer, you can double-click the data file object labeled PRDESC.LST. You then see a list of printer models and their associated printer drivers. You can use the Help menu item on the pop-up menu for the printer object and its printer driver to get information about the specific features that the driver supports.

To make changes to the settings notebook (including job properties) for your printer object, click the right mouse button on the printer object, open the object's settings, and modify the items on the notebook pages. The job properties settings appear on the notebook page labeled Printer driver.

Printing to a File

You can set up a printer object to produce a disk file containing your printouts instead of sending the printouts to a printer. You can use this operation if your computer is not connected to a printer, and you have to perform print operations on another computer that is connected to a printer. (This approach assumes that your computer is not part of a local area network with a shared LAN printer.) You begin this task on your computer by creating a printer object with a printer driver matching the characteristics of the printer that is attached to the other computer. In the printer object settings notebook, check the Output to File box.

Each time you print to a file, OS/2 asks for the name of a file to use in place of an actual printer. You can specify a drive letter and path to send the printout to a directory of your choosing. When you are ready to produce a printout of the file, copy the file to a disk and take the disk to the other computer. On the other computer, you can drag and drop the disk file onto a printer object, or you can copy the file to the appropriate printer port (LPT1, for example).

For Related Information

- "Understanding How OS/2 Expands upon DOS," p. 62
- "Using the Workplace Shell," p. 231
- "Introducing Presentation Manager," p. 234
- "Learning the Commands for Viewing and Printing Files," p. 329

Chapter Summary

In this chapter, you learned how OS/2 helps you make your printouts look their best. After surveying the basics of printing with OS/2, you learned how to configure OS/2's print-related options. The chapter presented information on printer objects, print jobs, and print job properties. After coming up to speed on fonts, you learned about the OS/2 system fonts, Adobe Type 1 fonts, and font cartridges.

You have explored various methods of printing with OS/2—from the command line, with a drag-and-drop action, or from within your applications. In this chapter, you saw how OS/2 notifies you of printer problems. You also learned how to look at the entries in the awaiting-print queue and how to manage those entries. You know how to set up multiple printer objects and how to use multiple printer objects to send printouts to a file rather than to a printer.

In Chapter 16, you learn more about working with DOS and Windows under OS/2.

Chapter 16

Running DOS and Windows Under OS/2

Many high-quality OS/2 applications are available, and more are being written each day. Still, tens of thousands of DOS applications exist, and you don't want to turn your back on them. Fortunately, you can run almost any DOS or Windows program under OS/2. In fact, if you have enough memory (or disk space), you can run up to 240 different DOS programs at one time. OS/2 runs DOS and Windows programs better than real DOS or Windows. Consider the following, for example:

- OS/2 can run several programs simultaneously. You can type a letter or memo in Word for Windows, recalculate a DOS spreadsheet in another window, and download a bulletin board file in the background with an OS/2 terminal program.

- If a DOS or Windows program crashes, you just close its session. No harm comes to the other programs you're running at the same time. You don't need to reboot the computer when one program goes astray, as is so often necessary with real DOS or Windows.

- DOS programs may actually run faster under OS/2 because OS/2 does a better job of managing disk files.

- OS/2 can make more total memory available to your DOS programs than you have actually installed in your computer. When OS/2 runs out of memory, it uses free disk space instead.

- Today's most powerful DOS applications use clever tricks to bypass the memory limitations of DOS. Configuring these applications properly can be a tough challenge. OS/2 configures these applications for you.

- Windows 3.1 is included. You do not have to buy it separately. In addition, Windows applications run on the Workplace Shell desktop, enabling you to get the advantages of the new user interface.

- Even if you find a DOS program that doesn't run well under OS/2, you can easily load your old copy of DOS.

This chapter is arranged so that you master one concept at a time and build on what you have learned. After a quick overview of DOS sessions, you see how to get to DOS's usual interface, the command line prompt. You then learn how to incorporate the advantages of the Workplace Shell interface by setting up your DOS and Windows applications on the desktop. Next, you explore options that increase your DOS session's memory and speed. The chapter concludes with a troubleshooting guide and a discussion of a few types of DOS programs that you cannot run under OS/2.

Understanding DOS Sessions

Imagine having several separate computers linked together so that they share one monitor and one keyboard, with each computer running a different DOS program. If one computer crashes, you reboot it while the other computers continue to run independently, unaffected by the mishap. This scenario is what DOS sessions under OS/2 are like. Each program runs in its own DOS session, and you can run several programs at a time. Although the programs share the resources of a single machine, each program functions as though it were running alone on a separate computer.

A DOS session under OS/2 is difficult to distinguish from DOS running by itself, which we call *real DOS* in this chapter for clarity. IBM engineers took great pains to make DOS sessions work the same as real DOS, testing OS/2's DOS support with dozens of popular applications. You can run almost any DOS or Windows program under OS/2, including applications that require expanded or extended memory, such as large spreadsheets. You can even play graphical DOS games, which run so smoothly that you might forget you're running OS/2.

Because DOS sessions run under OS/2, they can access files on a High Performance File System partition. All the features of this advanced file system are available except for long file names, which DOS programs cannot understand anyway. Even the File Allocation Table file system runs faster under OS/2 than under real DOS.

You must install DOS support before you can run DOS programs. Windows programs require additional support. If you did not load these options when you installed OS/2, add them now. See the description of Selective Install in Chapter 7, "Modifying Your OS/2 Configuration."

For Related Information
- "Matching OS/2 with DOS," p. 60
- "Understanding How OS/2 Expands upon DOS," p. 62

Opening a DOS Command-Line Session

Inside the OS/2 System object is a folder named Command Prompts. This folder contains objects that open command line sessions for DOS and OS/2, either windowed or full screen. A full-screen DOS session looks exactly like real DOS. A windowed session is similar, except that you usually see only part of the DOS screen in a window on the Workplace Shell desktop. Open a full screen session and a windowed session now to experiment with their properties.

Run the DIR command in each session. You may immediately notice one major difference: the full-screen session seems several times faster than the windowed session. Although the programs run at about the same speed, screen output in a windowed session is much slower because it runs in graphics mode. Full-screen sessions can use text mode, which takes advantage of fast video hardware to write a whole character at a time.

Making Sessions Full Screen or Windowed

Go to your windowed DOS session, hold down the Alt key, and press Home. The DOS session turns into a full-screen session. Pressing Alt-Home again returns you to the windowed session.

Having both options is convenient. Full-screen sessions have snappier video response and show you the whole screen at one time. Windowing, however, enables you to see more than one session at a time. Although you normally see only part of the application's screen in a window, you can view the entire screen if you maximize the window.

Moving among Sessions

As you learned in Chapter 10, "Managing the Workplace Shell," you can go from one session to the next by pressing Alt-Esc. Another combination keystroke, Alt-Tab, also enables you to go from one session to the next, but with one important difference. Alt-Tab cycles only between your windowed desktop applications and sessions. Alt-Tab does not switch to or from full-screen sessions.

When a windowed DOS or OS/2 session is active, pressing the Alt key alone reveals that session's system menu, shown in figure 16.1. From the system menu, you can use the Window lis**t** option to switch to another session or application. You can see from the list of menu options in figure 16.1 that several other choices are also available.

Fig. 16.1
A DOS session's system menu.

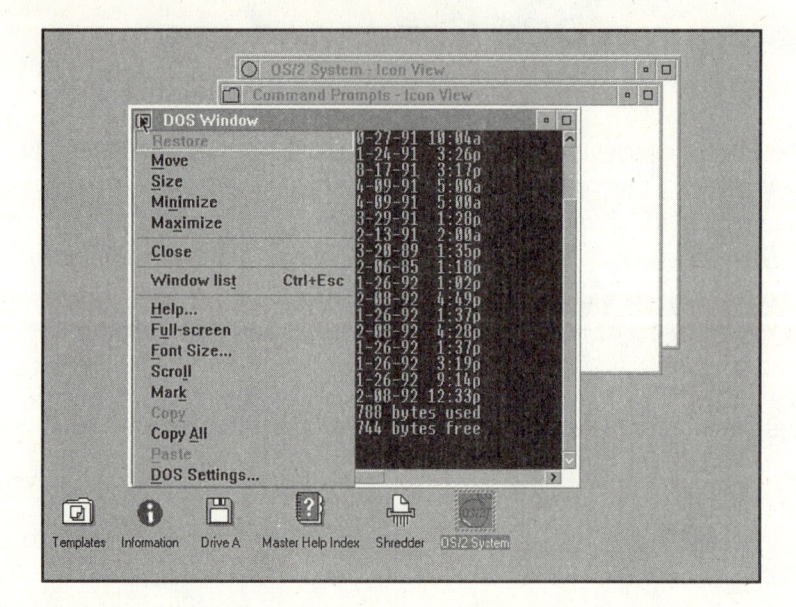

Starting a Windows Session

If you open the Windows Full Screen object in the Command Prompts folder, you see the Windows Program Manager, just as though you started Windows under real DOS.

The first release of OS/2 2.0 incorporated Version 3.0 of Windows, but OS/2 2.1 now includes Windows 3.1 support, as well. Many applications have been written for the Windows environment, and you can run these applications in addition to your DOS and OS/2 programs.

You have now learned everything you absolutely need to know in order to run most DOS programs under OS/2. You can start them by typing their names at the command line, the same as if you were running real DOS. You also know how to run Windows programs the way you are used to. In the rest of this chapter, you will become even more productive with your DOS and Windows applications as you learn how to do the following:

- Run applications from the Workplace Shell desktop, without using the command-line interface.

- Start an application by double-clicking one of its data files, such as a word processing document.

- Protect Windows sessions from each other so that if one terminates with an Unrecoverable Application Error, you do not lose work in other Windows applications.

- Cut and paste between sessions.

- Fine-tune sessions for maximum performance.

- Fix common problems.

- Leave OS/2 and boot real DOS.

For Related Information
- "Beginning the Command-Line Interface," p. 303

Adding DOS Programs

As you learned in Chapter 10, you can add DOS and Windows applications to the Workplace Shell desktop or to any folder. Automatic installation, using the Migrate Applications program in the OS/2 System folder, is the easiest way to add applications. If you want to add applications manually, however, complete the procedures provided in the following sections, which illustrate how to install Borland's Quattro Pro spreadsheet for DOS.

Creating a New Program Object

To create a new Program object, you drag a Program icon from the Templates folder to the desktop. Then you assign a program to that icon. To create an example Quattro Pro Program object, follow these steps:

1. Open the Templates folder by double-clicking it.

2. Select a Program icon by clicking it once with the left mouse button.

3. Hold down the right mouse button and drag the Program icon onto the desktop; then release the right mouse button, dropping the icon on the desktop.

   These steps create a new program object, whose settings notebook opens automatically. To move to a specific notebook page, you can click the tabs on the right side of the notebook.

4. Click the **G**eneral tab to open the General page.

5. Type in a title for the program, in this case **Quattro Pro**.

   Your new title appears underneath the Program object's icon.

Chapter 16—Running DOS and Windows Under OS/2

Telling OS/2 How to Run the Program

You now need to establish Program settings, which tell OS/2 how to run the program. Follow these steps:

1. Click the **P**rogram tab on the settings notebook.

2. Type the program's complete file name in the Path and file name field; for this example, type **C:\QPRO\Q.EXE**.

   You can specify any program here as long as its name ends in EXE, COM, or BAT.

3. Move to the Parameters field and type any options you need, such as switches that you would type after the program's name if you were running it from the DOS command line. Quattro Pro does not need any optional parameters.

4. Then fill in the Working Directory field, which tells OS/2 where to find the program's data files. For this example, you type **C:\QPRO**.

Figure 16.2 shows the completed Quattro Pro Program page.

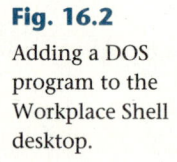

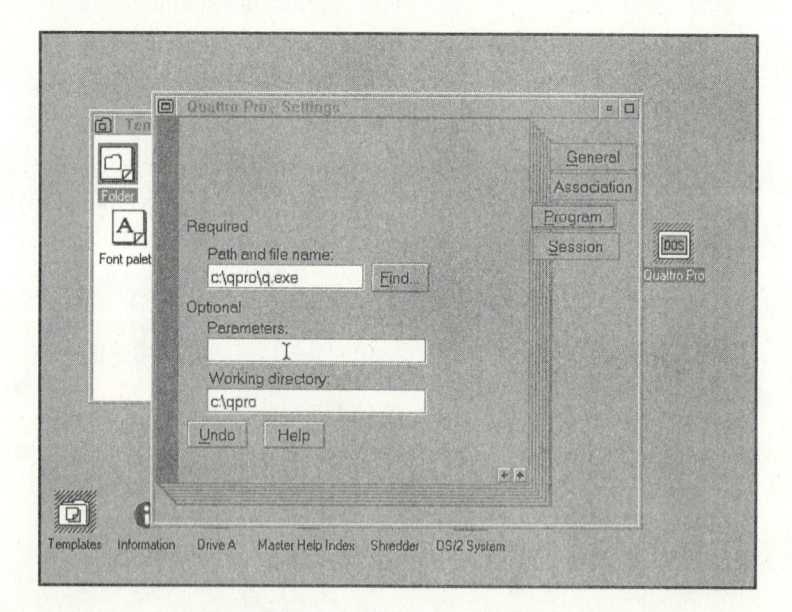

Fig. 16.2
Adding a DOS program to the Workplace Shell desktop.

Telling OS/2 How to Recognize Files

You can use the Association page to specify what sort of files the application uses. The built-in types are mostly for programmers, so you usually need to create your own.

Quattro Pro worksheets, for example, use the file extensions WQ1 and WQ!. Type ***.WQ1** in the New Name field, and choose A**d**d>> to move it to the Current Names field. Then do the same for the WQ! extension by typing ***.WQ!** in the New Name field, as shown in figure 16.3. The asterisk is a *wildcard* that tells OS/2 to associate, with the program, *any* file that has the specified extension(s).

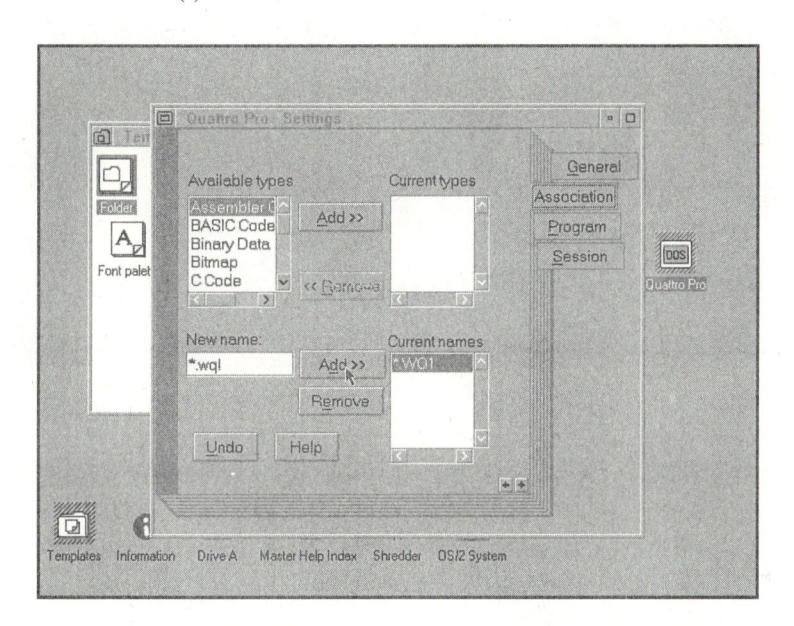

Fig. 16.3
Identifying a program's data files.

Whenever you double-click a spreadsheet's data file icon—for example, while viewing the working directory with the drive C object—this association tells the system to load the file into Quattro Pro. You don't need to start the spreadsheet program explicitly. You have already told OS/2 to associate Q.EXE (Quattro Pro) with any file that has an extension of WQ1 or WQ!.

Telling OS/2 What Kind of Session to Open

Figure 16.4 shows the settings notebook's Session page. As soon as you filled in the Program page, OS/2 analyzed the program file and determined that Q.EXE is a DOS program. Therefore, OS/2 only offers you a choice between windowed and full-screen DOS sessions. Click whichever button you prefer. For this program, full screen gives you the best performance. A windowed DOS session, on the other hand, enables you to see your program run in a window on your desktop, alongside other desktop windows.

Fig. 16.4
Types of DOS sessions you can choose.

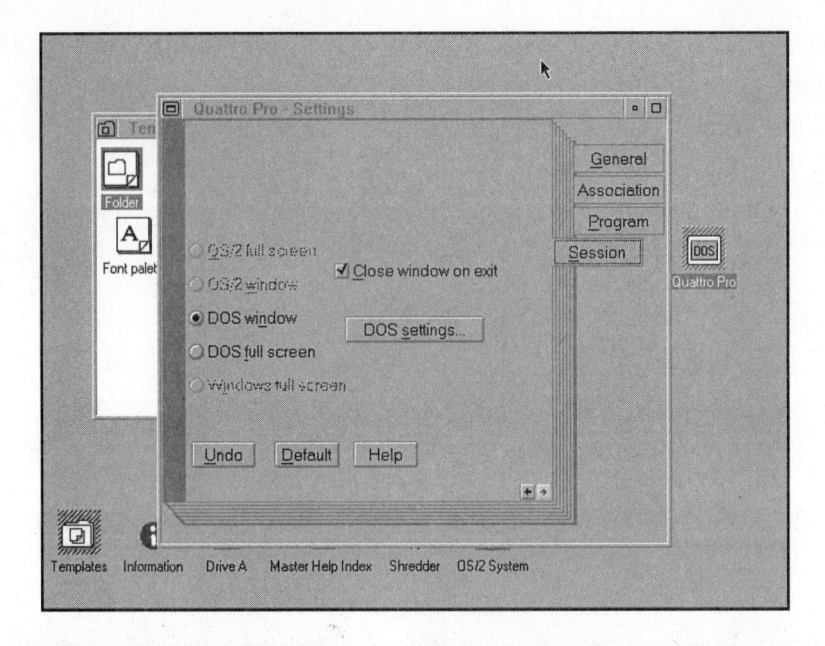

Sometimes, when you set up what you think is a DOS program, the Session page insists that you load it in an OS/2 session. This feature means that you have a *bound* program, which can run under either operating system, DOS or OS/2. Many Microsoft applications are bound programs. Running them in an OS/2 session yields better performance and fewer memory constraints.

The Close window on exit check box is automatically selected because you normally want to end the session when you leave the program. If you turn this option off, the session remains open when you exit from the program so you can view any last minute error messages the application might display upon exiting.

The DOS settings button offers you many options to tune the performance of the application. The next chapter, "Configuring Your DOS and Windows Sessions," discusses DOS Settings in detail. For now, close the settings notebook by pressing Alt-F4, or by choosing Close from the notebook's system menu.

Your new Program object is now an icon on your desktop. Before you store the Program object in a folder, explore some of the things you can do with the new object. Double-clicking the object runs the program. The clicking the right mouse button displays the object's pop-up menu.

Double-click the object to start the program now. If you chose to run the program in full-screen mode, use Alt-Home to window the DOS session on your desktop.

Using a DOS Session's System Menu

The system menu you saw in figure 16.1 has the usual items you would expect after reading Chapter 10, but some new choices also are present. Full-screen does the same thing as Alt-Home. DOS Settings enable you to customize many options that fine-tune DOS's performance, as detailed in Chapter 17, Configuring Your DOS and Windows Sessions.

Go to your windowed DOS session and pull down its system menu by pressing Alt. You see even more choices. Full-screen does the same thing as Alt-Home, and DOS Settings is again available. The other new choices control font size and enable you to cut and paste, as explained in the next few sections.

Controlling the Font Size. Windowed DOS sessions offer you a choice of character sizes. The largest characters are easiest to read, although the smaller fonts enable you to see an entire DOS screen in a small window. Figure 16.5 shows the options available when you load a DOS application, in this case Quattro Pro, and choose Font Size from the system menu.

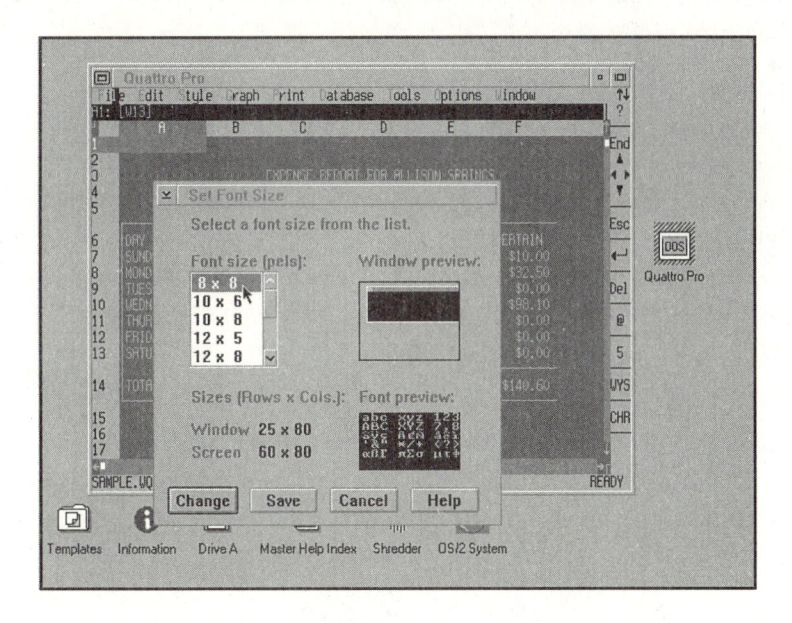

Fig. 16.5
Choosing a font size for a windowed session.

The Set Font Size window describes font sizes in terms of *pels* (sometimes called *pixels*), which are the tiny dots that make up each character. For example, with the 12 x 5 font, each character is 12 dots high and 5 wide. For comparison, the standard font you see in a full-screen DOS session is 14 x 8 on a VGA monitor. An additional column of blank dots always occurs between characters, to separate them.

The numbers beneath the Font size menu labeled Window tell you the size of your DOS window. The size is usually 25 rows of 80 characters, but many applications allow you to use 50 rows instead. Another pair of numbers, labeled Screen, tells the maximum number of character rows and columns that can be shown on-screen. This number depends on the font size, and it changes as you move through the various options with the up and down arrows. The Window preview area, which graphically shows how large an area the window would fill, also changes for each font size. And the Font preview gives you a snapshot of sample characters in each size.

After you have made your selection, press the Change button to activate it for the current DOS session. If you press Save instead, the selected font size becomes the default for all DOS sessions. Many people prefer the 12 x 5 font, which enables you see a whole screen in a small window, or the 18 x 8 font, which is the easiest to read.

Cutting and Pasting in DOS Sessions. In Chapter 14, you learned how to cut, copy, and paste text in the Enhanced Editor. You can use this feature in windowed DOS or OS/2 sessions, too. For example, you might want to cut or copy a table of numbers from a spreadsheet and paste it into a word processor document. But you cannot cut and paste between applications by using the handy shortcut keys you learned, like Ctrl-Ins. Remember, programs running in DOS sessions think that they are running on a separate computer of their own, so they don't know how to communicate with other sessions. For windowed DOS or OS/2 sessions, you need to use the session's system menu.

To mark a block of text that you want to copy, choose Mark from the system menu. If you want to use the keyboard, notice that the text cursor changed to a box shown in reverse color. Move this cursor to a corner of the block, hold down the Shift key, and use the arrow keys to highlight the whole block. Then release the Shift key.

You also can mark text with the mouse; its cursor changed to a picture of a box to let you know it is ready. Move the mouse cursor to a corner of the block you want to copy, hold down the left button, and move the mouse to highlight the whole block. Release the button when done.

After marking a block, press Alt to pull down the system menu again, and this time pick Copy. The text you selected is now in OS/2's Clipboard.

Finally, go to the session into which you want to copy the block, position the cursor where you want to insert it, and pick Paste from that session's system menu.

Closing a Session. Each session's local menu includes a Close option. Avoid using it except as a last resort. Instead, exit from the application as though you were running real DOS or Windows. Otherwise, the program doesn't have a chance to shut itself down properly, saving any files it has opened. But if the program crashes and you cannot get its attention even to terminate it, Close lets you end the session. This action is like rebooting the computer when you are running real DOS and a program locks up.

Running Individual Windows Applications

Under real DOS, you cannot run a Windows application directly; you must load Windows first. You open the Windows Full Screen object (in the Command Prompts folder) and run your application from the Windows Program Manager. If you're an experienced Windows user, you'll feel at home with the familiar interface. This method takes up less memory if you run several Windows applications at a time because only one copy of the Windows program code is loaded. But if you get an Unrecoverable Application Error in one Windows application, it can crash the whole Windows session, and other applications might lose data.

OS/2 gives you another option. You can create an OS/2 desktop object for your Windows application and run that application directly. The procedure is the same you used earlier to place Quattro Pro on the desktop. For example, to create a Word for Windows object, type **C:\WINWORD\WINWORD.EXE** on the top line of the Program screen in the settings notebook. OS/2 automatically recognizes Windows applications and installs the special support they need.

For Related Information
- "Using Microsoft Windows with OS/2," p. 70
- "Setting Up Other Applications," p. 264

When you open the Word for Windows object, it loads its own copy of the Windows code. Each Windows application runs in a separate Windows session. If you get an Unrecoverable Application Error in another session running a Windows spreadsheet such as Excel, for example, it does not harm the Word for Windows session. Running Windows applications in separate sessions consumes more memory, but that may be a small price to pay for the error protection OS/2 provides.

Switching between OS/2 and DOS with Dual-Boot

When you start a program, the operating system does the nitty-gritty work of loading it. But when you start an operating system, it must load itself—like pulling itself up by its own bootstraps. The colorful term "booting" describes this process.

You can switch back and forth between OS/2 and real DOS with the BOOT command. To start DOS, double-click the Dual-Boot icon in the Command Prompts folder, which is inside the OS/2 System folder; or in any OS/2 or DOS session, type the following command:

    C:\OS2\BOOT /DOS

For Related Information
- "Looking at DOS and OS/2 Incompatibilities," p. 71

To go back to OS/2, type the following at the DOS prompt:

    C:\OS2\BOOT /OS2

When you use Dual-Boot to switch from OS/2 to DOS, OS/2 goes through its normal shutdown procedure first.

Booting DOS without Leaving OS/2

For Related Information
- "Changing DOS Settings for Each Session," p. 418

Some finicky programs run only under a specific version of real DOS. If you want to run such a program at the same time as OS/2, you can boot that version of DOS from a floppy disk. Change the DOS_STARTUP_DRIVE setting in the OS/2 DOS Settings window to reflect the drive you are using, insert your DOS boot disk there, and start the DOS session. What you get is not the normal OS/2 emulation of DOS: it is actually real DOS. You cannot boot versions of DOS before 3.0, however. The next chapter covers the DOS_STARTUP_DRIVE and other DOS settings in more detail.

Learning What You Cannot Do in a DOS Session

OS/2 was designed to isolate sessions from each other so that a bug in one program could not crash the system. To protect programs from each other, OS/2 must take exclusive control of the hardware. This step means you cannot run DOS programs that try to take such low-level control themselves. But in most cases, OS/2 gives you another way to do the tasks for which these DOS programs were designed.

Preventing Viruses

Many DOS viruses cannot do their dirty work because of OS/2's protection. Because OS/2 is a nearly crash-proof operating system, it protects crucial parts of your disk and system memory, which these nasty programs often try to modify. You should continue to take your usual precautions, of course, such as obtaining programs only from legitimate retailers and quality bulletin boards, and running virus-check software regularly.

Using Disk Utilities

PC Tools and Norton Utilities include examples of low-level disk utilities that do not work under OS/2. Used improperly, such programs can crash your system, and OS/2 does not permit that. It does not even allow you to run the potentially dangerous commands in DOS itself. For example, while OS/2 is running, you cannot format the hard disk from which you booted OS/2.

You can still use most of the programs in these packages, such as PC Tools Shell and Norton Commander. Only programs like DiskFix and Norton Disk Doctor, which try to take complete control of the disk, are not allowed to execute. For the same reason, you cannot run Stacker in a DOS session under OS/2.

Many of the jobs these programs do are built into OS/2. For example, OS/2 includes an UNDELETE command that you can use to get back files that you accidentally erase and a cache program to speed up your hard disk.

> **Caution**
>
> Using a DOS disk cache under OS/2 is not safe. Many programs, such as Norton Cache, recognize that OS/2 is active and refuse to run anyway.

> **Caution**
>
> Do not use disk defragmenters (sometimes called disk organizers) like Speedisk, Compress, and Disk Optimizer. You can run them if you boot real DOS first, but they may damage the extended attributes of files you used under OS/2. Make sure you use a defragmenter compatible with OS/2.

Running Diagnostic Utilities

You can run DOS diagnostic programs like Norton Sysinfo or Quarterdeck Manifest, but they may crash or give incorrect information. Such programs usually rely on undocumented quirks of DOS and try to access the hardware directly. You may need to use Dual-boot to run plain DOS if you want to run such a diagnostic utility.

Working with Memory Managers

Most people who run DOS on 386 PCs use memory management software such as QEMM, 386MAX, or EMM386, which lets DOS applications access all the computer's memory. To accomplish this, they have to take full control of the 386 chip, and OS/2 does not permit that. You don't need these programs in DOS sessions because their function is built in into OS/2. Best of all, OS/2 takes care of memory management automatically, whereas configuring real DOS memory managers can be a time-consuming task even for experts.

Using Applications that Use Obsolete DOS Extenders

A few DOS applications still use an outdated technique to access memory beyond 640K. Their documentation should mention the words VCPI or Virtual Control Program Interface. This early DOS extender tries to get around the wall that OS/2 puts between DOS sessions. A bug in such a program can crash the computer, so OS/2 doesn't let the program run. OS/2 supports the modern DPMI DOS extender, and most software companies are upgrading their products accordingly.

Employing Windows Enhanced Mode

Almost all Windows applications run in *Standard* mode. Windows also offers an *Enhanced* mode, which can run several Standard mode programs simultaneously. As the name indicates, Windows accomplishes this step by taking exclusive control of the 386 chip. OS/2 does not let that happen, but it does enable you to multitask Windows applications by loading them in separate sessions. This step is an improvement over Windows because OS/2 protects these sessions from each other, whereas an error in one application can crash Windows Enhanced mode.

For Related Information
- "Looking at DOS and OS/2 Incompatibilities," p. 71

Chapter Summary

OS/2 applications are the wave of the future, but you don't have to leave behind your favorite DOS and Windows programs. In fact, they will run better than ever under OS/2. In Chapter 16, you learned how to run these programs from the Workplace Shell desktop. You also learned how to tailor your DOS sessions for maximum performance, and how to troubleshoot common problems.

The next chapter expands your knowledge of DOS and Windows sessions under OS/2.

Chapter 17

Configuring Your DOS and Windows Sessions

Most DOS applications work well without any special configuration changes. Some applications may benefit from extra memory, however, and any program is more fun to use if it runs faster. In the next few sections, you learn how to change global DOS settings by using CONFIG.SYS commands to get more memory and speed and how to fix common problems. You also learn how to modify the global settings to affect each DOS session.

Changing Default Settings in CONFIG.SYS

You will want to apply many settings in all your DOS sessions. The best approach is to place those settings in your system configuration file, CONFIG.SYS. You can edit this file with the Enhanced Editor discussed in Chapter 14, "Using the OS/2 Text Editors." Try editing your configuration file now, and follow the recommendations in the next few sections. Generally, the installation defaults are appropriate, but a few improvements are recommended.

Telling DOS to Make the Best Use of Memory

DOS normally can use only 640K of memory. Part of that space is occupied by DOS, which leaves less memory for your applications. You can free this space by loading DOS in *high memory*, memory beyond 640K.

Another special kind of memory, *upper memory*, enables DOS to load programs that run in the background. The AUTOEXEC.BAT file in your root directory, for example, contains the following line:

```
LOADHIGH APPEND C:\OS2;C:\OS2\SYSTEM
```

When you type LOADHIGH before the name of the APPEND program, DOS loads it into upper memory.

You don't need to know the technical details of high and upper memory. Just remember that this memory is outside the 640K where DOS loads your applications. You have more room to work in DOS if you tell DOS to use these special kinds of memory. To do so, make sure that your CONFIG.SYS contains this line:

```
DOS=HIGH,UMB
```

Delete any other line beginning with DOS=.

Setting the Number of Files DOS Can Use

DOS applications use disk files to store programs and data. The maximum number of files a DOS session can use is set in CONFIG.SYS. This maximum is set to 20 when you install OS/2. That number is enough for most applications, but some programs, such as Windows, occasionally may need more. Search through CONFIG.SYS for the line that says the following:

```
FILES=20
```

Change the number to 50.

Expanding the DOS Environment

The environment is part of DOS's 640K memory area, where programs can store information. DOS sessions normally set aside only 256 bytes for the environment, which is not enough for some applications. Find the following line in CONFIG.SYS:

```
SHELL=C:\OS2\MDOS\COMMAND.COM C:\OS2\MDOS /P
```

Change it to the following:

```
SHELL=C:\OS2\MDOS\COMMAND.COM C:\OS2\MDOS /E:1024 /P
```

The /E:1024 you added sets aside a full kilobyte—1024 bytes—for the DOS environment. This size is enough for almost any application that adds environment variables to your system.

For Related Information

- "Changing Your Configuration Settings," p. 153

- "Using CONFIG.SYS and AUTOEXEC.BAT," p. 162

Changing Settings in the System Menu

The changes you make to CONFIG.SYS apply to all DOS and Windows sessions, but several other settings enable you to customize each program's session to better fit its particular needs. You have the following two ways to access these settings:

- Click mouse button 2 on the program or command prompt object to open its settings notebook, and choose DOS or Windows Settings from the Session page.

- Press Alt when a windowed session is open, and pick DOS Settings from the local menu.

Some settings do not appear when you use the second method because they cannot be changed while the program is running.

Figure 17.1 shows the DOS Settings screen. When you move through the settings in the list box on the left side, the Description field is updated to give a brief explanation of the setting. More information is available by pressing the **H**elp Button. When you change one or more settings, press **S**ave to apply those changes to the object. The **D**efault button restores all settings to the values they originally had when you loaded OS/2.

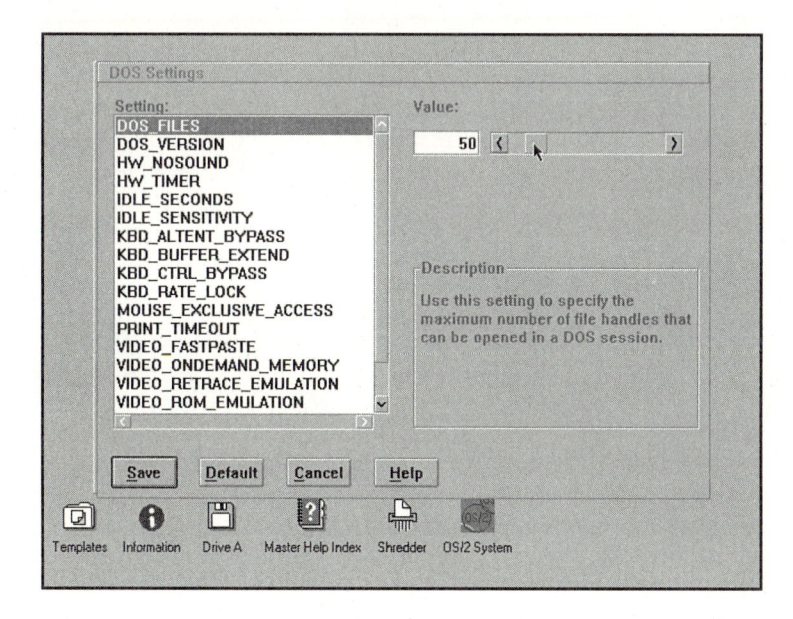

Fig. 17.1
The DOS Settings screen.

Using Special Kinds of Memory

Some DOS applications manage to break the 640K barrier and use all your computer's memory. These applications use several methods, known as EMS, XMS, and DPMI, to break this barrier; each method requires you to configure special support when running under real DOS. But with OS/2's DOS sessions, you don't need to wade through this alphabet soup of memory enhancements,

Chapter 17—Configuring Your DOS and Windows Sessions

because a couple of megabytes of each type of memory are automatically available to every program.

You might want to change the defaults to provide even more memory to a particular DOS program, or to strip out these extra features and streamline your DOS sessions. This section explains the techniques for determining which sort of memory your application requires and optimizing the settings.

> **Note**
>
> Software products from Borland International use a nonstandard method to detect DPMI memory. For Borland products, such as the Borland C/C++ compiler, you should set DPMI_DOS_API to ENABLED.

By looking for certain key words in your program's documentation, you can figure out which setting controls its use of extra memory:

- Use the XMS_MEMORY_LIMIT setting if the documentation mentions Extended Memory or XMS.

- Use the EMS_MEMORY_LIMIT setting if you find the words Expanded Memory, LIM, EMS, or EEMS.

- Use the DPMI_MEMORY_LIMIT setting if you see DOS Protected Mode Interface or DPMI.

No matter what type of memory your program requires, OS/2 provides all the memory the program asks for, up to 2M. You can change this limit. Increase the limit when you need more—for example, when you run out of memory when loading a large spreadsheet. On the other hand, some programs rudely grab all the extra memory they find, regardless of whether they need it. Tame these programs by experimenting with lower limits.

Most DOS programs don't use EMS, XMS, or DPMI. Turning all three options off is a good idea when you don't need them; change all their limits to zero. This step reduces the memory the DOS session takes up. DOS loads faster and leaves more room for other sessions.

To see how much EMS and XMS memory is available, run the MEM command from a DOS command prompt. As you can see in figure 17.2, this step also tells you how much regular memory DOS can use, and whether DOS was loaded in high memory by specifying DOS=HIGH in CONFIG.SYS.

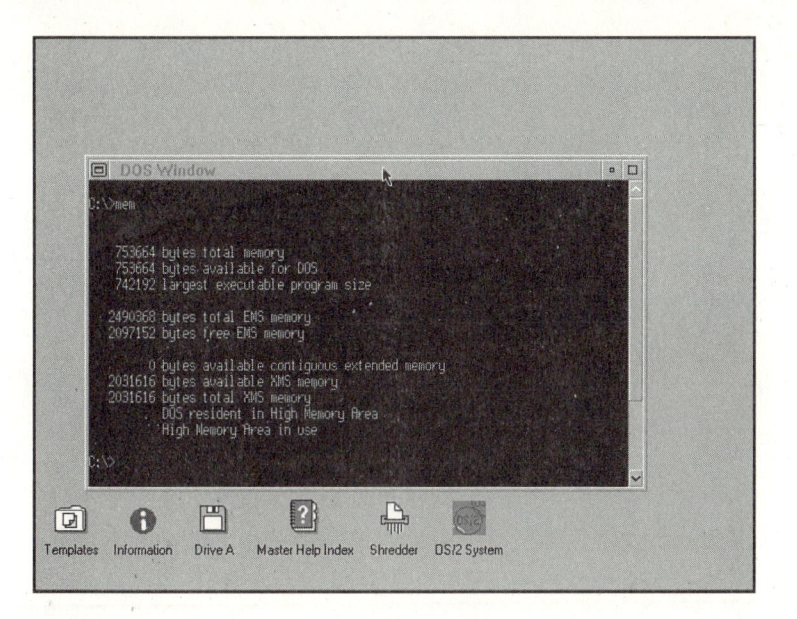

Fig. 17.2
Different types of memory a DOS Session can use.

Getting More than 640K of Memory for DOS

You have probably heard that DOS can access only 640K of memory—so why does figure 17.2 show more memory than that available? An OS/2 DOS session can get well over 700K, as long as you use only the normal 25-line text mode and very low resolution graphics. Just change the VIDEO_MODE_RESTRICTION setting to CGA.

The graphics capabilities are primitive, and you cannot use enhanced text modes that display 50 lines on-screen. These limitations may not matter to you, however. With the extra memory, you can run a combination of programs that would not fit in a normal 640K session.

Tuning the Priority of DOS Sessions

When a DOS program waits for input from you, it continually checks the keyboard, perhaps a thousand times a second. If you are running real DOS, this feature doesn't matter; DOS runs only one program at a time because it has no better use for your computer's resources.

Under OS/2, on the other hand, this approach is wasteful because OS/2 tries to speed up the programs doing useful work by giving relatively less attention to others. OS/2 continually checks whether a DOS program is sitting idle, waiting for input from you. It keeps track of how long a program has waited for input, and how much time a program spends checking whether you have pressed a key or moved the mouse. OS/2 uses this information to adjust the priority of each session.

Usually, this method gives you the best overall performance, but sometimes you don't care how fast programs run in the background, as long as the foreground program is responsive. Two settings enable you to adjust the idle checking, or even turn it off:

- *IDLE_SECONDS*. Normally, OS/2 gives a program a lower priority if it sits idle for three seconds. You can change this to any number of seconds you want. Setting the number to zero completely disables this checking.

- *IDLE_SENSITIVITY*. OS/2 reduces the priority of any program spending 75 percent or more of its time checking the keyboard. You can set this time period as you like. If you set this period to 100 percent, the system stops checking, and the program always runs at a high priority.

Choosing Performance Enhancements

The following settings affect the performance of your system. You can tune OS/2 to give you faster DOS sessions by experimenting with these settings.

- *HW_ROM_TO_RAM*. Deep inside your computer, built-in programs that control devices such as the keyboard and disk drive are stored on relatively slow, permanent memory chips. When you turn this option on, these programs are copied to the system's main memory, which is much faster. This step consumes about 100K of memory, but it does not come from DOS's 640K, and the speedup is usually worthwhile.

- *HW_TIMER*. This option gives DOS sessions direct access to the computer's timer chip. Turn this option on for applications that need precise timing control, such as music programs or action games. If you use this option in more than one session, the sessions may interfere with each other.

- *KBD_BUFFER_EXTEND*. You can type ahead when your DOS program is busy. Your keystrokes are saved in a buffer and played back when the program is ready for input. In real DOS, the buffer is only 17 characters long. OS/2 DOS sessions extend this buffer to 128 characters. Some programs, however, do an end-run around DOS and buffer keystrokes themselves, in a way incompatible with OS/2's keyboard buffer enhancement. If a particular program doesn't work correctly when you type ahead, try turning off this setting.

- *VIDEO_FASTPASTE*. When you paste text to a DOS session, the text is entered at about the rate that a fast typist can manage. If you turn this option on, text is pasted much faster. The option is off by default, however, because the high speed is faster than some programs can handle. Experiment to find out whether your application can benefit from the faster pasting speed.

- *VIDEO_ROM_EMULATION*. This setting tells the system to use fast OS/2 routines to move the cursor and scroll the screen. Turning this setting on usually speeds up your screen. Some fancy video cards have their own built-in routines, however, which are even faster. Try both ways to see which works better on your computer.

- *VIDEO_WINDOW_REFRESH*. DOS OS/2 draws the contents of on-screen windows usually every tenth of a second, almost as fast as the eye can see. Screen-update-intensive applications, however, may spend much of their time redrawing the screen and, on a slow computer, OS/2 may struggle to keep up with the changes to the screen. If this is a problem, increase the redraw delay to get a snappier response. If you increase the delay too much, though, the window may appear jerky.

Accommodating Special Needs

As you have seen, several keystroke combinations have special meaning with OS/2. Your DOS programs, therefore, cannot ordinarily use Alt-Home, Alt-Esc, or Ctrl-Esc. If you have a DOS program that must use these keystrokes, change the KBD_ALTHOME_BYPASS or KBD_CTRL_BYPASS settings. You cannot reassign both Alt-Esc and Ctrl-Esc to a DOS session because you need one key combination to switch to a different session if your DOS program crashes.

Some DOS programs work only if you load a specific device driver first. If you list the driver in CONFIG.SYS, the driver loads in every DOS session. To load the driver only for a particular program, open that program's settings and type the name of the driver in its DOS_DEVICE field. Be sure to include the driver's complete path and file name.

Troubleshooting DOS Settings. Although almost any DOS program runs in an OS/2 DOS session with the default configuration, you may encounter problems. The most common problems are listed here, along with the settings you should change to fix them.

The modem doesn't work with a DOS communications program.
Type the following line in the DOS session, before you start the communications program:

    MODE COM1:
    9600,,,,OCTS=OFF,RTS=OFF,DTR=OFF,ODSR=OFF,IDSR=OFF

Enter the actual communications port and data rate you are using. If you have a 2400-bit-per-second modem on the second port, for example, use the following:

    MODE COM2:
    2400,,,,OCTS=OFF,RTS=OFF,DTR=OFF,ODSR=OFF,IDSR=OFF

If your program then works, you may want to add the MODE command to the AUTOEXEC.BAT file in your root directory C:\.

The modem disconnects the line when you temporarily exit from a DOS communications program. Turn on the COM_HOLD setting. This step prevents OS/2 from reclaiming the modem port when you exit from the DOS program temporarily. Until you close the current DOS session, no other session can use the modem.

A DOS program uses the speaker, and you want the program to run quietly. Turn on the HW_NOSOUND setting.

After a certain DOS program runs, the keyboard speeds up or slows down in other sessions. Turn on the offending program's KBD_RATE_LOCK setting. Some programs change the keyboard speed, which is usually what you want. Leave this setting off unless the program interferes with other programs.

A program in a windowed DOS session has two mouse cursors. Turn on the MOUSE_EXCLUSIVE_ACCESS setting, and then click the mouse in the DOS window. The Workplace Shell desktop's cursor disappears. To get the cursor back, press the Alt key.

You print a report from a DOS application, such as a spreadsheet graph, and the report prints in several pieces. Increase the PRINT_TIMEOUT setting. The system normally assumes that your report is finished if nothing is sent to the printer for 17 seconds. But your program may take longer to format different parts of your printout.

When you switch between windowed and full-screen with Alt-Home, the screen is garbled, or it goes blank. Turn VIDEO_RETRACE_EMULATION off, and turn VIDEO_SWITCH_NOTIFICATION on. If the problem persists, turn VIDEO_ON_DEMAND_MEMORY off. This last setting should be necessary only with graphics programs. It usually fixes the problem, but uses more memory and makes your program load slower.

When you run a particular program, you get an error message as shown in figure 17.3. End the program and contact the developer of the application. The application contains a bug. Such problems often go unnoticed for a while under real DOS, until the problems eventually result in puzzling sporadic errors. OS/2 catches such problems before they can affect other applications. Usually, the error indicates that the computer program tried to change a location in memory when it had no right to do so. Many DOS programmers develop applications in OS/2 DOS sessions so that they can catch bugs before the bugs cause problems. Chapter 8, "Troubleshooting OS/2," contains more information about such bugs.

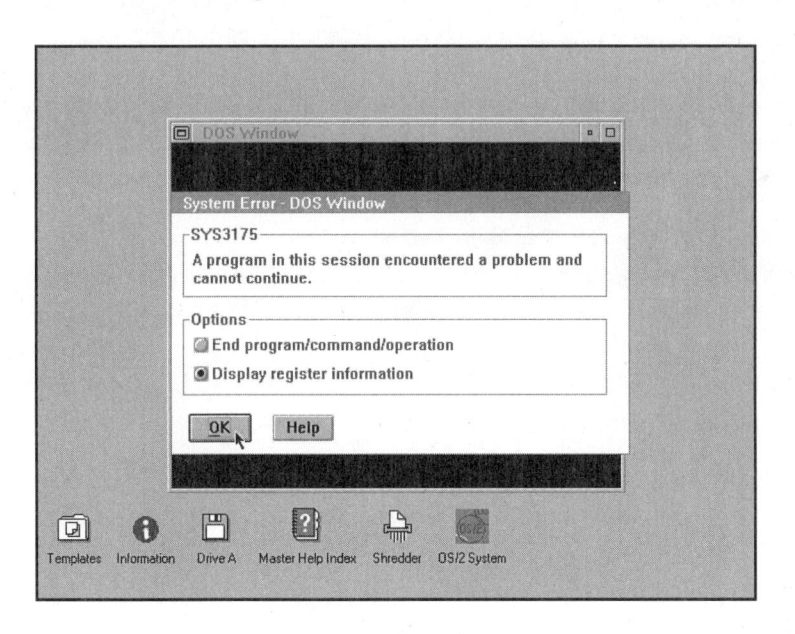

Fig. 17.3
OS/2 discovers a bug in a DOS application.

Changing DOS Settings for Each Session

The last section discussed global settings that you can make by using CONFIG.SYS commands. This section, however, details the configuration settings available for you to improve individual DOS sessions' performance and functioning capability. Refer to the earlier sections of this chapter for tutorial information on adjusting these settings and troubleshooting your DOS and Windows sessions.

The available configuration settings are divided into the following topics:

- Improving DOS session performance
- Configuring the keyboard, mouse, and touch screen
- Modifying display settings
- Maximizing available memory
- Using miscellaneous DOS settings for improving printing and Windows session performance, and controlling DOS environment parameters

Most DOS session settings are either ON or OFF. Adjust the settings by selecting a radio button in the settings window for the DOS session's icon. In some cases, you select a number, typically a time in seconds, for a setting.

Making DOS Sessions Perform Better

As a multitasking operating system, OS/2 divides the CPU time between each of the open sessions. To alter the proportion of time allocated to DOS sessions, OS/2's responsiveness to DOS sessions, and the way in which OS/2 redistributes time allocations to open sessions, you need to use the settings described in the following sections.

DOS_BACKGROUND_EXECUTION. When DOS_BACKGROUND_EXECUTION is ON, the default setting, a DOS session continues to operate in the background. When OFF, the DOS session in the background is suspended. The setting can be changed before or during the DOS session.

OS/2 can run multiple sessions (windows) at once; however, you can interact with only one of those sessions at a time. The currently active window is known as the *foreground session*, and all the others are *background sessions*. Use this DOS setting to alter the DOS session's behavior when it is a background session.

Suspending the DOS session in the background improves the performance of your other open OS/2 sessions because OS/2 does not have to allocate time to support it. In some situations, the suspension is appropriate because nothing happens unless you interact with the program.

If you type in a word processor and then switch it to the background, for example, nothing happens until you make it a foreground session again.

In other situations, however, you will want to switch the DOS session to the background as you perform other functions, and you will return to the session only when the action is complete. If you generate an index for a large document, in, say, the word processing example, you may want to use another program during the regeneration. In this case, you will not want the DOS program's operation suspended in the background.

Consider your actual use of a DOS application program before you switch this setting off. An electronic Rolodex or game program is a likely candidate for an off setting; a communications, network, Windows, or printing program is not a likely candidate.

HW_ROM_TO_RAM. *ROM* (read only memory) is an electronic memory chip that can store information even when your computer is off. The contents of the ROM are used, in part, when you boot your computer. *RAM* (random access memory) stores more temporary information; when power is removed, the data stored in RAM is lost. These two chip types are made in different ways, and, as a result, have different access times. (Typically, data can be retrieved from RAM ten times faster than from ROM.)

When you turn the HW_ROM_TO_RAM setting to ON, the ROM's data copies into the faster RAM; when your DOS program accesses this data, the data is retrieved from RAM rather than ROM. Your DOS session's performance may improve because your computer can access information stored in RAM faster than information stored in ROM. The default setting is OFF; you can change this setting only before you start a DOS session.

If your DOS program makes extensive use of the ROM contents, you will see a performance improvement in your DOS application. However, the percentage of time that your DOS application spends accessing ROM instead of performing other functions can be small, so the improvement may be minimal. In addition, you may experience compatibility problems, or your computer hardware may do this swapping automatically.

IDLE_SECONDS. OS/2 divides its time between all the open sessions and automatically adjusts the time allocation for each session. If OS/2 determines that a session is idle, perhaps waiting for you to type something, it gives the program less time until the program becomes active again.

Consider the action of pouring a cup of coffee as an analogy. If the person pouring says "Say when," that person continues to pour until you speak—like a program that awaits input, but continues to operate as it waits. OS/2 determines that it is waiting for your input, and reduces the time allocation for the program's session because it considers the program inactive. As a result, the rate of pouring coffee, or time allocated to the program, goes down. If this is undesirable, increase the IDLE_SECONDS value. OS/2 then delays checking whether the program is idle for the number of seconds specified.

The IDLE_SECONDS setting defines the number of seconds that OS/2 waits before it determines whether a DOS session is idle. You can choose a value between 0, the default value, and 60. This setting can change before starting or during a DOS session.

OS/2's idle detection can make your DOS program seem sluggish because your program appears idle when it is not, and OS/2 lowers the time allocation for the DOS session.

IDLE_SENSITIVITY. OS/2 allocates time to each open session automatically. To make each session operate more efficiently, OS/2 checks to see whether a session is idle and waiting for input. If a session is found idle, that session's proportion of time is reduced so that the remaining sessions operate more efficiently.

The IDLE_SECONDS value discussed in the preceding section delays the start of OS/2 to determine whether a session is idle; IDLE_SENSITIVITY determines how idle a session must be before it is judged as idle. The IDLE_SENSITIVITY setting is a percentage between 0 and 100, with a default value of 75 percent. OS/2 uses this value to determine when a DOS session is idle or only waiting for input.

A DOS session has a predetermined maximum *polling rate* (the number of times per second that the program checks for an input). When a program requires input, from say, a keyboard or a communications port, the program polls the input to see whether the input is ready, like checking a mail box to see whether mail has arrived. The polling rate is the number of times per second the input is checked. Because this polling is done by OS/2, OS/2 can determine how often a program polls the input. If the DOS session polls for input more often than the percentage of time given as a value for the IDLE_SENSITIVITY setting, OS/2 considers the program idle and reduces the time allocation for the DOS session.

If this setting is inappropriate, you may experience sluggishness with certain DOS sessions, most likely when a program waits for input but continues to operate. For example, if a program automatically increments a number on-screen and stops only when you press a key, you may find that the number increments more slowly than you would expect; OS/2 thinks the program is only waiting for you to press a key.

If you experience sluggish performance, try setting IDLE_SENSITIVITY to a higher percentage. If you do not see an improvement, however, return IDLE_SENSITIVITY to its previous value. You can change this value either before or during a DOS session.

> **Note**
>
> An IDLE_SENSITIVITY value of 22 is often best for all DOS and Windows sessions except those sessions that run communications programs. Try selecting a value of 22 for every DOS and Windows session, and a value of 100 for sessions the run communications programs, to see whether your system performs better.

Configuring the Keyboard, Mouse, and Touch Screen

Because DOS is not a multitasking operating system, DOS application programs almost always are written with the assumption that you have exclusive use of the keyboard and mouse. When you run these programs as DOS sessions under OS/2, the program shares the computer resources with other OS/2 applications.

In most cases, OS/2 can divide the resources so that the DOS session operates and "shares" without any problem. Some DOS application programs, however, may not work properly because those programs expect settings to remain constant or to have exclusive rights to a resource such as the keyboard. For example, OS/2 uses the Alt-Home key combination to switch between sessions. If your DOS application program uses the Alt-Home key combination, you need to alter a setting because the DOS program is not expecting OS/2 to use the Alt-Home key.

The other settings in this category alter the DOS session so that the DOS application program has access to the features it needs.

DOS_BREAK. Many DOS programs use Ctrl-C or Ctrl-Break as an interrupt or canceling command. To stop a BASIC program that is running, for example, you press Ctrl-C (or Ctrl-Break). To allow this interrupt, DOS must be prepared to receive the key combination even as it processes other information.

When the DOS_BREAK setting is OFF, the typical default setting, OS/2 does not continually check for the Ctrl-C or Ctrl-Break key combination used by many DOS programs to abort the current command or program. When DOS_BREAK is ON, OS/2 performs this check. Note that the line BREAK=OFF is placed in your CONFIG.SYS file during installation, unless you specify otherwise. If you change this setting, OFF will not necessarily be the default setting for BREAK. This setting must be made before you start a DOS session.

When running a DOS session under OS/2, it takes more overhead for OS/2 to be continually looking for this key combination. As a consequence, your programs can be very sluggish if you set DOS_BREAK ON.

If you set DOS_BREAK to OFF, you still can use the Ctrl-C and Ctrl-Break key combinations for keystroke input to your DOS program. These key combinations, however, do not act as interrupting keystroke mechanisms when your program is actually doing something else.

In general, unless you have a specific program in which you really need to use Ctrl-C or Ctrl-Break to interrupt the program, leave DOS_BREAK turned OFF.

KBD_ALTHOME_BYPASS. In OS/2, the key combination Alt-Home switches a session from a window to a full-screen session. Setting KBD_ALTHOME_BYPASS to ON means that within your DOS session you can use Alt-Home for other reasons. The default setting is OFF. You can change the setting either before or during a DOS session.

If you have a DOS application program that uses the Alt-Home key combination, you must set KBD_ALTHOME_BYPASS to ON. Otherwise, every time you try to press Alt-Home, OS/2 changes your window between a window and a full-screen session.

KBD_BUFFER_EXTEND. A *type-ahead buffer* is an area of memory that stores your keystrokes until your program is ready to process them. If you fill this buffer, your computer beeps each time you press a key until your computer can accept more keystrokes.

Most users, even those who type by hunting and pecking, take advantage of the keyboard type-ahead buffer. If you press a key to save a file in a word processor, you can anticipate that the program will next ask whether you want to overwrite the existing file, and press Y to speed the process. Most touch typists frequently overflow a 16-byte buffer. Consequently, increasing this buffer to 128 bytes, which enables you to type as quickly as you like, is a good idea in almost all cases.

The price you pay for the larger buffer, however, is that it uses memory—if you run a DOS program, these few extra bytes allocated to the type-ahead buffer rather than your DOS program can make the difference between being able to run your DOS program and not.

To allow your DOS program to increase the type-ahead buffer from 16 to 128 bytes, set KBD_BUFFER_EXTEND to ON, the default value. Set to OFF to prevent this increase. You can change this setting before or during a DOS session.

KBD_CTRL_BYPASS. In OS/2, by default the key combination Ctrl-Esc activates the window list, and Alt-Esc switches between sessions. Changing KBD_CTRL_BYPASS from the default NONE means that you can use either Alt-Esc or Ctrl-Esc within your DOS session for other reasons. You can change the setting either before or during a DOS session. If you select ALT_ESC, you can use Alt-Esc within your DOS session. If you select CTRL_ESC, you can use Ctrl-Esc within your DOS session.

If you have a DOS application program that uses the Alt-Esc key combination, set KBD_CTRL_BYPASS to ALT_ESC. Otherwise, every time you press Alt-Esc, OS/2 swaps to the next session.

If you have a DOS application program that uses the Ctrl-Esc key combination, set KBD_CTRL_BYPASS to CTRL_ESC. Otherwise, every time you try to press Ctrl-Esc, OS/2 displays the window list.

KBD_RATE_LOCK. When you press a key on your keyboard, the action is transmitted to the computer and recorded as a single keystroke. If you hold down the key instead of releasing it, after a delay—known as the *typematic delay period*—the computer automatically repeats the keystrokes until you release the key. The rate at which the keystrokes repeat is called the *keyboard repeat rate*, which can be altered by your programs.

Most DOS programs, however, do not alter this rate; even if they do alter it, they reset it again. In the rare event that you experience keyboard problems when you switch to another session after using a DOS session, consider altering the KBD_RATE_LOCK setting. The symptoms of a repeat rate problem show up when you press and hold down a key (the key's function repeats unusually slowly or rapidly).

To allow your DOS program to adjust the keyboard repeat rate, set KBD_RATE_LOCK to OFF, the default value. Set it to ON if you want to prevent this change. You can change this setting before or during a DOS session.

MOUSE_EXCLUSIVE_ACCESS. As a graphical user interface, OS/2 controls the mouse and mouse cursor, and shares this resource with all the open windows. DOS programs, which typically are not written to share the computer's resources with other programs, either do not use a mouse, or expect exclusive use of the mouse.

In many cases, a DOS program that uses the mouse controls the mouse's behavior as well as its position. For example, some programs use different mouse sensitivities so that you may have to move the mouse longer or shorter distances to make the mouse cursor move.

If your DOS program creates and manages its own mouse cursor, change the MOUSE_EXCLUSIVE_ACCESS default setting from OFF to ON. You can change the setting before or during a DOS session. When this setting is ON, click within the DOS session window to remove the Presentation Manager mouse cursor. Press Alt, Ctrl-Esc, or Alt-Esc to restore it.

Change MOUSE_EXCLUSIVE_ACCESS to ON for any DOS session that manages its own mouse. If you get two unsynchronized mouse pointers, one in OS/2 and one in your DOS session, for example, change the setting.

TOUCH_EXCLUSIVE_ACCESS. This setting is important only if you use a touch screen connected to a Personal System/2 mouse port. The setting prevents OS/2 from sharing the mouse port with other OS/2 sessions and allows your DOS program exclusive use of the touch screen.

If you experience problems with your touch screen in a DOS session, change the TOUCH_EXCLUSIVE_ACCESS default setting from OFF to ON. You can change the setting before or during a DOS session. When this setting is ON, the position you touch on-screen represents the position in the DOS session's window. Alter the DOS session's window size to full screen if you want the position you touch to match the DOS session's.

To avoid changing this setting, run your DOS sessions as full-screen sessions if you use a touch screen. Full-screen sessions are also preferable because of the connection between the position you touch on-screen and the displayed image. If you run a paint program in a window one-quarter the size of the screen, for example, your drawings would display at one-quarter their actual size, which might be a bit disconcerting.

Modifying Display Settings

DOS application programs are not designed to share resources such as the display, keyboard, or mouse. When you try to run these resources under OS/2, you may experience problems.

In the case of the display, problems usually arise because an OS/2 window overwrites the DOS session's window display or changes the video mode so that when the DOS application program runs, the video screen is corrupted. The DOS application program does not anticipate the change in the video screen because the application expects exclusive use of the computer's resources. Consequently, you may need to adjust the following settings to compensate.

VIDEO_8514A_XGA_IOTRAP. This setting is used only if you have an 8514/A or XGA board. To operate faster, many DOS programs that support these high-resolution video boards directly manipulate the hardware instead of using the operating system video services. When a program runs under DOS, this direct manipulation is good because the program is the only one running at the time. Under OS/2, however, many application programs can run at the same time, and the video is a shared resource; therefore, OS/2 must keep firm control so that all the programs work together. Consequently, your DOS program may operate more slowly than usual.

To regain speed, you can turn VIDEO_8514A_XGA_IOTRAP to OFF. When you switch back to the DOS program after working in another OS/2 session, however, this setting can be a problem. The DOS program probably will be unaware of any video mode changes and will not update your screen automatically. But if you set VIDEO_SWITCH_NOTIFICATION to ON, OS/2 notifies your DOS session that the screen needs updating when you switch back to the DOS session.

To allow your DOS program direct access to the 8514/A or XGA video adapter, change the VIDEO_8514A_XGA_IOTRAP setting from ON to OFF. Change this setting only before starting a DOS session. When you turn off this setting, change the VIDEO_SWITCH_NOTIFICATION setting to ON so that your screen is redrawn when you switch back to the DOS session. When VIDEO_8514A_XGA_IOTRAP is OFF, OS/2 also releases the 1M of memory normally reserved for video data in a DOS session.

VIDEO_FASTPASTE. When you copy or paste text information, the characters transfer between the session and OS/2's Clipboard. OS/2 uses the Copy command to transfer characters between a DOS session and the Clipboard, and the Paste command to transfer text characters between the Clipboard and a DOS session. OS/2 transfers that information faster than you can type it; and when you set VIDEO_FASTPASTE to ON, OS/2 sends the information even faster.

In most cases this speed increase is not a problem for your DOS program, which thinks you are typing fast. If the characters arrive too quickly in DOS programs that buffer keystrokes internally, however, you may fill the temporary buffer (storage area) where the keystrokes are being stored before processing. Your program may not be able to handle the overflow. Also, you will see no change from setting VIDEO_FASTPASTE to ON with DOS programs that directly monitor the keyboard interrupts. You also can try expanding the keyboard buffer by changing KBD_BUFER_EXTEND, but note that you use precious DOS memory to do this. (See the preceding section.)

The default value for this setting is OFF, and you can change the setting either before or during a DOS session.

VIDEO_MODE_RESTRICTION. A few DOS programs use only CGA or monochrome video modes. With these programs, the area of memory normally used to store video information for other video modes can be used for your application program, instead of keeping that memory reserved for video information.

You can use the VIDEO_MODE_RESTRICTION setting for programs that run only in CGA or monochrome text modes. If your DOS program uses these modes only, you can take advantage of the extra memory for your program. This method of gaining extra memory is useful on computers with limited memory and monochrome text or CGA video adapters. Your computer does not have limited memory by DOS standards, however; you would not be able to run OS/2 if it did. Your computer is also unlikely to only have a monochrome or CGA video board.

On the other hand, higher resolution video boards, such as EGA or VGA, emulate the CGA and monochrome text video modes, so in theory you could use this setting on most computers. The advantages, however, are negligible except with unusual (or very old) application programs that do not use any VGA or EGA video modes. Do not use this setting if your program uses any modes other than CGA or monochrome text modes.

The default setting is NONE, and you change this setting before starting a DOS session. If you choose CGA mode, 96K of memory space is added to low DOS memory. If you choose MONO mode, 64K of memory space is added to low DOS memory.

> **Note**
>
> DOS_RMSIZE must be set to 640 to use the VIDEO_MODE_Restriction setting.

VIDEO_ONDEMAND_MEMORY. One way OS/2 can handle multiple programs at the same time is by storing each program's current video image in memory as you view another session. When you switch from a full-screen session, OS/2 stores the image in memory and restores it when you return to the session.

If you run a DOS program that uses a lot of memory, or if you run many different programs at once, switching from the DOS session to another session, OS/2 may not have enough memory to enable you to switch back to another session without losing the current image. Your DOS session asks OS/2 for the memory, and the memory is not available. Consequently, the DOS session fails.

If your DOS program fails because of lack of memory when you switch from a full-screen view of the program, set VIDEO_ONDEMAND_MEMORY to OFF. The default value is ON, which allocates memory to the DOS program at the time you switch from the full-screen view instead of when you start the program. Adjust this setting either before or during the DOS session.

If you set VIDEO_ONDEMAND_MEMORY to OFF, the memory needed for the DOS session is allocated when you switch to the session. Your program is less likely to fail because of lack of memory, but there are disadvantages, too. The memory allocated to your DOS session is unavailable for other programs. Additionally, the time taken to switch to the DOS session increases because OS/2 has to reserve the memory before you start the program.

VIDEO_RETRACE_EMULATION. Setting VIDEO_RETRACE_EMULATION to OFF can improve the performance of your DOS session by causing OS/2 to retrace your DOS session's window at the speed of the DOS program's video mode instead of more frequently. Most DOS programs' speeds are unaffected by this OFF setting; for the exceptions, however, you do gain performance. Unfortunately, you may find that with the setting turned OFF, screen switching is not reliable. You can get incorrect palettes or even a blank screen.

The default setting is ON, and you can change that setting either before or during a DOS session.

VIDEO_ROM_EMULATION. When VIDEO_ROM_EMULATION is ON (the default setting), OS/2 provides emulation of the following text-mode video functions: full-screen scroll, WriteChar, and WriteTTY. When this setting is OFF, your programs use the equivalent routines supplied by your video board. You change this setting either before or during a DOS session.

In most cases, leaving this setting ON gives the best video performance because OS/2's emulation is faster than that of most video boards. Some manufacturers produce video boards whose routines are faster, however. If you have such a video board, selecting OFF enables you to scroll your screen and display text on-screen faster.

VIDEO_SWITCH_NOTIFICATION. When VIDEO_SWITCH_NOTIFICATION is ON, OS/2 notifies your DOS programs when you switch the session between foreground and background. If this setting is ON and your DOS program checks for screen switching, it saves or redraws the screen when you switch. You can change this setting either before or during a DOS session.

If you have one of the common video adapters, such as VGA, EGA, and CGA, you probably do not need this setting. Most video modes you can access with these adapters do not support screen-switch notification. To avoid getting a blank screen when you switch to the DOS session, however, you need to change the setting when you use VIDEO_ONDEMAND_MEMORY.

VIDEO_WINDOW_REFRESH. When you run a DOS session, OS/2 updates the screen at regular intervals, known as the *window refresh rate*. If you set this value too low, your screen is always current, but your program runs slowly because so much time is spent redrawing the screen instead of running your program. If you set this value too high, your screen is updated infrequently.

To choose the time interval in which OS/2 redraws a window, select a value between 0.1 second and 60 seconds for VIDEO_WINDOW_REFRESH. The default value is 0.1 second, but you can adjust the setting either before or during a DOS session.

Test the effect of altering this value by opening a DOS window and issuing a DOS command such as DIR or TYPE. Change the value and reissue the command. The appropriate value depends on the DOS program you run.

Maximizing Available Memory

Although OS/2 takes away the infamous 640K memory barrier, you may run into memory resource problems when you run DOS application programs under OS/2. Like the display, keyboard, and mouse settings, these problems typically arise because the DOS application program you run expects exclusive use of the computer's resources—in this case, memory. You can adjust the settings to give the DOS application program the memory resources it expects.

Many of these settings deal with memory specifications created to deal with the limitations of DOS, including expanded memory and extended memory. A large number of terms, such as upper memory blocks (UMB), high memory area (HMA), page frames, and handles relate to these specifications. OS/2 generally has eliminated the need to understand these terms unless you run a DOS program in a DOS session and need to use them. The following explanations briefly introduce the terms, but do not attempt a comprehensive explanation.

DOS_HIGH. The DOS_HIGH setting is equivalent to the DOS=HIGH directive available in DOS 5.0 and later versions. By allowing OS/2 to place DOS into high DOS memory, you have more memory available below 640K. Most programs allow this, but some do not work unless DOS is in low DOS memory (the more traditional location).

Change DOS_HIGH from its default value of ON to OFF so that OS/2 places DOS in low DOS memory rather than high DOS memory. You must change this setting before starting a DOS session.

DOS_RMSIZE. The DOS_RMSIZE value indicates the amount of memory available to DOS programs. The default setting is 640, but you can select between 128 and 640. The units are kilobytes. You must change this value before starting a DOS session.

You are unlikely to need to change this setting, because almost all DOS programs work best with 640K of memory. In exceptional situations, however, such as times when your video board uses some of the base memory, you need to change this value.

DOS_UMB. *Upper memory blocks* (UMBs), which are areas of memory between 640K and 1M, can be used to load DOS device drivers and DOS TSRs. One way to load these programs is to use DOS's features and add DEVICEHIGH and LOADHIGH statements to your DOS CONFIG.SYS file. In this case, DOS controls the UMBs and handles their creation and the loading and unloading of the data they contain.

An alternative method is to use a memory management program rather than DOS. Typically, the memory management programs have more features or are more flexible than DOS. In this case, the memory management program needs to control the UMBs. When running a DOS session under OS/2, change the DOS_UMB setting to OFF to allow the memory manager to control the UMBs. Change this setting before starting a DOS session.

DPMI_DOS_API. To overcome the 640K memory limitation, some DOS programs incorporate a DOS extender program for memory management. Many large DOS application programs, especially databases and CAD programs, include a DOS extender. These programs include their own memory management features. As you require more memory, the program organizes the available memory to accommodate. Some DOS programs (such as Windows), however, expect the operating system to supply these services. OS/2 can supply them, but you need to enable the DPMI_DOS_API setting.

If you run programs that include a DOS extender that conforms with the *DOS Protected Mode Interface* (DPMI), use the default DPMI_DOS_API setting of AUTO. Change the setting to ENABLED if you want the operating system to handle your program's requests for DOS services. Change the setting to DISABLED if your programs do not use DPMI. You must change this setting before starting a DOS session.

Software products from Borland International use a nonstandard method to detect DPMI memory. For Borland products, such as the Borland C/C++ compiler, you should set DPMI_DOS_API to ENABLED. The AUTO value is not sufficient.

If you do not know whether your programs can take advantage of DPMI, leave the default value; the services are then available, but not used if your programs do not support DPMI.

DPMI_MEMORY_LIMIT. This value limits the amount of memory available to your DOS session for programs that use DPMI services. Note that Windows uses DPMI services; you may want to increase this value if you run several Windows programs at once.

To make more or less memory available for DPMI memory allocation, change the DPMI_MEMORY_LIMIT from its default value of 2. Choose a number between 0 and 512, with the units in megabytes. You must set the value before you start a DOS session. The early 1994 Service Pack for OS/2 changes the default DPMI_MEMORY_LIMIT value to 4M. The devault value for Win-OS/2 is 64M.

See the other DPMI settings for further adjustments. If your DOS program does not use DPMI services, select zero for this setting.

DPMI_NETWORK_BUFF_SIZE. The DPMI_NETWORK_BUFF_SIZE controls the size of the buffer used when you transfer data across a network from programs using DPMI. This setting is important only if you are running on a network and using programs that take advantage of DPMI and transfer data across the network.

If you experience problems transferring data over the network from a DOS session, try increasing this buffer size. Change the default value of 8 (K); the available range is from 1 to 64. You must change the setting before starting a DOS session.

EMS_FRAME_LOCATION. Most DOS programs use the Lotus/Intel/Microsoft *Expanded Memory Specification* (EMS), which gives your DOS program access to more memory than 1M. The vast majority of these programs behave predictably, so you can ignore this setting. The operating system handles the allocation and deallocation of the areas of memory, known as page frames.

In a few rare cases, which may be due to your specific hardware configuration and/or your particular DOS program, you need to actually specify the page frame location. If you experience problems running programs with expanded memory, adjust EMS_HIGH_OS_MAP_REGION, and then change the EMS_FRAME_LOCATION if the problem is not resolved.

To designate the expanded memory specification page frame location instead of letting the session handle the memory allocation, adjust the default setting of AUTO for the EMS_FRAME_LOCATION to a different address. Choose a value from the list in the settings menu. You must change this setting before starting a DOS session.

EMS_HIGH_OS_MAP_REGION. Several versions of the expanded memory specifications exist. Most newer programs are written to the latest version of these specifications, which allows page frames to be larger than 64K. If you run into expanded memory problems with your DOS program, however, try limiting the page frame size to 64K by setting EMS_HIGH_OS_MAP_REGION to 0, which may clear up your program's confusion over memory allocation. If this fails, try explicitly specifying the expanded memory page frame location with the EMS_FRAME_LOCATION setting.

To allow your DOS programs to create EMS page frames larger than 64K, place a value for the EMS_HIGH_OS_MAP_REGION setting. The value can be between 0 and 96; the default value is 32. This number indicates the number of kilobytes larger than 64K that your page frames can be. You must change this setting before starting a DOS session.

EMS_LOW_OS_MAP_REGION. To allow your DOS programs to create EMS page frames in low DOS memory (memory below 640K), place a value for the EMS_LOW_OS_MAP_REGION setting. The value, which indicates the number of kilobytes of low DOS memory that can be allocated, can be between 0 and 576; the default value is 384. You must change this setting before starting a DOS session.

The page frame position is handled automatically by the operating system and should not be a problem for programs. If you find you need more expanded memory, however, try raising this value. Note that any memory allocated for expanded memory will not be available as low DOS memory.

EMS_MEMORY_LIMIT. The operating system automatically creates expanded memory page frames and handles their contents. The EMS_MEMORY_LIMIT indicates the maximum amount of expanded memory that can be allocated at once.

To specify the maximum amount of EMS memory your DOS programs can allocate, place a value for the EMS_MEMORY_LIMIT setting. This number indicates the number of kilobytes of EMS memory that can be allocated. The default value of 2048K (2M) may not be sufficient for some larger programs, such as large spreadsheets, but is adequate for most situations. You must change this setting before starting a DOS session.

Even though you can set a lower value, you typically do not need to do so; the memory is assigned only when needed. If your program does not use expanded memory or uses less than the assigned value, you will not reach this limit.

MEM_EXCLUDE_REGIONS. Your operating system automatically handles memory allocation and deallocation. In some cases, the operating system assumes that an area of memory is not in use when it actually is. This occurs most often with video boards with advanced features, which may require a larger area of memory than the operating system assumes.

If you experience problems with your hardware when you run a program using expanded memory or extended memory, or even when you copy the ROM contents to memory, you may have excluded the memory areas that the particular piece of hardware occupies. This information is usually specified in the hardware documentation.

To exclude specific areas of upper memory from being used for other purposes, such as expanded or extended memory, use the MEM_EXCLUDE_REGIONS setting. This setting has no default value. You must specify the addresses before starting a DOS session. Type the hexadecimal address for the range. Either specify the starting address for a 4K region, or type an address range separated by a hyphen. Specify multiple ranges by separating each range by a comma, but do not use spaces. To specify a range from B8000H to C0000H and a 4K region starting at C8000H, for example, type **B8000-C0000,C8000**.

MEM_INCLUDE_REGIONS. Your operating system automatically handles the allocation and deallocation of memory. Just as the operating system assumes that an area of memory is not in use when it actually is, the operating system may assume that an area of memory is in use when it is not.

You can improve program performance by finding additional areas of memory that it can use for expanded or extended memory. You need to be careful, however, that you do not specify an area used occasionally.

To allow specific areas of upper memory to be used for other purposes, such as expanded or extended memory, use the MEM_INCLUDE_REGIONS setting. This setting has no default value. You must specify the addresses prior to starting a DOS session. Type the hexadecimal address for the range. Either specify the starting address for a 4K region, or type an address range separated by a hyphen. Specify multiple ranges by separating each range by a comma, but do not use spaces. To specify a range from B8000H to C0000H and a 4K region starting at C8000H, for example, type **B8000-C0000,C8000.**

XMS_HANDLES. Each area of extended memory that the operating system generates has a unique name known as its *handle*. The XMS_HANDLES setting limits the number of different areas of extended memory to which your program can have access. In general, you do not need to change this setting; however, too large a number can slow your system.

The XMS_HANDLES value dictates the number of extended memory specification handles that can be assigned. Acceptable values range from 0 to 128, and the default setting is 32. You must change this setting before starting a DOS session.

XMS_MEMORY_LIMIT. The XMS_MEMORY_LIMIT value dictates the maximum amount of extended memory that can be assigned. Acceptable values range from 0 to **16384**; the default setting is 2048, and the values are in kilobytes. The maximum limit is equal to 16M. If you set too large a value for the extended memory limit, your system may slow. You must change this setting before starting a DOS session.

XMS_MINIMUM_HMA. The High Memory Area (HMA) is an area of memory—the first 64K immediately above 1M—that can be accessed as low DOS memory. You use this setting when you run multiple programs within a DOS session. In most cases, however, you can ignore this setting and allow the first program that wants HMA to have it. Consider opening another DOS session if you want a second program to use HMA memory.

Your DOS program must support HMA to be able to use it. Only one DOS program per session can use HMA, though, and you may want to restrict which program can access this memory. After this memory is assigned, all other programs are unable to use it. If the first program that requests HMA asks for only a couple of kilobytes, you are wasting the remaining 62K, so you may want to insist that a program ask for at least 20K. That way access to HMA is no longer given on a first-come, first-served basis; the first program that requests a value over your setting (over 20, in the example) would receive access.

To specify the minimum size of HMA that must be requested before it is allocated, change XMS_MINIMUM_HMA. Acceptable values are from 0 to 63; the default setting is 0 and the units are in kilobytes. You must alter this setting before starting a DOS session.

Tuning Other DOS Session Settings

OS/2 uses configuration settings comparable to those used by DOS. When you run a DOS session under OS/2, however, you may need to adjust the DOS session's settings so that you provide the DOS application program with the required settings.

For example, your DOS application program may need the LASTDRIVE setting changed or the DOS version changed. Alternatively, you may need to change Windows' operating mode if you run a Windows application program in OS/2.

COM_DIRECT_ACCESS. If your DOS program needs to have direct access to your serial ports (such as COM1 and COM2), you can change the COM_DIRECT_ACCESS default setting from OFF to ON. You must change the setting before starting a DOS session.

As a multitasking operating system, OS/2 typically controls any access to system resources, such as the serial ports, and shares these resources with all the open windows. Some DOS programs that were not written to share the computer's resources with other programs expect exclusive use of the serial ports.

Not only are some programs unwilling to share resources, but they also circumvent the operating system, DOS, and manipulate the hardware directly. The programs typically do this circumvention to improve performance or because the DOS features supplied are not adequate for their needs. When you then run these programs in a DOS window under OS/2, they do not operate correctly because OS/2 is limiting their access to the hardware. Change the COM_DIRECT_ACCESS setting to overcome the problem.

COM_HOLD. Some DOS communications products consist of multiple computer programs. Each program performs a different job, such as downloading a file. All the programs in the product may expect to be able to access a modem, through a COM port, at any time. However, if two or more programs try to send or receive information through a single COM port, OS/2 may deny access to the second attempt because OS/2 believes the first program still "owns" the COM port.

Note that most DOS communications products consist of just a single program (executable file), and OS/2 communications programs do not exhibit this problem.

If you communicate through a modem with an on-line service or bulletin board and your communications product consists of multiple DOS programs, you can use COM_HOLD to allow all computer programs in that session to access the modem. To give all software running in a DOS session exclusive use of a serial (COM) port, change the COM_HOLD setting from the default value of OFF to ON. You must change this setting before starting a DOS session.

COM_RECEIVE_BUFFER_FLUSH. Sometimes a DOS communications program seems to "freeze" because the program, waiting for a signal from the modem, misses the modem's signal. The DOS communications program waits forever for the modem and the communications port (COMx port) to send the signal and the associated modem character.

The COM_RECEIVE_BUFFER_FLUSH setting enables you to control how the communications program receives these signals from the modem and COM port. The setting has four possible values: *all*, *receive data interrupt enable*, *switch to foreground*, and *none*. Each value specifies when OS/2 will discard modem characters and signals. The values are explained in the following list:

- *All* specifies that OS/2 should discard pending (received inside the modem but not yet processed by the computer) modem characters and signals when you switch a program to the foreground or when the program enables the reception of modem signals.

- *Receive Data Interrupt Enable* specifies that OS/2 should discard any pending modem characters and signals when the program enables the reception of modem signals.

- *Switch to Foreground* specifies that OS/2 should discard pending modem characters and signals when you switch a program to the foreground.

- *None*, the default, specifies that OS/2 should not discard pending modem characters and signals for this session.

You can change COM_RECEIVE_BUFFER_FLUSH at any time.

COM_SELECT. To allocate a particular serial port (such as COM1 or COM2) to a DOS session, change the COM_SELECT default setting from ALL. You must change the setting before starting a DOS session. Compare this setting with COM_HOLD, which keeps the serial port assigned to the DOS session until the DOS session is ended.

When OS/2 is controlling your computer resources rather than DOS, it allocates the serial port use. When your DOS program stops using the serial port, OS/2 can assign it to another program wanting the port. Because most DOS programs are written to expect exclusive use of resources, however, you may run into problems with this reallocation; a subsequent DOS program may assume that it has control of the serial port when in reality it has been reassigned.

You may run a DOS communications program that has two parts, for example (one to establish the connection and another to do file transfer). The first program signals that the second can use the serial port at an appropriate time. Unless you have used the COM_SELECT setting, OS/2 may decide to reallocate the serial port to another session. The second DOS program, which does not expect to share a serial port, assumes that it has the serial port to itself and conflicts with the other program.

The available options are ALL, COM1, COM2, COM3, and COM4. Choose the port name from the list box in the settings window.

DOS_AUTOEXEC. When OS/2 starts a DOS session, it runs the AUTOEXEC.BAT file found in the root directory of the boot drive unless you specify the DOS_AUTOEXEC setting. Add a path and file name to the settings text box, indicating the location and name of the substitute AUTOEXEC.BAT. The default value is blank, and, obviously, you must set this value before starting a DOS session.

This setting is valuable for specifying different environments for different DOS sessions. If you want different environment variables in different sessions, for example, you can place them in different batch files, and then have OS/2 use a particular batch file for a particular DOS session.

DOS_DEVICE. When you boot your computer, OS/2 records any DOS device drivers in CONFIG.SYS. When you start a DOS session, these device drivers are loaded automatically. You can use the DOS_DEVICE driver setting to tailor the CONFIG.SYS device driver settings for a particular DOS session, however. When you start this DOS session, it then has the modified device driver values rather than those loaded by CONFIG.SYS when you booted the computer.

To change the device drivers for every DOS session, modify your CONFIG.SYS file. To modify the device drivers for only one session, use DOS_DEVICE. For example, if you need to load a device driver for your scanner, but you only want to do it when you run your desktop publishing program, use DOS_DEVICE to add the device driver. If you always want to have access to the scanner, add the device driver to CONFIG.SYS.

You can add, remove, or change any DOS device driver loaded with CONFIG.SYS by using the DOS_DEVICE setting. You must change this setting before starting a DOS session. To remove or change existing device drivers, select the driver from the list in the settings dialog box and modify. To add new drivers, type in the new value.

DOS_FCBS. When you run a program, DOS opens and closes small areas of memory called *file control blocks* (FCBs). If your program requests a file control block, DOS sets aside an area of memory for that program. The area cannot be used for anything else until DOS closes it. A larger number of open FCBs can improve your program's performance, but when running under OS/2, the overall performance of all the open sessions can deteriorate. OS/2 may be kept so busy handling all the open FCBs for a DOS session that your other background sessions, in particular sessions transmitting data across the network, do not have sufficient resources to be efficient.

To limit or expand the number of file control blocks that your DOS session can open at once, change DOS_FCBS. The acceptable range is from 0 to 255, and the default value is 16. You must change this setting before starting a DOS session.

If a program requests an FCB when the maximum number of blocks is open, your DOS session closes the least recently used FCB to free memory for the new one. (For information on preventing DOS from automatically closing FCB, see the section "DOS_FCBS_KEEP.")

DOS_FCBS_KEEP. The DOS_FCBS_KEEP setting tells DOS to keep a certain number of file control blocks (FCBs) open and not automatically close them. The valid range is from 0 to 255, and the default value is 8. You must change this setting before starting a DOS session. (See the preceding section, "DOS_FCBS," for more detailed information about file control blocks.)

You may want to prevent DOS from automatically closing an FCB when a program requests one more than the maximum FCB setting. After a program requests the number of FCBs stored in DOS_FCBS_KEEP, DOS does not automatically close an FCB to supply the program with an additional one. The program can continue to request FCBs up to the maximum specified in DOS_FCBS. If more FCBs are required, however, DOS can supply them only by closing existing ones, provided the value in DOS_FCBS_KEEP is equal to or higher than the number of open FCBs.

DOS_FILES. All DOS and Windows programs open multiple files at once, and in many cases you are unaware of the multiple file access. A word processor, for example, may enable you to work on two documents at once. When you have two documents loaded, you have at least three files open—the two documents and the word processing program (excluding the files STDIN, STDOUT, and STDERR which all DOS programs open). Many programs, however, do not just operate with a single program file, but use many other files as temporary storage and reference files and as places to hold less frequently used features. A word processor may keep backup files, allow user-generated dictionaries, and keep its graphics viewing features in separate files, all of which may be open at once.

The documentation for most DOS application programs specifies a minimum value for your FILES setting in DOS's CONFIG.SYS. To run that application program under OS/2, you need to set at least that value for the DOS_FILES setting.

This setting does not apply to your OS/2 sessions. As a multitasking operating system, OS/2 can keep many files open at once. To allow your DOS or Windows program to have access to as many files as it requires, however, you need to adjust the setting within the DOS session or Win-OS/2 session.

Change DOS_FILES to alter the number of files your DOS or Win-OS/2 session can have open simultaneously. Acceptable values are between 20 and 255. The default setting, which is also the minimum setting, is 20. You can change this setting before or during a DOS or Win-OS/2 session. In most cases, you will not need to change these values unless a particular application program instructs you to increase your DOS files setting.

DOS_LASTDRIVE. This setting is similar to using the LASTDRIVE setting in your CONFIG.SYS on a DOS-based computer, but its purpose on the OS/2-based computer is slightly different. OS/2 automatically enables you to access all drive letters up to Z. (You can use OS/2 settings to limit this choice.) Consequently, with OS/2 you do not need a LASTDRIVE setting for your DOS session.

On the other hand, you can restrict a DOS session's access to drives with this setting. If you do not want your DOS session to access network drives, for example, add a DOS_LASTDRIVE setting. Suppose that you have two hard disks on your computer (with drive letters C and D). To prevent them from accessing the network drives (with drive letters E and above), set DOS_LASTDRIVE to D.

Change DOS_LASTDRIVE to limit the last drive letter accessible to your DOS sessions. The default value is Z, and any setting between A and Z is acceptable; but you must include all drive letters physically in your computer. You must change this setting before starting a DOS session.

DOS_SHELL. One of DOS's flexible features is its capability to run an alternative command processor. As the name suggests, the command processor is the program that translates into instructions the commands you type at the command line, such as COPY, DEL, and DIR. You can purchase an alternative command processor, such as 4DOS, which typically includes all the DOS commands and adds functioning capability or speed. For example, 4DOS includes a directory deleting command that deletes the files in a subdirectory and removes the subdirectory. (With DOS you must use two commands for this action.)

On a DOS-based computer, you specify the alternative command processor in your CONFIG.SYS file; but on an OS/2-based computer, use the DOS_SHELL setting. You must change this setting before starting a DOS session. Type the full path and file name, along with any command-line switches, for the alternative command processor. The default value is as follows:

```
C:\OS2\MDOS\COMMAND.COM  /P
```

Although the alternative command processor's drive is not required if your processor is on the boot drive, you should still include the drive in this setting.

DOS_STARTUP_DRIVE. For most applications, OS/2's DOS emulation is suitable for your DOS programs. In certain cases, however, the emulation is inadequate. You may not be able to load a particular device driver into a normal OS/2 DOS session, for example, or a DOS program may not run properly. The DOS device driver software might function correctly in what OS/2 calls a specific version of DOS. In a specific-DOS session, you often can load device drivers and TSRs that don't work in an OS/2-emulated DOS session. OS/2 hosts the specific version of DOS.

Add the drive and path for an alternative version of DOS in DOS_STARTUP_DRIVE. Instead of allowing OS/2 to emulate DOS, use this setting to load a version of DOS between 3.0 and 5.0.

> **Note**
>
> The DOS_STARTUP_DRIVE setting is used for a different purpose from the DOS_VERSION setting. The DOS_VERSION setting lets a particular program assume that it is running a different version of DOS. The DOS_STARTUP_DRIVE setting is part of the method used to actually run a different version of DOS.

A specific-DOS session under OS/2 can start from either floppy disk or from an image of a floppy boot disk that you store on your hard disk. To use the DOS_STARTUP_DRIVE setting, you create a specific-DOS bootable floppy disk and, optionally, store that bootable floppy disk on your hard drive as an image file. You can use almost any version of DOS, including even Novell's DR-DOS product, in your specific-DOS session.

You first use DOS (not OS/2) to format a floppy disk with the /S parameter. The /S parameter tells FORMAT to make the floppy disk bootable. You then copy the files MOUSE.COM, EMM386.SYS, HIMEM.SYS, FSACCESS.EXE, and FSFILTER.SYS from your \OS2\MDOS directory to the floppy disk. MOUSE.COM enables the use of the mouse in the specific-DOS session. You use EMM386.SYS and HIMEM.SYS if you want to load the specific version of DOS, perhaps along with device drivers and TSRs, into high memory. Running FSACCESS enables you to use drive A after booting a specific-DOS version. FSFILTER lets the specific-DOS session access your hard drive while OS/2 is controlling the computer.

You can boot your specific-DOS session from the floppy disk you've thus created, or you can use the VMDISK utility to copy the floppy disk to an image file on your hard disk. If you boot from floppy, you use a DOS session program object that has a DOS_STARTUP_DRIVE setting of A:. (The OS/2 installation program puts such a program object in your Command Prompts folder for you.) If you boot from the image file on your hard drive, you put the name of the image file, including the drive letter and path, in the DOS_STARTUP_DRIVE setting for that DOS session. After you've opened the specific-DOS session, from floppy disk or the image file, OS/2 assigns the A drive to that session. Other sessions cannot access the A drive while the specific-DOS session is running. However, you can run the FSACCESS program in the specific-DOS session to end that session's allocation of the A drive. The specific-DOS session remains open, and other sessions can access the floppy drive.

DOS_VERSION. Similar to DOS 5.0's SETVER command, the DOS_VERSION setting enables you to run older programs that expect a particular version of the operating system to run. Suppose that a program uses a feature added only to DOS 3.0. That program may consult the operating system and determine that the DOS version number is 3.0 before it runs. If the DOS version is later, however, the program may run successfully because the feature is available, but it might not get past the version checking procedure. (Some programs include this check to avoid any potential incompatibility problems with later versions of the operating systems.) If you run DOS 5 before you install OS/2 and have program names in the SETVER region, you can add them to your OS/2 installation via this DOS_VERSION setting.

To change the DOS version number that a program encounters when operating in a DOS session, and to change the number of times OS/2 reports this version to your program, add that program to the DOS_VERSION setting. Type the program's executable file name, followed by the version number, a comma, the subversion number (two digits are required), a comma, and the number of times this version number can be reported to the program. A value of 255 for the latter parameter makes OS/2 report this simulated version number every time the program requests the information. If, for example, a program named WORDPROC.EXE requires DOS version 3.2, and you want the program to determine that the DOS version is 3.2 every time it asks, type **WORDPROC.EXE,3,20,255**.

HW_NOSOUND. Because DOS programs do not expect to share resources such as the speaker, they do not turn off the speaker when you switch to another session. You may want to hear the sound from another program, or you may have switched from the DOS session as the speaker was sounding and ended up with a continuous noise.

You can change the HW_NOSOUND default setting of ON to OFF. The OFF setting turns off the sound created by a DOS program. Remember to turn this setting back on to hear the sounds again. You can change this setting before or during a DOS session.

HW_TIMER. This setting is important for timing critical applications. The emulation supplied by OS/2 may not be suitable in all situations, and you may have to allow the DOS session to access the hardware timer directly.

Timing-critical applications require very precise time measurements. For example, a data acquisition program that samples data every millisecond must be able to time accurately, or your measurements are meaningless. The most common timing-critical programs are more frivolous than data acquisition, however, and include many game programs. A game program may use the time to determine how fast aliens are approaching, for example.

When you run a DOS session under OS/2, the operating system emulates the system's timer instead of allowing the program direct access to the hardware. This emulation allows multiple programs simultaneous access to timing features and is a feature of multitasking operating systems.

DOS programs, however, expect exclusive use of the timer. Because the OS/2 timer emulation does not and cannot include the time between the period when the program requested the time and when OS/2 actually determined the request, the time supplied to a program may not be completely accurate.

Change HW_TIMER from the default setting of OFF to ON to allow your DOS session to access the hardware timer ports. When set to OFF, OS/2 intercepts any hardware timer port requests and provides a timing emulation. You can change this setting before or during a DOS session.

INT_DURING_IO. If you want to permit the DOS programs to receive interrupts during a file read or write, change the INT_DURING_IO setting from its default of OFF to ON. You must change this setting before starting your DOS session.

In many situations, you do not want OS/2 to interrupt a DOS program while it is reading or writing a file to or from a disk; the program runs faster if it is not interrupted. However, some programs, in particular multimedia programs, need to receive interrupts during the process of reading or writing files. Some CD-ROM programs read data from the disk but are playing music or speech at the same time, for example. This is what the DOS program is doing when it processes interrupts while data is being read from the disk. You can think of it as if the program is reading the next thing to be said while the words are actually being spoken. Turning INT_DURING_IO on also can help some DOS communications programs perform file transfers (uploads and downloads) more quickly.

PRINT_SEPARATE_OUTPUT. Sometimes a single DOS program produces an entire report or other printout. However, sometimes you run a series of programs to produce one report. Each DOS program prepares a different section of the report. In this case, you need to disable some of OS/2's criteria for what makes one print job distinct from another.

PRINT_TIMEOUT. If you are running your DOS application program under DOS when you print from that program, the information is typically sent directly to the printer port. Under OS/2, print information is sent first to disk in a spool file; and then the OS/2 print spooler prints the file, allowing multiple sessions to print at once. The print spooler handles the printing sequence.

When you run a DOS session and print from the DOS program, OS/2 handles the print spooling. OS/2 waits a period of time defined by the setting in PRINT_TIMEOUT and then transfers the print data to a spooler file ready for printing. OS/2 senses the period of time elapsed since a computer program last sent data to the printer; if a period exceeding PRINT_TIMEOUT passes, OS/2 assumes that the computer program has finished printing.

You need to alter this setting if your program (perhaps processing slowly through a large file) takes longer than the specified time to create the print file. The symptom of too short a time is that your print job is divided. You may find that features such as fonts or highlighting are lost part way through a document because OS/2 treated the job as two print files rather than one.

To alter the time delay between the time when a DOS program starts to create a print file, and the time when the file is sent to OS/2's spool file, change the PRINT_TIMEOUT setting. The default value is 15, but values between 0 and 3600 seconds are acceptable. You can change this setting either before or during a DOS session.

Normally, OS/2 separates printouts into print jobs according to several criteria, as shown in the following list:

- The PRINT_TIMEOUT value
- Whether a program running in a different session created the printout
- Whether different programs in the same session send data to the printer
- Whether you have closed a session from which a program was printing

When you set PRINT_SEPARATE_OUTPUT to a value of OFF, you're instructing OS/2 to disregard that different computer programs are sending data to the printer. OS/2 then uses only the other criteria to sense when the end of the printout occurs. OS/2 does not signal the end of the print job just because a different computer program in that session begins sending data to the printer.

You must change the PRINT_SEPARATE_OUTPUT setting before opening that DOS session.

WIN_CLIPBOARD. You can use the OS/2 clipboard to transfer data (cut-and-paste or copy-and-paste) between programs running in several different combinations of sessions. You might, for example, copy data from a DOS session to an OS/2 session. You have a second clipboard in each Win-OS/2 session that you can use to transfer data between Windows programs running in that session.

The WIN_CLIPBOARD setting controls whether data in the OS/2 clipboard also flows into the Win-OS/2 clipboard and vice versa. You can turn WIN_CLIPBOARD off to keep each clipboard separate, or you can turn WIN_CLIPBOARD on to share data between programs running in different OS/2, DOS, and Windows sessions.

You can change this setting at any time.

WIN_DDE. You select the On or Off value for the WIN_DDE setting to control whether you want to create DDE links between Windows programs and OS/2 programs or between Windows programs running in separate sessions. You might turn WIN_DDE on, for example, if you have Lotus Ami Pro for Windows (your word processor) and Lotus 1-2-3 for OS/2 (your spreadsheet), and you use DDE links to transfer data between your word processor and your spreadsheet. The On value enables the creation of links between distinct sessions. The Off value allows DDE links to work only inside a particular session.

You can change this setting at any time.

WIN_RUNMODE. Microsoft Windows, depending on the type of CPU and amount of RAM in a computer, runs in either Standard or Enhanced mode. Most Windows programs do not care whether Windows is in Standard or Enhanced mode. A few Windows programs, however, use the additional memory allocation and other services that Windows offers when it is running in Enhanced mode. These programs do not run in Standard mode.

Win-OS/2 enables you to choose the mode in which that session runs. The choices are 3.1 Standard and 3.1 Enhanced Compatibility. In the latter mode, Win-OS/2 gives Windows applications almost the same memory allocation and other services that Microsoft Windows would. The only significant difference is that Win-OS/2, even in Enhanced mode, does not provide virtual device driver (VxD) facilities. Consult the manuals for your Windows application software to determine if you need to change this setting. As a rule, you can leave the setting at its default value.

You must change the setting before starting the Win-OS/2 session.

Chapter Summary

This chapter introduced each of the DOS and Windows session settings. Although some DOS application programs run with the default settings, you may need to make adjustments in particular instances because typically, your DOS applications were not written so that they could share your computer's resources, such as the screen, printer, or memory.

You can vary settings so that you can allocate more time to your DOS session; share computer resources, including keyboard, mouse, touch screen, display, and memory; alter the memory allocated to the DOS session; and adjust DOS settings commonly altered in CONFIG.SYS when you run DOS as the primary operating system.

Chapter 18
Batch-File Programming with OS/2

Batch files are to command-line sessions what macros are to spreadsheets. Batch files store a series of commands that, in combination, perform a useful task. You store the commands in a file and type the file name when you want to run that sequence of commands. This procedure is easier and more foolproof than typing each command individually. You may have noticed that some software products use batch-files to automate the products' installation processes; an INSTALL.BAT (or INSTALL.CMD) file enables you to use the software sooner than if you installed the product's components by hand.

You can create a batch-file easily with the Enhanced Editor, the System Editor, or some other text editor. Type the commands you want to execute, one to a line, exactly as you would type them at the command-line prompt. Save the file, in one of your PATH directories, with any name you choose. Use the extension BAT for a DOS batch-file; use the CMD extension for a batch-file you want to run in an OS/2 session. Batch file programming is that easy.

As you explore batch-files, you may find that you want the batch programs you write to do more than run commands, utility programs, and application programs. When this realization occurs, you are ready for more serious computer programming. OS/2 offers a higher-level batch-file programming environment called REXX. Chapter 19, "Programming with REXX," discusses this more advanced form of batch-file programming.

OS/2 and DOS batch-files can contain commands and directions in addition to commands and directions you type at a command-line prompt. You can combine regular DOS commands and these extra commands to create small, flexible programs that automate many of the tasks you perform on your computer. In this chapter, you learn how to save keystrokes and prevent typing errors by storing the DOS commands you frequently use in batch-files.

Learning Batch-File Program Basics

In DOS sessions, the operating system program COMMAND.COM executes the commands and statements in your batch-files. In OS/2 sessions, CMD.EXE executes the commands and statements. COMMAND.COM and CMD.EXE are the same operating system components that process the commands you enter at a command-line prompt. COMMAND.COM and CMD.EXE process your batch-file commands by simulating keyboard entry of those commands. Because the commands are stored in a text file, however, you don't have to worry about typing errors. This benefit is especially important if you use a long sequence of commands frequently or if one or more of the commands requires command-line parameters that are difficult to use.

The command processors in OS/2, for both OS/2 and DOS sessions, execute your batch-file programs one line at a time. The command processor begins with the first line of your batch-file. Unless you direct otherwise, the statements in your batch-file execute one after the other, from the top of the file to the bottom. You can use the GOTO statement to change the order in which the commands and statements execute.

In the next few sections, you learn to distinguish OS/2 and DOS batch-files, you discover ways to run batch-file programs, you explore using commands and statements in batch-files, and you create a simple, easy-to-understand batch-file program.

Distinguishing OS/2 and DOS Batch-Files

OS/2 batch-file programs have an extension of CMD. DOS batch-files use BAT. Most commands work the same whether you run the commands in a CMD file in an OS/2 session or run the commands in a BAT file in a DOS session. Some commands behave differently, however, or are not supported in one kind of session or the other. Part VI, the Command Reference, clearly spells out which commands work only in an OS/2 session or only in a DOS session. START, for example, is an OS/2-only command; MEM is an example of a DOS-only command. MKDIR, on the other hand, works the same in DOS and OS/2 sessions, assuming you use the same directory names in each session. You can create directories on an HPFS partition, with the OS/2 version of the MKDIR command in a CMD file, that taker advantage of HPFS long file names.

Running a Batch-File Program

You normally run batch-file programs that have a BAT extension in a DOS session, and you run CMD files in an OS/2 session. If you run a BAT file in an OS/2 session, OS/2 automatically starts a temporary DOS session for you and runs the BAT file in that session. The reverse is not true, however. You cannot run CMD files in a DOS session.

OS/2 and DOS search the directories in your PATH statement to find executable programs, including batch-file programs. You can explicitly name the directory from which OS/2 should run a program file. You can type the following command at a DOS or OS/2 prompt so that OS/2 searches your PATH prompt directories:

MYPROG

To avoid the searching of the PATH directories, you can type the following:

C:\BATDIR\MYPROG.BAT

You run BAT and CMD files at a command-line prompt the same way you run application and utility programs that have an extension of COM or EXE. You simply type the file-name portion without the extension and press Enter. If you have files with the same name that vary only in the extension (MYPGM.BAT or MYPGM.CMD, MYPGM.COM, and MYPGM.EXE, for example), both DOS and OS/2 run the program file with the COM extension. When the operating system looks for program files, the operating system finds COM files first, EXE files next, and BAT or CMD files last in the search order.

This makes naming a batch-file program the same name as a utility or application program difficult. OS/2 runs the COM or EXE file rather than the BAT (or CMD) file if the files are in the same directory. You can circumvent OS/2's (or DOS's) preference for COM and EXE files by putting your batch-file programs in a directory named earlier in your PATH statement than your other directories that contain programs.

OS/2 can represent a batch-file program as an icon (in a folder or on your desktop). You create such a program object in the same way that you create other program objects. Copy the PROGRAM object from the TEMPLATES folder by dragging the object onto the desktop while you press the right mouse button. In the Path and Filename field on the Program page of the settings notebook, you specify the drive, directory, file name, and extension of your batch-file program. You then can double-click the resulting icon to run your batch-file.

Using DOS and OS/2 Commands in Batch-Files

The batch-files you create can contain DOS commands, OS/2 commands, or a mixture of commands and invocations of computer programs. The DOS and OS/2 commands you are likely to use most often in batch-files are COPY, ERASE, MOVE, RENAME, XCOPY, CHDIR, MKDIR, RMDIR, CLS, and SET. The OS/2-only commands you are likely to use are START and DETACH. Note that many of these commands are file-oriented. You are not likely to find a use for the DATE or TIME commands in your batch-files.

Many office environments use a single tape drive to make backup copies of files on a local area network. To include your files in the office's backup procedure, you must copy files from your PC to the file server. Assuming your file server is drive F: and that you customarily put files in the F:\BACKUP directory so that the LAN tape drive can back up the files, you can automate your daily backup chores with the following batch-file program:

```
COPY C:\WP\*.DOC F:\BACKUP

COPY C:\123\*.WK1 F:\BACKUP

COPY C:\DATA\*.DAT F:\BACKUP
```

Although you can type each of these commands individually at a command-line prompt, you have to wait for one command to finish executing before you type the next command. A batch-file accomplishes all of the work of the several commands in one typing operation. You can insert these three lines with a text editor in a DOS batch-file (named SAVEWORK.BAT, perhaps) or an OS/2 batch-file (named SAVEWORK.CMD).

If you run this three-line batch-file program from a DOS-only (non-OS/2-based) workstation and if the files take a long time to copy, you must find something else to do while that computer runs the COPY commands. With OS/2, however, you can start the batch-file in one session and continue to work in other sessions.

Later sections of this chapter explain batch-file statements in detail. First, however, you create a simple batch-file program.

For Related Information
- "Storing Files and File Names," p. 45
- "Beginning the Command Line Interface," p. 303

Creating a Simple Batch-File Program

You can use a simple batch-file program to work around one of the limitations of DOS. The DOS PATH statement can contain up to 128 characters of information. The count of the characters that make up the drive letters, backslashes, directory names, semicolons, and file names in your DOS PATH must be less than 128. If you have many applications, you probably will find the 128-character limit constraining. (The OS/2 PATH statement does not have the 128-character limit; the limit applies only to DOS.) Several approaches enable you to work around this limit. Consider the following batch-file program, for example:

```
C:
CD \LETTERS
PATH C:\DOS;C:\WORDPROC
WORDPROC
PATH C:\DOS
CD \
```

This batch-file program, which is one of the most popular, makes the C drive current, changes to the LETTERS directory, modifies the PATH to indicate the DOS and WORDPROC directories, runs a program called WORDPROC, and restores the original PATH and root directory when you finish your word processing tasks. Although the file (WORDPROC) and directory names (LETTERS and WORDPROC) used in the preceding are fictitious, you can substitute directories and files used by your PC's setup.

You can begin the creation of a similar batch-file program by taking advantage of a characteristic of the PATH statement. If, at a command-line prompt, you issue a PATH statement with no parameters, DOS displays your current PATH, as shown in the following:

```
PATH=C:\DOS
```

Typing PATH with no parameters produces an executable PATH statement. You can redirect the display output of the PATH statement into a file. If you want to name your new batch-file program LETTERS.BAT and if you have a directory named DOS in your PATH, you can start your batch-file program by typing the following DOS command:

PATH >C:\DOS\LETTERS.BAT

Your DOS directory now contains the file LETTERS.BAT. When you type **LETTERS** at a DOS prompt, the new batch-file program issues a PATH command and the result is the same PATH in effect when you typed the name of the batch-file.

Use a text editor such as the System Editor to modify the LETTERS.BAT file. You can insert a PATH command to extend the number of directories in your PATH, insert a line that runs a program, and then insert a second PATH statement calling out the directories that were in effect before the first PATH command. After you save the file, you have a batch-file program that modifies your PATH, invokes an application, and restores your PATH when you exit the application. You can create other batch-file programs for your other applications that similarly set new PATHs for the duration of the application, and you won't have to worry about the 128-character limit imposed by the DOS PATH command.

Using Batch-File Program Statements

Batch file programs are not generally interactive; for example, you will not find an easy way to make a batch-file program ask questions while the batch-file executes. You can use display statements, however, to inform you of the progress of the batch-file.

You can insert reminders to yourself (*comments*) in batch-files. As your batch-file programs grow beyond the three-line example in the previous section, you may find these comments helpful to you or anyone who wants to use and modify your batch-files.

Batch file programs can make decisions and execute alternative sequences of commands based on the outcome of the decision. You, as the creator of the batch-file program, take three steps to insert decisions in your batch-files. You first analyze the requirements of the batch-file; you then determine what decisions the batch-file program should make; finally, you translate the decision-making process into a series of batch-file statements. You may think that this procedure sounds like computer programming, and for a very good reason: it is, indeed, a simple form of computer programming.

Batch files can contain programming language statements as well as DOS or OS/2 commands. The next few sections explain the programming statements you can use to make your batch-file programs clearer and more powerful.

Inserting Comments with the REM Statement

Comment lines you place in a batch-file program do not execute; the comments serve as documentation to explain what the batch-file program does and how the batch-file works. You use the REM statement to insert comments in your batch-files.

REM stands for remark. Your batch-files are easier to understand if you include remarks that explain what your programs do. To insert a remark, begin a line of the batch-file with the letters REM. Whatever you type on a line that begins with REM is not interpreted as a command. DOS and OS/2 just skip over REM lines. You might use the following statements, for example, to help document a batch-file program that starts the Lotus 1-2-3 application in a DOS session:

```
REM
REM    Always make C:\123 the current directory
REM    while 1-2-3 is running. The WK1 files are
REM    in the C:\123 directory.
REM
C:
CD \123
123
```

The REM statements document your preference for putting worksheet files in the 123 directory on the C: drive. The last three lines of this batch-file program make C the current drive, change to the 123 directory, and run 123.

Writing to the Screen with the ECHO Statement

When DOS or OS/2 runs a batch-file program, the command processor by default displays each line of the file on-screen. You can change this behavior—and tidy up your screen in the process—by typing ECHO OFF at the beginning of the batch-file program. When the command processor encounters an ECHO OFF statement, DOS or OS/2 stops echoing the lines of the batch-file. ECHO OFF does not affect the display of information generated by the commands and application programs you invoke in your batch-files; this command only affects the echo of the lines of the batch-file. Unfortunately, this command also hides your REM statements when you run the batch program. If you want your batch-file messages to appear on-screen while a batch program runs, use the ECHO command to explicitly display the messages, as shown in the following example:

```
ECHO OFF
CD \LETTERS
ECHO   You are now in the LETTERS directory.
```

You don't have to issue an ECHO ON at the end of a batch-file. DOS and OS/2 automatically revert to ECHO ON before running the next batch program.

Passing Parameters to a Batch Program

You can expand the usefulness of a batch-file program by supplying one or more parameters when you run the batch-file. Statements within the batch-file can access the parameters. Inside the batch-file program, each parameter is a *variable marker*. You can invoke a batch-file program named DELMANY.BAT, for example, by typing the following:

DELMANY *.TMP *.BAK *.JNK

If you write the DELMANY.BAT program to contain the following statements, DOS or OS/2 substitutes the parameters you supply to DELMANY (*.TMP, *.BAK, and *.JNK, in this example) in place of the %1, %2, and other variable markers:

```
ECHO OFF
ERASE %1
ERASE %2
ERASE %3
ERASE %4
ERASE %5
ERASE %6
ERASE %7
ERASE %8
ERASE %9
```

If you don't supply a parameter for every variable marker (which is the case in the following example; only three parameters appear), DOS and OS/2 substitute nothing for the extra markers. As the batch-file program in this example runs, the net result is the same as if you typed the following commands at a command-line prompt:

```
ERASE *.TMP
ERASE *.BAK
ERASE *.JNK
ERASE
ERASE
ERASE
ERASE
ERASE
ERASE
```

Although ERASE commands that are not followed by file names do no harm, each empty ERASE command produces the following error message in that DOS session:

```
Invalid number of parameters.
```

You learn how to test for the presence of batch-file parameters in a later section of this chapter, "Comparing Strings with the IF Statement."

DOS and OS/2 reserve the variable marker %0 for a special purpose. %0 contains the name of the currently running batch-file, without the extension. If you inserted ERASE %0 in a batch-file named DELZERO.BAT, DOS tries to ERASE the file named DELZERO.

Changing Program Flow with the GOTO Statement

You can use the GOTO statement to change the flow of execution of the lines of your batch-file program. You insert a *label* statement in your program to indicate to which line a GOTO statement should jump. A label begins with a colon (:) and can contain up to eight characters. When DOS or OS/2 encounters the GOTO statement, the command processor uses the line of the batch-file following the label as the next executable statement or command. The following batch-file program executes continuously until you press Ctrl-C:

```
ECHO OFF
:LINE2
GOTO LINE2
```

Such a batch-file, with its unconditional GOTO, isn't very useful. In the next few sections, you learn ways to test for situations in your batch-file programs and use the GOTO statement to execute different parts of the batch-file depending on the situation.

Testing File Existence with the IF EXIST Statement

You can make a batch-file program behave differently depending on the presence or absence of a file. The IF EXIST statement informs your batch-file program whether or not a certain file exists. You combine the IF EXIST statement with another command or statement. The command or statement after IF EXIST executes only if the file exists. The following example, which erases the file TEMP.DOC if the file exists, shows the use of a single command with IF EXIST:

```
IF EXIST TEMP.DOC ERASE TEMP.DOC
```

The next example shows an IF EXIST statement used in combination with a GOTO statement:

```
IF EXIST C:\OS2\BOOT.COM GOTO dualboot
ECHO    The Dual Boot facility isn't installed on this PC.
GOTO done
:dualboot
BOOT /DOS
:done
```

As the command processor executes this batch-file, one of two things happens. If the file BOOT.COM is in the OS2 directory, execution jumps to the dual-boot label, and the command processor then executes the BOOT program. If the file doesn't exist, however, the command processor executes the ECHO statement and the GOTO done statement. In the latter case, the command processor does not attempt to run the BOOT program because the batch-file has "jumped over" the lines that invoke BOOT.

Notice the use of the label in the last line of the batch-file. Using a label in this way is a common technique for naming the exit point of the batch-file program. You also can use the modifier word NOT in your IF EXIST statements. A batch-file line that contains the following line sometimes makes more sense and is more readable than an awkward form of IF EXIST:

```
IF NOT EXIST <filename> GOTO NotThere
```

Comparing Strings with IF

You can examine the variable markers in your batch-file programs by comparing strings. You use an IF statement to make the test. The command processor evaluates the IF statement to determine whether to execute the statement that you place on the same line as the IF. If the IF statement, as processed by the command processor, evaluates TRUE, DOS or OS/2 executes the indicated statement or command. Otherwise the command processor proceeds to the next line of the batch-file. A double equal sign ("==") denotes the test you want to make. The following example shows how IF works; in the example, the batch-file displays the message `Please use a filename as the first parameter to this batch-file` if you run the batch-file program with no command-line parameters. If you supply a parameter, the example batch-file erases the file named in the parameter.

```
IF "%1" == "" GOTO NoParms
ERASE %1
GOTO Done
:NoParms
```
Please use a file name as the first parameter to this batch-file.
```
:Done
```

If you don't supply a parameter, the "%1" parameter evaluates to a string containing no characters. The "%1" portion becomes back-to-back quotation marks, and the command processor interprets the first line of this batch-file as the following:

```
IF "" == "" GOTO NoParms
```

If you do supply a parameter (TEMP.DOC, for example) when you run the batch-file, the command processor interprets the first line as the following:

```
IF "TEMP.DOC" == "" GOTO NoParms
```

The preceding example is not a true statement. The command processor ignores the GOTO NoParms part of the first line.

Processing ERRORLEVEL in a Batch-File Program

Some utility programs and application software exit with a *return code* or *exit level*. A return code is a number that an application can give to the command processor as the application finishes and exits. (The documentation that comes with the utility or application mentions these return codes.) For these computer programs, you can make your batch-files behave differently depending on the computer program's return code. A return code of zero (0) usually means that the program encountered no problems and executed normally.

A return code value greater than 0 usually means that something went wrong. The problem may be that no files were found, for example, or that the program discovered an error in an input file. For programs that use return codes, you can use IF ERRORLEVEL to detect such problems. Your batch-file may use a GOTO statement to jump to a different section of batch statements depending on the result of the IF ERRORLEVEL test. The return code is available to you in ERRORLEVEL.

If the return code (ERRORLEVEL) from the utility or application is greater than or equal to the value you specify in the batch-file, the IF condition is true. Suppose that you run a program named COMPILE that returns 0 if the program runs without error. If COMPILE encounters errors, the COMPILE program returns the number 4 to the command processor. Your batch-file may resemble the following:

```
COMPILE datafile
IF ERRORLEVEL 4 THEN GOTO errors
GOTO done
:errors
ECHO    Compile ended in error!
:done
```

When you use a series of IF ERRORLEVEL statements (for programs that can return alternative exit levels), be sure to test for the highest ERRORLEVEL value first. The command processor considers an IF ERRORLEVEL statement true if the program's return code is greater than the value you specify.

Inserting FOR Loops in your Batch Programs

A FOR loop in a batch-file adds considerable power to your program in only a few lines. You use a FOR loop to make a particular command or statement execute as many times as the FOR loop specifies. A FOR loop enables you to invoke a utility program, DOS command, or OS/2 command for a group of files or drives. You may insert the following lines in a batch-file, for example, to make OS/2 perform a CHKDSK operation on drives A, C, and D:

```
FOR %%1 IN (A: C: D:) DO chkdsk %1
```

In a FOR loop, the %%1 variable takes on the value of each item in parentheses. In this example, the items are drive letters. You can use wild-card file names, drives, or paths as items in parentheses. The double percent sign keeps DOS (or OS/2) from treating the variable as a command-line parameter.

Calling Batch-Files from Other Batch Programs

For Related Information
- "Learning the Commands for Managing Directories," p. 305
- "Learning the Commands for Managing Files," p. 311
- "Command Reference," p. 717

You don't have to put all the commands and statements you want to execute into a single batch-file. You can modularize your programs by creating different batch-files for individual tasks. A main, or *primary*, batch-file can invoke batch-file modules with the CALL statement. The individual module performs its work and, when finished, returns to the main batch-file program. The main program continues execution at the statement following the CALL statement. The following batch-file shows an example of calling batch-files (notice the passing of parameters from one batch-file to the other):

```
MAIN.BAT
ECHO OFF
IF EXIST %1 GOTO ParmOkay
ECHO    Please supply a filename.
GOTO Done
:ParmOkay
CALL WORK %1
:Done

WORK.BAT

ERASE %1
REM    Control now returns to the MAIN.BAT program.
```

These batch-file programs, MAIN and WORK, operate in the following way. If you supply MAIN with a command-line parameter and that parameter is the name of an existing file, MAIN jumps (branches the flow of the program) to the ParmOkay label. If you do not supply a parameter or if the parameter isn't the name of a file, MAIN echoes the message `Please supply a filename`.

on-screen and jumps to the Done label. At the ParmOkay label, the MAIN batch-file calls the WORK batch-file program, supplying the same parameter to WORK that you supplied to MAIN as a command-line parameter. WORK simply erases the file whose name is the parameter.

Halting a Batch-File Program

A batch-file program finishes when execution reaches the last line in the batch-file. The batch program may execute statements and commands in sequential order, top to bottom. The batch program also may use a GOTO statement to alter the order in which the lines of the batch-file execute.

Occasionally, as you create a new batch-file program, you may find that you have put a GOTO statement in the wrong place. If your batch-file program appears to have gone into an *infinite loop*, never reaching the end of the batch-file, you can press Ctrl-C to stop the errant batch program. DOS or OS/2 returns you to the command-line prompt. You then can use your text editor to examine the logical flow of your batch program to analyze the problem.

Interacting with Batch-File Programs

You must use creativity when writing batch-file programs that interact with people during file execution. You may want to invoke a computer program, for example, that asks questions and sets ERRORLEVEL depending on the answer given. Your batch-file may use a GOTO statement to jump to a section of the batch-file appropriate to the given answer. The public domain utilities INPUT.COM and ASK.COM are especially useful in such a situation. Following is an example containing a series of batch-file programs that shows how you can create simple menus on your PC:

```
MENU.BAT

ECHO OFF
C:
CD \MENU
ECHO    DIRECTORY MENU
ECHO           1...Change to the LETTERS directory
ECHO           2...Change to the MEMOS directory
ECHO           3...Change to the DATA directory
PROMPT  Type the number (1-3) and press Enter:
```

```
1.BAT

ECHO OFF
REM    reset the prompt
PROMPT $P$G
CD \LETTERS

2.BAT

ECHO OFF
REM    reset the prompt
PROMPT $P$G
CD \MEMOS

3.BAT

ECHO OFF
REM    reset the prompt
PROMPT $P$G
CD \DATA
```

Note that MENU.BAT changes the DOS (or OS/2) PROMPT into an actual prompt, which asks the operator to enter a number and press Enter. When the operator types the number and presses Enter, he or she invokes a batch-file whose name corresponds to the number typed. The 1.BAT, 2.BAT, and 3.BAT files each reset the DOS PROMPT back to its usual value after changing the current directory to the value specified in each batch-file.

Using Startup Batch Programs That Run Automatically

You can create batch-file programs that run every time you start a DOS session or when you boot your computer. At boot time, you can have your batch-file program run before or after the Workplace Shell appears.

The AUTOEXEC.BAT file in the root directory of your boot drive (usually C:\AUTOEXEC.BAT) runs at the beginning of each DOS command-line session you start. You can change this by specifying a different batch-file in the DOS_AUTOEXEC setting for that session. DOS_AUTOEXEC is one of the DOS settings you can modify on the Session page of the settings notebook for that command-line session.

STARTUP.CMD runs each time you boot OS/2, not in each OS/2 session you start. OS/2 looks for STARTUP.CMD in the root directory of your boot drive.

Use these files for commands that you always want to run. If you want DOSKEY loaded at the beginning of every DOS session, for example, insert the appropriate lines in AUTOEXEC.BAT. If you want your computer to automatically log on to your local area network when you boot OS/2, put your log-in commands in STARTUP.CMD.

A STARTUP.CMD batch-file program in the root directory of your boot drive runs before the Workplace Shell displays your desktop. If you use the right mouse button to drag a CMD batch-file program into the STARTUP folder (which the OS/2 installation program puts in your OS/2 SYSTEM folder), however, your batch-file runs after the Workplace Shell displays your desktop.

Do not name the batch-file STARTUP.CMD because the batch-file program will run twice—once because of its special name and once because you moved the CMD file to the STARTUP folder. Give the batch-file some other name when you tell your text editor to save the file. Also, to prevent extra copies of the batch-file from taking up hard disk space, use the Create Shadow procedure described in Chapter 10, "Managing the Workplace Shell," to drag the CMD file into the STARTUP folder. You also can find a brief description of the Create Shadow procedure on the inside front cover of this book.

For Related Information
- "Customizing the Workplace Shell," p. 262
- "Setting Up Other Applications," p. 264

Chapter Summary

Batch file programs can save you many repetitious keystrokes. You can use batch-files to store long sequences of DOS or OS/2 commands or to store commands and parameters that are long or difficult to remember. Batch file programming is simple and easy. You don't have to be a professional programmer to create and use batch-files to make your day-to-day use of your computer more productive.

In the next chapter, you learn about OS/2's advanced features. You begin with an exploration of some of the little-known but useful utility programs that IBM supplies with OS/2.

Part V

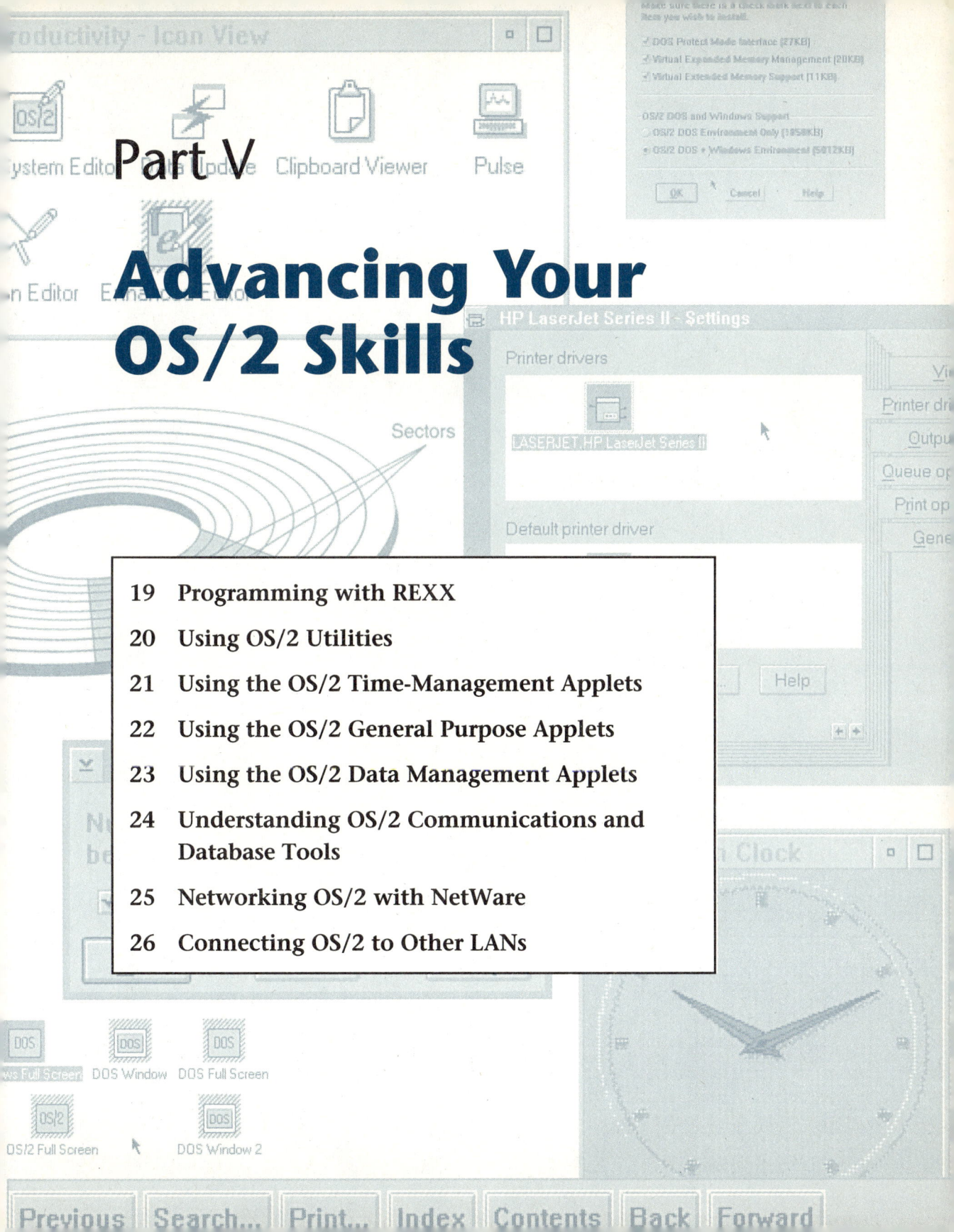

Advancing Your OS/2 Skills

- 19 Programming with REXX
- 20 Using OS/2 Utilities
- 21 Using the OS/2 Time-Management Applets
- 22 Using the OS/2 General Purpose Applets
- 23 Using the OS/2 Data Management Applets
- 24 Understanding OS/2 Communications and Database Tools
- 25 Networking OS/2 with NetWare
- 26 Connecting OS/2 to Other LANs

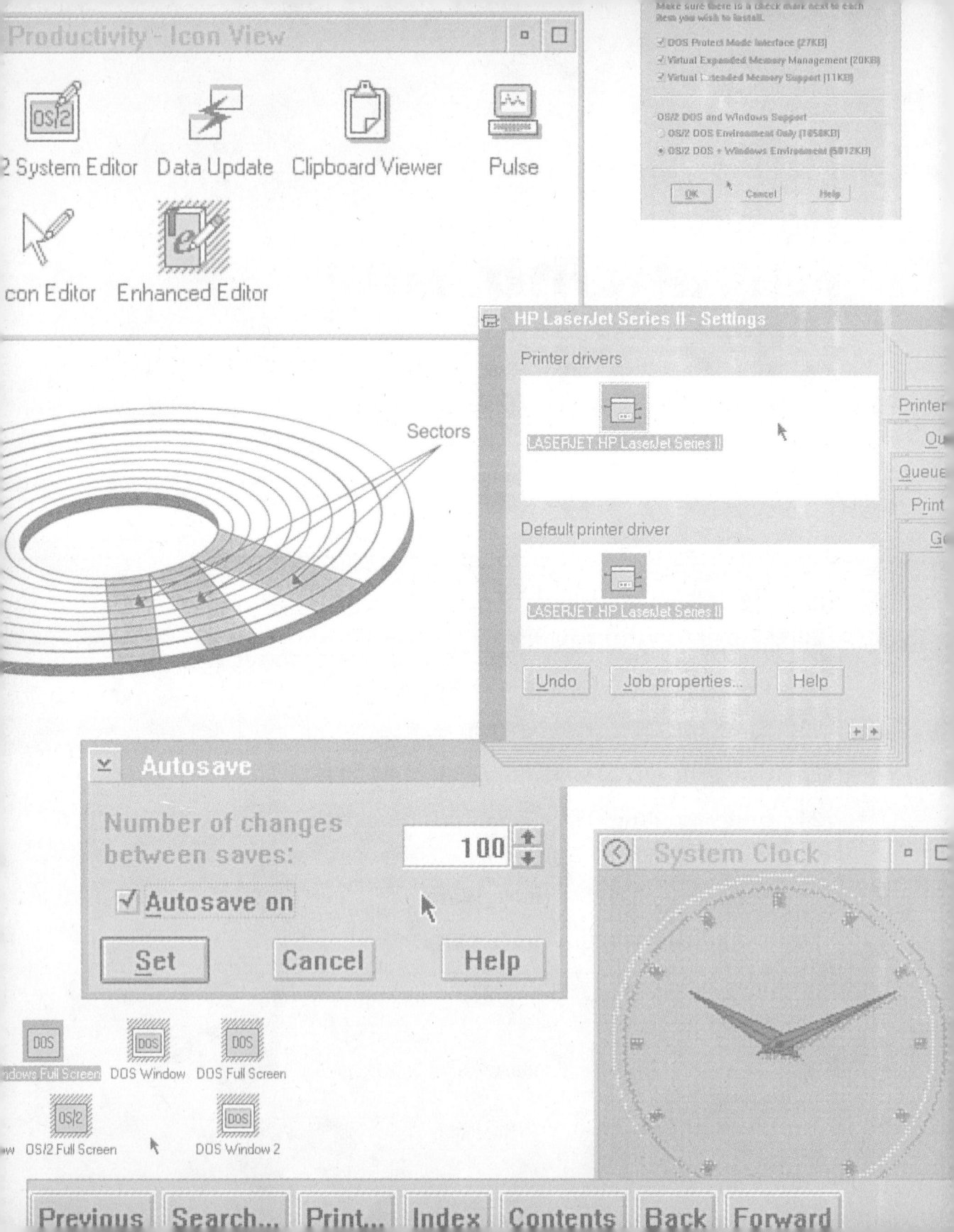

Productivity - Icon View

- OS/2 System Editor
- Data Update
- Clipboard Viewer
- Pulse
- Icon Editor
- Enhanced Editor

Make sure there is a check mark next to each item you wish to install.

- ☑ DOS Protect Mode Interface (27KB)
- ☑ Virtual Expanded Memory Management (20KB)
- ☑ Virtual Extended Memory Support (11KB)

OS/2 DOS and Windows Support
- ○ OS/2 DOS Environment Only (1050KB)
- ● OS/2 DOS + Windows Environment (5012KB)

[OK]   [Cancel]   [Help]

Sectors

HP LaserJet Series II - Settings

Printer drivers

LASERJET HP LaserJet Series II

Default printer driver

LASERJET HP LaserJet Series II

[Undo]   [Job properties...]   [Help]

Printer
Ou
Queue
Print
G

Autosave

Number of changes between saves: [100]

☑ Autosave on

[Set]   [Cancel]   [Help]

- Windows Full Screen
- DOS Window
- DOS Full Screen
- OS/2 Full Screen
- DOS Window 2

System Clock

[Previous] [Search...] [Print...] [Index] [Contents] [Back] [Forward]

Chapter 19

Programming with REXX

In the preceding chapter, "Batch-File Programming with OS/2," you learned to create your own DOS and OS/2 commands by building on the operating system's existing commands. To write a batch-file program, you create a text file with a text editor; each line of the text file runs a built-in command or computer program—just as if you had typed the command name or program name at a command-line prompt. A batch-file program is a named collection of commands and programs in a text file that has the extension BAT or CMD. You run the collection of commands and programs by typing the name of the batch file at a DOS command-line prompt (for BAT files) or at an OS/2 command-line prompt (for CMD files). OS/2 (or the DOS contained within OS/2) then executes each of the lines in the batch-file program. Chapter 18 also explained how to turn a batch-file program into a program object you can store in a folder or leave on the desktop.

When you master writing batch-file programs, you have much more control over your computer. You can use batch-file programs to customize your use of operating system commands, application programs, and utility programs. Batch-file programs don't offer a great deal of flexibility, however. A batch-file program can execute different commands or programs depending on whether a file exists, but a batch-file program cannot prompt the person running the program for information. Nor can the batch-file program perform calculations. The next logical step after simple batch-file programs is REXX—which provides these capabilities and more. REXX allows you to embed programming-language statements (as well as OS/2 commands and utilities) in batch-file programs. REXX programming is only slightly more complicated than batch-file programming.

In this chapter, you learn how to extend the usefulness of your batch-file programs with REXX. You first explore the basics of REXX programs: You learn how to use *variables* (data fields whose values you can modify), and you discover how to display information from within a REXX program. Then you learn several ways you can control the *flow of a program*—the order in which REXX executes the program statements you write. You learn how to compute results and how to manage *strings* (variables, such as a name or address, that contain textual information). You also learn how to build REXX programs that accept parameters. This chapter concludes with a discussion of how you can exercise your REXX programs in a test environment to make sure that the programs behave exactly as they should. If you plan to try out some or all the example REXX programs in this chapter, you may want to read the last section, "Testing REXX Programs," before you type the examples into your computer and run them. REXX includes some easy-to-use tools to help you test your hand-crafted software.

This chapter also looks at some visual REXX tools that create Presentation Manager (GUI) programs: VisproREXX, GPF REXX, and VX/REXX.

Understanding REXX Basics

A REXX program is an OS/2 batch file with special capabilities. You write a REXX program by using a text editor to create a text file with the extension CMD; the first line of this CMD file is a REXX comment line. A REXX comment starts with the two characters /* and ends with the two characters */.

> **Note**
>
> The first line of a REXX program *must* start with the characters /* and end with the characters */. If the REXX comment line is the second line of the text file (perhaps you left the first line blank), OS/2 does not treat the file as a REXX program.

You must install REXX support before you can run REXX programs. If you did not choose the REXX option during the installation process, refer to Chapter 7, "Modifying Your OS/2 Configuration," to selectively install REXX support. Also install the on-line documentation for REXX.

Mike Cowlishaw, who works for IBM, designed REXX. He had the help of over 300 other IBM people as he refined the REXX language. REXX is implemented in many types of IBM computing environments, from mainframes to PCs. Chapter 9, "Using Your Computer Screen as a Desktop," introduced you to IBM's System Application Architecture (SAA) standard. REXX is part of the SAA standard.

> **Tip**
>
> If you want more information about REXX than what this chapter provides, get Mike Cowlishaw's book *A Practical Approach to Programming REXX*. IBM offers entire books and technical references on REXX, including *OS/2 Procedures Language 2/REXX Reference* and *REXX User's Guide*. Additionally, you can read the REXX on-line documentation that is part of OS/2. This chapter explains how to use the most popular features of REXX, but you will need a separate reference if you find yourself writing serious REXX programs. REXX is a full-featured, complete programming language.

Most REXX implementations, including the one in OS/2, interpret your REXX program statements immediately rather than compiling and linking the program statements into an executable file. The interpreted nature of REXX allows you to use a text editor to create a REXX program, save the file, and immediately run the program at an OS/2 command-line prompt. You can conveniently develop, test, and run REXX programs right on your desktop by opening a text-editor window (perhaps the OS/2 System Editor or the OS/2 Enhanced Editor, both discussed in Chapter 14, "Using the OS/2 Text Editors") alongside an OS/2 windowed session. The OS/2 text editors are located in the Productivity folder; the OS/2 windowed session is an icon in the Command Prompts folder. Figure 19.1 shows one way you can configure your desktop to facilitate REXX program development.

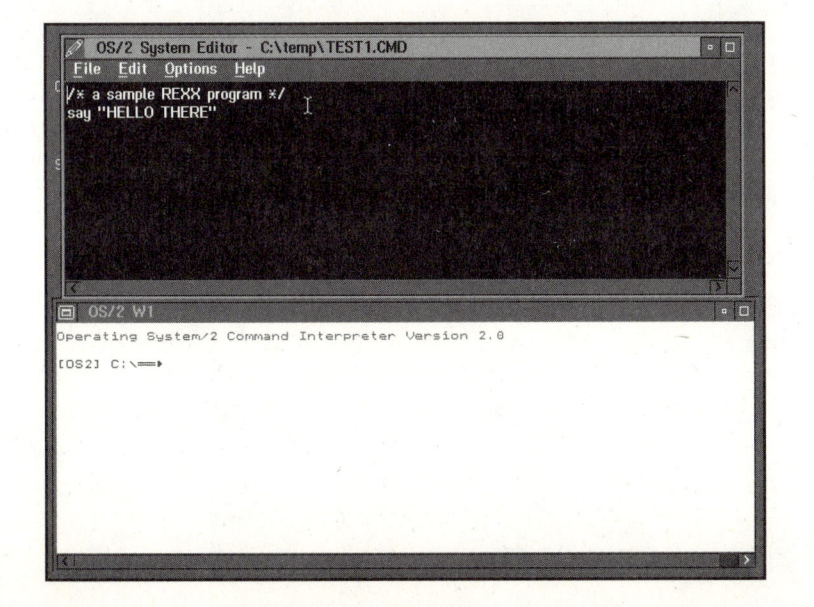

Fig. 19.1
(REXX-1) Using the System Editor and a windowed OS/2 session to create REXX programs.

REXX works by reading the text file, interpreting the lines of text, and performing whatever operations you specify. The OS/2 command-line processor, CMD.EXE, knows to invoke the REXX interpreter because the first line of the text file is a REXX comment (the /* and */ characters discussed earlier in this chapter). The OS/2 command-line processor treats a text file with the extension CMD as a normal batch-file program unless the first line of the file is a REXX comment.

> **Tip**
>
> The first time you run a new or changed REXX program, REXX examines and analyzes the REXX statements. REXX *tokenizes* the program source code and stores the result as a collection of Extended Attributes. (You learned about Extended Attributes in Chapter 3, "Learning OS/2 If You Know DOS.") Each time you run the REXX program after that, REXX uses the tokenized version. Subsequent executions of the program run faster because REXX doesn't have to reinterpret the source-code statements.

A REXX program can execute REXX program statements, OS/2 commands, and OS/2 applications. This chapter explains the REXX program statements from which you can construct REXX programs. *REXX program statements* let you interactively get responses from the person who runs the REXX program, display information to that person, perform calculations, and do other information-processing steps.

> **VREXX**
>
> Batch-file programs and REXX programs operate through the OS/2 command-line interface, which means that these programs cannot take advantage of Presentation Manager features such as windows, dialog boxes, and pushbuttons. However, IBM offers a companion product, called VREXX, you can use to give REXX programs a Presentation Manager interface. VREXX (Visual REXX for OS/2 Presentation Manager) consists of a library of OS/2 2.1 REXX functions. Although you can give REXX programs a Presentation Manager interface with VREXX, you do not have to be an expert in Presentation Manager programming to use VREXX. You simply incorporate VREXX functions into the REXX programs you write.
>
> VREXX includes functions for creating windows, drawing graphics, displaying text in multiple fonts, and displaying dialog boxes. The dialog boxes VREXX supplies let you perform filename selection, font and color selection, string input, and message display. VREXX also supplies dialog boxes you can use to present and select options through list boxes, tables, radio buttons, and check boxes.
>
> VREXX has on-line help and comes with sample REXX programs that show how easily you can add windows and dialog boxes to REXX programs. You can find VREXX on many bulletin boards and information services as file VREXX2.ZIP.

Displaying Information with REXX

You use the REXX statement SAY to display information to someone running the REXX program. The following example is a REXX program that displays the prompt Please enter the age of the computer: on-screen.

```
/* This first line, a REXX comment, makes this a REXX program. */

SAY "Please enter the age of your computer: "
```

This example REXX program displays a prompt and then exits back to the OS/2 command line. The next section explains how you can expand this example to obtain a response to the prompt from the person who runs the REXX program.

The SAY REXX command can display the value of a variable as well as the contents of a quoted text string. You learn about variables and other uses of the SAY command in later sections of this chapter.

Using the *PULL* and *PARSE PULL* Commands

When you want the person running a REXX program to type a response to a prompt so that the program can know and operate on the response, you use a PULL command. PULL gathers a line of typed characters that ends when the user presses the Enter key and stores the response in a variable. The following example asks the person running the REXX program to enter the age of the computer and then stores the response in a variable named *age*:

```
/* This first line, a REXX comment, makes this a REXX program. */
/* This example prompts for the age of the computer and stores */
/* the answer in a variable named age. */
SAY "Please enter the age of your computer: "
PULL age
```

The PULL command converts the person's keyboard response to uppercase. If you want PULL to store both uppercase and lowercase strings in a variable, use PARSE PULL.

Defining Variables in REXX

A *variable* is a data field, or symbol, containing a piece of information. The information in the variable can be a number or a text string. You use variables in REXX programs to hold numbers or text strings; you refer to the number or the text string by using the name of the variable. You can PULL or PARSE PULL information into a variable, you can SAY the value of a variable, and you can store calculated results in a variable.

A variable can hold different numbers or different text strings at different times while the REXX program executes. The following example assigns the numeric value 0.06 to the variable *TaxRate* and the numeric value 4700.00 to the variable named *Price*. The example calculates the sales tax based on the price and stores the sales-tax amount in a variable named *SalesTax*. The example then calculates the total price, reusing the *Price* variable, and displays the result as the number 4982.0000.

```
/* This first line, a REXX comment, makes this a REXX program. */
/* This example calculates a sales tax amount, using a tax rate */
/* of 6%. */
TaxRate = 0.06
Price = 4700.00
SalesTax = Price * TaxRate
Price = Price + SalesTax
SAY "Including tax, the price is " Price
```

When you name a variable, use names that suggest the meaning of the data contained in the variable. Although you can use names such as *A*, *B*, *X*, *Y*, and *Z*, your program will be difficult to understand in the future. Someday you will find it necessary to add enhancements to the program, and you will want the names you use in the program to immediately suggest what the program currently does. You can then change the program with some confidence. Computer programming isn't easy, but you can give yourself significant help by using meaningful variable names.

When REXX interprets and processes your program statements, REXX (which is actually a computer program itself) tests each word in the program text file to know which words are variable names. When REXX identifies the variables, it follows certain rules. The following rules dictate a variable name:

- The variable name begins with a letter
- The variable name cannot be the same as a REXX command (such as SAY)
- The variable name can contain a mixture of letters and numbers
- The variable name can contain both uppercase and lowercase letters

- The variable name can contain special characters, such as the underscore (_) character, that have no meaning to OS/2

- The variable name can be up to 50 characters long

These rules imply that names such as *123PROG*, *TEST<ONE*, *PROG&DATA*, and *PULL* are invalid variable names. *123PROG* begins with a number; *TEST<ONE* and *PROG&DATA* contain special characters that OS/2's command processor uses, and *PULL* is a verb in the REXX language. The variable names *SalesTax*, *SALESTAX*, *AmountCalculatedSoFar*, *PointsPerGame*, and *Lotus123* are all valid variable names, however.

The value contained in a variable is distinct from the variable's name. It is certainly valid for a variable to contain the strings *123PROG*, *TEST<ONE*, *PROG&DATA*, or *PULL*. Also note that the value of a variable before you store anything in that variable is the name of the variable itself.

REXX has three predefined variables: *RC*, *RESULT*, and *SIGL*. The *RC* variable is similar to ERRORLEVEL, which you learned about in Chapter 18, "Batch-File Programming with OS/2." *RC* contains the return code (exit code) of the most recently executed OS/2 command or computer program. *RESULT* contains a value set by a RETURN statement; you can use a RETURN statement to exit a REXX program that you have called from another REXX program. (The REXX CALL statement works much like the batch-file program CALL command you learned about in Chapter 18.) The RETURN statement allows you to communicate a value from the subprogram to the main (calling) REXX program. The *SIGL* variable contains the line number of the REXX program statement that caused the most recent jump to a label when an error occurs and you have used a SIGNAL statement to handle the error. (Until you become more experienced at writing REXX programs, you may want to skip using SIGNAL and *SIGL*. The on-line documentation for REXX explains error handling and can help you determine if and when you want to use SIGNAL and *SIGL*.)

Controlling Program Flow

REXX program statements execute sequentially, from the top of the REXX program to the bottom, unless you specify otherwise. You can control the flow of execution within a program with IF...THEN...ELSE statements, with SELECT statements, and with several forms of the DO statement.

You use an IF statement to determine whether the value of a variable or an expression has a certain relationship to another variable or expression. If the relationship (the test condition) you express is true, REXX executes the statement after the THEN but before an ELSE. If the relationship is not true, REXX executes the statement after the ELSE. ELSE is optional, however; if you don't specify an ELSE statement and the relationship is not true, REXX resumes execution at the statement following the IF.

As with many computer programming situations, the formal definition of what happens is more complicated than actually using an IF...THEN...ELSE statement. The following example, which shows how simple an IF...THEN...ELSE really is, sets the variable *TaxRate* to 0.08 if the variable named *State* contains the two-character string *NY* and sets *TaxRate* to 0.06 for any other *State* value:

```
<MS>/* This first line, a REXX comment, makes this a REXX program. */
<MS>IF State = 'NY' THEN
<MS>   TaxRate = 0.08
<MS>ELSE
<MS>   TaxRate = 0.06
```

Note that the ELSE clause is optional. The simplest form of the IF...THEN...ELSE statement is the following:

```
/* This first line, a REXX comment, makes this a REXX program. */
IF Computer = 'PC' THEN
   OperatingSystem = 'OS/2'
```

Perhaps the following syntax specifications for IF...THEN and IF...THEN...ELSE statements help clarify what happens when REXX executes an IF:

```
IF <condition> THEN <statement>
IF <condition> THEN <statement> ELSE <statement>
```

As your REXX programs get more complex, you may want to perform two or more tests in the <condition> portion of the IF statement. You can express *and* and *or* relationships with the & and | operators in REXX. The following example sets *TaxRate* to 0.06 for all states except New York, 0.08 for all parts of New York except New York City, and 0.09 for New York City:

```
/* This first line, a REXX comment, makes this a REXX program. */
IF State = 'NY' & City = 'New York City' THEN
   TaxRate = 0.09
ELSE
IF State = 'NY' THEN
   TaxRate = 0.08
ELSE
   TaxRate = 0.06
```

You may often want REXX to execute more than one statement as the result of an IF...THEN...ELSE test. You can encapsulate multiple statements with the DO and END commands. REXX treats the statements between DO and END as a single statement. The following example uses DO and END to set the variable *LongNames* to the string *TRUE* and the variable *Speed* to *FAST*, depending on a person's affirmative response to the question of whether a disk partition has been formatted with OS/2's High Performance File System:

```
/* This first line, a REXX comment, makes this a REXX program. */
SAY "Is the disk partition HPFS-based?"
PULL Answer
IF Answer = 'YES' | ANSWER = 'Y' THEN
    DO
    LongNames = 'TRUE'
    Speed = 'FAST'
    END
```

Several IF statements can follow one another when you want to determine the particular value of a variable, as the next example shows:

```
/* This first line, a REXX comment, makes this a REXX program. */
SAY 'Program Run Menu: 1)Lotus 123     2)Excel/PM     3)Quattro Pro'
PULL Response
IF Response = '1' THEN
    DO
    SAY 'You picked menu option 1'
    123
    END
ELSE IF Response = '2' THEN
    DO
    SAY 'You picked menu option 2'
    EXCEL
    END
ELSE
    DO
    SAY 'You must have picked menu option 3'
    QPRO
    END
```

The preceding example displays a simple menu prompt with SAY, uses PULL to assign the typed answer into the *Response* variable, and uses a series of IF statements to determine what was typed. If the menu offers many choices, the series of IF statements becomes quite long. At your discretion, based on how understandable and readable you feel the IF statements are, you can use a SELECT statement. The following example is exactly equivalent to the preceding example:

```
/* This first line, a REXX comment, makes this a REXX program. */
SAY 'Program Run Menu: 1)Lotus 123     2)Excel/PM     3)Quattro Pro'
PULL Response
SELECT
  WHEN Response = '1' THEN
    DO
    SAY 'You picked menu option 1'
    123
    END
  WHEN Response = '2' THEN
    DO
    SAY 'You picked menu option 2'
    EXCEL
    END
  OTHERWISE
    SAY 'You must have picked menu option 3'
    QPRO
END
```

Note

The menu-prompt REXX program examples reveal that you can execute OS/2 commands and run computer programs from within a REXX program. The menu-prompt examples run 123.EXE, EXCEL.EXE, or QPRO.EXE, depending on the response to the PULL statement. In fact, if you make a typing error in a program and ask REXX to do something it doesn't understand, REXX assumes that you want to execute a command or program and gives your typing error to the OS/2 command processor CMD.EXE to handle. When CMD.EXE cannot understand what you want it to do, OS/2 displays the following error message:

The name specified is not recognized as an internal or external command, operable program or batch file.

In addition to using IF statements to control the flow of execution of a program, you can use repetitive and conditional loops in REXX. A *repetitive loop* executes the statements within the loop a certain number of times (or forever, if you choose). A *conditional loop* executes the statements within the loop while or until a relationship is true.

To make one or more statements execute a certain number of times in REXX, you use DO *<number>*. The following example displays ERROR! on the screen five times:

```
/* This first line, a REXX comment, makes this a REXX program. */
DO 5
   SAY 'ERROR!'
END
```

You can make a set of statements execute without stopping by using the word FOREVER in place of <number> (DO FOREVER). Such a program is less than useful, however. To stop an infinite loop of statements in a DO FOREVER, you can press Ctrl+Break (this halts the REXX program completely) or use a LEAVE statement at an appropriate point inside the loop. The following example shows how you can use DO FOREVER and LEAVE to ensure that a person has typed a correct response to a prompt; the example loops until the person presses Y or N:

```
/* This first line, a REXX comment, makes this a REXX program. */
DO FOREVER
   SAY 'Log on to the network? (Y/N)==> '
   PULL Response
   IF Response = 'Y' OR Response = 'N' THEN LEAVE
   SAY 'Invalid response! Try again.'
END
```

You can use a variable in the REXX program to count the number of times through a loop. The variable's value increments for each iteration of the loop, starting with an initial value you specify. The syntax of this form of repetitive loop is as follows:

```
DO <variable> = <start value> TO <stop value>
<statements>
END
```

In a counted loop, REXX first sets the variable to <start value>. Then REXX evaluates the variable in the following manner:

1. If the variable's value is the same as <stop value>, leave the loop.

2. Perform the statements within the counted loop.

3. Increment the variable and go back to step 1.

The following example shows a counted loop that creates five directories named TMP1 through TMP5. Note that there is no space (blank) between the string *TMP* and *DirectoryNumber* (the name of the variable).

```
/* A REXX program that creates five directories */
DO DirectoryNumber = 1 TO 5
  MKDIR "TMP"DirectoryNumber
END
```

The REXX statements you use to perform conditional loops are DO <statements> WHILE <condition> and DO <statements> UNTIL <condition>. DO...WHILE and DO...UNTIL behave like the DO FOREVER statement explored earlier, but you can express the condition used to determine when to leave the loop without using separate IF and LEAVE statements. Use the DO...WHILE form of conditional loop when possible; in some cases, you do not need to execute the loop at all. Use the DO...UNTIL form to ensure that the statements within the loop execute at least once.

Computing Results with REXX

You can perform calculations inside REXX programs. When you assign a value to a variable, you can express the value to be assigned as the result of a computation. You can use simple arithmetic operators, such as + (addition), - (subtraction), * (multiplication), and / (division), and you can use the math functions built into REXX. (The REXX on-line documentation lists the built-in math functions.) If you use a combination of arithmetic operators, REXX evaluates the multiplication and division operations first, and then the addition and subtraction operations. You also can use parentheses to make REXX calculate results in a particular order.

The following example calculates sales tax at the rate of 6%, applies a discount of 25%, and stores the total price in the variable *TotalPrice*:

```
/* This first line, a REXX comment, makes this a REXX program. */
TaxRate = 0.06
Discount = 0.25
SAY 'Enter the price of the item==> '
PULL Price
/* calculate sales tax before applying any discounts */
TotalPrice = Price + (Price * TaxRate)
/* now apply the discount */
TotalPrice = TotalPrice - (TotalPrice * Discount)
SAY 'The total price is ' TotalPrice
```

Working with Strings in REXX

In REXX, a *string* is a group of characters contained by a variable; the characters appear within single quotation marks (') or within double quotation marks ("). When you have to use a single quotation mark inside a string (as an apostrophe, for example), enclose the string in double quotation marks.

To use double quotation marks inside a string, enclose the string in single quotation marks. The following two examples show how to embed quotation marks inside a string:

```
SAY "The file couldn't be opened"
SAY 'The file "SCRIPT.DOC" has been processed'
```

REXX includes several built-in functions to help you manipulate text strings. You can make one big string from two smaller strings (a process known as *concatenation*); you can translate lowercase strings into uppercase; you can make a smaller string by extracting part of a big string (that is, obtain a substring); you can determine the number of characters in a string; you can find a substring within a larger string; and you can remove leading and trailing spaces from a string. The following examples clarify how these string-manipulation functions work.

To combine two or more smaller strings to form one large string, type two string variable names one after the other. The same procedure applies if one or the other string is enclosed in quotation marks. REXX treats the *abutted* strings as one large string; by default, REXX inserts a blank between the string components. You can use the ¦¦ string-concatenation operator to eliminate the default blank REXX otherwise inserts. This example displays the string *Barry Nance* on-screen. Note the blank automatically inserted by REXX between the *FirstName* and *LastName* strings.

```
/* A sample REXX program */
FirstName = "Barry"
LastName = "Nance"
Name = FirstName LastName
SAY Name
```

The following string-handling example shows how you can override REXX's default insertion of spaces during concatenation of strings. This second example also displays the string *Barry Nance* on-screen—but the program explicitly inserts the space by using a variable named *Blank*. The program uses the ¦¦ operator to force REXX to use the strings exactly as specified, without inserting extra spaces.

```
/* A sample REXX program */
Blank = " "
FirstName = "Barry"
LastName = "Nance"
Name = FirstName ¦¦ Blank ¦¦ LastName
SAY Name
```

TRANSLATE is a REXX function that returns a string value. You use a *function* in REXX almost the same way you use a variable, but the function performs some processing as it takes on a value. In the case of TRANSLATE, you give the TRANSLATE function a string as an argument and TRANSLATE returns a copy of the string with all the characters in the string converted to uppercase. The following example demonstrates how you can ensure that a string contains only uppercase characters. The example converts the string *New York* to *NEW YORK*.

```
/* A sample REXX program */
StateName = 'New York'
StateName = TRANSLATE(StateName)
SAY 'After uppercase conversion, the StateName variable now contains ' StateName
```

SUBSTR is another useful REXX function. SUBSTR returns a portion of a string; you supply three arguments to SUBSTR to tell the function the string from which you want to extract a substring, the starting position of the substring, and the ending position of the substring. The following example extracts the substring *Barry* from the string *Barry Nance* and displays the substring.

```
/* A sample REXX program */
Name = 'Barry Nance'
StartPosition = 1
EndPosition = 5
FirstName = substr(Name, StartPosition, EndPosition)
SAY 'The substring is ' FirstName
```

If you omit the third argument to SUBSTR, the function returns a substring that begins at the starting position and extends through the end of the string.

The LEFT and RIGHT functions operate in a manner similar to SUBSTR. LEFT returns the leftmost portion of a string; RIGHT returns the rightmost portion of a string. You specify the number of characters. The following example assigns *Barry* to the FirstName variable and *Nance* to the LastName variable:

```
/* A sample REXX program */
Name = 'Barry Nance'
FirstName = LEFT(Name, 5)
LastName = RIGHT(Name, 5)
SAY 'First Name is ' FirstName
SAY 'Last Name is ' LastName
```

You can use the LENGTH function when the program needs to know the number of characters in a string. LENGTH requires a single argument: the string whose length you want to determine. The REXX program statement NumberOfChars = LENGTH('New York City'), for example, sets the variable NumberOfChars to a value of 13. Note that spaces (blanks) count as characters.

When you want to know the number of discrete words in a string, use the WORDS function. WORDS requires a single string argument and returns a numeric value. The REXX program statement `SAY WORDS('11711 North College Avenue')` displays the number 4 on-screen.

POS is another useful REXX function when you're dealing with string variables. You supply POS with two arguments: a substring to search for and a string that might contain the substring. If POS finds the substring within the second argument, POS returns the starting position of the substring. POS returns the value 0 (zero) if the string doesn't contain the substring you specify. For example, the REXX program statement `SAY POS('City', 'New York City')` displays the number 10 on-screen. The REXX function LASTPOS is similar to POS, except that LASTPOS returns the location in the string of the last occurrence of the specified substring.

The last string function this chapter discusses—but certainly not the last string function offered by REXX—is STRIP. When you want a copy of a string without leading or trailing spaces, use the STRIP function. STRIP examines its single string argument and returns that argument with leading and trailing spaces removed. The REXX program statement `SAY STRIP('   This string begins and ends with spaces   ')` displays `this string begins and ends with spaces` on-screen.

Reading and Writing Files in REXX

REXX programs can process information in text files on your hard disk in addition to strings you PULL from the keyboard. The LINEIN function requires a single argument consisting of the name of a disk file. LINEIN returns a string that is the next line of text from the file. Executing LINEIN repeatedly reads all the text lines in a file. Suppose that you have a file named PC.TXT whose contents are the following lines of text:

   IBM PS/2 model 57

   IBM PS/2 model 60

   IBM PS/2 model 70

   IBM PS/2 model 90

The first execution of `LINEIN(PC.TXT)` returns the string *IBM PS/2 model 57*. The second execution returns *IBM PS/2 model 60*. The third execution returns the third line of the file, *IBM PS/2 model 70*. The fourth execution of `LINEIN(PC.TXT)` returns the string *IBM PS/2 model 90*.

REXX programs can use the function `LINES` to determine whether there are more lines of text to read from a file. Like `LINEIN`, `LINES` requires a single argument consisting of the name of a disk file. `LINES` returns the numeric value 1 if more unread text lines exist in a file. `LINES` returns 0 if there are no more lines of text to be read. The following example uses the `LINES` and `LINEIN` functions to read every line of text in your CONFIG.SYS file and display the lines on-screen.

```
/* A sample REXX program */
FileName = 'C:\CONFIG.SYS'
DO WHILE LINES(FileName) <> 0
   Line = LINEIN(FileName)
   SAY Line
END
```

The `LINEOUT` function writes string values to a text file you name. Each string value that `LINEOUT` places in the disk file becomes a line of text. `LINEOUT` requires two arguments: the name of the file you want to write to and the string value to be written. If the file does not exist, `LINEOUT` creates a new file for you. If the file exists already, `LINEOUT` inserts your string values as lines of text at the end of the current file. `LINEOUT` returns the numeric value 0 if the write operation is successful. `LINEOUT` returns 1 if something went wrong. If `LINEOUT` returns a value of 1 as the program executes, it almost always means that the disk is full or that the first argument is not a valid OS/2 file name.

The following example copies the contents of your CONFIG.SYS file to a file named CONFIG.SAV:

```
/* A sample REXX program */
FileIn = 'C:\CONFIG.SYS'
FileOut = 'C:\CONFIG.SAV'
DO WHILE LINES(FileIn) <> 0
   Line = LINEIN(FileIn)
   Status = LINEOUT(FileOut, Line)
   IF Status = 1 THEN DO
      SAY 'Copy operation ended in error.'
      LEAVE
   END
END
```

Passing Parameters to REXX Programs

Chapter 18, "Batch-File Programming with OS/2," explained how you can use the variable markers %1 through %9 to retrieve and process individual command-line parameters supplied by someone running a batch-file program. REXX programs can similarly retrieve and process command-line parameters with the ARG statement. You specify with the ARG statement the names of the variables to receive the individual command-line parameters. Suppose that you have a REXX program named PARMTEST.CMD that contains the statement ARG Parm1 Parm2 Parm3 and you run this REXX program by typing **PARMTEST IBM COMPAQ Compudyne** at an OS/2 command-line prompt. The ARG statement stores the string *IBM* in the *Parm1* variable, *COMPAQ* in the *Parm2* variable, and *COMPUDYNE* in the *Parm3* variable. The following REXX program simply displays any command-line parameters supplied to the program:

```
/* A sample REXX program */
ARG CommandLine
SAY CommandLine
```

The ARG statement translates command-line parameters to uppercase before storing the parameters in the variable you specify. You can use PARSE ARG when you want to retain the original lowercase or uppercase values of the command-line parameters. When you need to know whether the person running the REXX program has supplied any parameters at all, you can use the ARG function (which is different and distinct from the ARG statement). The following example uses the ARG function to determine whether command-line parameters were entered and exits if none were used; it uses the ARG statement to specify two variables to hold the command-line parameters:

```
/* A sample REXX program */
IF ARG() = 0 THEN DO
   SAY 'You forgot to enter the command line parameters.'
   EXIT
END
ARG Parm1 Parm2
SAY 'The first parameter is ' Parm1
SAY 'The second parameter is ' Parm2
```

When you need to know the number of parameters supplied to a REXX program, use the following sample REXX statements:

```
/* A sample REXX program */
ARG CommandLine
NumberOfParms = WORDS(CommandLine)
SAY 'You typed ' NumberofParms ' parameters.'
```

Visual REXX Tools

Microsoft sells a Visual Basic for Windows product but doesn't offer Visual Basic for OS/2. (Microsoft almost released such a product. The unfinished Visual Basic for OS/2 project now gathers dust in the back of a file cabinet at Microsoft's headquarters in Redmond, Washington.) Visual Basic for Windows is a popular programming environment for casual programmers. Many businesses also use Visual Basic to write programs without contracting a team of professional programmers.

You'll be interested to know that not one but three visual programming tools exist for OS/2. Each is just as easy to use as Visual Basic for Windows, and each offers features and functions (such as multiple threads) that Visual Basic for Windows cannot provide. All three use REXX, not Basic, as a computer programming-language environment. The products are VisPro REXX, GPF REXX, and VX/REXX. All three are easy-to-use, productive programming environments; all three are relatively inexpensive.

VisPro REXX

A company named HockWare offers two editions of a REXX programming environment for creating Presentation Manager REXX programs: VisPro REXX Bronze and VisPro REXX Gold. The Bronze edition supports most Presentation Manager mechanisms for entering data, including radio buttons, pushbuttons, an assortment of list-box types, value sets, spin buttons, and text-entry areas. The Gold edition adds mechanisms such as containers, notebooks, and sliders. The Gold edition offers a business graphing tool and also supports programmatic access to databases such as DBM (from Extended Services) and DB2/2.

Figure 19.2 shows the VisPro REXX Gold edition's visual design tool. Both the Bronze and the Gold editions use a drag-and-drop programming paradigm. During the design of a program, you drop visual objects such as pushbuttons or text-entry areas onto a work area, called a *canvas*. You indicate which events (button clicks, list box selections, menu choices, and other user interface actions) you'd want your VisproREXX program to respond to by dragging and dropping objects. Each object represents an event that may happen while your program is running. For each such event, you can write REXX statements that execute when the event happens.

When you finish placing Presentation Manager objects and inserting REXX code, VisPro REXX compiles the program into a single executable file. You don't pay royalties to HockWare when you distribute your program.

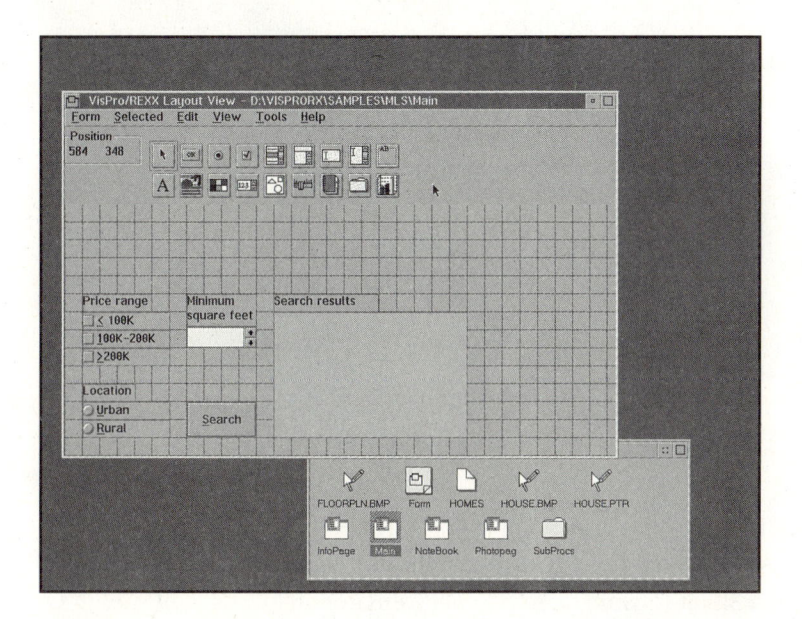

Fig. 19.2
The VisPro REXX Gold program design tool.

GPF REXX

The latest of the REXX visual programming environments, GPF REXX follows the form of the GUI Programming Facility (GPF) company's main product, called simply GPF. Like VisPro REXX Gold, GPF REXX programs can use a wide variety of Presentation Manager objects, including text-entry areas, pushbuttons, radio buttons, list boxes, sliders, spin buttons, notebooks, and containers. GPF REXX is "database-aware," which means that the design tool presents a list of database names it detects as available in either DBM or DB2/2. You choose the database you want your program to work with, if any, and GPF REXX helps you construct a REXX program to view or update that database.

In the GPF REXX visual design tool, shown in figure 19.3, you first concentrate on using drag-and-drop techniques to place your visual objects on the windows you want the program to display. You then open a separate program tool that you use to associate your custom REXX program statements with the objects and windows.

Fig. 19.3
The GPF REXX program design tool.

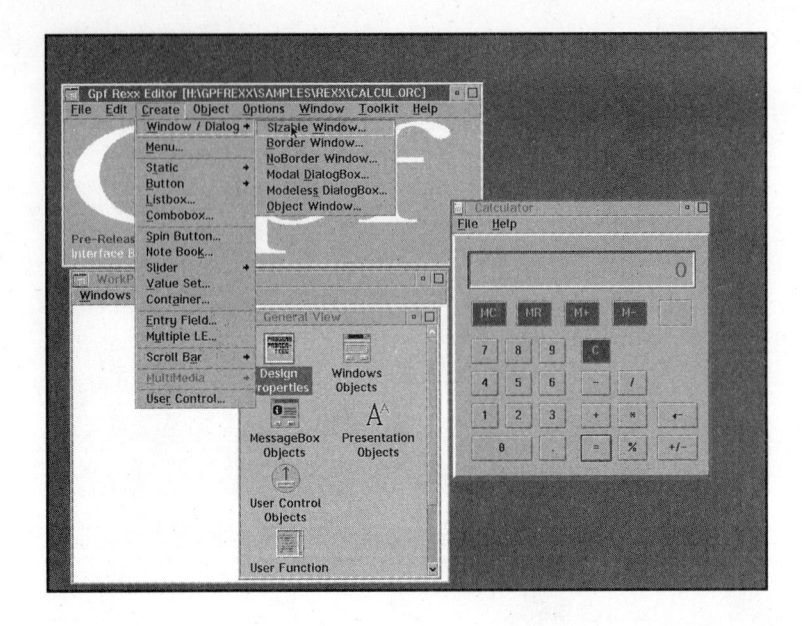

VX/REXX

The Watcom company, best known for its C compiler products (Watcom offers a 32-bit C compiler for the OS/2 environment), sells the VX/REXX visual design tool for producing REXX-based Presentation Manager programs. The VX/REXX design tool, shown in figure 19.4, lets you use drag-and-drop techniques to place Presentation Manager objects on the windows making up your application. You can access DBM and DB2/2 databases with VX/REXX, but the design tool doesn't list the database names and database layouts for you. VX/REXX is easy to program and offers a useful set of Presentation Manager objects for your program to display. These objects include radio buttons, pushbuttons, list-box types, spin buttons, and text-entry areas.

In VX/REXX, you attach the REXX statements right to the Presentation Manager objects you place in the windows by using the VX/REXX text editor or your own (external) text editor. Your REXX statements, object by object and function by function, become individual sections of the program you write. VX/REXX lists these sections in a separate window you can refer to whenever you like.

The VX/REXX manual is an excellent introduction to Presentation Manager programming concepts and a reference for VX/REXX itself.

You can write and distribute VX/REXX programs without royalty payment to Watcom. VX/REXX emits executable (EXE) files.

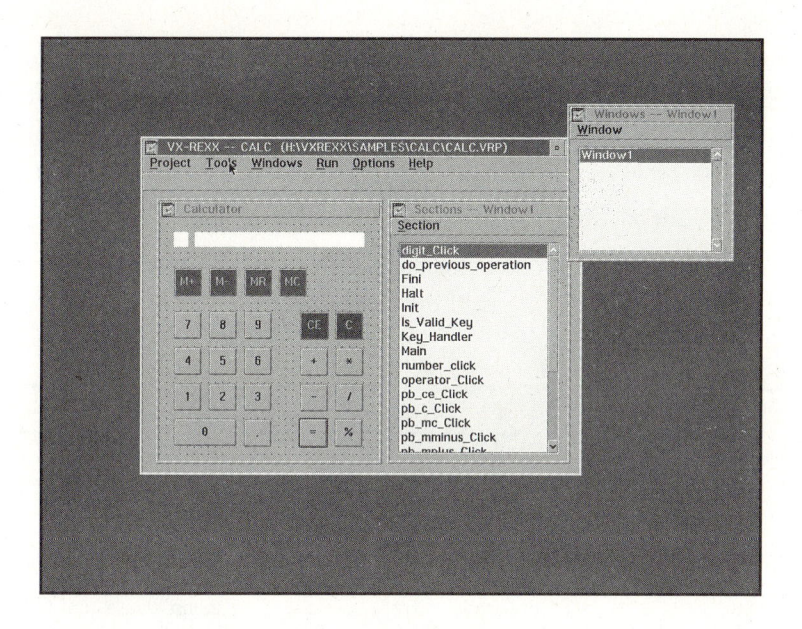

Fig. 19.4
The VX/REXX program design tool.

Testing REXX Programs

OS/2 gives you three tools to help you develop your REXX programs. Two of the tools are themselves computer programs you can use to help better understand REXX: PMREXX and REXXTRY. The third tool is a trace facility you can use in your REXX programs.

PMREXX is a Presentation Manager program that runs REXX programs in a Presentation Manager window on the OS/2 desktop. When you use PMREXX, the information displayed by the REXX program appears in a scrollable Presentation Manager window. You can use the vertical scroll bar at the right side of the window to browse back through previously displayed output. PMREXX allows you to select a font in which the output appears, and you can perform cut, copy, and paste operations on the information displayed in the PMREXX window. You invoke PMREXX by opening an OS/2 full-screen command-line prompt and typing **PMREXX** followed by the name of the REXX program and any command-line parameters the REXX program needs. The following example runs the REXX program REXXTEST.CMD in a Presentation Manager window; REXXTEST.CMD has two command-line parameters (Parm1 and Parm2) to process:

PMREXX REXXTEST.CMD Parm1 Parm2

Optionally, you can start PMREXX with a /TRACE parameter that turns on interactive tracing of the REXX program. You learn about tracing later in this section. To start PMREXX in TRACE mode, type **/T** before typing the name of the REXX program (for example, type **PMREXX /T REXXTEST.CMD Parm1 Parm2**).

When you run a REXX program inside PMREXX, you can use PMREXX's menus to control the execution of the program. The following table shows the PMREXX menu options:

Menu Choice	Options
File	Save, Save As, and Exit
Edit	Copy, Paste, Clear window display, and Select All lines
Options	Restart the process, Interactive Trace, and Set font
Actions	Halt procedure, Trace next clause, Redo last clause, and Set Trace off
Help	Help index, General help, Keys help, and Using help

REXXTRY is actually a REXX program. As with other REXX programs, you can run REXXTRY in an OS/2 full-screen session, an OS/2 windowed session, or inside PMREXX. REXXTRY lets you try out different REXX statements and observe the results. You interactively enter REXX statements at the REXXTRY prompt and REXXTRY executes your statements, one by one. You can quickly experiment with REXX and become familiar with REXX by running REXXTRY inside the friendly PMREXX environment.

The REXX TRACE facility allows you to watch how REXX evaluates expressions. While a REXX program executes, TRACE displays information that explains how REXX is interpreting the program. You can insert TRACE statements in a program in one of three formats: TRACE ?, TRACE <number>, or TRACE <action>. Issuing a TRACE ? statement toggles tracing off or on. Using TRACE <number> (TRACE 5, for example) causes REXX to skip over the specified number of debugging pauses that TRACE would normally do. The TRACE <action> format lets you indicate what you want TRACE to monitor. The following table lists the actions you can use in the TRACE <action> statement:

Action	What REXX Displays
All	All statements before execution
Commands	Each OS/2 command or utility before execution
Error	OS/2 commands with non-zero return codes
Failure	OS/2 commands that fail (same as the Normal option)
Intermediates	Intermediate results during evaluation of expressions
Labels	Labels encountered during execution
Normal	OS/2 commands that fail (default action)
Off	Nothing; tracing is turned off
Results	All statements before execution; REXX displays final results of each expression evaluation

Chapter Summary

When you want your computer to process information in a way existing applications do not provide for, you can use REXX to "do it yourself." REXX is simple to use; a few REXX program statements can do quite a bit of work. Computer programming is generally tedious and error prone; have patience if you expect to write working, useful software. However, REXX lets you develop programs quickly and productively. This chapter has shown you the REXX building blocks and visual programming tools you can use to create your own software.

Chapter 20
Using OS/2 Utilities

OS/2 includes several utility programs that help you customize, manage, and maneuver the OS/2 Workplace Shell, files, directories, programs, and other features while you work in the operating system. Some of these utilities aid in gathering information, others help correct system problems, and each is invaluable if used correctly.

IBM recommends that you use some of these utilities only with the help of a technical coordinator or a service representative. Before you type the utility command on the command line, be sure of your purpose for using the utilities and of the outcome you require.

This chapter discusses in detail the utilities listed in table 20.1. The sections that follow provide information about the purpose of each utility and instructions and examples for its use. In addition, specific warnings for several of the utilities are included. To make finding specific utilities easier, the utilities are organized alphabetically.

Table 20.1 OS/2 Utilities

OS/2 Utility	Description
BOOT	Enables you to switch between the DOS and OS/2 operating systems that are on the same hard disk
EAUTIL	Enables you to split (save) and join extended attributes from a data file to a hold file
FDISKPM	Enables you to create or delete a primary partition or a logical drive in an extended partition
MAKEINI	Re-creates the OS2.INI startup file and the OS2SYS.INI system file in your OS/2 operating system

(continues)

Table 20.1 Continued

OS/2 Utility	Description
PATCH	Enables you to apply software repairs and IBM-supplied patches
PMCHKDSK	Reads and analyzes files and directories, determines file system type, and produces a disk status report
PSTAT	Displays information about current processes and threads, system semaphores, shared memory for each process, and dynamic-link libraries
SETBOOT	Enables you to set time-out value, mode, and system startup index of Boot Manager
SORT	Sorts data from standard input by number or letter
SYSLEVEL	Displays the operating system name, version, ID, and current corrective service level
UNDELETE	Restores a file you recently erased
UNPACK	Restores compressed files on the OS/2 floppy to a form you can use
VIEW	Looks up a topic in an on-line help document

RETURN CODES are messages that some utilities display to signal the successful completion of a task, an error, message, or the reason for the termination of a task. A complete list of Return Codes for the utilities that follow appears at the end of this chapter.

Using BOOT

The BOOT utility enables you to switch between DOS and OS/2 when they are on the same hard drive. To use this utility, you must have installed OS/2 with the dual boot option. When you install Dual Boot, you add OS/2 to the same partition in which DOS resides. Installing OS/2 in this manner prevents you from operating DOS and OS/2 at the same time; however, you can switch between the two operating systems by using the BOOT command.

The following list explains the requirements and limitations of Dual Boot:

- You must have DOS version 3.2 or higher installed on your hard disk (drive C). For greater compatibility with OS/2, however, using DOS version 3.3 or greater is recommended.

- Your primary partition must be large enough to accommodate both the DOS and OS/2 operating systems.

- DOS uses the File Allocation Table (FAT) system only. Because OS/2 and DOS exist on the same partition, you cannot use the High Performance File System (HPFS) with the Dual Boot feature.

- If you formatted drive C during the OS/2 installation, you cannot use the BOOT command.

Instructions

You can run the BOOT utility in one of three ways: from an OS/2 command prompt, a DOS command prompt window under OS/2, or from DOS. To run the BOOT command, you first must activate the appropriate command prompt.

When you are using the OS/2 operating system, you access the OS/2 command prompt by following these steps:

1. Open the OS/2 System folder in Presentation Manager.

2. From the System folder, open the Command Prompts folder.

3. Open the OS/2 Window or the OS/2 Full Screen to access the command prompt [C:\].

If you are using the OS/2 operating system and want to access the DOS command prompt, follow these steps:

1. Open the OS/2 System folder in Presentation Manager.

2. Open the Command Prompts folder.

3. Choose either the DOS window or DOS Full Screen to access the command prompt C:\.

At the OS/2 command prompt, type the following, and then press Enter:

BOOT /DOS

OS/2 responds with the following message:

```
SYS1714: Warning! Make sure all your programs have completed or
data will be lost when the system is restarted.
You requested to start DOS from drive C:
Your system will be reset. Do you want to continue (Y/N)?
```

If you want your system to reboot to DOS, respond with Y. If you respond N, OS/2 remains the operating system.

When you are in the DOS operating system and want to switch to the OS/2 operating system, follow these steps:

1. To change from the DOS command prompt C:\> to the OS/2 directory, type the following and then press Enter:

    CD\OS2

2. To boot the OS/2 operating system, type the following and then press Enter:

    BOOT /OS2

    (Alternatively, you can combine the preceding two steps and type **OS2\BOOT /OS2**.)

    The system displays a warning similar to the warning displayed when you switch from the OS/2 operating system to DOS.

3. If you want your system to reboot to OS/2, press Y. If you want to cancel the operation, press N. DOS remains the operating system.

> **Tip**
>
> You can create a batch file, which you can use in DOS, to change the operating system to OS/2. Type the following in a file named OS2.BAT:
>
> **C:\OS2\BOOT /OS2**
>
> In addition, you can create a DOS or CMD batch file to use in OS/2 by typing the following in a file named DOS.BAT or DOS.CMD:
>
> **C:\OS2\BOOT /DOS**

Warnings

Before using the BOOT utility, be sure that you have completed all system operations and that you have stopped all programs; if you don't, you will lose data.

Return Codes

BOOT displays a return code of 0 for normal completion and an error message if a problem with the command occurs.

Using EAUTIL

The EAUTIL command enables you to *split*, or cut, extended attributes from a data file and save these attributes to a hold file, a file that contains the split attributes until you need them. You also can rejoin the split attributes to the original file or to another file.

An *extended attribute* is specific information attached by an application to a file or directory. Extended attributes describe that file or directory to another application, to the operating system, or to the file system program that manages the application. Some applications or file systems may not recognize or process extended attributes from another application. When this situation occurs, you can use the EAUTIL command to split the attributes from the file and save them in a hold file to prevent the attributes from being erased. The EAUTIL command also enables you to join those same attributes from the hold file to the file or directory.

Instructions
The syntax of the EAUTIL command is shown in the following:

> **EAUTIL datafile holdfile** /S /R /J /O /M /P

datafile specifies the name of the file that contains the extended attributes to be split.

holdfile specifies the name of the file that will hold the extended attributes.

/S splits the extended attributes from the data file and places the attributes in the hold file.

/R replaces the extended attributes in a hold file with new attributes you assign.

/J joins the extended attributes from the hold file to the data file.

/O overwrites extended attributes in the data file with the attributes in the hold file.

/M merges the extended attributes in the hold file into the attributes in the data file.

/P preserves extended attributes in the data file after a split or in a hold file after a join.

For Related Information
- "Introducing Presentation Manager," p. 234
- "Beginning the Command Line Interface," p. 303
- "Learning Batch File Program Basics," p. 448

Examples

To place extended attributes from a data file named MYFILES.TXT into a hold file named ATTRIBUT.EAU, use the following:

EAUTIL MYFILES.TXT ATTRIBUT.EAU /S

To join the extended attributes in the hold file ATTRIBUT.EAU with the data file MYFILES.TXT, use the following:

EAUTIL MYFILES.TXT ATTRIBUT.EAU /J

To replace the extended attributes in the hold file ATTRIBUT.EAU with attributes from a data file named MYNEWFIL.TXT, use the following:

EAUTIL MYNEWFIL.TXT ATTRIBUT.EAU /R /S

To merge the extended attributes in the hold file ATTRIBUT.EAU with attributes in a data file named MYFILES.TXT, use the following:

EAUTIL MYFILES.TXT ATTRIBUT.EAU /M /J

Warnings

Joining, merging, replacing, or overwriting extended attributes may create problems in your files. Applications attach their own unique extended attributes to files; if the files return to the application with the wrong attributes or with no attributes, the application may no longer be able to read or process the file.

Return Codes:

 0 Normal completion
 1 File not found
 2 Ended due to error

Using FDISKPM

FDISKPM enables you to create or delete a primary partition or a logical drive in an extended partition. FDISKPM is similar to FDISK except that you perform FDISKPM from the Presentation Manager; you use FDISKPM in OS/2 only. In addition, the presentation manager presents FDISKPM with menus and displays, which help you set up your hard disks. Help is also available from within FDISKPM.

Using FDISKPM 495

The Fixed Disk Utility window displays Partition Information about your present setup (see fig. 20.1). The information includes the number of partitions and an icon for each partition or logical drive within an extended partition. In addition, the window includes the following:

Element	Description
Name	The assigned name displayed on the Boot Manager menu
Status	Installable (a file system that uses a cache for quick access to large amounts of information), bootable (the partition is displayed on the Boot Manager partition), startable (the system restarts to this partition), or none of the above
Access	Accessible (the partition is available for use) and whether partition is primary or a logical drive within the extended partition
File System Type	FAT, HPFS, Unformatted, or Free Space
MBytes	Size in megabytes of the partition or free space

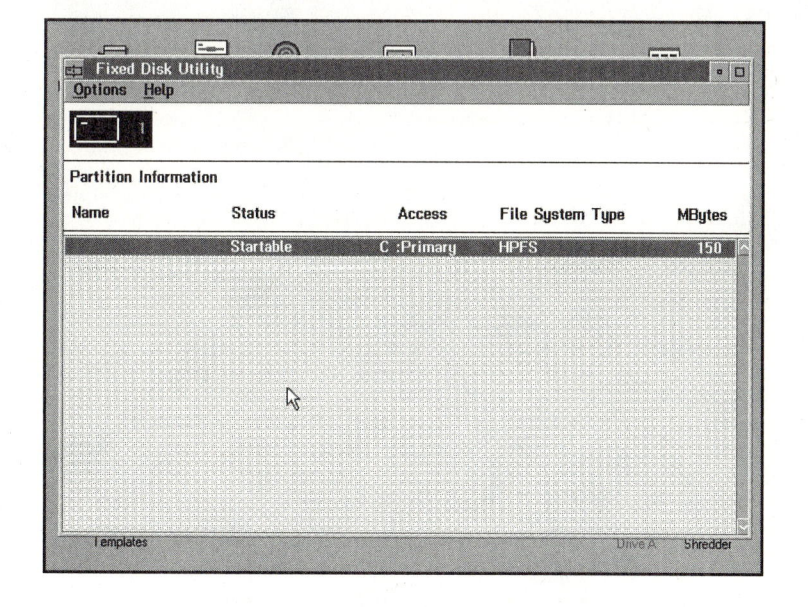

Fig. 20.1
The Fixed Disk Utility window showing partition information.

Two menu items are available: Options and Help. Figure 20.2 illustrates the Options menu. Only three of the commands from the menu are available to you at this point: Delete Partition, Set Installable, and Exit.

Fig. 20.2
The Options menu in the Fixed Disk Utility window.

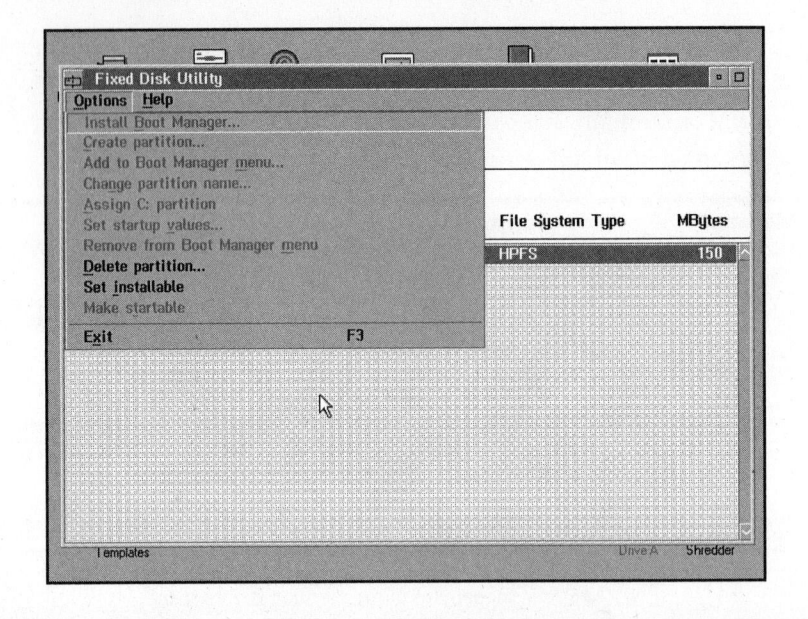

[Screenshot of Fixed Disk Utility window showing Options menu expanded with items: Install Boot Manager..., Create partition..., Add to Boot Manager menu..., Change partition name..., Assign C: partition, Set startup values..., Remove from Boot Manager menu, Delete partition..., Set installable, Make startable, Exit F3]

Table 20.2 Options and Help Menu Commands

Command	Function
Options Menu	
Install **B**oot Manager...	Installs the Boot Manager partition
Create partition...	Creates a primary partition or a logical drive
Add to Boot Manager **m**enu...	Adds a partition to Boot Manager
Cha**n**ge partition name...	Adds or changes an optional name to the partition
Assign partition	Assigns the accessibility of primary partitions
Set startup **v**alues...	Sets startup values like a default partition, selection time, or mode for the Boot Manager
Remove from Boot Manager **m**enu	Removes a partition from Boot Manager
Delete partition...	Deletes a primary partition or logical drive
Set **i**nstallable	Sets a primary partition as installable
Make s**t**artable	Specifies a primary partition as startable
E**x**it	Exits FDISKPM
Help Menu Help **i**ndex	Accesses information about FDISKPM window and descriptions within the window

Command	Function
General help	Provides access to OS/2 General help, search, and more
Using help	Explains how to use Help feature
Keys help	Uses the keyboard instead of the mouse
Product information	Provides information about FDISKPM utility

Instructions

The Boot Manager enables you to create up to four primary partitions on the hard disk. A *primary partition* cannot be shared, and only one primary partition can be active at one time. You can create an extended partition as one of the four primary partitions. You then can divide this partition into *logical drives*, which can be shared and can hold an operating system or data files.

When creating a partition, the Fixed Disk Utility prompts you to choose the type of partition (primary or extended with logical drives) and specify an optional name. You also are prompted to indicate whether the partition will be bootable, the type of files used with the partition (FAT or HPFS), the partition's accessibility, and so on.

You can use the FDISKPM utility in OS/2 only, at a command prompt. To access the OS/2 command prompt and run the FDISKPM utility from the command prompt, type the following and press Enter:

FDISKPM

The Fixed Disk Utility displays, and you may now set up partitions.

Warnings

If you have only one partition and delete that partition, you no longer have an operating system.

If you modify any partition, you delete its contents. Be sure to make back-up files before using the FDISKPM utility.

Read Hard Disk Information (found in your OS/2 Installation book or in the Command Reference folder) before you operate FDISKPM. In addition, be sure that you know what results you want from this utility and that you know exactly how to get them.

Using MAKEINI (OS/2 Only)

For Related Information
- "Adding a Hard Disk," p. 176
- "Understanding Disk Partitions and Disks," p. 43

The MAKEINI utility program re-creates the OS2.INI startup file and the OS2SYS.INI system file in your OS/2 operating system. The OS2.INI startup file contains system settings such as application defaults, display options, and file options. The OS2SYS.INI system file contains font and printer driver information. If either the system or startup file is corrupted, OS/2 cannot start. If you receive a message stating the OS2.INI file is corrupted, re-create both the OS2.INI and the OS2SYS.INI. Use the MAKEINI program from the command prompt to re-create the OS2.INI and the OS2SYS.INI files.

Instructions

Do not use the MAKEINI utility unless you receive a message from OS/2 that the system or user INI file is corrupted.

To re-create a new INI file, use the following syntax:

MAKEINI user system

user is the OS2.INI user file.

system is the OS2SYS.INI system file.

Example

You must first erase the old system and user files before re-creating the new ones. To create new user and system INI files, follow these steps:

1. Insert the Installation disk and reboot your system.

2. When the logo screen appears, remove the Installation disk and insert disk 1 into drive A. Press Enter.

3. When the Welcome screen appears, press Esc.

4. Change to drive C, by typing the following:

    C:

5. Change to the OS2 subdirectory by entering the following:

    CD \OS2

6. To erase the current, corrupted OS2.INI user file, type the following:

    ERASE OS2.INI

7. To erase the current OS2SYS.INI system file, enter the following:

    ERASE OS2SYS.INI

8. To re-create the new user INI file, enter the following:

    MAKEINI OS2.INI INI.RC

9. To re-create the new system INI file, enter the following:

    MAKEINI OS2SYS.INI INISYS.RC

10. Remove the floppy disk from drive A and reboot the computer.

This procedure re-creates a new user INI file and a new system ININ file on your hard drive, replacing the corrupted INI file.

Warnings

Use this command only if you receive an error message that says your OS2.INI or OS2SYS.INI file is corrupt, or if OS/2 fails to boot. The system INI and user INI files hold vital information that OS/2 needs to run on your computer.

Using PATCH

The PATCH utility enables you to apply software repairs and IBM-supplied patches. A *patch* is a correction or adjustment to the operating system files. Use this utility only if you completely understand the patch process and purpose. Two methods of applying patches to the OS/2 operating system exist: automatically and manually.

PATCH guides you through the process of changing the operating system's software with prompts. Selecting the /A option automatically applies a patch shipped by IBM. PATCH obtains the needed information from the patch information file supplied by IBM. An IBM-supplied patch verifies the problem and makes corrections to the codes. A non-IBM-supplied patch may not offer verification.

If you manually apply a patch, you must enter the command and supply an offset to direct the patch location. After you establish the location, you must enter the patch contents. You must enter both the contents and the offset in hexadecimal notations.

After you supply a hexadecimal offset, the operating system displays the 16 bytes at that offset. You can make changes to each byte by typing one or two hexadecimal digits. If you press the space bar, the byte remains unchanged. If you move your cursor past the 16th byte, the operating system displays the next 16 bytes. After you make your changes, press Enter.

Pressing Enter saves the patch information into memory, and the following message appears:

```
Do you want to continue patching filename (Y/N)?
```

If you answer Y, PATCH asks for an offset. When you have completed all patches, OS/2 displays the patches on-screen and asks for verification. If you respond with Y, the patches are written to disk in the same order in which you entered them.

Instructions

PATCH uses the following syntax:

PATCH path filename.ext /A

path is the location of the file to be patched.

filename.ext is the file to be patched; without /A, interactive mode is assumed.

/A is the option to apply the patch automatically.

Examples

To use the automatic mode from a PATCH information file named MYPATCH.TST that resembles

```
123456
```

enter the following into a patch file called MYFIX.FIL:

FILE MYPATCH.TST

VER 0 313233

CHA 0 343536

To apply the patch from the OS/2 command prompt, enter the following:

PATCH MYFIX.FIL /A

Warning

Use PATCH only if you understand the need for a patch, know how to make a patch, and understand the effect the patch has on the operating system. If you apply the wrong patch or apply the patch to the wrong offset, you can corrupt the operating system.

Return Code

PATCH issues a return code of 0 for normal completion.

Using PMCHKDSK

PMCHKDSK is similar to the CHKDSK utility, but PMCHKDSK works from the Presentation Manager. You can use the PMCHKDSK utility only in OS/2; the utility does not work from DOS. PMCHKDSK analyzes files and directories, determines file system type, and produces a disk status report. You can apply PMCHKDSK to the hard disk or a floppy disk.

Run PMCHKDSK to check for errors. If you choose to write corrections to disk when prompted by a dialog box, PMCHKDSK fixes errors when it finds them. PMCHKDSK also detects lost clusters on your disk. A *lost cluster* is a part of a file that the system did not save completely because of a power interruption. Lost clusters take up disk space. By choosing to write corrections to disk, PMCHKDSK automatically converts and deletes lost clusters.

> **Note**
>
> PMCHKDSK cannot write corrections to the hard disk if the hard disk currently has open files or separate partitions.

Instructions

To run PMCHKDSK from the OS/2 command prompt, follow these steps:

1. From the OS/2 command prompt, type the following and press Enter:

   PMCHKDSK

502 Chapter 20—Using OS/2 Utilities

2. The Check Disk dialog box appears, displaying the following message:

   ```
   Write corrections to disk
   ```

3. You can choose to check the disk without writing corrections to disk, check the disk and write corrections to disk, or cancel the process. To select Check Disk without writing corrections, press Alt-C or select the Check command button. To select Check Disk and write corrections to disk, press Alt-W and Alt-C. To cancel the process, press Esc.

   If you choose to check the disk but not write corrections to the disk, PMCHKDSK displays the warning message shown in figure 20.3 and does not correct the errors.

Fig. 20.3
The Check Disk - Results window with a warning message displayed.

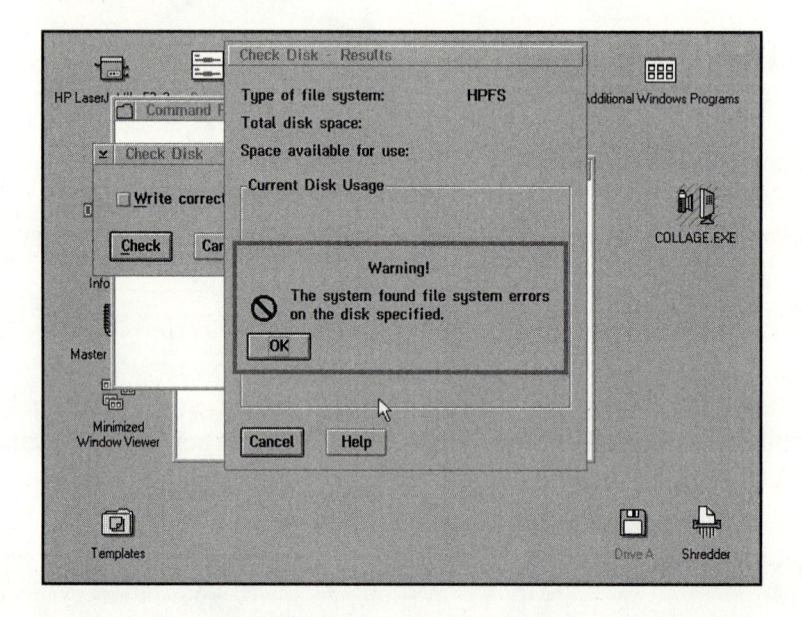

If you proceed with the process, the Check Disk - Results window appears (see fig. 20.4). The results include the following:

- *Type of file system.* This information indicates whether the FAT or HPFS file system is being used.

- *Total disk space.* This information informs you of the total number of bytes on the floppy or hard disk.

- *Space available for use.* This information indicates the number of bytes available for storage.

- *Current disk usage.* A color-coded pie chart displays how the disk is used by directories, files, unusable areas, extended attributes, and reserved space

- *Cancel.* Choose this option when you want to exit the window.

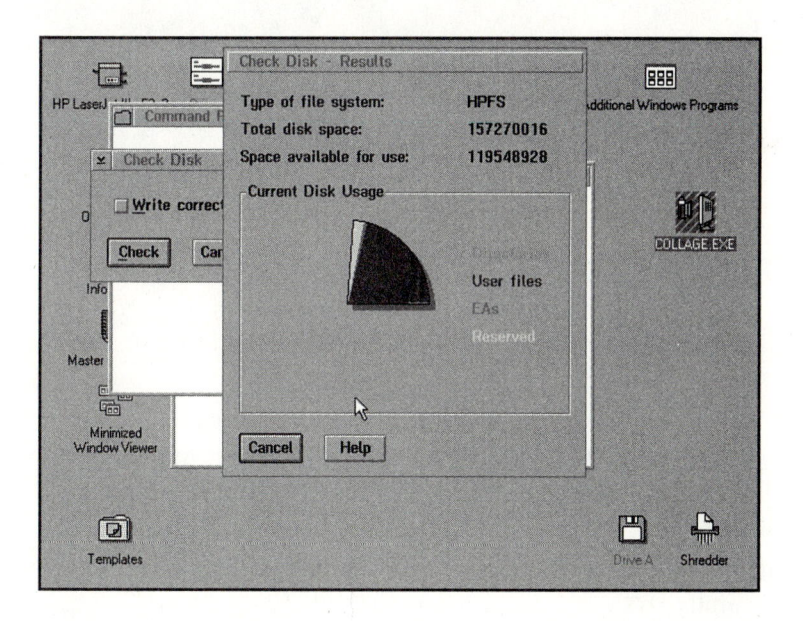

Fig. 20.4
The PMCHKDSK results.

When you finish viewing the disk information, choose Cancel. OS/2 returns to the Check Disk window. Choose Cancel from this window to return to the OS/2 command prompt.

Warning

To receive accurate information about your disk, use PMCHKDSK only when the hard disk is not in use. If the disk is in use, a warning appears when you run PMCHKDSK (see fig. 20.5). Choose OK to cancel the process.

Fig. 20.5
PMCHKDSK warning that the command cannot be completed.

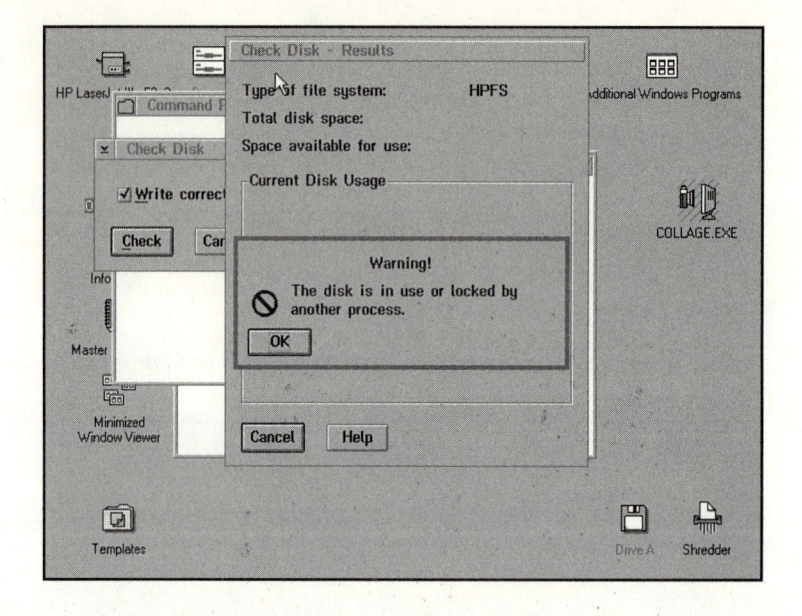

Using PSTAT (OS/2 Only)

For Related Information
- "Preparing for Trouble," p. 201

PSTAT displays information about current processes and threads, system semaphores (the method of transferring information betwen system components and programs API—Application Program Interface), shared memory for each process, and dynamic link libraries. Use PSTAT to help you determine which threads are running in the system, their current status, and their current priorities. PSTAT analyzes why a thread may be blocked or running slowly. In addition, PSTAT displays a process ID that you can use with the TRACE utility. PSTAT can be used only in OS/2.

Instructions

The PSTAT utility uses the following syntax:

   path PSTAT /C /S /L /M /P:pid

path specifies the location of the command

/C shows the current process and thread-related information. Use this parameter to display the process ID, parent process ID, session ID, and the process name for each process. **/C** also displays the thread ID, thread state, thread priority, and block ID for each thread.

/S shows the system-semaphore information on each thread. Use this parameter to display the process module name, process ID, session ID, index number, number of references, number of requests, flag (pace holder to indicate a procedure), and the name of the system semaphore for each thread.

/L shows the dynamic link libraries for each process. Use this parameter to display the process module name, process ID, session ID, and library list for each process.

/M shows shared information for each process. Use this parameter to display the handle (a number that identifies each standard device), selector (identifies the system level address), number of references, and the name of the shared memory for each process.

/P:pid shows information related to the ID of the specified process. Use this parameter to display the process ID, parent process ID, session ID, process module name, dynamic link libraries, and shared memory data for the ID of the specified process. */P:pid* also shows the thread ID, thread priority, thread status, block ID, and semaphore information for each thread associated with the process.

Examples

To display the current process and thread-related information, type the following and press Enter:

PSTAT /C

To display dynamic link libraries for the directory DATAFILE, type the following and press Enter after each line:

CD\DATAFILE

PSTAT /L

To display information related to the process ID 0004, type the following and press Enter:

PSTAT /P:4

Return Codes

Return codes are messages displayed at the completion of some OS/2 commands. A return code signals the normal completion of a task, error messages, or the reason for the end of the task. The most common return code for a command is 0, signifying normal completion. Table 20.3 provides a list of the commands that issue return codes and the meaning of those codes. Many commands that do not issue a return code may issue an error message describing a problem or error in completing the command.

Table 20.3 Return Codes

Command	Return Code	Description
ATTRIB	0	Normal completion
BACKUP	0	Normal completion
	1	No files found to back up
	2	Some files or directories not processed because of file errors
	3	Ended by user
	4	Ended because of error
	5	Not defined
	6	BACKUP was unable to process the FORMAT command
BOOT	0	Normal completion (displays error messages if command is not successfully completed)
CHKDSK	0	Normal completion
	1, 2, 5	Not defined
	3	Ended by user
	4	Ended due to error
	6	CHKDSK was unable to execute file system's CHKDSK program
COMP	0	Normal completion
	1	No files were found to compare
	2	Some files or directories were not processed because of file errors
	3	Ended by user
	4	Ended because of error
	5	Files did not compare OK

Return Codes

Command	Return Code	Description
DISKCOMP	0	Normal completion (displays error messages if command is not successfully completed)
DISKCOPY	0	Normal completion (displays error messages if command is not successfully completed)
EAUTIL	0	Normal completion
	1	File not found
	4	Ended due to error
FDISK	0	Normal completion (displays error messages if command is not successfully completed)
FIND	0	Normal completion
FORMAT	0	Normal completion
	3	Ended by user
	4	Ended due to error
	5	Ended due to NO response when user was prompted to format a hard disk
	6	FORMAT was unable to process another file system's format program
	7	Volume not supported by another file system's format program
GRAFTABL	0	No previously loaded character table exists and a code page is now resident
	1	A previously loaded character table exists; if new table was requested, it replaces previous table at its original location.
	2	No previously loaded character table exists; no new table is loaded
	3	Incorrect parameter
	4	Incorrect DOS version
LABEL	0	Normal completion
MORE	0	Normal completion
PATCH	0	Normal completion
RECOVER	0	Normal completion

(continues)

Table 20.3 Continued

Command	Return Code	Description
	1, 2	Undefined
	3	Ended by user
	4	Ended due to error
	5	Unable to read or write to one of the file allocation tables
	6	Unable to execute another file system's recover program
REPLACE	0	Normal completion
	1	No files were found to replace
	2	Some files not replaced due to file errors
	4	Ended due to error
RESTORE	0	Normal completion
	1	No files were found to restore
	2	Some files were not processed due to file errors
	3	Ended by user
	4	Ended due to error
SORT	0	Normal completion
TREE	0	Normal completion
UNPACK	0	Normal completion
	1	No files were found to unpack or copy
	2	Some files or directories were not unpacked or copied due to file errors
	3	Ended by user
	4	Ended due to error
XCOPY	0	Normal completion
	1	No files were found to xcopy

Command	Return Code	Description
	2	Some files or directories were not copied due to file or directory errors
	3	Ended by user
	4	Ended due to error

Using SETBOOT

SETBOOT helps you set up the Boot Manager. The parameters in the following section enable you to take full advantage of Boot Manager, which governs the startup of multiple operating systems. You can install the Boot Manager feature by using the FDISK utility program during installation. You can use the SETBOOT command only in OS/2.

SETBOOT is a utility that enables you to set the time-out value, the mode, and the system startup index of Boot Manager.

Instructions

SETBOOT uses the following syntax:

SETBOOT /T:x /T:NO /M:m /Q /B /X:s /N:name

/T:x sets the time-out value of the menu timer in Boot Manager; *x* represents the time in seconds.

/T:NO disables the menu timer so that the Boot Manager menu remains on-screen until you make a selection.

/M:m sets the mode for the Boot Manager menu. *m*=n is normal mode, which displays only the partitions that are selectable; *m*=a sets advanced mode, which displays additional information.

/Q queries the current startup environment.

/B performs a shutdown of the system and then restarts it.

/X:x sets the system startup index. *x*=0 sets the startup index to attended mode; *x*=3 sets the startup index to unattended mode.

/N:name sets the partition or logical drive by the name and its corresponding index value; *N*=0 assigns the specified name as the default operating system; *N*=1 to 3 specifies the name to be started when the corresponding index is started.

Examples

To set the Boot Manager selection timer to 15 seconds, use the following:

SETBOOT /T:15

To set the normal mode for the Boot Manager menu, use the following:

SETBOOT /M:n

To set the startup index to put the Boot Manager in attended mode, use the following:

SETBOOT /X:0

> **Caution**
>
> If you are unsure about using the SETBOOT command, consult your technical coordinator or a service representative before you use the command. You could cause damage to the operating system if you use SETBOOT incorrectly.

Using SORT

SORT reads and sorts data from standard input. You can sort data by letter or by number, and SORT rearranges the lines of text according to your instructions. For instance, you can sort the names in a mailing list in alphabetical order, or you can sort the Zip codes in a numerical sequence.

> **Note**
>
> The input and output files must have different names. The sorted version will not replace the original file.

Files are sorted according to the alphabet of the country you specify with the COUNTRY command. Upper- and lowercase letters are equivalent, and numerals precede letters.

Instructions
SORT uses the following syntax:

SORT <input-file >output-file /R /+n

<input-file is the name of the file to be sorted.

>output-file is the name of the file receiving the sorted data.

/R reverses the alphabetical sort (from Z to A).

/+n represents the column number where the sort starts. If you do not specify the parameter, the sort begins with column 1.

Examples
To sort alphabetically a file named MAILING and write the output to the file AMAIL, use the following:

SORT <MAILING >AMAIL

To sort a data file beginning in column 3 and send the output to the screen, use the following:

SORT /+3 <MAILING

To sort a mailing list in ADDRESS.DAT, which lists your customers' names in the first 20 columns, street addresses in the next 30 columns, and cities in the next 10 columns, and put the sorted output in SORTED.DAT, use any of the following:

To sort by customer name:

SORT <ADDRESS.DAT >SORTED.DAT

To sort ADDRESS.DAT by street address, which begins in column 21:

SORT <ADDRESS.DAT >SORTED.DAT /+21

To sort ADDRESS.DAT in reverse order by city, which begins in column 51:

SORT <ADDRESS.DAT >SORTED.DAT /+51 /R

Return Code
SORT issues a return code of 0 for normal completion.

Warnings

Large data files may take a few minutes to process.

The maximum file size you can sort is 63KB.

Using SYSLEVEL

SYSLEVEL displays the operating system name, version number, component ID, current corrective service level, and the prior corrective service level. You should run the SYSLEVEL utility before you install the PATCH utility; the SYSLEVEL information may prove helpful. SYSLEVEL is an OS/2-only command.

Instructions

SYSLEVEL uses the following syntax:

    SYSLEVEL

To access the OS/2 command prompt and run the SYSLEVEL utility from the OS/2 command prompt, type the following:

    SYSLEVEL

The message `Please wait...` appears. Then SYSLEVEL displays the current corrective service level.

Example

After SYSLEVEL determines the corrective service level, a message similar to the following appears on-screen:

```
C:\OS2\INSTALL\SYSLEVEL.OS2
IBM OS/2 Base Operating System
Version 2.10            Component ID 562107701
Type 0
Current CSD level:      XR02010
Prior CSD level:        XR02010
```

The explanation for each line is as follows:

`C:\OS2\INSTALL\SYSLEVEL.GRE` is the subdirectory and file containing the information.

`IBM OS/2 Base Operating System` is the system name.

`Version 2.10.1  Component ID 562107701` is the version number and the Component ID of the system.

```
Current CSD level:      XR02010 is the current corrective service level.

Prior CSD level:        XR02010 is the prior corrective service level.
```

Using UNDELETE

UNDELETE restores a file you recently erased. When you delete a file, OS/2 moves the file to a hidden area on your hard disk. If you act quickly, you can retrieve the file by using UNDELETE. If the file is recoverable, UNDELETE restores it to its original path.

Before you use the UNDELETE command, you must use the DELDIR environment available in CONFIG.SYS to define the path and maximum size of directories used to store deleted files, as shown in the following:

SET DELDIR= drive:\path, maxsize; drive 2:\path, maxsize

Path and maximum size values are separated by a comma; logical drive names are separated by a semicolon. When DEL or ERASE deletes a file, that file moves to the directory specified in the DELDIR statement for that logical drive. If you undelete a file that has the same name as another file, UNDELETE warns you and enables you to change the name.

The area for deleted files is limited in size. When this area fills up, the program discards the oldest files to make room for new files. Files that are available for UNDELETE are reported as used space on the disk.

Instructions

UNDELETE uses the following syntax:

UNDELETE dir\files /A /F /S /L

dir is the directory that you want to back up, and **files** specifies the files you want to back up. If you don't specify dir or files, UNDELETE looks for all deleted files in the current directory.

/A restores every deleted file in the directory.

/F tells UNDELETE to erase files completely so that no one can recover them.

/L lists the files that can be restored but does not actually restore these files.

/S restores every deleted file in a directory and its subdirectories.

Chapter 20—Using OS/2 Utilities

Examples

To display the names of the current directory's deleted files that can be restored, use the following:

> **UNDELETE /L**

To recover all deleted files without being prompted for confirmation on each file, use the following:

> **UNDELETE /A**

To erase your performance appraisal in C:\PERSONAL\REVIEW.DOC so that no one can recover it, use the following:

> **UNDELETE C:\PERSONAL\REVIEW.DOC /F**

Using UNPACK

Many of the files on the OS/2 distribution floppy disk are compressed so that they take up less room and require fewer floppy disks. The installation program automatically unpacks compressed files. If you accidentally lose one of OS/2's files and know which disk contains the file, however, you can use UNPACK to unpack the file. UNPACK restores compressed files on the OS/2 distribution floppy disk to a form you can use. Using UNPACK is easier than reinstalling OS/2.

On the OS/2 floppy disk, if the last character in a file's extension is @, the file is packed. Some packed files contain only one file. Other compressed files contain several files packed together and, when you use UNPACKED, the files may go to different directories. You can view the files' destinations on-screen during decompression.

Instructions

Use the following syntax: to unpack and direct the files to a specific target:

> **UNPACK packed-file target /N:filename** */V /F*

Use the following syntax to show the target path saved in the packed file:

> **UNPACK packed-file /SHOW**

packed-file is the name of the compressed file.

target is the drive and directory to which you want to copy the unpacked file.

/N:filename specifies the name of a single file that you want to extract from a bundle that contains more than one file.

/V verifies that the data was written correctly when it was unpacked.

/F specifies that files containing extended attributes should not be unpacked to a file system that doesn't support extended attributes.

/SHOW displays the names of the files that are combined in a packed bundle.

Do not specify an output file name; UNPACK uses the original file name as the destination file name.

Examples

To extract XCOPY.EXE from the file XCOPY.EX@ on a floppy disk in drive A and to write that file to the \OS2 directory on drive C, use the following:

UNPACK A:XCOPY.EX@ C:\OS2

To display the names of the files that are packed into the bundle GROUP.DA@ on drive A, use the following:

UNPACK A:GROUP.DA@ /SHOW

To extract FORMAT.COM from the floppy disk file BUNDLE.DA@ and to put the extracted file in C:\OS2, use the following:

UNPACK A:BUNDLE.DA@ C:\OS2 /N:FORMAT.COM

To verify that the compressed files are correctly written to disk, use the following:

UNPACK A:*.* C:\OS2 /V

To display the path and file name for every compressed file in the packed file, use the following:

UNPACK BUNDLE.DA@ /SHOW

Return Codes

    0 Normal completion
    1 No files were found to unpack or copy
    2 Some files or directories were not unpacked or copied due to file errors
    3 Ended by user
    4 Ended due to error

Using VIEW (OS/2 Only)

VIEW looks up a topic in an on-line document and displays files that have been compiled by the Information Presentation Facility (IPF) compiler as documents having a INF extension.

OS/2 comes with two on-line document files in its BOOK directory. Applications may add their own on-line document files. On-line document files usually contain specific help and perhaps instructions that are not included in the written documentation.

Instructions

VIEW uses the following syntax:

    VIEW path book topic

path is the drive and directory of the INF file to be displayed.

book is the help file with the extension INF.

topic is the subject you want to look up.

Examples

To look up the VIEW command in the on-line Command Reference, use the following:

    VIEW C:\OS2\BOOK\CMDREF VIEW

To find out how the REXX language uses loops, use the following:

    VIEW C:\OS2\BOOK\REXX LOOPS

The HELP command does the same thing and is easier to use. The two following commands yield the same results as the VIEW command; that is, the HELP command enables you to view specified on-line documents. In HELP VIEW, you see the on-line documentation for VIEW that explains the VIEW command and its uses. The HELP REXX LOOPS displays on-line references to LOOPS and how to use them.

> HELP VIEW

> HELP REXX LOOPS

If you do not specify book, then HELP assumes you mean CMDREF. With VIEW, you must always spell it out.

Chapter Summary

OS/2 provides several utility programs that help you while you work with the operating system. Most of the utilities reviewed in this chapter are safe to use and assist you with disk and file management, error detection and correction, and information gathering. A few utilities covered in this chapter, however, are dangerous to use unless you understand how they affect the OS/2 operating system. If you are unsure about using these utilities—SETBOOT, FDISKPM, MAKEINI, and PATCH, for example—consult your technical coordinator or a service representative.

Finally, a few utilities that you may be interested in are not only complicated commands, but could cause irreparable damage to your data files, programs, or operating system. IBM suggests these utilities—CREATEDD, LOG, TRACE, TRACEBUF, and TRACEFMT—be used only by a technical coordinator or service representative. For more information about these utilities, see your technical coordinator or service representative. Also, information on each utility is located in the Command Reference in OS/2 Presentation Manager.

Chapter 21

Using the OS/2 Time Management Applets

OS/2 includes a set of programs that work together to help you manage your time: Time Management applets. These programs perform all the functions of the appointment book that you might carry around with you, but are more powerful than a paper appointment book. Any entry you make using one program is immediately accessible to all the others. You can easily get summaries that show at a glance how you're spending your time.

The following list of Time Management applets will help you see how you can use these programs to make your time more productive:

- *Daily Planner* is like each day's page on your desk calendar. This is where you enter the day's schedule, including the time you set aside for each activity. When you finish each activity, you can check the activity off as completed.

- *Monthly Planner* summarizes the information you enter in Daily Planner so that you can see a couple of weeks at a glance.

- *Calendar* shows you an entire month at a time, without any detail. If you need to see the detailed schedule for a particular day, just double-click that day. Calendar also can give you a table of statistics on all your activities for a whole year.

- *Activities List* combines all the activities you have scheduled, no matter on what day they occur, into one list. Here you can easily see which activities are already completed and which remain to be done.

- *Planner Archive* is like a drawer where you keep the old pages you have torn off your desk calendar. Actually, Planner Archive is far better than that, because you can search through all your old activities for key words and phrases.

- *Alarms* works like an alarm clock, with ten independent alarms that are tied into your appointment calendar. You can use this applet, for example, to sound a warning a few minutes before you have to leave for an important meeting.

- *To-Do List* gives you a place to keep track of your most important tasks. You can pop it up any time to make sure you're focusing on the right things.

If you already use an appointment calendar to manage your time, take a look at what these programs can do for you. You might find them easier to use than your current time management tool. On the other hand, if you cannot be bothered to keep an appointment book because that takes more time than it's worth, these applets might be just what you need. Managing your time is easier when you harness the power of your computer, and this automated approach sure beats pencil and paper methods.

Starting Time Management Applets

To use the Time Management applets, you must first install the applets. If you left them out when you installed OS/2 on your computer, you can add the applets now by running the Selective Install program, which is inside the OS/2 System Setup folder. Chapter 7, "Modifying Your OS/2 Configuration," explains how to run that program.

After making sure that you have installed the Time Management applets, double-click the OS/2 System icon that is on the OS/2 desktop. Next, open the Productivity folder. Inside, you see icons for all the Time Management applets. To start any applet, just double-click the applet's icon. Try starting the Daily Planner applet now. Your screen looks like figure 21.1.

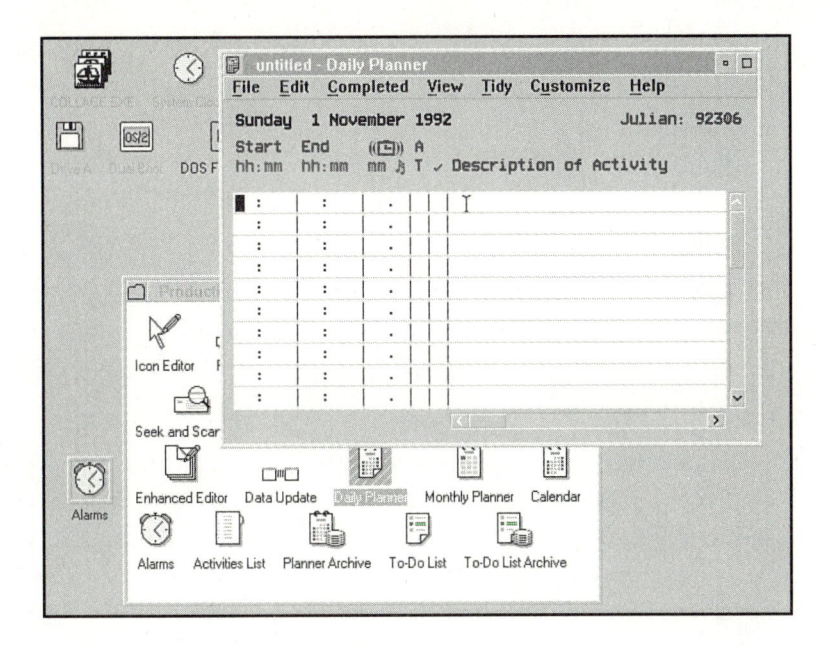

Fig. 21.1
The Daily Planner applet.

Using Daily Planner

Daily Planner's icon looks like a page from a desk calendar and works the same way. Daily Planner has one page for each day, and each page gives you space to write things to do, places to go, and people to see. Here you can write down everything you have to do each day and when you plan to do it.

Suppose that your day starts with a meeting from 10:30 to 11:00. Follow these steps to set up the Daily Planner applet:

1. Open Daily Planner by double-clicking its icon in the Productivity folder.

2. In the Start field, type **10** and then **30**.

3. Press the Tab key to go to the End field, and type **11**.

   Daily Planner assumes that the first activity you schedule is in the morning, but you can type the letter **P** after any time to indicate p.m.

For Related Information
- "Using The Workplace Shell," p. 231
- "Introducing Presentation Manager," p. 234

522   Chapter 21—Using the OS/2 Time Management Applets

4. Press the Tab key again to move to the Alarm field, which is indicated by a picture of an alarm clock. If you want OS/2 to sound an alarm five minutes before your meeting, type **5** here. If you type **15** instead, an alarm will go off at 10:15 to remind you of your meeting. Or just leave the field blank if you don't want a reminder. Later in this chapter, you learn how to customize alarms.

5. Every activity you schedule needs a description. If you press Enter now, Daily Planner pops up a window telling you that you haven't said what you plan to do at 10:30. Tab to the Description of Activity field and fill in a description.

   Each description can be up to 180 characters long. Only the first few characters appear on-screen at once, but you can drag the scroll bar at the bottom of the window to scroll through the entire description. If you enter more activities than fit on one page, you can use the scroll bar on the right to move through the entire day's plan.

Figure 21.2 shows what Daily Planner looks like with this one activity entered. The next step is to save this input, using commands you access from the menu bar.

Fig. 21.2
Entering an activity in Daily Planner.

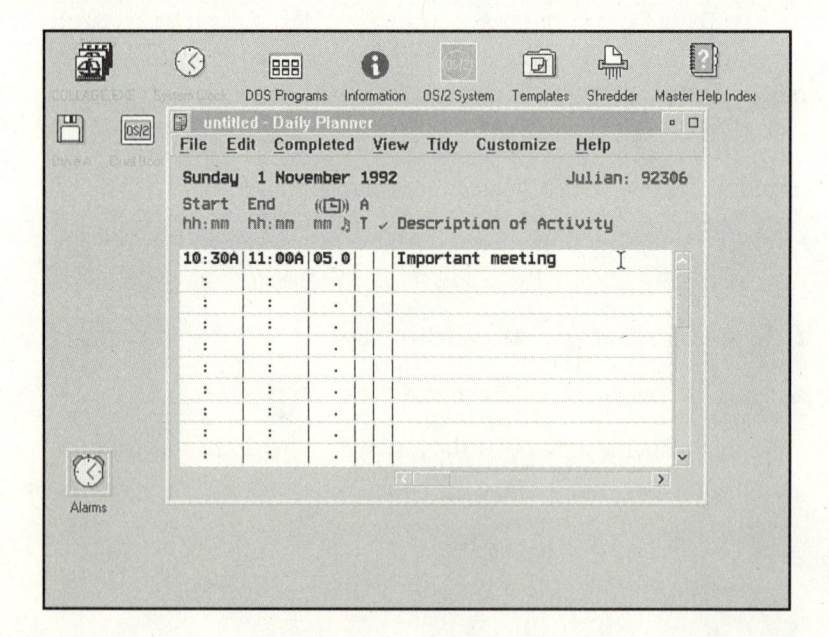

Using the File Menu

Pull down the File menu by clicking **F**ile; or activate the menu by pressing Alt-F. Choose Save to store the information you have entered. Daily Planner asks you to type the name of a file where you want to keep your calendar. Type any name you wish; for example, you might want to use your first name.

The File menu has several other commands. Use New to create a completely new Daily Planner file, or Open to access a file that already exists.

The Print command enables you to print a copy of your schedule. You can print your schedule directly on the printer, or save a copy of the schedule in any file you name. If you have installed more than one printer, you can pick which one you want to use. By default, the Print command prints seven days of your calendar, but you can change this number on the Print menu and print any number of days you want.

Using the Edit Menu

On the Edit menu, you see a variety of commands that help you manage your Daily Planner entries. The following list explains these commands:

- *Undo* gives you a chance to reverse the effect of the last change you made. This command is very handy when you accidentally delete an entry you want to keep.

- *Cut*, *Copy*, and *Paste* enable you to transfer text between Daily Planner and other applications, such as your word processor. These commands use the OS/2 clipboard, which you master in Chapter 21, "Using the OS/2 General Purpose Applets."

- *Clear Line* deletes everything you have entered on a line so that you can start over. *Clear All Lines* erases all the lines on the current day's list.

- *Activity Type* enables you to mark the day as a personal or national holiday. With this command, you also can mark activities that require you to be out of the office. The *Unmark* command allows you to reverse any incorrect Activity Type you have set by mistake.

- *Graphics* pops up a window with 32 different clip-art drawings. Double-click any drawing to copy it into the current activity's Description field. If an activity requires you to make a phone call, for example, you might want to label it with the telephone graphic.

- *Set Alarm Tune* gives you a choice of 26 tunes to play when an alarm is triggered.

- *Propagate/Delete Lines* allows you to schedule a recurring activity. If you have a staff meeting on the third Tuesday of every month, you can enter it once and then copy the entry to each month with a single command.

Using the Completed Menu

If you keep track of activities on your desk calendar, you probably cross them out when you complete them. Daily Planner enables you to do the same thing, but with more flexibility than a paper calendar.

Using the commands on the Completed menu, you can mark an activity as completed and leave the activity on the list. Or you can delete it from the list so that your calendar shows only the things you still haven't finished. You can mark or delete activities individually, or do a whole day's worth at once with a single command.

You probably would prefer to keep a separate record of completed activities, but that takes time with a paper calendar. Daily Planner does this chore for you automatically, however, by storing completed activities in an archive. The command you need is Archive All Completed Lines. This command puts a copy of every completed activity in a separate file. You can examine this separate file with the Planner Archive applet, which you learn about later in this chapter.

Using the View Menu

The View menu has commands that allow you to flip the pages in your Daily Planner calendar forward and backward. On the menu, you see that the shortcut keystrokes for these actions are Ctrl-+ (plus) and Ctrl-– (minus). If you have moved a few days ahead and want to move back to today, use the Today command, or just press Ctrl-T. The View menu provides no commands to move a month ahead or to go right to a particular date.

Another command on the View menu, View Complete Entry, shows you the entire description for an activity. This command is useful when you type a very long description and want to see it all at once. Figure 21.3 shows a description example.

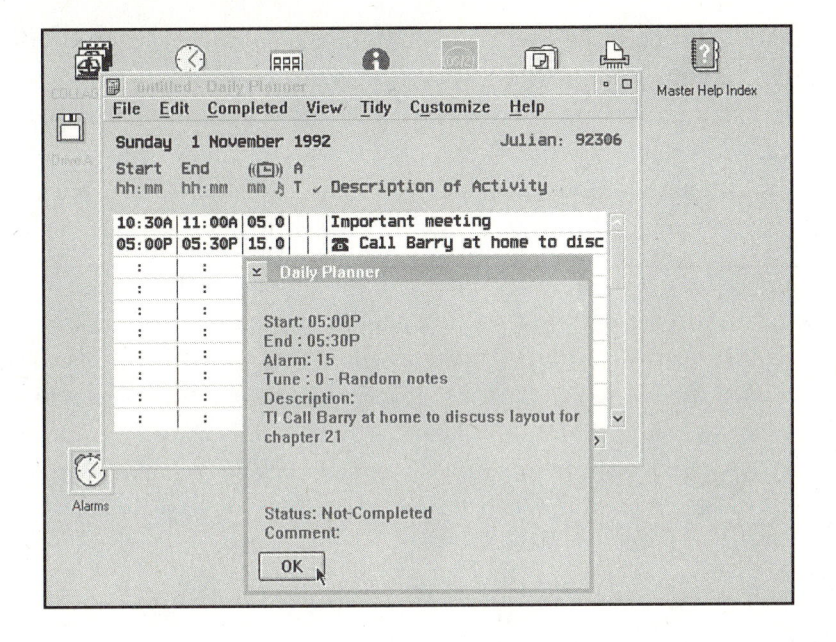

Fig. 21.3
Viewing a complete entry in Daily Planner.

Using the Tidy Menu

If you do not frequently use the Completed menu, your calendar can become cluttered. The commands on the Tidy menu let you clean it up all at once. The Tidy commands go through every previous page of your calendar, prior to the current date, and delete many activities with a single command. Before deleting old activities, you can save them in an archive. You can tidy up only the activities you have already marked as completed, or tidy every activity.

You may prefer to leave activities on your calendar for easy reference. In that case, avoid using the Tidy commands because they clear old calendar entries. After you clear old entries, you cannot get them back.

Using the Customize Menu

The Customize menu has two choices, Colors and Fonts. Choosing Colors pops up a window that enables you to pick your own colors for various areas of the Daily Planner window. You also can use special colors for completed activities so that a quick glance can show what you have accomplished and what remains to be done. You even have an option to pick a distinctive color for national holidays.

With the Font command, you can control the size of the characters used to display the Daily Planner window on-screen. Daily Planner starts with a default choice that matches the type of monitor and video card you have installed. You can pick any font size, no matter what equipment you have. But if you pick a font designed for a high-resolution XGA display when you have only a VGA monitor, the window may be too large to fit on-screen.

So far, you have learned how to enter activities into the Daily Planner, how to set alarms to prompt you a few minutes before important meetings, and how to tidy up old activities that you may no longer want on your calendar. In the next section, you learn how to manage the same list of activities in a different way, with the Monthly Planner applet. If you wish, you can close Daily Planner now, by pressing Alt-F4 or double-clicking the menu button at the upper-left corner of the Daily Planner window. If you have made any entries since you last saved the file, Daily Planner prompts you to save again before it closes.

Using Monthly Planner

As you have learned, the Daily Planner screen is like a page from your desk calendar. Monthly Planner is like the calendar for a whole month. It uses the same file as Daily Planner, but gives you a perspective of several weeks at a time. You can use the Daily Planner to enter appointments, meetings, and other events that you view with the Monthly Planner.

Open Monthly Planner now, by double-clicking its icon in the Productivity folder. Pull down the File menu and open the same file you used for Daily Planner. Your screen looks like figure 21.4. Each line represents one day, and you can see a couple of weeks at once. The current day is highlighted, as are weekends. All the activities you scheduled in Daily Planner are highlighted so that you can quickly see how much of your time is blocked out from day to day. The first letter or two of each Daily Planner description displays at the time scheduled.

Monthly Planner draws a box around the schedule for the current date. You can move this box forward or backward with the arrow keys or the scroll bar at right. Select any date and press Enter, and the Daily Planner for that date pops up. You are never more than a keystroke away from the greater detail that Daily Planner provides.

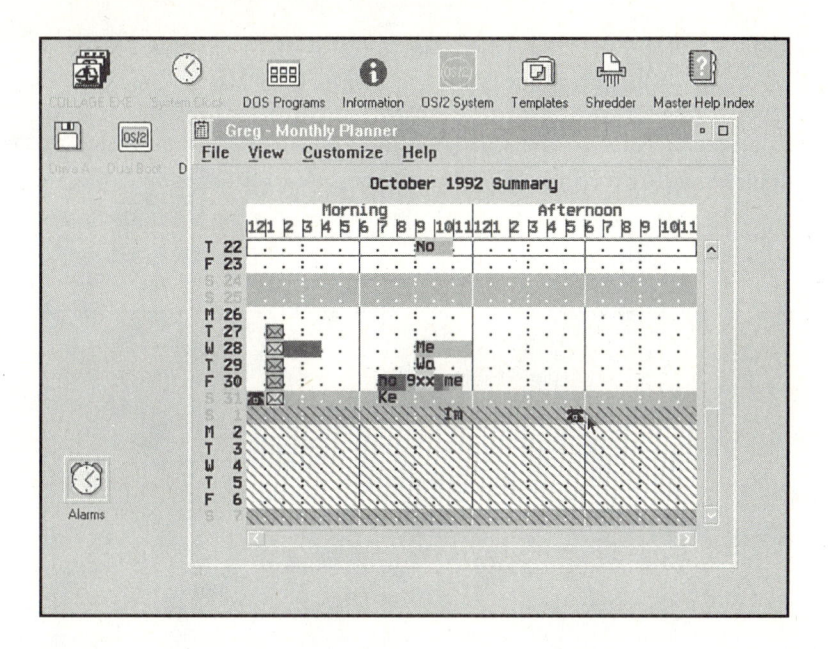

Fig. 21.4
The Monthly Planner applet.

Monthly Planner's File menu has only one choice, Open. No option to save is necessary because you can make schedule changes only in Daily Planner. Now that you have mastered the File menu, the following sections discuss useful commands available on Monthly Planner's View and Customize menus.

Using the View Menu

The View menu has commands that enable you to flip the pages in your calendar a month or a year at a time. The first choice, Month, pops up a list of all the months of the year. This command allows you to look at the calendar for any month instantly. Other options enable you to move forward or backward a month. The hot keys are Ctrl-+ (plus) and Ctrl-– (minus). These are the same hot keys you use for Daily Planner, but with Monthly Planner they move a whole month at a time, rather than just one day.

The Next Year and Previous Year options show you the calendar for the current month, one year in the future, or one year in the past. As with Daily Planner, the Return to Today option brings you right back to the present; its hot key is Ctrl-T.

Using the Customize Menu

The Customize menu has Color and Font options that work much the same as Daily Planner's. Monthly Planner's Color option also enables you to pick a

528 Chapter 21—Using the OS/2 Time Management Applets

different color for entries that trigger an alarm so that you can see which appointments you will be prompted to attend.

Shading is an additional Customize option in Monthly Planner, which allows you to pick shading for all dates outside the current month. You can use Shading in addition to Color to make the current month stand out clearly. Figure 21.5 shows the window that pops up when you choose Shading.

Fig. 21.5
The Shading Options window in Monthly Planner.

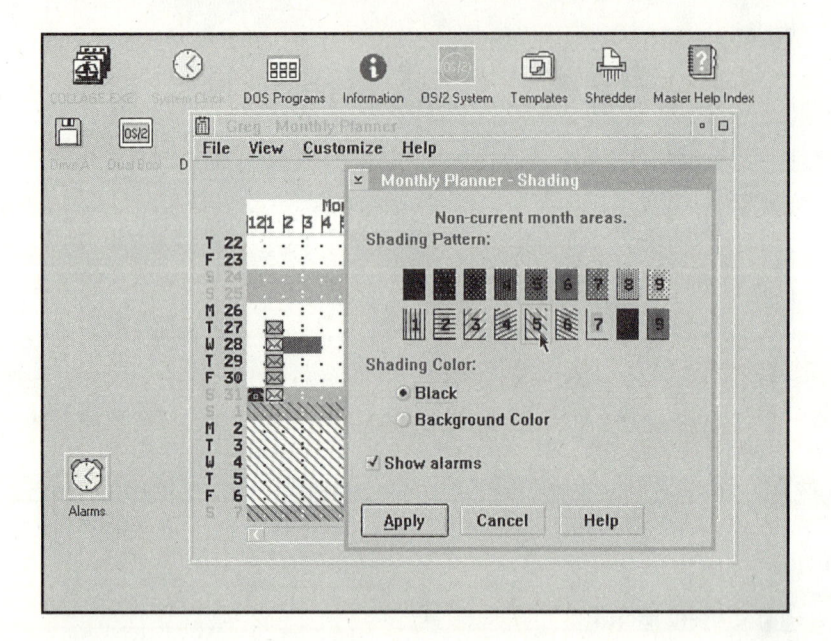

You can choose from among 20 different shading patterns by clicking a pattern with the mouse. A pair of radio buttons allows you to decide whether Shading should be in black or in the color that you have chosen for the window background. If you select the Show Alarms check box, any alarms you have set show up in a different color. When you're satisfied with the options you have chosen, click **A**pply to put them in effect.

Making Changes

While you are using Monthly Planner, you might notice a change you need to make—an appointment you forgot to enter, or perhaps a meeting that was cancelled. Follow these steps to make a change:

   1. Using the arrow keys, move to the date where you need to make a change, and then press Enter. Or if you're using a mouse, double-click the date. Either way, the Daily Planner for that date pops up.

2. Change the activity in Daily Planner.

   If you arrange your screen so that you can see both Daily and Monthly Planners, you will notice that the change isn't immediately reflected in Monthly Planner.

3. Now flip a page forward in Daily Planner—by using the Ctrl-+ hot key, for example. As shown in figure 21.6, a window pops up, prompting you to confirm the change you made. After you select Yes, the applet updates the Monthly Planner screen to reflect the change.

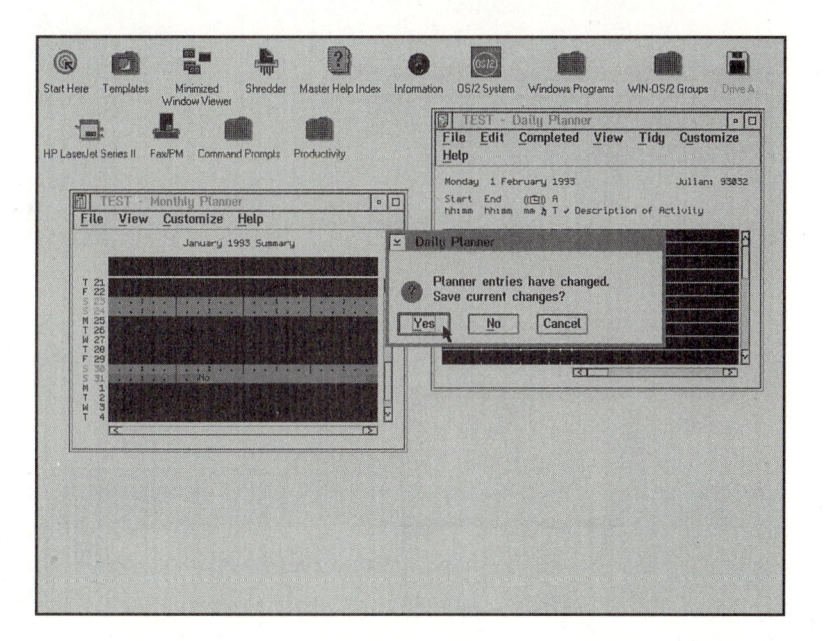

Fig. 21.6
New entries affect other applets only when you save them.

Using Calendar

Like Monthly Planner, Calendar uses the information you enter in Daily Planner, but gives you a broader view. Double-click the Calendar icon in the Productivity folder, and use the **O**pen command on its **F**ile menu to load the same file you used for your Daily Planner. Your screen resembles figure 21.7.

Calendar looks like a monthly wall calendar. Notice that weekdays are shown in a different color than weekends, and today's date is always a special color. If you have entered any Daily Planner activity for a particular date, Calendar draws a box around that date.

Fig. 21.7
The Calendar applet.

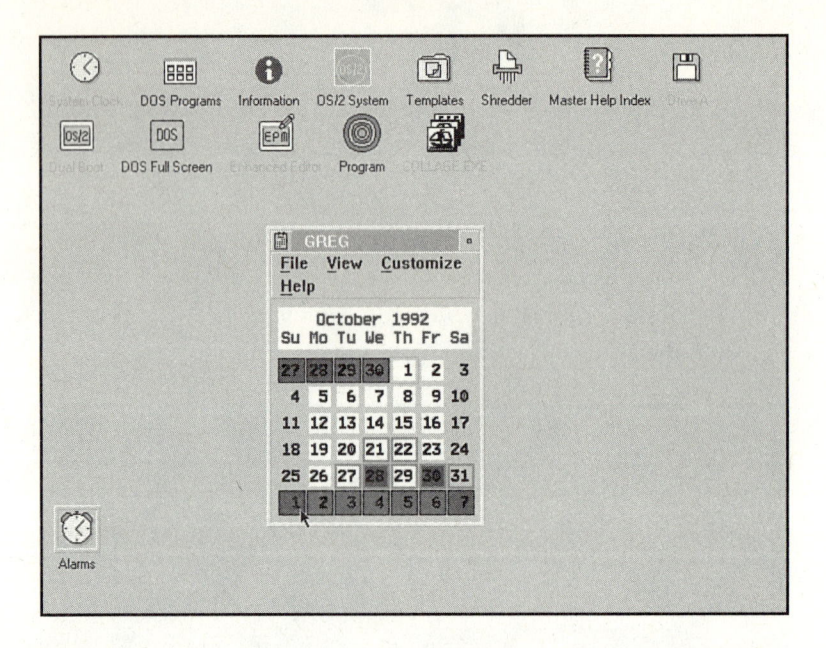

To pop up Daily Planner at any time, just double-click a date on the Calendar. You can enter or change activities only in Daily Planner, not in Calendar itself.

Similar to the other applets, Calendar has a menu bar, with many options that are familiar to you by now. In fact, the View and Customize menus are exactly the same as for Monthly Planner, so you have already mastered them. You also have already used the first option on the File menu, Open, to load your Daily Planner file. When you make a change in Daily Planner, use the second option, Refresh Current File, to update the Calendar.

The third option on the File menu is something new. This new option is Shows Statistics for the Current Year. The Statistics display gives you a convenient one-screen snapshot of the whole year. If your Daily Planner entries include graphics or activity types, they are summarized here. If you use the airplane graphic for each flight you schedule, for example, the Statistics screen shows you how many times you have flown this year and how many more flights you have planned. And if you use Activity Types to mark vacation days, you can see at a glance how much vacation you have already taken this year and how many days you have left. Figure 21.8 shows a sample Statistics screen.

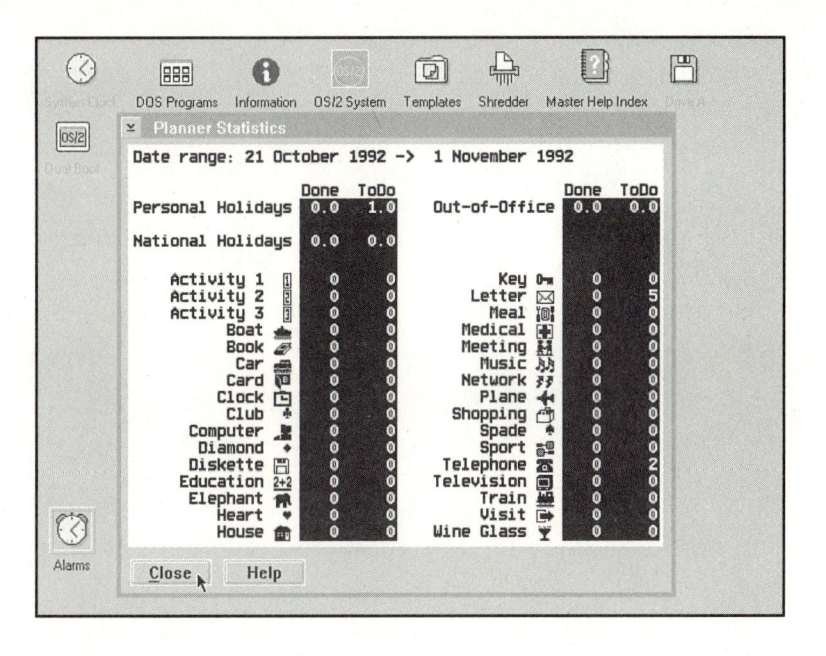

Fig. 21.8
The Calendar's Statistics screen.

Using Activities List

Activities List presents yet another view of the items you have entered into Daily Planner. As the sample screen in figure 21.9 shows, Activities List displays all the activities noted on your calendar. When you start Activities List by double-clicking its icon in the Productivity folder, it lists activities in date order, starting with today's date. Remember to load your Daily Planner file into Activities List, using the **O**pen command on the Activities List **F**ile menu.

You can examine past and future entries by scrolling the display with the PgUp and PgDn keys or the vertical scroll bar. Use the horizontal scroll bar to view any entries that are too long to fit on one screen. If you have set an alarm to remind you a few minutes before a scheduled activity, the alarm time appears. You also see a check mark next to each activity you have marked as completed. Various Activity Types, such as holidays and vacation days, are highlighted in color.

The menu bar contains commands that enable you to work with your schedule in ways that the other Time Management applets do not. The following sections cover these commands in detail.

Fig. 21.9

The Activities List applet.

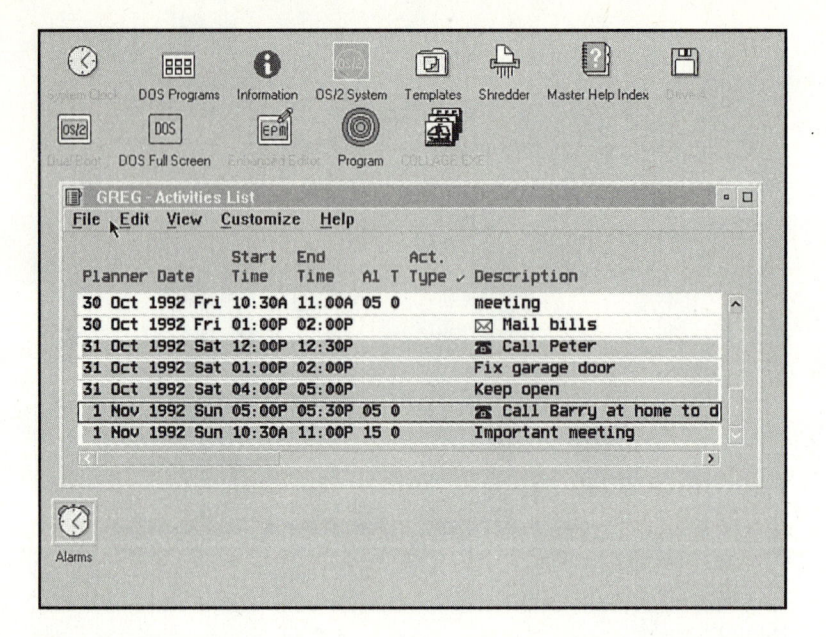

Using the File Menu

Along with the Open command that enables you to load your Daily Planner file, you see a Print command on the File menu. This command can print your entire list of activities. You can send the output to a file or to any printer that's attached to your system.

Using the Edit Menu

The Edit menu has two commands. Use the first command, Copy, when you want to copy the currently highlighted activity line to the OS/2 clipboard. You can then paste it into any other application, such as a word processor.

Figure 21.10 shows the Find command in use. This command searches through the description of every activity on the list and finds whatever string of characters you specify. In the figure, Activities List has found the word *Lunch*. The Find window remains on-screen so that you can look for other Lunch appointments by repeatedly pressing the Enter key. The Find command locates each occurrence in turn. When it gets to the end of the list, Find loops back to the beginning and restarts the search there.

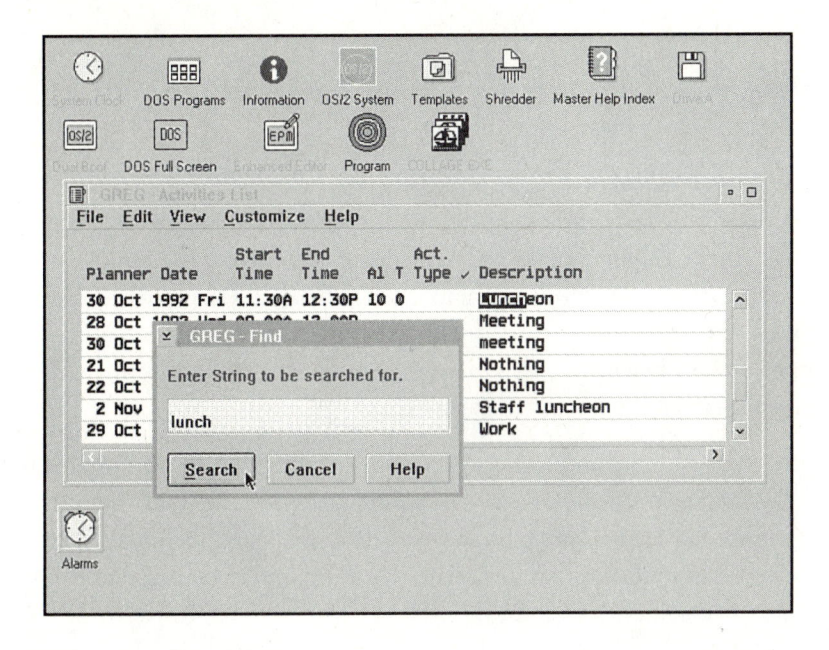

Fig. 21.10
Finding text in the Activities List.

Using the View Menu

The View menu has only one command, Sort. This command enables you to show activities in order by date or by description. Choosing Sort pops up a window that lets you sort in either of these two ways. In the First Field area, pick the button for the sort option that you want and choose the other, if you want, for the Second Field; then press Go. For example, do the first sort by description and the second by date. All appointments with the description *Lunch* are grouped together. And within this group, your lunch dates are sorted chronologically.

If you always want Activities List to be sorted in this particular way, press the Save button. Your preference are stored for future use, even after you turn the computer off. If you have an early release of OS/2 version 2.0, the Help button may not work.

Using the Customize Menu

The Customize menu has two options, Color and Font, that work the same as the corresponding options in the other Time Management applets. The Color option enables you to pick distinctive colors for holidays, days you are out of the office, or weekends, for example. These colors are not used unless you turn on the Color Lines option on this menu.

Using Planner Archive

You have already learned how to archive entries in Daily Planner, by using Daily Planner's Tidy menu, for example. Planner Archive is the Time Management applet that allows you to examine all the activities that you have ever archived. Try archiving an entry or two in Daily Planner, and then open Planner Archive by clicking its icon in the Productivity folder. Your archived entries display on-screen.

Planner Archive looks and works exactly like Activities list. As you can see in figure 21.11, the only difference is the spacing between the lines. The menus are identical, and the commands all work the same. Using the menu bar commands, for example, you can sort archived entries, print them out, or display a summary in a Statistics window.

Fig. 21.11
The Planner Archive resembles the Activities List.

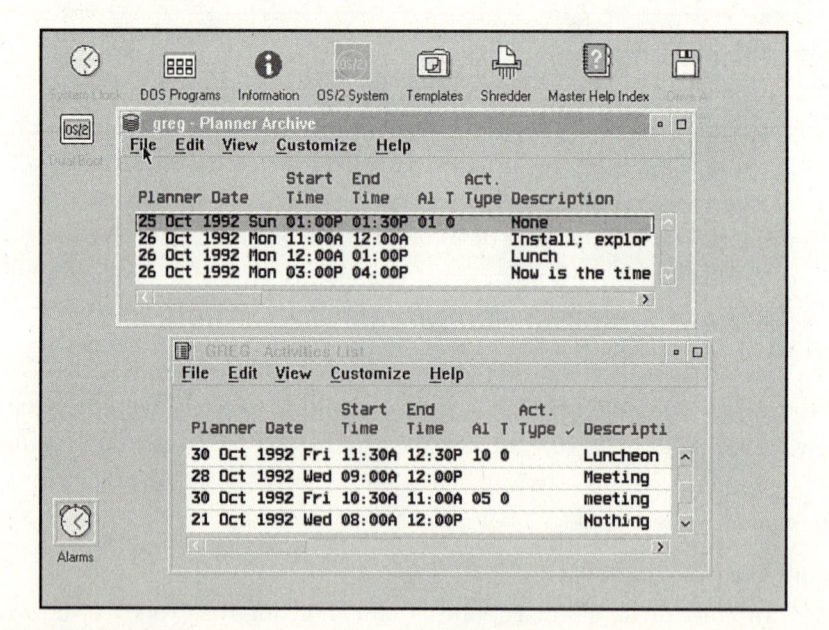

Using Alarms

You have already seen how to use Daily Planner to set alarms that warn you of impending meetings. The Alarms applet gives you precise control over the alarms you set. In this applet, you can turn alarms on or off, customize the message that displays at the time you set, and even make an alarm start a program of your choice.

The Alarms applet automatically starts running in the background whenever you open one of the other Time Management applets. (Alarms is like an alarm clock, which cannot go off unless you leave it plugged in all the time.) Daily Planner can set alarms, but Alarms must be running for the alarms to sound. If you have already run Daily Planner, find Alarms on the OS/2 Task List and maximize it. Your screen looks like figure 21.12.

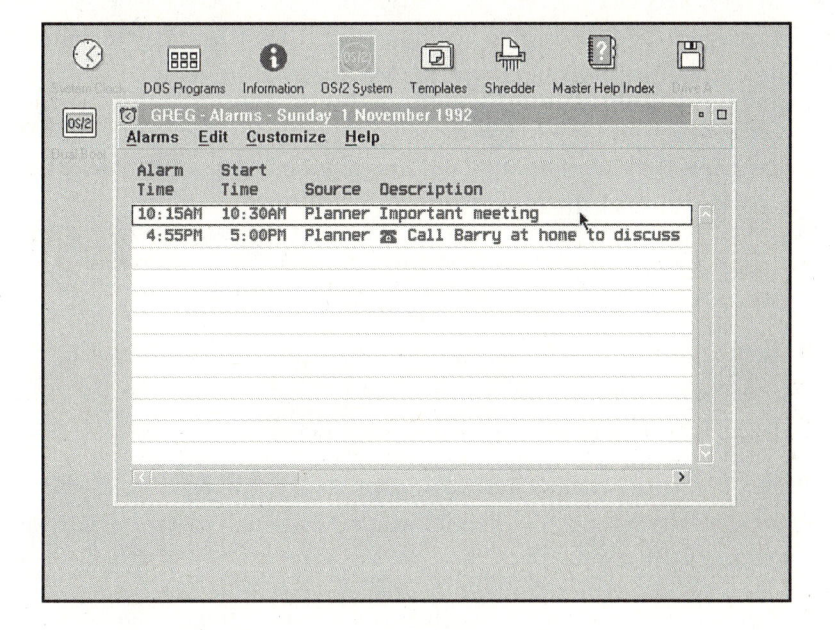

Fig. 21.12
The Alarms applet.

Using the Alarms Menu

Set Alarm is the option you most often use on this menu. Choosing this option pops up a window as shown in figure 21.13. The various fields here give you precise control over the alarms you set.

The following list explains the options available in the Alarms SetAlarm window:

- *Number* indicates the alarm with which you are working. Ten alarms are available, and you can set each independently of the others. You cannot type a number in this field, but you can change the number by clicking the arrows.

- *Status* can be On or Off. Usually it doesn't make sense to set an alarm without turning it on. After you have customized the settings for an alarm, however, you can turn it off without wiping out those settings, just in case you want to reactivate the alarm later. If an alarm's Status is Off, you cannot change any of the other settings until you turn the Status back on.

- *Setting* offers you four input fields. The first three enable you to pick the day, hour, and minute when the alarm should sound. The last field, Graphic, lets you choose a picture that pops up on-screen when the alarm goes off. If you set an alarm to remind you when it's dinner time, for example, you might choose the Meal graphic.

- *Comment* enables you to specify a line of text that displays on-screen in a window that pops up when the alarm sounds. This window pops up only if you check the PopUp box.

- *Tune* allows you to pick from a variety of tunes. The melody you choose plays when the alarm goes off.

- *Action* enables you to decide whether the alarm should sound only once, or every week. You can set an alarm to go off next Tuesday at 11:00, for example, or every Tuesday at 11:00.

- *PopUp* controls whether a window pops up over whatever work you're doing at alarm time. This pop-up window contains whatever you type on the Comment line.

- *Execute comment as command* allows you to start a program automatically at alarm time. Type the name of the program in the Comment field. It can be any program that you could run at an OS/2 session's command line. Be sure to specify the full path and name for the command.

Your alarm clock probably has a snooze button, which turns off the alarm temporarily, but tells it to sound again in a few minutes. The alarms you set in the Time Management applets also have a snooze feature, as you can see in figure 21.14. If you have selected the Snooze button and later decide you want to turn off the alarm before it sounds again, use the Cancel Snooze command on the File menu.

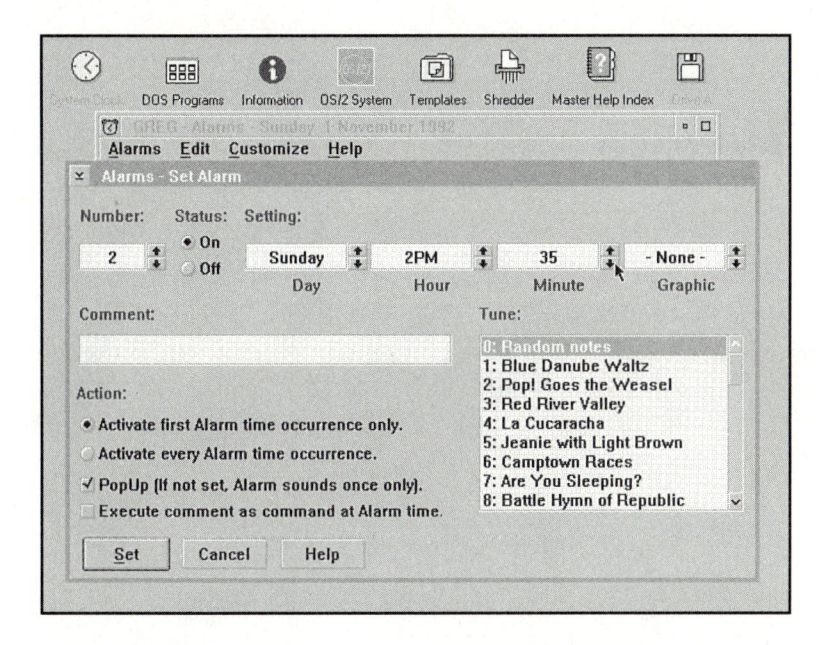

Fig. 21.13
The Set Alarm window.

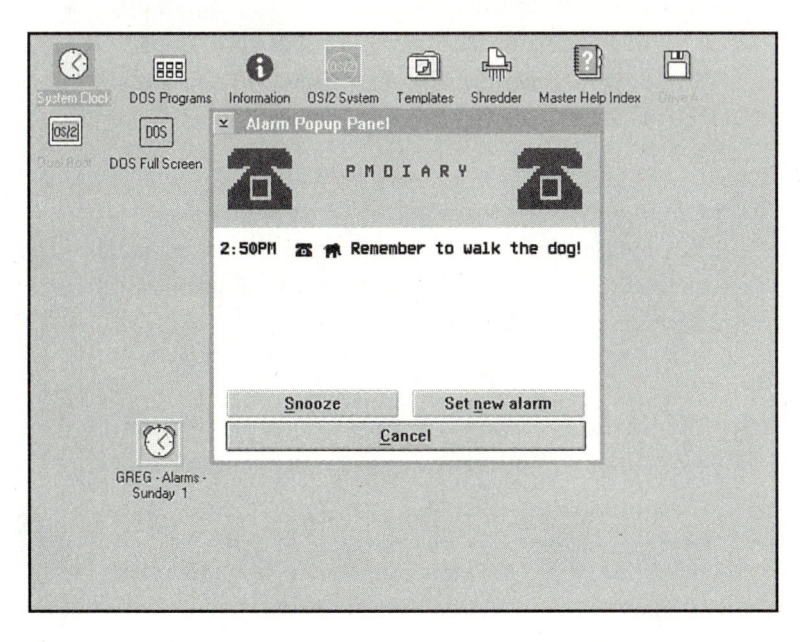

Fig. 21.14
An Alarm Popup Panel.

The last item on the File menu is the Print command. This command sends a copy of the Alarms window to whatever printer you choose. Alternatively, you can use this command to put the Alarms window into a file. This capability is useful if you want to use the list of alarms in another software package such as your spreadsheet.

Using the Edit Menu

Copy is the only choice on the Edit menu. This command puts a copy of the Alarms listing into the OS/2 clipboard so that you can paste it into another application.

Using the Customize Menu

The Font and Colors options on this menu work the same way as they do in the other Time Management applets. The choices you make apply not only to the Alarms screen, but also to the window that pops up at alarm time. You might want to pick bold colors for this pop-up window.

Another option on this menu, Sound Limit, controls the number of times an alarm tune plays before it stops. By clicking the arrows, you can vary the number from 0 to 30. If you choose 0, the tune does not play.

If you hit the Snooze button when an alarm sounds, the alarm stops temporarily, but it sounds again after a certain interval of time. The Snooze Period option on the Customize menu enables you to set the length of this time interval. Click the arrows to pick any period between 1 and 60 minutes.

The final option on the Customize menu is Set Master Planner File. You can use this option to tell Alarms to use a particular Planner file every time it starts. Pick this option, and take a moment now to tell it the name you chose earlier for your Daily Planner file. Then press the **S**et button, and Alarms will always examine that same file whenever it runs.

Setting a Default Planner File for All Time Management Applets

Perhaps you didn't mind using the Open command on the File menu each time you started one of the Time Management applets, and typing in the name of your Planner file each time. Or maybe you have already grown tired of this repetitive chore. At any rate, you don't want to go through all that trouble each time you want to run these programs. After all, their purpose is to save you time.

Here is a technique you can use to tell each of the Time Management applets to use the same Planner file every time you start the applets. Go through the

Setting a Default Planner File for All Time Management Applets

following series steps once for each applet: Daily Planner, Monthly Planner, Planner Archive, Calendar, and Activities List. Follow along with the example in figure 21.15, which shows how to set up Daily Planner.

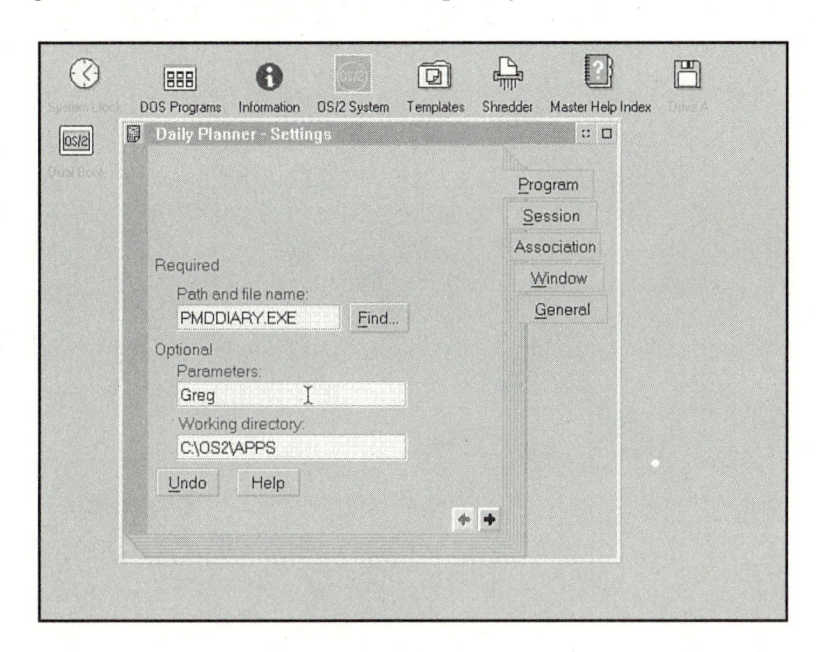

Fig. 21.15
Setting the default file for Daily Planner.

To set a default Planner file, follow these steps:

1. Make sure the Productivity folder inside OS/2 System is open.
2. Click mouse button 2 on Daily Planner's icon to pop up its local menu.
3. Click the arrow to the right of the **O**pen command, and pick **S**ettings from the pop-up window.
4. Click the Program tab of the settings notebook that now appears.
5. In the Optional Parameters field, type the name of your Planner file.
6. Double-click the menu button in the upper-left corner of the settings notebook to close it.

Repeat the preceding steps for each of the Time Management applets, and you will never have to open a Planner file again. For more information on managing the settings notebook, see Chapter 10, "Managing the Workplace Shell."

Using To-Do List

To-Do List looks a lot like Activities List, with one line for each activity. Open the list by double-clicking the To-Do List icon in the Productivity folder. Your screen looks like figure 21.16. You see that each task has a priority and a date. This applet keeps a count of the number of things you have to do and the number you have completed.

Fig. 21.16
The To-Do List applet.

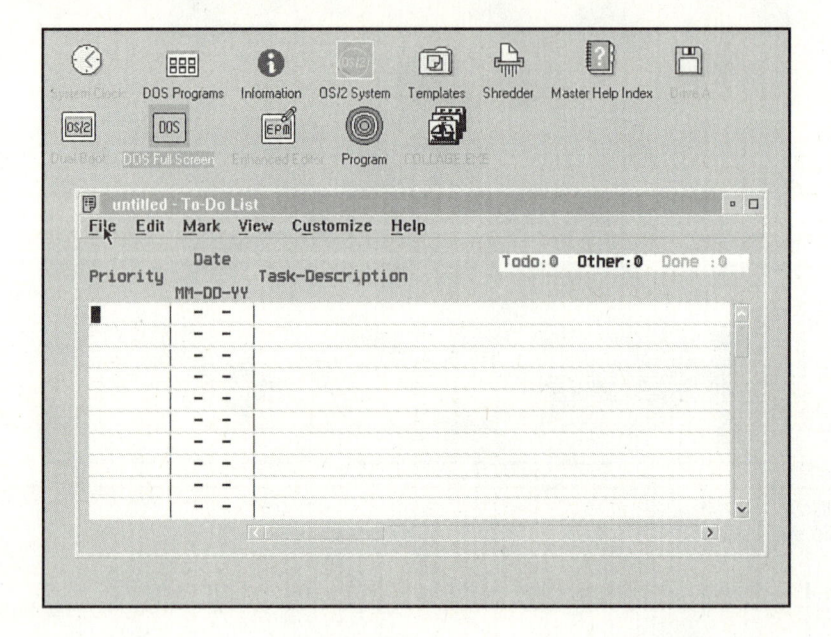

Unfortunately, To-Do List is not integrated with the other Time Management applets. Tasks you enter in To-Do List are not automatically copied to Daily Planner, or vice versa. If you want to copy entries back and forth, you can use the OS/2 clipboard, which is explained in Chapter 21.

However, many people who keep detailed appointment calendars also keep a separate list of critical things to do. And if you decide not to use the other Time Management applets, you may still find To-Do List helpful on its own. The next section shows how you enter tasks on your To-Do List.

Entering Tasks on To-Do List

To-Do List's screen has three fields for each item. The first field, Priority, indicates the relative importance of each item on the list. You can type one or two characters or numbers here, but you probably will want to use just a single number for simplicity. Use the number 1 for the most pressing task, 2 for the second most urgent, and so on.

The second field is Date. Enter the month, day, and year here. To enter today's date automatically, press Ctrl-C. You can use the date field to show the date on which you added an item to the list; or you might prefer to enter the date when you need to complete the task.

Type a description of the activity in the third field, Task Description. If your description is longer than the part of this field that you can see on-screen, just keep typing when you get to the end of the line. The field scrolls automatically to give you more room.

After you fill in all three fields, press Enter. Because you have not yet completed this task, it shows up in red. And the ToDo counter in the upper-right corner of the window now shows the number 1, to let you know you have one unfinished task on your list.

Now that you know how to enter tasks on the To-Do list, the following sections tell you how to compile and manage your own list of things to do each day.

Using the File Menu

Pull down the File menu by pressing Alt-F, or if you are using a mouse, just click File. Choose Save to store the information you have entered. To-Do List asks you for the name of a file where you want it to store your list. Your own first name will do nicely. You can use the same name for To-Do List that you used for Daily Planner; OS/2 stores the two files separately, with different file extensions.

You see several other commands on the File menu. Use New if you want to create a completely new To-Do List file, Save As if you want to store it under a different name, or Open if you want to load a file that already exists. If you always want to load the same file, type the file name into To-Do List's settings notebook, following the same procedure illustrated in figure 21.15 and the accompanying series of steps.

The Print command prints a copy of your To-Do List. You can print your To-Do List directly to any printer you have installed, or save a copy of the list in any file you name.

Using the Mark Menu

The most pleasant thing about a To-Do List is crossing off a task you have completed. The Mark menu has several commands that enable you to indicate which tasks are finished. Click a task you have entered, pull down the **M**ark menu, and choose Mark Current Item as Completed. The task's color changes from red to black. The number of things left to do, shown in the upper-right section of the window, goes down by one. And the displayed number of tasks completed increases by one.

Other options on the Mark menu allow you to delete lines when their tasks are completed (Add Line to Archive Then Delete), or move the lines to To-Do List's Archive (Mark Item & Add Line to Archive). Another command, Mark Item and Date Stamp, enables you to stamp a completed task with today's date. If you mistakenly mark an outstanding item as completed, you can correct the error by using the Unmark Line command. The last two menu items enable you to choose to Archive All Completed Lines, or to Archive All Completed Lines Then Delete.

Using the View Menu

The View menu has commands that enable you to see entries in their entirety, or to sort them in priority order. The first option, View Complete Entry, pops up a window that shows an entire entry all at once. This option is handy if some of your entries are so long that you cannot read them in the main window.

The other option on the View menu is Sort. You can sort tasks by priority, by date, or alphabetically by description. Choose up to three fields for sorting, specifying the most important one first.

The example in figure 21.17 shows one sort order that will probably suit your needs. The first sort is by Priority, and the second sort field is Date. These settings mean that all items with Priority 1 are listed first, and the items with this top priority display in chronological order. Priority 2 items, sorted by date, are listed next, and so on.

You probably want to choose Sort Completed Items to End of List so that the things you still need to do appear at the top. When the settings in this window suit your needs, press **G**o to apply them to To-Do List. Click **S**ave if you want to use the Sort options you have chosen every time you run To-Do List.

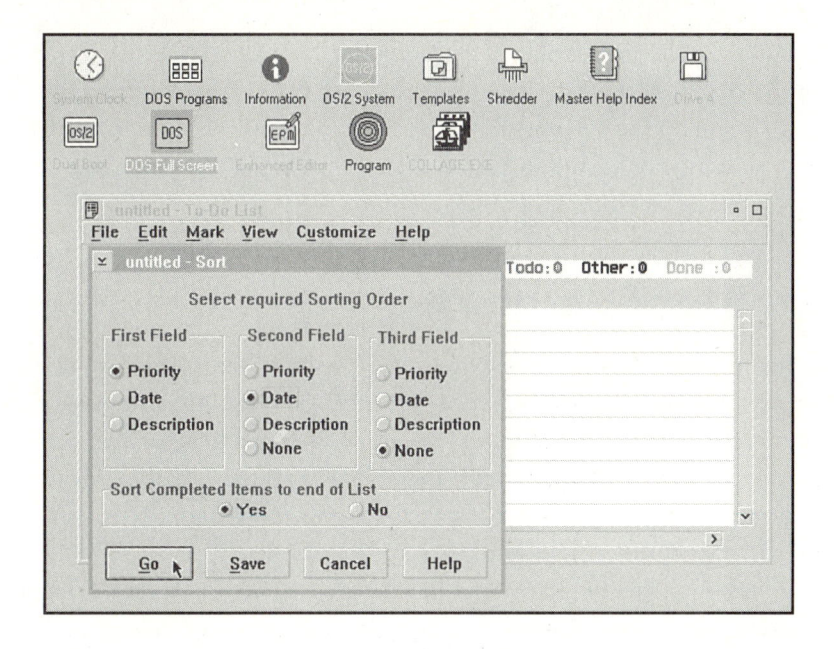

Fig. 21.17
Sorting your
To-Do List.

Using the Customize Menu

The Customize menu has two choices, Colors and Fonts. When you pick Colors, a pop-up window allows you to select your own colors for various areas of the To-Do List window. You can change the colors of the window background and border, and you can pick special colors to distinguish completed tasks from the items you still have to do.

The Font command works the same way as the Font command in the other applets you learned in this chapter. Using this command, you can make the characters in the To-Do List window larger or smaller. The default, based on the particular type of graphics card and monitor you are using, is usually best.

Using To-Do List Archive

When you use the commands on To-Do List's Mark menu, you can move tasks off the list and into an archive. This archive stores every task you have ever completed. In this way, the To-Do List Archive performs a function similar to that of the Planner Archive applet you learned in an earlier section.

In fact, To-Do List Archive's menu commands are exactly the same as the commands you have already mastered for Planner Archive. If you want to experiment with To-Do List Archive, you must first have saved a To-Do List file and archived at least one entry. Archiving the first entry creates the file that To-Do List Archive displays for you so that you can load it using the Open option on the File menu. If you plan to use To-Do List Archive often, set this file as your default, using the settings notebook technique illustrated in a preceding section.

Chapter Summary

For Related Information
- "Introducing Presentation Manager," p. 234

In this chapter, you learned how to use OS/2's Time Management applets. You saw that Daily Planner, Monthly Planner, Calendar, Activities List, Planner Archive, and Alarms work together, using the same files. You learned how to enter activities in Daily Planner, and work with those activities in various ways with the other applets. You now know how to set alarms that remind you of important meetings. And you have learned how to use To-Do List and To-Do List Archive to keep track of the important tasks you must accomplish each day.

In the next chapter, you master OS/2's General Purpose applets. These programs enable you to write notes and stick them anywhere on your desktop, find files on your hard disk, perform simple arithmetic, monitor usage of your computer's resources, create your own icons, and more.

Chapter 22

Using the OS/2 General Purpose Applets

In Chapter 20, you learned how to manage your time with an integrated group of applets that work closely together. In this chapter, you master other applets that serve very different functions, and are completely independent of each other. Each applet has its own section in this chapter, which gives a detailed description of the applet, instructions for using the applet's commands, and some useful hints. The following list tells what each of the General Purpose applets does. You can use it to decide which may be useful to you before reading on.

- *Calculator* looks and works exactly like the electronic calculator you probably have on your desk. With Calculator, you can perform arithmetic and print out your computations step by step.

- *Pulse* shows how much work your CPU is performing from one moment to the next by displaying a graph on-screen. If you don't want to clutter your screen with a large graph, you can tell Pulse to display this graph as an icon on the OS/2 desktop.

- *Clipboard Viewer* enables you to examine the text or graphic contents of the OS/2 Clipboard that you use to transfer information between programs. With this applet, you can move data between OS/2 and Windows programs, as well.

- *Icon Editor* is a drawing program that enables you to design your own icons. You can substitute an icon that you create for any application's default icon and give the OS/2 desktop a distinctive personal look.

- *Tune Editor* allows you to compose, play, and print your own melodies. The Alarms applet, discussed in Chapter 20, can use the tunes you write.

- *Seek and Scan Files* searches your hard disk for any file you specify. This applet is handy when you know the name of a file, but cannot remember the folder or directory where you stored it.

- *Sticky Pad* supplies you with little yellow notes that you can stick to windows on the OS/2 desktop. You can use these notes as reminders, the same way you use paper sticky notes on the documents and folders on your desk.

- *Notepad* gives you a stack of index cards that you can use to jot down ideas, using a different card for each topic.

If you choose to study only those applets that interest you, you should still read the first couple of sections of this chapter. Those sections show you how to start the applets, and they cover a few commands that are the same for most applets.

Starting the General Purpose Applets

You need to make sure you have installed the General Purpose applets before you can use them. To find out whether you have already installed these applets, open the OS/2 System folder and double-click Productivity. Inside the Productivity folder, you see an icon for each applet you have installed. If any applet that you want to learn about is missing, take a moment to install it now by using the Selective Install program that you see in the OS/2 System window. Complete instructions for running Selective Install are in Chapter 7.

For Related Information
- "Using the Workplace Shell," p. 231
- "Introducing Presentation Manager," p. 234

You start any General Purpose applet the same way you start any OS/2 application—by double-clicking its icon. Try starting the Calculator applet now. Your screen should look like figure 22.1. The next section uses the Calculator applet as an example to explain several commands that are common to many of the applets in this chapter.

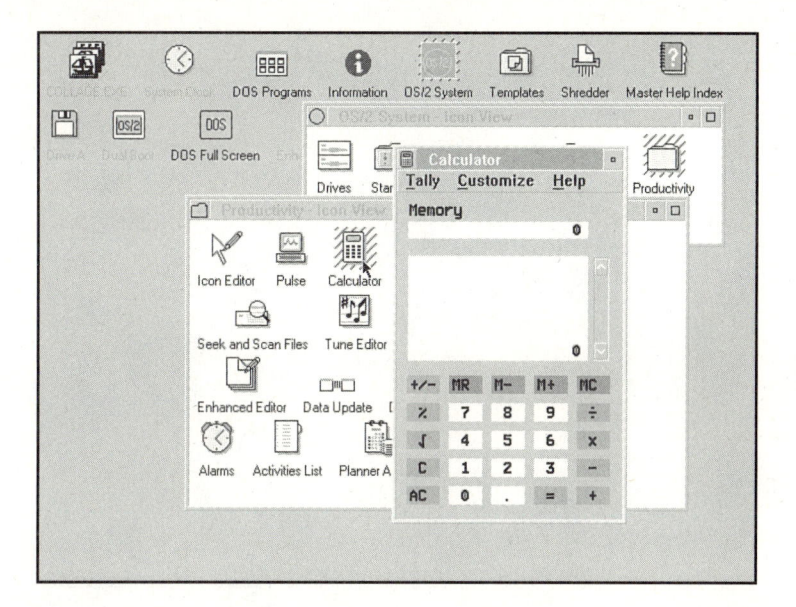

Fig. 22.1
The Calculator applet.

Learning Commands Shared by Most General Purpose Applets

Even though the General Purpose applets serve a wide variety of different functions, some of the commands on the applets' menu bars are the same; for example, each applet has a Help menu. You mastered the Help system in Chapter 13. The remainder of this section discusses the Colors, Font Size, and Print options that work the same way on most of the General Purpose applets.

Picking Colors

Figure 22.2 shows the Colors window for the Calculator applet. This window pops up when you choose Colors from the Customize menu. You can select a different hue for each part of the Calculator display. Pick one item from the list of Calculator window areas, select a color, and click Apply to see what the new color scheme looks like. In the figure, the color of the memory buttons is about to be changed to yellow.

Fig. 22.2
The Calculator's Colors window.

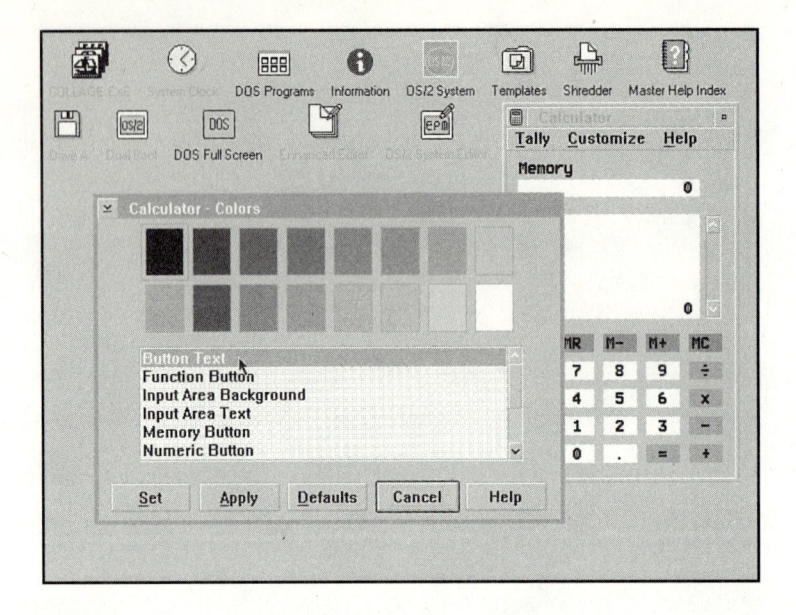

The Apply button shows you the new color scheme, but leaves the Colors window open. If you decide you don't like the new color you chose, you can pick another instead. When you are satisfied with your choices, click the Set button. Set applies your new colors and closes the Colors window. Set also saves your chosen colors so that they are used whenever you start the Calculator.

If you have changed many colors but aren't satisfied with the result, just click Defaults to get back the original color scheme. On the other hand, if you have experimented with a few color changes but decide to discard the changes you've made, choose Cancel.

Choosing a Font Size

OS/2 supplies a separate font for each of the most common video displays. By default, the General Purpose applets all use the font designed for your video card and monitor, but you can pick any of the other fonts. Moving to a larger font size, for example, makes each character in the Calculator window bigger. When you turn on your computer the next day and start Calculator again, it remembers the last font you set.

Figure 22.3 shows how the Calculator looks with an XGA font, displayed on a VGA monitor. The Font Size option on the Customize menu offers a menu of the fonts from which you can choose. The number next to each font's name tells how many little dots are used to draw each of that font's characters on-screen. XGA draws each character in a box 22 dots high by 12 wide, which is about 50 percent bigger than VGA's usual 14 by 8 dots. So using the XGA font makes the Calculator appear about 50 percent larger than it usually does on the VGA screen.

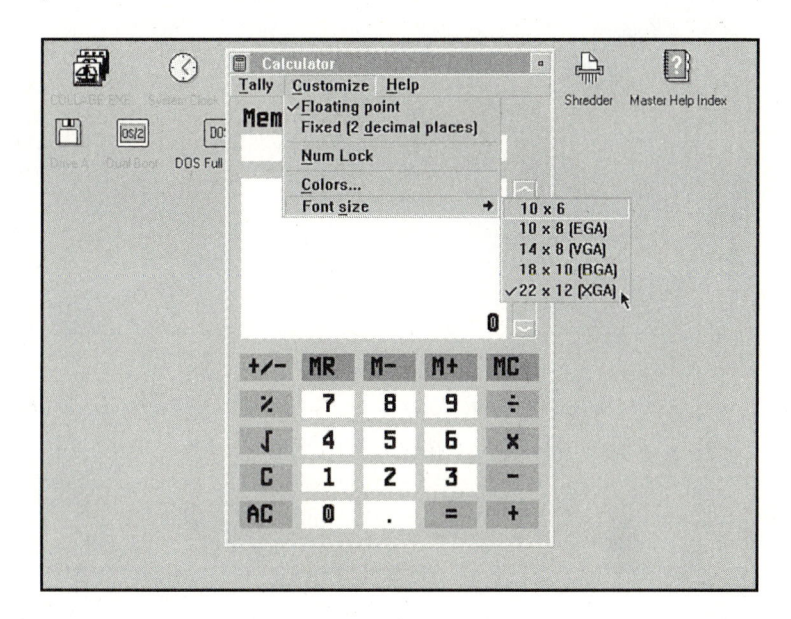

Fig. 22.3
A large font makes the Calculator window bigger.

Printing from a General Purpose Applet

Several of the General Purpose applets have a menu choice that enables you to print a copy of the work you have done in the applet. The Print option on the Calculator's Tally menu, for example, pops up a window that allows you to print the results of your computations. On other applets that offer it, the Print option is usually available on the File menu.

Figure 22.4 shows the Print option in action. The pop-up window enables you to choose between two different destinations for the printout. If you press the Printer button, the output goes directly to any printer you select from the choices offered. Of course, as the figure shows, this procedure does not work if you have not yet installed a printer. If you need to install a printer, refer to Chapter 7, "Modifying Your OS/2 Configuration."

Fig. 22.4
The Calculator's Print window.

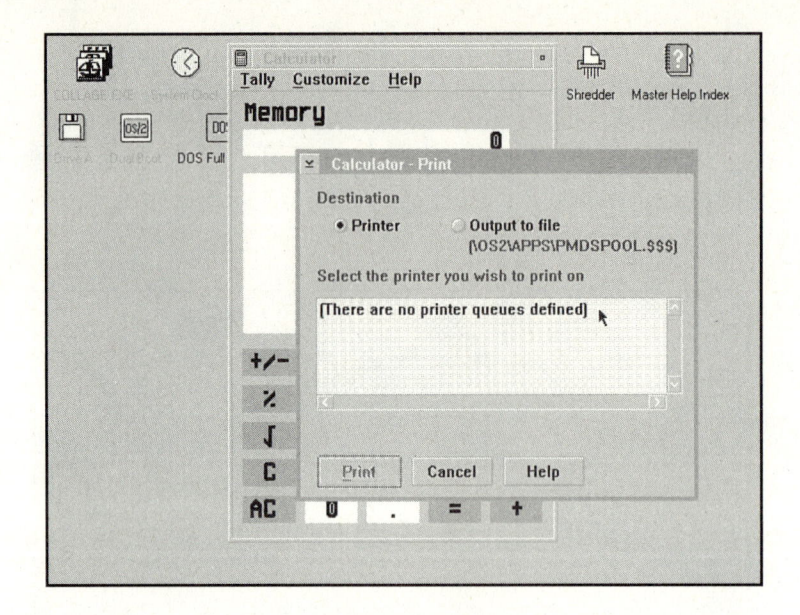

Even if you don't have a printer, you can use the Print option to copy your calculations to a file. To send the output to a printable file instead of a printer, click the Output to File button. This option can be handy if your printer is on a network, but the network is temporarily down.

Whichever destination or printer you pick, press the Print button at the bottom of the window to start the printout. Or choose Cancel if you decide not to print the calculation after all.

Now that you have mastered the commands that Calculator shares with other applets, you are ready to learn Calculator's arithmetic capabilities.

Using Calculator

For Related Information
- "Introducing Presentation Manager," p. 234

As you saw in figure 22.3, the Calculator applet looks exactly like the electronic calculator you probably keep on your desk. You can click the Calculator's keys with the mouse, or perform calculations by using the keyboard. Calculator has a percent key, a square root key, and a memory. Notice that the results of your calculation display step by step in the output area, which works like the paper tape in a desktop printing calculator. You can scroll this tape up or down with the scroll bar, or print it with the Print command on the Tally menu.

The next section tells you what the keys on the Calculator do. If you are already an expert at using your desk calculator, skip to the following section.

Doing Arithmetic on the Calculator

If you have ever used a desk calculator, you already know how to perform arithmetic with the Calculator applet. You can click the Calculator buttons with the mouse, or use the keyboard.

Suppose that you want to multiply 1728 by 50 percent. Using the mouse, follow these steps:

1. Enter **1728** by clicking the **1**, **7**, **2**, and **8** buttons in that order.

2. Click the button that shows a times sign (X), and then enter **50** by clicking **5**, then **0**.

   You see 1728 on one line, and 50 on the next.

3. Click the % button.

   The number .5 appears on-screen (.5 equals 50%).

4. Click the = button.

   Figure 22.5 shows that the answer is 864.

Or if you prefer to use the keyboard, follow these steps:

1. Press the Num Lock key until the Num Lock light on your keyboard comes on.

   This setting enables you to enter numbers from the keyboard's numeric keypad.

2. Type **1728**, and press the * (asterisk) key. The * key stands for multiplication.

3. Type **50**, and then press the % key.

4. Press Enter to see the answer.

Whether you use the keyboard or the mouse, the Calculator display looks the same as figure 22.5.

Fig. 22.5
Doing arithmetic in the Calculator.

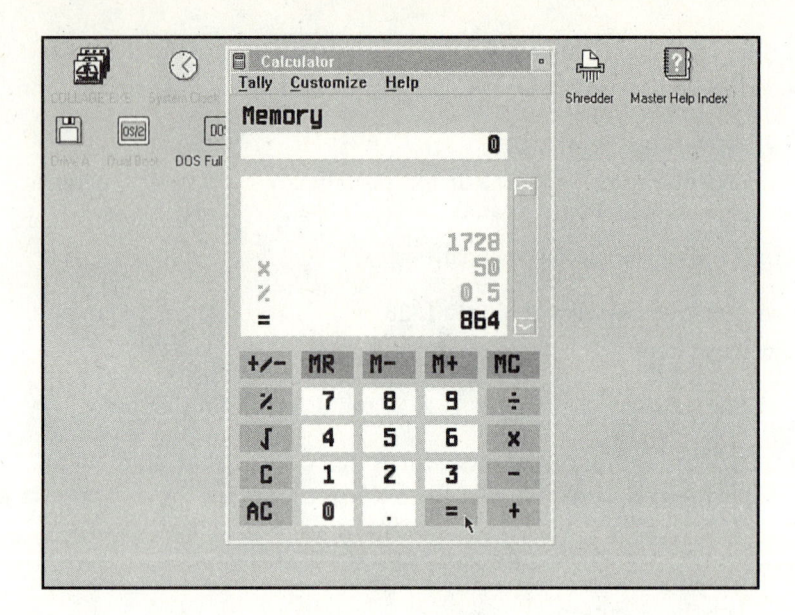

Every Calculator key you can click with the mouse has a keyboard equivalent. Table 22.1 shows the keystroke you use for each operation. Most people prefer to use the keyboard because this method is more like using a desk calculator and quicker than using the mouse.

Table 22.1 Calculator Keystroke Summary

Operation	Keystroke
Add	+
Subtract	-
Multiply	*
Divide	/
Equals	Enter
Square Root	S
Change Sign	T
Clear Entry	C
All Clear	A
Add to Memory	F7

Operation	Keystroke
Subtract from Memory	F6
Recall Memory	F5
Clear Memory	F8

Using the Tally and Customize Menus

On Calculator's Tally menu, you find the Print option, which is usually on the File menu of other applets. The other Tally option is Clear Tally Roll, which completely erases the calculator tape that shows the steps in each calculation.

The familiar Colors and Font Size options appear on the Customize menu, along with several other options. Two of these options, Floating Point and Fixed 2, work together. You can choose only one at a time. If you choose Floating Point, Calculator displays numbers using however many digits are required. The result of 1 divided by 3, for example, appears as .3333333333. On the other hand, if you choose Fixed 2, Calculator always shows exactly two decimal places so that one-third displays as .33. Any extra digits are rounded to the nearest hundredth.

The Customize menu also has a Num Lock command, which turns your keyboard's Num Lock light on or off. This option is equivalent to toggling the Num Lock key on your keyboard. When Num Lock is off, the keys in the separate numeric keypad move the cursor around. Turn Num Lock on when you want these keys to type numbers in the Calculator.

Using Pulse

The Pulse applet graphically displays how much of your computer's power is being used from moment to moment. You can see at a glance what proportion of your system's resources is demanded by the programs you are running. The closer the graph line is to the top of the window, the more resources the programs are using. This measurement gives you an idea how much available CPU power remains for other programs that you might want to run at the same time. With this applet, you can keep a finger on your computer's pulse.

For Related Information
- "Introducing Presentation Manager," p. 234

If you run Pulse while you have a DOS session open, the Pulse graph generally shows that all of your system's computing power is used. This reading is not an error—Pulse is telling you the truth. OS/2 is a multitasking operating system, designed to run several programs at once. But DOS is single-tasking, and a DOS application thinks it always owns the entire computer.

When an OS/2 program has prompted you for input and is waiting for you to type something, the program takes a brief nap and tells OS/2 to wake it up when you press a key or move the mouse. Meanwhile, other OS/2 applications that are running in the background can use the majority of the computer's resources. Pulse reflects the availability of this spare power.

But when a DOS program is waiting for input from you, it tells the system to check the keyboard continually. The DOS program thinks the computer has nothing better to do than to test the keyboard and see whether you have typed anything yet. OS/2 wrestles control away from the DOS program in order to make sure other programs have a chance to run. But DOS consumes every spare microsecond, so Pulse correctly reports a 100-percent load on system resources.

Setting Pulse Options

Aside from Help, Pulse has only one pull-down menu: Options. Figure 22.6 shows Pulse running, with its Options menu pulled down and its Background Color menu displayed.

Fig. 22.6
The Pulse applet and its Options menu.

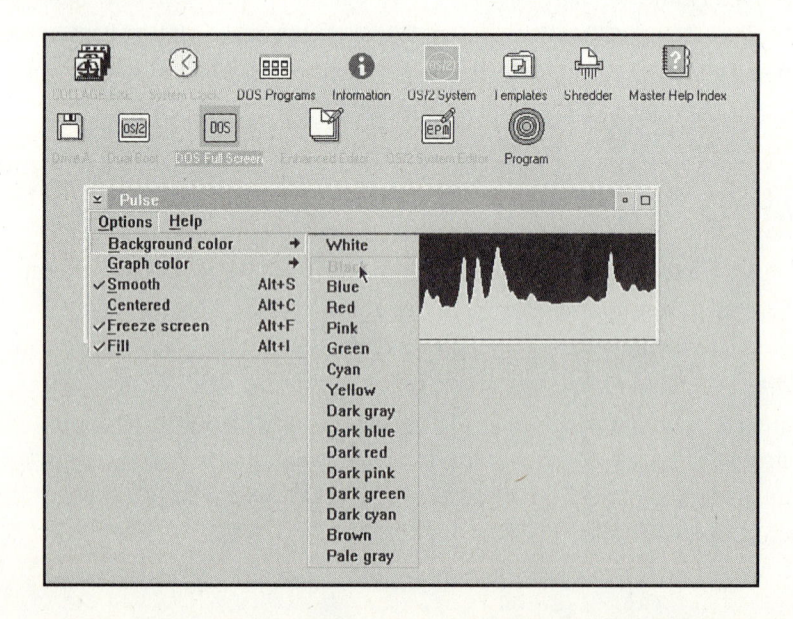

The following is a list of the Options commands and explanations of what each one does:

- *Background Color* gives you a choice of 16 colors for the main Pulse window.

- *Graph Color* enables you to choose any of 16 different colors for the graph. Don't choose the same color for Background and Graph, or else you will not be able to see the graph.

- *Smooth* makes the graph less jagged. Instead of displaying exact system usage at each instant, it shows a running average that doesn't jump around as much.

- *Centered* keeps the graph displayed inside the window's borders. You probably will want to turn Centered on so that the graph shifts back to the middle of the screen whenever it hits the right edge of the window. If you leave Centered off, the graph marches past the right side of a window, into an area where you can no longer see it.

- *Freeze Screen* tells Pulse to stop updating the graph, but leave it displayed on-screen.

- *Fill* colors the area under the graph with whatever graph color you choose. If you leave Fill off, the areas above and below the graph are the same color, and only the graph line itself is a different color.

Running Pulse as Graphically Changing Icon

Normally, if you minimize Pulse, you see only its default icon on-screen. This default icon is just a picture that always looks the same. You can set up Pulse, however, to keep updating its graph in a way that you can see even when Pulse is minimized. Figure 22.7 shows Pulse running minimized, with a constantly updated graph of system usage displayed inside the icon.

To configure Pulse this way, follow these steps:

1. Close Pulse if it is already running. Open the Productivity folder (OS/2 installs the Productivity folder in the System folder), and click the right mouse button on the Pulse icon.

2. Click the arrow to the right of **O**pen, and choose **S**ettings to open the settings notebook.

556   Chapter 22—Using the OS/2 General Purpose Applets

3. On the Program page of the settings notebook, type **noicon** in the Optional Parameters field.

4. Close the settings notebook by double-clicking the menu bar at the top-left corner.

5. Run Pulse, and minimize it.

Fig. 22.7
Pulse can graph the load on your system inside an icon.

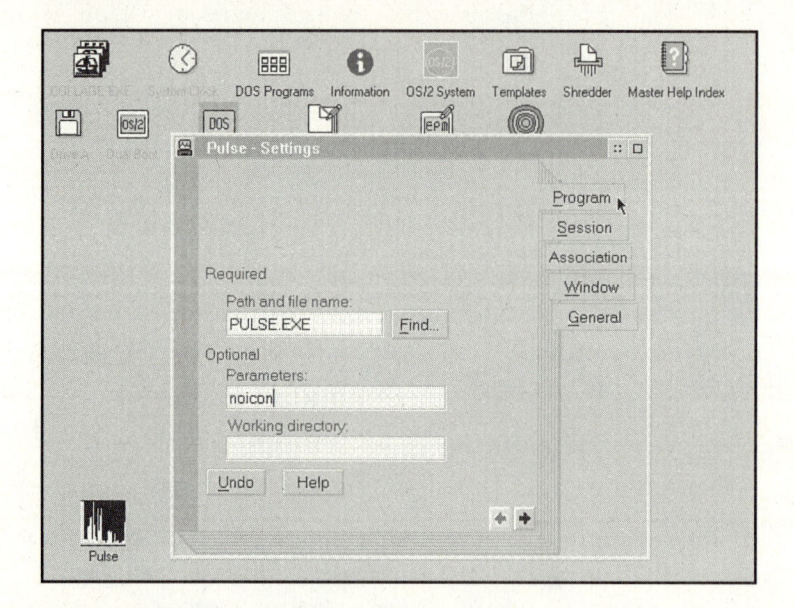

Using Clipboard Viewer

For Related Information
- "Introducing Presentation Manager," p. 234

As you learned in Chapter 20 and this chapter, OS/2's Clipboard enables you to transfer text or graphics within or between programs. When you use the Cut or Copy options on an application's Edit menu, for example, the information you highlighted is transferred to the Clipboard. After the text or graphic is on the Clipboard, you can paste it into another location or application.

Clipboard Viewer is minimized automatically when you start it. This makes sense, because you usually want the Viewer out of the way so that it doesn't clutter your screen. When you want to see what's on the Clipboard, double-click the minimized icon to restore the window.

Using Clipboard Viewer, you can display the contents of the Clipboard at any time. As soon as you copy data to the Clipboard, it appears in Clipboard Viewer, as illustrated in figure 22.8. The highlighted line of text in the

Enhanced Editor was selected with the mouse, and Ctrl-Ins was pressed to copy the selected line to Clipboard Viewer, where it appears instantly.

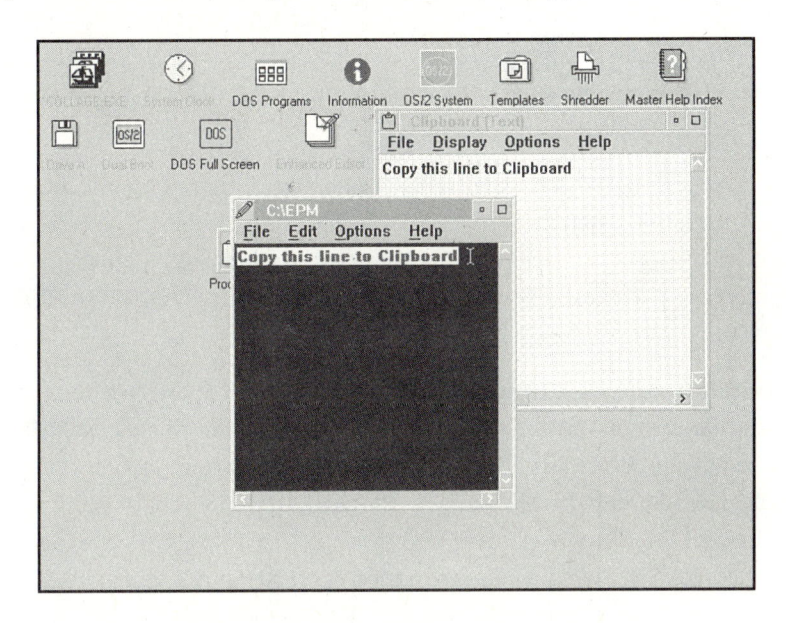

Fig. 22.8
Text cut from an application appears instantly in Clipboard Viewer.

Choosing a Display Format

Skip over the File menu for the moment and pull down the Display menu. This menu has only one choice: Render. When the Clipboard is empty, Render is dimmed and clicking it does nothing. After you copy something to the Clipboard, however, Render pops up a window that offers you a choice of ways to view the Clipboard's contents.

When the Clipboard contains graphics, you have several Render choices. Usually, Clipboard Viewer correctly guesses which one is appropriate. But if the display doesn't look right, try one of the other choices. When the Clipboard contains text, however, it doesn't make sense to Render it as graphics.

Sharing Information between Windows and OS/2

When you run Windows under OS/2, Windows has its own Clipboard which is usually separate from OS/2's Clipboard. You can share information between Windows and OS/2 programs in two ways. The following sections show you how to use each and how to pick the one that's best for you.

Sharing Information through a Public Clipboard. The easiest way to share information between Windows and OS/2 sessions is through a Public

Clipboard. Here, Public means shared: Windows and OS/2 use a common Clipboard. You can copy text or graphics from a Windows session and paste it directly to an OS/2 session, or vice versa. This approach is especially convenient when you are running Windows applications seamlessly so that they appear on the same screen as OS/2 applications. Refer to Chapters 16 and 17 for complete information on Seamless Windows.

The default Clipboard is Private instead of Public. To make it Public, pull down the **O**ptions menu on Clipboard Viewer and click Public. After you choose this option, a check mark appears next to the word Public on the Options menu. You can choose a Public Clipboard only when a Windows session is running under OS/2.

Sharing Information through a Private Clipboard. By default, the Public selection on the Options menu is not checked, which means that the Clipboard is Private. With this option, OS/2 and Windows have separate Clipboards. The system behaves exactly as though Windows were running on its own under DOS, completely insulated from OS/2. You might prefer this setup, for example, when you are running Windows in full-screen mode and using the Windows Clipboard to cut and paste graphics, while using OS/2's own Clipboard to move text between OS/2 programs.

The Windows Clipboard and the OS/2 Private Clipboard can communicate with each other, but this takes a little work on your part. To move information from Windows to OS/2, follow these steps:

1. Go to your Windows session. Select some text or graphics.

2. Press Ctrl-Ins to copy your selection to the Windows Clipboard.

3. Open OS/2's Clipboard Viewer. Pull down the **F**ile menu and choose Import.

   This command copies the contents of the Windows Clipboard to the OS/2 Private Clipboard. You now can paste your selection into any OS/2 application.

To transfer information in the opposite direction, from OS/2 to Windows, follow these steps:

1. Go to your OS/2 session. Select some text or graphics.

2. Press Ctrl-Ins to copy your selection to the OS/2 Private Clipboard.

3. Open OS/2's Clipboard Viewer. Pull down the File menu and choose Export.

   This command copies the contents of the OS/2 Clipboard to the Windows Clipboard.

You now can go to any Windows application and paste your selection there. Because of the extra effort required when the OS/2 Clipboard is Private, you will probably want to make it Public.

Using Tune Editor

Tune Editor enables you to create, save, change, print, and play simple melodies. Each tune can be up to 20 notes long. You can use melodies that you compose with Tune Editor in the Alarms applet that you mastered in Chapter 20. Tune Editor is easier to use if you already know how to read music. But you don't need any musical training to have fun with Tune Editor.

As an example, figure 22.9 shows the first four notes of Beethoven's Fifth Symphony in Tune Editor.

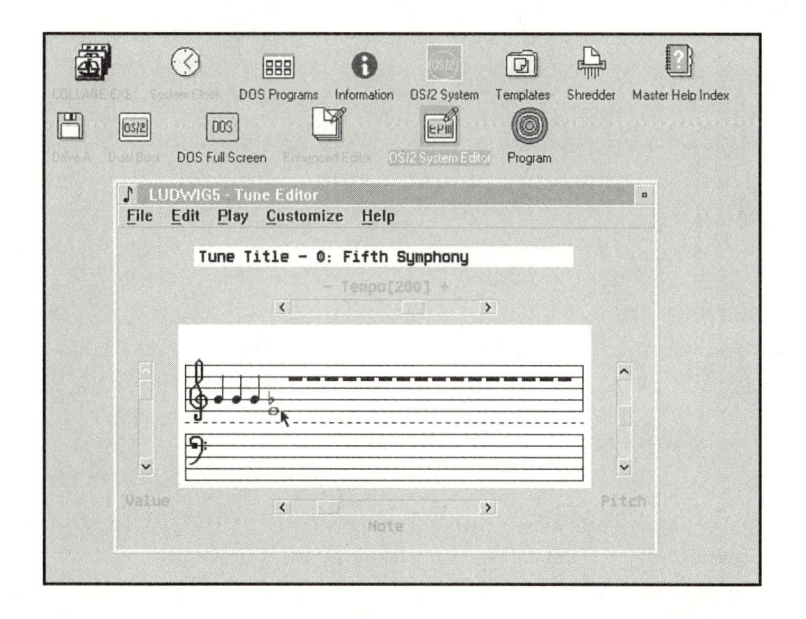

For Related Information
- "Introducing Presentation Manager," p. 234
- "Using the OS/2 Editors," p. 346

Fig. 22.9
Editing Beethoven's Fifth Symphony.

Entering a Tune

To enter a tune, you need to specify the pitch and duration of each note. Follow these steps:

1. Select a note that you want to enter or change, by clicking it with the mouse. Alternatively, you can move back and forth between successive notes with the keyboard arrow keys. The note currently selected displays in blue.

2. Choose the length of the note by moving the Value slider at left up or down. The top position of the slider gives you what musicians call a whole note. A whole note has the longest duration. Move the slider down one step at a time to get a half note, a quarter note, and so on. The current note instantly changes its appearance to the musical symbol for the type of note you have selected. As you continue moving the slider down, the notes change to rests, which take up time but make no sound.

3. Pick the pitch you want by moving the Pitch slider on the right up and down. The current note moves up or down on the music score to indicate the new pitch. An easier way to choose the pitch of a note is to click the mouse right on the score, at exactly the pitch you want. Rests make no sound so you cannot set their pitch.

Repeat these steps for each note in your tune. If you don't need all 20 available notes, make the ones you don't need into rests. Type the letter **P** at any time to play the tune you're working on. You can change the tune from slow to fast, or anywhere in between, by moving the Tempo slider that is above the musical score.

Notice that you cannot yet enter the exact melody shown in figure 22.9 because the fourth note is E flat. To enter that note, you need the flat symbol, which you learn when you study the menu commands in the sections that follow.

Using the File Menu

The commands on the File menu enable you to save the tunes that you have written in a file so that you can load them again whenever you want to play the melodies. These commands also enable you to change each tune's name and to print your tunes. Each file can contain up to 36 melodies. The following list explains the various File menu commands:

- *New* clears any tunes you have loaded in Tune Editor and gives you a book of blank pages to compose your own melodies. OS/2's Alarm tune is written on the first page of this book, just to get you started.

- *Open* allows you to load a file of tunes that you have previously saved.

- *Open Tune* enables you to select any of the 36 tunes in the file. This procedure is like flipping through the pages of your own songbook. The melody you select is drawn on the music score on-screen.

- *Rename* allows you to type the name of a tune. The name displays on-screen whenever you open that tune.

- *Save* is the command that stores a file of tunes. It saves your melodies in the tune file you currently have open.

- *Save As* stores the current tunes in a file you name.

- *Print* makes a copy of the current tune appear on the printer. You might be surprised, however, when you look at the printout. You do not get a graphical printout of the on-screen music score. Instead, you see a list of every note's pitch and duration, expressed as numbers.

Using the Edit Menu

The Edit menu displays commands that help you enter or modify a tune. You don't have to pull down the Edit menu to use any of these commands because every command has a hot key that's easier to use. The hot keys are all listed on the Edit menu.

The +, –, and = keys correspond to what musicians call sharps, flats, and naturals, respectively. A sharp looks like a pound sign next to a note, and it raises the pitch of that note slightly. Similarly, a flat, which looks a little like the letter b, lowers a note's pitch somewhat. The = sign cancels the effect of a sharp or flat.

When you need to set the duration of a note or rest, you may find that the slider is very sensitive to slight mouse movements. A quick way to pick a quarter note duration is to type the letter **C**, which stands for *crotchet*, a technical term for a quarter note. This command lets you rapidly change a rest into a note so that you can set the note's pitch. If you need to change a note to a rest, press **R**. Other durations, such as whole notes or sixteenth notes, do not have shortcuts.

To delete the current note, press the Del key. By analogy, you might suspect that the Ins key would insert a note, but actually the hot key to insert a note is the letter I. Pressing Ctrl-L deletes the entire current tune, replacing it with a blank score.

Playing Your Melodies

You can listen to your tunes with the commands on the Play menu. Here you see an option to play the current tune. You can always play the current tune just by pressing the shortcut key **P**. The other option, Play All Tunes, plays all the tunes in the current file.

The Alarms applet that you learned in Chapter 20 also can play your tunes. You can write your own melody and have Alarms play it automatically at any time of the day. But Alarms doesn't give you a choice of tune files. Alarms works only with the default tune file, which is named PMDIARY.$$A. To change the names and melodies of the tunes available to Alarms, you have to open PMDIARY.$$A in Tune Editor first and then make your changes and save them.

Using Seek and Scan Files

For Related Information
- "Introducing Presentation Manager," p. 234

As you learned in Chapter 10, folders and directories are useful tools for keeping your files organized. But sometimes you cannot remember the exact place where you stored an important file. If you can remember the file's name, or at least part of the name, then the Seek and Scan Files applet can sniff it out for you—no matter where the file happens to be on your hard disk.

You also can search files for a string of text. This option is handy if you do not recall the name or location of a file, but know a distinctive word or phrase that the file contains. The next section provides an example for searching for files.

Searching For a File

Suppose you have the chapters of this book stored in separate files somewhere on your hard disk. You don't know which directory holds them or remember the names of the files, but you know that the names of the chapter files all end with *DOC*. You need to find the chapter that discusses the Time Management applets, and you recall that somewhere this chapter contains the words "alarm tune." Seek and Scan Files comes to the rescue. Figure 22.10 shows the search example.

To access Seek and Scan Files, double-click the Seek and Scan Files icon in the Productivity window. Use the following steps to provide Seek and Scan Files the information needed to search for "alarm tune" in all the DOC files located on your hard disk:

1. In the File name to search for field, type ***.DOC**, which stands for all files with the DOC extension.

   This approach is faster than searching every file.

2. In the Text to search for field, type **alarm tune**.

   Seek and Scan files will scan each DOC file for this text.

3. Use the Drives to search check boxes to specify which disks the applet should scan. You can select each disk individually and even include floppy disk drives. In this case, you want to search fixed disk C, so check its box.

4. Choose the **O**ptions menu and ensure the option **I**gnore case has a check mark next to it. If there is not a check mark next to **I**gnore case, choose the option.

   Unless you know exact capitalization, you should generally search for text ignoring the case. Seek and Scan files will find "Alarm tune" or "Alarm Tune" or any other combination of capitalization.

5. After entering this information, press the **S**earch button.

   You hear the disk drive whirring as Seek and Scan Files looks for the misplaced chapter.

Fig. 22.10
Scanning files for a phrase.

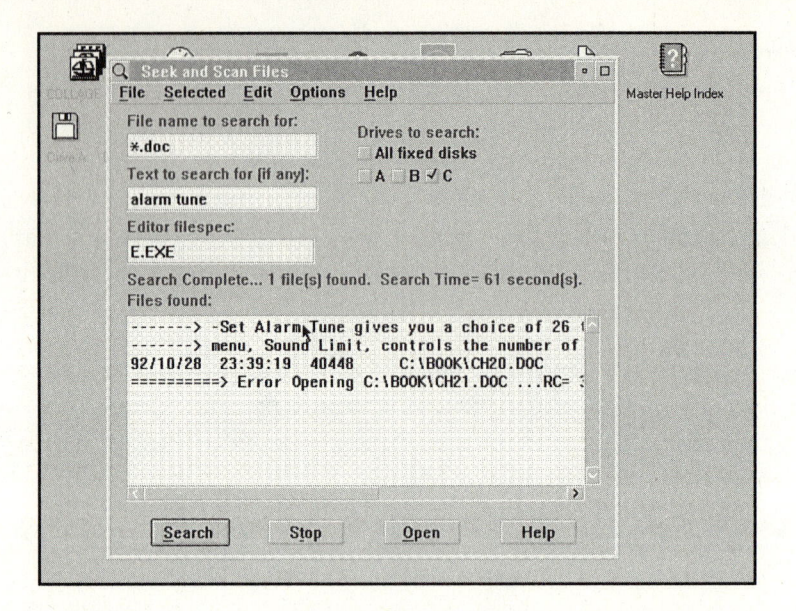

Each time the applet finds something of interest, it prints a message in the Files found box. Take a closer look at this output, which is explained in the following list:

- The first line clearly shows a successful search. You see the words Alarm Tune on-screen. Note that this phrase was found even though you didn't specify in the Text to search for field that the words should be capitalized. In a later section, you learn a command that tells the applet to require an exact match, including case.

- The second line reports another match, but the reason is not immediately obvious. The search text doesn't seem to be part of the line displayed. The answer to this riddle is that *alarm tune* really does occur later in this line, but only the first few characters of the line are displayed. When this happens, use the horizontal scroll bar to scroll to the right so that you can see the rest of the line.

- The third line gives the name of the file that contains the text shown in the first two lines. This line tells you that the file you seek is called CH20.DOC and is located in the C:\BOOK directory. The numbers tell you the date and time the file was saved and the number of characters it contains.

- You often see something like the fourth line. This line looks confusing at first. Why is Seek and Scan Files giving you an error message? The answer is that the file for Chapter 22 is being edited in a background window at the same time that the Seek and Scan Files applet is running. This file is locked while in use by the word processor, so the applet cannot examine it. This is a normal consequence of the steps OS/2 takes to protect the files an application owns from other applications. You see a similar error message when you try to examine any of OS/2's system files.

This fairly complicated example shows you the power of the Seek and Scan Files applet. Now that you understand what the applet can do, you learn how to use the menu commands in the following sections.

Using the File Menu

File searches can take a considerable amount of time, so you may want to save the results on disk. Saving the results is quicker than performing the search again. The Save command on the File menu puts the results of the search into a file you name. When you save the results of one search and then search for something else, you can use the Save As command to store the second set of results under a different file name that you specify.

Using the Selected Menu

When you have found a file that matches your search criteria, you may want to work directly with that file. You can do that without leaving Seek and Scan Files. Click the file of your choice in the Files found box; then pull down the Selected menu. The following options appear:

- *Open* loads the file into the editor of your choice. The default is OS/2's System Editor. You can specify any other editor by typing its name in the Editor filespec field. You may need to include the full path, for example C:\MM\MM.EXE if you want to use Multimate. The Open button at the bottom of the screen performs the same function as the Open command on the Selected menu.

- *Process* runs the file. This option works only if the file is an executable program, with file extension BAT, COM, or EXE.

- *Command* enables you to perform any OS/2 command on the file. If you want to delete the file you have found, for example, choose Command and then type **Erase** in the window that pops up.

Using the Edit Menu

The Edit menu offers two commands. The first, Copy, puts a copy of the line you have selected on the OS/2 Clipboard. You can then paste the line into any other location or application. The other command you see here, Clear List, erases the contents of the Files found box so that you can start a new search.

Using the Options Menu

The options available on this menu enable you to fine tune the way Seek and Scan Files works. A check mark appears next to each selected option.

- *Search Subdirectories* tells the applet to look in every file on the disks you have selected. If you do not check this option, the applet confines the search to files in the root directory or in any other directory you specify in the File name to search for field.

- *Display Found Text* instructs Seek and Scan Files to show each match in the Files found box when you have made an entry in the Text to search for field. This option is normally useful. But if you expect a lot of matches, you may want to turn the option off so that only the names of files containing the text display.

- *Ignore Case* indicates that the text you are searching for must be an exact match, including capitalization.

- *Clear on Search* means that the applet will clear the Files found box whenever you start a new search. Results of any previous search are erased.

- *Set Defaults* saves the current settings on the Options menu. Those settings become the defaults that the Seek and Scan Files applet uses whenever you run it. This command also saves the default editor that you have specified in the Editor filespec field.

Stopping a Search

Some searches take a long time. Even with a fast hard disk, it could take several minutes to seek a key word in every single file. When you see the file that you really need in the Files found box, choose the Stop button to keep Seek and Scan Files from continuing the search.

For Related Information
- "Storing Files and File Names," p. 45
- "Organizing Directories," p. 51
- "Introducing Presentation Manager," p. 234

Using Sticky Pad

The Sticky Pad applet enables you to write little yellow notes and attach them to windows on the OS/2 desktop. Minimize a sticky note, and it turns into an icon in the corner of the window. Minimize the window, and the sticky note stays attached. You can then double-click the sticky note to display its contents, without having to restore the minimized window to which you attached the note.

Use this applet the same way you use paper sticky notes. For example, imagine that you are working with your word processor when the phone rings. Your boss is calling to ask you to send a copy of last month's sales spreadsheet across the network—pronto. Write yourself a sticky note that tells what you were typing in the word processor, and then minimize the note and the word processor so that you can open up your spreadsheet and satisfy the boss's urgent request. When you have got that task out of the way, you see the sticky note attached to your word processor, and it reminds you of what you were doing before the interruption.

> **Caution**
> Don't close the applet, or the sticky notes vanish.

Attaching a Sticky Note

You can attach a sticky note to any open window. Just open the Sticky Pad applet, click the top sticky note's title bar, and drag it to the open window while holding either mouse button down. Release the mouse button when the sticky note is on top of the window, and the note sticks. If you drag the window around the screen, the sticky note moves along with it. And if you pop up OS/2's Window List with Ctrl-Esc, you can see the name of the window to which each sticky note is attached.

In figure 22.11, two notes are stuck to the Productivity folder. One of these notes is minimized, so it shows up as a little yellow square in the corner of the window.

568 Chapter 22—Using the OS/2 General Purpose Applets

Fig. 22.11
Sticky notes attached to a folder.

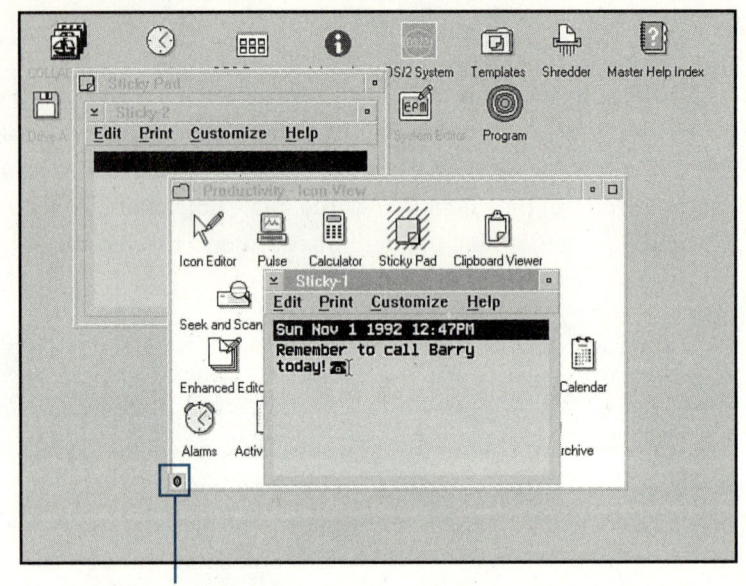

Minimized sticky note

If you close the Productivity window in this example, the sticky notes come unglued from the window, and show up on the OS/2 desktop. Closing the Sticky Pad applet clears all sticky notes. Menus available on each sticky note offer you useful commands that are discussed in the following sections.

Using the Edit Menu

Typing a sticky note is like typing in a word processor or an editor. The Edit menu provides commands that make it easier to enter notes. The first command on the menu, Undo, reverses the effect of the last change you typed, which is handy if you make a mistake like inadvertently erasing an entire note. You also see Cut and Paste commands that allow you to exchange information between a sticky note and any other Clipboard-aware application.

The Edit menu also provides commands that clear either a single line or the whole note. The menu also has a Delete Line command. The command to delete a line is only slightly different from clearing the line. Clearing gets rid of the contents of a line and fills in blanks instead, but deleting removes the line and closes up the space it occupied. In addition, the menu has two commands for adding new lines before or after the current line.

The remaining commands give you capabilities not normally available in other text editors. Reset Timestamp inserts the current time and date on the first line of the sticky note. Use this command whenever you modify a note and want to update the time. The Graphics command pops up a window that presents a choice of pictures that you can copy into a sticky note. You might use the telephone graphic in a note, for example, that reminds you to return a phone call.

Using the Customize Menu

In addition to the usual Colors and Font size options, Sticky Pad's Customize menu gives you a command to save the pad's position on-screen. Whenever you start Sticky Pad, it will appear in this same position. Icon is the other special option on the Customize menu. When you choose Icon, you see a menu that allows you to specify to which corner of a window your sticky notes will adhere. The Icon menu also offers you a command that stores this choice so that your sticky notes will always go in the same corner of any window to which you attach them.

Using Notepad

The Notepad applet is like a stack of index cards. There are five cards, and you can write something different on each one. You can use Notepad, for example, to jot down several separate lists of things you have to do during the day. You can have as many Notepad files as you like, with five cards in each. You might want to have a separate Notepad for each of your customers and use the cards to store information such as the customer's address, phone number, and names of key people.

For Related Information
- "Introducing Presentation Manager," p. 234

Creating Notes

To begin using the Notepad, you double-click the Notepad icon in the Productivity folder. You can type text on the card that's on top of the other cards, and then click one of the other cards to enter further information. You also can use the View menu, as explained in an upcoming section, to switch to a different card.

The five pages in each Notepad display in a stack (see fig. 22.12). You can always see the top line on each card, so you might want to use the top line to write down the subject of the notes that you write on each card. Clicking any card brings that card to the top of the stack so that you can view its entire contents.

Fig. 22.12
The Notepad applet.

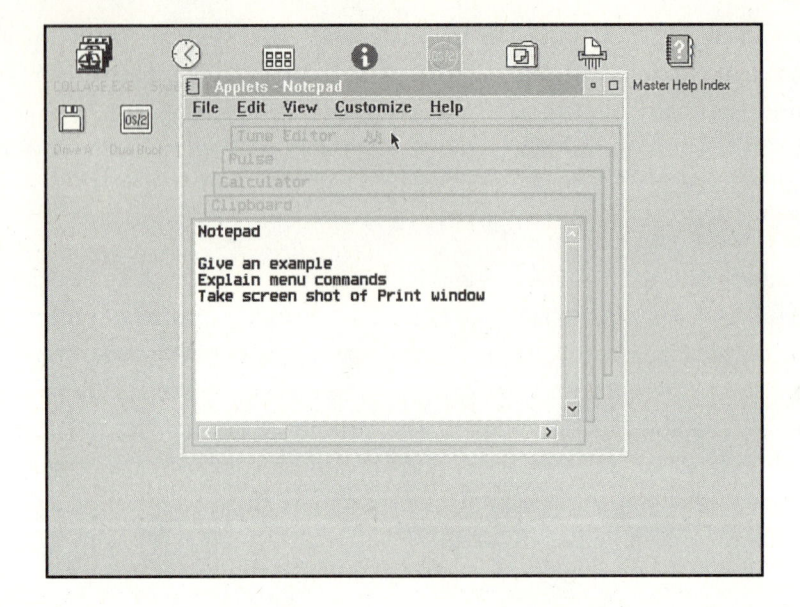

Through Notepad's menu bar, you access commands to load and save files, edit the text on a card, and view individual cards. You learn these commands in the next few sections. The commands on the Options and Help menus for Notepad are the same as for the other General Purpose applets.

Using the File Menu

You can save Notepad's contents in a file so that they are available whenever you need them. You can have several different Notepad files. The New command at the top of the File menu clears all the contents and gives you a fresh set of five blank cards so that you can start a new file.

To load an existing set of cards, use the Open command. The applet prompts you for the name of a card file. Notepad's files are saved in a special format, and you cannot load any other type of file into Notepad. For example, if you try to open the AUTOEXEC.BAT file that always exists in your root directory, Notepad beeps at you. You see the message, The requested path does not exist. The message could perhaps be clearer, but it really just means that you tried to load a file that wasn't created by Notepad.

The Save and Save As commands enable you to store the current Notepad in a file on your disk. The difference between these two commands is that Save As prompts you to type the name of the file, whereas Save stores the Notepad into the file currently open. The Save option is not available unless you have made a change to the Notepad contents since you last opened or saved a file.

You also can print the contents of the Notepad. Figure 22.13 shows the window that pops up when you chose the Print command from the File menu. Here you can select a printer and choose whether to send the output to a file or directly to the printer. You can decide whether to print every card or the top one only. The Include blank lines button allows you to print or suppress blanks. You can control the number of lines that print on each page by typing a number in the Lines to print field. Similarly, the Printer line length field enables you to control the number of characters that print on each line.

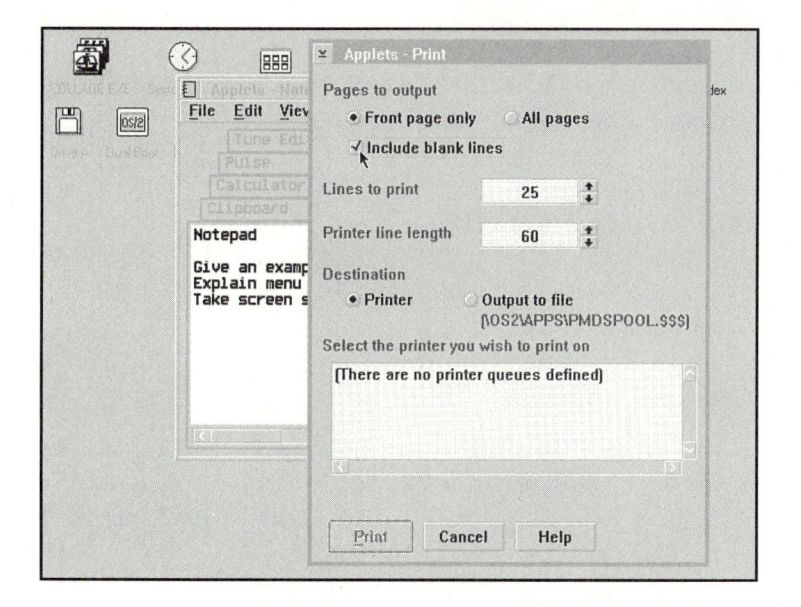

Fig. 22.13
Printing Notepad's contents.

Using the Edit Menu

The Edit menu gives you access to commands that modify the Notepad's contents. Here you see an Undo command, which cancels the last change you made. The Cut, Copy, and Paste commands permit you to transfer information between the Notepad and other OS/2 applications. The hot key for each of these commands is shown on the Edit menu; these hot keys—Shift-Del, Ctrl-Ins, and Shift-Ins—are the same ones you use for similar operations in other applications.

On the Edit menu, you also see commands to delete a line or clear a line, a card, or the whole Notepad. The Delete Line command is similar to the Clear Line command. Clearing a line turns it into a blank line, but Delete Line removes it completely. Other commands insert a blank line before or after the current line.

572 Chapter 22—Using the OS/2 General Purpose Applets

The last command, Graphics, pops up a window containing a variety of little icons. Double-click any of these icons to copy it to the current cursor position on the top card.

Using the View Menu

A line in the Notepad can be up to 160 characters long, but the screen isn't wide enough to show such a long entry all at once. To see the whole entry, choose the View Complete Line command. Double-clicking any line is a shortcut for doing the same thing.

The other commands on the View menu enable you to bring any card in the background to the top of the stack. An easy alternative method is to click the left mouse button once on the card you want to see on top.

Using Icon Editor

For Related Information
- "Introducing Presentation Manager," p. 234

Icon Editor is a paint program that you can use to design your own icons. You can substitute the icons you create for any of OS/2's default icons, or even modify OS/2's default icons. Figure 22.14 shows Icon Editor during the process of creating a new icon.

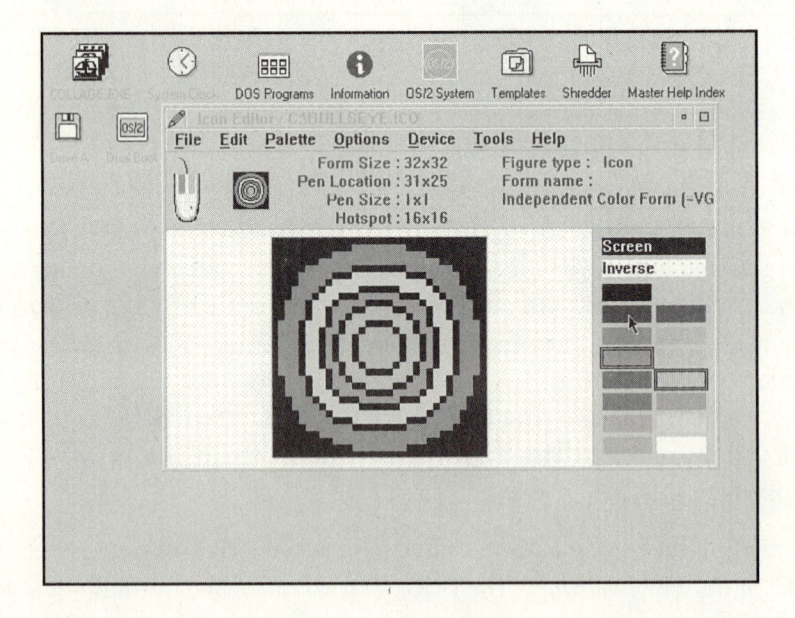

Fig. 22.14
Creating a new icon in Icon Editor.

Creating a New Icon

To draw a picture on-screen, you simply point the mouse to the spot you want to color and click. To draw with a different color, click any color shown in the palette at the right of the window. You can pick a different color for the left and right mouse buttons, for example; the current color for each is shown on the picture of a mouse near the upper-left corner of the window.

Icon Editor is quite a versatile paint program, with many options and commands available through its menus. The following sections show what you can do with each menu.

Using the File Menu

The New command on the File menu erases the current drawing and presents you with a blank screen for creating a new icon. If you want to change an icon you have already drawn, load your old icon with the Open command. Unfortunately, you cannot directly open the default icon for an OS/2 application. But later in this chapter you learn a technique to change even the System default icons.

Saving your work often pays; if you make a change that you don't like, you can just reopen the last version you saved. The Save command stores your icon in the file that is currently open. If you want to save your icon under a new name, use the Save As command.

Using the Edit Menu

The Edit menu gives you powerful commands for changing the icon on-screen. The first command, Undo, takes back the last change you made. The Cut, Copy, and Paste commands are used for transferring graphics between Icon Editor and other OS/2 applications. You can copy part of a picture from another program, for example, and paste it into Icon Editor, where it might form the basis of a new icon. And the Clear command erases the current drawing, in case you want to start with a blank screen.

Some commands work with a broad area of the drawing and require you to specify this area first with the Select command. To designate this area, choose Select, hold down the left mouse button on one corner of the area, drag the mouse to the opposite corner, and release the mouse button. This action surrounds the selected area with a black rectangle. If you want to select the entire icon, use the Select All command.

An example of a command that requires you to select an area is Stretch Paste. This command pastes the OS/2 Clipboard's contents into an area that you outline, stretching or shrinking the contents to fit. With a picture on the Clipboard, you select an area and then use Stretch Paste to insert the picture.

Another command that works on a selected area is Fill. Select an area, choose a color from the palette, and then pick the Fill command from the Edit menu. The entire selected area fills with that color, replacing whatever was in the area before. You also can reverse a selected portion from left to right, or up and down, with the Flip Horizontal and Flip Vertical commands. And the Circle command draws a circle that just fits inside the area you have selected.

Using the Palette Menu

The Palette is the group of colors on the right side of the screen. You can create different Palettes with colors that you blend yourself. If you have changed some colors and want to get the defaults back, pick the Load Default command on this menu. To access a Palette that you previously saved, use the Open command. After making changes to a Palette, use the Save command to store your updates, or the Save As command to store your modified Palette in a new file.

The Edit Color command pops up a window that enables you to mix your own custom colors, as you can see in figure 22.15. The three sliders control the amount of red, green, and blue that you blend into your new color. In the figure, the small, equal amounts of these three primary colors result in a dark gray.

Fig. 22.15
Blending a custom color in Icon Editor.

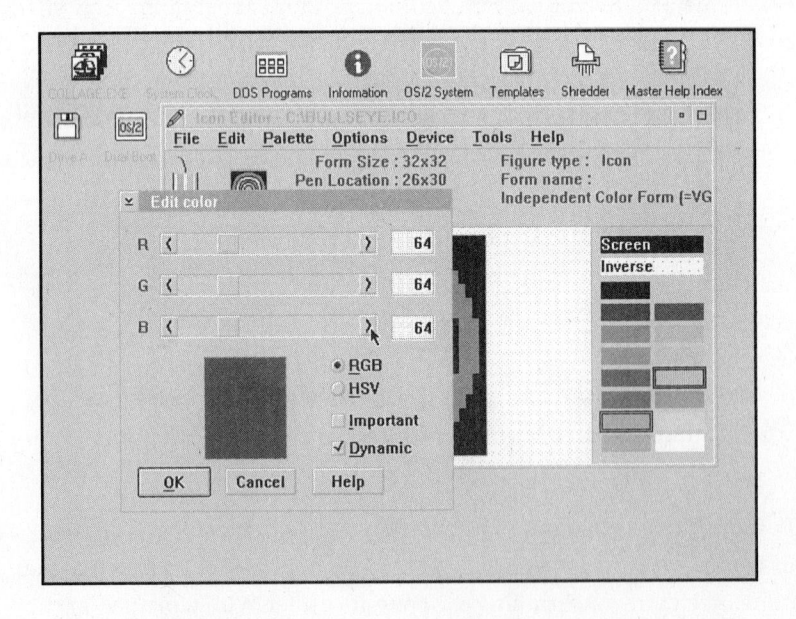

Two more commands complete the Palette menu. The Swap command exchanges the colors used by the left and right mouse buttons. And when you choose Set Default, your current modified Palette becomes the system default that loads whenever you start Icon Editor.

Using the Options Menu

This menu contains miscellaneous commands that enable you to control how the Icon Editor screen looks and how the drawing tools work. The following list describes these commands:

- *Test* substitutes the current icon for the mouse cursor.

- *Grid* draws a network of black lines that separate every picture element in the icon.

- *X Background* writes a little X on every picture element that you have not colored. When you use your icon to represent a program on-screen, these uncolored areas let the screen background show through.

- *Draw Straight* forces the mouse to move only in a straight line when you are holding the mouse button down. If your mouse is very sensitive, it can be difficult to draw a straight line without the help of this command.

- *Pen Size* brings up a menu that enables you to pick a width for the "pen" with which your mouse draws. By default, this pen is one picture element wide, but you can make it wider.

- *Preferences* allows you to modify and save the current settings of all your Icon Editor options.

- *Hot Spot* enables you to specify the icon's activation area.

Using the Device Menu

This menu offers two choices, which enable you to design icons for displays other than the one you have installed. This feature should not be important unless you are developing OS/2 programs that have to work on all types of video displays. The List option enables you to pick from among the different display types. The Edit Predefined selection gives you an opportunity to change the way these displays work by default. Use caution if you choose to experiment with these options.

Using the Tools Menu

The options on this menu change the way the mouse cursor works. When you pick Color Fill, clicking the mouse on any spot causes the whole area surrounding the icon to fill with the color you choose. The cursor changes to a picture of a paint bucket because this action is like spilling paint into a whole area. The other option, Find Color, turns the cursor into a question mark. When you click with this question mark on any spot on-screen, Icon Editor figures out what color is used at that spot and highlights that color in the Palette by drawing a box around it.

Associating Your Own Icon with a Program

After you have drawn and saved an icon, you will want to associate it with a program. Suppose that you have saved the icon drawn in figure 22.14 under the name Bullseye, and you want to use this icon for the DOS Window program in the OS/2 System Command Prompts folder. Follow these steps:

1. Open the Command Prompts folder in the system menu, and click the right mouse button on DOS Window.

   A pop-up menu appears.

2. Click the arrow to the right of **O**pen, and then choose **S**ettings.

   This step opens DOS Window's settings notebook.

3. Flip to the General page in the notebook, and click the **F**ind button.

   A Find window pops up, as shown in figure 22.16.

4. Click the **F**ind button here, and in a few moments you should see the Bullseye icon.

5. Click the Bullseye icon and press OK.

Your icon replaces DOS Window's default icon, as you can see by examining it in the Command Prompts folder on-screen.

Modifying an Application's Default Icon

As mentioned earlier in this chapter, there is no easy, direct way to open an application's default icon. But you can modify this icon if you start Icon Editor from the application's settings notebook.

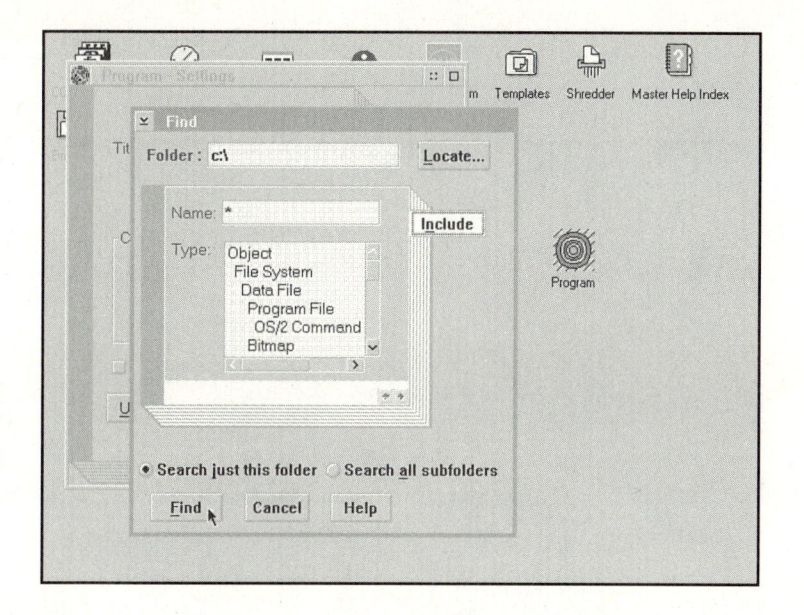

Fig. 22.16
Changing an application's icon.

The default icon for Enhanced Editor, for example, contains the letters OS/2. You might like to change those letters to EPM because, as you learned in Chapter 14, EPM is another name for the Enhanced Editor. Just follow these steps:

1. Open the Enhanced Editor's settings notebook to the General page, as explained in the preceding section.

2. Click the Edit button.

   Icon Editor appears on-screen. The default Enhanced Editor icon loads, and Icon Editor's title bar shows a temporary file name that OS/2 assigns to the editing session.

3. Using the painting techniques described earlier, cover up the letters OS/2 and draw the letters **EPM** instead.

4. Save the icon with the Save command on Icon Editor's File menu. Close Icon Editor, and then close EPM's settings notebook.

   You see the new icon appear on-screen inside the Productivity folder.

Fig. 22.17
Changing a default icon with the Icon Editor.

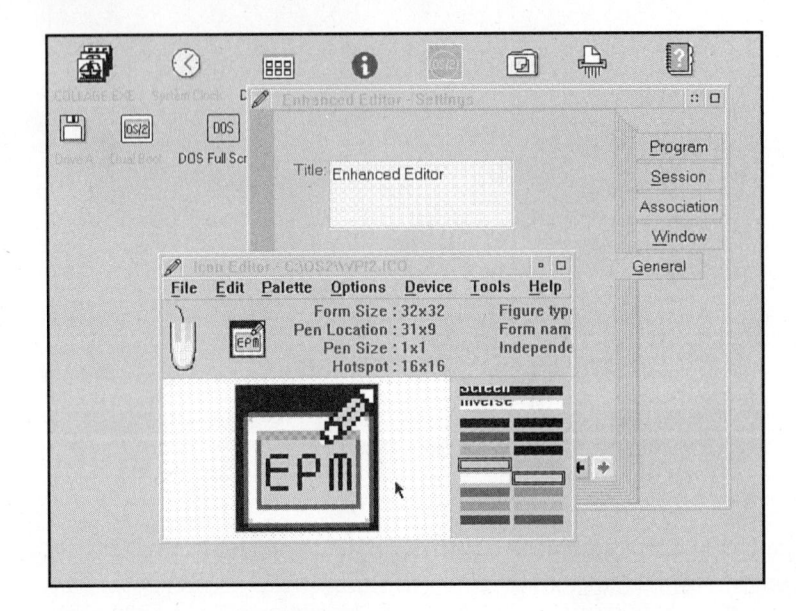

Figure 22.17 illustrates this process. If you have created any copies or shadows of EPM, they also display your revised icon.

Chapter Summary

For Related Information
- "Introducing Presentation Manager," p. 234

In this chapter, you mastered OS/2's General Purpose applets. You now know how to use these applets to do arithmetic, monitor system resources, manage the OS/2 Clipboard, and edit icons. You also learned how to write tunes, find lost files, and jot down ideas on sticky notes and note cards.

In Chapter 22, you study a group of applets that help you manage your data, using a spreadsheet, a chart program, a database, and a terminal program.

Chapter 23

Using the OS/2 Data Management Applets

Chapter 21 introduced the general purpose applets supplied with OS/2. This chapter covers the data management applets: Database, Spreadsheet, PM Chart, PM Terminal. While they are not full-blown application programs, these applets function adequately for small projects.

Database, as the name suggests, is a small database program where you can store lists of information. Database is comparable to an index card system where you store information about a particular topic on an index card and then have a series of cards in the collection.

Spreadsheet, also as its name suggests, is a small spreadsheet program for storing tables of information. Spreadsheet includes mathematical features, so you can use it for accounting or other arithmetic tables.

PM Chart is a small presentation graphics program that can make simple charts such as bar, line, or area graphs. You also can use PM Chart as a drawing program.

PM Terminal is a communications program for transmitting data to and receiving data from another computer by means of a modem. Although the applet is rather confusing to configure, it is very easy to use.

You probably will use these applets occasionally and will purchase OS/2 application programs with more features and capacities for a business. You can use Database to conveniently store a few names and addresses, for example, but you should buy a more powerful application to manage large mailing lists.

For each applet introduced in this chapter, you learn the following important features:

- Its purpose and typical application
- How to use the applet
- What the limitations are
- Examples of typical data entry and manipulation
- What data can be exchanged with other applets and how to make the exchange

Using Database

The Database applet is a small database program. In a database, you can store a series of lists of information. Each list is known as a *record*, and each item in a list is known as a *field*.

Database does not include the sophisticated sorting or reporting features that you can find in full-blown database applications. For small applications, such as keeping a few names and addresses, or for simple project tracking, however, Database is convenient and easy to use. The following table lists the menu options and their functions.

Menu	Menu Option	Description
File		
	9	
	Open	Open an existing database
	Save	Save your database
	Dialing function	Dial a phone number in the current record
	Print...	Print your database
	Print **l**ist format.	Arrange your printout's appearance

Menu	Menu Option	Description
Edit		
	Restore record	Restore your record
	Copy	Copy highlighted data
	Paste	Paste copied data
	Clear **l**ine	Clear the line in your database
	Clear **a**ll lines	Clear the record in your database
	Delete current record	Remove the current record
	Ca**n**cel edit	Undo all the edits made to current record
	Graphics...	Select a graphics image for your database line
	Edit line **h**eadings	Change or create headings for your database lines
	Add a new record	Add an additional record to your database
View		
	Line 1 through Line 8	A check alongside the heading name displays the relevant database line. "Line 1" is replaced by the line's name if you name your lines via Edit line headings in the Edit menu.
	Display statistics report	Lists statistics on your current database
	Print statistics report...	Prints statistic on your current database
Customize		
	Dial setup...	Adjust the dialing parameters
	Colors...	Change the colors for your database
	Font size	Change the font size
Help		

Purpose

The benefit of an electronic database over a series of index cards is found when you search through or organize your data. You can quickly find a database record containing particular information, and you can arrange the records in different sequences. These operations are much more time consuming when you are working with index cards.

Consider a database containing a list of names and addresses. A record is one name, along with its address and other associated data. You may store the first name, last name, street address, phone number and date of birth on one record, for example. You then can sort your records in alphabetical order by first or last name, by Zip code, or by date-of-birth order.

You can use the OS/2 Database as an electronic Rolodex; it can store up to 5000 records, each with eight fields of up to 30 characters. In addition to being able to store data, you can rearrange your database. You even can have your computer automatically dial a phone number stored in a record.

Understanding Database

OS/2 stores its applets in the Productivity folder. To access Database, open the OS/2 System folder and then open the Productivity folder. To open Database, double-click the Database icon. Figure 23.1 shows the Database opening window.

Fig. 23.1
Database opening window.

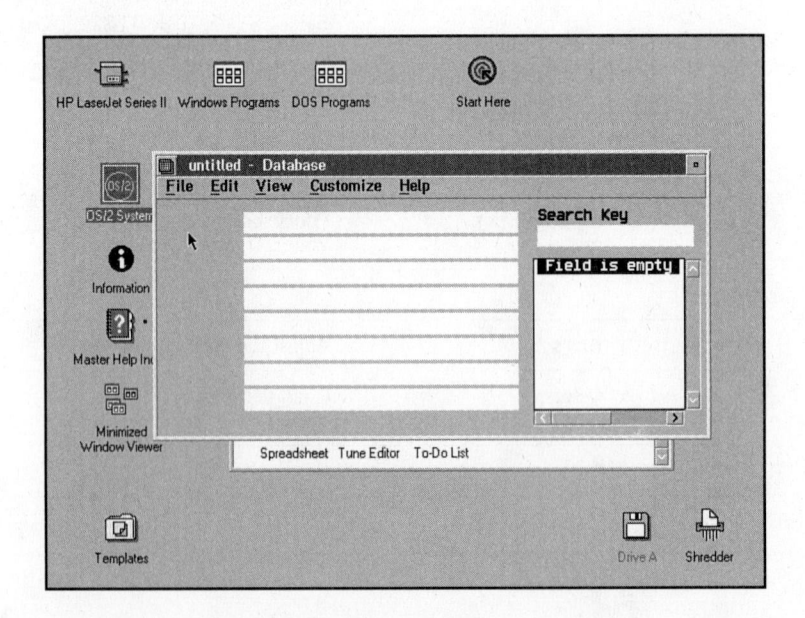

When you first open the database, no database is loaded and the title bar displays the word "untitled." When you save or reload a database, its name appears in the title bar.

The window area is divided into three sections. To understand these sections, you need to understand some database terminology. The terminology is easy to understand if you compare the database with a card index file, like a Rolodex, that contains names and addresses.

When you start Database, you are looking at one record in a database, the equivalent of looking at a particular index card. The left section of the window, which is blank when you have not loaded a database, shows the headings for each field in your database record. You can make these headings be First Name, Last Name, Phone Number, or Zip Code.

The center section has eight blank white bars where you enter your data. Each white bar is called a field. On your index card, this section is where you enter the data, which usually is different for each person in your card index file. The headings on every index card may be First Name and Last Name, for example, but the contents of each line, or field, will vary. Card number one may be for Jane Smith and card number two for John Jones. On card number one, a field name is First Name and the field's contents are Jane. On card number two, a field name is First Name, but the field's contents are John.

The right section of Database's window shows your current organization. The program arranges your database in an order based on a particular field, known as the *key field*. The database may be arranged by first names, for example. In this case, the First Name field is the key field. The list at the right of the window shows all the first names in alphabetical order. (If the fields' contents are numeric, the list places the fields in numerical order.)

To find a particular record based on the key field, you can scroll through the list until you find the record of interest, or you can type the field contents in the Search Key text box. You learn the procedures for retrieving records in later sections.

Because your database can contain up to 5000 records, this list is particularly important when you want to find a record. You can change the key field at any time, and the list is automatically updated. You can arrange the records in Zip Code order or in Last Name order, for example.

584 Chapter 23—Using the OS/2 Data Management Applets

Working with Database

To understand how to use the database, you can create a sample database of three records. First, you can set up the field name headings and the name of the database by following these steps:

1. Decide on names for your database fields. Each name can be up to eight characters in length.

2. To add headings to your fields, click Edit from the main menu bar and then click Edit line headings. Alternatively, you can press Alt-E to access the Edit menu and press H for the Edit line headings option. Figure 23.2 shows the window that appears.

Fig. 23.2
Editing Database headings.

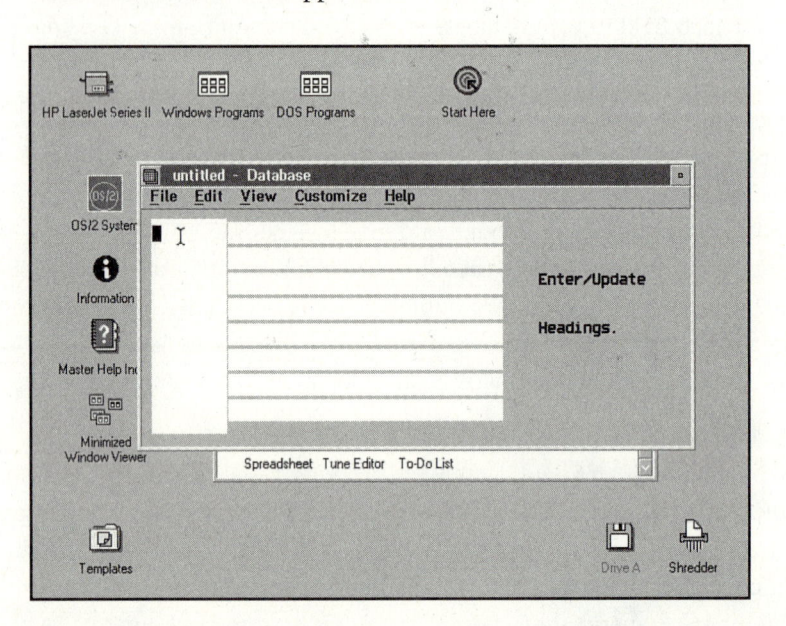

3. Type **First** for the First Name field in your database and press Enter. The flashing cursor moves to the next field heading. Continue entering the headings Last, Street, City, State, ZIP, Phone, and Comments.

   If you need to edit errors, click the field. You can use the typical editing keys such as Delete, Backspace, Insert, and the arrow keys to correct your headings.

Using Database 585

4. When you have entered the field names, click **F**ile and **S**ave to keep your headings or press Ctrl-S.

5. Type a database name, such as SAMPLE, in the Save as filename: text box and then click **S**ave to save the new database file. An empty sample database window appears (see fig. 23.3).

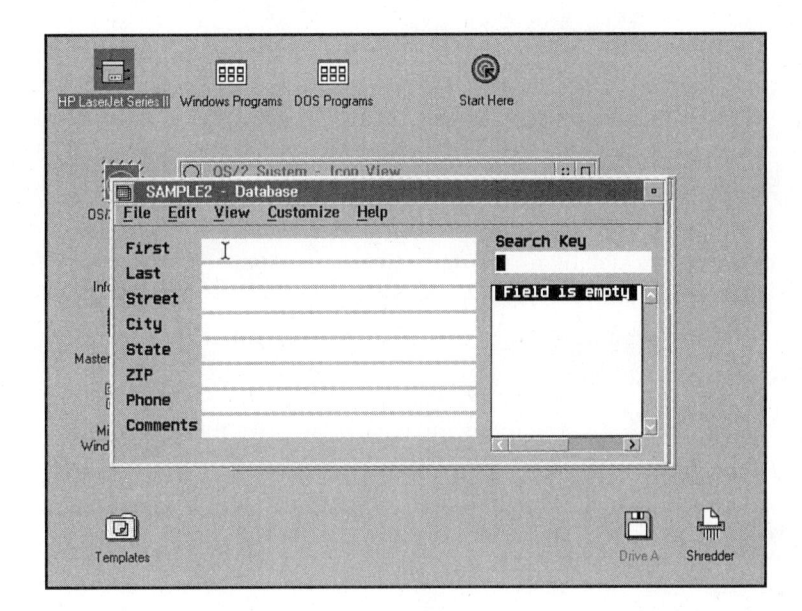

Fig. 23.3
Empty database record.

You screen shows the first record in your database. To enter data for this record, follow these steps:

1. Click the field area next to the heading First.

2. Type the name *Jane* and press Enter. You can use the arrow keys, Delete or Backspace key to correct any errors you make as you type.

3. Fill in the remaining blanks with the data in the table that follows.

Heading	Record 1
FIRST	Jane
LAST	Smith
STREET	123 Main St
CITY	Newtown

(continues)

586 Chapter 23—Using the OS/2 Data Management Applets

Heading	Record 1
STATE	IL
ZIP	60089
PHONE	708-123-4567
COMMENTS	new friend

4. When you have finished adding the data for the first record, click **F**ile and **S**ave to save the record or press Ctrl-S.

To add other records, choose **E**dit and then **A**dd a new record, or press Ctrl-A. Database displays a blank record ready for completion. When you have filled in the data, press Ctrl-S or click File and Save to save your file. If you decide not to add another record, press Ctrl-Q or click Edit and then Cancel Edit to cancel the record addition.

You can use the data in the following table to add two more records to the sample database.

Heading	Record 2	Record 3
FIRST	John	Sam
LAST	Jones	Ordinary
STREET	987 Side Rd	555 Primary Ave
CITY	Oldtown	Anytown
STATE	MD	MD
ZIP	21117	21246
PHONE	410-987-4321	301-999-1111
COMMENTS	old friend	business acquaintance

When you have completed entering the data, your screen should look like the one in figure 23.4.

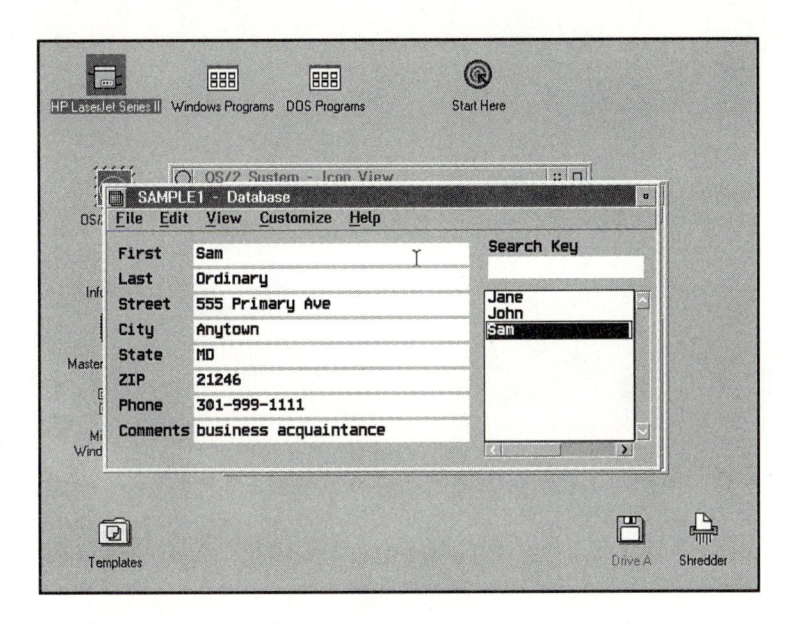

Fig. 23.4
Database with three records.

The center section of the window shows the current record, Sam. The right section shows a list of the records in your database. The key field is First and the list shows each first name. When you add more records, this list gets longer.

To find records containing the First Name you want, scroll through the list. To select the name from the list, double-click the desired name and your selection becomes the current record.

To find a record by using the Search Key field, click the text box immediately below the Search Key title and type the first letters of the name you are seeking. Database scrolls through the list automatically to find the record that matches your request.

In the sample database if you type **J**, the highlight moves from Sam to Jane. If you then type *o*, your window displays the John Jones record (see fig. 23.5).

If you want to change the key field (the field used to determine the sorting order), click **V**iew and then select the field name. If you want the records to be sorted by State, for example, click View and then click the field name State.

Fig. 23.5
The Search Key text box.

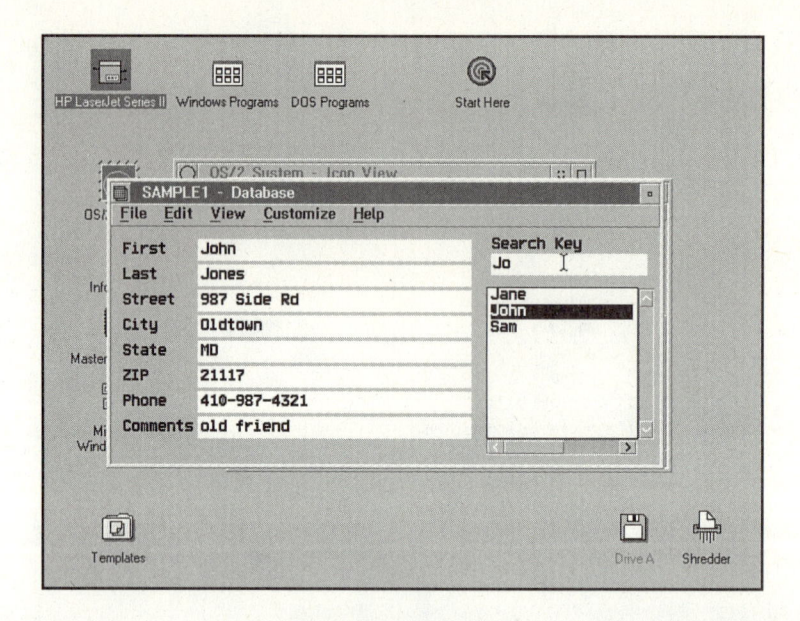

> **Note**
>
> If you have not added headings for your field names, the list in the view menu uses the titles Line 1, Line 2, and so on.

Figure 23.6 shows the sample database sorted by State. The list on the right shows the state names rather than the first names.

Fig. 23.6
Changing the sorting order.

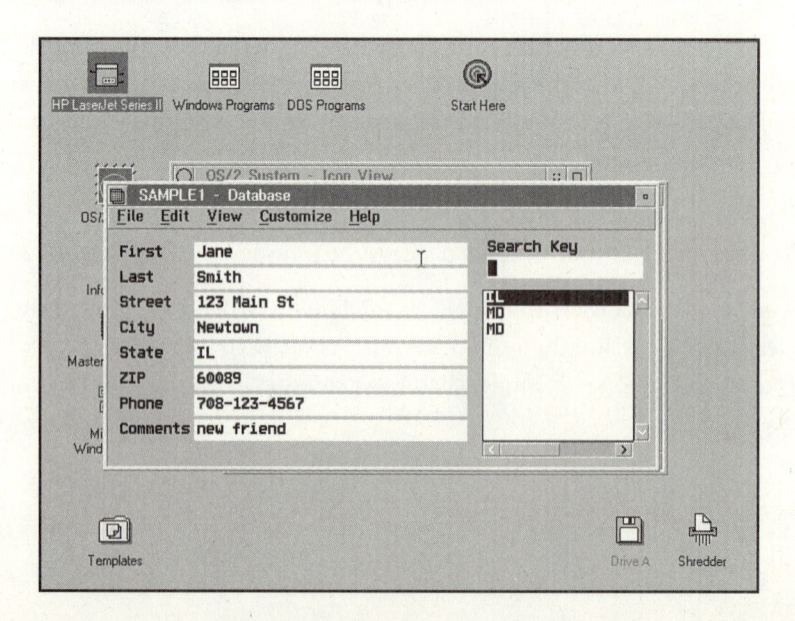

The Database printing features enable you to print the current record or the whole database. (Unfortunately, you cannot select a few records and print them.) To print a record, make it the current record by finding it in the list or by using the Search Key field. To print all records, you only need to load the database.

When Database displays the data you want to print, click **F**ile and then click **P**rint, or press Alt-F and then press P. Figure 23.7 shows the window that appears.

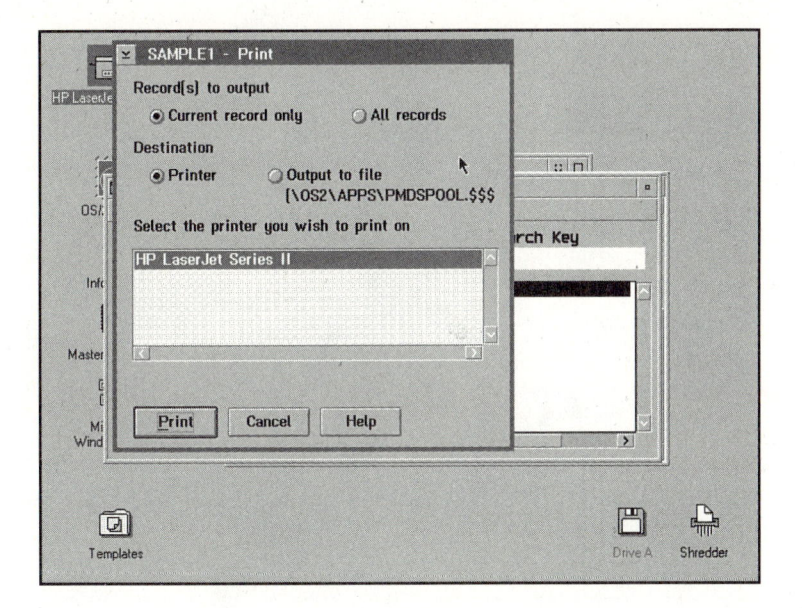

Fig. 23.7
Printing your database.

Click the radio button for outputting only the current record. If you want to print all records, click the other radio button for outputting all records. You then can choose between printing to your printer or to a file. After making your choices, click **P**rint.

Database includes a useful tool that uses your modem to dial a phone number from your database. (If you do not have a modem, you cannot use this feature.) Before you can use the automatic dialing, however, you must customize your configuration. Click **C**ustomize and then click **D**ial Setup, or press Alt-C and then D. The Dial Setup dialog box appears (see fig. 23.8).

Click the radio button for the serial port where your modem is attached. In the dialing control text box, you can type the control codes that your modem

590 Chapter 23—Using the OS/2 Data Management Applets

uses to start dialing. If you are using a Hayes-compatible modem, for example, you need to add the control codes that make the modem do the equivalent of taking the phone off the hook, perhaps pausing for a dial tone, and dialing any numbers to get an outside line. For the Hayes-compatible modem, you can add the codes ATDT; this code "wakes up" the modem and prepares it to dial a number by using tones rather than pulses. The codes you use vary with the modem. You may have a modem that is attached to a leased line and is permanently connected to another computer that requires different initial codes, for example.

Fig. 23.8
Dial Setup window.

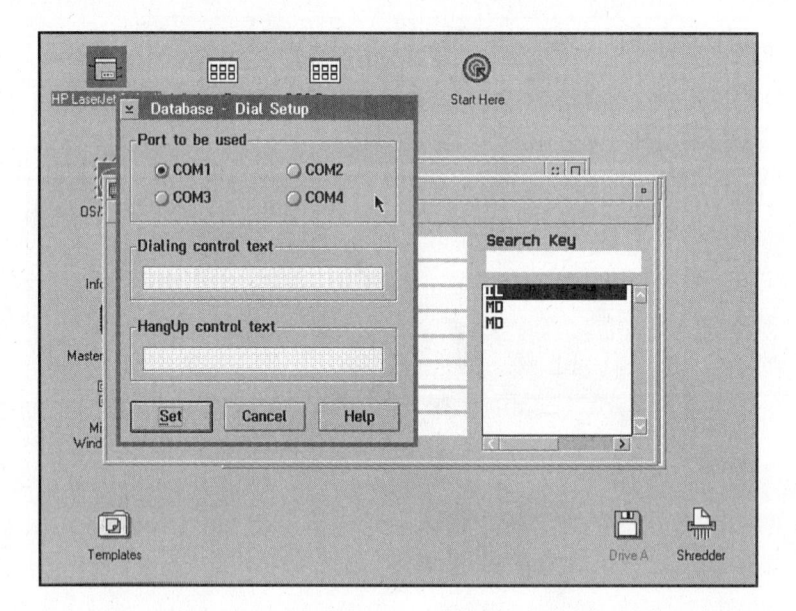

In the HangUp control text box, you can enter the codes your modem needs to break the connection. Again, the actual codes you use vary with the modem type. If you have a Hayes-compatible modem, you may include the hang up command ATH. Other modems have different requirements.

After you set the configuration, you can dial a number from your database record. Click **F**ile and then **D**ialing Function, or press Ctrl-D. The dialog box listing the dialing options from the current record appears (see fig. 23.9).

Database displays each field that starts with numbers from the current record. Choose the phone number you want the modem to dial. In this example, Database found three fields that begin with numbers and offers you the choice of each as a phone number to dial. Click the radio button alongside the phone number. Although the selection in this example seems ludicrous because you would not want to dial a house number or a Zip code, this feature allows you to have more than one field as a phone number. You can keep home and work phone numbers in your database, for example, and you can choose either number. When you have chosen the phone number, click **S**elect. The modem then dials the number.

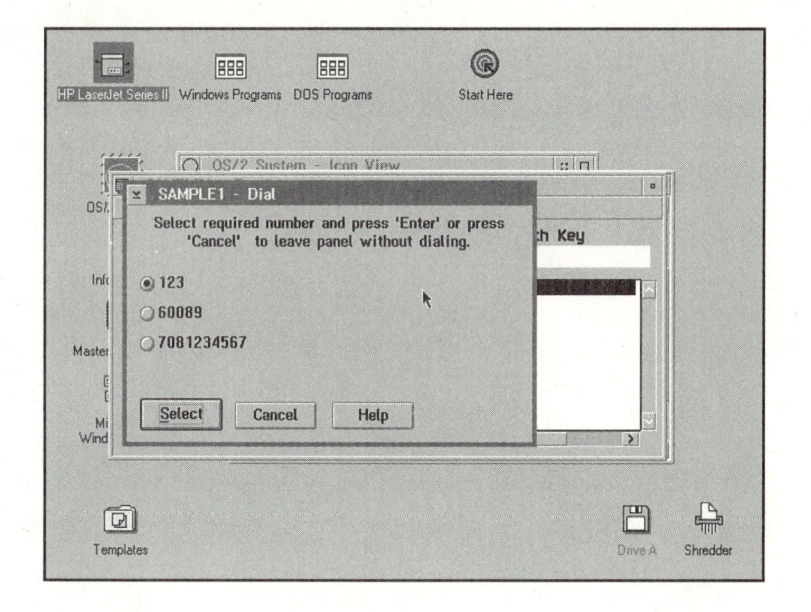

Fig. 23.9
The dialog listing the dialing options from the current record.

Understanding Database Limitations

Database has the following capacity:

- You can store up to 5,000 records in a database. Each record can contain up to eight fields, each with up to 30 characters. The field names can contain up to eight characters.

- You can sort your data records based on one field name.

- The printing features are fairly limited. You can print the current record or all records, but you do have some flexibility in the output format.

- You can have Database automatically dial a phone number stored in a record.

A full OS/2 database application includes the same features as Database but has far more flexibility. With a full OS/2 database application, you can have more fields, more records, and more options in field names. You can design a format for the presentation of your record. You can design a format, for example, that looks exactly like your current office forms.

The sorting features of a full database application also are more flexible. You can sort records using more than one key field, for example, sorting first by Last Name and then by First Name. You can display, print, or manipulate a subset of a full database—the records belonging to people living in a particular state, for example.

The output features of a full OS/2 database application allow you to design your output format, print a selection of records, and do numerical statistics. For example, a database of items that you sell may include prices. You could print out an order form listing several items and get a total price. You then can print out an order form listing several items and calculate the total price.

Full database applications also usually allow linking between databases. You can link a database containing parts lists, for example, with a customer database to create order entry screens, automatic invoicing, and packing list information.

Database is adequate as a simple Rolodex or other application that requires a short list of items. If you can imagine placing the database on a series of index cards, Database is a good starting application.

Sharing Database Information

As with all OS/2 applications, copying data from Database to another application requires a sequence of steps. To copy data from Database to another application, you highlight the area to be copied and then copy the data. You use the paste command in the other application to place the data into the new application.

To copy data from another application to Database, you highlight the data in the other application and use its copy command. You then use the paste command in Database to retrieve the data.

The final result of what is copied from one application to another depends on the applications being used. Database is a series of fields of data. You can highlight a single field or a series of fields for copying. When you place the data into a receiving application, however, the data is received as a single item, even if you copied multiple fields from your database. If you place the data in Sticky Pad, for example, the multiple fields are copied as a single item. If you place the data in spreadsheet, however, only one field is placed in a spreadsheet cell. You may have to copy each field individually for certain applications to get the expected results.

To copy all or part of a record to the Clipboard, follow these steps:

1. Move the cursor to the first character you want to copy.
2. Click and hold down the left mouse button.
3. Without releasing the mouse button, move to the last character you want to copy. A rectangle appears around the area.

When you release the button, the area is highlighted. If you want to select a different area, click the highlighted area to remove the highlighting.

Click **E**dit and **C**opy, or press Ctrl-Insert to copy the data to the Clipboard. In the receiving application, click the position where you want to place the data. Then choose **E**dit and **P**aste, or press Shift-Insert to place the data.

Using Spreadsheet

Spreadsheet is a table of information, typically mathematical. It is used most commonly for accounting applications. The table is divided into a series of rows and columns, and each location in the table is called a cell. A cell contains data—either text (such as a title), a number, or a formula. The formula relates the cell to other cells in the spreadsheet.

You can record business travel that can fit in a simple spreadsheet. The left column can contain dates; the next column, the activity; and the right column, the expense. A cell at the bottom can contain a formula totaling the expenses.

Spreadsheets are particularly powerful when they include formulas. If you alter an expense in the business travel report mentioned earlier, the cell containing the total expenses automatically updates to the new value. The following table describes the menu options available in Spreadsheet.

Menu	Menu Option	Description
File		
	New	Create a new spreadsheet
	Open	Open an existing spreadsheet
	Save	Save your spreadsheet
	Save **a**s...	Save your spreadsheet with a new name
	Print...	Print your spreadsheet
	Print **f**ormula/cell data...	Print the spreadsheet formulas and cell data
Edit		
	Copy	Copy highlighted data
	Paste	Paste copied data
	Clear input **l**ine	Clear the input line
	Home [go to cell A1]	Make the current cell A1
Recalculate		
	Recalc **c**urrent cell only	Recalculate the current cell
	Recalc **t**op->bottom, left->right	Recalculate starting at top and moving to the bottom and from the left moving to the right (cell A1 first, A2 second).
	Recalc **l**eft->right, top->bottom	Recalculate starting at left and moving to the right and from the top moving to the bottom (cell A1 first, B1 second).
	Auto recalculate	Recalculate after every edit
Customize		
	Colors...	Change the colors for your spreadsheet
	Font size	Change the font size
Help		

Purpose

Spreadsheet is a simple spreadsheet, allowing addition, subtraction, multiplication, and division operators in its formulas. Spreadsheet does not include more advanced mathematical operators such as statistical, trigonometrical, or engineering functions.

Typical applications for Spreadsheet include expenses, simple accounts, and record keeping. You can have up to 26 columns and 80 rows of data.

Understanding Spreadsheet

OS/2 stores all its applets in the Productivity folder. To access Spreadsheet, open the OS/2 System folder and then the Productivity folder. To open Spreadsheet, double-click the Spreadsheet icon. An untitled spreadsheet appears (see fig. 23.10).

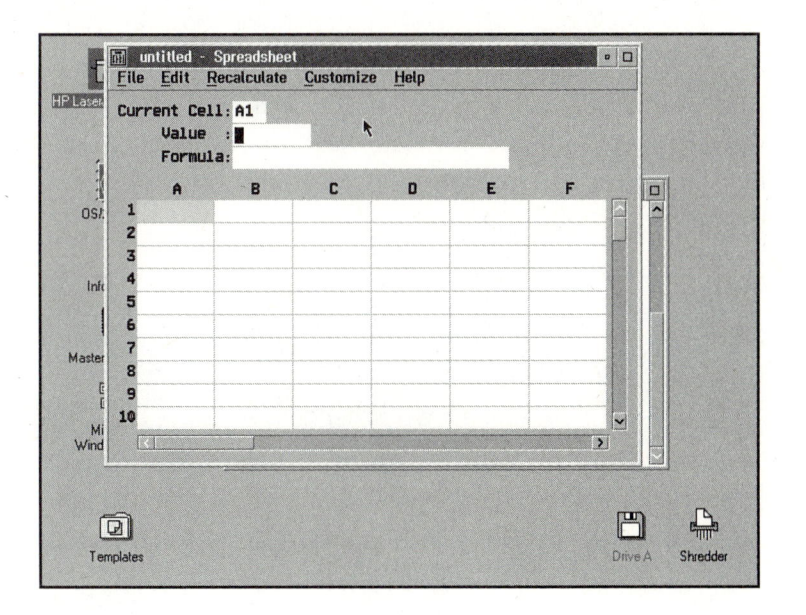

Fig. 23.10
The opening spreadsheet.

Spreadsheet numbers the rows and labels the columns with letters. To refer to a particular cell, you use its column letter and row number. Cell B3 is on the third row in the second column, for example. The cell where the cursor is currently located is known as the *current cell*.

When you start Spreadsheet, an empty spreadsheet appears. The title bar is labeled *untitled* until you save or reload a spreadsheet. The current cell is A1. Spreadsheet displays the contents of the current cell, along with its name, at the top of the window.

596   Chapter 23—Using the OS/2 Data Management Applets

A cell contains either a value or a value and a formula. A value can be a number or text. If the cell contains a formula, the value field is blank, but the result of the formula is shown in the spreadsheet cell.

You can move to any cell in the spreadsheet by clicking the cell or by using the scroll bars and clicking the required cell. To return to cell A1, known as the *Home cell*, press Ctrl-Home, or click Edit and then Home.

Working with Spreadsheet

If you want to practice entering data, labels, and formula, you can create a spreadsheet showing your utility expenses for the year. You can place the months of the year in the left column, column A and the total utility expense for the month in the next column, column B.

To insert the column titles into your spreadsheet, follow these steps:

1. Use the arrow keys to move to cell A2 or click cell A2.

2. Type **Month** and press Enter. The label Month appears in the spreadsheet in cell A2 (see fig. 23.11). Note that the word *Month* still appears in the current cell fields at the top of the window because cell A2 is the current cell.

Fig. 23.11
Spreadsheet contents.

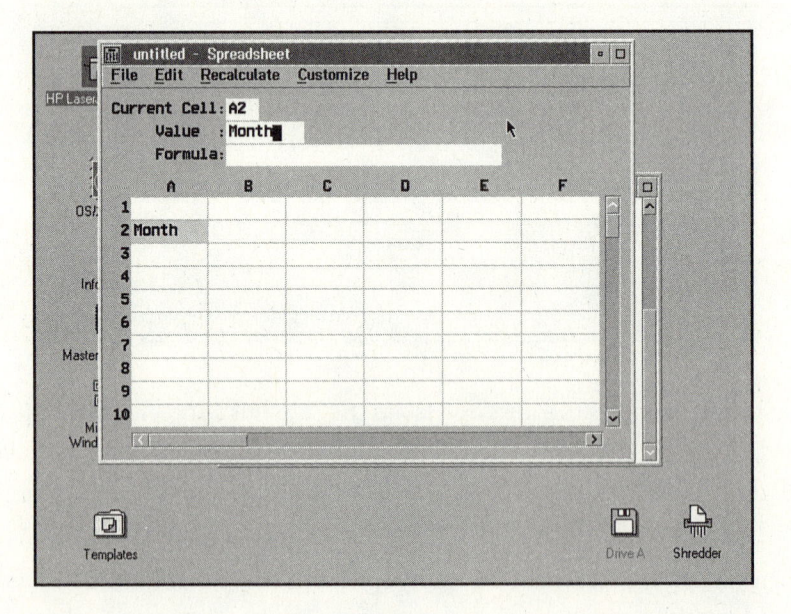

3. Use the down arrow key to reach cell A3 or click A3 with the mouse.

4. Type **Jan** and press Enter. Continue entering all the other months of the year until December is in cell A14. You must abbreviate the names of the month because you can only have up to eight characters in a cell.

5. Press Ctrl-Home to return to cell A1.

6. Move the cursor to cell B1 and type the title **Cost in$**. Then press Enter (see fig. 23.12).

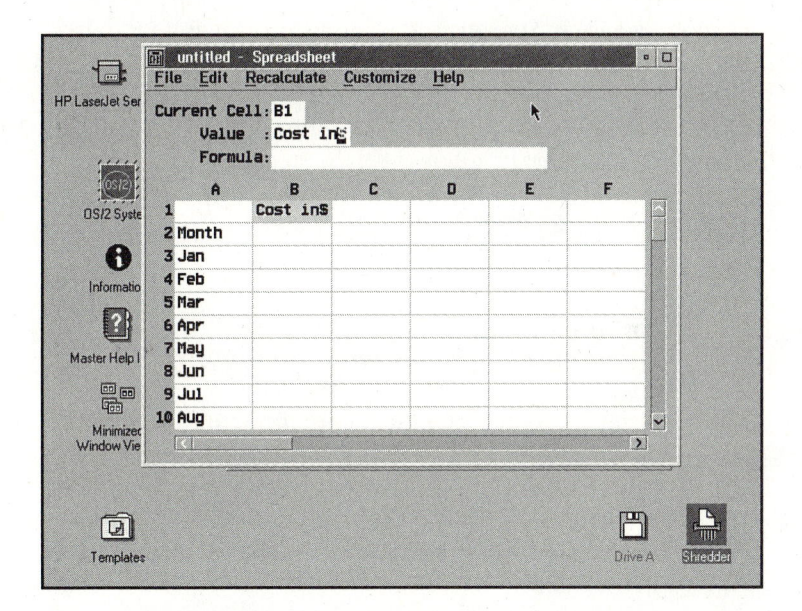

Fig. 23.12
Spreadsheet with labels.

7. Enter the following dollar amounts of the utility costs per month in cells B3 through B14: 65, 80, 105, 73, 46, 62, 92, 159, 94, 45, 43, and 58.

> **Note**
>
> A Spreadsheet cell can contain three types of information—a formula, text, or a number. If you enter a value that begins with a number, Spreadsheet considers it a number. If you start the value with a symbol such as the dollar sign, however, Spreadsheet considers the value as text.

With Spreadsheet, you can calculate the total annual and the average utility bill. Spreadsheet supports these arithmetic functions—addition, subtraction, multiplication, and division, using the symbols +, -, *, and / respectively. You also can use the @ symbol to add all the cells in a rectangular region. To multiply the contents of cell D4 by the contents of cell E5 and then to place the result in E6, for example, you enter the formula D4*E5 in cell E6.

To determine the total utility costs, Spreadsheet adds all the values found in cells B3 through B14 by using the formula B3@B14. More advanced spreadsheet programs include arithmetic functions such as average or square root. To calculate an average in Spreadsheet, you must use the full formula, B3@B14/12.

You can practice entering the formulas for totaling and averaging utility costs into the sample spreadsheet by following these steps:

1. In cell A16, enter the heading Total.

2. In cell A17 enter the heading Average.

3. Use the arrow keys to move to B16 or click the cell to make it the current cell.

4. Click the formula text box, or press Tab to move the cursor to the Formula text box.

5. Type **B3@B14** and press Enter. Do not leave any spaces between the characters. Your spreadsheet probably looks like the spreadsheet in figure 23.13.

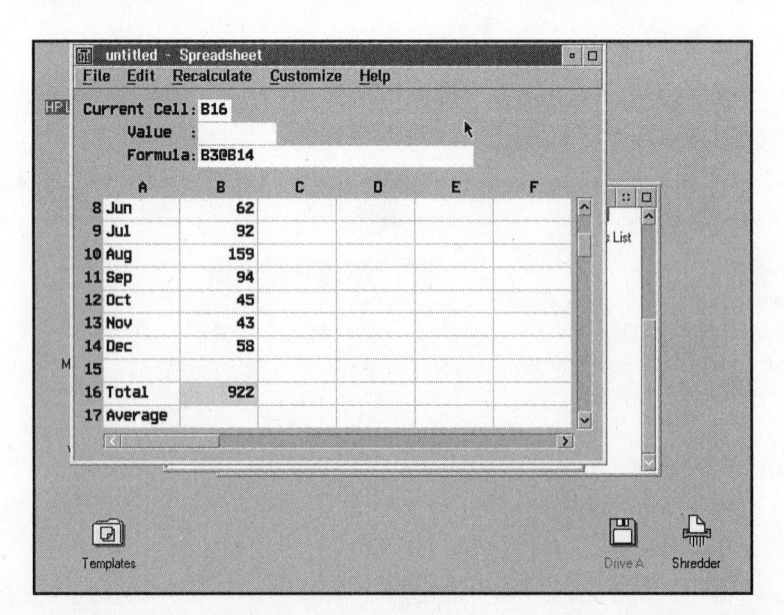

Fig. 23.13
Spreadsheet with a formula.

> **Note**
>
> You could have used the following formula:
>
> B3+B4+B5+B6+B7+B8+B9+B10+B11+B12+B13+B14
>
> The summation symbol @ is more manageable, however.

> **Tip**
>
> You also can use the @ symbol when you want to add more than one column at a time. You must define a rectangular area of the spreadsheet by first typing the cell name for the upper left corner of the area followed by @. Then type the cell name for the lower right corner of the area.

6. In cell B17, type the formula B3@B14/12 and press Enter. Spreadsheet calculates the average bill. Your spreadsheet probably looks like the spreadsheet in figure 23.14.

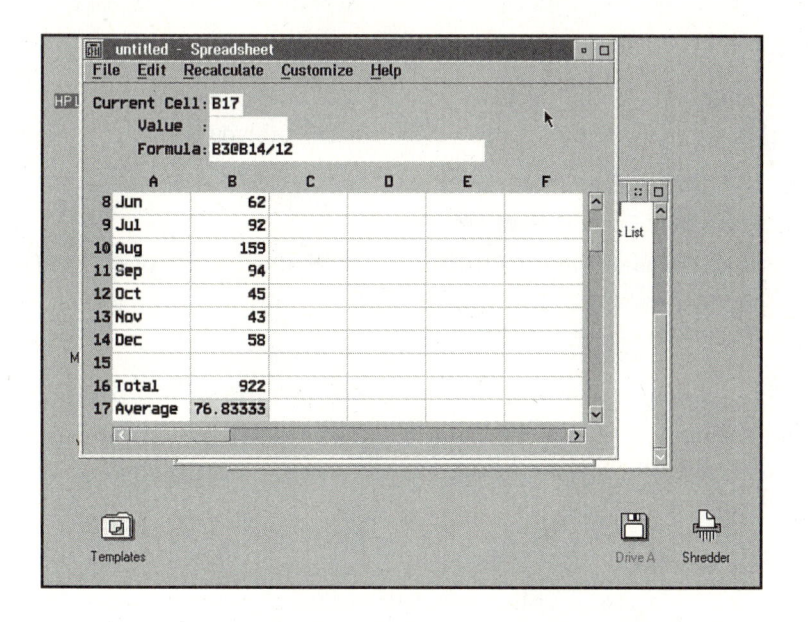

Fig. 23.14
The result of Spreadsheet's calculation, including all decimal places.

You also can use the formula B16/12, or the following formula:

(B3+B4+B5+B6+B7+B8+B9+B10+B11+B12+B13+B14)/12

Note that in the last OS/2 version you need to use parentheses to make Spreadsheet add all the numbers together before dividing by 12. Without the parentheses, the formula adds cells B3 through B13 and adds 1/12 of B14.

The value shown in B17 includes several decimal places. In other spreadsheet programs, you can alter the display format for the cell and only have the integer part displayed if you prefer. Spreadsheet does not include this formatting feature.

By default, Spreadsheet is set to automatically recalculate your spreadsheet values every time you edit a cell. On small or simple spreadsheets, the time taken to recalculate is minimal. As your spreadsheet becomes larger and includes more interrelated formulas, however, the recalculation time can become significant.

The Recalculate Menu offers alternatives. If you turn off Autorecalculate, Spreadsheet calculates new values only when you press Ctrl-C or Ctrl-R. Ctrl-C recalculates from top to bottom and from left to right; Ctrl-R recalculates from left to right and from top to bottom. Spreadsheet also can just recalculate the current cell.

You should leave Autorecalculate on until the time Spreadsheet uses in recalculation annoys you. By leaving Autorecalculate on, you reduce the chances of getting an incorrect value because you forgot to update the spreadsheet.

Understanding Spreadsheet Limitations

Spreadsheet has a maximum capacity of 26 columns and 80 rows. Each cell can contain a number or text with up to eight characters. A cell formula cannot exceed 30 characters.

You can do simple arithmetic using addition, subtraction, multiplication, division, and parentheses. No advanced functions such as trigonometric or statistical functions are supported. You can sum a rectangular area of cells, however, by using the @ symbol.

Sharing Spreadsheet Information

Copying data from Spreadsheet to another application requires the same sequence of steps as all OS/2 applications. To copy data from Spreadsheet, highlight the area to be copied and then choose **C**opy. Then paste the copied area into the new application. Remember that you can copy and paste within the same application. You can only copy one cell at a time in Spreadsheet, however.

To copy data from another application to Spreadsheet, you highlight the data in the other application and use the application's copy command. You then use the paste command in Spreadsheet to paste the data. The data you paste into Spreadsheet is placed in a single cell. Because a cell can only contain up to eight characters, however, you only get the first eight characters that you have copied.

To use Clipboard to copy a cell to another application, follow these steps:

1. Click the cell you want to copy with the left mouse button.

2. Click **E**dit and **C**opy, or press Ctrl-Insert, to copy the data to the Clipboard.

3. In the receiving application, click the position where you want to place the data.

4. Choose **E**dit and **P**aste, or press Shift-Insert, to place the data.

To copy information from Clipboard, click the cell where you want the data placed and press Shift-Insert or click **E**dit and **P**aste to place the data.

Using PM Chart

PM Chart is a presentation graphics program. You can use it to produce charts, such as bar charts or pie charts. You also can use it as a simple drawing program. PM Chart is the most fully featured data management applet in OS/2.

PM Chart enables you to create slides and charts for presentations. You can use the drawing tools to draw circles, ellipses, rectangles, lines, and even freehand objects. You can resize, move, copy, and edit your drawings. You can change the color of your lines and fill areas; you can produce quite complicated drawings.

The real power of PM Chart is its charting capabilities, however. You can chart the contents of a worksheet—a ledger sheet in PM Chart where you enter data to chart. You can type data into a worksheet in PM Chart or you can import data from another spreadsheet program, for example, Excel or Lotus 1-2-3. You cannot import spreadsheets created in the OS/2 Spreadsheet applet, however.

602 Chapter 23—Using the OS/2 Data Management Applets

After you have data in the worksheet, you select the information to graph. You also can add annotation to your graphs with the drawing tools and create presentation graphs rapidly and easily. The following table describes the menu options available with PM Chart:

Menu	Menu Option	Description
File		
	New	Create a new chart
	Open	Open an existing chart
	ClipArt...	View clipart
	Save	Save your chart
	Save **a**s...	Save your chart with a new name
	Print...	Print your chart
	P**r**inter setup...	Change your printer
Edit		
	Undo	Undo last command
	Cu**t**	Cut highlighted data
	Copy	Copy highlighted data
	Paste	Paste data
	Cl**e**ar	Clear
	Remove	Remove an object
Change		
	Align...	Align objects
	Combine	Combine objects
	Duplicate	Replicate objects
	Flip	"Turn over" objects
	M**o**ve to	Move objects
	R**o**tate	Rotate objects
	Smooth	Smooth a jagged object
	U**n**smooth	Return a smoothed object to original form

Using PM Chart

Menu	Menu Option	Description
	Colors/**S**tyle	Change colors and style of objects
Preferences		
	Cross**h**airs	Change mouse pointer to crosshairs
	Pa**g**es...	Configure page size, borders, and orientation
	Ru**l**ers/Grid...	Define rulers and drawing grids
	Screen **c**olor	Change screen colors
Help		

Understanding PM Chart

PM Chart is located in the productivity folder within the OS/2 System folder. Open the OS/2 System folder and then open the Productivity folder. To open PM Chart, double-click the PM Chart icon. Your screen will look like Figure 23.15.

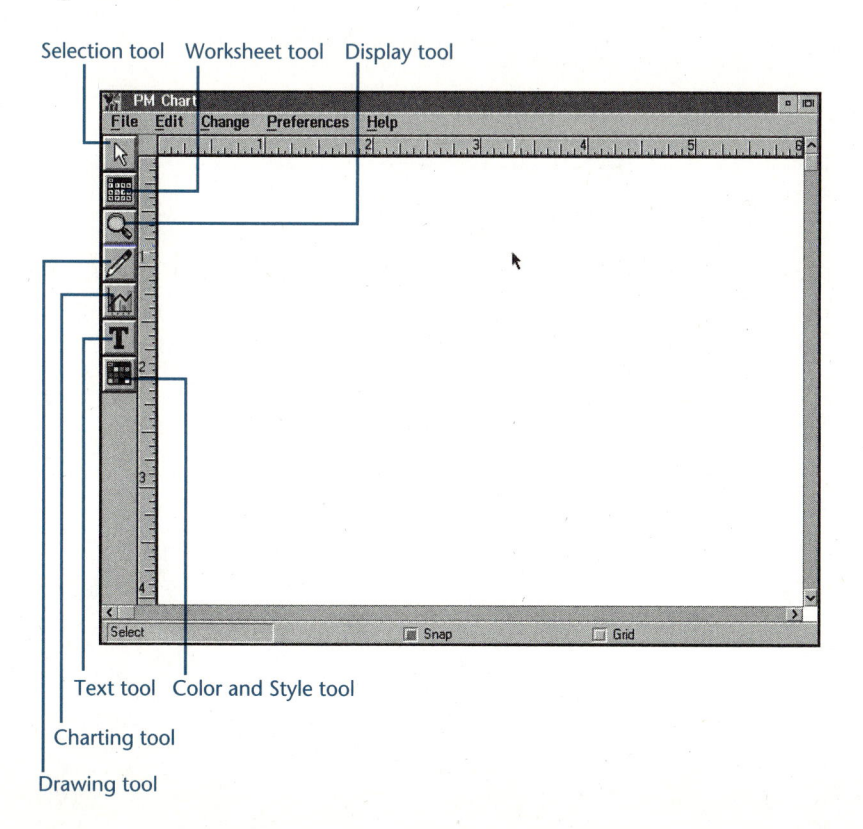

Fig. 23.15
The PM Chart window.

Labels: Selection tool, Worksheet tool, Display tool, Text tool, Color and Style tool, Charting tool, Drawing tool

To understand how to use PM Chart, you first should become familiar with the elements of PM chart that you see on-screen. The main area of the screen is your drawing area. As you might expect, this area is where you design charts.

On the left side of the screen is the toolbar. The toolbar contains seven tools that you use while creating your presentation. The seven tools and their descriptions are listed in the following table:

Tool	Description
Select arrow	Returns PM Chart to the default pointer tool.
Worksheet	Displays the PM Chart worksheet to load the data for charting.
View	Change your view of the presentation. For example, change from full-screen to full-page view.
Draw	Enables you to draw lines, circles, arcs, or freehand objects.
Chart	Accesses the chart options, such as pie chart, bar chart, or line chart.
Text	Enables you to create and adjust text, including changing fonts, styles and alignments.
Color/Style	Opens the Symbol-Color/Style dialog box to adjust colors and styles of objects.

PM Chart includes several options to help you place objects exactly where you want them. One of these options is the ruler (along the top and left sides of the drawing area). You can turn off the ruler or alter the division spacing by using the Preferences menu. Snap and Grid are two toggle settings that also help you place objects accurately. These settings are located at the base of the window.

When you have Snap turned on, the cursor "snaps" to the ruler divisions. You can place items only at each division on the ruler. If you turn Snap off, you can draw an item anywhere on-screen, which is good for freehand drawing; however, it makes aligning and positioning items, such as a series of circles, or the same size or drawing boxes, very difficult.

The Grid feature draws a grid of dots on-screen, making drawing on-screen equivalent to drawing on graph paper. The Grid is an aid for your drawing on screen. The grid does not appear on your finished presentation. As with the ruler, you can alter the position and spacing of the Grid with the Preference menu.

You also can change the cursor to make drawing easier. You can choose between the arrow cursor or the crosshair cursor. The arrow is the same arrow that you use throughout OS/2, enabling you to select objects. The crosshair is a vertical and horizontal line that extends the full width of the window. In some cases, the arrow is preferable (when you draw freehand, for example). In other cases, the crosshair helps guide accurate placement.

When you choose to use the crosshair, you do not lose the use of the arrow, however. The arrow appears on-screen when you move the crosshair outside the drawing area.

Working with PM Chart

The best way to learn to use an application is to work through an example using the applications. In this section, you will use sample information that accompanies PM Chart to learn how to create a chart.

First, you must open a worksheet data file that you can chart. Once the worksheet is open, you can make changes to the data and see how the changes affect the chart.

To load one of the sample worksheets, click File and then Open... Alternatively, you can press Alt-F and then O. The File - Open dialog box appears on the screen as shown in figure 23.16.

By default, you are shown a list of existing files with PM Chart's format, GRF. If you want to use another file format, such as Lotus 1-2-3's WKS or WK1 format, click the radio button to alter the selection list.

> **Note**
>
> PM Chart can import data from several different file formats such as Lotus 1-2-3 or Microsoft Excel. However, OS/2's Spreadsheet productivity application is not one of the file formats supported by PM Chart.

For this example, you want to read INVEST.DAT, a Micrografx Charisma data file. From the File - Open dialog box, click the DA**T** radio button. The list of files displays those files with the DAT extension.

606 Chapter 23—Using the OS/2 Data Management Applets

Select a file from the list by clicking it. For example, click INVEST.DAT. Click Open to load the data into the worksheet. When the data loads into PM Chart, click the Worksheet tool. Your screen will look like the one in figure 23.17.

Fig. 23.16
Loading a worksheet.

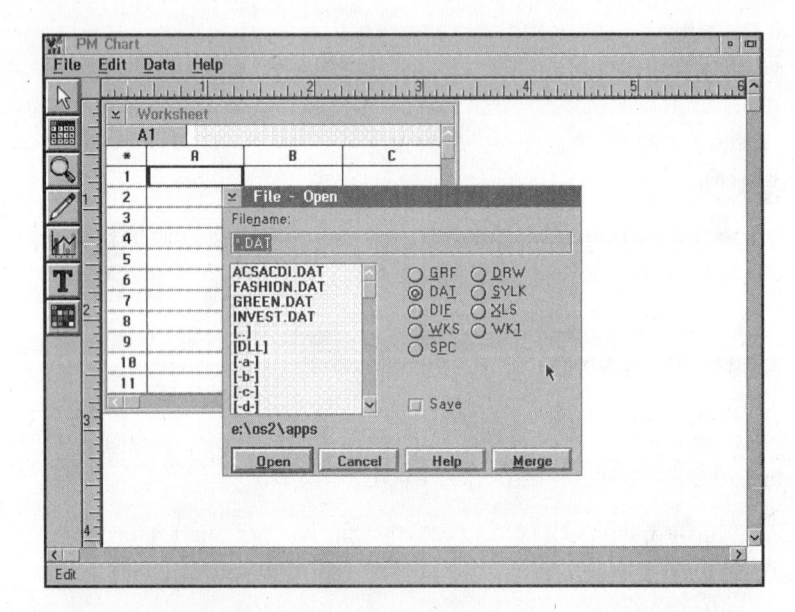

Fig. 23.17
Worksheet loaded with data.

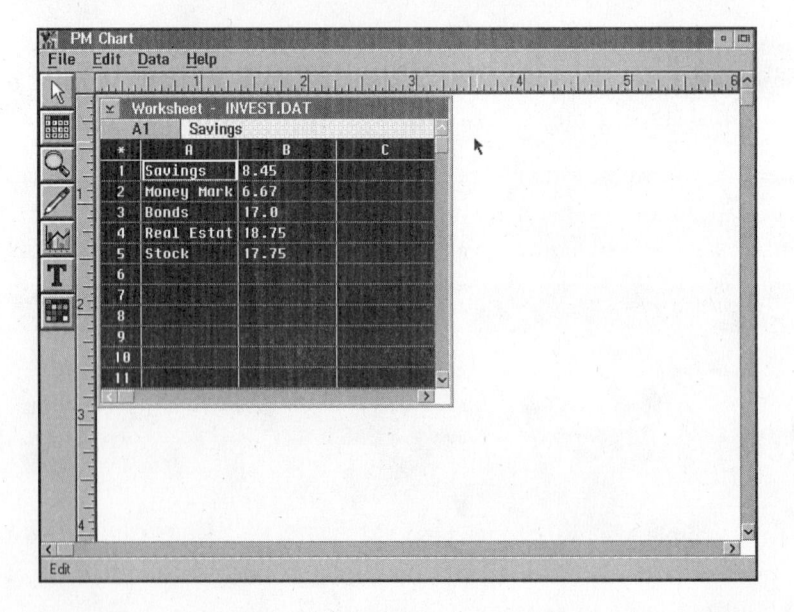

> **Tip**
>
> Another way to display the worksheet, besides clicking the worksheet tool, is to click the second button on the mouse, usually the right mouse button.

When you load the data into the worksheet, the data is highlighted and ready for charting. To remove the highlighting, click within the worksheet. To highlight a column or row, click in the name of the column or row. To highlight the whole worksheet, click the asterisk in the upper left corner of the worksheet.

With the data highlighted, you are ready to create a chart. Click the Charting tool. As shown in figure 23.18, a button bar displays to the right of the Chart tool.

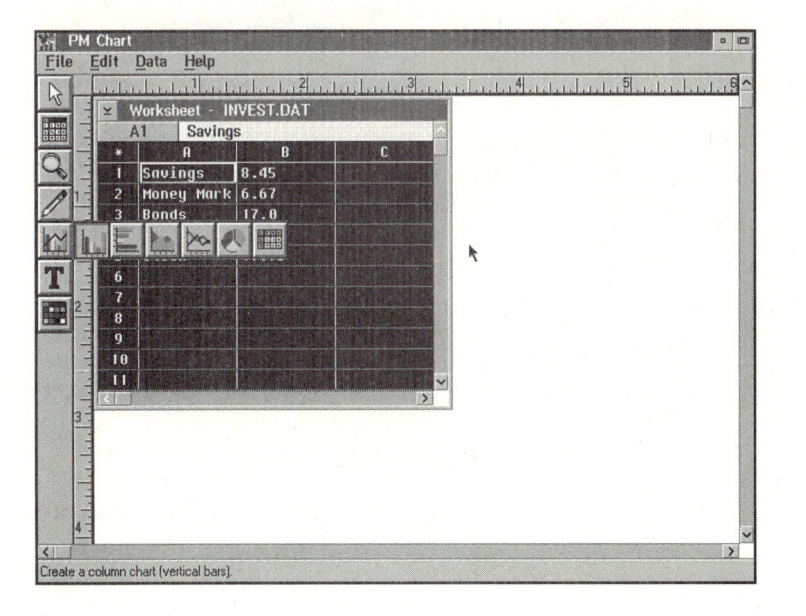

Fig. 23.18
Charting icon options.

In the button bar are buttons for choosing mixed bar and line, column (often known as bar or histogram), bar (often known as horizontal bar), area, line, pie and text charts. For this example, click the Column Chart icon (the button to the right of the chart tool.) The Column Chart dialog box appears as shown in figure 23.19.

608 Chapter 23—Using the OS/2 Data Management Applets

Fig. 23.19
Column Chart options.

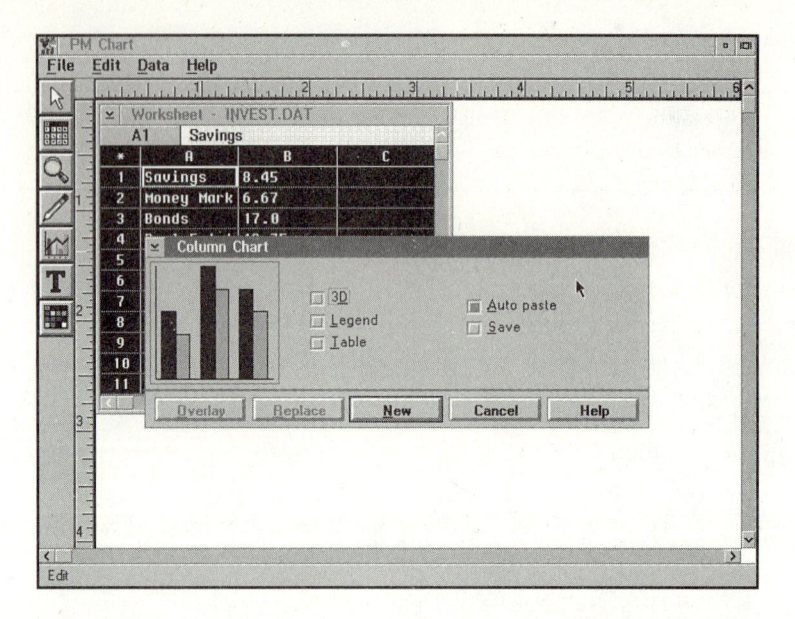

You adjust the options for your chart in the dialog box that opens after you choose the chart type. Each chart type has comparable options. Click the radio buttons to select the items of preference.

For example, in the column chart you can add a 3-D effect to your bars, and choose to add a legend and a table of the data. The Auto paste option, which is active by default, automatically creates a chart from the highlighted data and places it directly into your work area. If you turn Auto paste off, the chart is placed into the clipboard and you must use the Paste command to retrieve it into your drawing.

After adjusting the options, choose **N**ew to create a new chart. If you already have a chart on-screen, you can choose Overlay to add a second chart or to replace the current chart with a new chart. When you choose New for the sample chart and close your worksheet, your screen appears similar to figure 23.20.

PM Chart places the text labels as labels for the bars along the bottom of the chart and makes the bars the numerical values. You can make adjustments to the size and position of the chart. If your chart is not selected, click within the chart area (but not on a bar) with the select tool. Small squares, known as *object handles*, appear.

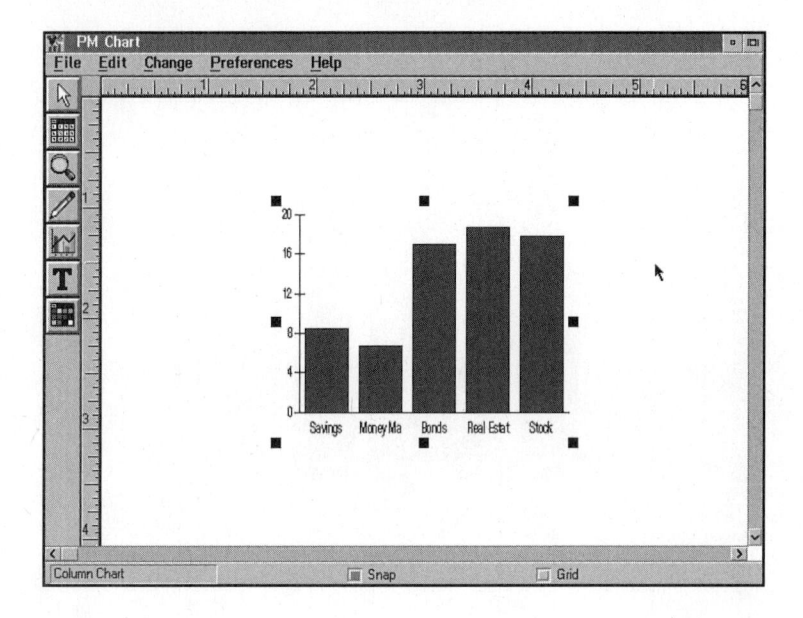

Fig. 23.20
Automatically created column chart.

If you click in the selected chart with mouse button and drag the mouse around, you move the whole chart. If you click a corner handle, you stretch the chart horizontally and vertically. Clicking a side or top handle stretches the chart horizontally or vertically, respectively.

Experiment with changing the position and size of the chart. Notice that if you increase the chart size, the bars increase in size but the text does not. When you increase the size, more room is created at the bottom of the bars for their labels.

Besides changing the entire chart, you can change elements within the chart. As with all the objects in PM Chart, you select the object and then pick the editing function. For example, click a bar within the chart. Your screen appears similar to figure 23.21.

Click the Color/Style tool at the bottom of the tool list. A dialog box appears showing the current color settings for the bars. You can pick a different fill color, change the line, text, or background color by using the radio buttons and selecting a color. First click Set so that PM Chart keeps the dialog box open until you have completed all your adjustments. For example, click the Fill radio button and double-click blue. Then click line and double-click red, and background (Bkg) and double-click light blue.

Fig. 23.21
Altering a bar.

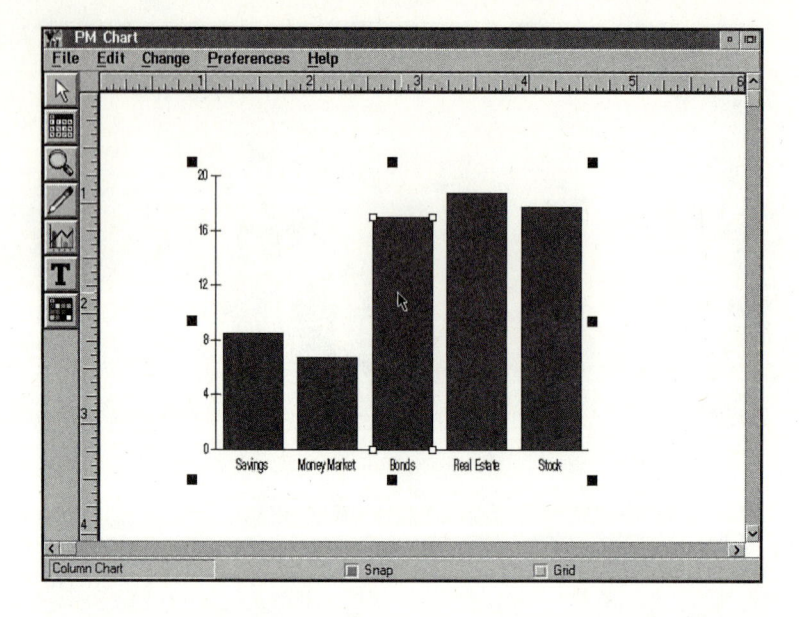

You also can alter patterns and fills by choosing patterns from the Style menu. Click Fill and then Style and Bitmap to alter the fill style. Choose a pattern from the dialog box and click OK to select it.

You can continue to alter your bar chart until it has the colors and form you like. You can alter the color palettes, that is the selection of colors, from the palette menu, add a gradient, where one color blends into another, or the style of the fill pattern, crosshatch or color with the style menu. You also can alter the text style, such as bold or underline, with the Style menu when you have the Text radio button selected.

When you have finished tailoring your chart, click Set and then OK to close the Style dialog box. Your screen appears similar to figure 23.22.

Use the other drawing tools to complete your chart. Use the Text tool, for example, to add a title. Put a frame around your chart by using the Rectangle or Rounded Rectangle drawing tool.

PM Chart includes many drawing features that make it particularly useful. If you have clip art, for example, you can add it to your chart from the Clip Art option in the File menu. You can create multiple pages, make them portrait or landscape and alter their borders by using the Preferences Page Options dialog box.

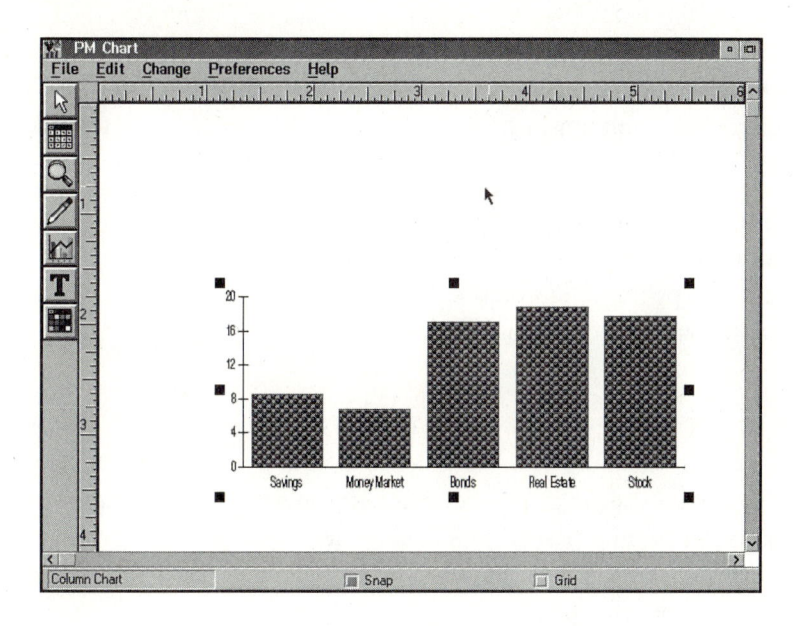

Fig. 23.22
Altered column chart.

In addition to manipulating objects with their handles, you can create a mirror image, combine multiple objects so that you can handle them as a single object, or copy objects with the change menu. You also can align objects from this menu.

Your work area is 34 inches by 22 inches and you can make as many pages at once as can fit into that size. If you make an A-size drawing (8.5 inches by 11), for example, you can create 12 pages at once. If you select a C sized drawing (17 inches by 22), you can only create two pages at once. The maximum size of the worksheet is 100 rows by 100 columns.

You can print the current displayed view, the current page, or all pages of your presentation from the File menu. Once you have made appropriate changes to your chart, you can save the chart using Save from the File menu.

Understanding PM Chart Limitations

PM Chart is the most advanced of the OS/2 applets. It can create multiple charts on multiple pages and has many control features to adjust the color and style of your charts and slides.

PM Chart is limited in that you only can produce a few chart types and each file can only contain a few pages. It also does not support Spreadsheet files. However, unless you are doing extensive presentation features, PM Chart is very suitable.

It does lack clip art and has limited drawing tools, but do not assume that PM Chart is as restrictive as the other OS/2 applets. Its worksheet can accept up to 100 rows and columns, which is more than adequate for most tables and charts.

Sharing PM Chart Information

You can cut and copy from both the worksheet and the drawing area. If you cut or copy from the worksheet the data is transferred to the Clipboard as text. If you cut or copy from the drawing area it is transferred to the Clipboard as a bitmap image.

The effect of pasting depends on the receiving application. If you paste into a text editor, for example, text is transferred as text. If you transfer into a field, such as in Database or Spreadsheet, however, only the first few characters are transferred. You must paste a bitmap image into an application that can accept bitmaps. For example, you can paste to another area of PM Chart or into a painting or drawing program.

Using PM Terminal

PM Terminal is a communications program that enables you to link your computer with other computers or terminals. You define a set of parameters, known as a *profile*, that contains the information needed to establish, maintain, and terminate a communications session. When you have established a session, you communicate with the remote computer by means of a session window that is displayed like a OS/2 application program's session window.

Each profile contains different information because you may need to connect with a variety of different other computers. You can link with a mainframe computer, for example, and may need your PC to emulate a terminal that the mainframe can understand. In another session, you may be connected to another computer by means of an asynchronous modem and regular telephone lines. Typical examples of networking include calling bulletin board systems (BBS), CompuServe, and the Dow Jones News Retrieval Service.

PM Terminal is easy to use if you know how to communicate with the remote computer. The applet is not particularly easy to configure because it requires some knowledge of your communications parameters.

Menu	Menu Option	Description
Session		
	S**t**art	Start a session
	Sto**p**...	Stop a session
	Add...	Add a session
	Change...	Change a session
	Delete...	Delete a session
	Setup **p**rofiles	Configure a session's profile
Options		
	Save window	Store the current session window information
	Minimize on use	Make the window an icon when used
Help		

Purpose

PM Terminal is intended to be configured by a knowledgeable communications person and then activated by an end user who does not need to know that the connection between a PC and a mainframe computer may be completely different than the connection linking two PCs by means of asynchronous modems. Other OS/2 communications programs probably offer more features and more flexibility, but PM Terminal offers the basic features many users need.

Understanding PM Terminal

To start PM Terminal, double-click the PM Terminal icon in the Productivity folder. Figure 23.23 shows the opening PM Terminal window.

The Session Manager window contains a list of named predefined sessions called profiles. After you define your sessions, you double-click on your selection on the list and PM Terminal starts establishing connections with another computer.

Note that most of the predefined profiles access on-line services to which you must subscribe. The profiles define only the information that is not unique to

614 Chapter 23—Using the OS/2 Data Management Applets

your particular account. This chapter gives an example of connecting to the Dow Jones News Retrieval Service but obviously does not include the unique information, such as an account number or regional phone number.

The second example in this chapter shows how to define your own profile. Because the telephone number and specific connection information is unique to a user and connection system, this information is again omitted.

Fig. 23.23
PM Terminal.

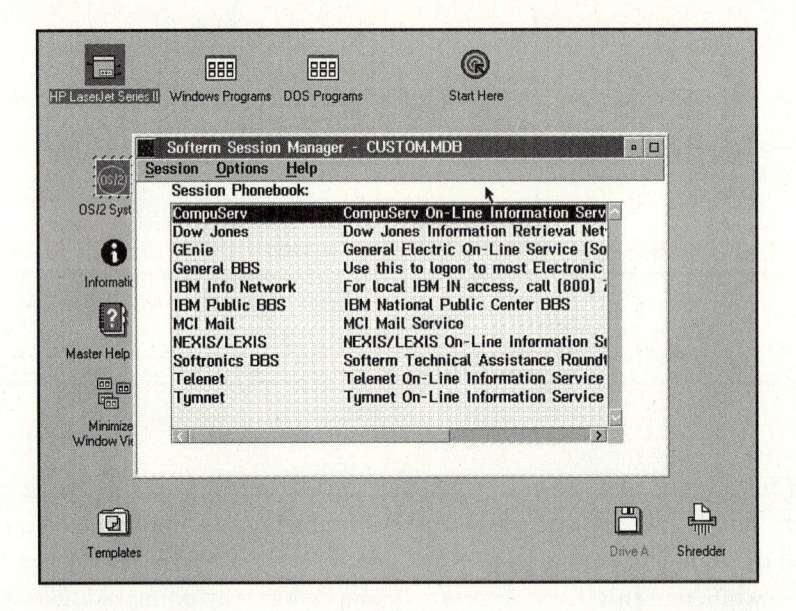

Working with PM Terminal

The first example shows the principle involved in connecting after a profile has been configured. If you select the Dow Jones Retrieval service and double-click the entry, for example, PM Terminal opens a session window and prompts you for connection details (see fig. 23.24).

This profile is configured so that it prompts you for admittance data before making the connection. Note that the button near the bottom of the window is checked, requiring that the dialog box appear. Another profile may already include this information and bypass this dialog box.

Using PM Terminal   **615**

In this window, you add the telephone number for the Dow Jones New Retrieval Service. The second line shows the information that PM Terminal must send when you connect with the remote computer. The third box, Telephone network profile name, is a list of all the different ways you can connect with an outside line. If you were to dial the number yourself, for example, you may dial a particular sequence of numbers to get an outside line from your company, another sequence of numbers to link to another division of your company, and perhaps other sequences to use different long distance companies.

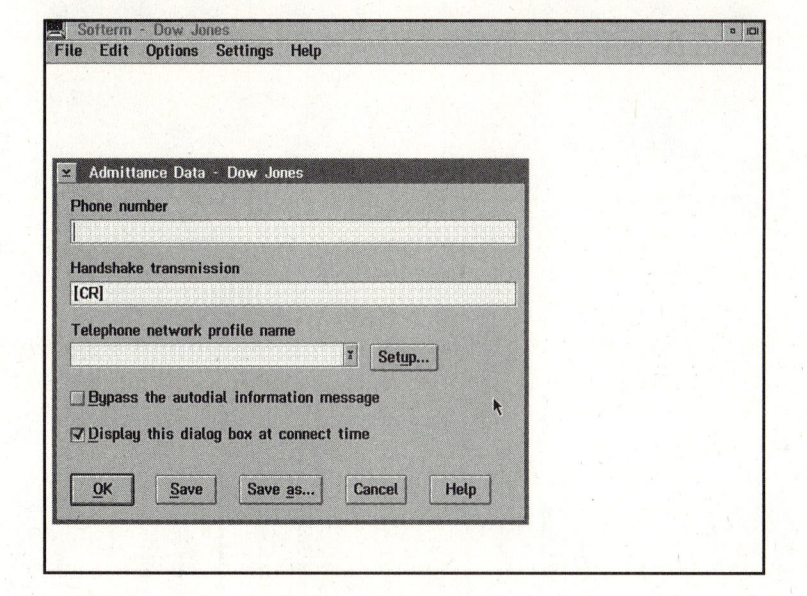

Fig. 23.24
A sample PM Terminal session.

This list does not include the part of the phone number or connection sequence that is unique to the Dow Jones Retrieval service, but contains the sequences that you may use for different connections. The idea is that you have access to the general connection lists within every profile, but only have access to the information unique to the particular profile within that profile.

When you have entered the required phone number and chosen a telephone network profile name, click OK to start the connection. When you start a connection, PM Terminal displays a session window comparable to the window in figure 23.25.

Fig. 23.25
PM Terminal
Session Window.

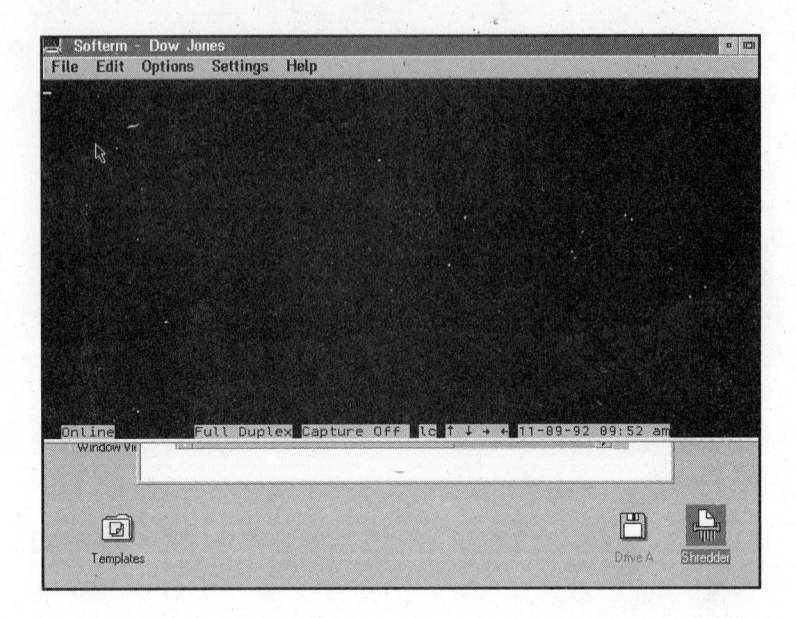

In the main area, you see messages from the remote computer. At the bottom on the session window is PM Terminal's status information. In figure 23.25, PM Terminal is using full duplex, is not capturing a record of information to a file, and shows the date and time of the connection.

You can adjust the settings for this session from the menu selections. You can turn on a capture file and have OS/2 capture data to a disk file or to the printer from a data capture selection in the File menu.

To give another example, you can send a file to or receive a file from the remote computer by clicking File and then sending or receiving a file. A dialog box prompts for the file transfer protocol and the file name. (A file transfer protocol, such as XMODEM, ASCII, or Kermit, defines the format of the file being transferred. File transfer protocol defines whether the file is sent in small or large groups, for example, and how each computer acknowledges or rejects the data being transferred.)

Remember that when you use PM Terminal and link with another computer, you have added a level of complexity to your user interface. You have to make both computers communicate with each other. When you want to transfer a file, for example, you have to prepare the receiving computer for file reception and the transmitting computer for transmittal. The methods used for this preparation as well as the actual transmission depend on the type of connection made, the computer software being run on both computers, and the configuration of that software.

If you can connect with a mainframe computer or a bulletin board system, for example, you use different syntaxes and commands for the two systems even though you are using the same computer running OS/2. The remote computers you are connecting with have completely different software and user interfaces.

When you have completed your communications session, click **F**ile and **D**isconnect to break the communications link. PM Terminal then disconnects you from the remote computer and frees the modem for another application program.

With PM Terminal you can have multiple communications sessions active at the same time. You cannot share a modem, however. When a session tries to use a modem that is already in use, PM Terminal displays a dialog box that asks if you want to try a different communications port. When all your modems are in use, you cannot run additional communications sessions simultaneously.

The easiest way to create your own profile is to base it on another profile that has been previously established. If you want to add a new profile for an on-line service, for example, you might use the GEnie, CompuServ, or Dow Jones News Retrieval Service as a template. If you are connecting with a bulletin board system, use the General BBS profile as a template.

To base your profile on an existing profile, you access the Setup profile dialog box after selecting a session. This chapter uses the General BBS profile as an example. Click General BBS and then click **S**ession and **C**hange, or press Ctrl-C. Figure 23.26 shows the Change Session dialog box that appears.

If you want to create your own profile from scratch, click **S**ession and **S**etup profiles or press Ctrl-P. You need extensive communications knowledge to use this approach.

This dialog box shows the currently selected subprofiles for the General BBS session. The top text box contains the comment that appears on the session list alongside the profile's name. The other four boxes shown the subprofiles. You need to select—or define and select—a terminal emulation, connection path, system environment, and file transfer profile.

Fig. 23.26
Change Session dialog box.

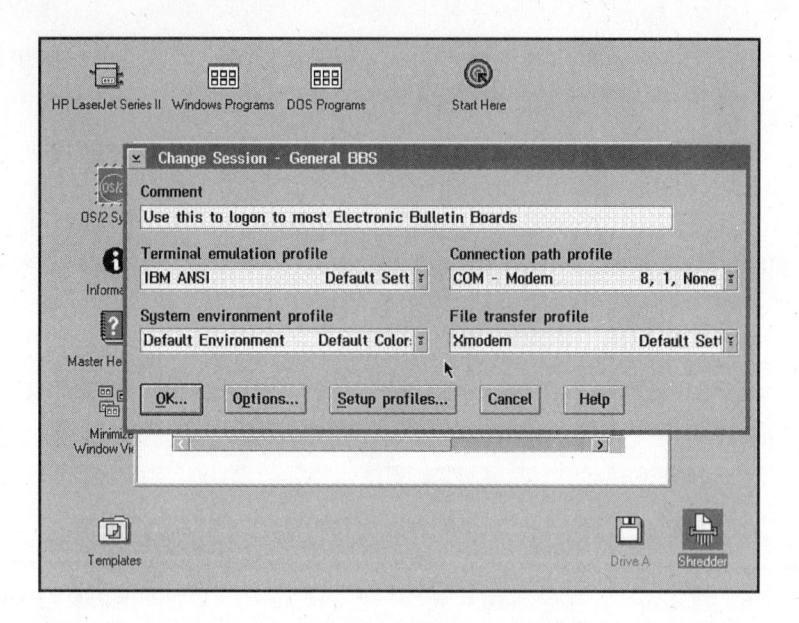

The terminal emulation profile defines how your OS/2 PM Terminal session looks to the connecting computer. A BBS usually can communicate with an ASCII terminal. PM Terminal emulates many other terminals. You may use an IBM 3101-10 terminal emulation, for example, when you are communicating with an IBM mainframe. Other emulations include DEC VT100 and TTY. To choose another emulation, click the list button beside the Terminal emulation profile text box and choose an emulation from the list.

To customize the emulation or to establish a new emulation, click **S**etup profiles and use the dialog boxes for setting up a terminal emulation. You need extensive communications knowledge for this procedure.

For a typical BBS, the ASCII terminal emulation is acceptable. When you register with the BBS, it probably will ask if you want ASCII terminal emulation as part of your registration procedure. Choose this emulation to make the BBS and PM Terminal communicate optimally.

Choose the other profiles from the lists, or define your own using setup profiles. The System Environment Profile defines such items as the disk file path, video code pages, your printers, nationality code page, and the window colors for your session. PM Terminal supplies only one profile, but you can create your own.

The Connection Path profile sets the communications parameters that OS/2 uses to communicate with the remote computer. You set the baud rate (the rate of communication) in this profile. You also define the serial port for your modem, the format of the text data, and other modem settings. This profile is most likely to be different for different types of sessions.

Examine the differences between the Dow Jones News Retrieval profile and the General BBS profile to see the two most commonly used connection path profiles. You can use other profiles if you have a faster modem and can connect with computers that also have faster modems. Similarly, if you have a slow modem, you may need to customize these profiles.

Note that the on-line services, such as Dow Jones News Retrieval Service, use seven data bits, one stop bit, and even parity. A BBS uses eight data bits, one stop bit, and no parity.

The File Transfer profile sets the default protocol for when you transfer files between computers. A typical communications session may have two different elements. For part of the session, you are typing and reading text from the remote computer. This data is sent one character at a time. The format for this character exchange is set by the number of data bits, stop bits, and parity that you choose from the connection path profile.

In the other part of the session, you may want to send a file to or to receive a file from the other computer. Rather than sending one character at a time, you want to send a whole file. The file transfer profile defines how that file is sent. A file normally is sent in sections, each of a particular size. Both computers must be set up to expect the data in a predefined format. They also must use the same format for acknowledging a section of data or for telling the sending computer that a section was corrupted during transmission. The computer industry uses various protocols for file transmission, and you choose one protocol from the file transfer profile text box.

With the profiles chosen, click OK to establish the admittance data. Figure 23.27 shows the Admittance Data form. If you complete this form when you define your profile, you can set it so that the form does not appear when the session starts.

Fig. 23.27
Admittance
Data Form.

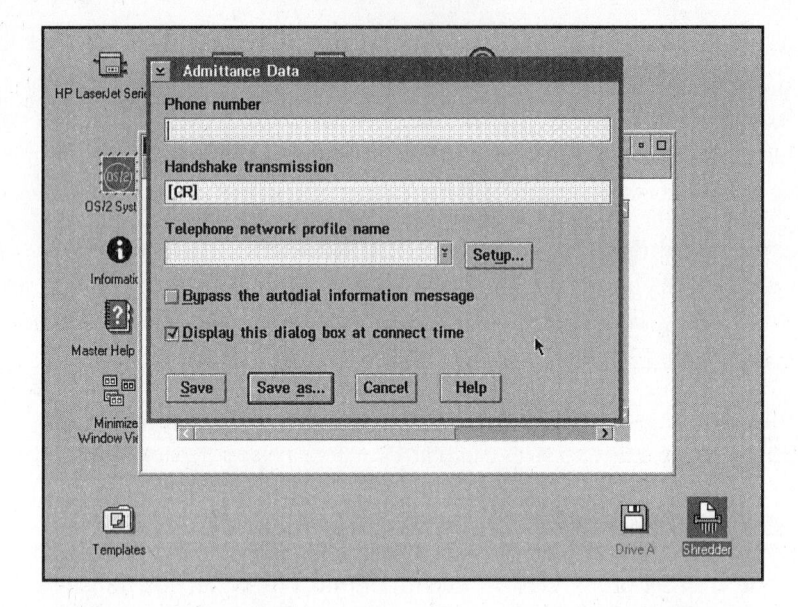

This dialog box makes up the second half of your profile for a communications session. You enter a phone number in the top text box and a telephone network profile name in the lower text box. As explained earlier, you can use different telephone network profiles if you use multiple long distance telephone companies or if you have special phone lines installed, such as lines linking different divisions within a corporation.

Click the **B**ypass the autodial information message, if you do not want the end user to see the autodialing information when they select this profile. This message is useful because it gives an intermediate status information while the connection with a remote computer is being made. If the end user does not realize that he or she is connecting with a remote computer, however, this message may be confusing. If the message is not present, the session gives the impression that the data is being loaded while the connection is being established.

The display this dialog box at connect time message is used if you want the user to enter information prior to the connection. For example, the Dow Jones News Retrieval example shown earlier did not include the necessary phone number, so the dialog box prompts users for the number when they select the session. If the information is the same every time, you can remove the check from this box to stop this dialog box's appearance when you choose the profile.

After making your selections, click Save **as** and choose a new session name for your profile. (Remember you were creating a new session based on an existing profile. You do not want to overwrite your template.) The new profile then appears on the session list.

Understanding PM Terminal Limitations

PM Terminal limits the number of concurrent sessions to 32. You are much more likely, however, to be limited by your hardware. Each communications session needs a communications port and modem. You are limited by the number of ports and modems available on your computer.

A typical PC is limited to four serial ports. You can purchase specialized adapter boards that increase the number of ports available, and you may be able to use these with PM Terminal.

PM Terminal does not emulate every terminal available. If you need a different terminal, you need to acquire a different program.

Sharing PM Terminal Information

PM Terminal does not support the Clipboard. To exchange information with other applets, you use file retrieval and saving methods.

You can save your communications session to a capture file. Additionally, by using the file transfer commands, you can transfer files to and from the remote computer. With the file transfer commands on your computer, you can use the file commands in other applets and application programs to access the file transfer commands.

Chapter Summary

This chapter introduced the data management applets supplied with OS/2. Database is a simple database program that can be used to store lists of information such as lists of names and addresses.

Spreadsheet is a simple spreadsheet program that supports basic arithmetic functions for creating tables of arithmetic information.

PM Chart includes many charting and drawing options for creating presentations of data. It is the most flexible of the data management applets.

PM Terminal is a communications program that enables you to link with remote computers. While relatively complex to configure, it fits many basic communications needs.

Chapter 24

Understanding OS/2 Communications and Database Tools

IBM and other companies, including Microsoft, market communications and database tools that complement and enhance OS/2. The IBM offerings presently consist of Communications Manager/2 (CM/2) and Database 2/2 (DB2/2). Until early in 1993, IBM bundled Communications Manager and Database Manager as a single product named *Extended Services*. The database software vendors Oracle, Ingres, and Gupta sell OS/2 versions of their products. And Microsoft—not wanting to lose customers—sells the OS/2-based SQL Server product. Even Microsoft realizes that OS/2 provides a good platform for multiuser access to relational databases.

The optional OS/2 product Extended Services (ES) and the current CM/2 and DB2/2 are valuable tools for specialized applications, but not everyone needs them. If you want to use these communications and database tools, you purchase them separately from OS/2. Extended Services consists of two primary components—Communications Manager and Database Manager—along with a collection of supporting utilities and drivers. Both Communications Manager and Database Manager are high-powered tools for dealing with complex connectivity issues and large amounts of data. The current CM/2 and DB2/2 products are compatible with the earlier Extended Services product but provide more features and more functions. IBM also made CM/2 and DB2/2 much easier to install.

Communications Manager provides your OS/2-based computer with the capability to connect to mainframes or other host computers through terminal emulators and System Network Architecture (SNA) links. Database Manager enables you to use Structured Query Language (SQL) to create, update, and report on relational database tables that contain information pertinent to your company or organization. You need these tools if your PC is connected to a mainframe computer or if you maintain a large collection of data in your computer. You don't need ES if you occasionally connect to a bulletin board system or only keep track of a few names and addresses with your computer.

What are SNA and SQL? You learn about these terms and more in this chapter. You begin your exploration of OS/2 database and communications technology by looking at the facilities and functions that Extended Services offers. You next cover the follow-on products CM/2 and DB2/2. You wrap up this chapter by learning about OS/2-based products such as Microsoft's SQL Server.

Defining the Facilities within Extended Services

IBM sold Extended Services as two products: *Extended Services with Database Server for OS/2* and the simpler *Extended Services for OS/2*. Both products contain Communications Manager and Database Manager. ES with Database Server also contains database-server software and a collection of database-client application enabler programs for use with DOS, Windows, and OS/2.

The database-server software enables a PC on a local area network (LAN) to share a *database*—a repository of relational tables. These tables, designed by you or someone in your organization, are files of information about customers, sales, products, employees, or other entities. The application enabler programs act as intermediaries, giving applications an interface to the relational tables in a database.

Learning Extended Server Basics

When you install ES, several new folders appear on your OS/2 desktop (see fig. 24.1). The Extended Services, Communications Manager, Database Manager, and User Profile Management folders contain program objects useful for performing ES tasks, as outlined in the following list:

- The program objects in the Extended Services folder help you install, maintain, and understand ES.

- The objects in the User Profile Management folder protect access to your databases by enforcing user-identification security.

- The Communications Manager folder objects are terminal emulation programs and connectivity diagnostics programs.

- The Database Manager folder contains program objects to help you create, repair, update, report, and inquire into your databases.

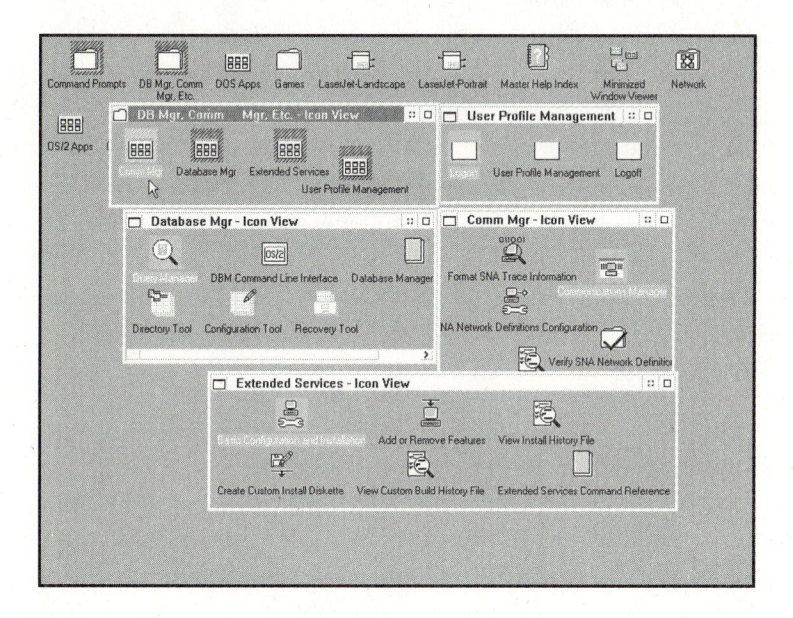

Fig. 24.1
The Extended Services folders and program objects.

During installation, you choose the Communications Manager and Database Manager components you plan to use in your application. If you install Communications Manager, for example, you choose terminal emulations DEC VT100 or IBM 3101 (for ASCII-based hosts), IBM 3270 (for mainframe or AS/400 hosts), or IBM 5250 (for AS/400 or System 36/38 hosts).

The Communications Manager component is especially complicated to install. To help prevent installation problems, read the IBM *Start Here* and the IBM *Workstation Installation Guide* carefully before configuring your computer to use any of the services and utilities within Communications Manager. Fortunately, IBM organized these manuals in the form of road maps that lead you through the installation and configuration processes. The Communications Manager configuration screens, however, are not CUA-compliant. (Chapter 9, "Using Your Computer Screen as a Desktop," discusses CUA compliance.)

You definitely need to refer to the IBM manuals the first time you run the Communications Manager configuration and verification tools. The configuration screens are difficult to navigate, and you may have trouble understanding the parameters you must set. If someone in your office has some experience with Communications Manager, by all means, ask that person for help during the configuration process.

Exploring Extended Services with Database Server

You can use Extended Services with Database Server to access a common database from multiple workstations on a network. The database operations (read, update, and search) reside in the database-server computer. Perhaps you have a local area network and want one of the PCs on the LAN to store a central database for the other workstations to share. You may have a file server, but you are concerned because response times are slow. The workstations request all or nearly all of the database from the file server each time a user performs a search. The transfer of records to the workstation performing the search consumes too much time. You believe response times can improve considerably if the search operation executes in the same computer that stores the database.

If you're willing to convert from a file-server environment to a database-server environment, your search operations can execute in the database-server computer. With this arrangement, workstations send search requests (or update requests) to the database server and receive the responses.

For Related Information
- "Using Device Support," p. 94
- "Upgrading Your Hardware," p. 169

You have two hurdles to overcome as you convert from one environment to the other. First, the installation and configuration of a database server requires significant effort on your part. Additionally, the software you use to access the database must be compatible with your new database server. You can ask the supplier of your database-oriented application software about compatibility of ES with Database Services. Most companies that sell off-the-shelf, shrink-wrapped database software (Borland International, Computer Associates, Gupta Technologies, and Microsoft, for example) offer ES with Database Services compatibility. If your organization has an in-house programming staff, you can ask one of the staff what plans exist to take advantage of database-server technology.

Securing Access to Your Data

Before you learn about Communications Manager and Database Manager, you need to understand how Extended Services helps you control access to your computer records. User Profile Management (UPM) is the Extended Services tool you use to protect the data in your computer from intruders. UPM consists of logon, logout, and user-account management facilities. Figure 24.2 shows the Logon screen UPM displays when you begin using Database Manager. In this screen, you must identify yourself to the computer before you can access Database Manager files. UPM does not control access to Communications Manager files.

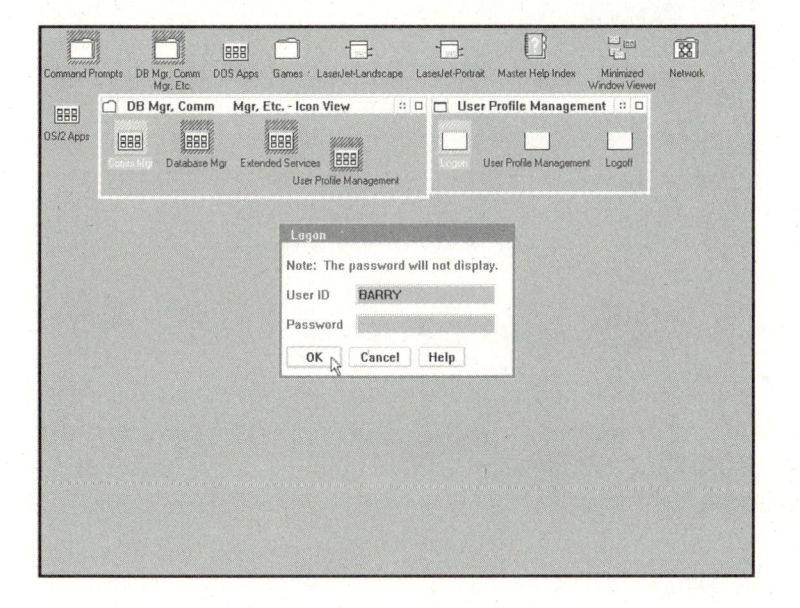

Fig. 24.2
The User Profile Management Logon screen.

You or another authorized person can set up account IDs for the users who need access to the files in Database Manager on your computer. You establish and maintain these account IDs through UPM. Figure 24.3 shows the screen you use to update user information. In this screen, you can establish the following identification components for each user:

- You can change a user's level of access (from lowest to highest levels of privilege, these are User, Local Administrator, and Administrator).

- You can permit or cancel a user's access to the database information (Logon Allowed or Denied).

For Related Information
- "Using CONFIG.SYS and AUTOEXEC.BAT," p. 162
- "Using the Workplace Shell's System Menu," p. 260

628   Chapter 24—Understanding OS/2 Communications and Database Tools

■ You can change a user's password or make the entry of a password unnecessary for a particular user.

Fig. 24.3
The Update User Information screen.

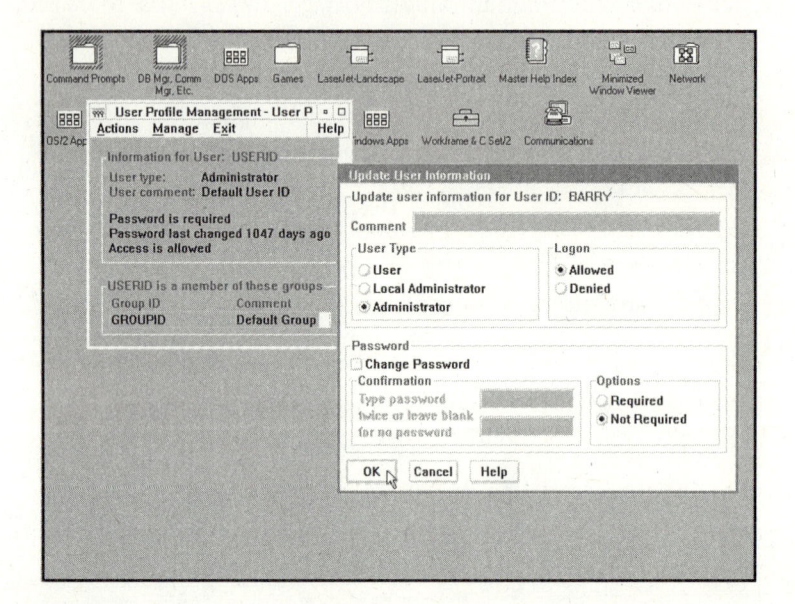

Using Communications Manager

The software modules that make up Communications Manager enable your PC to access another computer (typically an IBM mainframe, a DEC minicomputer, an IBM minicomputer, or another PC). You can exchange information with or use the resources of the other computer through Communications Manager. To use Communications Manager, your PC must be equipped with a serial I/O adapter, a Synchronous Data Link Control (SDLC) I/O adapter, or a network adapter.

You can use one of Communications Manager's connectivity options to open terminal emulation sessions with host computers. If you buy additional software, or if your organization has a staff of in-house programmers, you can establish other kinds of communication links between a PC running Communications Manager and a host computer. The programmers may design this link, for example, to transfer information automatically between the PC and the host at preset intervals.

Understanding Connectivity Options

Communications Manager supports four ways to connect your OS/2-based computer to other machines:

- SNA Gateway
- X.25 network
- Direct or modem-assisted
- Local area network

The next few sections explain these connectivity options.

Systems Network Architecture (SNA) Gateway. In most system setups, an SNA Gateway PC links an IBM mainframe host (System/370, System/390, ES/9000) to workstations on a local area network. The workstations on the LAN establish host sessions through the Gateway computer. To the host, the SNA Gateway computer is a single physical unit. To a workstation on the LAN, however, the host is directly attached to the workstation. The SNA Gateway maintains this illusion by distributing host messages to individual workstations and, in reverse, forwarding workstation messages to the host.

The Gateway PC carries on several host sessions on behalf of the workstations. The people at the workstations, through Communications Manager, use these 3270 terminal sessions to log on to the host and run mainframe software without any awareness that the SNA Gateway PC exists.

X.25 Network. X.25 is one of many standards established by the CCITT. CCITT is the Committee Consultatif International Telegraphique and Telephonique, or International Telegraph and Telephone Consultative Committee. CCITT is an international organization, headquartered in Geneva, that creates and maintains telecommunications standards for the whole world.

The X.25 network protocol defines how mainframes access packet-switching networks (*protocols*, also known as *conventions*, are discussed later in this chapter). *Packet switching* is a data-transmission method that sends computer information in messages (packets). The network routes the X.25 packets along the best possible path, in no particular order. Each X.25 packet contains information about itself that enables the receiver to reassemble and reorganize the packets to place the computer information in its original form. An X.25 network is an efficient means of routing computer information. If your company or organization uses an X.25 network, you can connect computers running Communications Manager to the network.

Direct or Modem-Assisted. Your computer may be directly connected to a host computer, or you may use modems and a telephone line to connect to the host. Direct connections may use a coaxial link to a mainframe, a twinaxial link to an AS/400, a Synchronous Data Link Control (SDLC) connection to a mainframe, or perhaps an asynchronous link to either a mainframe or minicomputer. Communications Manager supports serial I/O (COM1, COM2, COM3, or COM4) connectivity options through ACDI, the Asynchronous Communications Device Interface.

ACDI is a communications service within Communications Manager. The terminal emulators that operate through your COM ports (IBM 3101 or DEC VT100) use ACDI to set the baud rate and to send and receive information. Programmers can develop communications software using ACDI, producing customized computer-to-computer links between applications on different computers.

Local Area Network Connectivity. You can connect your OS/2-based computer, running Communications Manager, to other computers through a local area network. The LAN may use token ring network adapter cards, PC Network adapter cards, or Ethernet network adapter cards. IBM uses the name *ETHERAND* to refer to the Ethernet adapters it makes.

Communications Manager can interact with an SNA Gateway over a local area network. Communications Manager also contains drivers you can use to access other computers through specialized interfaces. These specialized interfaces are APPC (Advanced Program-to-Program Communication), APPN (Advanced Peer-to-Peer Networking), the Server-Requester Programming Interface, NetBIOS, and the IEEE 802.2 Protocol. Your programming staff can set up these interfaces and instruct you in their use.

IBM's Advanced Program-to-Program Communication (APPC) and Advanced Peer-to-Peer Networking (APPN) are, in essence, conventions computers use to exchange information. Computers need the guidance of conventions to send and receive information efficiently. Computers use the rules and specifications of conventions to determine, for example, which characters in a message denote the destination address and which characters represent incoming information. APPC and APPN are advanced conventions (also called protocols) because both enable computers to send and receive information as peers.

Long ago, before PCs, APPN, or APPC, host computers treated all devices as "dumb" because the peripheral devices did not execute applications. The host mainframe controlled the devices, and only the host mainframe could execute application software. The host accepted keystrokes from a terminal and sent screen data back to the terminal. The host mainframe recognized only those messages in the form of keystrokes from a terminal.

PCs and the interconnection of mainframes changed this device relationship. A PC can run application software and can act as a peer to the host mainframe. IBM invented APPC (also called *LU 6.2*) to enable computers to exchange information. The PC does not pretend to be a terminal (sending keystrokes and receiving screen data) with APPC. The PC and the host or hosts can establish a communications session and exchange information in the form of predefined fields, records, and files. A programmer defines the layout of these fields, records, and files.

Advanced Peer-to-Peer Networking (APPN) is a further enhancement to APPC. APPN provides for automatic best-path routing of messages in a network. An OS/2-based computer running Communications Manager can use APPC to communicate with other computers and can participate in APPN routing.

Using Terminal Emulations

For many users, the heart of Communications Manager is a terminal-emulator session with a host computer. Figure 24.4 shows the main Communications Manager screen from which you start or stop a terminal emulator session.

```
Message   Status   Advanced   Exit                    |F1=Help
─────────────────────────────────────────────────────────────
                Communications Manager Main Menu
Active configuration file . . . . . . . . : DEFAULT
Configuration file status . . . . . . . . :
  Verified
Press F10 to go to the action bar or
select an item below and press Enter.
1. Start emulators (3270, 5250, and ASCII)...
2. Stop emulators (3270, 5250, and ASCII)...
3. Transfer file
4. Specify new configuration file name default...
```

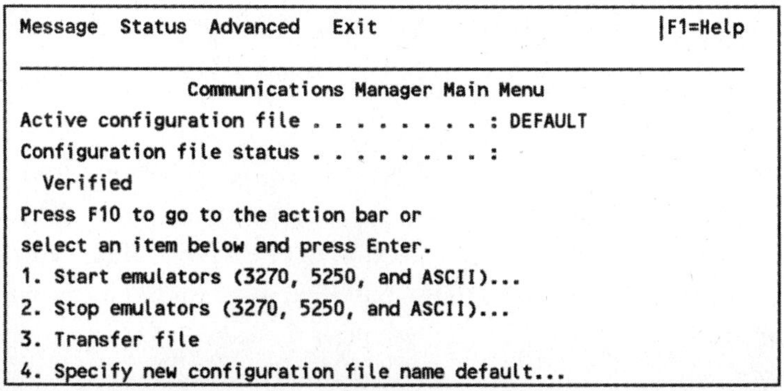

Fig. 24.4
The Communications Manager Main Menu screen.

The Communications Manager Main Menu is an OS/2 full-screen session you can leave running in the background. You bring the Main Menu session to the foreground (by using the Window List, for example) only in the following situations:

- When you want to start or stop a terminal-emulator session
- When you want to reconfigure Communications Manager
- When you want to terminate Communications Manager

When you install Communications Manager, you select the type of terminal-emulation sessions you plan to use: IBM 3270, IBM 3101, DEC VT100, or IBM 5250. Each of these is described in the following sections.

IBM 3270 Terminal Emulator. An IBM 3270 terminal is a device consisting of a screen and a keyboard. In most cases, the terminal is attached to a mainframe computer. A 3270 is a *block-mode device*: the terminal receives and sends entire screens of messages at once, rather than sending one character at a time. Each time you press the Enter key in a 3270 session, Communications Manager sends your typed data to the host computer. When Communications Manager receives the incoming host's response, the host's message appears on-screen.

You can configure the 3270 terminal emulator, using a screen such as the one shown in figure 24.5, to act as a *Distributed Function Terminal* (DFT). DFT is a 3270 mode of operation that enables multiple concurrent logical terminal sessions. You have one physical connection to the host computer(s), through which you can have more than one logical connection. You also can use the screen in figure 24.5 to configure the 3270 terminal emulator to use one of the connectivity options listed earlier in this chapter. As shown in figure 24.6, you can select and configure CICS (Customer Information Control System), VM (Virtual Machine), or TSO (Time Sharing Option) file transfer.

Communications Manager supports up to ten active 3270 sessions at one time. DFT enables five of these sessions; the other connectivity options can create up to five other sessions. Each active 3270 logical session runs in its own windowed OS/2 session. You can perform file transfers with the host computer; cut, copy, and paste information to or from the Clipboard; print locally or direct your print jobs to the host; and run customized computer programs that use Communications Manager services.

Using Communications Manager   633

```
            3270 Feature Configuration
DFT terminal/printer emulation
  1. DFT...
Non-DFT terminal/printer emulation (only one may be configured).
  2. SDLC...
  3. Token-Ring or other LAN type...
  4. X.25...
  5. IBM PC Network using Gateway...
  6. ETHERAND Network using Gateway...
DFT and non-DFT options
  7. 3270 color and alarm...
  8. 3270 file transfer...


Esc=Cancel    F1=Help    F3=Exit
```

Fig. 24.5
The 3270 Feature Configuration screen.

```
            Create/Change CICS Profile
Use the spacebar to select.
Profile name . . . . . . . . . . . . . . . . . . : M14
Comment. . . . . . . . . . . . . . . . . . . . .
   [MODEL PROFILE 3270 FILE TRANSFER   IBM HOST (CICS) TEXT FILES]
ASCII to/from EBCDIC translation . . . . . . . . . : Yes  No
Use CR/LF as record separator. . . . . . . . . . . : Yes  No
PC file code page. . . . . . . . . . . . . . . . . : [437 ]
Host file code page. . . . . . . . . . . . . . . . : [037 ]
IBM host file transfer command
   name . . . . . . . . . . . . . . . . . . . . . : [IND$FILE]
One-to-one character mapping . . . . . . . . . . . : Yes  No


Enter    Esc=Cancel    F1=Help    F4=List
```

Fig. 24.6
The Create/Change CICS Profile screen.

IBM 3101 Terminal Emulator. An IBM 3101 terminal is an ASCII device that connects to a host through an asynchronous (modem or direct-connect) link. The 3101 is one of the simplest terminals. The character sequences that control the 3101 screen (from the keyboard or from the host) are abbreviated versions of ANSI/DEC VT100 sequences. The 3101 is not compatible with ANSI or DEC VT100 protocols, however, because the 3101 character sequences for terminal commands are shorter and fewer in number. The 3101 offers both a block mode and a character mode of operation; most people operate the 3101 in character mode. Communications Manager supports the 3101 terminal in both modes.

You can use the 3101 emulator to access a bulletin board system or an information service such as CompuServe or MCI Mail. The 3101 isn't as popular as the DEC VT100, however, and you may find that you need to use the VT100 emulator to access these services. The 3101 terminal emulator runs in an OS/2 windowed session; you can use Clipboard-oriented cut, copy, and paste operations to manipulate host session information. You can transfer files with XModem, TSO, VM, or CICS file-transfer protocols.

DEC VT100 Terminal Emulator. Digital Equipment Corporation set an industry standard with the VT100 terminal. The VT100 device is a character-mode screen and keyboard that uses ANSI *escape sequences* to manage the appearance of the information on-screen and to indicate cursor-key and other special user operations at the keyboard. Figure 24.7 shows the VT100 terminal emulator as a windowed session on the desktop. You can use the VT100 emulator to access a bulletin board system, a DEC host computer, or an information service such as CompuServe, BIX, or MCI Mail.

Fig. 24.7
The Communications Manager's VT100 terminal emulator.

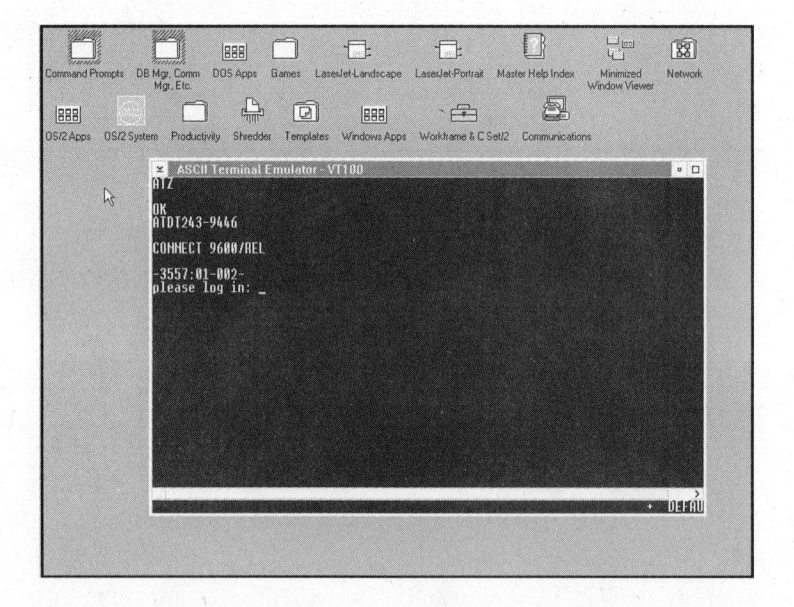

As with 3101 emulation, you can cut, copy, and paste information to and from the host session window. You can use the XModem, TSO, VM, or CICS file-transfer protocols to exchange files with the host computer.

IBM 5250 Terminal Emulator. If your host computer is an AS/400, System/36, or System/38 machine, you can access that host by emulating an IBM 5250 terminal from within Communications Manager. The 5250 Workstation

Feature of Communications Manager can operate through SDLC, token ring, Ethernet, X.25, or twinaxial connections.

The 5250 Workstation Feature manages up to five active terminal or printer sessions at one time. You can transfer files between your PC and an AS/400 host if you purchase PC Support/400, a separate IBM software product.

Learning Database Manager

The preceding sections of this chapter concentrated on the Communications Manager portion of Extended Services for OS/2 and the security features of User Profile Management. The discussion now turns to the other primary component of Extended Services: Database Manager.

Database Manager is easier to use than Communications Manager. Many functions within Database Manager make use of CUA-compliant screens under Presentation Manager to help you access information. In the following sections of this chapter, you explore the fundamentals of databases and learn about database services and database tools. These sections introduce you to Query Manager and teach you special techniques for accessing database files in a shared fashion from DOS, DOS-and-Windows, and OS/2 workstations.

Database Manager runs in a single-user (stand-alone) or multiuser (LAN) environment. The Database Manager portion of the Extended Services product consists of Database Services, Database Tools, Query Manager, Remote Data Services, and DOS and Windows Database Client support. You can use Database Manager in any of the following configurations:

- *Stand-Alone.* The databases you create exist only on your PC; other people cannot share your access to the files.

- *Database Client/Server.* You and others can share the databases that reside in your PC. You also can access databases on other database-server PCs.

- *Database Client.* You share databases that reside on other PCs (database servers); you have no local databases on your PC.

- *Database Client with Local Databases.* You share access to a database server in addition to having one or more local databases on your PC that only you can access.

For Related Information
- "Choosing the OS/2 Features You Want," p. 139
- "Using CONFIG.SYS and AUTOEXEC.BAT," p. 162

Understanding Database Manager Basics

Database Manager has many components and can do many tasks, but all the functions within Database Manager relate either to designing or manipulating databases. You specify the information you want to store when you design the database. You then add, change, and retrieve information when you use the database.

A database is a repository of relational tables that store information about entities. Each table is, in essence, a list of entities. At design time, you indicate what data fields the columns of the table are to hold. You also indicate the relationships among the tables.

Relational Databases. Database Manager uses the *relational model* of data. The software stores your information in table-oriented rows and columns. Each row is a different entity. Each column identifies a *data field*—a piece of information associated with each entity. You can designate one or more of the columns (fields) as indexes in the table. An *index* is a key that identifies each row of a table. A database can consist of one or more tables.

A simple example may help you understand relational database technology. Suppose that you work at a bank and want to use Database Manager to keep track of mortgage-loan accounts. You may at first design a single table, such as the following, for all customer data:

MORTGAGE CUSTOMERS

Name and Address   Account Number   Loan Amount   Monthly Payment

What if the same customer has several mortgages with your bank? You don't want the name and address information repeated several times in the database. To avoid this problem, you can design two tables in your database:

Table 1

MORTGAGE CUSTOMERS

Name and Address   Account Number   List of Mortgage Numbers (1 or more)

Table 2

MORTGAGES

Mortgage Number   Loan Amount   Monthly Payment

In this example, you can use Mortgage Number to relate the contents of one table to the other.

Structured Query Language (SQL). You use Structured Query Language (SQL) statements to store data in and retrieve data from relational tables. You can learn the details of SQL and issue your SQL statements explicitly. Alternatively, you can use Query Manager, or the facilities of another software product such as Borland International's Paradox, to formulate your SQL statements. Query Manager is a component of Database Manager that you learn more about later in this chapter.

SQL, pronounced *sequel*, is a language comparable to English. SQL statements occur in layers of increasing complexity and capability. You can learn SQL's basic features quickly, yet SQL provides programmers with considerable control over databases. With SQL, you can do the following:

- Create tables
- Store information in tables
- Select exactly the information you need
- Change the stored data
- Change the structure of the tables
- Combine data from multiple tables

In contrast to other data-manipulation languages, SQL is *nonprocedural*—you specify operations in terms of *what* SQL is to do, rather than *how* SQL is to do the operations. With a single command, you can update multiple rows of a table without knowing the location or other physical attributes of the rows.

Popular SQL statements are CREATE, SELECT, UPDATE, and INSERT. The following SQL statement creates a new staff member table in the database:

Create Table Staff	(Name)	Char(25),
	JOB_DESCRIPTION	CHAR(50),
	HIRE_DATE	DATE,
	SALARY	NUMBER(7,2));

This table is called STAFF and is to contain the name (25-characters wide), job description (50 characters), hire date (stored in date format), and salary (in #####.## format) for each staff member. The table is empty after the CREATE operation, ready to hold information about the people in your organization.

You use INSERT statements to populate the table with data, as shown in the following example:

```
INSERT INTO STAFF
VALUES ('JEFFREY', 'ADMINISTRATOR', 10/1/1982, 55000.00);
To update Jeffrey's salary, you issue the following UPDATE command:
UPDATE STAFF
SET SALARY = 57500.00 WHERE NAME = 'JEFFREY';
```

Finally, to obtain a list of all administrators and their salaries from the STAFF table, you use the following SELECT statement:

```
SELECT NAME, SALARY
FROM STAFF
WHERE JOB_DESCRIPTION = 'ADMINISTRATOR';
```

These examples show that SQL isn't difficult to use in its basic form. You can formulate much more complicated updates and queries with SQL. To help you in working with SQL, IBM supplies a complete *Structured Query Language (SQL) Reference* with the Extended Services product.

Using Database Services

Database Services is the part of Database Manager that actually manages the data stored in a database. Database Services provides record locking and transaction management. Database Services also ensures the integrity of the data in the database.

Database Services controls all access to the database; it performs database operations on your behalf (or those of a computer program you run) by processing SQL statements. You can interact with Database Services through the command-line interface, through Query Manager, through the Extended Services Database Tools, or through a computer program (written by your company's programmers) that issues SQL statements.

Preparing SQL Statements. Database Services accepts SQL statements from Query Manager, from the command-line interface, or from an application program. Database Services translates SQL statements into a sequence of internal operations. The translation process is called *preparing* or *binding*. Database Services must prepare all executable SQL statements before performing the operations called out by those statements.

If you use Database Services interactively, through Query Manager or the command-line interface, Database Services prepares the statements at runtime and then executes the statements. This method of operation is termed *dynamic SQL*. Some custom-written computer programs issue dynamic SQL, but most do not.

A computer programmer can use Database Services to prepare SQL statements before the program actually runs. The programmer runs an SQL precompiler; this mode of operation is termed *static SQL*. Static SQL statements, embedded in the application program, enable Database Services to bypass preparing the SQL statements at run time. The application program executes faster because Database Services has less work to do.

Programming SQL with REXX. You can use the REXX programming language to access Database Manager databases. REXX is the interactive, friendly programming environment you explored in Chapter 19, "Programming with REXX." Because REXX is interactive, the SQL statements in your REXX programs execute dynamically, not statically (there is no precompile step). You may not want to use REXX to create "mission-critical" software used in your day-to-day updating of the database, but you can certainly use REXX to quickly prepare ad-hoc queries that you run against your database. If you have the slightest inclination toward computer programming, you'll find REXX easier and faster to use than a tool such as Query Manager.

The following REXX program shows how you can access Database Manager (or DB2/2) with your own program statements. The REXX program uses `rxfuncadd` to load (add) the SQL functionality modules to the REXX environment, displays the message `Sample REXX database access program`, connects to the database with a `CONNECT TO` statement, issues an SQL `SELECT` statement, issues `PREPARE` and `DECLARE` SQL statements, fetches and displays table names, and disconnects from the database. Note that both Database Manager and DB2/2 come with reference manuals you can use to explore accessing your databases with REXX more fully.

If you have Database Manager or DB2/2 and if you created the sample database that comes with these database products (change to the SQLLIB directory and run SQLSAMPL to create it), you might want to try typing this small program into the OS/2 System Editor or Enhanced Editor. Save the file with a name such as MYSQL.CMD. Use the IBM-supplied DBM Command Line Processor to start the database and then type **MYSQL** at an OS/2 command-line prompt to run the program. The program displays a list of table names. The list you see follows the example REXX program.

```
/* REXX DATABASE ACCESS EXAMPLE PROGRAM */

if rxfuncquery('SQLDBS') <> 0 then
   rc = rxfuncadd( 'SQLDBS',   'SQLAR',  'SQLDBS'  );
if rxfuncquery('SQLEXEC') <> 0 then
   rc = rxfuncadd( 'SQLEXEC',  'SQLAR',  'SQLEXEC' );

say 'Sample REXX database access program'

call sqlexec 'CONNECT TO sample IN SHARE MODE';
if ( SQLCA.SQLCODE <> 0) then do
   say 'CONNECT TO Error:  SQLCODE = ' SQLCA.SQLCODE;
   exit
   end

st = "SELECT name FROM sysibm.systables WHERE name <> ?";
call sqlexec 'PREPARE s1 FROM :st';
call sqlexec 'DECLARE c1 CURSOR FOR s1';
if ( SQLCA.SQLCODE <> 0) then do
   say 'Error preparing statement:  SQLCODE = ' SQLCA.SQLCODE;
   call sqlexec 'CONNECT RESET';
   exit
   end

parm_var = "STAFF";
call sqlexec 'OPEN c1 USING :parm_var';
do while ( SQLCA.SQLCODE = 0 )
   call sqlexec 'FETCH c1 INTO :table_name';
   if (SQLCA.SQLCODE = 0) then
      say 'Table = ' table_name;
   end
call sqlexec 'CLOSE c1';
call sqlexec 'COMMIT';

call sqlexec 'CONNECT RESET';
Here is the output from the example program:
Sample REXX database access program
Table =   QRWSYS_OBJECT
Table =   SYSCOLUMNS
Table =   SYSDBAUTH
Table =   SYSINDEXAUTH
Table =   SYSINDEXES
Table =   SYSPLAN
Table =   SYSPLANAUTH
Table =   SYSPLANDEP
Table =   SYSRELS
Table =   SYSSECTION
Table =   SYSSTMT
Table =   SYSTABAUTH
Table =   SYSTABLES
Table =   SYSVIEWDEP
Table =   SYSVIEWS
Table =   ORG
```

Record Locking and Transaction Management. When you design your tables, you can express data relationships among the tables. You don't want these relationships destroyed by a sudden power failure in your building. Database Services uses the concept of a *unit of work* to ensure that the database is always in a consistent state. A unit of work is a transaction—a collection of updates to related tables. You want all the updates in the collection to be successfully applied. If only some of the updates happen and then a power failure occurs, you want the partial update to be "rolled back" so that the database returns to a consistent state.

To understand consistent and inconsistent database states, consider the tables you created earlier for the bank-mortgage records. When you use the MORTGAGE CUSTOMERS and MORTGAGES tables, you may issue SQL statements against the database to transfer a mortgage from one customer to another. After you remove the Mortgage Number from one customer's records, but before you add that Mortgage Number to the second customer's records, the database is in an *inconsistent* state. Only after you add the Mortgage Number to the second customer's records is the database *consistent* again.

Every time a computer program begins using a database, Database Services automatically starts a unit of work. The program can signal the end of the unit of work by issuing a COMMIT statement (that indicates successful completion of the update) or a ROLLBACK statement (that instructs Database Services to restore the database to the state it was in before the unit of work began). Note that the example REXX program you just examined contains a COMMIT statement. If the computer program disconnects from the database before successfully finishing the update, Database Services issues a ROLLBACK statement. While the unit of work is in progress, Database Services prevents other workstations in a multiuser environment from accessing the data you are updating.

Database Objects. Database Services objects include databases, tables, views, indexes, and packages. The following paragraphs describe these objects in detail and explain how Database Services groups the objects in the database.

In previous sections, you learned about databases and their tables. Database Manager considers a *database* to encompass not only the tables but also a set of system catalogs that describe the logical and physical structure of the data, a configuration file, and a recovery log file that contains information about ongoing transactions (updates in progress).

A *view* is an alternative representation of the data in one or more tables of the database. A typical view may include only some of the columns of the tables in a database and thus provide restricted access to the tables. You can create a view, for example, of only 20 or 30 fields that people can query and update, even though the entire table may contain hundreds of fields. You thus impose a measure of security and simplify people's access to the table.

An *index* is a key, a set of table columns you designate as fields that identify the entity stored in a row. You can specify whether the index value is unique or whether the table can hold duplicate indexes (keys).

A *package* is the result a programmer obtains when he or she prepares a set of SQL statements, in a computer language, for use with the database. The package contains all the information needed by Database Manager to process the programmer's specific SQL statements.

Database Manager groups objects in the database by *qualifier*. The qualifier is an identification code that can contain up to eight characters (numbers and letters). The qualifier identifies each person who accesses a database and helps Database Manager keep separate track of each person's database objects.

Exploring Database Tools

Extended Services offers three tools for configuring Database Manager and administering databases: the Configuration Tool, the Recovery Tool, and the Directory Tool. The following sections describe these tools and their uses.

Configuration Tool. You use the Configuration Tool to change Database Manager resources and database characteristics. You can allocate resources for the database buffer pool, the database log files, the number of applications that can use a database, and the size of the database sort buffer. You also can instruct Database Manager to use more memory for storage management.

The Configuration Tool also enables you to mark a database as a candidate for *roll-forward recovery* by the Recovery Tool. Roll-forward recovery is the update of the database by the application of changes recorded in the database log. The database log stores all pertinent information about each update operation during a unit of work (a transaction). Figure 24.8 shows the Configuration Tool screen.

Recovery Tool. You use the Recovery Tool to make backup copies of your databases and, when necessary, to restore your database files. You can specify that you want a backup of the entire database, or you can specify that the system copy only the changes and updates that are more recent than the last backup. The Recovery Tool can recover or restore a database as new, as a replacement for an existing database of the same name, or as a continuation of a recovery operation you previously started. Figure 24.9 shows the Recovery Tool screen.

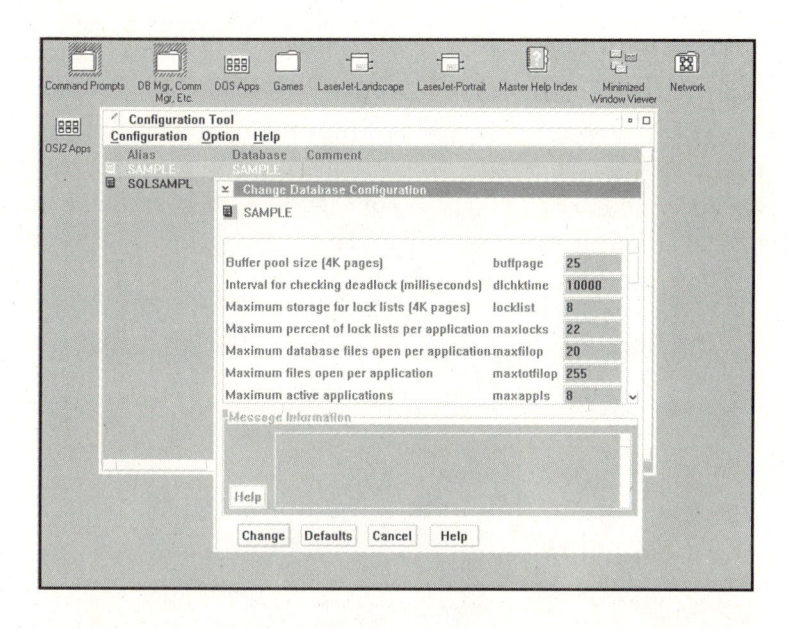

Fig. 24.8
The Configuration Tool screen.

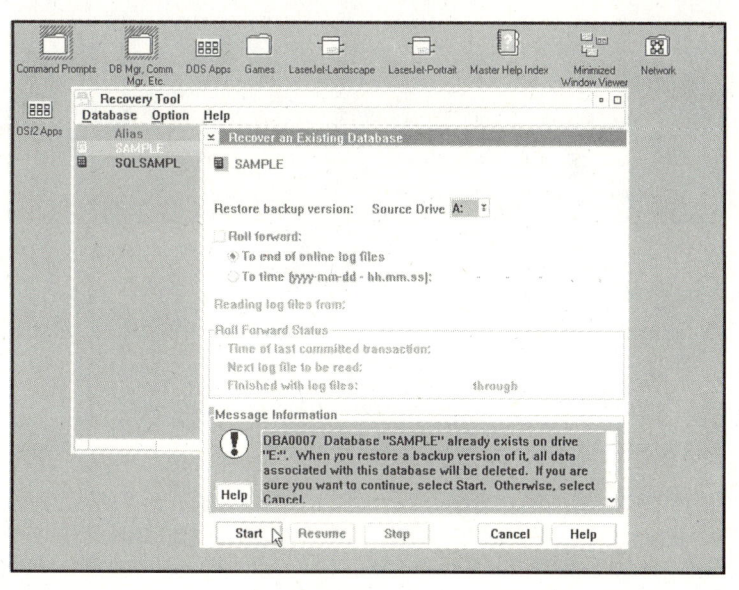

Fig. 24.9
The Recovery Tool screen.

Directory Tool. You use the Directory Tool to create database files and to specify who can access the databases. The Directory Tool can create a new database, catalog a local or remote database, and uncatalog a database. A *catalog* is a published description of the logical and physical structure of the data; other people can "see" a database on your PC if you have cataloged that database. The Directory Tool also can list all the local and remote databases cataloged in the system database directory, or list the volume database directories (the disk drives on which your databases reside). You can use the Directory Tool to catalog or uncatalog workstations (to enable or disable access to your databases) and to list the workstations cataloged on your computer. Figure 24.10 shows the Directory Tool screen.

Fig. 24.10
The Directory Tool screen.

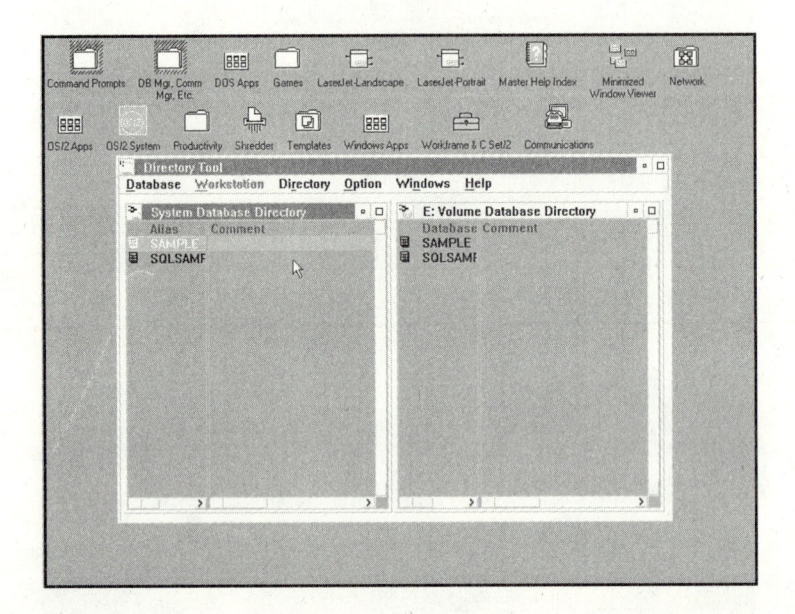

Using Query Manager

Query Manager is a Presentation Manager application that provides interactive access to your databases. You don't have to be an expert in SQL to use Query Manager. Query Manager's menus guide you through the steps of creating and executing SQL statements.

You can use Query Manager to create and define a database, request information from a database, review the operational status of a database, and change the authorizations that control who has access to specific database functions, tables, and views. You also can direct Query Manager to create a customized user interface through which users can gain access to your databases.

Creating and Defining a Database. After you double-click the Query Manager icon and identify yourself to the User Profile Management Services Logon screen, the Query Manager screen appears. You can choose a database from that screen's list or create a new database. Figure 24.11 shows the Query Manager screen.

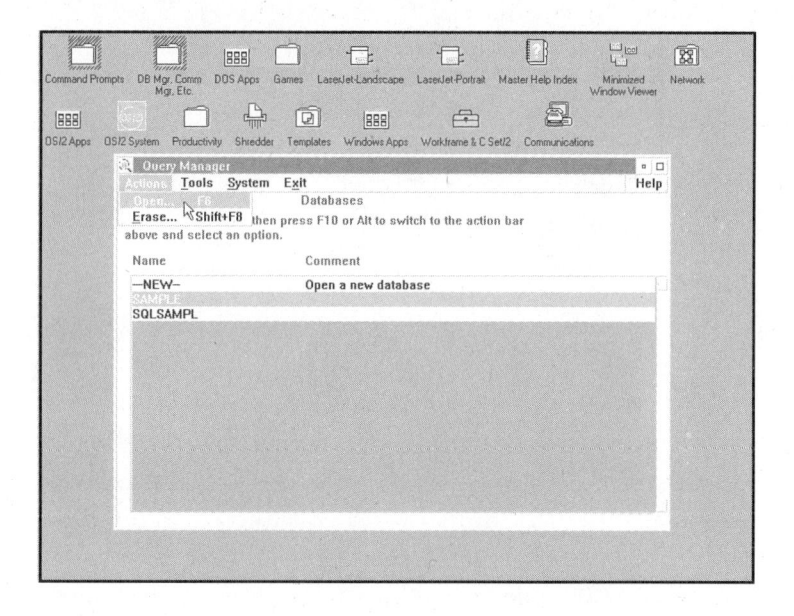

Fig. 24.11
The Query Manager initial screen.

After selecting a database, you use the Query Manager Main Selection screen, shown in figure 24.12, to begin working with that database. The following list describes the Query Manager options available on this screen:

- *Tables and Views.* Use this option to design tables or views, or update table data.

- *Queries.* Use this option to retrieve data from tables and display reports.

- *Forms.* Use this option to design reports.

- *Procedures.* Use this option to develop custom command sequences.

- *Panels.* Use this option to design custom data-entry screens.

- *Menus.* Use this option to design menus for data-entry screens.

- *Profiles.* Use this option to change default database names and other system defaults.

Fig. 24.12
The Query Manager Main Selection screen.

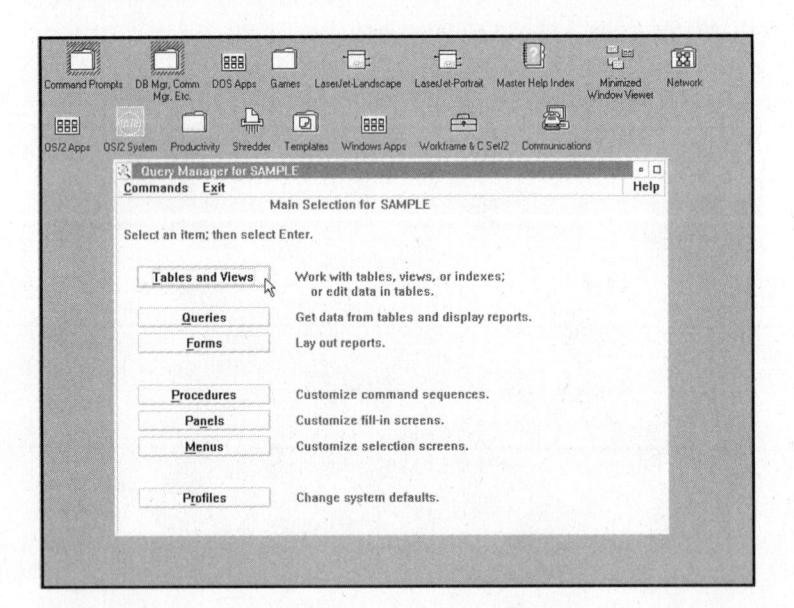

To add a column of information to a new or existing table, you use the Tables and Views option. This option brings up a Table screen, similar to the one shown in figure 24.13. On the Query Manager Table screen, you use menu options to add or delete columns from the table. The screen shows the current layout of the table.

Requesting Information from a Database. You can use Query Manager's menus to formulate a query. If you plan to use the same query several times, you can store the query for future reference. You start the process of building a query by selecting the Queries button on the Query Manager's Main Selection screen.

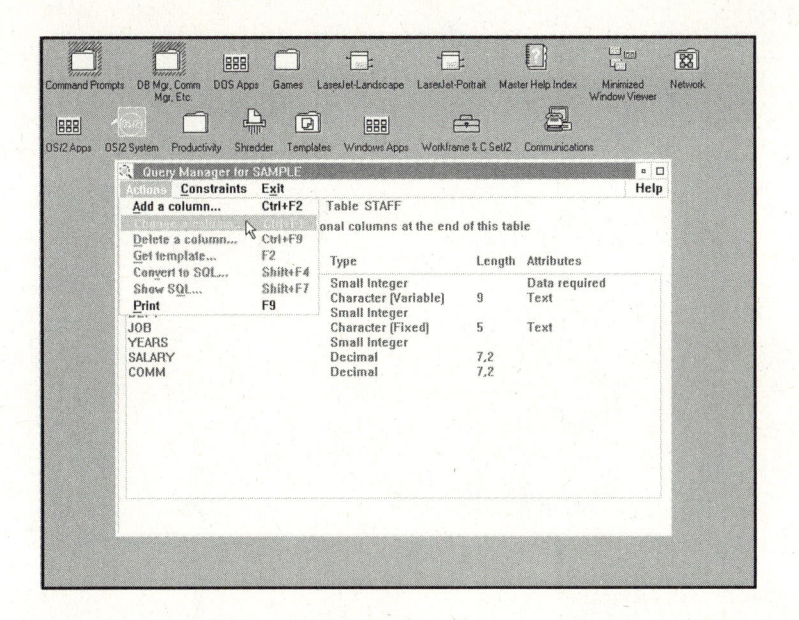

Fig. 24.13
The Query Manager Table screen.

You use Query Manager menus to build queries. In the menus, you select the columns the query is to display, the criteria for which rows the query displays, and the sort order of the final report. The first pull-down menu contains options for managing the query during the query-building process. You can run the query, save the query, get (load) a query, convert the query to SQL and show the result, and print the query.

Figure 24.14 shows a query under construction. In this example, the query is to display the columns (data fields) DEPT, SALARY, and COMM, and the expression SALARY+COMM. The *Row Conditions* entry of the query states IF DEPT Is Equal To 15, 20 OR 38. This query sorts information for departments 15, 20, and 38 in ascending order by DEPT.

When you run the query, Query Manager produces and displays a report containing the information you specified in the query construction. The on-screen report shown in figure 24.15 displays the query shown under construction in figure 24.14. Notice in the column headings that Query Manager named the combined SALARY+COMM column EXPRESSION 5. You can rename such expression-result headings.

Fig. 24.14
A query under construction.

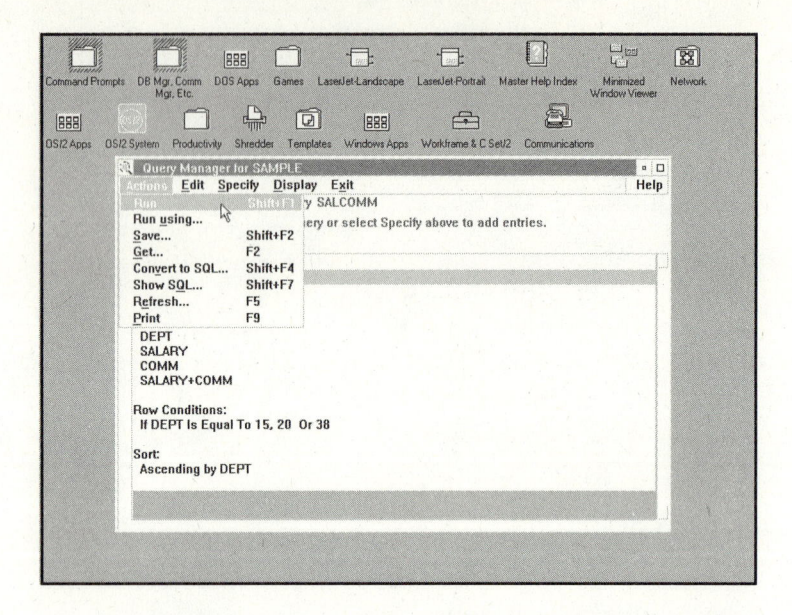

Fig. 24.15
Query Manager displays query results in report format.

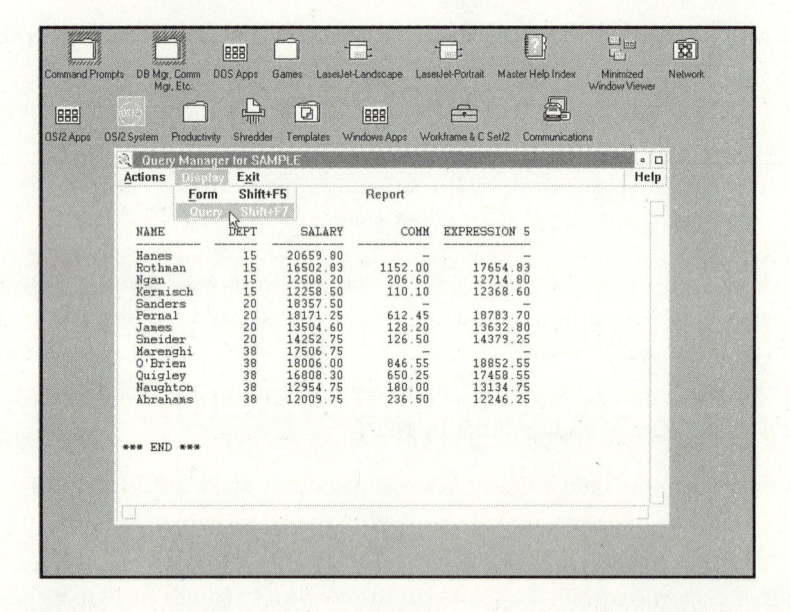

You use the Forms screen, shown in figure 24.16, to create reports containing data from the database. You can customize the appearance of Query Manager reports. You can change several options for the form, and you can specify Column Heading, Usage, Indent, Width, Edit Rules, and Sequence for each column in the report.

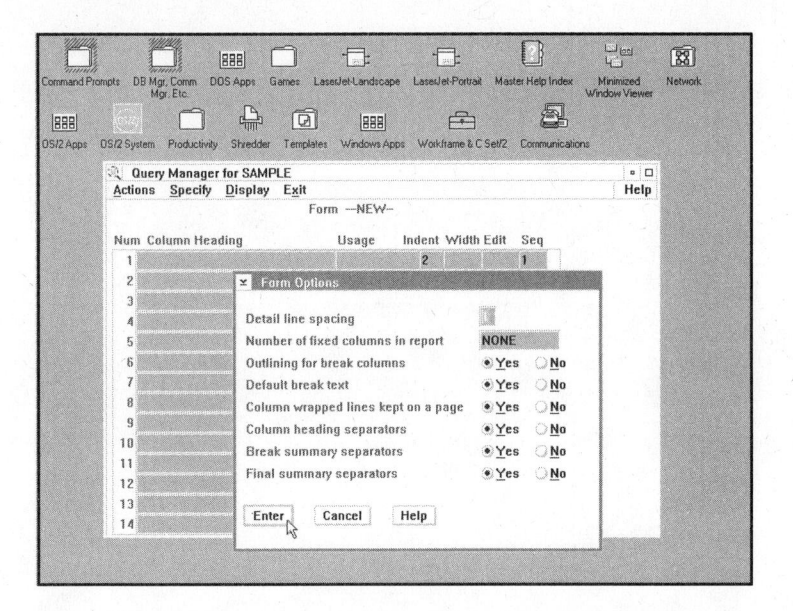

Fig. 24.16
The Query Manager Forms screen.

Reviewing the Query Manager Profile. Query Manager maintains a user profile for each account ID assigned to your database's users. The profile enables Query Manager to know the computer environment of each user when he or she accesses the database.

The profile contains *Sign-On Options* and *Printing Options*. The Sign-On Options indicate the default database name, the qualifier that Query Manager uses for this account ID, and the row-buffer size that Query Manager is to use for that account ID. The *qualifier* is a prefix that denotes a certain table in the database and allows a person to refer to that table without explicitly naming the table. The row-buffer size is a parameter that specifies how much memory is set aside for reading and writing rows of a table.

The Printing Options express the printer nickname (an alias by which you refer to the printer), lines per inch or centimeter, regular or condensed print, and number of copies. The Printing Options also include report-title configuration, which you use to indicate whether you want page numbers and the current date and time to appear on each report. Figure 24.17 shows the Query Manager Profile screen.

Using Customized Interfaces. You can use Query Manager menus to access your databases, or you can program Query Manager to present a customized interface to enable the same access. The interface you design can include

Chapter 24—Understanding OS/2 Communications and Database Tools

menus, data-entry screens, and simple procedures (in a simple computer programming language). You also can use the customized interface to print reports of your own design.

Fig. 24.17
The Query Manager Profile screen.

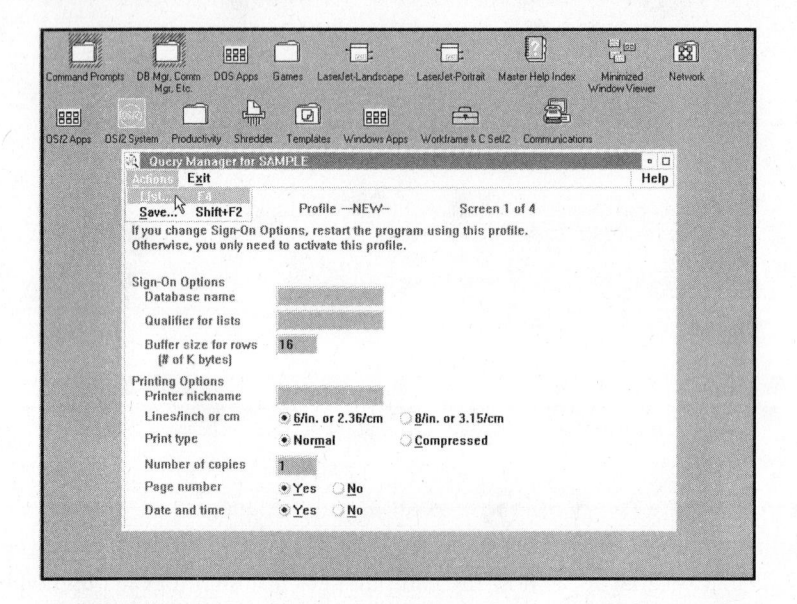

You design the custom interface menus with the Menu Actions screen (see fig. 24.18). You specify Action Text, a Mnemonic (which becomes a shortcut key), and a command for each menu option. The commands you list on this screen appear as Command options on your custom interface menu. When a user selects one of these options, Query Manager executes the designated Query Manager Procedure.

Figure 24.19 shows the Query Manager screen you use to design the panels of your customized interface. *Panels* is Query Manager's term for screens. You type procedural instructions that indicate the Query Manager processing that is to take place for a panel. You also designate panel search queries and names of procedures that are to execute under the conditions you specify.

Figure 24.20 shows the list of Panel Actions you can attach to each panel you design for the custom interface. Each action has a Mnemonic and an Action Key that users of your customized interface can invoke. You specify the Panel Operation/Command that executes when users invoke the Action. The Mode expresses whether the action is an Add, Change, or Delete operation.

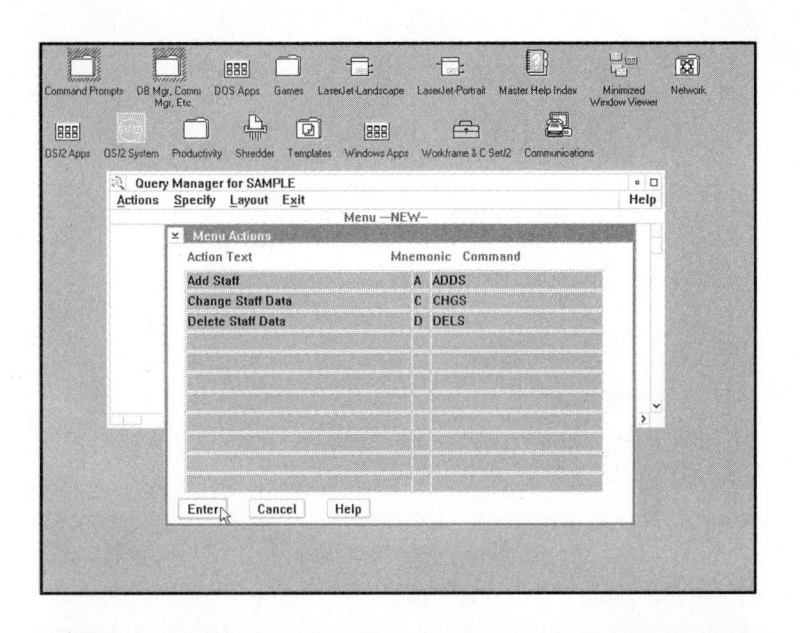

Fig. 24.18
The Query Manager Menu Actions screen.

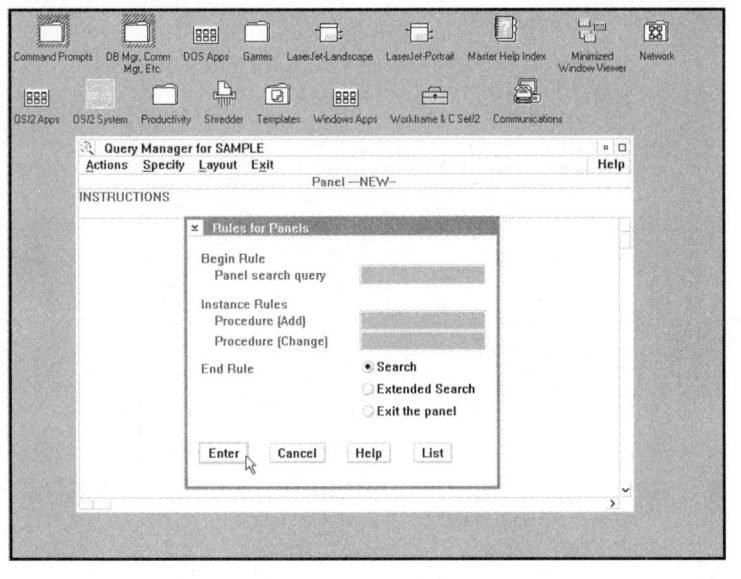

Fig. 24.19
The Query Manager Panel screen for designing customized interfaces.

Applying Remote Data Services

If you install and configure Database Manager as a networked, multiuser application, Extended Services also installs Remote Data Services on your computer. Remote Data Services enables multiple workstations to access a

652 Chapter 24—Understanding OS/2 Communications and Database Tools

shared, common database. Certain components of Communications Manager also install themselves on your computer to support Remote Data Services. You can use Remote Data Services through any one of the following connectivity options:

- A Token Ring-based LAN
- An IBM PC Network-based LAN
- An Ethernet-based LAN
- An SDLC adapter card
- An X.25 connection

Remote Data Services supplies the database-server and database-client functions; Communications Manager components supply the means of communicating database requests and replies to and from a remote database. After you establish catalogs of databases and remote workstations, you use Database Manager (through Query Manager, the command-line interface, or an application program) to access databases on the LAN in the same way you access databases on your local PC.

Fig. 24.20
The Query Manager Panel Actions screen.

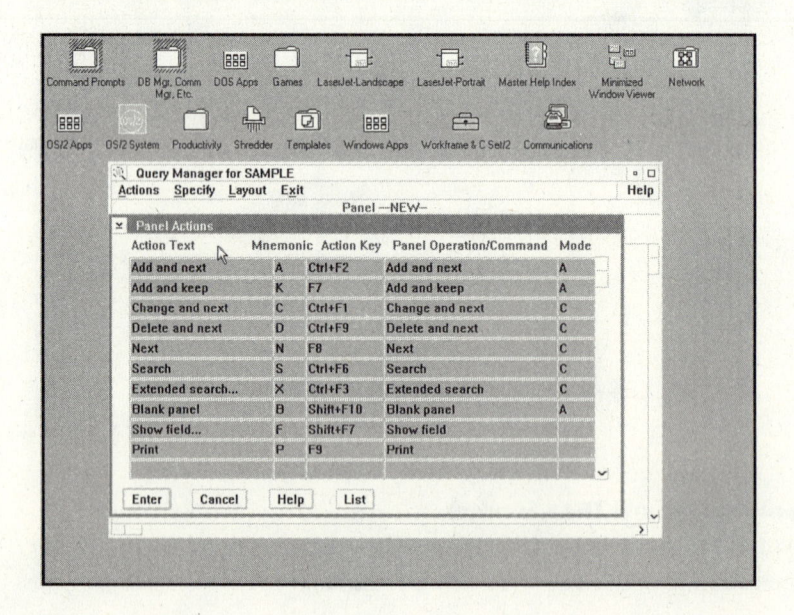

Understanding Client/Server Applications. You can use a network operating system such as IBM's LAN Server, Microsoft's LAN Manager, or Novell *NetWare* to turn a computer on the LAN into a file server. You then can put your databases on that file server.

The network operating system enables workstations to share the database file just as they share any other file. In a file-server environment, however, your database search operations take longer to execute and cause substantially greater LAN traffic. Your workstation must read the entire database from the file server to perform the search. If you have a database with a table of 5,000 entries and run a query that displays five rows of the table, for example, your workstation must read all 5,000 rows to find the five desired entries.

In a client/server environment, your workstation uses Remote Data Services to transfer your SELECT statement to the PC on which the database resides. Under the database conditions outlined in this example, the Database Manager running on that remote PC performs the search and returns the five table rows to your workstation. Remote Data Services processes the response through your own Database Manager. The faster running time is the only indication that the database is on a remote PC.

A *database-client workstation* requests access to resources made available by a *database-server workstation*. Applications your programmers develop, as well as software you buy, can take advantage of Remote Data Services. Such applications are client/server applications. Simple LAN workstation access to a file server involves the redirection of file read-and-write requests to and from the file server. On a busy LAN, the resulting LAN traffic flowing through the LAN cable and the demands placed on the file server can slow productivity. Database client/server technology involves sending SQL statements to a database server and receiving acknowledgments and possibly selected table rows from the database. In contrast to a file-server environment, the reduction in LAN traffic and the more intelligent use of the server computer in a client/server environment provide, overall, a higher capacity information-processing system.

A client/server environment puts each kind of information-processing chore—collecting information, searching through a series of files, updating files, and performing computations—on the LAN-attached PC that's best suited for that particular chore. A database server receives database query and database update requests, fulfills those requests, and returns a response to the workstation. A database server doesn't require a high-quality color monitor or a heavy-duty keyboard. The database server, however, does need a fast, large hard disk, a fast CPU, lots of RAM, and a high-quality network adapter. Database-client workstations, on the other hand, need color monitors, mice, and other user-interface amenities.

Making a Remote Database Seem Local. A database-client workstation uses either NetBIOS or Advanced Peer-to-Peer Networking (APPN) to communicate with a database server. NetBIOS is the default protocol for Database Manager and Remote Data Services, but you can use the Communications Manager configuration screens to work with either protocol.

Remote Data Services reads the Extended Services configuration and catalog files to know where each database resides. You or an administrator sets up these configuration and catalog files at Database Manager installation time or when your office designs and creates a new shared database.

Supporting DOS and Windows Database Clients

The Extended Services with Database Server product contains computer program "helper" modules that enable client workstations to access shared databases. Your organization's programmers can develop custom applications using these modules. The client workstations need not run OS/2 and Extended Services. Some of the workstations on the LAN can be DOS or DOS-and-Windows based, provided that at least one of the workstations runs Extended Services and OS/2. The DOS or DOS-and-Windows database-client workstations contain only NetBIOS and a database-access enabler. A user at a DOS workstation, for example, cannot use Query Manager to access a database.

For Related Information
- "Introducing Presentation Manager," p. 234

> **Note**
> Check with IBM about the licensing requirements for the database-client workstation-enabler software.

Moving Up to CM/2 and DB2/2

During 1993, IBM substantially improved the Communications Manager and Database Manager components of Extended Services. IBM released the new components as separate software products; IBM no longer sells Extended Services. If you presently use Extended Services, you can continue to get technical support from IBM, but consider upgrading to the new CM/2 and DB2/2 software. The next sections of this chapter explain the features and functions of CM/2 and DB2/2.

Communications Manager/2

This chapter's earlier discussion of Communications Manager cautioned you about the difficulty of installing and configuring that component of Extended Services. Although you may have gotten lost or confused while installing or configuring its predecessor, the new CM/2 product corrects virtually all the previous version's setup deficiencies. ES used a text-mode installation program, but CM/2 uses a series of Presentation Manager windows—with context-sensitive help available any time you need it—to install and configure itself. CM/2 can, at your option, remove an existing Extended Services component from your computer so that you don't have two CM products on your PC at the end of the installation process. You can buy CM/2 on floppy disk or CD-ROM media, and you can install CM/2 over the LAN cable if you have a local area network.

CM/2 offers much the same range of connectivity options as ES did, including coaxial, Synchronous Data Link Control (SDLC), asynchronous, Token Ring, Ethernet, PC Network, Fiber-Optic Data Distribution Interface (FDDI), twinaxial, and Integrated Services Digital Network (ISDN). In CM/2 you get 3270 terminal emulation, 5250 terminal emulation, LU 6.2 Advanced Program-to-Program Communications (APPC), and various application-programming interfaces for communications. These APIs include Emulator High-Level Language API (EHLLAPI), Server-Requester Programming Interface (SRPI), Asynchronous Communications Device Interface (ACDI), and an X.25 interface.

Database 2 for OS/2

IBM used to sell a diverse range of database-management products. If you owned an IBM mainframe, you installed DB2. If you owned an IBM RS/6000 RISC-based minicomputer, you may have installed Oracle's database manager. For AS/400 minicomputers, you accessed the relational database manager that's part of OS/400. On PCs, you may have installed Extended Services' DBM component.

IBM has consolidated this range of database-management products. You can now get DB2 for the mainframe, for the RS/6000, or for OS/2-based PCs. The database manager that's part of OS/400 is highly compatible with DB2. And IBM offers a product called Distributed Database Connection Services/2 (DDCS/2) that lets PC-based applications interact with DB2 on the mainframe. By simply plugging in DDCS/2, an application that connected to an Extended Services DBM database or a DB2/2 database can now connect to DB2 on the mainframe.

DB2/2 includes Database Services (the "engine" that uses the SQL statements your computer programs emit to manage the database); Remote Data Services, or RDS (the connectivity software that interfaces Database Services to the client workstations on a local area network); application-programming interfaces, or APIs (the specifications programmers use to develop DB2/2-aware software); database-management and administration tools; a command-line processor that accepts your typed SQL statements and gives them to Database Services; and Query Manager (a Presentation Manager window through which you can click and point to create your SQL).

DB2/2 is a collection of 32-bit computer programs. Although the 16-bit Extended Services ran on earlier versions of OS/2 as well as OS/2 2.x, DB2/2 runs only on OS/2 2.x. The move to a 32-bit architecture lets DB2/2 perform faster than Extended Services DBM did. IBM made other performance improvements in DB2/2 as well. The Database Services engine has been completely reworked.

To bring DB2/2 on the PC closer to the implementation of DB2 on the mainframe, IBM enhanced the SQL capabilities of DB2/2. The PC version of DB2 provides updated SQL syntax and processing for NOT NULL WITH DEFAULT table column definitions, for CONNECT statements, for CURRENT SERVER, for DECIMAL, INTEGER, and FLOAT scalar functions, and for the EXECUTE statement. DB2/2 also works with (and comes with) IBM's First Failure Support Technology product (FFST/2). FFST/2 lets programmers collect diagnostic information and determine the causes of problems so that the programmers can modify their computer software to run correctly.

IBM sells DB2/2 on floppy disk or CD-ROM media, and you can install DB2/2 over the LAN cable if you have a local area network.

Investigating Other OS/2-Based Products

Other database software companies, such as Oracle, Gupta Technologies, Ingres, and even Microsoft, recognize that OS/2 is a good environment for sharing databases on a local area network. All these vendors offer database technology that in some way uses OS/2. Client/server information processing, defined and described earlier in this chapter, generally works well when the database-server computer runs OS/2. Database-client workstations are also good candidates for running OS/2 because OS/2 provides a great number of network connectivity options and a friendly user interface.

Microsoft's SQL Server product, which was actually developed by a company named Sybase, is an interesting departure from the technology offered by Extended Services DBM and DB2/2. SQL Server runs on OS/2, like DBM and DB2/2, and client workstations can run DOS, DOS-and-Windows, or OS/2. Application software issues SQL statements to retrieve and update information in the database, just as with DBM or DB2/2. But application software that uses the programming interface of DBM and DB2/2 does not work with SQL Server. A programmer must write different programming statements to make a computer program work with SQL Server.

Although DBM and DB2/2 support both static and dynamic SQL, the SQL Server product supports only dynamic SQL. The application programmer does not precompile or bind a computer program to help the program work better against the database. SQL Server offers several significant extensions to Structured Query Language. Microsoft calls these extensions Transact-SQL. Ironically, most customers shy away from these extensions because they want their database accesses to comply with industry standards. Complying with standards makes migrating to a higher-capacity environment (such as the mainframe DB2) easier.

Chapter Summary

With this chapter, you gained an understanding of IBM's Extended Services product and its successors, DB2/2 and CM/2. You explored the features and functions of Communications Manager that let you link your computer to other computers. You learned how User Profile Management helps protect the privacy of your databases. You discovered the advantages of database access from within OS/2. And you briefly looked at other vendor's client/server database technologies running on OS/2.

In the next chapter, you turn your attention to networking OS/2 on a NetWare LAN.

Chapter 25

Networking OS/2 with NetWare

OS/2 is a natural computer environment for local area networks (LANs). The operating system and especially the Workplace Shell contain a number of LAN-aware features and facilities. Network operating system vendors such as Novell and IBM have taken advantage of these features and facilities to make their networks easy to install, administer, and use. You can access the network not only from a command-line session but also from the Workplace Shell's graphical interface.

You can use an OS/2-based PC as a workstation on a NetWare LAN or as a NetWare file server. Novell offers a NetWare Requester for OS/2 that turns your OS/2 computer into a workstation on a NetWare LAN. Novell also offers a relatively new product, NetWare for OS/2, which can turn an OS/2-based computer into a NetWare file server.

IBM offers its own LAN Server product to customers who want to run an IBM network operating system on an OS/2-based computer. Although in some respects LAN Server and NetWare are competing products, IBM sells both network software products. IBM entered into an agreement with Novell to resell NetWare under the IBM name. You learn more about LAN Server and other network operating systems in the next chapter.

This chapter gives you an understanding of how your OS/2-equipped PC functions on a NetWare-based local area network. You explore Novell's popular network environment, NetWare. You learn how to install and use the NetWare Requester for OS/2, and you cover using the OS/2 versions of Novell's NetWare utilities.

You can use OS/2 as part of a network in any of four ways:

- *You can dedicate an OS/2 PC as a file server.* OS/2 can be the platform on which you run a file-server operating system such as IBM's LAN Server, Microsoft's LAN Manager, or NetWare for OS/2. OS/2-based file servers use OS/2's file system, memory management, and multitasking capabilities as the basis for file serving.

- *You can use an OS/2 PC as a file server and a workstation at the same time.* Before version 4, NetWare required you to dedicate a separate PC as a file-server computer. Beginning with NetWare 4, Novell lets an OS/2 PC act as a NetWare file server even if that PC is also an application server, database server, communications server, or perhaps an ordinary workstation. (A file server that is also a workstation is termed *nondedicated*.) Naturally, if you ask the OS/2 machine to perform more tasks beyond the sharing of files, you need to use a faster, more capable PC.

- *You can use OS/2 as a client or networked workstation.* Workstations running OS/2, like their DOS counterparts, can access NetWare servers and use server disks to store and retrieve files. OS/2 workstations also can send print jobs to shared printers. DOS workstations use the NetWare workstation shell, but OS/2 workstations use the NetWare OS/2 Requester Version 2.01 or later. The first few sections of this chapter cover the OS/2 Requester.

- *You can incorporate OS/2-based devices into your network by using OS/2 to turn a PC into a specialized server that other workstations can access.* The most common example is the database server. Workstations send requests for database records to the database server. The database server processes the requests by searching a database for the records and returning the result to the workstation. Centralizing the search inside the database server is generally more efficient than having many workstations plow through a large shared file on a file server. For example, a workstation can send a single request to the database server and get back perhaps a few responses. If you used a file server to hold the searchable file, each workstation would have to read through the entire file (with redirected file I/O LAN packets) for each search operation.

Installing NetWare for OS/2 on an OS/2-based PC makes that PC appear on the LAN as a NetWare file server, just as if the machine were dedicated to

NetWare 4. Workstations log in to the OS/2 PC, map its drives, and share its printers exactly as they would with any other NetWare server. The OS/2 NetWare Requester is a different product from NetWare for OS/2. The Requester component turns an OS/2-based PC into a workstation on a NetWare LAN.

Looking at OS/2 Workstations on a NetWare LAN

The NetWare Requester for OS/2 enables a computer running OS/2 2.1 to become a workstation on a NetWare LAN. In the next few sections, you become familiar with the NetWare Requester for OS/2 product.

OS/2 is a multitasking operating system. You can start a long-running print job in one session under OS/2 and then switch your attention to another session to get other work done. The print job continues in the background while you work. If you start another print job in a different session, the OS/2 spooler and the network spooler work together to keep the printouts separate.

OS/2 and the LAN also work together to protect the integrity of your data files. If, for example, you edit a document with a word processor in one session and try to edit that same document from another session, you receive a `Sharing Violation` error message from OS/2. The same mechanism that protects multiple users on the LAN from editing the same file at the same time also protects your multiple OS/2 and DOS sessions from colliding.

Version 3.11 and 3.12 of NetWare supports several workstation environments. The server can store files from DOS, Macintosh, OS/2, UNIX, and OSI-based client workstations transparently. To do this, NetWare 3.11 sets aside special name spaces on the server. You load optional server modules (NetWare Loadable Modules—NLMs) to manage these name spaces. Each directory entry for a file holds a DOS-style name. The corresponding name-space entry (two 128-byte areas) contains machine-specific name information. A file that originates on an OS/2 workstation, for example, can retain its extended attributes (long name, creation date, and so forth). A Mac file uses the name space to hold the long name and Mac Finder (resource fork) information. An application running on a DOS workstation can access a file created by a Mac workstation, and vice versa.

The Macintosh, DOS, and OS/2 file-sharing features work well. After you load the NetWare for Macintosh NLM, you can create a Microsoft Word document on a Mac, revise the same file with Microsoft Word for Windows on a DOS-based or OS/2-based computer, and perform a final revision under Word/PM on an OS/2 workstation. In each case, you would not know that the file originated on a different kind of computer.

When you use Novell's NetWare Requester for OS/2 to turn your OS/2 computer into a workstation on a NetWare LAN, you notice the extra drive letters, the ability to print to the shared LAN printer, and many other LAN characteristics that DOS-based workstations are familiar with. The network software, however, does not use conventional memory under OS/2. With OS/2, you do not have to load the network software in DOS memory. You do not need a memory-manager product to reclaim usable memory.

Once you log in to the network and map your file-server drives as drive letters, each new DOS or OS/2 session you create has equal access to the file-server drives. A CAPTURE command issued in one DOS or OS/2 session affects all the other sessions. You can print from any environment in OS/2 after issuing the CAPTURE printer-redirection command.

Understanding NetWare Requester for OS/2

The NetWare Requester for OS/2 is an installable file system similar to HPFS. (Chapter 4, "Deciding How You Want To Use OS/2," discusses HPFS.) The file system you access through the Requester is in the file server rather than in your local PC. Through the Requester, you can share disk drives and printers, share files with other users, and send messages to people at other workstations.

NetWare Requester has several components. The components that enable you to access the file server are device drivers you load through your CONFIG.SYS file. The components you use to administer and manage the network are available as command-line utilities and also as Presentation Manager (PM) utilities. You can choose the command-line interface or the PM interface. The Requester product contains on-line help files that work in the same manner as OS/2's built-in help files.

The NetWare Requester enables you to access the file server and shared printer from any of your OS/2, DOS, or Windows sessions. Your DOS applications operate the same way in a DOS session, for example, as they operate on a plain DOS workstation. The DOS utility SHARE.EXE is always, in effect, under OS/2. You don't have to remember to load SHARE.EXE (which, under plain DOS, enables file-sharing) when you access the network.

Installing the NetWare Requester

The NetWare Requester is easy to install. The installation program is a PM application. Through a menu-driven interface, you copy the Requester files to your workstation and configure your workstation's networking parameters. Figure 25.1 shows the initial NetWare Requester Workstation installation screen. Follow the initial screen's step-by-step instructions to install the software that enables you, through your network adapter, to access the LAN.

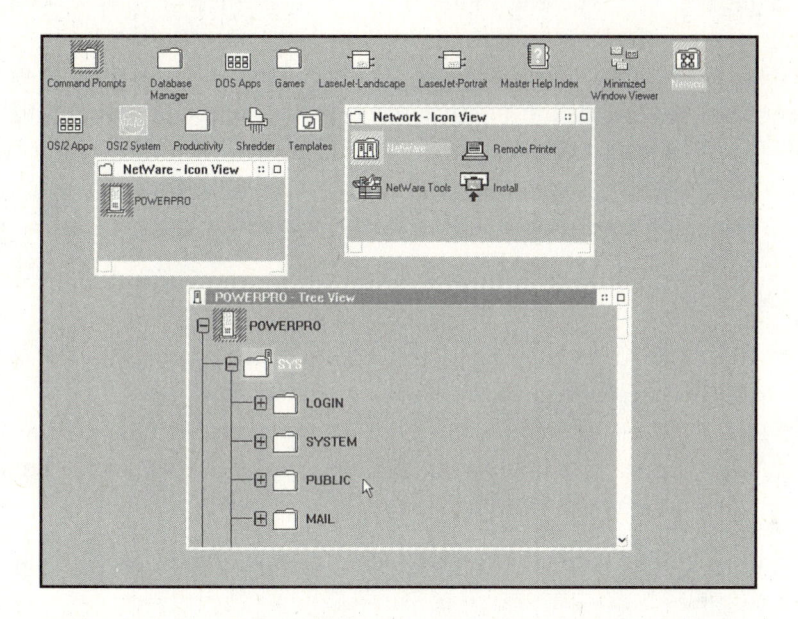

Fig. 25.1
The initial NetWare Requester for OS/2 installation screen.

Your organization's network administrator (an individual with supervisor privileges on your LAN) installs the OS/2 versions of the NetWare utility programs, such as SYSCON, PCONSOLE, and USERLIST. The installation process places these OS/2 utilities in the PUBLIC\OS2 directory on the file server. The OS/2 utilities have to be installed only once; your network administrator may have made the installation already. If you are the network administrator, use the Attach to a NetWare File Server screen to gain supervisor-level access to the file server once you install the Requester at a workstation and reboot that workstation.

The NetWare OS/2 Requester works with many but not all brands of network adapters. Some adapter manufacturers haven't yet programmed OS/2 device drivers for their adapter hardware. Consult the documentation that comes with your NetWare Requester, or check with your NetWare vendor to make sure that the NetWare OS/2 Requester supports the network adapter you plan to use. Another source of network-adapter device drivers for OS/2 is CompuServe, where additional drivers are added and updated regularly. Novell, IBM, and several network-adapter manufacturers (such as Thomas Conrad) have support forums on CompuServe. Appendix H, "Identifying Sources of OS/2 Information," mentions other electronic sources for driver software.

Installing the OS/2 Requester and the OS/2 utility files is a two-step process. A LAN administrator first installs the OS/2 versions of the OS/2 utilities; you then install the client software on each OS/2 workstation's boot disk. These client programs include the files that enable the workstation to connect to the server. The installation process can automatically update the CONFIG.SYS and NET.CFG files for you, or you can modify CONFIG.SYS yourself, by using a text editor, after completing the installation process.

To use the commands that activate the NetWare Requester, you must install the NetWare OS/2 Requester on each OS/2 workstation and update the CONFIG.SYS file for each workstation. Unless you are an experienced OS/2 and NetWare user, let the installation process automatically modify CONFIG.SYS to ensure that the Requester operates properly. The NetWare OS/2 Requester installation program does an excellent job of updating the rather complicated OS/2 CONFIG.SYS file.

Obtaining the Requester. There are three ways you can get the NetWare OS/2 Requester:

- Purchase NetWare 4.0 on CD-ROM, which ships with the NetWare OS/2 Requester Version 2.01.

- Purchase the NetWare OS/2 Requester kit and manuals from Novell separately by ordering one of the following part numbers:

    66264400-224 (for 3.5-inch disks)

    662644002217 (for 5.25-inch disks)

- Purchase NetWare 3.12 or NetWare 4 on CD-ROM. Download the NetWare OS/2 Requester kit from CompuServe. The files are located in the Client Kits section under NOVFILES (type **GO NOVFILES** at the CompuServe prompt and press Enter if you're using the CompuServe menus). You can also download the files from another electronic source (see Appendix H).

If you purchase the Client Kit directly from Novell, the disks are already created for you. However, if you obtain it in either of the other two ways—by downloading from CompuServe or by purchasing the NetWare 4.0 CD-ROM—you must create the installation disks manually.

There are three files in the Client Kit from CompuServe or other electronic sources:

WSOS21.EXE

WSOS22.EXE

WSOS2D.EXE

After you download these files, store them on your hard drive (if you have enough disk space). Then format three blank 3.5-inch floppy disks and label them as follows:

WSOS2_1

WSOS2_2

WSDRV_1

Next extract each file to its corresponding floppy disk. To do this, place in drive A the first formatted floppy, labeled WSOS2_1, and enter the command **WSOS21 -d A:** while in the directory in which the files are located. Repeat for the remaining files and disks. Here are the correlations for these files:

Floppy	Label	File	Command
1	WSOS2_1	WSOS21.EXE	WSOS21 -d A:
2	WSOS2_2	WSOS22.EXE	WSOS22 -d A:
3	WSDRV_1	WSOS2D.EXE	WSOS2D -d A:

This process creates the three installation disks you must use when installing the NetWare OS/2 Requester on your workstations.

The NetWare 4.0 and 3.12 CD-ROM also contains the NetWare OS/2 Requester files. To use these files to install the NetWare OS/2 Requester on an OS/2 workstation, you can use the CD-ROM itself or you can create the same three installation disks. If your OS/2 workstation has a CD-ROM drive, you don't need to create installation disks; you can install directly from the CD-ROM. If you must create the installation disks, you use a different procedure than the one used for working with files downloaded from CompuServe.

You must have three blank, formatted disks prepared ahead of time. The MAKEDISK.CMD command file labels the disks for you. To begin the process, open an OS/2 full-screen or windowed command-line session and change to the drive letter representing your CD-ROM drive. Change to the directory that contains the MAKEDISK.CMD command by entering the OS/2 command **CD \CLIENT\OS2**; then run the MAKEDISK.CMD file and follow the instructions on the screen.

When this batch file program is finished running, you have the same three installation disks you created from the downloaded files or that you get when you order the kit directly from Novell.

> **Note**
>
> These three disks have various names, including NetWare OS/2 Requester, Workstation Kit for OS/2, and NetWare Client Kit for OS/2. The terms *NetWare for OS/2* and *NetWare 4.01 for OS/2* are not the same as the Client Kit or Requester. *NetWare 4.01 for OS/2* refers to the portable version of NetWare 4.0x, which runs as an OS/2 server application rather than as the client portion. You may also find that Novell changes the internal disk labels (WSOS2_1, and so on) to other names from time to time. Check with your Novell reseller to make sure that you get the latest version of the Requester.

Now that you have the NetWare OS/2 Requester disks, you are ready to begin the installation process.

Performing the Installation. You can install the OS/2 Requester from the floppy disks you created in the preceding section or, if you have the NetWare CD-ROM, from the NetWare 4.0 CD-ROM disc.

To begin the installation process for the first time, boot the OS/2 workstation on which you want to install the NetWare OS/2 Requester. If you use NetWare 4 and are fortunate enough to have a CD-ROM attached to your workstation, you can install the Requester directly from the NetWare 4.0 CD-ROM, bypassing the requirement to create installation disks as described in the preceding section. Installing directly from the CD-ROM is faster because you don't have to insert and remove floppy disks. The installation program is located in the same directory as the MAKEDISK command file. If drive E is your CD-ROM drive, for example, the path name is E:\CLIENT\OS2

To install from CD-ROM, open an OS/2 command prompt, change to the E:\CLIENT\OS2 directory, and enter **INSTALL**. (With OS/2 2.1, you can move to the OS/2 command prompt by clicking the OS/2 System icon on the desktop. In the group window that appears, click the Command Prompts folder to open the Command Prompts group window. In the Command Prompts group window, click the OS/2 Window icon. This launches a windowed OS/2 command-prompt session.)

Another way you can launch the installation program is to use the Workplace Shell's object-oriented file system. To do this, open the OS/2 System folder and choose the Drives object. The Drives object consists of icons that represent each of the drive devices recognized by OS/2. When you choose the object that represents your CD-ROM device, a new window opens that displays a tree view of the contents of the NetWare 4.0 CD-ROM. Select the CLIENT subdirectory and then the OS2 subdirectory beneath it. Double-click the INSTALL.EXE file object to launch the installation program. This begins the installation process from the CD-ROM.

To begin the installation process from floppy disk (if you don't have a CD-ROM drive supported by OS/2), place the first installation floppy disk in drive A and open an OS/2 command prompt. Change to drive A and enter **INSTALL**. The installation program displays an opening message and a menu. Refer back to figure 25.1 to see the opening screen for the installation program.

Start the installation process by choosing Installation from the menu. From the pull-down menu that appears, choose Requester on Workstation. The dialog box shown in figure 25.2 appears and prompts you to enter the target directory for the NetWare Requester files.

By default, the Requester files are installed in a directory called NETWARE on drive C. To use a different directory, enter the directory name of your choice. Click OK when you are finished. Another dialog box appears and prompts you to choose from the four options shown in figure 26.3.

For an initial installation, choose the first option and click OK. This option copies all the Requester files and automatically edits the CONFIG.SYS file for you.

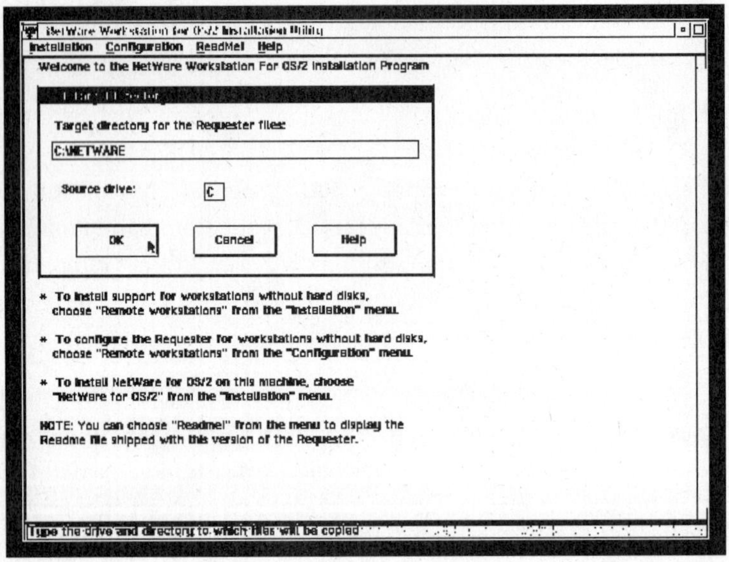

Fig. 25.2
Specifying the target directory on the OS/2 workstation.

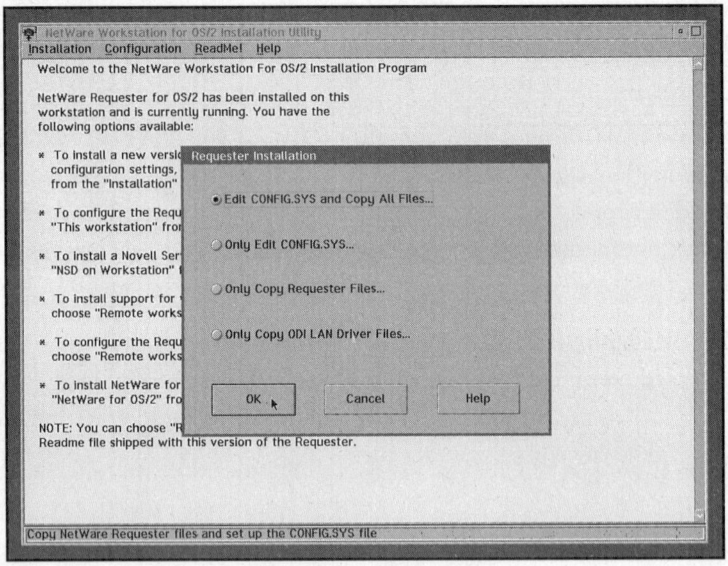

Fig. 25.3
Installation options for the OS/2 Requester.

The next dialog box, shown in figure 25.4, prompts you for the name of the device driver for your network adapter card. Specify the driver according to which network adapter type is installed in the OS/2 workstation. For example, if you are using an NE2000, click the down arrow next to the text-entry box and then highlight the appropriate network adapter type in the list that appears.

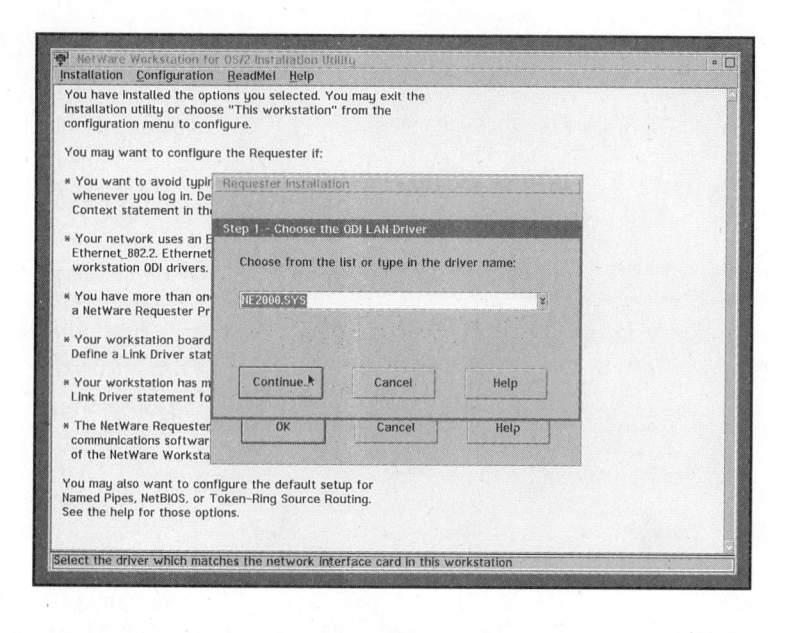

Fig. 25.4
Selecting your network adapter device driver.

Another dialog box appears to guide you through the choices for OS/2's DOS and Windows support. These choices affect the way a DOS or Windows session interacts with NetWare assignments and enables you to manually load a virtual NetWare shell for these sessions. Figure 25.5 shows the recommended selections for most cases. IPX support for DOS and Windows sessions is checked, as is the option for global NETX shell support.

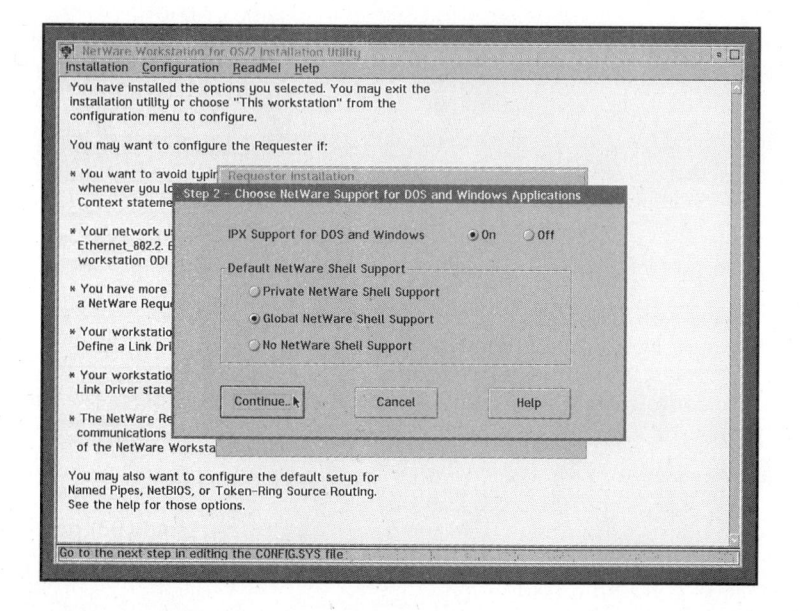

Fig. 25.5
Choosing private, global, or no NetWare shell support.

Private and Global Sessions

You can configure OS/2's DOS and Windows sessions to have global, private, or no NETX shell support. You set up the default configuration during installation of the OS/2 Requester. Later, after installation, you can change the configuration on a session-by-session basis.

The NetWare Requester for OS/2 distinguishes between two types of networked DOS and Windows sessions: *global* and *private*. By default, every DOS and OS/2 program runs in a global session. Private sessions are optional. A global session uses the login name and drive mappings you establish when you first log in to the network. A private session, on the other hand, can use a separate login name and set of drive mappings. The next few paragraphs explain the distinction more fully.

After you log in to the LAN, map your drives, and set up your access to shared printers, you can use network resources from any OS/2 session you start. Every DOS or Windows global session you start can also access the shared drives and printers. You have the maximum amount of memory available in your global DOS sessions because you don't have to load network TSR (terminate and stay resident) programs (such as IPX.COM or NETX.COM).

However, you may find, rarely, that some network utility programs do not work properly in a global session. An example of such a program is the freeware Pegasus E-Mail software product. If you use Pegasus Mail from an OS/2-based workstation, you must configure a private DOS session to run Pegasus Mail.

Novell supplies a version of the NETX.COM program you run in each private DOS session (don't run NETX in global sessions). After you run NETX, you must log in to the network from that session, remap the drives, and reestablish your access to shared printers. You then can run NetWare utilities such as USERLIST from that session, as well as programs that use IPX to do PC-to-PC communications. The disadvantages of a private session are the loss of some memory to the TSR NETX.COM program and the potential for confusion because you can have separate drive mappings in that private session.

You must next choose the options for installing protocol support for the OS/2 sessions. The protocol options screen, shown in figure 25.6, offers three options: SPX, NetBIOS, and named pipes.

Click the appropriate options. You should always choose SPX support because SPX enables some NetWare and OS/2 utilities to work and because SPX is one of NetWare's major protocols. NetBIOS emulation is required if the workstation must communicate with devices that use the NetBIOS protocol. Named-pipe support is used for some client/server applications, whether they are database or communications oriented; refer to the documentation provided with the application to determine whether this function is required.

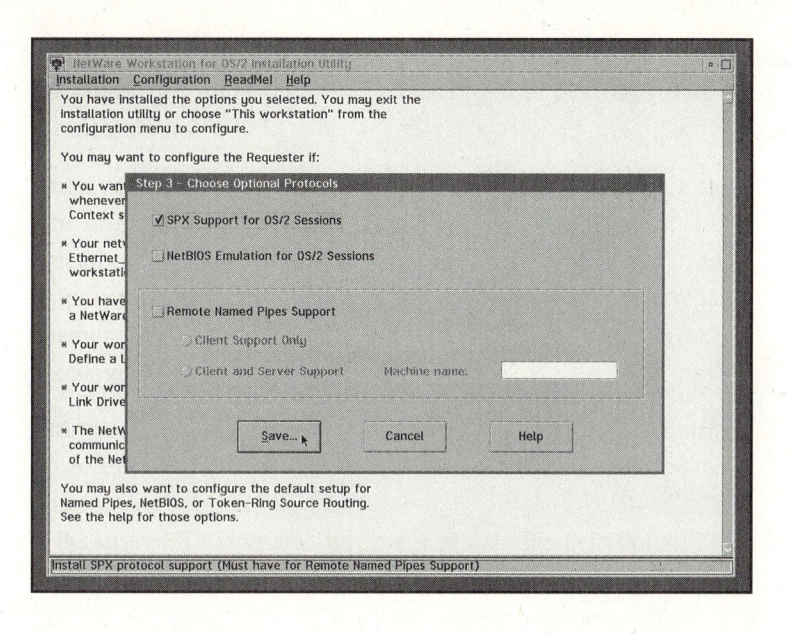

Fig. 25.6
Protocol options for the OS/2 Requester.

Click the box labeled Remote Named Pipes Support if you must access a server that uses named pipes to communicate (the Microsoft SQL server is the most common example of this type of server) or if the PC with which you are working is to be a named-pipes server. If you plan to use the PC as a workstation that accesses named-pipes servers, click the Client Support Only option. If the PC is to be a named-pipes server, click the Client and Server Support option; in the Machine Name text box, enter the name by which you want the PC to be known to other named-pipes devices. Figure 26.6 shows the recommended, most common protocol settings. You check the named-pipes or NetBIOS box only if you have applications that require these protocols. You don't need the named-pipes or NetBIOS protocol to simply access a NetWare file server.

From this point, continue through the remainder of the installation process until completion, accepting the defaults. This finishes the installation of the client portion of the NetWare OS/2 Requester. Don't forget to read the README file for the OS/2 Requester by selecting ReadMe! from the Installation menu.

Before you reboot the computer, consider some of the changes the installation process made to the computer. The next section explains these changes. You may also need to customize your NET.CFG file, as discussed in a later section.

Considering the Changes to the Computer. Based on your selection of options, the installation process adds the NETWARE directory name to the LIBPATH, PATH, and DPATH statements in the CONFIG.SYS file. The installation process also inserts statements that load the NetWare device drivers and installable file system (IFS) when you boot the computer. Following is an example of the changes to the CONFIG.SYS file:

```
LIBPATH=C:\NETWARE;
SET PATH=C:\NETWARE;L:\OS2;P:\OS2;
SET DPATH=C:\NETWARE;L:\OS2;P:\OS2;
REM --- NetWare Requester statements BEGIN ---
SET NWLANGUAGE=ENGLISH
DEVICE=C:\NETWARE\LSL.SYS
RUN=C:\NETWARE\DDAEMON.EXE
DEVICE=C:\NETWARE\NE2000.SYS
DEVICE=C:\NETWARE\IPX.SYS
DEVICE=C:\NETWARE\SPX.SYS
RUN=C:\NETWARE\SPDAEMON.EXE
REM DEVICE=C:\NETWARE\NMPIPE.SYS
REM DEVICE=C:\NETWARE\NPSERVER.SYS
REM RUN=C:\NETWARE\NPDAEMON.EXE
DEVICE=C:\NETWARE\NWREQ.SYS
IFS=C:\NETWARE\NWIFS.IFS
RUN=C:\NETWARE\NWDAEMON.EXE
DEVICE=C:\NETWARE\NETBIOS.SYS
RUN=C:\NETWARE\NBDAEMON.EXE
DEVICE=C:\NETWARE\VIPX.SYS
DEVICE=C:\NETWARE\VSHELL.SYS GLOBAL
REM --- NetWare Requester statements END ---
```

As the PATH statement suggests, the NetWare client files have been placed in the C:\NETWARE directory on the client workstation. The remainder of the OS/2 files, called *utility files*, are installed on the server during the installation of NetWare. These files are placed in the following directories:

```
SYS:LOGIN\OS2
SYS:PUBLIC\OS2
```

Figure 25.7 uses an OS/2 drives object, in both Icon View and Tree View, to show the OS2 subdirectory beneath the familiar PUBLIC directory on a NetWare file server.

Once you reboot and log in to the network, the new PATH statement lets you access the utilities and commands in the \PUBLIC\OS2 directory.

DOS utility files are in the LOGIN and PUBLIC directories; their OS/2 counterparts are stored in the LOGIN\OS2 and PUBLIC\OS2 directories. Under OS/2, be aware that the MAP command is always issued as a NetWare MAP ROOT command. This means that when a MAP command is issued under

OS/2, the drive assignments *appear* to be mapped to the root directory of the volume even though the drive is mapped to a specific directory of the volume. Under DOS, a drive letter is assigned to a given subdirectory, but you can always change to a lower level in the directory structure.

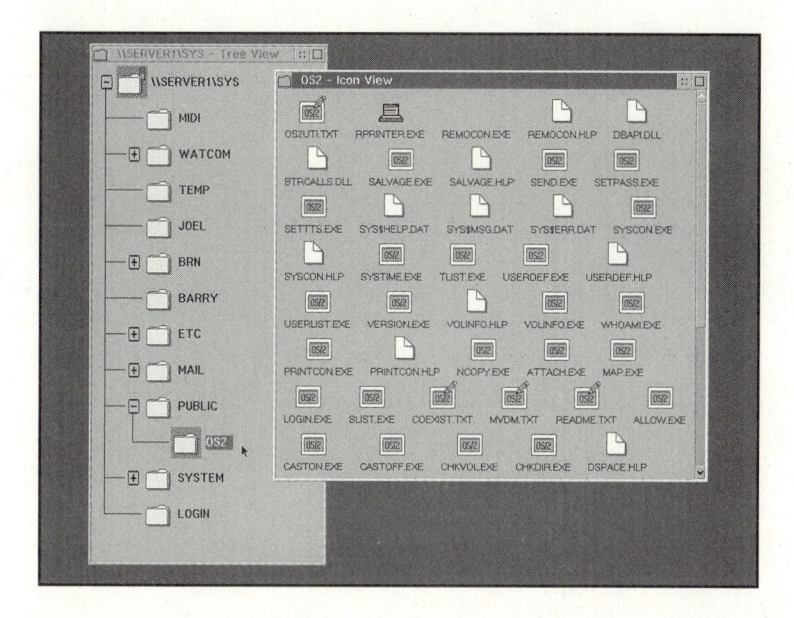

Fig. 25.7
An Icon View and Tree View of the \PUBLIC\OS2 directory.

Setting Up the NET.CFG File. During installation, the Requester installation program prompts you to set up your NET.CFG file. This file contains the parameters the workstation uses to control access to the LAN. The installation process, in true Presentation Manager form, presents a list of the parameters you can set and offers values for those parameters. You (or your network administrator) choose the parameters appropriate for your workstation. Assuming that the PC already has a network adapter in one of its slots, you merely reboot the computer after installing and configuring the Requester and you are ready to log in to the LAN.

Figure 25.8 shows the Requester installation program's screen for creating or updating a NET.CFG file on your workstation. As you highlight and click the items in the NET.CFG Options window, explanations of those items appear in the bottom window. You can select text from the explanations window (by using the mouse or the keyboard) and paste the result into the Current NET.CFG File Contents window. When you finish making your selections, choose the Save pushbutton to write your selected entries to the NET.CFG file. The Requester installation program provides you with useful on-line help as you work your way through the NET.CFG options.

Fig. 25.8
Constructing the NET.CFG file.

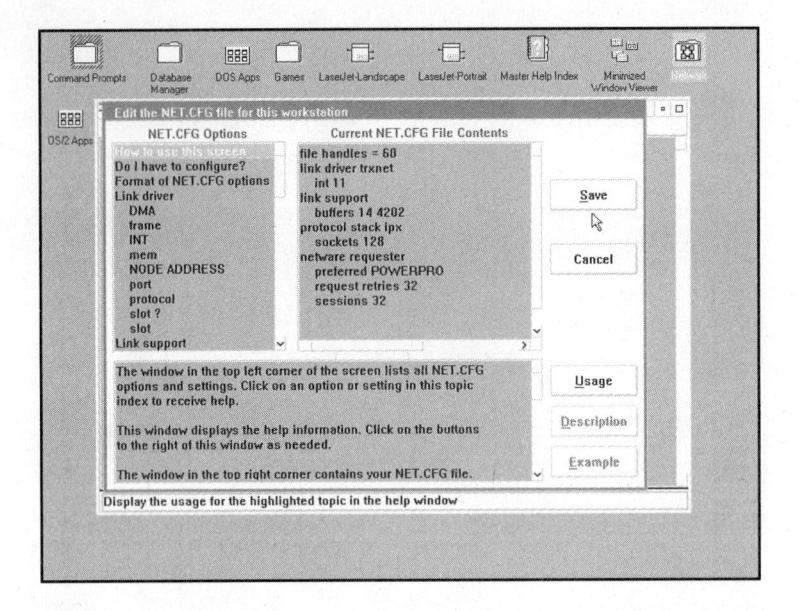

Finishing the Installation. After you have installed and configured the NetWare Requester, shut down and reboot the OS/2 workstation so that the CONFIG.SYS changes you made take effect. You can now log in to the network and begin executing NetWare utilities and other programs on the file servers your OS/2 workstation can now access. When you log in, remember to use an OS/2 session rather than a DOS session. Be sure to use the OS/2 version of the LOGIN program, located both in the LOGIN\OS2 directory and, on your workstation, in the newly-created NETWARE directory.

For Related Information
- "Using CONFIG.SYS and AUTOEXEC.BAT," p. 162.
- "Understanding DOS Sessions," p. 394

Figure 25.9 shows three new folders on your desktop. The NetWare Requester installation program put the Network and NetWare folders on your desktop. The Network folder contains the NetWare Tools, Remote Printer, and Install program objects. The NetWare folder contains an icon that represents a file server. And the Drives object Tree View in figure 25.9 shows a portion of NetWare's directory structure on the file server. You use the Drives object in the NetWare folder in the same way you use the OS/2 Drives object for your local floppy and hard disks, as explained in Chapter 11, "Using the Drives Object."

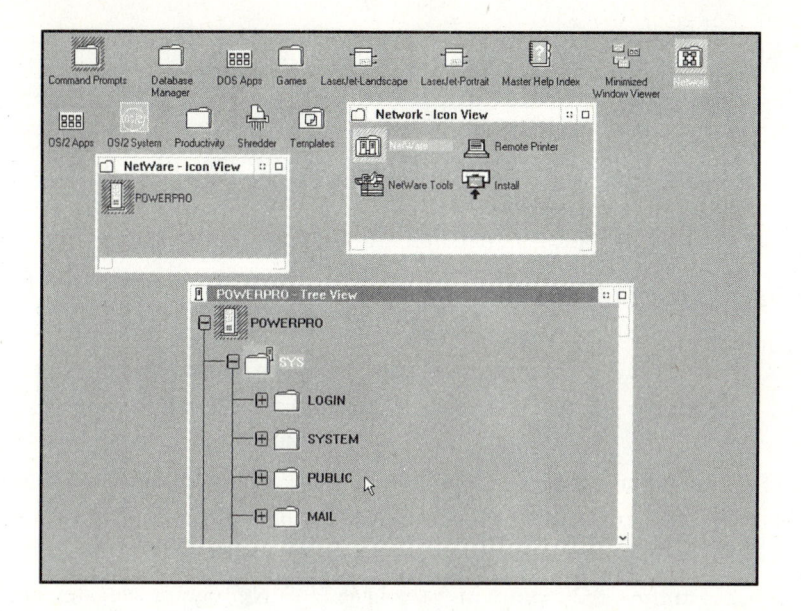

Fig. 25.9
The new NetWare Requester for OS/2 folders after installation of the Requester.

Logging In and Mapping Drives

You can perform the login sequence in a variety of ways with the NetWare Requester for OS/2. You can point and click your way onto the LAN through the NetWare Tools, you can log in manually at a command-line prompt, you can create a STARTUP.CMD file in the root directory of your hard drive to automate the login process, or you can create a program object (consisting of a CMD file that executes the LOGIN program) and place that program object in your Startup folder. The best way to accomplish the latter alternative is to use a text editor to create the CMD file, build your program object from the model in the Templates folder, and then do a Create Shadow operation to move the program object into the Startup folder. Chapter 10, "Managing the Workplace Shell," discusses how to create shadows of objects.

Issuing Commands To Log In

The OS/2 batch-file program CMD file you place in the Startup folder or that you name STARTUP.CMD likely contains entries similar to those in the following example:

```
L:
CD OS2
LOGIN BARRY
MAP G:=POWERPRO\SYS:
MAP L:=POWERPRO\SYS:PUBLIC\OS2
CAPTURE Q=LASERJET
```

Note that this login sequence is probably quite similar to the one you used under DOS, before you installed OS/2 (if you had a DOS workstation in the past). After you perform the login sequence (which you may have automated to happen at boot time by using the STARTUP.CMD batch file that runs when you start OS/2), you can access the shared network disk drives and printers from any application or command-line session you start.

Setting Up OS/2 Login Scripts

The LAN administrator may not want to store and maintain individual STARTUP.CMD files on each workstation. To make the mapping of drives consistent among several OS/2-based workstations, NetWare provides a login script facility. The LAN administrator merely updates the OS/2 system login script on the file server at the same time he or she updates the DOS system login script. The LOGIN.EXE program executes the entries in the login script when a person logs on to the network. The OS/2 LOGIN program executes statements in the OS/2 login script; the DOS LOGIN program executes statements in the DOS login script. NetWare supports both system and personal login scripts. To make maintenance of the scripts easier, you probably want to put commands into the system login script rather than your personal login script.

To update login scripts and map the appropriate drive assignments, the LAN administrator uses the OS/2 version of the SYSCON (for NetWare 2.x and NetWare 3.x) or the NETADMIN (for NetWare 4.x) utility. These utilities store OS/2 login scripts separately from DOS login scripts. To execute your new login script, you first must log out of the network and then log in again.

Your login script is a program that sets up your workstation's environment each time you log in. The script performs tasks such as mapping network drives, executing programs and starting applications, and attaching you to different file servers. Typically, the NetWare commands you include in a login script are ATTACH, MAP, and SET. You also can use IF...THEN statements in your script. The ATTACH command enables you to connect logically to other file servers while remaining logged in to your current file server. The SET script command sets environment variables. You might use SET as in the following example:

```
SET user="jwilson"
```

In a login script, IF...THEN statements are used to execute certain commands if a specified condition exists. The WRITE login script command writes messages to your screen as the login script executes. Following is an example that uses both WRITE and IF...THEN commands:

```
IF DAY_OF_WEEK = "Monday" THEN WRITE "AARGH..."
```

The NetWare login script for an OS/2 workstation can include statements similar to the following:

```
MAP L:=SYS:LOGIN
MAP P:=SYS:PUBLIC
```

The first statement assigns drive L to the login directory in the server's SYS volume. Likewise, the P assignment refers to the PUBLIC directory on the SYS volume of the server. To access the OS/2 versions of the NetWare utilities, the OS/2 PATH and DPATH statements point to a subdirectory (OS2) of these directories. For DOS sessions, the AUTOEXEC.BAT file refers to files in the *root* of these logical drive mappings and therefore executes the DOS version of the NetWare utility files.

For OS/2 sessions, the CONFIG.SYS file's PATH statement can specify a subdirectory (OS2) inside drives L and P to point to the OS/2 versions of the NetWare utilities:

```
SET PATH=C:\NETWARE;L:\OS2;P:\OS2;
SET DPATH=C:\NETWARE;L:\OS2;P:\OS2;
```

For DOS sessions, the AUTOEXEC.BAT file's PATH statement can specify drives L and P, without mentioning a subdirectory, to point to the DOS versions of the NetWare utilities:

```
SET PATH=L:.;P:.;
```

These statements ensure that each operating session, whether DOS or OS/2, selects the proper version of the NetWare utility commands.

> **Note**
>
> Under OS/2, you cannot use the NetWare facility for search drives; that is, you cannot issue MAP Sx: statements to add directories to the path dynamically. For OS/2 sessions, the installation process edits the CONFIG.SYS file to statically express the C:\NETWARE, SYS:LOGIN\OS2, and SYS:PUBLIC\OS2 directories in your PATH and DPATH statements. However, for DOS session support, you should use a text editor to add SYS:LOGIN and SYS:PUBLIC to the PATH statement—perhaps with the L: and P: drive-mapping convention just mentioned—in your workstation's AUTOEXEC.BAT file. Doing this ensures that DOS sessions launched under OS/2 can find and execute the DOS versions of the NetWare utilities.

Mapping Drives with NetWare Tools

Figure 25.10 shows the NetWare Tools screen. NetWare Tools is a Presentation Manager application that lists the network disk drives you currently have mapped. NetWare Tools also provides menu options for attaching to file servers, logging in to file servers, mapping drives, and sharing a LAN printer.

Fig. 25.10
The NetWare Tools screen.

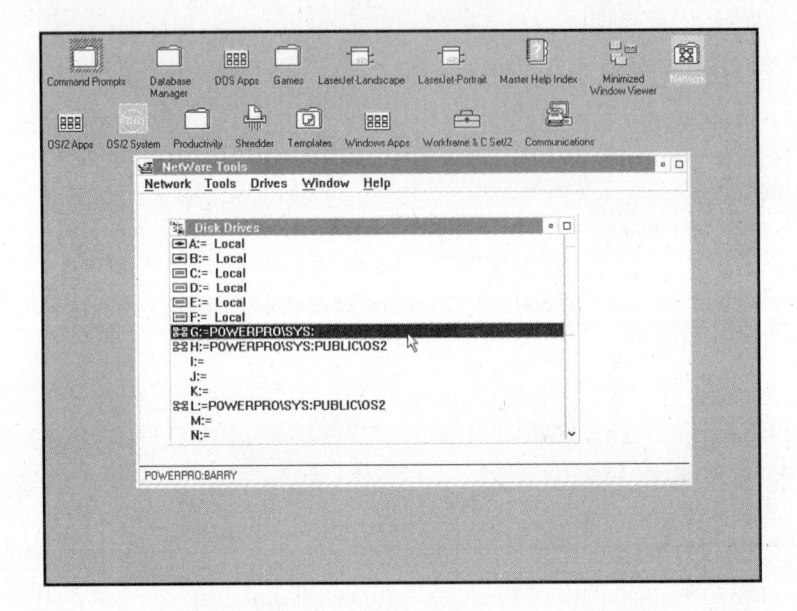

If you prefer using a PM interface (rather than a command-line interface) to map file-server volumes to drive letters, you can use the screen shown in figure 25.11. You double-click one of the disk drives in the list presented by NetWare Tools and then indicate the server, volume, and directory you want to map as that disk drive. You gain access to a shared LAN printer in a similar manner. Figure 25.12 shows the Add Remote Printer screen of NetWare Tools. You select the printer server and printer name from the lists and then click the Add pushbutton to share access to that printer.

In addition to the NetWare Tools PM utility, the NetWare Requester for OS/2 offers native OS/2 versions of the NetWare menu utilities and command-line utilities that DOS users have grown familiar with. You cover the NetWare utilities for OS/2 in more detail in the following sections of this chapter.

Logging In and Mapping Drives

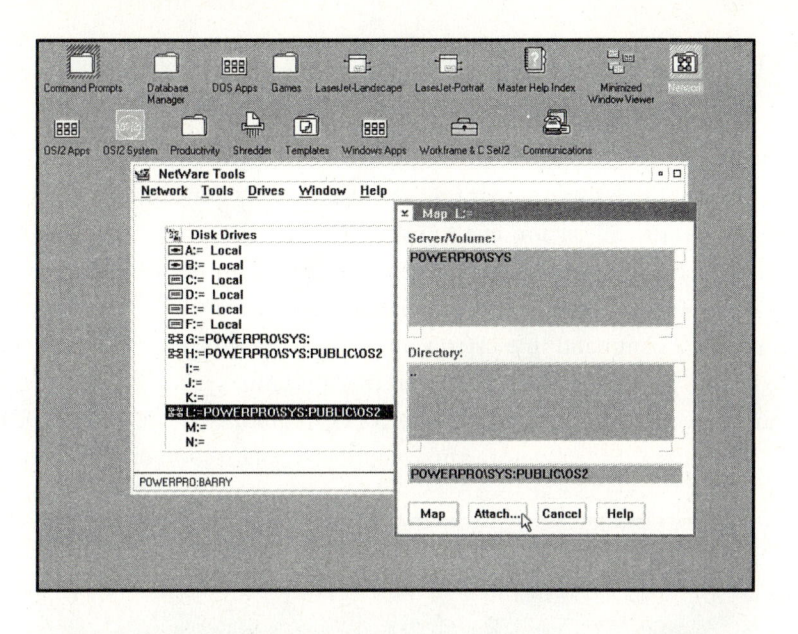

Fig. 25.11
Mapping drives with NetWare Tools.

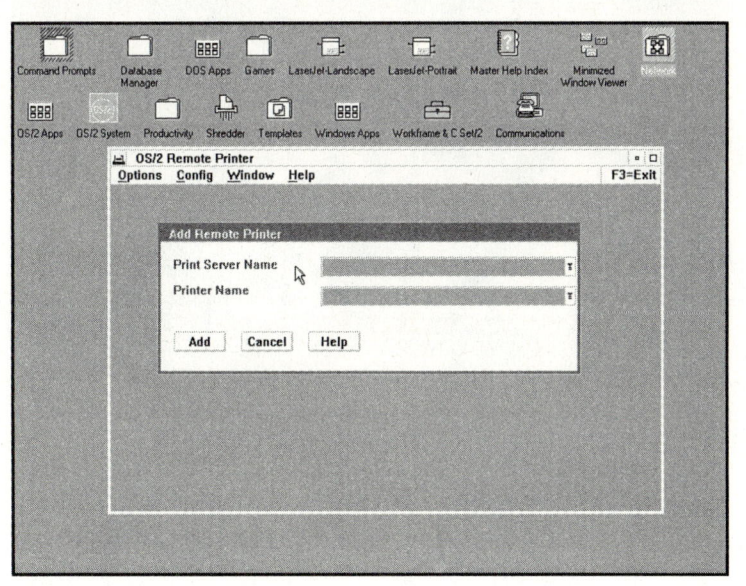

Fig. 25.12
Sharing a printer with NetWare Tools.

Using NetWare Utilities

You can use the OS/2 versions of the NetWare utilities in the \PUBLIC\OS2 directory from an OS/2 full-screen or windowed session. (A few of the utilities, however, expect to run in a full-screen session. OS/2 automatically changes a windowed session to a full-screen session when you run such a utility.) In an OS/2 session, you have full access to the network's resources and don't need to distinguish between global and private sessions. If you prefer using a command-line interface, you can run NetWare utilities such as USERLIST or WHOAMI in OS/2 sessions. Alternatively, you can use the PM interface provided by the NetWare Tools program. Figure 25.13 shows the NetWare utility SYSCON running in a windowed OS/2 session on the desktop.

Fig. 25.13
The NetWare utility SYSCON in a windowed OS/2 session.

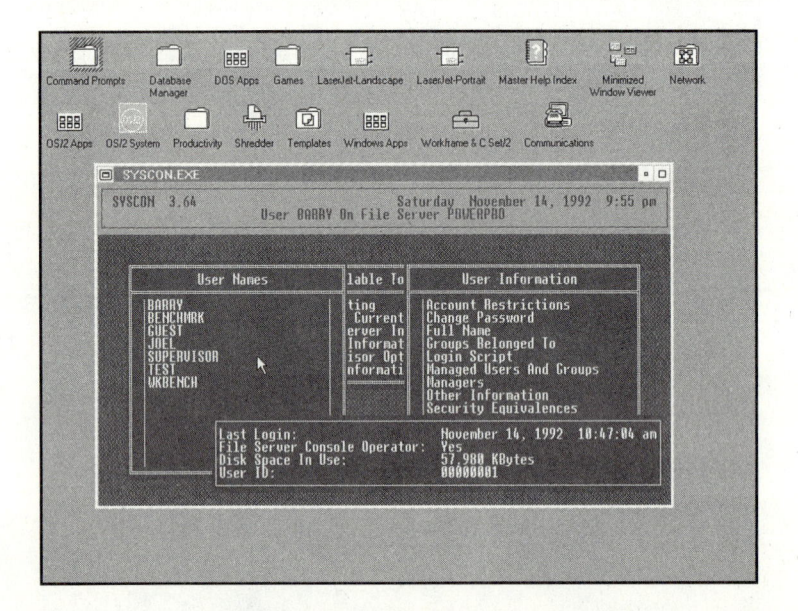

Figure 25.14 shows the User List, NetWare Tools' equivalent of the USERLIST display. NetWare Tools is an OS/2 Presentation Manager application that lists the network disk drives you currently have mapped. NetWare Tools also provides menu options for attaching to file servers, logging in to file servers, mapping drives, and sharing a LAN printer. If you prefer using a graphical user interface (GUI) rather than a command-line interface to map drives, you can use NetWare Tools to indicate your network commands and choices by simply pointing and clicking. For example, double-click one of the disk drives in the list presented by NetWare Tools, then indicate the server, volume, and directory you want to map as that disk drive. You gain access to a shared LAN printer in a similar manner.

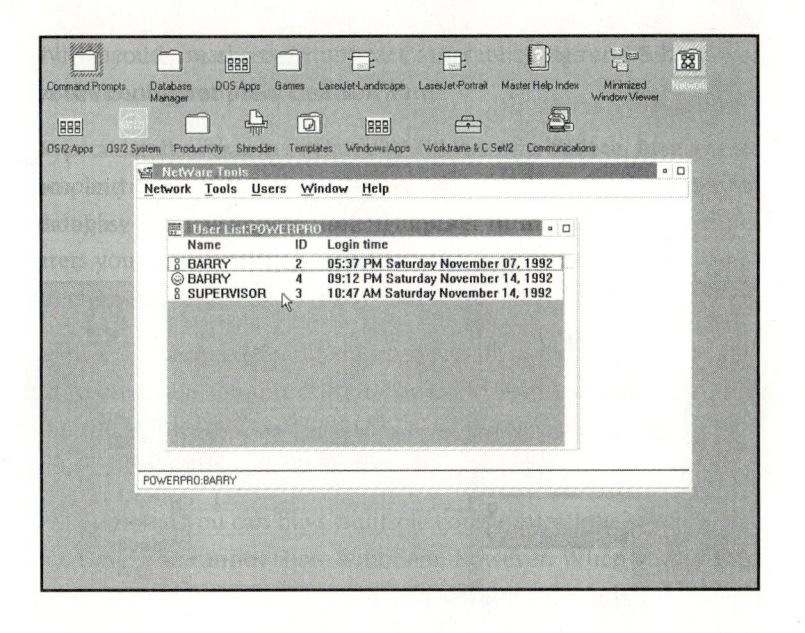

Fig. 25.14
Viewing logged-on users through NetWare Tools.

You use NetWare utilities to perform network tasks in OS/2 and DOS sessions. Some of the utilities are menu utilities; others are command-line utilities. Menu utilities enable you to perform network tasks by choosing options from menus. Command-line utilities enable you to perform tasks by typing commands at the OS/2 or DOS command line.

Using OS/2 Menu-Based NetWare Utilities

When you run a NetWare menu-based utility, such as FILER, you see the utility's main menu along with a screen header that shows the following information:

- The utility's full name
- The current date and time
- The directory path of the current directory (for most utilities)
- Your user name on your file server (for most utilities)
- Your connection number (for most utilities)

You can press Esc or the Exit key (usually Alt+F10) to leave a NetWare menu utility. Pressing Esc saves your changes; the Exit key abandons any changes you have made.

The Help (F1) key displays help screens. If you press F1, a help screen that applies to the task you are working on appears. The help screen describes all the options on the screen. To get help on a specific option, highlight the option and press Enter. If you press F1 twice, the utility lists your computer's function-key assignments.

Two typical menu-based utilities are SALVAGE and FILER, described in the next sections. You learn about PCONSOLE, a popular NetWare utility, in the section of this chapter on managing your printouts.

Salvaging Deleted Files. You can undelete files on a NetWare LAN with the SALVAGE utility. From the utility's menu, select View/Recover Deleted Files and specify whether you want to undelete a single file, multiple files you select from a list, or multiple files based on wild cards you supply. You can give the resurrected file a new name during the salvage operation, if you want.

Managing Your Network Files. You can use the OS/2 Drives object, an OS/2 or DOS command-line prompt, or a file-management utility to manage your network files. The NetWare menu-based utility FILER is in the last category. FILER is a text-mode utility that runs in windowed or full-screen OS/2 sessions. You use the menu options to choose a file server and navigate that server's directory structure. You can copy, delete, and rename files; you can also copy entire directories and directory structures with FILER.

Using OS/2 Command-Line NetWare Utilities

NetWare commands enable you to do single-purpose network tasks that do not need a menu. NetWare offers a multitude of such utilities. The installation process puts the OS/2 versions of these program files in a standard NetWare directory named PUBLIC\OS2. An explanation of two simple NetWare commands, NPRINT and TLIST, shows the similarity between NetWare and OS/2 commands.

The NPRINT command sends a text file to a LAN printer and is the NetWare equivalent of the DOS PRINT command. TLIST shows you the list of Trustees for a directory. Examples of the command formats for the NPRINT and the TLIST utilities follow:

```
NPRINT path [option...]
TLIST [path [USERS ¦ GROUPS]]
```

The *path* parameter for NPRINT specifies the path and filename of the file you want to print. You use the *option* parameter to specify how you want the file treated as it prints. For TLIST, the *path* parameter specifies the directory for which you want trustee information. You can use USERS or GROUPS to tell TLIST whether you are looking for single-user information or group information.

The following sections describe some of the many NetWare command-line utilities.

Sending One-Line Messages. You can communicate with other users on the network by sending messages from your workstation command line. Suppose that you want to send the following message to users MARK and HOLLY:

    Meeting at 1:30 today.

Also suppose that MARK and HOLLY are logged in to your default server. Use the SEND command, as shown in the following example, to notify Mark and Holly of the meeting:

    SEND "Meeting at 1:30 today." MARK, HOLLY

NetWare displays a confirmation message, telling you that it sent the message successfully to the two people.

If HOLLY is logged in to another file server called SERVER2, attach that file server and type, as in this example:

    SEND "Meeting at 1:30 today." SERVER2/HOLLY

As another example of NetWare's simple, one-line messaging facility, suppose that you are your company's accountant (or president) and want to tell all employees that the paychecks are ready. Because the NetWare group EVERYONE includes all users, you could type this command:

SEND "Paychecks are ready." EVERYONE

If you do not want to receive messages sent to you from any network stations, you can use the CASTOFF command. You see the following NetWare message:

    Broadcasts from other stations will now be rejected.

To allow your workstation to again receive messages from other network users, use the CASTON command.

Using the NetWare Login Command. To log in to your default server, type this command:

LOGIN servername/username

LOGIN is a NetWare command. Replace *servername* with the name of the file server you want to log in to. For *username*, use your login name. The LOGIN command prompts you for your password. To log out of the default server, type **LOGOUT**.

If you have multiple NetWare servers on the same LAN, you use the ATTACH command to logically connect your workstation to each server after the first. You then log in to the attached servers. You attach to another file server when you want to do any of the following tasks:

- Send messages to users on that file server
- Map a drive to that file server
- Copy a file or directory to (or from) that file server

You change your NetWare password with the SETPASS command. SETPASS asks you to type your old password and your new password.

Knowing Who Is Using a Workstation. To find out who is logged in to a workstation, use the WHOAMI command. You see a response displayed, similar to the following:

```
WHOAMI
You are user BARRY attached to server SERVER1, connection 12
Server SERVER1 is running NetWare v3.11.
Login time: Wednesday January 15, 1993 8:05 am
```

Find out the names of the file servers on your network with the SLIST command. To learn the user IDs of the other people who are logged in to the LAN, use the USERLIST command. The USERLIST display looks something like the following:

User Information for Server SYSTEMPRO

Connection	User Name	Login Time
1	THOMAS	1-06-1993 8:17 am
2	SUSAN	1-06-1993 8:19 am
4	*BARRY	1-07-1993 8:42 am

An asterisk (*) appears next to your user name.

Accessing Network Drives with the MAP Command. You can map an entire NetWare file server hard disk as a drive letter, and you also can map a subset of the hard disk (a directory and its subdirectories).

Mapped drives point to particular locations in the directory structure. NetWare distinguishes between *local drives* and *network drives*. Local drives are physically attached to a workstation. Network drives are the disk drives in the file server (often referred to as *volumes*). For a DOS workstation, another type of drive, called a *search drive*, enables you to execute programs (applications and utilities) in a directory other than the current directory. Search drives act as an extension of the DOS PATH statement. The NetWare Requester for OS/2 does not support search drives except in private DOS sessions.

To view the present status of your drive mappings, type the MAP command with no parameters. You see information similar to the following:

    DRIVE A: maps to a local drive

    DRIVE B: maps to a local drive

    DRIVE F:= SERVER1/SYS: /HOME/FRANK

    DRIVE G:= SERVER1/SYS2: /

    DRIVE H:= SERVER2/SYS: /APPS

Suppose that you want to map a network drive to a directory in which you have files. To see what network drive letters are available, first enter the MAP command. After choosing a drive letter that is not in use (such as J), run MAP again. This time, give MAP parameters that instruct the command to set up the new drive mapping. Suppose that your user name is FRANK and you want to map drive J to your home directory, which is on file server SERVER1 in volume SYS. Type the following command:

   MAP J:= SERVER1/SYS:HOME\FRANK

Using the NCOPY Command. The OS/2 (or DOS) COPY command is an inefficient way to copy files on the LAN if the same file server is both the source and target of the files. Because the COPY command executes at your workstation and because of the way file redirection works, the source file must flow into your workstation as a series of LAN message packets and then flow back to the server as yet another series of packets when you use COPY. The incoming packets represent the COPY command's read-file operations. The outgoing packets are the write-file operations. Why not tell the file server to do the copy operation internally, inside the server, and avoid the LAN traffic?

The NetWare NCOPY command does exactly this. When NCOPY determines that a file server is both the source and target of a file copy, the command sends a special message packet to the server instructing the server to do the file copy. If the copy operation involves different file servers, or a file server and a workstation, NCOPY does its job exactly like the COPY command.

Suppose that you want to copy a file called REPORT.DOC from your current, default directory on drive F to the MANAGERS directory. Both directories exist on volume SYS on the file server named SERVER1. Type the following:

```
NCOPY REPORT.DOC F:\MANAGERS\REPORT.DOC
```

Note that you can use the NetWare menu utility FILER to copy, delete, and rename files on the network.

Using the NetWare NDIR Command. Like the DOS DIR command, the NetWare NDIR command lists files in a directory. NDIR is NetWare-aware and knows how to display the additional file information that NetWare stores for each file and directory. NDIR also can traverse the file-server directory tree to look for a file. The NDIR utility searches all directories you have rights to on the server for a file you have misplaced. A typical **NDIR *.EXE** request looks like the following:

```
SYSTEMPRO/SYS:BARRY

   Files:          Size        Last Updated       Flags        Owner
   -----           ------      --------           ----         ----

   LANXPERT EXE    91,078      12-06-91  8:39p    [Rw-A--]     BARRY
   SHOW EXE         7,338       6-06-91  8:17p    [Rw-A--]     BARRY

    98,416 bytes in  2 files
   102,400 bytes in 25 blocks
```

Knowing Your Rights

You manage your network files and directories in a variety of ways. You can copy, delete, rename, view, write to, share, and print network objects. As you work with the LAN, NetWare's system of file and directory rights and file attributes makes sure that only authorized network users can access and update LAN files.

Both files and directories can have attributes on a NetWare file server. These attributes override the rights granted to the users on the LAN. Suppose that you have the right to rename files (the Modify right). The file you want to rename, however, is flagged with the Rename Inhibit attribute. The attribute prevents you from renaming the file, even though you have the right to do so.

To see what rights you have in the current directory, use the RIGHTS command. If, for example, you have all rights in the directory, you see the following display:

```
SYSTEMPRO\SYS:BARRY
Your Effective Rights for this directory are [SRWCEMFA]
You have Supervisor Rights to Directory.  (S)
 * May Read from File.  (R)
 * May Write to File.  (W)
   May Create Subdirectories and Files.  (C)
   May Erase Directory.  (E)
   May Modify Directory.  (M)
   May Scan for Files.  (F)
   May Change Access Control.  (A)
 * Has no effect on directory.
Entries in Directory May Inherit [SRWCEMFA] rights.
You have ALL RIGHTS to Directory Entry.
```

Printing with NetWare

Printing on a NetWare workstation is similar to printing on a stand-alone personal computer. When you send a print job to a network printer, however, the job is first routed through the file server and then delivered to the printer by the print server. The file server and print server may very well be the same computer.

Using CAPTURE To Print Screens

After you issue a CAPTURE command to redirect printer output to the shared LAN printer, you can use that printer port just as if a local printer were attached to it. You can even use the PrtSc key to print screens to the LAN printer.

Examining CAPTURE Options. The following chart lists some of the most common CAPTURE options:

Option	Function
L=*n*	Indicates which of your workstation's LPT ports (local parallel printing ports) to capture. Replace *n* with 1, 2, or 3. The default is L=1 (LPT1).

(continues)

Option	Function
nb	Specifies that you don't want a banner (job separator) page to print at the beginning of the printout.
nt	Specifies that you don't want CAPTURE to translate tab characters into space characters.
Q=*queuename*	Indicates the queue that the print job should be sent to. If multiple queues are mapped to a printer, you must include this option. Replace *queuename* with the name of the queue.
s=*name*	Supplies the name of the server whose print queue you want your printouts to go to. For example, you can put the following CAPTURE command in a batch file that you run as part of logging in: capture s=server1 q=laserjet.

> **Note**
>
> DOS-based workstations can use an additional CAPTURE timeout parameter, ti=*n*. When a computer program stops printing, CAPTURE counts the seconds of "print silence." When the number of seconds exceeds the value that replaces *n*, CAPTURE signals the end of the print job. On OS/2 workstations, CAPTURE uses the timeout parameter of the printer object instead of the CAPTURE command ti=*n* parameter.

ENDCAP is a NetWare command that undoes the printer redirection of the CAPTURE command. If you have sent something to the printer, ENDCAP sends your print job to the print queue without waiting for the time-out period to elapse. ENDCAP also ends the capture of your LPT port. You must issue another CAPTURE command to reenable printing to the LAN printer.

Managing Your Print Jobs. A *print queue* is a special directory in which print files are stored while waiting for printer services. To see which jobs are waiting in a queue to be printed, use the PCONSOLE NetWare menu utility. PCONSOLE is one of the NetWare utility programs that runs in a full-screen session. After selecting the Print Queue Information menu option and the name of the print queue, select Current Print Job Entries from the Print Queue Information list. The print job entries are displayed.

You can cancel your print job by deleting it from the print queue—even after the job has started printing. You can delete a print job only if you are the owner of the job or if you are the print-queue operator. Print-job removal is a function of the PCONSOLE utility supplied with NetWare: highlight the print job in a menu displayed by PCONSOLE, press the Del key, and confirm the deletion of the print job.

Once your OS/2 workstation has sent a print job to a network print server with an active CAPTURE command, you can use the menu-based PCONSOLE utility to see where in the LAN's print queues your job is. From the program's first menu, you select a file server, indicate that you want to view print-queue information, or choose to see print-server information. From the print-queue option, you can choose a print queue and view the list of jobs awaiting print for that queue.

If you feel more comfortable using a Presentation Manager-based utility to manage your print jobs, note that the NetWare Tools program, discussed earlier in this chapter, offers a print-queue menu item you can use.

Understanding NetWare Security

Office-wide (or company-wide) information, consisting of data files and programs, resides on the same file-server hard disk. Not all people in the office or company, however, should have access to all the information. Certain files contain confidential data and should be available only to certain users (such as payroll files). In addition, in applications that are not LAN-aware, you probably have data files that multiple people can update one person at a time. If two people access the same file at the same time, they may overwrite each other's work.

To prevent problems like these, NetWare provides an extensive security system to protect the data on the network. NetWare security consists of a combination of the following:

- Login security, which includes creating user names and passwords and imposing workstation, time, and account restrictions on users.

- Trustee rights that control which directories and files a user can access and what the user is allowed to do with those directories and files, such as creating, reading, erasing, or writing to those files.

- Directory and file attributes that determine whether the directory or file can be deleted, copied, viewed, or written to. These attributes also mark a file as shareable or nonshareable.

Each directory has a *maximum rights mask* that represents the highest level of privilege that any of the directory's trustees can be granted. The eight rights expressed by the rights mask are as follows:

- A user can read from open files.
- A user can write to open files.
- A user can open existing files.
- A user can create new files.
- A user can delete existing files.
- A user can act parentally—creating, renaming, or erasing subdirectories—and can set trustee rights and directory rights in the directory and its subdirectories.
- A user can search for files in the directory.
- A user can modify file attributes.

Assigning Types of Users

You can assign four levels of responsibility to people on a NetWare LAN:

- Regular network users
- Operators (file-server console operators, print-queue operators, print-server operators)
- Managers (work-group managers, user-account managers)
- Network supervisors

Regular network users are the people who work on the network. They can run applications and work with files according to the rights assigned to them.

Operators are regular network users who have been assigned additional privileges. A file-server console operator, for example, is a network user who is given specific rights to use FCONSOLE or the Remote Management Facility (RMF).

Managers are users who have been given responsibility for creating or managing other users. Work-group managers can create and manage users. User-account managers can manage, but not create, users. Managers function as supervisors over a particular group, but they do not have supervisor equivalence.

Network supervisors are responsible for the smooth operation of the whole network. Network supervisors maintain the system, reconfiguring and updating the LAN as necessary.

Using NetWare for OS/2

Until recently, when you used NetWare you had to set up a separate PC on the LAN to act as file server. In this configuration, the other PCs take the role of workstations. The file-server PC is dedicated to acting just as a file server. A new Novell product, NetWare for OS/2, enables you to install the NetWare file-server software on a computer running OS/2 2.1. You can choose to set this computer aside as just a file server, but you have the option of using OS/2 sessions on such a computer if you need OS/2 command-line access at the server. NetWare for OS/2 is based on Novell's "Portable NetWare" concept.

To the workstations on the LAN, NetWare for OS/2 is no different than any other NetWare server. The file-server PC, however, can do other tasks besides serve files. You can run a database-manager product (such as Oracle or IBM's Extended Services DB Manager) on the same computer that acts as file server. Such an environment is called *client/server computing*.

The NetWare component running on the OS/2 machine that lets the OS/2 machine act as a NetWare file server runs alongside OS/2. NetWare for OS/2 does not exist as a task for OS/2 to manage; rather, NetWare for OS/2 is a parallel operating system that shares the computer's resources with OS/2. The network software doesn't use OS/2 to access files and directories. NetWare for OS/2 installs onto a separate partition on the PC's hard disk and uses its own disk format to access the NetWare files in that separate partition.

The benefit of this parallel execution of two operating systems in the file server is primarily one of lower hardware costs. You can run OS/2, NetWare for OS/2, and even IBM's LAN Server network operating system in the same computer. The biggest drawback is one of performance. Running multiple server-based software products in the same computer is slower than if you ran the software in separate machines. Performance suffers even further if people use the server computer as a workstation in nondedicated fashion. One person, running CPU-intensive application software on the file server, can cause slowdowns for all the other people on the network who are trying to access the file server.

You install NetWare for OS/2 from two floppy disks and a CD-ROM disk. The CD-ROM disk contains NetWare version 4; the two floppy disks install NetWare 4 to run alongside OS/2. You also need driver software on floppy disk for the network adapter(s) in the computer. You don't want to install NetWare 4 entirely from floppy disk; the distribution floppy disk set from Novell consists of more than 250 floppies and takes more than 18 hours to install.

The installation of NetWare for OS/2 takes place in four steps. First, you prepare the hard drive in the computer by establishing separate partitions for NetWare and OS/2. Next, you install OS/2 (as explained in earlier chapters). If you want to use the OS/2 machine as both a server and a workstation, you also install the NetWare Requester for OS/2, as described earlier in this chapter. Finally, you use the two NetWare for OS/2 installation floppies to begin the installation of the network software. This final step copies files to both the NetWare and OS/2 partitions on the hard drive. You get network management utilities that you can access from an OS/2 session as well as the usual NetWare utilities that you access from a workstation on the LAN. Depending on the speed of your CD-ROM drive, the NetWare for OS/2 installation step takes about two hours.

Once the network software is installed and running, you can switch between OS/2's desktop and the NetWare console screen. Clicking the NetWare Command-Line icon switches to the server console; pressing Ctrl+Esc switches back to the OS/2 desktop. When OS/2 has control of the machine, the computer behaves just as described throughout this book (albeit a bit slower). When NetWare has control of the computer, however, the computer acts just like a NetWare 4 file server.

Chapter Summary

You have learned how to use OS/2 in a NetWare LAN environment in this chapter. You covered the installation of the Requester, you understand login scripts, you know how to map drives, and you are familiar with the Presentation Manager utility, NetWare Tools. You explored NetWare utilities and the NetWare concepts of rights and permissions. And you know about the NetWare for OS/2 file-server product.

In the next chapter, you turn your attention to using OS/2 with networks that aren't based on Novell NetWare.

Chapter 26

Connecting OS/2 to Other LANs

About 75 percent of local area networks use Novell NetWare, discussed in the previous chapter. Other network operating systems, from companies such as IBM and Microsoft, provide many of the same functions as NetWare. These other network software products, however, give the network a different appearance. You use different commands and utilities to manage the LAN, share disk drives, share printers, and even log in.

If you're familiar with NetWare, using a LAN based on OS/2 gives you the same ability to share files and printers. You learn to think of the LAN in different terms, but you quickly find the net result—shared disk space, shared files, and shared printers—not all that different from what you're accustomed to. LANs based on OS/2 use different means to achieve file and print I/O redirection, and they offer some extra capabilities difficult to implement in a NetWare environment.

This chapter focuses on LAN Manager (Microsoft's product) and LAN Server (IBM's product). Both products are growing in sales but lag behind Novell NetWare by a wide margin. Both network operating systems are high-quality software, but in this chapter you find out why Novell still sells better.

You learn what LAN Manager and LAN Server look like, how they operate, and what they offer in the way of functions and features. You explore, in depth, the procedures for logging in and mapping drives. You learn about OS/2 files, directories, and attributes. You see how your workstation behaves on an OS/2-based LAN, and you find out how print redirection works with these products.

After you become familiar with print-job management under LAN Manager and LAN Server, you look critically at the levels of security offered by these network operating systems. If you are thinking of installing LAN Manager, LAN Server, and NetWare on the same LAN but on different file servers, you find out about the potential problems you face.

Connecting an OS/2 workstation to a network based on the LANtastic, NetWare Lite, or Personal NetWare network operating system products isn't easy. This chapter discusses an approach you can take to accomplish this difficult feat.

Focusing on LAN Server and LAN Manager

Two server-based network operating systems from IBM and Microsoft, LAN Server and LAN Manager, run on various versions of OS/2 and share a common codebase—the IBM programmers in Austin and the Microsoft programmers in Redmond worked closely together to create the original first versions of these products.

NetWare 4.0 for OS/2 also runs on OS/2; however, NetWare for OS/2 lets workstations view the OS/2 server through NetWare commands such as LOGIN, MAP, and ATTACH instead of the LAN Server and LAN Manager commands LOGON, NET USE, and NET VIEW. Windows NT Advanced Server runs on NT; Microsoft will likely phase out LAN Manager running on OS/2 in favor of Windows NT Advanced Server. Of these products, all but NetWare for OS/2 use IBM's Server Message Block (SMB) protocol to do I/O redirection. NetWare uses Novell's proprietary NetWare Core Protocol (NCP) instead of SMB. In addition to using the same SMB-based I/O redirection protocol, the network software products LAN Server, LAN Manager, Windows for Workgroups, and NT Advanced Server also share the use of the Network Driver Interface Specification (NDIS) and the Network Basic Input/Output System (NetBIOS) protocols. You learn more about SMBs and NetBIOS later in this chapter. Because the network software products from both IBM and Microsoft use SMBs and NetBIOS to allow you to share hard drives and printers, you can often successfully intermix computers running LAN Server, LAN Manager, Windows-NT Advanced Server, Windows for Workgroups, and even the older PC LAN Program on the same local area network.

Both LAN Manager (LM) and LAN Server (LS) run on top of OS/2 versions 1.21 and higher. Workstations can run DOS versions 3.3 and higher or OS/2 versions 1.21 and higher. You can use an OS/2 LAN Manager or LAN Server file server as both a workstation and a server in a peer-to-peer arrangement, but you then incur security risks that your organization may not be willing to accept. As a rule, no one uses LAN Manager or LAN Server as the basis for a peer LAN.

Future LAN products from IBM will also use SMBs, on NetBIOS, to exchange redirected file and print data. At the PC Expo trade show in 1993, Lee Reiswig, President of IBM's Personal Systems Products Division, said his unit plans to ship a peer-to-peer LAN product in 1994. The IBM peer LAN product has an object-oriented interface and a clipboard that lets different workstations share information. IBM licensed some of the software for its new peer LAN from a company named Symbotics, Inc. IBM will position its peer LAN relative to OS/2 in the same way that Microsoft does with Windows for Workgroups and Windows 3.1.

IBM also offers a Transmission control Protocol/Internet Protocol (TCP/IP) for OS/2 products, which helps OS/2 act as a workstation on LANs with UNIX-based servers.

Considering LAN Server and LAN Manager

LAN Server 3.0 is a 32-bit network operating system that's been benchmarked by *BYTE* Magazine's National System Testing Laboratories (NSTL) as faster than NetWare 3.11. LAN Manager 2.1 uses many of the same commands and works internally much like LAN Server, but LAN Manager's days are probably numbered—in 1993, Microsoft released its new Windows NT Advanced Server product. LAN Server runs on OS/2 2.x, which you buy separately. Microsoft bundles OS/2 1.3 with LAN Manager, and you can, if you want, run Microsoft's LAN Manager on IBM's OS/2 2.1.

Both LAN Server and LAN Manager are excellent environments for client/server computing. It's relatively easy to program an OS/2 computer, even one that is already running as a file server. If you have a staff of programmers, or if the application software you buy already supports it, client/server architecture becomes a possibility. SQL Server, Oracle, and DB2/2 are examples of relational database managers that work well on OS/2-based LANs.

Exploring the IBM and Microsoft Team Effort

As Microsoft and IBM co-developed the OS/2 operating system, they realized that OS/2 could form the basis for a new, full-featured network operating system. With OS/2 running on the file server, the software modules of the network operating system could service file and print requests in a multitasking, threaded environment (threads enable different parts of the file-server software to execute concurrently; this enables the server to give the appearance of doing more than one thing at a time). The workstations, which could be using DOS, OS/2, or some other operating system, would see the benefit of the new high-performance environment. OS/2 file servers and a combination of OS/2-based and DOS-based workstations seemed like a natural, popular combination.

IBM and Microsoft have worked together on OS/2 since 1985. Each company markets its version of OS/2 differently, and each company has made slight changes to the operating system to customize it somewhat, but MS-OS/2 version 1.3 and IBM-OS/2 version 1.3 were essentially the same product. In 1985, the two companies added the writing of the OS/2 file-server software to their Joint Development Agreement (JDA). IBM's product is called LAN Server and Microsoft's is LAN Manager. Both share a common *codebase*, meaning that, like OS/2 itself, the network operating systems are the same software with only minor differences.

The first few versions of OS/2 were not greatly popular, despite the fact that OS/2 does not have a 640KB limitation or many of the other problems associated with DOS. Microsoft and IBM envisioned that OS/2 would replace DOS, but this did not happen. Application developers did not rush to market an OS/2 version of every DOS application, as Microsoft and IBM expected they would. The emulation of DOS within the early versions of OS/2 was limited in significant ways, and not every DOS application would run in the DOS box under OS/2. People kept using their DOS applications and purchased memory managers such as QEMM and 386MAX to give them more conventional memory in which to run their applications. Such purchases prolonged the life of the DOS applications, but people still complained when they ran out of room and bumped into the 640KB DOS limitation.

The current version of OS/2, the subject of this book, rectifies the situation by giving you multiple concurrent DOS sessions, each with about 620K of available conventional memory free for running your software. OS/2 2.x includes the Microsoft Windows environment and, of course, you can run OS/2 applications under OS/2. IBM calls OS/2 "...a better DOS than DOS, a better Windows than Windows, and a better OS/2 than ever before."

In the latter part of 1991, Microsoft and IBM split up and decided to go their own ways with OS/2 and their jointly developed network operating systems. Microsoft's LAN Manager still runs on OS/2 file servers, but Microsoft has redesigned its network operating system product to use Windows New Technology, sometimes called simply NT, in place of OS/2. Microsoft now is in the position of selling two network operating systems, LAN Manager (OS/2-based) and Windows-NT Advanced Server. IBM, however, remains firmly committed to OS/2. IBM believes that, with its new features, OS/2 2.x may yet replace DOS as the dominant operating system for personal computers.

In 1989 and again in 1990, Microsoft and IBM announced that the companies would merge LAN Manager and LAN Server into a single product. This has not happened, and the split between Microsoft and IBM makes it extremely unlikely that the merging of the products will ever take place.

With a history such as this, you begin to see why LAN Manager and LAN Server have not preempted Novell NetWare as the most popular network operating system. Novell has always sharply focused on building a better network operating system. People perceive IBM and Microsoft as being not quite as focused. The new OS/2 may very well "conquer the desktop" and eclipse DOS as the operating system of choice at the workstation. But at the file server, NetWare will continue to give OS/2 strong competition. As you learned in the previous chapter, you easily can turn a computer running OS/2 2.x into a workstation on a NetWare LAN.

Learning LAN Server and LAN Manager Terms

In LAN Server and LAN Manager terms, a *requester* is the software that lets a workstation log on to a domain and use network resources. Users have access to the network through the OS/2 LAN Requester program from OS/2 workstations and through the DOS LAN Requester program from DOS workstations. A server can share its files, printers, and even serial devices (such as modems) across the LAN. DOS requesters can't access a shared modem, but OS/2 requesters can share a file server's communications ports and modems.

During installation, the network administrator specifies a server to be a *domain controller* or an additional server. There is only one domain controller in a domain. A *domain* is a group of file servers and workstations with similar security needs. You can set up several domains on a large LAN Manager or LAN Server network. On a small LAN, a file server can also act as a domain controller. Domains provide a simple way for you to control user access to the network and the network's resources. A network user can have accounts in multiple domains, but he or she can log in to only one domain at a time. Additional servers cannot be started nor can users log in if the domain controller is not running. There can be several domains on the same LAN, each managed separately, but each file server belongs to only one domain. Domains are managed by network administrators who set up, maintain, and control the network, manage its resources, and support its users.

An *alias* is a nickname for a shared resource. On a server named ACCTING, an administrator can create an alias named OCTRCPTS to refer to the server's C:\RECEIPTS\OCTOBER directory. Workstations equate the OCTRCPTS alias to a drive letter, perhaps G, to gain access to the files in that directory. The alias specifies the server where the directory is located and the path to the directory so that people at workstations don't have to remember server names and directory structures. An alias remains defined after the domain controller is stopped and restarted, but a netname does not.

An administrator assigns a *netname* to a resource (disk directory, printer, or serial device) to define the resource temporarily. Like an alias, a netname identifies a shared resource on a server. However, to use a resource through its netname, you specify the server name in addition to the netname. Unlike an alias, a netname does not remain defined if the domain controller is stopped.

A UNC (*Universal Naming Convention*) name consists of a server name and a netname, which together identify a resource in the domain. A UNC name has the following format:

```
\\servername\netname\path
```

Note the use of the double backslash characters (\\) preceding the server's name.

If you assign LPT1 to a shared print queue, you override the local printer port and your print jobs go to the network printer. On the other hand, you can't override local drive-letter assignments. If you have a drive C on your computer, you must use other drive letters besides C to refer to file-server disk resources.

Understanding the Essentials of Security

User-level security on a LAN Manager or LAN Server network consists of logon security and permissions. Each user account has a password; the user specifies a user ID and the password to gain access to the network through a domain. A network administrator can limit a particular user's access to certain times of the day or the workstation(s) from which the user can log in. Permissions limit the extent to which a user can use shared resources. The network administrator, for example, can create a COMMON directory that everyone can use, and the administrator can create an UPDATE directory with files only certain people can modify but everyone can read.

The network administrator grants, restricts, or denies access to a shared resource by creating an access-control profile. Each shared resource can have just one access-control profile. An administrator can put individual logon accounts in an access-control profile, or the administrator can set up named groups of accounts and insert group names in the access-control profile. Group names are more convenient and they help keep the profile to a manageable size. Each individual or group name has a list of permissions and security restrictions the administrator can use. The access permissions allow or disallow these operations:

- Run programs
- Read and write data files
- Create and delete subdirectories and files
- Change file attributes
- Create, change, and delete access-control profiles

Contrasting LAN Server and LAN Manager

You tune LAN Server by using a text editor to modify the computer's CONFIG.SYS and IBMLAN.INI files. LAN Manager features autotuning, whereby the file-server software monitors its own activity and changes its initialization files automatically. To take advantage of autotuning, you merely have to stop and restart a LAN Manager file server periodically.

Persistent net connections are another feature of LAN Manager. By default, users get the same network connections they had in their last session each time they log on. You can enable or disable persistent connections with the /PERSISTENT= option on the NET USE command. You also can put entries in a user's LANMAN.INI file to turn persistent net connections on or off, or to freeze a certain set of network resources as shared by that user.

LAN Manager and LAN Server both use the concepts of domains and logon security, but in slightly different ways. If you want to use LAN Manager and LAN Server on the same physical network, you should set up separate domains for each network operating system. In one domain, all file servers should run either LAN Manager or LAN Server. You should ensure that workstations in a LAN Server domain log in to a LAN Server domain before trying to access LAN Manager file servers. Workstations in a LAN Manager domain, however, can log on in any domain.

LAN Server can use aliases (nicknames) for shared resources, but LAN Manager cannot. LAN Manager workstations must refer to the shared resources by their full name, not by the alias. Suppose that you have a LAN Server machine named PRODUCTION that shares a printer with an alias of REPORTS. The full name of the shared printer is \\PRODUCTION\PRINTER1. LAN Server workstations can share REPORTS, but LAN Manager workstations must use the full name \\PRODUCTION\PRINTER1 to access that printer.

LAN Manager and LAN Server interoperate well on a Token Ring LAN, but not on an Ethernet LAN. On Ethernet networks, you may need to modify both network operating systems' configurations. LAN Server supports both the Digital Intel Xerox (DIX) Version 2.0 protocol and the Institute of Electrical and Electronic Engineers (IEEE) 802.3 protocol; LAN Manager does not support DIX. On Ethernet, you need to switch LM and LS to use IEEE 802.3 so that workstations can use both kinds of file servers.

When you install OS/2 on the file-server computer, the installation process asks whether you want to use the High Performance File System. Because the computer is going to become a file server and you want the server to be as efficient as possible, you probably should answer Yes to the question. If you answer No, OS/2 uses the same type of file system that DOS uses, known as the FAT (file allocation table).

OS/2 offers a High Performance File System option especially designed for file servers: 386HPFS. OS/2 can access files in an HPFS partition much more rapidly than files in a FAT partition. The difference in performance is most dramatic for large files. HPFS gives you the ability to use long file names (up to 254 characters) and to include spaces and several periods in such a name. OS/2-based computers—either the file server or OS/2 workstations—can see and use files with long file names. DOS workstations cannot. The 386HPFS that comes with the IBM LAN Server Advanced Edition helps a file server respond to workstation file requests quickly. Using 386HPFS also lets you implement *local security* at a file server, which can keep a curious, unauthorized person from sitting down at the file server to view confidential, private files.

Demand Protocol Architecture (DPA) is a LAN Manager feature that Microsoft got from 3Com. The 3Com company bought a LAN Manager license from Microsoft and enhanced LM somewhat, but 3Com was never able to sell many copies of its enhanced network operating system. Microsoft bought the license back from 3Com when 3Com decided to get out of the business of reselling LAN Manager. Basically, Demand Protocol Architecture enables you to load and unload protocol stacks dynamically. You can use DPA to make occasional reference to a NetWare file server; DPA can temporarily load the Novell NetWare IPX and NETX software at the workstation. After you close your NetWare connection, DPA reclaims the memory used by IPX and NETX. In everyday use, people with both LAN Manager and NetWare file servers need more than temporary access to both kinds of file servers. DPA represents a technical feat, but one you will find not entirely useful or practical. LAN Manager comes with a special option called NetWare Connectivity to enable you to easily access both LAN Manager and NetWare file servers at the same time.

LAN Manager offers remote administration. As long as you have administrative privileges, you can add users, delete users, and do other administrative tasks from any OS/2 or LAN Manager Enhanced workstation. You do not have to visit the file server to make your changes.

With share-level security, a feature of LAN Manager, you can set up a single password to limit access to a shared resource or device. LAN Server does not support share-level security.

Both LAN Manager and LAN Server support Macintosh workstations as well as OS/2 and DOS workstations.

NetBIOS and SMBs

The network operating systems discussed in this chapter use NetBIOS to send and receive messages. The NetBIOS messages contain Server Message Blocks (SMBs) to carry file I/O requests and responses between servers and workstations. NetBIOS accepts communications requests from the file-redirection portion of the network operating system or from an application program (such as an electronic mail product). NetBIOS operations fall into four categories:

- *Name support:* Each workstation on the network is identified by one or more names. These names are maintained by NetBIOS in a table; the first item in the table is automatically the unique, permanently assigned name of the network adapter. Optional user names (such as BARRY) can be added to the table for the sake of convenient identification of each workstation. The user-assigned names can be unique, or, in a special case, can refer to a group of users.

- *Session support:* A point-to-point connection between two names (workstations) on the network can be opened, managed, and closed under NetBIOS control. One workstation begins by listening for a call; the other workstation calls the first workstation. The computers are peers; both can send and receive message data concurrently during the session. At the end, both workstations hang up on each other. LAN Server, LAN Manager, Windows for Workgroups, and NT Advanced Server establish sessions between workstations and servers.

- *Datagram support:* Message data can be sent to a name, a group of names, or to all names on the network. A point-to-point connection is not established and there is no guarantee that the message data will be received.

- *Adapter/session status:* Information about the local network adapter card, other network adapter cards, and any currently active sessions is available to application software that uses NetBIOS.

At the workstation, the requester software intercepts an application's file I/O operations and sends them across the network to the file server, using IBM's Server Message Block (SMB) protocol to accomplish the redirection. IBM defines four categories of SMBs:

- *Session Control:* Once a NetBIOS session is established between a workstation and the server, the workstation sends a Verify Dialect SMB to the server. This message contains data indicating the capabilities of the version of the PC LAN program running at the workstation. The server examines this message and responds to the workstation with information about itself and the capabilities the server supports. This exchange is then followed by one or more Start Connection SMBs used to create logical connections between the workstation and network resources at the file server. These logical connections are later terminated by the workstation when it sends End Connection SMBs to the server (or when the NetBIOS session is aborted by the occurrence of an error).

- *File Access:* The SMBs in this category are used by a workstation to gain access to the files on the server's hard disk. The functions included in this category allow the workstation to treat the server disk almost like a local hard drive—the workstation can create and remove directories, create, open, and close files, read from files, write to files, rename files, delete files, search for files, get or set file attributes, and, of course, lock records. The requester detects file operations intended for network files and converts the operation into one or more SMBs. The local operating system (DOS or OS/2) never sees file requests for network files. The server performs the file operation when it receives the SMB message and returns a response to the workstation's requester.

- *Print Service:* The SMBs in this category allow a workstation to queue files for printing by a server and to obtain print-queue status information. The workstation can create a spool file, write data to the spool file, close the spool file, and ask that the server return a Print Queue Status SMB.

- *Messages:* LAN Server and LAN Manager can use Message SMBs to route brief messages from workstation to workstation. Most people forgo the message-passing feature of LAN Server and LAN Manager, opting instead to purchase and use a complete electronic-mail software package.

Understanding LAN Server and LAN Manager

You install LAN Manager and LAN Server after you first install OS/2 on the file-server computer. Microsoft bundles MS-OS/2 version 1.3 with LAN Manager 2.1; IBM's LAN Server 2.0 requires you to purchase OS/2 separately. IBM now also offers the new 32-bit version 3.0 of LAN Server, which runs only on OS/2 2.0 or OS/2 2.1.

Because LAN Manager and LAN Server consist of pure OS/2 software, you need to disable OS/2's capability to emulate DOS when you install OS/2 on a file-server computer. A DOS session on a file server merely consumes memory. You give the network operating system more memory by disabling DOS emulation. The installation documentation for LAN Manager or LAN Server describes other configuration changes that help the OS/2 computer provide a better file-server environment.

On the OS/2 computer, LAN Manager or LAN Server runs in an OS/2 session. You have the option of running multiple OS/2 sessions on the file server. The LM or LS network operating system software does most of its work in the background. The file server shares its resources—files, directories, disk space, printer, and perhaps a database—across the network. The network operating system also performs administrative tasks such as recognizing workstations when LAN users log in and ceasing to recognize the workstations of users who have logged out.

You can use command-line entries or menus to perform administrative tasks on the network, including logging in and setting up your shared drive letters and printers.

When you set up a DOS-based personal computer to be a workstation on a LAN Manager or LAN Server network, you designate the workstation as having basic or enhanced capabilities. A *basic* workstation uses fewer commands, does not need to perform a login sequence to use the LAN, and cannot use menus. Although you do not have to log in from a basic workstation, you must provide a password to use each shared resource. An *enhanced* workstation offers menus and requires a login sequence that includes an account name and a password. OS/2 workstations on a LAN Server or LAN Manager network always use account names and passwords; an OS/2 workstation always operates in enhanced mode.

Taking Advantage of Client/Server Computing

LAN Server and LAN Manager are good environments for client/server computing. Programmability is the biggest reason that people talk about client/server in connection with these two OS/2-based network operating systems. OS/2 is easy to program, perhaps even more so than DOS.

Both LAN Manager and LAN Server can share the network adapter with other OS/2 application software running on the file-server computer. Under the control of OS/2's multitasking, one computer program—the network operating system—responds to file requests from workstations. Another computer program may be a database-server application. Your programming staff also may program the workstations to send and receive special requests and responses to and from the file server (or from a separate computer, for that matter). These custom-programmed requests and responses can carry, for example, SQL statements and relational database records.

OS/2 provides *named pipes* to programmers. The programmer treats a named pipe as if it were a file, but the named pipe actually contains message records. These message records travel from the workstation to the file server. On the file server, a custom-written application may do some record handling and other processing before returning a response to the workstation through the named pipe.

SQL Server is a Microsoft product that enables programmers to create client/server applications. SQL Server provides a relational database "engine" you install on an OS/2 computer on the network. Programmers write workstation software that sends SQL statements to SQL Server. SQL Server honors each request by sending back the appropriate records from within its database. Chapter 24, "Understanding OS/2 Communications and Database Tools," briefly discusses SQL Server.

Database Manager, a component of IBM's Extended Services, and Database 2/2 (which you also learned about in Chapter 24), provide functions similar to those of SQL Server.

Lotus Notes is yet another client/server application. Notes offers intelligent, group-oriented electronic-mail services. Notes enables the sophisticated storage and retrieval of messages; an index contains the subject, recipients, and other key data items related to the messages. Notes is particularly useful for large, geographically dispersed organizations in which people need to exchange information frequently, but work in different time zones or have conflicting schedules or work styles. Notes stores its data at a centrally located OS/2-based personal computer on a LAN. Workstations on the LAN or on a remotely attached LAN, through a wide area network, can interact with the central OS/2 Notes computer.

Building a LAN based on OS/2 can be a good investment. You'll find these database managers and other similar environments fertile ground for client/server applications. For example, you can save hardware and software dollars by running a database manager directly on the file server. You can create peer-LAN relationships on an OS/2 LAN. Or you can use one of these network operating systems as an application server on a LAN that's already running Novell NetWare. Novell has about 75 percent of the network operating system marketplace, and that percentage isn't likely to plummet significantly any time soon. However, you may find it advantageous to add LAN Server or LAN Manager to your Token Ring or Ethernet LAN.

Using LAN Manager or LAN Server

In the next few sections, you learn how to operate LAN Manager and LAN Server. You also see what these network operating systems look like on-screen. You first cover the menu interface these products offer and then the command-line interface. You learn about logging in to a LAN Manager or LAN Server network. You discover how to map drive letters, use files and directories, and print on the LAN. You learn how a computer operates when it becomes a workstation on a LAN Manager or LAN Server network, and you find out about the security features of these products.

Setting Up Workstations. One of the biggest reasons that Novell NetWare is more popular than LAN Manager or LAN Server is the disk space taken up by the LM or LS executable and configuration files. You generally need to use only from two to six relatively small files on a NetWare workstation to gain access to a file server. On a LAN Manager or LAN Server workstation, however, the installation process consumes from 1M to 3M of workstation disk space. You easily can create a bootable floppy disk that gets you onto the network with NetWare. With LM or LS, you may have difficulty creating a bootable floppy disk you can use to access the LAN. There are too many files.

On a DOS-based workstation, the memory usage of the LAN Manager and LAN Server workstation software is also greater than that for a NetWare-based workstation. Memory requirements vary according to the type of network adapter card and associated software drivers, but you can expect that LM or LS workstation software occupies about 90KB of RAM. Netware workstation software, on the other hand, usually occupies only 50KB to 60KB. On a workstation with an 80386 or 80486 CPU chip, you may be able to use a memory manager to load some or all of the network software into high memory. Chapter 6, "Installing OS/2," discusses memory managers and types of memory.

The workstation installation program copies files to your computer's hard disk and puts statements in your CONFIG.SYS and AUTOEXEC.BAT files to load the network software when you boot your computer. You can put the NET USE statements into a BAT file so that you do not have to retype them each time you reboot.

Using Menus. The LAN Manager or LAN Server menu interface appears when you use the NET command with no arguments. If you type characters following the word **NET**, the network operating system assumes that you want to use the command-line interface.

> **Note**
>
> On DOS basic (not enhanced) workstations, menus are not available.

The LM/LS menu screens operate in text mode, not graphics mode. The menu screens are only somewhat CUA-compliant. The LAN Manager and LAN Server menu interface enables you to do anything with menus that you can do by typing commands at a **DOS** prompt. You can log in to the LAN, log out, map drive letters, and redirect your printer port to the LAN printer. You can change your password, send short messages to other logged-in network users, and see lists of the file servers, disk drives, and printers on the LAN.

Using the Command-Line Interface. Especially after you have gained some experience with LAN Manager or LAN Server, you may feel more comfortable issuing network commands at the DOS command-line prompt of your workstation, or at the OS/2 command-line prompt at the file server. You invoke the network commands by running the NET command, but you avoid the menu screens by typing parameters after the word **NET**. The following is a list of the most important and most frequently used NET commands, with their parameters, that you use at a basic or enhanced workstation:

Basic Command	Function
LOAD	Loads a different network protocol
NET CONTINUE	Continues a paused service
NET HELP	Gets help for a command
NET NAME	Assigns a computer name
NET PAUSE	Pauses a connection to a network service
NET PRINT	Displays the print queue or prints a file
NET START WORKSTATION	Starts the network
NET USE	Displays shared resources or assigns a drive letter or device name to a new shared resource
UNLOAD	Unloads a LAN Manager network protocol

Enhanced Command	Function
LOAD	Loads a different network protocol
NET ACCESS	Views permissions
NET COPY	Copies network files
NET HELP	Gets help
NET LOGOFF	Logs off the network
NET LOGON	Logs on to the network
NET PASSWORD	Changes your password
NET PRINT	Controls print jobs and prints files
NET START	Starts a workstation or learns what workstation connections exist
NET TIME	Synchronizes the workstation's clock with the server's clock
NET USE	Displays shared resources or assigns a drive letter or device name to a new shared resource
NET VIEW	Displays a list of servers and server resources
NET WHO	Sees who is logged on
UNLOAD	Unloads a LAN Manager protocol

Using Utilities. The NET command performs most of the administrative duties you accomplish on a LAN Manager or LAN Server network. The network operating system comes with additional utility programs you may find helpful for accomplishing certain tasks. These computer programs enable you to schedule commands or programs to run at a specified date and time, make backup copies of the network's administrative (passwords and permissions) files, restore these files, verify a physical connection to a remote computer, and do other odd jobs on the LAN.

Logging In

You use the NET LOGON command to log on to the network. This command furnishes your user ID, password, and assigned domain to a domain controller for logon verification and authentication (you learn more about domains in the section of this chapter entitled "Ensuring Security"). The user ID and password identify you in a particular domain and grant you access to shared resources. You can use shared resources in other domains after you have logged in to the network. You need to perform the logon sequence on OS/2 workstations and on an enhanced workstation running DOS. On a basic DOS workstation, you supply a password to use a shared resource. You do not need to identify yourself on a basic workstation running DOS.

If you forget your password, your account may be locked out of the network. If you make repeated unsuccessful attempts at entering your password, the system disables your account. When this situation occurs, only the network administrator can reenable your account. This security feature helps keep intruders from gaining access to the LAN.

Mapping Drives

You use NET USE or the NET program's menus to map drive letters. Depending on how the network administrator has set up the file server's shared resources, your workstation's drive letter may refer to an entire server disk drive or to a single directory. The administrator decides the extent to which the workstations share the file server's resources. The system does not indicate, at the workstation level, whether the drive letter refers to an entire disk drive or to a single directory.

Following is an example of a NET USE command that sets up drive F. The network administrator has published the shared resource with the name NORTHEAST on the server named \\SALES.

```
NET USE F: \\SALES\NORTHEAST
```

You also issue a form of the NET USE command to cancel the use of a drive letter. The same NET USE command that sets up your network drive letters also can redirect your printed output to the LAN printer, as you learn later in this chapter.

After you establish the network drive letters your workstation can use, you work with your applications in the usual manner. Files on the LAN now are available to the computer programs you run, provided that you have permission to use those files.

If you do not have permission to read a particular file, you cannot access that file at all. Further, you may have read permission but not write permission on some files. You cannot save new data in files to which you do not have write permission. If you encounter strange error messages from the applications you run, talk to your network administrator to make sure that your permissions are correct and appropriate.

Printing with LAN Manager and LAN Server

In addition to providing network drive letters, the NET USE command redirects your printed output to the shared LAN printer. The network administrator assigns a name to the LAN printer in the same way that he or she assigns names to the file servers and to the shared resources that become drive letters at your workstation. The administrator may set up a printer named HP_LASER on the SALES file server, for example; you use the following NET USE statement for your printed output:

```
NET USE LPT1: \\SALES\HP_LASER
```

When you copy a file to the LPT1 device, or when you tell one of your applications to print, the network operating system creates a print job. The print job goes into the server's print queue to be printed when the printer becomes available. You can use the printer object in your Network folder, or the printer object directly on the file server, to view the queue of print jobs that are awaiting print. In addition to viewing your job's position in the queue, you can hold, release, and delete your own print jobs in the queue. You can also configure the network operating system to notify you when the print job is completed.

Ensuring Security

You organize file servers and workstations into *domains*. A domain is a group of file servers and workstations with similar security needs. You can set up several domains on a large LAN Manager or LAN Server network. Domains enable you to control user access to the network and the network's resources. A network user can have accounts in multiple domains, but he or she can log on in only one domain at a time.

User-level security on a LAN Manager or LAN Server network consists of logon security and permissions. Each user specifies a user ID and the password to gain access to the network through a domain. A network administrator can limit a user's access to certain times of the day or limit the workstation(s) from which the user can log on. Permissions limit the extent to which a user can use shared resources. The network administrator can create a COMMON directory that everyone can use, for example, and an UPDATE directory with files only certain users can modify but everyone can read.

The following table shows the permissions for files and directories you can assign, and what actions the permissions allow.

Permission	Allows
Change Attributes	Flag a file as read-only or read/write
Change Permissions	Grant or revoke access to other users
Create	Create files and directories
Delete	Delete files and remove directories
Execute	Execute a program file (EXE, BAT, or COM file) but allow reading or copying of that file
Read	Read and copy files, run programs, change from one directory to another, and make use of OS/2's extended attributes for files
Write	Write to a file

The OS/2-based network operating systems, LAN Server and LAN Manager, enable you to control access to the file server's keyboard and computer screen. In a special unattended mode, the file server enables users to view and manage print queues but not to modify user accounts or other administrative data. You must specify a password to use other screens.

Connecting OS/2 to LANtastic, NetWare Lite, and Personal NetWare

If you have a workstation on one of the DOS-based peer LANs from Artisoft (LANtastic) or Novell (NetWare Lite or Personal NetWare), you may have formed the habit of booting DOS, perhaps through the Dual-Boot feature, to copy some files from the network and then rebooting to use OS/2 to work on those files. Or you may simply have decided not to install OS/2 because you need a permanent connection to the LAN and you know that DOS sessions under OS/2 cannot access the network adapter in your PC.

However, you may be able to have the best of both worlds. You may be able to run OS/2 and still connect your computer to the peer LAN. Depending on the network adapter you use, the DOS network driver software may function correctly in what OS/2 calls a *specific version of DOS*. In a specific-DOS session, you can often load device drivers and TSRs that don't work in an OS/2-emulated DOS session.

A specific-DOS session under OS/2 can start from either floppy disk or from an image of a floppy boot disk stored on your hard disk. Chapter 17, "Configuring Your DOS and Windows Sessions," details the steps you take to create a specific-DOS bootable floppy disk and, optionally, store that bootable floppy disk on your hard drive as an image file. To recap briefly, you use DOS (not OS/2) to format a floppy disk with the /S parameter. The /S parameter tells FORMAT to make the floppy disk bootable. You then copy the files EMM386.SYS, HIMEM.SYS, FSACCESS.EXE, and FSFILTER.SYS from your \OS2\MDOS directory to the floppy disk. You use EMM386.SYS and HIMEM.SYS if you want to load the specific version of DOS along with device drivers and TSRs into high memory. Running FSACCESS lets you use drive A after booting a specific-DOS version. And FSFILTER lets the specific-DOS session access your hard drive while OS/2 is controlling the computer. You can boot your specific-DOS session from the floppy disk you created, or you can use the VMDISK utility to copy the floppy disk to an image file on your hard disk. If you boot from floppy, you use a DOS-session program object that has a DOS_STARTUP_DRIVE setting of A:. (The OS/2 installation program puts such a program object in your Command Prompts folder for you.) If you boot from the image file on your hard drive, you put the name of the image file, including the drive letter and path, in the DOS_STARTUP_DRIVE setting for that DOS session.

To access the network through the specific-DOS session, add whatever device drivers or TSRs that implement the network software at your workstation to the specific DOS CONFIG.SYS file or AUTOEXEC.BAT file. You should be able to log in to your peer LAN through the specific-DOS session you've created. Note, however, that other DOS and OS/2 sessions won't be able to use network services and shared devices.

> **Note**
>
> Novell and Artisoft have patches and updates for NetWare Lite and LANtastic that help their respective products work better in a DOS session under OS/2. Check with your vendor and review the information in Appendix H, "Identifying Sources of OS/2 Information," to obtain the latest patches that apply to you.

> **Tip**
>
> If you use VMDISK to create an image on your hard disk of the floppy boot disk, the image file is the same size as the capacity of the floppy disk. To save space on your hard drive, you can system-format a 720KB floppy disk rather than a 1.44MB floppy disk. The image file on your hard drive is smaller and you have the same features and functions as if you had used a floppy disk with greater capacity.

Following is a sample CONFIG.SYS file for a specific-DOS session you might create under OS/2:

```
DOS=HIGH,UMB
FILES=60
BUFFERS=40
STACKS=0,0
DEVICE=A:\FSFILTER.SYS
DEVICE=A:\HIMEM.SYS
DEVICE=A:\EMM386.SYS RAM NOEMS
DEVICE=A:\ANSI.SYS
SHELL=A:\COMMAND.COM A:\ /P /E:600
```

Chapter Summary

You looked at the almost-twin LAN Manager and LAN Server network operating systems in this chapter. These products from Microsoft and IBM look and behave alike, but have subtle differences you now know about. You understand why these products lend themselves to client/server architecture, you know why NetWare sells better, and you are familiar with the principles and concepts of LAN Manager and LAN Server. You have explored what these products look like, how they operate, and what they can offer in the way of advantages and benefits for your office. You also considered how to connect an OS/2 workstation to the popular DOS-based peer LAN products from Artisoft and Novell.

Part VI

Using the Command Reference

Productivity - Icon View

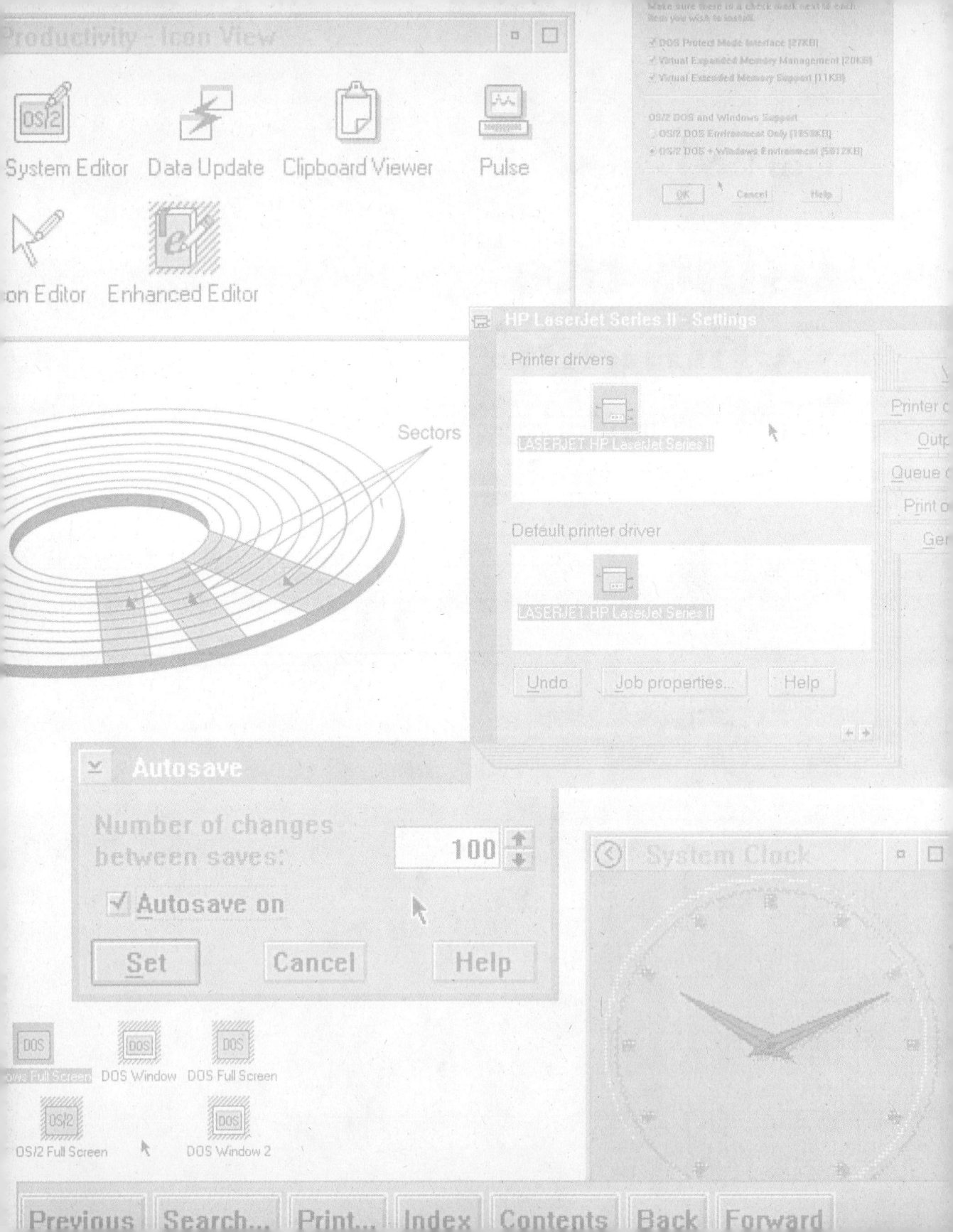

- System Editor
- Data Update
- Clipboard Viewer
- Pulse
- Icon Editor
- Enhanced Editor

Sectors

HP LaserJet Series II - Settings

Printer drivers

LASERJET HP LaserJet Series II

Default printer driver

LASERJET HP LaserJet Series II

Undo   Job properties...   Help

Make sure there is a check mark next to each item you wish to install.

- ☑ DOS Protect Mode Interface (27KB)
- ☑ Virtual Expanded Memory Management (20KB)
- ☑ Virtual Extended Memory Support (11KB)

OS/2 DOS and Windows Support
- ○ OS/2 DOS Environment Only (1858KB)
- ● OS/2 DOS + Windows Environment (5812KB)

OK   Cancel   Help

Printer o
Outp
Queue
Print o
Ger

Autosave

Number of changes between saves: 100

☑ Autosave on

Set   Cancel   Help

System Clock

- DOS Windows Full Screen
- DOS Window
- DOS Full Screen
- OS/2 Full Screen
- DOS Window 2

Previous Search... Print... Index Contents Back Forward

Using the Command Reference

OS/2 Version 2.1 includes more than 100 commands you can use at a command-line prompt in DOS or OS/2 sessions, full-screen or windowed. This section explains how to use the commands. First you find the commands summarized in logically related groups, and then you see each command discussed in detail. This section can be used, however, in conjunction with two other chapters in this book. Chapter 12 is a tutorial for the commands you use most often. It also contains a discussion of the on-line Command Reference that you may find helpful when you want to look up an OS/2 or DOS command.

Organization

The commands appear in alphabetical order. Most of them can be used in either OS/2 or DOS sessions; those that cannot are labeled *OS/2 Only* or *DOS Only*. Configuration commands, which you use only when you are fine-tuning your CONFIG.SYS file, are listed alphabetically at the end of this chapter.

Layout

Commands are a language you use to give instructions to OS/2 and DOS. A brief description follows the name of each command. Then you see up to four headings: syntax, switches, examples, and notes.

Syntax

Think of syntax as the grammar rules that tell you how to use each command. This book uses some simple conventions to make the syntax of each command clear and understandable.

For a command that operates on a file, the syntax for the command shows the following:

COMMAND *d:path***filename.ext**

This syntax tells you that *d:* represents a drive letter, *path* represents a single directory or a path of directories separated by backslashes (\\). The portion in italics, *d:path*, is optional. The portion shown in boldface, **filename.ext**, is required.

> **Note**
>
> When OS/2 cannot find the command you typed, the following message appears:
>
> ```
> The name specified is not recognized as an internal or
> external command, operable program, or batch file
> ```
>
> The problem in this example is that OS/2 needs a path to the command.
>
> You can tell OS/2 where to find the command by modifying your path, as explained later in this section. You also can explicitly tell OS/2 where to find the command by prefixing the command with the drive letter and path (directory) containing that command. Type the following command, for example:
>
> **C:\\BIN\\CHKDSK**
>
> This command directs OS/2 to look in the BIN directory on drive C for the CHKDSK command. OS/2 automatically sets up your PATH statement in the CONFIG.SYS file, however, to point to all the directories containing your OS/2 and DOS commands. If OS/2 informs you that it cannot find a command, the first thing to check is your spelling of the command. You rarely, if ever, need to prefix a command with the drive letter and directory containing that command.

This Command Reference shows literal text that you type in uppercase letters. Any variable text you replace with text of your choosing appears in lowercase letters. As an example, look at the syntax of the following entry:

FORMAT d:

This command means that you must type the word **FORMAT** if you want to format a disk. You replace **d:** with the drive letter of the disk you want to format.

Switches

Many commands have optional parameters that modify how they work. Switches start with a slash. If you erase a group of files by typing DEL *.* /P, for example, the /P switch tells the delete command to pause before erasing each file. With the pause, you can continue the process or cancel the operation.

Examples

Theory is fine, but concrete examples are often the quickest, simplest way to see how a command works. You will find many examples in this section.

Notes

You will find hints, background information, and—when appropriate—cautions in the Notes for a command.

Commands That Help You Work with Your Files

ATTRIB	Shows or changes a file's read-only, archive, hidden, and system attributes.
BACKUP	Backs up a hard disk to floppy disks or other media.
COMP	Compares files.
COPY	Copies or combines files.
DEL	Erases files.
ERASE	Erases files.
FIND	Searches for text in files.
MORE	Displays a file or directory contents one screen at a time.
MOVE	Moves files from one directory to another on the same drive.
PRINT	Prints files, or cancels printing.
RECOVER	Salvages files from a disk with bad sectors.

REN or RENAME	Changes a file's name.
REPLACE	Selectively replaces files.
RESTORE	Retrieves files from a backup.
TYPE	Displays a file on-screen or to a printer with redirection.
VERIFY	Checks that data is correctly written to a disk.
XCOPY	Copies directories or groups of files.

Commands That Help You Work with Your Directories

APPEND	Tells the system where to find data files.
CD or CHDIR	Shows or changes the current directory of a disk drive.
DIR	Lists the files in a directory.
MD or MKDIR	Creates a directory.
RD or RMDIR	Removes a directory.
TREE	Displays all directories on a disk and optionally lists files.

Commands That Help You Prepare and Maintain Disks and Floppy Disks

CACHE	Controls the disk cache on HPFS drives.
CHKDSK	Analyzes a disk and gives you a report; fixes disk problems.
DISKCOMP	Determines whether one floppy disk is an exact copy of another.

DISKCOPY	Duplicates a floppy disk.
FDISK/FDISKPM	Manages hard disk partitions.
FORMAT	Prepares a disk for use in OS/2, and reports any defects.
LABEL	Gives a name to a disk.
MEM	Displays the amount of used and free memory in DOS sessions.
VOL	Displays a disk's label and serial number.

Commands That Support National Languages

These commands work with the CONFIG.SYS commands CODEPAGE, COUNTRY, and DEVINFO.

CHCP	Switches between national alphabets.
GRAFTABL	Enables DOS programs to display line-drawing and national language characters on a CGA monitor in graphics mode.
KEYB	Tells the keyboard what national alphabet you want to use.

Commands That Give You Information about Your System or Let You Change How It Works

ANSI	Enables you to run OS/2 programs that require special support for the screen or keyboard.
ASSIGN	Tells DOS to pretend that one disk drive is another.

CLS	Clears the screen.
CMD	Starts a new copy of the OS/2 command processor.
COMMAND	Starts a new copy of the DOS command processor.
DATE	Displays or sets the date.
DETACH	Runs a noninteractive program in the background.
DDINSTALL	Enables you to install new device drivers after OS/2 has been installed.
EXIT	Terminates the current command processor.
HELP	Explains how to use a command, or what an error message means.
JOIN	Tells DOS to pretend that a disk drive is a directory of another drive.
KEYS	Controls command recall and editing.
MODE	Controls the communications port, screen mode, or parallel printer.
PROMPT	Sets the string of characters that is displayed at the command line.
SPOOL	Redirects a file that you send to one printer, so that it comes out on a different printer.
START	Runs another OS/2 program in another session.
SUBST	Tells DOS to pretend that a directory is a separate disk.
TIME	Displays or sets the time.
VER	Displays the version of OS/2 you are using.

Configuration Commands

These commands can be placed in the CONFIG.SYS file OS/2 reads each time it starts. CONFIG.SYS statements give information that OS/2 needs to control the computer and run programs. With the exception of the ANSI, PROMPT, SET, and PATH statements, you don't type CONFIG.SYS statements at a command-line prompt. Because you don't type these commands at a command prompt, they are listed separately at the end of the chapter.

ANSI	Enables you to run DOS programs that require special support for the screen or keyboard.
AUTOFAIL	Gives you a choice in dealing with certain hardware errors.
BASEDEV	Enables you to install a base device driver.
BREAK	Makes DOS programs stop sooner when you interrupt them by pressing Ctrl-Break.
BUFFERS	Sets aside a part of memory for moving data to and from disks.
CODEPAGE	Enables you to use the alphabets of various languages.
COUNTRY	Customizes your system for the country you live in.
DEVICE	Installs a device driver (a program that adds a function to the operating system) that is not on the device support diskette.
DEVICE (ANSI.SYS)	In DOS sessions, allows you to use extended keyboard and display support.
DEVICE (COM.SYS)	In OS/2 sessions, allows applications or system programs to use serial devices.
DEVICE (EGA.SYS)	Enables you to run DOS programs that control the Enhanced Graphics Adapter directly.

DEVICE (EXTDSKDD.SYS)	Enables you to access a disk that uses a logical drive letter.
DEVICE (MOUSE)	Enables you to use a mouse or trackball, but this command must be used with the POINTDD.SYS device driver.
DEVICE (PMDD.SYS)	In OS/2 sessions, provides pointer draw support.
DEVICE (POINTDD.SYS)	In OS/2 sessions, provides mouse support.
DEVICE (VDISK.SYS)	Installs a virtual disk.
DEVICE (VEMM.SYS)	In DOS sessions, provides Expanded Memory Manager.
DEVICE (VXMS.SYS)	In DOS sessions, provides Extended Memory Specification.
DEVICEHIGH	Loads a DOS device driver into upper memory, leaving more low memory available to run programs in DOS sessions.
DEVINFO	Sets the keyboard, printer, and screen for the country you live in.
DISKCACHE	Makes your hard disk seem faster by keeping the data you use most frequently in memory.
DOS	Runs DOS sessions and enables you to control how they use memory.
DPATH	Tells OS/2 programs where to look for data files.
FCBS	Supports File Control Blocks, a method of using files that was common in older DOS programs.
IFS	Installs a file system.

Configuration Commands

IOPL	Enables you to run programs that need to bypass OS/2 and work directly with hardware devices.
LASTDRIVE	Specifies the maximum number of logical drives your system can access in DOS.
LIBPATH	Tells OS/2 programs where to look for Dynamic Link Libraries.
LOADHIGH	Enables you to load DOS memory-resident programs into upper memory.
MAXWAIT	Makes sure that no program thread is put on hold forever, even when the system is very busy running other programs.
MEMMAN	Enables you to run time-critical processes more reliably by turning off virtual memory.
PATH	Tells OS/2 or DOS where to find programs.
PAUSEONERROR	Tells OS/2 to stop for a moment if it cannot process a line in CONFIG.SYS correctly.
PRINTMONBUFSIZE	Enables you to increase the size of the parallel port device-driver buffer.
PRIORITY	Tells OS/2 whether it should juggle the priority of different threads that are running at the same time.
PRIORITY_DISK_IO	Tells OS/2 the input/output priority for applications in the foreground.
PROTECTONLY	Tells OS/2 whether you want to be able to run DOS programs.

PROTSHELL	Loads OS/2's built-in command processor CMD.EXE or enables you to run a different one that you have purchased.
RMSIZE	Sets the amount of memory DOS can use.
SET	Assigns values to variables in the environment.
SHELL	Loads OS/2's built-in DOS command processor COMMAND.COM or enables you to run a different one that you have purchased.
SWAPPATH	Tells OS/2 where to create a swap file, which uses free disk space to let you run more programs than can fit in memory.
THREADS	Sets the number of different things OS/2 can do at a time; the maximum is 4096.
TIMESLICE	Sets upper and lower limits on the amount of time the computer spends on each thread.
VCOM	Enables you to use the communications ports for DOS sessions.
VMOUSE	Enables you to use a mouse or trackball in DOS sessions.

Other Commands

Two groups of commands are not discussed in this chapter. Because entire chapters are devoted to REXX and batch file programming, the following commands are not included here:

CALL ECHO ENDLOCAL EXTPROC FOR GOTO IF PAUSE PMREXX REM SET SETLOCAL SHIFT

The following commands are used only by technical-service people:

CREATEDD   LOG   SYSLOG   TRACE   TRACEBUF   TRACEFMT

ANSI   OS/2 Only

Enables you to run those OS/2 programs that require special support for the screen or keyboard. Most OS/2 programs don't require ANSI support.

Syntax

> **ANSI**

or

> **ANSI ON**
>
> **ANSI OFF**

Examples

To find out whether ANSI support is available:

> **ANSI**

or

> **ANSI ON**

To turn off ANSI support:

> **ANSI OFF**

Notes

This command affects only OS/2 sessions. The special support it provides is available in OS/2 sessions by default. You can turn the command off if you wish because very few programs require it. Similar support is available in DOS sessions only if you load the ANSI.SYS driver in CONFIG.SYS by using a DEVICE statement.

APPEND   DOS Only

Tells DOS programs where to find data files.

Syntax

> **APPEND** *dir1;dir2;...*

dir1 is a directory, such as C:\MEMOS.

dir2 is another directory.

The ellipsis (...) means that you can specify more directories. Use semicolons to separate the directories from each other.

Switches

/E restricts APPEND to DOS

/PATH:ON searches appended paths even if you have specified a path

/PATH:OFF searches appended paths, or all if you have not specified a path (default)

Examples

To tell DOS programs to look for data files in the directories C:\ and D:\DATA:

APPEND C:\;D:\DATA

To find out where the current APPEND statement tells DOS to look for data files:

APPEND

To cancel the APPEND command:

APPEND

Notes

Data files that are in the current directory are always available to a program, even if you do not include the current directory in the APPEND statement. APPEND enables DOS programs to access files in other directories you name, as though they were in the current directory. They will not search other directories if they find the files they need in the current directory.

You normally use APPEND in AUTOEXEC.BAT, although you also can type it in a DOS window. The list of directories you specify with APPEND cannot be more than 128 characters long.

APPEND works only in DOS sessions. The DPATH command works much the same in OS/2 sessions.

ASSIGN DOS Only

Tells DOS to pretend that one disk drive is another.

Syntax

ASSIGN *d1=d2*

d1 is the drive you specify.

d2 is the drive that DOS uses instead.

Do not type a colon after the drive letters.

Examples

To make DOS use drive C when it gets a command for drive A:

ASSIGN A=C

To cancel all previous drive assignments or to show assigned drives:

ASSIGN

Notes

ASSIGN hides the true device type from some commands; the following commands do not work in DOS sessions on drives that have the ASSIGN in effect: CHKDSK, DISKCOMP, DISKCOPY, FORMAT, JOIN, LABEL, PRINT, RECOVER, RESTORE, SUBST.

For the same result as ASSIGN, you can use SUBST.

SUBST A: C:

ATTRIB

Shows or changes a file's read-only and archive attributes.

Syntax

ATTRIB *+A -A -H +R -R +S -S* **file** */S*

file specifies the name of the file for which you want to display or change the attributes.

+A sets the archive flag, which means that the file has not been backed up.

-A turns off the archive flag.

+H hides the file.

-H no longer hides the file.

+R sets the read-only flag, which prevents the file from being changed or deleted.

-R turns off the read-only flag.

+S turns the system file attribute on.

-S turns the system file attribute off.

Switch

/S shows or changes attributes of files in all subdirectories.

Examples

To make sure that your CONFIG.SYS file cannot be accidentally erased or changed:

> **ATTRIB +R CONFIG.SYS**

To turn off the archive flag on a temporary database file so that an incremental backup will skip it, thinking that it has already been backed up:

> **ATTRIB -A MYDATA.DBF**

To find out which files in your \OS2 directory, and all its subdirectories, have not been backed up:

> **ATTRIB \OS2*.* /S**

This command lists every file, placing the letter A next to each one that has not been backed up.

To list every program on a disk, along with its attributes:

> **ATTRIB *.* /S**

Notes

Every file has several attributes—flags that store information about the file. OS/2 reserves most of them for its own use but allows you to change the backup and read-only flags. Avoid turning off the read-only flag on OS2's system files.

When you make an archival copy of a file by using the BACKUP command, the archive flag is turned off. When you make an incremental backup later on, it includes only files whose archive flag is not set.

If you remember a file name but cannot recall its location on a disk, use ATTRIB with the /S switch to find it.

ATTRIB issues a return code of 0 for normal completion.

BACKUP   OS/2 Only

Backs up a hard disk to floppy disks or other media.

Syntax

>   BACKUP d1:dir\files d2: /A /M /S /D:mm-dd-yy /T:hh:mm:ss /L:logfile /F:size

d1: is the hard disk you are backing up, such as C.

dir is the directory that you want to back up. The default is the root directory.

files specifies the files you want to back up. You can omit it if you want to back up all files in a directory.

You must specify at least one of **d1:**, **dir**, or **files**.

d2: is the letter of the floppy disk drive or other media to which you are backing up, such as A.

Switches

/A adds files to an existing backup disk, leaving old backup files intact.

/M backs up only files that you created or changed since your last backup.

/S backs up files in subdirectories of dir.

/D:mm-dd-yy limits BACKUP to files created or changed since a given date.

/T:hh:mm:ss limits BACKUP to files created or changed since a given time. Use this only with the /D switch.

/L:logfile creates a log that lists the name of every file that is backed up. The log file tells which floppy disk contains each file so that you can restore a single file without rummaging through all the floppy disks. The default log file is d1:\BACKUP.LOG.

/F:size formats floppy disks to the size you specify, chosen from the following table. Use this switch only if the floppy disks are not the default size for your drive.

Size	Description	Capacity
360	5 1/4-inch double density	360K
1200	5 1/4-inch high density	1.2M
720	3 1/2-inch double density	720K
1440	3 1/2-inch high density	1.44M
2880	3 1/2-inch ultra density	2.88M

Examples

To back up every file in every subdirectory on hard drive C to floppy disks in drive A, and create a log file:

BACKUP C: A: /S /L

To update a previous complete backup, adding only files that you have created or modified in the meantime:

BACKUP C: A: /A /M /S

To back up every file in C:\MEMOS that you have changed since noon on March 20, 1991:

BACKUP C:\MEMOS A: /D:3-20-91 /T:12:00

Notes

BACKUP may require a large number of floppy disks. You should format them first and discard any that have bad sectors. BACKUP formats them if you do not; it will assume they are the same default size as the drive, unless you specify a different size with the /F switch. Be sure to number the floppy disks as you use them because you will need to use them in the same order when you restore the backup.

The files that BACKUP writes onto floppy disks cannot be read by normal means. Use the RESTORE command to put the files back onto your hard disk.

OS/2's system files cannot be backed up. This safeguard means that if you restore a complete backup made with an earlier version of OS/2, you will not crash the system by writing over these critical files with obsolete versions.

The COUNTRY statement in CONFIG.SYS governs the national date-and-time format that the /D and /T switches use.

The following tables lists the return codes for BACKUP.

Return Code	Meaning
0	Normal completion
1	No files were found to back up.
2	Some files or directories were not processed because of file errors.
3	Ended by user.
4	Ended because of error.
5	Not defined
6	BACKUP was unable to process the FORMAT command.

CD or CHDIR

Shows or changes the current directory of a disk drive.

Syntax

CD *d1:*

CD *d1:dir*

d1: is the disk whose current directory you want to show or change. The default is the current disk.

dir is the directory you want to change to.

Examples

To find out the current drive and directory:

CD

To find out the current directory of drive D:

CD D:

To move to the \OS2\MDOS directory on the current drive:

CD \OS2\MDOS

To move to the same directory as in the last example, if the current directory is C:\OS2:

> **CD MDOS**

To move back to C:\OS2, if the current directory is C:\OS2\MDOS:

> **CD ..**

The double period is convenient shorthand for the parent directory, one level back from the current one.

To move from C:\OS2\MDOS to C:\OS2\INSTALL:

> **CD ..\INSTALL**

Notes

CD and CHDIR are different names for the same command.

When you specify a drive **d1:**, you show or change its current directory, but this does not make **d1:** the current drive. To make **d1:** current, type **d1: <ENTER>**.

CHCP

Switches between national alphabets.

Syntax

> **CHCP** *page*

page is the number of the code page for the alphabet you want to use.

Examples

To find out the number of the current code page:

> **CHCP**

To switch to the multilingual code page, assuming you loaded it in CODEPAGE and DEVINFO statements in your CONFIG.SYS file:

> **CHCP 850**

Notes

OS/2 stores many different national alphabets in code pages. You can load up to two pages through the CODEPAGE statement in CONFIG.SYS; only one national alphabet is active at a time. CHCP, Change Code Page, enables you to choose either one. You can find the number for each alphabet in the On-Line Command Reference, under the COUNTRY command.

If you work with people in other countries, they will have an easier time reading your files if you use the multinational alphabet, codepage 850. It includes most of the accented letters used in European languages. Stick to the letters A-Z and numerals 0-9 for file and directory names to prevent file access problems.

CHDIR
See CD.

CHKDSK
Analyzes a disk and gives you a report. This command also fixes disk problems. If OS/2 is open, CHKDSK conflicts with open files and cannot fix the boot drive.

Syntax
CHKDSK *d1:files /F /V*

d1: is the disk you want to analyze. The default is the current drive.

files specifies the files you want to analyze. CHKDSK checks whether each named file is stored all in one piece. The default CHKDSK checks all files but does not produce a report. Use *.* to get the report when checking all files.

Switches
The */C* and */F:n* parameters are only operable with the High Performance File System.

/C tells CHKDSK which files will be recovered if the file system was in an inconsistent state when the computer was started.

/F tells CHKDSK to fix any problems it finds.

/F:0 tells CHKDSK to analyze and display information about the disk but prevents the program from performing repairs.

/F:1 tells CHKDSK to resolve inconsistent file system structures.

/F:2 is the same as /F:1, plus checks the disk space not allocated by the file system and recovers file and directory structures when found. This is the default if you specify no recovery level.

/F:3 is the same as /F:2 plus scans the entire partition.

/V displays the name and path of each file as it is checked.

Examples

To analyze your drive C:

    CHKDSK C:

To analyze C and report any fragmented files:

    CHKDSK C:*.*

To analyze C and repair any problems found:

    CHKDSK C: /F

Notes

The files and directories on your hard disk can get scrambled if the power goes off while you are using your computer or if you turn it off without ending all applications first. Run CHKDSK from time to time to check for problems. You cannot use CHKDSK on a network drive.

CHKDSK reports useful statistics such as the number of files on a disk and the amount of free space. In DOS mode, CHKDSK also gives a summary of memory usage. If CHKDSK reports bad sectors, the sectors were marked as unusable when you formatted the disk so that they cannot be used to store files. The sectors are physically defective and cannot be repaired.

Ideally, a file's contents should all be kept together in one place. Over a period of time, however, the disk space becomes fragmented, and some files are spread over separate blocks. CHKDSK *.* tells you which files are fragmented. OS/2 can still work with them, but it will work more slowly.

CHKDSK may tell you it has found chains of lost clusters. These chains may be pieces of files that were improperly saved, for example, because of a bug in the program that created them. They also can be files that a background program was writing when you ran CHKDSK. You can rule out that possibility by running CHKDSK all alone with no background sessions.

If the problem persists, run CHKDSK with the /F switch and answer Yes when it asks your permission to fix the problem. CHKDSK collects every piece of stray data that looks like it belongs to a file and puts each piece in a separate file in the root directory. This comand creates distinctive file names; in FAT,

CHKDSK uses names like FILE0000.CHK and FILE0001.CHK; and in HPFS, names like FOUND.*xxx* (where *xxx* is the number of the file).

If you run CHKDSK with the /F switch and answer N (no), CHKDSK deletes these file parts without warning.

The following table lists the return codes for CHKDSK.

Return Codes	Meaning
0	Normal completion.
1	Not defined.
2	Not defined.
3	Ended by user.
4	Ended due to error.
5	Not defined.
6	CHKDSK was unable to execute file system's CHKDSK program.

CLS

Clears the screen.

Syntax

> **CLS**

Notes

OS/2 clears the screen and displays the prompt.

CMD   OS/2 Only

Starts a new copy of the OS/2 command processor, CMD.EXE.

Syntax

> **CMD** */C/K/Q/S command-line*

command-line is a program you want the command processor to run—an OS/2 command or a program with either a CMD or EXE extension, plus any optional parameters.

Switches

/C terminates the new copy of CMD.EXE after it executes the command line.

/K keeps the new copy of CMD.EXE active after it executes the command line.

/Q prevents commands from echoing to the screen.

/S prevents installation of a signal handler (such as Ctrl-C).

Example

To start a new copy of the OS/2 command processor, use CMD to run the CHKDSK program:

CMD /C CHKDSK

Notes

Terminate the additional copy of CMD.EXE with the EXIT command.

COMMAND   DOS Only

Starts a new copy of the DOS command processor, COMMAND.COM.

Syntax

COMMAND /C /E:size /K /P command-line

command-line is the program you want the command processor to run—a DOS command or a program with either a BAT, COM, or EXE extension, plus any optional parameters. If you specify a command-line, you must also use the /C switch.

Switches

/C passes **command-line** to COMMAND.COM. The new DOS command processor terminates after executing the command.

/E:size sets the size of the DOS environment in bytes. The default is 160 bytes, but you can set *size* to any higher value up to 32,768. The size is rounded up to the next multiple of 16.

/K does not return to calling command processor.

/P makes the new copy of COMMAND.COM permanent so that you cannot terminate it with the EXIT command. Use this switch only in the SHELL statement in your CONFIG.SYS file.

Examples

To start a new copy of the DOS command processor, use COMMAND to run the CHKDSK program:

COMMAND /C CHKDSK

To start a copy of the DOS command processor, with an 800-byte environment, from a DOS or OS/2 window:

COMMAND /E:800

Use the EXIT command to close this new DOS session.

Notes

You can use COMMAND /C inside a DOS batch file to run another batch file, but the DOS batch command CALL uses less memory to accomplish the same task.

COMP

Compares files.

Syntax

COMP file1 file2

file1 and **file2** specify the two files, or sets of files, you want to compare.

Examples

To determine whether CONFIG.SYS and CONFIG.OLD are identical:

COMP CONFIG.SYS CONFIG.OLD

To determine whether C:\MYFILE and A:\MYFILE are identical:

COMP C:\MYFILE A:

To determine whether all the files on A exactly match files of the same names on C:

COMP A: C:

Notes

COMP reads the contents of two files and tells you whether they are identical. If they are not identical, COMP reports the first 10 characters that do not match. This report uses a hexadecimal format. After 10 mismatches, COMP stops comparing.

Two files can be identical only if they are the same size. If they are not, COMP tells you if they are not the same size and gives you the option to proceed anyway, up to the length of the shorter file.

If you do not specify either of the files to compare, COMP prompts you for their names.

COPY (Combining Files)

Combines files together.

Syntax

COPY file1+file2... *target*

file1 and **file2** are the first two files you want to combine.

The ellipsis (...) means that you can specify more files. Use plus signs to separate them from each other.

target is the name of the file that combines the contents of all source files.

Examples

To combine the contents of FILE1, FILE2, and FILE3 into a file called COMBINED:

COPY FILE1+FILE2+FILE3 COMBINED

To append the contents of FILE2 and FILE3 to FILE1:

COPY FILE1+FILE2+FILE3

Notes

If you do not specify *target*, the contents of all the files are combined into **file1**.

COPY (Duplicating Files)

Copies files between disks or directories, optionally changing each file's name.

Syntax

COPY files /A /B **target** /A /B /V /F

files specifies the files you want to duplicate.

target is the name or location of the duplicates you create.

Switches

When used with a source filename:

/A treats file as ASCII. Data is copied to the first end-of-file character in the file.

/B treats file as binary and copies the entire file.

When used with the target file(s):

/A adds an end-of-file character as the last character.

/B does not add end-of-file character.

/V verifies that target file(s) were written correctly.

/F aborts the copy operation if the source files contain extended attributes and the destination file system does not support them.

Examples

To make a duplicate of MYFILE.TXT and name it MYCOPY.TXT:

    COPY MYFILE.TXT MYCOPY.TXT

To put a duplicate of MYFILE.TXT with the same name in the \DOCUMENT directory:

    COPY MYFILE.TXT \DOCUMENT

To copy all files with the extension TXT from the current directory to \DOCUMENT and change each file's extension to DOC:

    COPY *.TXT \DOCUMENT*.DOC

To copy every file in \MEMOS to a floppy disk in drive A:

    COPY \MEMOS*.* A:

To copy MYFILE.TXT to the printer:

    COPY MYFILE.TXT PRN

Notes

If you want to copy files to a different directory, first make sure that the directory exists. If a file that you tell COPY to create already exists, the old file is deleted first.

This command does not copy a file that is zero bytes long; you must use the XCOPY command.

DATE

Displays or sets the date.

Syntax

DATE *mm-dd-yy*

mm is the month (1-12).

dd is the day (1-31).

yy is the year (0-99, or 1900-1999).

Examples

To set the date to November 15, 1991:

DATE 11-15-91

To display and change (optional) the current date:

DATE

Notes

The computer remembers the date you set after you turn the power off. The COUNTRY command in CONFIG.SYS governs the way you format the date.

DDINSTALL   OS/2 Only

Enables you to install new device drivers after OS/2 has been installed.

Syntax

DDINSTALL

Enter the command (without a parameter) to begin the procedure to install device-driver files.

Example

    DDINSTALL

You are prompted to insert the Device Support diskette into drive A. After files are copied, you are prompted to insert the Installation diskette and restart the system. DDINSTALL automatically continues the installation procedure. When DDINSTALL is finished, press Ctrl+Alt+Del to restart the system.

Notes

The DDINSTALL program automatically adds necessary statements to the CONFIG.SYS and copies all necessary files to the appropriate directory on the hard disk.

DEL or ERASE

Erases files.

Syntax

    DEL files /P /N

files specifies the files you want to erase.

Switches

/P asks your permission before deleting each file.

/N suppresses the "Are you sure (Y/N)?" message displayed when OS/2 is deleting all files in a directory.

Examples

To erase the file PAYROLL.WK1 in the current directory:

    DEL PAYROLL.WK1

To erase every file with the extension DOC in the \WORDPROC directory:

    DEL \WORDPROC*.DOC

To modify the preceding example so that DEL displays each file name and asks your permission before erasing it:

    DEL \WORDPROC*.DOC /P

Notes

DEL does not erase the OS/2 system files or any files that you have protected by setting their read-only attribute with the ATTRIB command. DEL also does not erase directories; use the RD command to do that.

Using DEL with wild cards can be dangerous. If you use DEL to erase every file in a directory, OS/2 asks you to confirm the command first. If you want to see which files are to be deleted before OS/2 deletes them, use DIR, not DEL, with the same wild cards. If you accidentally delete files, use UNDELETE to recover them before you do anything else.

DETACH   OS/2 Only

Runs a program in the background while the command processor runs in the foreground.

Syntax

> **DETACH command-line**

command-line is the command you want to run in the background—an OS/2 command or a program with either a CMD or EXE extension, plus any optional parameters.

Example

To format a single floppy disk in the background:

> **DETACH FORMAT A: /ONCE**

Notes

The command must not require any input from the keyboard or mouse. You will not see anything the command tries to write to the screen. Because the command runs in the background, you can type another command without waiting for the first one to finish.

DIR

Lists the files in a directory.

Syntax

> **DIR** /F /N /P /W /A /B /O:sort-order /R /S /L *files*

files specifies the directory or files you want to list.

Switches

/F lists files with full drive and path information, omitting date, time, and size.

/N lists files on a FAT drive in the format used for an HPFS drive.

/P lists files one screen at a time.

/W omits date, time, and size information, and lists five file names across the screen so that you can see more file names.

/A lists only files with specified attributes (-H, H, S, -S, D, -D, A, -A, R, -R).

/B lists directories and files without heading and summary information.

/O: sort-order lists a directory in sort order. The following table lists the sort-order options.

Sort-Order Options	Type of Order
N	Alphabetic
E	Alpha by Extension
D	Date and Time oldest first
S	Size smallest first
G	Directories shown first

To reverse the order of a switch, place a minus sign in front of the switch.

/S searches all directories.

/R displays long file names in file systems that do not support them; in FAT, the /R switch shows FAT file names and the long file name to the right of the directory listing.

/L lists all file and directory menus in lowercase.

Examples

To list all files in the current directory of the current drive, showing each file's name, size in bytes, and date and time last modified:

DIR

To see the size, date, and time of \SALES\REGION1.WK1:

DIR \SALES\REGION1.WK1

To list only the names of all files with the extension SYS in the \OS2 directory across the screen and one screen at a time:

DIR /P /W \OS2*.SYS

Notes

DIR displays the volume label, directory name, number of files, and amount of space available on the drive, unless you use the /F switch. The /F and /W switches do not work together.

You can send the directory listing to your printer by typing:

DIR >PRN

DISKCOMP

Determines whether one floppy disk is an exact copy of another.

Syntax

DISKCOMP d1: d2:

d1: and **d2:** are the drives that hold the floppy disk to be compared. The command copies from d1: to d2:. The drives can be the same.

Examples

To compare a floppy disk in drive A to one in drive B:

DISKCOMP A: B:

To compare floppy disks by using only one drive:

DISKCOMP A: A:

Notes

DISKCOMP verifies the result of the DISKCOPY command. The command reports that two floppy disks are the same only if one is an exact clone of the other, with identical files in identical disk sectors. DISKCOMP ignores floppy disk serial numbers, however, because those numbers are always supposed to be different. To compare floppy disks that were not copied with DISKCOPY, use the COMP command.

DISKCOMP will not compare two floppy disks of different sizes. You cannot use the command to compare hard disks, even if they are the same size.

High capacity floppy disks can be compared in several passes if your computer does not have enough memory available to hold their contents all at once. If you are using a single drive, DISKCOMP prompts you to swap the floppy disk when necessary.

DISKCOMP issues a return code of 0 for normal completion or displays an error message if there was a problem.

DISKCOPY

Duplicates a floppy disk.

Syntax

DISKCOPY d1: d2:

d1: is the drive that holds the floppy disk from which to be copied.

d2: is the drive that holds the floppy disk to which to be copied. *d2* can be the same as d1:.

Examples

To copy a floppy disk in drive A to a disk in drive B:

DISKCOPY A: B:

To copy a floppy disk using only one drive:

DISKCOPY A: A:

Notes

DISKCOPY makes an exact duplicate of a floppy disk. If you have not formatted the floppy disk to which you are copying, DISKCOPY formats the floppy disk to which you are copying. If DISKCOPY finds defects while it is formatting, it reports the problem but continues copying anyway. To verify that the copy is accurate, use the DISKCOMP command.

Because DISKCOPY makes an exact clone, it will not copy between two floppy disks of different sizes. You cannot use it to copy hard disks, even if they are the same size.

High capacity floppy disks are duplicated in several passes, because your computer may not have enough memory available to hold their contents all at once. If you are using a single drive, DISKCOPY prompts you to swap the floppy disk when necessary.

Use DISKCOPY if you want to make a backup copy of your original OS/2 floppy disk.

DISKCOPY issues a return code of 0 for normal completion or displays an error message if there was a problem.

DOSKEY   DOS Only

Controls command recall and editing and creates macros.

Syntax

*dc:pathc***DOSKEY** */REINSTALL /BUFSIZE=N /M /H /OVERSTRIKE/INSERT macroname=macrotext*

dc:pathc refers to the disk drive and directory that hold DOSKEY.

macroname is the name of the macro to create.

macrotext is the command(s) contained by the macro name *macroname*.

Switches

/REINSTALL installs DOSKEY and clears the buffer.

/BUFSIZE=N specifies size of buffer in bytes.

/M lists all DOSKEY macro commands.

/H lists commands stored in memory.

/OVERSTRIKE turns Overstrike on.

/INSERT turns Insert on.

Examples

To experiment with command recall, first type:

DOSKEY

Next, list the contents of C:\OS2\MDOS:

DIR C:\OS2\MDOS

Then press up arrow once. You see the command again. Edit it by pressing Backspace three times:

DIR C:

Now press Enter to execute the modified command, which now lists files in the root directory.

Notes

After you have run DOSKEY (by typing DOSKEY and pressing Enter) you can press the up- and down-arrow keys to scroll through commands you have previously typed. You can edit a recalled command and then execute it by pressing Enter. You can use the previously mentioned switches and activate the DOSKEY at the same time to complete an action.

DOSKEY works only in DOS sessions, but you can get the same effect in OS/2 sessions by using the KEYS command.

ERASE
See DEL.

EXIT
Terminates the current command processor.

Syntax
> EXIT

Notes

If you loaded the current command processor from another one, you return to the program you shelled out of; otherwise, you return to Presentation Manager.

FDISK   OS/2 Only
Manages hard disk partitions.

Syntax
> FDISK

Notes

This command sets up partitions on your hard disk. Be careful when you use it because any changes you make to existing partitions will wipe out all your data.

Before you can use a hard disk, you must partition it. Each partition looks like a separate drive. If you have one physical hard disk divided into two partitions, for example, your system probably shows two hard drives—C and D.

FDISKPM is a Presentation Manager version of FDISK. Except for the appearance of the interface, the two programs are identical. The on-line menus give complete instructions. See more on this utility in Chapter 20, "Using OS/2 Utilities."

FIND

Searches for text in files.

Syntax

>   **FIND** /C /N /V /I **"text" file1** *file2*...

text is the string of characters you want to search for.

file1 is a file you want to search for text.

file2 is another file you want to search.

The ellipsis (...) means that you can specify more files to search. Separate the files from each other by using blank spaces. Alternatively, you can use wild cards (*.*) in your search.

Switches

/C tells you how many lines contain **text**, but does not display them.

/N displays each line that contains **text**, along with its line number.

/V displays all lines that do not contain **text**.

/I ignores uppercase or lowercase.

Examples

To show every line in CONFIG.SYS that contains the word "DEVICE":

>   **FIND "DEVICE" CONFIG.SYS**

To show every line in CONFIG.SYS that contains the word "DEVICE" along with the number of each line:

>   **FIND /N "DEVICE" CONFIG.SYS**

To count how many lines in CONFIG.SYS contain the word "DEVICE" without showing each line:

FIND /C "DEVICE" CONFIG.SYS

To show all lines in the files \BOOK\CHAPTER1.TXT and \BOOK\CHAPTER2.TXT that do not contain the lowercase letter e:

FIND /V "e" \BOOK\CHAPTER1.TXT \BOOK\CHAPTER2.TXT

Notes

The text for which you are searching must be surrounded by double quotation marks. FIND detects only exact matches unless your use /I. Uppercase and lowercase are different ("This" and "this" do not match). You cannot find a phrase that is split between two lines.

You have to list the full name of each file you want to search. Wild cards do not work with FIND.

You can combine the /V switch with either the /C or /N switch, but you cannot use /C and /N together.

FIND issues a return code of 0 for normal completion.

FORMAT

Prepares a disk for use and reports any defects.

Syntax

FORMAT d1: /ONCE /FS:file-system /L /V:label /F:size /4

d1: is the disk you want to format, such as A.

Switches

/ONCE formats a single floppy disk. If you format a floppy disk without this switch, FORMAT assumes that you will want to format another when you are finished. You can always just answer No when the command asks you to insert another.

/FS:file-system tells what file system you want to use. /FS:HPFS means the High Performance File System. The default, /FS:FAT, means the DOS-compatible File Allocation Table format.

/L formats an IBM read-write optical disk.

/V:label specifies a volume label. If you do not use the /V switch, FORMAT asks you to type a label anyway.

/F:size reports the capacity of the floppy disk you are formatting. If the capacity is the default for your drive, you do not need this switch; otherwise, you must specify a value from the following table.

Size	Description	Capacity
360	5 1/4-inch double density	360K
1200	5 1/4-inch high density	1.2M
720	3 1/2-inch double density	720K
1440	3 1/2-inch high density	1.44M
2880	3 1/2-inch ultra density	2.88M

/4 means the same thing as /F:360—that you want to format a double density, 360K 5 1/2-inch floppy disk in a 1.2M drive. Floppy disks formatted this way will not work reliably in lower-capacity drives.

Examples

To format a 1.44M floppy disk in a 1.44M drive A:

> **FORMAT A:**

To format just one 720K floppy disk in a 1.44M drive A:

> **FORMAT A: /F:720 /ONCE**

To format a 360K floppy disk in a 1.2M drive B:

> **FORMAT B: /4**

or

> **FORMAT B: /F:360**

To format hard drive D for the High Performance File System and give it the label HPFSDRIVE:

> **FORMAT D: /FS:HPFS /V:HPFSDRIVE**

Notes

FORMAT installs a file system on a disk and checks the surface for physical defects. If FORMAT finds defects, it locks the unusable sectors so that OS/2 will not place your data in them. You cannot use a disk until you have formatted it. If you reformat a disk that you have used before, all the data it holds is wiped out. You must partition a hard disk with FDISK before you can format it. You cannot format a network drive.

Most computers that can run OS/2 2.0 have high-capacity floppy disk drives. For best results, use high-density floppy disks in these drives. Never format a floppy disk to a higher capacity than it was designed for. Even if it appears to work fine today, it may fail six months down the road, or prove to be unreadable on someone else's computer.

If you format a 360K floppy disk in a 1.2M drive, you should use the disk only in 1.2M drives; it will not work reliably in a 360K drive. But 720K floppy disks formatted in a 1.44M drive with /F:720 work reliably in either 1.44M or 720K drives.

GRAFTABL   DOS Only

Enables DOS programs to display line-drawing and national language characters on a CGA monitor in graphics mode.

Syntax

    GRAFTABL ? */STA nnn*

nnn is the national language code page you want to use.

? lists the number of graphics code pages in use and lists code page options.

Switch

/STA lists the number of code pages in use.

Examples

To let DOS programs display line-drawing characters in graphics mode, according to the US code page:

    GRAFTABL 437

To see what other code pages you can specify with this command:

GRAFTABL ?

Notes

Use this command only if you have a CGA monitor.

HELP

Explains how to use a command or what an error message means.

Syntax

HELP ON

HELP OFF

HELP *command-name*

HELP *message-number*

command-name is the name of a DOS or OS/2 command.

message-number is the number of an error message.

Examples

To see which keys you can press to switch between tasks and how to use HELP:

HELP

To tell OS/2 or DOS to display at the top of the screen the keys you press to switch tasks:

HELP ON

To tell OS/2 or DOS not to show this information:

HELP OFF

To find out how to use the COPY command:

HELP COPY

To see an explanation of the OS/2 error message SYS0002:

HELP 2

Notes

Help on a command or an error message is available only for OS/2—not for DOS.

When you ask for help on an OS/2 error message, you do not have to type the letters SYS or the leading zeroes.

JOIN   DOS Only

Tells DOS to pretend that a disk drive is a directory of another drive.

Syntax

>   **JOIN d1: d2:***dir*

>   **JOIN d1:** */D*

d1: is the drive you specify.

d2:*dir* is the drive and directory that DOS uses instead. The drives d1: and d2: must be different.

Switch

/D cancels any previous JOIN command for d1:.

Examples

To show all current JOINs:

>   **JOIN**

To tell DOS to treat drive A as the subdirectory \DATA on drive C:

>   **JOIN A: C:\DATA**

To cancel the effect of the above JOIN command:

>   **JOIN A: /D**

Notes

If the directory already exists, it must be empty. If it does not exist, it is created. It must be a subdirectory of the root directory—not of any other directory.

You may need JOIN to make old programs that run from a floppy drive run from a hard drive. Otherwise, avoid using this command. JOIN is dangerous to use with many commands, such as CHKDSK, DISKCOMP, DISKCOPY, FORMAT, LABEL, and RECOVER.

KEYB   OS/2 Only

Tells the keyboard which national alphabet you want to use.

Syntax

KEYB nation *alternate*

nation is the country whose alphabet you want to use.

alternate is a number that selects an optional "enhanced" keyboard layout. It is available only if **nation** is Czechoslovakia, France, Italy, or the United Kingdom.

Examples

To switch to the Hungarian keyboard:

KEYB HU

To use the "alternate" Czechoslovakian keyboard:

KEYB CS 245

Notes

Run this command only in a full-screen OS/2 session. It affects DOS full-screen sessions and all OS/2 sessions—windowed and full screen.

KEYB enables you to switch quickly to another national alphabet. It works only if you have a DEVINFO statement in CONFIG.SYS. To change the default keyboard layout permanently, modify the DEVINFO statement. The number for each alphabet is in the on-line command reference, under the COUNTRY command.

KEYS   OS/2 Only

Controls command recall and editing.

Syntax

KEYS ON

KEYS OFF

KEYS LIST

Examples

To turn off command recall:

> **KEYS OFF**

To turn command recall on:

> **KEYS ON**

To find out whether command recall is on:

> **KEYS**

To see which commands are available for recall:

> **KEYS LIST**

To experiment with command recall, first list the contents of C:\OS2:

> **DIR C:\OS2**

Now press the up-arrow key once. You see the command again. Edit it by pressing Backspace three times:

> **DIR C:**

Now press Enter to execute the modified command, which lists files in the root directory.

Notes

When KEYS is ON, you can scroll through commands you have previously typed by pressing the up- and down-arrow keys. You can edit a recalled command and then execute it by pressing Enter.

DOSKEY works only in DOS sessions, but you can get the same effect in OS/2 sessions by using the KEYS command.

LABEL

Gives a name to a disk.

Syntax

> **LABEL** *d1:name*

d1: is the disk whose label you want to see or change, such as C. The default is the current drive.

name is what you want to call the disk—any combination of up to 11 letters and numerals.

Examples

To display and change (optional) the current drive's label:

LABEL

To display and change (optional) the label of drive D:

LABEL D:

To set the label of drive C to HARDDISK:

LABEL C:HARDDISK

Notes

If you run the FORMAT command on a hard disk that has a label, it prompts you for the label and will not continue if you do not type it. This command provides extra protection against formatting the hard disk by accident, which destroys your data. You should always LABEL your hard disk.

MD or MKDIR

Creates a directory.

Syntax

MD *d1:path***dir**

d1: is the disk where you want to create the new directory. The default is the current disk.

path is the parent of the new directory. The default is the current directory.

dir is the name of the new directory you want to create.

Examples

To make a directory \WORDPROC in the root directory:

MD \WORDPROC

To make a directory \MEMOS as a subdirectory of an existing directory \WORDPROC on drive D:

MD D:\WORDPROC\MEMOS

To make a directory \STUFF as a subdirectory of the current directory:

> **MD STUFF**

Notes

You cannot create a directory with the same name as a file that already exists in the same location.

MEM   DOS Only

Displays the amount of memory DOS can use and the amount of memory already in use.

Syntax

> **MEM**

Notes

This command tells how much conventional, expanded (EMS), and extended (XMS) memory is available for DOS programs. Chapter 16, "Running DOS and Windows Under OS/2," explains how to use these different kinds of memory.

MODE (Communications)

Controls the communications port.

Syntax

> **MODE COMx:rate,parity,databits,stopbits,P**

COMx is a communications port, such as COM1 or COM2.

rate is bits per second. The default is 1200. You do not have to type the last two zeroes of rate; 12 is the same as 1200, for example.

parity is a single character that tells how to verify that data is sent correctly. Use N for none, O for odd, E for even, M for mark, or S for space parity. E is the default.

databits is the number of bits used to represent one character. It can be 5, 6, 7, or 8. The default is 7.

stopbits is the number of bits added to mark the end of each character. It can be 1, 1.5, or 2. The default is generally 1.

P tells DOS to wait up to 30 seconds for the port to respond. *P* is available in DOS sessions only.

Examples

To see the current settings for the second communications port:

> **MODE COM2**

To set up the first communications port for 2400 bits per second, even parity, seven databits, and one stopbit:

> **MODE COM1:2400,E,7,1**

Notes

You must load support for communications ports by including COM.SYS in your CONFIG.SYS file before you use MODE to configure the ports.

You can leave out any item you do not want to change, but you must include the comma that would have followed that item unless it is the last one that you do want to change. To change to eight databits while leaving all previous settings alone, for example:

> **MODE COM1:,,8**

The *P* option, available only in a DOS session, tells the system to wait up to 30 seconds for the port to respond. This option is useful if you have a serial printer that may be busy.

MODE (Display) — OS/2 Only

Controls the screen mode.

Syntax

> **MODE** *CONx* **mode,lines**

CONx tells which monitor to control. If your computer has two monitors, the first is CON1 and the second is CON2. You do not need to use this parameter if you have only one monitor.

mode tells what kind of monitor you have.

lines is the number of lines to display on-screen. Choose 25, 43, or 50. The default is 25.

Examples

To show 50 lines on-screen on a monochrome monitor:

MODE MONO,50

To show 43 lines on your second monochrome monitor:

MODE CON2 MONO,43

Notes

This command works only for full-screen OS/2 sessions.

MODE (LPT#) OS/2 Only

Controls a parallel printer.

Syntax

MODE LPTx *char,lines,P*

LPTx tells which printer to set up. It can be LPT1, LPT2, or LPT3. You can use PRN as another name for LPT1.

char tells how many characters can be printed on one line. The number of characters can be 80 or 132.

lines tells how many lines to print per inch. The number of lines can be 8 or 6.

P tells OS/2 to keep trying to send each line until the printer responds. If you do not specify *P* and the printer is busy, OS/2 displays an error message.

Examples

To tell the first parallel printer to put 132 characters on a line and print 8 lines per inch:

MODE LPT1 132,8,,

You can leave out any item you do not want to change, but you must include the comma that would have followed that item unless it is the last one you do want to change. To tell the third parallel printer to keep trying to send each line until the printer responds without changing the width or spacing, for example:

MODE LPT3 ,,P

Notes

This command works only on parallel printers.

MORE

Displays a file one screen at a time.

Syntax

>   **MORE< file**

command file ¦ MORE

file is the file you want to view.

Example

To see \CONFIG.SYS one screen at a time:

>   **MORE< \CONFIG.SYS**

To get the same results by using the command and the pipe (split vertical bar):

>   **TYPE CONFIG.SYS ¦ MORE**

Notes

Think of the less-than sign as part of the command's name. You need to include it because MORE is a special type of program known as a *filter*. Filters is an advanced topic that this book does not cover.

MORE displays the file's contents one screen at a time. Press Enter when you want to go on to the next screen. If you do not want to see the rest of the file, press Ctrl-C.

MOVE   OS/2 Only

Moves files from one directory to another on the same drive.

Syntax

>   **MOVE files target**

files specifies the files you want move.

target is the new location for the files.

Examples

To remove all files with the extension DOC from the root directory and put them in \DOCUMENT:

    MOVE *.DOC \DOCUMENT

To modify the last example so that the extension of each file is changed to TXT:

    MOVE *.DOC \DOCUMENT*.TXT

To transfer OLDFILE.A from the current directory to \DATA, rename it as NEWFILE.B, and delete the original:

    MOVE OLDFILE.A \DATA\NEWFILE.B

To remove the \DOCUMENT directory (and any subdirectories and files it contains) and re-create it as a subdirectory of an existing directory \WORDPROC:

    MOVE \DOCUMENT \WORDPROC

To rename the \DOCUMENT directory as \DOC, assuming no \DOC directory already exists:

    MOVE \DOCUMENT \DOC

Notes

MOVE combines the functions of the COPY, RENAME, RD, MD, and DEL commands. MOVE enables you to prune a branch of the directory tree and to graft it onto another branch.

PRINT

Prints files.

Syntax

    PRINT *file1 file2... /D:LPTx*

    PRINT */C*

    PRINT */T*

    PRINT */B*

file1 and *file2* are files you want to print.

The ellipsis (...) means that you can specify more files to print. Separate them from each other by using blank spaces. You also can use wild cards.

Switches

/D:LPTx tells which printer to use. The first three printers are LPT1, LPT2, and LPT3; network printers can have higher numbers. The default is LPT1.

/C cancels whichever file is currently printing. Any other files you have sent to the printer still are printed.

/T cancels all files you have sent to the printer.

/B ignores <CTRL-Z> characters and does not interpret them as end-of-file markers so that the entire file prints.

Examples

To send the file \MAIL\LETTER1.TXT to the second printer:

PRINT \MAIL\LETTER1.TXT /D:LPT2

To print the files LETTER1.TXT and LETTER2.TXT in your \MAIL directory:

PRINT \MAIL\LETTER1.TXT \MAIL\LETTER2.TXT

To print all TXT files in the \MAIL directory whose names begin with LETTER:

PRINT \MAIL\LETTER*.TXT

Notes

PRINT works only with plain text files. If you PRINT a word processing document, you probably will not get what you want because most word processors use special formats. If you tell your word processor to save a file as plain text, however, you can PRINT the document.

You cannot use the /C or /T switch with a file name.

PROMPT

Sets the string of characters that is displayed at the command line.

Syntax

PROMPT *string*

string is a series of characters to display. You can use most characters that you can type from the keyboard and any of the following special codes:

Code	Meaning
$$	$
$_	New line
$a	&
$b		
$c	(
$d	Current date
$e	"Escape" character
$f	)
$g	>
$h	Backspace symbol
$i	Help information
$l	<
$n	Current drive
$p	Current drive and directory
$q	=
$r	Return code of last executed program
$s	Space
$t	Current time
$v	Version of the operating system

Examples

To set the prompt to show the current date and time on one line and the current drive and directory on the next:

PROMPT Date=date Time=time$_$p>

To restore the default prompt:

PROMPT

Notes

The default prompt in an OS/2 session is the DOS default prompt (current drive and directory); in a DOS session, $p>. The system stores the prompt as a string of characters in the environment. You can display it with the SET command.

RD or RMDIR

Removes a directory.

Syntax

RD *d1:path***dir**

d1: is the disk from which you want to remove a directory. The default is the current disk.

path is the parent of the directory to remove. The default is the current directory.

dir is the name of the directory you want to remove.

Examples

To remove the directory \WORDPROC\LETTERS from drive D:

RD D:\WORDPROC\LETTERS

To remove the directory \WORDPROC\LETTERS, if \WORDPROC is the current directory:

RD LETTERS

Notes

You can remove only an empty directory (a directory that contains no files and no subdirectories). You cannot remove the current directory or the root directory. If a directory appears empty but it will not allow you to remove it, use ATTRIB to check for Hidden files.

RECOVER

Partially salvages files from a disk with bad sectors.

Syntax

RECOVER *files*

files tells which files you want to salvage. You cannot use wild cards.

Examples

To salvage A:\MYFILE.TXT, placing whatever can be saved in the root directory with a name like FILE0000.REC, and then to delete the original file:

RECOVER A:\MYFILE.TXT

To wipe out the entire directory structure of a floppy disk in drive A:

RECOVER A:

Notes

As you probably gathered from the second example, RECOVER is a dangerous command. It attempts to read all the data in a file and puts it into a new file in the root directory with a name like FILE0000.REC, FILE0001.REC, and so on. If RECOVER cannot read the data in a particular sector, it substitutes zeroes. Then it deletes the original file. If the file is a program, it probably will not work because part of the code was replaced by zeroes.

Use RECOVER as a last resort and only on files that you know are unreadable. If you just specify a disk or directory, all the files it contains will be recovered, so always specify a file. The root directory can hold only a limited number of files, and if you try to RECOVER too many files at once, some may be lost. If you RECOVER a good file, it moves the file to the root directory and gives it an unrecognizable name. For safety, RECOVER does not work on a network drive.

REN or RENAME

Changes a file name.

Syntax

REN oldname newname

oldname is the original file name.

newname is the name you want to give the file.

Examples

To change the name of a file in the \PLANS directory on drive C from NEWPLAN.DOC to OLDPLAN.DOC:

REN C:\PLANS\NEWPLAN.DOC OLDPLAN.DOC

To change the name of JULIET1.DAT, JULIET2.DAT, and so on, to ROMEO1.TXT, ROMEO2.TXT, and so on:

REN JULIET*.DAT ROMEO*.TXT

Notes

You can specify a drive and path only for **oldname**. REN uses the same drive and path for **newname**, and it will not work if a file called **newname** already exists there. REM cannot change a subdirectory's name.

REPLACE

Selectively replaces files.

Syntax

REPLACE files target /A /F /P /R /S /U /W

files specifies the files you want to copy.

target tells the location to which you want to copy the files. The default is the current drive and path.

Switches

/A restricts the command to files that do not exist on target.

/F makes the command fail if you try to copy a file with OS/2 extended attributes to a drive that does not support them.

/P asks your permission before adding or replacing each file.

/R enables REPLACE to write over read-only files.

/S replaces files in all subdirectories of target.

/U replaces files only with newer versions.

/W waits for you to insert a floppy disk. Use this when you'll need to swap floppy disks.

Examples

To copy all files from C that do not already exist on A:

REPLACE A:*.* C: /A

To replace files in every directory of drive C with files of the same name from drive A:

REPLACE A:*.* C: /S

To replace every file on drive C named FINAL.TXT with the one in your \ULTIMATE directory:

REPLACE C:\ULTIMATE\FINAL.TXT C: /S

Notes

You cannot use the /A switch with the /S or /U switch. You cannot REPLACE OS/2's critical system files or any hidden files.

RESTORE   OS/2 Only

Retrieves files from a backup.

Syntax

RESTORE d1: d2:files */F /D /S /N /M /P /A:yy-mm-dd /L:hh:mm:ss /B:yy-mm-dd /E:hh:mm:ss*

d1: is the drive that holds the backup floppy disk you want to restore.

d2: is the hard drive to which you want to restore the backed up files.

files specifies the directory and files you want to restore. To do a complete restore, omit *files* and use the /S switch.

Switches

/F causes RESTORE to fail if the file contains extended attributes and the destination file system cannot support them.

/D lists the files on the backup that also exist of the target but does not restore them.

/S restores files in all subdirectories. If you do not use the /S switch, only files in the directory you specify will be restored.

/N restores only files that do not exist on the hard drive, for instance because you deleted them since making the backup.

/M ignores files that you have not modified since you made the backup. Only files that you have deleted or changed since then are restored. Use the /M switch if you have made accidental changes to your files, and want to put them back the way they were.

/P asks your permission before replacing any file that you have changed since you backed it up. This protects against accidentally wiping out the changes you have made since the backup.

/A:yy-mm-dd and /L:hh:mm:ss tell RESTORE to undo changes you made after a given date and time. Use the /L switch only with /A.

/B:yy-mm-dd and /E:hh:mm:ss tell RESTORE to undo changes you made before a given date and time. Use the /E switch only with /B.

Examples

To restore all the files from the backup floppy disk in drive A to drive C:

RESTORE A: C: /S

To restore all backed up files you have modified since 6:00 p.m. on March 1, 1991:

RESTORE A: C: /S /A:3-1-91 /L:18:00

To restore all Lotus worksheets in C:\123G:

RESTORE A: C:\123G*.WK*

Notes

This command restores files from a floppy disk backup you made with the BACKUP command. Because BACKUP wrote these files in a special format, commands like COPY cannot work with them; only BACKUP and RESTORE can. If the backup contains more than one floppy disk, RESTORE prompts you to insert the floppy disk in the right order.

You only can restore files to the same directory they were in when you backed them up. If the directory no longer exists, RESTORE creates it. You cannot restore files that OS/2 has locked because they are in use—for example, files used by programs that are running in the background. Because BACKUP will not copy OS/2's most critical system files at all, you cannot use RESTORE to create a bootable disk.

The COUNTRY statement in CONFIG.SYS governs the national date and time format that the /A, /B, /E, and /L switches use.

You cannot restore a backup made with any DOS version earlier than 3.3.

RMDIR
See RD.

SPOOL
Redirects a file that you send to one printer so that the file comes out on a different printer.

Syntax
   SPOOL */D:printer1 /O:printer2 /Q*

Switches
/D:printer1 is the printer to which you say you are sending a file. The printer can be any parallel printer such as PRN or LPT1 but not a serial printer such as COM1.

/O:printer2 is the printer to which the file really goes. It can be any parallel printer such as PRN or LPT1, or any serial printer such as COM1.

/Q queries existing device redirections.

Examples
To make any file you send to PRN come out on a serial printer on COM1:

   SPOOL /D:PRN /O:COM1

To cancel any SPOOL command that redirects LPT2 to another printer:

   SPOOL /D:LPT2 /O:LPT2

Notes
You must install COM.SYS in your CONFIG.SYS file before using the SPOOL command to direct files to a serial printer.

START   OS/2 Only
Runs a program automatically.

Syntax
   START **"title"** */C /K /N /B /F /PGM /FS /PM /WIN /DOS /MAX /MIN /I* **command-line**

"title" is the name that appears at the top of the program's window. It can be up to sixty characters and must be in double quotation marks.

command-line is the program's name plus any necessary parameters.

Switches

/C closes the window after the program terminates.

/K keeps the window open after the program terminates.

/N runs the program directly, without loading the OS/2 command processor CMD.EXE. The program must have an EXE extension.

/B runs the program in a background window.

/F runs the program in a foreground window.

/PGM indicates that the command-line is enclosed in double quotation marks.

/FS runs the program in a full-screen session.

/PM runs the program in a Presentation Manager window.

/WIN runs the program in a window.

/DOS runs a *bound* program—one that can run under DOS or OS/2-in a DOS window.

/MAX maximizes the window.

/MIN minimizes the window (makes it an icon).

/I allows the program to use the global environment rather than giving the program its own environment.

Examples

To open a windowed DOS session:

> **START /WIN /DOS**

To copy all the files from a floppy disk to your hard disk in a background window:

> **START "Copy files" /B COPY A:UL C:**

To run the OS/2 program C:\WP\WORDPROC.EXE and load the file MEMO.TXT in a maximized, foreground Presentation Manager window named WP that closes when you exit the program:

> **START "WP" /C /F /PM /MAX C:\WP\WORDPROC MEMO.TXT**

Notes

You normally use START in the STARTUP.CMD file that runs every time you turn on the computer. You can use the command to load the programs you run every time you use your computer.

SUBST   DOS Only

Tells DOS to pretend that a directory is a separate disk.

Syntax

SUBST d1: *d2:\dir*

SUBST d1: */D*

d1: is the drive you specify in a DOS command.

d2:\dir is the drive and subdirectory that DOS uses rather than **d1:**.

Switch

/D cancels any previous SUBST command for d1:.

Examples

To show all current drive substitutions:

SUBST

To tell DOS to treat the directory \DATA on drive C as though it were a separate drive Z:

SUBST Z: C:\DATA

To cancel the effect of the above SUBST command:

SUBST Z: /D

Notes

If you already have a physical drive d1:, it becomes unavailable while the SUBST command is in effect.

You may need SUBST to make old programs that run from a floppy drive run from a hard drive. Otherwise, avoid using SUBST. It is dangerous to use with many commands, such as CHKDSK, DISKCOMP, DISKCOPY, FORMAT, LABEL, and RECOVER.

TIME

Displays or sets the time.

Syntax

> TIME *hh:mm:ss.cc*

hh is hours (0-23).

mm is minutes (0-59).

ss is seconds (0-59).

cc is hundredths of a second (0-99).

Examples

To set the time to 5.98 seconds after 8:21 pm:

> **TIME 20:21:5.98**

To set the time to midnight:

> **TIME 0**

To display and change (optional) the current time:

> **TIME**

Notes

You must use the 24-hour clock. The computer remembers the time you set after you turn off the power. The COUNTRY command in CONFIG.SYS governs the way you format the time. You can omit the hundredths of a second (cc) when you change your system time.

TREE

Displays and lists (optional) all directories on a disk.

Syntax

> TREE *d1:* /F

d1: is the drive whose directory structure you want to see. The default is the current drive.

Switch

/F lists the name of every file in each directory.

Examples

To list all the directories on the default drive:

> **TREE C:**

To list all the directories on drive C and all the files in each directory:

> **TREE C: /F**

TYPE

Displays a file on-screen.

Syntax

> **TYPE file**

file specifies the file you want to display.

Example

To show the contents of \CONFIG.SYS on-screen:

> **TYPE \CONFIG.SYS**

Notes

If the file is too long to fit on one screen, the file scrolls by too rapidly to read. To overcome this problem, use the MORE command.

UNDELETE

Restores a file you recently erased.

Syntax

> **UNDELETE** *dir***files** */A /F /S /L*

dir is the directory that you want to back up.

files specifies the files that you want to back up.

If you don't specify dir or files, UNDELETE looks for all deleted files in the current directory.

Switches

/A restores every deleted file in the directory.

/F tells UNDELETE to erase files completely so that no one can recover them.

/L lists the files that can be restored but does not actually restore them.

/S restores every deleted file in dir and in all its subdirectories.

Examples

To display the names of the current directory's deleted files that can be restored:

> **UNDELETE /L**

To erase your performance evaluation in C:\PERSONAL\REVIEW.DOC so that no one can ever recover it:

> **UNDELETE C:\PERSONAL\REVIEW.DOC /F**

Notes

When you delete a file, OS/2 moves that file to a hidden area on your hard disk. UNDELETE enables you to restore the deleted file if you act quickly. The area for deleted files is limited in size. When this area fills up, the oldest files are discarded to make room for new ones.

Use the DELDIR environment available in CONFIG.SYS to define the path and maximum size of directories used to store deleted files, as follows:

> **SET DELDIR= drive:\path, maxsize; drive 2:\path, maxsize**

UNPACK

Restores compressed files on the OS/2 distribution floppy disk to a form you can use.

Syntax

> **UNPACK packed-file target** /N:filename
>
> **UNPACK packed-file /SHOW**

packed-file is the name of the compressed file.

target is the drive and directory to which you want to copy the unpacked file.

Switches

/N:filename specifies the name of a single file that you want to extract from a bundle that contains more than one file.

/SHOW displays the names of the files that are combined in a packed bundle.

/V enables you to verify a compressed file while you unpack it.

/F enables you to unpack a file without discarding extended attributes.

Examples
To extract XCOPY.EXE from the file XCOPY.EX@ on a floppy disk in drive A and write it to the \OS2 directory on drive C:

>**UNPACK A:XCOPY.EX@ C:\OS2**

To display the names of the files that are packed into the bundle GROUP.DA@ on drive A:

>**UNPACK A:GROUP.DA@ /SHOW**

To extract FORMAT.COM from the floppy disk file BUNDLE.DA@ that contains it and put the extracted file in C:\OS2:

>**UNPACK A:BUNDLE.DA@ C:\OS2 /N:FORMAT.COM**

Notes
Many of the files on the OS/2 distribution floppy disk are compressed so that they take up less room and fewer floppy disks are needed. The installation program automatically unpacks the files. If you accidentally lose one of OS/2's files and you know which disk contains it, however, you can unpack it yourself. Unpacking one file is easier than reinstalling OS/2.

On the OS/2 floppy disk, if the last character in a file's extension is @, then it is a packed file. Some disks contain only one file, but others are bundles of several files. You can tell what files a bundle contains by running UNPACK with the /SHOW option.

VER
Displays the version of OS/2 you are using.

Syntax
>**VER**

Example
To see what OS/2 version is running:

>**VER**

If you are using version 2.1, the system responds:

```
The Operating System/2 version is 2.10
```

VERIFY

Checks that data is written to a disk.

Syntax

VERIFY ON

VERIFY OFF

Notes

Although verifying disk writes sounds like a good idea, you should leave VERIFY OFF. If it is ON, OS/2 checks to make sure that something was written to the disk, but it does not guarantee that the right data was written. The slight benefit provided by VERIFY ON is not worth the extra time OS/2 takes to make the confirmation.

VOL

Displays a disk's label and serial number.

Syntax

VOL *d1:*

d1: is the drive whose label you want to examine. The default is the current drive.

Examples

To see the label of the current drive:

VOL

To see the label of drive C:

VOL C:

Notes

Every disk and floppy disk formatted with OS/2 have a serial number assigned by the system. You also should give it a label, which is any combination of up to 11 letters and numbers you choose. The VOL command displays both the serial number and the label.

If you run the FORMAT command on a hard disk that has a label, FORMAT prompts you for the label and will not continue if you do not type it, which provides extra protection against formatting the hard disk by accident.

OS/2 uses the serial number to keep track of your floppy disk. If a program is writing to a floppy disk and you change the floppy disk before the program finishes, the system can detect the change by comparing the serial numbers.

XCOPY

Copies directories, including all the files they contain.

Syntax

XCOPY dir *target* */S* */E* */D:mm-dd-yy*

dir specifies the directory you want to duplicate.

target is the location of the duplicate you create. If you do not specify it, XCOPY uses the current drive and directory.

Switches

/S copies files in dir and all its subdirectories as well.

/E can be used along with the /S switch to copy subdirectories even if they contain no files.

/D:mm-dd-yy copies only files created or changed since a given date.

/P prompts before copying.

/V verifies copying.

/A copies only archived files but does not clear the archive flag.

/M copies only archived files but also clears the archive flag.

/F halts copying if you are attempting to copy source files with extended attributes to a target that can't support them.

Examples

To copy every file in the \MEMOS directory of drive C to a floppy disk in drive A:

XCOPY C:\MEMOS A:

To copy the drive C:\MEMOS directory and each subdirectory of \MEMOS (whether or not it contains any files) to floppy drive A:

    XCOPY C:\MEMOS A: /S

Configuration Commands

The following commands can be added to your CONFIG.SYS file so that OS/2 reads and acts on the command. Do not type these commands at a command-line prompt.

AUTOFAIL   OS/2 Only

Gives you a choice in dealing with certain hardware errors.

Syntax

    AUTOFAIL=YES

    AUTOFAIL=NO

Notes

Suppose that you run a program that uses a file on a disk, but you forget to insert the disk. If you put AUTOFAIL=YES in your CONFIG.SYS file, OS/2 displays a dialog box describing the problem and asks you to choose a response. In this case, insert the disk and then tell OS/2 to try reading it again.

If you set AUTOFAIL=NO, then OS/2 will just tell your word processor that it was unable to read the file. The recommended setting is YES.

BASEDEV

Loads base drivers through the CONFIG.SYS file.

Syntax

    BASEDEV=driver <arguments>

driver is the name of the device driver file containing the code that the operating system needs to recognize the device and process information received from or sent to the device.

<arguments> specifies parameters of the base device driver.

Examples

To provide device support for a local printer (non-Micro Channel workstation):

BASEDEV=PRIN01.SYS

To provide device support for Micro Channel SCSI adapters:

BASEDEV=IBM2SCSI.ADD

Notes

The BASEDEV statement must not contain drive or path information; OS/2 cannot process this information during the startup sequence. OS/2 generates an error when the drive or path information is included in the statement.

BREAK   DOS Only

Controls how quickly DOS programs stop when you interrupt them by pressing Ctrl-Break.

Syntax

BREAK=ON

BREAK=OFF

Notes

You can stop many DOS programs by holding down Ctrl and pressing Break. With the default value, BREAK=OFF, DOS stops the program the next time it tries to read a character from the keyboard or to write to the screen or a printer. When you set BREAK=ON in your CONFIG.SYS file, DOS checks for Ctrl-Break more frequently. This extra checking, however, will make your programs run a little slower.

BREAK is OFF by default. You should leave this setting OFF unless you are having problems when you use Ctrl-Break to interrupt programs.

BUFFERS

Sets aside a part of memory for moving data to and from disks.

Syntax

BUFFERS=n

n is a number from 1 to 100 that tells how many disk buffers you want to use. Each buffer takes up 512 bytes.

Notes

When data moves to or from a disk drive, the data flows through a special area of memory called a buffer. If you use many different files at once, your system runs faster if each file has its own buffer. Each buffer takes up a small amount of memory, however, leaving a little less memory to run your programs.

The default, BUFFERS=30, usually works well. If you have plenty of memory and want to use some of it to speed up disk operations, increase the size of your disk cache (using the CACHE and DISKCACHE commands) instead of setting more BUFFERS.

CODEPAGE

Enables the computer to use the alphabets of various languages.

Syntax

CODEPAGE=primary,*secondary*

primary is a number that specifies your main national alphabet.

secondary is the number of another alphabet that you also want to use.

You can find the number for each alphabet in the on-line command reference, under the COUNTRY command.

Examples

To use the U.S. English alphabet and also have the multinational alphabet available:

CODEPAGE=437,850

To use the Icelandic alphabet only:

CODEPAGE=861

Notes

OS/2 stores many different national character sets in *code pages*. You can load up to two pages through the CODEPAGE statement in CONFIG.SYS; only the first page is active, unless you switch to the other page with the CHCP command. For a listing of the code pages supported by OS/2, see the OS/2 command reference on-line documentation.

If you do not put a CODEPAGE statement in CONFIG.SYS, your keyboard uses an alphabet based on the COUNTRY statement, but your screen and printer use their built-in defaults.

The multinational alphabet, CODEPAGE=850, includes most of the accented letters used in European languages. Stick to the letters A-Z and numerals 0-9 for file and directory names so that people in other countries can use them.

COUNTRY

Customizes your computer system for the country you live in.

Syntax

COUNTRY=nnn,file

nnn is a three-digit number that tells what country you live in. The number is usually the same as the telephone system's international dialing prefix for your country. You can find these numbers in the on-line command reference, under the COUNTRY command.

file is the file that contains information for your country. **file** is usually C:\OS2\SYSTEM\COUNTRY.SYS.

Example

To customize your system for the United Kingdom:

COUNTRY=044,C:\OS2\SYSTEM\COUNTRY.SYS

Notes

Dates, times, and numbers are formatted according to the custom of your country. In France, one tenth of a second before February 1, 1995, looks like this:

31/01/1995 23:59:59,90

The SORT command works according to the order of the letters in your national alphabet.

DEVICE

Install a device driver (a program that adds a function to the operating system) that is not on the device support diskettes.

Syntax

DEVICE=path\driver

path is the location of **driver**.

driver is the device driver file.

Example

To load the DOS ANSI driver:

DEVICE=C:\OS2\MDOS\ANSI.SYS

Notes

Device drivers are special programs that actually become part of OS/2 when you load them. Think of them as optional parts of OS/2. You need to load DOS.SYS, for example, if you want to run DOS. If you do not need DOS support, you do not need to load DOS.SYS. You can save space by loading only the device drivers that you need.

Mouse support is another example. OS/2 includes device drivers for six different types of mice, but you probably have only one mouse. You waste memory if you build in support for the other five types.

DEVICE (ANSI.SYS) DOS Only

Enables you to run the rare DOS program that requires special support for the screen or keyboard.

Syntax

DEVICE=path\ANSI.SYS /X /L /K

path is the location of the file ANSI.SYS. By default, it is C:\OS2\MDOS.

/X Enables you to redefine keys with extended key values.

/L prevents applications from overriding the number of rows you have set on-screen.

/K prevents ANSI.SYS from using the extended keyboard functions.

Examples

To load special screen and keyboard support and allow applications to set the number of rows on-screen, type this in CONFIG.SYS:

DEVICE=\OS2\MDOS\ANSI.SYS

To be able to redefine the extended key values, type this in CONFIG.SYS:

DEVICE=C:\OS2\MDOS\ANSI.SYS /X

Notes

This command affects only DOS sessions. The special support it provides is available in OS/2 sessions by default, although you can turn it off with the OS/2 ANSI command. Very few programs require this setting.

DEVICE (COM.SYS)

Enables you to use the communications ports for mice, modems, and serial printers.

Syntax

DEVICE=path\COM.SYS

path is the location of the file COM.SYS. By default, it is C:\OS2.

Examples

To make the communications ports available, type this in CONFIG.SYS:

DEVICE=C:\OS2\COM.SYS

You must list COM.SYS *after* any driver that uses the communications ports. Printer drivers must come before COM.SYS in CONFIG.SYS, for example.

DEVICE=C:\OS2\printer1.SYS

DEVICE=C:\OS2\printer2.SYS

DEVICE=C:\OS2\COM.SYS

Notes

Use COMDMA.SYS for IBM PS/2 Models 90 and 95 instead of COM.SYS. COM.SYS works for all other PS/2 models.

Both the COM.SYS and COMDMA.SYS support ports COM1, COM2, COM3, and COM4. COM.SYS does not provide support for devices that are attached to the COM port; application programs and system programs must provide the support. COM.SYS supports the asynchronous communications interface itself.

DEVICE (EGA.SYS)   DOS Only

Enables you to run DOS programs that control the Enhanced Graphics Adapter directly.

Syntax

    DEVICE=path\EGA.SYS

path is the location of the file EGA.SYS. By default, it is C:\OS2.

Examples

To load special EGA support, type this in CONFIG.SYS:

    DEVICE=C:\OS2\EGA.SYS

Notes

EGA.SYS must be installed for any application program that uses the EGA register interface.

If the mouse cursor leaves a trail on-screen or you see strange characters in a DOS window, try installing this device driver. Some DOS programs, such as games, control the EGA directly; the programs work better if you load EGA.SYS. In some cases, you may need EGA.SYS even if you have a VGA monitor because some programs treat EGA and VGA alike. Don't load EGA.SYS unless you have a problem, however, because the file takes up memory that your programs could use.

DEVICE (EXTDSKDD)

Enables you to use an external disk drive or specify the type of disks used in an internal drive.

Syntax

    DEVICE=path\EXTDSKDD.SYS /D:n /T /S /H /F:type

path is the location of the file EXTDSKDD.SYS. By default, it is C:\OS2.

/D specifies the physical drive number (0 to 255).

n is the number of the disk drive. The first internal drive, number zero, is the drive you normally call A, and the second drive (number one) is normally B. The first external drive is number two (D or E).

/T specifies the number of tracks per side (from 1 to 999); the default is 80.

/S specifies number of sectors per track (from 1 to 99); the default is 9.

/H specifies the maximum number of heads (from 1 to 99); the default is 2.

/F:type specifies the device type (from 0 to 9); the default is 2.

Type	Description	Capacity
0	5 1/4-inch double density	360K
1	5 1/4-inch high density	1.2M
2	3 1/2-inch double density	720K
3	8-inch	not used
4	8-inch	not used
5	hard disks	not used
6	tape drives	not used
7	3 1/2-inch high density	1.44M
8	RW Optical	not used
9	3-1/2-inch ultra density	2.88M

Examples

To tell OS/2 that you have an external 5 1/4-inch high-density disk drive:

> **DEVICE=C:\OS2\EXTDSKDD.SYS /D:2 /F:1**

To tell OS/2 to use an internal 1.44M A drive for 720K disks:

> **DEVICE=C:\OS2\EXTDSKDD.SYS /D:0 /F:2**

Now the same drive is a 1.44M drive when you call it A but a 720K drive when you call it B. If you have two internal disk drives, the 720K drive gets a higher letter, such as D.

Notes

You can use EXTDSKDD to tell an internal drive to use disks of a different density. Be careful because not every drive will work this way. Even if the command seems to work, the disks you write on may not be readable on a different computer. The value of *F:type* should be 0 or 1 for 5 1/4-inch drives, and 2, 3, or 4 for 3 1/2-inch drives.

The internal drive is still available as A or as B if you have two internal drives.

EXTDSKDD creates a new drive letter. It uses the first letter that was not already claimed. If you have two internal disk drives A and B, and hard drives C and D, for example, the new drive is normally E.

DEVICE (MOUSE)

Enables you to use a mouse or trackball.

Syntax

DEVICE=path\MOUSE.SYS TYPE=t *QSIZE=n*

path is the location of the file MOUSE.SYS. By default, it is C:\OS2.

t is the type of mouse. Choose one from the table below.

n is a number from 1 to 100 that tells how many mouse actions to save when you do things faster than the system can respond to. Clicking a menu item counts as one action. So does dragging a file to the Print Manager. The default, 10, is usually enough actions.

Examples

To tell OS/2 you have an IBM Personal System/2 Mouse:

DEVICE=C:\OS2\POINTDD.SYS

DEVICE=C:\OS2\MOUSE.SYS

To tell OS/2 that you have a Visi-On mouse:

DEVICE=C:\OS2\MOUSE.SYS TYPE=VISION$

Notes

The table below lists different mouse types and their special drivers:

Manufacturer/Model	Mouse Type T	Special Driver
Microsoft Bus	MSBUS$	(not needed)
Microsoft Inport	MSINP$	(not needed)
Logitec Pointing Devices	PCLOGIC$	PCLOGIC.SYS
PC Mouse Systems	PCLOGIC$	PCLOGIC.SYS
Visi-On	VISION$	VISION$.SYS

If you do not see your mouse or trackball listed here, a driver may be available from the manufacturer. If the manufacturer does not offer one, try installing your device as one of the types listed in the table.

To use a mouse in OS/2, you need to load several device drivers in CONFIG.SYS. OS/2 installation takes care of this for you, but the following steps are listed in case you want to make modifications yourself.

Load POINTDD.SYS.

Load the special driver shown in the table unless it indicates that you do not need one.

Load MOUSE.SYS.

If you have a serial mouse, load COM.SYS.

To install a PC Mouse System serial mouse on the second communications port, for example:

DEVICE=C:\OS2\POINTDD.SYS

DEVICE=C:\OS2\PCLOGIC.SYS SERIAL=COM2

DEVICE=C:\OS2\MOUSE.SYS TYPE=PCLOGIC$

DEVICE=C:\OS2\COM.SYS

For IBM PS/2 Models 90 and 95, be sure the final DEVICE= statement is:

DEVICE=C:\OS2\COMDMA.SYS

DEVICE (PMDD.SYS)　　　　　　OS/2 Only

Provides pointer draw support for OS/2 sessions. If the PMDD.SYS device statement is removed from your CONFIG.SYS, your system will not restart.

Syntax

DEVICE=path\PMDD.SYS

path is the location of the file PMDD.SYS. By default, it is C:\OS2.

Example

To load PM:

DEVICE=C:\OS2\PMDD.SYS

Notes

If your system does not start, insert the OS/2 Installation Program disk and proceed to the Welcome screen. Press Esc and then copy the file CONFIG.BAK into your root directory. You then can rename the CONFIG.BAK file to CONFIG.SYS. The PMDD.SYS statement is:

DEVICE=C:\OS2\PMDD.SYS

DEVICE (POINTDD.SYS)

Draws the mouse pointer on-screen.

Syntax

DEVICE=path\POINTDD.SYS

path is the location of the file POINTDD.SYS. By default, it is C:\OS2.

Example

To load mouse pointer support:

DEVICE=C:\OS2\POINTDD.SYS

Notes

Installing a mouse requires other drivers as well. See the explanation under the MOUSE command.

POINTDD.SYS provides draw support in all text modes (0, 1, 2, 3, and 7).

DEVICE (VDISK.SYS)

Makes a part of memory act like a fast electronic disk.

Syntax

DEVICE=path\VDISK.SYS *disk-size sector-size directories*

path is the location of the file VDISK.SYS. By default, it is C:\OS2.

disk-size (bytes) is a number from 16 to 4,096 that gives the size of the virtual disk in kilobytes. The default is 64.

sector-size is the number of bytes in a sector. Just like a real disk, a virtual disk is divided into sectors. The value must be 128, 256, 512, or 1,024. The default is 128 bytes.

directories is a number from 2 to 1,024 that tells how many directories you can put in the virtual disk's root directory. The default is 64.

Example

To create a 400K virtual disk with 256-byte sectors and a limit of 100 directories:

    DEVICE=C:\OS2\VDISK.SYS 400 256 100

If you want to use the default value of any parameter, use commas where the values should be:

    DEVICE=C:\OS2\VDISK.SYS 400 , ,

Notes

Virtual disks, also called RAM disks, act like real disk drives. Because virtual disks are part of the computer's memory, they are very fast. But virtual disks vanish when you turn the power off, and the memory they take up cannot be used for other purposes, such as running programs. You probably will not want a virtual disk unless you have over 4M of memory.

Try using a virtual disk to store files you read frequently, such as databases. You have to copy the database file to the RAM disk and then tell your database program to use the copy. This is safe if you only read the database to create reports. If you make any updates, however, you must copy the database back to your hard disk when you are finished. If you turn off the computer first or the power goes off, you lose your updates.

VDISK creates a new drive letter. It uses the first letter that was not claimed already. If you have two hard drives C and D, for example, the virtual disk usually is E.

Add up the space required for all the directories you want to put on the RAM disk, and set *disk-size* a little larger in case the files need more space.

If you use the virtual disk for large files, a *sector-size* of 1,024 gives the best performance; your options are 128, 256, 512, and 1,024. Because each file uses a whole number of sectors, a 100-byte file wastes 924 bytes. Use 128 for *sector-size* if you put dozens of very small files on the RAM disk.

Set *directories* (2 to 1,024) according to the number of files you want to use on the virtual disk. Add a few extra directories just in case. OS/2 usually rounds *directories* up to an even multiple of sixteen.

DEVICE=(VEMM.SYS)   DOS Only

Allows DOS applications to use expanded memory.

Syntax

    DEVICE=path\VEMM.SYS *n*

path is the location of the file VEMM.SYS. By default, it is C:\OS2.

n is the number of kilobytes of expanded memory available to each DOS session. It can range from 0 to 32,768. The default is 4,096, or 4M.

Example

To give each DOS session up to one megabyte of expanded memory:

    DEVICE=C:\OS2\VEMM.SYS 1024

Notes

Expanded memory, also called EMS or LIM 4.0, is a method for letting DOS applications use more than the usual 640K of memory. Most DOS spreadsheet programs use EMS to enable you to work with large amounts of data.

You can override the amount of EMS available to each DOS application when you add it to a group by changing the value of EMS Memory Size under DOS Options.

To load expanded memory support without giving any to DOS (unless you override it for a particular DOS session):

    DEVICE=C:\OS2\VEMM.SYS 0

Place VEMM and VXMS at the end of CONFIG.SYS. They need to know which areas in memory other device drivers have claimed so that they can make sure they do not try to use those same areas.

DEVICE (VXMS.SYS)   DOS Only

Provides extended memory emulation for DOS sessions.

Syntax

    DEVICE=path\VXMS.SYS

path specifies the drive and directory that contain VXMS.SYS. By default, it is C:\OS2.

Example

To provide XMS (Extended Memory Specification) emulation and to allow DOS applications to access more than 1MB of memory:

DEVICE=C:\OS2\MDOS\VXMS.SYS

Notes

Other parameters are available, such as system-wide maximum memory usage and setting the number of available handles in each DOS session. Consult the OS/2 command reference help file.

DEVICEHIGH   DOS Only

Loads a DOS device driver into upper memory, leaving more low memory available to run programs.

Syntax

DEVICEHIGH=path\driver

path is the location of **driver**.

driver is the device driver file.

Example

To load the ANSI driver into upper memory:

DEVICEHIGH=C:\OS2\MDOS\ANSI.SYS

Notes

DOS programs run in low memory, which is the first 640K. DOS device drivers normally load in low memory, leaving less space to run programs. When you load device drivers in upper memory (from 640K to 1,024K), you keep more low memory free and give DOS programs more space.

If the computer does not have enough upper memory to load the driver, it is loaded in low memory.

DEVINFO (Keyboard)

Sets the keyboard layout for the country you live in.

Syntax

DEVINFO=KBD,layout,path\KEYBOARD.DCP

layout is an abbreviation for your country, such as U.S. for United States. You can find these abbreviations in the on-line command reference.

path is the location of the file KEYBOARD.DCP, which tells what each key means. By default, it is C:\OS2.

Example

To use the US keyboard:

DEVINFO=KBD,US,C:\OS2\KEYBOARD.DCP

DEVINFO (Printer)

Tells the printer what country you live in.

Syntax

DEVINFO=printer,model,ROM=(font,0)

printer is LPT1, LPT2, or LPT3.

model is 4201 for the IBM Proprinter or 5202 for the IBM Quietwriter.

font is a three-digit number that tells what national alphabet you want. You can find these numbers in the on-line command reference, under the COUNTRY command.

Example

To set up an IBM Proprinter, attached to the second printer port, for the United States:

DEVINFO=LPT2,4201,C:\OS2\4201.DCP,ROM=(437,0)

DEVINFO (Screen)

Tells OS/2 what kind of screen you have.

Syntax

DEVINFO=SCR,type,path\VIOTBL.DCP

type is CGA, EGA, VGA, or BGA, depending on what kind of screen you have. BGA is the IBM 8514/A with memory expansion.

path is the location of the file VIOTBL.DCP, which tells what each character looks like. By default, it is C:\OS2.

Example

To tell OS/2 that you have a VGA monitor:

DEVINFO=SCR,VGA,C:\OS2\VIOTBL.DCP

Notes

To configure OS/2 to work with your monitor, you also must set a couple of environment variables. OS/2's Install program performs this complicated task automatically. If you change your monitor, run Install to update the settings.

DISKCACHE

Makes your hard disk seem faster by keeping the data you use most frequently in memory.

Syntax

DISKCACHE=n,*LW,t,AC:x*

n is a number from 64 to 14400 that tells how many kilobytes of memory to set aside for saving disk data.

LW (Lazy Writing) tells the cache to delay writing data to the disk until the system is not quite so busy. *LW* is the default.

t is a number from 4 to 128 that limits the number of disk sectors OS/2 reads or writes at one time. A sector is usually 512 bytes. The default value of *t* is 4.

AC stands for AutoCheck, and *x* is a drive letter. This option causes OS/2 to run CHKDSK/F at boot time.

Examples

To set up a 256K cache:

DISKCACHE=256

To get even better performance with the same settings:

DISKCACHE=256,LW,32

Notes

You probably use just a few programs and files at a time, which means that you are often reading the same parts of your hard disk over and over. A disk cache saves whatever you have most recently read in memory and reads it directly from memory when you need it again. A disk cache can make your hard disk seem much faster because retrieving data from memory is faster than retrieving it from disks.

As the cache becomes full, data that you have not used for some time is discarded. If you work with files that are larger than the disk cache, data can be discarded before you need to use it again.

To prevent this problem, you can limit the amount of data that is saved any particular time you read the disk by giving a value for *max*.

LW, or Lazy Writing, means that when a program needs to write data to the disk, the cache holds the data and actually puts it on the disk when the system is not busy. The system seems faster because programs do not have to wait for data to be written onto the disk. If you use *LW*, you must run the Shutdown procedure before turning off the computer or data that has not yet been written onto the disk is lost.

DISKCACHE works only on drives formatted with the FAT file system. For High Performance File System drives, use the CACHE command.

If your computer has less than 6M of memory, use a 6K disk cache. If you have more than 6M, use a cache size of 256K.

DOS (Control memory) — DOS Only

Enables you to control where DOS is loaded.

Syntax

DOS=where,upper

where tells whether DOS is loaded in high or low memory. It can be HIGH or LOW.

upper can be UMB or NOUMB. UMB allows DOS to run memory-resident programs in upper memory. NOUMB prevents this.

Example

To load DOS in high memory and let it run memory-resident programs in upper memory:

DOS=HIGH,UMB

Notes

DOS recognizes three different areas of memory. Low memory, from 0 to 640K, is where DOS programs, and DOS itself, usually run. With OS/2's special support, DOS programs also can run in upper memory, from 640K to 1,024K. High memory is the area from 1,024K to 1,088K; OS/2 can move DOS itself to high memory.

DOS is really just a program that runs under OS/2. If you run DOS in low memory, you have less room to run DOS programs there. To avoid this problem, run DOS in high memory.

If you specify UMB, you can run DOS memory-resident programs in upper memory, using the LOADHIGH command. You should normally use **DOS=HIGH,UMB** which leaves the lowermost memory free for applications.

DOS (Load DOS support)   DOS Only

Affects how DOS sessions work.

Syntax

DEVICE=path\DOS.SYS

path is the location of the file DOS.SYS. By default, it is C:\OS2\MDOS.

Example

To load DOS support:

DEVICE=C:\OS2\MDOS\DOS.SYS

Notes

DOS sessions will not start unless you have this command in CONFIG.SYS.

DPATH   OS/2 Only

Tells OS/2 programs where to look for data files.

Syntax

SET DPATH=dir1;*dir2;...*

dir1 is a directory, such as C:\MEMOS.

dir2 is another directory.

The ellipsis (...) means that you can specify more directories. Separate the directories from each other by using semicolons.

Example

To tell OS/2 programs to look for data files in the directories C:\ and D:\DATA:

> **SET DPATH=C:\;D:\DATA**

Notes

Data files that are in the current directory are always available to a program, even if you do not include the current directory in the DPATH statement.

The DOS APPEND command is similar to OS/2's DPATH. Unlike APPEND, DPATH works only with programs designed to use it, such as most commercial applications. Suppose that you have a file MEMO.TXT in the directory C:\MEMOS and that directory is on your DPATH. A word processing program in the C:\WORDPROC directory may be able to find the memo, but the OS/2 System Editor will not, unless you start it from the directory to which the file is saved or type in the full path name.

You normally set DPATH in CONFIG.SYS, although you can also set it in an OS/2 window. When you set a new DPATH, it replaces the old one.

FCBS   DOS Only

Supports File Control Blocks (FCBs), a method of using files that was common in older DOS programs.

Syntax

> **FCBS=max**,*protected*

max is the number of files, from 0 to 255, that can be used at one time with the FCB method.

protected is the number of FCBs that will not be closed automatically when a program needs more FCBs than are available. The number cannot be greater than **max**. The default is 16.

Examples

To give DOS 10 FCBs and to protect three from being closed:

> **FCBS=10,3**

To give DOS 255 FCBs and to tell DOS not to automatically recycle any of them if it runs out:

FCBS=255,255

Notes

You probably will not need to change the default, which is FCBS=16,16. Increase it to FCBS=255,255 if you have problems running DOS applications from the early 1980s.

If a program tries to open a file with an FCB, but all FCBs are already being used, the least recently used FCB is closed and given to the program. The file that was previously using the FCB is closed automatically, and any attempt to use it later will cause an error. If all FCBs are protected and they are all in use, a program that tries to open a file with an FCB will fail.

IFS

Enables you to use the High Performance File System (HPFS).

Syntax

IFS=path\HPFS.IFS */C:cache-size /AUTOCHECK:drives /CRECL:x*

path is the location of the file HPFS.IFS. By default, it is C:\OS2.

cache-size is the number of kilobytes of memory used as a disk cache. The default is 20 percent of total memory.

drives is a list of disks automatically checked for problems when you turn the computer on. Just give the letter of each drive; do not type a colon after the letter.

/CRECL:x specifies the maximum record size for caching (from 2K to 64K in multiples of 2K).

Example

To start the High Performance File System with a 128K cache, a maximum record size of 4K, and to check drives D and E for problems:

IFS=C:\OS2\HPFS.IFS */C:128 /AUTOCHECK:DE /CRECL:x*

Notes

If you formatted one or more of your drives with HPFS when you installed OS/2, the setup program placed an IFS statement in your CONFIG.SYS file. You need this statement to use an HPFS drive.

HPFS has a disk cache to improve performance. You probably use just a few programs and files at a time, which means that you are often reading the same parts of your hard disk over and over. A disk cache saves whatever you have most recently read in memory and reads it directly from memory when you need it again. A disk cache can make your hard disk seem much faster because memory is faster than disks. To use the HPFS cache, you need to use the /C switch and run the CACHE command.

The cache for HPFS drives, which you specify with the /C switch, is different from the cache for FAT drives, which you set up with the DISKCACHE command. Setting the cache too large can slow down your system because the memory the cache uses is not available for running programs. If you do not have enough room to run your programs, OS/2 swaps them to and from the disk, which negates the benefit of caching. A 128K cache is usually large enough.

The */AUTOCHECK* switch tells OS/2 to run the CHKDSK command when you turn the system on. This switch detects and tries to fix problems with the file system. Always use this switch with all HPFS drives; the safety is well worth the extra time it will take to start the system.

IOPL   OS/2 Only

Enables you to run programs that need to bypass OS/2 and work directly with hardware devices.

Syntax

    IOPL=YES

    IOPL=NO

    IOPL=list

YES means that all programs can access the hardware directly.

NO means that no program can access the hardware directly (the default).

list gives the names of specific programs that are allowed to work directly with the hardware. Programs not listed do not have this permission. Separate the names in the list with commas.

Examples

To prevent any program from working directly with the hardware:

    IOPL=NO

To prevent any program except PROGRAM1 and PROGRAM2 from working directly with the hardware:

    IOPL=PROGRAM1,PROGRAM2

Notes

OS/2 normally prevents programs from dealing directly with hardware such as the disk drive; one faulty program cannot crash the whole system. Setting **IOPL=YES** gives the best protection.

Some programs have to work directly with the hardware, in order to do things that OS/2 cannot do for them. If you have to run such a program, specify its name in the *list*.

LASTDRIVE — DOS Only

Specifies the maximum number of drives that are accessible.

Syntax

    LASTDRIVE=x

x is the number of the last valid drive that is recognized.

Example

To give your system access to 13 logical disks:

    LASTDRIVE=M

Notes

This statement has no effect in OS/2 sessions.

LIBPATH   OS/2 Only

Tells OS/2 programs where to look for dynamic link libraries (DLLs).

Syntax

LIBPATH=dir1;*dir2*;...

dir1 is a directory, such as C:\LIBRARY. Use a period to indicate the current directory.

dir2 is another directory.

The ellipsis (...) means that you can specify more directories. Separate the directories from each other by using semicolons.

Example

To tell OS/2 to look for DLLs first in the current directory, then in the directories C:\OS2\DLL and D:\DLL:

LIBPATH=.;C:\OS2\DLL;D:\DLL

The period following the equals sign means the current directory.

Notes

Many OS/2 applications place part of their program code in DLLs, which are program files with the extension DLL. To run these applications, OS/2 must know where to find their DLLs. Most applications come with an installation program that automatically adds the necessary LIBPATH to your CONFIG.SYS. Others may ask you to change the CONFIG.SYS manually.

LIBPATH is much like DPATH and PATH, but it can be used only in CONFIG.SYS. You do not use the word SET when specifying LIBPATH. OS/2 does not search the current directory for DLLs unless you include it, so starting LIBPATH with a period, as in the example, is a good idea.

LOADHIGH   DOS Only

Loads DOS memory-resident programs into upper memory.

Syntax

LOADHIGH path\program

path is the location of the memory-resident program.

program is the name of the memory-resident program. Follow **program** with any arguments you would use if you typed it at the command line.

Example

To load APPEND into upper memory with C:\OS2 and C:\OS2\SYSTEM as arguments:

LOADHIGH APPEND C:\OS2;C:\OS2\SYSTEM

Notes

Memory-resident programs, also known as TSRs, are DOS commands and applications that run in the background. Loading TSRs in upper memory leaves more lower memory free for other programs if the following statement is listed in your CONFIG.SYS:

DOS=HIGH,UMB

MAXWAIT   OS/2 Only

Makes sure that no program thread is put on hold forever, even when the system is very busy running other programs.

Syntax

MAXWAIT=n

n is the maximum number of seconds that a thread can be put on hold. The default is three seconds.

Example

To keep any thread from waiting on hold more than one second:

MAXWAIT=1

Notes

If you run several programs at once and a few of them grab most of the computer's attention, you still may want to be sure that even low-priority background programs make some progress. If a program has not gotten any attention for the number of seconds you set with MAXWAIT, OS/2 temporarily increases that program's priority.

The default, three seconds, is usually a good place to start. Try decreasing it to one if background programs run too slowly.

MEMMAN   OS/2 Only

Enables you to run time-critical processes more reliably by turning off virtual memory.

Syntax

MEMMAN=s,m,PROTECT

s is SWAP or NOSWAP.

m is MOVE or NOMOVE.

PROTECT allows memory to be compacted by using protected dynamic link libraries.

Example

To turn off virtual memory:

MEMMAN=NOSWAP,NOMOVE

Notes

OS/2 can run more programs and use more data than can actually be stored in memory at once. OS/2 does this by swapping chunks of memory to disk when they are not being used and by reading them back in when they are needed. This swapping is called *virtual memory*. Turn virtual memory on with SWAP or off with NOSWAP.

As programs run, they grab chunks of memory and then release them when they are no longer needed. After a while, memory gets fragmented into little pieces, slowing down the system. OS/2 can overcome this problem by combining these pieces together. You can turn this feature on by using MOVE or off by using NOMOVE.

The default, **MEMMAN=MOVE,SWAP,PROTECT**, is usually best. For some time-critical applications like controlling complex machinery in a factory, you cannot afford to let the computer divert its attention to moving or swapping for even a fraction of a second. In this case, specify NOMOVE and NOSWAP. This setting will increase the amount of memory needed to run the system.

PATH

Tells OS/2 or DOS where to find programs.

Syntax

    SET PATH=dir1;dir2;...

dir1 is a directory, such as C:\PROGRAMS.

dir2 is another directory.

The ellipsis (...) means that you can specify more directories. Separate the directories from each other by using semicolons.

Examples

To tell OS/2 to look for program files in the directories C:\ and D:\UTILITY, place this line in CONFIG.SYS or type it in an OS/2 window:

    SET PATH=C:\;D:\UTILITY

To tell DOS to look for program files in the directories C:\ and D:\UTILITY, place this line in AUTOEXEC.BAT or type it in a DOS window:

    SET PATH=C:\;D:\UTILITY

Notes

You can always run a program if you first use the CD command to change to the directory where you keep it. If that directory is on the PATH, however, you can always run the program from any directory without worrying about where you put it on the disk.

You normally set the OS/2 PATH in CONFIG.SYS, and the DOS PATH in AUTOEXEC.BAT. You also can use these commands in a DOS or OS/2 window. When you set a new PATH, it replaces the old one.

PAUSEONERROR   OS/2 Only

Tells OS/2 to stop for a moment if it cannot process a line in CONFIG.SYS correctly.

Syntax

PAUSEONERROR=YES

PAUSEONERROR=NO

Notes

The default, YES, is generally the better choice. If OS/2 has a problem running a line in CONFIG.SYS, it displays an error message and waits until you press Enter. If the setting is NO, the error message appears, but scrolls off the screen so quickly that you may not have a chance to read it.

PRINTMONBUFSIZE

Sets the buffer size for the parallel port device driver.

Syntax

PRINTMONBUFSIZE=x

x is the size of the buffer.

Example

To set the parallel port device driver buffer size for the LPT1 as 2,048 bytes:

PRINTMONBUFSIZE=2048

Notes

You can set a value for the LPT1, LPT2, and LPT3 by separating the x value with a comma.

PRIORITY

Tells OS/2 whether it should juggle the priority of different threads that are running at the same time.

Syntax

PRIORITY= DYNAMIC

PRIORITY=ABSOLUTE

Notes

You should normally use **DYNAMIC** priority. This setting allows OS/2 to vary the priority of threads, depending on how active they are. A thread running in the foreground has a higher priority so that the program with which you are currently working runs faster than a program running in the background.

In the rare case that you need to run a program that sets its own thread priorities, use **ABSOLUTE**.

PRIORITY_DISK_IO

Specifies disk input/output priority for foreground applications.

Syntax

PRIORITY_DISK_IO=YES

PRIORITY_DISK_IO=NO

YES allows an application running in the foreground to receive disk input/output priority.

NO allows background applications to receive disk input/output priority.

Example

To give the foreground application the disk input/output priority:

PRIORITY_DISK_IO=YES

Notes

If PRIORITY_DISK_IO is turned on, the foreground application has a better response time than the background applications.

PROTECTONLY   OS/2 Only

Tells OS/2 whether you want to be able to run DOS programs.

Syntax

PROTECTONLY=YES

PROTECTONLY=NO

Notes

YES means you want to run only OS/2 programs.

NO means you want to run both DOS and OS/2 programs.

PROTSHELL — OS/2 Only

Loads OS/2's built-in command processor CMD.EXE or enables you to run a different command processor.

Syntax

PROTSHELL=startup

startup is the statement used to start the command processor. It includes the full path, the file's full name including its extension, and various other parameters.

Examples

To use the built-in OS/2 command processor:

PROTSHELL=C:\OS2\PMSHELL.EXE C:\OS2\OS2.INI C:\OS2\OS2SYS.INI C:\OS2\CMD.EXE

To use Hamilton Laboratories' C Shell:

PROTSHELL=C:\OS2\PMSHELL.EXE C:\OS2\OS2.INI C:\OS2\OS2SYS.INI C:\OS2\BIN\CSH.EXE -L

Type these commands all on one line in CONFIG.SYS.

Notes

The OS/2 command processor, also known as a shell, is the program that makes OS/2 full-screen and window sessions work. You may want to buy a different command processor to replace the shell that comes with OS/2. If you choose to use a different shell, you can use the PROTSHELL command listed in the documentation for the new command processor.

PSTAT

Shows system information for current processes, threads, semaphores, shared memory, and dynamic link libraries.

Syntax

PSTAT /C /S /L /M /P:*processid*

Switches

/S displays system semaphore information.

/L displays dynamic link library information.

/M displays shared memory information.

/C displays the current process and other system thread information.

/P:processid displays process-related information for the process number you specify—for example, */P:4* displays information for process number 4.

Notes

PSTAT provides information about active processes in your system. By using this command without switches, you receive general information about current processes and threads, semaphores, shared memory, and dynamic link libraries. By using the switches with PSTAT, you receive specific system information.

RMSIZE   DOS Only

Sets the amount of memory DOS can use.

Syntax

RMSIZE=n

n is the number of kilobytes of memory DOS can use, up to 640.

Example

To limit DOS to 512 kilobytes:

RMSIZE=512

Notes

DOS normally can use up to 640K of memory. Many programs require this amount, so you usually should use **RMSIZE=640**, which is the default. A smaller value keeps you from running some programs, but makes more memory available to OS/2.

SET

Assigns values to variables in the environment.

Syntax

SET

SET var=value

var is the name of a variable in the environment.

value is what the name stands for.

Examples

To see the values of all environment variables, type this at the command line:

SET

To tell OS/2's on-line command reference that its files are stored in C:\OS2\BOOK:

SET BOOKSHELF=C:\OS2\BOOK

To tell OS/2 to look for its help messages in C:\OS2\HELP:

SET HELP=C:\OS2\HELP

To tell OS/2 to remember the commands you have typed and allow you to reuse them:

SET KEYS=ON

Notes

The environment is a part of memory where values are assigned to certain names. The command processor and your applications use these names for various purposes. The PATH variable tells OS/2 where to find programs, for example. DPATH, KEYS, and PROMPT also are environment variables. You can string paths together by using a semicolon between them.

SHELL   DOS Only

Loads OS/2's built-in DOS command processor COMMAND.COM or enables you to run a different command processor.

Syntax

SHELL=startup

startup is the statement used to start the DOS command processor. The statement includes the full path, the file's full name including its extension, and any optional parameters.

Examples

To use the built-in DOS command processor:

SHELL=C:\OS2\MDOS\COMMAND.COM C:\OS2\MDOS /P

To use JP Software's 4DOS shell, assuming you have installed it in the D:\4DOS directory:

SHELL=D:\4DOS\4DOS.COM /P

Notes

The DOS command processor, also known as a shell, is the program that makes DOS sessions work. You may want to buy a different command processor to replace the shell that comes with OS/2. If you choose to use a different shell, you can use the PROTSHELL command listed in the documentation for the new command processor.

If you use a different shell, you must add a line to CONFIG.SYS that sets the COMSPEC variable. This line gives the full path and file name of the new shell. For the 4DOS example above, add the following line to CONFIG.SYS:

SET COMSPEC=D:\4DOS\4DOS.COM

SWAPPATH   OS/2 Only

Tells OS/2 where to create a swap file, which uses free disk space to let you run more programs than can fit in memory.

Syntax

SWAPPATH=swapdir *minfree initial*

swapdir is a directory, such as C:\. The default is C:\OS2\SYSTEM.

minfree is a number from 512 to 32,767. It specifies the number of kilobytes of disk space that the swap file leaves free for other purposes. If 2,600K are free when you start OS/2 and *minfree* is 600, then the swap file cannot use more than 2,000K. The default for *minfree* is 512.

initial specifies the size of the swap file initially allocated by the operating system.

Example

To put the swap file in the \SWAP directory on drive D and allow it to use all available space on D except for 1,000K:

SWAPPATH=D:\SWAP 1000

Notes

For swapping to be active, MEMMAN must be in your CONFIG.SYS:

> **MEMMAN-SWAP**

If possible, put the swap file on a drive that has several (10 to 15) megabytes of free space. A large swap file enables you to run many programs at once.

THREADS   OS/2 Only

Sets the number of different things OS/2 can do at a time.

Syntax

> **THREADS=n**

n is the maximum number of threads, from 32 to 4,095.

Example

To allow up to 512 threads:

> **THREADS=512**

Notes

A thread is a part of a program that runs on its own, independently from the other parts. A spreadsheet might create a thread when you tell it to save a file. This thread runs like a program in the background, so you can continue entering numbers in the spreadsheet without waiting for the file to be saved. The default is 64, but you can try setting THREADS to 256 if you run several programs at once.

TIMESLICE   OS/2 Only

Sets upper and lower limits on the amount of time the computer spends on each thread.

Syntax

> **TIMESLICE** *min,max*

min is a number between 32 and 65,536. A thread gets the computer's attention and keeps it for at least *min* thousandths of a second. The default is 32.

max is a number between 32 and 65,535. A thread gets the computer's attention and keeps it for no longer than *max* thousandths of a second. The default is the value of *min*.

Examples

To set the minimum and maximum time slice to 32 and 500 thousandths of a second, respectively:

>   **TIMESLICE=32,500**

To set the maximum time slice to one second and use the default minimum value:

>   **TIMESLICE=,1000**

Notes

You should use 32 as the minimum value because OS/2 uses it for some special situations.

VCOM DOS Only

Enables you to use the communications ports for DOS sessions.

Syntax

>   **DEVICE=path\VCOM.SYS**

path is the location of the file VCOM.SYS. By default, it is C:\OS2\MDOS.

Example

To make the communications ports available to DOS, type this in CONFIG.SYS:

>   **DEVICE=C:\OS2\MDOS\VCOM.SYS**

Notes

List VCOM.SYS *after* COM.SYS in CONFIG.SYS. Older versions of OS/2 used a program called SETCOM40 to provide communications support to DOS sessions, but you should not use SETCOM40 with OS/2 Version 2.x.

VMOUSE   DOS Only

Enables you to use a mouse or trackball in DOS sessions.

Syntax

DEVICE=path\VMOUSE.SYS

path is the location of the file VMOUSE.SYS. By default, it is C:\OS2\MDOS.

Notes

Installing a mouse requires other drivers as well. See the explanation under the MOUSE command.

Appendix A

The Past, Present, and Future of OS/2

OS/2 has a checkered past, a successful present, and a closely guarded future (but one that is well in the works). In this appendix, you'll explore the past, present, and future of IBM's flagship operating system for desktop computers.

The Past

OS/2 began as a combined effort of IBM and Microsoft in 1985. In August of that year, the two companies signed a Joint Development Agreement that let them design and build a new operating system, to be named OS/2.

The agreement no longer exists; IBM and Microsoft no longer work together on OS/2. IBM has shouldered the work load itself. The companies still have a top-secret Cross-Licensing Agreement, however, that lets one company use the other's software. The Cross-Licensing Agreement covers DOS, Windows, OS/2, and even some future operating system designs, such as Microsoft's Windows NT. (Microsoft's development of Windows NT culminated in the release of NT late in the summer of 1993.)

IBM and Microsoft intended OS/2 to be a replacement for DOS. Software developers and end users alike had voiced their complaints about DOS. Specifically, people said they did not have enough memory in which to run applications (the infamous 640K limitation), that DOS did not support multiple concurrent applications, that DOS was too fragile, that DOS was too simple and rudimentary, and that DOS was too slow when applications accessed large files. In short, DOS was not industrial strength. People's biggest complaint about DOS, however, was that each DOS application had its own user interface and required too much training to make the DOS environment truly productive.

The new operating system addressed almost all these concerns. A consistent user interface (Presentation Manager) did not appear in the very first version of OS/2.

OS/2 1.0 shipped in December 1987. The first implementation of OS/2 had a single, small DOS Compatibility Box for running DOS applications. The first version of OS/2 did not contain or support a graphical user interface. The first version did offer up to 16M of memory, however, to applications rewritten to run under OS/2 instead of DOS.

Version 1.1 of OS/2—essentially the 1.0 product with the addition of Presentation Manager—appeared in the last quarter of 1988. Still saddled with a small DOS Compatibility Box, OS/2 1.1 was nonetheless a technical marvel. OS/2 1.1 allowed software developers to transcend the limitations of DOS if they rewrote their software. Unfortunately, few did.

At the same time that IBM and Microsoft released a Presentation Manager version of OS/2, IBM published a set of guidelines and standards, called *Systems Application Architecture* (SAA), to help the computer industry achieve some measure of consistency and coherence. IBM mentions its own products in the guidelines, but otherwise freely offers the guidelines as a set of suggested methods, interfaces, computer languages, and design techniques that software developers can follow. IBM reasons that consistency and coherence among software applications will encourage more people to use computers in more ways, more productively (and thus indirectly help IBM sell more hardware and software).

Microsoft and IBM also began offering an Extended Edition of OS/2. Called OS/2 EE 1.1, this special version contained a Communications Manager for computer-to-computer data transfer, a Database Manager based on IBM's *Structured Query Language* (SQL) standard for record keeping, and special support for local area networks. The regular version of OS/2 was called OS/2 Standard Edition (SE).

IBM and Microsoft enhanced OS/2 considerably and released OS/2 1.2 in October 1989. Version 1.2 added features that addressed many of the concerns that people expressed regarding version 1.1, including the capability to switch between DOS and OS/2 (Dual Boot), an installable file system (High Performance File System, or HPFS), and hardware compatibility with more kinds of personal computers. Unfortunately, IBM and Microsoft "broke" the print drivers in version 1.2, and many people had problems with their printouts with this version.

In December 1990, IBM and Microsoft released OS/2 1.3. Slimmed down considerably from earlier versions, OS/2 1.3 got the nickname "OS/2 Lite." You could run OS/2 1.3 on a computer with as little as 2M or 3M of memory. Version 1.3 did many things well for applications rewritten for OS/2, but it still had only a single, small DOS Compatibility Box. IBM did most of the development work for version 1.3. Version 1.3 was small, fast, reliable, and it printed. Its only drawback was its small DOS box.

Late in 1991, IBM and Microsoft stopped working together on OS/2, which became purely an IBM product (Microsoft went off on its own to develop other operating systems). With the Cross-Licensing Agreement still in effect, both companies still have access to each other's work. This situation is unusual, to say the least. The picture is further complicated because IBM and former rival Apple Computer have jointly agreed to develop enhancements to OS/2 and OS/2-like operating systems in the future. IBM and Apple started the Taligent company to produce the enhanced operating system, code-named "Pink." It will be several years before Taligent releases the follow-up to OS/2.

March 1992 saw the release of OS/2 2.0, the first version of OS/2 to support multiple DOS boxes. The key features of OS/2 2.0 are the following:

- Simple, graphical-user-interface installation
- System integrity protection
- Virtual memory
- Preemptive multitasking and task scheduling
- Fast, 32-bit architecture
- Overlapped, fast disk file access
- DOS compatibility
- More available memory for DOS applications (typically about 620K of conventional memory)

- Capability to run OS/2, DOS, and Windows software concurrently
- Multiple concurrent DOS sessions
- High Performance File System (HPFS)
- Presentation Manager (PM) graphical user interface
- The object-oriented Workplace Shell (WPS)
- National Language Support (NLS)
- Multiple Operating System Tool (MOST)
- Configuration tool for tailoring OS/2 to your preferences
- Small, easy-to-use applications (called *applets*) bundled with OS/2, such as notepad, diary, spreadsheet, presentation graphics software, and other productivity tools
- Interactive on-line documentation and help screens
- Capability to run OS/2 on both IBM and IBM-compatible hardware

OS/2 2.0 can run more than 2,500 OS/2 applications, 20,000 DOS applications, and 1,200 Windows applications. This makes OS/2 2.0 a versatile and flexible operating environment. By the end of 1992, IBM had sold approximately 3 million copies of OS/2 2.0.

A year after version 2.0 first became available, in March 1993, IBM released OS/2 2.1—the version this book discusses. Version 2.1 added the following features to the already capable version 2.0:

- Support for Microsoft Windows version 3.1
- Support for popular Super VGA video adapters, in a variety of resolutions, in both Presentation Manager and Windows sessions
- Support for more brands of printers
- Support for additional SCSI-based CD-ROM drives
- A CD-ROM installation capability
- Support for the Advanced Power Management (APM) specification (intended for notebook computers)

- Support for the Personal Computer Memory Card International Association (PCMCIA) specification
- Support for pen-based computers
- Multimedia support

In the fall of 1993, IBM released the OS/2 for Windows product. Targeted at people who already have Microsoft Windows 3.1 on their computers, OS/2 for Windows let IBM sell OS/2 without paying royalties to Microsoft for the Windows portion of OS/2. Indeed, the initial price of the CD-ROM edition of OS/2 for Windows was only $39.

The Present

IBM has sold more than 5 million copies of OS/2; the operating system is finding its way into large companies. The Travelers Insurance Company, for instance, uses OS/2 in many of its desktop computers and in many of its file servers (running IBM's LAN Server network operating system).

The Future

As with all future software releases, IBM has not publicly announced its plans for OS/2, but you can probably guess many of them. The enhancements you'll see in future versions of OS/2 are logical extensions of the features and functions in the existing product.

One not-so-secret enhancement is a separate version of OS/2 that runs on Symmetric MultiProcessor (SMP) computers. For high-end file-server environments, IBM has announced it will sell an OS/2 that can take advantage of multiple CPUs (two, four, or more 80486 or Pentium chips) in the same computer.

The following changes are likely to occur in the next release of OS/2:

- Replace slower 16-bit components with 32-bit modules
- Improve memory usage and handling, especially in a PC with only 4M of RAM
- Speed up program loading

- Execute concurrent tasks (such as two or more DOS programs) faster
- Compress files on-the-fly with built-in file compression
- Enhance the PCMCIA and APM functions
- Add more built-in fonts
- Support larger hard disks
- Support more types of hardware add-ons (video adapters, graphics files, audio adapters and sound cards, printers, CD-ROM drives, tape drives, and scanners)
- Integrate Taligent's object-oriented technologies into OS/2
- Add an intelligent CONFIG.SYS editor to OS/2
- Increase OS/2's support for different countries and languages
- Incorporate the virtual device driver (VxD) and Win-32 features of Windows in OS/2

What about the distant future? IBM has a sizable team of people working on a future operating system called Workplace OS. And Apple and IBM formed the Taligent company to explore the relationship of operating systems and object-oriented technology. These efforts are really extensions of the development of OS/2.

Eventually, perhaps by the end of this decade, OS/2 will grow to become a completely object-oriented, workplace-centric operating system. By that time, you'll speak to your computer, your computer will speak back, and your computer will show your data to you in a 3D holographic display in mid-air.

Appendix B
Workplace Shell Tasks and Keyboard Shortcuts

Many people find the Workplace Shell easy to use and intuitive. You don't use every task every day, however. The information in this appendix tells you how to correctly perform all the Workplace Shell tasks, especially the ones you use infrequently.

Workplace Shell Task	Do These Steps
Close a window	Double-click the Menu button in the upper left corner of the window.
Close a window or notebook	Point to (move the mouse cursor to) an object and click mouse button 2. Click the Close option.
Copy an object	Point to the object to be copied. Hold down the Ctrl key while you use mouse button 2 to drag the object to a new location.
Create a shadow of an object	Point to the object to be copied. Hold down the Shift key while you use mouse button 2 to drag the object to a new location.
Delete an object	Use mouse button 2 to drag and drop the object on the shredder.
Display object's System menu	Point to the object and click mouse button 2 or press and release the Alt key.
Display the window list	Point to an empty area on the desktop. Press both mouse buttons at the same time.

(continues)

Appendix B—Workplace Shell Tasks and Keyboard Shortcuts

Workplace Shell Task	Do These Steps
Drag-and-drop	Point to the object. Grab the object and move it by pressing and holding down mouse button 2 while you move the mouse. Release the mouse button when you have moved the object to its new location.
Dual-boot DOS	Double-click the OS/2 System folder, double-click the Command Prompts folder, and then double-click the Dual Boot icon.
Find an object	Display a folder's popup menu. Choose the Find option.
Maximize a window	Using mouse button 1, double-click the clock's title bar or click the Maximize button (the button with a large square) in the upper right corner of the window.
Minimize a window	Point to the Minimize button (the button with a small square) to the left of the Maximize button and click mouse button 1.
Move a window	Point to the window's title bar. Click and hold down either mouse button. Release the mouse button when you have moved the window to its new location.
Open an object	Point to the object and press mouse button 1 twice in rapid succession (a double-click).
Open settings notebook	Point to an object and press mouse button 2 once. Then click the Open menu option. Click the Settings option.
Open Workplace Shell's system menu	Click mouse button 2 on any blank area of the desktop. Opening this menu is a little more difficult with the keyboard.
Print an object	Drag and drop the object on the appropriate printer object.
Resize a window	Move the mouse cursor to any edge or corner of the window. When the cursor changes to a double arrow, hold down either mouse button and move the mouse to resize the window. Release the button.
Restore a window to its original size	Double-click the title bar or click the Restore button (a medium-size square between two vertical lines).
See an object's popup menu	Point to an object and click mouse button 2.
See the desktop's popup menu	Point to an empty area on the desktop and click mouse button 2.

Workplace Shell Task	Do These Steps
Select an object	Point to an object and click mouse button 1.
Shut down	Point to an empty area on the desktop and click mouse button 2. Then click the Shutdown option. Confirm the operation and then wait for OS/2 to indicate that you can reboot or turn off your computer.
Start a program object	Point to the object and double-click mouse button 1.

Workplace Shell Keyboard Shortcuts

Keystroke	Function
Alt-Esc	Switches to the next open window or full-screen session
Alt-Home	Switches a DOS program between window and full screen
Ctrl-Alt-Del	Restarts the operating system
Ctrl-Esc	Displays the Window List
Alt-PgDn	In a notebook, moves cursor to the next page
Alt-PgUp	In a notebook, moves cursor to the previous page
F1	Displays help for the active window
F5	Refreshes contents of the active window
F6	Moves cursor from one windowpane to another in a split window
F10	Moves the cursor to or from the menu bar
Alt-F4	Closes the active window
Alt-F5	Restores the window to previous size
Alt-F6	Moves cursor between associated windows
Alt-F7	Moves the active window or selected object
Alt-F8	Sizes the active window or selected object
Alt-F9	Minimizes the window

(continues)

Keystroke	Function
Alt-F10	Maximizes the window
Shift-Esc or Alt-Spacebar	Switches to or from the title-bar icon
Shift-F8	Starts or stops selecting more than one object
Shift-F10	Displays pop-up menu for the active object

Appendix C
Enhanced Editor Keystroke Guide

After listing the function key assignments for the Enhanced Editor, this appendix lists the other defined keystrokes by function and then by menu.

The following tables are included in this appendix:

- Function Key Keystroke Reference
- Basic Editing Keystroke Reference
- Cursor Key Keystroke Reference
- Mouse Cursor Reference
- Editing Keystrokes

    Basic editing and reformatting

    Selecting text (advanced mode)

    Altering selected text (advanced mode)

    Adding special characters

    Menu shortcut keys

- File Menu Keystroke Reference
- Edit Menu Keystroke Reference
- Search Menu Keystroke Reference

Appendix C—Enhanced Editor Keystroke Guide

- Options Menu Keystroke Reference
- Command Menu Keystroke Reference

For further information, see Chapter 14, "Using the OS/2 Text Editor."

Function Key Keystroke Reference

Key	Function	Function with Shift
F1	Help	Scroll left
F2	Save	Scroll right
F3	Quit (no save)	Scroll up
F4	Quit (with save)	Scroll down
F5	Open Dialog	Make current cursor position center line in window
F6	Select line draw command	None
F7	Rename file	None
F8	Edit additional line	None
F9	Undo last action	None
F10	Go to menu bar	None
F11	Previous file	None
F12	Next file	None

Key	Function with Alt	Function with Ctrl
F1	Draw sample box characters	Make word uppercase
F2	None	Make word lowercase
F3	None	Make selection uppercase
F4	Close window	Make selection lowercase
F5	Reopen window	Move cursor to beginning of word
F6	None	Move cursor to end of word
F7	Move window	Move selected area to left

Key	Function with Alt	Function with Ctrl
F8	Size window	Move selected area to right
F9	Minimize window	None
F10	Maximize window	None
F11	None	None
F12	None	None

Basic Editing Keystroke Reference

Cursor Key Keystroke Reference

Keystroke	Action
Left arrow	Left one letter
Ctrl-Left	Left one word
Right arrow	Right one letter
Ctrl-Right	Right one word
Tab	Right one tab stop
Shift-Tab	Left one tab stop
Up arrow	Up one line
Down arrow	Down one line
PgUp	Up one page
Ctrl-PgUp	Top of page
PgDn	Down one page
Ctrl-PgDn	Bottom of page
Home	Beginning of line
Ctrl-Home	Beginning of file
End	End of line
Ctrl-End	End of file

Mouse Cursor Reference

Mouse button and action	Result
Click button 1	Moves cursor to mouse position
Drag button 1	Selects the block
Drag button 2	Selects the lines; if in a selected area, moves the selected text
Ctrl key and drag button 1	Selects the characters
Ctrl key and drag button 2	If in selected area, copies the selected text
Double-click button 1	Unmarks text
Double-click button 2	Moves cursor to mouse position and selects the word

Editing Keystrokes

Key	Action
Basic Editing And Reformatting	
Backspace	Deletes character to left of cursor
Ctrl-Backspace	Deletes line
Del	Deletes character to right of cursor
Enter	Ends line
Ins	Toggles between insert and overwrite modes
Alt-J	Joins with following line
Alt-P	Reformats next paragraph
Alt-R	Reformats selected area
Alt-S	Splits line at cursor
Ctrl-D	Deletes word
Ctrl-E	Erases to end of line
Ctrl-K	Duplicates line
Ctrl-M	Inserts blank line
Ctrl-Tab	Adds tab character

Basic Editing Keystroke Reference

Key	Action
Selecting Text (Advanced Mode)	
Alt-B	Marks start or end of rectangular block
Alt-L	Marks start or end of lines
Alt-U	Unmarks selected text
Alt-W	Marks word
Alt-Z	Marks start or end of characters
Altering Selected Text (Advanced Mode)	
Alt-A	Moves marked text, leaving blank characters in the former location
Alt-C	Copies marked text
Alt-D	Deletes marked text
Alt-E	Moves cursor to end of marked text
Alt-M	Moves marked text
Alt-O	Moves marked text overwriting
Alt-T	Centers marked text
Alt-Y	Moves the cursor to the beginning of the marked text
Adding Special Characters	
Alt-F	Fills marked text area with selected fill character
Alt-N	Adds current filename to text
Alt-1	Edits file named on current line
Alt-0	Executes current line or selected area as commands
Alt-=	Same as Alt-0
Alt-—	Highlights cursor
Ctrl-Enter	Enter with no new line
Ctrl-2	Adds NULL character
Ctrl-6	Adds logical NOT character (ASCII 170)
Ctrl-9	Adds left brace character ({)

(continues)

Key	Action
Ctrl-0	Adds right brace character (})

Menu Shortcut And Command Keys

Key	Action
Shift-Del	Cuts marked text to Clipboard
Shift-Ins	Pastes block from Clipboard
Alt-Backspace	Undoes the last action
Ctrl-B	Lists the bookmarks
Ctrl-C	Searches and replaces next occurrence of search text
Ctrl-F	Finds next occurrence of search text
Ctrl-I	Opens command dialog box
Ctrl-L	Copies the current line to command line
Ctrl-N	Goes to next file in ring
Ctrl-O	Opens existing file
Ctrl-P	Goes to previous file in ring
Ctrl-Q	Swaps to or from ALL file
Ctrl-R	Starts or ends recording keystrokes
Ctrl-S	Searches for text
Ctrl-T	Plays back keystrokes into editor
Ctrl-X	Forces syntax expansion
Ctrl-Y	Chooses style (font and color) for file
Ctrl-Ins	Copies marked text to Clipboard

File Menu Keystroke Reference

Use after opening File menu by pressing F10, then F.

Key	Action
A	Saves current file with new name
I	Imports text file

Key	Action
N	Opens new file
O	Opens existing file
P	Prints file
Q	Closes window without saving file
R	Renames current file
S	Saves current file
U	Opens untitled file
V	Saves current file and closes window

Edit Menu Keystroke Reference

Use after opening Edit menu by pressing F10, then E.

Key	Action
A	Moves marked text, leaving its former location blank
B	Pastes block from Clipboard
C	Copies marked text
D	Deletes marked text
E	Chooses style (font and color) for file
I	Prints marked text
L	Undoes last action
M	Moves marked text
N	Unmarks marked text
O	Moves marked text, overwriting any existing text
P	Pastes lines from Clipboard
S	Pastes from Clipboard
T	Cuts marked text to Clipboard

(continues)

Key	Action
U	Undoes multiple actions
Y	Copies marked text to Clipboard

Search Menu Keystroke Reference

Use after opening Search menu by pressing F10, then S.

Key	Action
B	Opens bookmark menu
C	Finds and replaces next occurrence of search text
F	Finds next occurrence of search text
S	Searches for text
From Bookmark Menu?	
L	Lists bookmarks
N	Goes to next bookmark
P	Goes to previous bookmark
S	Sets a bookmark

Options Menu Keystroke Reference

Use after opening Options menu by pressing F10, then O.

Key	Action
A	Alters autosave settings
M	Displays program messages
N	Alters window appearance, such as menus and scroll bars
O	Saves current option settings
R	Alters settings, such as tabs and margins, advanced marking, or enable ring

Command Menu Keystroke Reference

Use after opening Command menu by pressing F10, then C.

Key	Action
C	Opens command dialog box
H	Halts command

Appendix D
OS/2 Games

After installation, OS/2 places games in a template within the OS/2 System window. (Refer to Chapter 6, "Installing OS/2," for installation instructions.) You can open the games template by double-clicking the OS/2 games icon. The following games are included:

- Cat and Mouse
- Jigsaw
- OS/2 Chess
- Reversi
- Scramble
- Klondike Solitaire

To start a game, double-click its icon. The following sections summarize the available games.

Cat and Mouse

The Cat and Mouse game called PMSeek helps you learn to use the mouse. The game is also handy for checking your mouse. When you start the game, a cat appears on the background and "chases" your mouse pointer. As you move the mouse pointer around, the cat follows. If it reaches the pointer, the cat sits down, washes, yawns, and then goes to sleep until you move the mouse again. The cat only appears in the background area and does not intrude into the open windows.

Settings and Options

When you first start the game, your screen looks like figure D.1. The open window displays a control panel where you can adjust the play time, speed, and step.

Fig. D.1
Cat and Mouse control panel.

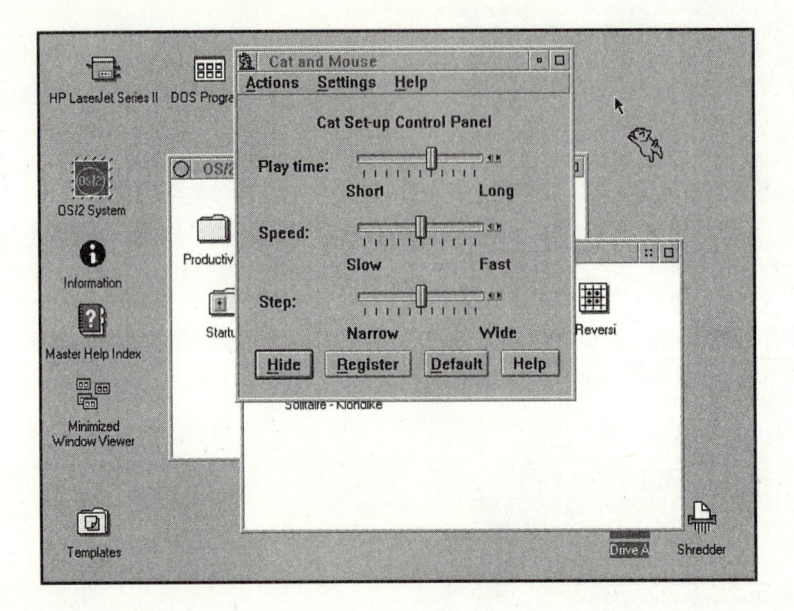

When you increase the play time, you lengthen the time the cat moves before resting. With a short play time, the cat follows the mouse without pausing.

The speed adjustment alters how fast the cat moves, and the step adjustment alters the size of the cat's step.

To save the new settings you select, choose **R**egister from the Control Panel or **S**ettings menu. To restore the default settings, choose **D**efault from the Control Panel or **S**ettings menu.

You disable or enable the cat without ending the program by using the **A**ctions menu. You also can remove all the windows from the screen by using this menu, making the cat run away from the mouse. When you choose **A**ctions and **H**ide or type F10 and I, the icons and windows disappear and you see a dialog box explaining that you can press Alt to redisplay your windows or click the cat. In this mode, the cat runs away from the mouse. You can chase the cat around the screen.

Jigsaw

The Jigsaw game displays a picture as a jigsaw puzzle. You assemble the pieces by dragging them with your mouse. Although OS/2 has only one bitmap sample image—the OS/2 logo screen, you can choose any OS/2 bitmap file as your puzzle's picture.

> **Note**
>
> You need a mouse to move the pieces around the screen. You cannot use a keyboard to assemble the puzzle.

Settings and Options

After starting Jigsaw, load a bitmap into the window by choosing the **F**ile menu **O**pen or by pressing F10 and then pressing O. Choose your image from the dialog box in the same way as you load files in most applications.

After loading the bitmap, choose the **O**ptions Menu **J**umble to mix up the pieces or press F10 and then J. If you maximize the window, your screen may look like the screen in figure D.2.

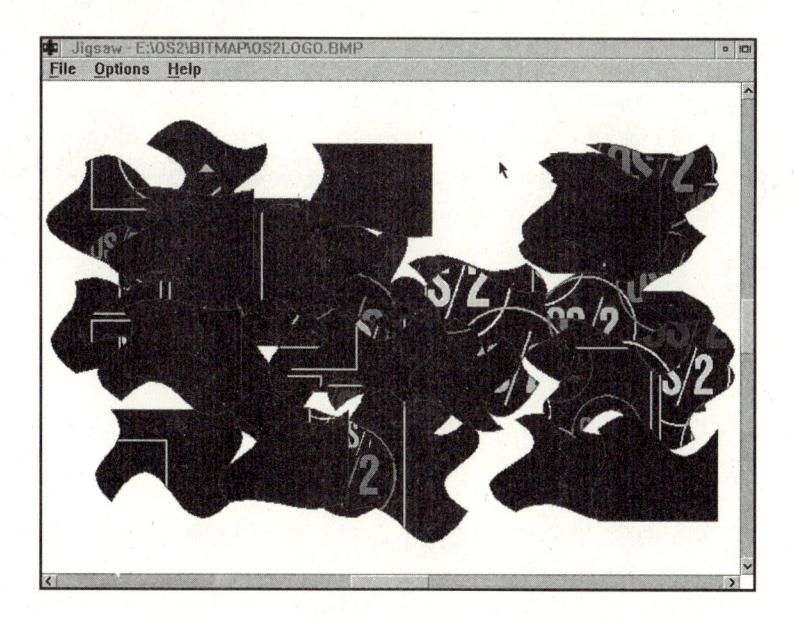

Fig. D.2
Jigsaw game.

You assemble the puzzle by pointing to a puzzle piece, pressing mouse button 1, and then dragging the piece to the desired position. You do not have to rotate the pieces. When you join pieces correctly, OS/2 beeps to show they are joined. You then can manipulate the joined pieces as a single piece.

> **Note**
>
> Listen for the beep that indicates that you have actually joined the pieces. Positioning the pieces exactly right on-screen is sometimes hard.

In addition to being able to change the picture by loading different bitmap images, you can change the size of the puzzle. Choose **O**ptions menu **S**ize and then choose from small, medium, large, or full size. This option does not change the number of pieces in the puzzle but alters the size of the displayed image.

OS/2 Chess

OS/2 Chess is a chess game for one or two players. If you are on a network, you can even play against someone at another workstation. When playing against the computer, you can choose the computer's experience level.

Settings and Options

When you start a chess game, OS/2 prompts you for the name of each player. You can choose between playing the game on your computer (against a human or your computer), or, if your computer is connected to a network, you can link with another user.

When you choose the computer as your opponent, you can choose among five skill levels, ranging from beginner to advanced. You also can select the book opening the computer uses. OS/2 offers nearly 50 openings.

Choose the options for each player and press OK. Figure D.3 shows the screen that appears.

The rules for this chess game are the same as conventional chess. You move pieces by dragging them across the board or by keyboard entry using algebraic chess notation. The help file includes rules and some elementary strategies. You can load save or delete games in progress, and you can print the current position from the File menu.

Fig. D.3
Chess Game.

The Options menu includes many selections for altering your screen's appearance and sounds. You can change the colors, turn the sound on and off, and enter moves from the keyboard. You can set up a game position, see the time taken for moves, and take back a move.

The View menu also includes selections that affect your screen's appearance, but these options are normally made during a game. You can rotate the board, see the possible valid moves, as well as get an analysis of these—your position, record of the moves made in the game, and captured pieces.

Network users can send a message indicating their move by using the Network menu. They also can disconnect from their opponent or get a list of users by means of this menu.

Reversi

Reversi, a game that you play against the computer, follows the rules of the board game Reversi. The object of the game is to place more red dots on an eight-by-eight square board than your opponent, the computer, places blue dots.

The rules for Reversi are simple, but the game is difficult to win. You place a dot in a square beside a blue dot. Try to choose a position so that a red dot at the other end traps the blue dot or dots. Trapped blue dots change to red. After you take your turn, the computer places a blue dot on the board.

842   Appendix D—OS/2 Games

If a horizontal row has a red dot and then two blue dots (moving from left to right), for example, you can place a red dot beside the right blue dot. The two blue dots then change to red.

Settings and Options

As you move the mouse around the board, the cursor changes from the shape of a pointer to a cross to show the valid moves. If you cannot make a valid move, you must pass. Figure D.4 shows a typical game in progress.

Options for playing the game include altering the computer's skill level between beginner, intermediate, advanced, or master and changing between two different starting positions. You can get a hint on the appropriate next move from the Moves menu.

Fig. D.4
Reversi Game.

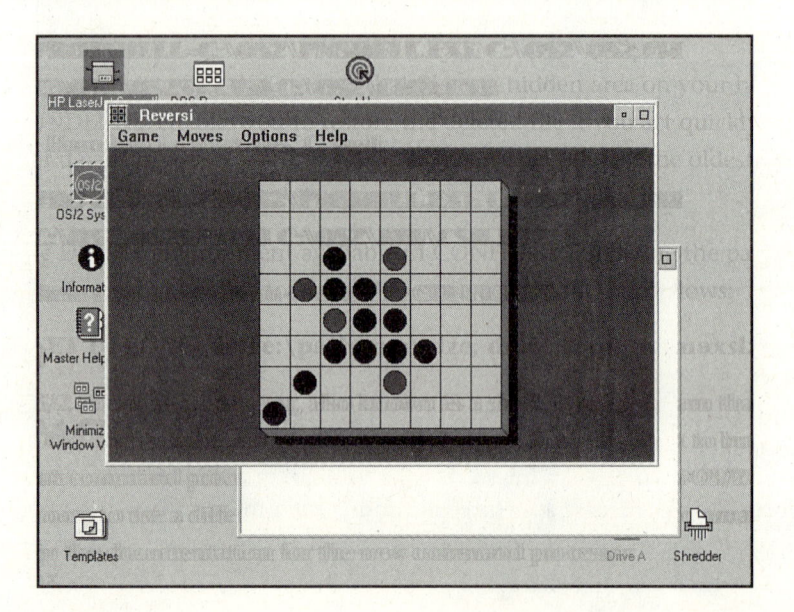

Scramble

Scramble is a tile-arranging game similar to games that have a series of numbered tiles or tiles with a portion of a picture. The tiles are in a frame, and you rearrange them in different sequences. Scramble has a four-by-four tile frame with 15 tiles (see fig. D.5).

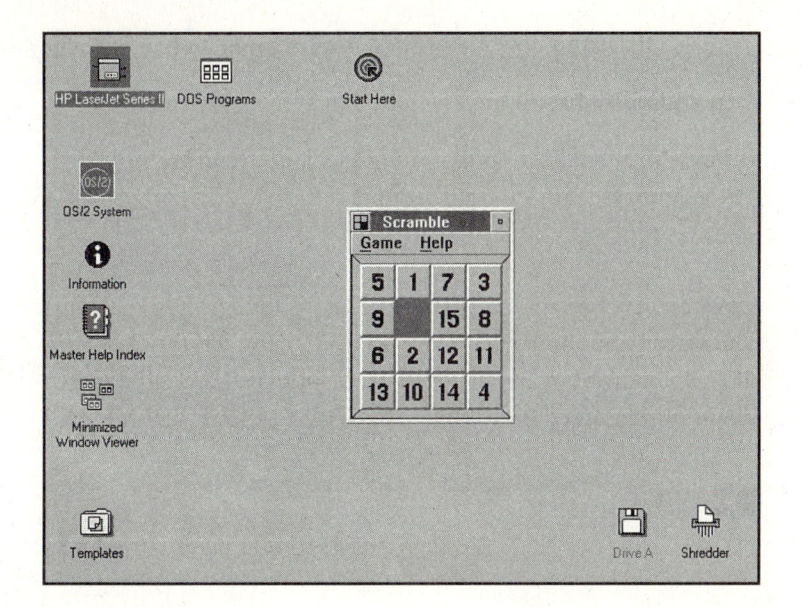

Fig. D.5
Scramble.

Settings and Options

The Open Game option offers three sets of tiles. One set numbers the tiles, another is a picture of cats (similar to the cat in the Cat and Mouse game), and the other is the OS/2 logo image.

You choose **S**cramble from the **G**ame menu to mix the tiles. You point to the tile you want to slide into the vacant tile position and then click button 1 to make the move.

Klondike Solitaire

OS/2 includes a version of the solitaire card game called Klondike. The object of the game is to place the cards in numerical order according to suits along the right edge of the window. You can build on the central stacks by alternating red and black cards in descending numerical order. Figure D.6 shows a game in progress.

Settings and Options

You can make the computer play on its own by choosing the **A**utoplay option in the **G**ame menu. Other options include turning the sound effects on and off, changing the cards' pictures, and altering the animation speed when the computer moves the cards. You can save and restore your preferred settings and turn the scoring on and off. As you play the game, you can take back a move, replay a move, or cheat.

Fig. D.6
Klondike.

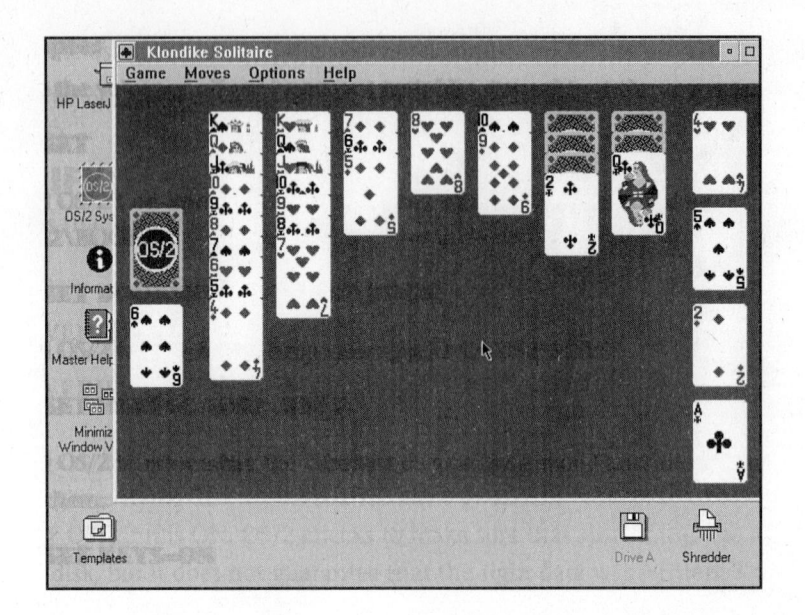

Appendix E
OS/2 Files by Function

File	Directory	Function
STARTMRI.DLL	\OS2\DLL	"Start here information" dynamic link library
STHR.EXE	\OS2	"Start here information," executable
8514.DLL	\OS2\DLL	8514 display dynamic link library
8514SYS.FON	\OS2\MDOS\WINOS2\SYSTEM	8514 font for WIN-OS2
8514OEM.FON	\OS2\MDOS\WINOS2\SYSTEM	8514 font for WIN-OS2
F80404.BIO	\OS2	Abios Patch File
F80403.BIO	\OS2	Abios Patch File
F80402.BIO	\OS2	Abios Patch File
F80700.BIO	\OS2	Abios Patch File
W050100.BIO	\OS2	Abios Patch File
F80600.BIO	\OS2	Abios Patch File
F80701.BIO	\OS2	Abios Patch File
W050101.BIO	\OS2	Abios Patch File
W020100.BIO	\OS2	Abios Patch File
W0F0000.BIO	\OS2	Abios Patch File
W060100.BIO	\OS2	Abios Patch File

Appendix E—OS/2 Files by Function

File	Directory	Function
W050000.BIO	\OS2	Abios Patch File
F80000.BIO	\OS2	Abios Patch File
000000.BIO	\OS2	Abios Patch File
W020101.BIO	\OS2	Abios Patch File
F80100.BIO	\OS2	Abios Patch File
F80702.BIO	\OS2	Abios Patch File
F80200.BIO	\OS2	Abios Patch File
F81000.BIO	\OS2	Abios Patch File
F80D00.BIO	\OS2	Abios Patch File
F80D01.BIO	\OS2	Abios Patch File
F81B00.BIO	\OS2	Abios Patch File
FC0403.BIO	\OS2	Abios Patch File
FC0500.BIO	\OS2	Abios Patch File
F88000.BIO	\OS2	Abios Patch File
FC0400.BIO	\OS2	Abios Patch File
F80903.BIO	\OS2	Abios Patch File
F80902.BIO	\OS2	Abios Patch File
F80A00.BIO	\OS2	Abios Patch File
F80904.BIO	\OS2	Abios Patch File
F80A01.BIO	\OS2	Abios Patch File
F80A02.BIO	\OS2	Abios Patch File
F80C00.BIO	\OS2	Abios Patch File
F80704.BIO	\OS2	Abios Patch File
F80703.BIO	\OS2	Abios Patch File
TOUMOU.BIO	\OS2	Abios patch file for touch devices
EXTDSKDD.SYS	\OS2	Access to an external drive

File	Directory	Function
AHA164X.ADD	\OS2\DRIVERS	Adapter device driver (Adaptec)
AHA174X.ADD	\OS2\DRIVERS	Adapter device driver (Adaptec)
AHA154X.ADD	\OS2\DRIVERS	Adapter device driver (Adaptec)
AHA152X.ADD	\OS2\DRIVERS	Adapter device driver (Adaptec)
FD16-700.ADD	\OS2	Adapter device driver (Future Domain)
FD850IBM.ADD	\OS2	Adapter device driver (Future Domain)
FD8XX.ADD	\OS2	Adapter device driver (Future Domain)
PMATM.DLL	\OS2\DLL	Adobe Type Manager dynamic link library
ATM.INI	\OS2\MDOS\WINOS2	Adobe Type Manager font support
README.ATM	\OS2\MDOS\WINOS2	Adobe Type Manager information
BASICA.COM	\OS2\MDOS	Advanced BASIC language interpreter
PMCHKDSK.EXE	\OS2	Analyzes hard disk
PMCHKDSK.DLL	\OS2\DLL	Analyzes hard disk dynamic link library
PATCH.EXE	\OS2	Applies fixes/patches to files
FIXWP.EXE	\OS2\MDOS\WINOS2	Applies WordPerfect patch
ASSIGN.COM	\OS2\MDOS	Assigns a drive letter to a different drive
BACKUP.EXE	\OS2	Backup files on hard disk
BKSCALLS.DLL	\OS2\DLL	Base keyboard calls
BMSCALLS.DLL	\OS2\DLL	Base monitor calls

(continues)

Appendix E—OS/2 Files by Function

File	Directory	Function
VIOCALLS.DLL	\OS2\DLL	Base video calls dynamic link library
BVH8514A.DLL	\OS2\DLL	Base Video Handler dynamic link library (8514A)
BVHCGA.DLL	\OS2\DLL	Base Video Handler dynamic link library (CGA)
BVHEGA.DLL	\OS2\DLL	Base Video Handler dynamic link library (EGA)
BVHMGA.DLL	\OS2\DLL	Base Video Handler dynamic link library (MGA)
BVHSVGA.DLL	\OS2\DLL	Base Video Handler dynamic link library (SVGA)
BVHVGA.DLL	\OS2\DLL	Base Video Handler dynamic link library (VGA)
BVHXGA.DLL	\OS2\DLL	Base Video Handler dynamic link library (XGA)
BVHINIT.DLL	\OS2\DLL	Base Video Handler Initialization DLL
BVHWNDW.DLL	\OS2\DLL	Base Video Handler window DLL
BVSCALLS.DLL	\OS2\DLL	Base Video System dynamic link library
BASIC.COM	\OS2\MDOS	BASIC language interpreter
KBDBE.DLL	\OS2\MDOS\WINOS2\SYSTEM	Belgian keyboard dynamic link library
BDCALLS.DLL	\OS2\DLL	Bidirectional support dynamic link library
BDBVH.DLL	\OS2\DLL	Bidirectional support dynamic link library
BDKBDM.EXE	\OS2\SYSTEM	Bidirectional support for keyboard

Appendix E—OS/2 Files by Function

File	Directory	Function
BDPRTM.EXE	\OS2\SYSTEM	Bidirectional support for printing
SWAN.BGA	OS2\BITMAP	Bitmap of a swan for 8514 displays
SETBOOT.EXE	\OS2	Boot Manager for a hard disk
KBDUK.DLL	\OS2\MDOS\WINOS2\SYSTEM	British keyboard dynamic link library
CACHE.EXE	\OS2	Caching program for HPFS file systems
MORTGAGE.BAS	\OS2\MDOS	Calculates a mortgage
CALIBRAT.DAT	\OS2	Calibrates touch screens data
CALIBRAT.EXE	\OS2	Calibration program for touch screens
CALIBRAT.TXT	\OS2	Information displayed while calibrating
KBDCA.DLL	\OS2\MDOS\WINOS2\SYSTEM	Canadian keyboard dynamic link library
NEKO.EXE	\OS2\APPS	Cat and Mouse applet
NEKO.DLL	\OS2\APPS\DLL	Cat and Mouse applet dynamic link library
NEKO.HLP	\OS2\HELP	Cat and Mouse applet help
CDROM.SYS	\OS2	CD-ROM device driver
CDFS.IFS	\OS2	CD-ROM installable file system
UCDFS.DLL	\OS2\DLL	CD-ROM utilities dynamic link library
UCDFS.MSG	\OS2\SYSTEM	CD-ROM utilities message file
CGA.DLL	\OS2\DLL	CGA display dynamic link library
CGA.RC	\OS2	CGA resource file used to create OS2.INI

(continues)

File	Directory	Function
FSACCESS.EXE	\OS2\MDOS	Changes access to the OS/2 file system from specific-version DOS sessions
OS2CHESS.BIN	\OS2\APPS	Chess applet
OS2CHESS.EXE	\OS2\APPS	Chess applet
CHESSAI.DLL	\OS2\APPS\DLL	Chess applet dynamic link library
OS2CHESS.HLP	\OS2\HELP	Chess applet help
CLIPVIEW.HLP	\OS2\HELP	Clipboard help file
CLIPOS2.EXE	\OS2\APPS	Clipboard program executable
CLOCK01.SYS	\OS2	Clock device driver for family 1 machines (non-MCA)
CLOCK02.SYS	\OS2	Clock device driver for family 2 machines
XLAT850.BIN	\OS2\MDOS\WINOS2\SYSTEM	Code page 850 for WIN-OS2
XLAT860.BIN	\OS2\MDOS\WINOS2\SYSTEM	Code page 860 for WIN-OS2
XLAT861.BIN	\OS2\MDOS\WINOS2\SYSTEM	Code page 861 for WIN-OS2
XLAT863.BIN	\OS2\MDOS\WINOS2\SYSTEM	Code page 863 for WIN-OS2
XLAT865.BIN	\OS2\MDOS\WINOS2\SYSTEM	Code page 865 for WIN-OS2
CMDREF.INF	\OS2\BOOK	Command reference help file
DISKCOMP.COM	\OS2	Compares contents of two diskettes
TESTCFG.SYS	\OS2	Configuration device driver
4202L.CFG	\OS2\SYSTEM	Configuration file for bidirectional support
4201.CFG	\OS2\SYSTEM	Configuration file for bidirectional support

File	Directory	Function
4019.CFG	\OS2\SYSTEM	Configuration file for bidirectional support
5204.CFG	\OS2\SYSTEM	Configuration file for bidirectional support
4019L.CFG	\OS2\SYSTEM	Configuration file for bidirectional support
5204L.CFG	\OS2\SYSTEM	Configuration file for bidirectional support
4216L.CFG	\OS2\SYSTEM	Configuration file for bidirectional support
4207.CFG	\OS2\SYSTEM	Configuration file for bidirectional support
5202-QL.CFG	\OS2\SYSTEM	Configuration file for bidirectional support
5201L.CFG	\OS2\SYSTEM	Configuration file for bidirectional support
5201.CFG	\OS2\SYSTEM	Configuration file for bidirectional support
4216.CFG	\OS2\SYSTEM	Configuration file for bidirectional support
5202-Q.CFG	\OS2\SYSTEM	Configuration file for bidirectional support
4208.CFG	\OS2\SYSTEM	Configuration file for bidirectional support
4208L.CFG	\OS2\SYSTEM	Configuration file for bidirectional support
5202.CFG	\OS2\SYSTEM	Configuration file for bidirectional support
4202.CFG	\OS2\SYSTEM	Configuration file for bidirectional support
5202L.CFG	\OS2\SYSTEM	Configuration file for bidirectional support
README	\	Contains latest release information about OS/2
VIOTBL.DCP	\OS2	Contains video mappings for all characters

(continues)

File	Directory	Function
CONVERT.EXE	\OS2	Converts OS/2 1.X applications to 2.0
MOVESPL.EXE	\OS2	Converts OS/2 1.0 applications to 2.x
DISKCOPY.COM	\OS2	Copies contents of one diskette to another
XCOPY.EXE	\OS2	Copies groups of files including subdirectories
COURIER.EGA	\OS2\DLL	Courier bitmap font
COURIER.PSF	\OS2\DLL	Courier postscript font
CREATEDD.EXE	\OS2	Creates a dump diskette for use with the Stand-alone Dump procedure
LABEL.COM	\OS2	Creates or changes a volume label
KBDDA.DLL	\OS2\MDOS\WINOS2\SYSTEM	Danish keyboard dynamic link library
DATABASE.DAT	\OS2\INSTALL	Database data file used in migrating applications to 2.1
DBTAGS.DAT	\OS2\INSTALL	Database data file used in migrating applications to 2.1
DATABASE.TXT	\OS2\INSTALL	Database text file used in migrating applications to 2.1
UNPACK.EXE	\OS2	Decompression program
CLEANUP.EXE	\OS2\INSTALL	Deletes extraneous files after installation
VTBL850.DCP	\OS2	Description profile table for code page 850
NOMOUSE.DRV	\OS2\MDOS\WINOS2\SYSTEM	Device driver for WIN-OS2 indicating there is no mouse attached to the system

Appendix E—OS/2 Files by Function   853

File	Directory	Function
DDINSTAL.EXE	\OS2\INSTALL	Device Driver Installation program executable
DDINSTAL.HLP	\OS2\HELP	Device Driver Installation program help
FSFILTER.SYS	\OS2\MDOS	Device driver that provides access to OS/2 disk partitions when running a specific version of DOS
VXMS.SYS	\OS2\MDOS	Device driver that provides extended memory specification from DOS sessions
HIMEM.SYS	\OS2\MDOS	Device driver that provides high memory support in DOS
DOS.SYS	\OS2\DLL	Device driver used to bring up DOS sessions
IBM2ADSK.ADD	\OS2	Device support for on-SCSI disk drives on MCA machines
DIGITAL.FON	\OS2\MDOS\WINOS2	Digital font for WIN-OS2
DISPLAY.DLL	\OS2\DLL	Displays dynamic link library
TREE.COM	\OS2	Displays all the directory paths found on specified drive
TRACEFMT.EXE	\OS2	Displays formatted trace records
TRACEFMT.HLP	\OS2\HELP	Displays formatted trace records help
HARDERR.EXE	\OS2	Displays hard error messages
VIEW.EXE	\OS2	Displays on-line documents created with IPF
VIEWDOC.EXE	\OS2	Displays on-line documents created with IPF

(continues)

File	Directory	Function
SYSLEVEL.EXE	\OS2	Displays operating system service level
SYSLEVEL.GRE	\OS2\INSTALL	Displays operating system service level for graphics engine
SYSLEVEL.OS2	\OS2\INSTALL	Displays operating system service level for OS/2
MORE.COM	\OS2	Displays output one screen at a time
PICVIEW.EXE	\OS2\APPS	Displays picture files
PICVIEW.HLP	\OS2\HELP	Displays picture files help
PSTAT.EXE	\OS2	Displays process, thread, system-semaphore, shared memory, and dynamic link library information
MEM.EXE	\OS2\MDOS	Displays the amount of used and free memory in DOS sessions
DOSCALL1.DLL	\OS2\DLL	DLL that contains entry points for base operating system
DOSRFICO.DLL	\OS2\DLL	DLL to refresh icons used during install
DRAG.DLL	\OS2\DLL	DLL used by Presentation Manager to allow drag/drop
DOSKRNL	\OS2\MDOS	DOS
GRAFTABL.COM	\OS2\MDOS	DOS command to load a table of characters into memory for graphics mode
EDLIN.COM	\OS2\MDOS	DOS line editor
COMDD.SYS	\OS2\MDOS	DOS serial port device driver
DEBUG.EXE	\OS2\MDOS	DOS system debugger

Appendix E—OS/2 Files by Function

File	Directory	Function
KBDNE.DLL	\OS2\MDOS\WINOS2\SYSTEM	Dutch keyboard dynamic link library
EGA.DLL	\OS2\DLL	EGA display dynamic link library
EGA40WOA.FON	\OS2\MDOS\WINOS2\SYSTEM	EGA font for WIN-OS2
EGAFIX.FON	\OS2\MDOS\WINOS2\SYSTEM	EGA font for WIN-OS2
EGAOEM.FON	\OS2\MDOS\WINOS2\SYSTEM	EGA font for WIN-OS2
EGA80WOA.FON	\OS2\MDOS\WINOS2\SYSTEM	EGA font for WIN-OS2
EGASYS.FON	\OS2\MDOS\WINOS2\SYSTEM	EGA font for WIN-OS2
EGA.RC	\OS2	EGA resource file used to create OS2.INI
EMM386.SYS	\OS2\MDOS	Enables extended memory support in DOS
EGA.SYS	\OS2\MDOS	Enhanced Graphics Support
DRAW.EX	\OS2\APPS	Enhanced PM editor
EPMHELP.QHL	\OS2\APPS	Enhanced PM editor
EPM.EX	\OS2\APPS	Enhanced PM editor
E3EMUL.EX	\OS2\APPS	Enhanced PM editor
GET.EX	\OS2\APPS	Enhanced PM editor applet
BOX.EX	\OS2\APPS	Enhanced PM editor applet
EXTRA.EX	\OS2\APPS	Enhanced PM editor applet
PUT.EX	\OS2\APPS	Enhanced PM editor applet
ETKE550.DLL	OS2\APPS\DLL	Enhanced PM editor dynamic link library
ETKR550.DLL	OS2\APPS\DLL	Enhanced PM editor dynamic link library
ETKTHNK.DLL	OS2\APPS\DLL	Enhanced PM editor dynamic link library

(continues)

Appendix E—OS/2 Files by Function

File	Directory	Function
EPM.EXE	\OS2\APPS	Enhanced PM editor executable
EPMLEX.EX	\OS2\APPS	Enhanced PM editor executable
EPM.HLP	\OS2\HELP	Enhanced PM editor help
HELPMGR.DLL	OS2\DLL	Entry points into the help manager
NPXEMLTR.DLL	\OS2\DLL	Entry points to convert floating point values
EAUTIL.EXE	\OS2	Extended attributes
ANSICALL.DLL	\OS2\DLL	Extended display and keyboard support dynamic link library
ANSI.SYS	\OS2\MDOS	Extended display and keyboard support in the DOS environment
ANSI.EXE	\OS2	Extended display and keyboard support in the OS/2 environment
FDISKPM.EXE	OS2	FDISK program
FDISKPM.DLL	OS2\DLL	FDISK program dynamic link library
FDISKPMH.HLP	\OS2\HELP	FDISK program help
COMP.COM	\OS2	File compare program
COUNTRY.SYS	OS2	File containing specific country information
MISC.FON	\OS2\DLL	File that contains system fonts
EA DATA.SF	\	File that holds all extended attributes in system
DRVMAP.INF	\OS2\MDOS\WINOS2\SYSTEM	File that maps WIN-OS2 printer drivers to OS/2 printer drivers
FIND.EXE	\OS2	Finds a string of text in file(s)

Appendix E—OS/2 Files by Function

File	Directory	Function
KBDFI.DLL	\OS2\MDOS\WINOS2\SYSTEM	Finishes keyboard dynamic link library
FFIX.EXE	\OS2\MDOS	Fixes for DOS touch and finds first APIs
SQ4FIX.COM	\OS2\MDOS	Fixes for Space Quest 4 game by Sierra
SYSFONT.DLL	OS2\DLL	Font dynamic link library
8514FIX.FON	OS2\MDOS\WINOS2\SYSTEM	Font file for 8514 displays
CARDSYM.FON	OS2\APPS	Font file for Solitaire Application
SCRIPT.FON	\OS2\MDOS\WINOS2\SYSTEM	Font for WIN-OS2
FORMAT.COM	\OS2	Formats a disk
PMFORMAT.EXE	\OS2	Formats a disk
PMFORMAT.DLL	\OS2\DLL	Formats a disk dynamic link libary
KBDFR.DLL	\OS2\MDOS\WINOS2\SYSTEM	French keyboard dynamic link library
FDISK.COM	\OS2	Full Screen FDISK
FKA.DLL	\OS2\DLL	Function key area dynamic link library
OS2DASD.DMD	OS2	General purpose device support for disk drives
OS2SCSI.DMD	OS2	General purpose device support for non-disk SCSI devices
IBM1FLPY.ADD	\OS2	Generic disk device driver for family 1 machines (non-MCA)
IBM2FLPY.ADD	\OS2	Generic disk device driver for family 2 machines
IBM2SCSI.ADD	\OS2	Generic SCSI device driver for family 2 machines

(continues)

Appendix E—OS/2 Files by Function

File	Directory	Function
IBM1S506.ADD	\OS2	Generic support for non-SCSI disk drives on non-MCA machines
KBDGR.DLL	\OS2\MDOS\WINOS2\SYSTEM	German keyboard dynamic link library
CHKDSK.COM	\OS2	Gives you information about your disk
GDI.EXE	\OS2\MDOS\WINOS2\SYSTEM	Graphics device interface for WIN-OS2
HELP.BAT	\OS2\MDOS	Help batch file for DOS
HELP.CMD	\OS2	Help batch file for OS/2
HELP.EX	\OS2\APPS	Help for Enhanced PM Editor
VIEWH.HLP	\OS2\HELP	Help for viewing on-line documentation
HPMGRMRI.DLL	\OS2\DLL	Help manager—"translatable strings" dynamic link library
HMHELP.HLP	\OS2\HELP	Help manager help file
HELV.BMP	\OS2\DLL	Helvetica font
HELVETIC.PSF	\OS2\DLL	Helvetica postscript font
HPFS.IFS	\OS2	High performance installable file system
UHPFS.DLL	\OS2\DLL	HPFS utilities dynamic link library
IBMINT13.I13	\OS2	IBM generic interrupt 13 device driver
KBDIC.DLL	\OS2\MDOS\WINOS2\SYSTEM	Icelandic keyboard dynamic link library
ICONEDIT.EXE	\OS2\APPS	Icon editor
ICONEDIT.HLP	\OS2\HELP	Icon editor help
IMP.DLL	\OS2\DLL	Imports dynamic link library

Appendix E—OS/2 Files by Function **859**

File	Directory	Function
INSTAID.CNF	OS2\INSTALL	Installation Aid configuration file
INACALL.DLL	OS2\DLL	Installation Aid dynamic link library
STXTDMPC.DLL	\OS2\DLL	Installation Aid dynamic link library
CPISPFPC.DLL	\OS2\DLL	Installation Aid dynamic link library
DTM.DLL	\OS2\DLL	Installation Aid dynamic link library
DMPC.EXE	\OS2\INSTALL	Installation Aid file used to create EZVU panels
INSTAID.LIB	OS2\INSTALL	Installation Aid library
ISPD.MSG	\OS2\INSTALL	Installation Aid message file
ISPM.MSG	\OS2\INSTALL	Installation Aid message file
INSTAID.PRO	OS2\INSTALL	Installation Aid profile file
INSTAIDE.EXE	\OS2\INSTALL	Installation Aid program executable
INSTAID.EXE	OS2\INSTALL	Installation Aid program executable
INSTALL.INI	OS2\INSTALL	Installation program configuration file
INSTALL.EXE	OS2\INSTALL	Installation program executable
INSTALL.HLP	OS2\HELP	Installation program's help
INSTSHEL.EXE	\OS2\INSTALL	Installation program's shell
KBDIT.DLL	\OS2\MDOS\WINOS2\SYSTEM	Italian keyboard dynamic link library
JIGSAW.EXE	\OS2\APPS	Jigsaw Applet (Puzzle)

(continues)

File	Directory	Function
JIGSAW.HLP	\OS2\HELP	Jigsaw Applet (Puzzle) help
KBD01.SYS	\OS2	Keyboard device driver for family 1 machines (non-Microchannel)
KBD02.SYS	\OS2	Keyboard device driver for family 2 machines
KEYBOARD.DRV	\OS2\MDOS\WINOS2\SYSTEM	Keyboard device driver for WIN-OS2
KEYBOARD.DCP	\OS2	Keyboard layout table for translating keystrokes into characters of each code page supported by the system
KBDCALLS.DLL	\OS2\DLL	Keyboards calls dynamic link library
KBDLA.DLL	\OS2\MDOS\WINOS2\SYSTEM	Latin keyboard dynamic link library
STARTLW.DLL	OS2\DLL	Lazy writer dynamic link library
DOSCALLS.LIB	\OS2	Library containing entry points for 1.X programs
LIGHTHOU.VGA	\OS2\BITMAP	Lighthouse bitmap for VGA displays
ABIOS.SYS	\OS2	List of all applicable ABIOS patch files
AAAAA.EXE	\OS2\BITMAP	Lists OS/2 developers' names
JOIN.EXE	\OS2\MDOS	Logically connects a drive to a directory
MINXOBJ.DLL	OS2\DLL	Master help index dynamic link library
MINXMRI.DLL	OS2\DLL	Master help index dynamic link library
MSG.DLL	\OS2\DLL	Message dynamic link library
HELPMSG.EXE	OS2	Message file to obtain help on system messages

Appendix E—OS/2 Files by Function

File	Directory	Function
DEV002.MSG	\OS2\SYSTEM	Message file used by CD-ROM file system
AAAAA.MET	\OS2\BITMAP	Metafile that has the background picture
MSNET.DRV	\OS2\MDOS\WINOS2\SYSTEM	Microsoft network device driver for WIN-OS2
MIGRATE.EXE	OS2\INSTALL	Migrates applications to OS/2 2.1
MIGRATE.HLP	OS2\HELP	Migrates applications to OS/2 2.1 help
PARSEDB.EXE	OS2\INSTALL	Migration database
OS2BOOT	\	Mini-operating system for booting other operating systems
MONCALLS.DLL	\OS2\DLL	Monitor calls dynamic link library
SYSMONO.FON	OS2\DLL	Monochrome bitmap font
MOUCALLS.DLL	\OS2\DLL	Mouse calls dynamic link library
MOUSE.COM	\OS2\MDOS	Mouse device driver for DOS
PDITOU01.SYS	\OS2	Mouse device driver for family 1 machines (non-Microchannel)
PDITOU02.SYS	\OS2	Mouse device driver for family 2 machines
PCLOGIC.SYS	OS2	Mouse device driver for PCLogic type pointing devices
MOUSE.DRV	\OS2\MDOS\WINOS2\SYSTEM	Mouse device driver for WIN-OS2
POINTDD.SYS	OS2	Mouse pointer draw support
NAMPIPES.DLL	\OS2\DLL	Named pipes dynamic link library

(continues)

File	Directory	Function
NLS.DLL	\OS2\DLL	National language support dynamic link library
NWIAPI.DLL	\OS2\DLL	Network API's dynamic link library
KBDNO.DLL	\OS2\MDOS\WINOS2\SYSTEM	Norwegian keyboard dynamic link library
KBDOLI.DRV	\OS2\MDOS\WINOS2\SYSTEM	Olivetti keyboard dynamic link library
SETCOM40.EXE	\OS2\MDOS	OS/2 1.1, 1.2, 1.3 compatibility file
LINK386.EXE	OS2	OS/2 386 linker
OS2CHAR.DLL	OS2\DLL	OS/2 character dynamic link library
CMD.EXE	\OS2	OS/2 command interpreter
CONFIG.SYS	\	OS/2 configuration file
OS2KRNLI	\	OS/2 kernel
LINK.EXE	\OS2	OS/2 linker
OS2LDR	\	OS/2 loader
OS2LDR.MSG	\	OS/2 loader message file
LOGDAEM.EXE	OS2\SYSTEM	OS/2 logging facility
OS2LOGO.BMP	OS2\BITMAP	OS/2 logo bitmap
OS2SM.DLL	\OS2\DLL	OS/2 session manager dynamic link library
LPTDD.SYS	\OS2\MDOS	Parallel port device driver for DOS
PMPIC.DLL	\OS2\DLL	Picture dynamic link library
PICVIEW.DLL	OS2\APPS\DLL	Picture viewer dynamic link library
PICV.DLL	\OS2\DLL	Picture viewer dynamic link library
PLASMA.DRV	\OS2\MDOS\WINOS2\SYSTEM	Plasma display device driver for WIN-OS2

Appendix E—OS/2 Files by Function

File	Directory	Function
BUTTON.DLL	\OS2\DLL	PM button control dynamic link library
PMCTLS.DLL	\OS2\DLL	PM controls dynamic link library
PMSDMRI.DLL	OS2\DLL	PM CUA control dynamic link library
PMDRAG.DLL	\OS2\DLL	PM drag/drop dynamic link library
PMWIN.DLL	\OS2\DLL	PM dynamic link library
PMGRE.DLL	\OS2\DLL	PM graphics engine dynamic link library
PMGPI.DLL	\OS2\DLL	PM graphics programming interface dynamic link library
PMBIND.DLL	\OS2\DLL	PM language binding dynamic link library
PMMLE.DLL	\OS2\DLL	PM multiline edit dynamic link library
SELECT.DLL	\OS2\DLL	PM selection control dynamic link library
PMSETUP.INF	OS2	PM setup information used for installing printer drivers
PMSHELL.EXE	OS2	PM shell
PMSHAPIM.DLL	\OS2\DLL	PM shell dynamic link library
PMSHAPI.DLL	OS2\DLL	PM shell dynamic link library
PMTKT.DLL	\OS2\DLL	PM shell dynamic link library
PMSHLTKT.DLL	\OS2\DLL	PM shell dynamic link library
PMSHELL.DLL	OS2\DLL	PM shell dynamic link library
PMVIOP.DLL	\OS2\DLL	PM dynamic link library

(continues)

Appendix E—OS/2 Files by Function

File	Directory	Function
PMVDMP.DLL	\OS2\DLL	PM virtual DOS machine private dynamic link library
FASHION.GRF	OS2\APPS	PMChart applet
MGXLIB.DLL	\OS2\APPS\DLL	PMChart applet
GREEN.GRF	\OS2\APPS	PMChart applet
FASHION.DAT	OS2\APPS	PMChart applet
MGXVBM.DLL	\OS2\APPS\DLL	PMChart applet
PMFID.DLL	\OS2\APPS\DLL	PMChart applet
INVEST.GRF	\OS2\APPS	PMChart applet
PMCHART.EXE	OS2\APPS	PMChart applet
PMCHART.HLP	OS2\HELP	PMChart applet
INVEST.DAT	\OS2\APPS	PMChart applet
GREEN.DAT	\OS2\APPS	PMChart applet
PMDMONTH.EXE	\OS2\APPS	PMDiary applet
PMDNOTE.EXE	OS2\APPS	PMDiary applet
PMSTICKY.EXE	\OS2\APPS	PMDiary applet
PMSTICKD.DLL	\OS2\APPS\DLL	PMDiary applet
PMDALARM.EXE	\OS2\APPS	PMDiary applet
PMDDARC.EXE	OS2\APPS	PMDiary applet
PMDIARYF.DLL	\OS2\APPS\DLL	PMDiary applet
PMDIARY.DLL	OS2\APPS\DLL	PMDiary applet
PMDCALEN.EXE	\OS2\APPS	PMDiary applet
PMDIARY.HLP	OS2\HELP	PMDiary applet
PMDCALC.EXE	OS2\APPS	PMDiary applet
PMMBASE.EXE	OS2\APPS	PMDiary applet
PMDTODO.EXE	OS2\APPS	PMDiary applet
PMDDIARY.EXE	\OS2\APPS	PMDiary applet

Appendix E—OS/2 Files by Function

File	Directory	Function
PMDLIST.EXE	OS2\APPS	PMDiary applet
PMDTARC.EXE	OS2\APPS	PMDiary applet
PMDIARY.$$A	OS2\APPS	PMDiary applet
PMSPREAD.EXE	\OS2\APPS	PMDiary applet (Spreadsheet)
PMDCTLS.DLL	OS2\APPS\DLL	PMDiary controls dynamic link library
PMDD.SYS	\OS2	Pointer draw support for OS/2 sessions
MOUSE.SYS	\OS2	Pointing device
KBDPO.DLL	\OS2\MDOS\WINOS2\SYSTEM	Polish keyboard dynamic link library
PARALLEL.PDR	\OS2\DLL	Port driver for parallel port (LPT)
SERIAL.PDR	\OS2\DLL	Port driver for serial ports (COM)
PSCRIPT.SEP	OS2	PostScript separator file
PMPRINT.QPR	OS2\DLL	Print queue processor
PRINT01.SYS	OS2	Printer device driver for family 1 machines (non-MCA)
PRINT02.SYS	OS2	Printer device driver for family 2 machines
PRINT.COM	\OS2	Prints files to default printer
QBASIC.EXE	\OS2\MDOS	QuickBasic program
QBASIC.HLP	\OS2\MDOS	QuickBasic program help
DOSKEY.COM	\OS2\MDOS	Recalls DOS commands, edits command lines, and creates macros
MAKEINI.EXE	OS2	Recovers user and SYSTEM.INI files

(continues)

Appendix E—OS/2 Files by Function

File	Directory	Function
RECOVER.COM	OS2	Recovers files from a disk that contains defective sectors
SPOOL.EXE	\OS2	Redirects printer output from one device to another
RIPLINST.EXE	\OS2\INSTALL	Remote IPL installation program
RIPLINST.HLP	\OS2\HELP	Remote IPL installation program help
UNFIXWP.EXE	OS2\MDOS\WINOS2	Remove WordPerfect patch for FIXWP.EXE
REPLACE.EXE	OS2	Replaces files from one drive to another drive
KEYB.COM	\OS2	Replaces the current keyboard layout
RCPP.EXE	\OS2	Resource compiler
RCPP.ERR	\OS2	Resource compiler
RC.EXE	\OS2	Resource compiler
OS2_13.RC	\OS2	Resource file used to create the 1.3 "look/feel"
OS2_20.RC	\OS2	Resource file used to create the 2.0 "look/feel"
8514M.RC	\OS2	Resource file used in creating OS2.INI file for monochrome 8514 display
VGA.RC	\OS2	Resource file used in creating OS2.INI for VGA displays
8514.RC	\OS2	Resource file used in the creation of the OS2.INI file
UPINI.RC	\OS2	Resource file used in updating 1.0 programs to 2.x
INI.RC	\OS2	Resource file used to create OS2.INI

Appendix E—OS/2 Files by Function **867**

File	Directory	Function
XGA.RC	\OS2	Resource file used to create OS2.INI file for XGA displays
PLASMA.RC	\OS2	Resource file used to create OS2.INI for plasma displays
INISYS.RC	\OS2	Resource file used to create OS2SYS.INI
WIN_30.RC	\OS2	Resource file used to create the Windows 3.0 "look/feel"
RSPDDI.EXE	\OS2\INSTALL	Response file device driver installation program
SAMPLE.RSP	\OS2\INSTALL	Response file for response file installations
RSPINST.EXE	OS2\INSTALL	Response file installation program
RSPMIG.EXE	\OS2\INSTALL	Response file migration program
RESTORE.EXE	OS2	Restores backed up files from one disk to another
REVERSI.EXE	OS2\APPS	Reversi applet
REVERSI.HLP	OS2\HELP	Reversi applet help
REXXAPI.DLL	OS2\DLL	REXX API dynamic link library
REXXTRY.CMD	OS2	REXX command file
REXX.INF	\OS2\BOOK	REXX documentation
REXX.DLL	\OS2\DLL	REXX dynamic link library
REXH.MSG	\OS2\SYSTEM	REXX help message file
REXXINIT.DLL	\OS2\DLL	REXX initialization dynamic link library

(continues)

File	Directory	Function
RXSUBCOM.EXE	\OS2	REXX language executable
RXQUEUE.EXE	OS2	REXX language executable
PMREXX.EXE	\OS2	REXX language interpreter
PMREXX.DLL	\OS2\DLL	REXX language interpreter DLL
PMREXX.HLP	\OS2\HELP	REXX language interpreter help
REX.MSG	\OS2\SYSTEM	REXX message file
REXXUTIL.DLL	\OS2\DLL	REXX utilities dynamic link library
SVGA.EXE	\OS2	Run Super VGA in DOS mode
SCRAMBLE.EXE	\OS2\APPS	Scramble applet
SCRCATS.DLL	OS2\APPS\DLL	Scramble applet dynamic link library
SCRLOGO.DLL	OS2\APPS\DLL	Scramble applet dynamic link library
SCRAMBLE.DLL	\OS2\APPS\DLL	Scramble applet dynamic link library
SCRAMBLE.HLP	\OS2\HELP	Scramble applet help
SCREEN01.SYS	\OS2	Screen device driver for family 1 machines
SCREEN02.SYS	\OS2	Screen device driver for family 2 machines
PMSEEK.EXE	\OS2\APPS	Searches one or more disks for files or text
PMSEEK.DLL	\OS2\APPS\DLL	Searches one or more disks for files or text (DLL)
PMSEEK.HLP	\OS2\HELP	Searches one or more disks for files or text help
TRACE.EXE	\OS2	Selects or sets the system trace

Appendix E—OS/2 Files by Function

File	Directory	Function
SAMPLE.SEP	\OS2	Separator file
COM.SYS	\OS2	Serial port device driver
SESMGR.DLL	\OS2\DLL	Session manager dynamic link library
APPEND.EXE	\OS2\MDOS	Sets a search path for data files that are outside the current directory
MODE.COM	\OS2	Sets the operation modes for devices
SHPIINST.DLL	\OS2\DLL	Shell installation file
PULSE.EXE	\OS2\APPS	Shows CPU usage
PULSE.HLP	\OS2\HELP	Shows CPU usage (help)
KLONDIKE.EXE	\OS2\APPS	Solitaire applet
KLONBGA.DLL	OS2\APPS\DLL	Solitaire applet dynamic link library
KLONDIKE.HLP	\OS2\HELP	Solitaire applet help
SORT.EXE	\OS2	Sorts files
SOUND.DRV	\OS2\MDOS\WINOS2\SYSTEM	Sound device driver for WIN-OS2
KBDSP.DLL	\OS2\MDOS\WINOS2\SYSTEM	Spanish keyboard dynamic link library
SPL1B.DLL	\OS2\DLL	Spooler dynamic link library
PMSPL.DLL	\OS2\DLL	Spooler dynamic link library
SPOOLCP.DLL	OS2\DLL	Spooler dynamic link library
SPLH.MSG	\OS2\SYSTEM	Spooler help message file
SPL.MSG	\OS2\SYSTEM	Spooler message file
START.HLP	\OS2\HELP	Starts help programs automatically

(continues)

File	Directory	Function
SUBST.EXE	\OS2\MDOS	Substitutes a drive letter for another drive and path
KBDSW.DLL	\OS2\MDOS\WINOS2\SYSTEM	Swedish keyboard dynamic link library
KBDSF.DLL	\OS2\MDOS\WINOS2\SYSTEM	Swiss French keyboard dynamic link library
KBDSG.DLL	\OS2\MDOS\WINOS2\SYSTEM	Swiss German keyboard dynamic link library
BOOT.COM	\OS2	Switches between DOS and OS/2 operating systems that are on the same hard disk (drive C)
E.EXE	\OS2	System Editor
EHXHP.HLP	\OS2\HELP	System Editor dynamic link library
EHXDLMRI.DLL	\OS2\DLL	System Editor dynamic link library
SYSLOGH.HLP	OS2\HELP	System error-log help
LOG.SYS	\OS2	System error logging using the SYSLOG utility program
SYSLOG.DLL	\OS2\DLL	System error-log dynamic link library
SYSLOGPM.EXE	\OS2	System error-log viewer
SYSLOG.EXE	\OS2	System error-log viewer
OSO001.MSG	\OS2\SYSTEM	System message file
OSO001H.MSG	OS2\SYSTEM	System message help file
SOM.DLL	\OS2\DLL	System Object Module dynamic link library
QUECALLS.DLL	\OS2\DLL	System queue calls dynamic link library
VTTERM.HLP	\OS2\HELP	Terminal emulation applet

Appendix E—OS/2 Files by Function

File	Directory	Function
SACDI.DLL	\OS2\APPS\DLL	Terminal emulation applet
SASYNCDA.SYS	\OS2\APPS	Terminal emulation applet
SACDI.MSG	\OS2\SYSTEM	Terminal emulation applet
SOFTERM.EXE	OS2\APPS	Terminal emulation applet
SOFTERM.HLP	OS2\HELP	Terminal emulation applet
OCSHELL.DLL	OS2\APPS\DLL	Terminal emulation applet
OVM.DLL	\OS2\APPS\DLL	Terminal emulation applet
OTTY.DLL	\OS2\APPS\DLL	Terminal emulation applet
OVT.DLL	\OS2\APPS\DLL	Terminal emulation applet
SASYNCDB.SYS	\OS2\APPS	Terminal emulation applet
XRM.HLP	\OS2\HELP	Terminal emulation applet
TTY.HLP	\OS2\HELP	Terminal emulation applet
OFMTC.DLL	\OS2\APPS\DLL	Terminal emulation applet
OCHAR.DLL	\OS2\APPS\DLL	Terminal emulation applet
OKERMIT.DLL	OS2\APPS\DLL	Terminal emulation applet
OCOLOR.DLL	\OS2\APPS\DLL	Terminal emulation applet
OIBM1X.DLL	\OS2\APPS\DLL	Terminal emulation applet
OCM.DLL	\OS2\APPS\DLL	Terminal emulation applet

(continues)

Appendix E—OS/2 Files by Function

File	Directory	Function
OKB.DLL	\OS2\APPS\DLL	Terminal emulation applet
OMCT.DLL	\OS2\APPS\DLL	Terminal emulation applet
ODBM.DLL	\OS2\APPS\DLL	Terminal emulation applet
SAREXEC.DLL	OS2\APPS\DLL	Terminal emulation applet
OKBC.DLL	\OS2\APPS\DLL	Terminal emulation applet
OIBM2X.DLL	\OS2\APPS\DLL	Terminal emulation applet
OLPTIO.DLL	\OS2\APPS\DLL	Terminal emulation applet
CTLSACDI.DLL	\OS2\APPS\DLL	Terminal emulation applet
ACDISIO.HLP	OS2\HELP	Terminal emulation applet
IBM31012.HLP	\OS2\HELP	Terminal emulation applet
CUSTOM.MDB	\OS2\APPS	Terminal emulation applet
ACSACDI.DAT	OS2\APPS	Terminal emulation applet
CTLSACDI.EXE	\OS2\APPS	Terminal emulation applet
OANSI.DLL	\OS2\APPS\DLL	Terminal emulation applet
OACDISIO.DLL	\OS2\APPS\DLL	Terminal emulation applet
OANSI364.DLL	\OS2\APPS\DLL	Terminal emulation applet
IBMSIO.HLP	\OS2\HELP	Terminal emulation applet
OSOFT.DLL	\OS2\APPS\DLL	Terminal emulation applet
IBM31011.HLP	\OS2\HELP	Terminal emulation applet

Appendix E—OS/2 Files by Function

File	Directory	Function
ANSI364.HLP	OS2\HELP	Terminal emulation applet
OSIO.DLL	\OS2\APPS\DLL	Terminal emulation applet
OPM.DLL	\OS2\APPS\DLL	Terminal emulation applet
OPCF.DLL	\OS2\APPS\DLL	Terminal emulation applet
OVIO.DLL	\OS2\APPS\DLL	Terminal emulation applet
OTEK.DLL	\OS2\APPS\DLL	Terminal emulation applet
OSCH.DLL	\OS2\APPS\DLL	Terminal emulation applet
OMRKCPY.DLL	OS2\APPS\DLL	Terminal emulation applet
OXMODEM.DLL	OS2\APPS\DLL	Terminal emulation applet
ANSIIBM.HLP	OS2\HELP	Terminal emulation applet
OPROFILE.DLL	\OS2\APPS\DLL	Terminal emulation applet
OXRM.DLL	\OS2\APPS\DLL	Terminal emulation applet
ORSHELL.DLL	OS2\APPS\DLL	Terminal emulation applet
TIMES.BMP	\OS2\DLL	Times/Roman bitmap font
TIMESNRM.PSF	\OS2\DLL	Times/Roman postscript font
FSGRAPH.DLL	OS2\DLL	Touch device dynamic link library
TCP.DLL	\OS2\DLL	Touch device dynamic link library
TOUCO21D.BIN	\OS2	Touch device file
TCP.HLP	\OS2\HELP	Touch device help

(continues)

Appendix E—OS/2 Files by Function

File	Directory	Function
TDD.MSG	\OS2\SYSTEM	Touch device message file
TDDH.MSG	\OS2\SYSTEM	Touch device message file
TDIH.MSG	\OS2\SYSTEM	Touch device message file
TDI.MSG	\OS2\SYSTEM	Touch device message file
TOUCH.SYS	\OS2	Touch devices—device driver
TOUCALLS.DLL	\OS2\DLL	Touch devices—dynamic link library
TOUCH.INI	\OS2	Touch devices—INI file
SYSTEM.TFF	\OS2\SYSTEM\TRACE	Trace file
SYSTEM.TDF	\OS2\SYSTEM\TRACE	Trace file
TRACEFMT.DLL	\OS2\DLL	Trace formatter dynamic link library
PMDTUNE.EXE	OS2\APPS	Tune editor applet
TUTORIAL.EXE	\OS2	Tutorial
ANMT.DLL	\OS2\DLL	Tutorial animation dynamic link library
ANIMAT.AMT	\OS2\HELP	Tutorial animation file
TUT.DLL	\OS2\DLL	Tutorial dynamic link library
TUTMRI.DLL	\OS2\DLL	Tutorial dynamic link library
TUTDLL.DLL	\OS2\DLL	Tutorial dynamic link library
TUTORIAL.HLP	\OS2\HELP\TUTORIAL	Tutorial help
UNDELETE.COM	\OS2	Undeletes files
KBDUS.DLL	\OS2\MDOS\WINOS2\SYSTEM	United States keyboard dynamic link library
KBDDV.DLL	\OS2\MDOS\WINOS2\SYSTEM	US-Dvorak keyboard dynamic link library

Appendix E—OS/2 Files by Function

File	Directory	Function
KBDUSX.DLL	\OS2\MDOS\WINOS2\SYSTEM	US-International dynamic link library
WINVER.EXE	\OS2\MDOS\WINOS2	Version of WIN-OS2 you are running
SWINVGA.DRV	OS2\MDOS\WINOS2\SYSTEM	VGA device driver for WIN-OS2
V7VGA.DRV	\OS2\MDOS\WINOS2\SYSTEM	VGA device driver for WIN-OS2
VGA.DRV	\OS2\MDOS\WINOS2\SYSTEM	VGA device driver for WIN-OS2
VGAMONO.DRV	OS2\MDOS\WINOS2\SYSTEM	VGA device driver for WIN-OS2
VGA.DLL	\OS2\DLL	VGA display dynamic link library
VGA865.FON	\OS2\MDOS\WINOS2\SYSTEM	VGA font for WIN-OS2
VGAFIX.FON	\OS2\MDOS\WINOS2\SYSTEM	VGA font for WIN-OS2
VGA861.FON	\OS2\MDOS\WINOS2\SYSTEM	VGA font for WIN-OS2
VGA863.FON	\OS2\MDOS\WINOS2\SYSTEM	VGA font for WIN-OS2
VGA860.FON	\OS2\MDOS\WINOS2\SYSTEM	VGA font for WIN-OS2
VGAOEM.FON	\OS2\MDOS\WINOS2\SYSTEM	VGA font for WIN-OS2
VGASYS.FON	\OS2\MDOS\WINOS2\SYSTEM	VGA font for WIN-OS2
VGA850.FON	\OS2\MDOS\WINOS2\SYSTEM	VGA font for WIN-OS2
VGAM.RC	\OS2	VGA monochrome resource file
ATTRIB.EXE	\OS2	View/Change attributes of a file
V8514A.SYS	\OS2\MDOS	Virtual 8514A device driver
VBIOS.SYS	\OS2\MDOS	Virtual BIOS device driver
VCDROM.SYS	\OS2\MDOS	Virtual CD-ROM device drive
VCGA.SYS	\OS2\MDOS	Virtual CGA device driver

(continues)

Appendix E—OS/2 Files by Function

File	Directory	Function
VCMOS.SYS	\OS2\MDOS	Virtual CMOS device driver
VDMA.SYS	\OS2\MDOS	Virtual direct memory access support device driver
VDSK.SYS	\OS2\MDOS	Virtual disk device driver
VDISK.SYS	\OS2	Virtual disk device driver (simulated disk)
VDPX.SYS	\OS2\MDOS	Virtual DOS extender for DPMI applications driver
VDMSRVR.EXE	OS2\MDOS\WINOS2	Virtual DOS machine server for WIN-OS2
VDPMI.SYS	\OS2\MDOS	Virtual DOS protect mode interface device driver
VEGA.SYS	\OS2\MDOS	Virtual EGA device driver
VEMM.SYS	\OS2\MDOS	Virtual expanded memory manager device driver
VFLPY.SYS	\OS2\MDOS	Virtual floppy device driver
VKBD.SYS	\OS2\MDOS	Virtual keyboard device driver
VMDISK.EXE	\OS2\MDOS	Virtual memory disk
VMONO.SYS	\OS2\MDOS	Virtual monochrome device driver
VMOUSE.SYS	\OS2\MDOS	Virtual mouse device driver
VNPX.SYS	\OS2\MDOS	Virtual NPX exulator device driver
VLPT.SYS	\OS2\MDOS	Virtual parallel port device driver
VPIC.SYS	\OS2\MDOS	Virtual picture device driver
VCOM.SYS	\OS2\MDOS	Virtual serial port device driver

File	Directory	Function
VSVGA.SYS	\OS2\MDOS	Virtual SVGA device driver
VTIMER.SYS	\OS2\MDOS	Virtual timer device driver
VTOUCH.SYS	\OS2\MDOS	Virtual touch device driver
VTOUCH.COM	\OS2\MDOS	Virtual touch program (touch screen applications)
VVGA.SYS	\OS2\MDOS	Virtual VGA device driver
VXGA.SYS	\OS2\MDOS	Virtual XGA device driver
SF4019.EXE	\OS2\MDOS\WINOS2\SYSTEM	WIN-OS2 4019 printer file
WIN87EM.DLL	OS2\MDOS\WINOS2\SYSTEM	WIN-OS2 80X87 emulator dynamic link library
8514.DRV	\OS2\MDOS\WINOS2\SYSTEM	WIN-OS2 8514 display device driver
WOS2ACCE.GRP	\OS2\MDOS\WINOS2	WIN-OS2 accessories group
ATM16.DLL	\OS2\MDOS\WINOS2\SYSTEM	WIN-OS2 Adobe type manager 16-bit dynamic link library
ATMCNTRL.EXE	\OS2\MDOS\WINOS2	WIN-OS2 Adobe type manager control file
ATMSYS.DRV	\OS2\MDOS\WINOS2\SYSTEM	WIN-OS2 Adobe type manager device driver
CGA.DRV	\OS2\MDOS\WINOS2\SYSTEM	WIN-OS2 CGA device driver
CGASYS.FON	\OS2\MDOS\WINOS2\SYSTEM	WIN-OS2 CGA font
CGA40WOA.FON	\OS2\MDOS\WINOS2\SYSTEM	WIN-OS2 CGA font
CGAOEM.FON	\OS2\MDOS\WINOS2\SYSTEM	WIN-OS2 CGA font
CGAFIX.FON	\OS2\MDOS\WINOS2\SYSTEM	WIN-OS2 CGA font
CGA80WOA.FON	\OS2\MDOS\WINOS2\SYSTEM	WIN-OS2 CGA font

(continues)

Appendix E—OS/2 Files by Function

File	Directory	Function
CLIPBRD.HLP	OS2\MDOS\WINOS2	WIN-OS2 Clipboard help file
CLIPWOS2.EXE	\OS2\MDOS\WINOS2	WIN-OS2 Clipboard program executable
CLOCK.EXE	\OS2\MDOS\WINOS2	WIN-OS2 clock program executable
COMMAND.COM	OS2\MDOS	WIN-OS2 command interpreter
CONTROL.EXE	OS2\MDOS\WINOS2	WIN-OS2 control file
CONTROL.HLP	OS2\MDOS\WINOS2	WIN-OS2 control program help
CONTROL.INI	OS2\MDOS\WINOS2	WIN-OS2 control program initialization file
COURF.FON	\OS2\MDOS\WINOS2\SYSTEM	WIN-OS2 Courier font for 8514 displays
COURA.FON	\OS2\MDOS\WINOS2\SYSTEM	WIN-OS2 Courier font for CGA displays
COURB.FON	\OS2\MDOS\WINOS2\SYSTEM	WIN-OS2 Courier font for EGA displays
COURE.FON	\OS2\MDOS\WINOS2\SYSTEM	WIN-OS2 Courier font for VGA displays
COURG.FON	\OS2\MDOS\WINOS2\SYSTEM	WIN-OS2 Courier font for XGA displays
VWIN.SYS	\OS2\MDOS	WIN-OS2 device driver
LANGDUT.DLL	OS2\MDOS\WINOS2\SYSTEM	WIN-OS2 Dutch language DLL
PMDDE.EXE	\OS2	WIN-OS2 dynamic data exchange program
DDEAGENT.EXE	\OS2\MDOS\WINOS2	WIN-OS2 dynamic data exchange program
EGA.DRV	\OS2\MDOS\WINOS2\SYSTEM	WIN-OS2 EGA display device driver
EGAMONO.DRV	OS2\MDOS\WINOS2\SYSTEM	WIN-OS2 EGA display device driver

Appendix E—OS/2 Files by Function

File	Directory	Function
EGAHIBW.DRV	OS2\MDOS\WINOS2\SYSTEM	WIN-OS2 EGA display device driver
LANGENG.DLL	OS2\MDOS\WINOS2\SYSTEM	WIN-OS2 English
WINOS2.COM	\OS2\MDOS\WINOS2	WIN-OS2 executable
WIN.COM	\OS2\MDOS\WINOS2	WIN-OS2 executable
LZEXPAND.DLL	\OS2\MDOS\WINOS2\SYSTEM	WIN-OS2 file decompression dynamic link library
LANGFRN.DLL	OS2\MDOS\WINOS2\SYSTEM	WIN-OS2 French
LANGGER.DLL	OS2\MDOS\WINOS2\SYSTEM	WIN-OS2 German
WINHELP.EXE	OS2\MDOS\WINOS2	WIN-OS2 help
WINHELP.HLP	OS2\MDOS\WINOS2	WIN-OS2 help
HELVF.FON	\OS2\MDOS\WINOS2\SYSTEM	WIN-OS2 Helvetica font for 8514
HELVA.FON	\OS2\MDOS\WINOS2\SYSTEM	WIN-OS2 Helvetica font for CGA
HELVB.FON	\OS2\MDOS\WINOS2\SYSTEM	WIN-OS2 Helvetica font for EGA
HELVE.FON	\OS2\MDOS\WINOS2\SYSTEM	WIN-OS2 Helvetica font for VGA
HELVG.FON	\OS2\MDOS\WINOS2\SYSTEM	WIN-OS2 Helvetica font for XGA
HERCULES.DRV	\OS2\MDOS\WINOS2\SYSTEM	WIN-OS2 Hercules card device driver
WINOS2.ICO	\OS2\MDOS\WINOS2	WIN-OS2 icon
WIN.INI	\OS2\MDOS\WINOS2	WIN-OS2 ini file
KERNEL.EXE	\OS2\MDOS\WINOS2\SYSTEM	WIN-OS2 Kernel
WOS2MAIN.GRP	\OS2\MDOS\WINOS2	WIN-OS2 main group
GOPM.EXE	\OS2\MDOS\WINOS2	WIN-OS2 mode to PM
MODERN.FON	\OS2\MDOS\WINOS2\SYSTEM	WIN-OS2 modern font
PRINTMAN.EXE	\OS2\MDOS\WINOS2	WIN-OS2 print manager

(continues)

File	Directory	Function
PRINTMAN.HLP	\OS2\MDOS\WINOS2	WIN-OS2 print manager help
PROGMAN.EXE	OS2\MDOS\WINOS2	WIN-OS2 program manager
PROGMAN.HLP	OS2\MDOS\WINOS2	WIN-OS2 program manager help
PROGMAN.INI	OS2\MDOS\WINOS2	WIN-OS2 program manager initialization file
OS2K286.EXE	OS2\MDOS\WINOS2\SYSTEM	WIN-OS2 real mode kernel
ROMAN.FON	\OS2\MDOS\WINOS2\SYSTEM	WIN-OS2 Roman fonts
LANGSCA.DLL	OS2\MDOS\WINOS2\SYSTEM	WIN-OS2 Scandinavian
COMM.DRV	\OS2\MDOS\WINOS2\SYSTEM	WIN-OS2 serial port device driver
SETUP.EXE	\OS2\MDOS\WINOS2	WIN-OS2 setup file
SETUP.HLP	\OS2\MDOS\WINOS2	WIN-OS2 setup file help
SETUP.INF	\OS2\MDOS\WINOS2\SYSTEM	WIN-OS2 setup file information file
WINSHELD.EXE	\OS2\MDOS\WINOS2	WIN-OS2 shield for command prompts
LANGSPA.DLL	OS2\MDOS\WINOS2\SYSTEM	WIN-OS2 Spanish
SYMBOLF.FON	OS2\MDOS\WINOS2\SYSTEM	WIN-OS2 symbol font file for 8514 displays
SYMBOLA.FON	OS2\MDOS\WINOS2\SYSTEM	WIN-OS2 symbol font file for CGA displays
SYMBOLB.FON	OS2\MDOS\WINOS2\SYSTEM	WIN-OS2 symbol font file for EGA displays
SYMBOLE.FON	OS2\MDOS\WINOS2\SYSTEM	WIN-OS2 symbol font file for VGA displays
SYMBOLG.FON	OS2\MDOS\WINOS2\SYSTEM	WIN-OS2 symbol font file for XGA displays
SYSTEM.DRV	\OS2\MDOS\WINOS2\SYSTEM	WIN-OS2 system device driver
SYSTEM.INI	\OS2\MDOS\WINOS2	WIN-OS2 system ini file

File	Directory	Function
WINSMSG.DLL	OS2\MDOS\WINOS2\SYSTEM	WIN-OS2 system message dynamic link library
TASKMAN.EXE	OS2\MDOS\WINOS2	WIN-OS2 task manager
TMSRF.FON	\OS2\MDOS\WINOS2\SYSTEM	WIN-OS2 Times/Roman font for 8514 displays
TMSRA.FON	\OS2\MDOS\WINOS2\SYSTEM	WIN-OS2 Times/Roman font for CGA displays
TMSRB.FON	\OS2\MDOS\WINOS2\SYSTEM	WIN-OS2 Times/Roman font for EGA displays
TMSRE.FON	\OS2\MDOS\WINOS2\SYSTEM	WIN-OS2 Times/Roman font for VGA displays
TMSRG.FON	\OS2\MDOS\WINOS2\SYSTEM	WIN-OS2 Times/Roman font for XGA displays
TOUCH.DRV	\OS2\MDOS\WINOS2\SYSTEM	WIN-OS2 touch screen file
USER.EXE	\OS2\MDOS\WINOS2\SYSTEM	WIN-OS2 user interface code
OASIS.DLL	\OS2\DLL	Windows compatibility dynamic link library
MIRRORS.DLL	OS2\DLL	Windows compatibility dynamic link library
WPCONMRI.DLL	\OS2\DLL	Workplace shell configuration dynamic link library
WPCONFIG.DLL	\OS2\DLL	Workplace shell configuration dynamic link library
PMWPMRI.DLL	OS2\DLL	Workplace shell dynamic link library
WPPWNDRV.DLL	\OS2\DLL	Workplace shell dynamic link library

(continues)

File	Directory	Function
PMWP.DLL	\OS2\DLL	Workplace shell dynamic link library
WPGLOSS.HLP	OS2\HELP\GLOSS	Workplace shell glossary help file
WPHELP.HLP	\OS2\HELP	Workplace shell help file
WPINDEX.HLP	OS2\HELP	Workplace shell index help file
WPMSG.HLP	\OS2\HELP	Workplace shell message help file
WPPRTMRI.DLL	\OS2\DLL	Workplace shell printable translation support
WPPRINT.DLL	OS2\DLL	Workplace shell printing dynamic link library
XGARING0.SYS	\OS2	XGA device driver
XGA.DRV	\OS2\MDOS\WINOS2\SYSTEM	XGA device driver for WIN-OS2
XGA.DLL	\OS2\DLL	XGA display dynamic link library
XGAOEM.FON	\OS2\MDOS\WINOS2\SYSTEM	XGA font for WIN-OS2
XGASYS.FON	\OS2\MDOS\WINOS2\SYSTEM	XGA font for WIN-OS2
XGAFIX.FON	\OS2\MDOS\WINOS2\SYSTEM	XGA font for WIN-OS2

Appendix F
The Default CONFIG.SYS File

If you use a text editor to make changes to your CONFIG.SYS file, you may make mistakes that will cause your system to no longer function. The advice in Chapter 8, "Troubleshooting OS/2," suggests that you make backup copies of your configuration files, including CONFIG.SYS. You may need the information in this appendix, however, to reconstruct a CONFIG.SYS file that you have made several changes to since you last backed up the file. Even if you don't get into trouble by editing your CONFIG.SYS file, you will find the following discussion of the default CONFIG.SYS file interesting. You can refer to this appendix whenever you want to know why a particular entry appears in the file.

The OS/2 installation process creates a CONFIG.SYS file on your computer similar to the file shown below. You may find differences between the entries you see here and the ones in your new CONFIG.SYS file. Options you select during installation and OS/2's detection of the hardware components of your computer can cause OS/2 to create a slightly different CONFIG.SYS file for your PC. Use the information in this appendix as a guide, and compare your own CONFIG.SYS file with the entries below to see where differences exist. You may want to pencil a few notes into the margins of these pages to indicate these differences, for future reference.

```
IFS=C:\OS2\HPFS.IFS   /CACHE:64  /CRECL:4
```

IFS stands for Installable File System. OS/2 loads High Performance File System support by default each time you boot your PC, even if you didn't choose HPFS during OS/2 installation. OS/2 anticipates that you may want to work with HPFS in the future; you need this entry in your CONFIG.SYS if you want to format a disk partition with HPFS.

    PROTSHELL=C:\OS2\PMSHELL.EXE

This line identifies the main Workplace Shell executable.

    SET USER_INI=C:\OS2\OS2.INI

    SET SYSTEM_INI=C:\OS2\OS2SYS.INI

    SET OS2_SHELL=C:\OS2\CMD.EXE

    SET RUNWORKPLACE=C:\OS2\PMSHELL.EXE

These four SET statements tell the Workplace Shell where to find certain OS/2 components. These components are the initialization files for OS/2, the OS/2 command processor, and the Workplace Shell executable.

    SET AUTOSTART=PROGRAMS,TASKLIST,FOLDERS

The Workplace Shell uses the AUTOSTART environment variable to determine how you want your desktop restored each time you start OS/2.

    SET COMSPEC=C:\OS2\CMD.EXE

The COMSPEC environment variable specifies the location of the OS/2 command processor.

    LIBPATH=.;C:\OS2\DLL;C:\OS2\MDOS;C:\;C:\OS2\APPS\DLL;

LIBPATH indicates to OS/2 where to find Dynamic Link Library (DLL) files. When you install an application comprised partly of DLLs, the application's installation procedure may modify this line of the CONFIG.SYS file. The default, which you see here, calls out the location of OS/2's DLL files.

    SET PATH=C:\OS2;C:\OS2\SYSTEM;C:\OS2\MDOS\WINOS2;C:\OS2\INSTALL;

    C:\;C:\OS2\MDOS;C:\OS2\APPS;

The PATH environment variable names the directories that OS/2 searches to find OS/2 executable files. The PATH statement in your AUTOEXEC.BAT file does the same job for DOS executable files.

    SET DPATH=C:\OS2;C:\OS2\SYSTEM;C:\OS2\MDOS\WINOS2;C:\OS2\INSTALL;

    C:\;C:\OS2\BITMAP;C:\OS2\MDOS;C:\OS2\APPS;

The DPATH environment variable indicates to OS/2 which directories to search for data files (rather than executable files). DPATH works like the DOS APPEND command.

```
SET PROMPT=$i[$p]
```

The default PROMPT for your OS/2 command line sessions indicates the current drive and directory, with the directory encased in brackets.

```
SET HELP=C:\OS2\HELP;C:\OS2\HELP\TUTORIAL;
```

```
SET GLOSSARY=C:\OS2\HELP\GLOSS;
```

The HELP and GLOSSARY environment variables tell OS/2 where to find on-line help files and the OS/2 glossary file.

```
PRIORITY_DISK_IO=YES
```

The default setting for PRIORITY_DISK_IO is YES, which means that foreground tasks receive speedier service from OS/2's disk access services.

```
FILES=20
```

The default maximum number of file handles in each DOS session is 20.

```
DEVICE=C:\OS2\TESTCFG.SYS
```

TESTCFG.SYS is a system configuration device driver.

```
DEVICE=C:\OS2\DOS.SYS
```

DOS.SYS is one of the OS/2 components that enable DOS sessions.

```
DEVICE=C:\OS2\PMDD.SYS
```

This device driver provides pointer drawing support in OS/2 sessions.

```
BUFFERS=30
```

The BUFFERS statement default is 30 sector buffers.

```
IOPL=YES
```

OS/2's default for allowing applications access to the PC's I/O port hardware is YES.

```
DISKCACHE=384,LW
```

The default disk cache is 384K, with Lazy Writing turned on.

```
MAXWAIT=3
```

The default value for MAXWAIT is 3.

```
MEMMAN=SWAP,PROTECT
```

OS/2 by default allows memory swapping to disk and provides protected memory to Dynamic Link Libraries.

```
SWAPPATH=C:\OS2\SYSTEM 2048 4096
```

OS/2 places the SWAPPER.DAT file in C:\OS2\SYSTEM. OS/2's default MINFREE value does not permit the SWAPPER.DAT file grow to leave less than 2048K (2M) of free disk space. Depending on the physical memory in your computer, OS/2 creates an initial 4096K (4M) SWAPPER.DAT file each time you boot OS/2.

```
BREAK=OFF
```

This DOS-related setting by default turns off the extra processing (in DOS sessions) for Ctrl-Break checking.

```
THREADS=256
```

The OS/2 default is 256 maximum threads.

```
PRINTMONBUFSIZE=134,134,134
```

OS/2's print buffers for LPT1, LPT2, and LPT3 is 134 characters each.

```
COUNTRY=001,C:\OS2\SYSTEM\COUNTRY.SYS
```

COUNTRY expresses the choice of country you made during installation.

```
SET KEYS=ON
```

The KEYS environment variable by default enables OS/2's command history recall feature in OS/2 command line sessions.

```
REM SET DELDIR=C:\DELETE,512;
```

OS/2 installation creates a DELDIR entry in the CONFIG.SYS file, but disables the entry by prefixing it with REM. You must remove the REM from the beginning of the line to enable undeletion of files.

```
BASEDEV=PRINT01.SYS
BASEDEV=IBM1FLPY.ADD
BASEDEV=IBM1S506.ADD
BASEDEV=OS2DASD.DMD
```

These four device drivers manage OS/2 access to the printer ports, floppy disk drive, and hard disk drive.

    SET BOOKSHELF=C:\OS2\BOOK

    SET EPMPATH=C:\OS2\APPS

The BOOKSHELF and EPMPATH environment variables are OS/2's way of remembering where certain help files and Enhanced Editor files are located.

    PROTECTONLY=NO

OS/2's default for PROTECTONLY allows DOS sessions.

    SHELL=C:\OS2\MDOS\COMMAND.COM C:\OS2\MDOS /P

SHELL indicates the location of the DOS command processor.

    FCBS=16,8

OS/2 provides by default 16 File Control Blocks in each DOS session. Eight of these FCBs are protected, which means OS/2 never closes and reuses FCBs in a way that leaves fewer than eight available. If you changed FCB values during installation, this setting reflects your choices.

    RMSIZE=640

The default size of each DOS sessions is 640K.

    DEVICE=C:\OS2\MDOS\VEMM.SYS

VEMM.SYS is a memory manager for DOS sessions.

    DOS=LOW,NOUMB

OS/2 defaults to loading DOS into conventional (low) memory rather than upper (high) memory. OS/2 also defaults to not making DOS a provider of upper memory blocks.

    DEVICE=C:\OS2\MDOS\VDPX.SYS

    DEVICE=C:\OS2\MDOS\VXMS.SYS /UMB

    DEVICE=C:\OS2\MDOS\VDPMI.SYS

These three device drivers are memory managers for DOS sessions. By default, VXMS is an upper memory block provider.

    DEVICE=C:\OS2\MDOS\VWIN.SYS

The VWIN device driver helps manage WIN-OS2 sessions.

```
DEVICE=C:\OS2\MDOS\VCDROM.SYS
```

VCDROM.SYS provides CD-ROM support in DOS sessions.

```
DEVICE=C:\OS2\MDOS\VMOUSE.SYS

DEVICE=C:\OS2\POINTDD.SYS

DEVICE=C:\OS2\MOUSE.SYS
```

These three device drivers provide mouse support. In particular, VMOUSE provides mouse support in DOS sessions.

```
DEVICE=C:\OS2\COM.SYS

DEVICE=C:\OS2\MDOS\VCOM.SYS
```

These two device drivers manage your serial (COM) ports.

```
CODEPAGE=437,850

DEVINFO=KBD,US,C:\OS2\KEYBOARD.DCP
```

These two statements reflected your choice of country and national language.

```
DEVICE=C:\OS2\MDOS\VVGA.SYS

SET VIDEO_DEVICES=VIO_VGA

SET VIO_VGA=DEVICE(BVHVGA)

DEVINFO=SCR,VGA,C:\OS2\VIOTBL.DCP
```

These four statements provide display (video) management.

Appendix G
Enjoying Multimedia Presentation Manager/2

The OS/2 operating system includes multimedia extensions you can install separately from the base operating system. These extensions are IBM's Multimedia Presentation Manager/2 (MMPM/2). With the proper hardware, you can produce interesting, enjoyable, and sometimes even useful sound and video effects from your computer.

This appendix gives you a working definition of *multimedia* and describes MMPM/2. It also identifies the hardware requirements of MMPM/2, explains how to install MMPM/2, and helps you begin exploring what you can do with MMPM/2.

Defining Multimedia and Multimedia Presentation Manager/2

Professional musicians have for years understood how to use desktop computers to enhance their music. You can find PCs in recording studios, theaters, and at concerts (especially rock-and-roll concerts). For example, Neil Diamond, the singer, uses no fewer than eight PCs in his concert tours. The PCs manage and control several aspects of the concert and even play some of the music you hear (Neil Diamond's voice, of course, is his own). The PCs connect to some of the musical instruments through a MIDI interface. MIDI stands for Musical Instrument Digital Interface. MIDI is both a way of storing music in digital form, inside a computer, and a way of communicating musical-event information from a computer to a musical instrument. A musician can create a disk file of musical events by playing a song on an instrument such as a synthesizer while running software that captures those events through a MIDI interface. The software even lets the musician edit mistakes after playing the song, much as you use a word processor to correct spelling after typing a letter or report.

Multimedia builds on the capabilities of MIDI. Through both sound and pictures, your computer uses multimedia to help you better understand information you otherwise would have to visualize for yourself in your mind's eye. Without multimedia (or for information not accompanied by sound and pictures), you have to read some text on your computer screen and hope that your understanding of the description you've read is correct. Multimedia makes understanding new concepts easier and more accurate. Your computer can use multimedia hardware and software to teach, explain, describe, and relate information to you. You can, for example, purchase encyclopedias, dictionaries, and almanacs on CD-ROM that use multimedia to present their information.

Multimedia Presentation Manager/2 is IBM's operating-system foundation for multimedia, and IBM bundles MMPM/2 with OS/2. OS/2's preemptive multitasking and capability to run sizable computer programs that process large amounts of information make multimedia possible under OS/2. (The memory constraints of DOS, covered in Chapter 3, "Learning OS/2 If You Know DOS," keep multimedia from working well in a DOS environment.)

MMPM/2 consists of components for showing digitized movies in a Presentation Manager window on your desktop and for playing music. You can use MMPM/2 to record, edit, and play music. You also can play music CDs (in addition to reading data CDs) if you have a supported CD-ROM drive.

Knowing the Hardware Requirements

MMPM/2 presently supports three sound cards: the IBM M-Audio Card, the Sound Blaster, and the Pro AudioSpectrum 16. To these sound cards (which themselves are quite capable) you can connect a synthesizer. You'll definitely want to attach the sound card to a good-quality amplifier and speaker combination. If you have a stereo component system, for example, you can have the computer play music through your stereo. You also need a CD-ROM drive supported by OS/2. Review Chapter 4, "Deciding How You Want To Use OS/2," for a list of such drives and their interface adapters.

IBM and several sound-card companies are busy developing support for additional sound cards. If you're thinking of buying a sound card, check with the manufacturer to see if an OS/2 driver is available.

You need an additional 5M of disk space to install MMPM/2 and at least 8M of RAM in your computer (2M beyond the recommended minimum for the base operating system).

Installing MMPM/2

Before you install MMPM/2, you must install OS/2. Chapter 6 covers the installation of the base operating system.

If you're installing from floppy disk, insert the first MMPM/2 disk in drive A. If you're installing from CD-ROM, insert the CD-ROM disc in the CD-ROM drive.

Open the Command Prompts folder and start an OS/2 full-screen or windowed command-line session.

Change to the drive from which you're installing MMPM/2. For example, if you're installing from drive A, type **A:** and press Enter.

Type **MINSTALL** and press Enter.

The installation program begins by asking you the drive letter on which you want to install MMPM/2 and letting you choose which MMPM/2 features you want to install. Select the drive on which you want to install MMPM/2 and choose from the MMPM/2 features that the installation program lists on your screen. If you have a CD-ROM drive, for example, you'll want to choose CD Audio.

Select the Install menu item and follow the instructions on your screen to complete the installation.

Finally, shut down OS/2 and reboot the computer. When your desktop reappears, it contains a new Multimedia folder. Inside the folder are icons labeled Multimedia Install, Multimedia Data Converter, Multimedia Setup, Volume Control, Digital Video, Digital Audio, MIDI, Compact Disc, and others.

Double-click the Multimedia Setup icon to configure MMPM/2 for your sound card and multimedia preferences. You're now ready to enjoy multimedia on your OS/2-based computer.

> **Note**
>
> If you later put a different type of sound card in your computer, run the MINSTALL program again.

Using MMPM/2

You can use MMPM/2 to associate sounds with system and program events. The OS/2 Sound Object in the System Setup folder provides this capability. You can use the Digital Audio program object to record sounds and music. The Digital Video program object can play movie files (MMPM/2 can display movies at a resolution of 320 x 240 and a speed of 15 frames per second). The Compact Disc application can play music CDs, and the MIDI program object can render MIDI files through an amplifier and speaker.

The best way to explore the objects in your Multimedia folder is to run each of them and enjoy watching and listening to the results.

Appendix H

Identifying Sources of OS/2 Information

You'll find several sources of information about OS/2, including shareware and public domain utilities and other computer programs, in this appendix. These sources include information services, bulletin boards, and the Internet. If you have a modem, you will not lack for information about OS/2.

Information Services

All the major information services have forums, conferences, or other discussion areas devoted to OS/2. IBM maintains an official presence on CompuServe. BIX is an excellent technical resource; you'll find on BIX an IBM OS/2 conference, downloadable files, and the online presence of the OS/2 Professional magazine. Other services, such as Prodigy, America Online, Delphi, and Genie, also have areas where you can discuss OS/2, get the latest information, and ask questions.

Bulletin Boards

Dave Fisher, who runs LiveNet, maintains a list of bulletin boards around the world that focus, to one extent or another, on OS/2. You can download Dave's list from many BBS's or from several locations on the Internet (you learn about the Internet later in this appendix). To save you some effort, we have printed the segments of Dave's list that deal with the United States, Canada, and the United Kingdom.

OS/2 BBS's ACROSS THE WORLD
This list is a compilation of OS/2 BBS's across the world. If you
wish to make an addition or correction to this list, please netmail
your BBS information to Dave Fisher at LiveNet, 1:170/110@fidonet.org.

This list is distributed to many FidoNet nodes found in this OS/2 BBS
listing via the Fernwood distribution system. All BBS's listed are in
alphabetical order by country, and then by BBS name. Unless otherwise
noted, all node addresses are FidoNet.

A current list can always be file-requested from LiveNet as 'OS2WORLD'.

-------------------------| Country: Canada |----------------------------
----

```
         BBS Name: BBS Council          Sysop: Herbert Tsui

Phone/Node/Modem: (604) 275-6883, 1:153/922, 14.4 V.32b/V.42b
Phone/Node/Modem: Same, 40:649/1008, Same
        Location: Richmond, BC, Canada
   Primary Focus: OS/2
    Last Updated: August 14, 1992
        Comments: Focus is mostly OS/2 with ibmNET technical support, some DOS
                : and WIN.
```

```
         BBS Name: Baudeville BBS        Sysop: Ian Evans

Phone/Node/Modem: (416) 283-0114, 1:250/304, 14.4 V.32b/V.42b
Phone/Node/Modem: (416) 283-6059, n/a, USR HST 9600
        Location: Toronto, Ontario, Canada
   Primary Focus: OS/2
    Last Updated: September 7, 1992
        Comments: Carry all the Fidonet OS/2 echos as well as the Usenet
                : newsgroups.  Also a member of SDSOS2 and OS2NEW.
```

```
         BBS Name: Bear Garden           Sysop: Tony Bearman

Phone/Node/Modem: (604) 533-1867, 1:153/920, USR HST DS 9600 V.32b/V.42b
        Location: Langley, B.C.
   Primary Focus: OS/2
    Last Updated: March 1, 1992
        Comments: First call access to everything; Freqs accepted from
                : anyone.
```

```
            BBS Name: CAGE, The                    Sysop: Brian P. Hampson

Phone/Node/Modem: (604) 261-2347, 1:153/733, USR HST DS 16.8 V.32b/V.42b
        Location: Vancouver, B.C., Canada
   Primary Focus: OS/2, Antivirus, echos
    Last Updated: June  1, 1992
        Comments: First time callers must go through a short application and
                : will have access to File and Message areas on second call.
                : The CAGE receives the file echo, OS2NEW.  We also
                : participate with IBM Canada in a support forum which
                : includes some IBM staff, and people who have already fought
                : through any wierd setups with OS/2.
                : Hours: 3am-1am Pacific Local Time (GMT-7, -8 in winter)
                : ibmNET address 40:649/1007.

---------------------------------------------------------------------------

            BBS Name: ECS Net                      Sysop: Evan Smith

Phone/Node/Modem: (403) 253-5996, 1:134/72, USR HST DS 14.4 V.32b/V.42b
Phone/Node/Modem: Same, 40:649/1013 (ibmNET), Same
        Location: Calgary, Alberta, Canada
   Primary Focus: Operating Environments
    Last Updated: July 28, 1992
        Comments: The intent of this system is to provide support for, and
                : promotion of new, robust operating environments.  The
                : primary focus at this time being on OS/2.
                :
                : This system runs on OS/2 2.0 using BinkleyTerm and Maximus/2

---------------------------------------------------------------------------

            BBS Name: Home Front BBS               Sysop: Chris Ange-Schultz

Phone/Node/Modem: (514) 769-5174, 1:167/256, Hayes V-Series 2400
        Location: Montreal, Que
   Primary Focus: OS/2
    Last Updated: March  1, 1992
        Comments: OS/2

---------------------------------------------------------------------------

            BBS Name: RT Labs                      Sysop: Peter Fitzsimmons

Phone/Node/Modem: (416) 867-9663, 1:250/628, USR HST 9600 V.32
        Location: Toronto, Ontario
   Primary Focus: OS/2
    Last Updated: March  1, 1992
        Comments: We like programmers.
                : No games or picture files allowed.
                : Maximus for OS/2 was born here.
                : Sponsored/Funded by Royal Trust.

---------------------------------------------------------------------------
```

Appendix H—Identifying Sources of OS/2 Information

```
         BBS Name: Sound Stage BBS              Sysop: Ken Kavanagh

Phone/Node/Modem: (604) 944-6476, 1:153/770, 2400
Phone/Node/Modem: (604) 944-6479, 1:153/7070, USR HST DS 16.8 V.32b/V.42b
        Location: Vancouver, BC, Canada
   Primary Focus: Music, Multitasking (OS/2)
    Last Updated: August 14, 1992
        Comments: ibmNET member (40:649/1006)  File Distribution site
                : Adultlinks (69:3600/123).  80 echos, special interests,
                : 100 megs of files.  Online concert listings for Vancouver.

---------------------------------------------------------------------------

         BBS Name: Telekon/2 BBS                Sysop: Joe Lindstrom

Phone/Node/Modem: (403) 226-1157, 99:9305/55@EggNet, USR HST DS 14.4 V.32b/V.42b
Phone/Node/Modem: (403) 226-1158, 99:9305/56@EggNet, 2400 MNP
        Location: Calgary, Alberta, Canada
   Primary Focus: OS/2, Echomail, sound+music
    Last Updated: August 14, 1992
        Comments: Running RemoteAccess BBS under OS/2 (DOS Sessions).  Online
                : Teleconference.  As many OS/2 file echos as I can glom onto,
                : even a few online games for those with lotsa spare time.

---------------------------------------------------------------------------

         BBS Name: The Idle Task                Sysop: Gerry Rozema

Phone/Node/Modem: (604) 275-0835, 1:153/905, USR HST 14.4 V.42
        Location: Richmond, British Columbia
   Primary Focus: OS/2
    Last Updated: March 1, 1992
        Comments: The Idle Task carries ONLY OS/2 related files and
                : discussions.  DOS files and discussion are not
                : welcome or tolerated.  First time callers get full
                : access.  File requests are accepted from anybody.

---------------------------------------------------------------------------

         BBS Name: The Locutory                 Sysop: Jerry Stevens

Phone/Node/Modem: (613) 722-0489, 1:163/182, QX/4232hs 9600 V.32/V.42b
        Location: Ottawa, Ontario
   Primary Focus: OS/2
    Last Updated: April 27, 1992
        Comments: Fernwood OS/2 library distribution.  Also carry Programmers
                : magazine sources.

---------------------------------------------------------------------------

         BBS Name: The Nibble's Roost           Sysop: Alec Herrmann

Phone/Node/Modem: (604) 244-8009, 1:153/918, USR HST 14.4 V.42
        Location: Richmond, BC (near Vancouver)
   Primary Focus: OS/2
    Last Updated: March 1, 1992
        Comments: Other foci on useful DOS utils, Windows apps (runs on
```

```
              : ver 2.0 !)  First time users can download and upload
              : files, and read echomail areas but not enter echomail
              : until verified.  All OS2 echoes carried as well as
              : others from FidoNet, and local BC networks.
              :
              : Software: OS/2 OS, Maximus 2.0 / Binkley 2.50 BBS
              : Hardware: 386-40 with 8MB RAM, 200MB IDE, 200MB SCSI,
              :           Wangtek QIC02 tape.
```

```
         BBS Name: University of Saskatchewan      Sysop: Kevin Lowey

Phone/Node/Modem: (306) 966-4857, 1:140/43, USR HST DS 14.4 V.32b/V.42b
        Location: Saskatoon, Saskatchewan
   Primary Focus: OS/2, MS-DOS, Windows
    Last Updated: March 1, 1992
        Comments: The U of S BBS is primarily a service to undergraduate
                : students at the University of Saskatchewan.  However,
                : anyone can call in and download files.
                :
                : Our files are stored on our campus VAX/VMS computers.
                : The BBS accesses it using the DEC Pathworks networking
                : software.  Access to the files can be slow, which means
                : that during a File Request your BBS might time-out while
                : my BBS is locating the files.
                :
                : The machine the files are stored on is down for backups
                : on Friday evenings, so don't try to get anything from me
                : Friday evenings.
                :
                : The files may soon be moved to a Unix computer on campus.
                : This should speed up the file access.  In addition, we
                : will likely make the collection available via anonymous
                : FTP on the Internet at that time.
```

```
         BBS Name: iKon View                       Sysop: Herbert Kowalczyk

Phone/Node/Modem: (416) 635-1400, 1:250/816, 2400
        Location: Toronto, Ontario
   Primary Focus: OS/2
    Last Updated: May 28, 1991
        Comments: Full OS/2 support for population of Toronto area.  About
                : 60 megs of OS/2 related files.  All FidoNet OS/2 Conferences
                : are here.  Fernwood (OS2NEW) library distributor.
```

Appendix H—Identifying Sources of OS/2 Information

```
-------------------------------| Country: UK |-------------------------------

-----------------------------------------------------------------------------

         BBS Name: MonuSci BBS                 Sysop: Mike Gove

Phone/Node/Modem: +44-0-454-633197, 2:252/10, USR HST 9600
        Location: Bristol, UK
   Primary Focus: OS/2 Developers, Users and Support Staff
    Last Updated: September 7, 1992
        Comments: Support centre for the International OS/2 User Group

-----------------------------------------------------------------------------

         BBS Name: MonuSci Opus                Sysop: Mike Gove

Phone/Node/Modem: +44-45-453197, 2:252/10, USR HST DS 9600 V.32b/V.42b
        Location: Bristol
   Primary Focus: ?
    Last Updated: March 1, 1992
        Comments: UK OS/2 User Group Support BB + DP Professional
                : File Areas

-----------------------------------------------------------------------------

         BBS Name: The TJD Support BBS         Sysop: Phil Tuck

Phone/Node/Modem: +44-535-665345, n/a, USR HST DS 9600 V.32b/V.42b
Phone/Node/Modem: +44-535-665345, n/a, USR HST 9600
        Location: England
   Primary Focus: OS/2 and TJD Software
    Last Updated: March 1, 1992
        Comments: OS/2 support mainly directed at programmers, and
                : support provided for TJD Software's shareware products.
                : Running Magnum BBS for OS/2.

-----------------------------------------------------------------------------

-------------------------------| Country: USA |------------------------------

-----------------------------------------------------------------------------

         BBS Name: Akron Anomoly, The          Sysop: Mark Lehrer

Phone/Node/Modem: (216) 688-6383, 1:157/535, USR HST DS 9600 V.32b/V.42b
        Location: Akron, Ohio
   Primary Focus: ?
    Last Updated: March 1, 1992
        Comments:

-----------------------------------------------------------------------------

         BBS Name: Alternate Reality           Sysop: Todd Riches

Phone/Node/Modem: (206) 557-9258, 1:343/118, Smart One 2400 MNP 2-7
        Location: Issaquah, Washington
   Primary Focus: DOS, OS/2, and Windows Utils/games/music
```

```
        Last Updated: August 14, 1992
            Comments: DOS, OS/2, and Windows File areas
```

```
            BBS Name: Ascii Neighborhood I & II    Sysop: Bob Morris

   Phone/Node/Modem: (203) 934-9852, 1:141/332, 9600 PEP
   Phone/Node/Modem: (203) 932-6236, 1:141/333, USR HST DS 9600 V.32b/V.42b
            Location: West Haven, Connecticut
       Primary Focus: General Purpose OS/2 and MS-DOS File Areas
        Last Updated: June  1, 1992
            Comments: Contains "Fernwood Collection" OS/2 Files.  Running
                    : BinkleyTerm and Maximus.  Many OS/2 related echos available.
```

```
            BBS Name: AsmLang and OS/2            Sysop: Patrick O'Riva

   Phone/Node/Modem: (408) 259-2223, 1:143/37, USR HST 14.4 V.42
            Location: San Jose, California
       Primary Focus: OS/2 and Assembly Language programming
        Last Updated: March  1, 1992
            Comments: 60+megs files (no games or GIF's).  Open Access policy
```

```
            BBS Name: Asylum BBS, The             Sysop: Bill Schnell

   Phone/Node/Modem: (918) 832-1462, 1:170/200, USR HST 14.4 V.42b
            Location: Tulsa, Oklahoma
       Primary Focus: OS/2 and Windows Support
        Last Updated: March  1, 1992
            Comments: F'reqable 23 hours.
```

```
            BBS Name: BBS/2                       Sysop: Scott Dickason

   Phone/Node/Modem: (918) 743-1562, 1:170/101, 2400
            Location: Tulsa, Oklahoma
       Primary Focus: OS/2, Windows 3.x, Music and Sound
        Last Updated: July 28, 1992
            Comments: Over 150 megabytes of shareware, including many Windows 3.x,
                    : Sound MIDI & Music, Cheats and Unprotects, and a growing
                    : OS/2 collection.  Many FidoNet Echos.  Open access policy.
```

```
            BBS Name: Backdoor BBS                Sysop: Thomas Bradford

   Phone/Node/Modem: (919) 799-0923, 1:3628/11, PM14400FXSA V.32b
            Location: Wilmington, North Carolina
       Primary Focus: OS/2
        Last Updated: August 14, 1992
```

Appendix H—Identifying Sources of OS/2 Information

```
         Comments: The Backdoor is an OS/2 oriented BBS that only carries OS/2
                 : shareware in the file areas and we also carry all the
                 : available OS/2 Fido echos.
```

```
         BBS Name: Bullet BBS                    Sysop: Steve Lesner

Phone/Node/Modem: (203) 329-2972, 1:141/260, USR HST 9600 V.32
Phone/Node/Modem: (203) 322-4135, 1:141/261, USR HST 9600 V.32
         Location: Stamford, Connecticut
    Primary Focus: OS/2, Lans, Programming
     Last Updated: May 14, 1992
         Comments: These boards focus on OS/2 and narrow in on running OS/2
                 : Novell Network Software.  Both nodes are running Maximus
                 : and have the ability to spawn a copy of Simplex.  Lots
                 : of PD files for DOS, Windows, and OS/2 as well as Novell
                 : software (much acquired from the CIS NOV forums).
```

```
         BBS Name: Byte Bus, The                 Sysop: Troy Majors

Phone/Node/Modem: (316) 683-1433, 1:291/13, Hayes V9600 V.32/V.42b
         Location: Wichita, Kansas
    Primary Focus: OS/2 Files, Messages, Information
     Last Updated: September 7, 1992
         Comments: Newly established and trying to grow.  Need OS/2 files and
                 : Information.  Member of OS2NEW (Fernwood) File Distribution.
```

```
         BBS Name: COMM Port One                 Sysop: Bob Juge

Phone/Node/Modem: (713) 980-9671, 1:106/2000, USR HST DS 14.4 V.32b/V.42b
         Location: Houston, Texas
    Primary Focus: OS/2 - DOS Communications
     Last Updated: June 1, 1992
         Comments: SDS Region 19 Coordinator, OPUSarchive
```

```
         BBS Name: Caddis OS/2 BBS               Sysop: Kerry Flint

Phone/Node/Modem: (702) 453-6687, 1:209/705, USR HST 14.4
         Location: Las Vegas, Nevada
    Primary Focus: OS/2 Files and Echos
     Last Updated: September 7, 1992
         Comments: Carry all available OS/2 file and message echos.  Running
                 : BinkleyTerm and Maximus under OS/2.  (Will soon be using a
                 : USR Dual Standard modem).  Freq FILES for file listings
                 : (except during ZMH).
```

```
       BBS Name: Caladan                    Sysop: Rob Schmaling

Phone/Node/Modem: (203) 622-4740, 1:141/243, USR HST 14.4 V.42b
        Location: Greenwich, Connecticut
   Primary Focus: OS/2
    Last Updated: August 14, 1992
        Comments: Running under OS/2 and Maximus 2.01.
```

```
       BBS Name: Capital City BBS           Sysop: Bob Germer

Phone/Node/Modem: (609) 386-1989, 1:266/21, USR HST DS 14.4 V.32b/V.42b
Phone/Node/Modem: Same, 8:950/10, Same
        Location: Burlington, New Jersey
   Primary Focus: OS/2, Word Perfect, Disabilities
    Last Updated: April 27, 1992
        Comments: Users who answer 10 question registration form get download
                : privileges on first call.  QWK format message download
                : supported.
```

```
       BBS Name: Catacombs, The             Sysop: Mike Phillips

Phone/Node/Modem: (317) 525-7164, 1:231/380, USR HST 9600
Phone/Node/Modem: Same, 8:74/1, Same
        Location: Waldron, Indiana
   Primary Focus: DOS, OS/2, Programming, Technical
    Last Updated: June  1, 1992
        Comments: Full access to first time callers, no FEE.  Open 24 hours,
                : File Requests honored 24 hours.
```

```
       BBS Name: Choice BBS, The            Sysop: Mark Woolworth

Phone/Node/Modem: (702) 253-6527, 1:209/710, USR HST DS 16.8 V.32b/V.42b
Phone/Node/Modem: (702) 253-6274, n/a, 9600 V.32/MNP
        Location: Las Vegas, Nevada
   Primary Focus: PD and Shareware files.  Message Echos, too.
    Last Updated: September  7, 1992
        Comments: Supporting OS/2, Windows, and DOS systems.  We also have
                : many of the file echos, SDN, PDN, OS2NEW, GEOWORKS, etc...
                : Over 100 file areas, and over 40 message areas, including
                : more than 10 OS/2 specific Fidonet echos.  Full access to
                : everything on your first call.  Both lines available 24
                : hours, 7 days (except ZMH).  Callers with 9600 baud or
                : slower modems are requested to call line 2 first, if busy,
                : then call line 1.  Over 400 megs online now, another 1.3
                : gigs next month!  BBS (Maximus/2) is run under OS/2 2.0.
                : FREQ available to unlisted nodes.
```

```
     BBS Name: Communitel OS/2 BBS         Sysop: Dennis Conley

Phone/Node/Modem: (702) 399-0486, 1:209/210, USR HST DS 14.4 V.32b/V.42b
        Location: Las Vegas, Nevada
   Primary Focus: OS/2 (Files/Messages/Information)
    Last Updated: March 1, 1992
        Comments: FREQ "FILES" for list of available list of files
                : to download or from BBS download "F209-210.ZIP".


--------------------------------------------------------------------

     BBS Name: Cornerstone BBS, The         Sysop: Dave Shoff

Phone/Node/Modem: (616) 465-4611, 1:2340/110, 14.4 V.32b/V.42b
        Location: Bridgman, Michigan
   Primary Focus: OS/2
    Last Updated: September 7, 1992
        Comments: Carry all OS/2 echos (except OS2PROG).  Member of OS2NEW
                : (Fernwood) File Distribution.


--------------------------------------------------------------------

     BBS Name: Cuerna Verde                 Sysop: William Herrera

Phone/Node/Modem: (719) 545-8572, 1:307/18 aka 1:307/1, 9600 V.32/V.42b
        Location: Pueblo, Colorado
   Primary Focus: OS/2 and conferences/files support for helping professions
    Last Updated: September 7, 1992
        Comments: Running Binkley/2 and Maximus/2 in the background on an
                : OPTI 486-25 with 8 meg RAM, 600 MEB on 2 IDE drives (Maxtor
                : 80, Fijitsu 520).  Both formatted HPFS.  Specialize in
                : OS/2 conferences and files, and also carry most health/
                : wellness type message areas on the backbone.


--------------------------------------------------------------------

     BBS Name: Dog's Breakfast, The          Sysop: Mike Fuchs

Phone/Node/Modem: (908) 506-0472, 1:266/71, USR HST DS 14.4 V.32b/V.42b
Phone/Node/Modem: (908) 506-6293, n/a, Intel 2400 MNP-5
        Location: Toms River, New Jersey
   Primary Focus: Business and Professional Microcomputer Users
    Last Updated: August 14, 1992
        Comments: Over 50 Networked Echomail conferences, and participation
                : in numerous File Distrubution Networks, including: OS2NEW,
                : WinNet, PDN, SDN, SDS, bringing in a continuous flow of the
                : latest in OS/2, Windows, Program development tools and code,
                : and high quality Shareware.  No fees.  First time callers
                : get full read-only access to EchoMail and all file areas.


--------------------------------------------------------------------

     BBS Name: Dugout BBS, The               Sysop: Shawn Haverly

Phone/Node/Modem: (817) 773-9138, 1:396/12, USR HST DS 16.8 V.32b/V.42b
Phone/Node/Modem: (817) 773-9140, n/a, 2400
        Location: Temple, Texas
   Primary Focus: DOS and OS/2
    Last Updated: August 14, 1992
```

```
         Comments: Running under OS/2 2.0 and Maximus/2 on a 340MB drive.
                 : Still supporting DOS heavily with OS/2 support up and coming
                 : on strong.
```

```
         BBS Name: Emerald Isle, The          Sysop: Mike Mahoney

Phone/Node/Modem: (602) 749-8638, 1:300/14.0, USR HST DS 14.4 V.32b/V.42b
         Location: Tuscon, Arizona
    Primary Focus: OS/2 Conferences from Fidonet, ibmNET and Usenet
     Last Updated: September 7, 1992
         Comments: OS/2 Version 2.0, BinkleyTerm 2.56, Maximus 2.01.
                 : Internet Gateway for Network 300
                 : A little bit of Ireland in the Desert
```

```
         BBS Name: Encounter, The             Sysop: Frank Ward

Phone/Node/Modem: (602) 892-1853, 1:114/95, USR HST DS 14.4 V.32b/V.42b
         Location: Gilbert, Arizona
    Primary Focus: UFO Research
     Last Updated: August 14, 1992
         Comments: The main focus of The Encounter is honest research into
                 : UFO's by a skeptic (me).  UFINET, PARANET, MUFONET, and
                 : others are but a few of the net's into this BBS.  Besides
                 : being a Hub (1:114/800), The Encounter is also state Host
                 : for Paranet, MUFON, UFInet and others.
```

```
         BBS Name: Excelsior, The             Sysop: Felix Tang

Phone/Node/Modem: (203) 466-1826, 1:141/222, USR HST DS 14.4 V.32b/V.42b
Phone/Node/Modem: (203) 466-1892, n/a, 2400
         Location: New Haven, Connecticut
    Primary Focus: OS/2, Amiga, Virtual Reality, DOS, Windows-in that order :-)
     Last Updated: April 5, 1992
         Comments: 820Mb online capacity.  OS2NEW (Fernwood) distribution.
                 : Running Maximus 2.01wb under OS/2 1.3 SE.
```

```
         BBS Name: Fernwood                   Sysop: Emmitt Dove

Phone/Node/Modem: (203) 483-0348, 1:141/109, USR HST DS 9600 V.32b/V.42b
Phone/Node/Modem: (203) 481-7934, 1:141/209, USR HST 14.4 V.42b
         Location: Branford, Connecticut
    Primary Focus: OS/2
     Last Updated: March 1, 1992
         Comments: Origin of the Fernwood Collection.  All first-time
                 : callers have full access and 90 minutes per call.
                 : All files are file-requestable - request OS2FILES for
                 : a listing of all OS/2-related files, or FWOS2INF.ZIP
                 : for a VIEWable listing.
```

```
        BBS Name: GREATER CHICAGO Online!! BBS  Sysop: Bill Cook

Phone/Node/Modem: (708) 895-4042, n/a, 9600
        Location: Chicago, Illinois
   Primary Focus: OS/2
    Last Updated: April 27, 1992
        Comments: Supporting OS/2 in the Chicago Metropolitan Area.  Home of
                : the Chicago OS/2 User Group.  Approximately 400 OS/2 files,
                : and around 200 active users.

-------------------------------------------------------------------------

        BBS Name: Gecko Control              Sysop: Rodney Lorimor

Phone/Node/Modem: (509) 244-0944, 1:346/26, 9600 MNP V.32
        Location: Fairchild AFB, Washington
   Primary Focus: OS/2
    Last Updated: June  1, 1992
        Comments: New convert to OS/2 and looking to grow.  Currently
                : receiving Fido OS/2 echos and Fernwood File distribution.

-------------------------------------------------------------------------

        BBS Name: Ghostcomm Image Gallery    Sysop: Craig Oshiro

Phone/Node/Modem: (808) 456-8510, 1:345/14, USR HST DS 14.4 V.32b/V.42b
Phone/Node/Modem: Same, 8:908/23 (RbbsNet), Same
        Location: Pearl City, Hawaii
   Primary Focus: Imaging and Graphics, OS/2, some Macintosh and MSDOS
    Last Updated: September  7, 1992
        Comments: Free access to OS/2 Fidonet conferences and OS/2 file areas.
                : File retievals from Internet ftp archives such as
                : ftp-os2.nmsu.edu are preformed on a daily basis.  Latest
                : patches and fixes from software.watson.ibm.com as they are
                : made available.  OS2NEW retrievals from zues.ieee.org.
                : Currently running in a DOS 5.0 boot image.

-------------------------------------------------------------------------

        BBS Name: HelpNet of Baton Rouge     Sysop: Stan Brohn

Phone/Node/Modem: (504) 273-3116, 1:3800/1, USR HST DS 9600 V.32b/V.42b
Phone/Node/Modem: (504) 275-7389, 1:3800/2, USR HST 9600
        Location: Baton Rouge, Louisiana
   Primary Focus:
    Last Updated: June  1, 1992
        Comments: Carry OS/2 files and downloadable programs.  The second line
                : is echos only.

-------------------------------------------------------------------------

        BBS Name: I CAN! BBS                 Sysop: Bogie Bugsalewicz

Phone/Node/Modem: (312) 736-7434, 1:115/738, USR HST DS 14.4 V.32b/V.42b
Phone/Node/Modem: (312) 736-7388, n/a, PP 2400SA MNP
        Location: Chicago, Illinois
   Primary Focus: Disability Topics
```

```
        Last Updated: April 27, 1992
            Comments: ADAnet Regional Hub (94:107/0).  Large collection of message
                    : bases (150) on assorted topics, including technical forums.
                    : Small OS/2 section, but growing.

-------------------------------------------------------------------------------

            BBS Name: IBM National Support Center    Sysop: IBM

Phone/Node/Modem: (404) 835-6600, n/a, 2400
Phone/Node/Modem: (404) 835-5300, n/a, USR HST DS 9600 V.32b/V.42b
        Location: Atlanta, Georgia
   Primary Focus:
    Last Updated: March 1, 1992
        Comments: Very active OS/2 conference areas.  Helpful IBM'ers
                : doing an outstanding job.

-------------------------------------------------------------------------------

            BBS Name: Information Overload         Sysop: Ed June

Phone/Node/Modem: (404) 471-1549, 1:133/308, USR HST 9600
        Location: Riverdale, Georgia
   Primary Focus: OS/2
    Last Updated: May 28, 1992
        Comments: Atlanta's OS/2 Users Group BBS.  First time callers have
                : full access, 90 minutes per day.  Carriers ALL OS/2 FidoNet
                : echos, along with the comp.os2... newsgroups from the
                : Internet.  Receives the Fernwood File Distribution.  No DOS
                : files, please!

-------------------------------------------------------------------------------

            BBS Name: Integrated Media Services    Sysop: Bill Taylor

Phone/Node/Modem: (503) 667-2649, 1:105/469, ZyXEL U1496E 14.4 V.32b/V.42b
        Location: Gresham, Oregon
   Primary Focus: General Purpose BBS
    Last Updated: September 7, 1992
        Comments: Carry FidoNet backbone OS/2 echos, SDSOS2, OS2NEW file echo
                : plus Windows, DV, and DOS files.  Runs under BinkleyTerm
                : and Maximus for OS/2.  Access to all but adult areas for
                : first time callers.

-------------------------------------------------------------------------------

            BBS Name: Kind Diamond's Realm         Sysop: Mikel Beck

Phone/Node/Modem: (516) 736-3403, 1:107/218, USR HST DS 14.4 V.32b/V.42b
        Location: Coram, Long Island, New York
   Primary Focus: OS/2 and VAX/VMS
    Last Updated: September 7, 1992
        Comments: Carrying the following Fidonet conferences:  OS2, OS2BBS,
                : OS2DOS, OS2HW, OS2PROG, OS2LAN.  Carrying the following
                : Usenet newsgroups: comp.os.os2.misc, comp.os.os2.programmer

-------------------------------------------------------------------------------
```

```
        BBS Name: Last Relay, The          Sysop: James Chance

Phone/Node/Modem: (410) 793-3829, 1:261/1120, 14.4 V.32b/V.42b
Phone/Node/Modem: Same, 100:904/0, Same
Phone/Node/Modem: Same, 100:904/1, Same
        Location: Crofton, Maryland
   Primary Focus: OS/2, Windows, and Desktop Publishing
    Last Updated: August 14, 1992
        Comments: Over 100 megs of OS/2 & Windows files, complete SDS
                : load


-----------------------------------------------------------------------


        BBS Name: Live-Wire                 Sysop: Robert McA

Phone/Node/Modem: (214) 307-8119, 1:124/5105, USR HST 9600 V.32/V.42b
        Location: Dallas, Texas
   Primary Focus: ?
    Last Updated: March  1, 1992
        Comments:


-----------------------------------------------------------------------


        BBS Name: LiveNet                   Sysop: Dave Fisher

Phone/Node/Modem: (918) 481-5715, 1:170/110, USR HST DS 16.8 V.32b/V.42b
        Location: Tulsa, Oklahoma
   Primary Focus: OS/2
    Last Updated: July 28, 1992
        Comments: Over 240 megabyes of OS/2 shareware, articles, and
                : technical information.  Request FILES via mailer or
                : ALLFILES.ZIP via BBS for complete files listing.  All
                : Fidonet OS/2 national echos carried and archived weekly for
                : downloading.  Also a Fernwood (OS2NEW) distribution site.
                : Access available to ibmNET echos and files.
                :
                : The OS2World BBS list is distributed from LiveNet.
                :
                : BBS access is temporarily restricted.  New accounts can be
                : requested via NetMail (please include a chosen password).


-----------------------------------------------------------------------


        BBS Name: Lonnie Wall               Sysop: Operand BBS

Phone/Node/Modem: (901) 753-3738, n/a, 2400
Phone/Node/Modem: (901) 753-7858, 1:123/58, Galaxy UFO 14.4 V.32b/V.42b
        Location: Germantown, Tennessee
   Primary Focus: OS/2, DOS, Windows 3.1, Adult GIF's and Animations
    Last Updated: September  7, 1992
        Comments: Running Maximus 2.01wb under OS/2 2.0


-----------------------------------------------------------------------
```

```
         BBS Name: Looking Glass, The         Sysop: Edward Owens

Phone/Node/Modem: (901) 872-4386, 1:123/81, SupraFax 14.4 V.32b/V.42b
        Location: Millington, Tennessee
   Primary Focus: OS/2 and C, C++, and Pascal Programming and OS/2 DN Files
    Last Updated: June  1, 1992
        Comments: Software running is BinkleyTerm and Maximus under OS/2.
                : Have lots of OS/2 files for downloads.  I am working on door
                : games that will run under OS/2 so you don't have to
                : interface to DOS and multiple other utilities.  Carry
                : Programming echos and files of all kinds.  Will be putting
                : in second node that will hunt from first line to keep up
                : with traffic.

--------------------------------------------------------------------------------

         BBS Name: Magnum BBS                 Sysop: Chuck Gilmore

Phone/Node/Modem: (805) 582-9306, n/a, USR HST DS 9600 V.32b/V.42b
        Location: California
   Primary Focus: OS/2
    Last Updated: March  1, 1992
        Comments: Support BBS for Magnum BBS software

--------------------------------------------------------------------------------

         BBS Name: Max's Doghouse             Sysop: Joe Salemi

Phone/Node/Modem: (703) 548-7849, 1:109/136, 2400 MNP
        Location: Alexandria, Virginia
   Primary Focus: OS/2
    Last Updated: March  1, 1992
        Comments: Also support LANs.

--------------------------------------------------------------------------------

         BBS Name: Monster BBS, The           Sysop: Bob Hatton

Phone/Node/Modem: (908) 382-5671, n/a, USR HST 9600
        Location: Rahway, New Jersey
   Primary Focus: OS/2
    Last Updated: March  1, 1992
        Comments: Running Magnum BBS software with drive storage of
                : 1.1G (not counting the system drive).  The BBS is
                : free limited access on node 1, all that is required
                : to be a regular user is an introduction message.
                :
                : Background tasks include File list creation, message
                : list creation (for offline editing,replying...), and
                : soon to be added- on-line FAX send/receive capability.
                :
                : The BBS is OS/2 based running a BETA 2.0, but DOS users
                : as well as Apple, Amiga, CoCo, and Commie users are
                : welcome.  Few games, lotsa files, and the Original
                : HotRod/Musclecar message base, as well as tech topics
                : and others.

--------------------------------------------------------------------------------
```

Appendix H—Identifying Sources of OS/2 Information

```
         BBS Name: Multi-Net                    Sysop: Paul Breedlove

Phone/Node/Modem: (503) 883-8197, n/a, USR HST DS 9600 V.32b/V.42b
         Location: Lakeside, Oregon
    Primary Focus: OS/2
     Last Updated: March  1, 1992
         Comments: Support BBS for Multi-Net BBS software and
                 : PM Comm communications software.
```

```
         BBS Name: Nibbles & Bytes              Sysop: Ron Bemis

Phone/Node/Modem: (214) 231-3841, 1:124/1113, USR HST 9600
         Location: Dallas, Texas
    Primary Focus: ?
     Last Updated: March  1, 1992
         Comments: Carry a number of BBS-related OS/2 utilities.
```

```
         BBS Name: OS/2 Connection              Sysop: Craig Swanson

Phone/Node/Modem: (619) 558-9475, 1:202/514, ZyXEL 14.4 V.32b/V.42b/MNP4-5
         Location: La Jolla, California
    Primary Focus: OS/2
     Last Updated: March  1, 1992
         Comments:
```

```
         BBS Name: OS/2 Connection              Sysop: Craig Swanson

Phone/Node/Modem: (619) 558-9475, 1:202/514, ZyXEL 14.4 V.32b/V.42b
         Location: La Jolla, California
    Primary Focus: OS/2
     Last Updated: August 14, 1992
         Comments: Our open access download areas have over 2100 OS/2 files
                 : totalling over 150MB, including the complete Fernwood
                 : collection as of January, 1992, plus many new files received
                 : over OS2NEW and Usernet's comp.binaries.os2.  We carry all
                 : OS/2 related Fidonet, Usenet, and OS/2 Shareware message
                 : areas, plus many other technical areas covering topics like
                 : hard disk drives, CD-ROM, SCSI, and modems.  No upload/
                 : download ratios are enforced, but bonus time is given for
                 : those who upload OS/2 files.
                 :
                 : Contributors receive additional time (90 minutes per call,
                 : 100 minutes per day) and will have access to a second BBS
                 : line for contributors only (which will be starting up soon).
```

```
         BBS Name: OS/2 Shareware               Sysop: Pete Norloff

Phone/Node/Modem: (703) 385-4325, 1:109/347, USR HST DS 9600 V.32b/V.42b
Phone/Node/Modem: (703) 385-0931, 1:109/357, USR HST DS 9600 V.32b/V.42b
```

```
           Location: Fairfax, Virginia
      Primary Focus: OS/2
       Last Updated: March  1, 1992
           Comments: Collection of over 2200 OS/2 specific files totalling over
                   : 100 megabytes.  Open access policy.
```

```
           BBS Name: OS/2 Woodmeister, The      Sysop: Woody Sturges

Phone/Node/Modem: (314) 446-0016, 1:289/27, USR HST DS 14.4 V.32b/V.42b
           Location: Columbia, Missouri
      Primary Focus: OS/2
       Last Updated: April 27, 1992
           Comments: Carry all the major OS/2 echos and files areas.  Free
                   : access, no ratios.
```

```
           BBS Name: OS2 Exchange                Sysop: Don Bauer

Phone/Node/Modem: (904) 739-2445, 1:112/37, ZYXEL 14.4 V.32b/V.42b
           Location: Jacksonville, Florida
      Primary Focus: OS/2
       Last Updated: August 14, 1992
           Comments: Over 40 megabytes of OS/2 shareware, articles, and technical
                   : information.  Open access policy.  Request FILES via mailer
                   : or OS2EXCH.LST via BBS for complete files listing.
                   : Automated file retieval from comp.binaries.os2 in addition
                   : to all FTP sites carrying OS/2 shareware.  We keep up with
                   : the latest drivers/fixes.
```

```
           BBS Name: Oberon Software             Sysop: Brady Flowers

Phone/Node/Modem: (507) 388-1154, 1:292/60, USR HST 14.4
           Location: Mankato, Minnesota
      Primary Focus: OS/2
       Last Updated: April  5, 1992
           Comments: User support BBS for Oberon Software products (TE/2,
                   : fshl, etc.) however everyone's welcome.
```

```
           BBS Name: Omega-Point BBS             Sysop: Unknown

Phone/Node/Modem: (714) 963-8517, n/a, 2400
           Location: California
      Primary Focus: ?
       Last Updated: March  1, 1992
           Comments: Home of Omega-Point BBS software
```

Appendix H—Identifying Sources of OS/2 Information

```
          BBS Name: Other World, The           Sysop: Troy Kraser

Phone/Node/Modem: (904) 893-2404, 1:3605/56, Cardinal 9600 V.32
        Location: Tallahassee, Florida
   Primary Focus: DOS and OS/2
    Last Updated: March 1, 1992
        Comments: Have file areas for both DOS and OS/2, hoping to focus on
                : the OS/2 sections by collecting new OS/2 shareware that is
                : released.  No registration requirements (except real
                : names).

---------------------------------------------------------------------

          BBS Name: PMSC OnLine Resource        Sysop: Paul Beverly

Phone/Node/Modem: (803) 735-6101, 1:376/32, 2400
        Location: Columbia, South Carolina
   Primary Focus: OS/2
    Last Updated: April 5, 1992
        Comments: First time callers have very limited access.  You must
                : follow the directions when you first call to gain access.
                : Fairly large OS/2 file collection which is growing rapidly.
                : File Requests welcome.  No file ratios.  Carry major OS/2
                : echos and USENET.

---------------------------------------------------------------------

          BBS Name: Padded Cell BBS, The        Sysop: Jim Sterrett

Phone/Node/Modem: (504) 340-7027, 1:396/51, USR HST DS 14.4 V.32b/V.42b
        Location: Marrero (New Orleans), LA
   Primary Focus: OS/2, Genealogy
    Last Updated: July 28, 1992
        Comments: OS/2 shareware, FileBon File Echo Hub, SDS, and SDN.
                : Open access policy.  Request FILES for complete file
                : listing.

---------------------------------------------------------------------

          BBS Name: Padded Cell BBS, The        Sysop: Jim Sterrett

Phone/Node/Modem: (504) 340-7027, 1:396/51, USR HST DS 14.4 V.32b/V.42b
        Location: Marrero (New Orleans), Louisiana
   Primary Focus: OS/2, Sysop Support
    Last Updated: September 7, 1992
        Comments: OS/2 shareware, FileBone File Echo Hub, SDS.  Open access
                : policy.  Request FILES for complete listing.

---------------------------------------------------------------------

          BBS Name: Play Board, The             Sysop: Jay Tipton

Phone/Node/Modem: (219) 744-4908, 1:236/20, USR HST 9600
Phone/Node/Modem: Same, 60:4800/1, Same
Phone/Node/Modem: Same, 60:3/220, Same
        Location: Fort Wayne, Indiana
   Primary Focus: OS/2
    Last Updated: June 1, 1992
```

        Comments: OS/2 support for Fort Wayne and contact point for Fort
                : Wayne's OS/2 users group. We carry most of the FidoNet OS/2
                : echos along with alinks and voyager echos.

         BBS Name: Psychotronic BBS   Sysop: Richard Lee

Phone/Node/Modem: (919) 286-7738, 1:3641/1, USR HST DS 9600 V.32b/V.32b
Phone/Node/Modem: (919) 286-4542, 1:3641/224, USR HST 9600 V.32
         Location: Durham, North Carolina
    Primary Focus: Echomail
     Last Updated: May 28, 1992
         Comments: We carry almost *every* FidoNet technical conference and
                : support the XRS, QWK, and Blue Wave offline readers. Member
                : of the Fernwood, Programmer's Distribution Net, HamNet, and
                : several other file distribution networks. PCPursuitable
                : (NCRTP), Starlinkable, and *always* 100% free.

         BBS Name: Quantum Leap   Sysop: Louis F. Ursini

Phone/Node/Modem: (215) 967-9018, n/a, 2400
         Location: Pennsylvania
    Primary Focus: ?
     Last Updated: March 1, 1992
         Comments: Running MAXIMUS 2.00 with OS/2 1.3 -- Not dedicated
                : to OS/2, but file areas for OS/2 growing. Currently
                : ordering a USR 14.4k modem.

         BBS Name: Roach Coach, The   Sysop: David Dozier

Phone/Node/Modem: (713) 343-0942, 1:106/3333, USR HST DS 14.4 V.32b/V.42b
         Location: Richmond, Texas
    Primary Focus: OS/2, echos, cooking
     Last Updated: June 1, 1992
         Comments: We carry FidoNet and Internet OS/2 echos. OS/2 files all
                : available for file request or first time download, everyone
                : is welcome.

         BBS Name: Rock BBS, The   Sysop: Doug Palmer

Phone/Node/Modem: (512) 654-9792, 1:387/31, ZyXEL 1496E
Phone/Node/Modem: (512) 654-9793, n/a, Boca M2400E
         Location: San Antonio, Texas
    Primary Focus: Religion, Debate, Literature and Techinical Issues
     Last Updated: July 28, 1992
         Comments: Two nodes, one High Speed, one 2400/ARQ. Over 100 echos
                : from all over the States. Multi-line chat available, some
                : files. Focus is on message traffic and religious issues.
                : Equipment: i486/33 20Meg RAM 428Meg HD, OS/2. Specializes
                : in Point support as well.

Appendix H—Identifying Sources of OS/2 Information

```
         BBS Name: RucK's Place/2           Sysop: Ken Rucker

Phone/Node/Modem: (817) 485-8042, 1:130/65, USR HST DS 14.4 V.32b/V.42b
        Location: Fort Worth, Texas
   Primary Focus: OS/2
    Last Updated: April 5, 1992
        Comments: All first-time callers have full access and 60 minutes per
                : call.  All files are files-requestable - request 130-65.ZIP
                : for a listing of all files, or RucK2BBS.ZIP for a VIEWable
                : listing.
```

```
         BBS Name: SandDollar, The          Sysop: Mark Wheeler

Phone/Node/Modem: (407) 784-4507, 1:374/95, USR HST 9600
        Location: Cape Canaveral, Florida
   Primary Focus: OS/2 and Windows 3.0
    Last Updated: March 1, 1992
        Comments: Carry a lot of OS/2 and Window programs
```

```
         BBS Name: SeaHunt BBS              Sysop: Michael Nelson

Phone/Node/Modem: (415) 431-0473, 1:125/20, USR HST DS 14.4 V.32b/V.42b
Phone/Node/Modem: Same, 8:914/501 (Rbbs-Net), Same
Phone/Node/Modem: (415) 431-0227, No mailer, BBS Only, USR HST 14.4
        Location: San Fransisco, California
   Primary Focus: OS/2, Programming, echos
    Last Updated: June 1, 1992
        Comments: Several Internet conferences, including several that are
                : OS/2 specific.  With a growing collection of OS/2 files.
                : Running on an i486/33, 650MB, under OS/2 2.0.  Maximus/2
                : OS/2 BBS Software and BinkleyTerm 2.55 OS/2 Mailer.
```

```
         BBS Name: Singer Bear BBS          Sysop: John Tarbox

Phone/Node/Modem: (302) 984-2238, 1:150/130, USR HST 9600
        Location: Wilmington, Delaware
   Primary Focus: Technical, including OS/2, Client/Server and programming
    Last Updated: June 1, 1992
        Comments: System has over 1700 files available for download by first
                : time callers.  Running BinkleyTerm and Maximus under OS/2.
                : On-line since 1988.  (Will soon be using a USR Dual Standard
                : modem)
```

```
         BBS Name: Sno-Valley Software Exchange  Sysop: LeRoy DeVries

Phone/Node/Modem: (206) 880-6575, 1:343/108, USR HST DS 9600 V.32b/V.42b
        Location: North Bend, Washington
   Primary Focus: Files and messages for OS/2
```

          Last Updated: June 1, 1992
             Comments: Hub distribution for FidoNet Backbone files.

             BBS Name: Socialism OnLine!   Sysop: Randy Edwards

Phone/Node/Modem: (719) 392-7781, 1:128/105, USR HST 9600 V.42b/MNP
             Location: Colorado Springs, Colorado
        Primary Focus: OS/2
         Last Updated: April 5, 1992
             Comments: Carrying a full line of OS/2 files -- along with the OS/2
                     : 'OS2NEW' file-echo, and over a dozen OS/2 echomail
                     : conferences.

             BBS Name: Soldier's Bored, The   Sysop: Art Fellner

Phone/Node/Modem: (713) 437-2859, 1:106/437, USR HST DS 9600 V.32/V.42b
             Location: Missouri City, Texas (Houston)
        Primary Focus: OS/2
         Last Updated: April 5, 1992
             Comments: First time callers have full access.

             BBS Name: Sorcery Board BBS, The   Sysop: B.J. Weschke

Phone/Node/Modem: (908) 722-2231, 1:2606/403, USR HST DS 9600 V.32b/V.42b
Phone/Node/Modem: (908) 704-1108, 1:2606/407, USR HST DS 9600 V.32b/V.42b
             Location: Bridgewater, New Jersey
        Primary Focus: File echos
         Last Updated: June 1, 1992
             Comments: Carry File Echos catering to any type of user up to and
                     : including OS/2. Also, have echos available on OS/2 BBSing.

             BBS Name: Space Station Alpha   Sysop: Scott Street

Phone/Node/Modem: (302) 653-1458, 1:2600/135, USR HST DS 14.4 V.32b/V.42b
             Location: Smyrna, Delaware
        Primary Focus: OS/2 and Programming OS/2
         Last Updated: July 28, 1992
             Comments: Primary focus on OS/2 FidoNet echos. Fernwood files are
                     : available.

             BBS Name: Storm Front - OS/2, The   Sysop: Chris Regan

Phone/Node/Modem: (203) 234-0824, 1:141/600, USR HST 9600
Phone/Node/Modem: Same, 1:141/565, Same
             Location: North Haven, Connecticut
        Primary Focus: OS/2

        Last Updated: June 1, 1992
           Comments:

           BBS Name: System-2 RBBS   Sysop: Ed Barboni

Phone/Node/Modem: (215) 631-0685, 1:273/714, 9600 V.32/V.42bis
Phone/Node/Modem: (215) 584-1413, 1:273/724, 9600 V.32/V.42bis
Phone/Node/Modem: Same, 8:952/4 (Rbbs-Net), Same
           Location: Norristown, Pennsylvania
      Primary Focus: ?
       Last Updated: March 1, 1992
           Comments: OS/2 is not the primary interest on the board,
                   : but growing!

           BBS Name: Systems Exchange, The   Sysop: Bill Andrus

Phone/Node/Modem: (703) 323-7654, 1:109/301, USR HST 9600
           Location: Fairfax, Virginia
      Primary Focus: OS/2
       Last Updated: March 1, 1992
           Comments: OS/2 ASYNC Comm software, with source. Also
                   : graphics conversion software, gobs of it. OS/2
                   : games, most with source.

           BBS Name: Treasure Island   Sysop: Don Dawson

Phone/Node/Modem: (203) 791-8532, 1:141/730, USR HST DS 14.4 V.32b/V.42b
           Location: Danbury, Connecticut
      Primary Focus: Something for everyone
       Last Updated: August 14, 1992
           Comments: 400+meg of files, including BBS, ANSI, OS/2, DV, Windows,
                   : SDS/SDN/PDN/WinNet/UtilNet. 200+ Fidonet echos. Running
                   : BinkleyTerm/Maximus/OS/2 under two phone lines.

           BBS Name: U.S. Telematics   Sysop: Richard A. Press

Phone/Node/Modem: (215) 493-5242, 1:273/201, USR HST 9600 V.32/V.42b
           Location: Yardley, Pennsylvania
      Primary Focus: Medical, Handicap, & Transportation Issues; OS/2 echos/files
       Last Updated: June 1, 1992
           Comments: Regional outlet for ADAnet. Running TBBS, TIMS, TDBS, and
                   : BinkleyTerm.

           BBS Name: WSI BBS   Sysop: Unknown

Phone/Node/Modem: (901) 386-4712, n/a, 2400
           Location: Memphis, Tennessee

```
        Primary Focus: ?
        Last Updated: March  1, 1992
            Comments: Wilkes Software -- author of Wilkes Database program

------------------------------------------------------------------------

            BBS Name: Zzyzx Road OS/2 BBS          Sysop: Michael Cummings
  Phone/Node/Modem: (619) 579-0135, 1:202/338, 9600 V.32/V.42b
            Location: El Cajon, county of San Diego, CA
       Primary Focus: OS/2 Message bases and files with some business echos
        Last Updated: September  7, 1992
            Comments: This BBS is online 24 hours daily 7 days a week and is a
                    : member of FidoNet (1:202/338) and BizyNet (70:1/15).  Our
                    : file areas are devoted to OS/2 shareware of all sorts and we
                    : carry a few business echos for those interested in
                    : conducting real business in a network environment.


-------------------------| End of BBS Listing |-----------------------------
```

The Internet

The Internet is a cooperative effort of educational institutions, corporations, people, and various government agencies. You can use the Internet to browse a university library's card catalog, get information on health and medicine, download recent weather maps, and send electronic mail. You can also get a wealth of information about OS/2 through the Internet.

Many Internet sites devote some attention to OS/2, but the primary sites you'll be interested in are software.watson.ibm.com, hobbes.nmsu.edu, and the popular Walnut Creek site — ftp.cdrom.com. If you have access to the Internet, you'll definitely want to browse Walnut Creek. Notice that Walnut Creek from time to time releases a CD-ROM disk containing its files; the CD-ROM is inexpensive.

When you use the **ftp** command to access ftp.cdrom.com, log in with an account name of **anonymous** and you use your Internet mail address as your password (I use **barryn@bix.com**, for example). This convention holds true for most Internet sites. To give you an idea of what you can download (or purchase on CD-ROM) from Walnut Creek, the following is a list of directories and files at that site.

```
        1_x/                 = OS/2 1.x-specific files
        2_1/                 = OS/2 2.1-specific files
        2_x/                 = OS/2 2.x files (32-bit)
        all/                 = Files for all versions of OS/2
        cdrom.txt          263 How to order the FTP-OS2 CD-ROM
        ibm/                 = Mirror of software.watson.ibm.com (129.34.139.5)
```

Appendix H—Identifying Sources of OS/2 Information

```
incoming/              -    Incoming - please put new submissions here
netware/               -
new/                   -    Recent additions - files stay here 1 week
old/                   =

1_x:
00index.txt         6916
comm/                  -    Communications programs/utilities (1.x)
drivers/               -    Device drivers (1.x)
editors/               -
graphics/              -    Graphics-related programs/utilities (1.x)
info/                  -    Various text/information files (1.x)
network/               -    Networking Utilities (1.x)
patches/               -    Corrective service diskettes (CSDs) and patches (1.x)
program/               -    OS/2 16-bit programming utilities
sysutils/              -    Various text mode & PM system-related utilities (1.x)

1_x/comm:
00index.txt          308
com03.zoo           3988    COM3 on an ATklone
compatch.txt        1744    Patch OS/2 1.x device driver for higher speed
nba.zoo            28800    NetBios broadcast agent (S)
ox2.zoo             7511    Support for auxiliary port
setbaud2.zoo       10341    Set baud rate up to 115200 baud

1_x/drivers:
00index.txt         1910
4019drvr.zoo      202662    IBM 4019 Laser Printer driver
aha_ibm.cip        33497
aha_ibm.zip        33497    ASW-1420/AT ASPI SCSI driver for AHA-154x
aha_ms.zip         57793    ASW-1420/1220 v1.21 BETA 1/18/90
ati256c1.zoo      205803    ATI VGA Wonder 256 color drivers
atios213.zoo      231461    ATI VGA Wonder/Integra OS/2 1.3 display drivers
atipm4_1.zoo       75515    75515  ATI VGA Wonder 800x600x16 display driver
bocapm12.zoo       58516    Boca SVGA 800x600x16 display driver
com16550.zoo       12334    Patch to allow more than 2 serial ports on non-PS/2s
crnrstne.zoo      185197    Cornerstone dual/single-page monitor display driver
ctmap098.lzh       35839    Extended memory manager for Chips & Tech
ctmap098.zoo       35365    Increase DOS Box memory up to 944K with C&T BIOS
digib141.zoo       21224    OS/2 1.x driver for non-intelligent Digiboards
espdisk.zoo        68453    Hayes ESP modem device driver (D)
et4000.zoo        211840    ET4000 chipset 800x600x16 & 1024x768x16 display driver
et400_1x.zip      156349    156349  OS/2 1.x drivers for Focus VGA4000 & VGA4000+
ev678os2.zoo       56889    Everex Viewpoint 800x600x16 OS/2 1.1 driver
ibmtrbm.zoo        56885    IBM Token Ring 16/4 Busmaster/A NDIS Device Driver
in2000.zoo          5842    Always IN-2000 SCSI driver for OS/2 1.3
orchidp2.zoo      313194    Orchid ProDesigner II 1024x768x16 & 800x600x16 drivers
os2laddr.zip      116641
paradise.zoo      236905    Paradise 800x600x16 & 640x480x16 OS/2 1.1 drivers
pcmou03.zoo         1985    Mouse Systems Bus Mouse driver for OS/2 1.3
plycom10.zoo       40040    COM driver allows multiple ports on same interrupt
trid256.zoo       437780    Trident video drivers for OS/2 1.3 (256 colors)
trid256a.zoo       77824    Patch for trid256.zoo
tridos2.zoo       186099    Trident 8900 16-color drivers for OS/2 1.x
tseng12.zoo       161247    TSENG ET4000+ 1024x768x16 & 800x600x16 display drivers
```

```
1_x/editors:
00index.txt         152
jove414s.zip     167187    Joes Own Version of Emacs (sources)
jove414x.zip     128367    Joes Own Version of Emacs (executables)

1_x/graphics:
00index.txt         715
animated.zoo      11547    Animated background
backdrp2.zoo      36216    Utility to make an image of a desktop background
backsrc.zoo       45614    PM background (S)
bgrid.zoo          6583    Put a background grid on PM display
deskpct.zoo      123817    A desktop picture/screen saver
desktop.zoo        8661    PM desktop background
eyecon.zoo        28911    A background floating eye
newdesk.zoo       59202    PM desktop 1.2
pmglobe.zoo       58706    Display a world globe, very nice (PM)
scapture.zoo       8915    Capture full-screen text mode snapshots
scrnbl13.zoo      18216    Screen Blanker (Screen Saver), version 1.3
silvrbal.zoo      15993    Background picture of two silver balls

1_x/info:
00index.txt         627
advos2.err        11163    Errata for Advanced OS/2 Programming, by Ray Duncan
dbmdemo.zoo     1228230    Online documentation & utils for Database Manager
ibmee13.ann       66588    Announcement: IBM Extended Edition 1.3
ibmse13.ann       57258    Announcement: IBM Standard Edition 1.3
mslan12.ann        5395    Announcement: LAN Enhancements for OS/2
msos212.ann        3584    Microsoft announcing OS/2 1.2
msov212.ann        2355    Microsoft announcing Office Vision for OS/2 1.2
saarexx.zoo      157837    Online docs for SAA REXX
techtips.zoo     263698    .INF file of tech tips for OS/2 1.2 and 1.3

1_x/network:
00index.txt         483
12req0.txt        11927    OS/2 Novell requester version 1.2 - Info
12req1.zoo       291071    OS/2 Novell Netware requester - Part 1
12req2.zoo       307379    OS/2 Novell Netware requester - Part 2
12req3.zoo       328905    OS/2 Novell Netware requester - Part 3
12req4.zoo       281748    OS/2 Novell Netware requester - Part 4
12req5.zoo       261816    OS/2 Novell Netware requester - Part 5
12req6.zoo       196476    OS/2 Novell Netware requester - Part 6

1_x/patches:
00index.txt         659
c286_b.zip       576384    Patches for WATCOM C (16-bit) - Part 1
c286_c.zip       226327    Patches for WATCOM C (16-bit) - Part 2
c286_d.zip       577568    Patches for WATCOM C (16-bit) - Level D
c286_e.zip       475672    Patches for WATCOM C (16-bit) - Level E
f286_b.zip       424651    Patches for Watcom Fortran 77 (16-bit) - Part 1
f286_c.zip       298870    Patches for Watcom Fortran 77 (16-bit) - Part 2
f286_d.zip       782614    Patches for Watcom Fortran 77 (16-bit) - Level D
f286_e.zip       324883    Patches for Watcom Fortran 77 (16-bit) - Level E
jr05151.zip      141201    Fix for APAR JR05151-HPFS probs affecting Comm Manager

1_x/program:
00index.txt         108
findseg.zip       31055    Segment Search Utility-great for diagnosing TRAP 000Ds
```

Appendix H—Identifying Sources of OS/2 Information

```
1_x/sysutils:
00index.txt        1307
bkupini.zoo       58403    Backs up menu and program list from OS2.INI
checklim.zoo      17801    Check to see how much memory OS/2 sees
ctmap098.zoo      35365    Increase DOS Box memory up to 944K with C&T BIOS
gridlock.zoo      21649    Sort icons along edges of screen
inishow.zoo        7901    Display OS2.INI file
iniut102.zoo      31350    INI file utility (PM)
killem10.zip      10899    Kill processes by name or ID
map55.zoo         32241    List running processes and threads (D)
metz.zoo          17125    Display date/time & free memory (PM)
newini.zoo         6290    Makes new .INI file active
os2alias.zoo      26483    CED for OS/2 sessions
os2prc.zoo        16382    Display processes
os2run.zoo        24467    Display/kill processes
osrm21a.zoo       74827    OS/2 Resource Manager version 2.1a
pm_mem.zoo         9962    Memory monitor (PM)
pmpref.zoo        43683    Resets PM preferences
pspm.zoo          40471    Display active processes (PM)
running.zoo       24467    Show/kill processes and resources
rwini.zoo         20532    Reads & writes INI (1.2)
snapdump.zoo     170082    Problem determination tool for OS/2 1.2 & 1.3
theseus.zoo      110420    Performance measurement tool-RAM usage (1.2 only)
thstat.zoo         6208    Display number of threads in various states

2_1:
00index.txt        3699
drivers/              -    Device drivers (2.1)
graphics/             -    Graphics-related programs/utilities (2.1)
info/                 -    Various text/information files (2.1)
mmedia/               -    Multimedia-related programs/utilities (2.1)
patches/              -    Corrective Service Diskettes (CSDs) and Patches (2.1)
program/              -
sysutils/             -    System utilities (2.1)

2_1/drivers:
00index.txt        1364
8514smal.zip     204971    Small font 8514/a display driver for OS/2 2.1
87os221.zip      586815    Oak-087 ProStar SuperVGA drivers for OS/2 2.1
actixs3.zip     1423902    Seamless S3 drivers for Actix Graphics Engine 32
ati32v11.zip     670036    ATI Mach8/Mach32 display drivers
bwos2-2m.zip    1162262    OS/2 2.1 display drivers for Spider BlackWidow VLB
dynamite.zip     951209    Hercules Dynamite Tseng ET4000-W32/W32i display drivers
fos221.zip      1202761    Orchid F1280 (plus), 1280-D, VA, 2.1 VGA drivers
ftdvr14.zip       12424    Tape driver for the BackMaster backup program
mvos2.zip        113298    PAS-16 promixer and SCSI Device drivers for MMPM
mvprodd.zip       30051    PAS-16 updated MMPM device driver
ncrvid21.zip    1061430    NCR 77C22/77C22E display drivers verion 1.01
p9os2140.zip    1059904    Sixgraph Wizard 900VL OS/2 2.1 display drivers
smldrv21.zip      81313    Small fonts/icons for 1024x768 SVGA display driver
speaker.zip       44737    Speaker audio device driver for MMPM/2
spider1m.zip     991003    Display drivers for Spider BlackWidow VLB w/1MB
stlos21.zip     1360117    Diamond Stealth VRAM (911) display drivers v1.0
summa.zip         11059    Driver for Summa MM1201 or compatible graphics tablets
trident.zip      411719    Trident OS/2 2.1 display driver (beta)
vpros21.zip     1085819    Diamond Viper display drivers
```

```
2_1/graphics:
00index.txt            104
vf03r2.zip           99253   Flexible Image Transport Systems (FITS) image viewer

2_1/info:
00index.txt            564
boot21.zip            8193   How to create an OS/2 2.1 boot disk
cnfgsort.zip          2643   Document: How to decrease OS/2's boot-up time
os2_pas.zip           2352   Questions and Answers for ProAudio Spectrum soundcard
os2ga.txt             7767   Announcement: OS/2 2.1
os2perf.zip         100035   OS/2 2.1 performance tuning for end-users
passetup.zip          5907   How to set up/use a Pro Audio Spectrum soundcard
retail.txt            3219   OS/2 2.1 hits retail shelves - article
unlshd.zip            2707   Announcement: 2nd printing of OS/2 2.1 Unleashed

2_1/mmedia:
00index.txt            167
repeat.zip            5620   Play a multimedia file multiple times (PMREXX)
systunes.zip         25182   System sounds for those without a soundcard

2_1/patches:
00index.txt            550
21optcl.zip           7111   Patch for Optical driver - fixes FORMAT problem
nts2fx.zip          136950   NTS/2 fixes for OS/2 2.1 and CID install
pj08734.zip         104448   Fix for AMI-PRO faults & Quicken Invoice overflow
pj08996.zip          62464   Fix for IPE running DOS
pj09122.zip         464896   Fix for IPE at ## 0160 with non-S3 video cards
pj09201.zip         304128   Fix for modal dialogs hanging desktop
pj10200.zip          71924   OS/2 2.1 fixes (8 Nov 1993), fixes many things
vdma.zip              5821   Virtual DMA patch for PAS-16

2_1/program:
00index.txt            288
gbase1.zip         1240017   Guidelines: Visual C++ GUI Tool 1 of 3
gbase2.zip         1398315   Guidelines: Visual C++ GUI Tool 2 of 3
gbase3.zip         1382980   Guidelines: Visual C++ GUI Tool 3 of 3
guidoci.zip         14772   Guidelines: Visual C++ GUI Tool Info file

2_1/sysutils:
00index.txt            171
bootd21.zip         796363   1.44M disk image of a single OS/2 2.1 boot disk
hstart02.zip         52052   An enhanced replacement for OS/2 start command

2_x:
00index.txt          74499
archiver/               -    Compressors/decompressors (2.x)
bbs/                    -    Bulletin board system programs/utilities (2.x)
comm/                   -    Communication programs/utilities
demos/                  -    Commercial Software Demos (2.x)
diskutil/               -    File/directory/disk utilities (2.x)
dos/                    -    DOS programs/drivers userful for OS/2 2.x
drivers/                -    Device drivers (2.x)
editors/                -    Editors and browsers (2.x)
educate/                -    Education-related programs (2.x)
games/                  -    Games (2.x)
graphics/               =    Graphics-related programs/utilities (2.x)
info/                   =    Various text/information files (2.x)
```

Appendix H—Identifying Sources of OS/2 Information

```
miscutil/            -   Miscellaneous utilities (2.x)
mmedia/              -   Multimedia related programs/utilities (2.x)
network/             =   Network drivers/programs (2.x)
patches/             -   Corrective Service Diskettes (CSDs) and Patches (2.x)
printer/             -   Printer utilities (2.x)
program/             =   32-bit programming utilities/source code (2.x)
sysutils/            -   System utilities (2.x)
unix/                =   Unix-related programs/ports (2.x)
win_os2/             -   Win-OS/2 programs/drivers (2.x)

2_x/archiver:
00index.txt          1357
av181.zip            313756   PM archive viewing/launching/maintenance utility
deboo100.zip         73487    Encode/decode binary files into printable files
funzip2.zip          36191    Filter unzip utility for Info-ZIP UNZIP
gtak212b.zip         551281   GTAK SCSI tape backup software, version 2.12
macutils.zip         299294   Utilities for Macintosh files, archives & fonts
rxdecode.zip         46894    Intelligent UU/XX-decoder
selfpr.zip           5371     Utility which unpacks archived files & creates icons
unarj241.zip         84237    UNARJ 2.41 ARJ-extractor
unz50x32.exe         116709   Info-ZIP UNZIP version 5.0 - 32-bit executables
uu_codes.zip         25211    Extract/create ASCII versions of binary files
uudoall.zip          81536    Decode multipart UUENCODED files from one large file
uuprep10.zip         28147    UUPREP - automatically extract c.b.os2 posts
varc10b3.zip         10077    Archive utility front-end, requires VREXX
zc300.zip            93387    Zip Chunker 3.00, a ZIP file splitter
zcp300.zip           104325   Zip Chunker Pro 3.00, ARC/ARJ/LHZ/ZIP file splitter
zip201x2.zip         119552   Info-ZIP ZIP version 2.01 - 32-bit executables
zipeng10.zip         45120    Front end for PM Zip/Unzip, req. VREXX & ZIP/UNZIP
zipme101.zip         94358    PM shell for INFO's [un]zip, 32 bit, multithreaded
zoo21-2.zip          299000   ZOO 2.1 (HPFS/FAT aware) - 32-bit version

2_x/bbs:
00index.txt          1197
1013tw2.zip          476984   Classic Trade Wars 2 BBS Door Game
arca130.zip          82288    ArcAnal - Archive Analysis BBS utility
atp07os2.zip         101149   ATP 1.42 QWK Reader for OS/2 - Freeware
elite.zip            185377   Elite multi-line information service software
kwq12d.zip           206591   32-bit PM-based .QWK mail reader
los233-1.zip         828174   Lora Bulletin Board System - Part 1 of 4
los233-2.zip         293789   Lora Bulletin Board System - Part 2 of 4
los233-3.zip         301607   Lora Bulletin Board System - Part 3 of 4
los233-4.zip         368729   Lora Bulletin Board System - Part 4 of 4
los233-5.zip         652988   Lora Bulletin Board System Part 5 of 7?
los233-6.zip         514254   Lora Bulletin Board System Part 6 of 7?
los233-7.zip         505649   Lora Bulletin Board System Part 7 of 7?
myed_09.zip          128167   PM FIDOnet-style message reader
offtag10.zip         96499    Offline file tagger for Maximus/2 BBS
pmqwkb07.zip         203881   PMQWK Offline Mail Reader, BETA Ver. 1.0/Rel. #7
timb9p.zip           115024   Timed BETA 9 Squish/*.MSG editor
uu_waf.zip           88250    Generate waffle compatible filenames w/UUPC for OS/2
uugat023.zip         138830   Complete Fidonet/Internet gateway

2_x/comm:
00index.txt          1112
am4pm05c.zip         56385    Answering machine for PM and ZyXEL 1496
linkr3.zip           107056   A LapLink-like file transfer program (beta 0.3)
lwb2.zip             204655   LiveWire 2.1 communications program beta release 2
```

ppi_os2.zip	3983	Hints on using high speed modems
psfax2.zip	333032	A utility for sending out faxes via a Supra FaxModem
satisfax.zip	80052	Tips & techniques for Intel SatisFAXion FAXmodem
sendrecv.zip	21248	Provide SEND/RECEIVE to DOS VMD & Comm Manager
upc12b21.zip	349117	UUPC/extended 1.12b OS/2 2.x executables (1 of 3)
upc12b22.zip	373756	UUPC/extended 1.12b OS/2 2.x executables (2 of 3)
upc12b23.zip	109272	UUPC/extended 1.12b OS/2 2.x executables (3 of 3)
upc12bad.zip	324805	UUPC/extended 1.12b documents and sample files
upc12bap.zip	318983	UUPC/extended 1.12b documents in PostScript format
upc12baw.zip	140653	UUPC/extended 1.12b Word for Windows document source
upc12bs1.zip	433324	UUPC/extended 1.12b source files (1 of 2)
upc12bs2.zip	49182	UUPC/extended 1.12b source files (2 of 2)

2_x/demos:

00index.txt	1542	
arcadia1.zip	538836	Arcadia Workplace Companion demonstration disk
biaf100d.zip	219264	Back In a Flash, backup utility demo
bmdemo1c.zip	207285	BackMaster QIC 40&80 tape backup utility demo
bocademo.zip	231010	System Sounds for OS/2 (demo)
cm250_11.zip	79140	Demo driver for Philips CM205 CDROM (expires 31-Dec-1993)
compass.zip	523763	Golden Compass Navigator for CompuServe demo
condemo.zip	177105	Conduit LAN Admin package demo
dcf2show.zip	393875	DCF/2 on-the-fly disk compression demo
demo21.zip	1263475	IBM OS/2 2.1 demonstration disk
descrb40.zip	1348070	Describe 4.0 word processor preview
dmdemo.zip	138409	Displaymaster-view multiple images, audio & DVI files
dms4demo.zip	269517	DMS/Intelligent Backup 4.0 for OS/2 & DOS
ibmcua_1.zip	1350454	IBM Common User Access demo, Part 1
ibmcua_2.zip	554962	IBM Common User Access demo, Part 2
mlginf.zip	490212	MicroLearn Game Pack volume 1 demo package
njoydemo.zip	347372	N/JOY demo - the world of objects
os201inf.zip	201685	Demo version of Using OS/2 2.0 Applications
osdemo.zip	162439	Open Shutter screen capture demo
rim21.zip	562348	RimStar Programmers Editor demo version
rwm212.zip	630048	Relish time manager working model - 32 bit
vpeval.zip	545982	Working evaluation version of VisPro/REXX visual REXX
wipeout.zip	388608	BocaSoft WipeOut screen saver demo
wp52demo.zip	1431408	WordPerfect 5.2 for OS/2 demo diskette

2_x/diskutil:

00index.txt	3076	
back2fat.zip	8099	Backup HPFS to a FAT partition (requires EABACKUP&ZOO)
backini.zip	20157	Make numbered backups of any file
bakitup.zip	103348	A front-end for using the OS/2 BACKUP command
bigname.zip	19670	Names files that do not obey DOS 8.3 convention
bsplit.zip	47634	Binary file splitter/combiner
cdir2.zip	64712	CDIR v1.00, color directory listing
dcopypm6.zip	144535	PM file copy utility
deltree2.zip	20158	Delete an entire directory tree, like MSDOS deltree
dhrff10.zip	36574	Directory list and file find version 1.0
dhrgcd.zip	38766	Global Change directory version 1.01
dsiz32.zip	15539	Directory size and file count utility
dsize10.zip	5994	Display file/directory space usage on drives (REXX)
dskst102.zip	32242	Display hard drive usage/swap file activity
dsplit.zip	41900	File splitting/joining utils for multiple platforms
extfs2.zip	14933	A utility which lists file extentions
fc2_016.zip	95831	File Commander/2 v0.16, Norton Commander clone

Appendix H—Identifying Sources of OS/2 Information

File	Size	Description
ff147.zip	24361	File find utility version 1.47, HPFS aware
filjet5e.zip	235375	Norton Commander/PCShell-like program
fit20.zip	23541	Multithreaded best-fit multi-disk copy
fm2_114.zip	252998	A powerful Workplace Shell file manager
fs2.zip	15744	OS/2 2.0 file size calculation and reporting utility
iostone.zip	45921	Disk, file I/O & buffer cache efficiencies benchmark
look2_21.zip	111325	Look, a full screen 32-bit file viewer
lstpm104.zip	103408	Oberon file lister/browser for PM
lx91.zip	46644	LX, a directory lister/file find utility
makedskf.zip	19340	Create diskette image file for LOADDSKF
nemo02.zip	97972	Captain Nemo 0.2, closely imitates Norton Commander (R)
ocln108.zip	290265	McAfee Virus Clean for OS/2 version 1.08
onet102.zip	221303	McAfee Network Virus Scan for OS/2 version 9.14V102
oscan109.zip	270898	McAfee Virus Scan for OS/2 version 1.09
pcd231.zip	48085	Paddys directory changer
pchash2.zip	25586	Display 16/32-bit CRC values for files
pgp22.txt	1946	How to get a free public key encryption program
pmdcopy.zip	41140	PM-based disk copier
pmscb11.zip	97472	PM Scrapbook - a tool for organizing files/info
pmund101.zip	51049	PM program for quick recovery of deleted files
qformat.zip	18329	Quick floppy formatter
shlong10.zip	3701	Lists non-FAT names on an HPFS drive (REXX)
strings.zip	13492	Print text strings found in binary/ASCII files
treesize.zip	23589	Text directory lister with "space/percentage" printout
unsdel10.zip	34157	Safe delete and undelete utilities (HPFS aware)
vundel2.zip	48309	Visual Undelete, find deleted files fast
whereis.zip	35829	Whereis 2.1, command line file-finder utility
wizos2.zip	26432	Wiz 1.14 directory changing utility
xeol10.zip	17351	End-of-line translation utilities for Mac/OS2/DOS/Unix

2_x/dos:

File	Size	Description
00index.txt	1832	
00readme.txt	1283	Readme file for DOS programs
16550doc.zip	25041	Do you need a 16550 UART? 16550 docs/utils
amos10.zip	67679	AMOS v1.0, access HPFS drives from pure DOS
boot2c.zip	13267	Force boot from hard disk even if floppy is inserted
bootfx.zip	10179	Fix OS/2 boot after DOS 6.0 installation
bp7-os2.zip	110830	Produce OS/2 programs w/Borland Pascal 7.x
bpos2api.zip	34726	OS/2 system API & replacement units for BP7-OS2.ZIP
chkchg.zip	2774	Check for proper recognition of changing floppies
dos5iso.zip	19350	IBM DOS 5.0 ISO font supplement
fossdumm.zip	43247	Dummy fossil server for OS/2 VDM sessions
hdk100a.zip	260394	Help Engine development kit (Part 1 of 2)
hdk100b.zip	225348	Help Engine development kit (Part 2 of 2)
hpfsr16e.zip	20615	Read HPFS-partitions under plain DOS
hpfsread.zip	39149	Read HPFS disks while running DOS, very primitive
mscdex2.zip	21286	Patched version of MSCDEX 2.21 - runs in DOS box
msvc_os2.zip	124034	Patch to allow Visual C++ to run under OS/2
os2speed.zip	1853	Allow Desqview-aware programs to give up timeslices
prntst.zip	8668	Determine if your LPT1 setup will conflict w/OS2
ptch70.zip	341783	Patches for Microsoft C/C++ 7.0, run 7.0 in DOS box
run110.zip	8686	Run OS/2 programs within DOS sessions
sfrename.zip	8833	Rename EA DATA. SF,WP ROO. SF for DOS defrag utils
vgasve11.zip	11604	Save/restore DOS session VGA screens correctly
viz423.zip	75764	DOS text mode video accelerator.
winicon.zip	21715	Convert Windows 3.x icons to OS/2 2.x
x00150.zip	105112	X00 Fossil serial driver for an OS/2 2.x DOS session
xgaibm.zip	3472125	IBM butterfly demo of XGA-1/XGA-2 capabilities

```
2_x/drivers:
00index.txt         3983
14os22x.zip        11547    Ultrastor 14F and 34F drivers for OS/2 2.x
24f-os2.zip        40394    Ultrastor 24F EISA SCSI control OS/2 drivers
24os220.zip        11732    Ultrastor 24F device driver for OS/2 2.x
34f-os2.zip        56414    Ultrastor 34F SCSI controller OS/2 drivers
4mmdrv.zip         34037    Systos Plus device driver for 2GB 4mm DAT
77os221.zip       548320    SVGA drivers for OAK 77 & 67 chips 2.0 + SP
8900bfix.zip       12811    Patch for using the Trident drivers with the 8900B
ati256c2.zip      191572    ATI VGA Wonder 256 color display drivers
bt-os2.zip         10240    OS/2 2.x driver for the BusLogic SCSI Host Adapter.
canon38.zip       184649    CaPSL printer driver for Canon LPT4/8III
cdsys.zip           5305    CD-ROM driver for more drives; OS/2 2.0 only
cdu535.zip          6400    Sony CDU-53x CD-ROM driver
clos216.zip       278461    16-color display drivers for Cirrus Logic boards
clos2256.zip      376629    256-color display drivers for Cirrus Logic boards
cm206cdr.zip       17902    Phillips CM206 CD-ROM Driver (beta)
et400_20.zip      389163    OS/2 2.0 drivers for Focus VGA 4000/VGA 4000+
et4_os2.zip       397044    Generic ET4000 16-color display drivers
f1280_30.zip      514184    Orchid Fahrenheit 1280 drivers v3.0
genoa7k.zip       431235    Display drivers for Genoa 7000 series
hpmouse.zip         9840    HP HIL mouse drivers (beta) for OS/2 2.0
hrdcd2xl.zip       14051    OS/2 2.0 Plus Hardcard IIXL Drivers
ibmprint.zip      168769    Several IBM printer drivers not shipped w/OS/2 2.0
in2kadd.zip         8038    IN2000 SCSI Adapter ADD driver (beta)
k542x-d1.zip      575704    Cirrus Logic display drivers (Disk 1 of 4) - DOS utils
k542x-d3.zip      428736    Cirrus Logic display drivers (Disk 3 of 4) - Windows
k542x-d4.zip     1239452    Cirrus Logic drivers (BETA) (Disk 4 of 4) - OS/2
lockdrv.zip         4650    Format DASD & r/w CD drives with FAT or HPFS
mitlu002.zip       12346    CD-ROM driver for Mitsumi lu005s/lu002 drive
ncr14.zip         607687    OS/2 2.x display drivers for NCR77C22E chipset
no9os2.zip       1877237    Number Nine GXE display drivers for OS/2
os2_tsl6.zip       76309    Trantor SCSI card drivers
os2spd.zip          1442    NEC Powermate 386/25si device driver for turbo mode
p9kos2-b.zip      432627    Beta display drivers for the Orchid P9000 board
pgos2_20.zip      263006    STB drivers for Tseng-based cards with STB BIOSes
pjet.zip           43997    HP PaintJet printer drivers
post32.zip        196932    32-bit Postscript printer drivers v21.389
proii4.zip        209764    Orchid 16 color display drivers (Tseng based cards)
proii8.zip        315003    Orchid 256 color display drivers (Tseng based cards)
promise.zip        16904    OS/2 2.x drivers for Promise Disk Accelerator (Beta 1.1)
qvision.zip       222166    Video drivers for Compaq QVision 1024/E & 1024/I
rodnt100.zip       64251    A better mouse driver - includes 3-button support
s3_dell.zip       803378    Display drivers for Dell S3 86C805 On-Board Video
s3altrix.zip      804743    Drivers for S3 cards w/911, 924, 80X, & 928 chipsets
sbcd2.zip          10240    Soundblaster 16/Pro CD-ROM drivers
sbcd2pan.zip       11904    Soundblaster drivers for Panasonic/Matsushita CD-ROMs
sio120.zip         80754    High performance serial drivers for OS/2
sony31a.zip        20665    Sony CDU-31A beta CD-ROM driver
spea_v7.zip      2313472    Spea V7-Mirage/V7-Mercury display drivers
st01_102.zip        7864    Device driver for Seagate ST01 SCSI adapter
stealth.zip      1034290    Diamond Stealth VRAM display drivers
systos.zip         44425    Mod 6157 device driver for Sytos Plus v1.35
tmv1scsi.zip       53141    IRQ driven CDROM drivers for the PAS-16
trid32.zip       1085395    32-bit display drivers for Trident TVGA series
v7mirage.zip     2914944    SPEA Video Seven-Mirage display drivers
vga800_1.zip      107152    Generic 800x600x16 drivers for SVGA cards
wkaa15.zip         14101    Sytos Plus driver for Wangtek PC02 QIC tape drive
x24os221.zip     1709908    Drivers for STB PowerGraph X24/VL24 video
```

924 Appendix H—Identifying Sources of OS/2 Information

```
2_x/editors:
00index.txt         906
autoquo.zip       55646    SmartQuotes macro for DeScribe 4.0
beav140.zip      204492    Beav 1.40 binary file editor
beav_2.zip       225353    Beav 1.33 binary file editor
browse.zip        14073    View text/binary files in ASCII/Hex
descrfax.zip        760    Describe macro for creating FAX cover sheets
dsb32env.zip      10133    Describe macro for printing envelopes
ehp11.zip        317339
ehp12.zip        357770    An editor written on a HP UNIX workstation ported to OS/2
epm_spel.zip     378458    Spell checker add-in for EPM editor
ftnote.zip        84494    Describe 4.0 macros to convert endnotes to footnotes
ked203.zip        80314    KED, OS/2 character mode text editor
l2_25.zip         36632    L2, a text file-viewer utility
te265os2.zip      93767    Fast, full-featured programmers editor
wplog32.zip       65441    WordPerfect for OS/2 macros to open/close sets of docs

2_x/educate:
00index.txt         649
biprob.zip        31499    Binomial probability calculator
clopt.zip         99840    Construct/display hierarchical trees
math.zip          23479    Math flash card program
pari138.zip     1490257    Calculator and library for number theory
pmchaos.zip       74933
pmmath24.zip     126377    Elementary school math quiz program version 2.4
pmspel22.zip      95540    Elementary school spelling program version 2.2
sonnet.zip        85168    Shakespeare sonnets in INF viewable format
spice2g6.zip     225815    Spice 2G.6 electrical circuit simulator
ssiim11.zip      595509    SSIIM, a sedimentation engineering simulation

2_x/games:
00index.txt        1576
anagram2.zip     109406    Utility for solving/decrypting anagrams
cdungeon.zip     324863    Port of famous dungeon game (w/src)
checkr12.zip      27107    PM checkers, version 1.2
craps3.zip        51618    Craps game, version 2.01
daleks.zip        84451    Daleks, a strategy game for OS/2 PM
dchess.zip        90405    Dungeon Chess version 2.0
dmine120.zip      92800    32-bit MineSweeper for OS/2
dum212.zip       236010    Dinkum3 v2.12 text adventure
entrtain.zip     106115    BG (V1.4), four (2.3), master (2.3). pegged (1.1)
flip.zip          26693    A PM dice game
greed.zip         55253    A PM implementation of the game Greed
jive_val.zip      46243    Jive and valley-speak text filters
mah21.zip        319441    Mah Jongg 2.1 (German version), many features
mah21e.zip       316251    Mah Jongg 2.1 (English version), many features
mine31.zip       544857    Multimedia PM Minesweeper
niknak.zip        26118    NikNak, Tic Tac Toe with a twist
number11.zip      64122    Numbers version 1.1, a PM quiz game
omega75.zip      281609    Omega adventure D&D-type game
os2moria.zip     178328    Moria 5.5 adventure D&D-type game
pmbots11.zip      28093    The classic UN*X robots game for OS/2 PM
pmics091.zip      82910    Play chess through Internet Chess Server
rollball.zip     120768    Roll the ball for points game for PM (S)
spew.zip          36442    Create National Enquirer headlines and more
tetris.zip        26355    32-bit Tetris for OS/2 2.x
trsh12.zip        53695    Transman - a game for OS/2 PM
xword.zip        154512    Crossword Puzzle game for PM
```

```
2_x/graphics:
00index.txt          5172
3dmaze.zip          59197   Generates 3-D mazes with solutions
blanker20.zip       47137   Screen Blanker 2.0 screen blanker for OS/2
bmpgif2.zip         10994   Command line BMP to GIF converter
chartbl.zip         41355   Display & print character tables of outline fonts
dkbos2.zip         305662   Dkbtrace raytracer 2.12 for OS/2 2.0
dkbpm2.zip         451926   Integrated graphical interface for DKB ray tracer
edgefx.zip          38779   Display marquee-style lights on your desktop
elephant.zip        11050   Icon-size animated dancing elephant
fbmp.zip            12930   Freeware 256-color PM bitmap viewer, source included
fredicn3.txt          599
fredicn3.zip      1068169   Now over 1000 16-color & 256-color OS/2 icons
galler.zip         145907   Galleria, a bitmap editor/converter
gbm.zip            394483   Generalized Bitmap module, supports many formats
gbmsrc.zip         215398   Generalized Bitmap module, sources
gif3210a.zip        69404   32bit SVGA GIF viewer. Multithreaded, with look-ahead
hexmaze.zip         67865   Display mazes with hexagonal rooms (PM)
icons/                  -   Icons for OS/2
imgarc13.zip        88004   Image Archiver - JPEG converter/viewer v1.03
imgtkit2.zip        77353   IBM Image Toolkit for OS/2
imshow.zip          87242   BMP/GIF/IM viewer with palette manager support
irit_os2.zip       428073   IRIT solid modeller for OS/2 2.0
joevw121.zip       262639   Image viewer with print, clipboard & slideshow
jpegv4.zip         100148   JPEG version 4.0 image compression software
life.zip            49536   Game of Life - screen saver w/source
magnify2.zip        34154   Screen Magnifier, require Image Toolkit (imgtkit2)
mazelock.zip        22023   Mouse and keyboard lock / screen saver
mpegplay.zip        97028   Full-screen 320x200 MPEG animation player
myplot.zip          49280   A simple and quick XY PM plotting program
nikon214.zip       110093   Nikon II, WPS screen capture program, version 1.4
os2magni.zip        34274   OS/2 magnification glass utility - from DAP CD
os2maze.zip         48412   Display 3D mazes without using PM
pbmplus.zip       1374839   PBMPLUS image format conversion utilities
pcd14.zip           58377   Show photo-CDs in a fullscreen session
pmdraw2.zip       1229115   PM Draw image editing software
pmfra2.zip         386604   FRACTINT version 17.2 fractal generation engine
pmjpg142.zip       212512   GIF/BMP/JPEG/PCX/Targa/TIFF viewer/converter
pmpovf.zip         652808   POVFrame, a PM shell for POV-Ray
pmview86.zip       231751   A fast GIF/BMP/JPEG/PCX/TGA viewer for OS/2 PM
pmvu85a.zip        139551   A fast GIF/BMP/JPEG/PCX/Targa viewer for OS/2 PM
povray2.zip        541966   Persistence of Vision Ray Tracer (POV-Ray)
povscn.zip         498563   Povray 2.0 example scene files
pvqos216.zip       137234   Persistence of Vision Quantiser Utils 1.6
pvquan16.zip       113106   Persistence of Vision Quantiser Utils (source)
rt.zip             403711   Andys CSG-RayTracer
s2f01.zip           22629   SBIG-ST4 to FITS image format converter
scale.zip            9305   Display grayscale using Palette Manager (source incl.)
shbmp212.zip        28659   ShowBMP - view BMP, ICO, or PTR files
ssaver11.zip       409990   Modular 32bit screen saver for OS/2 2.x
stplot12.zip       116067   Create/print ASCII graphics from numerical data
stshow16.zip       123212   View/convert/print BMP/PCX/GIF/PM/TGA files
view3d.zip         209187   Interactive 3D data set viewer/manipulator

2_x/graphics/icons:
00index.txt          1766
1700ico2.zip       341649   Another collection of icons for OS/2
256icons.zip        27954   A set of SDS Icons using up to 256 colors
```

Appendix H—Identifying Sources of OS/2 Information

File	Size	Description
3icons.zip	2004	3 icons
absicons.zip	20360	A collection of 48 icons with a Mac-like 3D look
folders.zip	27017	A set of icons for folders
fredicon2.txt	820	
fredicon2.zip	868107	Now over 910 16-color & 256-color OS/2 icons
gamesico.zip	32144	Several icons for various games
icns40.zip	13006	Forty icons for OS/2
icon1.zip	19593	A collection of DOS icons converted to OS/2
icon135.zip	82883	135 custom icons
icon_170.zip	55175	Icon Tool: Facilitates changing icons
iconbw.zip	15334	Icons for folders, includes abacus, quill, etc.
icones.zip	58748	Icon Ease - manage icon files efficiently
icons2.zip	396017	1,144 icons - be patient when unzipping.
iconsvx.zip	38483	73 icons - nice quality
joeicons.zip	31872	60 of Joe's favorite icons
ndwshred.zip	660	A replacement for the OS/2 Shredder icon
neaticnx.zip	172849	Some 256 color icons -- 8514 resolution
nexticon.zip	9613	Some icons ported for NeXT
os2_icon.zip	349553	A collection of over 1000 icons
os2icon4.zip	833269	A large collection of icons sorted into directories
os2icon7.zip	125680	More OS/2 icons
os2icon8.zip	142162	211 good-looking icons created by IBM employees
os2sicon.zip	166996	A select group of 500 icons converted from Windows
sdsicons.zip	51067	102 256 color Icons
sysicons.zip	41453	OS/2 2.0 systems icons in PMWP.DLL
trashico.zip	7735	Good looking icons for use as a trash can
wpsicons.zip	25445	Some nice icons for WPS, more subtle than most

2_x/info:

File	Size	Description
00index.txt	11330	
20readme.txt	74128	README file included with OS/2 2.0
amibios.txt	8475	AMI BIOS considerations
appbrf.zip	2541	Brief from ARA-how customers are using OS/2
appos2.zip	26963	OS/2 application list - updated 6/02/93
benchtec.txt	3224	BenchTech performance measurement tool press release
bigdsk.txt	5001	Procedure to use >1024 cylinders with SpeedStor
bootdisk.txt	4717	How to create an OS/2 2.0 boot disk
bwiz.zip	5450	Application for beta test of BackupWiz for SCSI tape
conf9108.txt	35582	CompuServe conference with Lee Reiswig (8/91)
cstore.zip	3962	The Corner Store OS/2 Catalog
dcf2info.txt	1698	Information on DCF/2 Disk Compression Facility
dispinst.txt	2373	How to manually install display drivers
epmkeys.txt	8639	Guide to EPM editor keys
erratadd.zip	6656	Errata for Writing Device Drivers in C-Mastrianni
eskimo02.zip	36590	Arctic Connection OS/2 Products Catalog
excel.txt	2406	Excel 3.0 macro problem and workaround
galciv.zip	106574	Announcement of Galactic Civilizations, an OS/2 game
games20a.txt	34142	Information on DOS settings for games
gw66v.zip	1638	How to install OS/2 2.0 on a Gateway 2000 4DX2-66V
ibm/	-	IBM OS/2 2.0 information and product announcements
iguide.zip	64111	OS/2 2.0 Information and Planning Guide (ASCII text)
iguideps.zip	153959	OS/2 2.0 Information and Planning Guide (Postscript)
iguidetx.zip	162711	OS/2 2.0 Information and Planning Guide (TeX/DVI)
infdisk.txt	470	Info on Chili Pepper Software Infinite Disk
isvbet.zip	29426	OS/2 32-bit Applications for Beta Testing
isvbeta.txt	96726	ISV/Customer Interaction program
ivleague.txt	9529	List of OS/2 support organizations/people

jmos2-10.zip	60343	Joe's OS/2 tips #10
joestips.zip	219364	Joe's OS/2 tips 1 - 8
laplink.txt	2075	Using LapLink Pro with OS/2
ljv.txt	1557	Announcement: LJV utilities for OS/2
newsltr/	-	Users Group Newsletters
os2_com.zip	52808	Information on COM ports under OS/2, hints & tips
os2_mou.zip	57466	Information on mouse/pointer devices, hints & tips
os2cdrom.txt	1939	Instructions for installing non-Toshiba CD-ROMs
os2cfg52.zip	21075	OS/2 CONFIG.SYS file explanation
os2flist.txt	148471	Listing/description of OS/2 system files
os2pro.zip	31701	Info on OS/2 Professional, a bi-monthly publication
os2prob.txt	8382	OS/2 2.0 Problem Report Form
os2show.zip	1270251	OS/2 2.0 32-bit showcase - listing of 32-bit progs
pasgim.zip	518342	Online Personal AS/2 General Information Manual
prnmap.txt	15541	Listing of printers with corresponding driver names
ps2ref.zip	448058	General PS/2 info
rdmeinf.zip	60189	OS/2 2.0 README in the .INF format
redsha.zip	1028	Announcement: Red Shark Nymbus Multimedia tool suite
stac.os2	4981	Announcement: Stacker for OS/2
svga20.txt	13191	OS/2 2.0 SVGA information from the net
svgabn.zip	28800	PM Benchmark Results for 1024x768 device drivers
t_3401.zip	1977	How to install a CD-ROM in a PS/2 Model 57 or 77
tapesw.doc	1145	List of OS/2 compatible tape backup software
teamos2.zip	142436	Vicci Conways TEAM OS/2 listing 05/31/93
tips/	-	Technical tips from the OS/2 Technical Support Team
tjbench.zip	4123	OS/2 2.0 Service Pak Benchmarks under DOS
tricks2.zip	122276	Stupid OS/2 Tricks #2 - OS/2 tips & tricks
unix20.txt	3712	Unix to OS/2 2.0 Migration Workshop Description&Survey
untiecom.zip	1244	Press release for UnTieCom for unleashing comm port
video2.zip	3514	Assessment of video cards with OS/2 2.x support
vmbfaq.zip	6021	How to set up a VMB (boot other versions of DOS), .INF
walnutcd.txt	1446	Get the entire ftp-os2 archive on CD-ROM!
winbench.txt	10194	Benchmarking WIndows and OS/2
windos.txt	11160	How to spawn a DOS shell from Win-OS/2
wpsguide.zip	65851	Guide to the OS/2 2.0 Workplace Shell
wpskeys.txt	13844	Information on Workplace shell keys & their functions
write.zip	15512	Form letters asking for OS/2 products/support
2_x/info/ibm:		
00index.txt	4105	
293187.ann	4067	Withdrawal: IBM Developers Migration Kit/2 Program
293188.ann	34296	Plantworks Start Services/2 & Display Services/2
293253.zip	5398	Announcement: IBM Device Driver Sourcekit
293328.zip	7293	Announcement: IBM Ultimedia Workplace/2
293329.zip	8430	Annoucnement: IBM Multimedia Builder/2
293330.zip	7169	Announcement: IBM Ultimedia Perfect Image/2
293340.zip	8107	Announcement: IBM Thesaurus Admin/2
293348.zip	7521	Announcement: IBM Continuous speech developers toolkit
393092.ann	3967	IBM C Set++ for OS/2 introductory promotion
authors.ann	2292	IBM announcement for OS/2 2.0 authors
cicsos.txt	1863	The CICS OS/2 v2.0 Early Introduction Program
cisconf.txt	39014	IBM OS/2 CompuServe Conference - April 1993
conos2.ann	45490	IBM Consumer Transaction Licensed Programs
csetann.zip	25361	C-Set++ Product Announcement/Promotion
dcetxt.zip	5720	Distributed Computing Environment Beta program
ddconf.txt	2138	OS/2 device driver converence -- announcement
ddkforms.zip	4178	Forms required to obtain Device Driver Devel. Kit

928 Appendix H—Identifying Sources of OS/2 Information

defect.ibm	3932	IBM Defect Report Process Information
demotm.zip	1764	IBM-PSP Support of Team OS/2 Events info
direct.ann	24977	IBM CICS OS/2 Version 2
fastos2.ann	28122	Fastservice for OS/2
ftn0113.zip	851619	FTN on LAN Network Mgr./:AN Station Mgr. Update
ftn0126.zip	304149	1/26/93 FTN: DB/2 information
ftn0211.zip	323925	2/03/93 FTN: Distributive Computing Services Info
ftn0225.zip	392133	2/12/93 FTN: System Performance Monitoring Utilities
ftn0311.zip	645098	3/11/93 FTN: Communications manager/2
fullmotn.txt	2407	IBM announces full motion video support for OS/2
homeos2.txt	115456	IBMs vision of OS/2 in home use
ibmpeopl.txt	5801	A listing of IBM Tech People w/email addresses
ibmplans.txt	18960	IBM plans for OS/2 through this fall
mmpm2ann.txt	39502	Multimedia Presentation Manager/2 Announcement
nls.txt	13063	199 international seminar for national lang. support
nwsec.ann	5688	IBM LAN Systems Statement on LAN Protocol Integrity
os220all.ann	124546	OS/2 2.0 ES/2,DDCS/2,Lan Server & Tools Announcement
os220q_a.ann	16970	OS/2 2.0 Questions and Answers
os220rel.ann	6687	OS/2 2.0 USA release announcement
os221ftn.zip	404080	05/11/93 FTN: OS/2 2.1
os22xpub.zip	123210	OS/2 2.x Publications Catalog in INF format
os2_qas.txt	35984	OS/2 2.0 Questions and Answers
os2br603.lis	37230	
os2fut.txt	11848	IBM future plans
os2goods.txt	7730	OS/2 Marketing Premiums
os2prob.txt	7312	Submit OS/2 problem reports electronically
os2v2.ann	6579	Announcement: OS/2 Version 2.0
os2v21.ann	39338	IBM OS/2 2.1 product announcement
os2v2_es.ann	3477	Announcement: OS/2 2.0 Extended Services
os2v2_ls.ann	5700	Announcement: OS/2 2.0 Lan Services
os2v2dev.txt	44701	OS/2 2.0 tools for application development note
os2you.ann	13317	OS/2 2.0 and You course from Skill Dynamics
pcmtab.zip	11994	List of OS/2 2.0 compatible PC systems
reswps.txt	10303	Restricted Workplace Shell service offering
rlapaper.zip	15681	IBM Remote LAN Access beta program
spm20.txt	2160	IBM Beta program for System Performance Monitor
strategy.zip	24153	IBMs product line & planned future directions
submit.txt	11904	IBM OS/2 Developer Magazine Submission Guidelines
tcp624.zip	21750	Graphics from OS/2 Enhanced Editor presentation
tcpip20.ann	75482	Announcement: IBM TCP/IP version 2.0
techsup2.txt	55456	IBM technical support answers to common questions
techupd.ann	1665	PS and OS/2 Technical Update Tuition Waiver Promotion
whyos2.doc	83897	Why OS/2?
wkset2.pro	3004	IBM Developers WorkSet/2 Promotion
wwdap.txt	8659	IBM Developer Assistance Program application

2_x/info/newsltr:

00index.txt	996	
mm0693.zip	89863	Mid Missouri OS/2 Users Group Newsletter, 06/93
mm0793.zip	86690	Mid Missouri OS/2 Users Group Newsletter, 07/93
mm0893.zip	145969	Mid Missouri OS/2 Users Group Newsletter, 08/93
mm0993.zip	211824	Mid Missouri OS/2 Users Group Newsletter, 09/93
mm1093.zip	199069	Mid Missouri OS/2 Users Group Newsletter, 10/93
mm1193.zip	84446	Mid Missouri OS/2 Users Group Newsletter, 11/93
mn0893.zip	41045	
mn0993.zip	37146	Minnesota OS/2 Users Group - 09/93 newsletter
mn1093.zip	39705	

```
sd9301.zip         112937    San Diego OS/2 Users Group - 01/93 newsletter
sd9302.zip         164599    San Diego OS/2 Users Group - 02/93 newsletter
sd9303.zip         269412    San Diego OS/2 Users Group - 03/93 newsletter
sd9304.zip         184762    San Diego OS/2 Users Group - 04/93 newsletter
tag1_1.zip          10331    L.A. Technical Architect Group newsletter
team1093.zip        39916    Team OS/2 News - October 1993

2_x/info/tips:
00index.txt          1839
bios.fax             7776    OS/2 2.0 Technical Tips - BIOS Level Information
cdrom.fax            4825    OS/2 2.0 Technical Tips - Configuring CDROMs in a VDM
cont.fax             3393    OS/2 2.0 Technical Tips - Aborted Installation
dosset.fax          49382    OS/2 2.0 Technical Tips - DOS Settings for VDMs
dosvmb.fax          40579    OS/2 2.0 Technical TIps - Setup up DOS Virt. Machines
hngtr.fax            4758    OS/2 2.0 Technical Tips - OS/2 Traps and Hang
insat.fax            5431    OS/2 2.0 Technical Tips - Install on AT Bus Machines
instmc.fax           4298    OS/2 2.0 Technical TIps - Misc. Install Problems
int66h.fax           1928    OS/2 2.0 Technical Tips - Resolving INT 66 errors
intrpt.fax          13966    OS/2 2.0 Technical TIps - Interrupt Level Information
lotus.fax            9692    OS/2 2.0 Technical Tips - OS/2 and Lotus 1-2-3
mouse.fax           17699    OS/2 2.0 Technical Tips - Mouse devices
multim.fax           1906    OS/2 2.0 Technical Tips - OS/2 Multimedia Compatibility
os2g2k.fax           2803    OS/2 2.0 Technical Tips - Gateway 2000 Machines
pcsup.fax            7028    OS/2 2.0 Technical Tips - Using IBM PC Support/400
print.fax            7487    OS/2 2.0 Technical Tips - OS/2 Print Troubleshooting
video.fax           10433    OS/2 2.0 Technical Tips - Video Related Problems
winclp.fax           7440    OS/2 2.0 Technical Tips - WIN-OS2 Clipboard
wincom.fax           7252    OS/2 2.0 Technical Tips - WIN-OS2 Communications
winmig.fax          10142    OS/2 2.0 Technical Tips - WIN-OS2 Application Migration
winprt.fax          14720    OS/2 2.0 Technical Tips - WIN-OS2 Printing
winscn.fax           1427    OS/2 2.0 Technical Tips - WIN-OS2 Scanners & Software
winsml.fax           9702    OS/2 2.0 Technical Tips - WIN-OS2 Seamless
wps.fax             16100    OS/2 2.0 Technical Tips - OS/2 Workplace Shell Info

2_x/miscutil:
00index.txt          3110
allinf.zip           5965    Creates a folder containing all .INF on system
alrmck28.zip       210120    Alarm clock/task scheduler for WPS, version 2.7
alrmpr.zip         340047    Alarm Pro 1.0 - Alarm Clock plus ToDo & Contact List
bigsrt42.zip        36492    Unlimited size SORT program, many options
bookshlf.zip          959    Creates a bookshelf of all .INF files on the system
chrtbl11.zip        42096    Character set display/print any font/codepage
cmdline.zip         25708    Run commands without opening a command line session
dkclock.zip         23713    PM-based configurable clock program
float.zip           14997    Keep windows floating on top of others
hazel11.zip         81645    Hazel, PM address book program
hpclc09.zip         48647    PM calculator similar to HP 41C, version 0.9
icpausa.zip       1294196    PM PS/2 configurator and pricer
infcnb79.zip       318449    Convert .INF files to ASCII text
infidx13.zip        44280    Dynamically create INF file objects
islite.zip         224404    Ispell-lite, text mode spell checker
jmode100.zip         6686    Change fullscreen font to 80x30
klcpu.zip           27008    CKLCPU, CPU speed tester
lbb2_121.zip       158493    Little Black Book/2 personal information manager
lower.zip           14119    Lower a windows z-order by clicking on it
memo11.zip          17434    Small list and reminder utility w/alarms
menumast.zip       226415    Multitask OS/2 sessions from text screens
```

930 Appendix H—Identifying Sources of OS/2 Information

miniapps.zip	59503	Time, date, and uptime applets, includes C++ source
more_20b.zip	42729	A better/faster replacement for OS/2 more
mousey10.zip	17029	Change the OS/2 mouse pointer to another bitmap
open.zip	11718	Open folders from the command line
pcard100.zip	38411	Personal Cards 1.0, store phone numbers easily
pmhoro.zip	159100	PM horoscope, a planetary calculator
pmstock.zip	135680	PM$tock stock analyzer for OS/2 2.0
rolodx23.zip	373546	
rolodx24.zip	385749	An OS/2 2.x rolodex program
sample.zip	37787	High speed sampling (700kB/s or more) from any I/O port
smartvu2.zip	19180	Enables the SmartVU display on Dell computers
sosutl12.zip	104637	Directory tree printer, process viewer, file finder
spl.zip	322807	Manage spells/spellbooks for role-playing games
sqledit.zip	253482	Edit data in ES 1.0 DBM w/SQL queries
starter.zip	27660	Start programs/command files at specified times
style.zip	114424	Various controls, styles, etc. good CUA91 demo
tasktime.zip	25380	Track time spent running different programs
tblcpy.zip	76303	SQL table copy between DBM, DBM2, or DB2 databases
timup121.zip	57180	Display time since last reboot
tkeep.zip	39120	Timekeeper - track the time you work on tasks
vhelp10.zip	20989	ViewHelp v1.0, PM tool for reading IPF-helpfiles
vol12n03.zip	96064	PC magazine utilities from vol 12 number 3
wages1.zip	48136	Wages - a personal wage calculator
xvgart2.zip	2332	Set refresh rate for XGA-2, for those having problems
yowza.zip	318229	A full-featured screen-saver for OS/2 2.0
2_x/mmedia:		
00index.txt	1162	
bigben.zip	127805	Big Ben on SB every hour, requires SBOS2.SYS
borgwa.zip	204050	A collection of Borg .WAV files from Star Trek
cdexpl20.zip	30236	IBM Compact Disc Explorer
cdtrack.zip	12970	Play specific track range of a CD
cplayv20.zip	104453	REXX script to play archived sound files.
cuckoo.zip	8364	Cuckoo Clock, beats hours, requires SBOS2.SYS
mlabex.zip	140288	Midilab/2: Midi music recorder and editor
mmos2nws.txt	8018	MMOS2 Source TidBits
modinfo.zip	17647	Generate information about Protracker modules
pmmix20.zip	10104	A great PM-based mixer for the Soundblaster Pro
rhythm.zip	13674	A metronome program that uses the speaker
sbos2new.zip	451409	Sound Blaster/Soundblaster Pro non-MMPM drivers
sbpmix.zip	28739	Soundblaster Pro mixer panel for MMPM/2
sbwave.zip	210636	Soundblaster audio files for MMPM/2 Toolkit Examples
soxv10.zip	145993	SOX sound file format conversion utility
track061.zip	96829	Tracker/PM MOD file player, requires SBOS2.SYS
trakv11.zip	64870	Command line MOD player, requires SBOS2.SYS
2_x/network:		
00index.txt	4589	
aplog100.zip	39178	Enhanced TELNETD for IBM TCP/IP for OS/2
bmr200.zip	31403	Novell Netware Broadcast Message Receiver
dirstat.zip	11850	Show Token-Ring adapter info in PM window
dumpgrp.zip	97357	Dumps newsgroups to a file; req. IBM TCP/IP & NNTP
elm23-2.zip	959912	ELM 2.3.11 mail front-end (req. UUPC)
fingerd.zip	12646	A finger server (req. TCP/IP & rxSock DLL)
ftprxfe1.zip	6513	Front end for TCP/Ip FTPPM (req. IBM TCP/IP & VREXX)
genfldr.zip	3903	NetWare WPS Folder/Program builder, version 1.4
hihoteln.zip	400013	Program which lists several internet services & sites

```
irc10h.zip          32744    Internet Relay Chat client (req. IBM TCP/IP)
lampop11.zip        90835    OS/2 LaMail POP Interface for IBM TCP/IP
lanadmn.zip         11849    PM interface for IBM LAN Server, needs VREXX 2.0
lanstart.zip        22755    Startup folder that only starts after network is up
lmos22.zip          203093   Beta Lan Manager 2.1 update for OS/2 2.0 client support
ltimes25.zip        129744   LA Times PM newsreader (req. TCP/IP and NNTP news)
mail19.zip          13245    Sen/Rcv/Fwd mail with TCP/IP, very configurable
mail22.zip          38662    Text mode mail reader for IBM TCP/IP
maxiftp2.zip        15830    MaxiFTP FTP client (req. IBM TCP/IP & rxFTP)
ndis/               -        NDIS drivers and information
netapi.zip          22406    Run selected Net API from the command line
nistime.zip         35703    Update time/date from NIST Internet server
nsd202.zip          390305   Novell Service Diskette (NSD #2) for Wrksta. Kit 2.0
ntp.zip             1122     REXX Network Time Protocol client (req. rxSock DLL)
ntwrtcp.zip         4744     Now to make Netware and TCP/IP coexist peacefully
os2gofer.zip        22463    Gopher client for OS/2 PM (requires VREXX & TCP/IP)
os2nosv4.zip        324464   TCP/IP for OS/2 (via SLIP) - text-based
os2wais.zip         234239   Wide Area Information Server client (req. IBM TCP/IP)
passwd.zip          56354    IBM TCP/IP passwd file maintenance utilities
pmnews.zip          186069   PMNEWS - PM front end for SNEWS/UUPC
pmnos11x.zip        421693   KA9Q TCP/IP for ax25 & SLIP, PM-based
pmnos1dx.zip        411266   TCP/IP for OS/2 (via SLIP) PM-based
restok.zip          3968     Token Ring Reset Program, for LSP use
rmtcpy.zip          97149    Remote host file utilitiy (requires TCP/IP)
rn38d.zip           85954    4th bugfixed version of IBM readnews (RN) 3.8
rxnew11a.zip        36234    RexxNews newsreader (req. IBM TCP/IP & rxSock)
shuffle.zip         46321    E-Mail separator/distributor (req. IBM TCP/IP)
slip2xv1.zip        144950   Better performing SLIP for IBM TCP/IP 1.2.1
tcpstart.txt        99704    Getting started with IBM TCP/IP 1.2.1 for OS/2 2.0
tin122.zip          176783   NNTP version of TIN newsreader (req. IBM TCP/IP)
tn_enh11.zip        121217   Enhancement for IBM OS/2 2.0 telnet daemon
trn_12.zip          763230   Threaded newsreader for use with UUPC
ur37165.zip         1552511  Lan Manager Version 1.0 updated for OS/2 2.0
vnwlog.zip          45630    Visual NetWare login - simple PM login
whois10c.zip        22981    Whois client for OS/2: Name lookup on the internet.
wsos21.zip          624031   Novell Netware Requester 2.01 for OS/2, Disk 1 of 3
wsos22.zip          710110   Novell Netware Requester 2.01 for OS/2, Disk 2 of 3
wsos2d.zip          686460   Novell Netware Requester 2.01 for OS/2, Disk 3 of 3
xgaripl.zip         295695   RIPL info for XGA-2 w/Service Pak from Lan Server 3.0

2_x/network/ndis:
00index.txt         1073
3c507.zip           60973    NDIS MAC drivers for 3Com Etherlink/16
3com_mac.zip        15976    NDIS MAC drivers for 3Com Etherlink
coax_mac.zip        12265    NDIS MAC drivers for IBM Lan-Over-Coax 3174
ethr_mac.zip        22023    NDIS MAC drivers for IBM Ethernet Adapter/A
hplanb.zip          28549    NDIS MAC drivers for HP 27245A, 27250A, 27247A
ndis_mac.zip        54329    Microsoft/3Com LAN Manager NDIS specification
ndisconc.zip        15365    NDIS COncepts (from 3Com Technical Journal)
ne2000.zip          23507    NE2000 ethernet card NDIS driver (req. for 2.1 GA)
norb200.zip         17781    OS/2 Requester Driver for Ethernet 800/8013
pcn_mac.zip         11992    NDIS MAC drivers for IBM PC Network
pcna_mac.zip        12032    NDIS MAC drivers for IBM PC Network/A
tkbm_mac.zip        18291    NDIS MAC drivers for IBM Token-Ring Busmaster
tok_mac.zip         13756    NDIS MAC drivers for IBM Token-Ring (except Busmaster)
ubas_mac.zip        26650    NDIS MAC drivers for Ungermann-Bas NIUpc
wdig_mac.zip        23887    NDIS MAC drivers for WD EtherCard PLUS & PLUS/A
```

Appendix H—Identifying Sources of OS/2 Information

```
2_x/patches:
00index.txt        4398
aolfix.zip         6254    OS/2 2.0 fix for Geoworks/America Online
basecsd.zip        2688739 IBM TCP/IP 1.2.1 CSD UN50427 - Base System
c32_a.zip          2243459 Watcom C/C++^32 patch level A
c386_a.zip         752654  Patches for Watcom C/386 (32-bit) - Part 1
c386_b.zip         626401  Patches for Watcom C/386 (32-bit) - Part 2
c386_c.zip         336976  Patches for Watcom C/386 (32-bit) - Part 3
c386_d.zip         409411  Patches for Watcom C/386 (32-bit) - Level D
c386_e.zip         411987  Patches for Watcom C/386 (32-bit) - Level E
cs000054.3v1       1473087 CSet/2 V1 (LoadDskF Diskette Image - 1 of 2)
cs000054.3v2       1421887 CSet/2 V1 (LoadDskF Diskette Image - 2 of 2)
cset050a.zip       1366096 IBM C-Set/2 (Version 1.0) CSD 50 (1 of 2)
cset050b.zip       640413  IBM C-Set/2 (Version 1.0) CSD 50 (2 of 2)
cset2hp.zip        2119    Fix for IBM C++-Set/2 Beta 4.0
csetc004.zip       2630339 IBM C/C++ C/C++ CSD #4 for both versions 2.0 & 2.01
csetl002.zip       1267338 IBM C/C++ Tools CSD #2 - Class Libs fixes
csetl003.zip       1268746 Cset++ Class Libraries CSD #3 (INTERIM) (Tools 2.0 Only)
csetm003.zip       2183565 Cset++ Class Libraries CSD #3 (INTERIM) (Tools 2.1 Only)
csetu002.zip       1915292 IBM C/C++ Tools CSD #2 - Utilities fixes
dbox2943.zip       163007  IBM TCP/IP DOS/Windows Access Kit Update (10/15/93)
dm2101.zip         259773  Deskman/2 patch for 1.00 -> 1.01
endvdm.zip         426     A patch which will close a bootable VDM via exit
f32_a.zip          1428193 Watcom Fortran/77^32 patch level A
f386_b.zip         766225  Patches for Watcom Fortran 77/386 (32-bit) - Part 1
f386_c.zip         682752  Patches for Watcom Fortran 77/386 (32-bit) - Part 2
f386_d.zip         778967  Patches for Watcom Fortran 77/386 (32-bit) - Level D
f386_e.zip         639976  Patches for Watcom Fortran 77/386 (32-bit) - Level E
flgpatch.txt       1313    How to patch Lotus Freelance for OS/2 2.0
instb.zip          1450264 Install 3 1/2" version of OS/2 2.0 from drive B:
instlfix.zip       1481    A fix for OS/2 2.0 installation problems on non-IBMS
link_v12.zip       212529  LINK386 version 12 from IBM
lptx.zip           6405    LPTX.SYS from Lexmark, corrects server lockups
lsm3csd.zip        461825  Patch for OS/2 Lan Server for Macintosh
netsrv.zip         2107    A fix for Novell Netware Lite 1.0
netwlsrv.zip       2107    Patch to allow NetWare Lite Server to run in a VDM
nfscsd1.zip        118997  IBM TCP/IP 1.2.1 CSD UN37900 - NFS Support
os2acad.zip        184217  Run AutoCAD Rel. 12 in a full-screen DOS session
palett.zip         24870   A fix for Lotus Freelance Palette problems
patch_1f.txt       1731    Patching Lotus Freelance to install on OS/2 2.0
patchs3a.zip       1333    Patch f1280 drivers to work with other S3 cards
pj04056.zip        12621   PJ04056, fix for problems w/2456 SCSI scanner
pj04405.zip        31259   PJ04405, OS/2 2.0 fix for trap on Ctrl-ESC w/GA+SP
pj06485.zip        297390  Fix for ALT+HOME problems with the Service Pak
pliifx.zip         44614   IBM PL/I Package/2 v1.1.1 installation fix
pmdpat.zip         20545   Patch to allow C-Set++ debugger to run after June 1
pmr4x565.zip       8707    Fix for loginunix.exe included with TCP/IP CSD UN37938
pmspl110.zip       93013   Patch for the PM Spooler (fixes certain obscure bugs)
pmwordu.zip        45782   OS/2 2.x Patch for MS PM Word 1.1a (or earlier)
pmxcsd1.zip        975338  IBM TCP/IP 1.2.1 CSD UN35990 - X Windows
progcsd.zip        193190  IBM TCP/IP 1.2.1 CSD - 32-bit Programming Toolkit
r201fx.zip         113665  OS/2 Novell Netware Requester 2.01 patch
scopart.zip        1984    A SCO Unix script which allows OS/2 2.0 to boot also
tbos2.zip          23822   Patched soundblaster driver for MV Thunderboard
tdgx.zip           593053  New tddebug.dll (1.01) for Borland TurboDebugger
tridfix.zip        103548  Latest fixes for Trident drivers (new)
vdmlink.zip        8564    Debug DOS programs in VDMs w/Watcom compilers
```

vxrx101.zip	1370748	Patch files to upgrade VX-REXX 1.00 to 1.01
vxrx101a.zip	21750	Patch files to upgrade VX-REXX 1.01 to 1.01a
vxrx101b.zip	507543	Ver 1.01b patch to Watcom VX-REXX Ver 1.01a
vxrx101c.zip	1644	Patch Watcom VX-REXX from Ver. 1.01b to 1.01c
wf2_0006.zip	923353	CSD #6 for IBM Workframe/2
x25csd.zip	47165	IBM TCP/IP 1.2.1 CSD UN30759 - X.25 Support
xga2dmqs.zip	22443	*UNSUPPORTED* DMQS files for the XGA-2 adapter

2_x/printer:

00index.txt	674	
40x9su33.zip	427699	Lexmark supplemental utilities for IBM LaserPrinter
flxtxt12.zip	67200	Print files in a variety of fonts and page setups
fontutls.zip	37924	PostScript Type 1 font conversion utilities
hex2prn.zip	18203	Send hex codes directly to your printer
lptmaze.zip	78318	Print mazes with hexagonal rooms
pm2col1c.zip	56320	Create multicolumn text and/or Postscript
prtf.zip	19661	
prtup2.zip	11092	Print 1 or 2 up on a variety of printers (HPFS aware)
ps_up241.zip	31835	Print ASCII text files on Postscript printers
psfix.zip	10596	Fix WINOS/2 postscript output

2_x/program:

00index.txt	9359	
alphal.zip	132332	Alpha version 1.5 source code browser
atccnr.zip	45509	Container sample-air traffic control container
bootdr.zip	3306	Source for properly determining the boot drive
bp7-os2.zip	121132	Patch to Borland Pascal v7.x to produce 16 bit OS/2 programs
bugalr.zip	66121	Unique debugger, provides info about PM windows/apps
call32.zip	27170	How to call 32-bit code from 16-bit apps
cdisk.zip	253952	Companion disk for Writing OS/2 Device Drivers in C
cenvi23.zip	252160	Cmm (C minus minus), a shareware C interpreter
chk_er.zip	21072	Error message check program for IBM C compiler
class.zip	26643	C++ classes for PM programming w/Mandelbrot example
cnradv.zip	129540	Container sample program that builds on CNRMENU
contain.zip	199618	Sample code for creating/using container classes
csetdoc.zip	4060355	Reformatted versions of PS IBM C-Set++ docs
ctrldes.zip	22218	Designing PM custom controls-OS/2 dev mag
curs13_3.zip	86652	PC Curses 1.3 for OS/2 2.0 with Watcom C/386 9.0
custct.zip	37888	Demystifying Custom Controls - source code
dde20s.zip	45754	Dynamic Data Exchange source code sample
dragin.zip	12758	Drag & Drop simulation program
e_edit.zip	159051	from issue #7 Brain Andersons uncut article
elistb.zip	12383	How to make an MLE into a multi column list box
essamp.zip	613644	ES Communications Manager sample programs
f2cb.zip	397525	Fortran to C translator for OS/2 2.0 for EMX/GCC2
f2cs.zip	344814	Fortran to C translator (source)
fchek261.zip	357520	Fortran checker version 2.6.1
forth025.zip	48132	An implementation of Forth (beta 0.25)
frmsub.zip	31160	Frame Window Subclassing Sample - tool bars/menus
gio-100.zip	26135	Gerns 32-bit multi-thread async I/O routines
gmd_os2.zip	1108614	GMD compiler toolbox w/src
gpfrex21.zip	1289316	Beta GpfRexx visual development tool - Disk 1 of 2
gpfrex22.zip	996052	Beta GpfRexx visual development tool - Disk 2 of 2
hookkbs.zip	32527	Hooking the keyboard & assigning hotkeys
hugelb.zip	25403	Owner-drawn listbox sample for hug lists (>64K)
icctee.zip	19502	IBM C compiler filter
icon88.zip	395502	Version 8.8 of the Icon programming language

Appendix H—Identifying Sources of OS/2 Information

File	Size	Description
inf02a.doc	20286	Description of the IPF .INF format
inf16bit.zip	412063	Documentation for 16-bit API functions (.INF format)
io386.zip	2061	How to do port I/O in 32-bit programs
iopl32.zip	23591	Demonstrates how to access I/O ports w/IBM C Set/2
iv-pm.zip	506214	Partial Port of InterViews 2.6
kdebug.zip	47081	OS/2 2.0 Kernel Debugger Enhanced Documentation
kwhelp.zip	12776	Replacement NDX for Ctrl+H for EPM, more complete
licc.zip	11993	Load C Set/2 Compiler into memory, speed up compiles
lr.zip	334592	Create grammars in minutes, better than LEX/YACC
lxexe.doc	79298	Linear Executable Module Format documentation
mkhkb2.zip	36096	How to monitor all keyboard activity
mkptypes.zip	28741	Generate prototypes for functions in C files
mltcol.zip	28999	Multi-column list box sample program
monte.zip	19107	Multithreaded OS/2 code examples shown at Phoenix conf.
nbbase.zip	38178	Shows basics of notebook control, from ColoradOS/2
nbload.zip	41503	Notebook control sample program, from ColoradOS/2
newsltr/	-	Programming-related newsletters/columns
nmake2.zip	47865	IBM NMAKE that supports HPFS long filenames
objlib.zip	16329	OS/2 .OBJ/.LIB formats
os2-yaca.zip	334527	LR parser generator, includes SQL V2.3 grammar
p2c_1_20.zip	719774	Pascal to C translator for gcc/emx 0.8f
pasos2b.zip	472701	A 32-bit Pascal compiler (req. MASM 6.0A/TASM)
physcolo.zip	6716	Show physical screen colors/how to use palette manager
pilot.zip	55468	Pilot CAI interpreter (old, ported to OS/2)
pmwalkr2.zip	19590	How to make an animated icon
portio2.zip	81040	Port I/O and IOPL examples for IBM C and Borland C++
pp002.zip	43847	Power Pascal/2 version 0.002 (req. MASM 6.00)
printq12.zip	140713	PRINTQ, a DLL for easy printing from PM apps
rb3730.zip	127588	Redbook sample code: Vol. 1: Control Program
rb3731.zip	133767	Redbook sample code: Vol. 2: DOS & Windows
rb3774.zip	344814	Redbook sample code: Vol. 4: Application Develop.
rebuild.zip	31528	Rebuild icons for IBM Toolkit, C-Set/2, Workframe/2
rexx/	-	REXX programs/source
rexxcobj.zip	5290	Information on how to create WPS objects using REXX
sherlock.zip	105600	Post mortum dump utility for debugging
shr93.zip	133672	Workplace shell sample program - address book
skel32.zip	4461	How to write a 32-bit program using TASM
slice.zip	5417	Give up time slices from DOS progs, w/TASM source
slidco.zip	52820	PM slider example-uses serial IOCTLs w/terminal
slider2.zip	31768	How to use sliders in PM
sml.zip	332293	Port of functional language ML (Edinburgh)
smlnj093.zip	1695095	Functional standard ML of New Jersey 0.93
som_nt.zip	11715	Introduction to Object Oriented Programming and SOM
som_ov.zip	3062	High level overview of SOM
som_qa.zip	12870	Some commonly asked questions on SOM
somcla.zip	8621	8621 A discussion of Class Objects in SOM
somcls.zip	8637	SOM Class Objects - article in OS/2 developer
somftn.zip	561080	Complete slides/documentation from SOM FTN
somint.zip	12425	SOM Introduction - article in OS/2 Developer
thread.zip	4754	A thread class for C++ under OS/2
thread2.zip	10941	A sample PM program illustrating how to multi-thread
tlc10.zip	44156	C source list program
tm1632.zip	6692	Examples of 32 <-> 16 thunks, w/Assembly source
tune.zip	2210	C example for reading files produced by Tune editor
vgalib.zip	107248	Preliminary full screen (non-PM) graphics package
vxtech01.zip	23306	How to build REXX/VX-REXX external functions in C
wfdoc.zip	210946	Workframe/2 interface docs and sample programs

```
wp2ipf2.zip        564102   Create .IPF/.INF files from WordPerfect 5.1 files
wpsdbg.zip          13108   SOM/WPS debugging tool
wpsprgm.zip         20591   Some small examples of Workplace Shell programming
wpz001.zip          18800   WPZIP - A Workplace Shell class for .ZIP files
xlibos2.zip        101863   Full screen VGA X Mode library w/demo
xscheme2.zip       162124   Scheme for OS/2 2.0 (with OOP extensions)

2_x/program/newsltr:
00index.txt          1518
cnradvtx.zip         5737   OS/2 Developer, Spring 1993, Container Control Examples
cnrbastx.zip         8380   OS/2 Developer, Winter 1993, Container Control Basics
edmi1.zip          136912   EDM/2 Issue #1 (March 1993)
edmi2.zip          118571   EDM/2 Issue #2 (April 1993)
edmi3.zip          178386   EDM/2 Issue #3 (May/June 1993)
edmi4.zip           51200   EDM/2 Issue #4
edmi5.zip          222087   EDM/2 Issue #5
edmi6.zip          169823   EDM/2 Issue #6
edmi7.zip          372362   EDM/2 Issue #7
edmsub.zip           6793   EDM submission guidelines
os2cneps.zip       275084   IBM OS/2 Compiler news - volume 4 - Postscript version
os2cnevm.zip       139730   IBM OS/2 Compiler news - vol 4 - list 3820 ver.
os2cnew1.zip        50411   OS/2 C/Set Newsletter #1
os2cnew2.zip       179005   OS/2 C/Set Newsletter #2
os2cnew3.zip       148764   OS/2 C/Set Newsletter #3
os2cnew4.zip       241464   OS/2 C/Set Newsletter #4
os2cnew5.zip       241170   OS/2 C/Set Newsletter #5
os2cnew6.zip       362389   OS/2 C/Set Newsletter #6
vol1n3.zip          10274   OS/2 Monthly, Volume 1.3 - Ultimate OS/2 Game (text)
vol1n4.zip          26586   OS/2 Monthly, Volume 1.4 - Ultimate OS/2 Game
vol1n5.zip          31417   OS/2 Monthly, Volume 1.5 - Ultimate OS/2 Game
vol1n6.zip          42816   OS/2 Monthly, Volume 1.6 - Ultimate OS/2 Game
vol1n7.zip          61011   OS/2 Monthly, Volume 1.7 - Ultimate OS/2 Game
vol1n8.zip          75292   OS/2 Monthly, Volume 1.8 - Ultimate OS/2 Game
vol1n9.zip          77676   OS/2 Monthly, Volume 1.9 - Ultimate OS/2 Game

2_x/program/rexx:
00index.txt          1070
bdsom1.zip          10179   Build SOM - a REXX procedure that creates WPS objects
chckdmns.cmd         2878   Monitors running processes, kill/restarts if necessary
datergf.zip         19307   REXX procedures for working with sorted dates
deskutil.zip        21664   Info on the REXX SysCreateObject functions (2 samples)
etools.zip          31406   a collection of REXX cmd files and misc tools
openfdr4.zip         4372   Open folders from a popup menu (req. REXX & 4OS2)
rexmenu2.zip        58624   Parse text file for menu selection
rexxobjv.zip         2973   REXX samples for use with OS/2 Object Vision
rexxtut.zip         47223   Some REXX tutorial documents
rexxutil.zip        27687   Information and samples for REXX utility functions
rxbks.zip            4249   Review of three REXX books
rxlogin.zip          3008   Rexx procedure that asks for a password
rxu11.zip          120064   Some REXX external functions
seldel.zip           2896   Selectively delete applets that come with OS/2
vopnfdr3.zip         4987   Open folders from a PM listbox (req. REXX & VREXX)

2_x/sysutils:
00index.txt          4894
4os232.zip         296832   4OS2/32 v1.11, OS/2 2.x alternative command line shell
9lives0d.zip        32782   9 Lives, get multiple desktops in the Workplace Shell
addico11.zip         5187   Add icons to program files from the command line
```

Appendix H—Identifying Sources of OS/2 Information

File	Size	Description
assoed02.zip	35216	Inspect/modify WPS file & type associations
blckh3.zip	35382	Portable Black Hole 3.0 - deletes things shredder cant
blkos207.zip	40682	BLKOS2 beta .7 command shell for OS/2 sessions
bootable.zip	10963	A method for creating DOS bootable disks under OS/2
cbtoolsx.zip	115872	Carlsberg tools-variety of system-related tools
cfged1b.zip	146719	PM-based configuration file (CONFIG.SYS) editor
clipbrd.zip	46226	Use the clipboard from the command line
clrclp20.zip	39828	A mini-app which clears the system clipboard
cpudriv2.zip	43620	Monitor disk and CPU utilization
cpyini2.zip	16059	Make a copy of OS2.INI/OS2SYS.INI, reducing their size
csed_10.zip	79168	System Config Editor, PM editor for startup files
dinfo13.zip	46389	Display swap file information (from IBM)
eabrws02.zip	40659	Browser/editor for extended attributes (beta)
go_12.zip	16529	List, switch to, and kill running processes
hswtch02.zip	32058	Text-mode task switch menu
inicnv.zip	30071	Convert OS/2 1.3 .INI data to OS/2 2.0
inimt21b.zip	357216	INI file maintenance utilities version 2.1b
inimt30.zip	495101	PM util to display/manage INI files
inios2.zip	20608	ALLINI 1.1 - edit and delete INI files
interc.zip	24704	Intercept/disable icon arrange and desktop lockup
kill.zip	21300	Kill running processes by Process ID (PID)
kill21.zip	18874	Killem 2.1, kill running processes by name
lockboot.zip	5948	Enable/disable system lockup upon bootup
makbtdsk.zip	4330	A REXX script which creates an OS/2 2.0 boot disk
makdoc.zip	8858	Utility for creating icons for .INF files
makeobj.zip	8532	Make WPS object via commandline or filetype assoc.
mdsk14.zip	33841	DeskMan - save/restore WPS settings - freeware
mem428.zip	11713	A utility to determine how OS/2 2.0 uses memory
mems204.zip	33437	Display amount of free memory and swap space
memsz210.zip	146612	Display running status of memory, swapfile, etc.
mnicon.zip	16657	WPS Icon class replacement for drag & drop
muser066.zip	65933	Multi-desktops (for multiple users)
nistp.zip	86272	Set system clock via a call to the NIST BBS
nocad.zip	24033	Disable/enable CTRL-ALT-DEL reset
nolist.zip	66660	Remove PM programs from window list & ALT-ESC list
nolist2a.zip	27363	Remove running programs from the window list
onexit.zip	7291	Runs a .cmd or .exe file during shutdown
pc2.zip	229637	Program Commander/2 DesktopMenu add-on version 1.50
peg001.zip	247347	Pegasus profiling tool-monitors a variety of activities
pmkill.zip	21870	PM point and shoot process killer
pmps.zip	35254	PM Process Status - graphical process display/kill
pmswitch.zip	13062	PMSwitch, switch quickly between program sessions
pmtree30.zip	101052	Display PM window hierarchy (from IBM)
pmvd021.zip	34216	PMVDesk virtual desktop screen manager
privf.zip	55617	Password protect private folders, v1.21
procs21.zip	18393	Displays a list of running processes
pspm2.zip	45214	Graphical display of processes, selective kill
qwik32.zip	76448	QwikSwitch hotkey and keyboard launching util
sdplus.zip	18668	System shutdown plus mini-app
se20boot.zip	25799	Create OS/2 boot disks (from IBM)
showini32.zip	41703	INI file editor/viewer/backup/restore (Rexx)
shutdown.zip	10471	Shutdown your system from the command line prompt
shutdwn5.zip	13033	Shutdown OS/2 from a batch file or icon
sp.zip	26095	Start OS/2 & DOS programs at a defined priority
startd.zip	25123	Start DOS programs with DOS Settings given in a file
startvdm.zip	14849	Start a DOS image (VDM) from the command line
sysinf.zip	54873	System information values in a handy notebook control

```
tl.zip                3419    A utility to keep the Task List in the same place
ultimate.zip         31408    Replace OS/2 icons and folders
wcat10.zip           47299    Recover from hung OS/2 (requires special HW)
wdog10.zip           24666    Shutdown cleanly after some types of system crashes
willutil.zip         19993    Alter NUMLOCK key state and other system settings
wpprgext.zip         36793    A replacement WPS class for WPProgram
wps2rexx.zip         63239    Convert Workplace Shell desktop to a REXX script
wpsbk202.zip         49790    WPS Backup - save/restore Workplace Shell settings
wptool10.zip        183442    A collection of INI-file and WPS maintenance tools

2_x/unix:
00index.txt           9666
32dudf11.zip         23201    Unix-like DU & DF commands w/HPFS support
bash.zip            417514    The bash shell for OS/2
byacc.zip           111304    Berkeley YACC parser generator
cal32.zip            33265    Berkeley cal ported to OS/2
compr412.zip         54557    Compress version 4.12
cron213.zip         110902    Unix cron with networking extensions
cvs13p4b.zip        287301    CVS 1.3, patchlevel 4 revision control system (requires rcs56)
cvs13p4s.zip        366234    CVS 1.3, patchlevel 4 revision control system (sources)
dired.zip           100178    A directory editor modeled after Dired Mode of Emacs
elvb18s2.zip        315412    Elvis 1.8c (beta) (sources + *roff docs)
elvb18x2.zip        210188    Elvis 1.8c (beta), a vi clone
elvis172.zip        307845    Elvis 1.7, a vi clone
emacs22/                 -    GNU Emacs 19.22 of OS/2 2.x
emx08h/                  =
feelx10.zip         379687    Simulates mouse usage of an X-Windows system
flex23_2.zip        191320    Fast lexical analyzer generator version 2.3
freeze_2.zip         83970    Freeze/Melt compression program
fudg_emx.zip        524557    General purpose data analysis and curve fitting
gawk213.zip         386182    GNU Awk version 2.13
gcc2_254/                -    GCC/2 native-OS/2 C/C++ compiler version 2.5.4
gmkexe.zip           72800    GNU make 3.6.2 (native)
gnuawk.zip          694798    GNU awk 2.13 patchlevel 2 using EMX; Kai Uwe Rommel
gnubc.zip           131142    GNU bc, interactive arithmetic language processor
gnubison.zip        213633    GNU Bison parser generator
gnucpio.zip         153044    GNU cpio 2.0
gnudbm.zip          151703    GNU dbm database routines
gnudc.zip           134653    GNU dc, desk calculator
gnudiff.zip         581794    GNU Diff 2.6
gnudosck.zip        109752    Check filenames for DOS (and SYSV) compatibility
gnufind.zip         240438    GNU find, version 3.8; Kai Uwe Rommel
gnufutil.zip        512887    GNU file utilities (ls,cat,mv,etc.)
gnugdbm.zip         207725    GNU GDBM 1.7.1
gnugrep.zip         179799    GNU Grep 2.0
gnuindnt.zip        248428    GNU indent version 1.3
gnuinfo.zip         885751    GNU TeXinfo version 2.16
gnum4.zip           335241    GNU m4 macro language processor version 1.0
gnumake.zip         500835    GNU Make 3.65
gnuman.zip           44610    GNU man 1.0 (for use with groff)
gnupatch.zip        208257    GNU patch
gnuperf.zip         111367    GNU perf - generate perfect hash functions
gnuplt35.zip        388792    Gnuplot 3.5 - a graph plotting program
gnused.zip          265387    GNU sed
gnusutil.zip        350457    GNU Shell utilities 1.9
gnututil.zip        423644    GNU Text utilities 1.9
```

Appendix H—Identifying Sources of OS/2 Information

```
grep20.zip          206882   GNU Grep 2.0
groffexe.zip        911548   GNU groff document formatting system (executables)
groffsrc.zip        906713   GNU groff document formatting system (sources)
gs261os2.zip        602455   Ghostscript 2.6.1 without PM support (currently)
gsf261_1.zip       1178865   Ghostscript fonts for Ghostscript 2.6.1 - Part 1 of 2
gsf261_2.zip        570518   Ghostscript fonts for Ghostscript 2.6.1 - Part 2 of 2
gspm25.zip         1935645   Ghostscript 2.5.2 (Postscript) interpreter
gspm25b.zip         151717   Patch for Ghostscript 2.5.2 problems w/OS/2 2.1
gspm26.zip          370625   Ghostscript 2.6.1 with a PM driver
gz124-32.zip         76749   GNU zip compression utility version 1.24
hpgl312.zip         356334   HP-GL conversion utility
isp3009b.zip        663815   Ispell v3.0.09b, OS/2 version 19-APR-93
iv31pm.zip          775831   InterViews 3.1, GUI toolkit
joe.zip             397276   GNU JOE editor v 1.0.8
ksh48.zip           326781   The Korn shell for OS/2 (32-bit)
less_2.zip          170521   Less, a better more (KAI Uwe Rommel)
lsqrft13.zip        143501   Non-linear least-squares fit (req. Gnuplot)
lsqrft14.zip        237825   Non-linear least-squares fit (req. Gnuplot)
mawk_os2.zip        480362   Port of M. Breannas fast AWK
memacs32.zip        486903   MicroEMACS 3.12
mmv32.zip           106570   Move/copy/append lines/multiple files w/wildcards
oraperl2.zip        349929   Oraperl, Oracle DBMS variant of Perl
patch2u6.zip        129201   Patch kit version 2.0
perl4036.zip        915327   Perl 4.0 patchlevel 36 language interpreter
plbin.zip          1205622   SWI Prolog for OS/2
ps2fax.zip          779664   Ghostscript 2.6.1-based PS to PCX/DCX for faxing
qutil2.zip          108251   A collection of Unix-like utilities
recode32.zip        281503   GNU recode 3.2.4 convert text to other character sets
rev.zip              80105   Print filter for reversing pages, double sides, etc.
sc621.zip           352598   SC Spreadsheet 6.21 for OS/2 2.x with Watcom C/386 9.0
tex/                   -     TeX typesetting language
tr100.zip            35315   Unix TR - translate characters and more
twcp120.zip          40262   Mark, Copy and Paste to/from windows like X-Windows
xfeel11.zip           7730   A utility to make PM behave like X-Windows

2_x/unix/emacs22:
00index.txt            755
HISTORY             106738   History of changes for GNU Emacs (19.22 version)
README               48226   GNU Emacs 19.22 README
e22el1.zip         1197401   Emacs Lisp files (source), part 1
e22el2.zip          690460   Emacs Lisp files (source), part 2
e22info.zip         534512   Emacs info files (online help)
e22lib1.zip         896148   Emacs Lisp library (base set, compiled)
e22lib2.zip         364878   Emacs Lisp library (remaining files, compiled)
e22man.zip          694634   Emacs documentation files ( mostly TeX )
e22min.zip          894473   Minimum set of files for running GNU Emacs
e22more.zip         318587   Additional files for running Emacs
e22rest.zip         932996   Remaining files for running Emacs
e22src.zip          969033   Emacs source files

2_x/unix/emx08h:
00index.txt           2003
INSTALL.DOC          13679   EMX 0.8h Installation Guide
README.DOC            8936   Introduction to EMX 0.8h
bsddev.zip           23719   BSD libraries (curses, etc.)
bsddoc.zip           48096   Documentation for BSD libraries
bsdsrc.zip           79529   Source for BSD libraries
```

```
contrib/                   -       Contributions
emxample.zip           17433       Sample programs
emxdev.zip            801785       EMX development system (without compiler)
emxlib.zip            398515       EMX library sources
emxrt.zip             151918       EMX runtime package
emxsrc1.zip           126857       Source for emxomf, emxomfar and emxomfld
emxtest.zip            83889       Test programs (used for testing emx and the libraries)
emxview.zip           244731       EMX documentation in OS/2 .INF format
gassrc.zip            180404       Patched GNU sources (GAS 1.38.1)
gccsrc1.zip          1176878       Patched GNU sources (GCC 2.5.7, part 1)
gccsrc2.zip          1142664       Patched GNU sources (GCC 2.5.7, part 2)
gccsrc3.zip           280989       Patched GNU sources (GCC 2.5.7, part 3)
gdbsrc1.zip           825119       Patched GNU sources (GDB 4.11, part 1)
gdbsrc2.zip           457357       Patched GNU sources (GDB 4.11, part 2)
gnudev.zip           1076416       GNU development tools compiled for EMX
gnudoc.zip            806052       Documentation for GNU programs (texinfo sources)
gnuinfo.zip           192957       GNU texinfo (includes info file browser)
gnupat.zip             79653       Patches for GNU sources
gnusrc.zip            374722       Patched GNU sources (ld, ar, nm, size, etc.)
gnuview.zip            22467       GNUDEV.INF (gnudev.doc in OS/2 .INF format)
gobjcdev.zip          525222       GNU programs and files for compiling Objective C
gppdev.zip           1040420       GNU programs and files for compiling C++
gppsrc.zip           1025366       Patched sources of libg++ 2.2

2_x/unix/emx08h/contrib:
00index.txt              289
dbmalloc.zip          210683       Debugging malloc library for EMX
emxfont.zip            11821       Small font package for use with EMX/GCC
svgakt14.zip           30135       SVGA high-res fullscreen graphics library for EMX
vesa14.zip             23693       VESA interface for EMX, used by svgakit

2_x/unix/gcc2_254:
00index.txt             1136
base254.zip           366053       GCC/2: REQUIRED binaries, dlls, and docs
c254.zip              563923       GCC/2: GNU C Compiler - req. for C development
cplus254.zip          827465       GCC/2: GNU C++ Kit - Required for C++ development
dev254.zip            781485       GCC/2: REQUIRED libraries and include files
gccfiles.txt            1913
glibp115.zip           37427       GCC/2 object file librarian
glibs115.zip           37427       GCC/2 object file librarian (source)
man254.zip           1031402       GCC/2: Optional manual pages for Standard C library
news.txt                 315
objc254.zip           642340       GCC/2: GNU Objective C Kit - Req. for ObjC work
pminfo21.zip          178381       Source for PMInfo and PMMan
sampl254.zip           66605       GCC/2: SOURCE - Example C, C++, Obj-C code
sgas138.zip           336912       Source for GAS/2
sgcc254.zip          6343151       GCC/2: SOURCE for GCC/2 2.5.4
sgmk362.zip           247108       Source for GNU Make
slib254.zip           536379       GCC/2: SOURCE for Standard C library
slibg251.zip         1765422       Source for GNU C++ library
sutil254.zip           13354       GCC/2: SOURCE for GCC/2 utility programs
texi254.zip           604946       GCC/2: Optional manuals for C/C++ compilers

2_x/unix/tex:
00index.txt              999
bm2fon20.zip          603237       BitMapTOfont - convert pictures into TeX fonts
cmtex330.zip          992175       Common TeX add-in for emTeX (HPFS/no memory limits)
```

```
cweb_2_8.zip      241152   CWEB programming language documentation program
dvips.zip         463826   DVIPS 5.516-DVI to Postscript converter for emTeX
epmtex13.zip       23507   Add Tex support to menu bar of OS/2 EPM v5.51
funnel_s.zip      583017   Funnel, a literate programming tool (sources)
funnel_x.zip      280022   Funnel, a literate programming tool (executables)
latexinf.zip       32833   LaTeX command reference and help file for EPM
pmtex22i.zip       57553   TeX shell for OS/2 presentation manager
spider.zip        461763   Spider - generate tangle/weave for other languages
texas11.zip       156719   TEXAS, a version of big Tex for OS/2
texi2ipf.zip       50147   texinfo to ipf converter
texpert.zip       148664   A text-mode shell for emTeX
txi2ipf1.zip      165269   Yet another TeXinfo to .ipf (.INF) translator

2_x/win_os2:
00index.txt         1385
amiuos2-1.zip    1327614   Ami Pro 3.0 to 3.01 upgrade for Win-OS2 Part 1 of 3
amiuos2-2.zip    1426091   Ami Pro 3.0 to 3.01 upgrade for Win-OS2 Part 2 of 3
amiuos2-3.zip    1407498   Ami Pro 3.0 to 3.01 upgrade for Win-OS2 Part 3 of 3
l4wn30.zip        415501   HP LaserJet 4 Win 3.0 driver
maudio.zip         91989   Multimedia driver for IBM M-Audio Adapter
opl3.zip           15395   WIN-OS/2 OPL driver fixes for ProAudio Spectrum 16
os2win31.zip      366750   Run MS Win 3.1 in Standard Mod in a DOS VDM
sb_wu.zip         207487   Latest Soundblaster family drivers for Windows
sbupdate.zip      393106   Update replaces drivers for all Creative Lab's Cards.
seamwin3.zip        9573   Load seamless Windows programs quickly
speaker.zip         8745   Multimedia driver for PC Speaker (no soundcard)
thunwin.zip        19465   Windows multimedia driver for MediaVision Thunderboard
upc12bw1.zip       69002   UUPC/extended 1.12b Windows executables (1 of 3)
upc12bw2.zip      207280   UUPC/extended 1.12b Windows executables (2 of 3)
upc12bw3.zip       35595   UUPC/extended 1.12b Windows executables (3 of 3)
videodr5.zip       53039   Win-OS/2 full screen video driver changer
winfonts.zip      234091   Extra ATM fonts for WIN OS/2
wnbff14a.zip       15934   A port of Unix biff for use with UUPC & Windows
xgawin21.zip      469218   XGA-2 Windows/WINOS2 full screen drivers version 2.1

all:
00index.txt        71590
archiver/              -   OS/2 compression/decompression archive programs
bbs/                   -   OS/2 bbs programs and utilities
comm/                  -   OS/2 communications programs/utilities
demos/                 -   Commercial product demos for OS/2
diskutil/              -   OS/2 disk utilities
drivers/               -   Device drivers for OS/2
editors/               -   OS/2 text/binary file editors
educate/               -
fonts/                 -   OS/2 fonts (ATM, PFM, etc.) and utilities
games/                 -   OS/2 games
graphics/              =   OS/2 graphics programs and utilities
info/                  =   Various OS/2-related information files
miscutil/              -   Miscellaneous utilities for OS/2
mmedia/                -   Multimedia-related drivers/programs
network/               =   Network-related programs for OS/2
patches/               -
printer/               -   OS/2 printer-related programs/utilities
program/               =   Programming tools/information for OS/2
sysutils/              -   OS/2 system utilities
unix/                  =   Unix-related ports and utilities for OS/2
```

```
all/archiver:
00index.txt              1063
arc521_2.zip           165155   ARC version 5.21
av109.zip               66601   1.x PM archiver viewing/launching/maintenance util
lh2_222.zip            114258   LHARC version 2.22 (16 and 32-bit versions)
ncdc_os2.zip            46615   A fast/intelligent XX/UU encoder/decoder
pkz102_2.exe           258176   PKZIP 1.02 (P/D/SFX)
pmzip10.zip             67161   Front-end for PKZIP (PM)
rxship24.zip            29818   Convert archive to self-extracting REXX script
unarj210.zip            84791   .ARJ file extractor version 2.10
unz50x16.exe           102097   Info-ZIP UNZIP version 5.0 - 16-bit executables
uugrab16.zip            40940   Easily extract multi-part comp.binaries.os2 posts
x_os2_18.exe            80896   Unzip/UnArc/UnLZH
xbin.zip                46421   Macintosh BinHex-format unarchiver (S/D)
zip201.zip             245702   Info-Zip ZIP version 2.01 - sources
zip201x1.zip           106061   Info-Zip ZIP version 2.01 - 16-bit executables
zipv101.zip             17427   Zip file viewer
zoo210e.exe            119554   ZOO 2.1 (HPFS/FAT compatible) - Executables
zoo210s.zip            196730   ZOO 2.1 (sources)

all/bbs:
00index.txt              2706
afp_120.zip             49093   Area Fix 1.20 - Alter BBS files remotely
ahatch21.zip             6897   Automated hatch procedure for Tick release
binkp256.zip           172914   BinkleyTerm 2.56 EchoMail processor
bos2_258.zip           188371   Binkleyterm version 2.58 beta for OS/2
btp_eebe.zip           273730   BinkleyTerm OS/2 2.5 (Extended Edition)
bubba03.zip            206008   Offline mail reader for the IBM NSC BBS
catqwk.zip              15048   Combines two or more QWK files together
dwnsrs57.zip           100150   Maximus Downsort 5.7 source material
dwnsrt57.zip           244226   Maximus CBCS DOWNload file SORT and List V 5.7
fan_120.zip            109593   File Announcement Utility, echo mail via TIC file
fdsyn103.zip            16029   Sychronize system clock for Front Door under OS/2
insp110p.zip           347697   InspectA - file, archive, and FidoNet mail manager
max200_1.zip           301476   Maximus 2.00 Part 1 (Necessary only for DOS)
max200_2.zip           162595   Maximus 2.00 Part 2 (Necessary only for DOS)
max200_3.zip           136529   Maximus 2.00 Part 3 (Necessary for DOS and OS/2)
max200_4.zip           284774   Maximus 2.00 Part 4 (Necessary for DOS and OS/2)
max200p1.zip           346196   Maximus 2.00 Part 1 (Necessary only for OS/2)
max200p2.zip           163879   Maximus 2.00 Part 2 (Necessary only for OS/2)
maxcom22.zip             4153   Updated/fixed MAXCOMM.DLL for MAX/2
maxipc2.zip             11927   Maximus IPC Creator
maxlog20.zip           114687   Trims Max/Squish log files by # of days
maxp201b.zip           476089   Maximus/2 2.01 beta (requires 2.00 installed first)
mnum416b.zip            16150   Msgnum, a utility for deleting excess BBS messages
mr2_151.zip            191774   MR/2, a QWK compatible mail reader (text only)
mrpm099b.zip           138238   A QWK compatible mail reader (PM based)
msq2_1p.zip            108565   FTSC + Squish compatible message editor
newsdesk.zip            40522   BBS news login screen designer
plst_133.zip            37429   ParseLst, a program for processing a FidoNet nodelist
ptktexe0.zip           334920   Complete POINT kit
qwklay15.zip            17437   A complete description of the qwk format
qwklay16.zip            18820   QWK Mail Packet File Layout information
qwkp9211.zip            19234   A listing of QWK-format products
simplex2.zip           460453   Simplex bulletin board system
sqlnk120.zip            38784   Squish message base MSGID/REPLY linker
sqshp101.zip           271184   EchoMail tosser, processor version 1.01 for OS/2
```

Appendix H—Identifying Sources of OS/2 Information

```
sqst10a.zip         61492   SQUISH.LOG Statistics Reporter
tickp210.zip       112503   Tick, a BBS mail/file handler
upname.zip           7178   Inserts uploaders name into description for Maximus
vbbs2_b1.zip       828416   A port of Virtual VBBS 5.60 (beta)
yabp120.zip        186496   Yet Another Binkly Outbound Mail Processor

all/comm:
00index.txt          2672
at2_14a.zip         26258   Send AT commands to your modem from the command line
cko5a189.zip       515955   Latest ckermit port for OS/2 from Columbia U.
ckote2.txt           4293   How to use CKERMIT with TE/2
ckpm5xe.zip        238060   C-Kermit (PM)
clink140.zip        76228   External SEAlink 1.40 communications protocol program
com16550.zip        13478   Replacement COM drivers for high-speed UARTs
comm_m.zip          15219   Monitor characters flowing between two comm devices
comtalk.zip         48663   Communications program (S/PM)
hptdemo.zip         48546   Demo version of Personal TSO
kermte2.zip         13527   Kermit protocol add-in for TE/2
log230.zip          96480   Logicomm version 2.30 communications program
m2z214.zip         106831   External Zmodem protocol program
magcom22.zip        84596   MagCom 2.20 telecommunications program
magcomgr.zip       116704   MagCom 2.20 telecommunications program (German version)
os2com15.zip        25259   A simple OS/2 communications program (w/source)
os2ftp15.zip        50771   External file transfer protocols - X/Y/Z-modem
os2you27.zip       235326   Run an OS/2 text session remotely, version 2.7
phoneat4.zip        21710   Incoming telephone call alerter/dialer
pm2ub12.zip        704108   PM2You version 1.2 (beta) remote session package
pm2you11.zip       646723   Run PM/Windows/full screen session remotely
pmac10.zip          34595   A few small utilities for PM COMM
pmcom110.zip       224697   PM COMM communications package (PM)
pmqvt.zip           60582   PM VT200 terminal emulator
setbaud2.zip         8223   Set baud rate up to 115200 baud
snaaos2.zip         90240   SNA Async communcations program from IBM
softos2.zip       1319112   Softerm Plus for OS/2 communications program
te2_124.zip        524293   TE/2 communications program version 1.24
term2b23.zip       168717   Terminal program that works with os2you (PM)
ths403.zip         121094   TNC2 (WA8DED) Packet radio terminal program
upc12b11.zip       182972   UUPC/extended 1.12b OS/2 executables (1 of 3)
upc12b12.zip       205746   UUPC/extended 1.12b OS/2 executables (2 of 3)
upc12b13.zip        59444   UUPC/extended 1.12b OS/2 executables (3 of 3)
upc12bad.zip       324805   UUPC/extended 1.12b documents and sample files
upc12bap.zip       318983   UUPC/extended 1.12b documents in PostScript format
upc12baw.zip       140653   UUPC/extended 1.12b Word for Windows document source
upc12bs1.zip       433324   UUPC/extended 1.12b source files (1 of 2)
upc12bs2.zip        49182   UUPC/extended 1.12b source files (2 of 2)
xfer.zip            22353   Easel file transfer local app supporting x/ymodem
xhs400.zip         157775   PK232 Packet Radio terminal program (hostmode)

all/demos:
00index.txt           280
describe.zip       873789   Describe word processor demo
lmu2demo.zip       286290   IBM Lan Management Utilities/2 2.0 demo diskette
openwi.zip         444316   OpenWin Demo Application, 4GL GUI
sztdem.zip          12946   Canon LBP scaleable fonts program demo
```

```
all/diskutil:
00index.txt       5067
2coldir.zip       9217    Directory listing in two columns
absshare.zip     73556    File encryption utilities for OS/2 and DOS
aw.zip           18288    Find a file anywhere
back01.zip       21768    Text mode backup utility similar to FIT and FILL
bcsutil.zip      12528    File finder, file size, and key utilities
bootany.zip      34084    Boot manager program
chdirc20.zip      8481    An enhanced cd utility
compupd.zip      59491    Compare and update file utilities
contrast.zip     57794    A really nice file comparison program
ctree.zip        30177    Replacement for OS/2 tree command
d53.zip          66159    An enhanced dir utility
dbls.zip          8212    Doubles finder, file finder utility
ddir0_10.zip     21067    Two column directory listing
ddump001.zip     34657    Dual dump file utility, similar to cable
delpth11.zip     10363    Delete a directory path and all its subdirectories
dirman21.zip    137796    PM Directory Manager 2.01f for OS/2
diskmap.zip      26956    Produces a map of all disk drives
diskut.zip       84759    PM clock/data display w/disk & file utilities
dlabel.zip       18044    Disk label utility
drsz10.zip       20031    Shows the amount of space used for all dirs in a path
dskarc13.zip     38692    Archive disk images to file and vice-versa
dskcpy2a.zip     15687    Fast disk copy replacement
dskst101.zip     26968    Display contiually updated disk drive stats
dualboot.zip     17159    Dual boot OS/2 and MS-DOS
dump.zip         11349    File dump program
dx.exe           22016    Display DLL and EXE file information
dxp230.zip      204451    Disk Express — create disk images
eabk202.zip      85204    Backup/restore HPFS extended attributes, version 2.02
fa10.zip          7835    Norton-like file attribute changer
fc.zip           42616    File Commando, a file utility like Norton Commander
ff11.zip          9017    File find utility
ffff.zip          7098    Fast false floppy formatter, DOS format /q for OS/2
fill_os2.zip     10386    Disk copy filling program
finder.zip       19399    Search multiple disks and directories for files
findstr2.zip     22496    Find strings on disk
fitt101.zip      13520    A smart COPY, optimally fit files on a diskette
fj606e.zip      285258    File manager for OS/2 & DOS
flexboot.zip     14837    Allows multiple partition boot options
flist58.zip     119963    File and directory manipular, Zip shell, etc.
forall70.zip     31700    A file finder
gtak100.zip     207242    GTAK SCSI tape backup software, version 1.00
gtak100s.zip    156184    GTAK SCSI tape backup software (source)
hexdisp.zip      23370    Hex & ASCII display (S)
jcd21.zip        18197    Intelligent CHDIR-partial match, across drives
lcd.zip          27110    Less change directory ver 6.0
lf37.zip         22603    Multi-featured directory lister
list10h.zip      24641    File browser
list75h.zip      18767    Port of Buergs popular file lister
look2.zip        58113    Text mode file viewer and directory browser
mmv_2.zip        81475    Utility for moving/copying/appending/linking files
mrfilepm.zip    259596    A very good file manager for PM (16/32 versions)
oback793.zip     75313    Obackup v1.4 - backups up floppies with compression
obkup340.zip     71073    OBACKUP 3.40 multi-threaded backup utility
os2tree.zip       5688    Seetree for OS/2
os2utils.zip     54746    Scan files, dir list, etc.
```

Appendix H—Sources of OS/2 Information

os2utl10.zip	92765	Various file utilities
osfindr.zip	19399	File finder utility (PM/S)
ov143.zip	70116	Overview, a hard disk and file maintenance utility
pgp22.txt	1946	How to get a free public key encryption program
phoenix.zip	23807	Undelete for FAT and HPFS
pmdc101u.zip	20556	A PM utility for copying/comparing disks
pmflp202.zip	82239	Read floppy disk into a disk image file
pmfrmt15.zip	33748	PM Format, a PM front end for formatting disks
rh2os2.zip	60824	A file finder program
sde.zip	111078	PCTools-like multifunction program
sdfl.zip	3441	Sorted double directory listing program (HPFS aware)
showfrag.zip	30196	Display the fragmentation of FAT drives
sliceit.zip	15058	A utility for chopping up files to fit on disks
state.zip	9795	Checks existence of a file
substp00.zip	21749	DOS SUBST command ported to OS/2
tcan20.zip	37144	A trashcan for OS/2 PM
trans.zip	21564	Newline/Backspace conversion (Unix file exchange)
ts.zip	17470	Seek text files for a pattern
vc132.zip	71565	Visual compare, file comparison util for programmers
vcd10.zip	30539	An enhanced change directory (CD) program
vszap10.zip	6577	Subdirectory & file remover
vv097exe.zip	197970	Binary<->ASCII converter for emailing binary files
whereis2.lzh	13254	A file finder
wipedisk.zip	8431	Save ext. attributes when deleting files on floppies
wiper.zip	15638	Deletes directory trees
xl2271.zip	235250	X-List/2 2.71, a file/directory utility

all/drivers:

00index.txt	1623	
42xx.zip	231898	OS/2 IBM 42xx Printer driver v1.354
52012.zip	58629	IBM 52012 printer driver v1208
52xx.zip	192219	IBM 52xx printer driver v1.289
ati_11.zip	231028	ATI VGAWonder display drivers (work with OS/2 2.0)
atibeta3.zip	619102	OS/2 video drivers for most ATI cards
bj6osv12.zip	86784	Canon BJ-200/230/300/330 & BJC-600/800 printer drivers
cdd2.zip	4912	Get a command prompt to fix a broken CONFIG.SYS
com01a.zip	6575	AST 4-port communications adapter device driver
cyrix.zip	8447	Driver for Cx486DLC cache hardware
dlos2.zip	2096	Driver to boot DSI Connection 96+ SoftModems
ecomon12.zip	22115	Driver for using monochrome screen as a 2nd monitor
epson.zip	82259	Epson printer driver v13.384 (5/24/93)
hpdjet.zip	96420	OS/2 HP DeskJet family printer driver v13.380
lbpcap.zip	190388	Canon OS/2 LBP4/8 printer driver version 2.1
ljos2.zip	273545	Beta Laserjet PCL 5 drivers (supports Laserjet 4)
necpin.zip	111715	OS/2 1.3 and 2.0 drivers for NEC Pinwriters
null.zip	55290	IBM Null Printer Driver v1208
os2matrx.zip	208418	IBM 42xx printer driver 1.306, incl. ExecJet/InkJet
pause.zip	1092	Device driver which pauses so you can read boot screen
post16.zip	206075	16-bit Postscript printer drivers v13.389
scangs1.zip	7450	GS4500 hand scanner driver/software for OS/2
uos2144.zip	170224	Digiboard drivers v1.4.4 for "intelligent" cards
vga132.zip	92417	PM/WPS display driver for VGA - 664x480x16

all/editors:

00index.txt	1782	
ae.zip	141714	Andys editor, a small, powerful folding editor
aedit.zip	72576	A small editor, from PC Magazine

ana015.zip	33587	Binary file analysis tool
bb2_120.zip	170105	Blackbeard/2 programmers editor
beav132x.zip	228136	Binary editor and viewer, version 1.32 (S)
browse2.zip	65703	File Browser (PM)
config2.zip	42999	PC Magazine config.sys editor (non-PM)
dedump.zip	33337	Hexadecimal dump utility (PM)
dscb_env.zip	9957	Describe 3 macro for printing envelopes
e2_v321.zip	158419	Rand editor for DOS & OS/2
ed.zip	29816	Unix-like ed editor executables
ed_s.zip	32367	Unix-like ed editor sources
elv15bin.zip	317928	Elvis 1.5, a full-screen vi clone (executables/docs)
elv15src.zip	215551	Elvis 1.5, a full-screen vi clone (sources)
flip1os2.zip	34194	Convert Unix-style text files to OS/2 & vice-versa
fsb.zip	1951	Browser by Charles Petzold
heditorp.zip	157285	Binary editor
levee.zip	33693	Levee - a vi clone for OS/2
memo.zip	14049	Notepad type editor
pminfo.zip	325506	PM hypertext manual browser (includes gcc manual)
pmview5b.zip	80571	Latest version of PC Magazine PMText-view text files
sed106.zip	90961	A stream editor
sedt2.zip	178921	SEDT (VMS EDIT-like) text editor
stvi369g.zip	194742	Stevie vi-clone
te25.zip	115293	Technical Editor - handles up to 32MB files
tedp090.zip	10507	A tiny editor, great for that emergency boot disk
theos2_e.zip	80353	THE full-screen text editor, based on VM/CMS XEDIT
we12.zip	56818	The Wilkes editor, version 1.2
zviewos2.zip	144558	ZiffNet text viewer utility
all/educate:		
00index.txt	461	
catsmeow.zip	294037	Cats Meow, a collection of recipes (.INF format)
cptut22.zip	188418	Coronado Enterprises C++ tutorial (ASCII text)
cptut22g.zip	164404	Coronado Enterprises C++ tutorial (GNUINFO format)
pspice.zip	1190276	Spice electrical circuit simulator
spring.zip	25906	Demonstrates the behavior of a spring using graphs
typefast.zip	43302	A typing exercise game—type the falling words
all/fonts:		
00index.txt	14498	
0index.txt	19297	
0pfm2afm.zip	25061	
0refont.zip	27045	
aachen.zip	37207	
aarco1.zip	18474	ATM font - novelty font, looks like static electricity
adjutant.zip	40381	
adlib_t1.zip	18891	ATM Font - Adlib
afract.zip	25854	
afutblk.zip	33000	
agate.zip	33776	
agateb.zip	33498	
agatei.zip	33970	
albatros.zip	45865	
alger_t1.zip	34560	ATM Font - Algeria
alison.zip	24288	
ambro.zip	21305	
amuncial.zip	55857	
andrmeda.zip	34375	
animal.doc	23156	

```
answer1.zip      22901
antique.zip      41557
aplnorma.zip     39441
arabian.zip      36316
architec.zip     27663
archmed.zip      12304
arcti.zip        21915
arcturt1.zip     15652   ATM Font - Architectura
arctxt.zip       33114   ATM font - ArchiText, an architectural type
ariston.zip      55007
arnold.zip       40350
ashley.zip       21772
atm-flor.zip     40285   ATM font - "FLORENCE"
atm_ball.zip     27809   ATM font - "BALLEENG"
atm_flor.zip     38570   ATM font - "FLORENCE"
atm_murl.zip     21967   ATM font - "Murle"
atm_otwn.zip     33035   ATM Font - Old Town
atm_rabb.zip     17828   ATM font - Rabbit
avanthin.zip     36535
avntgard.zip     34922
balleeng.zip     29084
barcod39.zip     19606   ATM Font - BarCode39
baskvl.zip       45737
baskvlb.zip      46002
baskvli.zip      48599
bauheav.zip      34740
baulite.zip      36583
bauthin.zip      34456
bebop_t1.zip     17089   ATM Font - Beebop
becker.zip       33821
bedrock.zip      21307   ATM Font - Bedrock-Light
beffle.zip       31897
bengbold.zip     42408
benglite.zip     42263
benjacap.zip     16883   ATM font - BenjaminCaps
blackcha.zip     26101
blackfor.zip     26525
bladder2.zip     24877
blippo.zip       37455
blkcha.zip       26097   ATM font - Black Chancery
bodacius.zip     45064
bodidlyb.zip     31676
bodnoff.zip      29133
bodoni.zip       44897
bodonib.zip      44710
bodonii.zip      46760
boecklin.zip     53260   ATM font - Boecklin
boldface.zip     44181
broadway.zip     48442
brushscr.zip     59457
busor_t1.zip     16590   ATM Font - Busorama
caligu.zip       29912   ATM Font - Caligula - like calligraphy
caligula.zip     29916
camberic.zip     22174
capri.zip        13874
carawbol.zip     23750
carricap.zip     35759
```

carta.zip	44797	
cartwrig.zip	20383	ATM Font - Cartwright
cascade.zip	34631	
caslite.zip	41388	
caslonop.zip	56721	ATM Font - Caslonop
casopen.zip	63815	
cavemann.zip	15619	
centlite.zip	40552	
centthin.zip	43206	
chancery.zip	43606	
charlcha.zip	36302	ATM Font - Charlie Chan
cheq.zip	32633	
chicago.zip	21486	
chilipep.zip	41350	
chitown.zip	31379	ATM Font - ChiTown-Light
chpsf301.zip	56373	ATM Font - Hanzi-Kaishu (Chinese)
chrlychn.zip	21991	
civtyp.zip	36070	ATM font - Civtyp, based on Civilite
classhvy.zip	32198	
cloister.zip	39611	
cocacola.zip	20193	ATM Font - CocaCola
coliseo.zip	35365	
comaro.zip	14390	
cooprblk.zip	54747	
cop-goth.zip	32656	ATM Font - Engraver-Light
coronet.zip	34029	
crackfir.zip	32055	ATM font - CracklingFire, novelty font
crakfir.zip	54331	
crill.zip	42123	ATM Font - Crillee
crillee.zip	46321	
csdblock.zip	27190	
csdchalk.zip	32772	
csdjersy.zip	29292	
ctnwood.zip	54151	
cunefrm.zip	29816	
cunei.zip	19875	
cyrillic.zip	145814	ATM Font - Cyrillic (various)
dabkc.zip	57974	
davysrib.zip	78663	
delegate.zip	40495	
diego1.zip	50393	ATM Font - Diego1-Light
dingbats.zip	51322	
dobkin.zip	24266	
domcas.zip	45821	
domcasul.zip	29190	
dragon.zip	19592	
dragonwi.zip	19636	
dubielit.zip	40687	
durango.zip	18644	ATM Font - Durango
eastside.zip	25142	
elann.zip	25458	
elite.zip	40267	
englisht.zip	33094	
engravrl.zip	32600	
eras.zip	33663	
erasb.zip	33709	
erasblkb.zip	34281	

Appendix H—Sources of OS/2 Information

eraselt.zip	33388	
erasltra.zip	34528	
erasmed.zip	33626	
essay.zip	40713	
eurobold.zip	41565	
fargo.zip	28716	
farqufre.zip	19560	ATM font - Farquharson
faustus.zip	19524	
fetfrak.zip	51565	
fettefrk.zip	34644	
flemish1.zip	65119	ATM Font - Flemish normal & shadow
flora-b.zip	50356	
flora.zip	49509	
florence.zip	36307	
fr-b.zip	37726	
fr-n.zip	37820	
frankhvy.zip	35833	
franklte.zip	35665	
franktim.zip	36299	
frcnd-b.zip	37401	
frcnd-n.zip	37612	
frcndo-b.zip	37981	
frcndo-n.zip	38169	
frext-b.zip	38040	
frext-n.zip	38407	
frexto-b.zip	38425	
frexto-n.zip	38678	
frnkftt1.zip	48340	ATM Font - Frankfurt
fro-b.zip	38217	
fro-n.zip	38332	
frquad.zip	37816	
frquadb.zip	37776	
ftpstrps.zip	27386	
fusion-b.zip	39265	
fusion.zip	38564	
futur-bl.zip	44616	ATM font - Futur-bl
futur_bl.zip	41066	ATM font - Futur-bl
futura1.zip	33480	
futura2.zip	34554	
futura3.zip	34191	
futura4.zip	34633	
future.zip	45580	
garmnd.zip	48666	
garmnd1.zip	47538	ATM Font - Garmond-Normal
garmndmi.zip	48762	
garrett.zip	57908	ATM Font - ElGarrett
genoaita.zip	23207	
genoarom.zip	22809	
glypict1.zip	14052	ATM Font - Glypic
gocm.zip	105257	
goudymed.zip	21122	
goudyo.zip	56195	
goudyob.zip	60079	
goudyoi.zip	58314	
grafikt1.zip	37166	ATM Font - Graphik & Graphik Shadow
gralig.zip	29587	ATM Font - Graphic Light
graphlig.zip	28417	

```
greencap.zip     13156    ATM font - GreenCap, ported from the Mac
harqu.zip        19777
harri.zip        22060
harting2.zip     73105
heidelbe.zip     40733    ATM Font - Heidelberg-Light
helvblak.zip     35562
helvblk2.zip     34610
helvcond.zip     34511
helvins.zip      35105
helvlite.zip     35014
hobo.zip         48009
holt.zip         44789
horstcap.zip     15742    ATM font - HorstCap, ported from the Mac
hotshot.zip      14230
houters.zip      27918
howrdfat.zip     30442
hwrdlite.zip     30697
ibmklone.zip     38949
iglesia.zip      52370    ATM Font - Iglesia-Light
igloolas.zip     19040
inkwe.zip        21968
inkwell.zip      17035
ironwood.zip     45506
isado.zip        19366
judas.zip        21747
juniper.zip      43407
kabel_t1.zip     18024    ATM Font - Kabel
kafka.zip        35314
karkode.zip      82738
kashmir.zip      30206    ATM Font - Kashmir
kathlita.zip     30839
kaufmann.zip     34953    ATM font - Kaufmann
key-top.zip      73159
klinz.zip        10957
kochread.zip     28090
konankap.zip     27081    ATM font - KonanKap, ported from the Mac
kornital.zip     39943
kornlite.zip     38509
koshgar.zip      20874
kramer.zip       38124
latinwid.zip     34255    ATM font - Latinwid
latinwyd.zip     45796
leftycas.zip     25567
lemiesz.zip      29096
libbyscr.zip     26107
light.zip        45596
lincoln.zip      39044
linotext.zip     52122
lithost1.zip     18371    ATM Font - Lithos
livia.zip        16795    ATM font - Livia
liviread.zip     19037
lnoscrpt.zip     52871
lombardc.zip     10516
lombardi.zip     28574    ATM Font - Lombardic (letters only)
loopdelo.zip     19007
lowereas.zip     55148    ATM font - Lower East Side
lowerwes.zip     25579    ATM font - Lower West Side, a vibrating novelty face
```

Appendix H—Sources of OS/2 Information

```
ltrgothc.zip     35040
lumpa.zip        25340
luxem.zip        19355
luxembrg.zip     16054
machine.zip      30584
machineb.zip     19800    ATM Font - Machine Block
machumai.zip     33681
maidsscr.zip     25006
maidston.zip     22144    ATM font - Maidstone Script
manzanit.zip     23726
marriage.zip     59347
mazama.zip       23828
mesozic.zip      70107
miami.zip        30799
miamib.zip       30686    ATM Font - MiamiBeach-Light
middleto.zip     59632
minipics.zip     35608    ATM font - Minipics
mistral.zip      36412    ATM font - Mistral
monobold.zip     37366
monot.zip        30047
mortbats.zip     38956
muriel.zip       23199
mystical.zip     65570
nauert.zip       37660
nbskrvl.zip      42472
newsgoth.zip     39118
nordi.zip        16857
nouveau.zip      18996
nwsgth-b.zip     39275
old-town.zip     34263    ATM font - Old Town
old_town.zip     32990    ATM font - Old Town
oldcnd-r.zip     40285
oldext-r.zip     40648
oldtwn-r.zip     40452
oldworld.zip     45478
optima.zip       39028
oregdry.zip      16083    ATM Font - Oregon Dry
oswaldbl.zip     33938
paint_t1.zip     32885    ATM Font - Paintbrush
palathin.zip     44496
palatino.zip     43084
palladam.zip     38871    ATM Font - Palladam (Tamil)
papyrus.zip      45713
paradox.zip      47592
paris.zip        42546
parismet.zip     13938
parkave.zip      49841    ATM font - Park Avenue
pceir.zip        18452
pceire.zip       18365
pclip_t1.zip     44328    ATM Font - Paper Clip
pcmir.zip        19590
pcorn.zip        39773
pcrou.zip        26958
peiglite.zip     33714
peigmed.zip      37295
peignot.zip      35268
pfm2afm.zip      23861    Convert Windows AFM files to OS/2 .PFM files
```

phoenix1.zip	29982	
pica.zip	41956	
pig_nose.zip	35072	
pignoset.zip	32030	
pixel.zip	100054	
pixiefon.zip	21008	ATM font - Pixiefon, converted from the Mac font
playbill.zip	59822	ATM Font - Playbill
polo-sem.zip	18845	
polosems.zip	20221	
postanti.zip	29983	
postcr.zip	42564	ATM font - PostCrypt, bleeding letters
postcryp.zip	39089	
present.zip	48094	
presento.zip	40131	
prestige.zip	38260	
ransonot.zip	50419	
recycle.zip	28003	ATM Font - Recycle
redlette.zip	35819	ATM Font - RedLetter
refont.zip	27294	Convert Mac type 1 fonts to Windows and ATM
relief.zip	24655	ATM font - ReliefDeco, has an embossed look
revue.zip	33261	
reynocap.zip	13832	ATM font - ReynoldsCap, ported from the Mac
rhyolite.zip	11188	
riversid.zip	18384	
rodchenk.zip	26605	
roissy-b.zip	39916	
roissy.zip	39992	
roosthea.zip	20069	
rothm.zip	12251	
rothman.zip	13953	ATM font - Rothman, an Art Deco font
rsalison.zip	30895	
rsandrom.zip	37978	
rscanai.zip	34544	
rscavema.zip	15469	
rschacha.zip	20571	
rschasli.zip	30035	
rschitow.zip	28354	
rscunfon.zip	17844	
rsdayton.zip	42761	
rsdeusex.zip	17529	
rselgarr.zip	36216	
rsflifon.zip	18549	
rsfutbol.zip	22696	
rsfutura.zip	17651	
rsgordon.zip	17934	
rsgralig.zip	26173	
rsheidel.zip	28713	
rsjackso.zip	32413	
rskathli.zip	40639	
rslaslon.zip	27092	
rsmanzan.zip	25000	
rsmianig.zip	19181	
rsmoroma.zip	30720	
rsparhav.zip	20271	
rssanser.zip	22055	
rsslainf.zip	16936	
rsstyle.zip	17893	

Appendix H—Sources of OS/2 Information

rsstymie.zip	23309	
rstempus.zip	34018	
rstimmir.zip	38630	
rstoulau.zip	26313	
rstoyblo.zip	32031	
rsultlin.zip	16460	
rudel.zip	21036	ATM font - Rudel, converted from the Mac font
rudelsbe.zip	21066	
safatt.zip	48450	ATM Font - SafariPlain and more
saintfra.zip	21848	
saloon.zip	38630	ATM Font - SaloonExt
sanserif.zip	51697	ATM font - Sanserif, based on the Corel Draw font
savannah.zip	23412	ATM Font - SavannahFatsPlain
schwawal.zip	22389	
script.zip	44033	
scriptit.zip	44060	
secretco.zip	14977	
shaloold.zip	20683	
shaloscr.zip	19980	
shalosti.zip	17233	
sharktoo.zip	25616	
shelley.zip	164305	ATM font - Shelley, based on the Corel Draw font
shellyal.zip	53873	
shellyan.zip	49080	
shellyvo.zip	53680	
shohl.zip	20489	
show.zip	46400	ATM Font - Show-Light
showboat.zip	47297	ATM font - Showboat, a port of the Mac font
silic.zip	11889	
sinaloa.zip	19995	ATM font - Sinaloa, similar to Capri
slabface.zip	17297	ATM Font - SlabFace
slogan.zip	42431	ATM font - Slogan, based on the Corel Draw font
sntfra.zip	21844	ATM font - Apple Computers San Francisco font
snydersp.zip	34367	ATM Font - Snyder Speed
souvenir.zip	49378	ATM font - Souvenir, based on the Corel Draw font
squir_t1.zip	16226	ATM Font - Squire
starb.zip	41687	
stencilc.zip	16695	ATM Font - StencilCut
stfranci.zip	30427	ATM Font - Saint Francis
stop_t1.zip	14904	ATM Font - Stop
sunset.zip	15565	
sydne.zip	12577	
symbol.zip	38998	
techpho.zip	61942	
tekton.zip	29470	
tempofon.zip	36116	
tempoita.zip	35128	
thomas.zip	32260	
tiempo.zip	50164	ATM Font - MicroTiempo-Normal
tif_b.zip	20664	
tif_e.zip	20777	
tiffhevy.zip	48946	
tiffthin.zip	49179	
title.zip	39765	
trekfont.zip	91477	ATM Font - Various Star Trek Typefaces
tribe.zip	28341	ATM Font - Tribeca
tribeca.zip	42701	

```
typwrite.zip      53667
ultrabla.zip      15071   ATM Font - UltraBlack
umbrathn.zip      41545
uncial.zip        41935   ATM font - Uncial
univers.zip       38498
univlite.zip      34158
unvrsblk.zip      34705
uppereas.zip      27871   ATM font - UpperEastSide (parisian face)
upperwes.zip      71594
upreas.zip        25669   ATM Font - Upper EastSide
upsil.zip         12107
usps_bar.zip      16341   ATM Font - USPS BarCode
vaground.zip      40338
varahcap.zip      49340
vicsec.zip        20784
video_ps.zip      24770   ATM Font - Video Terminal Screen
vireofon.zip      21565   ATM Font - VireoFont
wedgie.zip        25342
western.zip       40684
westsd.zip        79909   ATM Font - UpperWestSide
windsord.zip      40698
zalescap.zip      16617   ATM Font - ZaleskiCaps (based on Art Deco)
~readme.fonts     23156

all/games:
00index.txt        2215
adventf.zip       77297   The original Adventure game
aster221.zip      24990   Asteroids (PM)
battle.zip        12658   Battleship (PM)
bj21.zip          16648   Blackjack 21 (PM)
checker4.zip      47058   Checkers for PM, from Microsoft Systems Journal
chomp.zip         18979   Pac Man (PM)
connect4.zip      17175   A network version of the Connect 4 game
cube10.zip        32607   Rubiks cube game (PM)
cw35Bos2.zip     194593   Czar Wars version 3.58
dfa200.zip        58363   Death from above, multi-player cannon game
drmwld21.zip     209398   The Dreamworld Trilogy, full-screen text adventure
football.zip      39819   American football (PM)
fortunes.zip     333077   Full screen fortune teller with DeskPic module
fractal.zip       69090   Fractal background for PM
jigsaw.zip        64086   Make jigsaw puzzles of .BMP files (PM)
maze_100.zip      22920   Excellent 3D maze game
mine.zip          34777   Minesweeper for OS/2 PM
mjs_11.zip        49570   Mahjongg (PM)
nh311os2.zip     706125   NetHack version 3.11 - D&D-type game
npm.zip           36484   Shows path of planets around stars (PM)
os2cooki.zip      57565   Fortune Cookie
patience.zip       9509   Classic solitaire
pmbio.zip         47941   Biorhythm Chart Maker
pmchess.zip       76403   Chess (PM)
pmdcrypt.zip      11100   Crypto (PM)
pmeyes.zip        19249   Eyes follow your mouse curosr (a la X Windows)
pmfrac.zip       208540   Fractal generator (PM)
pmfrsc.zip       332555   Fractal generator source (PM)
pmmandel.zip      21965   Create Mandelbrot sets
pmmaze1a.zip      14736   Solve the maze (PM/S)
pmnim1.zip        11758   Nim (PM)
```

Appendix H—Sources of OS/2 Information

pmttt.zip	8079	Tic-tac-toe (PM)
poker110.zip	31416	Poker Solitaire
reversi.zip	12100	The ubiquitous reversi (a la Windows 3.0)
sirtet.zip	33171	Tetris (PM)
tangram.zip	23227	A PM game
taquin.zip	8243	Slide the tiles around
tetris13.zip	24014	Full screen text mode tetris, runs in a BBS door
wor.zip	50673	Wizard of Wor: 2 player PM action game
yatzynet.zip	64965	A network-aware version of the Yahtzee game
zapped2.zip	34053	PM game-save the trees from lightning, version 2.0

all/graphics:

00index.txt	5016	
2monitor.zip	33565	Dual monitor (MDA & CGA/EGA/VGA) utilites
banner16.zip	8564	Simple full screen banner printing program
bmp/	-	.BMP images/utilities
clipedit.zip	47291	PM clipboard editor/viewer/printer
collage.zip	18986	An ever-changing graphical collage
cvbmp.zip	9357	Converts Windows 3.0 bitmaps to PM bitmaps
cvtico.zip	18296	Convert Windows 3.0 icons to OS/2 icon format
dbwbound.zip	257800	DBW-Render 1.02 ray tracing
deskp132.zip	93676	Deskpic screen-saver version 1.32
display2.zip	47927	Convert DBW-render images to the GIF format
dskpicds.zip	58160	Lots of deskpic blanking screens
earthani.zip	28772	Deskpic animation of a spinning Earth
ekdss.zip	25460	3 more DeskPic screen save modules
fatbits3.zip	5559	Magnify a portion of the PM screen
foto102.zip	19232	Snapshot utility for text mode screens
gif2bmp.zip	14712	Convert a .GIF file to a .BMP file
icons_hs.zip	7250	PM icons for DOS apps
jpeg4_16.zip	115083	JPEG version 4.0 image compression software (16-bit)
neko111b.zip	25320	Neko the mouse-cursor-chasing cat
nikon11.zip	14592	A PM screen capture utility
os22boun.zip	4681	Deskpic picture - bubbling OS/2 champagne bubbles
os2bounc.zip	4376	Deskpic picture - bouncing OS/2 logo
os2gif.zip	23693	Non-PM .GIF viewer 320x200x256
os2icon1.zip	111284	Assorted PM icons
os2icon2.zip	28879	More PM icons
os2maz.zip	47635	Display 3D mazes on VGA without PM
pmbench.zip	52167	PM Benchmark
pmcap14.zip	30211	Capture Pm screens version 1.4
pmdraw3.zip	110515	PM Draw version 3.0 - bitmap creation tool
pmfli100.zip	33994	Autodesk Animator file player
pmfract.zip	332783	PMFRACT Release 3.0 fractal program for PM
pmgif.zip	27092	PM GIF viewer
pmguts.zip	19090	PM Guts - a graphic demo for OS/2 PM
pmp1201.zip	22015	Pmpaint paint program that creates metafiles
pmpant12.zip	18581	Paint program
pmtopm.zip	32563	Convert 256-color .BMP files to 16-colors
pmwalker.zip	6511	Silly little walking icon
present.zip	46485	A PM tool for creating simple slide shows
presparm.zip	13291	PM combo box examples
qrt15os2.zip	171193	Quick Ray Tracing rendering package
qrtinput.zip	11003	Quick Ray Tracing addition images
showbmp.zip	49497	Show .BMP images (PM/S)
small.zip	14251	Small fixed-width bitmap PM font
smarties.zip	3768	Deskpic picture - smarties candies fill screen

```
spview13.zip       132320  Super Previewer for monochrome graphic images
swarmdss.zip         4866  Deskpic picture - swarm of bees
tpv.zip             12773  Idle graphics display
vfont2.zip           5992  Replacement VGA text mode fonts
viewgif1.zip        40250  GIF picture viewer version 1.60
worm.zip             4513  Deskpic picture - colorful worms erase screen

all/graphics/bmp:
00index.txt          1994
1701_d.bmp         308278  Starship Enterprise from the Next Generation
b1.zip              54766  B1 landing BMP
backgrnd.zip      1059301  Three colorful 1024x768 background bitmaps
bckgrnds.zip      1059301  Bitmaps created to display well as WPS backgrounds
bmpfake1.zip      1166234  Some surreal .BMP files (part 1 of 3)
bmpfake2.zip      1318150  Some surreal .BMP files (part 2 of 3)
bmpfake3.zip       797935  Some surreal .BMP files (part 3 of 3)
bmppics1.zip       155048  A collection of .BMP images
borg.zip           116736  Borg Ship holding the Enterprise in a tractor beam
dinobmp.zip        250096  4 bitmap pictures for the TV show Dinosaurs
dunes.zip          127650  Dunes BMP
ebscuba.zip        165534  The Energizer Bunny Scuba Diving!
ebunny.zip          62335  A collection of Energizer Bunny BMPs
frcbmp.zip         189667  Fractal bitmap desktop background 800x600x256
ibmlogo.zip          4352  Bitmap of a white IBM logo next to an OS/2 logo
junglbmp.zip        70656  OS/2 BMP of a jungle scene sharp and colorful
lupin3.zip         229379  BMP of a picture of LUPIN III cartoon
nt_not.zip           2061  Background bitmap which says NT...Not!
ntreal.zip         101847  Not too real: a strange surrealistic image (256 colors)
os2_bmp.zip       1220142  A few 256 color background bitmaps
os2bmp.zip          26208  2 bitmaps of the OS/2 logo done in gray relief
os2tile.zip          4224  The champagne bubble OS/2 logos adjusted
porsch.zip          48423  Porsche 944 BMP
redskin.zip          4895  Washington Redskins BMP
roman.zip          132603  Roman columns & arches desktop background
textures.zip       716215  100 24-bit BMPs converted from Mac for backgrounds
tilos2.zip          14700  Several tiled backgrounds
tree.zip            22206  A background picture of a tree in moonlight
winkill.zip         19880  A .BMP picture of the enterprise killing Windows
xmaps1.zip         205862  BUMPS and PASTEL backdrop bitmaps
yoda4.zip           56918  Yoda with sunglasses

all/info:
00index.txt          6560
16550.doc           17959  Information on using high speed 16550 UARTS for OS/2
apar5100.zip        39227  .INF file listing fixes in CSD WR05100 for OS/2 1.3
belowzro.zip       285876  Below Zero, the cool computer company, OS/2 catalog
cdbook.zip           1728  Contents of the IBM OS/2 Online Book Collection
comhack.txt         10506  How to hack a COM port to use a high IRQ
csp2ad.txt           1126  Free Demo of IBM CSP/2AD available
cua91.txt           19812  IBM SAA Common User Access Controls Library/2
faq/                    -  OS/2 Frequently Asked Questions
forum/                  -  OS/2 discussion forum archive
ftnguide.nat        16954  IBM Field Television Network broadcast guide
galciv.zip         106574  Announcment — Galatic Civilization OS/2 game
hobbes.ps            8184  Description of the Walnut Creek CDROM Hobbes OS/2 disc
➥(PostScript)
hobbes.txt           3277  Description of the Walnut Creek CDROM Hobbes OS/2 disc
```

Appendix H—Sources of OS/2 Information

```
hpfs.zip              65718   Microsoft Journal technical info on HPFS
ibcat10.zip          122351   Catalog for Indelible Blue in Raleigh, NC
jargn299.zip         785712   A series of .INF files which explain computer jargon
mousepat.txt           1281   Move the mouse port to some other IRQ than 3/4
os2.inf               68044
os2_apps.txt         176616   IBMs list of all 16-bit OS/2 applications
os2books.txt          13863   A list of programming-related OS/2 books
os2dinfo.txt           2560   IBM OS/2 Developer Magazine information
os2mag.txt             3354   IBM OS/2 Developer Magazine Circulation
os2tcpip.zip          46446   Information on IBM TCP/IP 1.2
os2traps.txt           1385   Likely causes for the mysterious Trap messages
os2world.zip          63578   OS/2 BBSes around the world
quatec.txt             8870   Info on Quatech communications adapters
s3info.zip             6447   Info on 16-bit S3 display drivers
startkit/                 -   COMP.BINARIES.OS2 starters kit
strategy.txt          64291   IBM Personal Software Products: Product Line Update
tcpip12.ann           39898   Announcement: IBM TCP/IP 1.2 for OS/2
tcpip121.txt           2857   How to get IBM TCP/IP 1.2.1
tinf34.zip           649216   Listing of OS/2 programs (.INF format) version 3.4
xgaps2.ann            70656   Product Announcement: IBM PS/2 XGA-2 Display Adapter/A

all/info/faq:
00index.txt             800
faq19g.zip            47787   OS/2 Frequently Asked Questions, for OS/2 1.3
faq201.zip           137619   OS/2 Frequently Asked Questions, release 2.01
faq21c.zip           213809   Frequently Asked Questions for OS/2 2.1, release C
faq21d.zip           229932   Frequently Asked Questions for OS/2 2.1, release D
os2winfq.zip           3553   Frequently Asked Questions about Win-OS/2
ostechsp.faq           5612   OS/2 2.0 Technical Support FAQ
pfaq20as.zip          20629   OS/2 Programming FAQ v2.0 (ASCII Version)
pfaq20in.zip          38495   OS/2 Programming FAQ v2.0
pfaq21as.zip          69758   OS/2 Programming FAQ v2.1 (ASCII Version)
pfaq21in.zip         114505   OS/2 Programming FAQ v2.1 (INF version)
pfaq22.zip           116682   OS/2 Programming FAQ v2.2
pfaq221.zip          190598   OS/2 Programming FAQ v2.21

all/info/forum:
00index.txt            3048
frm9201.01            42647   OS/2 Discussion Forum, Volume 9201 Issue 01
frm9201.02            21073   OS/2 Discussion Forum, Volume 9201 Issue 02
frm9201.03            39618   OS/2 Discussion Forum, Volume 9201 Issue 03
frm9201.04            42619   OS/2 Discussion Forum, Volume 9201 Issue 04
frm9202.01            30947   OS/2 Discussion Forum, Volume 9202 Issue 01
frm9202.02            23768   OS/2 Discussion Forum, Volume 9202 Issue 02
frm9202.03            23768   OS/2 Discussion Forum, Volume 9202 Issue 03
frm9202.04            17617   OS/2 Discussion Forum, Volume 9202 Issue 04
frm9203.01            20995   OS/2 Discussion Forum, Volume 9203 Issue 01
frm9203.02            39610   OS/2 Discussion Forum, Volume 9203 Issue 02
frm9203.03            39610   OS/2 Discussion Forum, Volume 9203 Issue 03
frm9203.04            33656   OS/2 Discussion Forum, Volume 9203 Issue 04
frm9203.05            31269   OS/2 Discussion Forum, Volume 9203 Issue 05
frm9204.01            44246   OS/2 Discussion Forum, Volume 9204 Issue 01
frm9204.02            38882   OS/2 Discussion Forum, Volume 9204 Issue 02
frm9205.01            50653   OS/2 Discussion Forum, Volume 9205 Issue 01
frm9205.02a           38342   OS/2 Discussion Forum, Volume 9205 Issue 02a
frm9205.02b           32973   OS/2 Discussion Forum, Volume 9205 Issue 02b
frm9205.02c           38792   OS/2 Discussion Forum, Volume 9205 Issue 02c
```

```
frm9205.03       25461   OS/2 Discussion Forum, Volume 9205 Issue 03
frm9205.04       31391   OS/2 Discussion Forum, Volume 9205 Issue 04
frm9206.01       91418   OS/2 Discussion Forum, Volume 9206 Issue 01
frm9206.02       44669   OS/2 Discussion Forum, Volume 9206 Issue 02
frm9206.03       34770   OS/2 Discussion Forum, Volume 9206 Issue 03
frm9206.04       27587   OS/2 Discussion Forum, Volume 9206 Issue 04
frm9206.05       65874   OS/2 Discussion Forum, Volume 9206 Issue 05
frm9207.01       56046   OS/2 Discussion Forum, Volume 9207 Issue 01
frm9207.02a      36025   OS/2 Discussion Forum, Volume 9207 Issue 02a
frm9207.02b      41055   OS/2 Discussion Forum, Volume 9207 Issue 02b
frm9207.02c      12275   OS/2 Discussion Forum, Volume 9207 Issue 02c
frm9207.03a      34259   OS/2 Discussion Forum, Volume 9207 Issue 03a
frm9207.03b      40291   OS/2 Discussion Forum, Volume 9207 Issue 03b
frm9207.03c       7448   OS/2 Discussion Forum, Volume 9207 Issue 03c
frm9208.01       59456   OS/2 Discussion Forum, Volume 9208 Issue 01
frm9208.02       41936   OS/2 Discussion Forum, Volume 9208 Issue 02
frm9208.03       32291   OS/2 Discussion Forum, Volume 9208 Issue 03
frm9209.01       78134   OS/2 Discussion Forum, Volume 9209 Issue 01
frm9210.01      138425   OS/2 Discussion Forum, Volume 9210 Issue 01
frm9210.02       35713   OS/2 Discussion Forum, Volume 9210 Issue 02
frm9210.03       35686   OS/2 Discussion Forum, Volume 9210 Issue 03
frm9212.01a      38768   OS/2 Discussion Forum, Volume 9212 Issue 01a
frm9212.01b      35125   OS/2 Discussion Forum, Volume 9212 Issue 01b
frm9212.01c      42769   OS/2 Discussion Forum, Volume 9212 Issue 01c

all/info/startkit:
00index.txt        432
booz.exe         25651   A simple ZOO 2.1 file extractor
policy.txt        5590   Rules for Comp.binaries.os2 submissions
rxdecode.zip     43621   An intellgent UU/XX-decoder
startkit         43754   Starters kit, comp.binaries.os2
startkt.2a       55547
startkt.2b       27733
startkt1         26356
startkt2         82583
uudecode.exe     16400   UUDECODE
uuencode.exe     14800   UUENCODE

all/miscutil:
00index.txt       2410
aclock2.zip      18979   Analog clock with alarm
acts11.zip        8339   Set system date/time from ACTS mainted by NIS
alpm15.zip      126593   "Active life" planning/calendaring program version 1.5
apptype.zip       9884   Determine .EXE file type (OS/2, Windows, etc.)
ask.zip          24760   Command-file prompt and response
billbrd.zip      17175   Displays billboard message after bootup
chkbkpm.zip      59161   Checkbook program (PM)
clkcal.zip       32991   Displays clock & calendar
clockpm.zip      31592   Clock including alarams and chimes (PM)
cpm.zip          74941   CP/M emulator (D)
cshell2.zip      43105   Text mode shell runs fullscreen OS/2 in <4MB
icontalk.zip      3688   Display messages below icons/in title bars
itsnow11.zip     37724   Displays time/date in a variety of formations (PM)
jargon.zip       25188   PM/WPS hypertext browser for the jargon file
katcal.zip       58337   Programmable calculator (PM)
klock2d.zip      37148   Set/unset Num/Caps/Scroll-lock from OS/2 & DOS
mailmind.zip    111649   Network NetBIOS protocol mail reminder
```

Appendix H—Sources of OS/2 Information

```
mushp71.zip       288694   Mail Users Shell
na10se.zip         39348   Numerical Assistant, scientific calculator
nsort.zip          28262   New Sorting Utility
odomtr10.zip       24367   A mouse odometer
os2exec.zip        24764   Execute OS/2 programs from a DOS session (v1.1b)
par141.zip         70654   A paragraph reformatter
pcalc.zip          20194   Calculator (PM)
pmcardsr.zip       56081   Cardfile for Presentation Manager
pmpopup.zip         2536   Write a short message to the screen in a dialog box
pmworld1.zip       45437   Display map of the world with time zone clocks
remin310.zip      382590   Sophisticated reminder (and calendar) program
row2r01.zip        12936   Set the number of rows displayed for text programs
sc621.zip         395319   Spreadsheet Calculator sc 6.21
scrutl18.zip       20960   Screen blanker, also show free memory & date
sfos2.zip           5956   OS/2 utility for Northgate Omnikey keyboard
split.zip          24487   File Splitting Utility
times21.zip        96403   TimeStar 2.1 time scheduler
ux_alarm.zip        2725   Unix-like alarm (S)
vfont2.zip         29312   Change your VIO fonts
vgasync.zip         2429   Utility to keep VGA sync polarities negative
view.zip            6926   Display text file in a window
wd30.zip          161987   Database program
wlo10.zip        1320057   Windows libraries for OS/2 with Windows applets

all/mmedia:
00index.txt          162
mpudd103.zip       61392   Generic MIDI MPU-401 drivers, version 1.03
os2sn2.zip         30911   OS/2 sound sample player through speaker

all/network:
00index.txt         5961
3c507_92.zip      346703   3Com EtherDisk for EtherLink 16 & 16 TP Adapters
3com.zip           92513   OS/2 drivers for 3com ethernet cards (incl. elnk3)
bmr_110.zip        28648   Broadcast Message Receiver for Netware
btng2exe.zip      833279   Beholder, an RMON compliant ethernet monitor
btng2src.zip      896002   Beholder, an RMON compliant ethernet monitor (sources)
cd_shr.zip          1458   How to share a CD-ROM on a LAN Server (3.0) system
cnfgls13.zip       63019   Tuning aid for LS 1.3 - Lotus/Excel spreadsheets
conman.zip        119385   Graphically display available PM Lan network resources
connect/              -    The IBM TCP/IP Connection newsletter
elm23exe.zip      446896   ELM 2.3 mail processor executables (requires UUCP)
elm23src.zip      504374   ELM 2.3 mail processor sources
fsp2_03b.zip      257177   Port of FSP for OS/2 (req. IBM TCP/IP)
gg243890.zip      359806   NetWare Related Protocols - BookManager document
gg243893.zip      389491   Netware in TCP/IP environments - BookManager file
lantasti.zip        2321   How to install LANtastic on an OS/2 machine
lsshdo.zip         21760   OS/2 Lan Server command-line shutdown utility
nbr11.zip         381420   Eight Layer Systems NDIS Serial Bridge
ndis/                 -    NDIS device drivers
ne2000.zip         25452   Using IBM Lan Server 2.0 with Novel NE2000 Adapter
netwar.zip          1406   Integrating NetWare and OS/2
nwibm.zip           3552   NetWare IBM Coexistence Guidelines
odinsp.zip        212774   Support NDIS protocol in a NetWare configuration
osrm216.zip       485446   Osrm2 LAN System version 1.3.15
pmnews.zip         75246   PM front-end for snews
rxlan10.zip       188124   REXXLAN/2, REXX API extension for LAN Server networks
slipcall.zip        7663   Source to IBM TCP/IP 1.2.1 SLIPCALL program
```

The Internet

```
snews_20.zip      341011  Simple threaded news reader for OS/2 with UUPC 1.11
tune.zip           65891  Configure Lan Server 1.3 via an Excel spreadsheet
tune05.zip         58785  Spreadsheet to generate configs for LAN Server 3.0
xutil091.zip       51520  Nodelist Net lister, node extractor
yatzynet.zip       64965  A network-aware version of the Yahtzee game

all/network/connect:
00index.txt          356
tcpnewc1.txt       11506  The IBM TCP/IP Connection - Issue 92-01
tcpnewc2.txt       10377  The IBM TCP/IP Connection - Issue 92-02
tcpnewc3.txt        8658  The IBM TCP/IP Connection - Issue 92-03
tcpnewc4.txt        8563  The IBM TCP/IP Connection - Issue 92-04
tcpnewc5.txt        9332  The IBM TCP/IP Connection - Issue 92-05

all/network/ndis:
00index.txt         3413
depca12c.zip       18341  DEPCA driver w/NIF working w/IBM TCP/IP 1.2.1 LAPS
depcao.zip         16099  DEPCA, DE100, DE200, and DE210 drivers
domain.arc         19436  Microsoft Primary Domain Istallation Program
elnkiio.zip         9122  NDIS drivers for the 3Com Etherlink II
elnko.zip           7589  Ndis drivers for the 3Com EtherLink boards
elnkplo.zip        10971  Ndis drivers for the 3Com EtherLink Plus
ethiieo.zip         7919  NDIS drivers for the Nokia Data Ethernet IIe
everexo.zip         6626  NDIS drivers for the Everex SpeedLink /PC16
exp16.zip          15519  NDIS drivers for Inter EthernetExpress 16 v.2.36
hpfserr.zip         2964  Text file explaning HPFS386 Internal Errors
hplano.zip          9371  NDIS drivers for the HP Ethertwist PC LINK(8,16 & MCA)
ibmnetao.zip        8217  NDIS drivers: IBM PC Network Adapter II/A (MCA)
ibmneto.zip         8176  NDIS drivers for the IBM PC Network (Baseband) Adapters
ibmtoko.zip         9477  NDIS drivers: IBM Token-Ring Adapter(II, /A, 16/4(A)
ibmtrdb.zip        63215  NDIS driver for IBM LANStreamer Token-Ring card
mac586o.zip        12173  NDIS Drivers for the DCA 10BASE cards
macwdo.zip         10102  NDIS drivers: Western Digital EtherCard Plus(/A)
msarco.zip         10337  NDIS drivers: Standard Microsystems SMC Arcnet PC130E
ncrslano.zip       14579  NDIS drivers for the NCR StarCard 8-bit ISA Card
ncrtrno.zip         9727  NDIS drivers for the NCR 4mb Token-Ring Adapter
ndis.txt            3553
ndis.zip           22974  1990 LanServer NDIS upgrade: new netbind.exe
ne1000o.zip         9534  NDIS drivers for the Ne1000 card
ne2000o.zip        10085  NDIS drivers for the Ne2000 card
ne3200o.zip        10165  NDIS drivers for the Ne3200 card
ni5210o.zip         7393  NDIS drivers for the Racal Interlan NI5210
ni6510.zip          9326  NDIS drivers for the Racal Interlan NI6510
ni6510o.zip        16538  OS/2 NDIS drivers: Racal Interlan NI6510
ni9210o.zip         7434  NDIS drivers for the Racal Interlan NI9210
npafddid.arc       15935  DOS NDIS drivers:Network Peripherals NPI-ISA
npafddio.arc       15960  OS/2 NDIS drivers:Network Peripherals NPI-ISA
npefddid.arc       16478  DOS NDIS drivers:Network Peripherals NP-EISA
npefddio.arc       16596  OS/2 NDIS drivers:Network Peripherals NP-EISA
olitoko.zip        61652  NDIS drivers for the Olicom 16 Bit ISA Token card
olmgloss.zip       45469  OS/2 Lan Manager Version 2.00 Glossary List
olmindex.zip       46140  OS/2 Lan Manager 2.00 Index List
s12960.zip          8587
s12963.zip          7434
s12965.zip          7393
s12967.zip         16158
s13389.zip          6687
```

Appendix H—Sources of OS/2 Information

```
s13393.zip          11599
s13395.zip           5912
s13397.zip           8622
s13399.zip          20071
s13401.zip          19775  NDIS drivers for Ungermann Bas NICps2 ethernet card
spidero.zip          8929  NDIS drivers:Spider Communications SC-100E
tccarco.zip          7550  NDIS drivers for the Thomas Conrad TC6145
tlnko.zip            8083  NDIS drivers for the 3COM TokenLink (3C603)
tokwdo.zip          10050  NDIS drivers for the Western Digital WD8005TR(15TR)
tsbethro.zip         8218  NDIS drivers for the Toshiba ToshibaLan adapter
ubneio.zip          20198  NDIS drivers for the Ungermann-Bass PC2030 cards
ubneps.zip          26088  NDIS driver for Ungermann Bass NICps2 ethernet card
wavelano.zip        15788  NDIS drivers for the NCR WaveLan adapter

all/patches:
00index.txt           217
c16_a.zip         1680567  Watcom C/C++^16 patch level A
f16_a.zip          680703  Watcom Fortran/77^16 patch level A
jr07011.zip        124545  Extended Services V1.0 APAR JR070011 for hostprint

all/printer:
00index.txt          1337
2upprt.zip          10696  Print 2UP or 1UP on laser printers - version 2.4
a4print.zip         38552  Prints very compact listings on HP LaserJets
addlpt.zip           2679  Add LPT3-LPT9 to the OS/2 Print Manager selection menu
cprint.zip          22008  Intelligent printing for dot-matrix printers
dcfvba.zip          44431  Converts HPPCL streams to IBM DCF (Script/US)
dlst.zip            20973  Print compact listings on HP Laserjet Series II
hex2prn.zip         17841  Send hex codes directly to the printer
lj2os2.zip          64367  Print 2-up on an HP Laserjet series printer
lj2up.zip           26063  Prints 2-up on HP LaserJets
nec95_10.zip         5040  Switch NEC Silentwriter 95 through emulation modes
nec95mon.zip         8439  NEC Silentwriter 95 print monitor
nensc113.zip        63384  Nenscript 1.13 ASCII—>Postscript translator
pmenv.zip           28139  Envelope printer (PM)
poslp.zip           14876  Prints listings in PostScript
posprint.zip        26028  Prints text in PostScript
pr.zip              29635  Print formatter
prpcx2.zip          27946  Print PCX files on a Postscript printer
prtcal.zip          15508  Print monthly planning calendar
ps_up237.zip        27461  Print ASCII text files on Postscript printers
sw50.zip            23126  Sideways printing on NEC/Epson dot-matrix printers

all/program:
00index.txt          6281
aclinf.zip           8406  Information about how PM translates accelerators
asdt.zip           104269  A great debugger for OS/2 1.3
avbrowse.zip        29961  Dialog Box usage sample source code
bitblt.zip           6569  Demo blitter routines
c7os2.zip         2158080  OS/2 hosted add-in for Microsoft C/C++ 7.0
cb.zip              11723  C beautifier
cdecl.zip           27981  Converts C declarations to English and back
combo.zip           14892  Combo Box support routines
common.zip         264831  Common/2 Subroutine Library version 1.0
cpr34src.zip        21303  C cross reference utility (S)
cprt102.zip         54966  A C source code printing system (family mode)
```

File	Size	Description
cs69.zip	89758	Compiler shell for Microsoft languages, Bison, and Flex
cserial.zip	1849	C program fragment for accessing serial port
curs13_2.zip	135915	A port of Curses to OS/2
cursor.zip	5966	Sample file to illustrate usage of make
datpatch.zip	17994	Change the current date/time in an executable module
dayfield.zip	29738	A subclass for handling day-of-the-week input
dbaseos2.zip	10362	Example code for reading dBase III .dbf files
dentist.zip	24947	Resource extractor version 1.1
dlghigh.zip	17120	Sample code for Listbox programming
dmake38x.zip	106378	Dmake version 3.8
dx.zip	14905	Shows makeup & dependency info about EXE/DLL modules
ef_wday.zip	29738	PM code subclass for days of the week input
f77_draw.zip	43821	Full screen (non-PM) graphics library for Fortran
fchk261.zip	333122	Fortran checker version 2.6.1
forth.zip	20200	A Forth interpreter
gamept.zip	6479	Sample source for using a joystick (w/driver)
grafdemo.zip	17013	Demo/source code for programming non-PM graphics
hlpdk80.zip	354683	RL help engine, support for DOS,OS/2,DESQview & Win3.x
hrtimer.zip	20708	Sample code/driver for a high resolution timer
icon8_0.zip	257014	Icon programming language
icon8doc.zip	468376	Icon documentation (Postscript and ASCII)
indent.zip	40349	C source code formatter
invoke10.zip	4837	Drag and drop interface sample code
ipfcpp.zip	34289	IPFC Preprocessor (INF files) version 1.11
ipfcpp10.zip	27665	A preprocessor for the IPF compiler (.INF files)
j_os2.zip	121583	J, an APL-like programming language
jcldoc.zip	123639	App for documenting/flowcharting MVS JCL
jrcpp.zip	184686	ANSI C porting preprocessor
m_ext23.zip	29869	Extensions for the Microsoft Editor
makemb.zip	2157	A utility for binding message files to executables
midisrc.zip	6658	Source for an OS/2 MIDI driver
msjournl/	-	Microsoft Systems Journal program listings
os2_nls.zip	24851	Some OS/2 programming examples
os2lint.zip	26317	Some C programming tools - lint
os2xlisp.zip	91464	A Lisp interpreter for OS/2
oxlexe.zip	110564	XLisp for OS/2
pamake18.zip	64887	PAMAKE-a public domain make program
patch212.zip	148310	Larry Walls patch program
pctjos2.zip	15864	PC Tech Journal dual-boot code
pdcurs20.zip	225323	Public Domain curses version 2.0 for OS/2 & DOS
pipes.zip	11148	Named Pipe Client/Server Debugging Utility
pmdvl2.zip	38787	An integrated programming shell for PM
ppos2.zip	24316	ASM source for power program
proc.zip	8557	Info about undocumented functions to get process info
rexx/	-	Rexx source code/utilities
runpli1a.zip	103840	PL/I interpreter
scalc.zip	40857	SourceCalc, programmers calculator
sde.zip	110162	Systemax development environment
setl2.zip	681000	Setl/2 programming environment
spy4v12.zip	49603	Message and queue spy version 1.2 (PM)
sqzh102.zip	23032	SQZh v1.01 - a C header file compressor
tagos2.zip	7683	Public domain version of MARKEXE
trac_099.zip	94392	Software development tracking system, req. OS/2 EE
tracer10.zip	23620	Debugging tool (PM)
zfrms110.zip	288915	Z-Forms text window libs, supports 16/32-bit compilers

Appendix H—Sources of OS/2 Information

```
all/program/msjournl:
00index.txt         1558
msjhello.zoo       12598   Sample Hello program
msjmesg.zoo         1275   Utility showing to create .MSG files
msjpms2.zoo        12766   Presentation Manager Application Skeleton 2
msjqueue.zoo        5226   How to use OS/2 queues from compiled BASIC
msjtask.zoo         4817   Sample utility to remove the Task Manager
msjv2_2.zoo         5779   Vol 2; Issue 2; May 1987
msjv3_1.zoo        14628   Vol 3; Issue 1; January 1988
msjv3_12.zoo        4338   Vol 3; Issue 1; January 1988 Part 2
msjv3_2.zoo         4194   Vol 3; Issue 2; March 1988
msjv3_3.zoo         6520   Vol 3; Issue 3; May 1988
msjv3_32.zoo        2534   Vol 3; Issue 3; May 1988 GPI Examples
msjv3_33.zoo        1497   Vol 3; Issue 3; May 1988 Semaphore Examples
msjv4_6.zoo        38440   Vol 4; Issue 6; October 1989
msjv5_1.zoo       155450   Vol 5; Issue 1; December 1989
msjv5_2.zoo       112008   Vol 5; Issue 2; April 1990
msjvpms.zoo        12670   OS/2 Presentation Manager Application Skeleton
s12331.zoo         16435
s12349.zoo         28335
s12362.zoo         23932
s12364.zoo          9213
s12380.zoo          1227
s12381.zoo          1816
s12405.zoo          9238
s12408.zoo          4059
s12409.zoo         18758
s12410.zoo        110412
s12411.zoo         66776
s12442.zoo         39095
s12444.zoo         13319
s12447.zoo          6799
s12518.zoo         46517
s12519.zoo         57636
s12546.zoo         23516
s12547.zoo         24752
s12602.zoo         23217
s12626.zoo          3870
s12629.zoo          8982
s12720.zoo          9921

all/program/rexx:
00index.txt          520
color.zip           3948   Set screen colors for OS/2 text sessions
defprn.cmd           569   A REXX script which determines the default printer port
deldir.zip          1910   A REXX script with deletes an entire directory subtree
prxutl10.zip       70331   A collection of REXX utilities/functions
rexxtacy.zip      154782   REXXTACY - REXX to C translator
rxps17.zip          1707   Rexx Process Report Command version 1.7
timeset.zip         2381   Set time base on Naval Observatory clock (REXX)

all/sysutils:
00index.txt         4300
4os216.zip        266752   4OS/2 16 v1.11, OS/2 1.x alternative command line shell
alias11.zip        38733   Command line editor
ameval1.zip       243065   Applications Manager - Part 1 (executables)
ameval2.zip        92788   Applications Manager - Part 2 (bind file for database)
```

ameval3.zip	40926	Applications Manager - Part 3 (sample files)
ameval4.zip	76994	Applications Manager - Part 4 (documentation)
appt.zip	17707	A Unix port of an appointment calendar program
atkey.zip	2386	Turns off NumLock key if it is on
atrgf21.zip	39969	Run commands at specified dates/times - REXX
calendar.zip	13836	Calendar display (PM)
checklim.zip	13631	Displays what OS/2 thinks your memory limit is
chkansi2.zip	24681	Checks for viruses in ANSI text files
choose.zip	4235	Allows menus in .CMD files
chron23.zip	46763	Schedule programs to run at any date/time
clip11.zip	42012	Schedule programs to run at any date/time
clipit10.zip	22422	An OS/2 text mode clipboard utility
clonboot.zip	5736	Patch for AT clones to allow installation disk to boot
color.zip	5951	Change full screen text colors
cpuload.zip	5147	PM CPU Load monitor
cpumeter.zip	48940	Display percentage CPU activity in a window
cpumon3.zip	75618	OS/2 system performance monitor
cputach.zip	13366	Shows CPU load on an analog meter (PM)
dates1a.zip	33259	Edit dates/times into a command line & execute it
dhrymon.zip	12559	Displays a graph of CPU load measured in dhrystones
freetime.zip	24645	A screen blanker/CPU graph
fshl125.zip	85962	F-Shell version 1.25, CMD.EXE enhancement
globen.zip	58826	Global Environment Package
gone.zip	3565	Keyboard lock (PM)
iplpau.zip	12672	Put a pause between boot and PM startup
kbd.exe	4736	Control the repeat rate and LEDs of MF2 keyboards
kernrev.zip	1034	Print major/minor revision # of your OS/2
map57.zip	33569	List running processes and threads (D)
memsz162.zip	144455	Display running status of memory, swap file, etc.
menumin3.zip	51943	Choose among multiple configs for convenience/security
mole.zip	17222	Mole, view/terminate badly behaved/crashed programs
mon120.zip	21911	Displays CPU activity as a graph
os2free.zip	5353	Shows RAM, date and time
os2stat.zip	2239	Prints global environment table
oshexdec.zip	18605	Hex<->Decimal converter
osrm202.zip	19127	OS/2 resource monitor program
phymem.zip	7252	Show memory
pmalarm.zip	8833	Pop up at a specified time
pmasc.zip	5638	ASCII code table display (PM)
pmfree.zip	21367	Shows free/claimed memory/disk space (PM)
pmlock.zip	6593	Lock out use of the keyboard
pmquick.zip	7080	A program starter
pmsleuth.zip	54236	Window snooper for PM (S)
pmtest.zip	45268	Application Regression testing tool (PM)
qsystem.zip	23850	Query system-display hardware config info
qwkswi12.zip	14731	QuickSwitch 1.2—switch between apps via hotkeys
ramscop2.zip	22999	Show any part of OS/2 memory
reboot.zip	9497	Program to reboot OS/2
setpri.zip	7773	Set the priority/delta of running programs
size.zip	1692	Set the number of lines displayed in VIO windows
spawn203.zip	59130	New command-processor for DOS & OS/2
stats.zip	2597	Show OS/2 system statistics
swapdcp.zip	19640	Change the keyboard layout as you see fit
swapsz11.zip	3811	Displays running status of OS/2 swap space
switch10.zip	7357	Remove tasks from ALT-ESC round robin
syscols2.zip	50595	Set colors for desktop-includes several color schemes
sysinfo.zip	44717	Various system info in a window

Appendix H—Sources of OS/2 Information

```
timeline.zip      29545   Display date and time in a window (PM)
udesktop.zip      30693   Manage the OS/2 desktop from the command line
vswitch.zip       13179   A text mode-based task switch for OS/2
wait.zip           3442   Sleep for a while
wheel1.zip        97811   V1.1 select PM colors DLL
wl.zip            14607   Lock out keyboard use
xtime0.zip        21368   Start a program at a future time

all/unix:
00index.txt        5573
awf.zip           23641   NROFF-like program
cal29a.zip        50057   Matulichs enhanced Unix-like cal[endar]
cawf.zip         100189   NROFF-like text formatter
compress.zip      42290   Compress 4.0
cronrgf11a.zip    32272   UNIX cron - REXX
cvs13bin.zip     231394   CVS 1.3 revision control system (requires rcs56)
cvs13src.zip     453390   CVS 1.3 revision control system (sources)
fgrep11.zip       49901   GNU fgrep, version 1.1
file39a.zip      211833   Darwin's file ( 1 ) command - guesses file type
flex23.zip       208467   Fast lexical analyzer version 2.3
flip1os2.zip      34194   Convert Unix text files to OS/2 & vice-versa
gawk211.zip      201146   GNU AWK version 2.11
gawk215.zip      601333   GNU awk 2.15 - Hankerson
gnubc.zip        186423   GNU arbitrary precision calculator
gnudbm.zip       225475   GNU database manager libraries (Microsoft lib format)
gnudiff.zip      225400   GNU DIFF and DIFF3 utilities, version 1.15
gnufu.zip        778889   Many Unix file utilities like head, cat, ls, etc.
gnuindnt.zip     163128   GNU indent - C source code formatter
gnuinfo.zip      465200   GNU hypertext/online-help tool
gnum4.zip        203669   GNU m4 macro processor
gnutar.zip       217589   GNU tar (HPFS aware)
grep15.zip       269665   GNU e?grep - fast lazy-state deterministic matcher
gz124-16.zip      73963   GNU gzip file compression
gzip-2.zip       212631   GNU gzip, replacement for compress
gzip124.zip      266474   GNU gzip file compression (sources)
less177.zip      218915   Less 1.77, an enhanced more
ms_sh21c.zip     149216   MS-SH 2.1c, an SH shell for OS/2 and DOS
newshar.zip       21892   Shar and Unshar: Create and Extract Shell Archives
nice10.zip        19855   Unix nice = give up timeslices to other programs
pdmake.zip        26120   Unix-0like public domain make
perl4019.zip     929909   Perl programming environment
pmload11.zip      11180   A port of xload - display graph of system load
pushd21.zip        5226   REXX programs for implementing csh pushd/popd/dirs
rcs56exe.zip     882095   RCS 5.6 - resource control system (executables)
rcs56src.zip     922531   RCS 5.6 - resource control system (sources)
rh2os2.zip        60824   RawHide - recursive file finder
sed106.zip        91205   GNU sed - stream text editor
shar349.zip       84740   Unix shar/unshar v 3.49
strings.zip       21104   Print the strings in executable files
sum.zip            8069   Unix checksums
tar.zip           53622   Tar file archiving utility
tex/                  =   TeX typesetting language
ue312ins.zip     846868   MicroEMACS 3.12 for DOS, Windows and OS/2
which210.zip      50185   A clone of the Unix locate command
```

```
all/unix/tex:
00index.txt        2876
betatest/             -
bonus/                -
psfonts/              -
texdisk1.zip     913476
texdisk2.zip    1199335
texdisk3.zip    1161230
texdisk4.zip    1200867
texdisk5.zip    1168170
texdisk6.zip    1129983
texfonts/             -
utils/                -
zemtex/               -

all/unix/tex/betatest:
00index.txt         433
README.TST         3937
btexb8.zip       464422
dvidrv87_14s.zip
                 448181
dvidrv_14s.zip  1033814
dvispell_01b.zip  52171
emtexwps.doc       4508
maketcp.zip       26335
mfb1.zip         957225
mfjob11l.zip      99304
mfpm.zip          12216
pkeditpm.zip      87230
tex386b8.zip     219721
texb5.zip        419511
texit.cmd          2163
texit2.cmd          446

all/unix/tex/bonus:
00index.txt         416
bm2font.zip      526163
drivers.zip      609128
dvips.zip        463842
dvipssrc.zip     391983
dviwin.zip       197751
emtex.bon          3368
emtex.ps         141548
emtex.tex         45275
morebin.zip      205093
moremf.zip       318363
moresty.zip      315211
newlatex.zip    1039144
ps2pk12.zip      313140
psnfss.zip       209093
seminar.zip      146495

all/unix/tex/psfonts:
00index.txt         338
README.PS          6201
fonttst1.tex       2666
fonttst2.tex        955
```

Appendix H—Sources of OS/2 Information

```
lj.cnf                334
newfonts.sub          820
ps_0.fli         1260136
ps_1.fli          318265
ps_2.fli          485093
ps_3.fli          515917
ps_4.fli          631781
ps_5.fli          726233
ps_h.fli          290905

all/unix/tex/texfonts:
00index.txt          904
README.fx_med_fonts
                    1025
fx_med_0.fli      332733
fx_med_1.fli      378921
fx_med_2.fli      436317
fx_med_3.fli      508265
fx_med_4.fli      597645
fx_med_5.fli      716081
fx_med_h.fli      353621
fxfonts1.zip      934202
fxfonts2.zip      898863
fxfonts3.zip      820056
fxfonts4.zip      728688
itofont1.zip      775355
itofont2.zip      596666
itofont3.zip      860343
ljfonts1.zip      865921
ljfonts2.zip      951969
ljfonts3.zip      979845
ljfonts4.zip      824288
ljfonts5.zip      462315
p6hfont1.zip      941776
p6hfont2.zip      938987
p6hfont3.zip      992289
p6hfont4.zip      823568
p6hfont5.zip      980518
p6hfont6.zip      984536
p6lfont1.zip      911797
p6lfont2.zip      784378
p6lfont3.zip      950418
p6mfont1.zip      855837
p6mfont2.zip      978061
p6mfont3.zip      935513
p6mfont4.zip      764579

all/unix/tex/utils:
00index.txt          182
detex25a.zip      146646
dvidvi.zip         58727
dvips551.zip      515518
dvips55s.zip      347015
lachec18.zip       61246
pmtex.zip          50028
```

```
all/unix/tex/zemtex:
00index.txt          208
lj1990.cnf           388
lj1992.cnf           426
lj_amsz.fli       251222
oz.tex             44919
texinput.zip       17676
tfm.zip            14283
zemtex11.doc        6965

ibm:
00index.txt        37768
epm/                   -    Enhanced Presentation Manager Editor Files
ews/                   -    Employee Written Software
info/                  -    IBM product announcements and OS/2 maintenance info
lanserv/               -    Lanserver Software
misc/                  -    Miscellaneous information and drivers
neworg.os2           574    How the ibm archive is organized
os2fixes/              -    OS/2 Patches and Drivers
readme.os2           419    Licence agreement for ibm files
servpak/               -    2.0GA service pack: 32bit GRE and bug fixes
tcpip/                 -    TCPIP patches: NFS, Xserver, X.25, ect

ibm/epm:
00index.txt         1161
ebooke.zip        513661    EPM add-on: facilitates creating tagged source files
epmapp.zip        162034    Application Files: Unzip into \os2\apps
epmasi.zip         38765
epmatr.zip         27618
epmbbs.pck          2429
epmbbs.txt          7647
epmbk.zip         398245    BOOKSHELF help files: Unzip into your BOOKS directory
epmdll.zip        287672    dlls required to run epm
epmhlp.zip         88639    EPM help files
epmmac.zip        290962    5.51 Macro Compiler: Unzip into its own directory
epmrex.zip         10549    Sample Rexx Macros to run with the Rexx shell
epmsmp.zip         66891    Sample macro code
etkbbs.pck          3376    OS/2 2. E Toolkit Documentation and Samples - INFO
etkbbs.txt          2118
etkdia.zip          7386    Sample C files: How to imbed an E-MLE in a dialog box
etkdlg.zip          8899    Sample dll with functions to create dialog boxes
etkdoc.zip        194057    INF and postcript E-Toolkit documentation
etkexp.zip         15929    Header files for use with the Toolkit
etksim.zip          5708    Sample C file: simple control window
lampdq.zip         13286    Files for sharing information with a host

ibm/ews:
00index.txt         5578
20memu.pck          1218
20memu.zip         91553    Displays Memory allocation and system storage usage
21memu.pck          1033
21memu.zip         13278    Replacement dll for 20menu for version 2.1
alphal.pck          1072
alphal.zip        260849    Code browser and Analysis Tool
aping.pck           1398
aping.zip         105472    APPC test program: Connection stats and viability
arexec.pck          1156
```

Appendix H—Sources of OS/2 Information

File	Size	Description
arexec.zip	89437	APPC Remote Command Execution program
atell.pck	1087	
atell.zip	89585	APPC Tell Program: Similar to UNIX write
autodi.pck	950	
autodi.zip	14642	Gives a Graphical Display of APPN resources
bn2src.pck	1052	
bn2src.zip	23825	Convert binary data to high level language structures
boot20.pck	1192	
boot20.zip	28639	Program to create an OS/2 2.0 boot diskette
boot2x.pck	1064	
boot2x.zip	48529	Program to create an OS/2 v2.x boot diskette
cbook.pck	1153	
cbook.zip	55391	C language field formatter for BookMaster
cdexpl.pck	1090	
cdexpl.zip	36515	A compact Disc Digital Audio Explorer
cidsetup.zip	99440	Create CID Code servers for SRVIFS, LAD/2, etc.
clokgs.package	993	
clokgs.pck	1006	
clokgs.zip	30907	A simple digital clock for your PM desktop
clpsrv.package	1195	
clpsrv.zip	32961	
colrpt.pck	1074	
colrpt.zip	41120	Shows the color under the mouse pointer
cpost.pck	957	
cpost.zip	58705	C language file formatter for PostScript
cstepm.pck	1067	
cstepm.zip	150457	Add an ACTIONS menu to EPM to extend functionality
dbmrpw.pck	931	
dbmrpw.zip	31971	OS/2 2.0 and ES 1.0 Remote Password Administrator
dinfo.pck	2268	
dinfo.zip	50847	Monitors SWAPPER.DAT and bytes left on the swap disk
dirsta.pck	1007	
dirsta.zip	31271	Displays Lan information
edtini.pck	1021	
edtini.zip	20686	OS2 .INI profile modifier (text only)
elep2f.pck	1295	
elep2f.zip	158070	Entry Level 3270 Emulation program
elepht.pck	1041	
elepht.zip	14927	Animated Elephant Icon
ewscat.txt	55279	
ewscat.package	818	
ewscat.pck	818	
ewscat.text	61219	The IBM EWS Catalog version 1.28
ewscat.txt	44098	The IBM EWS Catalog version 1.28
exdesk.pck	1060	
exdesk.zip	45989	WPS DLL to extend functions of Desktop
exemap.package	1088	
exemap.zip	45853	
gfoldr.pck	1109	
gfoldr.zip	103757	Group Folder: Creates subsections within a folder
gopher.pck	1073	
gopher.zip	93363	PM client for the Internet Gopher Client
goserv.pck	1352	
goserv.zip	55644	A Gopher Server protocol for OS/2 2.x
hexdmp.pck	1202	
hexdmp.zip	26874	bin2hex and hex2bin tool
ipfcpp.pck	1459	

The Internet

ipfcpp.zip	27171	IPFC Pre-Processor
l40bat.pck	970	
l40bat.zip	38706	L40sx Battery condition Program v2.20
l40tem.pck	1285	
l40tem.zip	38854	L40sx Temperature indicator program
loaddf.pck	1604	
loaddf.zip	26171	Utility to save and restore diskette images
lp3820.pck	1201	
lp3820.zip	283371	Prints AFP (IBM's own format) docs on a laser printer
lp382f.pck	1171	
lp382f.zip	849195	Fonts for use with lp3820 HP-PCL and 4019 PPDS modes
ltrnam.pck	1066	
ltrnam.zip	10231	Change title text of Comm Manager LT session
megads.pck	1042	
megads.zip	63698	Megadesk, a virtual desktop overviewer
os2cdr.pck	1216	
os2cdrom.zip	172640	OS/2 Cdrom device drivers (BETA)
pcswocid.pck	1402	
pcswocid.zip	85943	Patch to run PC/3270 for Win under WIN-OS/2
pmcam2.pck	1278	
pmcam2.zip	155173	PMCamera: An OS/2 Presentation Manager Screen Grabber
pmftrm.pck	2078	
pmftrm.zip	87409	ASYNC Terminal Emulator:ANSI, VT100, TTY and FTTERMC
pmgb32.pck	1503	
pmgb32.zip	113229	An OS/2 Presentation Manager World Globe
pmprtf.pck	1358	
pmprtf.zip	36804	32-bit printf() support for PM and OS/2 apps
pmtree.pck	1387	
pmtree.zip	113421	Tree display of the PM window hierarchy
prntps.pck	1211	
prntps.zip	4774	Print text on a PostScript printer
qconfg.pck	1019	
qconfg.zip	185593	System Configuration Report Utility
rxappc.pck	1014	
rxappc.zip	30303	REXX/APPC Function interface pck
rxd.pck	975	
rxd.zip	149595	PM source level debugger for Rexx
rxftp.package	1000	
rxftp.zip	85899	
rxmath.pck	1237	
rxmath.zip	32434	Basic Math function add on for OS/2 2.0 REXX
rxnetb.pck	992	
rxnetb.zip	21277	REXX/NETBIOS Function interface pck
rxsock.pck	1078	
rxsock.zip	53932	Rexx Function pck for using TCP/IP Sockets
shftrn.pck	1664	
shftrn.zip	21392	Hit shift key to run program before PM comes up
tap2demo.package	1228	
tapdem.zip	1578122	
tinyed.pck	923	
tinyed.zip	71943	Small editor (DOS and OS/2 versions) — boot disk must
tuneup.package	1141	
tuneup.zip	127666	
txt2ps.package	1581	
txt2ps.pck	1295	
txt2ps.zip	57625	Print monitor that allows either text or PostScript
vrexx2.pck	1250	
vrexx2.zip	202532	Visual REXX library for Presentation Manager

Appendix H—Sources of OS/2 Information

```
ibm/info:
00index.txt          2769
badlan.txt           1264   Problems with the Lan Fix Modules - LS20FX & LS13FX
bbs.announce          955
bbslist.txt         20736   Latest List of BBS's with OS/2 software
bbsnames.txt        11664   Another OS/2 BBS list
bbstext.txt          3159   Request for removal of first Service Pack from BBSes
compusrv.pck          202
compusrv.zip        11987   March Beta Compuserve Discusion Transcript
confer.zip          11987
dosinfo.txt          6272   How to create Installation Disks from CDROM
dsn3ga.zip          60026
dsn3gi.zip         119022
dsn3gp.zip         172407
dsn93a.zip          48564   IBM Developer Support News - Issue 1
dsn93b.zip          45859   IBM Developer Support News - Issue 2
dsn93c.zip          59025   IBM Developer Support News - Issue 3
dsn93d.announce      3268
dsn93d.zip          45429   IBM Developer Support News - Issue 4
dsn93e.announce      2790
dsn93e.zip          26826   IBM Developer Support News - Issue 5
dsn93f.inf         119280
dsn93f.zip         134436
dsn93fex.announce    2443
dsn93g.announce      2562
dsn93g.zip          59901
dsnews.93d         140446
dsnews.93e          77526
dsnews.93f         135640
dsnews.93g         179155
idapi.wp            23600   Integrated Database Application Programming Interface
lsesserv.nws         4313   Lanserver extended services news group transcript
newsfl.txt           2553   Original 2.1 Beta testing announcement
omf.pck               936
omf.zip             79792   OS/2 2.0 Object Module and Linear Executable format
os2beta.not          1701   March Beta Announcement
os2cnew1.3820       55926
os2cnew1.ps        274965
os2cnew2.3820      592510
os2cnew2.ps       2091556
os2cnew3.3820      161665
os2cnew3.ps        807664
os2cnew4.3820      737227
os2cnew4.ps       2562972
os2cnew5.3820      649394
os2cnew5.ps       2305276
os2cnews.pck         2508
os2fax.txt           2216   IBM Automated Fax Service Information
os2grwin.txt         2835   Announcement of October Beta
os2tnd.zip          83530   Tips and Techniques: 9-15-92
os2tni.zip         129045   Tips and Techniques: 9-15-92 INF format
os2tnt.pck           1249
pcmtab.zip          31883
pcmtable.txt        82892   List of OS/2 compatible machines
pdkann.txt            869   Announcement of the March PDK
problm.txt           8504   How to submit an OS/2 Bug report
ps2ast.package       3709
```

```
ps2ast.zip          2095992  PS/2 Assistant - OS/2 information, 78th Edition
rlapaper.txt          49923  LAN remote Access information
spann.txt             24057  Service Pack Early Announcement
spapar.txt           149647  Summary of APARs: 5-22-93
svcpak3.asc             642  Information on update to the Service Pack: October '92
touch.pck               979
touch.zip             43459  Information on IBM's Touchscreen DOS and OS/2 API calls

ibm/lanserv:
00index.txt            1135
7005cid.tip            3750
db22.zip             161186
ip06030.lbl            1445
ip06030.pck            1405
ip06030a.lbl           1210
ip06030a.pck           1342
ip07001.announce      13881
ip07001.lbl             978
ip07001.pck            1498
ip07001a.lbl            976
ip07001a.pck           1494
ip07003.announce       5671
ip07003.pck            1224
ip07003.zip          417814
ip07005.avail          2614
ip07005.package        1772
ip07005.zip          379027
ip07006.avail          4334
ip07006.package        2041
ip6030b1.dsk        1204265  Lan Server 2.0 Service Pack 5.25" Disk 1
ip6030b2.dsk        1497218  Lan Server 2.0 Service Pack 5.25" Disk 2
ip6030b3.dsk        1501700  Lan Server 2.0 Service Pack 5.25" Disk 3
ip6030b4.dsk         601987  Lan Server 2.0 Service Pack 5.25" Disk 4
ip6030d1.dsk        1467904  Lan Server 2.0 Service Pack 3.5" Disk 1
ip6030d2.dsk        1472512  Lan Server 2.0 Service Pack 3.5" Disk 2
ip6030d3.dsk        1443394  Lan Server 2.0 Service Pack 3.5" Disk 3
os220.zip            691526
os221.zip            595435
us7001b1.dsk        1454080
us7001b2.dsk         326656
us7001d1.dsk        1214464
us7001d2.dsk         562176

ibm/misc:
00index.txt            1888
21d1ht.package         1165
21d1ht.txt             7611
bga1bmps.zip         800508  Extra BGA bitmaps: Place in your Bitmap directory
bga2bmps.zip         789676  Extra BGA bitmaps: Place in your Bitmap directory
bgabmaps.pck            846
cidsetup.pck           1568
cidsetup.zip          99440  CID Code Server setup program for SRVIFS and LAD/2
dbprep.pck             1285
dbprep.zip            28815  Install the Dual Boot Feature after Install
dcf2ct.package         1258
dcf2ct.zip            76025  DCF/2 (de)compression test utility (CTU)
dcf2ut.exe           106944
```

```
dsn93g.announce        2562
dsn93g.zip            59901
dsnews.93g           179155
fixini.pck              774
fixini.zip            73821  INI correction program: 2.0 only
ftpbeta.inf             546  IBM request to not place the March 2.1 beta up for ftp
mitfx.package          1057
mitfx.zip             14932
os2beta.not            1701  March Beta announcement
os2ccp.pck             1139
os2ccp.zip            24957  OS/2 2.1 Compression Compatibility Package
prcp.pck                874
prcp.zip             411828  Missing Reference Manuals sections in 2.0 Toolkit
redbk1.zip           472449  Red Book vol 1: Control Program (.INF)
redbk2.zip           724504  Red Book vol 2: Dos and Windows Environment (.INF)
redbk3.zip           436082  Red Book vol 3: Presentation Manager and WPS (.INF)
redbk4.zip           467551  Red Book vol 4: Application Development (.INF)
redbooks.pck           1652
sbmmpm.pck              983
sbmmpm.zip           189762  Sound Blaster drivers for OS/2 2.1 MMPM
sp506.pck              1077
sp506.txt               405
spb506.pck             5444
spb506.zip           170495  OS/2 2.0 beta driver for ST506 drives
ultimoti.pck           1229
ultimotn.zip        1554818
vgabmps.pck             816
vgabmps.zip          526810  OS/2 2.0 extra Bitmaps for VGA systems
wr07020.avail          5110
wr07020.package        1444
wr07020.zip          891421

ibm/os2fixes:
00index.txt           18034
20apr1.zip           835603
20apr2.zip           785913
20apr3.zip           770454
20apr4.zip           778536
20apr5.zip           163598
20fixes.txt           29177  List of IBM fixes as of 12/07/92
21apr1.zip           770520
21apr2.zip           359772
21cmd.pck               922
21cmd.zip             27776  OS/2 2.1 Dec Beta fix for DOS_AUTOEXEC DOS setting
21d1ht.package         1165
21d1ht.txt             7611
21dfct.pck             1157
21dfct.zip           883050  OS/2 2.1 Defect Reports in INF format
21disk.package         1421
21disk.zip            69428
21gt16.pck             1623
21gt16.zip           489680  OS/2 2.1 fix for >16MB on machines
21kbi1.pck             1191
21kbi1.zip            40720  OS/2 2.1 fix for NEC Ultralight
21krnd.pck             1136
21krnd.zip           888071  OS/2 2.1 Debug version of Slowdown fix kernel
21krnl.pck             1972
```

The Internet

```
21krnl.zip      802229   OS/2 2.1 March Beta Slowdown fix kernel
21rexx.pck        1059
21rexx.zip      130836   Replacement REXX.DLL for the March 2.1 beta
21ripl.pck        1791
21ripl.zip      394239   2.1 March Beta Lan RIPL fixes
21wpsf.pck        2388
21wpsf.zip      152100   Fixes for OS/2 2.1 WPS
360k.zip         37200   Adds 360k drive support to OS/2 2.0
360kfix.pck       1018
4019.zip        267861   IBM 4019 Printer Driver
4029p.pck         1031
4029p.zip        16720   OS/2 2.0 4029 Printer fix for prompting of .DRV files
42xx.zip        231898   Patched version of IBM 42XX printer driver
52012.zip        58629   IBM 52012 Printer Driver
52xx.zip        192219   IBM 52XX Printer Driver
addprt.pck         977
addprt.zip       72800   Fix to allow Printer Setting to be changed under WINOS2
b8514a.pck        1084
b8514a.zip      299011   Beta 8514a 32 bit display drivers
blkico.pck         995
blkico.zip      432918   Fix for OS/2 2.0 GA Black Desktop Icons
bmouse.pck        1043
bmouse.zip       14147   Logitech 3 button mouse & hot plug fix for March beta
bvhsvga.pck       1080
bvsvga.zip       12620   OS/2 2.0 BVHSVGA.dll:Fixes C00005 prob on 1MB SVGA
cmapr1.zip      188491
commga.pck        1682
commga.zip       72734   New com drivers for OS/2 2.0GA
dbapr1.zip       34185
deskjet.abs       2240
dpmi.pck           950
dpmi.zip         27600   OS/2 2.0 DPMI fix for Microsoft C 7.0
dspins.pck         965
dspins.zip      160875   OS/2 2.1 Beta fix for ATI Ultra switch from 8514 2 VGA
ebooke.zip      513661   Tagged file editor: use with Bookmaster and others
epmapp.zip      151676   Enhanced Editor: Application files
epmasi.zip       38765   Enhanced Editor: Tools for editing C, Pascal,E source
epmatr.zip       27618   Example of attribute support in EPM
epmbbs.pck        1500
epmbbs.txt        7146
epmbk.zip       439610   EPM documentation files in INF format
epmdll.zip      287232   EPM DLL files needed for installation
epmhlp.zip       88045   EPM help files
epmmac.zip      284434   Sample configuration files for EPM
epmrex.zip       10549   Sample Rexx macros for EPM
epmsmp.zip       66891   Sample macros for EPM
epson.zip        82259   OS/2 Epson Printer Driver
esapr1.zip      559951
goodlan.txt       2086   Lanserver patch announcement 9/25/92
gt16mb.pck        1128
gt16mb.zip       61042   Fix for OS/2 2.0 on systems with Greater Than 16 MB
hpdjet.abs        3305
hpdjet.anc        2835
hpdjet.pck        1087
hpdjet.zip       96420   HP deskjet OS/2 2.0 drivers
hpfs.pck          1110
hpfs.zip         70378   OS/2 2.0 HPFS fix for Swapper.dat and chkdsk problems
```

Appendix H—Sources of OS/2 Information

```
hpfs21.pck         1262
hpfs21.zip        71857    March Beta HPFS Patch
hpljw.pck          1091
hpljw.zip        165922    Replacement HP LaserJet Windows Drivers for OS/2 2.0
ibm1flpy.add      24080    360k floppy fix for OS/2 2.0GA
ibm2flpy.add      16384    ADD file required for PMTAPE to run in OS/2 2.0
ibm2flpy.pck        975
ibm3852.zip       51688    IBM 3852 Printer driver
ibm5152.zip       51117    IBM 5152 Printer driver
ibm5182.zip       54460    IBM 5182 Printer driver
ibm52011.zip      38664    IBM 52011 Printer driver
ibm5216.zip       38678    IBM 5216 Printer Driver
inftxt.pck         1076
inftxt.zip        75782    A collection of files for problem determination in 2.0
ins21l.pck         1401
ins21l.zip      1891068    OS/2 2.1 install from B for BLUE GA code
ins21m.pck         1401
ins21m.zip      1934345    OS/2 2.1 install from B for SALMON GA code
l40pwr.pck         1136
l40pwr.zip        12715    OS/2 2.1 L40SX power management files
lampdq.zip        13286    Interface to execute commands on a VM host through EPM
lapdll.pck         1145
lapdll.zip        68511    March Beta patches for NTS/2
ljet.zip         266025    Beta 2.1 HP LaserJet driver: new 4 series support
loaddf.pck          984
loaddf.zip        10382    Utility to create diskettes from IBM .DSK images
loaddskf.exe      13634    Utility to create diskettes from IBM .DSK images
lotus3.pck         1484
lotus3.zip       519779    Fixes problems with Lotus 123 and the 32 bit2.0SP GRE
ls13fx.pck         5351
ls13fx.zip       112000    OS/2 1.30.2 DOS Lan Requester fixes
ls20fx.pck         6101
ls20fx.zip       255600    OS/2 2.0 DOS Lan Requester fixes
lsapr1.zip       523900
m21com.pck         1046
m21com.zip        16339    OS/2 2.1 March Beta COM.SYS driver replacement
m21shp.pck         2915
m21shp.zip       900258    OS/2 2.1 March Beta .INI patches 4/16/93
migrat.pck          912
migrat.zip        50558    March Beta Migrate Trap 000D patch
mitfx.package      1057
mitfx.zip         14932
mmapr1.zip        25916
mmpmcs.dsk      1190953
mmpmcs.package     1190
mouse.pck          1047
mouse.zip         10772    OS/2 2.0 Uncontrollable Mouse pointer fix
mvpro.pck          1024
mvpro.zip         27798    OS/2 2.1 March Beta drivers for MediaVision cards
ntapr1.zip        71456
null.zip          55290    IBM Null printer driver 3/19/93
nwapr1.zip        47671
oapar1.zip       684503
oapar2.zip       714378
oapar3.zip       774307
oapar4.zip       793334
oapar5.zip       245341
```

```
oapar6.zip         458632
oapar7.zip         607186
oapar8.zip         599642
omf.pck               936
omf.zip             65205  2.0 Object Module and Linear Executable format .INF
os220fix.pck         1089  List of fixes for OS/2 2.0GA
os2apar1.zip       848172  List of OS/2 2.x Bugs reported to IBM (.INF) Disk 1
os2apar2.zip       884460  List of OS/2 2.x Bugs reported to IBM (.INF) Disk 2
os2apar3.zip       960148  List of OS/2 2.x Bugs reported to IBM (.INF) Disk 3
os2apar4.zip       980672  List of OS/2 2.x Bugs reported to IBM (.INF) Disk 4
os2apar5.zip       299106  List of OS/2 2.x Bugs reported to IBM (.INF) Disk 5
os2apar6.zip       543512  List of OS/2 2.x Bugs reported to IBM (.INF) Disk 6
os2apar7.zip       754015
os2apar8.zip       863229
os2apars.packa       1163
os2apars.package     5349
os2apars.pck         1163
os2fl.zip           16988  Chart of descriptions of OS/2 files
os2flist.pck         1068
os2flist.txt       144626
os2krn.zip         455907  2.0GA Kernal fix for growing swap file
os2krnl.pck          1114
os2pdrvr.ann         2835
os2pdrvr.annou       2835
os2pdrvr.packa       1353
os2pdrvr.pck         1384
os2prntd.packa       1444
os2prntd.pck         1569
p120apr1.zip      1044329
p120apr2.zip       981800
p120apr3.zip       964024
p120apr4.zip       974710
p120apr5.zip       129790
p121apr1.zip       969785
p121apr2.zip       103812
p1cmapr1.zip       186263
p1dbapr1.zip        41179
p1esapr1.zip       700803
p1lsapr1.zip       658414
p1mmapr1.zip        30656
p1ntapr1.zip        88414
p1nwapr1.zip        58588
p1tcapr1.zip       214949
p1tkapr1.zip       180559
pcmtable.zip         8193
pjet.zip            46341  OS/2 Paintjet Printer Driver
plotqp.zip          58348  OS/2 PM Plot Queue Processor
plotr.zip           79108  OS/2 Plotter Print Drivers
plotr2.zip          90014
post16.zip         206075
post32.zip         196932
prnfix.txt          12903  Living document of revisions to OS/2 printer drivers
prnmap.txt          14914  List of printer names w/corresponding drivers
progcsd.pck          1897
pscrpt.zip         196163  OS/2 2.x PostScript Printer Driver
readme.zip           6447
rexx20.pck           1072
```

Appendix H—Sources of OS/2 Information

```
rexx20.zip          175065   Rexx Language patch for 2.0GA
s3-16m.dsk         1326121
s3-16m.package        4046
s3-256.dsk         1203753
s3-256.package        2682
s3-256.pck            2359
s3-64k.dsk         1209897
s3-64k.pck            2260
s3.dsk              763139   S3 display card drivers for OS/2 2.1
s3.zip             1128411
s3_16m.dsk         1420841
s3_16m.package        1486
s3bdd1.zip          805214
s3bdd2.zip          984899
s3driver.packa        1225
s3ibm.pck             3519
s3ibm.txt              324
s3ndd1.zip          666709
s3ndd2.zip          808741
s3sdd1.zip          805540
s3sdd2.zip          983962
sbmmpm.pck            1065
sbmmpm.zip          189121   Sound Blaster MMPM/2 drivers
set2_1.pck            1435
set2_1.zip            3894
sndblast.package       917
sndblst.zip         106126
somfix.pck            1354
somfix.zip          945360   Replacement SOM.dll for 2.0GA
sony31.pck            1160
sony31.zip           19451   Sony 31a CDROM drivers
sp016.avail            891
sp016.avl              891
sp016.cmd             9600
sp016.doc             5680
sp016.pck             1091
sp016.zip            84240   Adds EHLLAPI support to WinOS2 and DOS
sp16mb.pck            1089
sp16mb.zip           47157   Service pack - Greater than 16 MB fix 2/1/93
spdstr.pck            1090
spdstr.zip           59443   Diamond Speedstar Sync problem patch
svga16.pck            1502
svga16.zip         1104046
tcapr1.zip          173418
tcpipcsd.packa        3102
tkapr1.zip          190956
turbo.pck             1153
turbo.zip              778   Patch for NEC Turbo machines that ran slow with 2.0GA
uhpfs.pck              991
uhpfs.zip           104306   UHPFS.DLL that fixes the cps extents not found error
us6035b1.dsk       1462272
us6035b2.dsk       1471488
us6035b3.dsk       1471488
us6035b4.dsk       1209344
us6035d1.dsk       1201152
us6035d2.dsk       1221632
us6035d3.dsk       1217536
```

```
us6035d4.dsk      1201152
us6035d5.dsk       784384
vbios.pck            1337
vbios.zip            5534  OS/2 2.0GA VBIOS.SYS fixes hangs on some OEM machines
vsvga.pck            1205
vsvga.zip           97803  2.0GA video driver patches for SVGA
wr06001.pck          1327
wr06001.zip        712203  OS/2 ES 1.0 Database Manager SelectPak 1
wr06002.pck          1256
wr06002.zip        120741  OS/2 ES 1.0 Database Manager SelectPak 2
wr06003.pck          1248
wr06003.zip        272532  OS/2 ES 1.0 Database Manager SelectPak 3
wr06004.pck          1250
wr06004.zip        119142  OS/2 ES 1.0 Database Manager SelectPak 4
wr06014.pck          1296
wr06014.zip        845166  OS/2 ES 1.0 Database Manager SelectPak 14
wr06015.pck          1210
wr06015.zip        336478  OS/2 ES 1.0 Database Manager SelectPak 15
wr06035.label        1708
wr06035.package      1474
wr06035a.label       1466
wr06035a.package     1410
wr07008.avail        6160
wr07008.package      1399
wr07008.zip        890695  OS/2 NTS/2 LAPS Services Refresh (WR07008 U.S)
wr07020.avail        5110
wr07020.package      1444
wr07020.zip        891421
wrc6001.pck          1466
wrc6001.zip        706948  OS/2 ES 1.0 Fr-Canadian Database Manager selectpak 1
wrc6002.pck          1394
wrc6002.zip        124186  OS/2 ES 1.0 Fr-Canadian Database Manager selectpak 2
wrc6003.pck          1386
wrc6003.zip        276113  OS/2 ES 1.0 Fr-Canadian Database Manager selectpak 3
wrc6004.pck          1366
wrc6004.zip        120988  OS/2 ES 1.0 Fr-Canadian Database Manager selectpak 4
wrc6014.pck          1434
wrc6014.zip        848986  OS/2 ES 1.0 Fr-Canadian Database Manager selectpak 14
wrc6015.pck          1363
wrc6015.zip        339578  OS/2 ES 1.0 Fr-Canadian Database Manager selectpak 15
wrf6001.pck          1463
wrf6001.zip        706932  OS/2 ES 1.0 Database Manager selectpak 1 French Version
wrf6002.pck          1391
wrf6002.zip        124174  OS/2 ES 1.0 Database Manager selectpak 2 French Version
wrf6003.pck          1383
wrf6003.zip        276125  OS/2 ES 1.0 Database Manager selectpak 3 French Version
wrf6004.pck          1363
wrf6004.zip        120991  OS/2 ES 1.0 Database Manager selectpak 4 French Version
wrf6014.pck          1431
wrf6014.zip        849004  OS/2 ES 1.0 Database Manager selectpak 14 French Version
wrf6015.pck          1360
wrf6015.zip        339574  OS/2 ES 1.0 Database Manager selectpak 15 French Version
wrg6001.pck          1463
wrg6001.zip        706882  OS/2 ES 1.0 Database Manager German selectpak 1
wrg6002.pck          1391
wrg6002.zip        124071  OS/2 ES 1.0 Database Manager German selectpak 2
wrg6003.pck          1383
```

Appendix H—Sources of OS/2 Information

```
wrg6003.zip      275959    OS/2 ES 1.0 Database Manager German selectpak 3
wrg6004.pck        1363
wrg6004.zip      121167    OS/2 ES 1.0 Database Manager German selectpak 4
wrg6014.pck        1431
wrg6014.zip      848891    OS/2 ES 1.0 Database Manager German selectpak 14
wrg6015.pck        1360
wrg6015.zip      339600    OS/2 ES 1.0 Database Manager German selectpak 15
wrh6001.pck        1469
wrh6001.zip      706384    OS/2 ES 1.0 Database Manager Holland (NL) selectpak 1
wrh6002.pck        1397
wrh6002.zip      123742    OS/2 ES 1.0 Database Manager Holland (NL) selectpak 2
wrh6003.pck        1389
wrh6003.zip      275434    OS/2 ES 1.0 Database Manager Holland (NL) selectpak 3
wrh6004.pck        1369
wrh6004.zip      120668    OS/2 ES 1.0 Database Manager Holland (NL) selectpak 4
wrh6014.pck        1437
wrh6014.zip      848486    OS/2 ES 1.0 Database Manager Holland (NL) selectpak 14
wrh6015.pck        1366
wrh6015.zip      339194    OS/2 ES 1.0 Database Manager Holland (NL) selectpak 15
wri6001.pck        1464
wri6001.zip      706882    OS/2 ES 1.0 Database Manager Italian selectpak 1
wri6002.pck        1392
wri6002.zip      124214    OS/2 ES 1.0 Database Manager Italian selectpak 2
wri6003.pck        1384
wri6003.zip      275987    OS/2 ES 1.0 Database Manager Italian selectpak 3
wri6004.pck        1364
wri6004.zip      121134    OS/2 ES 1.0 Database Manager Italian selectpak 4
wri6014.pck        1432
wri6014.zip      848944    OS/2 ES 1.0 Database Manager Italian selectpak 14
wri6015.pck        1385
wri6015.zip      339752    OS/2 ES 1.0 Database Manager Italian selectpak 15
wrl6001.pck        1464
wrl6001.zip      706831    OS/2 ES 1.0 Database Manager Finnish selectpak 1
wrl6002.pck        1392
wrl6002.zip      124036    OS/2 ES 1.0 Database Manager Finnish selectpak 2
wrl6003.pck        1384
wrl6003.zip      275835    OS/2 ES 1.0 Database Manager Finnish selectpak 3
wrl6004.pck        1364
wrl6004.zip      120922    OS/2 ES 1.0 Database Manager Finnish selectpak 4
wrl6014.pck        1432
wrl6014.zip      848783    OS/2 ES 1.0 Database Manager Finnish selectpak 14
wrl6015.pck        1361
wrl6015.zip      339370    OS/2 ES 1.0 Database Manager Norwegian selectpak 15
wrn6001.pck        1466
wrn6001.zip      706315    OS/2 ES 1.0 Database Manager Norwegian selectpak 1
wrn6002.pck        1394
wrn6002.zip      125037    OS/2 ES 1.0 Database Manager Norwegian selectpak 2
wrn6003.pck        1386
wrn6003.zip      277447    OS/2 ES 1.0 Database Manager Norwegian selectpak 3
wrn6004.pck        1366
wrn6004.zip      123967    OS/2 ES 1.0 Database Manager Norwegian selectpak 4
wrn6014.pck        1434
wrn6014.zip      849030    OS/2 ES 1.0 Database Manager Norwegian selectpak 14
wrn6015.pck        1363
wrn6015.zip      341321    OS/2 ES 1.0 Database Manager Norwegian selectpak 15
wrp6001.pck        1467
wrp6001.zip      706846    OS/2 ES 1.0 Database Manager Portuguese selectpak 1
```

```
wrp6002.pck          1395
wrp6002.zip        124169    OS/2 ES 1.0 Database Manager Portuguese selectpak 2
wrp6003.pck          1387
wrp6003.zip        271738    OS/2 ES 1.0 Database Manager Portuguese selectpak 3
wrp6004.pck          1367
wrp6004.zip        118698    OS/2 ES 1.0 Database Manager Portuguese selectpak 4
wrp6014.pck          1435
wrp6014.zip        848925    OS/2 ES 1.0 Database Manager Portuguese selectpak 14
wrp6015.pck          1364
wrp6015.zip        335779    OS/2 ES 1.0 Database Manager Portuguese selectpak 15
wrs6001.pck          1464
wrs6001.zip        706964    OS/2 ES 1.0 Database Manager Spanish selectpak 1
wrs6002.pck          1392
wrs6002.zip        124276    OS/2 ES 1.0 Database Manager Spanish selectpak 2
wrs6003.pck          1384
wrs6003.zip        276059    OS/2 ES 1.0 Database Manager Spanish selectpak 3
wrs6004.pck          1364
wrs6004.zip        121055    OS/2 ES 1.0 Database Manager Spanish selectpak 4
wrs6014.pck          1432
wrs6014.zip        849033    OS/2 ES 1.0 Database Manager Spanish selectpak 14
wrs6015.pck          1361
wrs6015.zip        339655    OS/2 ES 1.0 Database Manager Spanish selectpak 15
wru6001.pck          1460
wru6001.zip        719585    OS/2 ES 1.0 Database Manager U.K selectpak 1
wru6002.pck          1389
wru6002.zip        126463    OS/2 ES 1.0 Database Manager U.K selectpak 2
wru6003.pck          1381
wru6003.zip        278256    OS/2 ES 1.0 Database Manager U.K selectpak 3
wru6004.pck          1364
wru6004.zip        122832    OS/2 ES 1.0 Database Manager U.K selectpak 4
wru6014.pck          1429
wru6014.zip        851655    OS/2 ES 1.0 Database Manager U.K selectpak 14
wru6015.pck          1347
wru6015.zip        340687    OS/2 ES 1.0 Database Manager U.K selectpak 15
wrw6001.pck          1464
wrw6001.zip        706158    OS/2 ES 1.0 Database Manager Swedish selectpak 1
wrw6002.pck          1392
wrw6002.zip        123507    OS/2 ES 1.0 Database Manager Swedish selectpak 2
wrw6003.pck          1384
wrw6003.zip        275258    OS/2 ES 1.0 Database Manager Swedish selectpak 3
wrw6004.pck          1364
wrw6004.zip        120409    OS/2 ES 1.0 Database Manager Swedish selectpak 4
wrw6014.pck          1432
wrw6014.zip        848245    OS/2 ES 1.0 Database Manager Swedish selectpak 14
wrw6015.pck          1361
wrw6015.zip        338882    OS/2 ES 1.0 Database Manager Swedish selectpak 15

ibm/servpak:
00index.txt          6063
06100b1.dsk       1168384    OS/2 2.0 ServicePak XR06100 3.5" - Disk 1 of 17
06100b10.dsk      1474048    OS/2 2.0 ServicePak XR06100 3.5" - Disk 10 of 17
06100b11.dsk      1474048    OS/2 2.0 ServicePak XR06100 3.5" - Disk 11 of 17
06100b12.dsk       702976    OS/2 2.0 ServicePak XR06100 3.5" - Disk 12 of 17
06100b13.dsk      1223168    OS/2 2.0 ServicePak XR06100 3.5" - Disk 13 of 17
06100b14.dsk       982016    OS/2 2.0 ServicePak XR06100 3.5" - Disk 14 of 17
06100b15.dsk      1466880    OS/2 2.0 ServicePak XR06100 3.5" - Disk 15 of 17
06100b16.dsk      1148928    OS/2 2.0 ServicePak XR06100 3.5" - Disk 16 of 17
```

```
06100b17.dsk      536064   OS/2 2.0 ServicePak XR06100 3.5" - Disk 17 of 17
06100b2.dsk      1455416   OS/2 2.0 ServicePak XR06100 3.5" - Disk 2 of 17
06100b3.dsk      1474048   OS/2 2.0 ServicePak XR06100 3.5" - Disk 3 of 17
06100b4.dsk      1474048   OS/2 2.0 ServicePak XR06100 3.5" - Disk 4 of 17
06100b5.dsk      1474048   OS/2 2.0 ServicePak XR06100 3.5" - Disk 5 of 17
06100b6.dsk      1473536   OS/2 2.0 ServicePak XR06100 3.5" - Disk 6 of 17
06100b7.dsk      1474048   OS/2 2.0 ServicePak XR06100 3.5" - Disk 7 of 17
06100b8.dsk      1474048   OS/2 2.0 ServicePak XR06100 3.5" - Disk 8 of 17
06100b9.dsk      1474048   OS/2 2.0 ServicePak XR06100 3.5" - Disk 9 of 17
06100d1.dsk       995840   OS/2 2.0 ServicePak XR06100 5.25" - Disk 1 of 19
06100d10.dsk     1228288   OS/2 2.0 ServicePak XR06100 5.25" - Disk 10 of 19
06100d11.dsk     1228288   OS/2 2.0 ServicePak XR06100 5.25" - Disk 11 of 19
06100d12.dsk     1228288   OS/2 2.0 ServicePak XR06100 5.25" - Disk 12 of 19
06100d13.dsk     1228288   OS/2 2.0 ServicePak XR06100 5.25" - Disk 13 of 19
06100d14.dsk     1115648   OS/2 2.0 ServicePak XR06100 5.25" - Disk 14 of 19
06100d15.dsk     1221120   OS/2 2.0 ServicePak XR06100 5.25" - Disk 15 of 19
06100d16.dsk      979968   OS/2 2.0 ServicePak XR06100 5.25" - Disk 16 of 19
06100d17.dsk     1192960   OS/2 2.0 ServicePak XR06100 5.25" - Disk 17 of 19
06100d18.dsk     1086464   OS/2 2.0 ServicePak XR06100 5.25" - Disk 18 of 19
06100d19.dsk      849920   OS/2 2.0 ServicePak XR06100 5.25" - Disk 19 of 19
06100d2.dsk       981504   OS/2 2.0 ServicePak XR06100 5.25" - Disk 2 of 19
06100d3.dsk      1227264   OS/2 2.0 ServicePak XR06100 5.25" - Disk 3 of 19
06100d4.dsk      1228288   OS/2 2.0 ServicePak XR06100 5.25" - Disk 4 of 19
06100d5.dsk      1228288   OS/2 2.0 ServicePak XR06100 5.25" - Disk 5 of 19
06100d6.dsk      1228288   OS/2 2.0 ServicePak XR06100 5.25" - Disk 6 of 19
06100d7.dsk      1228288   OS/2 2.0 ServicePak XR06100 5.25" - Disk 7 of 19
06100d8.dsk      1228288   OS/2 2.0 ServicePak XR06100 5.25" - Disk 8 of 19
06100d9.dsk      1228288   OS/2 2.0 ServicePak XR06100 5.25" - Disk 9 of 19
os220s2a.label      3064   OS/2 2.0 Service Pack #2 - Label file
os220s2a.package    3282   OS/2 Version 2.0 Service Pak Number 2 - information
sp16mb.zip         49280   Over 16 megabyte fix for OS/2 2.0 + SP
sp2301.dsk       1474560   OS/2 2.0 Service Pack #2, 3.5" - Disk 1 of 17
sp2302.dsk       1474560   OS/2 2.0 Service Pack #2, 3.5" - Disk 2 of 17
sp2303.dsk       1474560   OS/2 2.0 Service Pack #2, 3.5" - Disk 3 of 17
sp2304.dsk       1474560   OS/2 2.0 Service Pack #2, 3.5" - Disk 4 of 17
sp2305.dsk       1474560   OS/2 2.0 Service Pack #2, 3.5" - Disk 5 of 17
sp2306.dsk       1474560   OS/2 2.0 Service Pack #2, 3.5" - Disk 6 of 17
sp2307.dsk       1474560   OS/2 2.0 Service Pack #2, 3.5" - Disk 7 of 17
sp2308.dsk       1474560   OS/2 2.0 Service Pack #2, 3.5" - Disk 8 of 17
sp2309.dsk       1474560   OS/2 2.0 Service Pack #2, 3.5" - Disk 9 of 17
sp2310.dsk       1474560   OS/2 2.0 Service Pack #2, 3.5" - Disk 10 of 17
sp2311.dsk       1474560   OS/2 2.0 Service Pack #2, 3.5" - Disk 11 of 17
sp2312.dsk       1474560   OS/2 2.0 Service Pack #2, 3.5" - Disk 12 of 17
sp2313.dsk       1474560   OS/2 2.0 Service Pack #2, 3.5" - Disk 13 of 17
sp2314.dsk       1474560   OS/2 2.0 Service Pack #2, 3.5" - Disk 14 of 17
sp2315.dsk       1474560   OS/2 2.0 Service Pack #2, 3.5" - Disk 15 of 17
sp2316.dsk       1474560   OS/2 2.0 Service Pack #2, 3.5" - Disk 16 of 17
sp2317.dsk       1474560   OS/2 2.0 Service Pack #2, 3.5" - Disk 17 of 17
xr06100.avail       2838   OS/2 2.0 ServicePak XR06100 - Avail. information
xr06100.cidtip      6276   OS/2 2.0 ServicePak XR06100 - RIPL install info.
xr06100.fixes      35275   OS/2 2.0 ServicePak XR06100 - List of APARS fixed
xr06100.label      15633   OS/2 2.0 ServicePak XR06100(5.25") - Disk Labels
xr06100.package     2914   OS/2 2.0 ServicePak XR06100 (5.25") - Package info
xr06100a.label     13203   OS/2 2.0 ServicePak XR06100(3.5") - Disk Labels
xr06100a.package    2714   OS/2 2.0 ServicePak XR06100 (3.5") - Package info
xr06110.avail       1207   OS/2 2.0 Developers Toolkit ServicePak Info
xr06110.label       6237   OS/2 2.0 Devel. Toolkit ServicePak(5.25")-Disk Labels
```

```
xr06110.package        1883    OS/2 2.0 Devel. Toolkit ServicePak(5.25")-Package Info
xr06110a.label         5508    OS/2 2.0 Devel. Toolkit ServicePak(3.5")-Disk Labels
xr06110a.package       1809    OS/2 2.0 Devel. Toolkit ServicePak(3.5")-Package Info
xr6110b1.dsk        1473536    OS/2 2.0 Devel. Toolkit ServicePak (3.5"), Disk 1 of 6
xr6110b2.dsk        1475072    OS/2 2.0 Devel. Toolkit ServicePak (3.5"), Disk 2 of 6
xr6110b3.dsk        1474048    OS/2 2.0 Devel. Toolkit ServicePak (3.5"), Disk 3 of 6
xr6110b4.dsk         936448    OS/2 2.0 Devel. Toolkit ServicePak (3.5"), Disk 4 of 6
xr6110b5.dsk        1156096    OS/2 2.0 Devel. Toolkit ServicePak (3.5"), Disk 5 of 6
xr6110b6.dsk        1177600    OS/2 2.0 Devel. Toolkit ServicePak (3.5"), Disk 6 of 6
xr6110d1.dsk        1227776    OS/2 2.0 Devel. Toolkit ServicePak (5.25"),Disk 1 of 7
xr6110d2.dsk        1229312    OS/2 2.0 Devel. Toolkit ServicePak (5.25"),Disk 2 of 7
xr6110d3.dsk        1228288    OS/2 2.0 Devel. Toolkit ServicePak (5.25"),Disk 3 of 7
xr6110d4.dsk        1228288    OS/2 2.0 Devel. Toolkit ServicePak (5.25"),Disk 4 of 7
xr6110d5.dsk         454144    OS/2 2.0 Devel. Toolkit ServicePak (5.25"),Disk 5 of 7
xr6110d6.dsk        1154048    OS/2 2.0 Devel. Toolkit ServicePak (5.25"),Disk 6 of 7
xr6110d7.dsk        1175552    OS/2 2.0 Devel. Toolkit ServicePak (5.25"),Disk 7 of 7

ibm/tcpip:
00index.txt            449
basecsd.zip        2688739    IBM TCP/IP 1.2.1 CSD UN50427 - Base System
dbox2943.zip        163007    IBM TCP/IP DOS/Windows Access Kit Update (10/15/93)
nfscsd1.zip         118997    IBM TCP/IP 1.2.1 CSD UN37900 - NFS Support
pmxcsd1.zip         975338    IBM TCP/IP 1.2.1 CSD UN35990 - X Windows
progcsd.zip         193190    IBM TCP/IP 1.2.1 CSD - 32-bit Programming Toolkit
x25csd.zip           47165    IBM TCP/IP 1.2.1 CSD UN30759 - X.25 Support

incoming:
00index.txt           6616
4os2.txt               241
4os216-20.txt           59
4os216-20.zip        82367
4os232-20.zip       111795
4os232.zip          296809
4os2b.zip           292321
4os2upgr.upload        424
4os2upgr.zip          3350
750aud11.txt           190
750aud11.zip        953252
ADU22D.TXT             348
ADU22D.ZIP          135176
LOTUS.FAX             9692
MR2_157.TXT            477
NikNak11.txt           389
NikNak11.zip         28101
Nim120.txt             389
Nim120.zip           35535
README                3996
Sorry.txt              357
Sorry.zip            30107
UPDATES.OLD          21250
UPDATES.TXT           2118
UPDATES.TXT~          2805
aedit.txt              365
amos101.txt            371
amos101.zip          70129
aplus.zip           119975
artsub.txt             449
```

artsub.zip	7063
askit100.txt	53
askit100.zip	24285
assoed03.txt	332
assoed03.zip	37013
bash-112.txt	470
bash-112.zip	1369864
bibdayo1.txt	695
bibdayo1.zip	72607
bigben2.txt	576
bigben2.zip	67219
bmpat101.txt	1428
bmpat101.zip	150665
boulder.txt	541
boulder.zip	188130
bsys098.txt	0
bsys098b.txt	0
bsys098b.zip	155378
btcookie.txt	723
btcookie.zi2	53852
btcookie.zip	0
cawf405.txt	1413
cawf405.zip	154470
cdu8002.txt	0
cdu8002a.txt	418
cdu8002a.zip	23000
chaos11.txt	726
chaos11.zip	84682
cnfgsort.txt	441
cnfgsort.zip	2643
csedit.txt	443
csedit.zip	342496
cset2g.ini	133
cset2i.ini	133
cvs13p4.txt	719
cvsdos2.txt	689
cvsdos2b.zip	286295
deskext.txt	1017
deskext.zip	35328
dm101.txt	775
dm101.zip	109900
dm2120.txt	30215
dm2120.zip	992372
dm2demo1.txt	526
dm2demo1.zip	175219
dmpv270.zip	3072
doomicon.txt	533
doomicon.zip	5739
drgmon.txt	290
drgmon.zip	121905
dsn93i.txt	383
dsn93i.zip	43279
dsnews.93i	127277
eabrws02.txt	821
emxfix01.txt	459
emxfix01.zip	234655
flex245-2.txt	493

```
flex245-2.zip      388770
flxtxt22.txt          429
flxtxt22.zip       101210
fm2_115.txt           290
fm2_115.zip        256869
fmapp11b.txt          677
fmapp11b.zip       139794
fourpm.txt            384
fourpm.zip          72213
games21a.txt          414
games21a.zip        11911
geog1219.txt          373
geog1219.zip       318734
gfoldr.txt            393
gfoldr.zip          92118
gi.txt                499
gi.zip             172631
gspm261.txt           669
gspm261.zip       1863909
hstart03.txt          381
hstart03.zip        52169
ic06257.zip         23099
il2hdk31.zip        33269
inimt30b.txt          380
inimt30b.zip       472069
int_e.lzh            1998
int_e.txt               0
int_e.txt.new         758
joevwb4.txt           654
joevwb4.zip        315785
ked206b.txt           679
ked206b.zip         83414
latexinf.txt         2181
latexinf.zip       223448
lbb2_123.txt          201
lbb2_123.zip       166249
loaddskf.exe        14145
loaddskf.txt          399
lstpm105.txt          308
lstpm105.zip       122769
lw21.txt              683
lw21.zip           257184
memsz220.txt          405
memsz220.zip       158849
mr2_157.txt           419
mr2_157.zip        204966
mshell2.txt           296
mshell2.zip         86940
os2dd311.txt          394
os2dd311.zip       173151
os2sp200.txt          332
os2sp200.zip         2166
ot-100.txt            346
ot-100.zip          13521
pc2ps.txt             370
pc2ps.zip           30871
pclogic.doc          2005
```

pclogic.doc.2	196
pclogic.zoo	3314
peg007.txt	412
peg007.zip	276748
peg008.txt	284
peg008.zip	277316
pj10200.txt	12311
pmdu13.txt	324
pmdu13.zip	32448
pmed32.txt	381
pmed32.zip	38740
pmjpeg15.txt	2082
pmjpeg15.zip	196054
pmmixer.txt	639
pmmixer.zip	12891
pmnews.txt	452
pmnews.zip	129242
pmpstat.txt	493
pmpstat.zip	65664
pmund111.txt	1724
pmund111.zip	70269
presto.txt	1082
psrt_11b.txt	478
psrt_11b.zip	111873
repeat.txt	352
repeat.zip	11114
run160.txt	805
run160.zip	17726
runit.exe	18400
rxu13.txt	455
rxu13.zip	135210
sio124.txt	333
sio124.zip	129537
softwin.txt	819
sqed087.lzh	219390
sqed087.txt	389
ssiim12.txt	4103
ssiim12.txt2	326
ssiim12.zip	724112
svgakit1_5.txt	494
svgakit1_5.zip	29993
tclock.txt	401
tclock11.zip	87424
tclock2.zip	451502
term2b23.txt	791
term2b23.zip	198182
theos215.txt	1809
theos215.zip	151980
thesrc15.txt	1810
thesrc15.zip	311082
thewall.zip	210854
threads.txt	291
threads.zip	10941
tracker.txt	860
tracker.zip	148081
trash081.txt	3260

trash081.zip	8939
treesz11.txt	2438
treesz11.zip	23267
tshell.txt	451
tshell.zip	44197
tstdev.txt	350
tstdev.zip	22082
uucode10.txt	340
uucode10.zip	41970
uucode101.txt	401
uucode101.zip	42370
vaspibeta.txt	2261
vaspibeta.zip	8766
vesa_emx1_5.txt	576
vesa_emx1_5.zip	41419
vt100.text	42
vt100.tst	3189
vxga-fix.txt	1767
vxga-fix.zip	13525
wbo132s.txt	365
wbo132s.zip	82995
wf10_7.txt	4312
wf10_7.zip	926505
wf21_1.txt	2862
wf21_1.zip	472128
wor.txt	435
wor.zip	94097
wpfld15.txt	542
wpfld15.zip	28670
wpfld18.txt	528
wpfld18.zip	34600
wpfldext.zip	28756
wpfolder.txt	531
wpfolder.zip	28756
wpnewf.txt	458
wpnewf.zip	55260
wpprg15.txt	617
wpprg15.zip	35866
wpprg18.txt	607
wpprg18.zip	40476
wptool11.txt	424
wptool11.zip	186397
xcppinst.exe	217472
yaos02.txt	2089
yaos02.zip	52272
yrn2-051.txt	343
yrn2-051.zip	183284
yrn2-052.txt	378
yrn2-052.zip	185791
zipbrand.txt	403
zipbrand.zip	27363
zoc100.txt	479
zoc100.zip	231512
zocdev.txt	466
zocdev.zip	50781

wpfld18.txt 528 — Cset++ Class Libraries CSD #3 (INTERIM) (Tools 2.1 Only)

Appendix H—Sources of OS/2 Information

```
netware:
00index.txt          26

new:
cshell2.zip          43105     Text mode shell runs fullscreen OS/2 in <4MB
dcopypm6.zip         144535    PM file copy utility
pari138.zip          1490257   Calculator and library for number theory
trn_12.zip           763230    Threaded news reader for use with UUPC

old:
00index.txt          7631
2_1/                 =
2_x/                 =

old/2_1:
00index.txt          163
drivers/             -

old/2_1/drivers:
00index.txt          101
ati32beta.zip        661139    ATI Mach32/Mach8 32-bit beta drivers for OS/2 2.1

old/2_x:
00index.txt          7334
drivers/             -
games/               -
unix/                =

old/2_x/drivers:
00index.txt          98
f1280_20.zip         326302    Orchid Fahrenheit 1280 drivers v2.0 (12-11-92)

old/2_x/games:
00index.txt          124
mine25.zip           42587     A port of Windows Minesweeper for PMA port of Windows
Minesweeper for PM

old/2_x/unix:
00index.txt          6948
emacs19/             -         GNU Emacs 19.19 of OS/2 2.x
emx08f/              =
emx08g/              =
gcc2_233/            -         GCC/2 native-OS/2 C/C++ compiler version 2.3.3
gnumk362.zip         254752    GNU Make 3.65
grep.zip             181279    Unix Grep - version ??
grep15.zip           154673    Unix Grep - version 1.5
less177.zip          238795    OS/2 emx 0.8f port of less 1.77
make363c.zip         65530     GNU make 3.6.3c

old/2_x/unix/emacs19:
00index.txt          818
README               45984     GNU Emacs 19.17 for emx README
e19el1.zip           1208547   Emacs Lisp files (source), part 1
e19el2.zip           610811    Emacs Lisp files (source), part 2
e19info.zip          484931    Emacs info files (online help)
e19lib1.zip          856040    Emacs Lisp library (base set, compiled)
e19lib2.zip          338128    Emacs Lisp library (remaining files, compiled)
```

```
e19man.zip          653120   Emacs documentation (mostly for TeX)
e19min.zip         1107812   Emacs executables (minimal set of files)
e19more.zip         304960   GNU Emacs - Additional files
e19rest.zip         642064   GNU Emacs - Remaining files
e19src.zip         1207082   GNU Emacs - sources
emacmail.zip         17874   Routines to hook emacs 18 and 19 to OS/2 sendmail.
tempbuf.zip           5669   Dynamically sized temp buffers for Emacs 19

old/2_x/unix/emx08f:
00index.txt           2342
bsddev.zip           21872   BSD libraries (curses etc.)
bsddoc.zip           48096   Documentation for BSD libraries
bsdsrc.zip           79532   Source for BSD libraries
contrib/                 -
emxbk.zip           363349   EMX documentation (INF format)
emxdev.zip          619559   EMX development system (without compiler)
emxdl08f.zip         63269
emxfmtdv.zip         40373   EMX formatted documentation (Postscript)
emxlib.zip          358355   EMX library sources
emxptchs/                -
emxst37.zip          11622   A guide to the EMX GNU software development system
emxtest.zip          76166   Test programs for emx and the libraries
gassrc.zip          180376   Patched GNU sources (GAS 1.38.1)
gccsrc1.zip        1169746   Patches GNU sources (GCC 2.3.3 part 1)
gccsrc2.zip        1158957   Patched GNU sources (GCC 2.3.3 part 2)
gdbsrc.zip          871289   Patched GNU sources (GDB 4.7)
gnudev.zip          873393   GNU development tools compiled for EMX
gnudoc.zip          513872   Documentation for GNU programs (texinfo sources)
gnuinfo.zip         314773   GNU texinfo (includes info file browser)
gnupat.zip           82813   Patches for GNU sources
gnusrc.zip          243753   Patched GNU sources (ld,ar,nm,size,strip,objdump,term)
gobjcdev.zip        426378   Additional GNU programs for compiling Objective C
gppdev.zip          944529   Additional GNU programs for compiling C++
gppsrc.zip          967066   Patched GNU sources of libg++ 2.2
readme.doc            6190
whlinf8f.zip        814040   Whole info for EMX-0.8f

old/2_x/unix/emx08f/contrib:
00index.txt            240
emxfn10.zip         116902   INF version of emx/gcc 0.8f function reference
svgakt13.zip         29835   SVGA high-res fullscreen graphics library for EMX
vesa13.zip           23605   VESA interface for EMX, used by svgakit

old/2_x/unix/emx08f/emxptchs:
00index.txt            571
patch01               1955   Patch #1: removes an error in history .doc
patch02               2049   Patch #2: _dt_read() bug under DOS
patch03                520   Patch #3: fix for v_delline()
patch04               2344   Patch #4: fix for _ea_get
patch05               1845   EMX 0.8f patch #5: fixes for os2emx.h
patch06               1549   EMX 0.8f patch #6: video.h and winmgr.h with C++
patch07               3958   EMX 0.8f patch #7: os2emx.h, Prf*()
patch08                496   EMX 0.8f patch #8: ctype.c
patch09                883   EMX 0.8f patch #9: GDB, redirection

old/2_x/unix/emx08g:
00index.txt           1917
INSTALL.DOC          13107   EMX 0.8g Installation Guide
```

Appendix H—Sources of OS/2 Information

```
README.DOC           6810      Introduction to EMX 0.8g
bsddev.zip          21875      BSD libraries (curses etc.)
bsddoc.zip          48096      Documentation for BSD libraries
bsdsrc.zip          79532      Source for BSD libraries
contrib/               -
emxample.zip        18158      Sample programs
emxdev.zip         650270      EMX development system (without compiler)
emxlib.zip         370550      EMX library sources
emxrt.zip          138668      EMX runtime package
emxsrc1.zip         95692      Source for emxomf, emxomfar and emxomfld
emxtest.zip         69550      Test programs (used for testing emx and the libraries)
emxview.zip        219797      EMX documentation in OS/2 .INF format
gassrc.zip         180376      Patched GNU sources (GAS 1.38.1)
gccsrc1.zip       1213243      Patched GNU sources (GCC 2.4.5, part 1)
gccsrc2.zip       1076749      Patched GNU sources (GCC 2.4.5, part 2)
gccsrc3.zip        156270      Patched GNU sources (GCC 2.4.5, part 3)
gdbsrc.zip        1112983      Patched GNU sources (GDB 4.9)
gnudev.zip         986278      GNU development tools compiled for EMX
gnudoc.zip         769656      Documentation for GNU programs (texinfo sources)
gnuinfo.zip        188872      GNU texinfo (includes info file browser)
gnupat.zip          88496      Patches for GNU sources
gnusrc.zip         373768      Patched GNU sources (ld, ar, nm, size, etc.)
gnuview.zip         21141      GNUDEV.INF (gnudev.doc in OS/2 .INF format)
gobjcdev.zip       482460      GNU programs and files for compiling Objective C
gppdev.zip         970508      GNU programs files files for compiling C++
gppsrc.zip         966996      Patched sources of libg++ 2.2

old/2_x/unix/emx08g/contrib:
00index.txt           288
dbmalloc.zip       210683      Debugging malloc library for EMX
emxfont.zip         11821      Small font package for use with EMX/GCC
svgakt14.zip        30135      SVGA high-res fullscreen graphics library for EMX
vesa14.zip          23693      VES interface for EMX, used by svgakit

old/2_x/unix/gcc2_233:
00index.txt          1374
gcc_inf.zip        465257      ASCII text documentation for GCC/2 2.3.3
gccbin.zip        1468582      GCC/2 2.3.3 C & C++ compiler executables
gccdll.zip          62080      GCC/2 Dynamic linked C library
gccdoc.zip          13374      GCC/2 2.3.3 documentation
gccincl.zip        842844      GCC/2 2.3.3 include files
gccinfo.zip        519698      GCC/2 hypertext manuals
gcclib.zip         290818      GCC/2 link libraries
gdb_inf.zip        152087      GNU Debugger documentation in INF format
glibp115.zip        37427      GCC/2 object file librarian
glibs115.zip        37427      GCC/2 object file librarian (source)
news.txt             1329      Feature list of the latest gcc/2
readme.1st           2375      What you need to install gcc/2
s_gas138.zip       336357      GCC/2 assembler
s_gcc233.zip      4394799      GCC/2 SOURCE: GNU C/C++ compiler gcc-2.3.3
s_ld.zip             2718      GCC/2 SOURCE: ld - Unix interface to link386
s_lib.zip          554628      GCC/2 SOURCE: C library for GCC under OS/2
s_mk362.zip        114023      GCC/2 SOURCE: GNU make 3.62 compilation utility
s_o2obj.zip          9755      GCC/2 SOURCE: os2obj-COnvert a.out object code to obj
s_pminfo.zip        73201      GCC/2 SOURCE: pminfo 2.0-hypertext gnuinfo reader
s_speed.zip          1201      GCC/2 SOURCE: gccspeed-loads gcc into memory
s_tst.zip           11866      GCC/2 compiler test cases
samples.zip          6460      GCC/2 example source code
```

Index

Symbols

& (ampersand) in REXX programs, 472
" " (double quotation marks) in REXX programs, 476
' (single quotation mark) in REXX programs, 476
* (asterisk)
 in REXX programs, 466, 476
 wildcard, 282, 313, 399
+ (plus sign)
 REXX programs, 476
 Tune Editor, 561
- (minus sign)
 REXX programs, 476
 Tune Editor, 561
/ (slash) in REXX programs, 466, 476
: (colon) in label statements, 455
= (equal sign) in Tune Editor, 561
== (double equal) in IF statements, 456
? (question mark) wildcard, 313
_ (underscore) in variable names, 471
{ (left brace) character, 831
| (vertical bar) in REXX programs, 472
|| string concatenation operator, 477
} (right brace) character, 832
32-bit architecture, 66
386HPFS, 702
8514/A video adapter, 118

A

accessing DOS, 491
accessing networked drives, 685
ACDI, 630
action bars, 237
active windows, 234
Activities List, 519, 531-534
Activity Type command (Edit menu), 523
Adapter/session status (NetBIOS), 704
Add to boot Manager menu... (Options menu), 496
Adobe Type Manager fonts, 384-385
Advanced Power Management (APM), 97-98
Akron Anomoly, The (BBS), 898
Alarm page (System Clock), 189
Alarms, 520, 534-538
aliases, 256, 700
allocating hard disk partitions, 43-45
alt key, 17
Alternate Reality (BBS), 898
AMI BIOS, 112
ampersand (&) in REXX programs, 472
An error occurred when System Installation tried to ... error messages, 198
ANSI command, 729
ANSI.SYS, 68
APM (Advanced Power Management), 97-98

APPC (Advanced Program-to-Program Communications), 630-631
APPEND command, 729-730
appending applications to desktop, 190
applets, 100, 579-621
 Database, 580-593
 General Purpose applets
  Calculator, 545, 550-553
  Clipboard Viewer, 545, 556-559
  commands, 547-550
  font size, 548-550
  Icon Editor, 545, 572-578
  Notepad, 546, 569-572
  printing, 549-550
  Pulse, 545, 553-556
  Seek and Scan Files, 546, 562-566
  starting, 546
  Sticky Pad, 546, 567-569
  Tune Editor, 546, 559-562
 operating systems, 24
 PM Chart, 601-612
 PM Terminal, 612-621
 Spreadsheet, 593-601
 Time Management applets
  Activities List, 519, 531-534
  Alarms, 520, 534-538
  Calendar, 519, 529-530
  Daily Planner, 519-526
  Monthly Planner, 519, 526-529
  Planner Archive, 520

990   applets

Planner file default, 538-539
starting, 520
To-Do List, 520, 540-544
applications, 393-394
   32-bit architecture, 66
   appending to desktop, 190
   associating files, 292-297
      by name, 293-294
      by type, 292-293
      pop-up menu method, 294-297
   bound programs, 400
   DOS sessions, 63-65, 394-397
   Drive objects, 265-266, 271-300
   folder setup, 264-265
   Help, 337-340
   installing, 397-404
      file recognition, 398-399
      new program objects, 397
      program settings, 398
      session type, 399-401
   migrating, 190, 264
   multitasking, 34
   object-oriented interfaces, 66
   print jobs, 67
   program errors, 211-213
   return codes, 457
   running Windows applications, 403-404
   starting, 401
   threads, 66
   troubleshooting, 220-221
   see also software, 31
applications setup (Workplace Shell), 264-266
APPN (Advanced Peer-to-Peer Networking), 630-631, 654
APPS directory, 208
ARC files, 48
Archive All Completed Lines command (Completed menu), 524
archiving To-Do List, 543-544
ARG function, 481
ARG statement, 481
arithmetic operations (Calculator applet), 551-553
arranging icons, 258
ASC files, 48
ASCII files, 346
Ascii Neighborhood I & II (BBS), 899
ASK.COM utility, 459
ASM files, 48

AsmLang and OS/2 (BBS), 899
ASSIGN command, 731
Assign partition command (Options menu), 496
assigning
   file attributes, 297-298
   user types (NetWare), 690-691
associating files with applications, 292-297
Association page (applications), 190
Asylum BBS, The, 899
ATI Technologies VGA Wonder XL adapter, 174
ATM (Adobe Type Manager) fonts, 384-385
ATTACH command, 684
ATTRIB command, 506, 731-733
attributes (files), 277-278, 489, 493-494
AUTOEXEC.BAT file
   executing statements, 168
   installing OS/2, 158
   running batch files automatically, 460
AUTOFAIL command, 68, 88
automatic application setup, 264
Autosave command (File menu), 358
autosave settings, 834
autotuning, 701

B

Backdoor BBS, 899
background changes (windows), 259
Background Color command (Options menu), 555
background images, 182-183
Background page (desktop), 181
backing up files, 40-41, 202-206
   CONFIG.SYS file, 202
   hard disks, 323-329
   installing OS/2, 127, 130
Backspace key, 17, 350
BACKUP command, 324-327, 506, 733-735
BAK files, 48
BAS files, 48

BAT file, 48, 448, 465
batch files, 447-448, 465
   batch file modules, 458-459
   changing operating systems, 492
   commands, 450
   creating programs, 451-452
   halting programs, 459
   hiding lines, 453
   icons, 449
   infinite loops, 459
   interacting with programs, 459-460
   OS/2 vs. DOS, 448
   parameters, 454-455
   programming, 101-102
   return codes, 457
   REXX programming language, 466-487
   running batch file programs, 449-450
   running programs automatically, 460-461
   SETVGA.CMD, 174
   statements, 452-459
      CALL, 458-459
      ECHO, 453-454
      FOR loops, 458
      GOTO, 455
      IF, 456-457
      IF ERRORLEVEL, 457
      IF EXIST, 455-456
      label statements, 455
      REM statement, 453
   see also REXX programming language
Baudeville BBS, 894
BBS (bulletin board systems), 612, 893-915
BBS Council, 894
BBS operations, 617-621
BBS/2, 899
Bear Garden (BBS), 894
BIN files, 48
BIO files, 48
bit-map fonts, 384
BITMAP directory, 208
bitmaps, 99, 153, 178
BMP files, 48
BOOK directory, 208
bookmarks, 832-834
BOOT command, 68, 404, 506
Boot Manager, 62, 82-83, 121, 127, 131-133, 159-160, 490, 509-510
boot problems, 215-218, 224

boot sectors, 36
BOOT utility, 489-492
booting
    BOOT command, 404
    Boot Manager, 82-83
    DOS from OS/2, 404
    Dual Boot, 82
    installation disk, 127-128
    operating systems, 24
    OS/2 command-line prompt, 129
borders (windows), 238
bound programs, 400
BREAK option, 92-93
buffers, 85
bugs, 39
Bullet BBS, 900
Byte Bus, The (BBS), 900

C

C files, 48
CACHE command, 68
caches, 86
Caddis OS/2 BBS, 900
CAGE, The (BBS), 895
Caladan (BBS), 901
calculations in REXX programs, 476
Calculator, 545, 550-553
    arithmetic operations, 551-553
    Customize menu, 547-548, 553
    fonts, 548-549
    Tally menu, 553
Calendar, 519, 529-530
calendar operations, 304
CALL statement, 458-459
Cancel Snooze command (File menu), 536
canceling
    file selection, 286
    icon operations, 257
Capital City BBS, 901
CAPTURE command, 687
capture files, 621
cascaded menus, 247
case-sensitive text search, 355
CASTOFF command, 683
CASTON command, 683
Cat and Mouse game, 149, 837-838
Catacombs, The (BBS), 901
CBL files, 48

CCITT (Committee Consultatif International Telegraphique and Telephonique), 629
CD command, 308-309, 735-736
CD-ROM, 83-84, 123, 126, 142, 176
Centered command (Options menu), 555
CFG files, 48
CGA (Color Graphics Adapter) video adapter, 94, 116-117
Change partition name... command (Options menu), 496
CHCP command, 68, 736-737
CHDIR command, 308
check boxes, 242
Chess, 150
CHKDSK command, 68, 506, 737-739
Choice BBS, The, 901
CHP files, 48
Circle command (Edit menu), 574
Clear command (Edit menu), 573
Clear Line command (Edit menu), 523
Clear on Search command (Options menu), 566
Clear Tally Roll command (Tally menu), 553
clearing
    screens, 305
    text (System Editor), 352
clicking mouse, 18, 830
client area, 238
client database support (Database Manager), 654
client/server computing, 691
    Database Manager, 653
    LAN Server/Manager, 706-707
Clipboard, 352, 832-833
Clipboard Viewer, 545, 556-559
Close window, 400
closing
    DOS sessions, 403
    windows, 249, 828, 833
CLS command, 305, 739
CMD command, 739-740
CMD files, 48, 448, 465
CNF files, 48

colon (:) in label statements, 455
color, 94-95
Color Fill command (Tools menu), 576
Color Graphics Adapter video adapter, *see* CGA
Colors command
    Customize menu, 525, 547
    Options menu, 359
COM files, 48
COM_DIRECT_ACCESS setting, 434
COM_HOLD setting, 416, 435
COM_RECEIVE_BUFFER_FLUSH setting, 435-436
COM_SELECT setting, 436
combination boxes, 242
combining files, 319-320
COMM Port One (BBS), 900
COMMAND command, 740-741
command history/recall, 102
command keys, 832
Command menu keystrokes, 835
Command Prompts folder, 26, 395
Command Reference (on-line documentation), 146
Command Reference utility, 340-343
command-line based utilities (NetWare), 682-686
command-line parameters (REXX programs), 481
command-line sessions
    batch files, 447-448
    Help system windows, 334-335
    LAN Manager/Server, 709
    OS/2, 303-305
COMMAND.COM file, 137
commands, 301-331
    Alarms menu, 535-538
    ANSI, 729
    APPEND, 729-730
    ASSIGN, 731
    ATTACH, 684
    ATTRIB, 506, 731-733
    AUTOFAIL, 68
    BACKUP, 324-327, 506, 733-735
    batch files, 450
    BOOT, 68, 404, 506
    CACHE, 68

commands

CAPTURE, 687
CASTOFF, 683
CASTON, 683
CD, 308-309, 735-736
CHCP, 68, 736-737
CHDIR, 308
CHKDSK, 68, 506, 737-739
CLS, 305, 739
CMD, 739-740
COMMAND, 740-741
COMP, 506, 741-742
Completed menu (Daily Planner), 524
COPY, 317-321, 387, 742-744
COUNTRY, 510
Customize menu
   Activities List, 533-534
   Alarms, 538
   Calculator, 547-548, 553
   Daily Planner, 525-526
   Monthly Planner, 527-528
   Sticky Notes, 569
   To-Do List, 543
Database applet, 580-581
DATE, 303-304, 744
DDINSTALL, 744-745
DEL, 56, 315-316, 745-746
DETACH, 746
Device menu (Icon Editor), 575
DIR, 47, 312-315, 395, 746-748
DISKCACHE, 68
DISKCOMP, 507, 748-749
DISKCOPY, 55, 127, 507, 749-750
Display menu (Clipboard Viewer), 557
DO, 473
DOSKEY, 750-751
DPATH, 68
Edit menu
   Activities List, 532
   Alarms, 538
   Daily Planner, 523-524
   EPM, 364-366
   Icon Editor, 573-574
   Notepad, 571-572
   Seek and Scan Files, 566
   Sticky Notes, 568-569
   System Editor, 358
   Tune Editor, 561-562
END, 473
ENDCAP, 688

ERASE, 56, 315-316, 454, 745-746
error messages, 210
EXIT, 305, 751
FDISK, 507, 751-752
File menu
   Activities List, 532
   Daily Planner, 523
   EPM, 363-372
   Icon Editor, 573
   Notepad, 570-571
   Seek and Scan Files, 565
   System Editor, 356-358
   To-Do List, 541
   Tune Editor, 560-561
file-oriented, 721-722
FIND, 507, 752-753
Find menu (System Editor), 353
FORMAT, 160, 507, 753-755
GRAFTABL, 507, 755-756
halting, 835
HELP, 30, 68, 335, 517, 756-757
help availability, 341-343
Help menu, 496
HELP OFF, 334
HELP ON, 334
IFS, 68
IOPL, 69
JOIN, 757
KEYB, 758
KEYS, 69, 758-759
LABEL, 507, 759-760
LIBPATH, 69
LOGIN, 684
login sequence (NetWare), 675-676
MAP, 685
Mark menu (To-Do List), 542
MAXWAIT, 69
MD, 307-308, 760-761
MEM, 761
MEMMAN, 69
MKDIR, 307
MODE, 761-764
MORE, 329, 507, 764
MOVE, 56, 69, 764-765
NCOPY, 685
NDIR, 686
NPRINT, 682
Options menu, 496
   EPM, 367-371
   FDISK, 132, 133
   Icon Editor, 575
   Pulse, 554-555

Seek and Scan Files, 566
   System Editor, 359-361
OS/2 compared to DOS, 61
Palette menu (Icon Editor), 574-575
PAUSEONERROR, 69
Play menu (Tune Editor), 562
PM Chart, 602-603
PM Terminal, 612-613
PRINT, 329-330, 387, 765-766
PRIORITY, 69
PROMPT, 766-768
PROTECTONLY, 69
PROTSHELL, 69
PULL, 469, 473
RD, 309-310, 768
RECOVER, 507, 768
REN, 316
RENAME, 56, 316-317
REPLACE, 508
RESTORE, 327-329, 508
RIGHTS, 687
RMDIR, 768
RMSIZE, 69
RUN, 69
SAY, 469
SAY command, 473
Search menu (EPM), 366-367
Selected menu (Seek and Scan Files), 565
SEND, 683
Services menu, 338
SETBOOT, 69
SETVGA.CMD, 174
SLIST, 684
SPOOL, 69
Spreadsheet applet, 593-594
SWAPPATH, 69
switches, 721
syntax, 719-720
system-oriented, 723-724
Tally menu (Calculator), 553
THREADS, 69
Tidy menu (Daily Planner), 525
TIME, 304-305
TIMESLICE, 69
Tools menu (Icon Editor), 576
TREE, 508
TYPE, 127
UNDELETE, 405
updated, 67-69
VIEW, 69

View menu
    Activities List, 533
    Daily Planner, 524
    Monthly Planner, 527
    Notepad, 572
    To-Do List, 542
VMDISK, 715
WHOAMI, 684
XCOPY, 321-323, 508
COMMIT setting (MemMan), 91
Common User Access interface, *see* CUA
Communications Manager, 628-635
    connectivity options, 629-631
    installation, 625
    terminal emulation, 631-635
Communications Manager/2 (CM/2), 623, 655
communications ports, 97
Communitel OS/2 BBS, 902
COMP command, 506, 741-742
comparing strings, 456-457
Completed menu commands, 524
compressed files, 490, 514-516
CompuServe, 612
computer magazines, 42
concatenating strings, 477
conditional loops, 474-475
CONFIG.SYS file, 63
    backing up, 202
    changing statements, 163-165
    default, 883-888
    DOS session configuration, 409-410
    installing OS/2, 158
    migrating statements, 167
    specific-DOS sessions, 715
    updating statements, 167
configuration commands, 724-728
configuration settings, 153-154
Configuration Tool, 642
configuring
    DOS sessions, 421-425, 434-445
    Drives object display, 278-279
    hard disks, 201
    OS/2 preferences, 161-191

Confirmations page (System page), 184
connectivity options (Communications Manager), 629-631
controller cards, 114-115
conventional memory, 63, 151
COPY command, 317-321, 387, 742-744
Copy command (Edit menu), 358, 523
copying
    directories, 321-323
    files, 55-56, 127, 138-139, 287, 317-321
    floppy disks, 55, 127, 291-292
    objects, 256-257
    text, 352, 832-833
    to/from devices, 320-321
Cornerstone BBS, The, 902
counted loops, 475
COUNTRY command, 510
Country object customization, 186
country settings customization, 263
COUNTRY.SYS file cannot be found error message, 199
Cowlishaw, Mike, 467
CPI files, 48
CPUs, 105-110
    80386 chip, 108
    80486 chip, 109
    MaxWait option, 90
    Pentium chip, 109
    Priority option, 91
    threads, 91
crashing system, 405
Create Another Printer window, 390
Create command (Options menu), 133
Create partition command (Options menu), 496
cross-linked extended attributes (drives), 218-219
Ctrl key, 17
CUA (Common User Access), 14, 229-231
Cuerna Verde (BBS), 902
current cell, 595
current directory, 53, 306
cursor keys, 17, 829

cursors
    highlighting, 831
    mouse cursor, 349
    text cursors, 348-349
Customize menu
    Activities List, 533-534
    Alarms, 538
    Calculator, 547-548, 553
    Daily Planner, 525-526
    Monthly Planner, 527-528
    Stick Notes, 569
    To-Do List, 543
customizing
    AUTOEXEC.BAT, 168
    CONFIG.SYS file, 163-167
    desktop, 98-99, 178-190
    DOS/Windows settings, 165-166
    hardware upgrades, 169-176
        fonts, 172-173
        hard disks, 176
        mouse, 173
        printers, 169-172
        video, 173-175
    icons, 576
    Install object, 176-178
    keyboard, 99, 188-189, 262
    monitor, 98-99
    mouse, 99, 186-188, 262
    national language support, 186
    palettes, 263-264
    sounds, 185
    STARTUP.CMD, 168
    System Clock, 189
    System object, 184-185
    windows, 263
    Workplace Shell, 262-264
Cut command (Edit menu), 358, 523
cutting
    DOS sessions, 402-403
    text (System Editor), 352, 832

D

Daily Planner, 519, 521-526
DAT files, 49
data entry fields (dialog boxes), 243
Database 2/2, *see* DB2/2
Database applet, 580-593
    commands, 580-581
    copying/pasting data, 592-593, 600-601

Database applet

limitations, 591-592
modem use, 589
operations, 584-591
Database Manager, 635-654, 707
   client database support, 654
   Configuration Tool, 642
   Database Services feature, 638-642
   Directory Tool, 644
   operations, 636-638
   Query Manager, 644-650
   Recovery Tool, 642
   Remote Data Services, 651-654
Database Server, 626
Datagram support (NetBIOS), 704
DATE command, 303-304, 744
Date/Time page (System Clock), 189
DB2/2, 623, 655-656, 707
DBF files, 49
DCP files, 49
DCT files, 49
DDINSTALL command, 744-745
DEC VT100 terminal emulation, 618, 634
defaults
   Icon Editor, 574
   modifying default icons, 576-578
   Planner file, 538-539
deferring print operation, 378
defining variables in REXX programming language, 469-471
DEL command, 56, 315-316, 745-746
Del key, 17, 350
DELETE directory, 207
Delete partition... command (Options menu), 496
deleting
   files, 207, 315-316
   fonts, 386
   partitions, 494-497
   text, 350, 833
desktop
   appending applications, 190
   bitmaps, 99
   customizing, 98-99, 178-190
   Details view, 181
   Icon view, 179-180
   page settings, 181-182

restoring, 204-206
saving arrangement, 261
screen color/background, 182-183
System object, 184-185
Tree view, 180
Workplace Shell, 94
DETACH command, 746
Details View (desktop), 181
   Drive objects, 276-278
   print job list, 380
DEV files, 49
device drivers
   ANSI.SYS, 68
   mouse, 173
Device menu (Icon Editor), 575
device support disks, 158
diagnostic utilities, 177, 406
dialog boxes
   command, 835
   opening, 239, 832
   Presentation Manager options, 239-243
DIF files, 49
Digital Audio program, 892
Digital Intel Xerox (DIX) Version 2.0 protocol, 702
DIR command, 47, 312-315, 395, 746-748
direct connectivity, 630
directories, 21, 51-53, 208
   changing, 308-309
   copying, 321-323
   creating, 52-53, 307-308
   DELETE, 207
   Drives object, 27
   listings, 279-281
   maximum rights mask, 690
   outlines, 51-53
   PATH, 449
   removing, 309-310
   rights (networks), 686-687
   searching, 566
   WINSTALL, 125
Directory Tool, 644
DISKCACHE command, 68
DISKCOMP command, 507, 748-749
DISKCOPY command, 55, 127, 507, 749-750
disks
   AUTOFAIL option, 88
   buffers, 85
   caches, 86
   CD-ROM, 83-84

defragmenters, 406
file compression, 87
lazy writes, 86
partitions, 489
RAM Disk utility, 87-88
utilities, 405-406
   see also Drives objects; floppy disks; hard disks
display adapters, 173-175
Display Found Text command (Options menu), 566
Display menu (Clipboard Viewer), 557
display settings (DOS sessions), 425-428
displaying files on-screen, 329
DLLs (Dynamic Link Libraries), 49, 91, 164, 208
DO command, 473
DOC files, 49
documentation, 100
Documentation feature, 176
Dog's Breakfast, The (BBS), 902
domains, 699-700, 712
DOS (disk operating system)
   applications, 63-65, 264
   batch files, 448, 451
   boot disks, 202, 225
   booting from OS/2, 404
   BREAK option, 92-93
   command comparison, 61
   command-line prompt, 33
   customizing settings, 165-166
   DOS sessions, 394-397
      closing, 403
      cutting and pasting, 402-403
      extender, 406
      full-screen sessions, 395
      navigating, 395-396
      starting Windows, 396
      system menus, 401-403
      windowed sessions, 395
DPMI (DOS Protected Mode Interface), 151
Dual Boot, 82, 131, 136-138, 404
FATs (File Allocation Tables), 84
file comparison, 60
installing applications, 397-404
   file recognition, 398-399
   new program objects, 397

program settings, 398
session type, 399-401
memory management, 151
memory managers, 406
non-Windows applications, 14
printing, 389
ProtectOnly option, 93
Pulse applet, 554
Real Mode Size (RMSIZE) option, 93
software, 25
starting, 404
switching to OS/2, 404, 489-492
VDM (Virtual DOS Machine), 25
viruses, 405
DOS file comparison, 60
DOS sessions
CONFIG.SYS changes, 409-410
CONFIG.SYS configuration, 410-411
configuration, 421-425
configuring general settings, 434-445
display settings, 425-428
memory, 411-413, 428-434
performance enhancements, 414-415, 418-421
priority, 413-414
troubleshooting, 415-417
DOS support, 60-61, 177
DOS_AUTOEXEC setting, 436
DOS_BACKGROUND_EXECUTION setting, 418
DOS_BREAK setting, 422
DOS_DEVICE setting, 437
DOS_FCBS setting, 437
DOS_FCBS_KEEP setting, 438
DOS_FILES setting, 438
DOS_HIGH setting, 429
DOS_LASTDRIVE setting, 439
DOS_RMSIZE setting, 429
DOS_SHELL setting, 439
DOS_STARTUP_DRIVE setting, 440-441
DOS_UMB setting, 429
DOS_VERSION setting, 441
DOSKEY command, 750-751
dot-matrix printers, 22, 375
double equal (==) in IF statements, 456
double quotation marks (") in REXX programs, 476

Dow Jones News Retrieval Service, 612
downloadable character sets, 375
DPA (Demand Protocol Architecture), 703
DPATH command, 68
DPMI (DOS Protected Mode Interface), 151, 412
DPMI_DOS_API setting, 430
DPMI_MEMORY_LIMIT setting, 430
DPMI_NETWORK_BUFF_SIZE setting, 431
dragging
icons, 255
mouse, 830
objects, 232
templates, 264
Draw Straight command (Options menu), 575
drives, 113
controller cards, 114-115
mapping, 678
Drives object, 27, 265-266, 271-300
details view, 276-278
directory lists, 279-281
display configuration, 278-279
finding files, 282-284
tree view, 275-276
views, 271-279
drop-down list boxes, 242
dropping icons on other icons, 257
DRV files, 49
DSPINSTL utility, 174
DTA files, 49
Dual-Boot, 82, 131, 136-138, 404, 490-491
Dugout BBS, The, 902
duplexing, 23
dynamic SQL, 639

E

EA DATA. SF file, 207
EAUTIL utility, 493-494, 507
ECHO statement, 453-454
ECS Net (BBS), 895
Edit Color command (Palette menu), 574

Edit menu
Activities List, 532
Alarms, 538
Daily Planner, 523-524
EPM, 364-366
Icon Editor, 573-574
Notepad, 571-572
Seek and Scan Files, 566
Sticky Notes, 568-569
System Editor, 358
Tune Editor, 561-562
Edit menu keystrokes, 833-834
editing
keystrokes, 830-835
Monthly Planner, 528-529
multiple text files (EPM), 369
Notepad, 569-570
text (System Editor), 347-356
To-Do List, 540-541
Tune Editor, 560
EGA (Enhanced Graphics Adapter) video adapter, 94, 116-117
Emerald Isle, The (BBS), 903
EMS (expanded memory)memory, 64, 412
EMS_FRAME_LOCATION setting, 431
EMS_HIGH_OS_MAP_REGION setting, 431
EMS_LOW_OS_MAP_REGION setting, 432
EMS_MEMORY_LIMIT setting, 432
Emulator High-Level Language API (EHLLAPI), 655
Encounter, The (BBS), 903
END command, 473
end key, 17
ENDCAP command, 688
Enhanced Editor, *see* EPM
Enhanced Editor keystroke, 827-835
Enhanced Graphics Adapter video adapter, *see* EGA
Enhanced mode (Windows), 406
Enhanced Small Drive Interface (ESDI) disk drive, 113
enhancing system performance, 223-224
enter key, 17

EPM (Enhanced Editor for
  Program Manager), 27, 149,
  346-347, 361-362
    editing multiple files, 369
    fonts, 365, 369
    margins, 369
    menus, 362-372
      Edit menu, 364-366
      File menu, 363-372
      Options menu, 367-371
      Search menu, 366-367
    message line, 371
    modifying default icon, 577
    printing files, 364
    redefining keystrokes, 369
    Settings Notebook, 368
    starting, 362
    tabs, 369
    undoing changes, 365
    window display, 370
equal sign (=) in Tune Editor,
  561
ERASE command, 56, 315-316,
  454, 745-746
erasing files, 315-316
error messages, 210
    HELP command, 335
    installing OS/2, 124, 138
    Invalid number of
      parameters, 454
    Unrecoverable Application
      Error, 403
errors
    AUTOFAIL, 88
    PauseOnError, 88-89
    printer errors, 389
    see also troubleshooting
esc key, 17
ESDI (Enhanced Small Drive
  Interface) disk drive, 113
Ethernet adapters, 630
Ethernet-based LANs, 652
EUATIL utility, 489
Excelsior, The (BBS), 903
EXE files, 49
EXIT command, 305, 751
Exit command (Options
  menu), 496
expanded memory (EMS), 64,
  151
extended attributes
    drives, 73-74, 218-219, 493
    files, 298-299
Extended Graphics Array
  video adapter, see XGA
Extended memory (XMS), 64,
  151

Extended Memory
  Specification (XMS), 151
Extended Services, 623-624,
  654
    Communications Manager,
      628-635
      connectivity options,
        629-631
      terminal emulation,
        631-635
    Database Manager, 635-654
      client database support,
        654
      Configuration Tool, 642
      Database Services feature,
        638-642
      Directory Tool, 644
      operations, 636-638
      Query Manager, 644-650
      Recovery Tool, 642
      Remote Data Services,
        651-654
    Database Server interaction,
      626
    installing, 624-626
    security, 627-628
extensions, 46-50
extracting files, 515

F

FAT (File Allocation Table),
  44, 84, 130, 134
FCONSOLE utility, 690
FDISK command, 507,
  751-752
FDISK unsuccessful error
  message, 198
FDISKPM utility, 489, 494-497
Fernwood (BBS), 903
fields, 580, 584-585
File Access SMBs, 705
File Allocation Table, see FAT,
  44
File menu
    Activities List, 532
    Daily Planner, 523
    EPM, 363-372
    Icon Editor, 573
    Notepad, 570-571
    Seek and Scan Files, 565
    System Editor, 356-358
    To-Do List, 541
    Tune Editor, 560-561
File menu keystrokes, 832

File pages (desktop), 182
files, 21
    * (asterisk) wildcard, 282
    ANSI.SYS, 68
    appending Help information
      to, 338
    associating with
      applications, 292-297
        by name, 293-294
        by type, 292-293
        pop-up menu method,
          294-297
    attribute information,
      277-278
    AUTOEXEC.BAT, 158
      executing statements,
        168
      running batch files
        automatically, 460
    backing up, 40-41, 127, 130,
      202-206
    batch files, 447-448, 465
      batch file modules,
        458-459
      changing operating
        systems, 492
      commands, 450
      creating programs,
        451-452
      halting programs, 459
      icons, 449
      infinite loops, 459
      interacting with
        programs, 459-460
      OS/2 vs. DOS, 448
      parameters, 454-455
      programming, 101-102
      REXX programming
        language, 466-487
      running, 449-450,
        460-461
      statements, 452-459
    canceling selections, 286
    capture files, 621
    CMD.EXE, 448
    combining, 319-320
    COMMAND.COM, 137
    commands, 721-722
    compressed file restoration,
      514-516
    compressed files, 490
    CONFIG.SYS, 158
      backing up, 202
      changing statements,
        163-165
      default, 883-888

games 997

DOS session configuration, 409-410
  migrating statements, 167
  updating statements, 167
CONFIG.SYS file, 715
copying, 55-56, 127, 138-139, 287, 317-321
deleting, 207
deleting/erasing, 315-316
directories, 51-53
displaying on-screen, 329
DOS sessions, 410
EA DATA. SF, 207
extended attributes, 73-76, 298-299
extensions, 46-50
file compression, 87
finding, 282-284
flags, 297-298
Hidden attribute, 206
hold files, 489, 493
HPFS names, 703
importing, 832
Internet file listing (Walnut Creek site), 915-988
IPF (Information Presentation Facility), 516-517
listing by function, 845-882
message files, 209
moving, 286-287
naming, 46-47, 84, 828, 833
NET.CFG, 673
opening, 285, 832-833
OS/2 compared to DOS, 60
OS2.INI, 73, 498-499
OS2SYS.INI, 73, 498-499
Planner file default, 538-539
print queues, 688
printing, 329-330, 833
printing to disk, 390-391
read-only, 278
README.INS, 127
recovering deleted files, 682
renaming, 316-317
restoring, 327-329, 490, 513-514
rights (networks), 686-687
saving, 832
searching, 563-565
selecting, 285-286
SETVGA.CMD batch files, 174
shadowing, 288
sorting, 511

STARTUP.CMD
  executing statements, 168
  running batch file automatically, 460
styles, 832
SwapPath option, 92
SWAPPER.DAT, 64
System attribute, 206
text files
  editing, 347-350
  REXX programs, 479-480
UNDELETE command, 405
utility files, 672
wildcards, 47, 313-315
WPROOT. SF, 207
fill character, 831
Fill command (Edit menu), 574
Fill command (Options menu), 555
Find Color command (Tools menu), 576
FIND command (Edit menu), 358, 507, 752-753
Find menu commands (System Editor), 353
finding
  files, 282-284
  text, 353-356
Fixed 2 command (Customize menu), 553
flags (files), 297-298
flat files, 346
Flip Horizontal command (Edit menu), 574
Flip Vertical command (Edit menu), 574
Floating Point command (Customize menu), 553
floppy disks, 19-20, 45, 106
  copying, 55, 127, 291-292
  DOS boot disks, 202, 225
  formatting, 54, 289-291
  hard disk backups, 324-327
  installing OS/2, 126-127
  OS/2 2.1, 123
  PMCHDSK utility, 501-503
  reformatting, 289
  volume labels, 326
FNT files, 49
folders
  creating, 264-265
  menus, 258-259
  opening, 266
  settings notebook, 259
FON files, 49

Font command (Customize menu), 526
Font Installer window, 386
Font Palette, 172
fonts, 22, 96-97, 360, 369, 383
  Adobe Type Manager fonts, 384-385
  deleting, 386
  EPM, 365
  font cartridges, 375
  Font Palette, 386
  General Purpose applets, 548-550
  IBM Core Fonts, 384
  installation, 382-386
  installing, 172-173
  installing OS/2, 146
  printing, 375
  size, 401-402
Fonts command (Options menu), 360
Fonts feature, 176
FOR loops, 458
FORMAT command, 53-54, 160, 507, 753-755
formatting disks, 53-54, 289-291
Frame Controls command (Options menu), 370
Freeze Screen command (Options menu), 555
frozen systems, 38
full-screen DOS sessions, 399-401
function keys, 17, 828-829
functions (REXX)
  ARG, 481
  LEFT, 478
  LENGTH, 478
  LINEIN, 479
  LINEOUT, 480
  LINES, 480
  POS, 479
  RIGHT, 478
  STRIP, 479
  SUBSTR, 478
  TRANSLATE, 478
  WORDS, 479

G

games, 100-101, 177, 837
  Cat and Mouse, 837-838
  installing OS/2, 148-149
  Jigsaw game, 839-840

998 games

OS/2 Chess, 840-841
Reversi, 841-842
Scramble, 842-843
GammaTech Utilities (GammaTech), 75-76
garbled screen, 221
Gecko Control (BBS), 904
General help command (Help menu), 497
General page
    desktop, 181
    mouse, 188
    System Clock, 189
    System page, 184
General Purpose applets
    Calculator, 545, 550-553
        arithmetic operations, 551-553
        Customize menu, 547-548, 553
        fonts, 548-549
        Tally menu, 553
    Clipboard Viewer, 545, 556-559
        Display menu, 557
        Private Clipboard, 558-559
        Public Clipboard, 557
    commands, 547-550
    font size, 548-550
    Icon Editor, 545, 572-578
        customizing icons, 576
        Device menu, 575
        Edit menu, 573-574
        File menu, 573
        modifying defaults, 576-578
        Options menu, 575
        Palette menu, 574-575
        Tools menu, 576
    Notepad, 546, 569-572
        creating notes, 569-570
        Edit menu, 571-572
        File menu, 570-571
        View menu, 572
    printing, 549-550
    Pulse, 545, 553-556
        Options menu, 554-555
        updating graph, 555-556
    Seek and Scan Files, 546, 562-566
        Edit menu, 566
        File menu, 565
        Options menu, 566
        searching files, 563-565
        Selected menu, 565
        stopping searches, 566

    starting, 546
    Sticky Notes
        Customize menu, 569
        Edit menu, 568-569
        inserting, 567-568
    Sticky Pad, 546, 567-569
    Tune Editor, 546, 559-562
        Edit menu, 561-562
        editing, 560
        File menu, 560-561
        Play menu, 562
GEnie, 617
Ghostcomm Image Gallery (BBS), 904
global sessions (networks), 670
GOTO statement, 455
GPF REXX, 483
GRAFTABL command, 507, 755-756
Graph Color command (Options menu), 555
graphical user interface (GUI), 24
graphics, printing, 23
Graphics command (Edit menu), 569
    Daily Planner, 523
graphics mode (monitor), 19
GREATER CHICAGO Online!! BBS, 904
Grep search function, 366-367
Grid command (Options menu), 575
GUI (graphical user interface), 24
GUI Programming Facility (GPF), 483

H

halting commands, 835
hard disks, 19, 106
    allocating partitions, 43-45
    backing up, 323-329
    boot sectors, 36
    clusters, lost, 501
    configuring, 201
    controller cards, 113-115
    extended attributes (drives), 218-219
    formatting, 53
    HPFS (High Performance File System), 84-85, 129
    installing, 176
        OS/2, 135, 138

MemMan (Memory Management), 90-91
partial backups, 327-329
PMCHDSK utility, 501-503
repartitioning and reformatting, 129-139
restoring from backups, 327-329
REXX programs, 479
utilities, 74-76
volume labels, 326
hardware
    device support disks, 158
    directories, 21
    keyboard, 15-17
    monitor, 18-19
    mouse, 18
    printers, 21-23
    requirements, 105-107
    upgrades, 169-176
        fonts, 172-173
        hard disks, 176
        mouse, 173
        printers, 169-172
        video, 173-175
    video adapters, 141
Headland Technology VRAM II adapter, 174
HELP command, 30, 68, 335, 517, 756-757
HELP directory, 208
help function key, 828
Help index command (Help menu), 496
Help menu commands, 496
HELP OFF command, 334
HELP ON command, 334
Help system, 333-344
    appending information to files, 338
    available detail in table of contents, 340
    Command Reference utility, 340-343
    command-line window, 334-335
    commands, 341-343
    on-line documentation, 100, 145
    Presentation Manager, 333, 336-340
        Help system, 336
        menu options, 336-337
HelpNet of Baton Rouge (BBS), 904
Hidden attribute, 206
high memory area, 151

installation

High Performance File System, *see* HPFS
highlighting text, 351
HLP files, 49
HockWare, 482-483
hold files, 493
Home Front BBS, 895
Home key, 17, 348
Hot Spot command (Options menu), 575
HPFS, 44, 72-73, 84-85, 121, 127-129, 134-135, 152, 159-160, 177, 702
HW_NOSOUND setting, 416, 442
HW_ROM_TO_RAM setting, 414, 419
HW_TIMER setting, 414, 442

I

I CAN! BBS, 904
IBM
   3101 Terminal Emulator, 633
   3101-10 terminal emulation, 618
   3270 Terminal Emulator, 632
   5250 Terminal Emulator, 634-635
   Core Fonts, 384
   M-Audio Card, 890
   software support, 193
IBM National Support Center (BBS), 905
IBM PC Network-based LANs, 652
IBM-compatible computers, 104-107
Icon Editor, 545, 572-578
   customizing icons, 576
   Device menu, 575
   Edit menu, 573-574
   File menu, 573
   modifying defaults, 576-578
   Options menu, 575
   Palette menu, 574-575
   Tools menu, 576
Icon view (desktop), 179-180, 380
icons, 19, 254-258
   arranging, 258
   batch files, 449
   canceling operations, 257
   copying, 256
   dragging, 255

   dropping on other icons, 257
   in-use emphasis, 255
   installing OS/2, 156
   keyboard operations, 258
   minimized views, 257
   moving, 255
   name changes, 257
   OS/2 System, 246
   selecting, 255
   shadows, 256
   views, 255
IDLE_SECONDS setting, 420
IDLE_SENSITIVITY setting, 420-421
IDX files, 49
IF ERRORLEVEL statement, 457
IF EXIST statement, 455-456
IF statement, 456-457, 472-473
IFS command, 68
IFS files, 49
Ignore Case command (Options menu), 566
Ignore case search function, 366
iKon View (BBS), 897
IMG files, 49
Import Text File command (File menu), 364
importing files, 364, 832
in-use emphasis (icons), 255
inactive windows, 234
Include page (desktop), 181
indexed help, 337
indexes, 642
INF files, 49
infinite loops, 459
Information Overload (BBS), 905
information services, 893-942
   BBSes, 893-915
   Internet, 915-988
INI files, 49, 73-74
INIMAINT utility (Carry Associates), 76
initializing Workplace Shell, 159
INPUT.COM utility, 459
Input/Output Privilege Level (IOPL), 89
ins key, 17
inserting
   Sticky Notes, 567-568
   text, 349-350
Install Boot Manager... command (Options Menu), 496

INSTALL directory, 208
Install Most... command (Options menu), 132
installation, 121-123
   applications, 100-101, 397-404
      file recognition, 398-399
      new program objects, 397
      program settings, 398
      session type, 399-401
   backing up files, 127, 130
   bit maps, 153
   Boot Manager, 121, 127, 131-133, 159-160
   booting installation disk, 127-128
   CD-ROM, 123, 126, 142
   configuration settings, 153-154
   copying files, 138-139
   device support disks, 158
   disks, 224
   DOS, 150-152
      DPMI (DOS Protected Mode Interface), 151
   DOS-formatted machines, 131
   Dual Boot, 490-491
   Dual-Boot, 131, 136-138
   errors, 195-200
      error messages, 124, 138, 197-200
      symptoms, 196-197
   Extended Services, 624-626
   failure, 128
   files
      AUTOEXEC.BAT, 158
      CONFIG.SYS, 158
   floppy disks, 126-127
   fonts, 146, 172-173, 382-386
   formatting hard drive, 130-139
   games, 148-149
   hard disk space, 135
   hard disks, 176
   HPFS (High Performance File System), 121, 127-129, 134-135, 152, 159-160
   icons, 156
   Install all features option, 140
   Migrate Applications, 156
   mouse, 137-140, 173
   Multimedia Presentation Manager/2, 891
   NetWare Requester, 663-674

non-formatted machines, 131
on-line documentation, 145
options, 143
OS/2 for Windows, 125, 152, 157
partitioning hard drive, 130-139
printer objects, 374
printers, 169-172
README.INS file, 127
REXX programming language, 153, 466
selective, 176-178
Selective Install, 124, 140
serviceability and diagnostic aids, 153
system configuration, 140-143
    peripherals, 142-143
    serial devices, 141
    video adapters, 141
text mode, 128-139
threads, 123
tools, 148-149
utilities, 147
video upgrades, 173-175
Institute of Electrical and Electronic Engineers (IEEE) 802.3 protocol, 702
INT_DURING_IO setting, 442
Integrated Media Services (BBS), 905
Intel 80386 chip, 108
Intel 80486 chip, 109
Internet, 915-942, 943-988
Invalid number of parameters error message, 454
IOPL (Input/Output Privilege Level), 89
IOPL command, 69
IPF (Information Presentation Facility), 516-517

J

Jigsaw game, 149, 839-840
JOIN command, 757
joining
    extended attributes, 494
    lines, 350

K

K (kilobyte), 21
KBD_ALTHOME_BYPASS setting, 422
KBD_BUFFER_EXTEND setting, 414, 422-423
KBD_CTRL_BYPASS setting, 423
KBD_RATE_LOCK setting, 416, 423
key fields, 583
KEY files, 49
KEYB command, 758
keyboard, 15-17
    arithmetic operations (Calculator), 551
    compatibility, 115
    customizing, 99, 188-189, 262
    failure, 222
    icon operations, 258
    Presentation Manager options, 234-235
    shortcuts (Workplace Shell), 823-826
    special keys, 17
KEYS command, 69, 758-759
Keys help command (Help menu), 497
keystrokes
    command keys, 832
    Command menu, 835
    cursor keys, 829
    Edit menu, 833-834
    editing, 830-835
    File menu, 832
    function keys, 828-829
    Options menu, 834
    playing, 832
    recording, 832
    Search menu, 834
    selecting text, 831
    special characters, 831
kilobytes (K), 21
Kind Diamond's Realm (BBS), 905

L

LABEL command, 507, 759-760
label statements, 455
LAN connectivity, 630-631

LAN Manager (Microsoft), 695-713
    client/server computing, 706-707
    command-line interface, 709
    compared to LAN Server, 701-705
    installation, 705-706
    logging on, 710-711
    mapping drives, 711
    menus, 708-709
    printing, 712
    security, 701, 712-713
    terminology, 699-700
    utilities, 710
    workstation setup, 708-709
LAN Server (IBM), 695-713, 697
    client/server computing, 706-707
    command-line interface, 709
    compared to LAN Manager, 701-705
    installation, 705-706
    logging on, 710-711
    mapping drives, 711
    menus, 708-709
    printing, 712
    security, 701, 712-713
    terminology, 699-700
    utilities, 710
    workstation setup, 708-709
landscape orientation, 23
LANtastic (Artisoft), 713
laptop computers, 15
laser printers, 21-22, 375, 384
Last Relay, The (BBS), 906
lazy writes, 86
left brace ({) character, 831
LEFT function, 478
LENGTH function, 478
LET files, 49
LIB files, 49
LIBPATH command, 69
LIM 4.0 Specification, 64
LINEIN function, 479
LINEOUT function, 480
LINES function, 480
lines/arrows (railroad diagram), 343
list boxes, 242
listing files, 47, 312-315
Live-Wire (BBS), 906
LiveNet (BBS), 906
Load Default command (Palette menu), 574

local drives, 685
locking up systems, 260
Lockup pages (desktop), 182
LOG files, 49
log on (LAN Server/Manager), 710-711
logical drives, 497
login (NetWare)
    commands, 675-676
    scripts, 676-677
LOGIN command, 684
Logo page (System page), 184
Lonnie Wall (BBS), 906
Looking Glass, The (BBS), 907
lost extended attributes (drives), 218-219
Lotus Notes, 707
LST files, 49

M

M (megabyte), 21
MAC files, 49
Magnum BBS, 907
Make startable command (Options menu), 496
MAKEINI utility, 489, 498-499
manual application setup, 264
MAP command, 685
MAP files, 49
mapping drives, 678
    LAN Server/Manager, 711
Mappings page
    keyboard, 188
    mouse, 187
margins, 834
Mark command (Edit menu), 358
Mark menu commands (To-Do List), 542
Marked area function, 366
marking text blocks, 351
maximizing memory, 428-434
maximizing windows, 235, 247-267, 829
maximum rights mask, 690
Max's Doghouse (BBS), 907
MAXWAIT command, 69
MaxWait option, 90
MD command, 307-308, 760-761
MDOS directory, 208
megabytes (M), 21
MEM command, 761

MEM_EXCLUDE_REGIONS setting, 432
MEM_INCLUDE_REGIONS setting, 433
MemMan (Memory Management), 90-91
MEMMAN command, 69
memory
    DOS sessions, 409-413
        maximizing, 428-434
    DOS-based appplications, 63-64
    LIM 4.0 Specification, 64
memory management (DOS), 151
memory managers, 406
Menu bar (System Editor), 356
menu based utilities (NetWare), 681-682
menu interface (LAN Manager/Server), 708-709
Menu page (desktop), 182
menus, 246-249
    cascaded, 247
    EPM (Enhanced Editor for Program Manager), 362-372
    folders, 258-259
    System Editor, 356-361
    Workplace Shell, 260-261
merging extended attributes, 494
message files, 209
message line, 371
Message SMBs, 705
MFM (Modified Frequency Modulation) disk drive, 113
MIDI (Musical Instrument Digital Interface), 889
Migrate Applications, 156
migrating applications, 190, 264
migrating CONFIG.SYS statements, 167
minimized views (icons), 257
minimizing windows, 248-267, 829
minus sign (-)
    in REXX programs, 476
    in Tune Editor, 561
MKDIR command, 307
MODE command, 761-764
modem-assisted connectivity, 630
modems, 589

Modified Frequency Modulation (MFM) disk drive, 113
modifier keys, 17
monitors, 18-19, 106
    8514/A, 118
    CGA, 116-117
    color, 94-95
    customizing, 98-99
    EGA, 116-117
    graphics mode, 19
    resolution, 94-95
    Super VGA, 116-119
    text mode, 19
    VGA, 116-117
    XGA, 116-117
Monster BBS, The, 907
Monthly Planner, 519, 526-529
    Customize menu, 527-528
    editing, 528-529
    View menu, 527
MonuSci BBS, 898
MORE command, 329, 507, 764
mouse, 18, 107, 115-116
    arithmetic operations (Calculator), 551
    Cat and Mouse, 149
    clicking, 830
    cursor, 349, 830
    customizing, 99, 186-188, 262
    dragging, 830
    installing, 173
    installing OS/2, 137-140
    Presentation Manager options, 236
    troubleshooting, 222
MOUSE_EXCLUSIVE_ACCESS setting, 416, 424
MOVE command, 56, 69, 764-765
moving
    files, 286-287
    icons, 255
    text, 833
    text blocks, 351-352
    text cursor, 348
    windows, 249-267, 828
MSG files, 49
Multi-Net (BBS), 908
Multimedia Presentation Manager/2 (MMPM/2), 889-892
multiple Extended Attributes, 74

multiple object views
    (Window List), 253-254
Multiple Operating System
    Tool (Boot Manager), 82-83
    see also Boot Manager
multiple printer objects, 390
multitasking, 34
    DOS-based apppications, 65
    MaxWait option, 90
    threads, 89-90

N

Name support (NetBIOS), 704
named pipes, 707
named-pipe support, 670
naming
    files, 46-47, 833
    variables, 470-471
National Language Support
    (NLS), 62, 186
navigating
    cursor keys, 829
    DOS sessions, 395-396
    windows, 252
    Workplace Shell, 233-234
NCOPY command, 685
NDIR command, 686
NDX files, 50
NET.CFG file setup, 673
NetBIOS, 704
    emulation, 670
netnames, 700
NetWare (Novell), 659, 713
    local drives, 685
    login
        commands, 675-676
        scripts, 676-677
    mapping drives, 678
    network drives, 685
    one-line messages, 683
    OS/2 version, 691-692
    printing, 687-689
    security, 689-690
    user accounts, 690-691
    utilities, 680-686
        command line, 682-686
        menu based, 681-682
    workstations, 661-674
        NetWare Requester,
            663-674
        Requester, 662
NetWare Core Protocol (NCP),
    696

NetWare OS/2 Requester kit,
    664
NetWare Requester, 663-674
network adapters, 663
Network Basic Input/Output
    System (NetBIOS), 696
Network Driver Interface
    Specification (NDIS), 696
networking, 659-693
networks
    accessing drives, 685
    drives, 685
    rights, 686-687
NETX.COM program, 670
New command (File menu),
    357
    EPM, 363
Nibbles & Bytes (BBS), 908
non-formatted machines, 131
Norton Utilities (Symantec
    Corporation), 74, 405
NOSWAP setting (MemMan),
    91
NOT character, 831
Notepad, 546, 569-572
    creating notes, 569-570
    Edit menu, 571-572
    File menu, 570-571
    View menu, 572
NPRINT command, 682
NULL character, 831
Num Lock command
    (Customize menu), 553
Num Lock key, 16-17
numeric keypad, 16

O

Oberon Software (BBS), 909
OBJ files, 50
object handles, 608
object view (Window List),
    253
object-oriented interfaces, 66
objects, 70
    copying, 256-257
    dragging/dropping, 232
    shadows, 256
    viewing, 250-252
    Workplace, 231
    see also files; folders;
        programs
occasional backups, 40
OLD files, 50
Omega-Point BBS, 909

on-line documentation, 100,
    145
on-line documents (VIEW
    utility), 516-517
one-line messages (NetWare),
    683
Only some files were copied
    error message, 197
Open command (File menu),
    357
    EPM, 363
Open Tune command (File
    menu), 561
Open Untitled command (File
    menu), 363
opening
    command dialog box, 835
    dialog boxes, 239, 832
    files, 285, 828, 832
    folders, 266
    windows, 828
operating systems, 24, 33-36
    applications support, 34-35
    Dual-Boot, 82
    Multiple Operating System
        Tool (Boot Manager), 82-83
    switching, 489-492
    SYSLEVEL utility, 512-513
    system management, 35-36
    UNIX, 132
Options menu, 496, 834
    Icon Editor, 575
    EPM, 367-371
    FDISK, 132-133
    Pulse, 554-555
    Seek and Scan Files, 566
    System Editor, 359-361
OS/2
    development, 698-699
    DOS support, 60-61
    file listing, 845-882
    historical overview, 817-822
    IBM software support, 193
    information services,
        893-988
    Windows support, 70-71
OS/2 2.1, 59, 67-69
OS/2 Chess, 840-841
OS/2 Connection (BBS), 908
OS/2 EE 1.1, 818
OS/2 for Windows, 152
    desktop, 157
    installing, 125
OS/2 Shareware (BBS), 908
OS/2 System icon, 246
OS/2 Woodmeister, The (BBS),
    909

OS2 Exchange (BBS), 909
OS2.INI file, 73, 489, 498-499
OS2SYS.INI file, 73, 489, 498-499
Other World, The (BBS), 910
OVL files, 50
OVR files, 50

P

packages, 642
Padded Cell BBS, The, 910
PAK files, 50
Palette menu (Icon Editor), 574-575
palettes, 263-264
parallel cables, 22
parameters (batch files), 454-455
partial backups, 327
partitions
   allocating, 43-45
   creating, 489, 494-497
PAS files, 50
Paste command (Edit menu), 358
   Daily Planner, 523
pasting
   windowed DOS sessions, 402-403
   text, 832-833
      System Editor, 352
PATCH utility, 490, 499-501, 507
PATH directories, 449
paths, 306
   railroad diagram, 343
Pause key, 17
PauseOnError, 88-89
PAUSEONERROR command, 69
PC Tools, 405
PCL printer control language, 23
PCMCIA (Personal Computer Memory Card International Association, 97-98
PCONSOLE utility, 688
PCX files, 50
peer LANs, 713-715
Pen Size command (Options menu), 575
Pentium chip, 109
performance enhancement, 414-415, 418-421

peripherals, 142-143
permissions, 712-713
Personal Computer Memory Card International Association (PCMCIA), 97-98
Personal NetWare (Novell), 713
Personal Productivity, 149
PgDn key, 16, 348
PgUp key, 16, 348
Phar Lap Software, 151
PIF files, 50
placing extended attributes, 494
Planner Archive, 520
Planner Archive command (Tidy menu), 534
Planner file default, 538-539
Play Board, The (BBS), 910
Play menu commands (Tune Editor), 562
playing keystrokes, 832
playing melodies (Tune Editor), 562
plus sign (+)
   in REXX programs, 476
   in Tune Editor, 561
PM applications printing, 387
PM Chart applet, 149, 601-612
   commands, 602-603
   copying/pasting data, 612
   limitations, 611-612
   operations, 605-611
PM Terminal applet, 612-621
   capture files, 621
   commands, 612-613
   limitations, 621
   operations, 614-621
PMCHKDSK utility, 490, 501-503
PMREXX, 485-486
PMSC OnLine Resource (BBS), 910
polling rate, 420
pop-up menus, 294-297
ports, 97
POS function, 479
POST (Power-On Self Test), 36
Postscript, 23
power surges, 40
power users, 39
Power-On Self Test, *see* POST
power-on sequence, 36-37
A Practical Approach to Programming REXX, 467
predefined variables (REXX), 471

Preferences command (Options menu), 368, 575
Presentation Manager, 14, 24, 70, 229, 234-243, 336-340
   dialog boxes, 239-243
   Help, 333, 337-340
      Help system, 336
      menu options, 336-337
   keyboard operations, 234-235
   mouse operations, 236
   PMCKDSK utility, 501-503
   PMREXX, 485-486
   VisPro REXX, 482
   VREXX (Visual REXX), 468, 482
   VX/REXX, 484
   windows, 237-239
   Workplace Shell, 24, 30
primary partitions, 497
PRINT command, 329-330, 387, 765-766
Print File command (File menu), 364
Print Manager, 373
print queues, 688
Print Screen (System page), 185
Print Service SMBs, 705
PRINT_SEPARATE_OUTPUT setting, 443-444
PRINT_TIMEOUT setting, 416, 443-444
printed help, 338
Printer Configuration window, 388
printers, 21-23, 96-97, 375-376
   downloadable character sets, 375
   downloadable fonts, 383
   fonts, 2, 375, 383
   installation, 143, 169-172
   soft fonts, 385-386
   PCL printer control language, 23
   printer objects, 29, 374-378
      multiple printer objects, 390
   printer drivers, 377
   queue drivers, 377, 380
   viewing print jobs, 380
printing, 67, 375-382
   Alarms window, 537
   changing job status, 381
   COPY command, 387
   Daily Planner, 523
   Database Manager, 649

printing

deferring print operation, 378
disk files, 390-391
DOS applications, 389
drag and drop, 387
duplexing, 23
errors, 389
files, 329-330
fonts
   Adobe Type Manager fonts, 384-385
   Font Palette, 386
   OS/2 system fonts, 384
General Purpose applets, 549-550
graphics, 23
LAN Server/Manager, 712
landscape orientation, 23
multiple applications, 375
NetWare workstations, 687-689
Notepad, 571
PM applications, 387
PrtSc key, 17
Spooler, 375, 380
To-Do Lists, 541
troubleshooting, 222-223
tunes, 561
viewing print jobs, 380
Widows Print Manager, 388
Windows applications, 388
printing files, 833
priority (DOS sessions), 413-414
PRIORITY command, 69
Priority option, 91
Private Clipboard, 558-559
private sessions (networks), 670
PRN files, 50
Pro AudioSpectrum 16, 890
PRO files, 50
Process command (Selected menu), 565
Product information command (Help menu), 497
productivity aids, 177
Productivity folder, 27, 347, 362, 467
professional backups, 41
profiles, 612
program flow
   conditional loops, 474-475
   IF statement, 472-473
   repetitive loops, 474-475
program objects, 397
Program Template, 190

programming languages, 146, 153
programs
   closing windows, 249
   Digital Audio, 892
   FORMAT, 53-54
   maximizing windows, 247-267
   menus, 246-249
   minimizing windows, 248-267
   moving windows, 249-267
   NETX.COM, 670
   resizing, 249-267
   restoring windows, 248-267
   starting, 246
   see also applets; applications
PROMPT command, 766-768
Propagate/Delete Lines command (Edit menu), 524
PROTECT setting (MemMan), 91
PROTECTONLY command, 69
ProtectOnly option, 93
PROTSHELL command, 69
PrtSc key, 17
PS files, 50
PSF files, 50
PSTAT utility, 490, 504-505
Psychotronic BBS, 911
Public Clipboard, 557
PULL command, 469, 473
Pulse, 149, 545, 553-556
pushbuttons, 241

Q

qualifiers, 642
Quantum Leap (BBS), 911
Quarterdeck Office Systems, 151
Query Manager, 644-650
queue drivers, 377, 380
Quit command (File menu), 364
quitting with function key, 828

R

radio buttons, 241
railroad diagrams, 342-343
RAM Disk utility, 87-88
RC files, 50

RC variable, 471
RD command, 309-310, 768
read-only files, 278
README.INS file, 127
Real Mode Size (RMSIZE) option, 93
rebooting, 36
recording keystrokes, 832
records, 580
records locking (Database Manager), 640-641
RECOVER command, 507, 768
recovering files, see salvaging
Recovery Tool, 642
redefining keystrokes (EPM), 369
Redo command (Edit menu), 358
reformatting
   floppy disks, 289
   hard disks, 129, 130-139
reinstalling OS/2, 218
relational databases, 636-638
REM statement, 453
Remote Data Services, 651-654
Remove from Boot Manager menu command (Options menu), 496
removing directories, 309-310
REN command, 316
RENAME command, 56, 316-317
Rename command (File menu), 364, 561
renaming files, 316-317
Render command (Display menu), 557
repairing software, 499-501
repartitioning hard disks, 129, 130-139
repetitive loops, 474-475
REPLACE command, 508
replacing extended attributes, 494
replacing text, 354
Requester (NetWare workstations), 662
requesters, 699
Reset Timestamp command (Edit menu), 568
resizing windows, 249-267
resolution, 94-95, 173-175
restarting system unit, 37-39
RESTORE command, 327-329, 508

restoring
    compressed files, 514-516
    desktop, 204-206
    files, 327-329, 490, 513-514
    windows, 248-267
RESULT variable, 471
Return Codes, 457, 490, 505-509
    PATCH utility, 501
    SORT utility, 511
    UNPACK utility, 516
Reverse search function, 366
Reversi, 149, 841-842
REXX Operating System/2, 177
REXX programming language, 101-102, 146, 153, 465-466, 639-640
    /* (slash asterisk) in comments, 466
    ARG statement, 481
    calculations, 476
    command-line parameters, 481
    displaying prompts, 469
    DO command, 473
    END command, 473
    executing OS/2 commands, 474
    functions
        ARG, 481
        LEFT, 478
        LENGTH, 478
        LINEIN, 479
        LINEOUT, 480
        LINES, 480
        POS, 479
        RIGHT, 478
        STRIP, 479
        SUBSTR, 478
        TRANSLATE, 478
        WORDS, 479
    GPF REXX, 483
    installing REXX support, 466
    PMREXX, 485-486
    program flow, 471-476
        conditional loops, 474-475
        IF statement, 472-473
        repetitive loops, 474-475
    PULL command, 469, 473
    REXX program statements, 468
    REXX TRACE, 486-487
    REXXTRY, 486
    SAY command, 469, 473

strings, 476-479
text editors, 467
text files, 479-480
variables, 466, 469-471
    naming, 470-471
    predefined variables, 471
VisPro REXX, 482-483
VREXX (Visual REXX), 468, 482, 484
RFT files, 50
right brace (}) character, 832
RIGHT function, 478
rights (networks), 686-687
RIGHTS command, 687
RLL (Run-Length-Limited) disk drives, 113
RMDIR command, 768
RMSIZE command, 69
RMSIZE option, 93
Roach Coach, The (BBS), 911
Rock BBS, The, 911
ROM BIOS, 110-112
rotate buttons, 371
RT Labs (BBS), 895
RucK's Place/2 (BBS), 912
RUN command, 69
Run-Length-Limited (RLL) disk drives, 113
running
    batch file programs, 449-450, 460-461
    REXX programs in Presentation Manager, 485
    Windows applications, 403-404

S

SAA (System Application Architecture), 14, 229, 467, 818
salvaging deleted files, 682
SandDollar, The (BBS), 912
SAV files, 50
Save and Close command (File menu), 364
Save As command (File menu), 356
    EPM, 364
Save command (File menu), 358
    EPM, 364
Save Options command (Options menu), 371

saving
    attributes, 489, 493-494
    desktop arrangement, 261
    files, 832
    function key, 828
    icon palettes, 574
    Notepad, 570
    To-Do Lists, 541
    tunes, 561
SAY command, 469, 473
SCR file extension, 152
Scramble, 149, 842-843
screen colors, 182-183
screen display, *see* monitor
scripts (NetWare login sequence), 676-677
scroll bars, 239, 371
Scroll Lock key, 17
SCSI (Small Computer System Interface) disk drive, 113
SDLC adapter cards, 652
SeaHunt BBS, 912
Search and Scan tool, 149
Search commands (Services menu), 338
search drives, 685
Search menu command (EPM), 366-367
Search menu keystrokes, 834
Search Subdirectories command (Options menu), 566
searching files, 563-565
searching help topics, 338
searching text, 832
security
    Extended Services, 627-628
    LANs, 701
    LAN Server/Manager, 712-713
    NetWare, 689-690
Seek and Scan Files, 546, 562-566
    Edit menu, 566
    File menu, 565
    Options menu, 566
    searching files, 563-565
    Selected menu, 565
    stopping searches, 566
Select All command (Edit menu), 573
Select command (Edit menu), 573
Selected menu commands (Seek and Scan Files), 565

1006 selecting

selecting
  files, 285-286
  icons, 255
  text, 831
selection emphasis, 255
selective installation, 176-178
Selective Install, 124, 140
Selective Install object, 178
SEND command, 683
serial cables, 22
serial device support, 177
serial devices, 141
serious backups, 40
Server Message Block (SMB) protocol, 696
Server-Requester Programming Interface (SRPI), 655
Services menu commands, 338
Session Control SMBs, 704
Session support (NetBIOS), 704
Set Alarm command (Alarms menu), 535
Set Alarm Tune (Daily Planner), 524
Set Default command
  Options menu, 566
  Palette menu, 575
Set Font Size window, 402
Set installable command (Options menu), 496
Set Master Planner File command (Customize menu), 538
Set startup values... command (Options menu), 496
SETBOOT command, 69
SETBOOT utility, 490, 509-510
setting alarms, 536
setting up NET.CFG file, 673
Settings Notebook, 368
  desktop, 178, 181-182
  folders, 259
  printer object, 377
  undoing changes, 252-253
  viewing, 250
Setup page (mouse), 186
SETVGA.CMD batch file, 174
Shading command (Customize menu), 528
shadowing files, 288
shadows (objects), 256
SHARE.EXE, 662
shortcut keys, 339

Shows Statistics for the Current Year command (File menu), 530
Shredder, 257
shut-down (system unit), 37
shutting down systems, 260-261
SIGL variable, 471
simple Extended Attributes, 74
Singer Bear BBS, 912
single quotation mark (') in REXX programs, 476
sizing windows, 829
slash (/) in REXX programs, 466, 476
slider boxes, 242
SLIST command, 684
Small Computer System Interface (SCSI) disk drive, 113
SMBS (Server Message Block) categories, 704-705
Smooth command (Options menu), 555
SNA (System Network Architecture) links, 624
SNA Gateway, 629
Sno-Valley Software Exchange (BBS), 912
Snooze Period command (Customize menu), 538
Socialism OnLine! (BBS), 913
soft fonts, 383-386
software, 23-31
  application software, 31
  autotuning, 701
  device support disks, 158
  directories, 27
  DOS, 25
  erasing, 15
  memory managers, 406
  operating systems, 24
  Presentation Manager, 24
  printer driver, 376
  Printer object, 29
  repairing, 490, 499-501
  requesters, 699
  ROM BIOS, 110-112
  utilities, 27-29
  utilities incompatibility, 71-76
    hard disks, 74-76
    HPFS (High Performance file systems), 72-73

INI files/extended attributes, 73-74
Workplace Shell, 24, 30
Soldier's Bored, The (BBS), 913
Solitaire-Klondike, 149
Sorcery Board BBS, The, 913
Sort command (View menu), 542
Sort page (desktop), 181
SORT utility, 490, 508, 510-512
sorting files, 511
Sound Blaster, 890
sound cards, 890
Sound Limit command (Customize menu), 538
Sound Stage BBS, 896
sounds, 185, 263
source disks, 291
Space Station Alpha (BBS), 913
Special Needs page keyboard, 188
specific-DOS sessions, 713-715
spin buttons, 142, 241, 251
splitting lines, 350
SPOOL command, 69
Spooler, 375, 380
Spreadsheet applet, 593-601
  commands, 593-594
  limitations, 600
  operations, 596-600
SPX support, 670
SQL (Structured Query Language), 624, 637-638
SQL Server (Microsoft), 657, 707
SQL statements
  preparing, 638
  programming with REXX, 639-640
starting
  applications, 401
  Database applet, 582
  DOS, 404
  EPM (Enhanced Editor for Program Manager), 362
  General Purpose applets, 546
  MAKEINI utility, 498-499
  PM Chart applet, 603
  PM Terminal applet, 613-621
  programs, 246
  Spreadsheet applet, 595
  Time Management applets, 520
  Windows, 396

Startup Values command
 (Options menu), 133
STARTUP.CMD file
    executing statements, 168
    running batch file
      automatically, 460
    statements
      batch files, 452-459
      CALL, 458-459
      ECHO, 453-454
      FOR loops, 458
      GOTO, 455
      IF, 456-457
      IF ERRORLEVEL, 457
      IF EXIST, 455-456
      label statements, 455
      parameters, 454-455
status line, 371
Sticky Notes
    Customize menu, 569
    Edit menu, 568-569
    inserting, 567-568
Sticky Pad, 546, 567-569
stopping searches, 566
Storm Front - OS/2, The (BBS), 913
Stretch Paste command (Edit menu), 573
strings
    comparing, 456-457
    REXX programs, 476-479
STRIP function, 479
Structured Query Language (SQL), 818
STY files, 50
subdirectories
    copying, 322
    searching, 566
SUBSTR function, 478
Super VGA video adapter, 95, 116, 118-119
Swap command (Palette menu), 575
Swap File, 91-92
SWAPPATH command, 69
SwapPath option, 92
SWAPPER.DAT file, 64
switches (commands), 721
switching between OS/2 and DOS, 404, 489-492
symbol sets, 383
Symmetric MultiProcessor (SMP) computers, 821
syntax (commands), 719-720
SYS files, 50
SYS1475 error message, 199

SYS2025 error messages, 200
SYS2026 error mesages, 200
SYS2027 error message, 200
SYS2028 error message, 200
SYS2029 error message, 200
SYS2030 error messsage, 200
SYS3146 error message, 200
SYS3147 error message, 200
SYSLEVEL utility, 490, 512-513
System Application Architecture, *see* SAA
System attribute, 206
System Clock, 189, 250-251
system configuration
    installing OS/2, 140-143
    peripherals, 142-143
    serial devices, 141
    video adapters, 141
SYSTEM directory, 208
System Editor, 346, 361-362
    clearing text, 352
    color, 359
    copying text, 352
    deleting text, 350
    finding text, 353, 355-356
    inserting text, 349-350
    joining lines, 350
    marking text blocks, 351
    menus, 356-361
      Edit menu, 358
      File menu, 356-358
      Options menu, 359-361
    mouse cursor, 349
    moving text blocks, 351-352
    pasting text, 352
    replacing text, 354
    splitting lines, 350
    text cursor, 348-349
    undoing changes, 358
System Installation failed trying to load a module into memory message, 198
system lockup, 260
system management, 35-36
system menus, 401-403
    closing sessions, 403
    CONFIG.SYS configuration, 410-411
    cutting and pasting sessions, 402-403
    font size, 401-402
System object, 184-185
system requirements, 59
System Setup folder, 124

System Setup utility, 29
system shutdown, 260-261
system unit
    power-on sequence, 36-37
    restarting, 37-39
    shut-down, 37
system utilities, 177
System-2 RBBS (BBS), 914
system-oriented commands, 723-724
Systems Editor, 352
Systems Exchange, The (BBS), 914

T

table of contents (Help), 340
Tabs command (Options menu), 369
Tally menu commands (Calculator), 553
target disks, 291
TCP/IP (Transmission control Protocol/Internet Protocol), 697
Telekon/2 BBS, 896
Template Folder, 190
templates, 264
Templates folder, 397
terminal emulation
    Communications Manager, 631-635
    PM Terminal applet, 618
Terminal Emulator, 149
Test command (Options menu), 575
text
    copying, 832-833
    cursor, 19, 348-349
    cutting, 832
    deleting, 833
    moving, 833
    pasting, 832, 833
    searching, 832
    selecting, 831
text editors, 467
text files
    clearing text, 352
    color, 359
    copying text, 352
    cutting text, 352
    deleting text, 350
    editing multiple files, 369
    finding text, 353, 355-356
    fonts, 360

text files

importing, 364
inserting text, 349-350
joining lines, 350
margins, 369
marking text blocks, 351
mouse cursor, 349
pasting text, 352
printing, 364
replacing text, 354
searching (EPM), 366
splitting lines, 350
tabs, 369
text cursor, 348-349
undoing changes, 358
word wrap, 361
text mode
installing OS/2, 128-139
monitor, 19
The Idle Task (BBS), 896
The Locutory (BBS), 896
The Nibble's Roost (BBS), 896
The TJD Support BBS, 898
threads, 66, 89-91, 123, 504-505
THREADS command, 69
Tidy menu commands (Daily Planner), 525
TIF files, 50
TIME command, 304-305
Time Management applets, 520
Activities List, 519, 531-534
  Customize menu, 533-534
  Edit menu, 532
  File menu, 532
  Planner Archive command, 534
  View menu, 533
Alarms
  Customize menu, 538
  Edit menu, 538
Calendar, 519, 529-530
Daily Planner, 519-526
  Completed menu, 524
  Customize menu, 525-526
  Edit menu, 523-524
  File menu, 523
  printing, 523
  Tidy menu, 525
  View menu, 524

Monthly Planner, 519, 526-529
  Customize menu, 527-528
  editing, 528-529
  View menu, 527
Planner Archive, 520
Planner file default, 538-539
starting, 520
To-Do List, 520, 540-544
  archiving, 543-544
  Customize menu, 543
  editing, 540-541
  File menu, 541
  Mark menu, 542
  View menu, 542
TIMESLICE command, 69
Timing page
keyboard, 188
mouse, 186
title bars, 237, 240
TMP files, 50
To-Do List, 520, 540-544
archiving, 543-544
Customize menu, 543
editing, 540-541
File menu, 541
Mark menu, 542
View menu, 542
Token Ring-based LANs, 652
tools, 100-101
installing OS/2, 148-149
Tools menu (Icon Editor), 576
TOUCH_EXCLUSIVE_ACCESS setting, 424
trackballs, 18
Transact-SQL, 657
transaction management (Database Manager), 640-641
transferring data
  Private Clipboard, 558-559
  Public Clipboard, 557
TRANSLATE function, 478
TRAPxx error message, 199
Treasure Island (BBS), 914
TREE command, 508
tree view (Drives object), 275-276
Tree view (desktop), 180
Trident Microsystems 8900 adapter, 174
troubleshooting, 193-225
accessing message files, 209
application program errors, 211-213
applications, 220-221

backing up files, 202-206
boot problems, 215-218, 224
configuring hard disks, 201
DOS boot disks, 202, 225
DOS sessions, 415-417
extended attributes (drives), 218-219
garbled screen, 221
installation, 195-200
  error messages, 197-200
  symptoms, 196-197
keyboard failure, 222
mouse, 222
performance problems, 223-224
printing, 222-223
Tseng Laboratories ET4000 adapter, 174
TST files, 50
TTY terminal emulation, 618
Tune Editor, 546, 559-562
Edit menu, 561-562
editing, 560
File menu, 560-561
Play menu, 562
tutorial, 146, 159
TXT files, 50
TYPE command, 127
typefaces, 383

U

U.S. Telematics (BBS), 914
UNC (Universal Naming Convention), 700
UNDELETE command, 405
UNDELETE utility, 490, 513-514
underscore (_) in variable names, 471
undo function key, 828
Undo command (Edit menu), 358
  Daily Planner, 523
  EPM, 366
undoing
  changes, 365, 358
  Settings Notebook changes, 252
University of Saskatchewan (BBS), 897
UNIX operating system, 132
Unmark Line command (Mark menu), 542
UNPACK utility, 490, 508, 514-516

Unrecoverable Application Error, 403
updating
 CONFIG.SYS statements, 167
 login scripts, 676
 Pulse graph, 555-556
upgrading hardware, 169-176
 fonts, 172-173
 hard disks, 176
 mouse, 173
 printers, 169-172
 video, 173-175
upper memory, 151
user accounts (NetWare), 690-691
User Profile Management (UPM), 627
Using help command (Help menu), 497
utilities, 100-101, 177, 489-490
 ASK.COM, 459
 BOOT, 489, 490-492
 diagnostic utilities, 406
 disk utilities, 405-406
 DSPINSTL, 174
 EAUTIL, 489, 493-494, 507
 EPM (Enhanced Editor for Program Manager), 27
 FCONSOLE, 690
 FDISKPM, 489, 494-497
 GammaTech, 75-76
 INIMAINT (Carry Associates), 76
 INPUT.COM, 459
 installing OS/2, 147
 LAN Manager/Server, 710
 MAKEINI, 489, 498-499
 NetWare, 680-686
  command line, 682-686
  menu based, 681-682
 operating systems, 24
 PATCH, 490, 499-501, 507
 PCONSOLE, 688
 PMCHKDSK, 490, 501-503
 PSTAT, 490, 504-505
 Return Codes, 490, 505-509
  BOOT utility, 492
  PATCH utility, 501
  SORT utility, 511
  UNPACK utility, 516
 SALVAGE, 682
 SETBOOT, 490, 509-510
 SHARE.EXE, 662
 SORT, 490, 508, 510-512
 SYSLEVEL, 490, 512-513
 System Setup, 29

UNDELETE, 490, 513-514
UNPACK, 490, 508, 514-516
VIEW, 516
utilities incompatibility, 71-76
 hard disks, 74-76
 HPFS (High Performance File Systems), 72-73
 INI files/extended attributes, 73-74
utility files, 672

V

variables
 command-line parameters, 481
 naming, 470-471
 predefined variables, 471
 REXX programming language, 469-471
VCPI (Virtual Control Program Interface) memory, 151
VDM (Virtual DOS Machine), 25
vertical bar (|) in REXX programs, 472
VESA (Video Electronics Standards Association), 95, 105, 116
VGA (Video Graphics Array) video adapter, 116-119
VGA resolution, 174
video adapters, 141
Video Electronics Standards Assocation, see VESA
Video Graphics Array video adapter, see VGA
video RAM (VRAM), 95
video upgrades, 173-175
VIDEO_8514A_XGA_IOTRAP setting, 425
VIDEO_FASTPASTE setting, 415, 426
VIDEO_MODE_RESTRICTION setting, 426-427
VIDEO_ONDEMAND_MEMORY setting, 427
VIDEO_RETRACE_EMULATION, 427
VIDEO_ROM_EMULATION setting, 415, 428
VIDEO_SWITCH_NOTIFICATION setting, 428

VIDEO_WINDOW_REFRESH setting, 415, 428
VIEW command, 69
View menu commands
 Activities List, 533
 Daily Planner, 524
 Monthly Planner, 527
 Notepad, 572
 To-Do List, 542
View page (System Clock), 189
VIEW utility, 516
viewing
 objects, 250-252
 print jobs, 380
 Settings Notebook, 250
views
 databases, 641
 Drives object, 271-279
 icons, 255-257
Virtual Control Program Interface memory (VCPI), 151
Virtual DOS Machine, see VDM
viruses, 405
VisPro REXX, 482-483
VMDISK command, 715
volume labels, 326
volumes, 685
VRAM, 95
VREXX (Visual REXX), 468, 482
VT100 Terminal Emulator, 634
VX/REXX, 484

W

Walnut Creek (Internet site), 915-988
warm boots, 36
Watcom, 484
Western Digital Paradise adapter, 174
WHOAMI command, 684
wild cards, 47, 313-315
 * (asterisk), 282
WIN_CLIPBOARD setting, 444
WIN_DDE setting, 444
WIN_RUNMODE setting, 445
window backgrounds, 259
Window List, 253-254
 multiple object views, 253-254
 object view, 253

Window page
    desktop, 182
    System page, 184
windowed DOS sessions, 399-401
    system menus, 401-403
        closing sessions, 403
        cutting and pasting sessions, 402-403
        font size, 401-402
Windows (Microsoft Corporation)
Windows, 80-81
    applications, 264
    customizing settings, 165-166
    desktop, 157
    Enhanced mode, 406
    installing OS/2, 152
    installing OS/2 for Windows, 125
    Migrate Applications, 156
    printing, 373, 388
    running applications, 403-404
    sessions (CONFIG.SYS), 410-411
    starting, 396
    transferring data to OS/2
        Private Clipboard, 558-559
        Public Clipboard, 557
    transition to Presentation Manager, 14
windows, 19
    action bars, 237
    borders, 238
    client area, 238
    Close, 400
    closing, 249, 828, 833
    Create Another Printer, 390
    customizing, 263
    EPM, 363-372
        display, 370
        multiple files, 369

Font Installer, 386
maximizing, 235, 247-267, 829
minimizing, 248-267, 829
moving, 249-267, 828
navigating, 252
opening, 828
Presentation Manager, 237-239
Printer Configuration, 388
resizing, 249-267
restoring, 248-267
scroll bars, 239
Set Font Size, 402
sizing, 829
title bars, 237
Windows support, 70-71, 177
WINOS2 directory, 208
WINSTALL directory, 125
WK1 files, 50
WK3 files, 50
WKS files, 50
Word Wrap command (Options menu), 361
WORDS function, 479
Workplace Shell, 19, 24, 30, 70, 231-234, 245-267
    applications setup, 264-266
    customizing, 262-264
    dragging/dropping, 232
    initializing, 159
    installing applications, 397-404
        file recognition, 398-399
        new program objects, 397
        program settings, 398
        session type, 399-401
    keyboard shortcuts, 823-826
    menus, 260-261
    navigating, 233-234
    objects, 231
    tasks, 823-826
    VDM (Virtual DOS Machine), 25

Workplace Shell desktop, 94
workstation setup (LAN Manager/Server), 708-709
workstations
    domains, 712
    NetWare based, 661-674
        NetWare Requester, 663-674
        Requester, 662
WP ROOT. SF file, 207
WQ1 files, 50
WSI BBS (BBS), 914

X-Y-Z

X Background menu (Options menu), 575
X.25 connections, 652
X.25 Network standard, 629
XCOPY command, 321-323, 508
XGA (Extended Graphics Array) video adapter, 116-117
XMS (Extended Memory Specification), 64, 151, 412
XMS_HANDLES setting, 433
XMS_MEMORY_LIMIT setting, 433
XMS_MINIMUM_HMA setting, 434

ZIP files, 50
Zzyzx Road OS/2 BBS, 915

GO AHEAD. PLUG YOURSELF INTO
PRENTICE HALL COMPUTER PUBLISHING.

Introducing the PHCP Forum on CompuServe®

Yes, it's true. Now, you can have CompuServe access to the same professional, friendly folks who have made computers easier for years. On the PHCP Forum, you'll find additional information on the topics covered by every PHCP imprint—including Que, Sams Publishing, New Riders Publishing, Alpha Books, Brady Books, Hayden Books, and Adobe Press. In addition, you'll be able to receive technical support and disk updates for the software produced by Que Software and Paramount Interactive, a division of the Paramount Technology Group. It's a great way to supplement the best information in the business.

WHAT CAN YOU DO ON THE PHCP FORUM?

Play an important role in the publishing process—and make our books better while you make your work easier:

- Leave messages and ask questions about PHCP books and software—you're guaranteed a response within 24 hours
- Download helpful tips and software to help you get the most out of your computer
- Contact authors of your favorite PHCP books through electronic mail
- Present your own book ideas
- Keep up to date on all the latest books available from each of PHCP's exciting imprints

JOIN NOW AND GET A FREE COMPUSERVE STARTER KIT!

To receive your free CompuServe Introductory Membership, call toll-free, **1-800-848-8199** and ask for representative **#597**. The Starter Kit Includes:

- Personal ID number and password
- $15 credit on the system
- Subscription to CompuServe Magazine

HERE'S HOW TO PLUG INTO PHCP:

Once on the CompuServe System, type any of these phrases to access the PHCP Forum:

GO PHCP   **GO BRADY**
GO QUEBOOKS   **GO HAYDEN**
GO SAMS   **GO QUESOFT**
GO NEWRIDERS   **GO PARAMOUNTINTER**
GO ALPHA

Once you're on the CompuServe Information Service, be sure to take advantage of all of CompuServe's resources. CompuServe is home to more than 1,700 products and services—plus it has over 1.5 million members worldwide. You'll find valuable online reference materials, travel and investor services, electronic mail, weather updates, leisure-time games and hassle-free shopping (no jam-packed parking lots or crowded stores).

Seek out the hundreds of other forums that populate CompuServe. Covering diverse topics such as pet care, rock music, cooking, and political issues, you're sure to find others with the sames concerns as you—and expand your knowledge at the same time.

Complete Computer Coverage

Que's 1994 Computer Hardware Buyer's Guide

Que Development Group

This absolute must-have guide packed with comparisons, recommendations, and tips for asking all the right questions familiarizes the reader with terms they will need to know. This book offers a complete analysis of both hardware and software products, and it's loaded with charts and tables of product comparisons.

IBM-compatibles, Apple, & Macintosh

$16.95 USA

1-56529-281-2, 480 pp., 8 x 10

Que's Computer User's Dictionary, 4th Edition

Bryan Pfaffenberger

This compact, practical reference contains hundreds of definitions, explanations, examples, and illustrations on topics from programming to desktop publishing. You can master the "language" of computers and learn how to make your personal computer more efficient and more powerful. Filled with tips and cautions, *Que's Computer User's Dictionary* is the perfect resource for anyone who uses a computer.

IBM, Macintosh, Apple, & Programming

$12.95 USA

1-56529-604-4, 650 pp., 4¾ x 8

que

To Order, Call: (800) 428-5331

Enhance Your Personal Computer System with Hardware and Networking Titles from Que!

Upgrading and Repairing PCs, 3rd Edition

Scott Mueller

This book is the ultimate resource for personal computer upgrade, maintenance, and troubleshooting information! It provides solutions to common PC problems and purchasing decisions and includes a glossary of terms, ASCII code charts, and expert recommendations.

IBM PCs and Compatibles

$34.95 USA
1-56529-467-X, 1,312 pp.

Introduction to Personal Computers, 4th Edition

White & Schafer

IBM, Macintosh, & Apple

$19.95 USA
1-56529-275-8, 512 pp.

Introduction to PC Communications

Phil Becker

IBM PCs

$24.95 USA
0-88022-747-8, 500 pp.

The CD-ROM Book

Sloman & Bosak

IBM, Macintosh, & Apple

$34.95 USA
1-56529-292-8, 480 pp.

Que's 1994 Computer Hardware Buyer's Guide

Bud Smith

IBM-compatibles, Macintosh, & Apple

$16.95 USA
1-56529-281-2, 480 pp.

Que's Speed Up Your Computer Book

David Reed

DOS 5

$29.95 USA
0-88022-761-3, 350 pp.

Using Novell NetWare 4, Special Edition

Que Development Group

Through Version 4

$35.00 USA
1-56529-069-0, 1,100 pp.

---

que

To Order, Call: (800) 428-5331
OR (317) 581-3500

Using WordPerfect Is Easy When You're Using Que

Using WordPerfect Version 6 for DOS, Special Edition
Que Development Group
The classic, #1 best-selling word processing book—only from Que! Includes tear-out command map, icons, margin notes, and cautions.
WordPerfect 6
$27.95 USA
1-56529-077-1, 1,200pp., 7³/₈ x 9¹/₈

WordPerfect 6 QuickStart
Que Development Group
A graphics-based, fast-paced introduction to 6 essentials! Numerous illustrations demonstrate document production, table design, equation editing, and more.
WordPerfect 6
$21.95 USA
1-56529-085-2, 600 pp., 7³/₈ x 9¹/₈

WordPerfect 6 Quick Reference
Que Development Group
Instant reference for the operations of WordPerfect 6. Alphabetical listings make information easy to find!
WordPerfect 6
$9.95 USA
1-56529-084-4, 160 pp., 4³/₄ x 8

Easy WordPerfect for Version 6
Shelley O'Hara
The perfect introduction for new WordPerfect users—or those upgrading to Version 6.
WordPerfect 6
$16.95 USA
1-56529-087-9, 256 pp., 8 x 10

Check Out These Other Great Titles!

Using WordPerfect 5.1, Special Edition
Que Development Group
WordPerfect 5.1
$27.95 USA
0-88022-554-8, 900 pp., 7³/₈ x 9¹/₈

WordPerfect 5.1 QuickStart
Que Development Group
WordPerfect 5.1
$21.95 USA
0-88022-558-0, 427 pp., 7³/₈ x 9¹/₈

WordPerfect 5.1 Quick Reference
Que Development Group
WordPerfect 5.1
$9.95 USA
0-88022-576-9, 160 pp., 4³/₄ x 8

WordPerfect 5.1 Tips, Tricks, and Traps
Charles O. Stewart III, Daniel J. Rosenbaum, & Joel Shore
WordPerfect 5.1
$24.95 USA
0-88022-557-2, 743 pp., 7³/₈ x 9¹/₈

Easy WordPerfect
Shelley O'Hara
WordPerfect 5.1
$19.95 USA
0-88022-797-4, 200 pp., 8 x 10

WordPerfect 5.1 Office Solutions
Ralph Blodgett
Version 5.1
$49.95 USA
0-88022-838-5, 850 pp., 8 x 10

que To Order, Call: (800) 428-5331 OR (317) 581-3500